PROFESSIONAL

Access® 2013 Programming

PROFESSIONAL
Access® 2013 Programming

Teresa Hennig
Ben Clothier
George Hepworth
Dagi (Doug) Yudovich

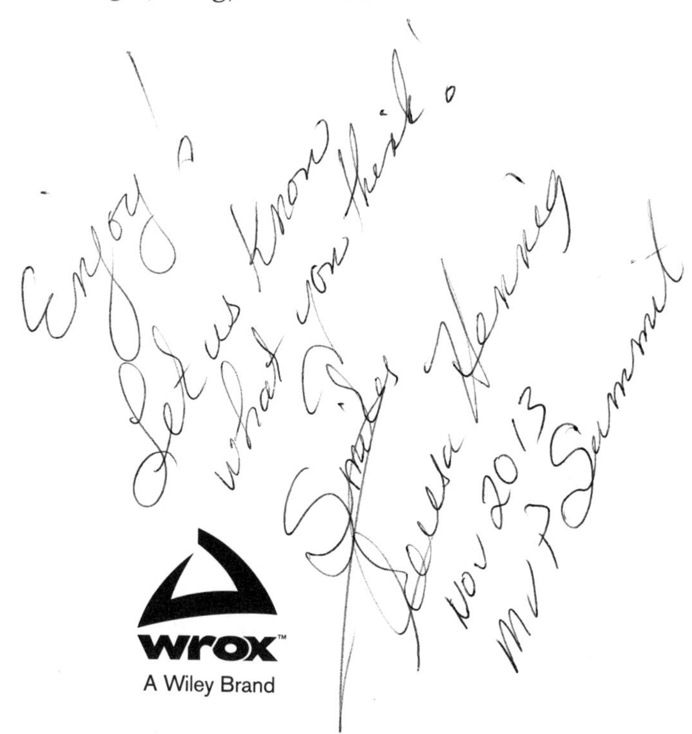

Professional Access® 2013 Programming

Published by
John Wiley & Sons, Inc.
10475 Crosspoint Boulevard
Indianapolis, IN 46256
www.wiley.com

Published simultaneously in Canada

ISBN: 978-1-118-53083-2
ISBN: 978-1-118-53082-5 (ebk)
ISBN: 978-1-118-78961-2 (ebk)

Manufactured in the United States of America

10 9 8 7 6 5 4 3 2 1

Library of Congress Control Number: 2013907974

To my family and my dearest friends — you are my inspirations, role models and mentors. Whatever I am facing, I can find strength and guidance by thinking of what my Mom, Papa, Dad, or brother might say or do. Every day I have reasons to say thank you for teaching us to work, to accept responsibility for our actions, to do the right thing, and to help others. You taught us to do what we enjoy and to do our best. What a great formula to be happy, energized, and resilient, and to appreciate all that we have! You set the foundation for me to embrace the thrills, lessons, and adventures in life. And, throughout life, to be compassionate and to give generously — especially laughter and smiles, a hug or a helping hand.

—Teresa Hennig

To Suzanne and Harry, for being just plain awesome. I couldn't have done it without you two!

—Ben Clothier

I want to dedicate my part in this book to my mother and father, who not only brought me into the world, but showed me how to live properly once I got here. Family comes first, but that is easy when you have a family like mine. To my siblings, JoAnna, Tom, Sam, Jack, Nancy, and Jane: Your encouragement (and unusually high tolerance for bad jokes, lies, and war stories) helps keep me going. Thanks. I promise I'll update the family website again soon. I also need to make special mention of my daughter, Lyndsey; you give me reason to be proud every day. Love ya, sweetie. We'll make up for the missed weekend dinners soon.

—George Hepworth

To my wife, Lisa, who still patiently picks up the slack as I dive head-first into new adventures. None of it would have been possible without you. I love you.

—Dagi Yudovich

CREDITS

EXECUTIVE EDITOR
Robert Elliott

PROJECT EDITOR
Christina Haviland

TECHNICAL EDITORS
F. Scott Barker
Jerry Dennison
Jerry Wood

PRODUCTION EDITOR
Christine Mugnolo

COPY EDITOR
Nancy Rapoport

EDITORIAL MANAGER
Mary Beth Wakefield

FREELANCER EDITORIAL MANAGER
Rosemarie Graham

ASSOCIATE DIRECTOR OF MARKETING
David Mayhew

MARKETING MANAGER
Ashley Zurcher

BUSINESS MANAGER
Amy Knies

PRODUCTION MANAGER
Tim Tate

VICE PRESIDENT AND EXECUTIVE GROUP PUBLISHER
Richard Swadley

VICE PRESIDENT AND EXECUTIVE PUBLISHER
Neil Edde

ASSOCIATE PUBLISHER
Jim Minatel

PROJECT COORDINATOR, COVER
Katie Crocker

PROOFREADER
Sarah Kaikini, Word One New York

INDEXER
John Sleeva

COVER DESIGNER
Wiley

COVER IMAGE
© iStockphoto.com/PhekThong Lee

ABOUT THE AUTHORS

TERESA HENNIG has been an Access developer and business consultant since 1997, when she decided to start her own business on the second day that she used Access. Her company's name, Data Dynamics Northwest, aptly reflects her dynamic personality and her innate ability to quickly grasp a situation, formulate and implement a solution, and motivate others. With a strong background in business and project management, Teresa focuses on providing intuitive, cost-effective solutions that support all levels of an organization. One of her favorite aspects of being a consultant is working with an endless variety of businesses across many industries and in numerous locations.

As a self-taught developer, Teresa quickly became involved with the Seattle Access Group and has been the President since 1999. It wasn't long before she was asked to help run, and then became President of, the Pacific Northwest Access Developer Group. Her first book *Access 2003 Programmer's Reference* (Wiley, 2003) opened the door to new opportunities to help fellow developers share their passion and expertise with the community. Over the past 10 years, Teresa has helped dozens of colleagues to become authors, editors and contributors. This is her sixth book, and she already has requests to do more.

Teresa has been recognized as a Microsoft MVP continuously since 2006, and has twice earned INETA's National Community Champion award. Teresa thrives on challenges, project management, and creating cost-effective solutions. Her skills for motivating and helping others are reflected in her contributions to the developer community and support of numerous non-profit organizations. She is expanding her reach by doing presentations and offering customized training, mentoring, and consulting for database development as well as business and project management. You can contact Teresa at Teresa@DataDynamicsNW.com to learn more about any of these services. You can also read about some of her adventures and charitable endeavors by visiting her website, `www.DataDynamicsNW.com`.

BEN CLOTHIER is a Lead Developer with IT Impact, Inc., a premier Access and SQL Server development shop based in Chicago, Illinois. He has worked as a freelance consultant with notable shops including J Street Technology and Advisicon, and has worked on Access projects from small, one-man solutions to company-wide line-of-business applications. Notable projects include job tracking and inventory for a cement company, a Medicare insurance plan generator for an insurance provider, and order management for an international shipping company.

Ben is an administrator at UtterAccess and was a coauthor, with Tim Runcie and George Hepworth, on *Microsoft Access in a SharePoint World* (Advisicon, 2011), and a contributing author for *Access 2010 Programmer's Reference* (Wiley, 2010). He is a certified MySQL 5.0 Developer and a Microsoft Certified Technology Specialist for SharePoint 2010 configurations. He has been a Microsoft MVP since 2009.

Ben lives in San Antonio, Texas with his wife, Suzanne, and his son, Harry.

GEORGE HEPWORTH began his Access career by creating tools to track sales and exam results for his business, which created and sold training and exam materials. Realizing that Access databases were more interesting and rewarding than writing training materials, he soon transitioned to full-time Access development and started his company, Grover Park Consulting (`www.GPCData.com`), specializing in resuscitating "owner-built" Access databases for small- and medium-sized organizations. As a self-taught developer, George believes that any day on which he doesn't learn at least one new thing is a day wasted.

George is a database developer for Data and Domains, a development organization near Bellevue, Washington, creating Access and Access/SQL Server solutions for clients in the Puget Sound region. George is part of the administrator team, and a regular contributor, at UtterAccess, the most popular Access support site on the Internet. He is the author or contributor to several books on Access, and a presenter at the Pacific Northwest Access Developer Group and Seattle Access Group.

George holds a BS in English and an MA in TESL from Utah State University. And now, George's daughter and his money go to Seattle University.

DAGI (DOUG) YUDOVICH is the Assistant Director of Departmental Computing for the University of Washington School of Medicine. One of the department's primary BI responsibilities is developing database solutions using Access and SQL Server.

Doug is an Administrator on UtterAccess forums and the UtterAccess wiki. Doug was a contributing author to *Microsoft Access Small Business Solutions* and the *Access 2010 Programmer's Reference*. Additionally, Doug is an active member of the Pacific Northwest Access Developers Group (PNWADG) and a presenter in the Seattle Access Group (SAG). Doug has been awarded the Access MVP award since 2009.

ABOUT THE TECHNICAL EDITORS/ CONTRIBUTORS

JERRY DENNISON has over 20 years of professional experience in the design and development of Microsoft Access database applications. He was one of the coauthors of *Microsoft Access 2010 Programmer's Reference* (Wiley, 2010) and a contributing editor on other Access books. Jerry was a four-year recipient of the Microsoft Office Access MVP award and is considered by his peers to be one of the foremost experts on the forms of data normalization.

Jerry is the owner of TradeIt! Software Support Services, where he provides database consulting for businesses and other Access developers. He is an automation engineer at Rexam Healthcare Packaging, where he has worked for 22 years providing design, installation, and service support for automated inspection and test systems.

Jerry lives with his wife of 24 years in Hixson, Tennessee.

PATRICK WOOD is the founder of Gaining Access Technologies, which provides consulting and custom software development. Originally a minister with a bachelor's degree in biblical studies, he decided one day while he was between churches to develop an application to manage the many tasks involved with small- to medium-sized churches. That sparked his interest in Microsoft Access development, which led to the founding of his company. He learned ASP.NET to build the company website, and began developing SQL Server and Azure SQL databases. Pat's articles about cutting-edge technology software development have been featured on several websites. He received the MVP Award for Microsoft Access in 2011.

Pat still preaches at a small country church and enjoys taking walks, playing the guitar, hunting and fishing, and spending time with his wife and three young grandsons.

F. SCOTT BARKER is the owner of AppsPlus, where he develops software for industries ranging from government agencies, insurance companies, banks, medical analysis firms, and even for Microsoft. Scott is a former Microsoft MVP and Microsoft employee, and was a member of the original Access team. He is also the author of a number of books on programming techniques using Microsoft technologies.

LEO (theDBguy™) is an Access MVP and moderator of the UtterAccess (UA) Forums. Since joining UA in 2007, Leo has made over 50,000 posts responding to questions and solving worldwide database dilemmas. Leo is a renowned Access expert with over 17 years of experience creating complex and intuitive Access solutions. He currently works as a Knowledge Manager for the Navy and manages the SharePoint portal for his command, which supports over 1500 sites and more than 5500 users.

Leo's free time is dedicated to his family and to helping others leverage the powers of Access. In addition to being an active member and presenter at the Access User Group of San Diego, he also shares his expertise through his website at `www.accessmvp.com/thedbguy` and his blog site at `www.thedbguy.blog.com`.

TECHNICAL CONTRIBUTORS

GREG LINDHORST is the Principal Program Manager for Microsoft Access. He has been a member of the Microsoft Access engineering team since 2006, specializing in Access web apps and the programming model. Greg is a 20-year veteran at Microsoft, where he has worked on a wide range of application development tools in Office and Visual Studio.

TOM VAN STIPHOUT is an Access MVP and the software development manager for Kinetik I.T. (`www.kinetik-it.com`), a premier provider of website design, SEO Internet marketing, software development, and computer network services and solutions in Phoenix, Arizona. Tom can be reached at `tom7744@cox.net`.

JACK D. LEACH is an Access MVP with a strong background in the manufacturing business. He runs Dymeng Services (`www.dymeng.com`), a software development company in upstate New York, specializing in database and website solutions for small businesses. Jack can be found on `www.utteraccess.com` as jleach and at `jeach@dymeng.com`.

PETER DOERING is an Access MVP from Bamberg, Germany and an expert on migrations to SQL Server as well as SQL Azure and Office 365. He's been an independent developer on international projects for over 20 years. Peter is an acclaimed speaker at developer conferences in Europe and can be reached at `mvp@doering.org`.

GLEN KRUGER is an Access MVP and the Developer/Owner of KNK Consulting, assisting clients using Access and Visual Basic. Glen graduated from NAIT's Computer Systems Technology (CST) program. He is an administrator of the UtterAccess Forums, and can also be reached at `krugerglen@hotmail.com`.

RIK HEPWORTH is a Microsoft vTSP and is the IT Director and head of the SharePoint Practice at Black Marble in the UK. With over 20 years in IT, Rik has worked in nearly every aspect of computing. As a technology evangelist, Rik is a regular presenter at events around the UK and Ireland. He is easiest to find on Twitter as `@rikhepworth`.

JONATHAN SAMPSON is an IE MVP and the Director of Support at AppendTo (`appendTo.com`). Jonathan is a full-stack developer who participates on stackoverflow.com and produces content for sampson.ms. Jonathan can be found on Twitter at `@jonathansampson`.

ACKNOWLEDGMENTS

AS A TEAM, WE WOULD LIKE TO EXPRESS our respect and appreciation for all of the people who contributed to the content, editing, and production of this book. This project truly epitomizes the concept of team work and community — especially the MVP community. We wanted this book to reflect a wide perspective of expertise, but we didn't anticipate the extent that would become. We reached around the world to leverage the expertise and passion of more than a dozen MVPs and experts from multiple disciplines. They invested an unprecedented amount of time, research, and resources to create this book and all of the supporting files and examples. Much like creating a solution for your clients, the team has invested hundreds of hours to create or enhance developer tools that you can incorporate directly into your files.

Over the course of a number of months, we conquered many hurdles, forged new connections, and helped to expand the functionality for Access web apps. We couldn't have done it without the timely and invaluable efforts of our editors and technical contributors. These guys stepped up the moment they were called upon — and yes, that often meant at a point of near panic and urgency! Whether it was to resolve a version conflict, expand into associated technologies, or to share tools and techniques, they generously shared their expertise and passion with the community and you, the readers. Please take a moment to read about our contributing editors and technical contributors.

Of course, we wouldn't have anything to write about if it weren't for the incredible people on the Microsoft Access team. Their passion, dedication, and commitment to continuously expand and enhance Access are truly remarkable and inspiring. And we wouldn't have a book without all of the editors and teams at Wiley — Bob, Rosemarie, Mary Beth, Nancy, and so many more. Plus a very special thank you to Chris Haviland for her remarkable skills, attitude, and encouragement while guiding us through months of reviews and production. Hmm, we've lost track of all the IOUs, but suffice it to say they should include a spa day, margaritas, chocolate dipped strawberries, and many massages!

—The Authors

FIRST AND FOREMOST, I WANT TO EXPRESS heartfelt appreciation to my family and dearest friends. I am immensely grateful for the opportunities, encouragement, and support that you continue to give me — personally, professionally, and for so many charitable endeavors. From the summit of Mt. Rainier to Uganda, and from fundraisers to books, you help me to stay focused, energized, and positive. Life can take us on quite a roller coaster ride filled with excitement, challenges, accomplishments, and lessons. People and life have so many facets to relish and cherish; thank you for sharing the adventures. I also want to thank my colleagues, especially my MVP family, and everyone working on this book.

This project has been like no other. When we started planning over 12 months ago, no one could have foreseen the amount of time and effort, or the extensive and ongoing changes, that would be involved. On behalf of myself and the entire Access community, I want to thank Ben and George for their vision, perseverance, and dedication to not only proving that an Access 2013 web app can be a robust business solution, but also providing a model and guide for others to follow. At critical moments, we also gained the invaluable expertise of Greg, Rik, and Jonathan. And to ensure that the traditional Access solutions demonstrate multiple perspectives and significant new approaches, Doug and I incorporated content and tips from several of our MVP colleagues. Their involvement was also instrumental in completing a second round of technical reviews and testing; with many thanks to the Herculean efforts by Leo, who reviewed nearly all of the web chapters!

Over the months, the team has undergone major transitions. Starting with a team of four authors, we added more than a dozen experts with a seeming exponential increase in coordination tasks. (Talk about lessons in project management!) Fortunately, those challenges also enriched my life with new friends as they joined our team. In working countless hours with Leo, Glen, Jack, and Pat, I gained the utmost respect for their expertise and dedication. Similarly, it is always a pleasure to work with my treasured colleagues, Tom, Peter, Jerry, and Scott. Your contributions helped make our book a truly remarkable and invaluable resource for all Access users. I am grateful for being able to share both the opportunity and the credits with so many. In recognition of the invaluable part that they played, we have designated a new role, *Technical Contributor.* These are remarkable people, so please take a moment to read their bios. This is truly a team effort and it epitomizes the spirit of the MVP community.

With all of the turmoil on the book, I essentially took a 4+ month hiatus from consulting to support the team. So I also want to thank my clients for understanding the delays and for working with me to prioritize and schedule tasks so that we could meet their immediate needs and defer others. THANK YOU!

I must also express very special, heartfelt appreciation to Christina Haviland — for her patience, guidance, humor, and compassionate understanding. Thank you for doing whatever it took to pull all of the pieces together to get everything to production and print! Your entryway should be overflowing with gift baskets, massage certificates, and a lifetime of gratitude.

This project has tested and strengthened us individually and collectively. We did this for you, the Access community. Our greatest reward is helping you to help others, so it is with great pride that we present this book. As you benefit from this compilation of resources, we hope that you too will realize that it is indeed priceless.

This demonstrates yet again that life is filled with opportunities — celebrate them all!

—TERESA HENNIG

WITHOUT THE HELP OF MANY WONDERFUL PEOPLE, this book would not have happened. Thank you, Greg Lindhorst, for helping us to set the parameters and providing guidance. Thank you, Rik Hepworth and Jonathan Sampson, for your excellent contribution when we found ourselves deep in the new and brave world of SharePoint and web development. I'm indebted to Jerry Dennison, Patrick Wood, and Leo theDBGuy™ for their meticulous diligence. Thank you, Christina Haviland and Teresa Hennig, for your guidance in the project. And most importantly, thank you, George Hepworth, for putting up with me!

—BEN CLOTHIER

THE CONTRIBUTIONS OF VARIOUS PEOPLE have been of great help in this journey. Greg Lindhorst, Access Program Manager at Microsoft, was an early and on-going source of key information about Access web apps. His help was invaluable. Later, when it became clear we had ventured some distance into the SharePoint realm, we were fortunate to obtain the assistance of Rik Hepworth in shoring up that part of the narrative. We also appreciate Jonathan Sampson for his important contributions in reviewing some of the JavaScript code. I also want to thank the partners at Data & Domains, Eric Change and Frank Wilson, for their generosity in allowing me time off to work on this book. We also want to acknowledge the contributions of Leo "theDBGuy" and Jerry Dennison for their excellent reviews and comments that helped make the book better.

—GEORGE HEPWORTH

SPECIAL THANKS to my coauthors — Teresa, Ben, and George. It's been a wild ride, but riding along with you made it all worthwhile. Your support during the project was nothing short of amazing. Extra thanks to Teresa for leading the project with an unlimited amount of energy and enthusiasm.

To my fellow MVPs and friends, Tom van Stiphout and Peter Doering — thank you for your help, insight, and input. Your knowledge seems boundless, and I've learned a lot from you. I'd also like to thank Pat Wood for taking the time to solve the puzzle after finding a missing piece.

To Chris, our project editor, thank you for your patience and guidance throughout the project and for being a calm port in the storm. To the technical editors, technical advisors, and anyone else who helped iron out the wrinkles — thank you.

—DAGI YUDOVICH

CONTENTS

INTRODUCTION

THANK YOU FOR BUYING THIS BOOK. We wrote it with you (the developer, the manager, the business owner) in mind to provide valuable tips, techniques, and tools applicable to a wide spectrum of experience, expertise, and industries. Each time you use one of the tools that we've provided, you've more than recouped the price of the book.

As the most popular database system in the world, Microsoft Access keeps getting better with each new version. The new Access 2013 provides significant new features that will enhance your experience of building web-based and traditional database applications. This book shows you everything you need to get started immediately, and it guides you through exploring a multitude of programming tools and techniques for building Access 2013 solutions.

Written by a team of Microsoft Access MVPs, this book leverages our expertise and passion for Access. In expanding the reach of Access, we incorporated the knowledge and experience of over a dozen experts to consult, test, and provide examples working with SharePoint, SQL Server, .NET, and web development. And to make sure that we could provide a model for a robust business solution, we worked closely with the Microsoft Access team to be at the forefront of defining, testing, and implementing the new features for Access 2013 web apps.

In creating the demo apps and writing this book, our team pushed the limits of what was provided and helped to delineate the required functionality. We not only blazed the way into a new frontier, but we also expanded the horizon. In doing so, we created an application that will guide you on a successful journey to create and deploy your own Access web apps. With the countless variations of platforms and configurations, there are unprecedented opportunities for security and other issues that you might encounter. To help you avoid and resolve such challenges, we have also provided a list of some of the potential issues you may encounter.

The chapters in Part II, "Client Server Design and Development," draw from resources far beyond the author team. We wanted to ensure that we addressed the needs of developers from a wide spectrum of expertise and industries. To that end, we enlisted the contributions of fellow MVPs from around the world. That culminated in providing you with tools, tips, techniques, and examples that incorporate the experience, style, and perspective of more than a dozen developers.

The emphasis is on creating cost-effective solutions based on real-world scenarios. The techniques in this book focus on rapid development, stability, and automation. They will help you to work more effectively with multiple data sources and integrate with other programs, leverage SQL Server, and deploy polished, professional solutions.

In addition to demonstrating how to enhance and work with Access's built-in features, we also discuss critical changes that may affect legacy programs — such as the deprecation of ADPs. Our book clearly communicates these changes and future alternatives so that developers and businesses can make informed decisions about how to move forward and how to maintain their applications when incorporating the new features.

This book encompasses thousands of hours of development, testing, writing, and reviews. We designed it to serve as a learning manual, a reference, and a means to expand your expertise that will pave the way to new opportunities. The more you use it, the greater your rewards.

WHO THIS BOOK IS FOR

Professional Access 2013 Programming is a complete guide to the latest tools and techniques for building Access 2013 applications for both the web and the desktop. The information and examples are structured so that developers and businesses can make decisions and move forward with confidence. Whether you want to expand your expertise with client-server deployments or start developing web apps, you will find this book to be an invaluable manual, companion, and reference.

Access 2013 web applications are completely new, so the material is new to everyone. The web section starts with the basic fundamentals and lays a strong foundation. The subsequent chapters then provide a step-by-step process to build the structure resulting in a robust web application.

In the client-server section, the premise is that readers have been using Access and have some familiarity with VBA, so we breeze through the fundamentals to provide a foundation and then quickly dig into features, development techniques, and examples that you can relate to. The emphasis is on cost-effective solutions that address rapid development, stability, working with multiple data sources, integration with other programs, automation, and leveraging SQL Server.

The book is also an informative guide for decision makers who are seeking to identify and evaluate available options to make informed decisions and invest in solutions that will support their current and anticipated needs. You will see solutions to real-world scenarios that have strong correlations to your activities and needs.

WHAT THIS BOOK COVERS

This book is the professional developer's resource for Access 2013 web apps and traditional client solutions. As the training manual and proving ground for Access 2013 web apps, this book shows you everything you need to immediately start developing new solutions, upgrading existing projects, and planning future enhancements. It uses real-world scenarios to demonstrate how to use Access to provide custom solutions — whether you are working with a traditional client-server, web, or hybrid application.

The book is structured to support the two major deployment environments for Access 2013: Web applications and the traditional client-server (desktop) solutions. But regardless of your current needs or focus, you will find invaluable tips and techniques in both sections.

In a nutshell, this book:

- Explores the new development environment for Access web apps
- Focuses on the tools and techniques for developing robust web applications

- Explains how to use macros to create solutions that will run in a web browser and perform tasks on SQL Server
- Discusses the Office Store and using it to monetize your apps
- Demonstrates how to use SQL Server effectively to support both web and client solutions and to synchronize data across multiple SQL Servers.
- Provides examples for adding professional polish to traditional desktop application development
- Shows you how to automate other programs using macros, VBA, API calls, and more
- Illustrates how to use data macros to simplify enforcement of business rules and automate data processing tasks. And it provides a tool for managing data macros
- Demonstrates features and techniques using real-world examples that can easily be modified and incorporated into your custom solutions
- Provides several full featured examples and databases that can easily be incorporated into your solutions

Part I: Access Web Application Design and Development

With Access 2013, Microsoft introduced a new architecture for authoring database applications that can be provisioned to the web. One major feature of the new architecture is that it's now based on SQL Server. This opens up many opportunities for developing robust, full-featured web applications, as well as a means of quickly creating prototypes that can easily become the foundation for the final solution.

The web section is targeted toward the professional developers and content experts who want to create a rich application that is focused on solving business problems. But at the same time, you want to avoid getting lost in the tedious plumbing that is typically involved in the traditional web development process.

A major challenge for people who are experienced with building powerful Access solutions is transitioning their current database design skills over to the web. The structure and code is just one aspect. Web apps also require a new approach to designing the user interface. This book facilitates the mental transition from traditional client development to web development. It focuses on building the conceptual foundation and points out the differences between the two approaches.

To help reinforce the concepts, the book incorporates a running example throughout the web section. The example uses a hypothetical professional maid services company that needs to efficiently manage the maids, customers, and jobs. As one of their tools, the maids use their tablets to record the progress and status of their jobs.

As you follow along, you will progressively build a full-featured application, adding ever richer functionalities. In addition to creating a functional solution, the example will help you envision the power of the Access web app and how it can be used to solve common business problems. For instance, you can make the application accessible to more than just internal users, such as a remote data entry operator or external partners.

Part II: Client Server Design and Development

The second section of the book is devoted to traditional client-server solutions, primarily using Access as the front end with Access or SQL Server as the data source. The emphasis is on providing you with tools and techniques to add the functionality and professional polish that you expect to find in a really great Access application. Each chapter includes several examples that you can easily incorporate into your existing or new Access solutions.

The client-server section is based on the premise that readers have some familiarity with Access and VBA, so after a brief introduction to build a foundation, each chapter quickly gets into features and development techniques. They introduce and demonstrate how to use the key features, and provide examples and tips that are fundamental to creating and deploying professional-caliber solutions. The emphasis is on helping you to provide cost-effective solutions that leverage Access's rapid development environment with multiple data sources, including Access, SQL Server, and other formats.

As you delve into SQL Server, you will learn how to use SQL Server Management Studio and SQL Server Migration Assistant. You will learn how to use T-SQL syntax and other techniques to effectively leverage SQL Server's features.

You will also learn how to integrate with and even automate other programs from Access. As you work through the examples, you will create documents in Word, Excel, Outlook, and PowerPoint. After that, you will use PKZip as a model to demonstrate how to automate non-Office programs.

In addition to examples and code in the book, you can download database files that contain full-featured forms and reports that provide key functionality to support real-world scenarios. You'll find intuitive search and filter forms that incorporate a variety of techniques and tools to enable users to specify criteria fields and grouping to customize reports. Among the standalone tools, you will receive a fully functioning solution that will fill in PDF forms with data stored in Access. Another program allows you to tap online resources to display maps and directions in Access forms, and there is a program to help you manage data macros across multiple database files.

Online Material

The book also has three "appendixes" available online at `www.wiley.com/go/proaccess2013prog.com` that are packed full of tips, functions, tools, and sample files as well as lists of time-saving shortcuts. These materials supplement and support the material in the chapters, by covering a wide spectrum of other topics, such as managing data, preventing duplicate records, using alternative approaches to form controls, and much more.

Professional Access 2013 Programming is a complete guide to the latest tools and techniques for building Access 2013 applications for both the web and desktop. As you will quickly discover, the book more than pays for itself with each use.

HOW THIS BOOK IS STRUCTURED

The following is a detailed chapter-by-chapter overview of what you can expect to find in this book. It is divided into two main parts, web apps and traditional client-server solutions. Chapters 1 through 14 introduce, explain, and walk through the steps to design and deploy an Access web application. Chapters 15 through 21 and three online "appendixes" delve into traditional client-server solutions.

In Chapter 1, you will review what has changed for Access 2013 and new features introduced to Access 2013. In addition, you will get an overview of Office 365 and how it makes SharePoint accessible for small businesses and how they can leverage the power of SharePoint without involving expensive IT resources. You learn how to create an Office 365 account as you follow the example in the web section.

In Chapters 2, 3, 4, and 5, you learn about the fundamental building blocks for creating new web apps. Casual users and professional developers will appreciate comprehensive coverage of the new architecture and information about how it will influence the design choices that may be made. You will learn about new paths that lead to successful development experience and identify paths that are fraught with roadblocks. The chapters also provide a good comparison and contrast with client design that may be familiar to you but may not translate to the new web architecture. The chapters are ordered in generally the same workflow that you will naturally follow when building new web apps, which differs from the typical order seen in developing client Access solutions.

Access development always starts with tables, so in Chapter 2 you learn about the deep integration of Access with SQL Server and how tables are built and represented in SQL Server. You will see how the new features such as Nouns and Import Data make it easier and faster to design new tables.

Once you've built the tables, you move to Chapter 3 where you start to explore the new interface. You will become familiar with the new design surface and begin to internalize the differences in designing and working with web apps as compared to the client database. You also learn about *Tiles* and *View Selectors*, which represent a new approach to navigation. You will quickly appreciate how Tiles and View Selectors greatly simplify the navigation with minimal effort.

Building on that orientation, Chapter 4 explores the new *views*, which are web counterparts to a traditional Access form. Once you are familiar with designing views, you will move to Chapter 5, where you will learn about queries and new functions. You will see how to use the expressions that you can now incorporate into your queries, controls, and macros.

In Chapter 6, you learn how to use the new Macro Designer and experience the process of creating macros. The emphasis is on helping you understand the nuances that can make a big difference in whether you have a productive design experience when building macros. You also learn about how data macros and UI macros differ, as well as how and when to leverage each.

In Chapters 7, 8, and 9, you begin to apply your new knowledge as you work with the new objects introduced in prior chapters to building more sophisticated solutions for different business problems. The chapters emphasize identifying common design patterns that you may have experienced in traditional Access development. The focus is on highlighting the design choices and ramifications, whether it's a familiar design pattern you've used in client applications or something new that works seamlessly with the new web app architecture.

In Chapter 7, you study the data types closely and learn more about how the tables are defined within SQL Server. You then explore the changes to validation rules and calculated types and learn how to use them to help solve business problems.

In Chapter 8, you concentrate on identifying efficient design principles. You then apply the principles to build an intuitive navigation system and learn how the new Tiles and View Selectors can be used efficiently in lieu of traditional popup forms. Using these web design principles, you will do a deep dive into building a full-featured query by form component. Mastering the concepts and techniques for building the query by form are pivotal to making the transition from the traditional client to the web approach. They provide the foundation for creating rich custom solutions.

As you proceed into Chapter 9, you will expand on those views by incorporating macros that simplify common workflows. You will see how to use macros to provide filtering and perform data operations.

In Chapters 10, 11, and 12, the focus shifts from working within the Access environment to looking at how the Access web app is provisioned on SharePoint using SQL Server as a back end. You'll also see how to integrate the data stored in the web app's database with other applications or processes. You will discover how to use tools from other programs, such as SQL Server and SharePoint, to create powerful solutions. Seeing the benefits will provide incentives for developers to gain competency with those tools and to leverage them in parallel with Access. With that in mind, the book covers the fundamentals to get you started. We supplement the material in the book by suggesting additional resources in these areas.

In Chapter 10, you learn about authoring solutions in SharePoint and SharePoint Designer and integrating the solutions with your Access apps. You will discover a new world of web services and APIs available to deliver rich content to your apps without requiring you to build a web application from the ground up. You will see how to integrate charting and also see how easy it can be to associate e-mails with database records.

The next step is to access the web app's database directly. In Chapter 11, you will see how you can use familiar tools such as the Access client or SQL Server Management Studio to manage the data and perform additional data operations against the database. You learn techniques to effectively access and query the data.

In Chapter 12, you learn how you can work with multiple web apps and how to create templates so that you can efficiently apply branding and standards as you are building new web apps. You also use an app catalog and document library.

In Chapters 13 and 14, you learn about web app security and deployment considerations, respectively. You will review how the architecture of web apps uses a completely different approach to security. You will see how to leverage SharePoint's built-in security to effectively manage access. You learn how to provide granular access for both web apps and Access client files that are linked to the web app database without sharing the password for linking.

You then learn about new avenues to distribute your web apps. In Chapter 14, you see how the new app architecture simplifies deployment, including how you can use the Office Store and app catalogs. You also learn some of the ways that you can implement version and upgrade options, as well as some of the ramifications. With this information and tools you should have a broad view of what you can expect to achieve with Access, and you can start building awesome Access web apps! Much of the content discussed in the web app chapters is also applicable to Access client solutions. And that provides a good transition to the next section of the book.

The Access client section starts by discussing techniques for connecting Access with data that is stored in other programs. In Chapter 15, you learn about using ODBC to connect and work with different external data sources, especially SQL Server, to harness the power of Access as a FE tool to provide data management and reporting. You also learn about the Extract, Transform, Load (ETL) process and how to use ETL to import data to your database. When the data is loaded, we show you how to clean and reformat the data to conform to the structure of the tables in your solution.

As you read through Chapter 16, you will learn to enhance your VBA code by creating User Defined Functions (UDF) to efficiently process and report data. There is also a database to demonstrate how to include robust error handling routines and to identify pending issues such as reoccurring errors. The demo includes a table for capturing the errors so that you can track, trend, correct, and prevent recurrences. There is also a discussion of the differences between 32-bit Access and 64-bit Access, including the modifications that will be required in your VBA code if you end up working with the 64-bit version of Access.

Chapter 16 also presents a variety of query techniques that you can use to manage and mine your data. It covers concepts such as *sargable* queries to leverage indexes and improve performance, and `Upsert` queries simultaneously insert and update data. You also learn how to use Query by Form (QBF) to let your users set the criteria for form and reports. And you can use the code in the sample database to learn how to construct the correct syntax and as a starting point for your own samples. You will see complex implementations of QBF in Chapters 17 and 18.

Chapter 16 then takes it a step further to show you how to use API calls to extend the reach of your VBA code, including how to pass *nulls*, how to use *scalable pointers*, and more. The final section of Chapter 16 expands on working with macros, especially data macros. This supplements the material in Chapters 6 and 8 on macros in the UI and using macros to implement business rules. You will also learn how to use macros to enforce data integrity, create an audit trail, and to provide actions comparable to SQL Server triggers.

Chapters 17 and 18 are all about the user interface forms and reports, respectively. They provide several examples and demo files that address real-world scenarios. Each chapter provides a basic foundation to the key concepts as well numerous techniques and tips that you can use to enhance the user experience and add professional polish to your database solutions. The download files include several powerful tools you can incorporate directly into your solutions.

As you go through the examples in Chapter 17, you will see several ways to work with image files and attachments. To consider this in a real-world scenario, the example discusses presenters and attendees at a conference. You will see how to add an image on a personal bio to provide information about a speaker. You see how to leverage the `datasheet` view to quickly provide a search form that allows users to open and compare several bios. And for the show-piece, we have created an impressive report customization tool that offers users the ability to tailor their reports to their individual needs. The user can specify which fields will have selection criteria, define the criteria, select the report format, and add custom report headers.

Chapter 18 starts by covering some of the fundamentals to build a foundation for the ensuing examples. You'll learn how to create multipurpose reports, how to use forms and reports as subreports, and how to incorporate both bound and unbound reports. The examples walk you through several common tasks, such as printing name badges, creating conference schedules, and customizing report criteria.

Chapters 17 and 18 include complex techniques that have been generously shared by our Access MVP colleagues. A couple of the more complex tools include the forms to allow users to create custom grouping for their reports, and the database that is used to fill in a PDF form using data from Access. You will find the tools and examples in the database files for the chapters.

Chapter 19 shows you how to automate other Office applications using menus, macros, VBA, and more. We begin with a discussion of Excel and demonstrate simple exports. Then we move on to the creation of pivot tables and charts, with the option of displaying them in Access forms and reports. Next, you see different ways to work with Word. After reviewing some basic approaches, you learn how to create a Word document with attractive formatting. The example walks you through the use of data from a table and the creation of a report in a Word document.

Chapter 19 then moves on to PowerPoint. You learn how to automate the process to incorporate data from Access into your PowerPoint presentations. You might use this to dynamically update narrative content, such as for an online training company, or to update project status reports. The example walks you through the process of creating and updating a presentation.

Chapter 19's final Office example works with Outlook. We begin by discussing how to send e-mail using macros or VBA, and then we explain how to automate your reading and moving of e-mail. You also learn how to create Tasks, Contacts, and Appointments from Access.

Chapter 19 wraps up with an example using a third-party program. With this, you learn how to automate PKZip to compress and decompress files. You can use similar techniques to automate other programs.

After you are done with development, you can use the content in Chapter 20 to learn how to deploy your database solution. You will review various methods of deployment and some of the available options, for both initial deployment and updating existing solutions. Among the techniques covered, you will learn how to use checksums and deploy updates to the back-end files. You will then complete the process by setting up an automated backup solution to provide a means of recovering from a disaster. The chapter includes several references to additional tools and resources.

In addition, your clients can benefit from securing and managing access to the database. In Chapter 20 you learn different methods for creating a security matrix to control what each user can do. You will also see how to customize a ribbon to match a security role. The sample database has the code to get you started in your own products.

Chapter 20 also explains how to use an audit trail to track changes to the data. You learn two methods, VBA and *data macros*, to capture the information you need to track. You can use the sample database for the audit trail to see how to implement the two methods.

Chapter 21 shows you when you need to upsize the database engine of your solution to SQL Server. It covers the various options that are available during the process as well as different ways to upsize. You will also learn about some of the issues that you should watch for when upsizing.

Chapter 21 also presents some of the fundamentals to help you work more effectively with SQL Server. The chapter goes through different objects available in SQL Server such as *views* (not to be confused with the views used in Access web apps in Chapters 4 and 7); Stored Procedures (SProcs); User-Defined Functions (UDF), which are also distinct from VBA UDFs as discussed in Chapter 16; triggers and more. In addition to learning about the tools, you will learn about some of the common issues you might encounter and some techniques that will help you troubleshoot your SQL Server database. You can use the chapter database to learn about and experiment with using SQL Server as data source.

Additionally, you learn how to leverage passthrough queries to utilize the processing power of the server for faster response time. You also learn the differences between T-SQL and Access SQL when composing queries, contrasting `IIF()` and `CASE`, and comparing concatenation characters such as `&` versus `+`. You will also be pleased to learn that as of SQL Server 2012, you can now use the `IIF()` function in SQL Server.

The three online "appendixes" are packed full of tips and demo databases that were generously shared by our Access MVP colleagues. Appendix A provides numerous tips to enhance forms and manage data. Examples include datasheet views, tab controls, and continuous forms. Additional discussions cover the use of bound and unbound forms, preventing duplicate data, and a few of the under-used built-in features. Plus, you'll see a few useful functions that can quickly be added to your solutions.

Appendix B provides a data macro tool that is nicely packaged in a database. The Data Macro Tools utility (DMT) provides an efficient way to manage and update data macros. This gives you an easy way to view and edit groups of data macros. The DMT also allows you to define standardized, reusable macros with XML and table fields for common macro tasks such as providing a timestamp or an audit trail.

Appendix C provides a comprehensive list of keyboard shortcuts that can be used to time and minimize errors. It also includes two short lists of our favorites: one for developers and one for users. The lists are also provided in a Word document so that you can easily customize the lists to share with your clients and users.

The examples and demo files are included in the download files for each chapter. You can easily use them to follow the processes described in each chapter. Plus, you can copy the objects and code into your files to quickly incorporate the techniques into your solutions.

WHAT YOU NEED TO USE THIS BOOK

If you are reading this book from the perspective of a decision maker who is seeking information, then you can gain a better understanding of the capabilities of Access web and client solutions by selectively reading or perusing the chapters. And you can supplement the examples and images by reviewing some of the online application templates and demos provided by Microsoft and others.

If you are an Access developer, all you need is Access 2013 to work through most of the examples in the Access client section of the book (Chapters 15–21). Of course, to follow the SQL Server example, you will need a version of SQL Server, but that doesn't mean that you have to purchase SQL Server. You can use SQL Server Express, Microsoft's free version. If you want to automate other programs, you need those programs as well.

Some of the examples demonstrate how to work with image files. For those examples to work as currently designed, you will need to store the images in the specified directory. Alternatively, you can store the images in the location of your choice and modify the path accordingly.

Also, if you want to learn about web apps as covered in the web section, you will need an Office 365 account or you will need to have access to an on-premises installation of SharePoint 2013 with Access Services 2013 enabled. However, this does not mean that you have to purchase Office 365. You can utilize Microsoft's offer for a free 30-day trial and select the Small Business Plan (P1).

It is important to note that not all Office 365 plans include the Access Services 2013. If you intend to follow along with the examples, you will also need to install SQL Server Management Studio and SharePoint Designer to work with some of the chapters. Again, these do not require a purchase as they are provided as a free download from Microsoft.

> **NOTE** *Please note that some network and security configurations may prevent the downloaded files from functioning as designed. This is most commonly associated with files that are downloaded from the Internet. In order for the functions to work properly, the files and the location need to be trusted and enabled. If you still have problems after enabling and trusting the files and locations, you might try copying the objects into a new container. Beyond that, you may need to consult with your help files, IT, or online resources.*

Additionally, working on the web presents numerous opportunities for security considerations to impact your ability to work effectively with Access web apps, as well as traditional Access databases. Some of the issues that might impact functionality include:

- In some organizations, JavaScript is not enabled; therefore, any web app or functionality that relies on JavaScript may not run.
- Some organizations place restrictions on the use of network resources. You may find that such limitations impact your ability to use or deploy Access solutions.
- In many organizations, end users are prohibited from installing programs or may be limited to a list of approved programs. This may impact you or your users' ability to use programs needed by a solution described in the book.
- Under Internet Explorer, you may need to add SharePoint sites to your local intranet group to allow some features, such as security, to work. Other web browsers may also have security settings that affect functionality.
- In order to sign into Office 365, invited external users need an account to which their credentials can be assigned. This is often a Microsoft account, but it can also be a

non-Microsoft account, such as Gmail. The account must be linked to a Live account or the equivalent.

- On Office 365, permissions for Account owners differ from those of other account users. This may create confusion and questions from users if they cannot find something. This may be due to lack of permissions and SharePoint may not make it clear that they lack the permissions.
- While Office 365 tends to perform well on most major browsers, your experience may vary based on the browser, versions, and settings. You can find additional information about browsers and other issues in Microsoft's statement regarding software requirements for Office 365 for Business at `http://office.microsoft.com/en-us/office365-suite-help/software-requirements-for-office-365-for-business-HA102817357.aspx`.

The source code for the samples is available for download from the Wrox website at:

```
www.wiley.com/go/proaccess2013prog.com
```

CONVENTIONS

To help you get the most from the text and keep track of what's happening, we've used a number of conventions throughout the book.

> **WARNING** *Warnings hold important, not-to-be-forgotten information that is directly relevant to the surrounding text.*

> **NOTE** *Notes indicates notes, tips, hints, tricks, or asides to the current discussion.*

As for styles in the text:

- We *italicize* new terms and important words when we introduce them.
- We show keyboard strokes like this: Ctrl+A.
- We show filenames, URLs, and code within the text like so: `persistence.properties`.
- We present code in two different ways:

```
We use a monofont type with no highlighting for most code examples.
```

`We use bold to emphasize code that's particularly important in the present context.`

SOURCE CODE

As you work through the examples in this book, you may choose either to type in all the code manually, or to use the source code files that accompany the book. All the source code used in this book is available for download. Specifically for this book, the code download is on the Download Code tab at:

`www.wiley.com/go/proaccess2013prog.com`

You can also search for the book at `www.wrox.com` by ISBN. A complete list of code downloads for all current Wrox books is available at `www.wrox.com/dynamic/books/download.aspx`.

Throughout each chapter, you'll find references to the names of code files as needed in listing titles or within the text.

Most of the code on `www.wrox.com` is compressed in a .ZIP, .RAR, or similar archive format appropriate to the platform. Once you download the code, just decompress it with your preferred compression tool.

ERRATA

We make every effort to ensure that there are no errors in the text or in the code. However, no one is perfect, and mistakes do occur. If you find an error in one of our books, such as a spelling mistake or faulty piece of code, we would be very grateful for your feedback. By sending in errata, you may save another reader hours of frustration, and at the same time you will be helping us provide even higher quality information.

To find the errata page for this book, go to:

`www.wiley.com/go/proaccess2013prog.com`

and click the Errata link. On this page, you can view all errata that has been submitted for this book and posted by Wrox editors.

If you don't spot "your" error on the Book Errata page, go to `www.wrox.com/contact/techsupport.shtml` and complete the form there to send us the error you have found. We'll check the information and, if appropriate, post a message to the book's errata page and fix the problem in subsequent editions of the book.

P2P.WROX.COM

For author and peer discussion, join the P2P forums at `http://p2p.wrox.com`. The forums are a web-based system for you to post messages concerning Wrox books and related technologies and interact with other readers and technology users. The forums offer a subscription feature to e-mail you topics of interest of your choosing when new posts are made to the forums. Wrox authors, editors, other industry experts, and your fellow readers are present on these forums.

At `http://p2p.wrox.com`, you will find a number of different forums that will help you, not only as you read this book, but also as you develop your own applications. To join the forums, just follow these steps:

1. Go to `http://p2p.wrox.com` and click the Register link.
2. Read the terms of use and click Agree.
3. Complete the required information to join, as well as any optional information you wish to provide, and click Submit.
4. You will receive an e-mail with information describing how to verify your account and complete the joining process.

> **NOTE** *You can read messages in the forums without joining P2P, but in order to post your own messages, you must join the forum.*

Once you join, you can post new messages and respond to messages other users post. You can read messages at any time on the web. If you would like to have new messages from a particular forum e-mailed to you, click the Subscribe to this Forum icon by the forum name in the forum listing.

For more information about how to use the Wrox P2P, be sure to read the P2P FAQs for answers to questions about how the forum software works, as well as many common questions specific to P2P and Wrox books. To read the FAQs, click the FAQ link on any P2P page.

PART I

Access Web Application Design and Development

1

Introduction to Access Web Apps and Architecture

WHAT'S IN THIS CHAPTER?

- Defining an app
- Examining how apps are structured
- Identifying methods for distributing apps
- Listing deprecated components and new tools

With the release of Office 2013, Microsoft introduced major changes to the Office architecture, and Access is no exception. To make Office more accessible to an increasing number and variety of users, devices, and platforms, Microsoft continues to expand, provisioning Office "in the cloud" with an emphasis on making a seamless transition when running on different devices. One major frustration with traditional hosted environments has been that you had to accept everything out of the box; custom applications or code might not run in a hosted environment or might run only in a restricted mode. New to SharePoint 2013 and Office 2013, the *Cloud App Model* (subsequently referred to as *app* in this book) is Microsoft's answer to the longstanding problem of enabling people to write and create custom solutions that can run in the cloud without the usual complexities that come with a client installation. With the new model, we now can create a new app, which is essentially a web application that has been prepared and packaged in a specific way. Apps can take many different forms, but essentially they are all web pages containing custom code and content that is integrated into Office, typically using Office 365. Access 2013 can create an app that can be used in the cloud. In this chapter, you'll learn how the new app architecture can allow you to distribute, deploy, and integrate custom solutions.

First, you will quickly review what has changed in Access 2013, starting with features that have been deprecated. Then you'll move into the anatomy of an app, and wrap up with a brief look at how an Access web app functions.

DEPRECATED COMPONENTS

As with every new release, one of your first tasks is to review the possible impacts on existing Access solutions and tools if they are migrated to or integrated into environments using the new version. Features that depend on deprecated components will typically need to be modified in order for the application to work using Access 2013. The following discussion identifies the components that were deprecated for Access 2013 and offers suggestions to accommodate the changes.

With the vast quantity of legacy files being used for storing data, it can be helpful to know what features are deprecated or compatible with each new release. The `.accdb` file format was introduced with Access 2007 so the lists will start with that release. The following lists are for your convenience and to assist with troubleshooting and converting files.

The following features are no longer available, as of Access 2007:

- *Designing* Data Access Pages (DAPs)
- Microsoft Office XP Web Components
- Replication
- User-Level Security and Workgroup Administrator
- The UI for import and export of older file formats

The following features are no longer available as of Access 2010:

- *Opening* Data Access Pages (DAPs)
- Snapshot format for report output
- Calendar control (`mscal.ocx`)
- ISAM support, including Paradox, Lotus 1-2-3, and Jet 2.x or older
- Replication Conflict Viewer

The following features are no longer available as of Access 2013, and each is discussed further in this section:

- Access Data Projects (`.adp`)
- Jet Replication
- Menus and Toolbars
- Import/Export/Link to Jet 3.x and dBASE files

- PivotTables and PivotCharts
- Collect Data via E-mail
- SharePoint Workflow
- Source Code Control Extension
- Packaging Wizard
- Upsizing Wizard
- Creating Access Web Databases

Access Data Projects

Introduced in Access 2000, the Access Data Project (`.adp`) file format allowed for Access solutions to be built with SQL Server, bypassing the Jet engine entirely. The `.adp` file format also enabled you to create and edit SQL Server objects (for example, tables, views, and stored procedures) within Access. Unfortunately, the object designers were version-dependent; if the SQL Server instance to which the `.adp` connected was upgraded to a later version, Access Designer for those objects would no longer function and it was necessary to use T-SQL to edit those objects. Moreover, `.adp` uses OLEDB and ADO to connect with SQL Server, and SQL Server 2012 is the first version to start deprecating OLEDB as a first-class provider. Microsoft now recommends ODBC instead of OLEDB. Since the release of Access 2007, Microsoft recommends creating new Access solutions using the `.accdb` file format rather than the `.adp` file format. In Access 2010, there was no quick button to create a new `.adp` file format. While we believe that a SQL Server back end for an Access solution is a wonderful combination, the combination is best delivered via the linked table method made available in both `.mdb` and `.accdb` file formats. It's better to design the Access solution with server-client architecture from the start. In the second half of this book, we will look into this architecture more deeply. Furthermore, the new Access web apps, which we will discuss, are now based on SQL Server; so in a sense, Access web apps can be said to be a more modern replacement for the `.adp` file format. We will also look at how this is achieved in the first half of the book.

For those wanting to migrate an `.adp` file, we recommend that you start from scratch in an `.accdb` file format; import the forms, reports, and modules; and then create linked tables referencing the tables and views in SQL Server. Refitting the code will be necessary to get the forms and reports to work correctly in the `.accdb` file format. Keep in mind that you can continue to use ADO as the connection technology in `.accdb`, but because forms default to DAO, it will be necessary to write the code needed to bind a form to an ADO recordset. For reports, passthrough queries will be the recommended method for binding a report to a SQL Server object output. Modules require review and may require modifications to verify that the code will function correctly, especially for those depending on an `.adp`-specific context such as the `CurrentProject.Connection` object.

Jet Replication

Since the introduction of the `.accdb` file format in Access 2007, Microsoft has been recommending against creating new Access solutions based on Jet Replication. The new `.accdb` file format did not support Jet Replication. However, Access 2007 and Access 2010 did continue to support Access solutions that used the `.mdb` file format and Jet Replication. Access 2013 ends this support entirely. Jet Replication is a technology that allows for offline synchronization of data and was more relevant when Internet availability and speed were not as good as today. However, the effort required to manage a replicated Access database usually made it quite daunting and required considerable specialized knowledge. Furthermore, with the new `.accdb` file format and SharePoint integration, working offline using SharePoint lists is much simpler and requires none of the administrative work that Jet Replication required. Thus, if you have a solution that uses Jet Replication, we recommend that you look at SharePoint lists as replacements for providing offline synchronization of the data, and remove the replication from the Access file prior to upgrading to Access 2013.

Menus and Toolbars

Since Office 2007, Microsoft has moved away from menus and toolbars and has largely replaced them with ribbons. In prior versions of Access, it was possible to create custom menus and toolbars that could then be added to an Access solution. Access 2007 and 2010 continued to support the use of those custom menus and toolbars by displaying them in the ribbon's Add-Ins tab. Alternatively, by hiding the ribbon, you could get the original menu back. However, it was awkward and not without problems.

Access 2013 no longer supports displaying menus and toolbars from older versions, though you can continue to import the legacy menus and toolbars with the understanding that they can only be used via the ribbon's Add-Ins tab. You can continue to use shortcut menus as always. For those who rely on custom menus and toolbars, here are a few recommendations:

- Customize the ribbon.
- Create macros to create your shortcut menus and/or create the shortcut menus programmatically. Refer to *Ribbon X: Customizing the Office 2007 Ribbon* (Wiley Publishing, Inc., 2008) for the details the details on creating a shortcut menu.
- Create controls on your forms to provide the needed navigation in lieu of the ribbon.

Any of these recommendations will work and, if appropriate, may be mixed and matched. Only you can decide what is best for migrating your Access solutions with custom menus and toolbars. Figure 1-1 shows the Customize Ribbon pane in Access 2013.

Since Access 2010, creating custom ribbons has been much easier because there are two panes: Customize Ribbon pane and Customize Quick Access Toolbar pane; in the Access Options, which also supports importing and exporting of the customization. You can use the import/export functionality to quickly build the ribbon as you need it, and then either fine-tune the resulting XML or put it into the ribbon table so that at distribution your users get the ribbon just as you specified it.

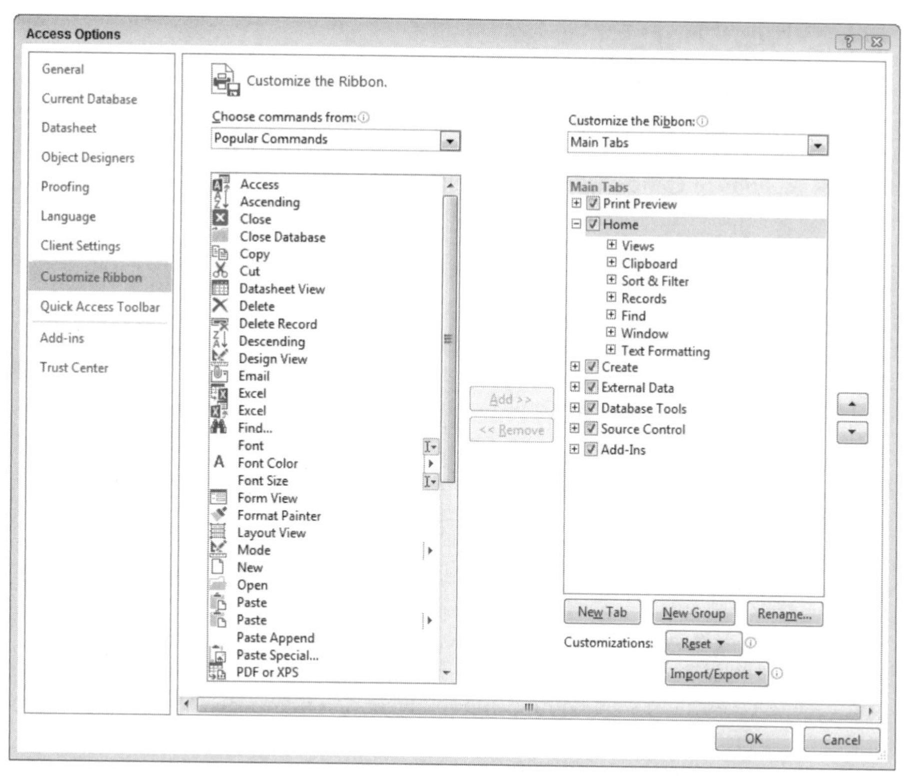

FIGURE 1-1: Customize the Ribbon pane

Import/Export/Link to Jet 3.x and dBASE Files

In Access 2010, we saw deprecation for support of Jet 2.x (Access 2.0 `.mdb` file format), Lotus 1-2-3, and Paradox files. Those were removed as those formats were quite old and rarely used. Likewise, use of Jet 3.x files (Access 95 and 97 `.mdb` file format) and dBASE has dwindled and thus does not merit continued support. As was the case in Access 2010, if you have files of those types, we recommend that you upgrade them using a previous version of Access that still supports importing/exporting from those file formats. This will enable you to complete the upgrade to Access 2013. If you do not have a previous version of Access available to you, the alternative is to export the source file using the original program into another file format, such as text file or Excel spreadsheet, which Access 2013 still supports for import and/or linking operations.

> **NOTE** *For cases where you need to use an* `.mdb` *file based on Jet 3.x or earlier and do not need to use Access, an option to consider is to use Jet 4.0, which is usually already installed with the Windows operating system, to open the database. You could then use DAO automation and a private* `DBEngine` *object to upgrade the file or access the data.*

PivotTables and PivotCharts

In previous versions, Access forms could be configured to show data in PivotTable and/or PivotChart view, which was effective for displaying multi-dimensional data or for rendering aggregated data in a visual manner. Both relied on Microsoft Office Web Components, which has already been deprecated in previous versions of Office. Excel has since refined and enhanced its PivotTable/PivotChart capabilities, but those enhancements aren't available to Access directly.

To upgrade Access solutions that make use of PivotTables or PivotCharts, you have two possible approaches:

1. Add an ActiveX control referencing "Microsoft Office XX.0 PivotTable" and/or "Microsoft Office XX.0 Chart" where XX.0 may be either 10.0 or 11.0, and update all VBA references to PivotTable/PivotChart events and properties from the form to the added ActiveX control.
2. Instead of rendering the data in Access, automate Excel to build a PivotTable and/or PivotChart and use Office Data connection to enable Excel to query the data directly from the source table/queries.

Collect Data via E-mail

Introduced in Access 2007, this feature made it possible to build an e-mail template based on a table, send e-mail requests out to recipients, process their replies via Outlook, and convert the replies into rows in the table. While it seemed like a good idea when it was introduced, this feature required that the e-mail be formatted as HTML, or created as an InfoPath form. Also, it generally worked best with Microsoft Outlook. These limitations made it impractical for situations where you had no control over whether the e-mail would be viewed as HTML or text, or over which e-mail client would be used.

If your Access solution requires input from external users, we generally recommend that you make use of a service that can provide web pages for filling out and submitting data to you. One good example of such a service is `www.surveymonkey.com`. This service is more accessible in the sense that you need only send people a link to the survey URL. They can use their favorite web browser to fill in their responses, and you can extract the data out of a downloaded Excel spreadsheet.

Furthermore, there is no guarantee that you need only a single table to store the responses; normalization may require multiple tables for a single "survey." For this reason, you would still have to transform the responses, whether you were using the Collect Data via Email feature or a linked Excel spreadsheet.

SharePoint Workflow

In Access 2007, as part of enhanced integration with SharePoint, it was also possible for Access to initiate a SharePoint workflow that was associated with a SharePoint list. Figure 1-2 demonstrates how to start a new workflow in Access 2010.

However, adoption of workflows was not easy because the programmability was quite limited, required that you work in SharePoint or use associated tools such as SharePoint Designer rather than Access, and called for considerable knowledge of how SharePoint Workflow works.

Furthermore, there were no events to facilitate scripting actions when a workflow was started, progressed, and finished. For those reasons, the adoption of Workflow has been slow.

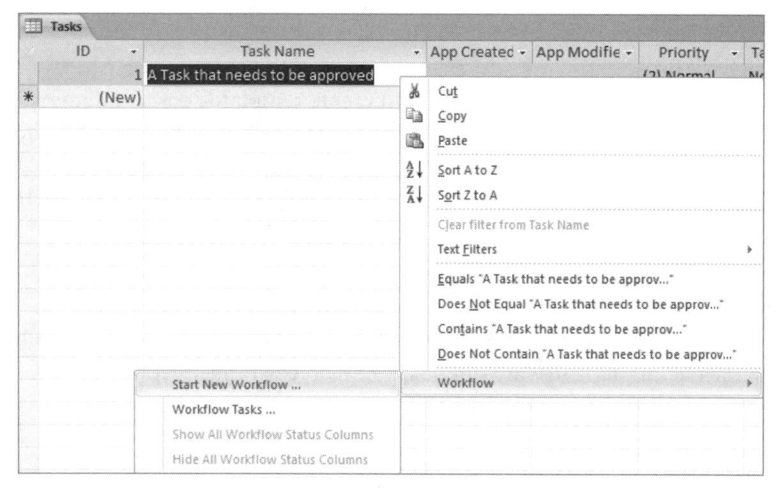

FIGURE 1-2: Starting a new workflow in Access 2010

For those who use workflows, better solutions can be discovered via two possible workarounds:

1. Use forms and VBA to perform the work that was done by the workflow. VBA is fully capable of performing automation (for example, generating a report, creating and sending an e-mail) and is more flexible than SharePoint Workflow, which is scripted using a flowchart.
2. Use table event macros to perform a custom action based on insert/update/deletion of data.

Source Code Control Extension

Access has long supported the Microsoft Source Code Control Interface (MSSCCI), which allowed Access to work with source code control client applications such as Visual SourceSafe, Team Foundation Server, and several other third-party software packages, providing control over the source code in your databases. The source control model has not changed much. It is based on a locking model where one must first obtain an exclusive lock on an Access object before editing it. Because Access Form objects and Report objects are technically binary objects, it is not possible for two or more developers to edit the same Form objects or Report objects concurrently. Only VBA modules can be edited concurrently. The source code control model has since evolved to support a merging model as well as decentralized repositories.

If you want to migrate to Access 2013 and continue to use source code control, then you should adopt an approach that involves manually exporting and importing Form and Report objects as text using the undocumented `SaveAsText` and `LoadFromText` methods. You would then perform the update/commit activities in the filesystem rather than within Access.

Alternatively, you could explore using plugins that do not rely on MSSCCI and automate the `SaveAsText/LoadFromText` process for you. OASIS-SVN, a commercial product is one example of such a plugin that can be used in Access 2013.

Packaging Wizard

Since Access 2007, it has been easier to create an installer to distribute easy installs of custom Access solutions to users. The Packaging Wizard can be used to create templates describing how to build a Windows installer that incorporates the source Access files, additional files needed for the application, and any registry entries that needed to be set. Furthermore, the Packaging Wizard can create a bootstrapper to determine whether the Access Runtime is installed on the target computer, and if not, to download it from the web.

In theory, this seemed like a godsend, but in practice, complex Access solutions were usually the ones that needed an installer. More often than not, a solution would require installation of additional components, something that the Packaging Wizard did not help with. Thus, it was still necessary to obtain a third-party packaging software application. Choices ranged from freeware, such as Inno Setup, to high-end InstallShield, to developer-centric Wix.

BOOTSTRAPPER AND SETUP.EXE

When installing software, people instinctively know to go for a `setup.exe` file. However, they may not realize they are actually running a bootstrapper. Windows Installer (aka `.msi` files) is not able to determine the prerequisites, download the needed files, verify privileges, and so forth. For this reason, a small executable is needed to "bootstrap" the install by performing those tasks before executing the `.msi` files to perform the actual installation.

Upsizing Wizard

In earlier versions of Access, Microsoft developed the Upsizing Wizard to make it easier to transform Access tables into SQL Server tables. This provided an easy-to-use GUI for selecting tables and specifying additional options that should be performed when the tables were upsized. However, the Upsizing Wizard has not been updated for several versions. In the interim, a new tool, called SQL Server Migration Assistant for Access (SSMA), was introduced and has matured into a powerful tool for not simply uploading, but also transforming several Access-specific options such as the Allow Zero Length property, into their SQL Server analogues. Furthermore, SSMA also makes intelligent recommendations on what changes may be needed, such as adding a `rowversion` column to tables that may benefit from having one.

> **ROWVERSION BY ANY OTHER NAME...**
>
> In earlier versions of SQL Server, the data type was called `timestamp` but that term is quite confusing because it does not reference an actual timestamp but rather identifies when a version of the row was updated relative to the creation of the database. Since SQL Server 2005, this data type has been called `rowversion`, which accurately describes its functionality. Unfortunately, even into SQL Server 2012, SQL Server Management Studio's designer and scripting continue to use the older term `timestamp` even though Microsoft has stated that it is deprecated and will be removed in future versions of SQL Server.

Because SSMA is a far more modern solution, there is no reason to continue to use the Upsizing Wizard. SSMA can be downloaded for free from the Microsoft download center. Alternatively, as you will discover later in this book, Access web apps make it very easy to import Access data into SQL Server tables without the configuration steps that either SSMA or the Uploading Wizard required of you.

Creating Access Web Databases

Access 2010 introduced us to Access web databases. Web databases are still supported in Access 2013 and can be opened and edited just like in 2010. However, to encourage people to use the new app architecture, Microsoft does not provide a way to create a new web database in Access 2013. As Figure 1-3 shows, you can work around this limitation by creating a new web database via a SharePoint site, but we feel that you'll find that the new format in Access 2013 has more to offer than Access 2010 web databases did. Note that the availability is contingent on whether the SharePoint farm has the Access 2010 Services running.

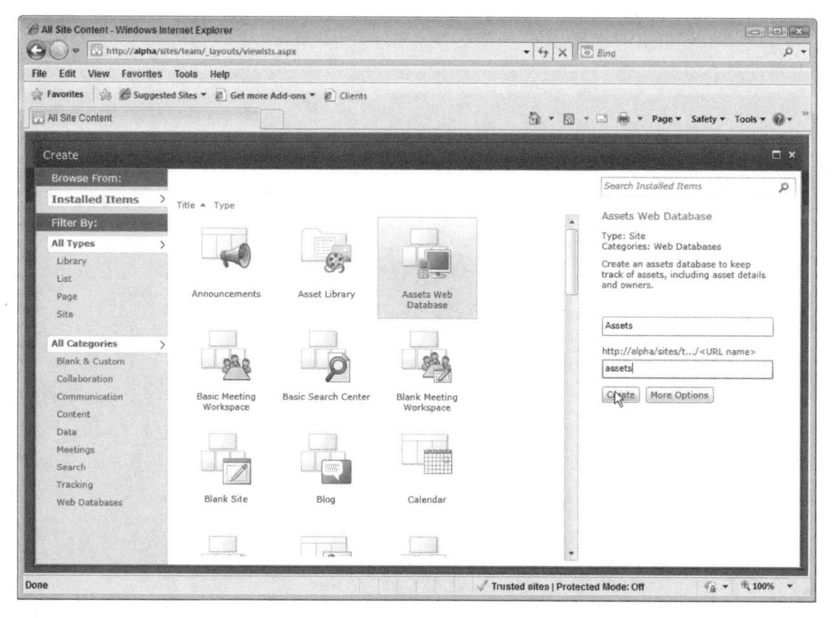

FIGURE 1-3: Creating a 2010-style web database in SharePoint 2013

NEW COMPONENTS ADDED

While the first part of this book will focus on Access web apps, we want to point out new additions to Access that are also relevant to Access solutions migrating from previous Access versions. Microsoft has emphasized strengthening the manageability of both Access databases and Excel spreadsheets. Because these are files, they have a tendency to proliferate. An organization can easily find itself awash in hundreds, if not thousands, of Excel and Access files, and not just different files but also multiple versions of the same file. Even if you don't suffer from file management challenges, the new 2013 tools may prove beneficial for managing your Access solutions. Two are most relevant to Access: the Database Compare tool and the Audit and Control Management Server.

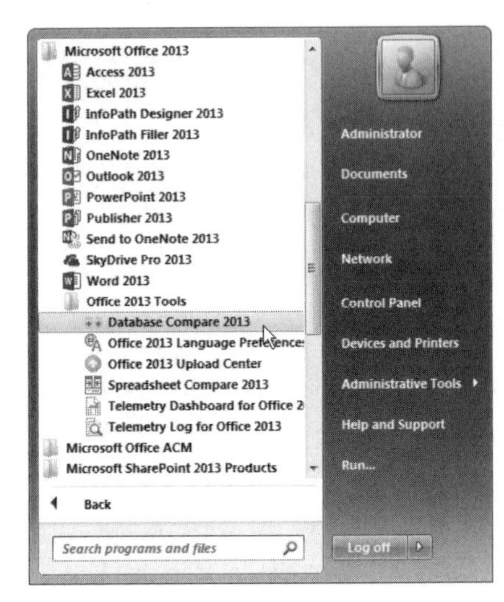

FIGURE 1-4: Database Compare

Database Compare

To help address the common problem of identifying what has changed in two similar Access desktop files, Microsoft has introduced Database Compare, as shown in Figure 1-4.

It is common to copy Access solutions as part of distribution; however, opening an Access file immediately changes its last modified timestamp. This can lead to confusion when trying to identify the latest version. To alleviate this problem, we can now turn to the Database Compare tool, which allows us to compare two Access files. In Figure 1-5, you can choose which type of objects to compare and the desired level of granularity.

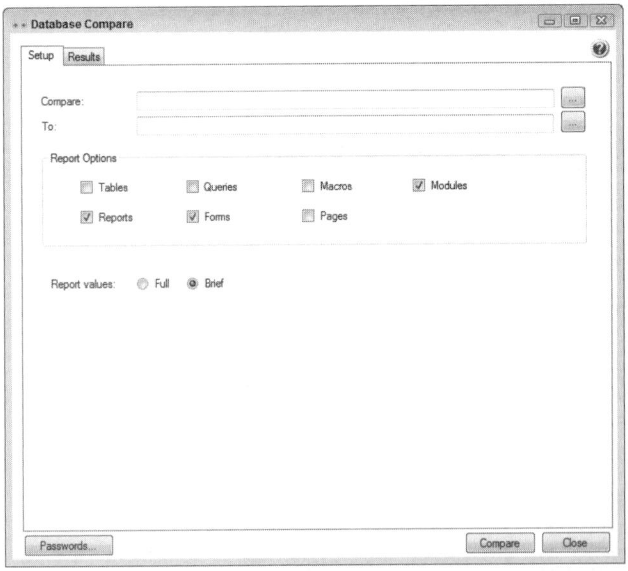

FIGURE 1-5: Selection screen

Once the comparer has finished the analysis, you get a report listing all differences. With this, you can quickly zero in on the changes and ensure that all desired updates are included in your final selection.

Audit and Control Management Server

For organizations with large numbers of Access and/or Excel solutions, Audit and Control Management (ACM) Server can be very useful in tracking the usage of Access and Excel solutions organization-wide, and Figure 1-6 provides an idea of what it can do.

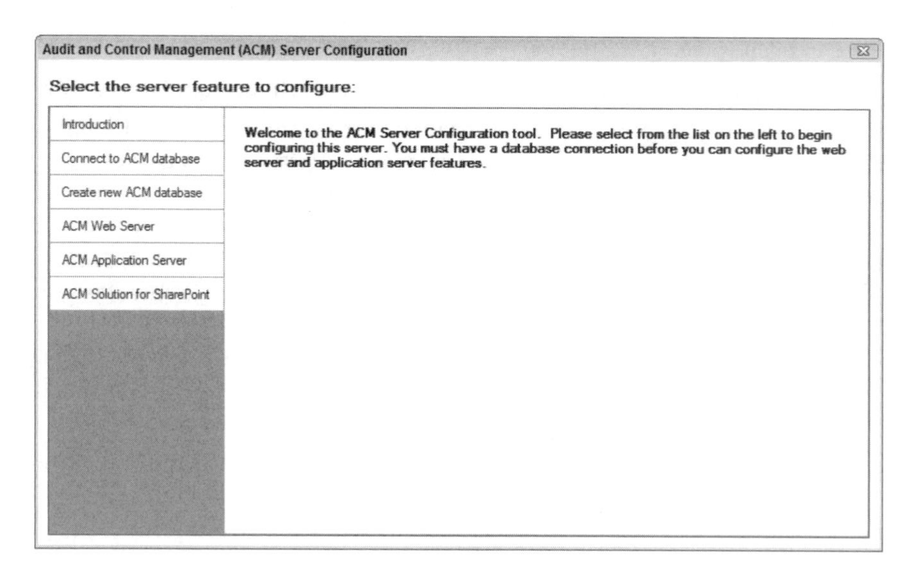

FIGURE 1-6: Audit and Control Management Server

ACM Server will provide data on when the file was last used and how often it was used, which can be useful in supporting decisions about organizing the files and whether that activity requires additional support. ACM Server is available on certain Office 365 plans and Office 2013 Professional Plus.

WHAT IS AN APP?

Having reviewed the deprecated features and new components added to Access 2013, you are now ready to explore the underlying foundation that enables you to use Access in a web browser. Understanding the foundation will be beneficial in assessing and identifying appropriate solutions for deploying and distributing Access web apps.

As noted at the start of the chapter, a longstanding problem with a hosted environment is that customization is inherently limited or even outright banned. This is a regrettable, but logical, conclusion when we consider that the overriding requirement is maintaining a stable hosted environment that won't go down when someone introduces a custom solution that doesn't work as expected.

But this is not the only problem the app architecture is intended to solve. With mobile devices becoming more widespread, it can be a daunting task to create an application that can be consumed on a wide variety of hardware, operating systems, and software.

Many mobile devices come with their own specialized repository, commonly referred to as an *app store*, for distributing, downloading, or purchasing applications. The advantages of such repositories are numerous. For one, consumers can have some level of assurance that the application listed in the repository has at least been reviewed and deemed safe for use. For another, the process of buying and acquiring an application is greatly simplified in this environment — there is a single process to check out and pay for the applications. This eliminates the uncertainty inherent in entering into a transaction with an unknown merchant. Furthermore, distribution and installation are now as simple as downloading and deploying.

Another problem that app architecture attempts to solve is to make the melding of disparate business needs easier. In a given organization, it is likely that you use several different software packages, and other types of solutions in different languages, that may perform one business function very well. But suppose you need to integrate those business processes? What if you had QuickBooks for accounting, but you need to be able to get the relevant transaction information out of a SQL Server database for a web order? The usual approach has been to find the appropriate bridge, such as ODBC for QuickBooks, or maybe custom scripting, or one of many other possible solutions. The common factor in these solutions is that they are one-time glue, are not easy to reuse for other similar problems, and don't necessarily scale well. It can be quite frustrating when an organization is constantly refining its processes but does not want to dedicate resources for significant software engineering required to achieve specific tasks.

You are probably very much aware that this is why Access works so well on a worker's desktop; it makes it very easy to perform common automation. This is what Microsoft expects to achieve with Access web apps in a web browser.

To help unify this experience for Office applications, Microsoft will use the app architecture, along with the Office Store, to facilitate cross-platform distribution and in the process simplify development greatly.

There are two major classes of apps:

1. Apps for SharePoint
2. Apps for Office

Let's consider Apps for Office first. They are akin to Add-Ins, with which you are probably familiar. However, their major advantage is that Apps for Office are written in JavaScript and render their output as HTML5, meaning they will work on any platform, including Office Web Apps. Apps for Office are, by definition, client-side scripting and can be used to extend or enrich a document. For example, a Word document could have an app to render a page from Wikipedia with additional content regarding a word used in the document.

Because Apps for Office already come with a means of distribution and deployment, the process is greatly simplified in comparison to the steps required to distribute an Add-In for Office. Installing an Add-In would potentially require elevated privileges and additional components such as Visual Studio Tools for Office runtime and other dependencies. In contrast, an App for Office is simple to install — whether it's free or not — and distribution and installation is all done via Office Store and/or App Catalog. Furthermore, Apps for Office enable some object model access so they can be used to perform some simple automation tasks.

In the preceding introduction to the current environment for Access and the new app architecture, you should have gained some insight into why apps are potentially exciting. However, we should be clear on what you are going to be doing. Although Access is an Office product, it does not generate Apps for Office; it actually generates Apps for SharePoint, which we will now examine in detail.

Apps for SharePoint have all the functionality we've discussed regarding Apps for Office and, in addition, can have server-side code written and executed as part of the process. Because apps integrate into SharePoint, we have a rich environment that enables us to focus on solving business problems, rather than getting all the plumbing done as you would need to do when patching together disparate software. An app can be designed to work with SharePoint, other apps, and even Apps for Office.

HOW IS AN APP HOSTED?

There are three different models for an App for SharePoint. In the first two, the app has server-side code. For simpler cases where there is no custom code, the app can be hosted entirely within SharePoint. Like Apps for Office, HTML5 and JavaScript are used with the SharePoint client libraries to provide the functionality in the app. SharePoint provides a safe sandbox for those apps, called "app web." Suppose we have a SharePoint farm with the address `http://contoso.com`, or, perhaps a hosted O365 site with the address `http://contoso.sharepoint.com`, and we install an App for SharePoint named "SuperCalc." The URL for web hosting the app may then end up as: `http://app-XXXXXXXXXXXXXX.appcatalog.contoso.com/` or `http://app-XXXXXXXXXXXXXX.contoso.sharepoint.com` where the Xs are strings of hexadecimal characters randomly generated when the app is provisioned. We'll look into what this means for security later in the chapter.

> **NOTE** *Note that for some environments, SharePoint administrators can customize the location of the app and therefore provide custom prefixes and a different domain to store the apps, so the URL may be formed differently than shown in the book. However, in all cases, each app will get its own unique URL no matter what SharePoint environment it has been provisioned to.*

When an App for SharePoint contains custom code, you can choose between auto-hosted or provider-hosted models. When an app is "auto-hosted," SharePoint will deploy the needed components using Windows Azure Web Sites and/or SQL Azure.

With a provider-hosted model, your organization provides a dedicated server that the app can reach to execute custom code outside the SharePoint environment, in similar fashion to how we would use a remote web service. Of course, you can mix the models, such as by using ASP.NET hosted on your server to execute custom action based on inputs from a SQL Azure database (an auto-hosted component).

In the context of Access web apps, however, there is no custom code, at least not in the usual sense of writing lines of instructions in your preferred language. All custom code you will author for an Access web app is in the form of macros. Even so, an Access web app technically does generate custom code, usually by converting macros into T-SQL objects (for example, stored procedures or views). It hosts the data in a SQL Server database. Because of its dependency on a separate SQL Server database, an Access web app falls in the category of an auto-hosted App for SharePoint.

For those needing more customizations beyond what macros can provide, Access web apps also support the web browser control introduced in Access 2010. The web browser control enables consumption of additional apps or other web components, which you'll learn about in later chapters. For those who choose to run SharePoint on-premises or subscribe to dedicated hosting services where you have access to the SQL Server used to store Access web apps, you may choose to perform additional customizations in T-SQL directly. Obviously, such customizations would be unsupported by Microsoft, and they would not be practical for a hosted environment. We briefly look at those options later in the book as well.

HOW IS AN APP DISTRIBUTED?

As we alluded to in earlier discussions, app architecture helps simplify distribution by building the channels of distribution into the architecture so you don't have to worry about figuring out how to distribute an app and deal with a plethora of installer problems such as overcoming antivirus programs, getting all dependencies right, and numerous other complications.

App Marketplace for Publicly Available Solutions

Let's start with public distribution. Learning from the success of application repositories for mobile devices, Microsoft will be providing an Office Store, hosted at `http://office.microsoft.com/store/`. Instead of having to host your own website, manipulating search engines to get good rankings, and marketing your app, you can place your app in the Office Store. That greatly simplifies the effort to get exposure for your app. Instead of scouring the entire Internet for potential buyers who may or may not have Office 2013, you can focus your marketing on people who already have Office 2013 and later and thus can take advantage of app architecture in your solution. Furthermore, it is possible to set up licensing arrangements, which helps enormously in simplifying the transaction made between your potential buyers (if you choose to sell an app) and yourself. Thus, the Office Store provides you with new opportunities to monetize, or at least popularize, your solutions with much less effort.

App Catalogs for Internal-Facing Solutions

You are no doubt familiar with the fact that many available Access solutions are not designed to be public-facing; they're rarely meant to be used by the public, but rather by employees or other "insiders" in an organization. For organizations that wish to manage internal-facing apps, SharePoint can provide an internal repository called an App Catalog. A SharePoint administrator can deploy App Catalogs, which then become repositories for installing apps to any site within the

SharePoint farm. This is useful in ensuring that you don't clutter the farm with apps that may not be applicable to everyone but may be needed by more than one site.

App Catalogs can also function as a mechanism for requesting apps from an Office Store. In cases where a given app requires payment, it is more likely that the person wanting the app isn't the same person signing the checks for the organization. Or perhaps the app is free but the administrators would prefer to review and evaluate whether the app is appropriate for the internal App Catalog. In this case, the person submits a request, which queues the app for review by administrators. Once review is completed, the app approved, and the licensing fee, if any, is paid, the app from the Marketplace becomes available on the App Catalog for internal consumption. Furthermore, the App Catalog can also function as a licensing server for apps that have a licensing model based on per-seat or per-site, enabling the organization to optimize assignment of the app.

On the other hand, creating an app doesn't always require presence of an App Catalog or going to the Office Store. When you want to use the app for a single site out of an entire farm (or entire Internet), you can just create an app directly on the site. SharePoint Document Libraries, SharePoint Custom Lists, Access web apps, and many more are examples of apps that do not need to go through an App Catalog or Office Store because you can create them directly on your SharePoint site, as demonstrated in Figure 1-7 and Figure 1-8.

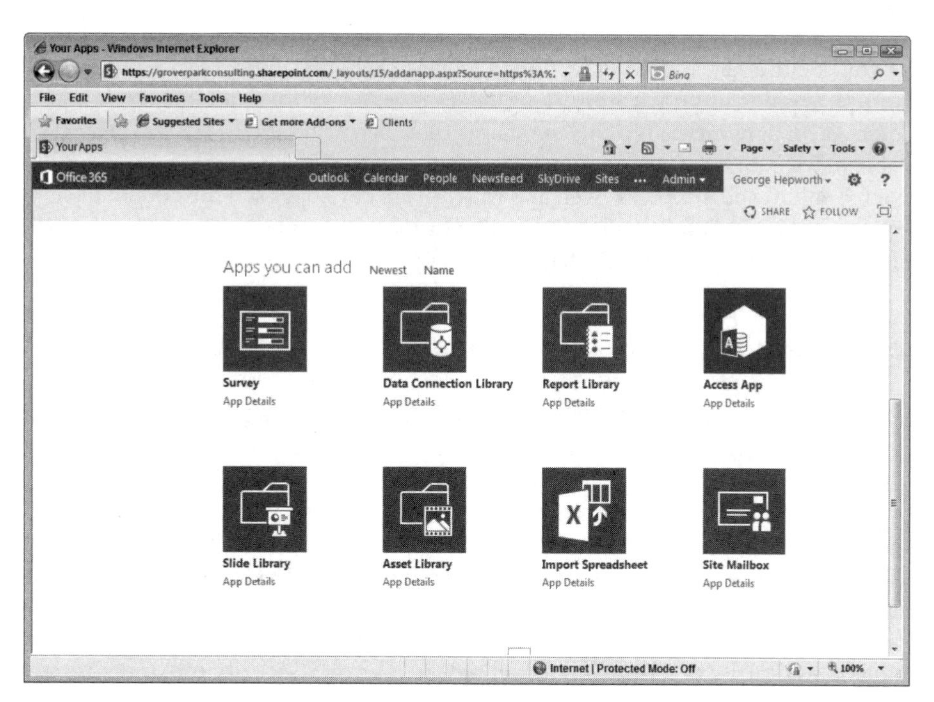

FIGURE 1-7: Creating an app via the SharePoint Site Contents page

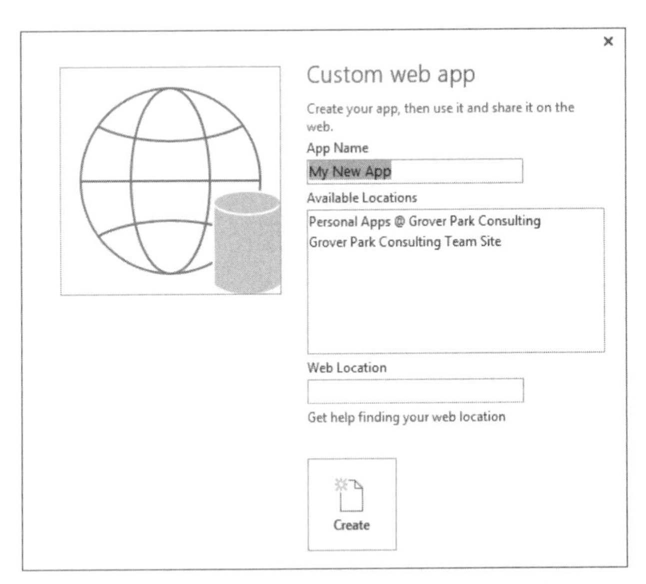

FIGURE 1-8: Creating an Access web app in Access 2013

By default, when you create a new app in Access 2013, you are actually adding a new app without going through an App Catalog or Office Store. This makes it very easy for you to deploy a new app. However, the downside of apps created in this manner is that there is no lifecycle management. If you want to be able to back up, perform upgrades, or monitor usage in various sites, then it may be more desirable for you to add an Access web app to a private developer site for development and then add the subsequent App Package to an App Catalog or the Marketplace. We will explore the issues surrounding lifecycle management in Chapter 14.

HOW ARE SECURITY AND TRUST MANAGED IN APPS?

One major enhancement SharePoint 2010 introduced to client libraries was that authentication was totally abstracted away. As long as you had a reference to a context object variable in the code, the authentication was already taken care of. Before you even get to run any SharePoint component, you have to log in, which establishes the security context. Because of this, there is no need to explicitly initiate an authentication process when invoking a web service within SharePoint. This continues into SharePoint 2013 and the new app architecture. SharePoint itself is very versatile in supporting different methods for authenticating users into the farm. A full discussion of different authentication protocols supported by SharePoint is beyond the scope of this book. However, it is sufficient to know that you do not necessarily need to plan on rolling out your own security for your Access web apps. In fact, you will need to resist the temptation to carry over the habit of rolling out your own access control from traditional Access development and get used to relying on SharePoint to provide the security context. In later chapters, we examine how you can effectively leverage the user context in SharePoint to provide access control and thus secure your Access web app.

However, our story does not end with merely authenticating the users. You also need to authenticate the app itself. Because an App for SharePoint may require additional privileges so it can interact with the rest of a SharePoint farm, it may be necessary to make an explicit trust to grant the app sufficient permissions to access other parts of SharePoint. Access web apps are no exception as you can see in Figure 1-9.

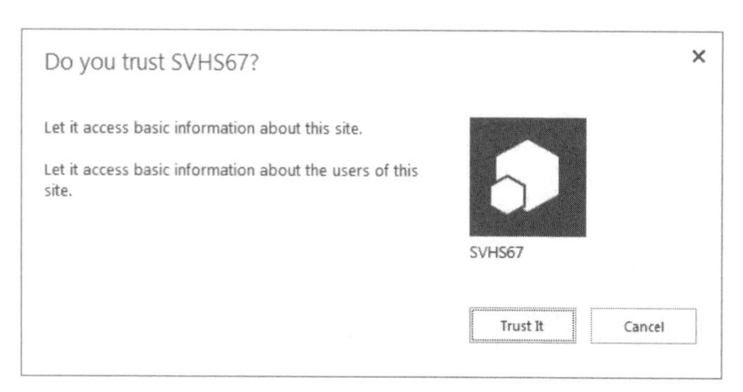

FIGURE 1-9: Trusting an Access web app

Typically, an Access web app needs to be able to access information about the SharePoint site to which it has been published, and to get information about the users of the site, as shown in Figure 1-9. Thus, installing an Access web app will require explicit trust. This step adds a layer of protection in that you will always know what an app needs to function, and you can decide if it is a reasonable request, especially when dealing with third-party apps. This provides a bit more transparency in contrast to traditional installer software, which is a black box in contrast. With a traditional installer, it was hard to know exactly what was installed. With the extra transparency, it becomes easier for administrators to make informed decisions, which is beneficial for you as Access developers interested in distributing an app.

In the preceding sections, you looked at different hosting models. We should make it explicit that there is a reason the hosting model is largely governed by what custom code is involved in an app. For a complex app, where reviewing the custom code can be difficult, providing a dedicated server apart from the SharePoint farm guarantees that custom code does not execute on the hosted SharePoint farm. An explicit trust decision is required when adding a provider-hosted app. Another enhancement introduced into apps is support for OAuth. OAuth is an open standard for authentication that allows servers to trust a user based on credentials provided by a specified third-party. OAuth also enables cross-domain authentication, which expands the reach of an app. If you need to invoke an external web service in a different domain without raising red flags, this can provide you with the means to build a secure app that is easy to trust without having to package everything in one monolithic domain. We hope this illustrates how app architecture makes manageability of custom solutions much easier.

Setting Up a SharePoint Site for Your Apps

As you just learned, Access web apps are not like Access desktop files, which are primarily under the developer's control. An app is not a file that you create and save on your local hard drive or network share. It is a web application created on the SharePoint platform and stored within the SQL Server database. Consequently, there is no way to create a new Access web app without access to a SharePoint 2013 server. Furthermore, SharePoint 2013 must be running the Access Services 2013 service application to enable creation of new Access web apps.

So, before we move on to discuss the specifics of creating web apps, let's take a quick look at some of the prerequisites when using the SharePoint 2013 server.

For small businesses, buying a SharePoint license is rarely practical. A much better solution is to consider a hosted environment. Microsoft offers Office 365, which is SharePoint hosted by Microsoft and can support Access web app solutions. There may be third-party hosting solutions available as well.

> **NOTE** *All Office 365 plans support Access, which means you can obtain a license to run Access 2013 and use your traditional Access solutions (i.e., client databases) with Access 2013 from Office 365. But if you want to host Access web apps on Office 365, then you must select a plan such as:*
>
> - *Office 365 Small Business Premium*
> - *Office 365 ProPlus*
> - *Office 365 Enterprise*
>
> *There may be other plans available. For up to date listings, refer to the Technet Article, "SharePoint Online Service Description"* at `http://technet.microsoft.com/en-us/library/jj819267.aspx`.

The move to a hosted environment, especially for application development tasks, can be a stumbling block for experienced Access developers who have frequently found themselves working outside the scope of the IT department. Frequently, Access solutions arise out of the necessity to meet a departmental need in the absence of IT department support or because of the inability of IT to respond to and act on business needs in a timely manner. Access web apps require involvement of an IT team, whether directly as an internal department or as support from a hosting provider in order to administer the SharePoint server. This is a profound change in the role played by many Access developers, so you should understand why this is happening.

Traditionally, Excel workbooks and Access databases have been problematic for IT departments. With Excel and Access files, there are many questions that IT departments cannot readily answer:

- Which version(s) of a given document is current?
- How many people use those documents?
- How are those documents secured?

Without answers to these questions, it's practically impossible to effectively manage the documents and assess what is required to provide adequate support. All too often, IT departments cannot budget sufficient funds to projects that need it the most, cannot prioritize projects properly, and so on. Microsoft is trying to solve manageability problems like these with enhancements in Office 2013 Apps.

Now, if you're thinking, "But those are enterprise problems; my clients are small businesses, and if they're lucky enough to have an IT department, it's probably a one-person department," you certainly are not alone. When you assess what a typical Access solution requires in terms of IT resources, it's rare that it's something that can be correctly implemented by non-IT personnel. For example, the best practice for sharing an Access desktop file is to split it, place the back end on a network share, and deploy a copy of the front end to each user's desktop. This requires some planning and configuration. If, like most Access developers, you're getting new clients today who are still sharing unsplit Access files among their users, that should indicate the problem is not trivial. Furthermore, it doesn't end at splitting; once the Access database is split, you must deal with the problems of distributing updates, making changes safely, maintaining backups, and more.

More important, users are no longer confined to a physical office. More and more people are working outside an office for various reasons. In the past, the solution to the problem of the traveling salesman was to use Jet Replication. However, replication certainly was not something that could be configured with a click of a button. It required even more careful planning and considerable expertise to deploy successfully.

Cross-platform usage is still another consideration. More people expect to be able to use an application on different platforms, so you can no longer assume you can count on a Windows-only solution. To address that requirement, Access web apps are based on HTML5 and JavaScript, which are accessible to a wide variety of hardware and operating systems, and thus you can build an application that can be used on any device — from a smartphone to a standard desktop computer.

Microsoft's answer for those small business owners who can't justify having an IT department, or even a full time IT person, is Office 365. Small business owners can shift the responsibility for securing, backing up, and managing their IT resources from themselves to Microsoft by signing up for a subscription service on Office 365. The Office 365 service is not limited to Access web apps; it also enables managing of Excel and Word documents. This helps make Office documents accessible to any authenticated and authorized user on any device. In addition, complex installation that would come with an on-premise SharePoint Server is abstracted away. Office 365 is meant to completely change how a small business manages its IT resources. Although the focus in this book is on Access web apps, the scope of Office 365 itself is not limited to Access solutions.

Setting Up an Office 365 Trial Account

For those who want to use Office 365 to host their Access web apps, the following section may be useful in getting a new Office 365 plan set up quickly. While the details of customizing and configuring Office 365 are beyond the scope of this book, these instructions will be useful when you want to follow the examples in the book to build your own Access web app. Those who already have access to an on-premises SharePoint server, an Office 365 plan, or another hosted provider can skip to the next section. Note that the specific steps provided may change as Microsoft frequently updates their site.

1. Using your preferred web browser, go to `http://office.microsoft.com/`.
2. Click Try it for free as shown in Figure 1-10.
3. Click the Try now link, as shown in Figure 1-11.
4. Enter the required information on the page.

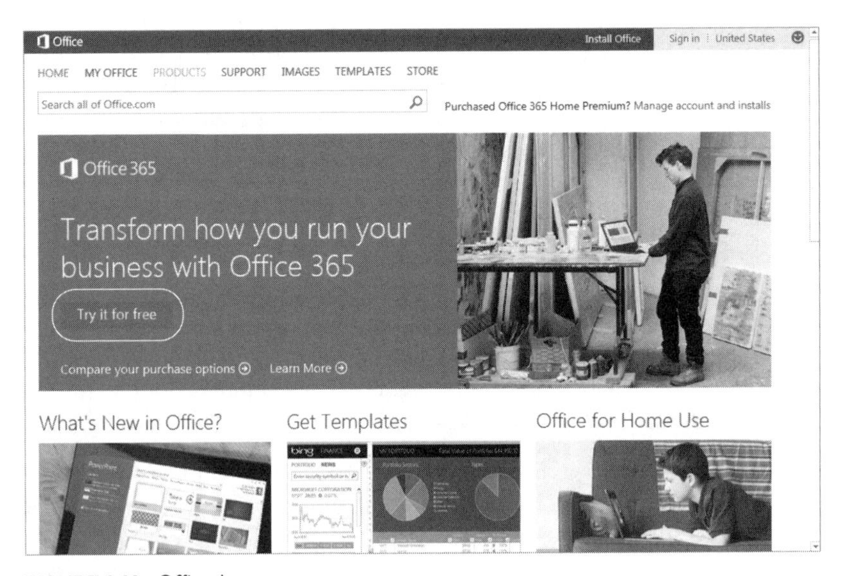

FIGURE 1-10: Office homepage

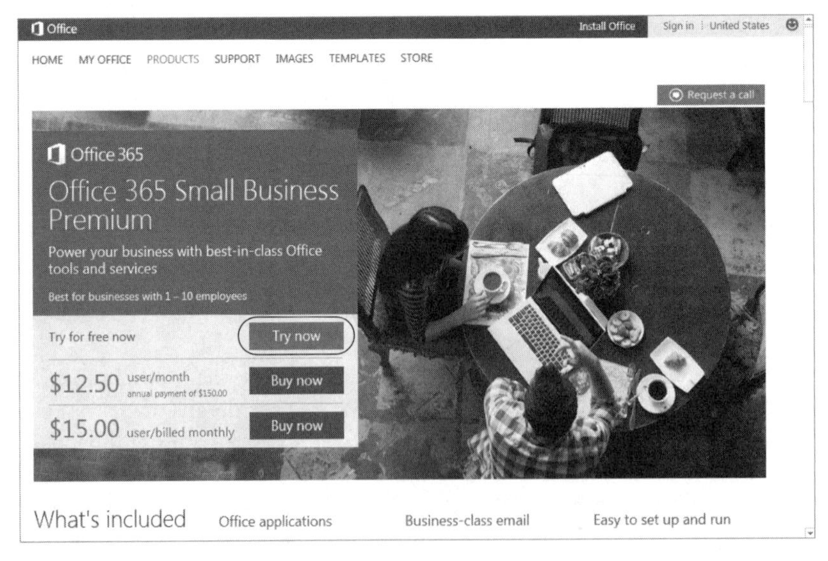

FIGURE 1-11: Trial page

> **NOTE** *You need to be aware of the difference in how e-mail addresses and site addresses are handled on Office 365. When you choose an organization ID such as "RedBarn," your e-mail address to sign into Office 365 will be* `yourname@redbarn.onmicrosoft.com`.
>
> *However, your Office 365 site, where your Access web apps would be discovered, would be hosted at* `www.redbarn.sharepoint.com`. *Don't be confused by this difference. Of course, it is possible to customize your e-mail address and site URL, but that is beyond the scope of this book.*
>
> *Furthermore, if you are using Windows 8, and your Windows login is linked to a Microsoft account such as a Hotmail account, the steps may differ because your Microsoft account already has you linked.*

5. Click create my account.
6. You'll be signed in and asked to provide a mobile number and e-mail address to which a forgotten login or password can be sent. Enter a mobile phone number (it must accept text messages) and the e-mail if not already filled in, and click Save and continue.
7. Click software.
8. Click Set up your software link. Ensure Office is selected so you see a page as depicted in Figure 1-12.

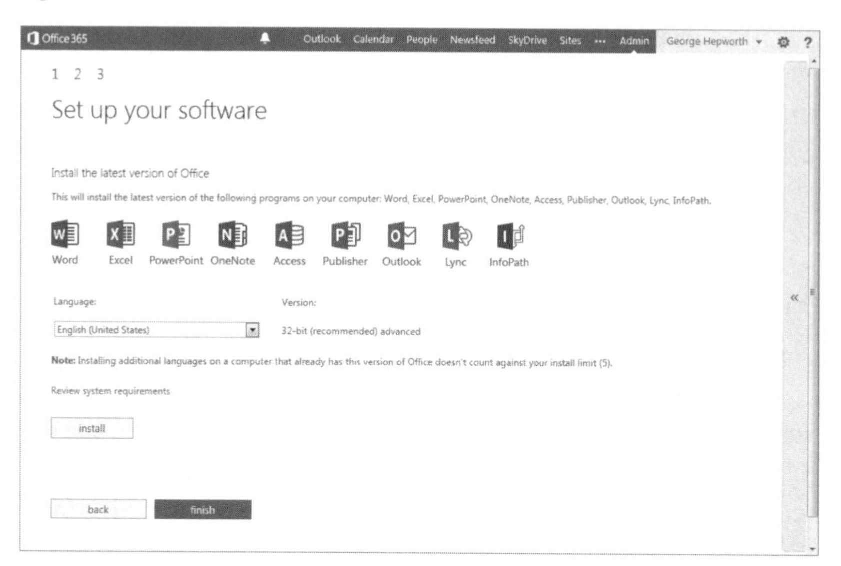

FIGURE 1-12: Office download page

9. You may need to wait until Office is ready. When you see an install button, click it.

Office installer will start streaming applications to you. Wait until you see Access 2013 listed in your Start menu. Then you're ready to create new Access web apps.

In the next chapter, where you learn about creating web apps and tables, you'll rely on the information you just learned here.

SOLVING BUSINESS PROBLEMS

Because we believe a sample application is a good way to introduce you to creating Access web apps, we'll have you build one to solve a real-world business problem and use it to illustrate the components of the web app as we discuss them. The following is a summary of the purpose of the database that you will build throughout the book. The complete app, `MaidToOrder.app` is available for download.

THE MAID TO ORDER WORK SCHEDULE DATABASE

Maid To Order is a ficitional private company that provides cleaning and maintenance services to commercial and private clients throughout its geographic region. Teams of professionally trained Maid To Order cleaners visit client sites to provide cleaning services contracted by the client. You will build a database application that supports the following features:

- Maid To Order managers will use the Work Schedule database to manage staff assignments and client requests.
- Maid To Order cleaning staff will use the Work Schedule database to stay informed of their assignments and report on completion of their assignments.
- Maid To Order customers will use the Work Schedule database to request and schedule cleaning services.
- The Maid To Order Work Schedule Database will support these requirements through both an in-house database and a web app via browser or mobile devices.

At appropriate points in the discussion, you'll learn the details of the database requirements and specifications. You will then learn how to complete the steps required to build the application.

SUMMARY

This chapter began with a review of the changes that Access 2013 introduced, starting with features that were deprecated and other features that were added. It also looked at the new tools included with Office 2013 to help effectively manage large numbers of Access solutions. You then turned to the anatomy of an app and looked at how it helps solve several problems encountered in traditional client and web solutions. You considered the channels of distribution available to apps, from the Marketplace for public distribution to App Catalogs for organizations.

The chapter concluded with an overview of security and trust for apps. With this information, you should now have a solid overview of the foundation Access web apps are built on, which will be very relevant in our subsequent discussions on building an Access web app. In the next five chapters, you will become familiar with basic operations in the new architecture, such as creating tables and queries that are different from client counterparts and identifying the difference. In subsequent chapters, you will look at building a complete solution. In the next chapter, you will learn how to create tables in and for Access web environments and how that differs from traditional table creation for client databases.

2

Designing Tables

WHAT'S IN THIS CHAPTER?

- Reviewing the new process of creating tables
- Using Nouns
- Importing from external sources
- Linking SharePoint lists
- Identifying changes in data types

One major change Microsoft introduced in the new Access web app architecture is that the tables for each app are contained in a SQL Server database created exclusively for that app. Because of that tight linkage between the app and the database, the structure and design of Access web app tables need to have one-one parity with SQL Server tables. In the past, when you linked to SQL Server tables from an Access client solution, you would have to account for differences between SQL Server and the JET/ACE database engine. This is no longer the case in an Access web app, which means you need to know how things have changed so you can use the SQL Server tables to their best advantage.

Another thing Microsoft introduced in Access web apps was the ability to quickly create commonly used tables for a new app. This new functionality is called "Nouns." The idea behind Nouns is that common entities — such as people — have common attributes such as first name, last name, and date of birth, which are frequently a part of a table. Instead of searching for an existing Access file template from which to retrieve prebuilt tables, or building common tables from scratch, you can select templates for tables by Nouns that reference them. For example, you can use a people noun to add a new table representing people. With that table set up for you, you can quickly customize the table to the particular solution needed for the current app, perhaps adding a field or two for particular attributes needed in that app.

You still have the ability to create tables as you have in the past; Nouns are available in addition to the traditional methods of creating tables. You'll get a chance to try out both methods in this chapter. But first, you need to create the web app into which the tables will be inserted.

In Chapter 1, you had a quick overview of the steps required to set up and configure your Office 365 account; refer back to that section if you need a refresher before continuing with the task of creating tables for your first new app.

CREATING A BLANK APP

Once you have access to a SharePoint server account, whether on-premises or in a hosted environment, you can create a new blank Access web app using the following steps:

1. Launch the Access 2013 client program.
2. Click Custom web app as shown in Figure 2-1.

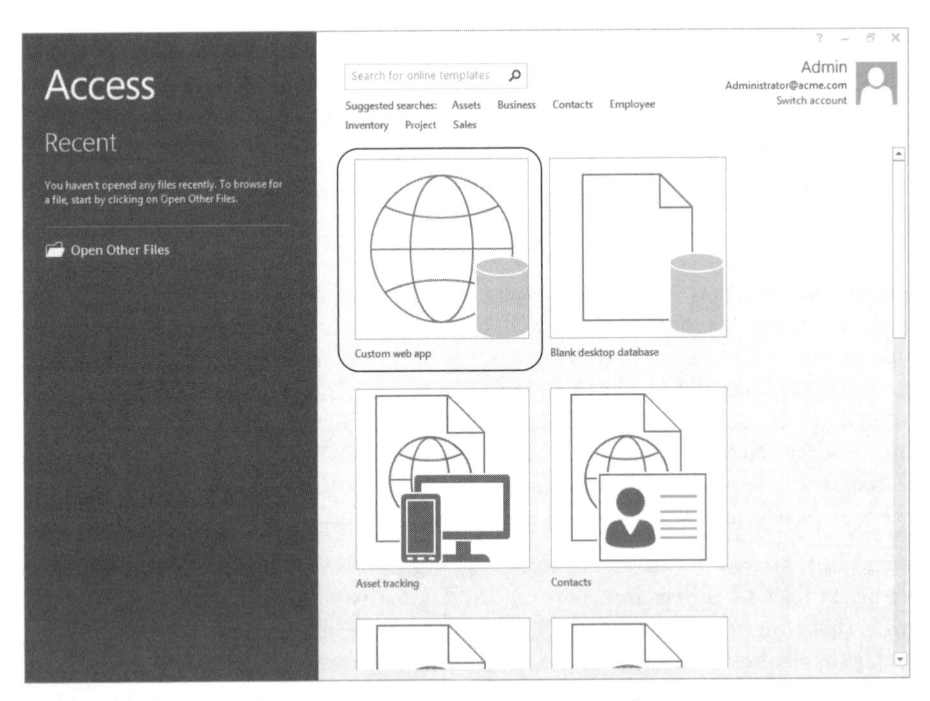

FIGURE 2-1: Custom web app

3. Name the new app as shown in Figure 2-2.
4. Enter the URL of a SharePoint site where you have permission to create new apps.

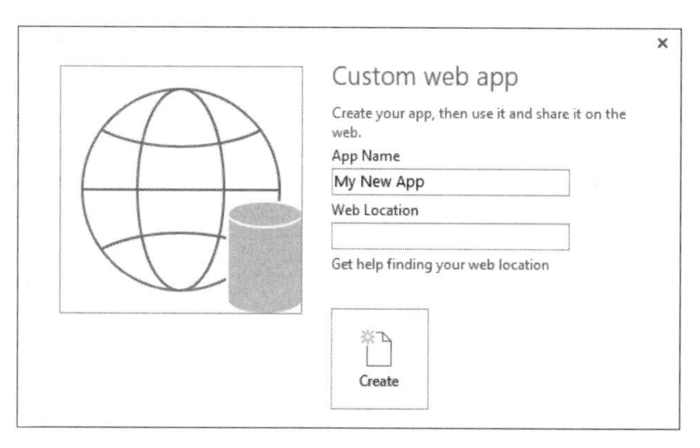

FIGURE 2-2: Custom app dialog box

5. If prompted, provide the login information needed to connect to your SharePoint account.

This will present you with a new blank app and you can get started building apps. We will turn to creating tables next.

KEEPING YOUR LOG INS STRAIGHT

Note that when you use an Office 365 plan to host your Access web app, the login will be different from what you would see for an on-premises SharePoint server. Instead of using your login for your Windows machine, you need to use the Live ID or Organization profile assigned to you for the SharePoint account. If you set up an Office 365 trial account as described in the previous section, you would use your Organization Profile and enter the e-mail address that you created during the Office 365 setup.

If you want Access 2013 to remember the site URL used to create Access web apps, you need to ensure that you are already signed in before you create a new blank app. To do this:

1. Launch the Access 2013 client program.
2. At the opening screen, select a SharePoint Account to use by clicking the link in the upper-right corner, as shown in Figure 2-3.
3. Figure 2-4 shows where Access offers you a choice between two types of accounts: personal or organization (work or school). You'll use the latter to create an Access web app. Most of the time, you will use organization accounts; if you created your Office 365 account, you created an organization account as part of the setup.

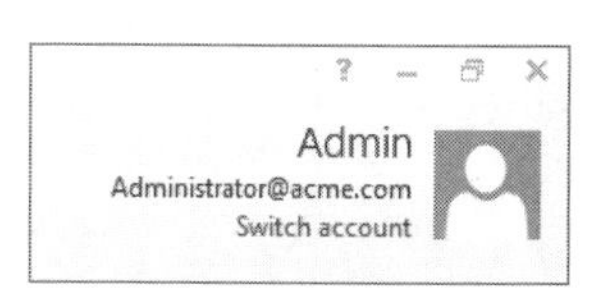

FIGURE 2-3: Signing into an existing account

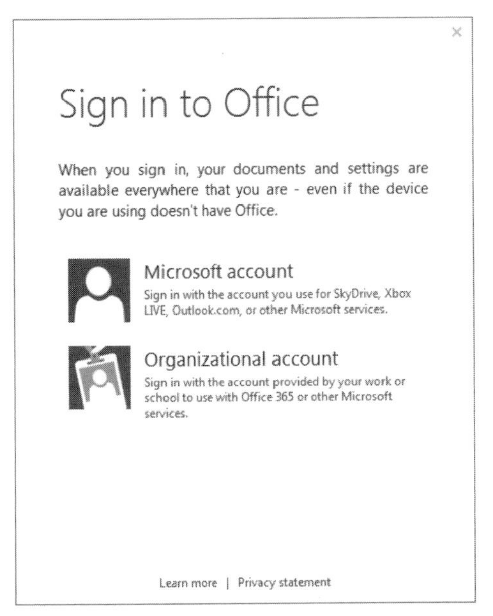

FIGURE 2-4: Selecting the account type

FIGURE 2-5: Entering and saving credentials

4. Enter your credentials and click "Sign in," as shown in Figure 2-5. Make sure you select the option to keep yourself logged in.
5. Once you are logged into your account, you can create a new web app, using the icon for Custom web apps illustrated in Figure 2-6.

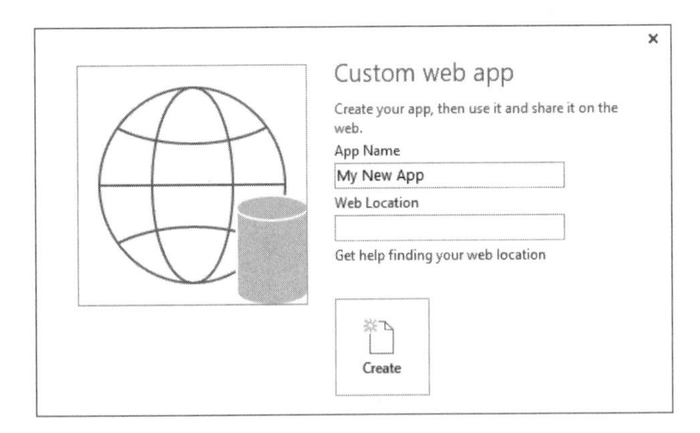

FIGURE 2-6: Creating a custom web app

6. You need to give your new web app a name and tell Access where to store it (see Figure 2-7). App names can't be changed, so choose carefully at this step.

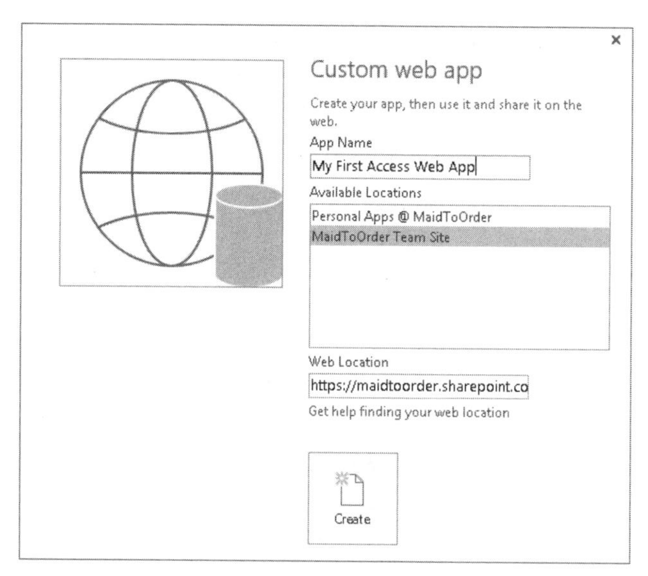

FIGURE 2-7: Naming your app and selecting a storage location

You can save your app to a Personal Apps location or to a Team Site. The choice of locations depends, in part, on whether and how you want to share the app. Saving it to a Personal Apps location makes it available to you through your Personal Apps location which is accessible via the SkyDrive. Saving it to your Team Site allows you to manage it as an app for members of your Team Site. The latter makes more sense for the majority of business apps.

With your new app created, you're ready to create tables for it.

CREATING TABLES

Once Access has created the app for you, you are ready to start creating your tables. In the following section, you will look at three primary methods of creating tables and how you can best leverage them:

1. Using Nouns
2. Importing from external data sources
3. Creating a blank table

You will then see other tasks Access also performs in the process of creating tables.

Creating Tables Using Nouns

Microsoft has added a new feature, Nouns, to help speed up creation of common table designs; the idea is that you use Nouns to describe what a table should be and you get a listing of possible table templates with fields prepopulated. When you have a blank app, you will be presented with an

Add Table page, where you can enter noun(s). When you enter a noun, you will get a listing of possible Nouns, or table templates, that will match the noun you searched on. As you can see in Figure 2-8, there are four broad Noun categories suggested underneath the search box.

1. Person
2. Order
3. Service
4. Sell

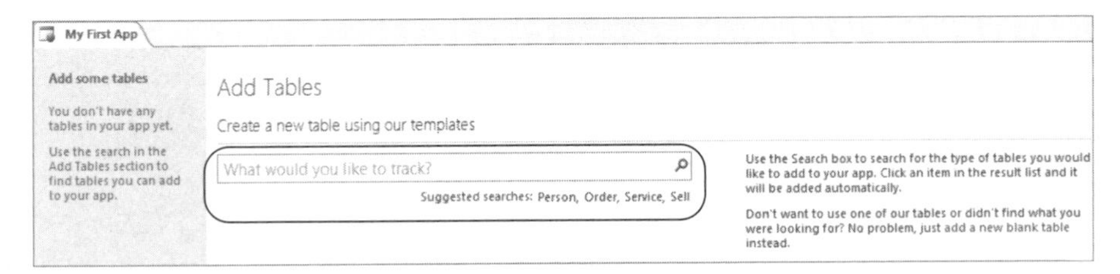

FIGURE 2-8: Using Nouns to create tables

Clicking one of the Noun links opens a drop-down list of more specific Nouns, as shown in Figure 2-9.

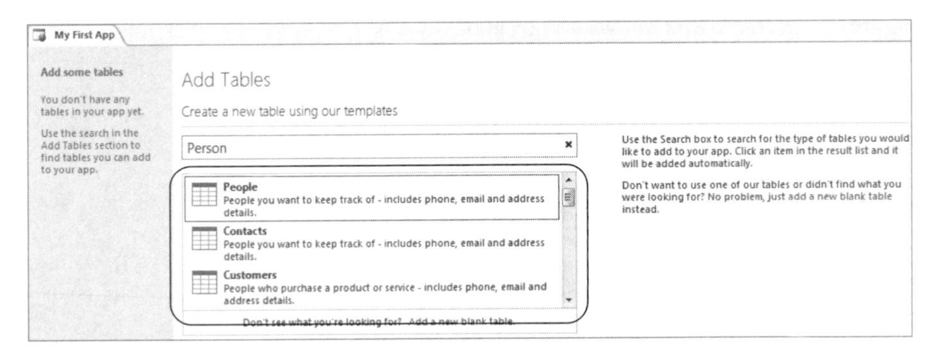

FIGURE 2-9: Selecting specific Nouns

Nouns are not limited to the four categories offered on the start page. For example, you can enter **Real Estate**, which will then list tables that have some similarities pertaining to real estate management such as **Properties**, **Tenants**, and so forth.

Nouns and Their Attributes

The basic attributes for each Noun are the same. In many cases, only the name of the resulting table is different. Therefore, it's important to plan ahead for the tables you need. It would be very easy to create overlapping tables, such as People, Employees, and Vendors, all of which contained identical fields. Your experience developing relational databases with Access will guide you here. Once you know which tables you'll need, you can select one or more Nouns to set up the commonly used tables, being careful to select only those you need.

Simply click the name of a Noun to create that table. In some cases, Access will also create related tables that are commonly required for that type of table. For example, if you select Orders as the Noun, Access creates not only the Orders table but an Order Details table, a Product table, and a Category table. This design intelligence makes creating tables with Nouns a much quicker and easier task. You can readily identify whether more than one table will be created by noticing that the icon for the Orders has cascading tables, while icons for other Nouns show only one table as shown in Figure 2-10.

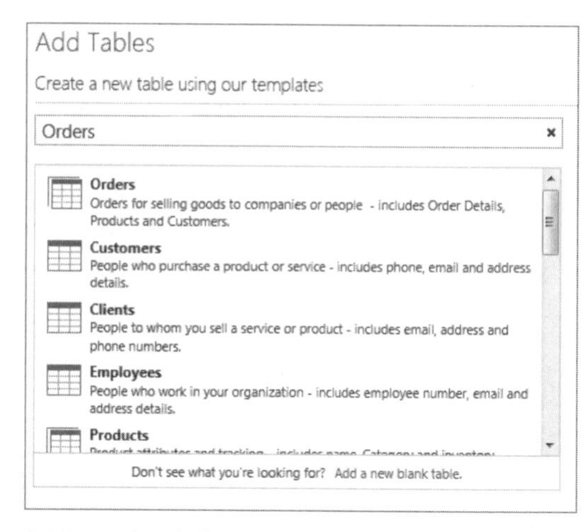

FIGURE 2-10: Different Noun icons

Creating Tables from Imported Data Sources

A second way to quickly and easily create new Access tables is to import the data from an existing external data source. You've always had that ability in Access, so this method should be familiar to you. The main difference is that Access 2013 makes it more obvious and easier to get to, as shown in Figure 2-11.

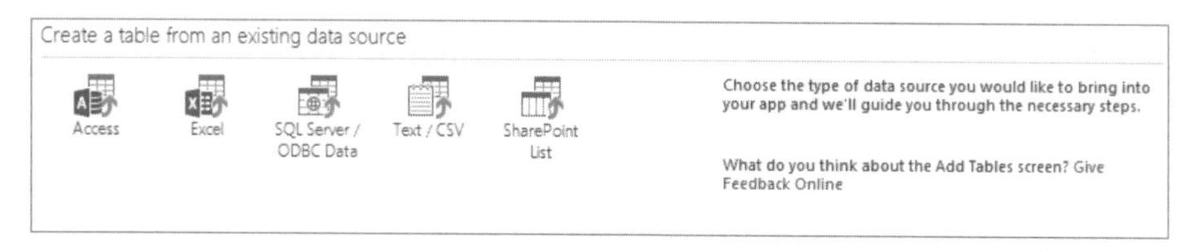

FIGURE 2-11: Creating a table from an external data source

Figure 2-11 illustrates your options for importing external data, which appear at the bottom of the main Access opening screen. You can import data from:

- Other Access databases
- Excel files
- SQL Server or other ODBC data sources
- Text or csv files
- SharePoint lists

You'll recognize the import wizards, which handle the import process for each type of data source. They are similar to the import wizards in previous versions of Access. For Access, however, there's only one tab for tables. There is no mechanism for importing other objects from `.accdb` files because of the way such objects are created and stored in the SQL Server database.

See Figure 2-12, for example, which illustrates importing an Access table from another Access database. Obviously, you could import multiple tables in a single step by selecting them from the list. This is similar in concept to the way you've always been able to import Access tables. Only the end result is somewhat different.

Figure 2-13 shows the table structure of the source table being imported for this example, which has an AutoNumber primary key and five additional attribute fields.

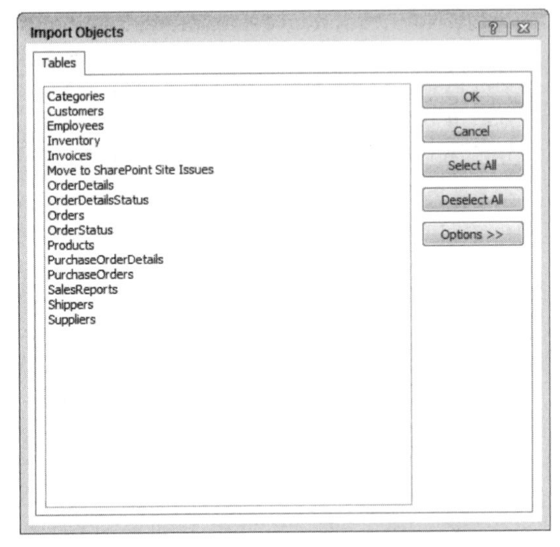

FIGURE 2-12: Importing an Access table

TblCourses

Field Name	Data Type	Description (Optional)
CourseID	AutoNumber	the internal course number
CourseTitle	Short Text	
CourseDescription	Long Text	
CatalogueDescription	Long Text	Catalog descriptions for the Learning Center Descriptions
Active	Yes/No	
ContactHours	Number	

Field Properties

General | Lookup

Field Size	Long Integer
New Values	Increment
Format	
Caption	Course Number
Indexed	Yes (No Duplicates)
Text Align	General

A field name can be up to 64 characters long, including spaces. Press F1 for help on field names.

FIGURE 2-13: Source Table structure

Figure 2-14 shows the resulting table after it is imported to Access 2013 for a web app. As you can see, it looks very much like the source table, with one obvious exception. In the General properties tab, there is no `Field Size` displayed for the AutoNumber field, which has been designated as the primary key. Autonumbers in Access web apps can only be integers because they are also defined as an identity field in a SQL Server table. Therefore, you don't have the other options for autonumbers as you would in a client table.

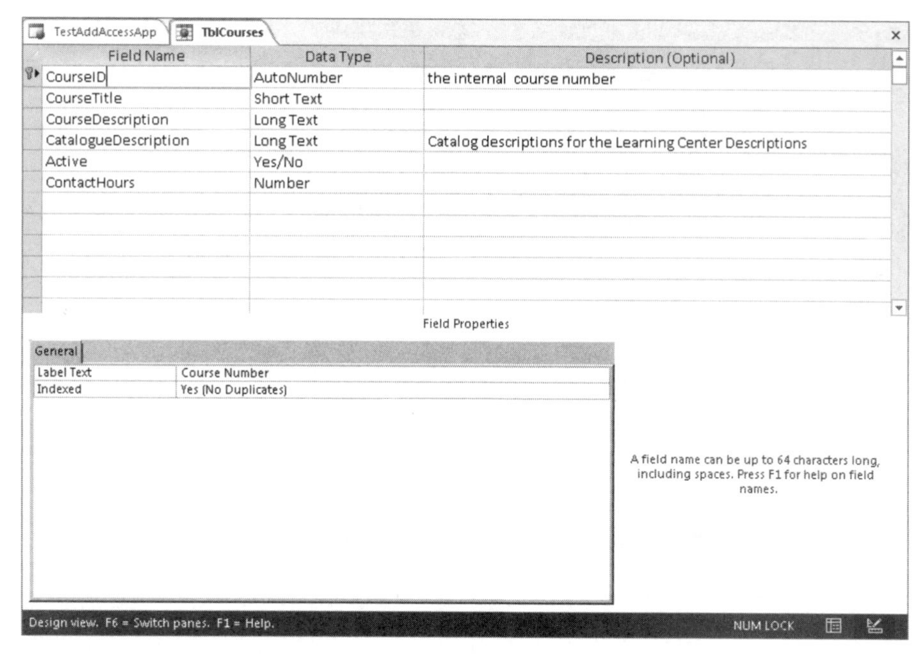

FIGURE 2-14: Imported Access table in a web app

Design Requirements for App Tables

Note that certain rules, which apply to all app tables, are enforced on the tables we just created for this Access web app:

- The primary key in each table must be an AutoNumber data type. If there is no qualifying primary key, Access creates one during import.
- Web app tables do not support compound primary keys.
- Relationships are defined using Lookup Fields, as was the case with Access 2010.

If an imported table doesn't conform to those requirements, Access may either fail to import the table, import it with errors, or add the required primary key field.

For the sake of comparison among import types and to illustrate how these restrictions are applied, let's look at the same table, exported from Access into an Excel worksheet, and then reimported into your Access web app.

Figure 2-15 shows what happens when Access can't identify an AutoNumber field to use as the primary key in the imported table. When the table was exported to Excel and reimported, the original Course ID field was converted to a floating point number, which Access couldn't use for a primary key. So, Access added a new ID field, using the AutoNumber, and made it the primary key for the table as demonstrated in Figure 2-16.

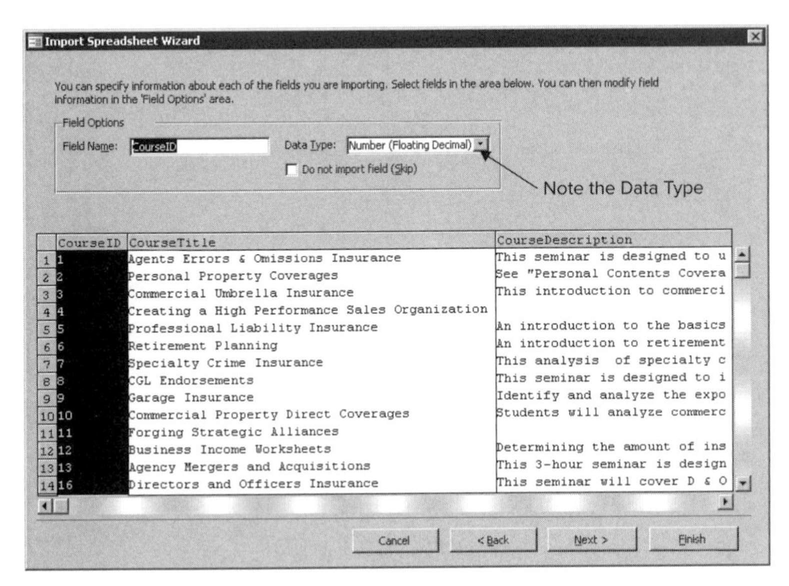

FIGURE 2-15: Import Spreadsheet Wizard dialog

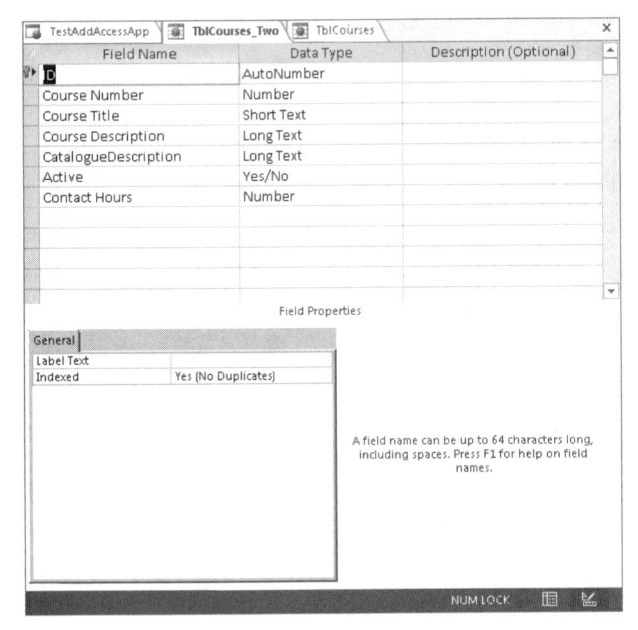

FIGURE 2-16: AutoNumber primary key added

Course ID, which would have been an AutoNumber and the primary key in the original source file, did not qualify to be the primary key in the new Access web app table — it's the wrong data type after being exported to Excel. If you are not going to import additional, related tables, you might repair this table simply by deleting the old Course ID field and retaining the new ID field, perhaps renaming it as CourseID, following the original naming convention. However, if you will be importing additional tables, which need to be related to this table via a primary and foreign key, you'll need to fix up the tables first.

Here's an example of such a table as it originally appeared in Access. You'll import it directly from Access, so you can see in Figure 2-17 how the import process modifies fields to conform to the app restrictions.

This table has a compound primary key on State, CourseID and ApprovalDate. When you import it into an Access web app, that's going to change, as shown in Figure 2-18.

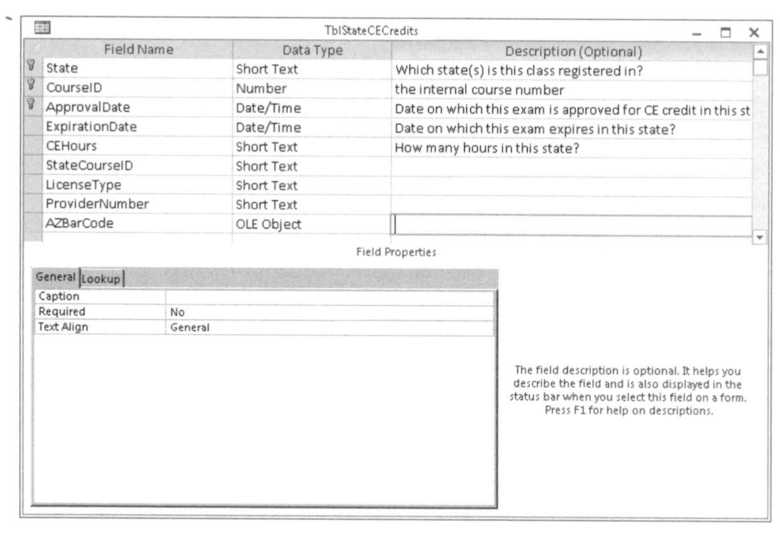

FIGURE 2-17: Related table with compound primary key

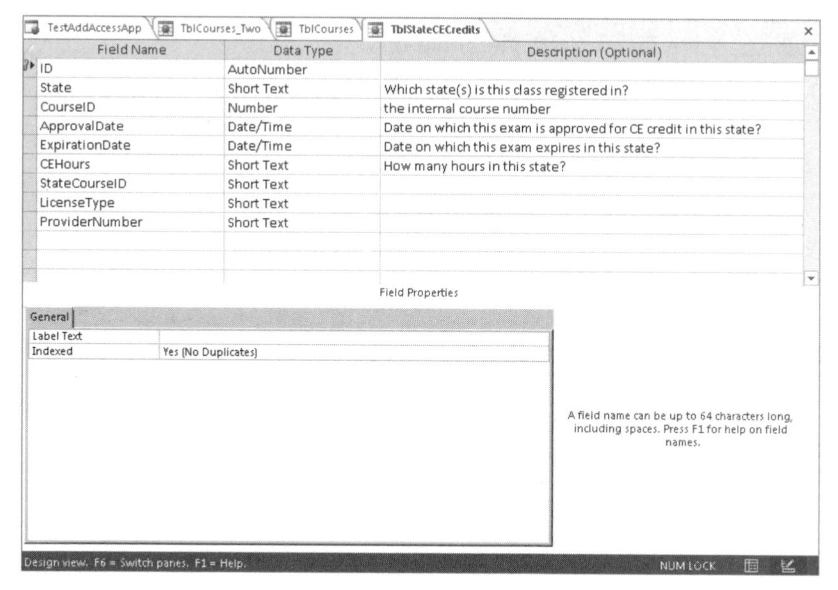

FIGURE 2-18: Imported table with changes to primary key fields

As you saw in the table imported from Excel, Access needed to add a new AutoNumber field to be the primary key and it removed the existing compound primary key. At this point, we want to emphasize that though this may look like a loss of functionality on the surface, that is not the case. If you have compound primary keys, you can get the equivalent functionality by creating compound indexes on the same set of columns and ensuring individual columns do not allow nulls. To illustrate how you would do this, you would use the Indexes button on the Table Design tab of the ribbon to open up the Indexes dialog shown in Figure 2-19 and add the fields as shown. Note how the second column is blank for the index name, indicating that it is part of the same index as the row above it.

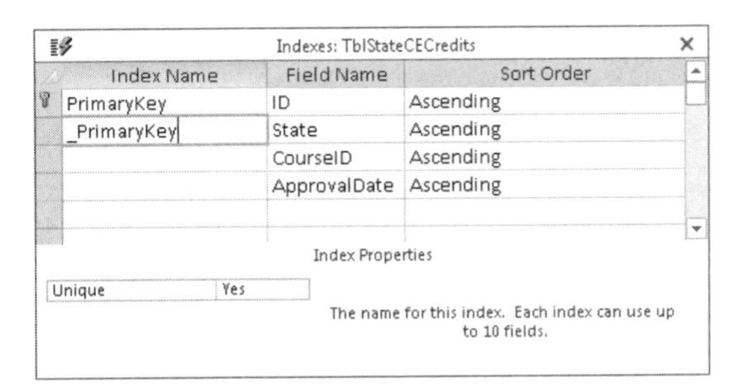

FIGURE 2-19: Indexes dialog

Be sure to also set the Unique property to Yes to ensure the index will be unique. As you can see in Figure 2-19, when Access added the new Primary Key, it kept the original Primary Key as a unique index, with the prefixed dash to distinguish it from the new Primary Key Index. Note that you can easily rename the indexes, if you want to make them more identifiable.

You may notice a few changes in the data types as well; you'll consider data types in the next section.

Creating Tables the Traditional Way

You can create tables just as you have always done with Access, subject to a few restrictions, as noted previously. Locate the link to create a new table, as illustrated in Figure 2-20. Note that in Figure 2-21, Access web app tables always start out with the ID field defined.

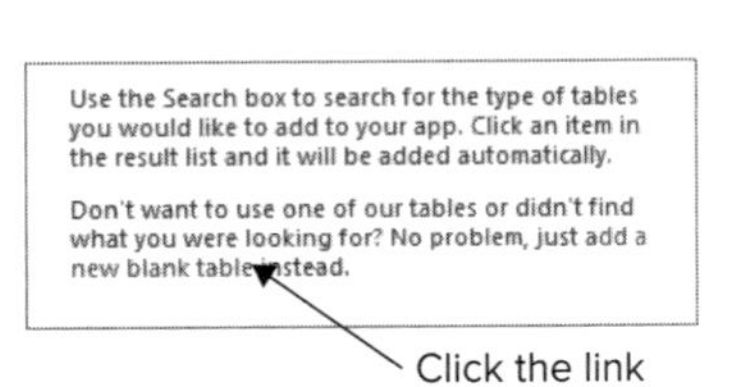

FIGURE 2-20: Creating a new table from scratch

My First App | Table1

Field Name	Data Type	Description (Optional)
ID	AutoNumber	

FIGURE 2-21: Template table with predefined primary key

Access requires an autonumbering primary key so Access inserts it for you by default. You can rename it to fit your naming convention.

From here, you will follow your usual practices for creating new fields in your table, with the caveat that Text fields will either be Long or Short Text, as you will learn later in the chapter.

You have now learned three ways you can create new tables in an Access web app, and in the case of importing, how you can populate the new table(s) with existing data from the source table(s). Next you'll learn about a new feature in Access web apps — views for tables.

Tables and Their Related Views

Access goes further than simply creating tables. It also creates the related views for the tables. You learn more about creating and editing views in a later chapter. For now, just take a look at the example in Figure 2-22.

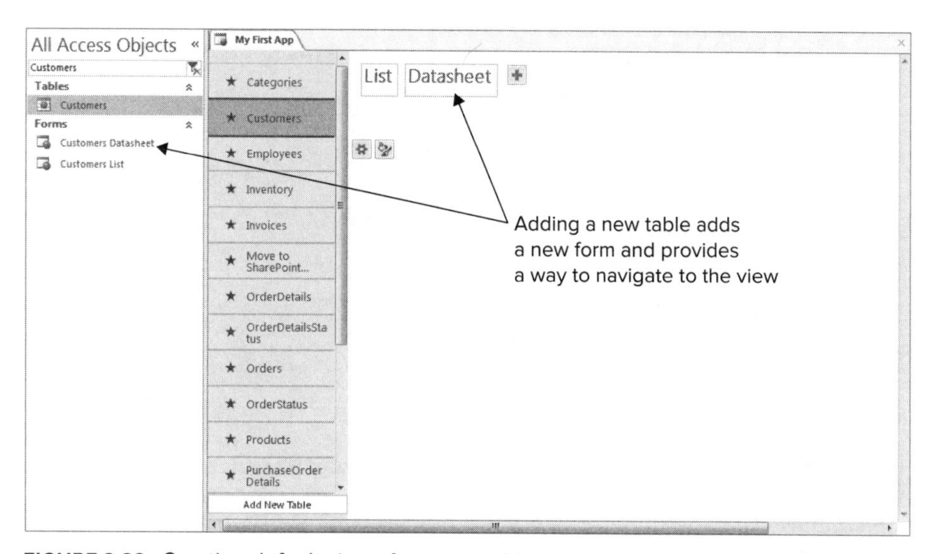

FIGURE 2-22: Creating default views for a new table

You probably realize from looking at Figure 2-22 that, in the Access web app environment, a view is very much like a form in a client database. In fact, Access web app views serve the same function as forms have served in client databases.

Access creates both a Datasheet view and a List view when it creates each new table. Although we get into the specifics in a later chapter, you might appreciate knowing that you can customize, copy and repurpose, or even delete the default views.

There is another important ramification; related views are bound to a specific table and cannot exist without a table. Therefore, if you decide to delete a table, all related views will also be automatically deleted. In later chapters, you will look over strategies for managing views when making structural changes that involve deleting tables but keeping views.

DATA TYPE CHANGES FROM PREVIOUS VERSIONS

You may already have noticed that data types in our example tables are different from previous versions of Access. Let's quickly review the new labels for data types and identify which SQL Server data type they map to. The following table summarizes the data types available to you in an Access web app:

ACCESS DATA TYPE	SUBTYPE	SQL SERVER DATA TYPE
Number	Whole number (no decimal places)	`int`
	Floating-point number (variable decimal places)	`float`
	Fixed-point number (6 decimal places)	`decimal(28,6)`
Currency	<No subtype>	`decimal(28,6)`
Short Text	<No subtype>	`nvarchar(1)` to `nvarchar(4000)`
Long Text	<No subtype>	`nvarchar(MAX)`
Date/Time	Date	`date`
	Time	`time(3)`
	Date with Time	`datetime2(3)`
Yes/No	<No subtype>	`bit`
Hyperlink	<No subtype>	`nvarchar(MAX)`
Image	<No subtype>	`varbinary(MAX)`
Calculated	<Not applicable>	Varies, depending on the result of expression
Lookup	<Not applicable>	`int`

Let's talk about the ramifications of these changes. One of the most important changes in table design is that, because of tighter binding between the table design and form design, several properties that you may have traditionally ignored in previous versions of Access become more relevant, affecting the UI behavior.

Text Data Type

Long Text loosely corresponds to the Memo data type in previous versions of Access, while Short Text loosely corresponds to the previous version's Text data type. However, there are important differences both in the length of the fields and in the default enter key behavior, enough differences to make comparisons very useful.

Text Field Lengths

A Long Text field can be of "unlimited" length, or they can be limited to a specific number of characters. Of course, "unlimited" really isn't unlimited. To understand how that works, you need to remember that Access web app tables are created in a SQL Server database, and therefore, the data types are determined by SQL Server data types. In the case of Long Text, the underlying data type, `varchar(MAX)`, can hold up to 2,147,483,647 characters. Technically that's not unlimited, but for all practical purposes, it probably amounts to the same thing.

For Short Text fields, the maximum length is 4,000 characters; this is quite different from Access desktop database's Text, which is limited to only 255 characters.

Enter Key Behavior

The other difference between Short and Long Text fields is in the default Enter key behavior. For Short Text fields, pressing the Enter key moves the cursor to the next field. For Long Text fields, pressing the Enter key inserts a carriage return into the field.

Additional Considerations

There is one confusing aspect that needs to be pointed out — both Short Text and Long Text have both a *Limit Length* property and *Character Limit* property. By default, Short Text's Limit Length property is set to **Yes** while Long Text has it as **No**. However, you are allowed to flip the settings, which effectively changes the underlying data type from `nvarchar(n)` to `nvarchar(MAX)` and vice versa. Therefore, you could have a Short Text field of virtually unlimited length and a Long Text field with limited length. When Limit Length is set to Yes, you can see the Character Limit property and enter a number between 1 to 4000. The Limit Length property also affects the Enter key behavior. So for practical purposes, Short Text and Long Text are basically identical data types with different defaults for length.

Also it's important to note that Access web apps impose a limitation on indexing text fields. If you want to create an index, whether unique or not, on a text field, you are limited to text that's 220 characters or less. Therefore, a text field that allows for 255 characters cannot be indexed. So if you're importing data from desktop database files, you may need to plan on truncating the length if you need to keep indexes.

Hyperlink Fields

Hyperlink is internally another text data type. If you enter `google.com` into a hyperlink field, the raw value is `google.com#http://google.com`, which is similar to how Access desktop databases have handled the hyperlink data type. Because this is saved as text in the database, if you link to the table containing a Hyperlink data type, it will be necessary to ensure that the data type is correctly handled within the client application.

Numeric Data Type

One important thing to note is the change in the default value for the numeric data types. In versions prior to Access 2007, adding a numeric data type would add a default value of zero. In versions 2007 and 2010, the default value was left blank. In Access 2013, however, the default value now will be zero, for better or for worse. If you want to require users to explicitly enter a number, even a zero, to disambiguate a case of truly having zero amount of something versus not having any data at all, then it will be necessary to manually clear the default as you may have done for earlier versions of Access.

Note that if you want to dictate the number of decimal places for your numeric fields, you will need to first set the Display Format property to some value other than General Number which will in turn display another property named Display Decimal Places.

Date/Time Data Type

If you've worked with Access solutions where date expressions were problematic, you will no doubt be delighted to see that you finally have a true Date-only & Time-only data type. If you're importing data from existing data sources, you definitely will want to review and update the data type for your date/time fields to ensure maximum fidelity.

In an Access desktop database, the date/time data type had granularity of one second. With an Access web app, when we use time and/or date/time, the granularity is now a millisecond, but for practical usage we can only resolve time up to one second. The primary reason for this is that all date/time fields have a display format, which affects how the data can be entered and stored. Changing a display format by itself does not alter the underlying values, but when a user enters seconds to a date/time field using a display format that allows for minutes, the seconds are truncated and only minutes and higher granularity are stored. Therefore, you should take care to set the correct display format in addition to correct date/time data type.

Image Data Type

You should also note that even though the Image data type maps to `varbinary(MAX)` data type, Access web apps will allow you to store only graphic files and not any kind of BLOBs even though the underlying data type can be used in this manner. If you need to be able to store files or other BLOBs (or Binary Large Objects), we recommend you use the SharePoint Document Library for this functionality — it's specially designed to handle documents effectively and comes with several other features. In Chapter 8, we look at leveraging this functionality. This also leads you into the next section where you learn how to link SharePoint lists and libraries to the Access web app.

Lookup Data Type

Lookup fields are internally an integer, which is expected given that the primary keys are always auto-incremented integers and lookups need to be of the same data type. However, lookups also allow you to select another column from the foreign table for display and this display value may be a different data type. This also has ramifications for how you will perform joins in queries, a topic covered in Chapter 5.

FIELD PROPERTIES

The Access client offered a set of properties for tables and their fields. Access web apps do not have customizable properties for tables but do still offer properties for fields which can be set. A number of common properties such as `Indexed`, `Required`, `Validation Rule`, and `Validation Text` are carried over from the client into web apps.

As you learned in earlier discussions about field properties for text and number, you will want to keep in mind that, unlike client versions, not all properties will be immediately visible and you will want to become familiar with properties that may allow other properties to be available for further editing, as noted in the chapter.

One often ignored property in the Access client was `Caption` which allowed you to define a user-friendly labeling of a field name for a table's fields. In the past, it proved more problematic because it also changed how you would reference the fields in programming, which was undesirable. However, in Access web apps, you will find that the new property, `Label Text`, has equivalent functionality to help save time in customizing the associated label when adding those fields to a new view. Unlike its `Caption` predecessor, filling in `Label Text` does not affect how you reference the field in programming and it is limited strictly to only the associated label that is added at design time, making it more attractive.

LINKING SHAREPOINT LISTS

Access web apps allow you to not only import SharePoint lists but also link to them. When you choose SharePoint lists as the data source for creating a table, you have the option to choose between importing and linking, as shown in Figure 2-23.

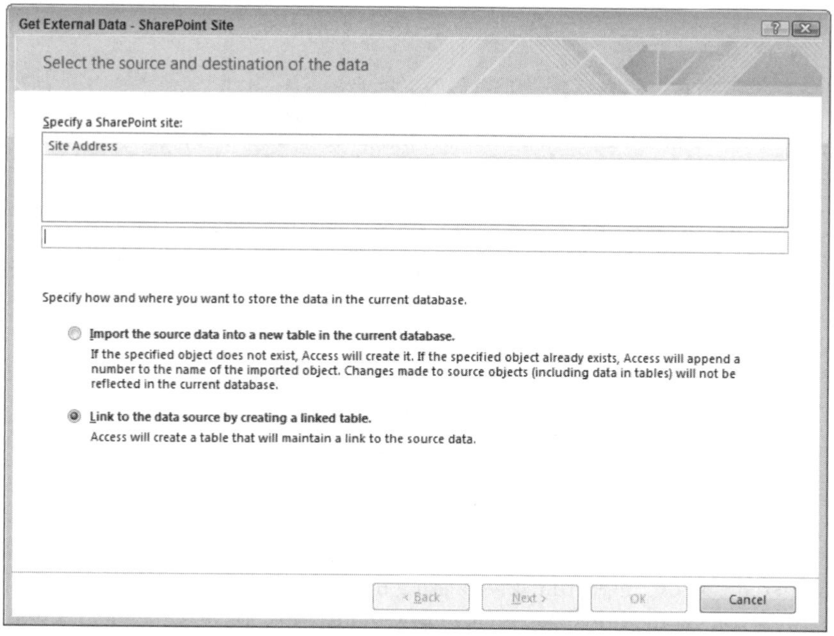

FIGURE 2-23: Linking option for SharePoint list

When you link a SharePoint list, you can use it as a query source, joining it with your Access app's tables and so forth. Linked SharePoint lists are always read-only, so if you need to edit content in SharePoint lists, you can leverage Access app's web browser control to reference a SharePoint form to edit the contents accordingly.

As you can see in Figure 2-24, you can enter a URL that points to a SharePoint site, which may be the same site where you host your Access web app. You can then click Next to get a list of SharePoint lists and document libraries available on the site.

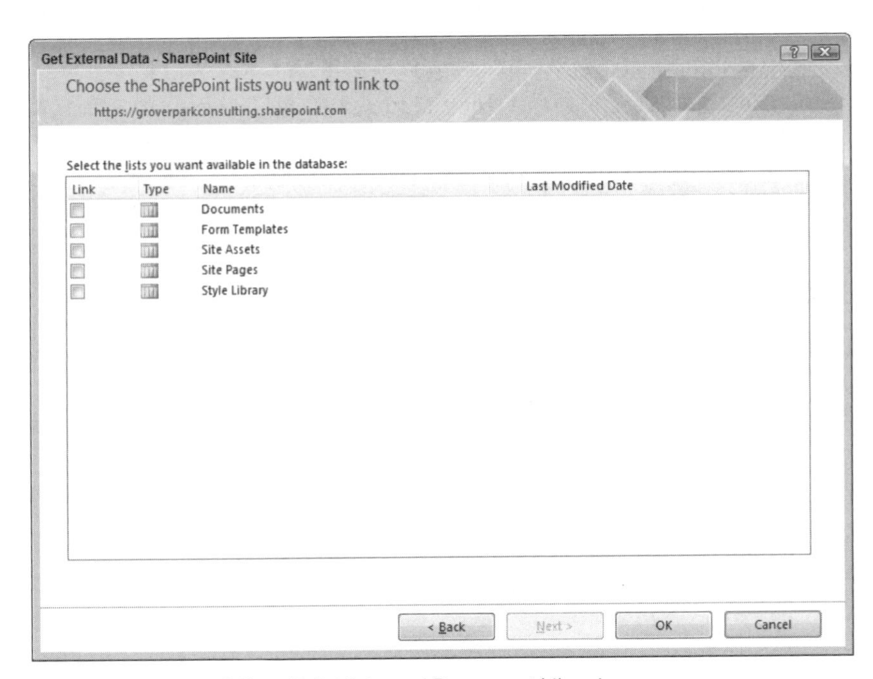

FIGURE 2-24: List of SharePoint lists and Document Libraries

Unlike Access 2010 web databases, you are not restricted to lists on the same site. As long you are authorized to do so, you can link to SharePoint lists located on subsites or sibling sites. Furthermore, you can link to a document library as well as a standard SharePoint list. Just like any other tables, Access will automatically create read-only views for any linked SharePoint lists.

SUMMARY

In this chapter, we reviewed the changes made to the processes of designing tables and importing existing data. You learned about the new tools to make building tables quicker. You may be familiar with the need to clean data before importing any existing data to ensure smooth transition, and saw what was changed and you should now have an idea of what to look for in achieving a smooth import operation. We also reviewed the changes to data types and some ramifications especially with text data types. You also saw how Access web apps can link to SharePoint lists and document libraries from other sites or subsites within the same SharePoint farm.

It's important to remember that in Access web apps, the design of tables is tightly bound with their views, so the design decisions you make with a table, whether you're creating from scratch or importing, have a more significant effect than in a desktop database. In upcoming chapters, we cover the ramifications arising from different table design and data types. One benefit of the new Access web apps over Access 2010 web databases is that you no longer need to sacrifice good database design and normalization for better performance, which makes it much easier to provision a database solution as an Access web app. Therefore, you should feel more confident in proceeding forward with your database design just as you would have with the desktop database. Simply note the differences in the data types and some table properties. Now that you've looked over the table designs, you will study what has changed on the design surface for building queries, forms, and macros and get a feeling for the new environment.

3

Understanding the New User Interface

WHAT'S IN THIS CHAPTER?

- Becoming familiar with web navigation
- Understanding the new approach to layout
- Identifying the different types of views
- Become familiar with the new ribbon
- Explore the backstage
- Getting acquainted with SharePoint and Office365
- Understanding layout in mobile devices

In this chapter, you become familiar with the new approach to the user interface introduced in Access 2013 web apps. As you learned in previous chapters, almost everything about web apps is a departure from prior versions of Access. This clean break from the past permitted Microsoft to refocus on how users interact with their apps in the browser and create an experience more in line with their expectations for web apps. You analyze the elements of the web interface, including both the surface and control elements in the web page, and the working surface. You see how the approach to layout in an Access web app adheres to design patterns and restrictions in the web interface. Along the way, you learn how web navigation is supported by the new elements and features of the user interface.

This chapter provides an introduction to the types of views available and how they relate to user interface requirements, although a more in-depth discussion of designing those views is reserved for Chapter 4. In the final sections of this chapter, you see how the backstage has changed from the previous version of Access. You learn how to exploit the tools and features it offers. And we end with a review of the Access 2013 ribbon, with special emphasis on the reduced elements for Access web apps.

WEB NAVIGATION

Although there are significant differences between navigation on the web and navigation in a client database, it is worth starting out with an acknowledgement that, in at least one way, they share common features, which you'll leverage from your Access experience. First, of course, the objective of all navigation is to enable a smooth flow between working functions in the database, with a minimum of mouse-clicks. Second, a good navigation framework helps users stay "grounded" within the application, so they know where they are at any point and how to get back to a prior place when they need to. Third, navigation should reinforce the overall structure and organization of the application. And finally, the navigation framework should follow well known, or at least intuitive, patterns so that users don't need to spend precious time trying to work out how to do their tasks. As you look at the navigation framework for Access web apps, try to keep these features in mind.

Navigation Tools

Design patterns for navigation in a web environment include the following elements. We list them first, then discuss the ones found in Access web apps, and then give you a chance to see how they are implemented in Access web apps.

- Navigation bar
    - Top horizontal
    - Side vertical
- Search navigation
- Tab navigation
- Breadcrumb navigation
- Tags navigation
- Fly-out menu and drop-down menu navigation
- Faceted or guided navigation
- Footer navigation
- Combined navigation

You'll notice that none of the web navigation methods resemble the kind of switchboard with multiple command buttons for which Access is infamous. Many experienced developers moved away from the switchboard approach some time ago, but again, the web environment makes it more important to use navigation tools that both support your workflows and present users with a navigation system consistent with their other web experiences.

Also, as we discuss each navigation tool, keep in mind that Access web apps are data-driven and primarily transactional. In that context, some navigation tools, such as a tag cloud, offer less utility than other tools. So, although we've included them for completeness, and to help you get a broader perspective of the art of web navigation, we don't think you'll implement tag clouds very often.

Navigation Bars

Although modern websites have adopted more sophisticated designs and graphics, much website navigation is still based on navigations bars, either horizontal or vertical. Consider the examples highlighted in Figures 3-1 and 3-2.

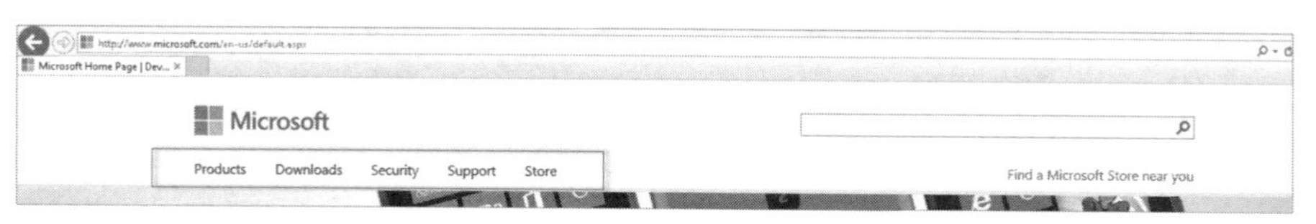

FIGURE 3-1: Horizontal navigation bar

FIGURE 3-2: Vertical navigation bar

Now compare these navigation features to those in an Access web app, as shown in Figure 3-3. Note that these navigation features are "out-of-the-box" with web apps. Although you'll determine the specific content within them, you don't have to do anything to create them.

Although it is fair to say that the design element you'll use to develop the vertical menu is not the same as you would find in a standard page, the visual and functional impact is very much in line with most users' experience and expectations for the web. The horizontal links are closer to the hyperlinks they resemble, but they are still unique to web apps. We talk more about the vertical menu in the next section. You learn how to manage the vertical and horizontal navigation pieces in your web app views later in this chapter.

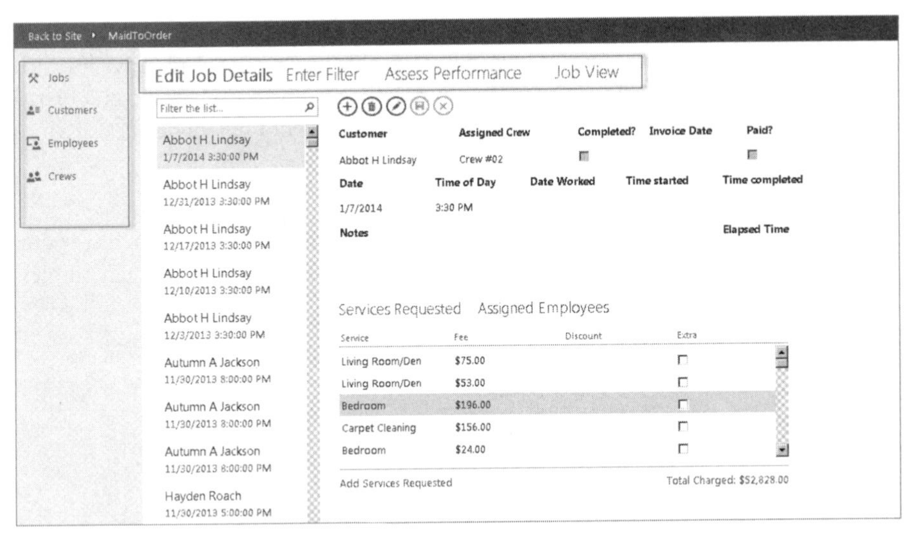

FIGURE 3-3: Horizontal and vertical navigation bars in a web app

Search Navigation

Search navigation is a very powerful way to navigate within a website (or even outside it, depending on the implementation), without having to build a structured menu system to enumerate all of the possible linked pages and sections. In most cases, it works by entering a key word or phrase in a text box and clicking the associated search button. This returns a list of all potentially matching locations or words within the site. It can be structured in different ways on different websites. Figure 3-4 shows one popular search tool.

FIGURE 3-4: Search navigation in a typical web implementation

Notice that the search box begins to offer suggested matches as you type into it. Clicking one of those links takes you to that page within the site. The concept is one you should be comfortable with from using this type of search on other sites, such as Bing or Google. If you click the magnifying glass icon at any point, the currently highlighted list item becomes the search term.

FIGURE 3-5: Search navigation in an Access web app

Search Navigation in an Access Web App

Within an Access web app, search navigation serves a narrower purpose and is implemented in a somewhat different way, but the overall process is similar. In addition, as mentioned previously, search navigation is built into certain web app views.

Consider the search box in Figure 3-5 as implemented for an Access web app's List view. One of the items in the list can be searched for and selected by clicking. Clicking the selection moves focus to that item in the current view. Note that the page itself doesn't change, only the content within it updates. The controls on the page are also static. That's another important navigation element, which we return to in a later section.

Search navigation in an Access web app has the following features, which you can see are similar to search in other web contexts, but different in ways specific to the web app context.

- Most obvious is the fact that the list pane which supports searching is limited to a closed domain of possible matches. The list pane is based on a table or a query that includes the items to be searched.
- The list pane is structured, giving the user strong cues about possible selections. There is both a primary and secondary element in each search term, giving the user additional information on which to make a selection. In Figure 3-5, that is the name of the customer with his or her company affiliation below.
- The search is not prefiltered as you type. Because the list is being filtered from a table in the database, interactive filtering would initiate a series of round-trips to the database to update the list on each keystroke, a potentially very expensive method. Instead, the search is run when the user clicks the magnifying glass.
- The filtered list pane offers the "x," which you click to remove the current filter and restore the full list. See Figure 3-6.

You have, no doubt, used combo boxes in your client applications to create functionality similar to the search navigation in an Access web app. One thing you should appreciate about the search in web apps is that it requires no work to create. When you create a List view or Summary view, the list pane for searching is already included and then automatically configured based on Access's best guess as to what you'd want to search on from the linked table. Of course, you can edit it if you need to.

FIGURE 3-6: Clear the filter on a web app search

We are confident that you'll find the search navigation in web apps to be one of the more useful new features. You learn more about creating and updating them in later chapters, when we focus on building interfaces.

Tabbed Navigation

You're familiar with tabbed navigation from tab controls you have used in your client databases. It is a set of buttons, or tabs, usually horizontal. Because such tabs have a border or container, they often feature a background color or even icons that complement the color scheme and graphic design of a web page. A tab set usually is attached to or slightly protrudes from a container. Typically, the selected button in a tab set is shaded darker or lighter than the unselected buttons. Refer to the highlighted areas in Figure 3-3, which share these tab features. The vertical Tile Pane functions like a vertical menu, while the horizontal View Selector functions like a horizontal menu.

The Tile Pane in Figure 3-3 resembles a vertical navigation bar in one way, with text links to different sections of the web app, and also a tabbed navigation bar, although the presence of the icons tends to suggest the latter is a closer match. In either case, the key lesson is that navigation in an Access web app adheres to good web design practice and the default design patterns support that without additional work on your part.

Breadcrumb Navigation

Named for the Hansel and Gretel fable, breadcrumb navigation usually refers to the trail of previously visited links displayed at the top of a page. It shows the path followed by the user within the site to get to the current page. It can also be based on a page hierarchy leading from the current page back up through the parent page to the highest page level. In either case, it is a good way to keep the user oriented to where they are within the site. Clicking any crumb in the string takes the user back to that page. Because the general path through a transaction within a web app follows a regular workflow, and because the tiles are always present to orient the user, breadcrumbs are not standard in Access web apps themselves, although they do appear in SharePoint navigation.

Tags, Fly-Out and Drop-Down Menus, Faceted or Guided Searches, and Footer Navigation

In this section, we consider the next group of web navigation tools as a group; they are more useful in large content-driven websites, where navigation between pages or sections is not likely to be as structured as a workflow in an Access web app, which is data-centric and transactional type of application type of application. And, of course, we don't implement most of them, at least not in the sense you do so in an Access web app. Again, for the sake of completeness of coverage, and to help you grasp the larger context in which web navigation occurs, we briefly comment on them.

Many sites have so much content scattered across dozens or even hundreds of pages that it would be hard to construct a menu to navigate it. A "tag cloud" is a visual representation of the possible links to other content. Usually the font size or color of a tag is an indication of its relative importance. It should be clear that relatively unstructured tag navigation would probably not be as useful in a transactional app as it would be elsewhere.

Fly-out and drop-down menus are useful in more deeply layered websites, where drill-down to a lower content level is desirable. As we illustrate in a later chapter, the drill-down functionality is available through other elements of the interface.

Faceted or guided searches are typically found on e-commerce sites, where the user selects from a number of "facets" of a product in order to navigate through a catalog to a smaller number of products. It can be thought of as a custom search. We show you the method by which you can create similar searches in your web apps in Chapter 8, when we show you how to create Query by Form functionality in an interface.

Footer Navigation

Essentially, this means navigation is incorporated into the footer in addition to, or instead of, the main navigation within a website. While there are good reasons for doing so in many websites, it doesn't serve a useful purpose in an Access web app; we don't need to consider it further.

Combined Navigation

As the name indicates, you can combine two or more of the navigation methods described in the previous section in a website. And, as you saw in Figure 3-3, Access web apps almost always incorporate both vertical and horizontal navigation. The point to take away from this observation is that, in order to take the best advantage of the navigation possibilities with Access web apps, you need to pay attention to how Access provides the topmost levels of navigation for you while you design your own navigation functions to correlate with the overall approach to navigation in web apps. Thus, planning your application design around the navigation design established by Access will make a big difference in the development experience. You can add your own elements on top of the framework provided by Access, of course, as needed.

In the next section of this chapter we look at the new approach to layout introduced for forms with Access web apps.

The New Approach to Layout

We've mentioned this before, and will repeat it again — Access web apps are, in many ways, a clean break from the past. Layout in views is one place you can see this quite well. You can think of layout in web apps as a macro design task, as opposed to a micro design task. In other words, micro control over pixel placement for individual controls is not possible in views in a web app. On the other hand, what you get in return for working at a more comprehensive level is assisted rapid design capability, where Access automatically manages the positioning and size of elements on a view to accommodate existing controls. Consider the layout of the editing surface in Figure 3-7.

First, you can see the list pane on the left, and the horizontal Action Bar, with command buttons, along the top of the page, both of which are automatically added to a List Detail view like this one, as you have learned. However, we want you to pay most attention to the controls in the body of the view. As you can see, there's no grid and no HTML table. Controls are not randomly placed, however, as Figure 3-7 indicates. Access maintains the column and row orientation of controls on the view to keep the overall layout in shape.

That frees you from trying to nudge elements into place or having to alter grids or cells in a table to get decent layout. Instead, elements slide smoothly into place when you drag them into position.

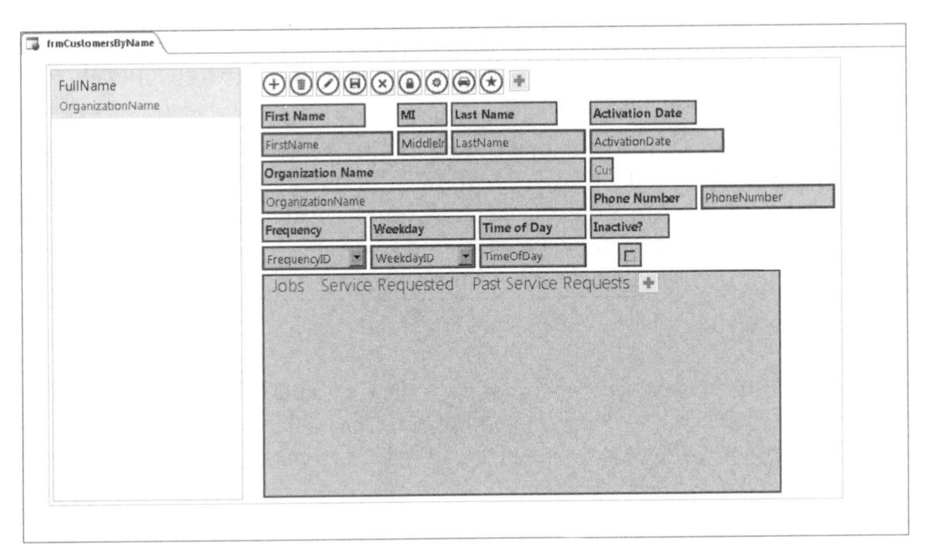

FIGURE 3-7: Controls on the layout surface

Layout also honors relative vertical and horizontal positions, so you no longer need to worry about alignment at the micro scale. You can also increase or decrease the size of most controls relative to others on the view. As you can see in Figure 3-7, for example, `MiddleInitial` has been narrowed, compared to the `FirstName` and `LastName` fields. Compare that to what happens when the `MiddleInitial` field is widened, as illustrated in Figure 3-8. Controls to the right are moved to accommodate the increased width.

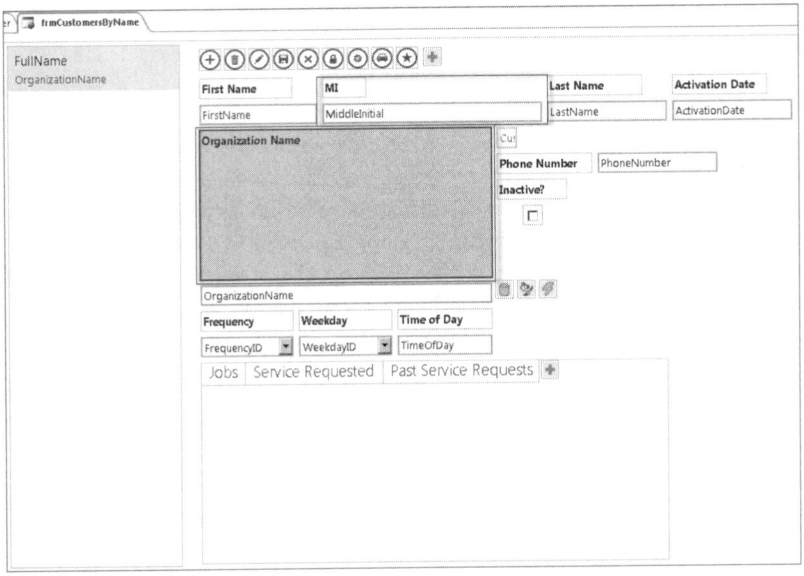

FIGURE 3-8: Controls self-adjust to accommodate changes

Figure 3-8 also shows the impact of increasing a control height vertically. Controls below it are smoothly moved to make room for it. As you can see, Access automatically changes the layout of each view as it reacts to your modifications, speeding the task of designing the layout while giving you considerable freedom in creating an effective overall layout.

In later chapters, you have a chance to try working with controls in layouts on views and also learn how to add controls to the view, using the redesigned ribbon.

Types of Views Available

Let's review the types of views available. There are four, and each serves a specific purpose.

List View

List views can be considered the workhorses in most situations. The views you've seen in this chapter are List views. They include the list pane which supports search. It's the richest and most flexible view. The name may be a bit confusing at first because the view itself is closer in appearance to the standard "single view form" of client databases. It takes its name from the list pane that appears on the left side of the view. The list pane is used to filter and navigate the records contained in the view. You learned about this feature earlier in this chapter. We often refer to the functionality it provides as *search* rather than list, which seems a bit too generic, but it is the same thing.

Another feature of List views you will find useful, in addition to the layout support mentioned earlier, is the existence of a built-in action bar. Again, you get some standard actions for free on the Action Bar whenever you create a list view (see Figure 3-9).

FIGURE 3-9: Action bar with both default and custom buttons

The default buttons, on the left in Figure 3-9, are quite intuitive: add a new record, delete a record, edit a record, save edits, and cancel. The four buttons on the right side are custom actions. They were created to perform additional tasks needed by the application. We show you how to create and use them in Chapter 8, on interface design, later in this book.

One significant change you will discover is that unlike past Access behaviors, you cannot just edit away on a record in a web app. You must click the Edit button to enable editing of a record and, once you're finished, explicitly save the record. This can be good in the sense that you have more control over how the record may be edited and whether the record is in a consistent state before allowing saving.

Blank View

The blank view, as its name suggests, is an empty canvas on which you can place controls, including images. Blank views offer the most flexible layout choices, and they can be unbound. On the other hand, they have no built-in filtering. They are a good choice for views where you need to present static information or when you need to present only a single record. The range of functionality a blank view has to offer is basically identical to the list view, *sans* the search functionality.

Datasheet View

In some ways, the Datasheet view is most similar to its counterpart in the client database. It should, therefore, be the most familiar to Access developers. It has more filtering options, which can include multiple columns in a filter, than a List view. However, it is not as rich or flexible as a List view. They lend themselves well to reporting situations where you need to give users a set of records which they can filter and sort as they need.

Another thing to note is that the Datasheet view is not as picky in restricting editing as List view and Blank views. You do not need to explicitly initiate an edit and commit changes with a save operation. That makes updates to several records very easy but presents you with less control over the workflow.

Summary View

Summary view supports summary and drill-through information, which can be filtered but it is very limited in layout design. It has a list pane that works similarly to the one on the List view, but unlike List view, which displays a single record at a time, the Summary view's list pane lists each group with aggregate statistics. For each group entry in the list pane, you can then see the individual records that make up the group listed on the body of the Summary view. You can additionally click a record to open a popup view that provides the full detail of that single record.

To put it in more concrete terms, suppose you have a group of orders, and you want to know the total dollar value of each order. Each single order appears in the Summary view's list pane, along with a dollar total. When you click an order, you are presented with a list of the products in that order which contribute to the order's total. You can click an individual product to open a popup form showing full details on that product. This gives you a drill-through capability that has not been built in to Access up to now.

Choosing a View Type

In thinking about the four view options, you can probably see where you'd use one over the others in an app. For example, many of the data entry tasks in an app would probably work best in a List view, which supports the search function via the list pane, and which can be tailored to present information the user is most likely to be interested in. You'd most likely use the Blank view as the basis for a splash screen, popups exposing a single record, or a dialog box to accept inputs. Datasheet view would be good for tasks in which you want to show the user a set of records, which they can filter in multiple ways to get the information they need. As you will learn in Chapter 8, you can modify the standard elements of the views you just learned about to create a rich, custom app.

The New Ribbon

The new ribbon in web apps also reflects the fact that layout and design are exclusively web oriented. Elements of the ribbon that pertain to client databases are not needed when we open a web app. For example, there is no icon to open VBA, no icon to relink tables, and no icon to switch between design and form view of an object. Those actions would pertain only to a client app. The ribbon is trimmed down to present only actions that matter in designing a web app. Although you'll have a chance to learn to use the ribbon in designing views in later chapters, we'll show it to you here, in a close-up view (see Figures 3-10 and 3-11).

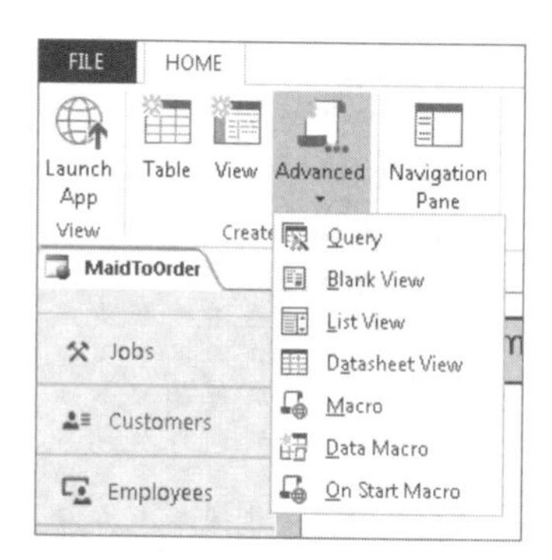

FIGURE 3-10: Context-sensitive ribbon with single tab

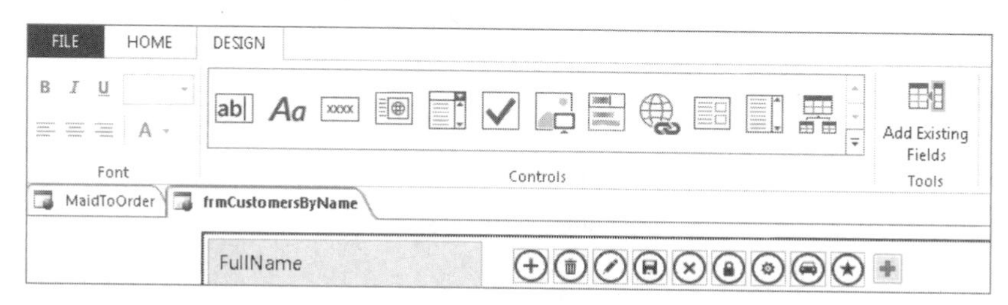

FIGURE 3-11: Context-sensitive ribbon with two tabs

As you can see, the number of tabs is smaller in the ribbon for a web app, they are context sensitive, and the actions available are all directly based on tasks needed to create and publish your web apps.

As you work through the book, you'll get a more hands-on view of all of the ribbon and layout choices now available, and you'll also learn how to use them.

The Backstage

The concept of the backstage is familiar to everyone from Access 2010, but as you'd expect, when you create a web app, the options become more focused on the tasks appropriate to the web app. The initial view of the backstage has familiar functions, such as the option to create a new database or open an existing database. Clicking the Options button takes you to the Options pane, which applies to client databases. However, we are interested in the options to create a new web app. As you'll see shortly, the options for web apps are limited.

As you can see in Figure 3-12, there are templates for both web apps and client apps. Web app templates are clearly indicated by the wire-frame globe in the icon. Clicking Custom Web App opens the dialog box shown in Figure 3-13. In Chapter 2, you learned how to proceed from here to create a new web app.

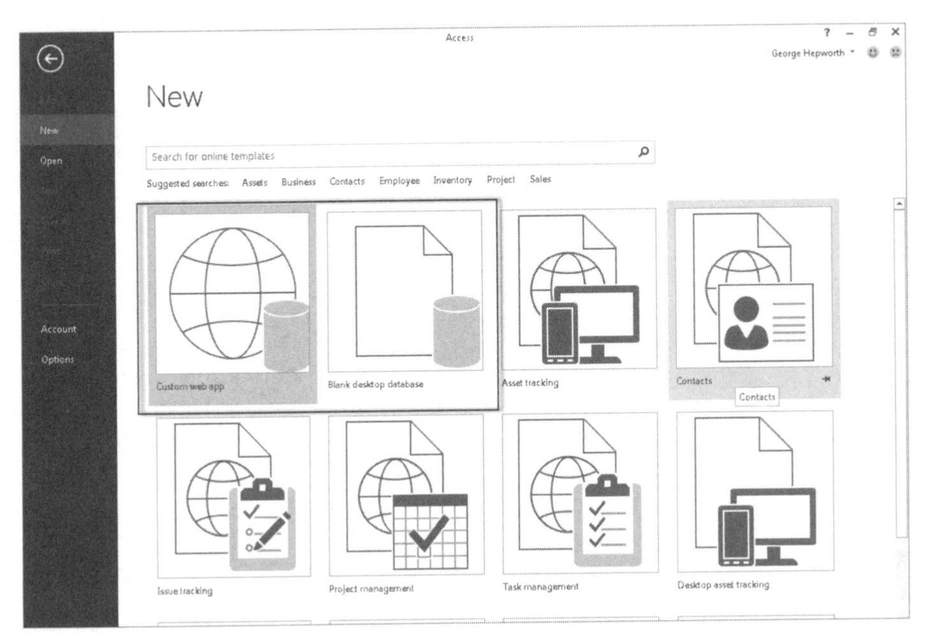

FIGURE 3-12: Backstage offering templates for web apps and client databases

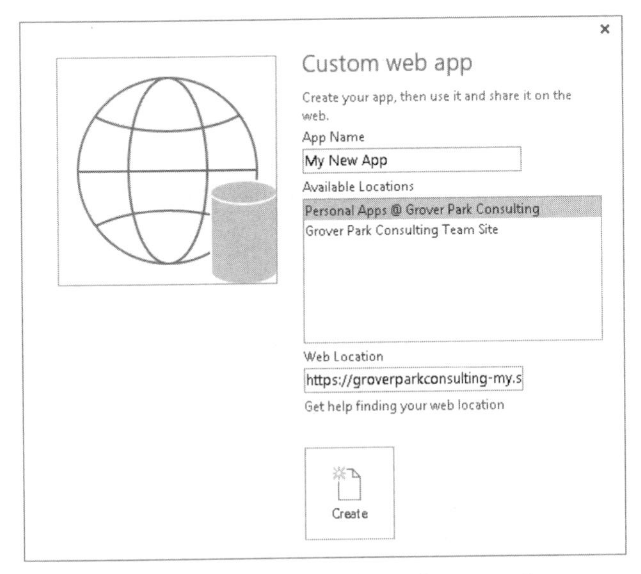

FIGURE 3-13: Dialog box after selecting Custom web app

Info Page

Once you have created a web app, the backstage opens. Figure 3-14 shows the Info tab where you find connection information for the SQL Azure or SQL Server database.

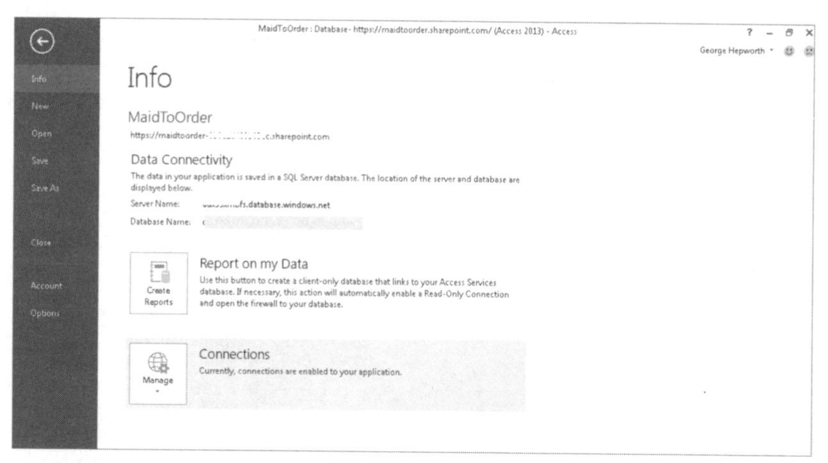

FIGURE 3-14: Backstage for a web app

Later in this book, when we talk about external connections in Chapter 11, you learn more about using the data connection information exposed in the backstage. However, to give you an idea of the significance of the connection information shown in Figure 3-14, it means that you can connect to the SQL Server database or the SQL Azure database behind your web app from a local Access desktop database. That, in turn, means you can create a hybrid application with both web and client interfaces. We're sure you'll be excited by that possibility. You learn more about the details in Chapter 11.

Let's walk through the other elements of the backstage for a web app. Where the element is unchanged from previous versions, or intuitive, such as the New link, we'll just give it a quick mention for completeness.

New

New opens the opening page where you can create a new database or app.

Open

As in other versions of Access, *Open* presents a page with options for selecting and opening an existing app or database. There are some additional choices here, however, as shown in Figure 3-15.

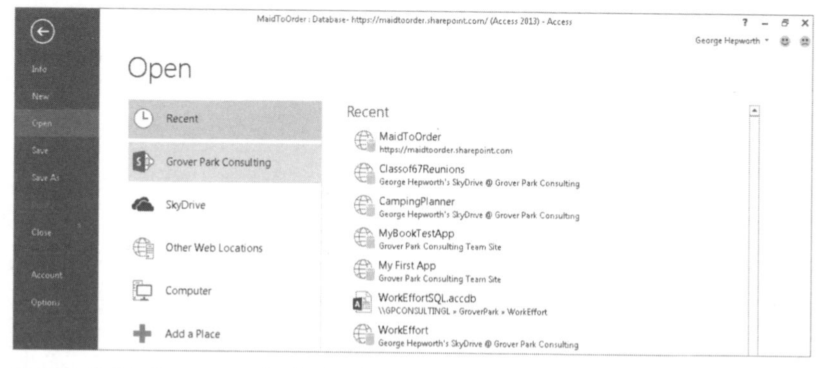

FIGURE 3-15: Open page in the backstage

First, note that the list of locations available to search includes both the local computer — including network locations when available — and cloud options, including the user's SkyDrive and Office 365 account, if available. In addition, the user can select `Other Web Locations`. That would include different Office 365 accounts to which the user has permissions. Figure 3-15 shows several such locations in the `Recent` list on the right side of the page.

Save and Save As

Save works as it has in all prior Access versions. *Save As*, however, offers two choices, one of which, *Save As Package*, is unique to Access web apps (see Figure 3-16).

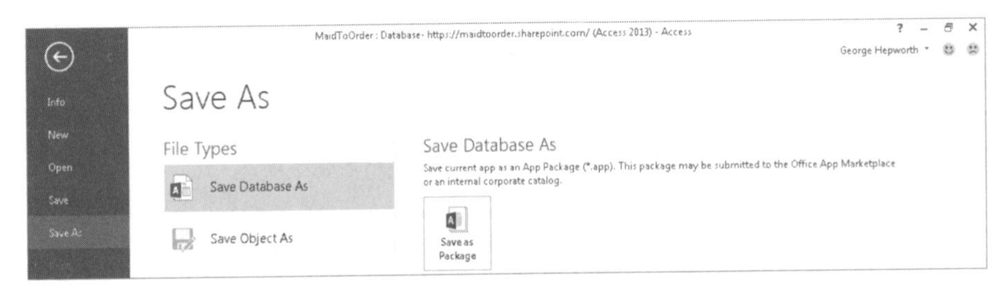

FIGURE 3-16: Save Database as App Package

Save As Package allows you to make a local app package containing the components of the web app, which can include the data. There are a couple of reasons for doing so. First, it can be seen as a backup mechanism. During development, you'll want to make regular app packages, just as you do now with your client databases. Second, it can be used as a mechanism to transfer an existing web app to a new database. You learn more about app packages in Chapter 14.

Save Object As works very similarly to the way it does in Access client; provided you have a focus on an opened object such as a table, a query, a view, or a macro, you can use *Save As* to make a copy of the object.

> **NOTE** *This is the* only *place where you can make copies of objects within web apps. You cannot customize the ribbon to display a* Save As *action, nor is it available via a right-click context menu. Thus, it may appear that you cannot save a copy of existing objects but in actuality it's available in the backstage.*

Close

As you'd expect, *Close* closes an open database.

Account

New to Access 2013, you will use the *Account* page, shown in Figure 3-17, to manage your Office 365 account(s). We dig more deeply into the use of the Account page in later chapters, when you learn how to set up and use your Office 365 account.

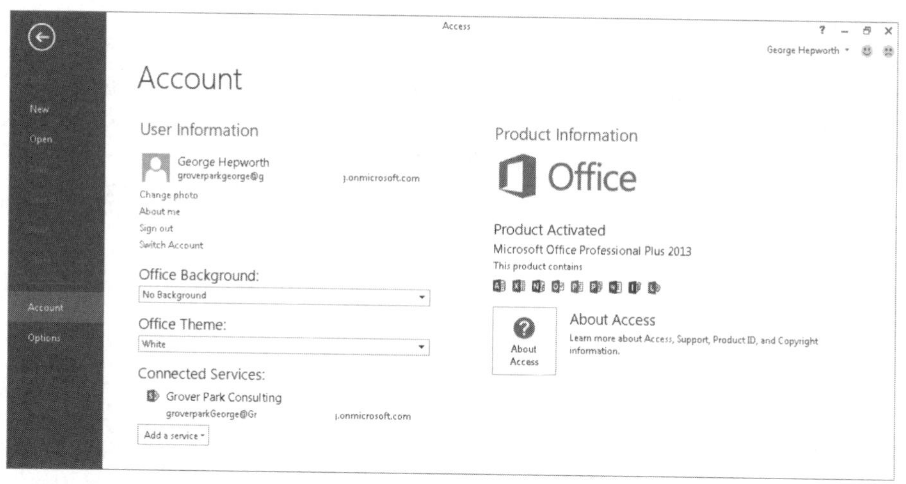

FIGURE 3-17: Account page

Options

The *Options* dialog is another place where you'll see how the web app environment has freed us to work with the reduced set of elements appropriate to the task at hand. Consider, for example, Figure 3-18, which shows the three options available, and the reduced list of settings under the *General* page.

Access Options
General
Language
Trust Center
General options for working with Access.
User Interface options
ScreenTip style: Show feature descriptions in ScreenTips
Show shortcut keys in ScreenTips
Disable hardware graphics acceleration
Creating databases
Default file format for Blank Database: Access 2007 - 2013
Personalize your copy of Microsoft Office
Office Background: No Background
Office Theme: White
OK
Cancel

FIGURE 3-18: Reduced option list for web apps

Language and Trust Center pages, now shown, are very similar to those you are familiar with. The remaining properties on the General page are those that pertain to the Access container itself.

At this point, you've surveyed the new ribbon for web apps and the changes to the backstage for web apps. In the next section, we turn our attention to the layout features important to mobile devices.

MOBILE DEVICES SUPPORT

Another factor driving the need to build Access applications that are accessible on the web is the proliferation of mobile devices. Microsoft is actively building the foundation within Office to work with mobile devices, notably with a touch screen interface. Within Office 2013, a new Touch mode is exposed to support using Office with mobile devices. Contrast Figure 3-19 with Figure 3-20, which shows Access with a Northwind application open in default mode and touch mode, respectively.

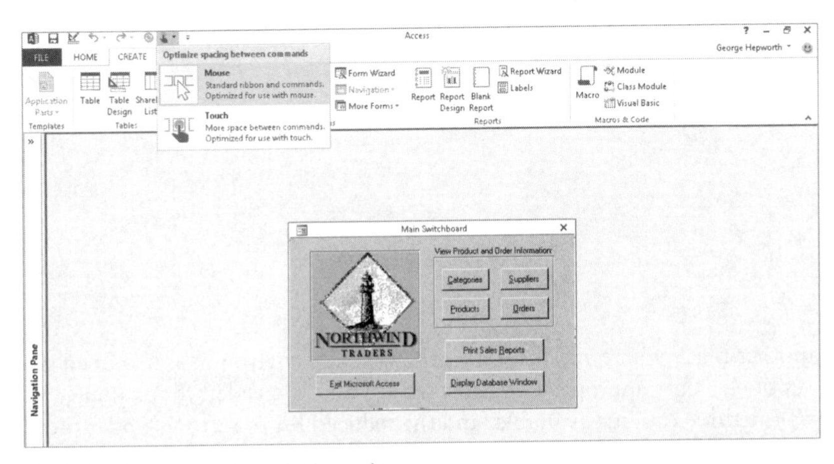

FIGURE 3-19: Access in default mode

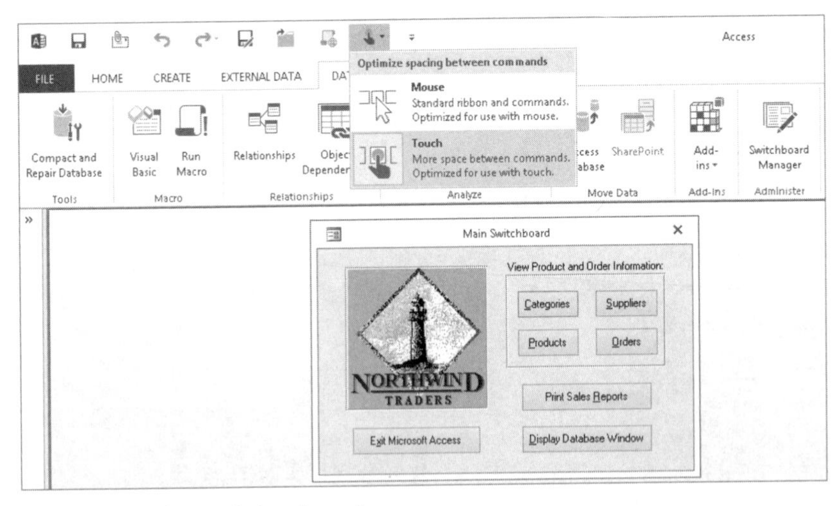

FIGURE 3-20: Access in touch mode

Office 2013 makes it possible to work with applications on a touch screen device that can run Windows. As you can see in Figure 3-20, this mode primarily works for the application's chrome. It will not affect the existing Access forms. Controls within the form remain unchanged. Although the touch mode is a client feature, it should illustrate the steps Microsoft is taking to make Office accessible on mobile devices.

> **NOTE** *Chrome means the surface surrounding the area that users directly interact with. Chrome is where you have your back, forward, refresh buttons, and address bar as well as status bar. You'll learn more about it in Chapter 10.*

As such, it is the first Office to try and move beyond traditional PCs. It goes without saying that Microsoft has invested considerable resources to ensure that a typical Access web app will run well on any mobile device. To run on different devices with different operating systems, browsers, and form factors is a monumental challenge and is not without its hazards.

To help you be informed when designing your first web app, we want to demonstrate some mobile devices to illustrate the experiences and help form realistic expectations when you are writing down design specifications.

Generally speaking, you can expect to have fairly good experiences using tablets with 4-inch screens or larger. Figures 3-21 and 3-22 illustrate the space available and a drop-down displayed on an iOS and an Android tablet, respectively.

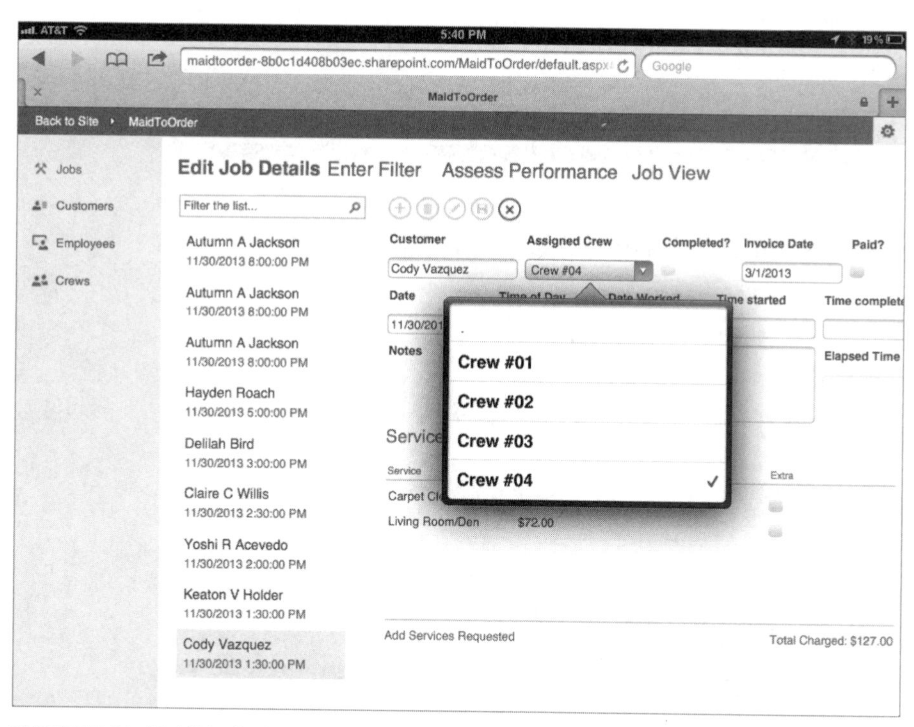

FIGURE 3-21: Maid To Order application on an iOS tablet with drop-down

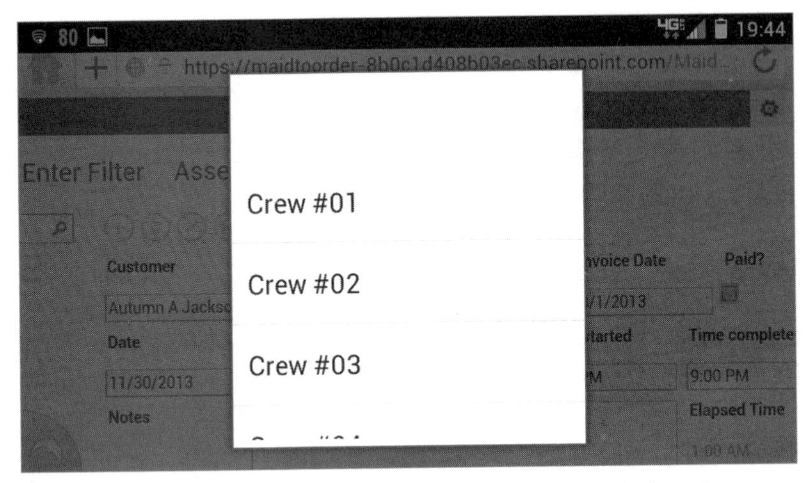

FIGURE 3-22: Maid To Order application on Android tablet with drop-down

If you look at the right side of Figure 3-21, you can see that the view is slightly too wide and requires some horizontal scrolling. Also, take into account the space that may be taken by an on-screen keyboard, as shown in Figure 3-23 (an iOS tablet) and Figure 3-24 (an Android tablet).

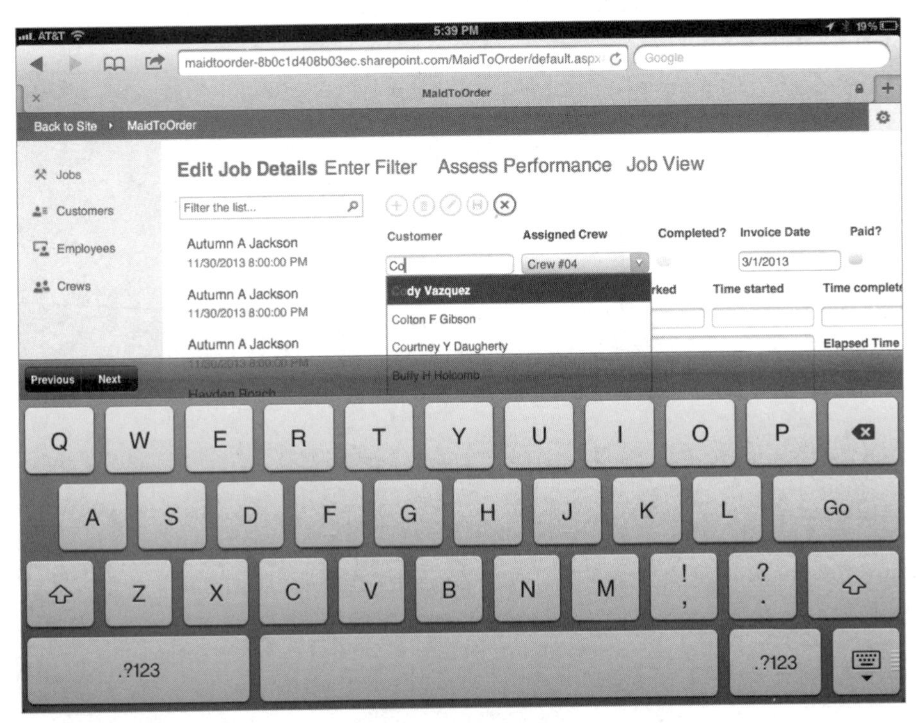

FIGURE 3-23: Maid To Order application on iOS tablet with keyboard displayed

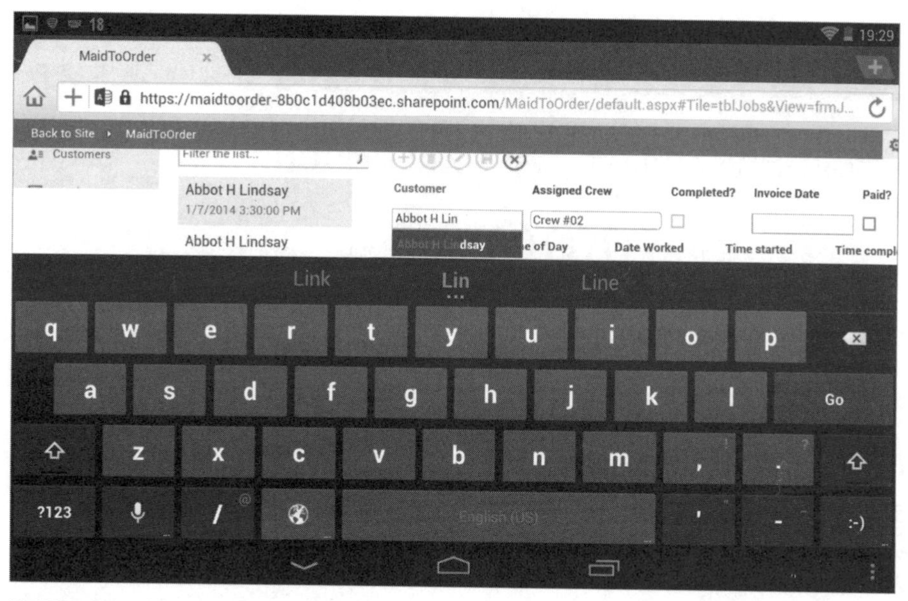

FIGURE 3-24: Maid To Order application on Android tablet with keyboard displayed

You can see that the user can continue to use features such as AutoComplete to select from a list of users. AutoComplete is partially obscured by the on-screen keyboard, which the user can hide once he is finished typing and ready to make a selection.

Therefore, when you plan to develop a web application that will target people using tablet forms, you have a reasonable expectation that it will be functional, provided you are conservative in how much space you use. One other major consideration is keyboard entry. Using an on-screen keyboard on a touch device is much slower in comparison to selecting from a list. Therefore, a well-designed web app would likely make more use of AutoComplete, Combobox, and Date Calendar popups to aid in data entry via a touch screen device. You may want to ensure that your buttons are sized similarly to the size of tiles and links on the web apps to accommodate the larger target area required by a finger compared to a mouse pointer.

You may find that not all browsers in different tablets will support the full range of functionalities required by the web app. In fact, you may find the design experience reminiscent of the days when inability to agree on standards led to compromises like the label on websites, "Best viewed in Internet Explorer," which nobody really liked. The frontier has now moved into browsers on tablets and, consequently, you may need to take additional time to plan the scope with your end users to determine what devices the web app should work for, and then design specifically for the selected device(s). You may need to consider alternatives to using the web app in a mobile device.

For smartphones or any other mobile devices of similar form factor, compare Figures 3-25 and 3-26.

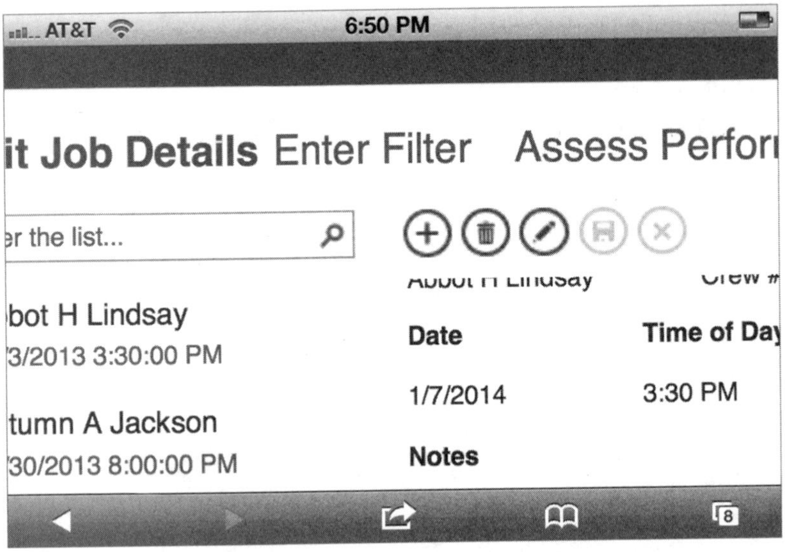

FIGURE 3-25: Maid To Order application on iOS smartphone

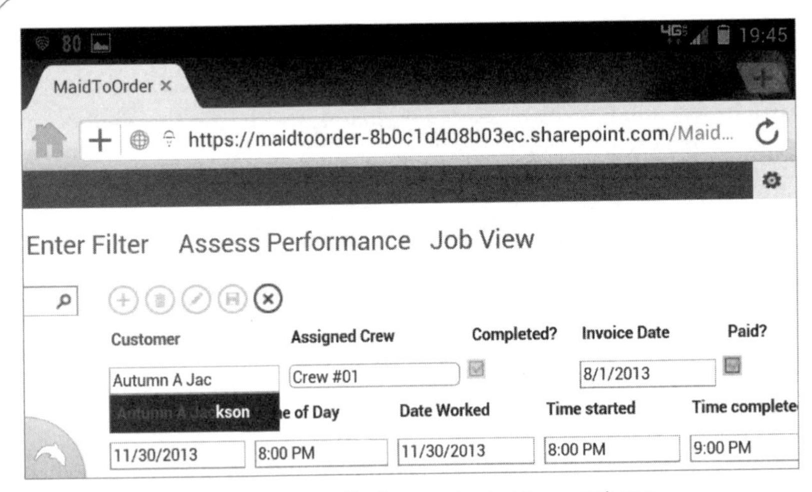

FIGURE 3-26: Maid To Order application on Android smartphone

As you can see, the smaller form factor makes it quite a challenge to deploy a web app targeting those devices. Views designed to work well with PC layouts are unlikely to work well on mobile devices. At any rate, the use of smartphones with the web app for the present will be a niche, although not for too long. As you may recall, the web app is based on the same architecture used broadly with SharePoint and there is considerable interest in using mobile devices.

In later chapters, you learn how the Maid To Order application is developed. Also, you will recall that one of our design goals is to enable maids to use their tablets or other mobile devices to maintain immediate records at the job site.

For the rest of the web app part of this book, we will look at designs that work well on any desktop PC and on any tablet. We consider additional components that we may be able to use with mobile devices in Chapter 10.

SHAREPOINT AND OFFICE 365

So far, we've looked at the Access client and how the design experience changes for web apps. To work effectively with web apps, it is necessary to have some familiarity with the SharePoint site where the web apps will be hosted. In Chapter 1, you learned how to create a new Office 365 account. When you log into your Office 365 account via your favorite web browser, you usually will land on the team site, illustrated in Figure 3-27.

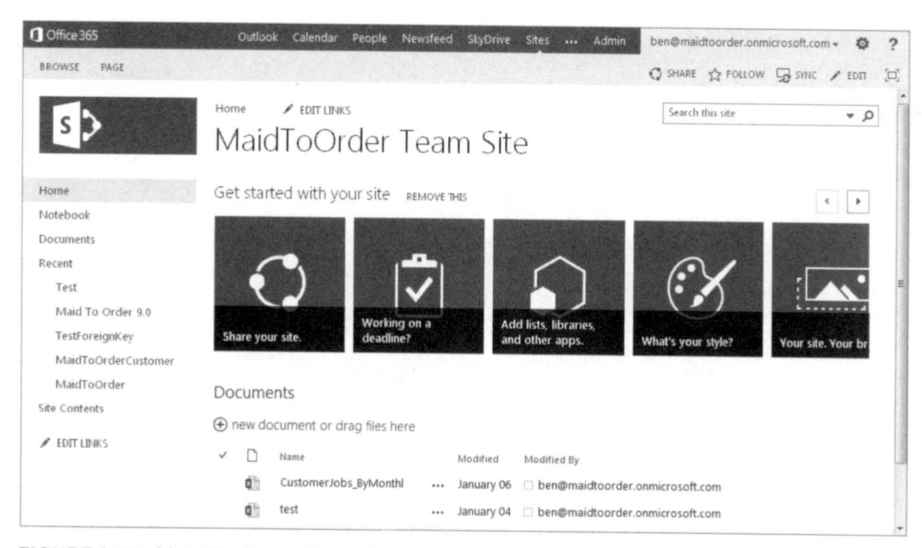

FIGURE 3-27: Maid To Order Team Site

The team site is not only a great place to publish your web apps but it also provides a place for you to share documents, different kind of SharePoint apps, and lists. You also can customize web pages with additional content as appropriate for your specific needs. A full discussion of SharePoint's many features is beyond the scope of the book. However, we want to point out a few that will be relevant for building apps.

If you've already tried to create a new web app from the Access client, you may have noticed that you had a choice between a team site and a creating a Personal App that will be available from your SkyDrive site associated with the Office 365 account, as in Figure 3-28.

You may wonder how to choose between a team site and a personal site. The short answer is that the team site by default makes an object available to any other member of the site who has sufficient permissions. On the other hand, a personal site is private by default unless you explicitly share it out to others. Because the intention of creating an Access web app is typically to allow for other people to use it, it usually makes sense to use a team site rather than a personal site to host your web apps.

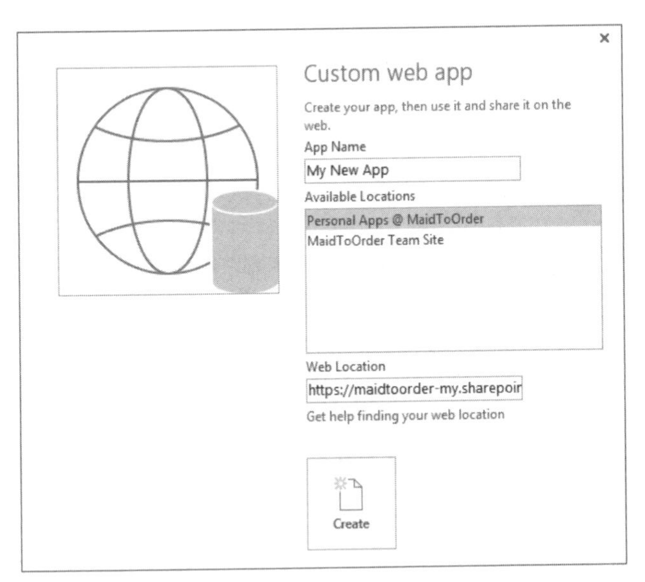

FIGURE 3-28: Dialog box listing sites available for creating a web app

> **WARNING** *Be aware that Office 365 plans provide SkyDrive as part of their offerings, which also includes additional features that are not available when you have only a SkyDrive account without an associated Office 365 plan. Thus, having a freestanding SkyDrive account will not enable you to create a web app to this account. You still need an Office 365 plan. Of course, you might have another site available to you, depending on what kind of plan you have chosen and whether you've created additional sites. In those cases, you are, of course, free to use different sites or maybe designate a specific subsite as the sole repository for hosting your web apps. So, a team site is an excellent choice for a simple deployment but is not the only choice available to you.*

Regardless of where you actually plan to deploy the web app, you may want to note that all apps will be easily found via the Site Contents link, which is typically listed on the left sidebar, as shown in Figure 3-29.

This provides you with a list of all installed apps, lists, and any subsites associated with the team site. It also provides the ability to add new apps or subsites, as illustrated in Figure 3-30.

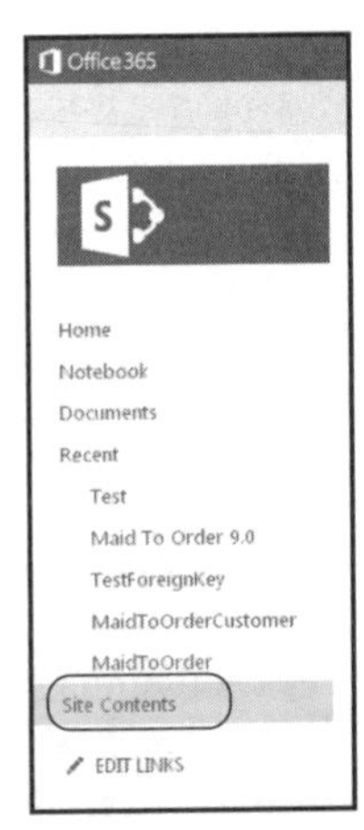

FIGURE 3-29: Site contents link

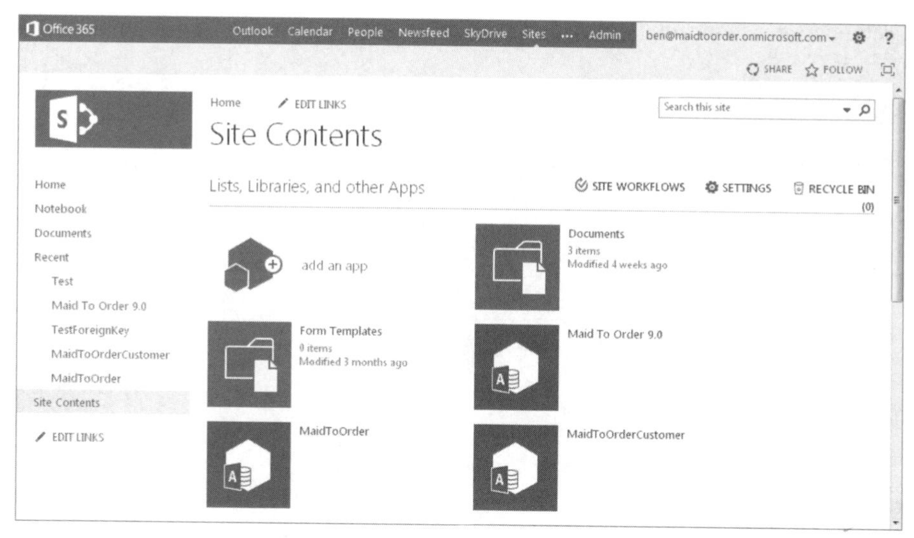

FIGURE 3-30: Site Contents page

Creating a Web App via Team Site

Because Access web apps are just SharePoint apps, you can also use this page to create an Access web app from the app store, rather than create it via the Access client. When you click the "add an app" link shown in Figure 3-30, you are presented with a popup listing different kinds of apps that may be built into a default SharePoint or Office 365 installation in addition to any other custom apps that may be available. Figure 3-31 shows a blank Access web app for you to add to a site.

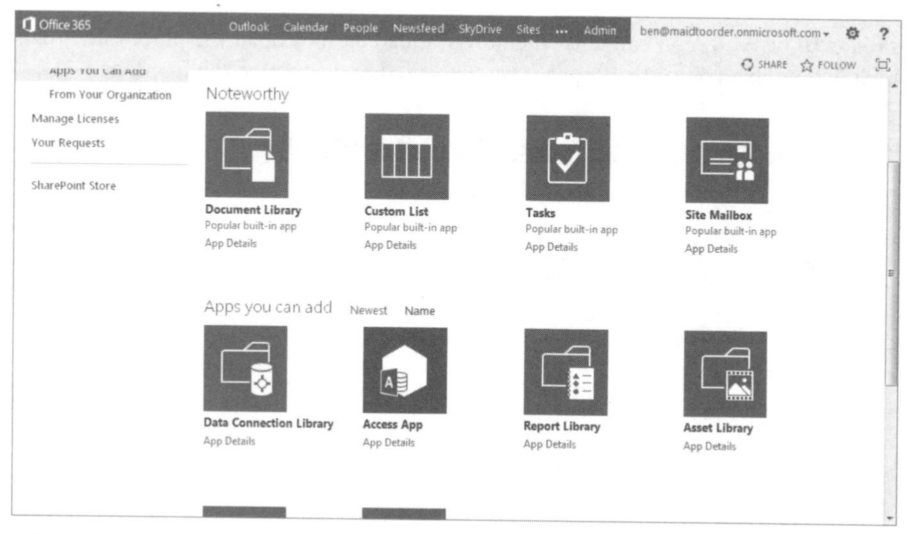

FIGURE 3-31: Adding Access web app

As Figure 3-32 demonstrates, you simply provide a new name for the app, which is then processed, as shown in Figure 3-33.

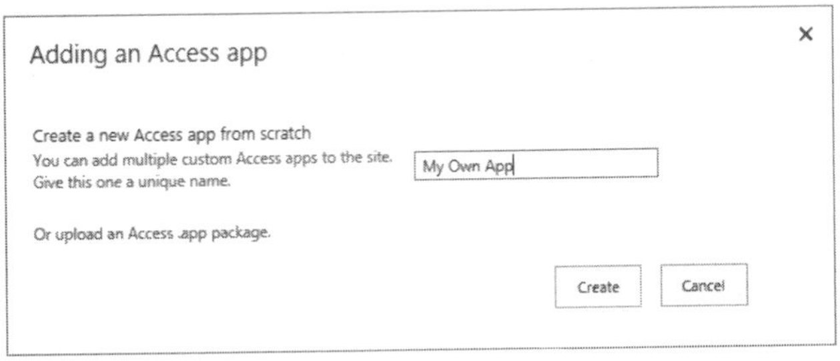

FIGURE 3-32: Providing a name for the new app

FIGURE 3-33: App being added to the site

> **WARNING** *Note that unlike the Windows filesystem, you are not prevented from creating multiple apps with the same name within the same site, which can quickly lead to confusion over which is the correct version. Therefore, you should be diligent in how you name your Access web apps so that they are unique, at least within that site.*

Once the app is ready to be used, you can click the newly added icon to open the placeholder page in Figure 3-34, which will enable you to then open Access to further customize the blank app.

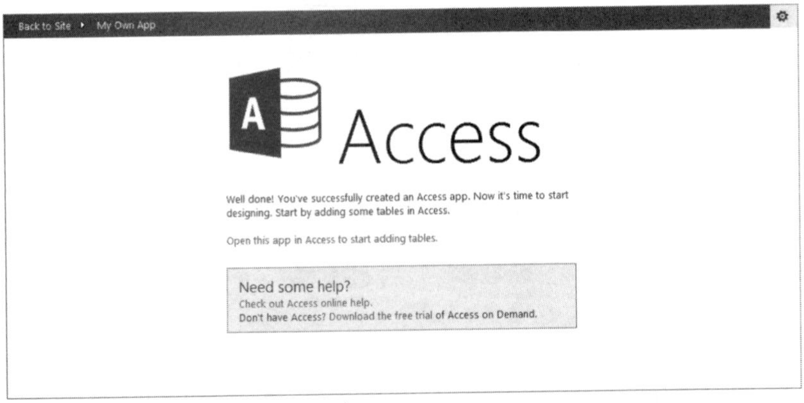

FIGURE 3-34: Placeholder page for blank Access web app

So you now have an alternative approach for creating new Access web apps outside of the Access client. Note that the process we discussed can also be used to deploy a developed web app, a topic we delve into in more detail when we get to Chapter 14, on deploying web apps.

Note that even after you've customized your new Access web apps, the gear button on the right side of the ribbon remains available, providing you with an easy way to launch the Access client if you want to further customize the web app, as illustrated in Figure 3-35.

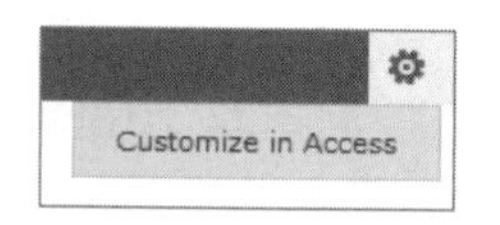

FIGURE 3-35: Gear button to customize Access web app

Deleting Web Apps

Sometimes you need to delete a web app. Because the web app is not a file that simply needs to be trashed, as was the case with an `.accdb` file, you must perform the deletion via the delete function on the site hosting the web app. When you click the ellipsis shown to the right of an app (see Figure 3-36), you are provided with a dialog box to manage the app, Delete being one of the options.

FIGURE 3-36: Open the App Properties dialog

You only need to click Delete to remove it. The deletion will be handled asynchronously; while the process continues, you may see the message indicating that the app is being deleted, as shown in Figure 3-37.

Once the deletion is complete, the app will be removed from the Site Contents page. Though SharePoint provides a Recycle Bin functionality, it does not help recover a deleted app. Therefore, you might want to make a backup via the Access client, as discussed earlier in the chapter before you perform the deletion.

FIGURE 3-37: Deleting an app message

Sharing Web Apps with Others

Access web apps are not always restricted to single users, so it naturally follows that you would want to share the app with others, particularly people who may not necessarily be a member of the team site. When you set up an Office 365 account, you set up an arrangement to pay for a specific number of users who will get access to the same team site, in addition to their personal site among other things, depending on the particulars of the Office 365 account you choose.

However, at times you may want to make your Access web app available to additional people who aren't a part of your Office 365 account. This could include customers, group members, and so forth. Unlike the first version of Office 365, you are allowed to share up to a certain number of external users without having to pay a subscription fee for those users. They can access your Access web app.

To share the web app with such users, use the Share link, which may be available to members of the site but will require approval of the owner, as shown in Figure 3-38.

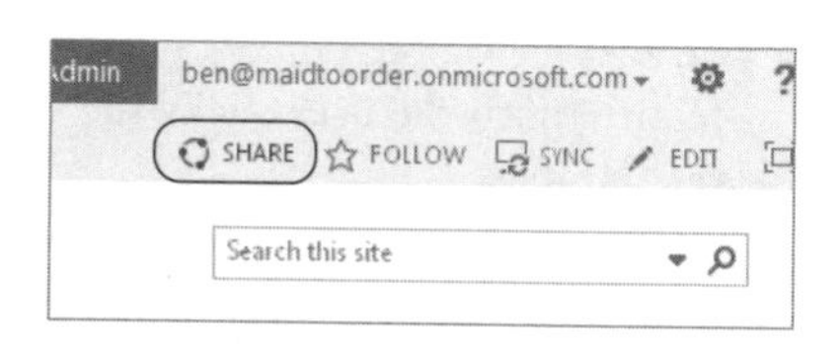

FIGURE 3-38: Share link on Team Site

Clicking Share opens a dialog box where you can enter a list of e-mail addresses to invite people, along with a message that will be included in the e-mail invitation sent to those users, as shown in Figure 3-39.

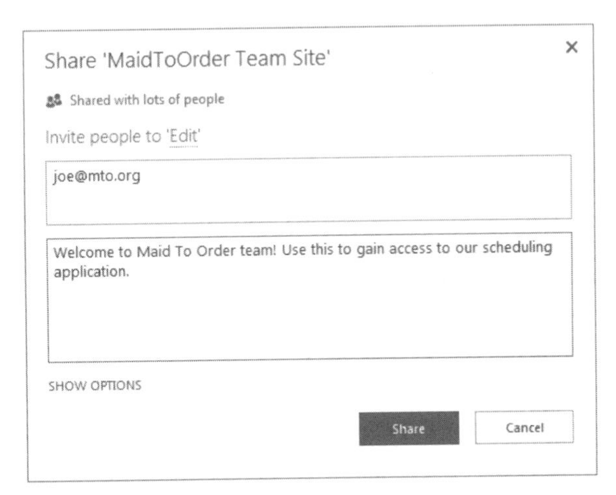

FIGURE 3-39: Share dialog box

You typically will want to specify a certain level of permissions for the invited users to define a set of allowable actions. Note in Figure 3-39 that the default permission is displayed as Edit, and if you hover the cursor over the permission, you can get a control tip listing permissions given, as in Figure 3-40.

You can choose a different permission by clicking Show Options, shown in Figure 3-39, which then exposes the permission drop-down shown in Figure 3-40. Figure 3-41 lists groups that are included by default in a typical SharePoint or Office 365 installation.

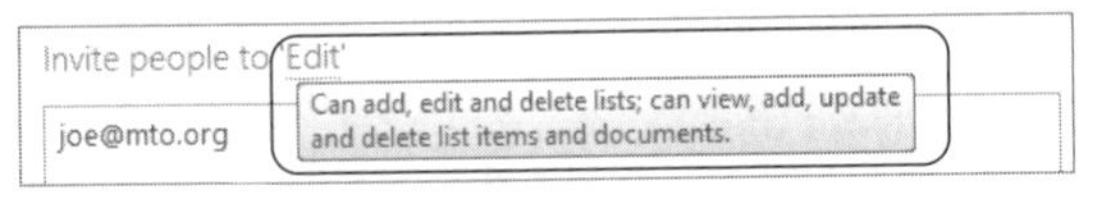

FIGURE 3-40: Permissions listed in a control tip

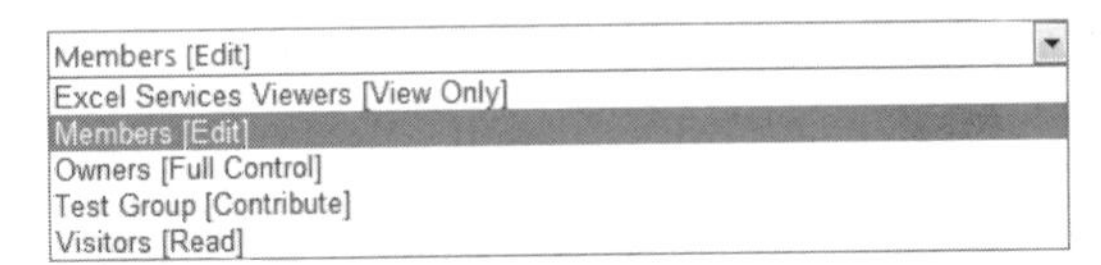

FIGURE 3-41: Default SharePoint groups

You delve into more details about the permissions and the various ramifications of each choice when you learn about security in Chapter 13.

SUMMARY

In this chapter you had your first close look at the layout and navigation principles that make Access web apps work well in the browser environment. We started by orienting you to the principles of web navigation, showing you how built-in web app features support good web navigation using both vertical and horizontal navigation elements.

We looked at one of the key new features in Access web apps, search navigation using the list pane on List views. Search navigation is customized for the data-driven web app by delaying the "match" feature until the user clicks the search icon, which preserves resources consumed by round-trips to the database.

Next, we identified the different types of views used in web apps and briefly previewed their appropriateness for different tasks such as data entry or rapid filtering and sorting. We then learned about the web-specific characteristics of the new ribbon, primarily the fact that it is trimmed down to the icons appropriate to web app design.

After that, we toured the backstage and took note of the pages within it that you will use to create new web apps and open existing web apps from whatever location holds them. You also got your first look at the tools for managing data connections to the web app database from a local `.accdb` or other file.

Finally, we took a quick look at layout in mobile devices. You saw that the limited form factors make designing web apps for mobile devices a bit more challenging.

Looking forward to Chapter 4, you'll dive deeper into the task of creating views for a web app.

Designing Views

WHAT'S IN THIS CHAPTER?

- Becoming familiar with the new view designer
- Understanding how tiles, links, and views work together
- Identifying new controls
- Recognizing what has changed about familiar controls
- Exploring the kind of views you can create and how to use them

Microsoft has introduced a new type of object, which it chose to call "views," as Access 2013's answer to viewing and manipulating data on the web. Unlike Access 2010 web databases and Data Access Pages, where Microsoft tried to preserve the same design model between the client side and the web side, Access 2013's view is a clean break from the design model for forms and reports in the Access client.

We believe that the clean break is a move in the right direction because fundamentally, designing objects for consumption on the web is a totally different proposition from designing objects for consumption within a client on a Windows desktop. It boils down to the fact that a web application must deal with much more limited scripting functionality, cannot run a database engine inside a web browser, and cannot rely on APIs from the operating system to do some of the more advanced stuff we have come to expect in a client object. Furthermore, web design requires an architecture that is totally disconnected from the database in contrast to Access's traditional approach wherein opening a bound form held open a connection to the database and maintained a pointer on a record within the recordset at all times.

At the risk of oversimplifying things, you could say that web browsers do not have an easy way to support storing session data from one page to the next. For example, a web page doesn't have any way of knowing whether any given browser instance is still actively viewing a page, or session state, or site. Also, when a new page is loaded, no information from the previous page, or session state, is available to that new page without explicit programming. With the advent of Asynchronous JavaScript And XML (AJAX), the task of managing session state is much easier but still relatively difficult in comparison to using client-based technology, be it Access, Silverlight, Flash, Java, and so forth. Moreover, the proliferation of mobile devices also calls for the ability to run your apps anywhere to a far greater degree than back in the 1990s when now-defunct Sun Microsystems promised a "compile once, run anywhere" platform that didn't go nearly as far.

In spite of the limitations inherent in web architecture, AJAX, HTML5, and other new web technologies have opened many new possibilities, and Access 2013 is certainly one of those new possibilities. Unlike Access 2010, where forms were built in Access and then translated into web components such as XAML and JavaScript, Access 2013 views are directly built as a web component, with no translation. What this means for you as an Access developer moving into web app development is that you are guaranteed 100 percent fidelity between how a form, or view, is dictated to behave in design view and what it actually will do in normal view when run in the browser. This eliminates one major pain point in Access 2010's web databases, where several elements were apparently compatible in both contexts, but in actuality would run only in the client and not on the web as a result of an inability to fully express the desired end result in terms of web components.

This chapter is aimed at getting you up to speed quickly with the new view designer, helping you to become productive with the new design surface, providing you with an orientation to the existing tools available to you, helping you sort out how designing a user interface has changed and, especially, introducing you to the new tools now available.

You will start with the primary elements of the design surface itself — the ribbon, field list, and the new interface for editing properties, called *popup buttons*. You then learn how to expose views for consumption on the web and to manipulate the surface of views. You will move on to the Action Bar and see how you can leverage it in your designs. You will then learn about controls on the design surface, what controls are still there and how they may have changed. You will see new controls and conclude with a brief list of controls that are no longer available in the web environment and possible substitutions for them.

VIEW DESIGN SURFACE

The view design surface is quite different from the traditional design view of forms and reports you might be accustomed to when building client objects. Figures 4-1 and 4-2 give you some idea of what is visually different between the designers.

As we progress through the chapter, you will learn in detail what those differences are and how to work best with them in designing views for your web apps.

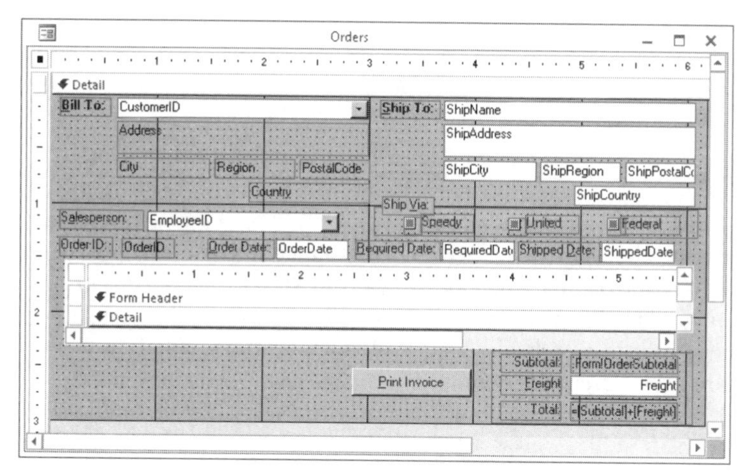

FIGURE 4-1: Client form in design view

FIGURE 4-2: Web app's view in design view

Ribbon

The ribbon should be familiar to you, as it was introduced in Access 2007. In the web app designer, however, the ribbon is quite simplified in contrast to the versions in either Access 2007 or Access 2010 when a form is open for design. At all times, you will have the File and Home tabs displayed. We'll focus on the contextual Design tab that is exposed when you have a view opened for design. It's shown in Figure 4-3.

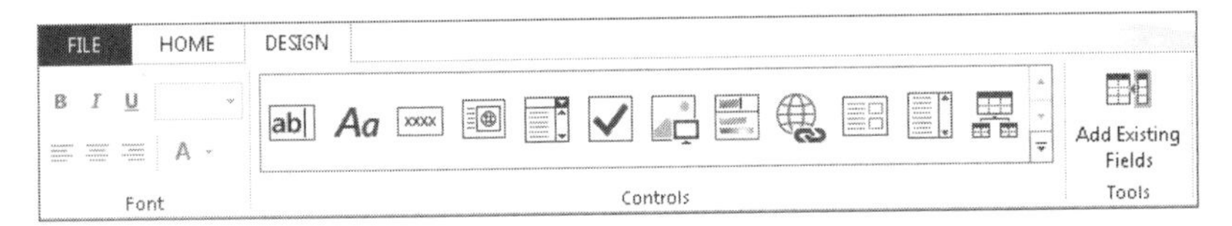

FIGURE 4-3: Design tab for a list view

As you see in Figure 4-3, you have some basic formatting options grouped under Font, mainly for usage with text controls and a list of controls that you can add to your view. The controls group contains many of the controls you are familiar with from Access client databases, including textboxes and labels, combo boxes, and the web browser control, among others. You'll have a chance to look at each one in more detail later in this chapter.

The set of controls available to you does vary with the type of view you have opened. As you may recall from Chapter 3, Blank and List views have the full range of controls available, whereas Datasheet view has only a subset of those controls and the Summary view none at all. Refer to Figure 4-4 for an example of the controls available to a Datasheet view.

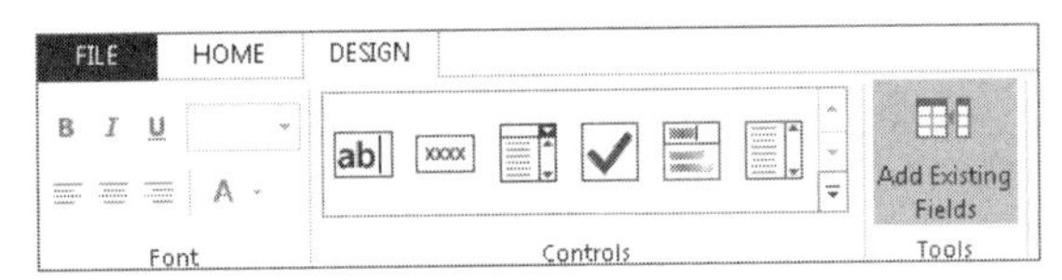

FIGURE 4-4: Controls available in Datasheet view

Datasheet views support controls such as Textbox, Label, Combobox, Yes/No checkboxes, AutoComplete, and Multiline Textbox. If you think about how datasheet views work, you should see that this list covers the controls you're most likely to want, and there's no reason to show other controls that you don't need, such as a web browser. Again, this increased level of context-sensitivity in offering only relevant controls reflects the clean break strategy taken with web apps.

Note that the rightmost button in Figure 4-3 is Existing Fields, which you may be familiar with from previous versions of Access. Clicking the Existing Fields button pops up a list of fields available to select and add to your design view. You learn more about field lists later in this chapter.

If you're looking for a property sheet icon on the ribbon, don't bother. There is no longer a separate property sheet for views or controls on views — we will talk more about the replacement in the "Popup Properties" section.

Tiles

In Chapter 2, you saw how tables and tiles are related. Creating a table creates a tile, and one cannot exist without the other. We want to call your attention to three additional properties of tiles, which are relevant to designing views.

Relabeling Tiles

First, you are free to relabel your tiles using a user-friendly name. This is useful if you need to have your tables adhere to a certain naming convention that would be annoying to your end users if they had to see it while using the app. Figure 4-5 shows how you can rename your tile via a right-click context menu.

Figure 4-6 shows what happens when you select Rename, enabling you to enter a new label for this tile. In this case, you would change the caption *tblForTestingOnly* to something more appropriate.

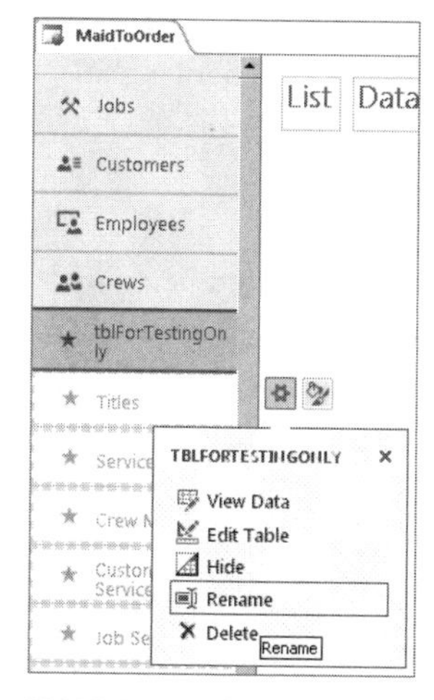

FIGURE 4-5: Choosing Rename for a tile via a right-click context menu

FIGURE 4-6 Renaming a tile

Note also that renaming the tile doesn't affect the name of the table to which it is linked.

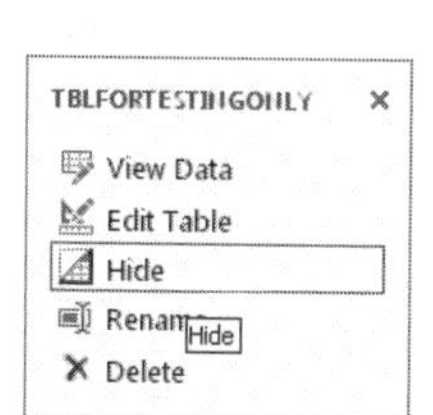

FIGURE 4-7: Hiding/unhiding tiles via a right-click context menu

Hiding and Showing Tiles

Next, you can choose to hide or show a tile. This is useful in cases where you want to hide supporting tables that are not meant for direct consumption by users. Figure 4-7 illustrates how you can hide and unhide a tile via a right-click context menu.

At the risk of calling attention to the obvious, hiding tiles only changes their behavior in the browser.

Figure 4-8 highlights how you can identify the difference between a hidden and a visible tile, in similar fashion to how you differentiate an enabled control from a disabled control. The visible tile, Crews, has a shaded background, whereas the hidden tile, Titles, has a plain background. Hidden tiles are grayed out, but remain visible.

FIGURE 4-8: A visible tile and a hidden tile

Tiles, Views, and Recordsources

Last, but not least, you want to be aware of the ramifications when you select a view for a tile. In the next section, you learn how to add a new view to a tile. Tiles do not merely function as an organizing tool but are also linked to tables. Therefore, any views bound to the tile are also linked to the same table. The view's recordsource must include the table; the only exception is to set the recordsource to `[No data source]`. Even if a tile-bound view has a blank recordsource, it is still linked to the tile's table and will be deleted should the tile's table be deleted. Figure 4-9 shows which tables or queries are available as a recordsource when you add a new view to a tile linked to the Jobs table using the [+] button. Note that the list of available queries roughly corresponds to whether the queries include the table to which the tile is linked. If the table is not selected within the query, then the query won't be listed.

While you can subsequently change a view's recordsource to something different, doing so in such a way that there is no connection to the tile and its linked table may cause unexpected behaviors or problems. Generally speaking, there needs to be a relationship between a view and the tile it is linked to.

Links and Creating Views

As you may have noticed, a tile can have any number of links — referred to as *View Selectors* in web apps — added to it. Each View Selector maps to a specific view. When you create a View Selector, you bind a view to a tile. For the rest of the book, we will disambiguate between a view that appears as a View Selector in *tile-bound view* versus a view that may be standalone. Standalone views are typically used as popup views or in subview controls.

As mentioned in the previous section, tile-bound views' recordsource must be related to the underlying table in some way.

To add a new tile-bound view, you would use the [+] button, as illustrated in Figure 4-9. Note also that you determine the type of view as part of the process of adding a tile-bound view.

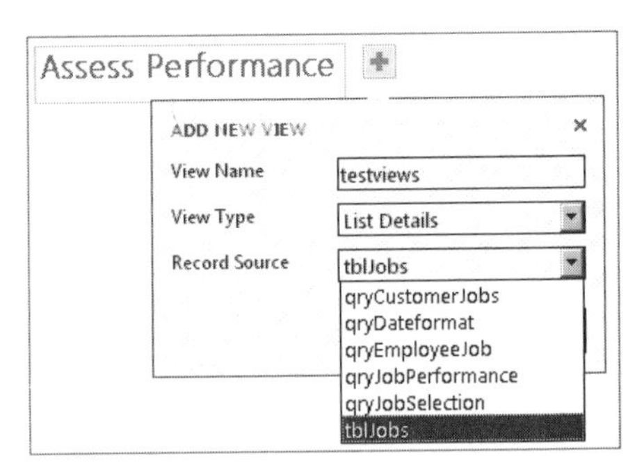

FIGURE 4-9: Available recordsources for a view

> **WARNING** *The choice of view type is irrevocable once made. When you consider that you also have no copy-and-paste functionality for individual controls, this becomes very important. While you can duplicate a whole view, you cannot change a view from one view type to another. You would need to replicate all controls, Action Bar buttons, and any associated macro actions on the other view. Therefore, make the decision carefully. If you're not sure which view you actually want, recall that for purposes of functionality, only blank views and list views are equivalent, whereas datasheets have only a subset of controls and summary views have almost none at all. To help you decide between a blank and list view, consider prototyping without doing any extensive layout. Then you can make the decision based on how the view works in your workflow and minimize the effort required to build up to the same level of functionality. Note that you still can copy and paste macro actions between different controls' event handlers but you can't copy and paste the controls or their layout arrangement at all.*

In similar fashion to tiles, you can name your views following your preferred naming convention, but also relabel the link for that view to a more user-friendly label. Figure 4-10 shows the context menu when you right-click a link on the View Selector, with Rename selected.

You can then relabel the View Selector in a fashion similar to what you did for tiles. You also can see in Figure 4-10 how you can open the associated view in design view or launch it in the browser. Launching it in the browser is a good way to test your changes without having to navigate manually to the link to the view from the starting page in the web browser.

> **NOTE** *Later in this book, you will learn about the On Start macro. Be aware that if your app has an On Start macro that navigates to another view, it will run every time you land on the app's site, so in this scenario, Launch Browser is of limited value.*

Note that you have the option to Duplicate or Delete the view as well, as you can see in Figure 4-10. You will read more about duplicating a bit later in this chapter but for now, you want to know that the Delete button does not delete just the link from the tile surface but also its associated view. We will consider this factor in greater depth later in the chapter.

In many situations, you may need a standalone view, not associated with a View Selector. You can create a standalone view via the Advanced menu shown in Figure 4-11. You can provide a means of accessing the view 3 ways: via an OpenPopup macro action, via the Popup view property of certain controls, or as a source object in a Subview control. You will see examples later in this chapter and again in Chapter 8.

FIGURE 4-10: A View Selector's right-click context menu with Rename selected

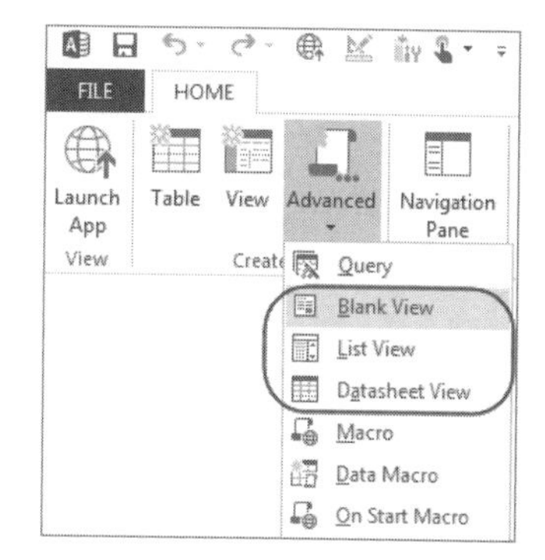

FIGURE 4-11: Creating a standalone view.

Field List

If you've previously worked in Access 2007 or 2010, the Field List should be familiar to you. It is largely unchanged from either version. The Field List also existed in earlier Access versions but was much simplified. Note that by default, the Field List is hidden, but you can pop it up by clicking the Add Existing Fields icon on the ribbon, as shown in Figure 4-12.

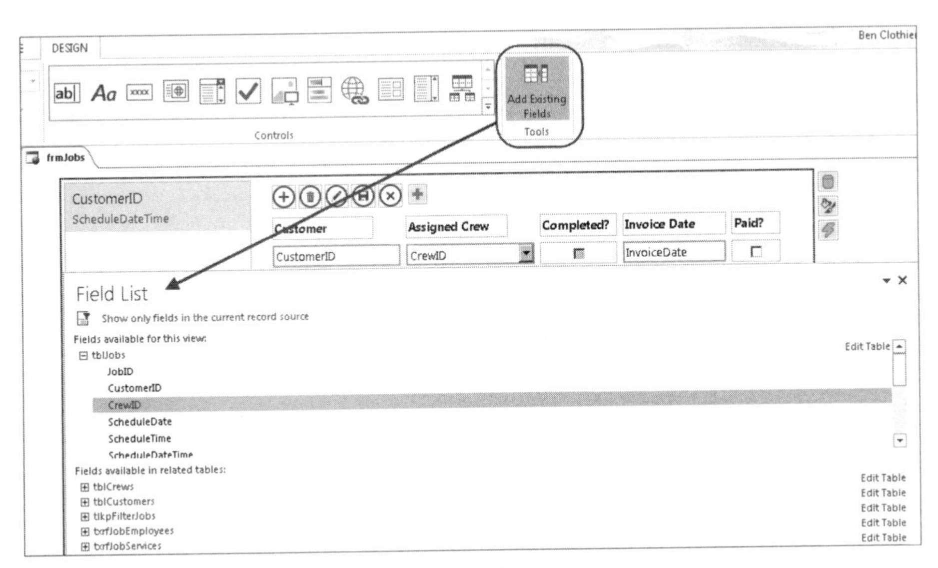

FIGURE 4-12: Add Existing Fields button on the ribbon

As you may expect, you can perform two operations with the Field List. First, you can use it to quickly add a control to the current view. Doing so in this way also creates an accompanying Label control with the caption inherited from the field's Display Text property. That can be a time-saver. Figure 4-13 shows the result of either double-clicking or dragging fields from the Field List to the open view.

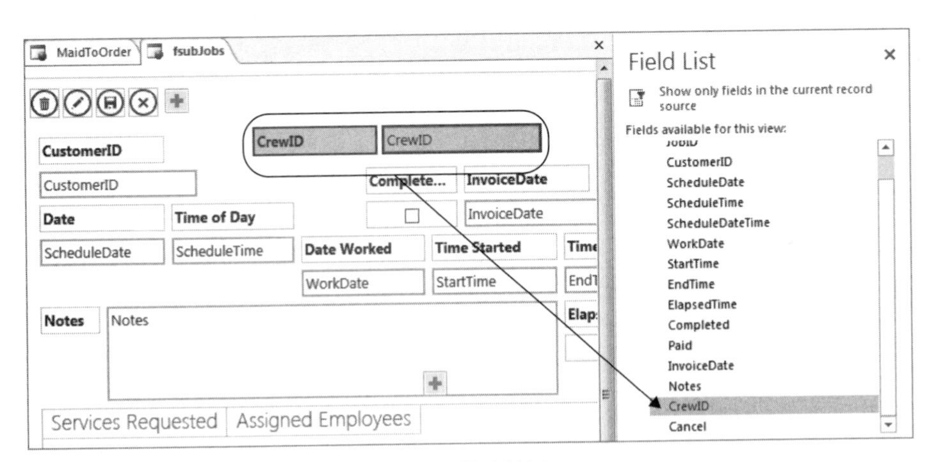

FIGURE 4-13: Result of adding a field via the Field List

One enhancement introduced in Access 2007 and carried over into 2013 is the ability to also see other tables that are related to the view's recordsource, and to add their fields. You can even add fields from other tables that are not related. Figure 4-14 lists the other tables' fields, grouping the related tables and all other tables separately.

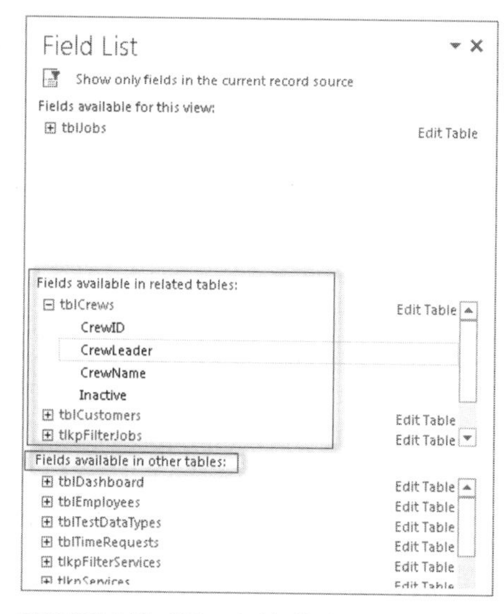

FIGURE 4-14: Other table listing in Field List

The tables included in the Related Tables group are primarily those used in the recordsource for your view and whether the source tables have any Lookup fields that join to the table in the view.

If your view is based on a table or an embedded query and you opt to add a field from a table that's not already selected in the view's recordsource, Access automatically adds the field and, if needed, the table into the view's recordsource. In cases where you add a field from a table that has no known relationship to the view's current table, you will see the dialog box shown in Figure 4-15, which asks you to describe the join.

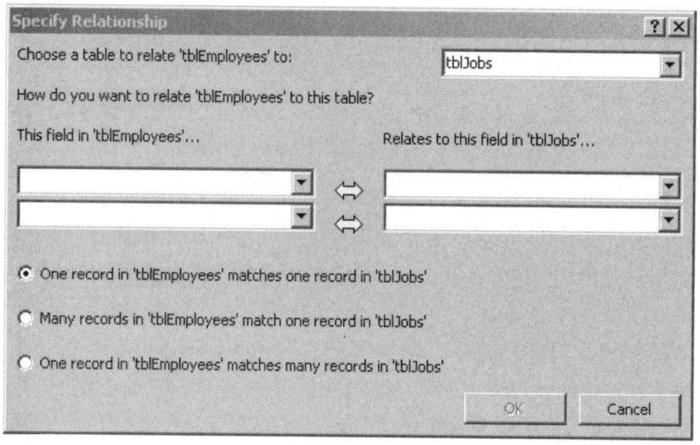

Specify Relationship
Choose a table to relate 'tblEmployees' to: tblJobs
How do you want to relate 'tblEmployees' to this table?
This field in 'tblEmployees'... Relates to this field in 'tblJobs'...
One record in 'tblEmployees' matches one record in 'tblJobs'
Many records in 'tblEmployees' match one record in 'tblJobs'
One record in 'tblEmployees' matches many records in 'tblJobs'
OK Cancel

FIGURE 4-15: Message box displayed when adding field not directly available

You can specify up to two fields to join between two tables. Most of the time, you'd just specify the key columns in each table. The radio buttons have no effect so you can ignore the radio buttons and click OK to add the table. However, because we should be using Lookup fields to define relationships between tables, you shouldn't see that dialog box. If it appears, it should indicate a potential design issue you need to resolve.

Let's consider what happens when you do add fields from a related table that you saw in Figure 4-14. If you have a view that uses a query as its recordsource, as shown in Figure 4-16, you may see that there is one Lookup field, `CrewLeader` from the table selected as one of the fields in the query.

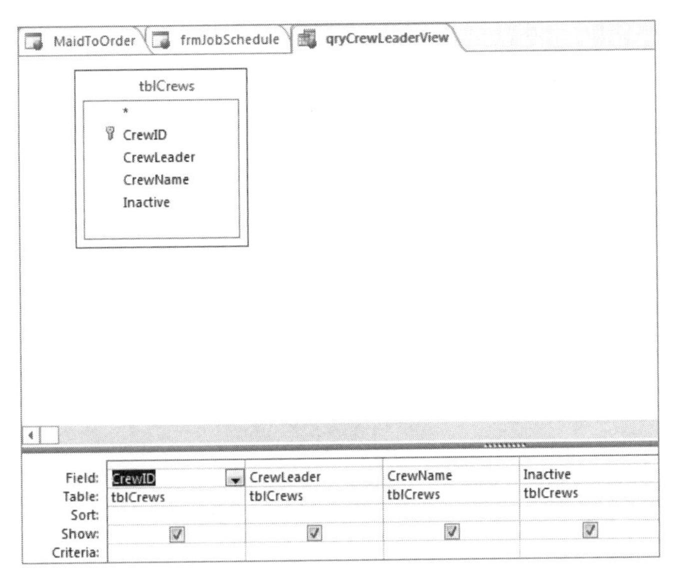

FIGURE 4-16: Query design view of a view's recordsource

Suppose you try to add the `FullName` field that's listed in the lookup table, `tblEmployees`, from the Field List. Doing so will show a message box to confirm the choice, as shown in Figure 4-17.

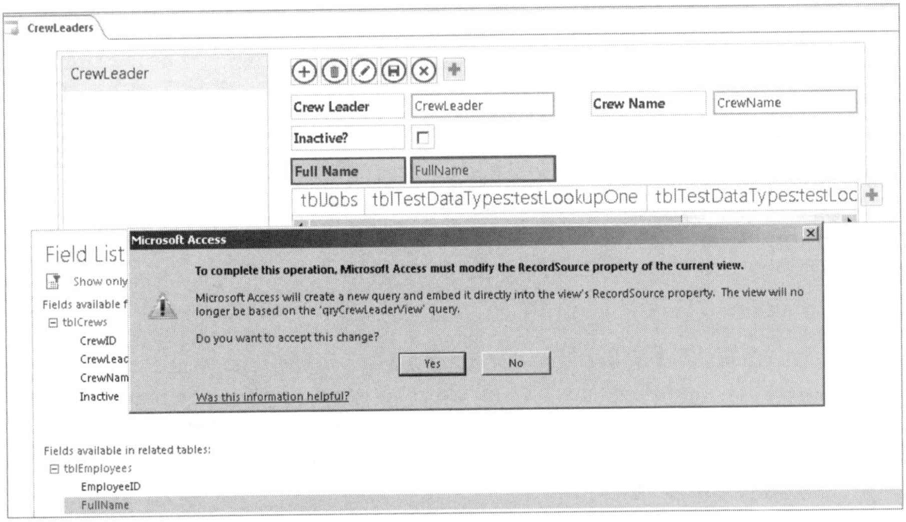

CrewLeaders

CrewLeader

Crew Leader | CrewLeader | Crew Name | CrewName

Inactive?

Full Name | FullName

tblJobs | tblTestDataTypes:testLookupOne | tblTestDataTypes:testLoc

Field List

Show only

Fields available f

tblCrews

CrewID

CrewLeac

CrewNam

Inactive

Microsoft Access

To complete this operation, Microsoft Access must modify the RecordSource property of the current view.

Microsoft Access will create a new query and embed it directly into the view's RecordSource property. The view will no longer be based on the 'qryCrewLeaderView' query.

Do you want to accept this change?

Yes | No

Was this information helpful?

Fields available in related tables:

tblEmployees

EmployeeID

FullName

FIGURE 4-17: Selecting a related table's field

Because the field isn't directly selectable in the current query, Access needs to add the related table where the field is found and create the join. Figure 4-18 shows the changed query after you click Yes to the message box shown earlier.

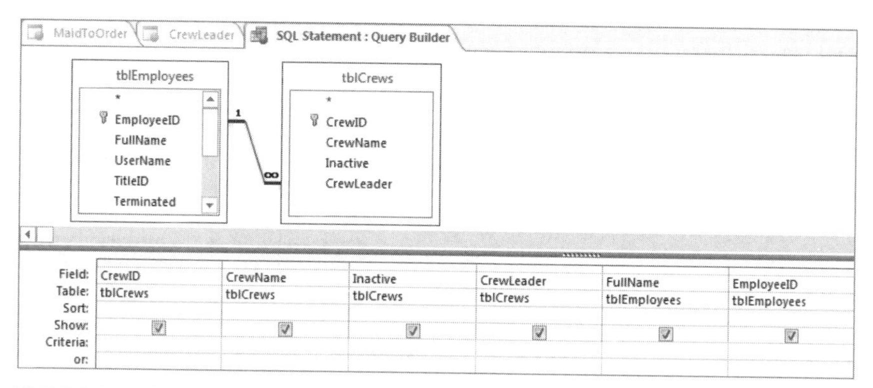

FIGURE 4-18: Modified query after adding the related field

This query is now saved with the view as an embedded query, rather than as the previously used named query. You can see this in Figure 4-19.

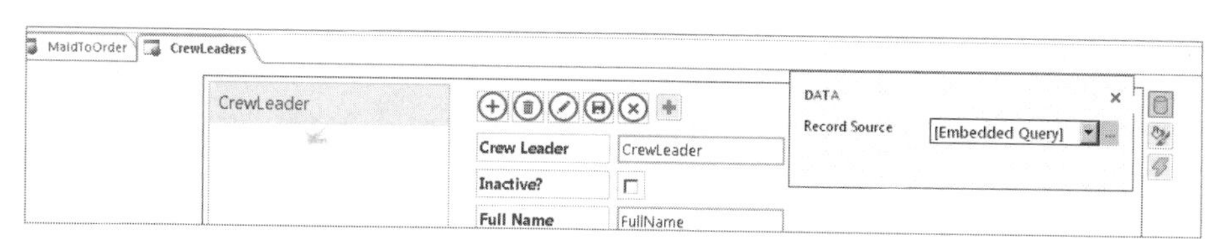

FIGURE 4-19: Embedded query replaces named query

This was a simple example because the original table had only one Lookup field. Access uses Lookup fields to determine how tables are related and thus was able to guess correctly. As you might expect, in more complicated setups where you might have more than one Lookup field, and especially when they come from the same table twice, it is important for you to double-check the modifications to the query suggested by Access to make sure they're what you expected.

FIGURE 4-20: Link to toggle between displaying only available fields versus all tables' fields

By default, you see all tables listed as you saw in Figure 4-14. However, if you want to show only fields that are in the current recordsource for easy reference, you can click the link shown in Figure 4-20 to toggle between the default listing and the restricted listing.

Lastly, the Field List provides a quick link to open the table in design view, as illustrated in Figure 4-21.

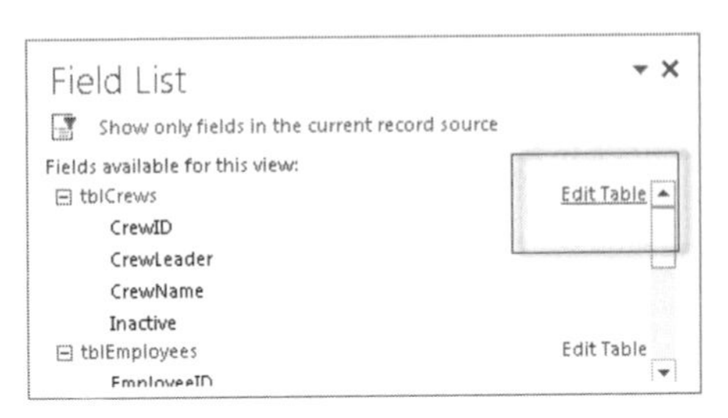

FIGURE 4-21: Edit Table link in Field List

Popup Properties

The interface for managing properties of objects has undergone another major transformation. You may recall that Access 2003 and prior versions used a free-floating dialog box to list an object's properties, as shown in Figure 4-22.

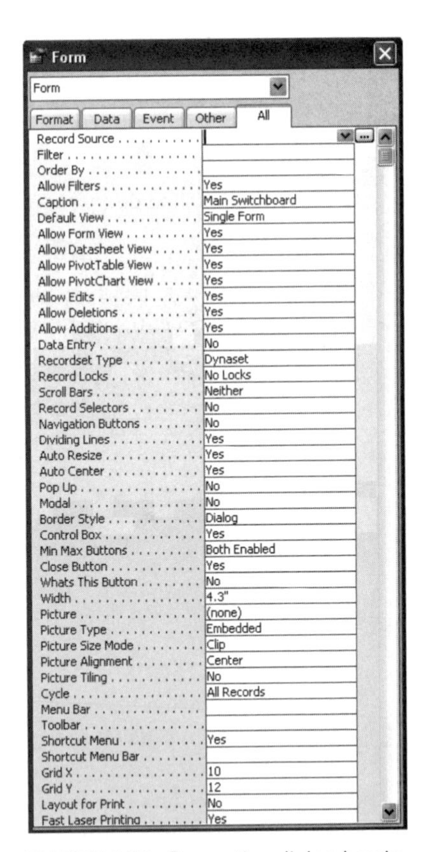

FIGURE 4-22: Properties dialog box in Access 2003

In Access 2007 and 2010, the Properties dialog was docked by default, which eliminated a common complaint with the free-floating dialog box; it would be in the way while working in design view and you had to move it around, requiring a fair amount of window management to keep your workspace uncluttered.

However, this brought on a new complaint — the docked sheet always took up the entire vertical area and although it could be resized, took away from the workspace. The loss of working area was also compounded by the introduction of the Navigation Pane, as Figure 4-23 illustrates.

Another complaint was that you couldn't display the Field List and the Properties Sheet simultaneously since both occupied the same space on the right side, regardless of whether you had ample screen area for both. That remains true even if you had detached the sheet from the right-side dock.

In an attempt to provide the best features from a freestanding dialog box and a docked sheet, Microsoft has revamped the interface. Instead of a dialog box or a sheet, the design surface presents a number of buttons, as demonstrated in Figure 4-24, which shows the buttons for the view on the right side.

Those buttons roughly correspond to the tabs that you would have seen on the Properties Sheet or Properties Dialog. This also presents an opportunity to introduce another change in the design interface.

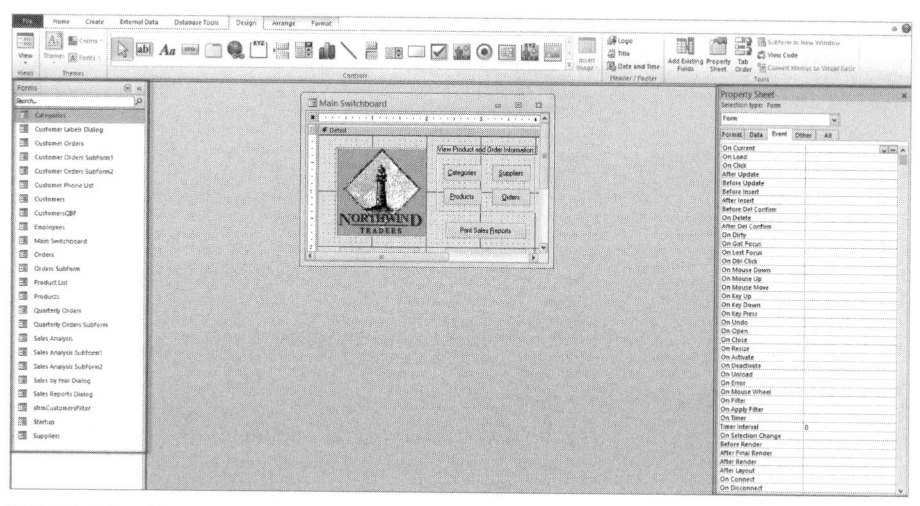

FIGURE 4-23: Narrow workspace with Navigation Pane and Properties Sheet displayed

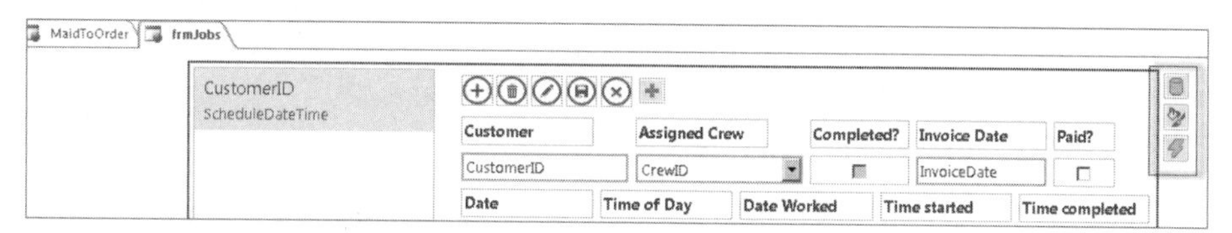

FIGURE 4-24: Properties button

DIFFERENT BUTTONS FOR DIFFERENT OBJECTS

You may have noticed that some objects outside the view's design surface have different buttons from what you saw in Figure 4-24. The buttons for tiles, shown in Figure 4-5, and views, shown in Figure 4-10, function more like a menu than a Properties Sheet, as is being discussed here.

Instead of consuming space with text, the design surface presents several icons; each icon always has a control tip to describe what that icon represents, as demonstrated in Figure 4-25.

FIGURE 4-25: Tooltip for Data properties button

As you can see in Figure 4-25, you have the Data button on the left, the Formatting button in the middle, and the Actions button on the right. Note that for views and some objects, those buttons may be arranged vertically, but in the same order from top to bottom, as you can see in Figure 4-26.

Clicking one of those buttons opens a context menu. Note further that not all three buttons are displayed for some objects. For example, if a control has no events attached to it, the button will not be available. Figure 4-27 shows the relevant properties for a combo box's Data button.

FIGURE 4-26: Vertical arrangement of the controls

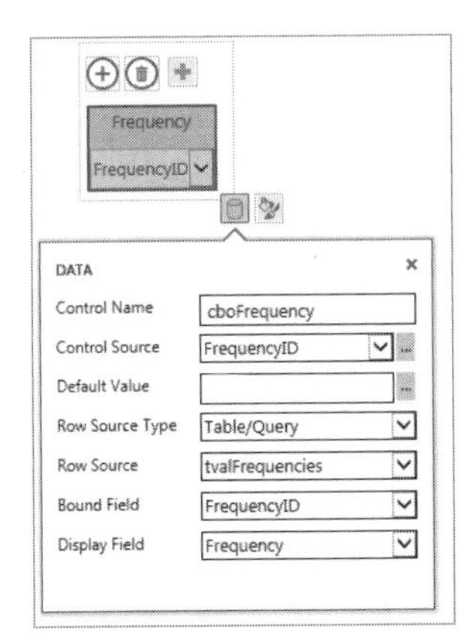

FIGURE 4-27: Data Properties popup

One other key thing you need to understand is that the properties popup will not show you all available properties. As you saw in Figure 4-28, you only have a RowSource property. You're probably wondering where you set the Bound Field property and edit the displayed fields in the combo box. The answer is that action buttons are even more context sensitive than in previous versions. You must set a RowSource to some other value than `[No Data Source]`, as in Figure 4-28, to expose those additional properties shown in Figure 4-29.

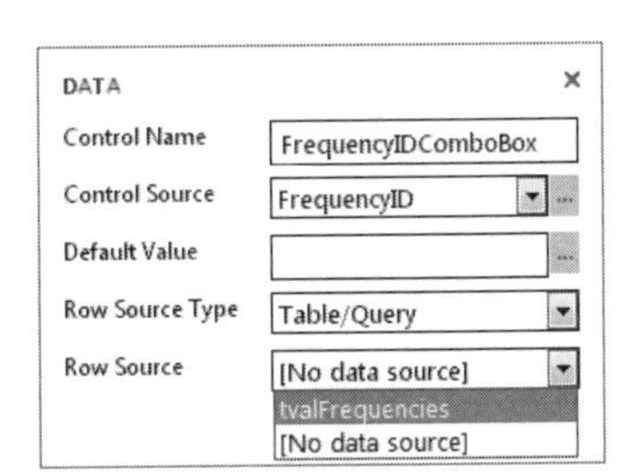

FIGURE 4-28: Selecting a rowsource

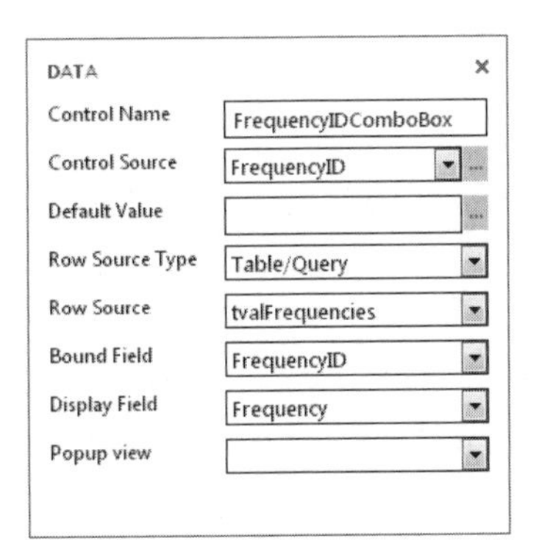

FIGURE 4-29: Additional properties shown after rowsource selection

The preceding figures should illustrate that the new popup buttons and their respective dialogs are much more context-sensitive than either the Properties dialog or Properties sheet was. On the one hand, this can be a good thing because you only see properties that are actually relevant, which saves you from wading through a sea of empty or inapplicable properties, as you had to with the Properties dialog and Properties sheet. On the other hand, it can make discovering properties a bit harder until you become more familiar with the new design surface. Therefore, when working with the new properties popups, it is a good idea to experiment with different properties to discover what additional properties are made available for those contexts.

The [icon] popup button deserves an additional mention. In previous versions of Access, you would refer to the Events tab on the Properties dialog or sheet to set up event handlers for objects. In Access 2013 web apps, the nomenclature has changed from "Event" to "Action." Also, recall that in a default installation of previous versions of Access, when you added a new event handler to an object, you would be presented with a dialog asking you to choose between macro, expression, or code to build the event handler, as in Figure 4-30.

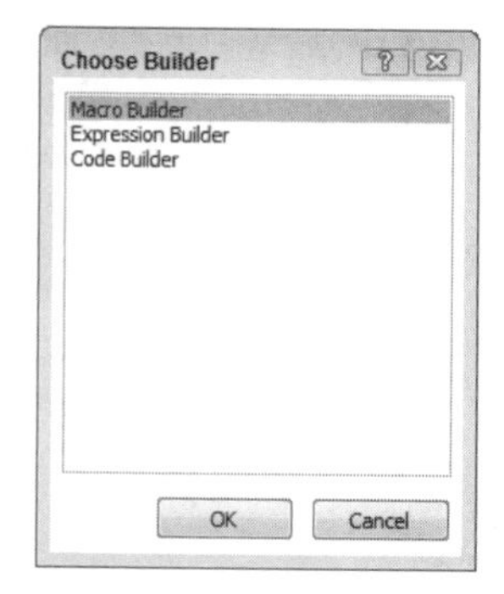

FIGURE 4-30: Dialog box for choosing the format of an event handler

Some longtime Access developers, possibly including yourself, have been annoyed with that constant request and may have gone out of their way to make sure the event handler defaults to using VBA. Although sometimes there were advantages in using macros or expressions instead of VBA, it was not very common and having to make the choice every time got old. Access 2013 simplifies this. Since all actions are macro driven, Access 2013 just presents you with a button for each available event, as shown in Figure 4-31.

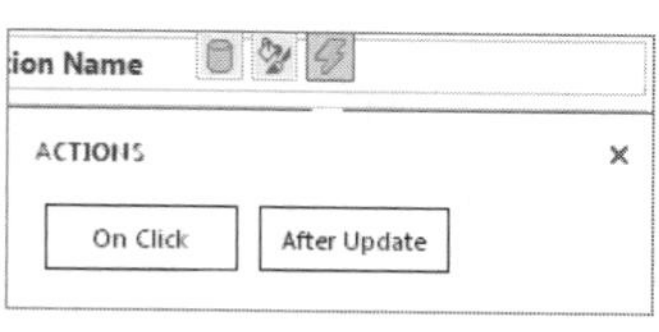

FIGURE 4-31: Actions properties popup

You can tell whether an event has any macro actions attached by the color of the button. A button turns green when it has a macro action attached, as you can see in Figure 4-32.

As you learn later in Chapters 6 and 9, you can call other macros from the event handler you create for an event, so we think you'll agree that this is a good simplification in general. We will revisit some more common properties in the three buttons later in this chapter in the "Common Properties" section.

To manipulate the properties of a view itself, you would click the blank area or outside the view's design surface. This then presents the three buttons just outside the view's design boundary, as shown in Figure 4-33.

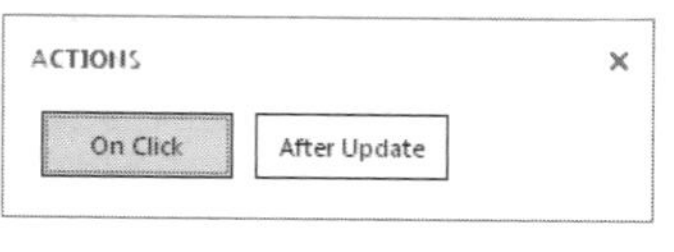

FIGURE 4-32: Event button highlighted indicating macro actions

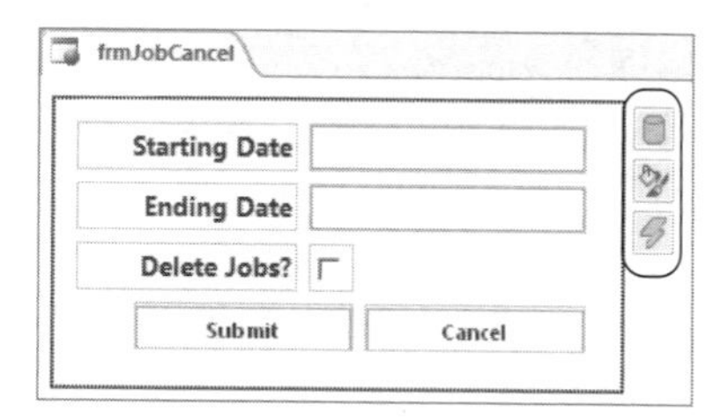

FIGURE 4-33: View properties buttons

> **NOTE** *If your screen is quite small or the view is too wide for the display, the form properties buttons will appear in the upper-right corner of the workspace.*

Furthermore, note that some objects, such as the List Pane for List views, or summary workspace on the Summary view, have their own sets of properties distinct from the view's properties. The List Pane is straightforward and works just like a control, as you can see in Figure 4-34.

However, Summary view can be a bit misleading because the workspace occupies the entire usable design area for the view. Figure 4-35 shows the properties exposed for the summary workspace. Contrast the buttons' placement with Figure 4-33.

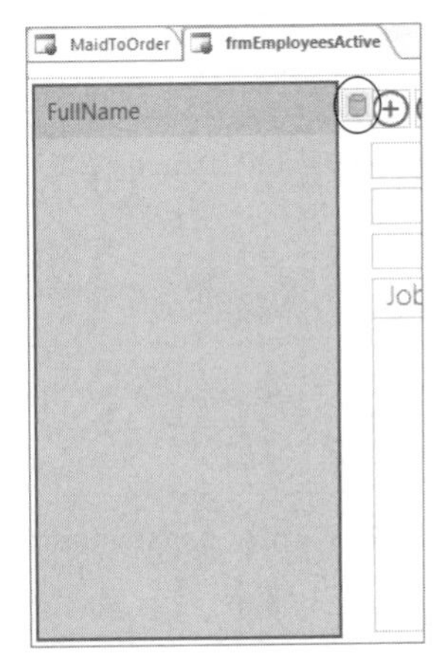

FIGURE 4-34: Clicking a List Pane to show the properties button

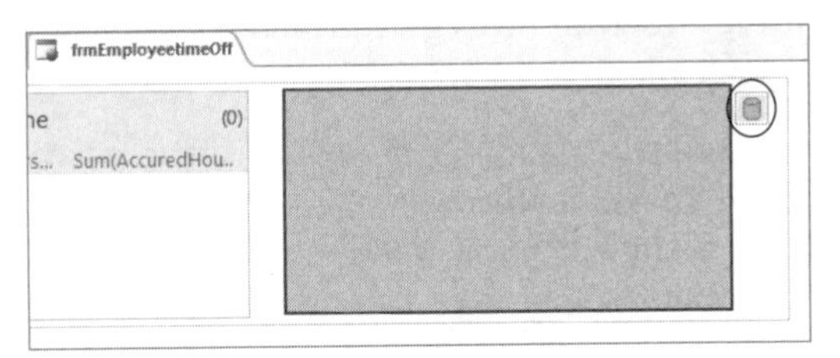

FIGURE 4-35: Summary workspace properties

> **NOTE** *As mentioned earlier, whenever you need to access form properties, click outside the design area, which is always delimited by a border, to bring the form's properties into focus.*

Refer to Chapter 3 for an explanation of what Summary views are; you will also learn more about how to use them in Chapter 9.

Manipulating Control Placement

Microsoft also has revamped the layout placement design. Starting with Access 2007, there has been support for creating an HTML table on a form, which made it easy to add and manage placement of controls, as you can see in Figure 4-36.

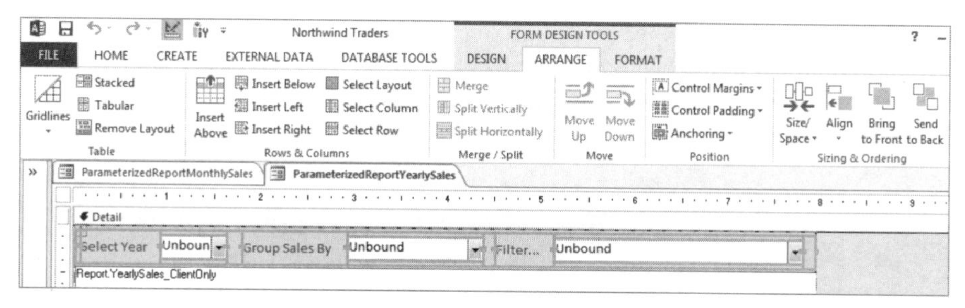

FIGURE 4-36: HTML table in a form design view

When building an Access 2010 web database, the HTML table was the only way to place and arrange the controls on it. You couldn't have pixel-perfect placement at all. Figure 4-37 illustrates a web form from a 2010 web database where the HTML table permeates the whole form surface.

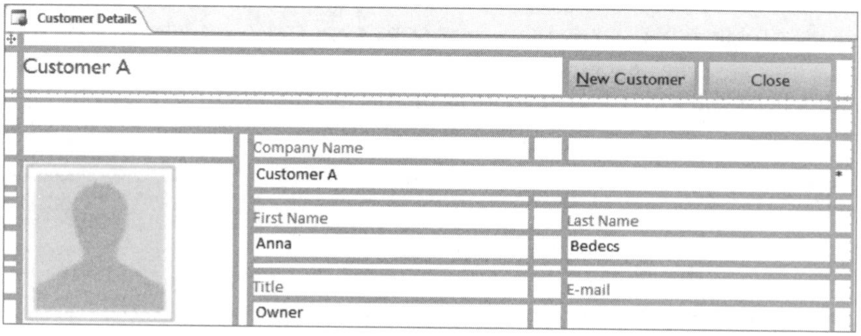

FIGURE 4-37: HTML table on an Access 2010 web form

Understandably, the requirement to work in an HTML table was very frustrating and restrictive for many developers. More importantly, it took more time to manipulate the placement of controls. While adding HTML tables to Access client forms was very helpful, especially for continuous forms, forcing it on the entire form and for all forms made it very hard to build forms that would accommodate different sized controls without adversely affecting several other controls in the process of resizing one control. There was a facility to merge and split cells, but it was quite cumbersome and time-consuming.

Adding a Control to a View and Resizing the Control

In light of those shortcomings, Microsoft has moved away from a rigid table-like layout and provided a new snap-in layout. Figure 4-38 shows how you can drag a control anywhere you please, whereas Figure 4-39 shows what happens when you drop the control, snapping it into the nearest invisible cell.

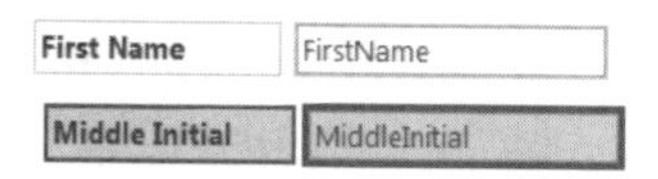

FIGURE 4-38: Dragging a control over the form design area

As you can see in Figure 4-39, you still have an essentially table-like layout, where is a minimum width and height a control can occupy. If you resize the control's width just wide enough, as in Figure 4-40, you'll see it snap to the next width, as Figure 4-41 shows.

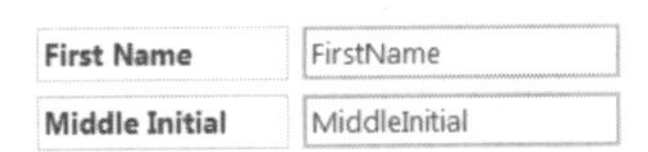

FIGURE 4-39: Control snapped into place after dropping

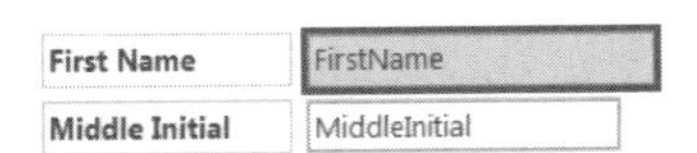

FIGURE 4-40: Dragging the control's width to resize

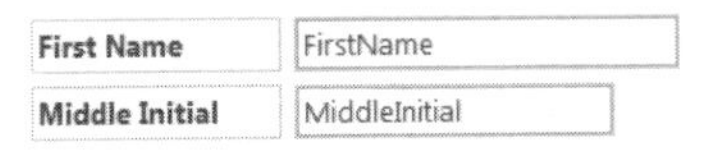

FIGURE 4-41: Result of resized control

To get a better idea of what sizes you can achieve, refer to Figure 4-42.

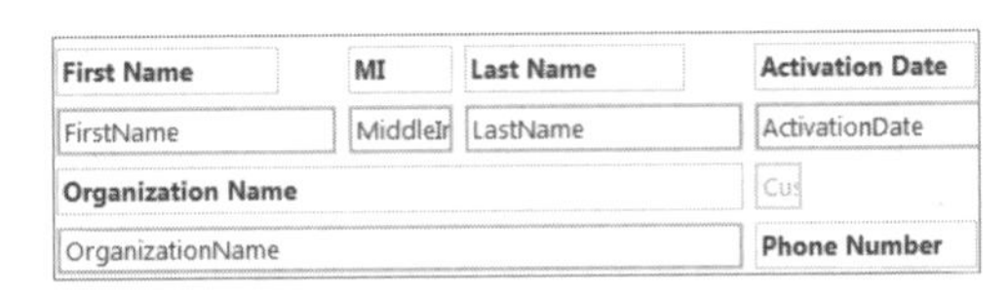

FIGURE 4-42: Collage of different sized controls

Unlike the rigid table layout in Access 2010 web forms, however, a resized control does not necessarily affect other controls. Figure 4-43 shows a view's layout before the Middle Initial control's resizing, while Figure 4-44 shows the changed size only for the Middle Initial control, leaving other controls unaffected.

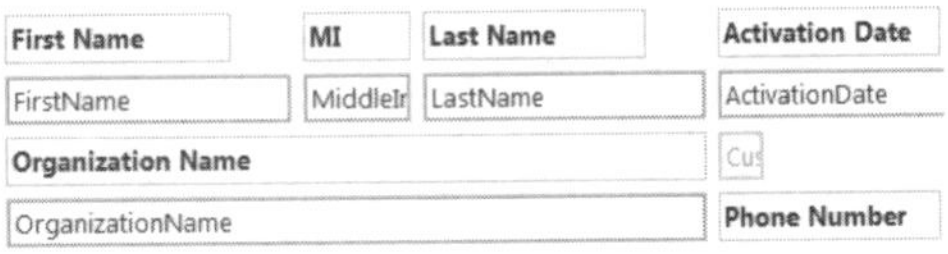

FIGURE 4-43: View's original layout before resizing

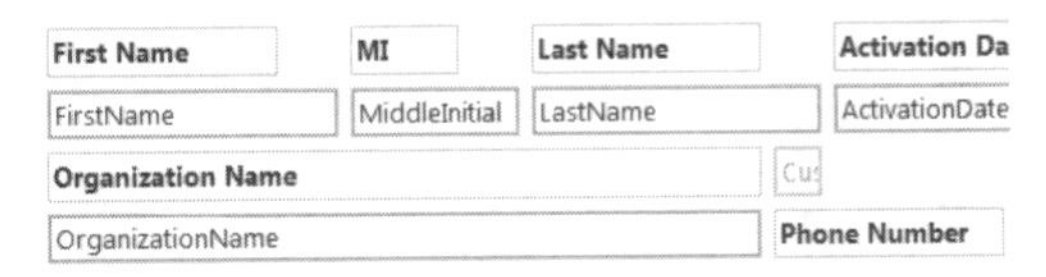

FIGURE 4-44: Result of resizing a control in the middle of a series of controls

As you can see, although you don't have pixel-perfect placement, the new snap-in layout is much easier to work with. Another major advantage of the new layout design is that it's auto-aligning; we think you'll like that. With client forms, where pixel perfection is possible, you would frequently have to align controls to ensure they were spaced and positioned correctly. This is no longer needed with the new snap-in layout.

Adding Controls over Existing Controls or Resizing into Another Control's Space

There are a few additional issues to consider with the new layout design. In a client form, you could have controls overlap each other. Overlapping is not possible in the app's view. Figure 4-44, shown previously, illustrates the controls' placement prior to dragging another field, and Figure 4-45 shows what you'd see when you drag the control into the same area as an existing control, which pushes it downward.

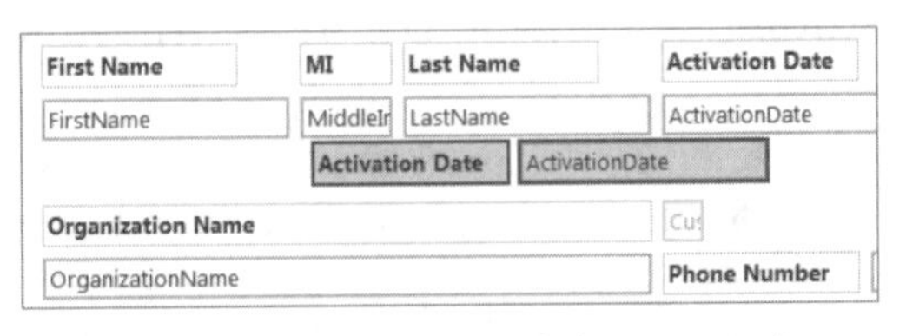

FIGURE 4-45: Modified control placement when a control is being dragged above another control

Generally speaking, controls will be pushed downward. However, if you hover over the left area of the existing control's original placement, the existing control will be pushed to the right instead. Furthermore, note that the control's movement is to some extent influenced by whether there is an associated label that will try to stick with the control.

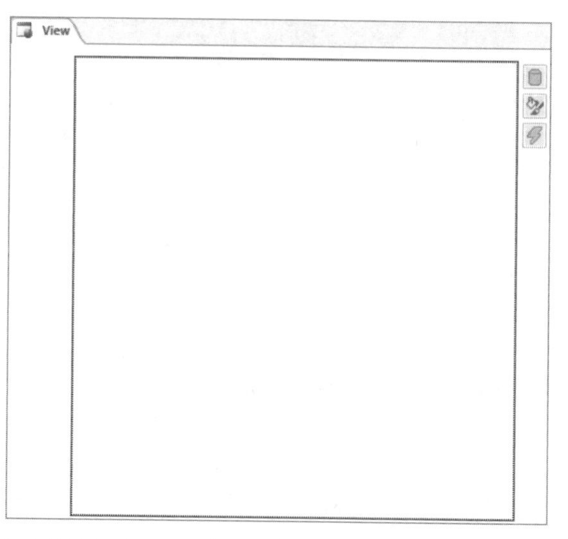

FIGURE 4-46: Default area defined for a new Blank view

Resizing the View's Surface

Unlike client forms, where you can specify an absolute size, views do not have a fixed width and height. When you create a new view, you are presented with a certain default design area, as shown in Figure 4-46.

However, if you were to save the Blank view immediately, close it and reopen, it would resize to the smallest area possible, as shown in Figure 4-47.

Instead of dragging the view's border to resize it, as you would with a client form, you'd have to add a control, and then resize the control to the size you want. The view itself will automatically resize to accompany the resized control's new dimensions, as you can see in Figure 4-48.

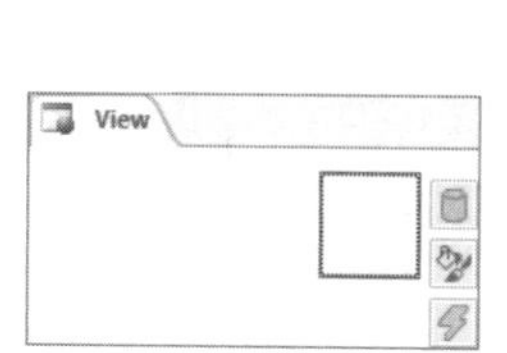

FIGURE 4-47: Blank view resized to smallest area

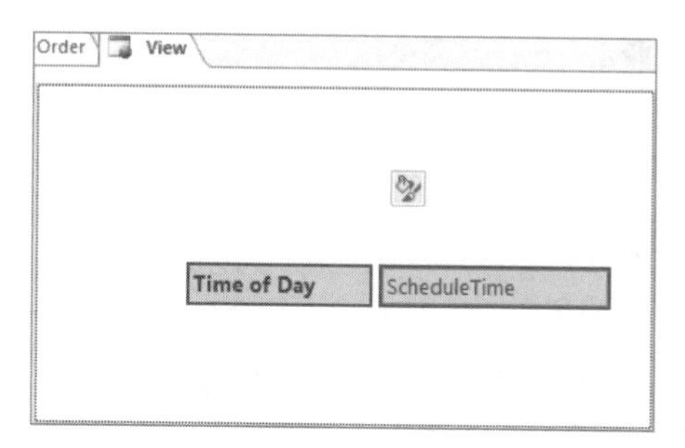

FIGURE 4-48: View being resized as control is resized

Manipulating a Group of Controls

As in the Access client, you can manipulate a group of controls collectively by clicking and dragging a selection area over controls or holding down Ctrl and Alt keys to select controls. As you're likely to be familiar with the process, we'll just point out two things and move on.

First, as you would expect, when you have multiple selections, you can only modify shared properties, as you can see in Figure 4-49.

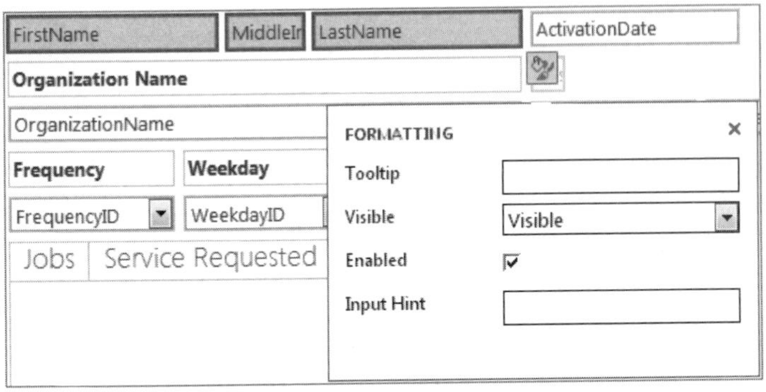

FIGURE 4-49: Shared properties displayed

Note that the button cannot be used in any multiple selections because each action is specific to the control to which it belongs.

Second, it's very useful to use arrow keys to move the controls as a group. Moving controls as a group makes it easy to keep your customized layout while making space for controls you want to add. Using arrow keys is also an easy way to move just the right number of units you need without dealing with the guesswork that dragging and dropping may entail.

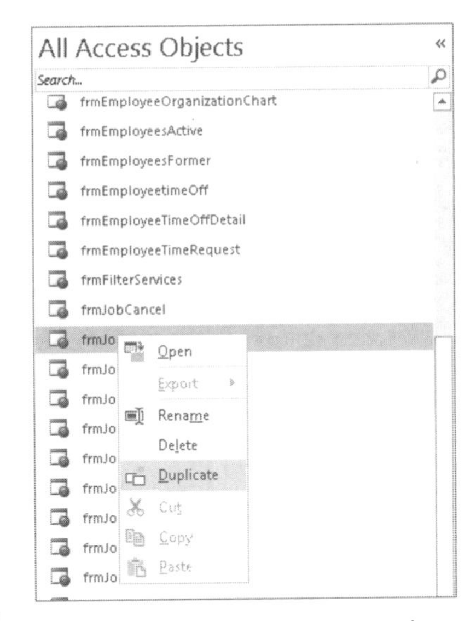

FIGURE 4-50: The navigation pane's right-click menu for a view with Duplicate selected

Duplicating a View

As we have noted a few times in this book so far, you cannot cut, copy, or paste controls in a view. For this reason, you will need to use the Duplicate View method to roughly approximate functionalities you'd otherwise have had via cut, copy, and paste functionalites.

To duplicate a view, you can either use the button for the link to that view on the View Selector, as you saw in Figure 4-10, or use the right-click menu in the Navigation Pane, as Figure 4-50 illustrates.

Selecting Duplicate presents a dialog box that enables you to select a different destination table/tile and create a new name for the duplicated view, as shown in Figure 4-51.

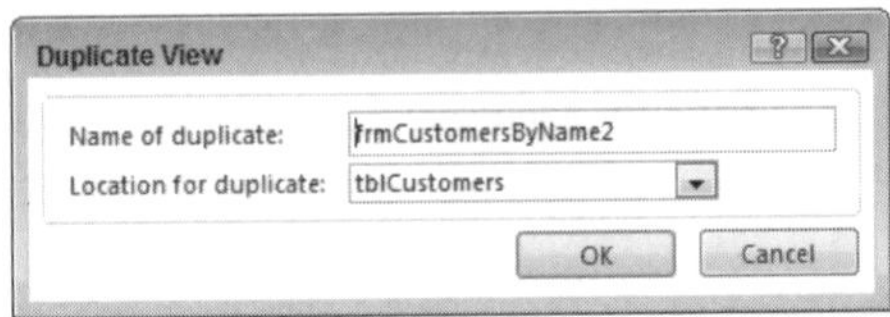

FIGURE 4-51: Duplicate View dialog box

You should see that you can use Duplicate View as a handy way to transfer a view from one tile to another without losing all the customization you've put into the view. This gives you some latitude in backtracking during the development stage where you're still trying to decide which tiles you want to expose and which views you want on each tile. Note that you can likewise duplicate a view as a standalone/popup view.

USING DUPLICATE VIEW TO CREATE A TEMPORARY BACKUP

When you are planning a major revision and/or enhancement to a view, Duplicate View can be a simple way of creating a backup of the view before you start working, providing you with a way to quickly revert without needing to restore from an `.app` file (which is a type of backup file you'll learn about in Chapters 8, 12, and 14). Should you choose to adopt this technique, be sure to use a good naming convention to disambiguate between production copy, working copy, and backup copy.

NOTE *The drop-down in Figure 4-51 shows tiles by table names rather than the tiles' labels. Since there is a one-to-one correlation between a table and a tile, you'd select the appropriate table to associate the duplicated view with the desired tile.*

ACTION BAR AND ACTION BAR BUTTONS

In client forms, you used a combination of objects such as navigation bars, windows buttons, command buttons, custom menus or ribbons to provide a system for initiating operations such as adding a new record, saving a record, opening another form, and so forth. Microsoft has provided a new interface that more or less replaces all of those. Because we will display our finished work in a web browser, it is necessary to present an interface that's simple, accessible, and consistent across all pages. The answer is the Action Bar, illustrated in Figure 4-52.

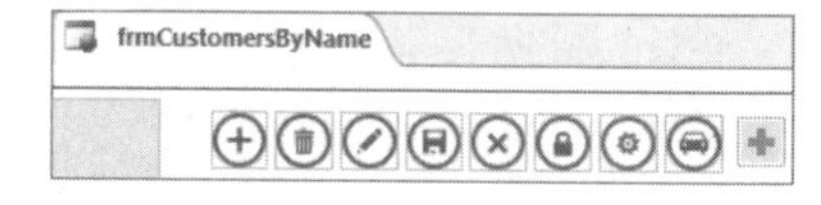

FIGURE 4-52: Action Bar on a view

In this section, you learn a bit more about the Action Bar and contrast the default Action Bar that is provided whenever a view is created with a custom Action Bar you can create.

One difference you will come to appreciate about the Action Bar is that it's much more customizable compared to the navigation bar. It is also easy to implement in comparison to custom menus and ribbons. We think this offers you the best features from various tools you used to support navigation and other operations for your client forms.

Action Bar Button Properties

A custom action button has four properties available shown in Figure 4-53:

1. Control Name
2. Tooltip
3. Icon
4. Click event

We want to emphasize that, because you cannot have a caption for an action button, you should never leave the tooltip property blank. Tooltips appear much sooner compared to the control tip on the client form so users are not going to have to wait as long in comparison. If all of your custom actions are consistently labeled, users will quickly learn to hover over the action buttons to get more details on what an action button does.

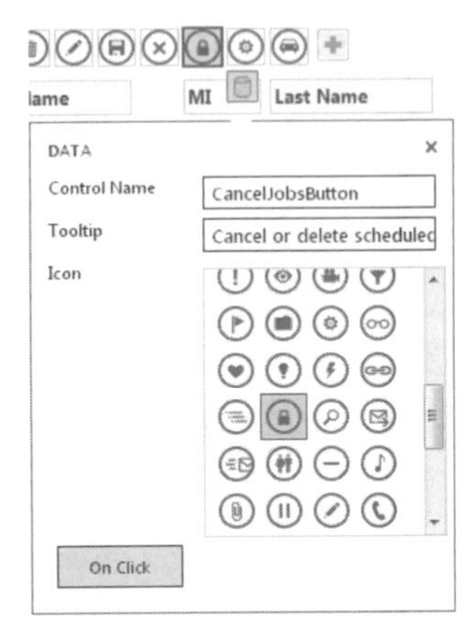

FIGURE 4-53: Action button properties popup

> **NOTE** *Note that throughout the book, we will use control tip to refer to this feature labeled as Tooltip in Figure 4-53 to remain consistent.*

You also need to factor in icon selection. First, even if you opt not to use the default Action Bar at all, your users may be exposed to different Access web apps and come to expect default icons to be used in a certain way. Therefore, it is essential that you are consistent in how you use icons throughout the app. It can be unsettling to users if you use a trash icon to delete a single record in one view and in another view use the same icon to delete all records. Microsoft has provided 72 icons for you to select from. Generally speaking, you shouldn't need so many different types of action buttons. It also becomes daunting for users to track and remember a larger number of icons. It is best to keep the number of action buttons as small as possible and use command buttons for more specialized operations.

You can attach macro actions to action buttons to perform actions such as opening a popup, performing a record operation, or moving to another view. You will learn more about using macros in general in Chapter 6 and behind action buttons in Chapter 9.

Default Action Button

Whenever you add a List view or Blank view, you will be presented with five default buttons, as shown in Figure 4-54.

FIGURE 4-54: Default action buttons for blank or list views

Datasheet view has only two default buttons, shown in Figure 4-55.

FIGURE 4-55: Default action buttons for datasheet views

The default action buttons for Datasheet views are identical in functionality to their counterparts in Blank and List views, so for the rest of this discussion, we'll refer to the default buttons in Blank and List views with the understanding that the functionality for their Datasheet counterparts is the same. Summary views cannot have an Action Bar at all, so we don't need to consider Summary views for this discussion.

FIGURE 4-56: Customizing properties not available for a default button

When you click one of the default buttons, you'll see that you cannot customize its properties, as illustrated in Figure 4-56; there is no button for you to click.

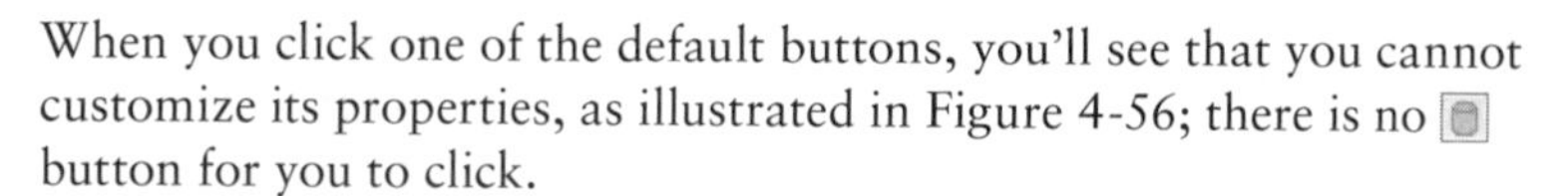

Perhaps you're thinking, "What's the big deal? I can just delete it and put in my own custom button that replicates the functionality." We need to caution you here. While it is indeed true that you can replace a default button with your own, functionality won't be identical between the two. Suppose that you create an Add button to add a new record to the default Add button, as demonstrated in Figure 4-57.

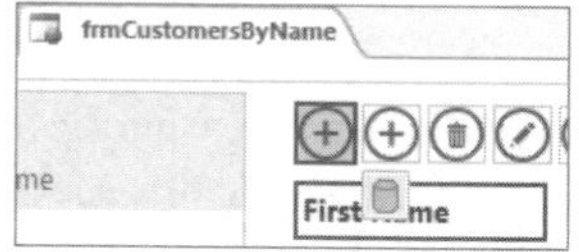

FIGURE 4-57: Default add action button and custom add action button, which is highlighted

Note that the leftmost button in Figure 4-57 is a custom action button; you can tell by the fact that there's a Data properties button while the second leftmost button is a default Add button.

Suppose you open the view in a web browser and land on a new blank record. You would see the difference between the default action button, as shown in Figure 4-56, and the custom button in Figure 4-58.

FIGURE 4-58: Availability of Action buttons on a new record

Landing on a new record automatically disables the default Add action button, whereas you would have to perform additional programming to replicate the enabling/disabling functionality for your custom Add button. The other default buttons have similar, behind-the-scenes functionalities, which disable and enable them for appropriate contexts.

You can see that you have to replicate not simply the action of buttons, but also control their availability when you replace an original default button with a replacement custom action button. And that brings us to the next point.

You are allowed to delete a default action button. However, doing so is an irrevocable action. You cannot restore a deleted action button. If you are trying to decide whether you want to use your custom action to replace the functionality provided by default action buttons, it usually is a good idea to duplicate the views before you delete the default action buttons so you have a means of reverting without having to rebuild the entire view again.

Custom Action Buttons

As alluded to earlier, you can add your custom action buttons, whether you place one or more buttons in among the existing default buttons or replace the default buttons with an entirely customized set of buttons. To add a new custom action button, click the button, as shown in Figure 4-59.

Unlike the button used to add new views to the View Selectors, clicking it for an action button doesn't open a popup and the addition is immediate. By default, the new action button added has a star icon, as illustrated in Figure 4-60.

FIGURE 4-59: Adding a new action button

You can, of course, customize the button, as you saw in Figure 4-57, via its button, changing its default name and icon and providing a control tip. You almost certainly will need to attach macros to the Click event; you learn how to do that in Chapters 6 and 9.

FIGURE 4-60: New custom action button with default star icon

CONTROLS

The set of controls available in Access 2013 apps has been revised, and although a large portion of the controls will be familiar to you from previous versions, it is essential that you go through the differences from familiar controls and familiarize yourself with the new controls. For your reference, we will list all properties for each control with a brief discussion about each control.

As you saw earlier in our discussion about popup properties, not all properties are available in all contexts. For this section, we will give you a table listing all properties from each group and indicate what they are named, when they are available, and what default values they may have. Note that the default values may differ when you add fields using Field List; the default values listed are based on when you add a control from the ribbon.

We will conclude with a more detailed discussion on some common properties.

Changed Controls

The most obvious change you may notice is the greatly simplified feature set for all controls in comparison to their client counterpart. This is partially a consequence of working in a web browser where the need for cross-platform and browser compatibility dictates you provide experience that will work the same across different environments.

On the other hand, some controls gained some new properties never seen before in the client. You will see them listed as we go through controls.

Label

One interesting change is that a Label control now has a Control Source property, which allows you to use Label controls as read-only controls for data from tables. This is a good solution when you don't want to disable textboxes to prevent users from being able to select and copy the content within.

Another property you may appreciate is that you can specify which control a given label is associated with. This makes the process of associating a label to a control more straightforward than in the client. Table 4-1 illustrates this.

TABLE 4-1: Label Properties

PROPERTY NAME	AFFECTED BY	DEFAULT VALUE
Data Properties		
Control Name	N/A	Context-dependent
Control Source	N/A	[No Data Source]

Formatting Properties		
Caption	Control Source	Context-dependent
Tooltip	N/A	
Visible	N/A	Visible
Label For	N/A	
Action Properties		
Click	N/A	

Textbox

One significant change for textbox controls is the new Input Hint property, which we'll discuss later. Otherwise, the properties are more or less what you'd expect for a textbox.

Another important change is that you can no longer use the textbox for multiple lines of text. You learn more about the multiline textbox later in the chapter and will learn more about how this has changed in Chapter 7 as well.

As alluded to in our discussion of the Label control, the Locked property, which you might have used to prevent editing, is no longer available. If you do not want to use the Enabled property, you can opt to use a Label control instead. You can see these properties in Table 4-2.

TABLE 4-2: Textbox Properties

PROPERTY NAME	AFFECTED BY	DEFAULT VALUE
Data Properties		
Control Name	N/A	Context-dependent
Control Source	N/A	[No Data Source]
Default Value	Control Source	
Formatting Properties		
Tooltip	N/A	
Visible	N/A	Visible
Enabled	N/A	Yes
Format	Control Source	
Decimal Places	Control Source, Format	Auto

continues

TABLE 4-3 *(continued)*

PROPERTY NAME	AFFECTED BY	DEFAULT VALUE
Input Hint	N/A	
Currency Symbol	Control Source, Format	
Action Properties		
Click	N/A	
After Update	N/A	

Combobox

The Combobox control is quite pared down from its client counterpart. You may be used to specifying multiple columns, showing headers, and applying arbitrary sorting to the rowsource. None of those apply any longer.

The sort order for the values listed is determined by the Display Field and is always ascending. If you need to show more than one column, you will need to resort to alternatives, such as concatenating those values into a single column for use in a Display Field.

On the other hand, the Popup view may be a useful property that you may want to leverage for easy editing of lists where appropriate. We talk more about that later in this chapter. Combobox properties are shown in Table 4-3.

TABLE 4-3: Combobox Properties

PROPERTY NAME	AFFECTED BY	DEFAULT VALUE
Data Properties		
Control Name	N/A	Context-dependent
Control Source	N/A	[No Data Source]
Default Value	Control Source	
Row Source Type	N/A	Table/Query
Row Source	Row Source Type	[No data source]
Bound Field	Row Source	[No data source]
Display Field	Row Source	[No data source]
Popup view	Row Source	

Formatting Properties		
Tooltip	N/A	
Visible	N/A	Visible
Enabled	N/A	Yes
Action Properties		
After Update	N/A	

Button

Though the feature set of a button is simpler, there is not that much of practical difference between the client and web versions. See the Button properties in Table 4-4.

TABLE 4-4: Button Properties

PROPERTY NAME	AFFECTED BY	DEFAULT VALUE
Data Properties		
Control Name	N/A	Context-dependent
Formatting Properties		
Caption	N/A	
Tooltip	N/A	
Visible	N/A	Visible
Enabled	N/A	Yes
Action Properties		
Click	N/A	

Checkbox

One omission is that the Click event is no longer available for a checkbox. Practically speaking, that should be no large loss as you still have the After Update event; that would usually have been the event you'd use in an Access client application anyway. Checkbox properties are shown in Table 4-5.

TABLE 4-5: Checkbox Properties

PROPERTY NAME	AFFECTED BY	DEFAULT VALUE
Data Properties		
Control Name	N/A	Context-dependent
Control Source	N/A	[No data source]
Default Value	N/A	No
Formatting Properties		
Tooltip	N/A	
Visible	N/A	Visible
Enabled	N/A	Yes
Action Properties		
After Update	N/A	

Hyperlink

In addition to being able to specify a default URL for a new record, you can also specify a default display text for hyperlinks. You also get to control whether clicking a hyperlink should open a new window or tab in the user's web browser or navigate away from your app to another site.

However, using hyperlinks to navigate to other parts of your application won't work — you use macro actions for that. You will learn about that in Chapter 6. For now, be aware that you'd primarily use hyperlinks to reference sites outside the app.

As you will see in the discussion in Chapter 7 on hyperlink data type, the Hyperlink control also provides a built-in popup to add a new URL. See Hyperlink control properties in Table 4-6.

TABLE 4-6: Hyperlink Properties

PROPERTY NAME	AFFECTED BY	DEFAULT VALUE
Data Properties		
Control Name	N/A	Context-dependent
Control Source	N/A	[No Data Source]
Default URL	N/A	
Default Display Text	N/A	

Formatting Properties		
Tooltip	N/A	
Visible	N/A	Visible
Open in	N/A	New Windows Tab
Action Properties		
Click	N/A	
After Update	N/A	

Image

You can use the Image control primarily in two ways. You can refer to an Image field on a table, or you can refer to pictures stored externally (for example, another site, a SharePoint library, and so on). When you use the Image control in the latter manner, you can additionally specify how to display the picture. Table 4-7 shows Image control properties.

TABLE 4-7: Image Properties

PROPERTY NAME	AFFECTED BY	DEFAULT VALUE
Data Properties		
Control Name	N/A	Context-dependent
Control Source	N/A	[No Data Source]
Picture URL	Control Source	
Formatting Properties		
Tooltip	N/A	
Visible	N/A	Visible
Picture Tiling	Control Source	None
Size Mode	Control Source	Zoom
Horizontal Alignment	Control Source	Middle
Vertical Alignment	Control Source	Middle
Action Properties		
Click	N/A	

Subview

One primary difference between a subview and subform, as you knew it in the Access client, is that a subform allows you to link on multiple fields between each master and child. Because composite keys aren't supported in web apps and every table must have an identity field, there is really no benefit to being able to link on multiple fields. Thus, you can specify only one field to link on for the Master/Child. On the other hand, as with client subforms, you can reference a control instead of a field in the parent view as your master field, offering you some flexibility over how you manage the linking.

However, it is also essential to note a couple of limitations. You cannot refer to a subview's content from the parent view. Nor can you refer to the parent view's content within the subview. For all practical purposes, the Link Master/Child Field property is your only connection between two views. Therefore, you must design within that constraint and not plan on additional references outside those two properties. Table 4-8 shows Subview control properties.

TABLE 4-8: Subview Properties

PROPERTY NAME	AFFECTED BY	DEFAULT VALUE
Data Properties		
Control Name	N/A	Context-dependent
Source Object	N/A	
Link Master Field	N/A	
Link Child Field	N/A	
Formatting Properties		
Visible	N/A	Visible
Action Properties		
N/A	N/A	N/A

Web Browser

The web browser control will be discussed in detail in the section, "Web Browser Control," later in the chapter, so we'll just list the properties here. You can see Web Browser control properties in Table 4-9.

TABLE 4-9: Web Browser Control Properties

PROPERTY NAME	AFFECTED BY	DEFAULT VALUE
Data Properties		
Control Name	N/A	Context-dependent

Control Source	N/A	[No Data Source]
Default URL	N/A	
Show Scrollbars	N/A	When Needed
Formatting Properties		
Visible	N/A	Visible
Action Properties		
N/A	N/A	N/A

New Controls

For Access web apps, three new controls were introduced: the Multiline Textbox, AutoComplete, and Related Items controls. We'll review them in turn.

Multiline Textbox

In an Access client database, you used textboxes for any kind of text and simply resized them and modified their properties if you wanted to allow for extended text entry. Microsoft has decided that it is necessary to separate out different methods of text entry. They provided a separate control to enter multiple lines of text and insert returns in your text. Therefore, you'd likely use a Multiline textbox for long text fields. You learn more about this in Chapter 7.

With that in mind, the properties listed for this control are very similar to what you'd see for the Textbox control with only one difference: Display Decimal Places is not available.

Finally, unlike textboxes, Multiline textboxes have scrollbars, which are displayed only when there is more text than can be displayed. Figure 4-61 illustrates the Multiline textbox. Table 4-10 lists the properties of the Multiline textbox.

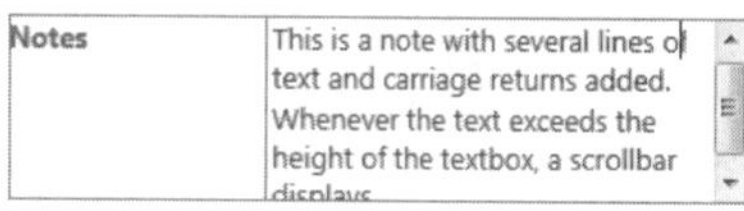

FIGURE 4-61: Multiline textbox

TABLE 4-10: Multiline Textbox Properties

PROPERTY NAME	AFFECTED BY	DEFAULT VALUE
Data Properties		
Control Name	N/A	Context-dependent
Control Source	N/A	[No Data Source]
Default Value	Control Source	
Formatting Properties		
Tooltip	N/A	

continues

TABLE 4-10 *(continued)*

PROPERTY NAME	AFFECTED BY	DEFAULT VALUE
Visible	N/A	Visible
Enabled	N/A	Yes
Format	Control Source	
Input Hint	N/A	
Currency Symbol	Control Source, Format	
Action Properties		
Click	N/A	
After Update	N/A	

AutoComplete

If you've ever written VBA code to dynamically filter a combo box's rowsource as the user types in it, you'll be delighted to know that you can have that functionality without coding by using the AutoComplete control. Not only is it appropriate for binding to a large list, it will filter matching entries using "contain" searches, enabling users to type a set of letters or a word from the middle of a string to select the desired value rather than forcing them to match by the first few letters as a combo box would. Figure 4-62 illustrates the power of matching in the AutoComplete control.

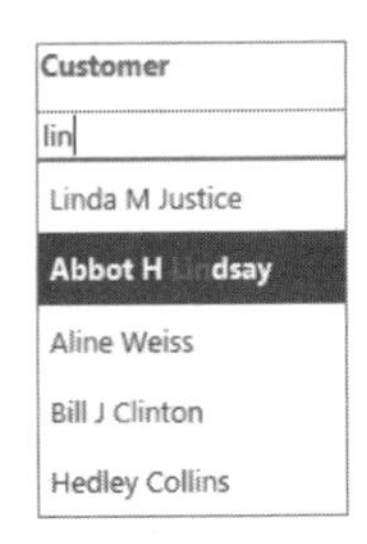

FIGURE 4-62: Auto Complete's list matching a user's input

Unlike combo boxes, you can have two fields displayed in an AutoComplete Control, although the matching will use only the first display field. You can use the second field as a more detailed differentiation between similar items in the primary level, such as multiple locations for an organization. AutoComplete control properties are shown in Table 4-11.

TABLE 4-11: AutoComplete Properties

PROPERTY NAME	AFFECTED BY	DEFAULT VALUE
Data Properties		
Control Name	N/A	Context-dependent
Control Source	N/A	[No Data Source]
Default Value	Control Source	
Row Source	N/A	
Bound Field	Row Source	[No data source]

Primary Display Field	Row Source	[No data source]
Secondary Display Field	Row Source	[No data source]
Formatting Properties		
Tooltip	N/A	
Visible	N/A	Visible
Enabled	N/A	Yes
Input Hint	N/A	
Action Properties		
Click	N/A	
After Update	N/A	

Related Item

When building complex forms in an Access client database, you might use a main form to list master records, with a tab control containing several subforms on different tabs. Each subform contains the related child records from one of the related tables. This is essentially what the Related Items control (or Relic) is, as demonstrated in Figure 4-63.

You can create as many tabs as you need to show related records from one or more related tables for a given master record. Unlike a subview, you don't attach a separate view in the Related Item control, but rather specify a list of the fields you want displayed in the tab. Access automates the display of those fields for you.

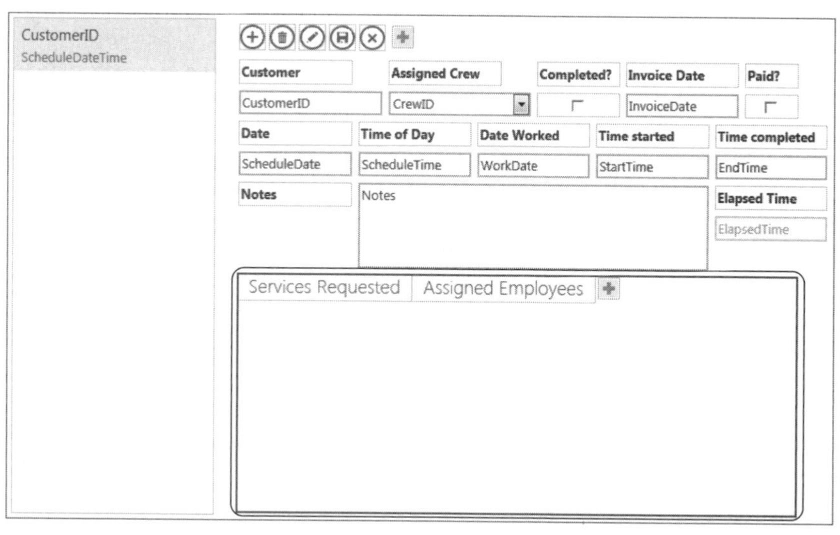

FIGURE 4-63: Related Items control

When you need to add or edit items from within a related item control, you can specify a popup form for that purpose. We believe that you'll find that this approach gives you a simple way to quickly display all related data while also giving users a powerful view to edit records. The popup form is made accessible via double-clicking a row or clicking the link, as shown in Figure 4-64.

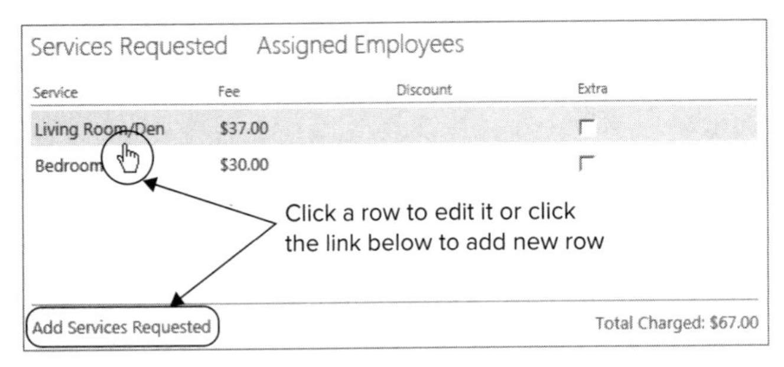

FIGURE 4-64: Edit items in a Related Items Control

In addition, you can display a calculation on one of the fields in the tab, which is useful. As also shown in Figure 4-64, you can have it display a sum of a field to provide a quick summary view. Do note, however, that the only calculations available are sum, count, and average. Those are typically sufficient for most scenarios you'll encounter. Note that all properties for calculations appear in their own popup button, which is represented by a Σ button in the place where you'd see the button.

There are no properties for the Related Items control itself; the only button provided is the + button, which pops up a form for you to add a new tab, where you can specify the caption and select the related tables. With a tab added, you can then edit the tab's properties by selecting the tab, as illustrated in Figure 4-65.

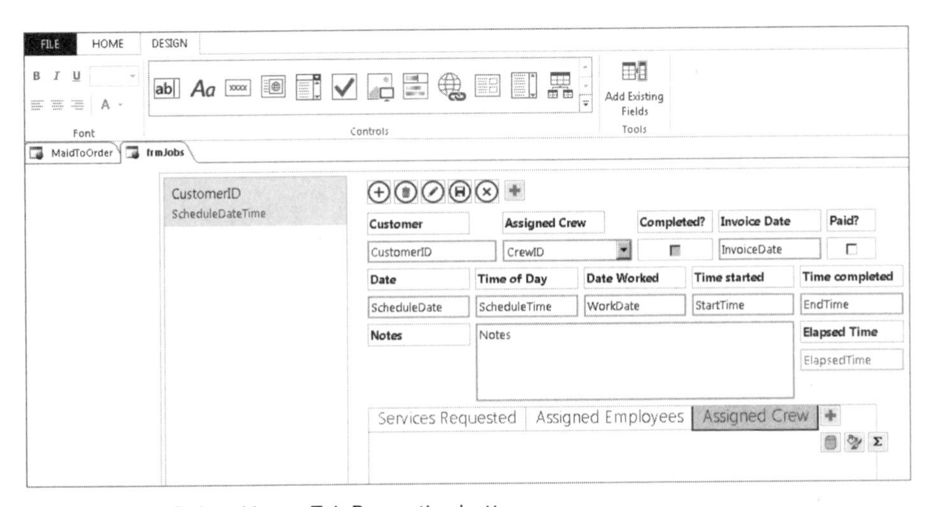

FIGURE 4-65: Related Items Tab Properties buttons

As noted earlier, you don't see an [icon] for tabs, but a Σ instead. See the properties of the Related Item Tab in Table 4-12.

TABLE 4-12: Related Item Tab Properties

PROPERTY NAME	AFFECTED BY	DEFAULT VALUE
Data Properties		
Data Source	N/A	Context-dependent
Related Field	N/A	[No data source]
First Field	N/A	[No data source]
First Caption	First Field	
Second Field	N/A	[No data source]
Second Caption	Second Field	
Third Field	N/A	[No data source]
Third Caption	Third Field	
Fourth Field	N/A	[No data source]
Fourth Caption	Fourth Field	
Popup view	N/A	
Sort Field	N/A	[No data source]
Sort Order	Sort Field	Ascending
Formatting Properties		
Caption	N/A	Context-dependent
Calculation Properties		
Calculation	N/A	Sum
Field	N/A	[No data source]
Calculation Caption	N/A	
Calculation Visible	N/A	Visible
Control Name	N/A	Context-dependent

Common Properties

As you studied the lists of properties for each control, you may have noticed that a number of similar controls use the same properties. Some of them are also familiar from the client environment, but we want to call your attention to some ramifications of using those common properties.

As you might expect, the Control Source and Default Value properties are common to many controls. With few exceptions, you still can use an expression in lieu of a field from a table for either property. In such cases, you can assign an expression by clicking the ellipsis button to open the Expression Builder. Unlike the client, however, you cannot enter the expression directly in the property.

Text controls such as Textbox and AutoComplete have a new property called Input Hint, in which provides a grayed out instruction for users, telling them how to fill in the control as seen Figure 4-66.

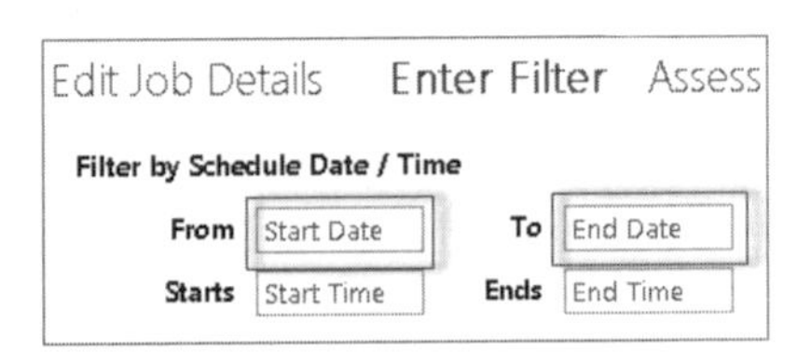

FIGURE 4-66: Input Hint property

As you can see, an input hint works much like some search boxes, especially in web pages. It provides a hint on what input is expected, and does so without requiring the user to hover over a control to see a tooltip. It is a very useful feature to leverage in your applications.

Another feature is that the Format property does more than you may be accustomed to in a client database. In an app, Format not only displays data in a certain way but it also provides some validation. Figure 4-67 shows what happens when a user enters an invalid date format into a textbox with its Format property set to one of the date formats.

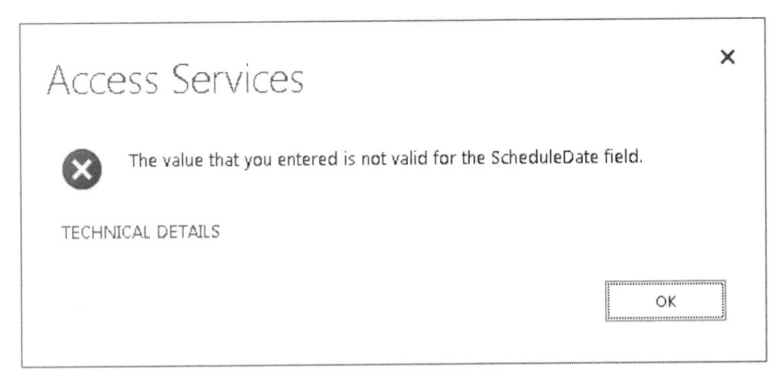

FIGURE 4-67: Invalid data entered into a textbox formatted for dates

Thus, you don't have to write any code to perform validation; simply set the Format property according to your requirements and Access will do it for you. Note, however, that Access does not actually prevent users from leaving the invalid data in the control. This is good and bad: good because users won't be intimidated by error messages disrupting their data entry, bad because users may not return and clean up their errors. Generally speaking, this behavior is not a problem because attempts to save the invalid data will still fail. The only time this may be an issue is if the input ends up in a text field rather than in a date/time or numeric field. Inserting a badly formatted date in a text field wouldn't raise an error. However, that's a design issue that you need to correct, anyway.

The Popup view is a property that you may see on Lookup controls. Generally speaking, if you want to enable users to add or edit values to the underlying tables driving the lookup, you'd set the Popup view for that lookup to a view you create for that purpose. This provides you with a codeless version of the NotInList event for which you would have had to write VBA. Better yet, because you get to build the popup view, you're still in control of how the data may be added or edited. Figure 4-68 illustrates how to access the popup view.

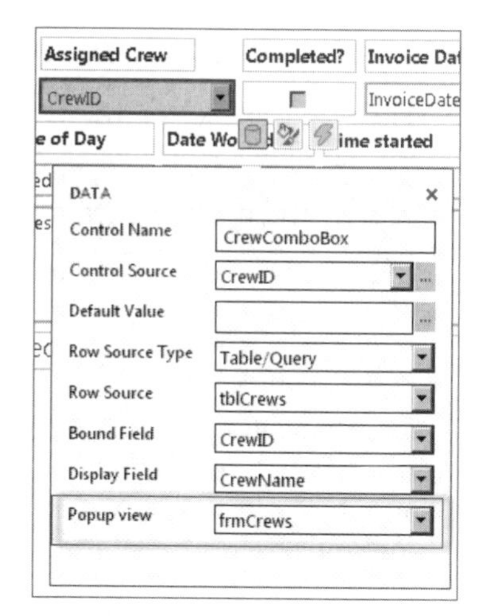

FIGURE 4-68: Popup view link

Client Controls with No Counterparts

For the sake of completeness, we've quickly listed controls that you may have worked with in the Access client that do not have a counterpart in the new apps environment. We've also listed some possible substitutions where they exist. Your experience will guide you in making the right selection when designing your new app views. Table 4-13 shows controls that are not available in Access web apps, though you still can use them in Access clients.

TABLE 4-13: Controls Not Available for Apps

CONTROL TYPE NAME	POSSIBLE SUBSTITUTIONS
Listbox	List view, Combobox, AutoComplete, Related Items Control
Option Group	Combobox, AutoComplete
Tab Control	Related Items Control
Navigation Control	Tiles & Link
Chart	None*
Toggle Button	Checkbox
Line	None
Rectangle	None
Attachment	Image for graphics, none otherwise*
Radio Button	Checkbox
OLE/ActiveX Control	None

*Note that charting and attachments are discussed in Chapter 10. You need to go outside the Access environment to incorporate those elements

Web Browser Control

The Web Browser control requires additional discussion because a web browser has additional uses beyond simply providing `iframe` elements on your Access web app. There are three main possible uses:

1. Delivering content such as news headlines, announcements, or tasks
2. Providing views into external tools such as Internet maps, currency converters, ZIP code lookup, time zone converters, or stock market tickers
3. Referencing images or attachments for a catalog or inventory listing

You probably can think of other possible uses for a Web Browser control but as you can see just from those three suggestions, the Web Browser control has the potential to enrich your Access web apps far beyond what you can do with macros. You learn more about integrating other web-hosted tools in Chapter 10.

In this section, you will learn how to configure the Web Browser control, starting with a simple hard-coded URL, graduating to modifying parts of a URL, and finishing up with a discussion on restrictions on placing content in an iframe element. For this discussion, we'll refer to the Maid To Order application where users can use Google Maps to locate a customer's residence and get driving directions.

Using a Static URL

This is the most straightforward method. Add an unbound web browser to the view, set its default URL to a valid HTTPS address, and you're done. To match what you see in Figure 4-69, use the following expression as the input:

```
https://maps.google.com/?ll=41.00,-98.00&spn=39.00,69.00&t=m&z=5&output=embed
```

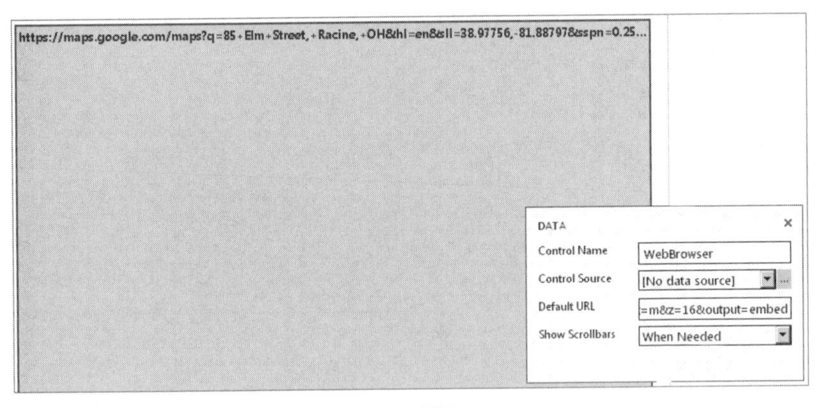

FIGURE 4-69: Web browser using a static URL

Obviously, this isn't flexible and is generally more appropriate for static content or a static URL that doesn't need to be modified.

Using a URL from a Table Field

One straightforward method to provide a bit more dynamic content is to bind the URL to a field in a table. For this usage, you can add a hyperlink field called `CustomerGoogleURL` and bind the web browser control to it. You can then train your user to use Google Maps, manually locate the address, obtain the URL, and save the URL into the field. From then on, the web browser control pinpoints the address automatically as in Figure 4-70.

```
https://maps.google.com/maps?q=85+Elm+Street,+Racine,+OH&hl=en&sll=38.97756,
-81.88797&sspn=0.255686,0.426407&oq=85+elm+street+&hnear=85+Elm+St,+Racine,+Ohio+45
771&t=m&z=16&output=embed
```

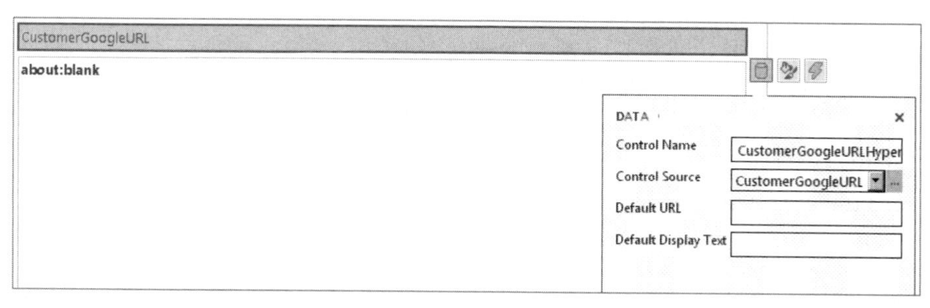

FIGURE 4-70: Setting the web browser control's content based on a field's value

The downside is the Google Maps URL must have `&output=embed` appended in order to work correctly. However, you could append it automatically via an After Update macro or via a table event. You'll learn more about macros and table events in Chapters 6 and 9.

Using a URL Built Dynamically

One more alternative to consider is that, instead of storing the whole URL, you can build a URL dynamically using macro actions. You cannot set the web browser directly via a macro but you can set the web browser's Control Source property to refer to a macro variable and perform a SetVariable macro action when you need to display a new URL. You'll learn more about macros and variables in Chapters 6 and 9, but Figure 4-71 illustrates how a SetVariable macro action on the Load event of the form can be used to supply the URL.

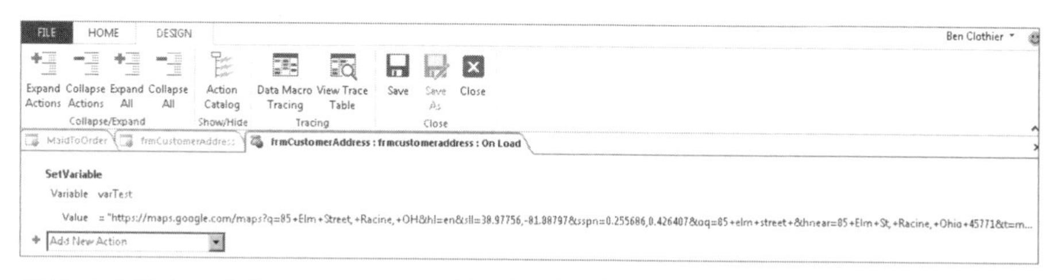

FIGURE 4-71: View's Load event executing SetVariable macro action

Figure 4-72 shows how you'd set the Web Browser control's Control Source via the Expression Builder. Recall that you cannot enter a variable directly in the Control Source property; you have to do so by opening the builder first.

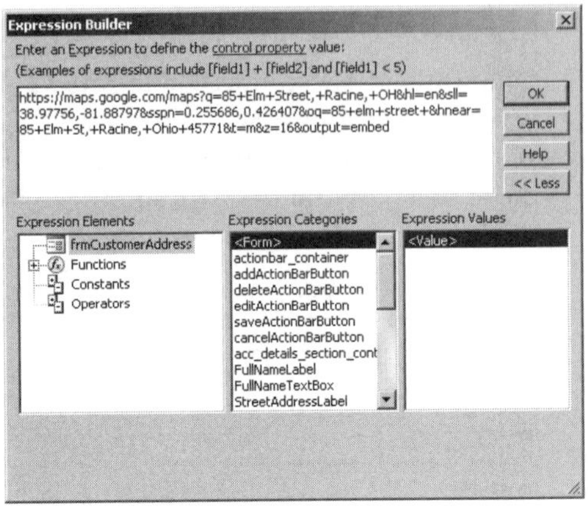

Obviously, this is an oversimplification because in a practical use you'd be performing other actions to concatenate and build a URL string to ultimately assign to a variable. Once you learn more about macro actions and available function sets in Chapters 6 and 9, you will be able to assess if you want to assemble URLs dynamically via macro actions rather than storing them in a table field.

FIGURE 4-72: Setting the web browser control's Control Source property in Expression Builder

Query String Parameters

Before we conclude this discussion, we want to call your attention to a feature in URLs that may help explain why you may want to build URLs dynamically instead of storing the full URL in a table field. If you look toward the end of any given URL, you may notice that they have a `?`, which is then followed by pairs of name and value. Look at the URL we used earlier for Google Maps to pinpoint an address:

```
https://maps.google.com/maps?q=85+Elm+Street,+Racine,+OH&hl=en…
```

The ? indicates the start of *query string parameters*, which is a convention used by all web browsers and scripting to pass parameters in addition to the URL. This is how Google Maps can "know" that you want a particular address. For each query string parameter, you must provide a key-value pair, which is separated by a `=` character. For each additional parameter you want to include, you add an `&` character to delimit each key-value pair. To help illustrate this in VBA terms, the following is conceptually equivalent:

```
Debug.Print GetMap(q:="85+Elm+Street,+Racine,+OH", hl:="en"…)
```

As you can see, it's as if you're calling an API function that accepts a set of parameters; the difference is that you "locate" an API function by supplying a URL, and then provide the arguments you want the API functions to take.

Although a full treatment of URL handling is beyond the scope of this book, we wanted to point out that this gives you a handy method for building dynamic content by modifying values for the query string parameters. There are several web tools with documented APIs that you can then leverage and incorporate in your specific applications. You will see some of that in Chapter 10. This also represents one major paradigm you may need to consider — instead of doing everything in VBA in your client apps, you may need to consider using web services to deliver rich content for the applications; the web browser control will be your primary vehicle to do so.

Security Considerations and Inline Frame Issues

You may have noticed in examples provided so far in this section that we used HTTPS rather than HTTP and that we had to consistently append `output=embed` to URLs. If we did not use HTTPS, the Web Browser control would refuse to display the content, as illustrated in Figure 4-73.

Next, if we simply naively copied and pasted from Google the URL meant to be used as a link instead of using the URL from inline code, Google will refuse to serve the content, as Figure 4-74 illustrates.

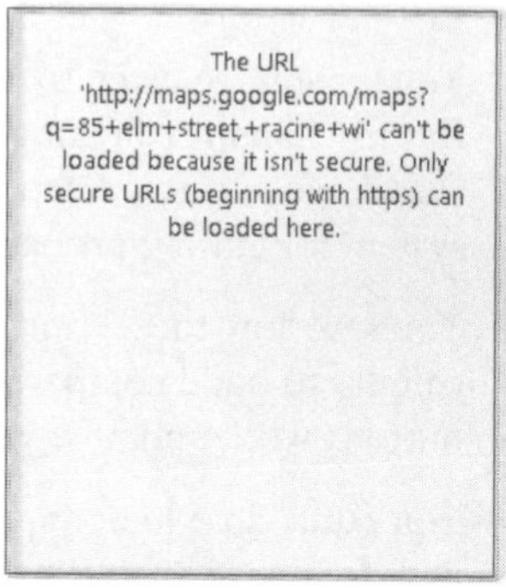

The URL 'http://maps.google.com/maps?q=85+elm+street,+racine+wi' can't be loaded because it isn't secure. Only secure URLs (beginning with https) can be loaded here.

FIGURE 4-73: Result of a web browser control referencing an HTTP address

Google has made it a convention to allow you to inline its content by appending `output=append`. Other web services may have their own convention or simply not support inlining at all. You'll learn about inlining in more detail in chapter 10. It is ultimately your responsibility to determine which web services allow you to inline their content and ensure that you use the correct URL for doing so.

All of this is done in the name of security. Whenever a web application displays inline content, there is most likely some kind of scripting being run. While you may trust Google to serve up your mapping requests, users' browsers have no way of knowing that. Therefore, by default, the Access web browser control will require that you use only HTTPS addresses so that the identity can be validated and that the owner of the site allows you to inline their content. When you think about it, it is not possible for any single entity to guarantee that information is protected over HTTPS if the web browser is allowed to mix content over HTTP and HTTPS. When the content is also your own (for example, you have a set of documents hosted on another part of your team site to which you want your app to refer), then you are responsible for enabling that content. You'll see how to enable that for your other sites in Chapter 10. For content outside Office 365 and/or SharePoint entirely, you need to determine the required steps as specified by the site owner — which may be you or someone else — to allow for inlining.

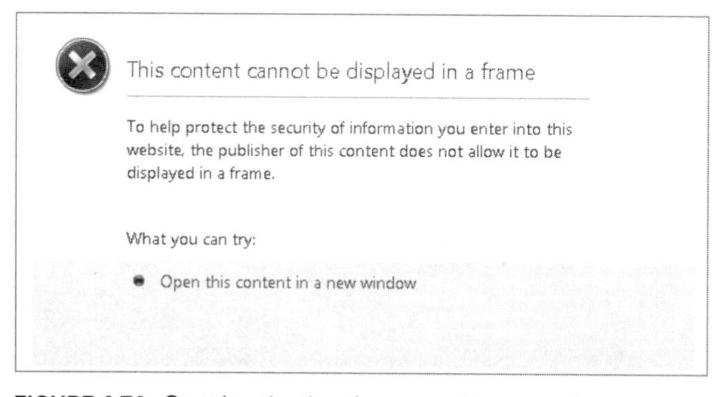

FIGURE 4-74: Google rejecting the request to serve the content

Therefore, if you plan to incorporate Web Browser controls in your app, you should ensure that you have accessible URLs and web services that you can actually consume before you do any work toward implementing this in Access.

SUMMARY

You were introduced to views in Chapter 3 and got to see different types of views available to you. In this chapter, you got a closer look at your workspace for designing a new view. You reviewed the design surface, starting with the ribbon, and familiarized yourself with the new popup buttons system for editing properties and the navigation system which uses tiles and views.

You saw how the Action Bar offers you much more customization than the old navigation bar. It is simpler to build compared to custom ribbons and menus, and you looked a bit at how default action buttons work and how you can create your own custom action buttons.

You got a close look at all of the controls available to you for building your views and discovered how familiar controls have changed and what new controls are available to you. You looked over some common properties and how they are relevant to your design. Finally, you looked closely at the web browser control in particular, and saw how it enables you to augment your app with additional content outside your app.

With those fundamentals, you can move into query design to enrich your views' recordsource and learn about new functions available to you in Chapter 5.

5

Creating Queries and Writing Expressions

WHAT'S IN THIS CHAPTER?

- Understanding how queries are created and stored
- Examining what has changed in Query Designer
- Using parameters in a query
- Enumerating query capabilities
- Identifying new functions, operators, and constants for query and macro expressions

Of the various components in Access, queries are probably the least changed; therefore, many query features should be familiar to you if you're coming from client Access. You still have the same query designer that allows you to add tables, join them in certain ways, select fields to display, and apply sorting and filtering just as you've always done. You may also be pleased to find that in comparison to support for web queries in Access 2010 web databases, the feature set for queries created in Access web apps is larger. While the feature set is still smaller than in the Access client, this chapter assesses the new architecture driving the creation of queries. Though the query designer looks familiar, you will learn how queries themselves are stored as SQL Server objects and how the designer is used to create and modify them. We will guide you through actions that are different from the client query designer, such as saving and previewing results from a query. Finally, we'll come to the biggest change presented in queries: new SQL syntax, expressions, and functions. By the end of this chapter, you should have all the tools you need to make the transition from the SQL dialect you use in client Access databases to the SQL dialect you will use in Access web apps.

Keep in mind that the primary focus of this chapter is not only to point out changes but also to familiarize yourself with the default behavior of Access. The samples provided in this chapter reflect the default behavior of Access. When we proceed to later chapters, you'll see how we can customize it more.

QUERY ARCHITECTURE

Because Access web app tables are now tables in SQL Server, it should come as no surprise to you that, when you create queries in a web app, Access will create the SQL objects needed to support the query. Normally, simple Access queries are saved as SQL Server views while Access parameterized queries become SQL Server inline table-valued functions.

SQL Server Views

When you work only via Access 2013 web apps, you do not have to worry about the particulars of how Access 2013 manages the queries' SQL Server object counterparts. However, in scenarios where you connect to the SQL Server database containing your web app's data from another interface, such as a client database, it may be useful to take note of those particulars.

First, although an Access client query allows you to define sorting as part of the query, this is not normally a part of a SQL Server view. Compare the query design shown in Figure 5-1, which sorts on `LastName, FirstName`, with the query design in Figure 5-2, showing the view definition in SSMS without sorting.

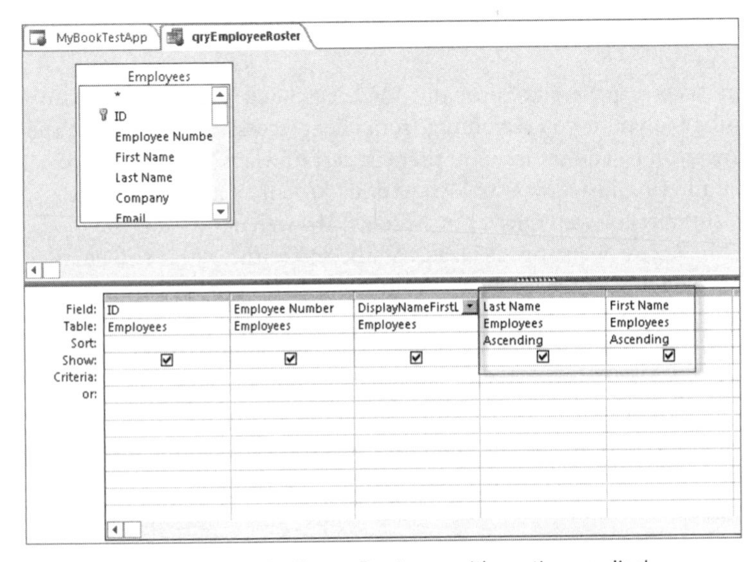

FIGURE 5-1: Basic query in Query Designer with sorting applied

```
/****** Object:  View [Access].[qryEmployeeRoster]    Script Date: 1/12/2013 3:11:12 PM ******/
SET ANSI_NULLS ON
GO

SET QUOTED_IDENTIFIER ON
GO

CREATE VIEW [Access].[qryEmployeeRoster]
AS
SELECT
    [Employees].[ID],
    [Employees].[Employee Number],
    [Employees].[DisplayNameFirstLast],
    [Employees].[Last Name],
    [Employees].[First Name]
FROM
    [Access].[Employees]

GO
```

FIGURE 5-2: SQL View for the query in SQL Server without sorting described

When a user opens an Access web view bound to this query, Access will specify the sorting when it runs the SQL Server view. When you connect to the SQL Server from an Access client database, the onus is on you to reapply the sorting missing from the view.

> **WARNING** *Note that there are two distinct uses for the term 'view' depending on the context. SQL Server views are distinct from Access web app views. A web app view is more like an Access client form, providing an interface to the data from either tables or queries. An Access web app query may be based on a SQL Server view and then used as a recordsource for an Access web app view.*

Table-Valued Functions

When you add a parameter to a query, it no longer can be expressed as a SQL Server view. Therefore, Access creates a table-valued function instead. You'll learn more about parameterized queries later in the chapter but for now, compare Figure 5-3, which shows a parameterized query, with the equivalent table-valued function in Figure 5-4.

Table-valued functions have the same restriction as SQL Server views; sorting does not normally comprise a part of the definition. However, you cannot link to table-valued functions in client Access, so you will find it necessary to use passthrough queries if you want to bind an Access client form to a table-valued function. You learn more about passthrough queries in Chapter 15 and Chapter 21.

Although this has been an all-too-brief introduction, we hope the discussion will illustrate some of the additional work that Access performs for you behind the scenes, not just with the SQL Server objects but also the objects used in serving up web content to a user's web browser and tying it back to the underlying SQL Server table. If you have no plans to connect to the SQL Server database outside the Access web apps, then you don't need to worry much about this. Otherwise, you learn more about techniques you can adapt in Chapter 21.

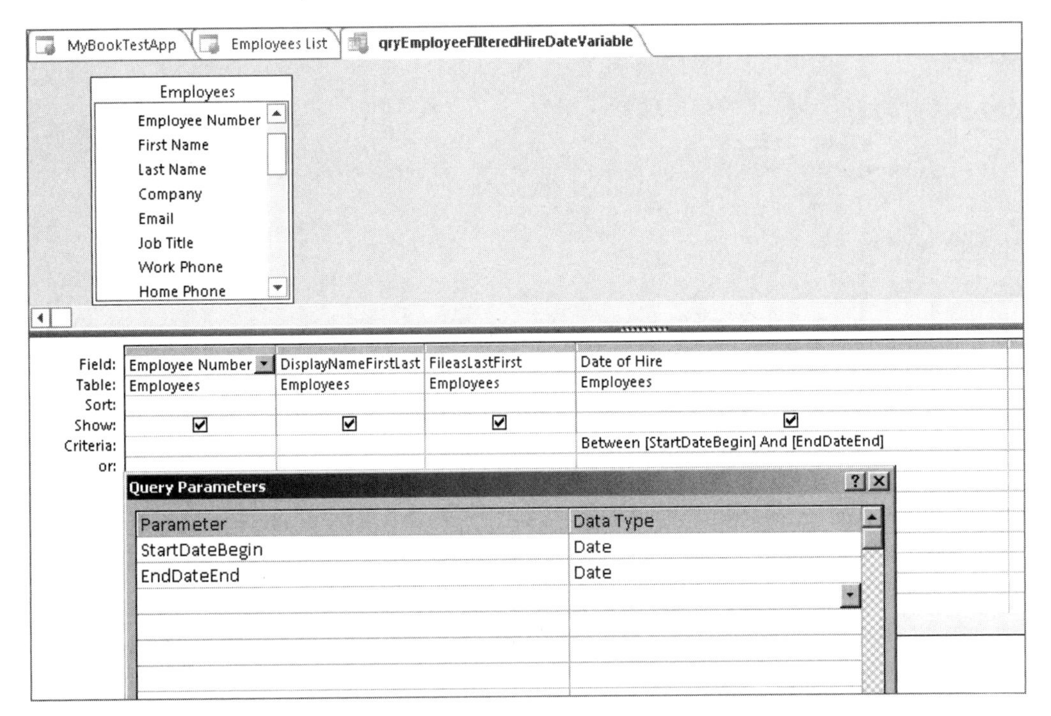

FIGURE 5-3: Parameterized query in Access

```
/****** Object:  UserDefinedFunction [Access].[qryEmployeeFIlteredHireDateVariable]    Script Date: 1/12/2013 6:29:44 PM ******/
SET ANSI_NULLS ON
GO

SET QUOTED_IDENTIFIER ON
GO

CREATE FUNCTION [Access].[qryEmployeeFIlteredHireDateVariable]
(
    @StartDateBegin Date,
    @EndDateEnd Date
)
RETURNS TABLE
AS
RETURN
(
    SELECT
        [Employees].[Employee Number],
        [Employees].[DisplayNameFirstLast],
        [Employees].[FileasLastFirst],
        [Employees].[Date of Hire]
    FROM
        [Access].[Employees]
    WHERE
        [Employees].[Date of Hire] BETWEEN @StartDateBegin AND @EndDateEnd
)
```

FIGURE 5-4: Table-valued function in SSMS

CHANGES IN THE QUERY DESIGNER

The main process of building queries is basically the same as it has been in previous versions of Access, so we'll focus on differences to help ease the transition from what you're used to in the client query designer to what you can do in the web app's query designer.

Creating, Editing, Saving, and Previewing Queries

The process of creating a new query hasn't changed significantly in web apps. You still have a few different ways to create one. The ribbon for web apps is much simplified compared to the client. Thus, the Query button has moved to the Advanced drop-down on the ribbon, as indicated in Figure 5-5.

You also can create a new query via the recordsource in a web app view. By default, the query gets saved as an embedded query in the view, as shown in Figure 5-6, but you can use Save As in the Query Designer to make it a brand new query that can be accessed in the navigation pane (see Figure 5-7).

FIGURE 5-5: Query button on the ribbon

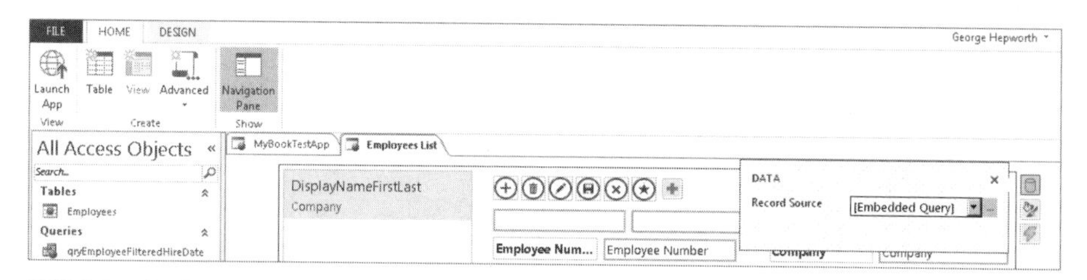

FIGURE 5-6: Creating an embedded query as a recordsource for a view

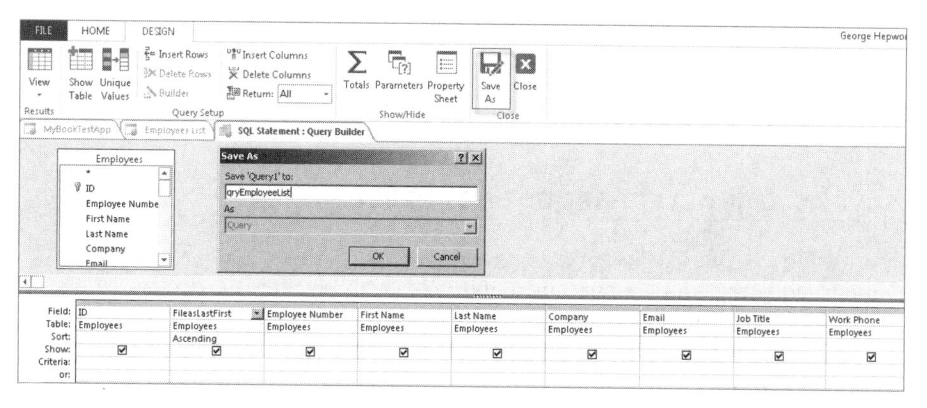

FIGURE 5-7: Save As button on the ribbon

The process of adding tables and fields to a query should be familiar to you. When you create a new query via the build button shown in Figure 5-6, you will also notice that you have the Save As button available on the ribbon, as shown in Figure 5-7.

As you can see in Figure 5-7, an embedded query can be saved as a standalone query. However, after you save the query as a new standalone query, it no longer can be saved as another query. The Save As button is removed from the ribbon for all standalone queries. The same is true if you create the query directly in the navigation pane via the Query option on the ribbon, as shown earlier in Figure 5-5. The Save As button is not available in these queries

Also note that there is no simple way to copy and paste queries as new copies. As Figure 5-8 shows, the ability to copy and paste is disabled when you right-click a query on the navigation pane.

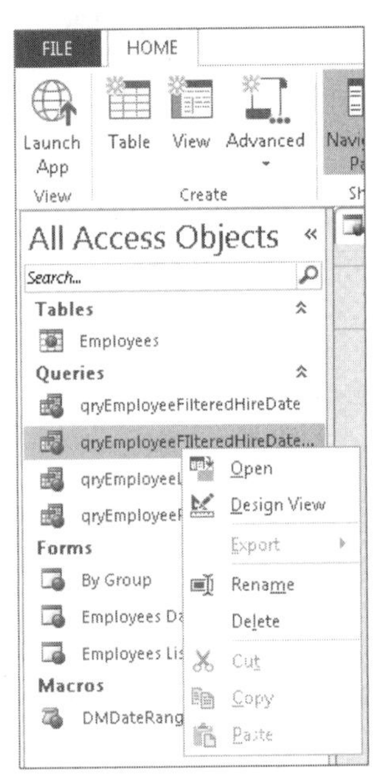

FIGURE 5-8: Copy and Paste disabled on the right-click menu for queries

WHY IS SAVE AS AVAILABLE THERE BUT NOT HERE?

It may appear arbitrary, but because every query is saved as a SQL object, when you create an embedded query, you are creating a SQL Server object that is not available for consumption outside the view where that query is embedded. The Save As functionality in embedded queries actually renames the SQL Server object and also makes it available to other views and/or other objects for consumption. As you can see, that's not a true Save As in the sense that a new copy of the object would be created. It merely transforms a hidden object to a visible object.

Manually Copying Queries

In scenarios where you need to replicate a query, there is a process you can use to ease the pain of copying one or more fields. Suppose you have a query that selects fields from three tables, as shown in Figure 5-9.

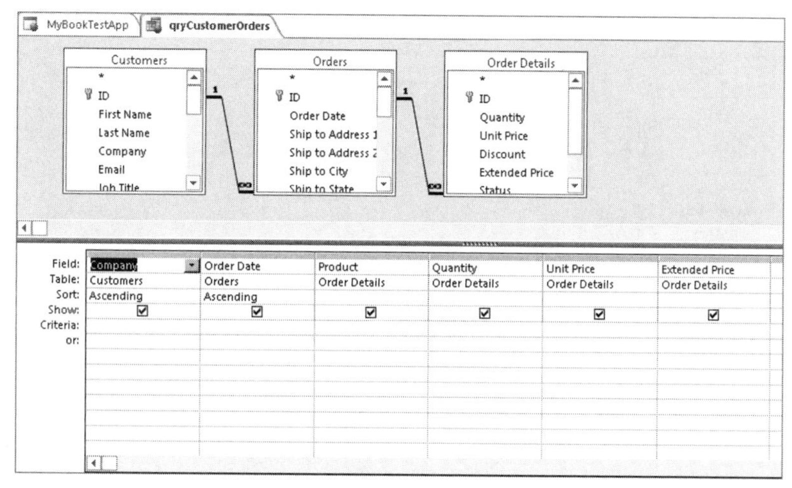

FIGURE 5-9: Query with three tables

You could create a new query, perhaps using the ribbon as illustrated in Figure 5-5. You would have to manually select the same three tables and, if necessary, specify the joins between them. That would give you a second query with no fields, like the one in Figure 5-10.

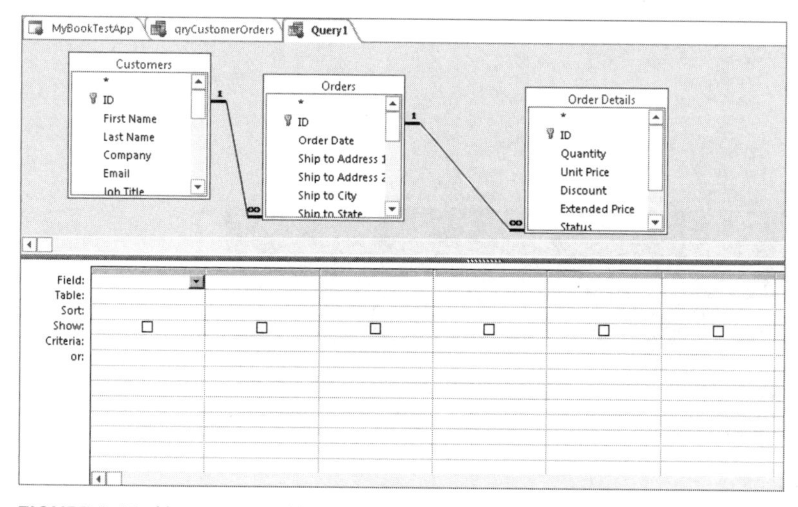

FIGURE 5-10: New query with tables added

In the first query shown in Figure 5-9, select one entire column, as shown in Figure 5-11. Hover the mouse over the column header for the field; you'll note how the cursor changes to a downward arrow. Click to select the column.

Move the cursor to the last column on the right side of the query, hold down the Shift key, and click to select the last column. That will select all columns between the first and last, as in Figure 5-12.

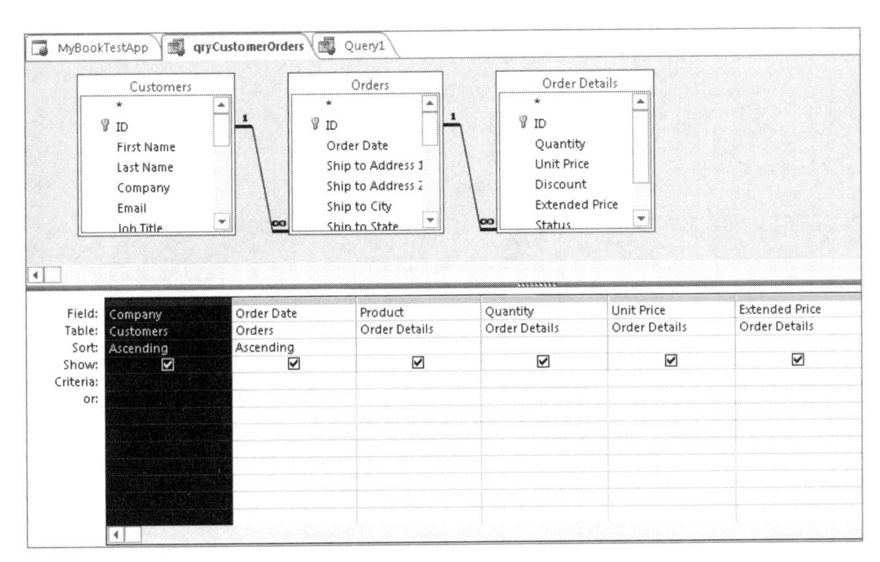

FIGURE 5-11: Selecting a column

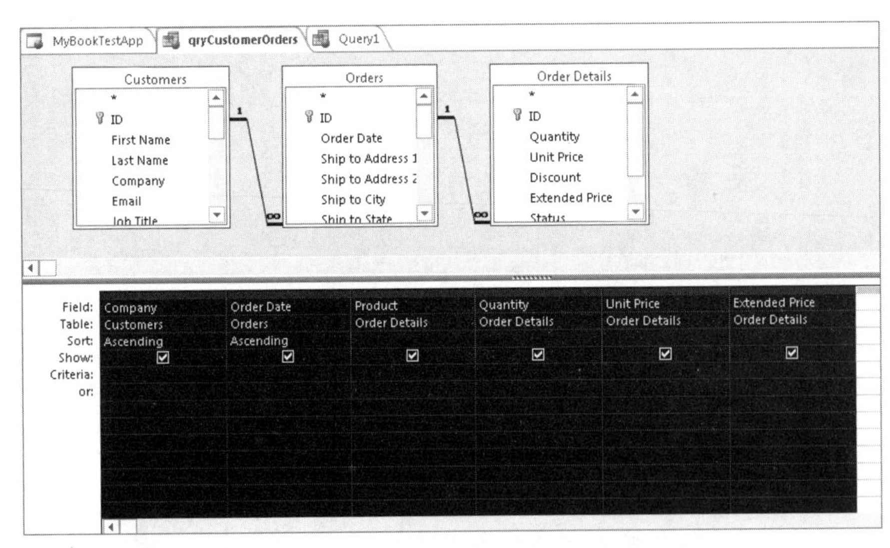

FIGURE 5-12: All columns selected

You can then press Ctrl+C to copy the selection. Go over to your new query and select the first column in that second query in the same manner you did to select the entire column, as illustrated in Figure 5-11. You can then press Ctrl+V to paste the contents from the first query into the second one, providing you with all the fields from the first query in your new query. Your second query should then be identical to the original query shown in Figure 5-9. Though not as convenient as actually copying the whole query as you could in the client, this method is better than entering fields one by one.

Previewing Query Results

One other notable change you may run into is that you'll be prompted to save the query after each change, even if it's only a change in the width of a column, as illustrated in Figure 5-13.

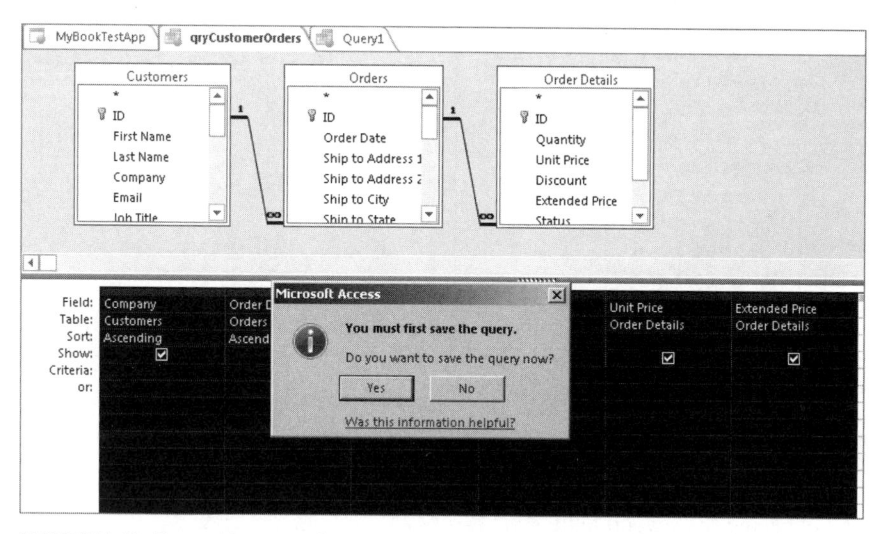

FIGURE 5-13: Prompt to save changes to a query

If you're like the authors of this book who make generous use of the query preview capability to check our work as we go, you might find that a bit cumbersome. However, this is a limitation of the new architecture; it is not possible to run a query without saving it first. During the building of sample apps, the authors found it useful to create and reserve a query named `qryTest` for creating one-shot queries for testing purposes or for sanity checks during the development process. You may want to adopt this approach to help avoid proliferating temporary queries that really shouldn't be part of the final application.

One other change is in how results are rendered in preview mode. Suppose you had a query that returns one field and you open the query in preview mode for the first time, as shown in Figure 5-14.

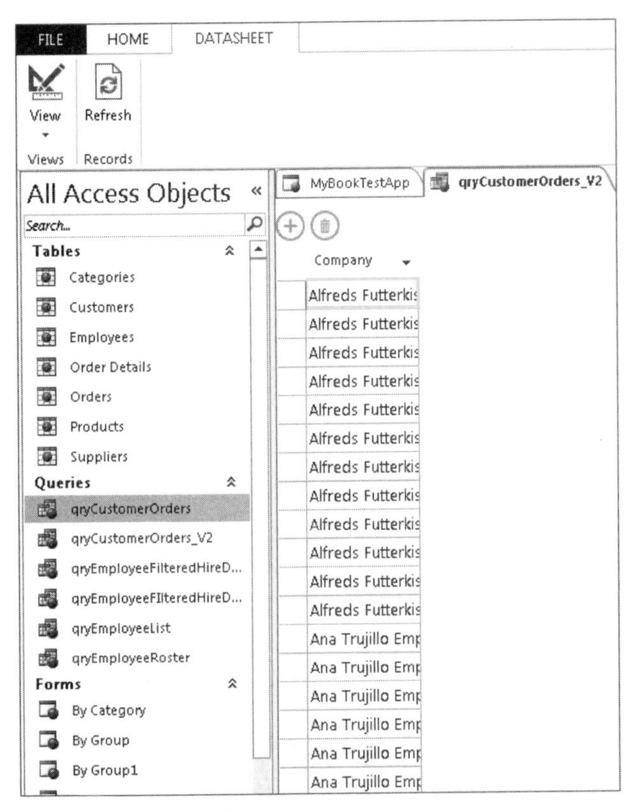

FIGURE 5-14: Previewing the query

You then go back to the Query Designer and add one more field, save the change, and preview the change again. Instead of seeing the second field you just added, you get the same output you saw before, as shown in Figure 5-14. Because queries are coming from a remote server, Access 2013 caches the results of query output, for better or worse, until you refresh it. Fortunately, you can quickly get the latest result by clicking Refresh on the ribbon, as demonstrated in Figure 5-15.

After clicking the Refresh button, you get the expected result showing the recently added field, as shown in Figure 5-15.

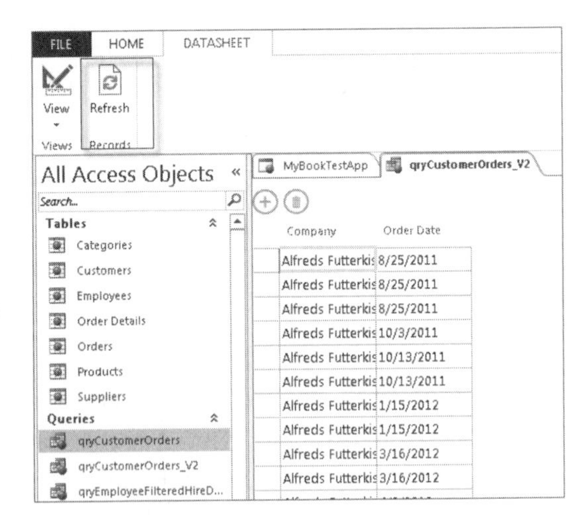

FIGURE 5-15: Refresh button on the preview

Action Queries

As with Access 2010 web databases, there are no action queries. In Chapter 6, you will learn about data macros, which allow you to insert, update, or edit records. If you have to perform regular bulk operations where performance will matter, consider using an Access client database to perform those bulk operations instead. You learn about using external connections to the SQL Server database for your web app database with an Access client database or SQL Server Management Studio in Chapter 11.

It is unlikely that people using web browsers, and especially those working on a mobile device, will need to work with bulk processes. Even if they needed to do so, it would be too cumbersome to do it in the browser. The capability to perform bulk operations is one of the primary reasons we think you'll appreciate the ability to connect to the SQL Server database directly from a client database.

Parameterized Queries

If you're like us, you've probably used parameterized queries a couple of times but generally avoided them. However, in Access 2013 parameterized queries definitely merit a second look. SQL Server has a much more sophisticated optimizer that works very well with parameters. Because all parameterized queries are created as inline table-valued functions, that query optimizer is able to plan in advance the optimum execution plan to return results quickly even for varying inputs.

Unlike in client queries, you cannot create implicit parameters in a web app query. You must explicitly declare parameters you want to use in your query, a feature we think you definitely will welcome. No doubt, you've seen one too many "Too few parameters" errors in client queries caused by a misspelled field name. Adding parameters is fairly straightforward and almost identical to the client version. To create a parameter, you click the Parameter button on the ribbon, as in Figure 5-16.

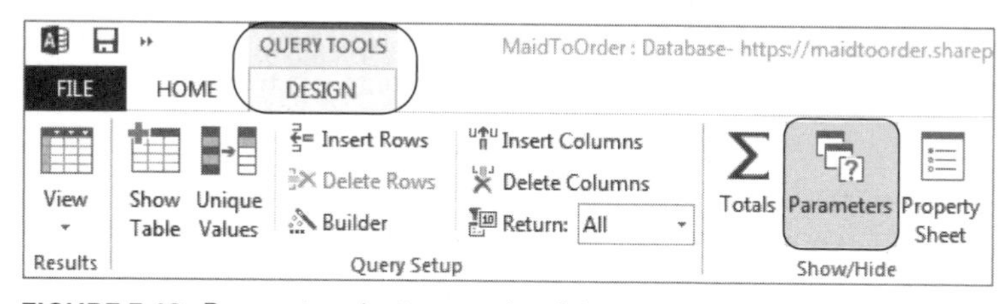

FIGURE 5-16: Parameters button on the ribbon

Access will present you with a parameter dialog box. As you may expect, the listings for data types are different, which you can see in Figure 5-17.

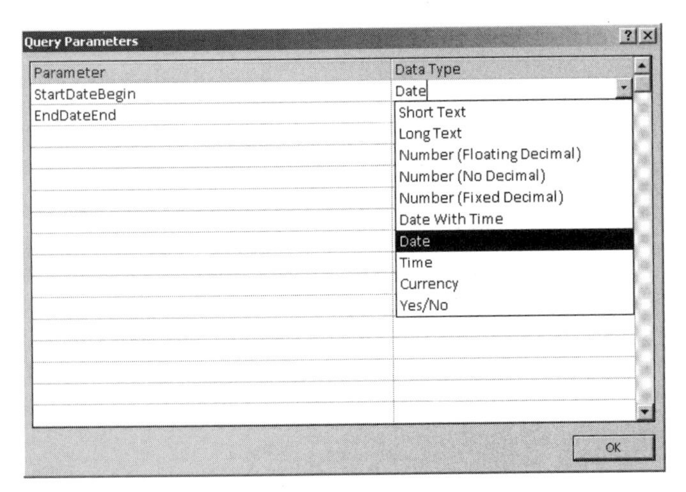

FIGURE 5-17: Parameter dialog box with data type drop-down displayed

You can add as many parameters as you need for a particular query. Of course, it may behoove you to follow a good naming convention, as discussed in Chapter 8. Referencing a parameter works the same way as it has always worked in the Access client; simply take care to bracket the parameter's name to ensure Access does not try to treat it as a string. In the Functions and Expressions section later in this chapter, you will see some examples of parameters being used.

One additional way you can take advantages of parameters is to filter a nested query. When a query contains another query as a source and both have a parameter of the same name, the same value supplied is re-used in both queries. You will see an example of this in Chapter 8.

Aggregates, Unique Values, and Top Values

Unlike Access 2010 web databases, web apps do support aggregate queries, with the familiar aggregate functions you have in client queries. Not only are they much faster to build and view than equivalent data macros, but you can also use them as sources for data macros, which you will see in Chapters 6 and 9.

As you may expect, you still can specify whether a query should return only distinct values or restrict the numbers of rows returned. Those options are available on the ribbon, as shown in Figure 5-18.

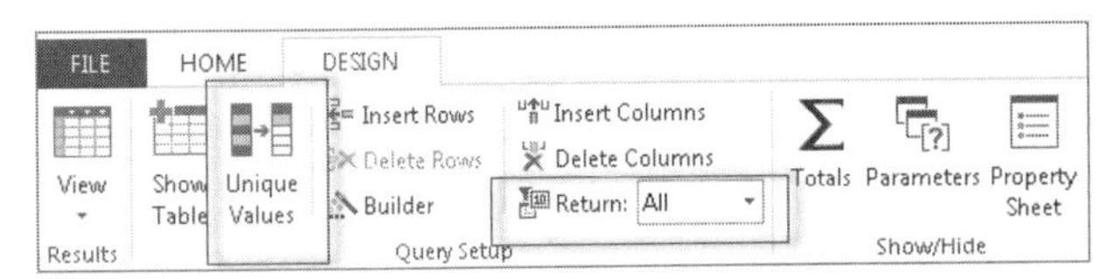

FIGURE 5-18: Totals, Unique Values, and Return controls on the ribbon

As in the client version, you can also specify a percent rather than an absolute value for the number of records allowed to be returned.

Query Properties

Like client queries, web app queries have a Property Sheet, which is hidden by default. You expose it by toggling the button on the ribbon, as shown previously in Figure 5-16.

Three main properties are available in web app queries, two at the query level and one at the table level:

1. Description
2. Top Values
3. Alias

As in the client, the Description property provides a customized text description of what a query does. The Top Values property has the same value as shown on the Return dropdown on the ribbon illustrated in Figure 5-18, so it's just an alternate method of entering a top value parameter.

The Alias property, which applies to tables in the query, is usually more useful when you are performing a self-join or joins from the same table multiple times. Typically, you might want to disambiguate what each joined table should represent in the query. Figure 5-19 shows a query where `tblEmployees` is self-joined using the default alias from Access.

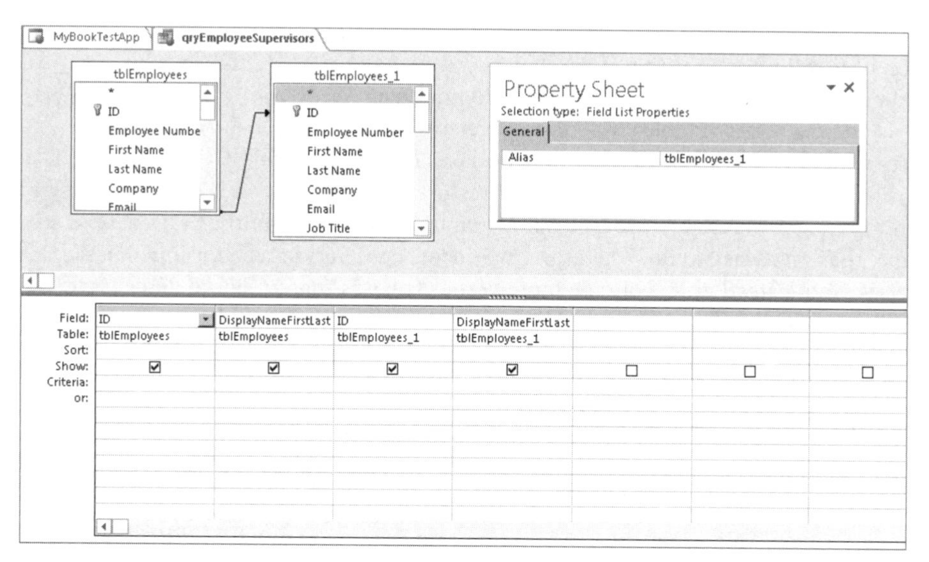

FIGURE 5-19: Self-joined query using default alias

Suppose you want to make it more explicit whether you're reading from a field from the employee's record or from the employee's supervisor. To accomplish that, you could change the default aliases from `tblEmployees` and `tblEmployees_1` respectively to `tblEmployees_Employee` and `tblEmployees_Supervisor`, as shown in Figure 5-20.

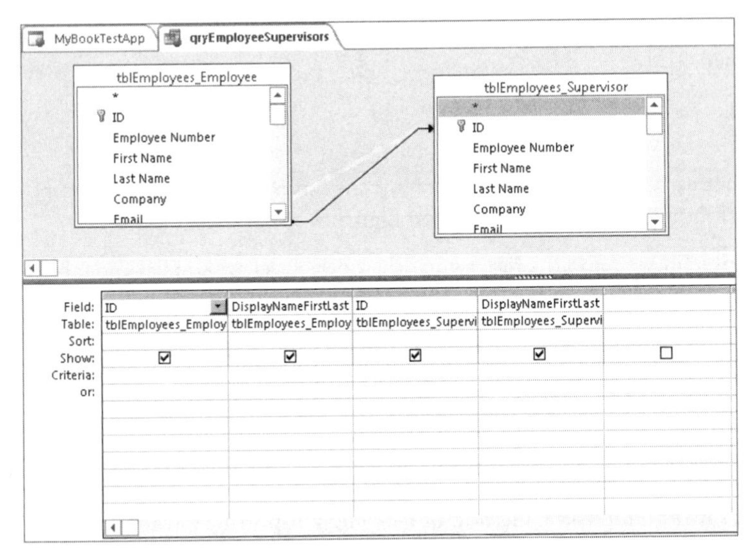

FIGURE 5-20: Changed aliases

We want to call your attention to one important caveat. Attempting to remove the alias field generates the error shown in Figure 5-21.

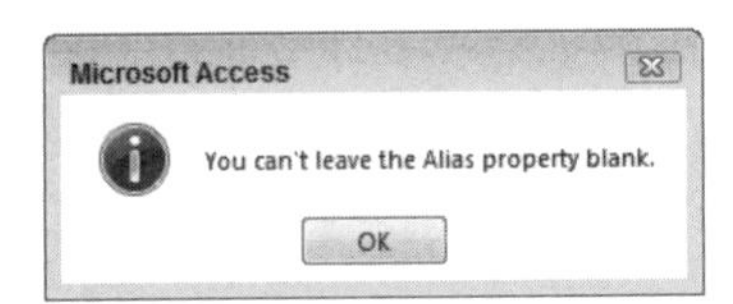

FIGURE 5-21: Error displayed after removing the Alias property

The ramification of this limitation is that if you have used a small number of letters as an alias to expedite typing, you do not have an easy way of seeing the original table name, nor of getting it back. Developers who have a practice of using short aliases to make typing easier may find this to be a problem. To restore it, you would need to re-enter the original source name manually, and without the SQL view to see that source name, that's not easy to do. Therefore, we encourage caution when using aliases in this manner for queries, and instead we encourage more verbose aliases that are more descriptive, as illustrated in the previous example.

FUNCTIONS AND EXPRESSIONS

While the process of building queries is largely unchanged, you will find that expressions are quite different from what you may be used to writing in client queries. Because the same expressions are also used in macros and validation rules in addition to queries, you will find the following discussion applicable in subsequent chapters. Some functions are unchanged; however, for the sake of completeness, we will list all functions.

Because functions and expressions are more or less based on T-SQL functions, and often have less to do with functions you might have used in the client, you will need to take note of the changed syntax, constants, and expected parameters for the functions in your web apps. To help ease the transition, we will review those functions and discuss their intended usage. We'll also provide an example for each and, when applicable, note the analogue functions in Access client. Of course, it goes without saying that even when a function in the Access client has the same name as the one in web apps, it may not behave exactly the same way. Our goal here is to identify the client analogue and note significant differences, rather than to provide complete specifications. For a full technical specification of each function, bookmark this URL in your web browser: `http://msdn.microsoft.com/en-us/library/office/jj583221.aspx`.

While building sample apps for the book, we usually found it easier to consistently write expressions as we would write them in T-SQL, even though Access could handle the translation smoothly. One rationale for doing so is to help set up the mental framework that you're not using the same familiar functions anymore, and to encourage you to be diligent in recognizing and observing differences in parameters and syntax. Thus, in the rest of this book, you'll primarily see examples where we tend toward the T-SQL dialect.

Delimiters

Although queries are now SQL objects, Microsoft has put considerable effort into enabling you to continue to use the same delimiters you've previously used to disambiguate a string and/or date/time from numbers. For example, you can continue to use either double or single quote marks to delimit the string literals and the octothorpe, or pound sign, to delimit date/time literals. Behind the scenes, Access will format the T-SQL generated for your expressions to return the literal in the same data type.

Operator Differences

Several of the operators used in expressions should be familiar, so we'll focus primarily on operators that were either removed from web apps or changed from their counterparts in the Access client, as well as the replacements for those operators, where appropriate.

Concatenation Operator

In the Access client, you've used the `&` operator to concatenate strings. If you try to use the same operator in web apps, you will get an error indicating that Access web apps could not find the function. Therefore, you need to use the `Concat()` function, as discussed later in the section, to get the equivalent behavior. Note that you still can use `+` operator to concatenate strings but like in the Access client, this is not a null-safe operation. As you'd expect, a null input for any single operand in the concatenation will yield a null result. The `Concat()` function is, therefore, the preferred choice.

Integer Division Operator

On occasion, you may have performed an integer division between two numbers using the \ operator, as opposed to standard division using the / operator to get an integer result, regardless of whether the dividend and divisor had fractional parts or not. To perform an integer division, you must explicitly cast both dividend and divisor to integers in web apps. Alternatively, you could use `Round()`, `Floor()`, or `Ceiling()` as appropriate to approximate the functionality.

In and Exists Operator

When building queries, you might have used the `In` operator to evaluate whether a value matches any one of the values in a list or from a subquery. We might typically use it to filter a query. In client Access, we can set it up using SQL where clauses like these:

```
WHERE [FirstName] In ('Joe', 'Brian', 'Bill')
WHERE [FirstName] In (SELECT SelectedNames FROM tblUserSelections)
```

The first version, using hard-coded values, is still supported in Access web apps. However, the second version, where a subquery is written in the `In()` function, is no longer supported in web apps. Similarly, the `Exists` operator is not available at all in web apps since it also requires a subquery. On one hand, this is no large loss because typically you can get the same filtering by simply joining on the appropriate tables. A query using joins usually outperforms equivalent query filtering using the `In` operator anyway. The `Exists` operator, on the other hand, usually has a good use; it will not change the number of rows returned by the query whereas joining could. This can be approximated by doing a `DISTINCT` on the joined query first. Unfortunately this option is not without a potential performance penalty. We believe that for typical web app scenarios, you shouldn't need to rely on `Exists`; you can always use it in a client query connecting to the web app's database.

Like Operator

You might have used the `Like` operator to compare strings using wildcard matches. A typical usage in Access client might look like this:

```
WHERE [FirstName] Like "Ja*"
```

This filter returns all customers whose first name starts with the letters *Ja*. However, if you copied and pasted it into a web app, you'd get no results. Because they're based on T-SQL, the `*` and `?` characters are not metacharacters which are interpreted as wildcards; they're just ordinary characters. You have to use the same metacharacters that T-SQL uses:

```
WHERE [FirstName] Like 'Ja%'
```

Consult the help file on the full listing of metacharacters that you should use in Access web apps to maximize the `Like` operator's functionality.

ANSI-89 AND ANSI-92

If you're familiar with ANSI specifications, you may know that T-SQL is closer to the ANSI-92 specification, whereas ACE SQL defaults to ANSI-89. This is why metacharacters for the `Like` operator, among other things, are different between Access client and SQL Server. If you want to be able to write queries in ANSI-92 rather than the default ANSI-89, you can set this in the Access client's options. However, this is really practical only when starting a new client application as it changes the behavior of all queries. A possible alternative is to use the `ALike` operator instead of the `Like` operator, which allows you to use ANSI-92's metacharacters without changing all other queries that are using ANSI-89's metacharacters with the `Like` operator.

Other Operators

The following operators are rarely used, but for the sake of completeness we will quickly list operators that are available in client Access but not in web apps:

- ^ (Power operator)
- `Eqv`
- `Imp`
- `Xor`

Note that the ^ operator has an equivalent replacement in web apps; you call the `Power` function instead, as you'll see later in this chapter.

New Constants

There are several new constants that you will use in conjunction with some functions. In the following discussion, we point out where they are used. Note that although you may be using functions that look very similar to the version in T-SQL, you cannot use T-SQL constants; they are not recognized as valid constants in the Access environment. For example, you shouldn't use the `int` constant, which is valid when writing T-SQL. In Access queries, you should use the `Integer` constant.

Basic Constants

Note that you no longer have `True` and `False` constants. You use `Yes` and `No` constants instead. Here are the basic constants:

- `No`
- `Null`
- `Yes`

Data Type Constants

You typically use the following constants as parameters to various data type conversion functions, which you will read about in the next section. Here are the Data Type Constants:

- `Currency`
- `Date`
- `DateWithTime`
- `Float`
- `Integer`
- `LongText`
- `ShortText`
- `Text`

- `Time`
- `YesNo`

Date Part Constants

You typically use date part constants as parameters for various date and time functions, which are discussed later in this chapter. Here are the date part constants:

- `Day`
- `DayOfYear`
- `Hour`
- `ISO_Week`
- `Millisecond`
- `Minute`
- `Month`
- `Quarter`
- `Second`
- `Week`
- `Weekday`
- `Year`

Data Type Inspection and Conversion

The set of functions used to inspect data types and perform data type conversion is significantly different from what you may be used to in the Access client. However, you'll find that you also have more flexibility than what you had with the Access client.

Cast()

The Client analogues include:

- `CLng()`
- `CDbl()`
- `CDec()`
- `CCur()`
- `CStr()`
- `CDate()`

To convert one data type to another, you can use the `Cast()` function. This is useful if you have no control over incoming data types and need to extract a value and make it suitable for use in other places. An example of such use would be to cast a decimal number as an integer so you can use it for addition with other integers to ensure consistent results:

```
Cast(3.00, Integer)
```

You can also use the `Cast()` function when you need to ensure all components are of the same data types for consistent results before performing other operations on them.

You can see that, instead of using a different function for each data type, as you would have done in client Access, you specify the desired data type using one of the data type constants.

Try_Cast()

There are no Client analogues for `Try_Cast()`.

`Try_Cast()` works very similarly to `Cast()` but offers you an advantage. Perhaps you've been frustrated in the Access client when using various `C<data types>()` functions which fail when the input value is null or otherwise invalid. You will definitely appreciate the `Try_Cast()` function. Unlike the `Cast()` function and the analogue client functions, when an input that cannot be converted to the desired data type is passed into `Try_Cast()`, the return value is null. Compare these two expressions:

```
Cast('A', Integer)
Try_Cast('A', Integer)
```

The first will cause a run time error because the letter *A* isn't a number, while the second returns a `Null`. Thus, you may find `Try_Cast()` very useful in scenarios where you can't control the purity of the data and would rather show nulls instead of throwing run time errors. For example, let's say you have to process the string "3 Oranges" and enter a new record indicating a quantity of three oranges. Further, assume you are able to extract the digit "3" out of that string. In this case, you'd use `Try_Cast()` to convert it to a number, or return a null.

```
Try_Cast('3', Integer)
```

In this example, the integer returned would be 3, just as with the `Cast()` function. When you use an expression like this in a query where you expect to be able to cast most, but not all, possible values in a column, the `Try_Cast()` function is handy.

Parse()

There are no Client analogues for `Parse()`.

`Parse()` is similar to `Cast()` but is more appropriate for converting a string in a certain format to numbers or date/time. The difference is that `Parse()` can use the current regional setting, which is determined by the server, not the client. So, if your web app is on a server that's configured using the UK regional setting, this expression will output April 10, 2013.

```
Parse('10/4/2013', Date)
```

If the same expression is evaluated on another server that's using the U.S. regional setting, the expression would instead return October 4, 2013. There is no means of governing culture from the client side. Because of that limitation, we feel that `Parse()` and `Try_Parse()` have limited value and you are better off using `Cast()` and `Try_Cast()`.

Try_Parse()

There are no Client analogues for `Try_Parse()`.

Similar to `Try_Cast()`, you'd use `Try_Parse()` when you cannot guarantee that all possible inputs can be converted into the desired data types and would prefer to get null returned instead of run time errors.

Coalesce()

There are no client analogues for `Coalesce()`.

`Coalesce()` takes in a variable consisting of several parameters and returns the first non-null parameter value. If all parameters in the expression are null, `Coalesce()` will return null. This offers you a few possible uses.

The first possible use is to replace a value that may be null with a non-null value. For example you might want to display a zero instead of null for a currency column:

```
Coalesce([CurrentBalance], 0)
```

Thus `Coalesce()` can be a substitute for the `Nz()` function, which you're familiar with from the client. Unlike the `Nz()` function, however, you can include multiple possible substitutions. For example, you might want to show the outstanding balance first before ending with 0:

```
Coalesce([CurrentBalance],[OutstandingBalance],0)
```

In this case, when the value in `CurrentBalance` is not null, you'd get it back. When `CurrentBalance` is null and `OutstandingBalance` is not null, you'd get the value in the `OutstandingBalance` field. If both `CurrentBalance` and `OutstandingBalance` are both null, then you get the final option, zero. That cuts down on the number of `Nz()` functions you would have had to wrap; plus it is more readable than nested `Nz()`s.

One other possible use for `Coalesce()` is to ensure that a set of expressions has at least one value. For example, you might want to require that a customer enter at least a first name, or a last name or preferably both, but never no name at all. Thus for a validation rule expression you might enter:

```
Coalesce([FirstName], [LastName]) Is Not Null
```

`Coalesce()` is a good way to implement a rule that "none of those fields can be left blank." Ultimately, `Coalesce()` is a very versatile function and we think you'll find many other uses for it.

Format()

The client analogue is `Format()`.

The `Format()` function should be familiar. You probably used it many times to return a value in a custom pattern. A common example is converting a string of 10 digits, `1234567890`, to something that people recognize as a standard phone number, `(123) 456-7890`.

However, this is a case where it looks and walks like a duck but hops like a frog. For one thing, you cannot use strings that look like numbers with the `Format()`; you can only use numbers or dates. Furthermore, consider this familiar expression you might have used in the client:

```
Format(#1/1/2013#,'yyyy-mm-dd')
```

You might expect it to return `2013-01-01` but it actually returns `2013-00-01`. Contrast that to the expression,

```
Format(#1/1/2013#, 'yyyy-MM-dd')
```

which returns the correct value. What's going on? The answer is that we're not using the same metacharacters you're familiar with from the Access client. Unlike the client version, lettercase matters in the web app environment, which is based on SQL Server expressions; to request month formatting, you must use `MM`, not `mm`. There are additional differences as well. You will need to consult the Access help file or search on the web using keyword "Access web app 2013 Format function", familiarize yourself with all metacharacters, and be mindful of the lettercasing in expressions you write. Chapter 7 discusses this further.

DateFromParts()

The client analogue is `DateSerial()`.

Sometimes you want to return a date that's built up from a set of numbers. Instead of concatenating a string that only looks like a date, you can create a `Date` data type via `DateFromParts()`. To obtain January 23, 2013, for example, you could use this expression:

```
DateFromParts(2013,1,23)
```

TimeFromParts()

The client analogue is `TimeSerial()`.

Similar to `DateFromParts()`, but unlike the client version returning a `Date` data value with a display format indicating time, you get a true `Time` data type. To build a variable of the `Time` data type representing 1:23:05 in the morning, you would enter:

```
TimeFromParts(1,23,5)
```

DateWithTimeFromParts()

There is no client analogue.

When you need a variable with both date and time, you can call `DateWithTimeFromParts()` instead of calling `DateFromParts()` and `TimeFromParts()` separately. As you may expect, you get a `DateTime` variable as the result. To put together the date and time from the previous two examples, you would use the following:

```
DateWithTimeFromParts(2013,1,23,1,23,5)
```

This returns January 23, 2013 1:23:05 AM as the output.

String Functions

The set of string functions for web apps differs more from their client analogues than the preceding list, but you'll find that, in some cases, they are the same functions going by different names. The following section introduces some new string functions.

CharIndex()

The client analogue is `InStr()`.

Sometimes you need to determine if a piece of text is located within a larger string of text. For instance, you might want to locate where the word "Resolutions" starts in a paragraph-long text:

```
CharIndex('Resolutions', [Notes])
```

If the word passed to the function is present, you get an integer result indicating where the word starts in the Notes field if it's present. However, the value returned is 0 if it's not present, just like the `InStr()` function in the client. Additionally, you can specify whether to search from somewhere in the middle of the searched string by passing in a third parameter. This example illustrates how you can locate the word "Goals" in all notes. For notes with the word "Resolutions" in them, the position will be returned only if the word "Goals" comes after the word "Resolutions" because the third argument specifies the search start there.

```
CharIndex('Goals', [Notes], CharIndex('Resolution', [Notes]))
```

One limitation to the `CharIndex()` function is that it doesn't work on Lookup fields. Remember that the Lookup field actually stores the integer which is the primary key for the related table, not the displayed value, so the comparison doesn't return anything on these fields. You may need to use a separate query for this operation using the table that the Lookup field referenced.

> **NOTE** *Recall that you can use the* `Like` *operator instead of* `CharIndex()`, *which in some cases can offer better query performance. A* `Like` *operator has the potential to use an index (though it may not be able to in all cases) whereas* `CharIndex()` *will never be able to use an index.*

Concat()

The client analogue is the `&` operator

To concatenate various values of different data types and not worry about nulls causing the output to be null as well, you would use the `Concat()` function instead of the `&` operator as you did in the Access client.

```
Concat(Null, 'Hello', Null, ', ', Null, 'World!')
```

Despite the nulls interspersed in the example, you get "Hello, world!" as the output.

Left(), Right()

Client analogues include the following.

- `Left()`
- `Right()`

As in the client version, you can use the `Left()` function to extract a substring from a string starting from the first character on the left and cutting at a specified position. This is frequently done in conjunction with `CharIndex()`. A possible example would be extracting the last name from a string consisting of names entered as First, Last.

```
Left([PersonName], CharIndex(',', [PersonName]) -1)
```

If `[PersonName]` contains the value `O'Mallory, Amber`, the expression would return "O'Mallory".

The `Right()` function works similarly, starting from the right and taking off the right portion of the string. Continuing with the example:

```
Right([PersonName], Len([PersonName])-CharIndex(', ', [PersonName]) -1)
```

Note that `Len()`, discussed next, is needed in order to calculate the length from the right, not the position counting from the left.

Len()

The client analogue is `Len()`.

This function returns the length of a string. However, unlike the client version, if there is one or more trailing spaces, they will not be counted. The expression that follows will return 9 instead of 14, which would be returned by `Len()` in the Access client:

```
Len('Goldstein     ')
```

If you want to count trailing spaces, and get 14 as the result, you can concatenate a non-whitespace character to the end of the string and take one off the `Len()` as in this expression:

```
Len(Concat('Goldstein     ',';'))-1
```

Lower(), Upper()

Client analogues are as follows:

- `LCase()`
- `UCase()`

Sometimes you may have text entered in varying letter case and need to make the text all the same letter case. You can use either `Lower()` or `Upper()` to convert each alphabetic character to its desired letter case.

```
Lower('Hello, World!')
Upper('Hello, World!')
```

These expressions return "hello, world!' and "HELLO, WORLD!" respectively.

LTrim(), RTrim()

The client analogues include the following:

- `LTrim()`
- `RTrim()`

Typically, text is stored with trailing spaces removed, but if you want to ensure that there are no leading spaces in front of the input, you would use `LTrim()`. `RTrim()` may be useful in situations where you are dealing with strings that still have trailing spaces not already stripped away.

```
LTrim('  Hello, World!  ')
RTrim('  Hello, World!  ')
```

The expressions will return "Hello, World! " and " Hello, World!" respectively. In the Access client, you had the `Trim()` function, which does not exist in web apps, but which can be approximated by wrapping both `LTrim()` and `RTrim()` around the string:

```
LTrim(RTrim('  Hello, World!  '))
```

Replace()

The client analogues is `Replace()`.

When you need to substitute a part of a string with something else, you can use `Replace()`, which is the same as in the Access client. Unlike the client version, however, you cannot specify when to start replacing or limit the number of occurrences to replace. The `Replace()` function will replace all occurrences of the supplied argument within the supplied string. For more granular replacement, consider using the `Stuff()` function instead, as discussed shortly.

A likely use for `Replace()` is to clean up a string by enforcing consistent use of double quote marks for an input string like this:

```
Replace([Notes],"'","""")
```

This enables you to ensure that even if a user types in single quote marks, they will be converted to double quote marks.

Replicate()

The client analogue is `String()`.

If you need to create repeating patterns, such as a number of spaces to create indentations, you can use `Replicate()`. Unlike `String()` in the client, you are not limited to a single character and can use a string with any number of characters.

```
Replicate('   ', [varNumberOfIndentations])
```

If `varNumberOfIndentations` has a value of 3, the output will be nine spaces.

Stuff()

There are no client analogues.

As mentioned when examining `Replace()` earlier, if you have a situation where you need to replace only a single occurrence of a string within another string, you may find `Stuff()` to be suitable. Suppose you want to replace the word "Goal" with "Resolution" but only for the first occurrence of the word "Goal". This is the expression you'd write:

```
Stuff([Notes], CharIndex('Goal', [Notes]), Len('Goal'), 'Resolution')
```

`CharIndex()` enables you to specify where to start the insertion and `Len()` governs how much of the original string should be deleted, which in this case is the length of the word "Goal." The string to the right of "Goal" will not be altered. Even if `[Notes]` has multiple instances of "Goal," you'll see "Resolution" replacing only the first instance of "Goal."

> **WARNING** *Note that if the arguments specifying the start and length for the* `Stuff()` *function are excessive or negative, the return will be null.*

SubString()

The client analogue is `Mid()`.

Whenever you need to extract a string from within another string, you can use `Substring()`, which, despite its name, behaves very similarly to the `Mid()` function in the client. You specify the string to be searched, the starting point for the selection, and the ending point for the selection. For example, if you want to extract the second sentence out of a paragraph using the first period as the starting point and the second period as the ending point, this is how you'd write the expression.

```
LTrim(SubString([varInput],CharIndex('.',[varInput],1)+1,CharIndex('.',[varInput],-
 CharIndex('.',[varInput],1)+1)-CharIndex('.',[varInput])))
```

Note that unlike `Mid()`, which allows the length parameter to be optional, you must explicitly enter a value for the length to the `Substring()`. If you want to use the `Substring()` to give you the remaining part of a string after a starting point, you could use `Len()` of the string, which will guarantee that you'll get the entire portion.

Date and Time Functions

One drastic difference between date and time functions for web apps compared to the equivalent functions in the client is that you no longer use a string to describe the date parts. Rather, you use one of the date part constants you saw earlier in this chapter. The examples in the following section illustrate the differences.

Note that you already saw the `DateFromParts()`, `TimeFromParts()`, and `DateWithTimeFromParts()` functions in the "Data Type Inspection and Conversion" section earlier in the chapter.

DateAdd()

The client analogue is `DateAdd()`.

As you already know, adding a range of intervals to dates is quite complicated, what with varying numbers of days per month and uncertainty over which day of the month falls on what weekday. As in the Access client, you can use `DateAdd()` to describe how you want to change an input date with a specified number of intervals. For example, to get the date that's 15 days after February 25, 2013, you would write the expression as,

```
DateAdd(Day,15,#2/25/2013#)
```

which would return March 11, 2013.

> **WARNING** *Note that there is a function* `Day()`, *not to be confused with the date part constant* `Day`. *Take care to not include parentheses when specifying a date part constant.*

Note that you don't pass in `Day` as a string to the `DateAdd` function as you might have done in the client. Contrast this with the equivalent expression in the Access client:

```
DateAdd("d",15,#2/25/2013#)
```

DateDiff()

The client analogue is `DateDiff()`.

When you need to extract the number of intervals between two dates, you've probably used `DateDiff()` in client databases. This is very similar. To return the number of days between the dates used in previous examples use the following expression:

```
DateDiff(Day,#2/25/2013#,#3/11/2013#)
```

DatePart()

The client analogue is `DatePart()`.

Sometimes you want to extract some part out of a date/time expression for use in other calculations. Sometimes you may use it in conjunction with the `DateFromParts()`, `TimeFromParts()`, or `DateWithTimeFromParts()` function to decompose and reassemble a different date. For example, you might want to convert a date to another date representing the 10th of the same month:

```
DateFromParts(DatePart(Year, [varInputDate]), DatePart(Month, [varInputDate]),10)
```

If you used July 20, 2013 as the input for the `varInputDate` variable, the result would be July 10, 2013 because the hard-coded `10` is passed into the day part. The year and month are extracted out of the `varInputDate` using the Year and Month expressions.

> **NOTE** *Note that in Access web apps, you have more date parts than you had in the client. For example, you now can store and extract milliseconds in your* `DateTime` *or* `Time` *expressions. Such granularity was not directly supported in the client Access.*

Day(), Month(), Year()

Client analogues are as follows:

- `Day()`
- `Month()`
- `Year()`

This set of functions is effectively a shortcut for the `DatePart()` function, with the date part specified for you as part of the name. Therefore, you can use those in the equivalent expression from the previous example:

```
DateFromParts(Year([varInputDate]),Month(varInputDate]),10)
```

Because you don't have to specify the `Year` and `Month` date part constant, the expression becomes shorter. However, note that you have only those three shortcuts; if you're going to use date parts other than those three date parts, you would need to use `DatePart()` and, as a matter of style, mixing shortcut functions and `DatePart()` may be an issue. Your mileage may vary.

EOMonth()

There are no client analogues.

If you've had a need to figure out the last day of a month, you've no doubt had to come up with a complicated expression in a client database. One possible client expression would be advancing to the first day of the following month and taking off a day:

```
DateAdd("d",-1,DateAdd("m",1,DateSerial(Year(Date()),Month(Date()),1)))
```

If you run that expression on April 15, 2013, you get April 30, 2013 as the result. This messy sort of calculation all goes away with this web expression:

```
EOMonth(Today(),0)
```

The `0` indicates that you want the end of the same month as the date specified. You can also specify the last day of other months by using a different number for the second argument. For example, you might want to get the last day of the third month after a given date:

```
EOMonth(Today(),3)
```

Again, assuming that this expression runs on April 15, 2013, you'd get July 31, 2013 as the result.

Now(), Today()

The client analogues are the following:

- `Now()`
- `Date()`

As you saw in previous examples, `Now()` and `Today()` give you today's date and you can use `Now()` to give you both date and time at the instant the function is called. The behavior is identical to the client version, other than a name change for the `Date()` function. You might want to use `Now()` as a way to timestamp a record when it's inserted and/or updated.

Math Functions

As a class, math functions are least changed between client and web versions so you should be quite comfortable with this set of functions. There are a few new functions that didn't exist in the client version, which we identify in the section that follows.

Abs()

The client analogue is `Abs()`.

To obtain the magnitude of a value, without a sign, you can use `Abs()`,

```
Abs(-100)
```

which returns 100.

Ceiling()

There is no client analogue.

`Ceiling()` returns the next greater integer based on a decimal number. This is useful when you want to always round up a decimal number, regardless of how small the fractional part is. An example is determining how many containers you need to fulfill an order even though one of the containers may be only partially full.

Both of the following expressions return 2:

```
Ceiling(1.3)
Ceiling(1.7)
```

Contrast `Ceiling()` with `Floor()`, which is discussed later in this section.

Exp()

The client analogue is `Exp()`.

If you're performing logarithmic calculations, you may need to use the value of *e*. The `Exp()` function returns the value of *e*. This expression is equivalent to getting the value of e^2:

```
Exp(2)
```

Floor()

There is no client analogue.

You might want to always round a decimal number down to an integer, irrespective of the fractional part. These two expressions both return 1:

```
Floor(1.3)
Floor(1.7)
```

You saw how `Ceiling()` can be helpful in telling you how many containers you need to fulfill the order; you can use `Floor()` to tell you how many full containers there will be.

Log(), Log10()

The client analogue is `Log()`.

`Log()` provides logarithmic evaluation defaulting with natural logarithm as the base. The following expression returns 1.609:

```
Log(5)
```

You can specify a different base by passing in a second parameter. To evaluate $\text{Log}_2(5)$, you can express it as:

```
Log(5, 2)
```

This returns 2.322. You also can use `Log10()` as a shortcut for evaluations using 10 as the base. These two expressions are equivalent:

```
Log(5,10)
Log10(5)
```

Both expressions return 0.699.

Pi()

There is no client analogue.

If you need to perform geometrical calculations with circular or spherical figures, you call on `Pi()` to return the value of π. `Pi()` takes no parameters. The expression allows you to get the area of a circle of a certain radius.

```
Pi() * ([varRadius] * [varRadius])
```

Power()

The client analogue is the ^ operator.

To raise a number to a specified power, you use a function instead of an operator, as you did in the Access client. To express 7^2 and get 49 as the result, you would use the following:

```
Power(7,2)
```

Rand()

The client analogue is `Rand()`.

`Rand()` provides pseudo-random numbers, which may be useful in performing a random selection of records, such as to simulate a lottery. As in the Access client, it returns a number between 0 and 1 and can take a seed value. Note that if the same seed is provided in different calls to the function, the same result is returned, for better or worse. Unlike the Access client, there is no corresponding `Randomize()` to set the seed; you may want to always provide a seed that will change to ensure you get random output at all times. This expression illustrates how you can sort records in random order based on a timestamp field on the table while keeping all records inserted on the same day grouped together:

```
Rand(DateDiff(Day,0,[DateModified]))
```

Round()

The client analogues are the following:

- `Round()`
- `Int()`
- `Fix()`

This is one function that is quite different from the client version of `Round()`. One difference is that you can pass in parameters that change how it behaves and, therefore, you can have it truncate instead of rounding, which gives you similar behavior to `Int()` or `Fix()`. Furthermore, you can round on the left side as well the right side of the decimal point. To better illustrate all the differences, consider the results shown in Table 5-1.

TABLE 5-1: Results of Round Expression on Different Values

WHEN *X* IS . . .	ROUND(X,1)	ROUND(X,1,1)
1.43	1.4	1.4
1.47	1.5	1.4
1.53	1.5	1.5
1.57	1.6	1.5
–1.43	–1.4	–1.4
–1.47	–1.5	–1.4
–1.53	–1.5	–1.5
–1.57	–1.6	–1.5
1.45	1.5	1.4
1.55	1.6	1.5
1.65	1.7	1.6
1.75	1.8	1.7
–1.45	–1.5	–1.4
–1.55	–1.6	–1.5
–1.65	–1.7	–1.6
–1.75	–1.8	–1.7

The `Round()` expression takes three arguments: 1) the number to be rounded, 2) the precision of the rounding, and 3) whether the result should be truncated. In Table 5-1, the expression for the second column indicates that the number should be rounded to a single decimal. In the third column, the expression indicates that the number should be truncated. Review the results shown to see how they reflect those arguments.

Note that unlike the Access client version of `Round()`, which uses banker's rounding, this version uses the more standard rounding scheme. You can also see that when you pass in a nonzero value for the third parameter, you have the same behavior as the client's `Int()` function or `Floor()` function.

In some scenarios where you have a large number and you want to round off the smaller portion in order to report numbers in thousands or millions, you can put in a negative value for the second parameters. The following expression will give you 2000 as output:

```
Round(1743,-3)
```

Sign()

The client analogue is `Sign()`.

You can use this function to determine if you have a negative number, a zero, or a positive number. The expressions shown here will return –1, 1, and 0 respectively:

```
Sign(-38.27)
Sign(38.27)
Sign(0)
```

Sqrt()

The client analogue is `Sqr()`.

You use this function if you need to find a square root of a number. Note the difference in spelling between the client and web apps versions.

The following expression returns 6:

```
Sqrt(36)
```

Other Functions

The functions mainly used for program flow or SQL aggregating are unchanged. For completeness, we list them here. Even though SQL Server may have extensions to some of the SQL aggregate functions, they are not exposed in Access 2013, so the functionality is on par with the client version.

- Program flow
  - `IIf()`
  - `Choose()`
- SQL aggregate
  - `Avg()`
  - `Count()`
  - `Max()`
  - `Min()`
  - `StDev()`
  - `Sum()`
  - `Var()`

> **NOTE** *As you may expect, SQL aggregate functions such as* `Sum()` *and* `Count()` *are not available for use in expressions outside of queries.*

Availability by Context

You have now learned about all of the functions and expressions available in web apps; however, not all of them are available in all contexts. For example, T-SQL functions such as `Cast()` and `CharIndex()` are not available in UI macros. Table 5-2 shows which functions and expressions are available by context, that is, in a query expression or data macro; in a UI macro; or in a calculated field.

TABLE 5-2: Availability of Functions and Expressions

FUNCTION	AVAILABLE IN...		
	DATA MACRO & QUERY EXPRESSION	UI MACRO	CALCULATED FIELD
`Abs()`	Yes	No	Yes
`Cast()`	Yes	No	No
`Ceiling()`	Yes	Yes	Yes
`CharIndex()`	Yes	No	Yes
`Choose()`	Yes	Yes	Yes
`Coalesce()`	Yes	Yes	Yes
`Concat()`	Yes	Yes	Yes
`DateAdd()`	Yes	Yes	Yes
`DateDiff()`	Yes	Yes	Yes
`DateFromParts()`	Yes	Yes	Yes
`DatePart()`	Yes	Yes	Yes
`DateWithTimeFromParts()`	Yes	Yes	Yes
`Day()`	Yes	Yes	Yes
`EOMonth()`	Yes	No	Yes
`Exp()`	Yes	No	Yes
`Floor()`	Yes	Yes	Yes
`Format()`	Yes	No	No
`IIf()`	Yes	Yes	Yes
`Left()`	Yes	Yes	Yes
`Len()`	Yes	Yes	Yes

`Log()`	Yes	No	Yes
`Log10()`	Yes	No	Yes
`Lower()`	Yes	Yes	Yes
`Ltrim()`	Yes	Yes	Yes
`Month()`	Yes	Yes	Yes
`Now()`	Yes	Yes	No
`Parse()`	Yes	No	No
`Pi()`	Yes	No	Yes
`Power()`	Yes	No	Yes
`Rand()`	Yes	No	No
`Replace()`	Yes	Yes	Yes
`Replicate()`	Yes	Yes	Yes
`Right()`	Yes	Yes	Yes
`Round()`	Yes	Yes	Yes
`RTrim()`	Yes	Yes	Yes
`Sign()`	Yes	No	Yes
`Sqrt()`	Yes	Yes	Yes
`Stuff()`	Yes	Yes	Yes
`SubString()`	Yes	Yes	Yes
`TimeFromParts()`	Yes	Yes	Yes
`Try_Cast()`	Yes	No	No
`Try_Parse()`	Yes	No	No
`Update()`	Table Event Only	No	No
`Upper()`	Yes	Yes	Yes
`UserDisplayName()`	No	Yes	No
`UserEmailAddress()`	No	Yes	No
`Year()`	Yes	Yes	Yes

NOTE *You will learn about table events and the* `Update()` *function in Chapter 6. You will also learn about* `UserDisplay()` *and* `UserEmailAddress()` *in Chapters 9 and 13.*

SUMMARY

This chapter reviewed the features of the Query Designer, noting how it has changed. You learned some techniques for working effectively with the modified Query Designer , and you now know what to expect when building new queries. You also got a glimpse under the hood of creating a query and how it is represented in a SQL Server database.

We then turned to expressions, and you reviewed a list of constants, operators, and functions. You are now equipped to identify which function(s) you want for specific purposes, and you have some idea of which function you need even though it may not be named the same or it may behave a bit differently from the client analogue.

You will see more of these expressions in later chapters; expressions are not only used in queries but also in macros and validation rules.

Creating Macros

WHAT'S IN THIS CHAPTER?

- Why we need macros
- Identifying differences between UI and data macros
- Understanding the scope of macros and variables
- Using the new Macro Designer effectively
- How data macros work with web apps

Macros in Access web apps fulfill a couple of critical functions. First, they allow you to enforce your business rules and automate many tasks to support data entry and management. In addition to enforcing business rules, macros also handle the necessary plumbing between the web client and the server. In order to provide the best possible coding experience for non-developers, without requiring that they learn multiple programming languages, Microsoft has created a set of macro actions to abstract away the underlying structure.

If you have been using VBA to augment your Access client solutions, you may have avoided macros in favor of VBA's greater power, especially in previous versions. However, to create a rich web app, you will need to delve into macros and put them to the best use.

Macros are an essential element of quality custom web apps. You must know how to develop quality data macros that make your web apps powerful and flexible enough to meet the needs of businesses and individuals. Your ability to create quality web apps depends upon being able to leverage the power of the Macro Designer, which is the tool you'll use to create macros. You learn about the Macro Designer in the first part of this chapter.

After you become familiar with the new Macro Designer, you'll study how macros are classified. You then learn the steps involved in creating macros. In Chapter 9, you will get to apply the building blocks discussed in this chapter to build a full-bodied web app.

WHY WE NEED A NEW WEB-COMPATIBLE MACRO LANGUAGE

Access web apps have presented Access developers with a whole new set of paradigms for thinking about our jobs. One of the more significant changes is the coding language dedicated to building web apps. Although many Access developers would love to be able to continue using VBA in their Access web apps, those apps must run in the browser environment, which quite simply doesn't support VBA. Fortunately, we have an alternative language to create web apps that run in all the major browsers. That alternative, the Macro Action Catalog, provides most of the functionality you'll need to create powerful web apps, even though it is undeniably less flexible than VBA. While there is a significant divide between VBA and macros in some ways, a quick look back at where we've been in the recent past should help you understand why a major change in direction was needed to ensure Access's continued success as the database development tool of choice for experienced and novice developers alike.

Where We've Been

A number of years ago, Microsoft developed VBScript as a coding language for web pages. Very similar to VBA, VBScript, which can manage data in Access databases, open recordsets, and do many of the tasks that we do with VBA, appealed to developers accustomed to using VBA in their client database applications. However, fatal flaws with VBScript sped its demise as a mainstream coding language. Most critically, VBScript could only be used in Internet Explorer and was never supported by the other major browsers. Keeping in mind that one of the major objectives for Access web apps is cross-platform compatibility, you can easily see why the VBScript path was not viable for web apps.

Moreover, classic ASP web pages became notorious for "spaghetti code" that was very difficult to debug. Even before the introduction of Access web apps, Developers had largely abandoned VBScript and classic ASP web pages for other platforms such as ASP.NET.

Another factor to consider in choosing how to implement coding for Access web apps is the inescapable fact that Access has had too many security weaknesses to gain the trust of the majority of ASP.NET developers. For years, there was no secure and accepted way to put Access databases on the Internet.

Then a revolution grew, with faster Internet speeds and the increasing popularity of smartphones and tablets which led to growing pressure by clients and developers to put Access databases on the Internet. Microsoft answered this demand by providing Access 2010 Web Services. However, they had the experience with VBScript to guide them in choosing a better coding language to support it. Macros developed in the Access design environment are implemented as JavaScript. Unlike VBScript, JavaScript is widely supported.

Obviously, neither VBA nor VBScript were good choices as the coding language for web apps, for the reasons just outlined, among others. But equally important, in our view, is the way macros fit so well with Access's dominant position as the "database tool of first choice" for inexperienced novices as well as seasoned developers. Access achieved dominance as the most important desktop database development tool because it is a low-risk introduction to databases for even complete newcomers.

A key feature of Access has always been that almost anyone could install the Access application and immediately create a usable database — even if it could be considered flawed by professional development standards. Newcomers starting out with macros and simple forms quickly learned how to create databases that almost always worked. If Access web apps are ever going to be successful, they must also be accessible to inexperienced non-developers in that same way. The macro approach to creating functions is a big part of that.

Access's Traditional Role as Tool of First Choice

And that leads to a final point with regard to other possible choices to replace VBA as the coding language in web apps. Quite simply, professional development languages, like C#, are beyond the reach of nearly all non-developers. It would have been a crippling mistake to expect the primary Access audience of non-programmers and novice developers to embrace development based on C# or JavaScript, or one of the other programming languages.

Given those considerations, you can see why Microsoft elected to make the Macro Action Catalog the basis for creating web apps in the next generation of Access databases.

Microsoft replaced the existing Macro Designer with a new, more powerful and flexible Macro Designer, which enables developers to create the new macros they need to build applications that run in the browser. The new catalog of macro actions provided a reasonable level of flexible and robust programming, which could transform an Access database into web pages consisting of HTML and JavaScript that run in all the major browsers.

Microsoft continued the innovations by making exceptional improvements in Access 2013 web apps. Access 2013 web apps work much differently behind the scenes than Access 2010 web databases. Access 2010 stores both the schema and the data of web databases in SharePoint servers as SharePoint objects. The new Access 2013 web apps save both the schema and data in a Microsoft SQL Server database, a much more suitable platform for managing and storing data than SharePoint lists and objects. The Access 2013 web app's database can be hosted on either a SQL Azure or SQL Server. The macros, tables, views (forms), and queries are stored in various forms in the same SQL Server database that contains all the data in regular SQL Server tables. The web pages continue to be hosted on SharePoint servers.

One of the most significant advantages of the Access 2013 web apps platform is the much greater speed the platform provides. Unlike SharePoint, SQL Server databases and the servers on which they are hosted are designed to handle large amounts of data with speed and efficiency. The power and speed they provide are significantly greater than that provided by SharePoint and Access 2010 web databases, especially when working with a large number of records.

MACRO DESIGNER

Access 2010 introduced a newly redesigned Macro Designer, which in many respects was an improvement over the old design surface of previous versions of Access. If you've skipped using macros in Access 2010, you will want to get familiar with them when building macros for web apps. Even if you've worked with the Macro Designer, you may be delighted to learn that the newest version of designer offers some UI features that make it easier to work with macros.

Because the Macro Designer is much more structured than what you may be used to in the Visual Basic Editor, we will lead you through the process of building a macro in the Macro Designer to help you understand how it is set up. You will see that it enables you to use the powerful combination of data blocks, data actions, and program flow blocks to create powerful data macros. With these tools, you can use queries, parameters, values returned from other macros, filters, expressions, and more. You can use the Macro Designer to incorporate complex business logic in your web apps. In this chapter, you learn the basics of using the Macro Designer so you will have the knowledge and skills necessary to create custom macros that meet your needs. In Chapter 9, you will learn practical ways to use macros to develop highly functional web apps that incorporate complex business logic.

As you can see in Figure 6-1, the Macro Designer is a bit closer to the VBA editor in comparison to the old Macro Designer.

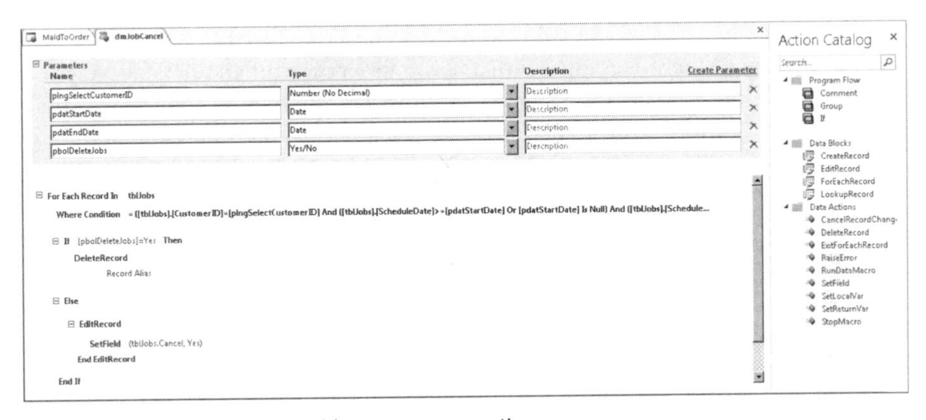

FIGURE 6-1: Macro designer with some macro actions

Still, the designer is much more structured compared to the VBA editor. Instead of typing out freehand text that forms a valid VBA syntax, you select an action and, where appropriate, provide the inputs needed for that action. Some inputs may be an expression, which you learned about in

Chapter 5, while other inputs expect an object such as a control, a view, or another macro.

Action Catalog

To provide assistance to people unfamiliar with which options are valid, the macro designer comes with an Action Catalog, illustrated in Figure 6-2.

The Macro Designer is context sensitive, so the actions you see are those that are valid for the macro you're currently designing. That helps to reduce the guesswork that was needed in the VBA editor: "Is this action a valid thing for me to do now?"

A search box at the top of the Macro Action Catalog filters the list of actions to those that meet your requirements. The matching actions are filtered in the catalog as you type in the search box.

You can add a macro action from the catalog to the body of a macro in a couple of ways. Double-clicking on the macro action inserts that action into the macro at the point which currently has focus in the macro. You can also add a macro action by clicking it and dragging it onto the Macro Designer, which allows you to add a macro action in the middle of other macro actions.

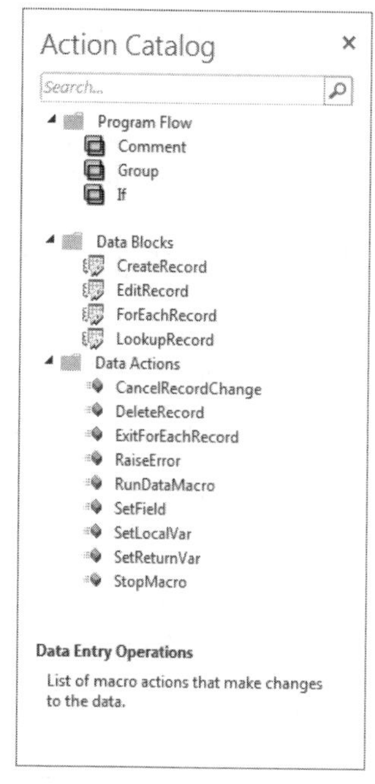

FIGURE 6-2: Action Catalog

Expressions and Expression Builder

For some inputs, an expression is always expected. You can spot them by the presence of the equal sign outside the textbox, as demonstrated in Figure 6-3.

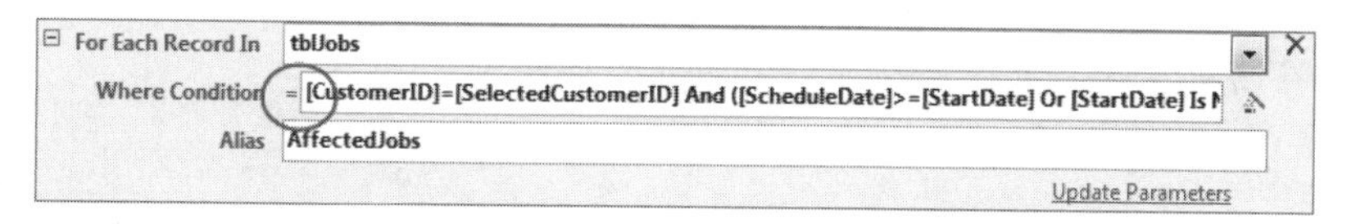

FIGURE 6-3: Equal sign outside the textbox indicates the expression is expected at all times

Some inputs expect literal values by default, but will accept expressions when preceded with an equal sign. Note that when you add an equal sign, the wizard button appears, as shown in Figure 6-4.

FIGURE 6-4: Equal sign inside a textbox to enable the expression

Of course, clicking the wizard button will bring up the Expression Builder, which should be familiar to you from previous versions of Access. This Expression Builder includes new functions that you reviewed in Chapter 5, as shown in Figure 6-5.

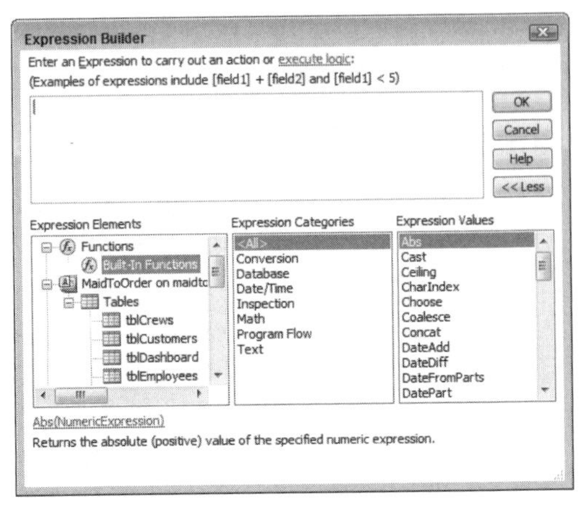

FIGURE 6-5: Expression Builder

Data Macro Tracing

One substantial improvement over the Access 2010 macro designer is the ability to toggle data macro tracing and its associated command to view the trace table on the ribbon, as Figure 6-6 shows.

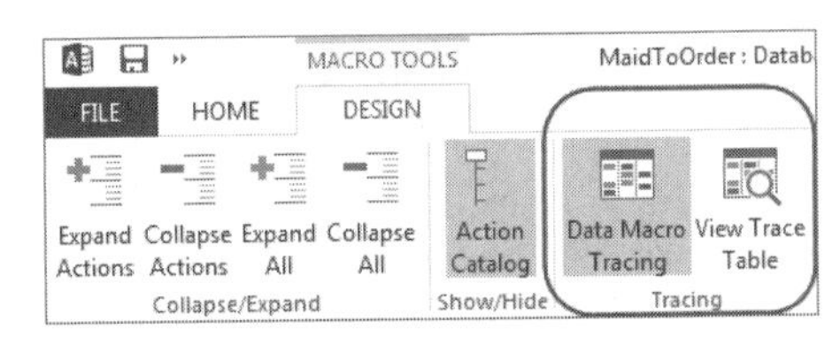

FIGURE 6-6: Data macro tracing buttons on the ribbon

Unlike the Application Error Log used in Access 2010 web databases, which simply reported errors, the trace provides step-by-step descriptions of the data macro's running and the various values, as Figure 6-7 illustrates.

This has a couple of advantages. It removes the need for you to manually add macro actions to log events to the application error log in order to debug a macro. It also makes analyzing errors much simpler, especially errors that only happen intermittently. Using the Trace table in a query to analyze errors is straightforward. You can use the Trace table as a source in a query and add filter criteria to filter results down to the actual issue behind a problem in the current data macro.

ID	MacroName	ActionName	Operand	Output	TargetRow	Timestamp	RuntimeErrorMessage
133695	dmFilterClearAll	ForEachRecord	tlkpFilterJobs;W			1/16/2013 3:04:	
133696	dmFilterClearAll	ForEachRecord	tlkpFilterService			1/16/2013 3:04:	
133697	dmFilterClearAll	ForEachRecord	tlkpFilterJobs;W			1/16/2013 3:05:	
133698	dmFilterClearAll	ForEachRecord	tlkpFilterService			1/16/2013 3:05:	
133699	dmFilterClearAll	ForEachRecord	tlkpFilterJobs;W			1/16/2013 3:05:	
133700	dmFilterClearAll	ForEachRecord	tlkpFilterService			1/16/2013 3:05:	
133701	dmFilterClearAll	ForEachRecord	tlkpFilterJobs;W			1/16/2013 3:05:	
133702	dmFilterClearAll	ForEachRecord	tlkpFilterService			1/16/2013 3:05:	
133703	dmFilterClearAll	ForEachRecord	tlkpFilterJobs;W			1/16/2013 5:27:	
133704	dmFilterClearAll	ForEachRecord	tlkpFilterService			1/16/2013 5:27:	
133705	dmFilterClearAll	ForEachRecord	tlkpFilterJobs;W			1/16/2013 6:07:	
133706	dmFilterClearAll	ForEachRecord	tlkpFilterService			1/16/2013 6:07:	
133707	dmFilterClearAll	ForEachRecord	tlkpFilterJobs;W			1/16/2013 6:17:	
133708	dmFilterClearAll	ForEachRecord	tlkpFilterService			1/16/2013 6:17:	
133709	dmFilterClearAll	ForEachRecord	tlkpFilterJobs;W			1/16/2013 6:29:	
133710	dmFilterClearAll	ForEachRecord	tlkpFilterService			1/16/2013 6:29:	
133711	dmFilterClearAll	ForEachRecord	tlkpFilterJobs;W			1/16/2013 6:31:	
133712	dmFilterClearAll	ForEachRecord	tlkpFilterService			1/16/2013 6:31:	
133713	dmFilterClearAll	ForEachRecord	tlkpFilterJobs;W			1/16/2013 6:33:	
133714	dmFilterClearAll	ForEachRecord	tlkpFilterService			1/16/2013 6:33:	
133715	dmFilterClearAll	ForEachRecord	tlkpFilterJobs;W			1/16/2013 6:33:	
133716	dmFilterClearAll	ForEachRecord	tlkpFilterService			1/16/2013 6:33:	

FIGURE 6-7: Trace table

More important, tracing is enabled and disabled by a single click of a button, which is faster than using 2010's application error log. Unfortunately, a UI macro cannot be traced in like manner. However, as you'll see later in the section on creating and editing UI macros, UI macros are generally limited in scope so the debugging requirement for UI macros is not as complex as it is for data macros.

Parameter Box

For data macros only, the Macro Designer also provides a way to pass parameters to the macro. They are set apart in a box, as shown in Figure 6-8.

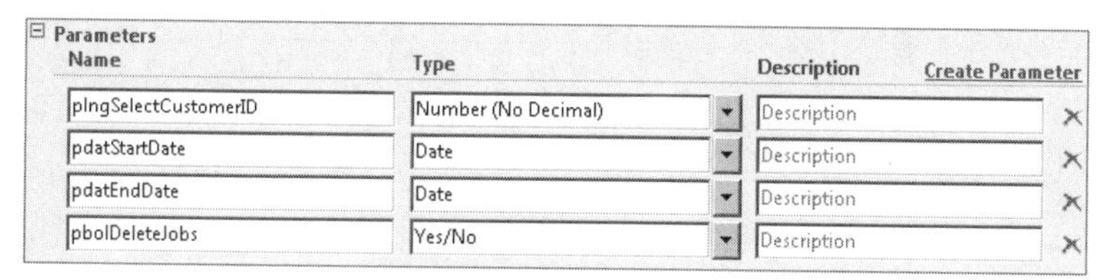

FIGURE 6-8: Parameters box in Macro Designer

You supply the name, data type and an optional, helpful description for each parameter. You define as many parameters as necessary to perform the data macro. You learn more about using parameters later in the chapter, and in more detail in Chapter 8.

Macro Links

Some macro actions and parameter boxes provide links to bring up additional features associated with the macro action or the parameter box. Figure 6-9 illustrates such links.

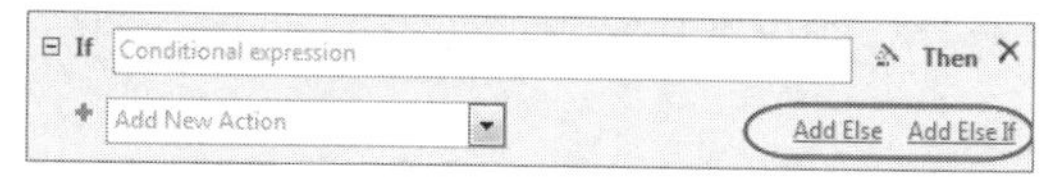

FIGURE 6-9: Add Else If and Add Else links

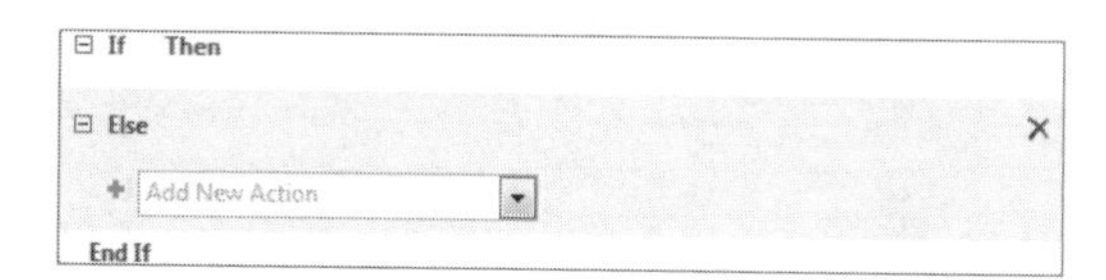

FIGURE 6-10: Add Else Link clicked, and focus moved away from the If . . . Then block

Note that, in keeping with the context sensitivity of the Macro Designer, links are displayed only when the associated macro action or parameter box has the focus. If you need to use a link for a certain macro action, you will need to click the desired macro action to set the focus to that action. That makes the links available for you to add. Depending on the logic of a macro action, some links, such as the Add Else link, can be used only once while other links can be repeated. Figure 6-10 shows what happens when you click the Add Else link and move the focus away from the If . . . Then macro action.

Interacting with the Macro Designer

The Macro Designer also supports dragging and dropping, which enables you to rearrange the macro actions as needed. Likewise, you can drag and drop a new macro action from the Action Catalog to insert between existing macro actions, as Figure 6-11 shows.

The macro designer also supports copying and pasting macro actions. When you copy a macro action, the data is saved to the clipboard as XML, which you can then paste into any text document. Consider Figure 6-12, which shows you the macro actions copied to Notepad.

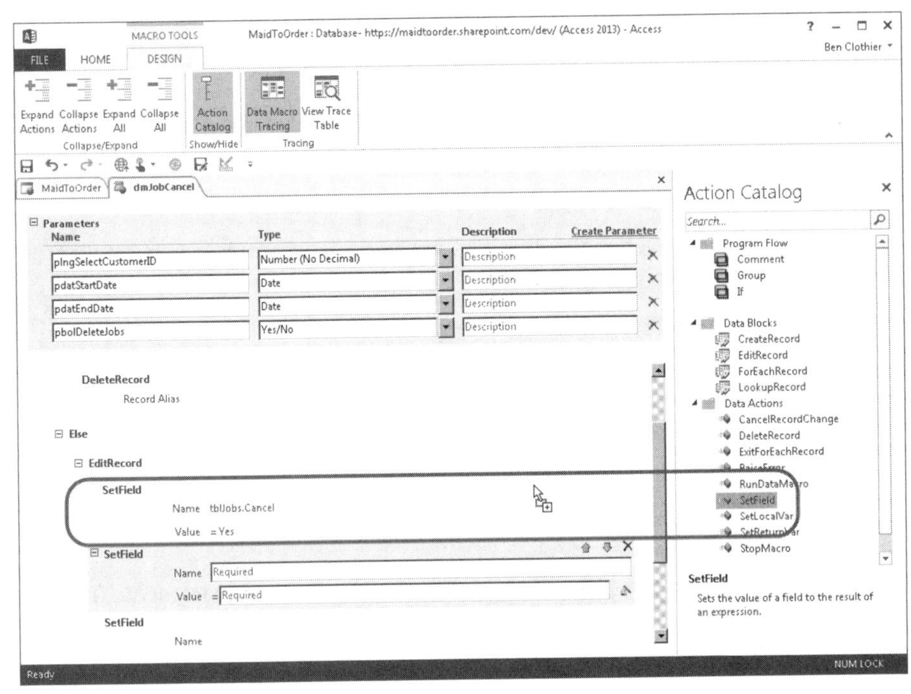

FIGURE 6-11: Dragging and dropping a macro action

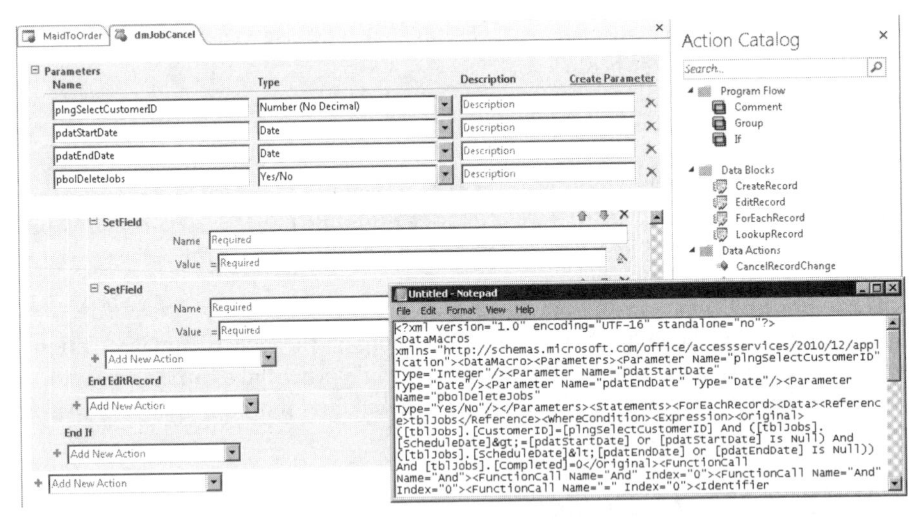

FIGURE 6-12: Macros copied to Notepad

This capability to paste between text and macro actions offers you the option of saving common macro actions as text for easy accessibility when working with different Access web app projects and also can be used to paste into other macros within the same project.

With this introduction, you've had a good overview of the Macro Designer's capabilities. Now we can get down to the macros themselves for the rest of this chapter. Later in the chapter, you will see how to use other features of the designer.

DIFFERENT TYPES OF MACROS

Access 2013 web apps support two types of macros: *user interface* (UI) macros and data macros. UI macros are used with views (called forms in previous versions of Access) and can be embedded macros or standalone macros. Data macros also come in two types, embedded table event data macros and the new standalone data macros. Table 6-1 summaries how the various types of macros may be used in a web app.

TABLE 6-1: UI Macros and Data Macros

TYPE	UI MACROS	DATA MACROS
Embedded	Views or Control Events	Table Events
Standalone	Called by embedded UI macros	May be called by any other macros

UI Macros

You use UI macros to perform actions with views or their controls. UI macros also enable you to use a number of operations with records such as navigating to a record in a view, modifying a control's properties, requerying views, running standalone UI macros and standalone data macros, and implementing a number of other user interface actions.

Data Macros

You use data macros primarily to manage data. You can perform actions such as looping through records, saving records, undoing changes to records, executing certain table events, and ensuring complex validation is done.

Together, the various kinds of macros provide you with a substantial assortment of actions. You can use them to perform a wide variety of tasks in your web apps. We feel that there is an impressive array of practical examples that will help you leverage the full potential of macros in your web apps, some of which you will learn about in Chapters 8 and 9.

Data Macro Architecture

When saved in the SQL Server database, data macros are changed into SQL Server database objects. Different types of macros are converted to different SQL Server objects. Standalone data macros are saved as stored procedures and event data macros are saved as `AFTER` table triggers in the SQL Server database. SQL Server developers routinely use these objects to develop applications.

> **NOTE** *You can read more about how macros are handled in the following blog post:* `http://blogs.msdn.com/b/windowsazure/archive/2012/11/06/microsoft-access-2013-a-cool-new-rapid-development-tool-for-the-cloud.aspx`.

The stored procedures and table triggers created from data macros run directly in the database where the data is stored. Being close to the data means they take advantage of the server's processing power with minimum network traffic. Moreover, stored procedures are optimized by the SQL Server database to run more quickly. While SharePoint — which was the basis for Access 2010 web apps — is well suited for many tasks, it was never intended to do the work of a high-performance relational database. Using a Microsoft SQL Server database or SQL Azure database is a far more efficient and optimal way to manage data in web apps.

You can use three types of table events in web apps, each attached to an event on the table. They are After Insert, After Update, and After Delete events. As the names for each event imply, they fire when you add a new record, modify an existing record, or delete a record, respectively. If you want the same data macro to be executed from more than one table event, consider using a standalone data macro and calling it in each table event.

> **NOTE** *Though the table events are labeled "After", you still can cancel such events by raising an error within the table event which will then prevent the action, be it inserting, updating or deleting, from completing.*

Generally speaking, a data macro is usually executed when a UI macro invokes the data macro via a RunDataMacro macro action or via one of the table events. You will learn how to use the RunDataMacro macro action, and how to use table events in Chapter 9.

Context in Data Processing

In a standalone data macro, it is necessary to first establish the context in order to do data modifications. What this means is that you must specify the table on which the data macro will make changes. You will learn more about this later in the chapter. On table events, the context is usually already established and you can have your macro act directly on the current record. In the case of an update or delete event, you also have access to the `old` virtual table, which contains the original data from the affected row of the table. You will see more about how you can use the `old` virtual table later in Chapter 9.

Changes Made to Data Macros Since Access 2010

As you may know, data macros were introduced in Access 2010. Access 2013 has made some changes to how data macros work compared to Access 2010. Note that Access 2013 desktop databases continue to use the same data macros as Access 2010, so the differences described here are specific to Access 2013 web apps. The new standalone data macros are more flexible than the named data macros of Access 2010. As their name implies, standalone data macros are not embedded in tables as was the case for named data macros, which are not supported in web apps. You can use standalone data macros both in your UI macros and table events. They can also be nested in other standalone data macros.

If you worked at all with web databases in Access Web Services under 2010, you may be familiar with the Before Change and Before Delete macros. However, they had limited functionality and had a complicated design. They are not needed in, and have been removed from, web apps because the table events in web apps can now be used to accomplish the tasks usually performed in the Before Change and Before Delete macros.

UI Macro Architecture

Generally speaking, a UI macro is transformed into a JavaScript snippet, which is then downloaded as a part of the document along with HTML and other elements to the web client. As indicated earlier, UI macros can either be embedded as a part of a control's event or be standalone. Standalone macros must be called by some embedded macro which may be behind a control's or view's event. Because a UI macro runs as a JavaScript snippet, it takes on all of the characteristics of a JavaScript code, which we will consider next, starting with the management of variables and the scope of the code.

There are two important conceptual differences to realize when using variables in UI macros. First, all variables created in any UI macro have global scope. Also, their lifetime is for the remainder of the session while the web browser is interacting with the Access web app. Variables will not be destroyed or reset until the web browser has left the web app, whether by navigating away or closing the window or tab or quitting, or when the user chooses to refresh the page. To put it in VBA terms, it's as if the only way for you to declare variables is to use the `Public` modifier; the `Private` and `Dim` modifiers simply do not exist. In Chapter 9, you will look at how we can manage the scope of UI macros, but for now, it helps to keep in mind that you need to be judicious with how many variables you can manage and be sure that you do not reuse variables for different purposes.

Second, JavaScript doesn't have strong data-typing, so all variables created in UI macros are more or less equivalent to VBA's `Variant` data type. When you pass a variable created in a UI macro to a data macro where strong data-typing exists, you will need to ensure the value within the variable can be converted to the appropriate data type expected by the data macro's parameter for that variable. Access will perform the data conversion implicitly so there is no need to explicitly perform data conversion, but you will need to take steps to ensure the value is valid.

Next, macros do not use objects in the same way you are used to in VBA. That means that at any time, there can be only one active view. You cannot build a UI macro that will act upon different objects; it can only act upon the current active object and its members. Therefore, when you create a standalone UI macro, you are relying on the fact that references you make from the standalone UI macro already exist and are part of the active view when you call the standalone UI macro.

To put it in more concrete terms, if you have a subview loaded, you cannot reference across the containing view into the subview, or from a subview into the containing view. You can only refer to other controls or fields in the current view where the user has set the focus. Your design of UI macros must take this restriction into consideration.

Block Macro Action

Block macro actions are different from other macro actions in that a block macro action can contain other macros within the block. A block macro action can appear in both data and UI macros. As you will learn later in the chapter, the If . . . Then block is one example (see Figure 6-13).

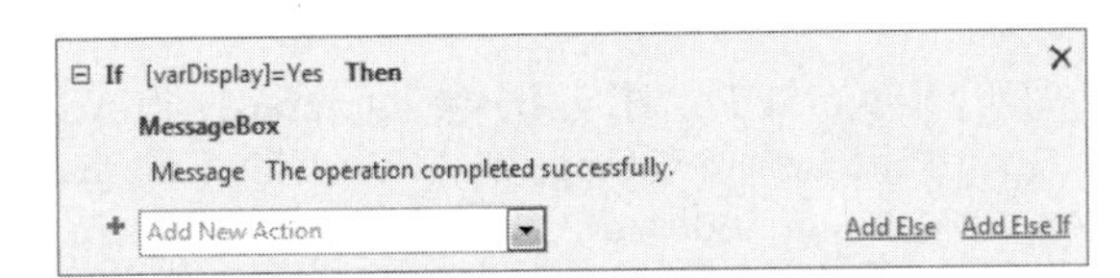

FIGURE 6-13: An If . . . Then block with macro actions within

As you can see, the block contains additional macros, which are indented from the rest, just as you'd usually indent your VBA code inside the true part of an If . . . Then block.

> **WARNING** *Indentation of the macro action indicates the scope the macro action currently is in. You will want to study how blocks may nest other macro actions and contain other blocks to ensure that macro actions behave in the way you expect them to.*
>
> *For some blocks, there are additional scoping considerations, which we explore in detail later in the chapter.*

CREATING AND EDITING DATA MACROS

So far in this chapter, we've looked at the design surface in the Macro Designer and pointed out various macro functionalities. You should now be ready to build a data macro. We'll walk you through a number of examples that will help you become familiar with different nuances of the building process. We will not touch all possible macro actions but, for the sake of completeness, we will provide a table of macro actions usually available in a data macro with a brief description. Once you have studied the examples in this chapter and Chapter 9, you should be able to extrapolate the lessons learned for other macro actions not specifically covered. We've summarized the macro actions by category in Table 6-2.

TABLE 6-2: Macro Actions by Group

MACRO ACTION	MACRO PURPOSE
Program Flow Actions	
Comment	Provide helpful comment
Group	Use to logically group macros
If	Provide If . . . Then functionality
Data Block Actions	
CreateRecord	Insert a new record into a specified table
EditRecord	Update a selected record from a table
ForEachRecord	Iterate across records in a table and/or query, selecting a record at a time
LookupRecord	Search and select a single record
Data Actions	
CancelRecordChange	Discard any edits made to a selected record
DeleteRecord	Delete the selected record
ExitForEachRecord	Leave the ForEachRecord block immediately
RaiseError	Return an error to the client with a custom error message, stopping the macro immediately. If fired in a table event, the event itself is cancelled and the operation prevented.
RunDataMacro	Execute another data macro
SetField	Select a field to edit within the selected record
SetLocalVar	Assign a value to a variable
SetReturnVar	Assign a value to a variable that is then returned from the data macro to the calling macro
StopMacro	Terminate the data macro immediately

NOTE *The If action and all actions under Data Blocks are all block macros.*

Creating a Standalone Data Macro

Let's create your first standalone data macro. Click the Advanced button on the Home tab in the ribbon to create a standalone data macro. Then click Data Macro in the drop-down list, as shown in Figure 6-14. This opens a new macro in the Macro Designer.

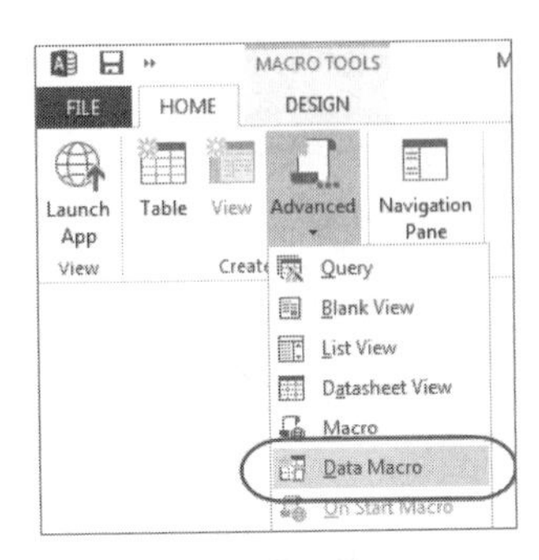

FIGURE 6-14: Creating a Standalone data macro

Using the Action Catalog

When you open or create a new macro, the Action Catalog shows at a glance a list of all of the data blocks and macro actions available. You can toggle visibility of the catalog by clicking the Action Catalog button on the Design tab in the ribbon, as shown in Figure 6-15.

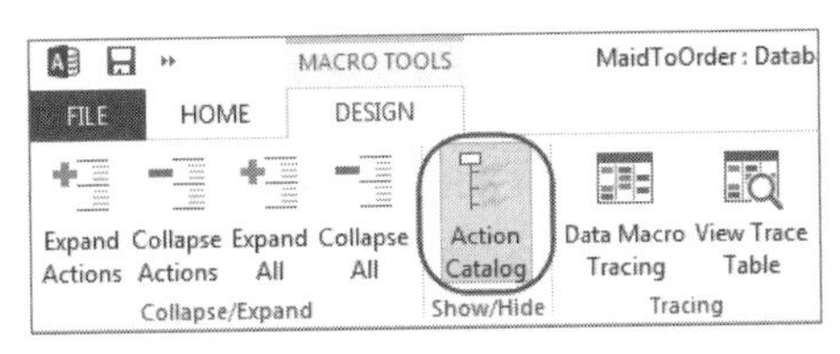

FIGURE 6-15: Displaying the Action Catalog

Being able to see all of the data blocks and macro actions in the catalog at a glance is very helpful. When you click a data block or a macro action, information about what the item does is displayed at the bottom of the catalog (see Figure 6-16).

Using the Add New Action Drop-Down

You can easily add a new action to your macro by using the Add New Action drop-down box, which is always available in the Macro Designer. The list in the drop-down is automatically filtered to show only those actions available to you at that place in the macro. Figure 6-17 shows a new action drop-down that has not yet been clicked, ready to accept your selection.

You can add Comments, a Group macro block, or an If . . . Then . . . Else macro block to your macros by using the Program Flow Action list. Refer to the illustration in Figure 6-16 if you need to locate the Comments macro block. In the next section, you learn more about how to do that.

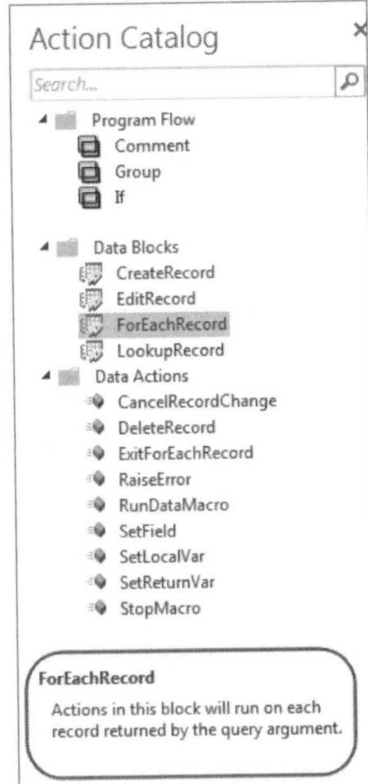

FIGURE 6-16: Using the Action Catalog

Using Program Flow Actions

The If . . . Then . . . Else macro block is one of the most important macro blocks you will use. When you think about it, all programming involves conditionals of this sort, regardless of the specific language you use to program. You can nest these blocks within other If . . . Then . . . Else blocks for even greater programming functionality. Let's learn how to create a data macro with an If . . . Then . . . Else macro block using a very simple expression so you can focus on the design of the macro rather than its contents.

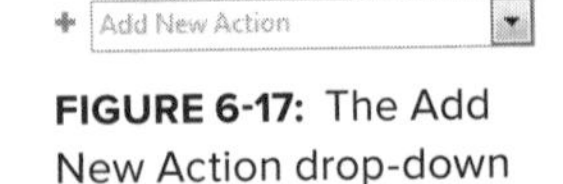

FIGURE 6-17: The Add New Action drop-down

To insert an If . . . Then . . . Else macro block into a data macro, go to the Home tab on the ribbon, click the Advanced button, and select Data Macro from the list, as you saw in Figure 6-14. A new blank macro opens in the Macro Designer. At the top of the macro you will see the Create Parameter link. Your first data macro will not use parameters, so you can leave it blank. We will show you how to create and use parameters later in this chapter. Next, click the Add New Action drop-down and select `If` from the list, as shown in Figure 6-18.

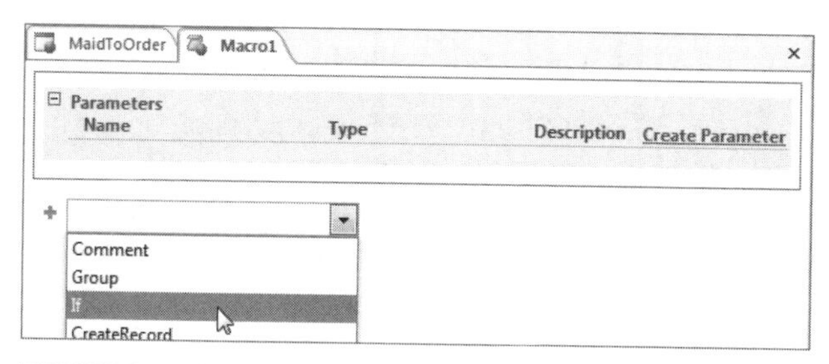

FIGURE 6-18: Insert the If . . . Then . . . Else macro block

This will insert an If . . . End If block in your macro. At this point, your cursor will be inside an Expression input box between If and Then. For our purposes in this simple example, enter `1>2` in the box. Because the If input expects an expression, we do not enter an = before `1>2`.

Next, you need to add an action to perform when your expression is true. We will take this opportunity to show you how to set a local variable using the SetLocalVar macro action. LocalVars retain their value only within the current macro. Click the Add New Action drop-down inside the If . . . End If block and select `SetLocalVar`. Be sure to use the drop-down box *within* the If . . . End If block. As you can see in Figure 6-19, the macro designer offers the same Add New Action drop-down both inside the block and after it. If your SetLocalVar is not within that block, the action will run after the If . . . End If block is finished, and the variable will not be set to the desired value. Enter `varExample` as the name of the LocalVar and enter `"1>2 is True"` with the quotes in the Expression input box, as shown in Figure 6-19.

FIGURE 6-19: SetLocalVar

> **WARNING** *The quotes are necessary because we want to indicate that the value is a string literal, not a variable or an expression. By default, Access treats a keyword that is not delimited as a reference to a variable.*

To continue to develop this conditional block, click `Add Else If`, highlighted in Figure 6-19. This time enter `1=2` in the Else If . . . Then Expression box. Within the Else If block that appears for this part of the conditional, use `SetLocalVar` as you did before. Give the variable the same name, `varExample`, and enter `"1=2 is True"` in the Expression input box with the quotes.

Next, add another Else If block. This time enter `1<2` in the Else If . . . Then expression box. The expression will be evaluated as True. Again, add a `SelectLocalVar` action, using `varExample` for the name. In the `SetLocalVar` Expression box enter `"1<2 is True"`. Because this section of the conditional will be evaluated as true, this is the value that `varExample` will be given when the macro runs.

Finally, click `Add Else` to add a final Else option to the macro block. Once more, add a `SetLocalVar` action, naming it `varExample`. In the Expression box, enter `"None of the Expressions was True."`. This is the value that would be given to the `LocalVar` if none of the expressions in the If . . . Then . . . Else macro block were true. Your macro should look like Figure 6-20.

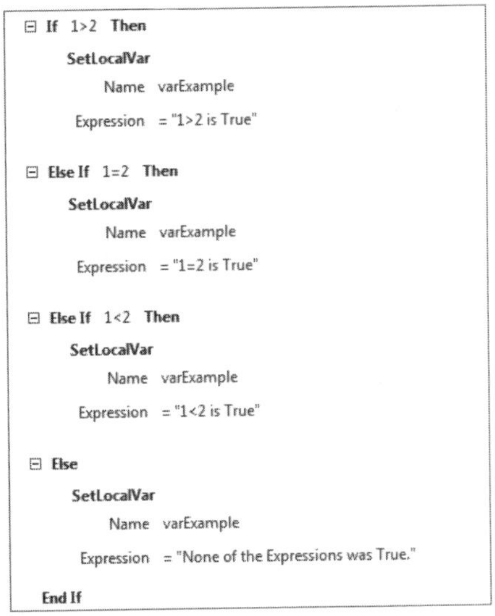

```
⊟ If 1>2 Then
    SetLocalVar
        Name  varExample
    Expression  = "1>2 is True"

⊟ Else If 1=2 Then
    SetLocalVar
        Name  varExample
    Expression  = "1=2 is True"

⊟ Else If 1<2 Then
    SetLocalVar
        Name  varExample
    Expression  = "1<2 is True"

⊟ Else
    SetLocalVar
        Name  varExample
    Expression  = "None of the Expressions was True."

End If
```

FIGURE 6-20: Finished If . . . Then . . . Else block

Now you know how to use the If . . . Else . . . Then block in the Macro Designer, which provides vital programming flexibility. The fact that you can nest one or more If . . . Else . . . Then blocks within each other makes it an even more useful feature. You have also learned how to use the SetLocalVar macro action. They are both very important tools that you can use to develop highly functional Access web apps.

The program flow blocks also include Comments that you can use to document your macros, making them easier to read and understand. As with other macro actions, you can add a Comment in several different ways; select the `Comment` action from the drop-down list, double-click `Comment` in the catalog, or click `Comment` in the catalog and drag it onto the macro designer. A multiple-line textbox opens for you to enter your comments. When you have finished entering your comments, they appear as green text surrounded by `/*` and `*/` delineators. A simple example can be seen in Figure 6-21. Only the first line of a comment is displayed, even though you can use up to 1,000 characters.

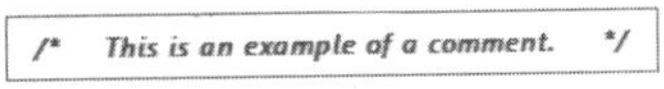

```
/*  This is an example of a comment.  */
```

FIGURE 6-21: A Comment macro block

As its name suggests, the Group macro block allows you to define a block of actions that you want to handle as a logical group. Within a Group macro block, you expand and collapse that section of a macro. It has no effect on how the macro works, but you can add a description to your block as well. You can use a group block to help organize your macro and make it easier to understand and work with. When you group your macros within a Group block, you can collapse/expand the Group block, making it easy to manage a complex macro with several actions.

How to Use the LookupRecord Data Block

The LookupRecord data block applies actions to a record from a table or a query matched by the specified condition, returning the first record with the matching value. Keep in mind, this will only operate on the first matching record. For example, you can use it to get the name of the crew leader of Crew #03. To do this, create a new data macro as you did before. In the Add New Action drop-down, select `LookupRecord`.

Next, you will enter the name of the table where you will look up the record. For this example, we assume there is a table named `tblCrews`. Begin typing `tblCrews`. IntelliSense provides a drop-down list filtered by what you type. Select `tblCrews` from the list.

You can make things even easier by using an alias for the name of the table. An alias works only within the block in which it was created. To use an alias, skip the WhereCondition block for now and click the Add Alias link. Note that the focus actually moves to the next Add New Action drop-down. Click the newly revealed alias input box to put focus back to it. Enter C in the alias input box. Now you can use the alias in the Where Condition input box. Enter `C` and double-click C from the IntelliSense dropdown list or hit the Tab key to select C. Next, add a dot (period) and then `[CrewName]`, which should result in `[C].[CrewName]`. After that, enter `= 'Crew #03'` and include the quotation marks so you should have `[C].[CrewName] = 'Crew #03'`. This will get the record with the field CrewName containing `Crew #03`.

Now that the macro will look up the record, you can get the value of any field in that record. To demonstrate this, use the Add New Action drop-down *within* the LookupRecord data block and select `SetLocalVar`. Enter `varCrewLeader` as the Name. In the Expression input box, enter `[C].[CrewLeader]` to set the value of `varCrewLeader`. The macro can now provide the name of the `CrewLeader` in the selected record, as shown in Figure 6-22.

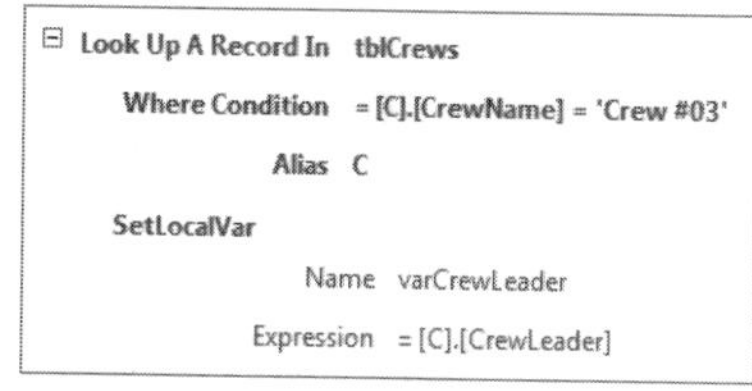

FIGURE 6-22: LookupRecord

How to Use ForEachRecord and EditRecord

The ForEachRecord macro block provides a way to loop through records in a table or query. You use the Where Condition expression to filter the records to specify the set of records you want. For example, you can get a list of all Customers that are not active in Oregon by using a ForEachRecord macro block. If you have just started expanding your business into Oregon, you need to change your potential Customers there from Inactive to Active.

You can use a ForEachRecord macro block to loop through the records you need to edit. To try this out, create a new data macro and use the Add New Action drop-down to select `ForEachRecord`. Enter `[tblCustomers]` for the source table, or select it from the drop-down list. You can again use `C` as an alias, but this time it represents `tblCustomers`. In the Where Condition input box enter `[C].[Inactive] = Yes And [C].[State] = 'OR'`. This will select all inactive customers in Oregon.

Use the EditRecord macro block to edit the records. Be sure to open it *inside* the ForEachRecord macro block. Within the EditRecord macro block, use the drop-down to select the `SetField` action. `SetField` can only be used within the CreateRecord or EditRecord data blocks. For the Field Name input box, enter **`C.Inactive`**. Enter `No` for the action's Value input box. With each iteration, a potential Customer in Oregon will be made active. Your macro should look like the one in Figure 6-23.

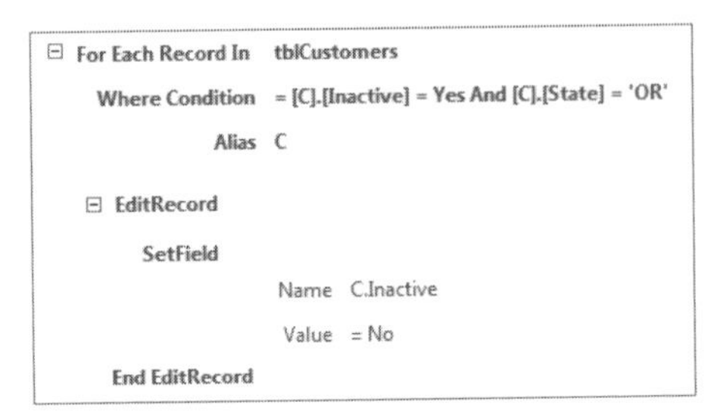

FIGURE 6-23: ForEachRecord and EditRecord

How to Use DeleteRecord

```
⊟ For Each Record In   tblCustomers
    Where Condition   = [tblCustomers].[State] = 'AL'
    DeleteRecord
        Record Alias
```

FIGURE 6-24: DeleteRecord

The DeleteRecord action deletes the current record. You must use it within a macro action block to identify what record should be deleted. Usually you will use either the ForEachRecord or the LookupRecord macro blocks. You could use the DeleteRecord action if you decided to stop doing business in a particular state that generated losses instead of profits. Typically, you would simply set the `Inactive` field for the appropriate customers to `Yes`. To give you an example, let's say you want to delete the records, using `DeleteRecord`, of all customers that reside within that state, as shown in Figure 6-24.

To create this macro, open a new data macro and insert a ForEachRecord macro action using the Add New Action drop-down. Select the `tblCustomers` table from the ForEachRecord drop-down list. For the Where Condition expression enter `[tblCustomers].[State] = 'AL'`. Next, use the drop-down within the ForEachRecord macro block and select `DeleteRecord`. We are not using the alias expression for this macro. When the macro is run, it will delete all customers that reside in the specified state.

> **NOTE** *Figure 6-24 illustrates that you don't have to specify an alias. However, when you have multiple nested data blocks, and you need to be explicit about which source you want to affect, using aliases will be required to provide the appropriate context. For this reason, it may be a good habit to consistently add aliases.*

CREATING AND EDITING UI MACROS

Many things you learned earlier about creating and editing data macros are also applicable to UI macros. The main difference with UI macros is the list of actions available to you and the more limited scope in which you can operate. We will start by listing the available actions (see Table 6-3) and then look at some specific examples for you to follow.

TABLE 6-3: Macro Actions and Their Functions

MACRO ACTION	FUNCTION
Program Flow	
Comment	Provide helpful comment
Group	Use to logically group macros
If	Provide If . . . Then functionality
Data Entry Operations	
DeleteRecord	Delete the current record
EditRecord	Enable the user to edit the current record
NewRecord	Send the user to a new record
SaveRecord	Commit the user's changes to a current record
UndoRecord	Discard the user's changes on the current record
Database Objects	
GoToControl	Set focus to a selected control
GoToRecord	For consistency, move the user to another record
SetProperty	Edit a control or view property
Filter/Query/Search	
RequeryRecords	Refresh listing of records returned to the user using same or different criteria
Macro Commands	
RunDataMacro	Invoke a data macro
RunMacro	Invoke a standalone UI macro
SetVariable	Declare a new variable and assign value
StopMacro	Stop a UI macro immediately
User Interface Commands	
ChangeView	Move the user to a different tile-bound view and stops the macro
ClosePopup	Close the currently open popup and stop the macro
MessageBox	Display a simple message to the user
OpenPopup	Open a view in a popup window, pass in any parameter if applicable, and stops the macro

Note that the only block macro action in UI macro actions is the If block. Some macro actions, such as the EditRecord action, are fundamentally different from the data macro action of the same name. The UI macro version merely enables editing on the screen for the user, rather than performing any actual editing as is done in the data macro version. This also suggests another mindset adjustment you may need to make — although you may have edited values via an Access form's controls in VBA, you will want to avoid doing that in a web app. Use a data macro instead. We address this particular issue in the next section but for now, let's look at some common UI macro tasks.

How to Use SetProperty

You will certainly want to manipulate the appearance of controls at run time as part of providing feedback to the users as they work through the views. Whenever you want to do this, you will be doing so via the SetProperty macro action. The SetProperty macro action sets six different properties, as listed in Table 6-4.

TABLE 6-4: SetProperty Macro Action Options

PROPERTY	EXPECTED DATA TYPE
Enabled	Boolean
Visible	Boolean
ForeColor	HTML Color
BackColor	HTML Color
Caption	String
Value	String

WHERE'S THE LOCKED PROPERTY?

If you've used the Locked property to prevent editing of data while allowing for selection and copying of values, recall that you can now bind a Label control, which offers you the same functionality as a locked textbox.

Suppose you have a pair of textboxes and you want to signal to the users that if they enter data in one of the textboxes, they must also fill in data in the other textbox by setting the textbox's backcolor to yellow. As Figure 6-25 shows, there is already a label on the form that informs users that they must fill in all yellow-colored textboxes, which will be highlighted dynamically as you will see shortly when creating UI macros.

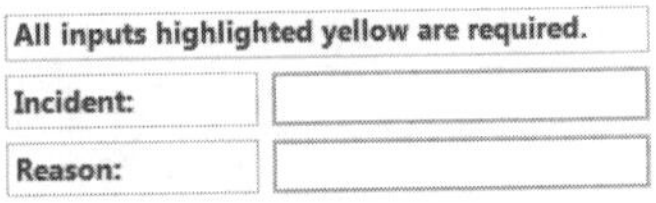

All inputs highlighted yellow are required.
Incident:
Reason:

FIGURE 6-25: A view with a pair of textboxes and label

You can create this functionality by attaching macro actions to the first textbox's AfterUpdate event. Figure 6-26 illustrates how you add macro actions to a click event handler.

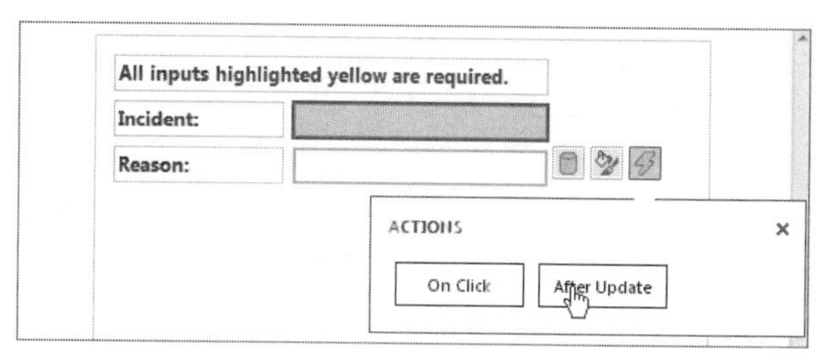

FIGURE 6-26: Creating a new event handler by clicking the After Update button

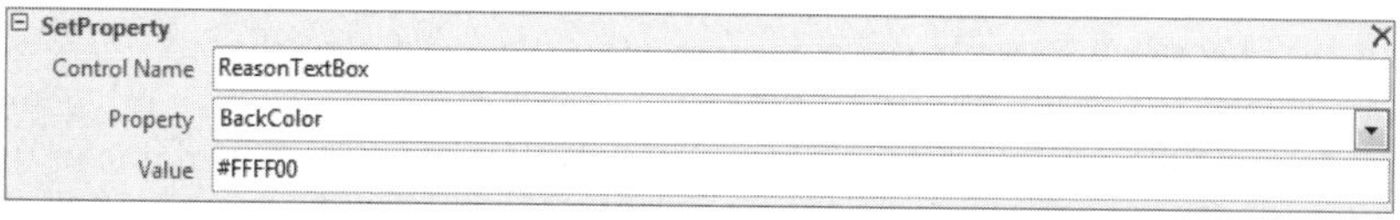

As you would expect, the Macro Designer opens with a new blank macro surface for you to add actions. Let's add the SetProperty macro action. Figure 6-27 shows how you would fill in the inputs to the SetProperty macro action.

FIGURE 6-27: Filling in the SetProperty macro action

When you save the event handler and the view, and then try to fill in the data, you'll see the result of the macro action running in a web browser, as Figure 6-28 demonstrates.

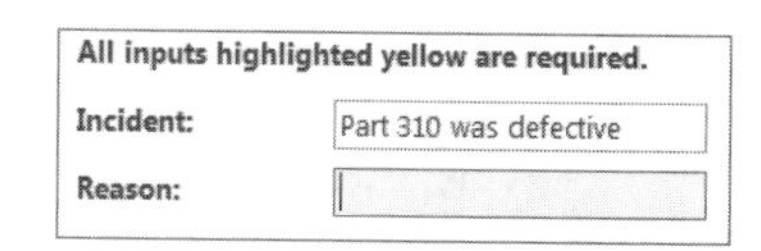

FIGURE 6-28: Result of the SetProperty macro action executed via the AfterUpdate event

How to Use ChangeView and OpenPopup

A common operation performed in data entry is to switch from one view to another, whether as a popup or to another view on the same or a different tile. The OpenPopup macro action handles the first task, and the ChangeView macro action handles the second. In Chapter 4, you learned about the difference between a tile-bound view and a popup form; you will see more applications in Chapter 8.

You also may optionally pass additional filtering and ordering parameters to be applied to the view being opened. Let's suppose you want to enable moving from a Customer view to an Order view in order to view the last few orders that a customer placed. You could add a new custom action button to the Customer view and add a new click event handler as in Figure 6-29.

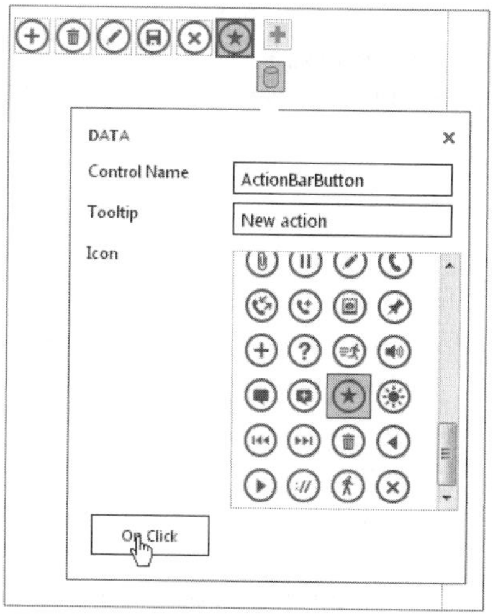

FIGURE 6-29: Custom action button with click event handler

Figure 6-30 illustrates how you would fill in the ChangeView action.

ChangeView
Table tblOrders
View frmOrders
Where = [tblOrders].[CustomerID] = [CustomerIDTextBox]
Order By

FIGURE 6-30: ChangeView macro action

There are few things to note here. First, ChangeView needs to establish which tile will be displayed before it can set the view from that tile. After all, if you manually performed the action, you would have to click the tile first, and then the view second. As you can see, both table and view arguments must be filled in. Furthermore, note that although you may rename tiles to something other than the associated table's name, you must reference the tile via the associated table's name, not the tile's name.

The next thing to note is that for the Where clause, you must use a two-part identifier to refer to fields. You cannot simply refer to the `CustomerID` field even when the view is based on a table, not a query, so there is no chance of ambiguous reference. If you attempt to omit the table name in the reference, you will get a run time error, as shown in Figure 6-31.

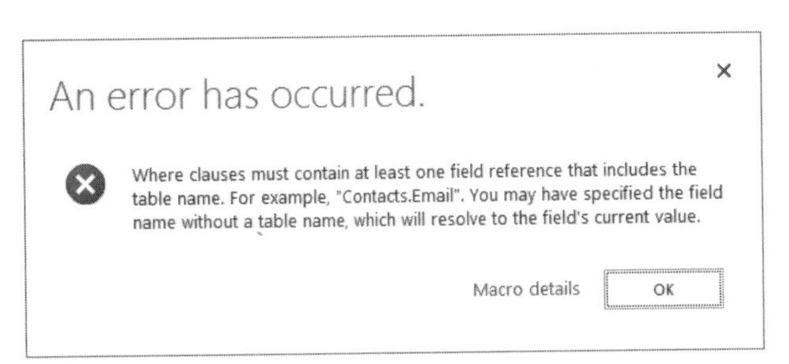
An error has occurred.
Where clauses must contain at least one field reference that includes the table name. For example, "Contacts.Email". You may have specified the field name without a table name, which will resolve to the field's current value.
Macro details
OK

FIGURE 6-31: Run time error with unqualified field reference in Where clause

As you can see in Figure 6-31, having a two-part qualifier removes the ambiguity over whether you want to refer to the current record's value for the field in question or to a field on the table.

Both Where and Order clauses work similarly to what you may expect from traditional approaches in filtering and sorting in Access. There is one additional exception that bears repeating — you are not putting in a string but rather a SQL snippet. That means you cannot use a string to represent a SQL snippet as you might have done in Access client. You must enter a valid SQL snippet.

The OpenPopup macro action is quite similar to the ChangeView macro action, but also supports the use of parameters. As discussed in Chapter 4, popup forms can be based on a query with parameters, whereas tile-bound views cannot. The OpenPopup macro action offers you the opportunity to supply the parameters for such popup forms. Refer to Figure 6-29 for creating an action button with custom event handler; then turn to Figure 6-32 to see how you can supply a parameter via the Parameters section.

FIGURE 6-32: OpenPopup macro action with parameters

How to Use RequeryRecords

The RequeryRecords macro action has a misleading name — if you are thinking about the `Requery` method on an Access client form, that is not all it can do. Rather, the functionality it offers is more akin to the Recordsource property in Access client forms, where you can modify the Where and Order part of the form's recordsource. This not only simplifies the process of searching and filtering but also provides you with a means of changing the sort at run time.

Generally speaking, you might want to use RequeryRecords in conjunction with other controls for users to input the filter and sort value. You may want to hard-code a filter for an Action button for quick access to common requests such as viewing today's schedule. To illustrate this, you can refer to Figure 6-29 for adding a new action button and adding a click event handler. Figure 6-33 shows you how to fill in RequeryRecords to set the current view to show only today's records.

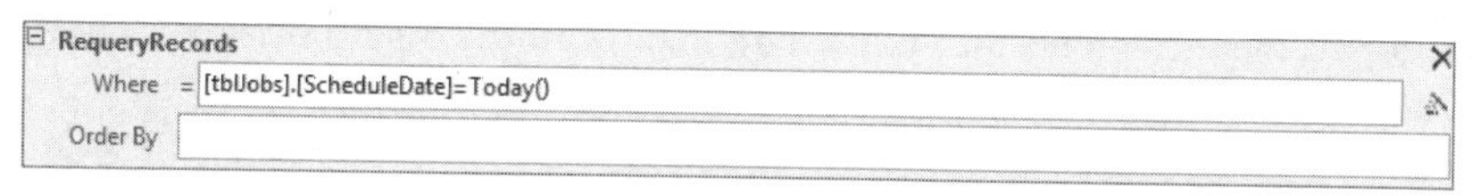
RequeryRecords
Where =
[tblJobs].[ScheduleDate]=Today()
Order By

FIGURE 6-33: RequeryRecords macro action with Today() filter

> **WARNING** *At the time of this writing, the RequeryRecords macro action will not function correctly if you supply a two-part qualifier to the Order clause. Although it is legal to use a two-part qualifier for the Order clause with other macros that have similar parameters, such as ChangeView, you must remember to remove the table name from the qualifier in order to use the Order clause for the RequeryRecords macro action.*

As you can see, the Where and Order clauses in RequeryRecords work similarly to the Where and Order clauses in ChangeView and OpenPopup actions, and are otherwise quite straightforward.

How to Use Data Entry Operations

As you learned in Chapter 4, you can create custom Action Bar buttons to perform custom macros. In cases where you need to customize a replacement for a default action button, you will use one of the data entry operations normally performed by the default Action Bar button.

To create an action button and add a click event handler, as shown in Figure 6-29, you would typically use one of the Data Entry Operations macro actions. Figure 6-34 shows an EditRecord macro action inserted.

FIGURE 6-34: EditRecord macro action

There are no parameters for those actions because the actions always act upon the current record of the active view.

USING UI AND DATA MACROS TOGETHER

Often, you will find that you need to use both UI macros and data macros in tandem to accomplish the tasks you need to perform. You can use parameters to supply inputs from the web client and collect outputs via ReturnVars. We will look at how you can design and use both parameters and retrieve outputs.

How to Create and Use Parameters

When you create a standalone data macro, you have the option to create one or more parameters for the macro. To create a parameter, you need to use a data macro. In the macro designer, click the Create Parameter link, as shown in Figure 6-35.

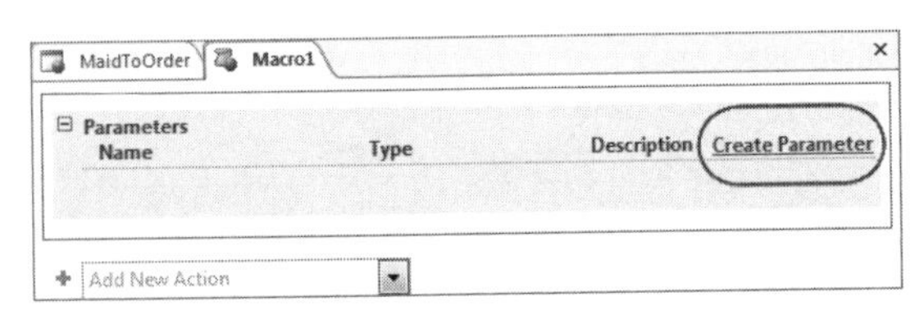

FIGURE 6-35: Create Parameter

If you want to get information about Jobs that occur on a certain date, you can use parameters to supply the date. Enter `pdatDateOfJob` in the Parameter Name textbox. For the Data Type, select `Date` from the Type drop-down. You can enter a description for the parameter, if you want to, and save your macro, naming it `dmGetJobsByDate`. Your macro thus far should look like Figure 6-36.

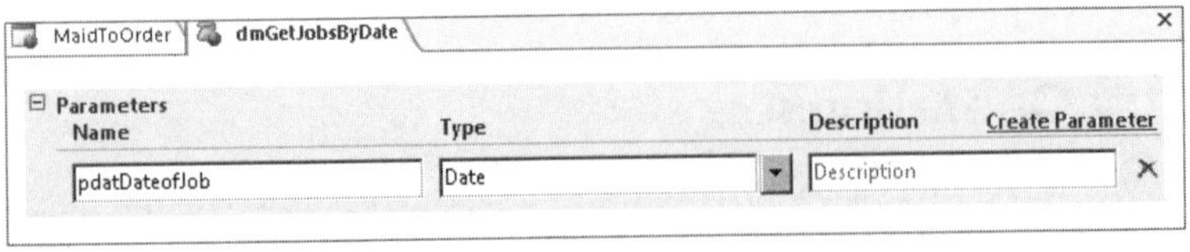

FIGURE 6-36: Parameter settings

You can use the macro to list all the Jobs on the date passed into the macro via that parameter. The next step is to create a variable to hold the IDs of the Jobs found and initialize it to a zero length string. It's called `vstrJobID`.

Next, use the Add New Action drop-down to select `ForEachRecord`. Select `tblJobs` from the list of tables and queries. Enter `[tblJobs].[JobDate]=pdatDateOfJob` as the WhereCondition expression to use the date provided by the parameter. Within the ForEachRecord data block, select `SetLocalVar` from the drop-down list. For this example, you will get the Job IDs for all jobs starting at a specific time. Enter the LocalVar `varJobIDs` previously created. For the expression, enter: `Concat(vstrJobID, [tblJobs].[JobID],';')` which will get the IDs of the Jobs on the date provided by the parameter. Use the `Concat()` expression to add each job ID to the variable as it is found by the macro. Your macro should look like Figure 6-37.

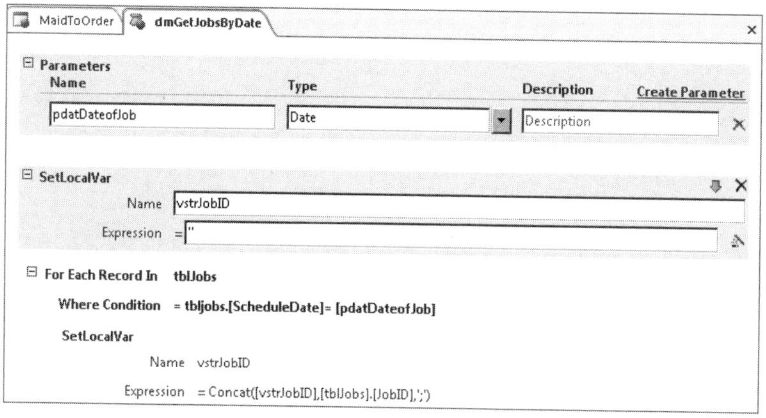

FIGURE 6-37: Macro parameters

You supply the Parameter value by calling this macro from another macro. To do this, create a new data macro and select `RunDataMacro` from the Add New Action drop-down. Next, select your `dmGetJobsByDate` macro from the list. The list of parameters will appear, which in this case will be only one, `DateOfJob`. You can enter any date you want to get the job's information on that date, but for this example, enter the `Today()` function so that it always finds the jobs for the current date. Your macro should look like Figure 6-38.

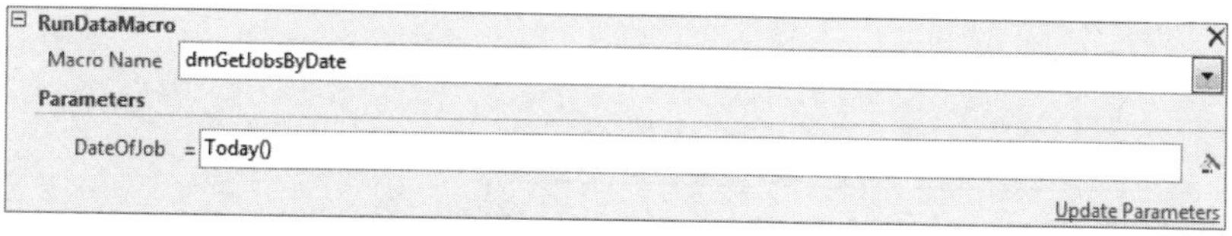

FIGURE 6-38: Using a parameter

You can save that macro and run it to get the times of the jobs scheduled for the parameter you provide. Parameters provide you with the flexibility to use one macro repeatedly instead of having to create many macros to get the results you need.

How to Return Values

Sometimes you need to supply values back to the UI macro actions that originally invoked the data macro in question. To continue with the `dmGetJobsByDate` example, you add one more action at the end, `SetReturnVar`, as in Figure 6-39.

```
MaidToOrder | dmGetJobsByDate

Parameters
  Name                    Type        Description
  pdatDateofJob           Date

SetLocalVar
        Name  vstrJobIDs
  Expression  =''

For Each Record In  tblJobs
  Where Condition  = tbljobs.[ScheduleDate]= [pdatDateofJob]
  SetLocalVar
          Name  vstrJobID
    Expression  = Concat([vstrJobIDs],[tblJobs].[JobID],';')

SetReturnVar
        Name  rstrJobIDs
  Expression  =vstrJobIDs
```

FIGURE 6-39: SetReturnVar macro action

As you can see, `SetReturnVar` is similar to SetLocalVar and SetVariable; you provide a name and expression to be passed back to the calling macro. Save the data macro and close. Create a new UI macro via the Advanced menu on the ribbon and select Macro, as illustrated in Figure 6-40.

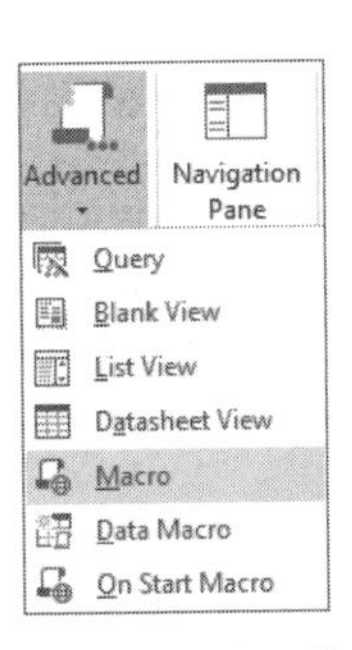

FIGURE 6-40: Creating a standalone UI macro

Add a RunDataMacro macro action and select the `dmGetJobsByDate` data macro, again providing `Today()` as the parameter. Note that you have an additional field to set the name of a new variable to accept the returned value. Enter `vstrReturnedJobIDs` in that field, as shown in Figure 6-41.

Add a MessageBox macro action and enter `=vstrReturnedJobIDs` as the expression, as shown in Figure 6-42.

```
RunDataMacro
  Macro Name  dmGetJobsByDate
Parameters
  pdatDateofJob  =today()
  SetLocalVar    vstrReturnedJobIDs   = rstrJobIDs
                                       Update Parameters
```

FIGURE 6-41: Setting a local variable to accept returned values

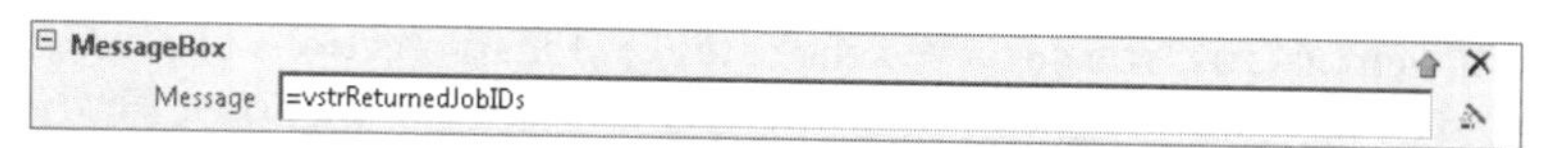

FIGURE 6-42: MessageBox macro action

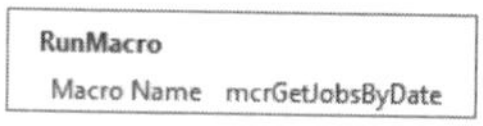

Save the UI macro, give it a name such as `mcrGetJobsByDate`, and then call it from one of the buttons on the view via a RunMacro action, as illustrated in Figure 6-43.

RunMacro
Macro Name mcrGetJobsByDate

FIGURE 6-43: RunMacro macro action

When you click the button on the view, you get a messagebox reporting the IDs of today's jobs. You can also see how you can use Parameters and SetReturnVar macro action in parallel to marshal data between the web client and the server and hook it up with other controls to support collecting inputs from users and displaying the output to the user.

Unlike other variables set with the SetVariable macro action, the ReturnVar variable is scoped to only the calling macro. If you need to keep the value that was returned by the data macro beyond the current macro, then you need to do a SetVariable and assign the value from local variable into the global variable created or edited by the SetVariable macro action.

For those familiar with the ReturnVars collection from Access 2010 web databases, you can continue to use the ReturnVars collection. However, we feel that 2013's revision to collecting the ReturnVar variable is a better approach, which removes potential errors due to mistyping names or referencing the ReturnVar out of scope.

SUMMARY

In this chapter, you learned why the programming language in web apps is based on macros, rather than one of the other possible candidates. You also learned about the new Macro Designer in Access 2013 web apps, which is a structured environment with context-sensitive support and IntelliSense to speed your coding work.

You then learned about the catalog of macro actions and how to use them to create macros that encode the business rules you need to make your web apps powerful and flexible tools for your users. You also learned about troubleshooting tools to aid in creating macros.

You learned about the categories of macros: UI macros, which can be embedded in events for views, or its controls, or be standalone. Likewise, data macros could be embedded behind table events or be used standalone. UI macros provide tools to make your interface interactive. You use data macros to manage records and data.

The Macro designer enables you to write business rules with a single language. Behind the curtains, UI macros are converted to JavaScript. Likewise, standalone data macros are saved in SQL Server as stored procedures and event data macros are saved as `AFTER` table triggers in the SQL Server database. Access then handles the setup to allow UI macros and data macros to be called by appropriate events automatically for you.

To fill out your introduction to web macros, you surveyed the catalog of macro actions provided for web apps. You then spent some time working with data and UI macros, learning how to use common actions, including program flows, looking up and editing records, and managing elements of the user interface. You learned how to use macro actions to do bulk operations on records with the ForEachRecord macro action and delete records as needed.

You finished up by creating parameterized macros to get familiar with their construction and use, alone or in combination with other macros. In Chapter 9, you will read up on practical examples of using macros and apply what you learned in this chapter.

In Chapter 7, you turn your attention to table design.

Designing the Table Structure

WHAT'S IN THIS CHAPTER?

- New and changed data types
- Using validation rules
- Leveraging calculated fields

WROX.COM CODE DOWNLOADS FOR THIS CHAPTER

The code and sample downloads for this chapter are found at `www.wiley.com/go/proaccess2013prog.com` on the Download Code tab. They are in the Maid To Order Sample App download. Refer to the Readme.txt file also located there for installation instructions.

Tables and the fields in them are the basic building blocks of all databases, of course. Table structures and field data types in Access have been quite stable over time, with the exception of Unicode compression, which was introduced in Microsoft Access 2000. In Chapter 2, you learned the basics of table creation in the web app environment. However, the 2013 version of Access also includes changes in data types that you'll find useful, particularly when creating web apps. In this chapter, we concentrate on those changes and how you can use them to optimize your table designs.

Also, although normalization is at the center of all good table structures, we think it's safe to assume that your experience as a developer will guide you in that area; good relational table schema hasn't changed. Instead, we direct your attention to the new and changed elements you'll be using in fields in tables in 2013 to implement your table designs. You learn how to define relationships between tables with the lookup field mechanism, which was first used for that purpose in version 2010, and which has been improved for use in web apps.

In this chapter, we also introduce you to some special tables you'll find very useful in the web app environment. We show you how to create a tally table and a utility table. These tables, like lookup tables, may already be familiar to you, but their importance in web apps makes it worthwhile to explore them in some detail.

Before we get to relationships between tables, let's examine the new and changed data types in those tables.

NEW DATA TYPES

Data type changes for 2013 include the following:

- Text fields — Web apps and client apps
- Number — Web apps
- Date/Time — Web apps
- Currency — Web apps
- Yes/No — Web apps
- Hyperlink — Web apps
- Image — Web apps (OLE Objects in client apps)
- Calculated — Web and client apps (each has a different set of functions allowed in the expression)
- Lookup — Web apps

As the list indicates, however, most of the changes apply to fields in tables in web apps. In the client, only text fields are significantly different from previous versions. Note that in the case of calculated and lookup fields, both versions have their own data types that work similarly, but which are not identical.

Short and Long Text Fields

One of the more interesting changes to data types is the replacement of the text and memo data types with two variations of text fields: *Short Text* and *Long Text*. The relabeling partly reflects the fact that text columns are based on SQL Server's text field in the web app environment, where memo doesn't exist as a data type.

In the web app environment, Short and Long Text also have different characteristics from the client side. Let's start by reviewing the client versions. Then you'll see how the new data types better support web apps.

Behavior of Short and Long Text Fields in Client Forms

The default behavior of Short differs from that of Long Text fields in forms in the client environment. When pressing the Enter key in a Short Text field, the default behavior is to advance the cursor to the next control in the form's tab sequence. Pressing the Enter key in a Long Text field, on the other hand, creates a return at that point in the text. The cursor remains in the control for further text entry.

In both types of Text field, this behavior is controlled by the Enter Key Behavior property of the textbox, which toggles between the two options. Changing this property setting swaps the Enter key behavior from the default to the opposite behavior. Regardless of the property setting, however, you can paste a string of text containing more than one line into either type of text field. That could be confusing, especially when the Enter Key Behavior is set to a value of Default and a textbox control bound to the field is only a line tall; it would appear to the user that there is only one line in the field, when in fact there's more than one line, accessible only by using arrow keys to move the cursor around.

Short Versus Long Text Character Limits in a Client Table

In a client table, Short Text fields can hold up to 255 characters, just as with text fields in previous versions of Access. You can, of course, set the limit to any number from 1 to 255. Other than the name change, Short Text fields are the same as the previous text field data type.

Long Text fields, which take the place of Memo fields, are not limited to a specific number of characters, just as Memo fields were not. Long Text is basically a name change for the memo field in client tables. Contents of Long Text fields are Unicode text, which can be formatted as either plain text or rich text.

So, while you may find the name changes slightly confusing at first, you'll quickly get used to the behavior and properties of Short and Long Text fields in client tables. That's not true, though, for tables in web apps, as you'll see next.

Short Versus Long Text in a Web App Table

The first thing to remember about web apps is that all tables are SQL Server tables, either SQL Azure in Office 365 or SQL Server in an on-premises installation. In the rest of this discussion we mean both versions when referring to SQL Server, unless a distinction is needed. That makes for several differences, including the way Short Text and Long Text data types are implemented in the table. The data types available to us in our web app tables are those provided by SQL Server — `nvarchar(xxxx)`, as explained in the discussion that follows. Text fields are exposed as Access data types in the design interface, but you must keep in mind that you are actually working with SQL Server fields. The following discussion is based on that fact.

Under the covers (i.e., in SQL Server tables) the actual data type for text fields is `nvarchar(xxxx)`, where *xxxx* is the number of characters — such as 2 or 255 or 4,000 — or `nvarChar(MAX)`, which stores up to 2,147,483,647 characters. So, while "Short" and "Long" are relative terms, and while *client* table Short Text fields hold a maximum of 255 characters, the rules are different for our web tables. Let's dive into the details.

The properties available for Long Text fields in a web table are illustrated in Figure 7-1.

Both Short and Long Text fields have a Limit Length property, which defaults to `No` for Long Text fields, as you can see in Figure 7-1. Unlimited Long Text fields are implemented as the `nvarchar(MAX)` data type in SQL Server tables, which means they are not really "unlimited." However, the amount of text they can hold is large enough to be considered unlimited in a practical sense for most situations you are likely to encounter.

Contrast that to what happens when you change the Limit Length property to `Yes`, as shown in Figure 7-2.

When Limit Length is set to `Yes`, the default for Long Text fields is 220 characters, as you can see in Figure 7-2. In case you are wondering, yes, there is a reason that it's 220 and not 255: Access 2013 allows indexing on a maximum of 220 characters on a text field. However, you can enter any value you want, up to 4,000 characters.

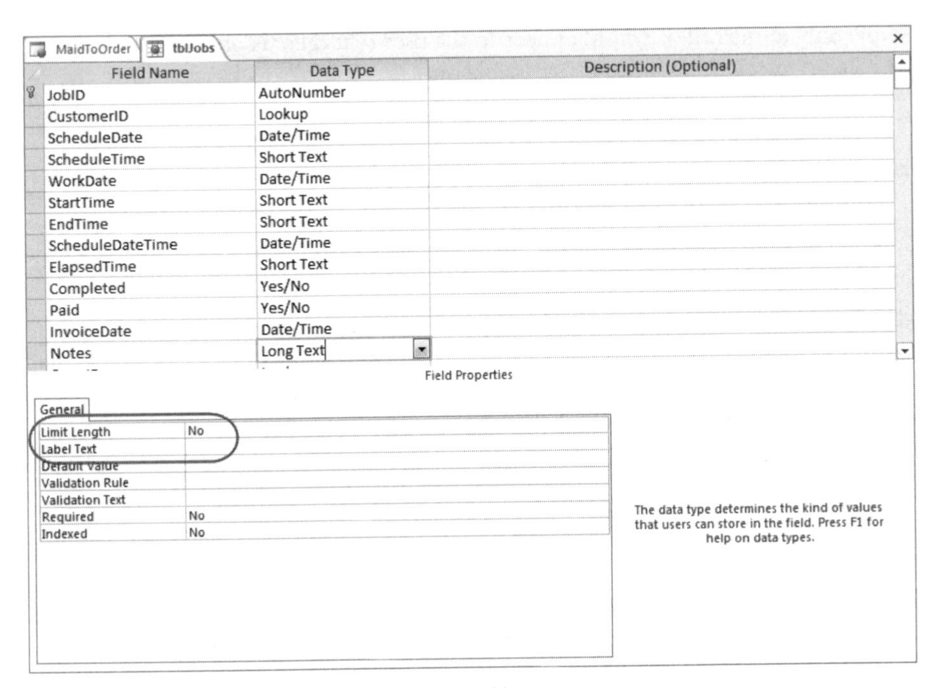

FIGURE 7-1: Long Text Field Limit Length set to No

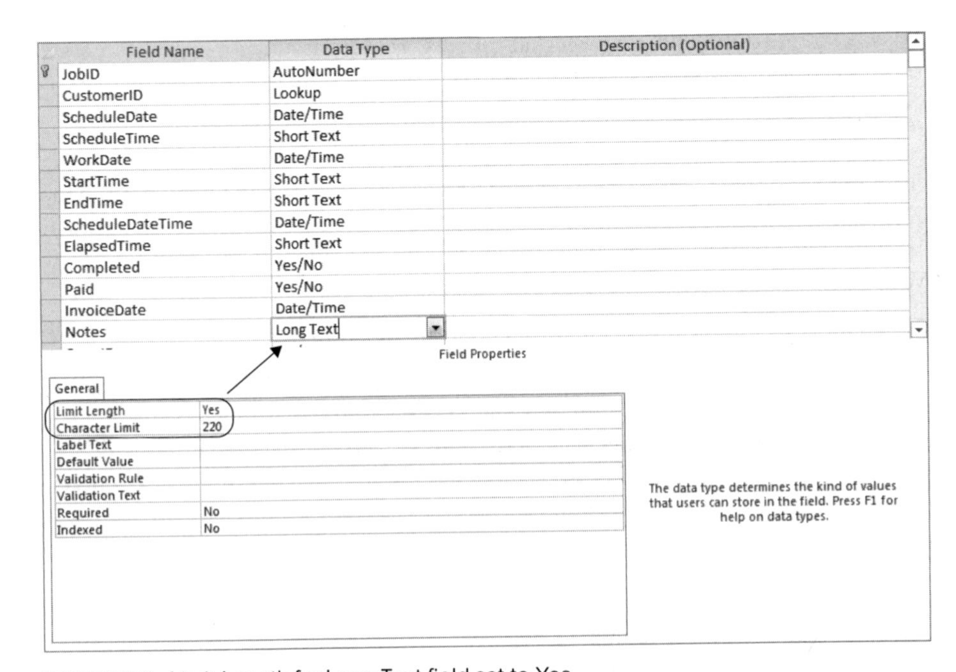

FIGURE 7-2: Limit Length for Long Text field set to Yes

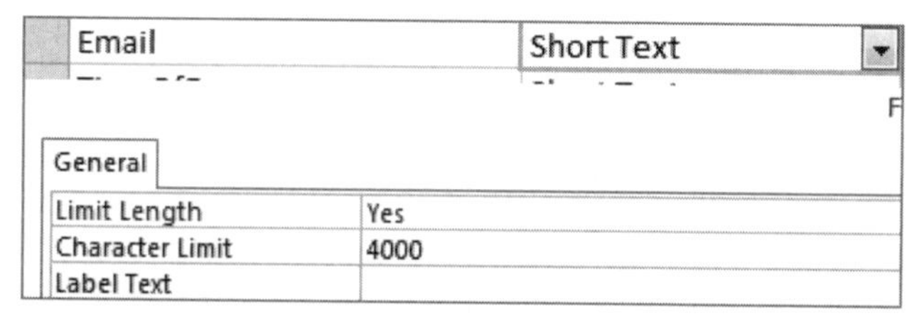

FIGURE 7-3: Short Text Field Limit Length set to Yes

As you can see in Figure 7-3, Short Text fields are really not that different from Long Text fields. They have a Limit Length property, which defaults to 220 characters, but which can be set to allow up to 4,000 characters, exactly like Long Text fields.

Now, compare this to Figure 7-4, where we've set the Limit Length property to `No` for the Short Text field. In terms of implementation, then, there's no practical difference between Long and Short Text in the web app environment, other than the default properties when they are first created.

The SQL Server Management Studio view of the table, pictured in Figure 7-5, shows how that field looks in SQL Azure, where it is implemented as an `nvarchar(MAX)` field.

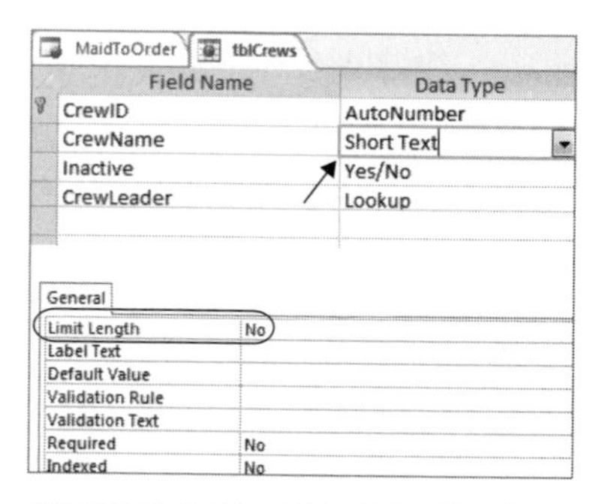

FIGURE 7-4: Short Text Field Limit Length property set to No

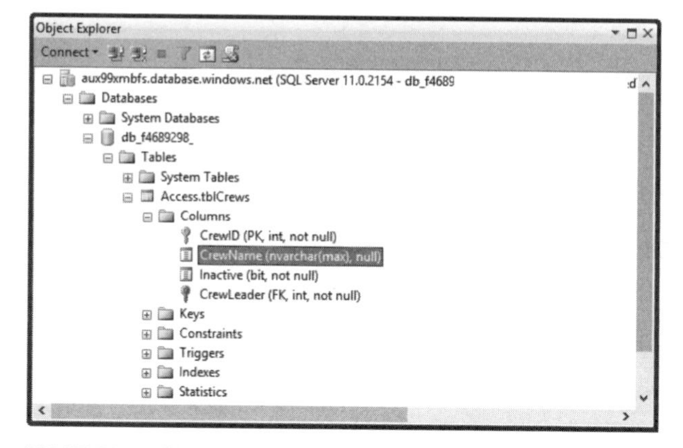

FIGURE 7-5: Short Text field implemented as nvarchar(MAX)

Interface Behavior of Short and Long Text Fields in Web Forms

In the web interface, pressing the Enter key in a Short Text field doesn't advance the cursor to the next field; nor does it insert a return line. Pressing the Enter key in a Long Text field inserts a return line. This behavior can't be toggled for either type of field as it can in client forms. It is enforced whether you use a single-line Textbox control or a Multiline Textbox control for either text field.

When you add it all up, in web apps Short and Long Text fields differ primarily in their default behavior in the interface, which is fairly counterintuitive in contrast to traditional Access development where interface behavior was mainly determined by the controls being used and the properties set for them, rather than the data type of the bound field and its properties. You will definitely want to keep that in mind and keep the difference between the web and client clear.

Number Fields

In client tables, Number fields are the same as in previous versions: for example, Double and Single, Integer and Long Integer, Byte, Decimal, and Replication ID. With Access 2013 web apps, Microsoft adopted the simplifying strategy that three numeric data types, in addition to the Currency data type, are sufficient.

In web tables, the data type for number fields also partially reflects their underlying implementation as SQL Server fields. In a web table, numbers can be one of three data types, as you can see in Figure 7-6:

1. Whole numbers, which are implemented as integers in SQL Server
2. Floating point numbers with variable decimal places
3. Fixed-point numbers with six decimal places

Field Name	Data Type
EmployeeID	AutoNumber
FullName	Short Text
UserName	Short Text
TitleID	Lookup
Terminated	Date/Time
AnnualOffHours	Number
HireDate	Date/Time
SupervisorID	Lookup
HierarchyPath	Short Text
Email	Short Text

Field Properties

General

Number Subtype	Fixed-point number (6 decimal places)
Display Format	
Label Text	
Default Value	
Validation Rule	
Validation Text	
Required	No
Indexed	No

Number Subtype options
Whole number (no decimal places)
Floating-point number (variable decimal places)
Fixed-point number (6 decimal places)

FIGURE 7-6: Number data types in a web app

Whole Numbers

SQL Server Integers (actually referred to as `int`) correspond to Long Integers in Access, as you may already know. They are identified as Whole Numbers in Access web apps. You'll use them in any situation where integers are appropriate.

One place where you could use Whole Numbers is in an order detail table where you need to record the quantity of an item sold. Unlike previous versions, however, where you might give consideration to whether a 16-bit integer or 32-bit Long Integer data type is the best choice, web apps only gives you the choice of Whole Numbers, which are always 32-bit.

Floating-Point and Fixed-Point Numbers

Floating-point numbers correspond to the Single and Double data types with which you should be familiar. Floating-point numbers are implemented as the `float` data type in the web app database, which is equivalent to Double data type. Floating-point and fixed-point numbers differ in that there will always be six decimal places in the fixed-point numbers, with 0s padding out the number, when needed, to the full six places. Fixed-point numbers are implemented as the decimal data type.

With the reduced set of choices and your experience as an Access developer, you should be able to select the most appropriate one for your application.

Number Field Formats in Web Tables

In addition to the data types you can assign to numbers, you have four formatting options for numbers:

1. General numbers
2. Fixed
3. Standard
4. Percent

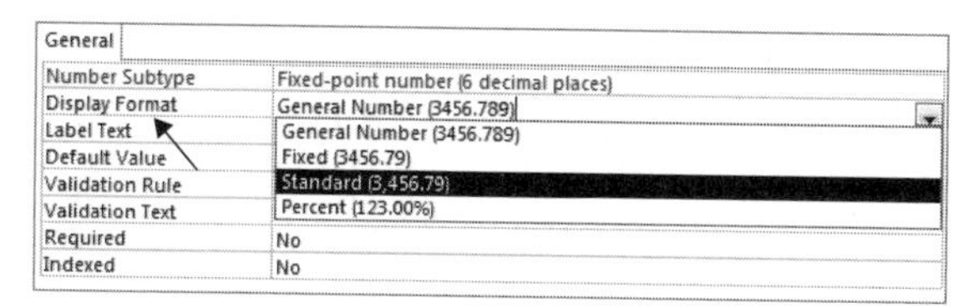

FIGURE 7-7: Number Formats web app

These formats are similar to those you are familiar with in previous versions (see Figure 7-7). Again, some simplifying assumptions were made about the range of formats needed in this environment.

Note that there is an additional property, Display Decimal Places, that is displayed when you choose Fixed, Standard, or Percent format. This property may be useful for enforcing the display of the same number of decimal places globally for a particular field.

Also, keep in mind that the format property of a number field affects only how values are displayed, not how values are stored. You can apply other formatting options via the interface if the four basic selections don't meet your needs.

One final thing to mention concerning number fields is that, as in previous versions of Access, you can also set a property to control the number of decimal places. As there isn't anything new there, we'll leave exploration of that property to you.

Date/Time Fields

For Date/Time fields you can choose between Date, Time, and Date with Time as subtypes (see Figure 7-8).

FIGURE 7-8: Date Formats in web apps

The good news for long-time Access developers is that SQL Server supports all three data types directly. You've probably gotten used to working around the fact that Access stored all date fields with both the date and time components, which could lead to complications in trying to filter date ranges, for example. Consider the actual date and time fields stored in SQL Server, as shown in Figures 7-9 and 7-10.

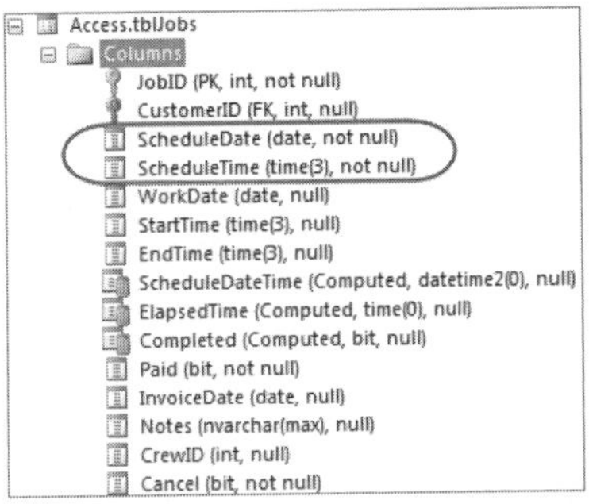

FIGURE 7-9: Date field and time(3) field in a SQL Azure table design view

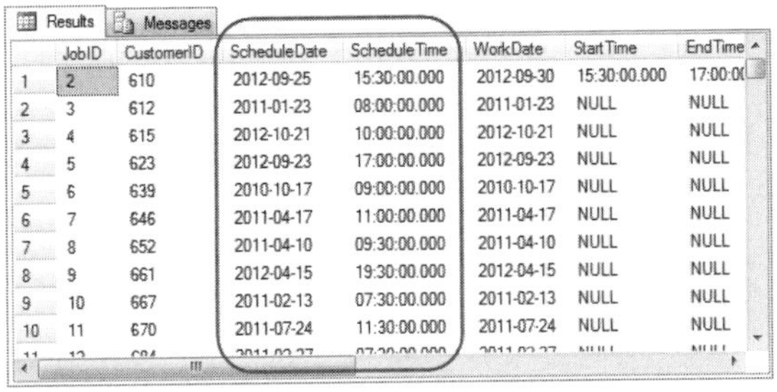

FIGURE 7-10: Date field and time(3) field in a SQL Azure table datasheet view

Dates are stored in SQL Server defaulting to ISO format as YYYY-MM-DD. Likewise, times are stored in a 24-hour format, also known as military time. You'll also see in Figure 7-10 that you can specify the number of digits for the fractional part of the seconds; it's 3 in the ScheduleTime field used in our example web app. This can be an integer from 0 to 7, but within a web app, it is always 3 and you cannot change the precision.

Formatting Dates and Times for Display

As you can see in Figure 7-10, dates and times are stored internally in a format that you probably don't want to show to your users, who are used to seeing them in the format specific to their location — for example, 12/29/2012 in the United States, or 29/12/2012 in many other countries. Therefore, you have the ability to specify the display formats for your date and time fields, as shown in Figure 7-11.

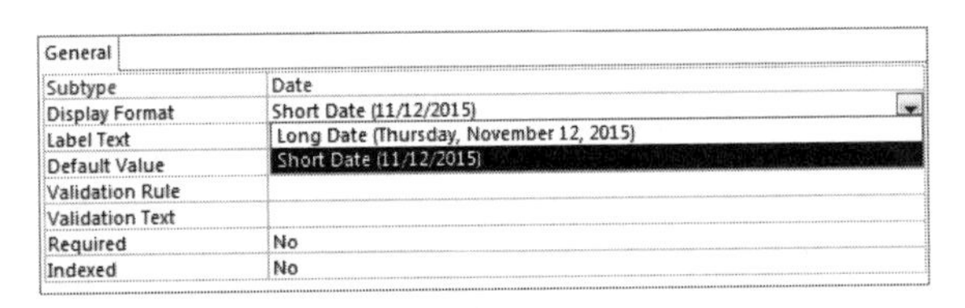

FIGURE 7-11: Short and Long Date display formats

Regional date formats are controlled by server settings. Those shown in Figure 7-11 are for the United States. Figure 7-12 shows format options for time fields.

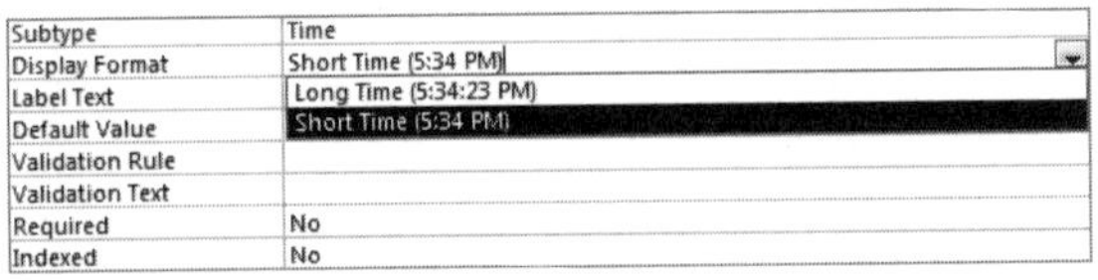

FIGURE 7-12: Time Display formats

You can display times with seconds (Long Time) or without seconds (Short Time). Time formats are more standard around the world, so you'll find the time options a bit more straightforward in practice than dates. However, in both cases, you can apply other formats using the `Format()` function. You can see examples of this in Figure 7-13.

To create the "special date" for this example, we used the `Format()` function with arguments `Format([ScheduleDate],"yy/MM/dd")`.

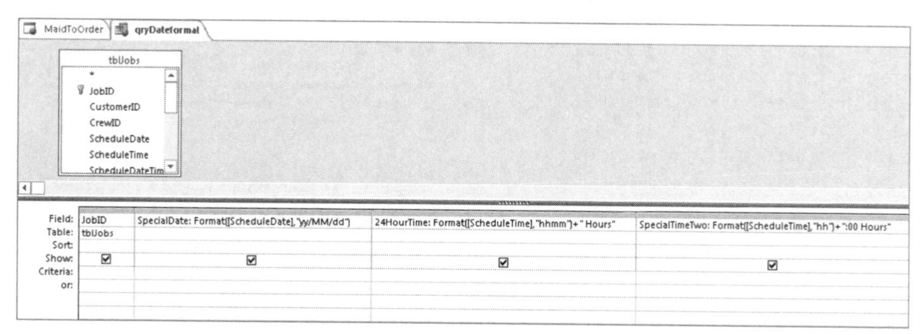

FIGURE 7-13: Query in Design view with special formatting applied to date and time fields

Figure 7-13 actually illustrates two important points about formatting in web apps. First, you can specify any sequence you need in order to create the display format; this one is two-digit year, two-digit month, and two-digit day:

```
SpecialDate: Format([ScheduleDate],"yy/MM/dd")
```

This format could support sorting dates by newest to oldest, for example.

Second, as you can see, the two-digit month literal is capitalized, whereas the year and day are not. As we've pointed out before, your web app tables are SQL Server tables. That means you must specify formatting that obeys rules for SQL Server, where date literals are case-sensitive. This is quite different from the Access client, where you can enter date literals as either lowercase or uppercase for the most part. You may also have realized that Access will convert date literals entered either way to the appropriate case, depending on context. In addition, Access will also respond to context and convert `"hh:mm:ss"` to `"hh:nn:ss"` where `n` is the proper literal for minutes while `mm` is the literal for months. Your Access web apps won't do that for you so you'll have to be much more careful about typing in the right date literals so the results are returned in the format you require (see Figure 7-14).

SQL server supports a wide range of options for formatting dates and times, which you should familiarize yourself with because, as you just learned, Access is not going to help with context-sensitive conversions. In fact, things can get fairly complicated quite quickly with dates and times. Rather than get sidetracked into a lengthy discussion, however, we'll show you the basic set of date literals you'll need to use and offer some suggestions on usage. Take a look at the SQL Statement in Figure 7-15, which illustrates several different `Format()` results.

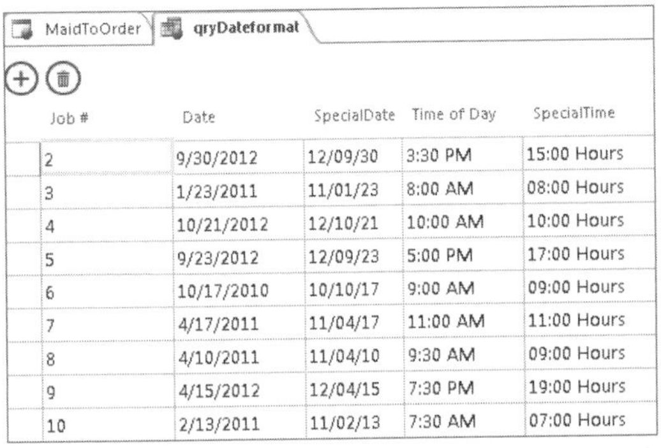

MaidToOrder | qryDateformat

Job #	Date	SpecialDate	Time of Day	SpecialTime
2	9/30/2012	12/09/30	3:30 PM	15:00 Hours
3	1/23/2011	11/01/23	8:00 AM	08:00 Hours
4	10/21/2012	12/10/21	10:00 AM	10:00 Hours
5	9/23/2012	12/09/23	5:00 PM	17:00 Hours
6	10/17/2010	10/10/17	9:00 AM	09:00 Hours
7	4/17/2011	11/04/17	11:00 AM	11:00 Hours
8	4/10/2011	11/04/10	9:30 AM	09:00 Hours
9	4/15/2012	12/04/15	7:30 PM	19:00 Hours
10	2/13/2011	11/02/13	7:30 AM	07:00 Hours

FIGURE 7-14: Query in Datasheet view with special formatting applied to date and time fields

SQLQuery1.sql - aux99xmbfs.database.windows.net.db_f4€

```
select top 10
format(scheduledate, 'yyyy/MM/dd') as 'yyyy/MM/dd',
format(scheduledate, 'YYYY/MM/DD') as  'YYYY/MM/DD',
format(scheduledate, 'yyyy/mm/dd') as 'yyyy/mm/dd',
format(scheduletime,'hhmm')  as 'hhmm',
format(scheduletime,'hhmmss')  as 'hhmmss',
format(scheduletime,'hhmm') + ' Hours'  as 'hhmm Hours'
from tbljobs
```

	yyyy/MM/dd	YYYY/MM/DD	yyyy/mm/dd	hhmm	hhmmss	hhmm Hours
1	2012/09/30	YYYY/09/DD	2012/00/30	1530	153000	1530 Hours
2	2011/01/23	YYYY/01/DD	2011/00/23	0800	080000	0800 Hours
3	2012/10/21	YYYY/10/DD	2012/00/21	1000	100000	1000 Hours
4	2012/09/23	YYYY/09/DD	2012/00/23	1700	170000	1700 Hours
5	2010/10/17	YYYY/10/DD	2010/00/17	0900	090000	0900 Hours
6	2011/04/17	YYYY/04/DD	2011/00/17	1100	110000	1100 Hours
7	2011/04/10	YYYY/04/DD	2011/00/10	0930	093000	0930 Hours
8	2012/04/15	YYYY/04/DD	2012/00/15	1930	193000	1930 Hours
9	2011/02/13	YYYY/02/DD	2011/00/13	0730	073000	0730 Hours
10	2011/07/24	YYYY/07/DD	2011/00/24	1130	113000	1130 Hours

ndows... | db_f4689298_1035_4588_... | db_f4689298_1035_4588_... | 00:00:00 | 10 rows

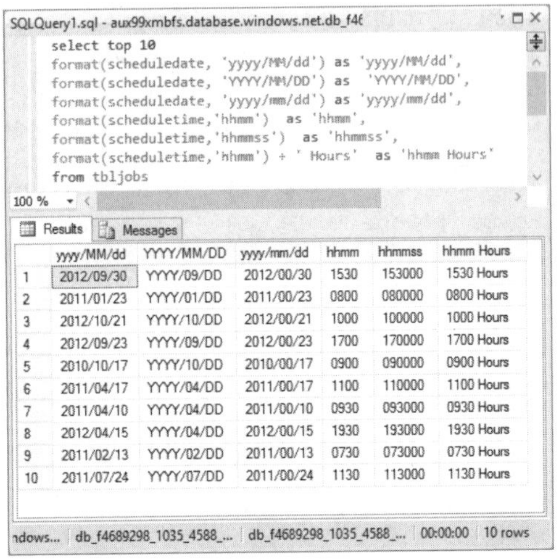

FIGURE 7-15: SQL with alternate formatting applied to date and time fields

The most important thing to note in Figure 7-15 is that date/time literals are case-sensitive in SQL Server, as previously stated. SQL Server returns the invalidly cased literal as the letter itself, as you can see for `format(scheduledate, 'YYYY/MM/DD')`. The month value is returned correctly in that format because `MM` is the proper literal, while the year and day are not because they are improperly cased. You can also see that `format(scheduledate, 'yyyy/mm/dd')`, also improperly cased, returns 00s because `mm` *is* the valid literal for minutes.

As you can see, properly formatting dates in your web apps will require caution and a good knowledge of date and time literals in SQL Server. Table 7-1 is a selected list of some of the more commonly used format specifications for dates. Note that examples in this table are U.S. regional formats. The full list of date and time formats is available at `http://msdn.microsoft.com/en-us/library/office/jj737650.aspx`.

TABLE 7-1: Format Specifications

FORMAT SPECIFICATION	DESCRIPTION
d	Displays the day as a number without a leading zero (for example, 1). Use %d if this is the only character in your user-defined numeric format.
dd	Displays the day as a number with a leading zero (for example, 01).
ddd	Displays the day as an abbreviation (for example, Sun).
dddd	Displays the day as a full name (for example, Sunday).
M	Displays the month as a number without a leading zero (for example, January is represented as 1). Use %M if this is the only character in your user-defined numeric format.

MM	Displays the month as a number with a leading zero (for example, 01)
MMM	Displays the month as an abbreviation (for example, Jan).
MMMM	Displays the month as a full month name (for example, January).
y	Displays the year number (0-9) without leading zeros. Use %y if this is the only character in your user-defined numeric format.
yy	Displays the year in two-digit numeric format with a leading zero, if applicable.
yyy	Displays the year in four-digit numeric format.
yyyy	Displays the year in four-digit numeric format.

> **WARNING** *The Format() function behaves differently from the way it does in the Access client. Whereas you can format strings in the client, such as Format([PhoneNumber],"(@@@) @@@-@@@@"), Format() only works on dates and numbers in a web app. You will need to devise another approach to formatting strings, perhaps using a combination of Left(), Mid() and Right() within Concat(). Or, cast the strings that look like numbers into numeric data types with Cast() function.*

Currency

The main difference with the currency data type in the Access interface in web apps is that you have a wide choice of currency symbols for displaying currency values, as you can see in Figure 7-16.

The important difference in the database, however, is that the values are stored as decimals. You can see this in Figure 7-17.

Figure 7-18 shows how it looks in a query on SQL Server.

There are three important things to remember about the currency data type. First, the fact that currency values are stored with six digit precision means that any math involving currency will reflect that level of precision, not the four digit precision you are used to in the Access client. Second, unlike for the client side of Access, currency is not a viable option for situations where you want to have a specific accuracy that isn't supported by double or single floating-point data types and want to avoid problems that come with the Decimal data type as implemented in the client. That's because in the web app, the display option for Currency will always include a currency symbol. This may make it difficult, if not impossible, to use this data type as a substitute for Decimal data type in your web apps. And finally, the data type stored for Currency is no different from numbers stored as fixed-point numbers. Currency fields are formatted to display the currency symbol and two decimals. Otherwise, there is no difference as far as the database is concerned.

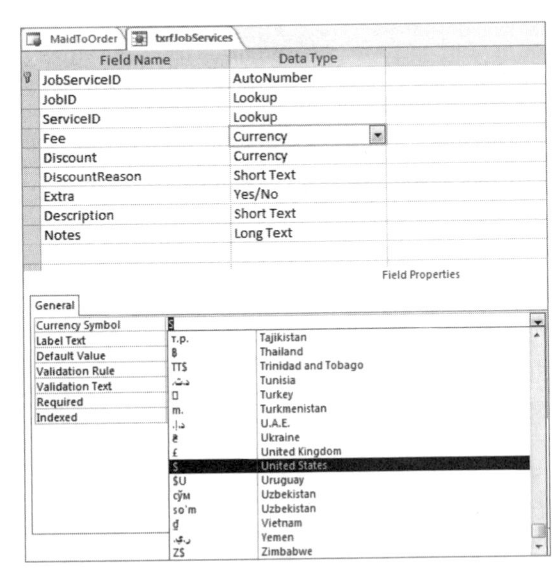

FIGURE 7-16: Currency symbol choices

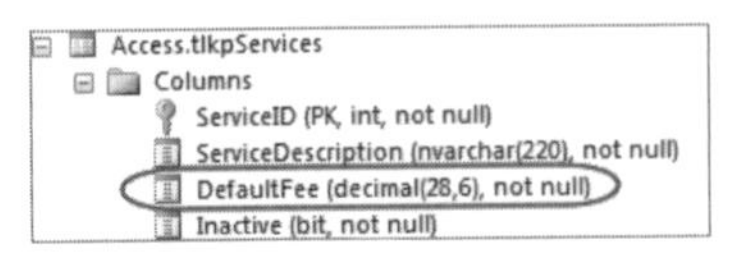

FIGURE 7-17: Decimal data type for values defined as currency in the web app design surface

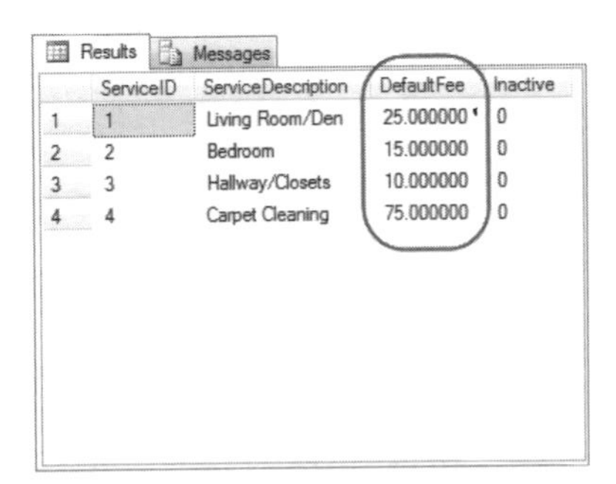

	ServiceID	ServiceDescription	DefaultFee	Inactive
1	1	Living Room/Den	25.000000	0
2	2	Bedroom	15.000000	0
3	3	Hallway/Closets	10.000000	0
4	4	Carpet Cleaning	75.000000	0

FIGURE 7-18: Decimal data type for values defined as currency in the web app design surface

Therefore, if you habitually used Currency data types in your client applications to work around the Access database engine's weak support for the Decimal data type or VBA's lack of a Decimal data type, which required you to use the Variant data type, you need to move away from that approach when moving into web apps.

Yes/No

As you would expect by now, Yes/No fields are different in web apps because they are stored in a SQL Server table as a data type found in SQL. In SQL Server, that data type is `bit`. Yes/No fields store values of `0` for `No` and `1` for `Yes`, and they don't support `Nulls`. In the Access web app itself, all values are displayed as `Yes` or `No`, and you'll use those terms in macro expressions, not `True` and `False` as you might be used to doing in Access client databases. In queries, `0` and `1` work as filters on Yes/No fields.

Hyperlink

The primary difference in hyperlink fields is the way users interact with hyperlinks in the browser. Look at Figure 7-19, which shows the popup view opened to edit or add a hyperlink to a hyperlink field in the view.

Clicking the Add or Edit button displays the Edit Hyperlink icon, which, when clicked, opens the Hyperlink editing popup. You can copy/paste a URL or type it in directly.

In the Access client, editing Hyperlink forms hasn't changed. You learn a lot more about Hyperlink fields in Chapter 17.

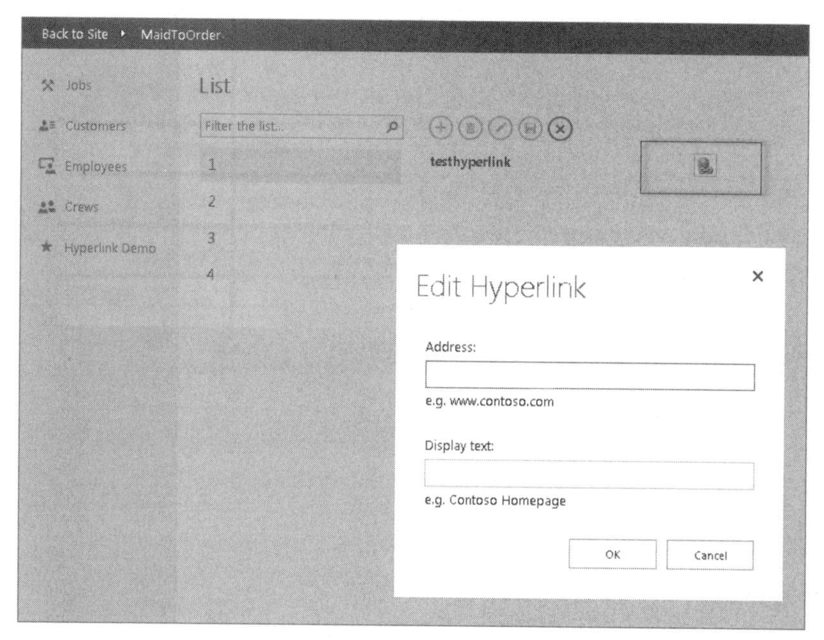

FIGURE 7-19: Popup to edit a hyperlink

Image

In Access web apps, the image data type has replaced the OLE Object data type for storing images. As you would probably expect by now, the actual data type in the SQL Server table is different; these fields are stored as `varbinary(MAX)` (see Figure 7-20).

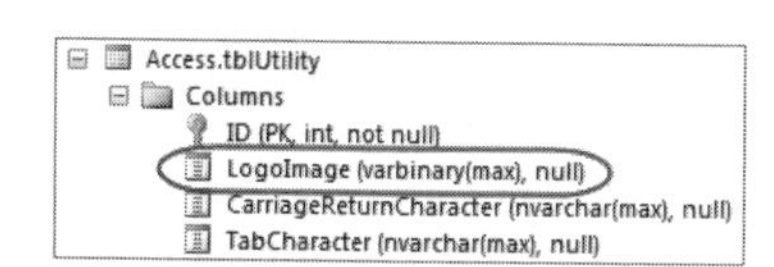

FIGURE 7-20: Image stored as varbinary(MAX) data type

A full discussion of the `varbinary(MAX)` data type in SQL Server is beyond our scope here, and knowing about it in depth is not critical to understanding how to use Image data types in web apps. Just be aware that the Image data type you see in your web app is stored in a modern data type in the underlying table. For those aware of other uses for `varbinary(MAX)` data type, note that in Access web apps, the data type can be used only with images; storage of anything else, although supported at the SQL Server level, is not supported in the Access web app.

You will also interact with the Image field differently from the way you have done in previous versions. You can add images through the run time environment only, not in the design surface. Figures 7-21 and 7-22 show you how to do this.

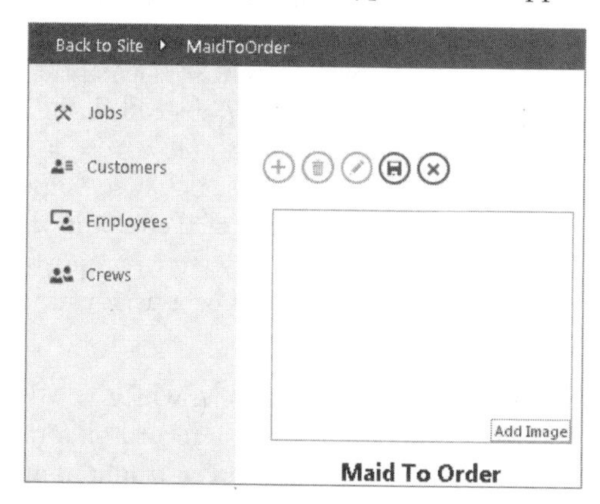

FIGURE 7-21: Add an image

> **NOTE** *Note that Figure 7-21 shows the Action Bar for this page. We enabled it to illustrate how you would add or change an image in an Image field. In the actual web app, you would hide the Action Bar because you don't want users changing your app's logo!*

As shown in Figure 7-21, click the Add Image link to open the Change Image popup. From here, you can navigate to the image you want to display in the view.

FIGURE 7-22: Edit an image

You can upload the image file from your local hard drive, for example, or from a location on your SharePoint Server from which the image is accessible. In either case, the binary for the image ends up in the SQL Server table to which the image control is bound.

Calculated Fields

Calculated, or computed, fields were introduced in version 2010, but they have been around in SQL Server for a while. Because your web app tables are also SQL Server tables, you have access to them in your web apps. They are very helpful in many situations, such as when you want to display the "full name" for a person, instead of the component fields. Traditionally, we've done this with a calculated field in a query. However, doing it in a calculated field in the table is a "once and done" process that exposes the calculated value whenever you need it. These fields are recalculated on the fly when any one of their components is modified. Note that the calculated fields are also stored the same as if they were regular fields. Unlike 2010, however, you can index the result of a calculation, which can be a performance advantage when you need to refer to calculated results for your filtering needs.

There are some limitations, which you'd expect. Calculated fields can only concatenate or calculate fields from within a single record on a table, i.e. `FullName` from `FirstName` and `LastName` in a person table, or `SalesPrice` from `Quantity * UnitPrice * Discount`, where all three are fields in a sales detail table.

Second, as you would expect by now, expressions used in creating calculated fields are based on SQL Server functions, which may differ from those you are used to. Consider, for example, the `Concat()` function illustrated in Figure 7-23.

Figure 7-24 illustrates a more familiar expression. It uses the `IIf()` function to calculate the completed status value for jobs, based on whether there are dates and times in the relevant fields. As noted previously, the calculation is redone any time one of the underlying fields is modified, so the value displayed will always represent the current status of any job.

You'll learn a bit more about leveraging Calculated fields in your web apps in a later section, after you learn about the final field type that has changed in Access web apps.

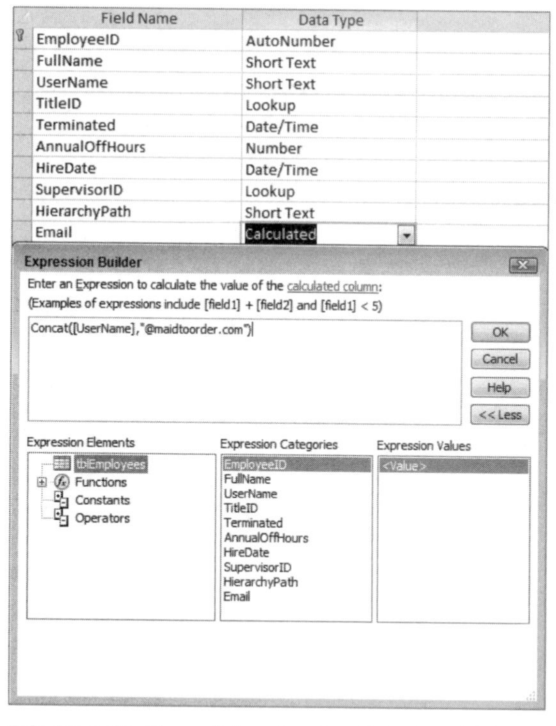

FIGURE 7-23: Concat() function in a Calculated field

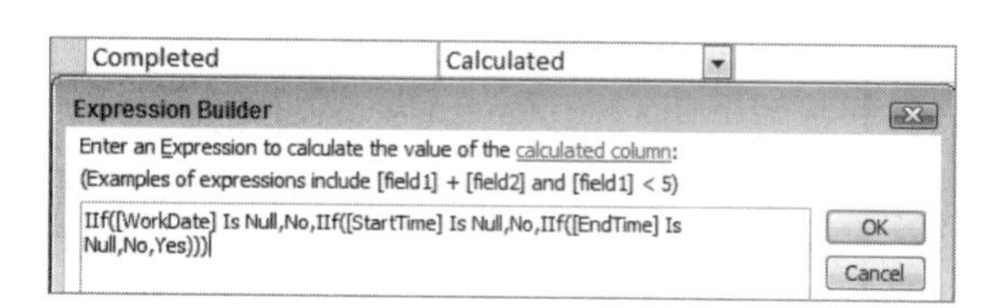

FIGURE 7-24: IIf() function to calculate Completed status

Lookup Fields

Many Access developers have held a negative opinion of Lookup fields in tables; admittedly, we used to agree. However, the Access web app environment is quite different from traditional client databases. We all need to take a fresh look at Lookup fields because they are now an integral part of how you will work with web apps, replacing completely the relationship window provided in client databases.

Lookup fields are the mechanism through which you define relationships between tables. There is no longer a relationship window. If you have worked with Access 2010 web databases, you'll be familiar with the basic Lookup field mechanism. However, in Access web apps, the process has been greatly improved.

The idea behind Lookup fields is that you define a relationship between two tables by creating a lookup field in the child table. In this lookup field, you store the foreign key from the parent table (where it is, of course, the primary key), which allows Access to define and enforce the foreign key constraint in the SQL Server tables.

Figure 7-25 illustrates several important points. Let's examine each in turn, starting with the option to create a lookup between tables, or to use a value list. That's the top section of the Lookup Wizard.

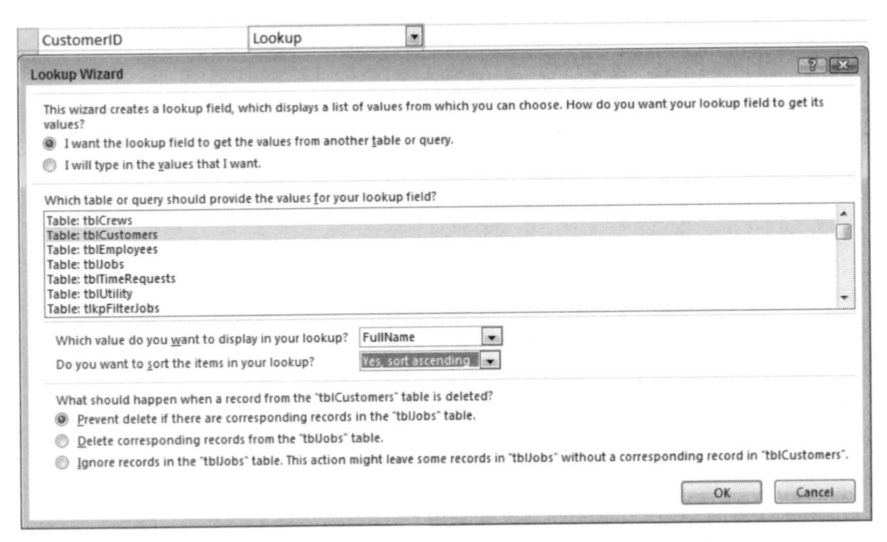

FIGURE 7-25: Defining a lookup field to enforce a Foreign Key constraint

You will use the same data type for lookups that use a value list as you do for lookups to a related table. Value lists are useful when you have a short, highly stable list of options that do not necessarily call for a Lookup table. Days of the week, or months of the year come to mind. Value Lists may also be a way to avoid a separate call to the server to fetch data for the lookup values, which could be a benefit in the web app. Otherwise, if the domain of possible values for the field is at all dynamic, you'll want to create a lookup table. Because you're defining a relationship between tables with this lookup field in Figure 7-25, the value list option is not relevant.

A side note on lookup tables is in order here. We assume you've used lookup tables many times. As you have seen previously, all tables in a web app have an ID field, defined as an Autonumber, which is implemented as an Identity field in the SQL Server table. Therefore, any lookup table you create follows this design as well. If you've been in the practice of creating lookup tables with value fields only, you'll quickly adapt to the new rules for web apps.

In the middle section of the Lookup Field Wizard, you'll define how values are displayed in the table and in views bound to it. Referring to the Lookup Field Wizard in Figure 7-25, you can see that you select both the table to which the relationship refers and a field from that table to display. It is not necessary to display a value field from the lookup table; if it makes you more comfortable, you can choose to display the ID or key field only. However, the web app environment may be better suited to displaying a value field because it can help make interface design simpler. This is another way in which you'll need to reconsider your approach to application design.

The bottom section of the Lookup Field Wizard, where you establish rules for referential integrity, is much improved over previous versions in Access. You can clearly see your options for enforcing Referential Integrity. The Lookup Field Wizard doesn't use that term, but you can easily see that's what you are doing here. As you'd expect, your options are:

- Prevent deletion of a parent record when child records exist for it.
- Delete child records when the parent record is deleted.
- Allow parent records to be deleted, potentially leaving orphans in the child table.

As is always the case, your experience will guide you and your clients to the appropriate choice.

Finally, as you can clearly see, although the process by which you define relationships is different from the relationship windows you are accustomed to in previous versions of Access, and even in SQL Server, the concepts of relationships and referential integrity are very much the same.

In the rest of the chapter, you'll be introduced to some additional considerations about using calculated fields and some configuration tables that you will find useful in the web app environment.

VALIDATION RULES AND TEXT

One significant change you will want to account for in your table design, and more generally in your application design, is the fact that there is no BeforeUpdate event in web app views. If, like many Access developers, you've used the client form's BeforeUpdate event to validate data, you'll need to adapt your approach in two different ways:

1. Using validation rules
2. Using table events

Because table events are based on macro actions, you'll learn more about using table events in Chapter 9. Even so, you should note that inserting a new record and updating an existing record trigger two different table events. If you need a business rule enforced at all times, you may find it necessary to use the same macro for both table events. However, writing macros for table events may be more work than setting a validation rule. For simple business rules contained in only a single field or a single record, you may want to consider using validation rules instead of using table events and associated data macros.

We'll go over the field-level validation rule and then turn our attention to the record-level validation rule and look at design considerations when creating and maintaining validation rules.

Field Level Validation

Suppose that Maid To Order has dictated that no customers can be activated using a future date. We can use a field-level validation rule to enforce this rule. Validation rules should be familiar to you as they are the same as in the Access client, although they will play a larger role now. Open the `tblCustomers` table in design view and select the `ActivationDate` field. Enter the expression `[ActivationDate]<=Today()` in the Validation Rule property and specify a message in the Validation Text property, as shown in Figure 7-26.

As you'd expect, whenever a user enters a future date for an activation date, that user gets a message from Access displaying the message you provide via the Validation Text property, as shown in Figure 7-27.

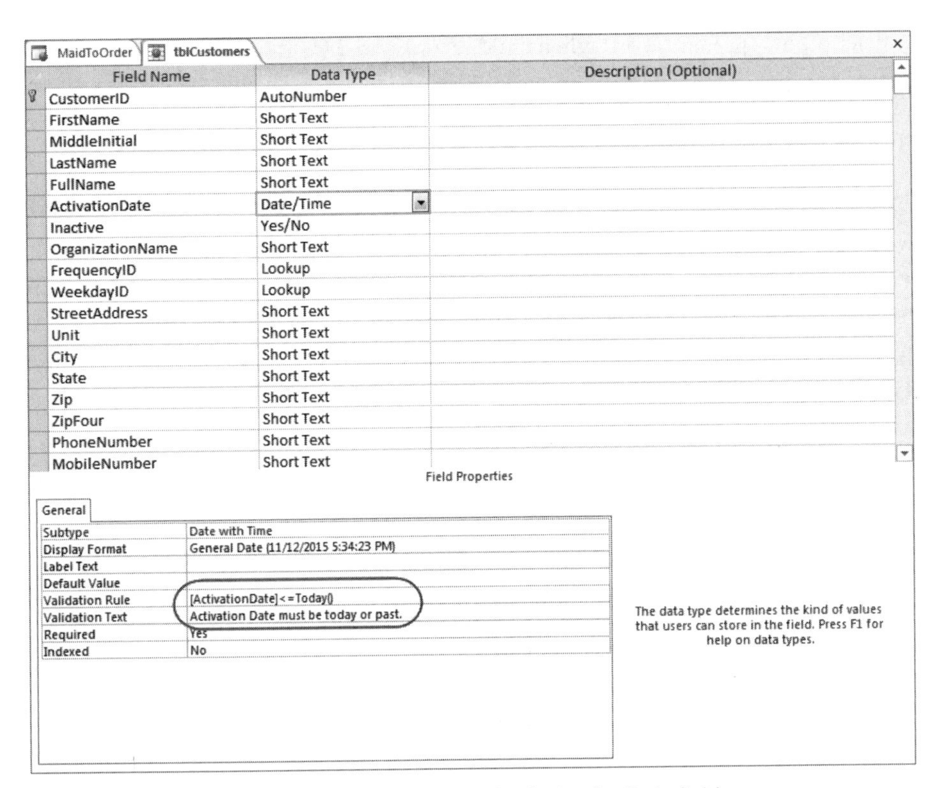

FIGURE 7-26: Validation Rule and Message for the ActivationDate field

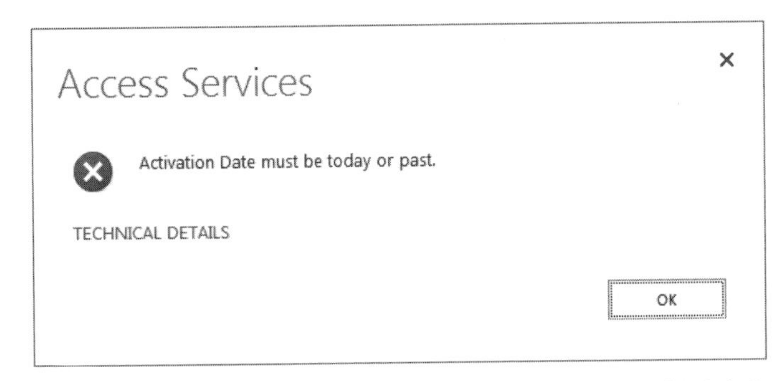

FIGURE 7-27: Error message displayed after a validation rule violation

As in the Access client, if you don't supply a validation message, users will get a fairly ugly message, as shown in Figure 7-28.

Therefore, when specifying validation rules, you will always want to provide a message.

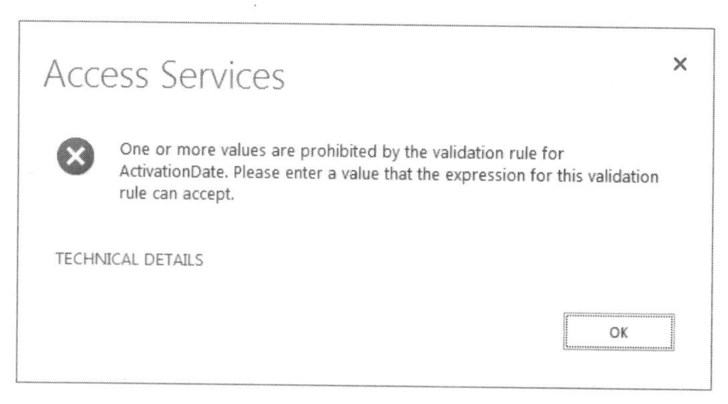

FIGURE 7-28: Default validation message displayed

> **WARNING** *Note that it is possible for you to enter a totally unrelated field level validation rule into a field. Doing so will not appear as a record level validation rule and will obfuscate the table design. Ensure that when using field level validation rules, you are entering the rules for the field it should act upon and not any other fields, or use record level validation when multiple fields are involved.*

Record Level Validation

Sometimes the rule isn't about a single piece of data. Maid To Order says that the customer must specify a weekday whenever he or she requests weekly, biweekly, or monthly services but not if it's a daily or one-time service. This rule involves two fields, `WeekdayID` and `FrequencyID`. Therefore, you'll need to use the Validation Rule button from the ribbon, shown in Figure 7-29.

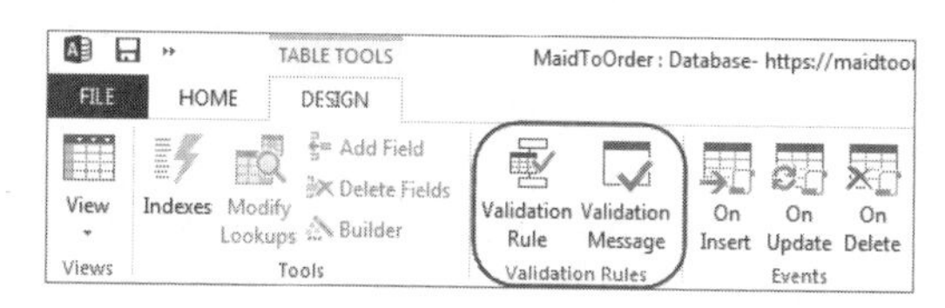

FIGURE 7-29: Validation buttons on the Table Design tab

Click the Validation Rule to open the Expression Builder and enter the following expression:

```
([FrequencyID] Is Not Null And [WeekdayID] Is Not Null) Or ([FrequencyID] In
(1,5) And [WeekdayID] Is Null)
```

Once you save the expression, you can see that the validation rule button lights up on the ribbon, indicating that it is in effect. This gives you a slight advantage over the field-level validation rule, for which you'd have to inspect each single field to discover the rules.

Editing Validation Rules with Existing Data

When you edit or add a new validation rule to a table that has existing data, you would be presented with a messagebox asking if you'd like to enforce the rule for existing data, as in Figure 7-30.

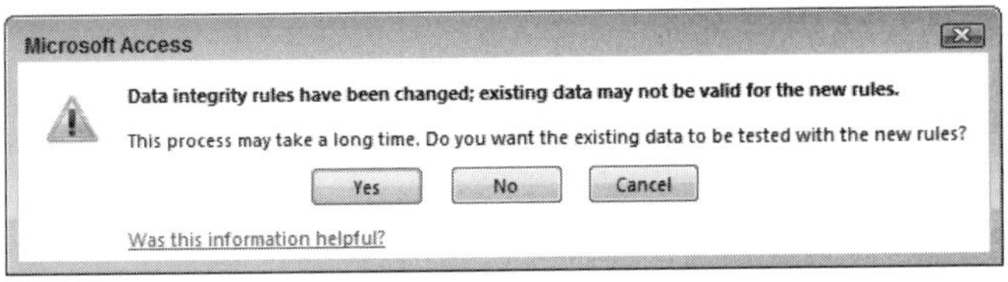

FIGURE 7-30: Messagebox asking to verify existing data

If you want to enforce the validation rule only for new data and ignore the existing data, which may be in violation, you can click No in the messagebox. However, there is one important consideration that didn't exist in the Access client. Clicking No prevents SQL Server from being able to consider the validation rules during its query optimization. This means that your queries may run slower than if you enforced the new validation rule on the existing data because SQL Server cannot trust a constraint that hasn't been validated against the entire data set and therefore is not able to discover optimizations that constraints may offer.

Generally speaking, you should avoid clicking No when presented with the choice and, if necessary, reconcile your data prior to implementing the new rules.

Validation Rules Design Consideration

One design issue to note is that once a user receives an error message after a validation rule violation, the focus may not fall on the offending control. Therefore, it is important that your validation message is clear in identifying which field was violated so the user can identify the offending control and correct the data.

In addition, validation rules are evaluated one by one. Therefore, for a table with more than one validation rule, data entry can become a frustrating experience for the users because they will see only one validation rule violation at a time, correct it, and then try to save again only to be told there's another violation. In this situation, you may want to consider either using record-level validation rules and providing a generic catchall validation message detailing all data requirements, or using data macros and table events so that you can perform all validation at once. This usually works well for a small set of strongly related fields but for more than 3 fields, it can be very difficult for the users to track down where they made the mistake and you should consider alternatives.

Finally, if you have any table events, those will not be invoked until all validation rules on a table have been satisfied. Because of the precedence, we don't recommend implementing checks on business rules in both validation rules and in table events. The recommendation is mainly to avoid situations where one version of a business rule is enforced as a validation rule and another version of the same business rule is enforced in a table event, each producing different results, again creating a frustrating user experience.

> **WHY NOT USE UI MACROS TO VALIDATE DATA?**
>
> If you're wondering why you can't attach validation checks to UI macros — perhaps by creating your custom Save button or using After Update events of each field — there are a few considerations. First, UI macros have a tendency to work only for single views, which can be a problem if you plan to present multiple views on the same data or if you allow connections to the SQL database via the Access client or other programs.
>
> Furthermore, while Blank and List views require you to explicitly start editing a record and explicitly save, that is not true for datasheet view, meaning you cannot hope to enforce business rules in a datasheet view, which means that you either need to make all your Datasheet views read-only or eschew use of Datasheet views altogether.

LEVERAGING CALCULATED FIELDS

One of the more significant changes you will find in designing web apps as opposed to client databases is that your toolkit is both different and somewhat limited in some ways. While you can create queries with calculated fields, you may find that reusing queries with different views is not always as straightforward as it can be in the client. Therefore, the power and usefulness of calculated fields in tables is a more significant advantage. We showed you the example of the e-mail field in Figure 7-23. As you can see, defining it once, as a field in the employee table, makes that value available anywhere else in the web app where we need it, without our having to re-create the concatenation each time. As the calculation becomes more complicated, as in Figure 7-24 where there are nested `IIfs` to contend with, the benefits of a single calculated field are more obvious. It's "once and done."

Creating Concatenated Fields

Let's look at a couple of examples of concatenation that greatly simplify your life as a developer. This expression uses two standard name fields to calculate a field called `Fullname`. The `Concat()` expression creates a string from the arguments supplied, which are delimited by commas:

```
Concat([FirstName],' ',[LastName])
```

You could add additional arguments, as appropriate, to create other variations, such as `FileAs`, in which the person's last name is first, to support sorting by last name in lists:

```
Concat([LastName],', ',[ FirstLastName])
```

Including a comma within the single quotes in the middle argument results in strings such as, "Nix, Stevie" or "Bocelli, Andrea".

More complex situations may call for other approaches. Suppose, for example, that your data might be incomplete, where the first names of some people are missing. The preceding expression would result in a slightly irregular appearance, as you can see in Figure 7-31. Note the space in front of the FullName field in the third record.

FirstName	LastName	FullName	FilesAs
Stevie	Nix	Stevie Nix	Nix, Stevie
Andrea	Bocelli	Andrea Bocelli	Bocelli, Andrea
	Wanz	Wanz	Wanz,

FIGURE 7-31 Missing value in a concatenated field

An even more obvious problem is the `FileAs` field, where the name appears with the comma but no first name. That's because `Concat()` puts all arguments specified for it into the string, including the comma and space, whether the argument in front of it or behind it is null or not. This may not be what you want.

If you need a more sophisticated concatenation, you can use the `IIf()` function. In the case of names, where either a first or last name could be missing, you'd construct the `IIf()` to include or exclude spaces and commas to generate consistent results. Of course, making sure your data is complete is an even better solution. Sometimes, however, you have to work with the data available.

Let's look at a different example of an expression using `IIf()` to display the completed status of jobs. You saw this expression in Figure 7-24. Here's a closer look:

```
IIf([WorkDate] Is Null,No,
  IIf([StartTime] Is Null,No,
    IIf([EndTime] Is Null,No,Yes)
  )
)
```

The logic encapsulated here is that, if there is no `WorkDate` entered for a job, that means it has not been started, so the `Completed` Status is `No`. If the `WorkDate` has been entered, but there is no `StartTime`, that means the job is on the schedule for that date, but not yet started, so the `Completed` Status is again `No`. If the `StartTime` has been entered, but there is no `EndTime`, the job is underway but not completed. Only if there are values in all three component fields can you say that the `Completed` Status is `Yes`. The field in the table, and therefore a control on a view bound to that field, will always display the `Completed` Status of all jobs because the field recalculates each time a value is added or modified in one of the component fields.

Codeless Maintenance of Values

You may have realized that using calculated fields in this way means you do not have to create code to update those fields. It all happens within the table.

And as a final example, here's a concatenation of date and time components to provide a display value. The components are separate in the table because you want to be able to search for a range of dates or for jobs occurring at a particular time of day. However, when searching across a midnight boundary, having a concatenated expression is easier.

```
DateWithTimeFromParts(
  DatePart(Year,[ScheduleDate]),
  DatePart(Month,[ScheduleDate]),
  DatePart(Day,[ScheduleDate]),
  DatePart(Hour,[ScheduleTime]),
  DatePart(Minute,[ScheduleTime]),
  DatePart(Second,[ScheduleTime])
)
```

`DateWithTimeFromParts()` is, as the name suggests, a way to create exactly the sort of calculated field you want. It takes six arguments — year, month, day, hour, minute, and second — and returns a date and time variable like:

```
9/30/2012 3:30:00 PM.
```

Rather than calculating this value in different queries or views, you need to create it only once in the table. When one of the underlying components is changed, it also updates the calculated field to display the new values.

A second way to use calculated fields is to display math calculations such as the following, which applies a discount from the `Discount field` to the Base Fee from the `FeeBase field` to return the calculated Discounted Fee:

```
[FeeBase]-([FeeBase]*[Discount])
```

A slightly more complicated calculation is the calculation to compute a line item price by multiplying unit quantity by unit price and applying a sales tax amount:

```
([UnitQuantity]*[UnitPrice])+ ([UnitQuantity]*[UnitPrice])* [SalesTax]
```

In all such calculations, you are taking advantage of the fact that calculated fields are always updated at the table level when one or more components are updated.

In the last section of this chapter, you'll be introduced to a couple of configuration tables, which you should find useful in supporting your web apps. You'll learn more about creating these specific tables when you actually need to use them in creating the sample app for this book, in Chapter 9.

Configuration Tables

Keeping in mind that the web app environment is somewhat more limited than the client database side, you should be open to using these tables, and others that you may design, in specific situations in your own database work. We will show you a tally table and a utility table here.

Tally Table

Because we do not have action queries in the web app environment, all actions that affect more than one record must be processed in a ForEachRecord action that processes each record in turn. The problem is that you need a way to tell Access how many times to repeat that action. The solution is a tally table. A tally table is a common concept among SQL Server developers. A tally table contains a range of sequential values that can be used to determine the number of iterations needed for each operation where it is called. Users do not use tally tables directly. You, the developer, use them within macros to provide a loop construct. For our purposes in this book, you'll learn how to construct a tally table with values from 1 to 10,000, as shown in Figure 7-32.

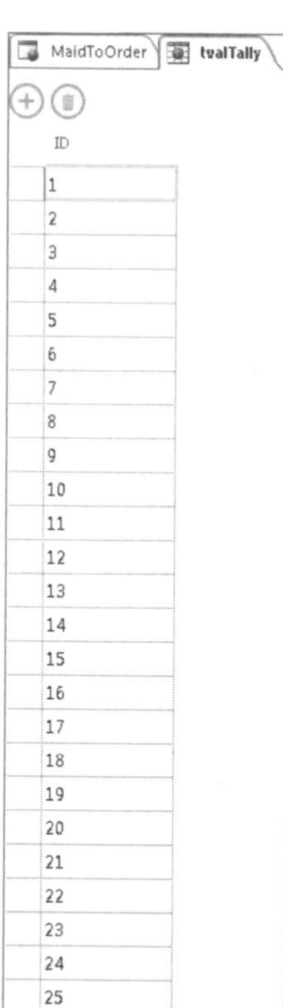

FIGURE 7-32: The first 25 rows in a tally table

You'll learn how to create tally tables in Chapter 9. For now, just note that tally tables have a single field, sequentially numbered, which you can create with an `AutoNumber` field.

Utility Table

The other configuration table you'll want to incorporate into your web apps is what we have chosen to call a Utility table. You may have created similar tables and used different naming conventions for them, such as usysConfig. In an Access Client database, the prefix "usys" indicates that it is a user-defined configuration table, a type of table which Access does not display in the Navigation Pane by default. Because that is not a factor in web apps — users never see the Navigation Pane — we chose a friendlier name for this table in our web app. Figure 7-33 shows our utility table, which contains only four fields for this web app.

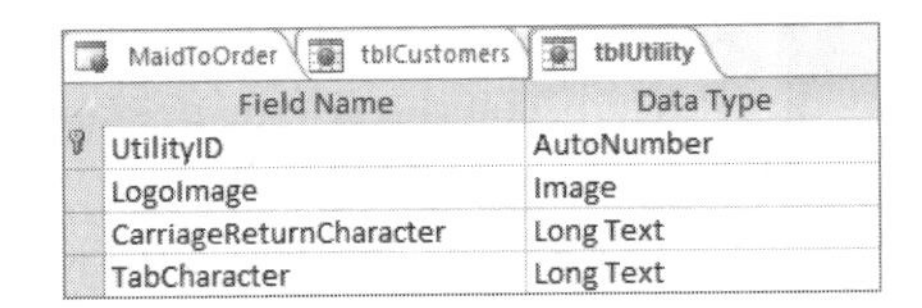

FIGURE 7-33: Utility table

There is only a single row in this table at all times. Each of the values found in the fields in that record are needed to manage processing tasks that can't be done in the web app interface or, as with the application logo, to supply application-wide values. As you can see in Figure 7-33, we need a way to insert the carriage return character and the tab character in certain text fields. Because there is no way to do that within a macro action, we supply the needed values from the utility table and reference them when needed within a macro. You'll also learn how to build, populate, and use the fields in the utility table in Chapter 9.

SUMMARY

In this chapter, you've learned about the new or modified data types for tables in Access 2013. You learned that the majority of changes are on the web app side, and that there are minimal changes in the client side, with the exception of the text data types.

You learned that text and memo fields have been replaced by Long Text and Short Text fields. In the client, the main difference is in the naming and Enter Key Behavior in a control bound to one of these fields. In the web app, Short and Long Text fields are essentially the same, except for the default properties set when they are first created.

You learned that the set of data types for numbers in a web app have been simplified, and are limited to Whole Numbers, Fixed Point numbers, and Floating Point number subtypes. You can format each data type for display, again using a simplified set of options. Although the options have been reduced, you should find that all, or nearly all, of your requirements will be adequately met.

You also learned about the changes to currency fields in web apps, which are stored as decimals but displayed with one of many possible currency symbols in the interface.

In addition, you saw the changes to Yes/No fields, stored as bytes and displayed as `Yes` or `No`. You saw the changes to image fields, stored as `varbinary(MAX)` in the SQL Server table. Image fields, as you learned, must be populated through the web interface. You learned that hyperlink fields are easily edited through the web interface.

Then, we turned your attention to the Lookup field mechanism with which you define relationships between tables in the web app environment. You saw that the improvements to the Lookup Field Wizard make it much easier to correctly define relationships and select appropriate options for enforcing referential integrity.

And finally, you got a brief introduction to the use of configuration tables in web apps and two of the tables created for the sample web app on which this book is based: tally tables and utility tables.

You are now ready to move into the tasks of creating your own application, beginning with the use of macros to solve typical business problems.

Designing the User Interface

WHAT'S IN THIS CHAPTER?

- Organizing tiles and links, emphasizing discoverability and accessibility
- Understanding how different types of Views can be used and maximizing their advantages
- Identifying techniques for building user-driven filtering, using either built-in tools and/or supplementing with macros
- Recognizing which control best fits the requirement
- Describing how queries can be used to expand the form's capabilities

WROX.COM CODE DOWNLOADS FOR THIS CHAPTER

The code and sample downloads for this chapter are found at `www.wiley.com/go/proaccess2013prog.com` on the Download Code tab. They are in the Maid To Order Sample App download. Refer to the Readme.txt file also located there for installation instructions.

One of the challenges to productivity in building web components for your Access web applications is learning how to work with the new programming model to create functions like those you've come to rely on in your client databases. If you've been building Access databases for long, you have doubtless developed several techniques to solve common problems such as enabling user-driven filtering and pulling additional information from related sources to provide users with information pertinent to the process. However, with the new user interface for web apps, you have to approach many tasks differently. This chapter equips you with new tools that work well in the web environment, enabling you to build Access web apps just as productively as you've done for Access desktop databases.

NAMING CONVENTION FOR WEB APPS

In this chapter, you will be implementing the techniques learned from earlier chapters as well as the utility table and tally table previously discussed, you will need to follow a more formal naming convention. As you will see, the authors chose to extend the tried and true Reddick VBA convention for use throughout later chapters. Let's review the extensions.

First, scoping is more important in web apps; it can be easy to lose track of which variables are local or global. The authors chose to prefix a single letter to indicate the scope of a variable:

- `v`—Local variable scoped to current macro
- `p`—Parameters passed in from a calling macro block or to a referencing query
- `g`—Global variable (Note that all UI macro variables are global)

The next difficulty is that there are no data typing at all within UI macros, while data macros have data typing. Following the original convention rigidly, it would be correct to use the `var` prefix to indicate that the variable is a variant. However, the authors found that doing so made it hard to identify the intended data type. For this reason, all variables, regardless of whether they are strongly typed or not, will have a prefix using the conventional Reddick convention. One advantage of this approach is demonstrated by this:

```
glngEmployeeCode = "abc"
```

Because it's prefixed with `lng`, it is apparent that we are assigning a string to a variable that is meant to take integers, which helps in preventing data type mismatch errors.

You may have already noticed that the authors chose to use `frm` prefix for views. Here is a list of prefixes the author made up for the new controls and objects.

- `acm`—AutoComplete control
- `mtx`—Multiline Textbox control
- `tab`—Related Items control's tab
- `web`—Web Browser control
- `lnk`—Hyperlink control
- `dm`—Data Macro

We encourage you to give your naming convention careful thought and be consistent. It is much more important in web apps and will make development much easier.

PLANNING THE USER INTERFACE

The following discussion is based on the premise that the client has indicated they want the following forms — views in the new environment — in their web app:

- For managers to track progress for today's workload from each crew
- For managers and employees to report on performance, hours accumulated, and duties performed
- For employees to submit work reports at the completion of the job

You've already built the queries needed to support those views so we will focus on construction of web app views, along with macros that don't need to be standalone. In Chapter 4, you saw how the design surface and construction for web apps are different. This chapter focuses on identifying effective methods to use those new tools.

Before we wade in, we want to discuss one technique that will help greatly in simplifying the development. As you learned in Chapter 4, there is no functionality to copy and paste individual controls, which makes it hard to re-use some functionality you may have already built somewhere. You also know that once a view is created, its type cannot be changed. However, instead of having to choose whether you want a List view or a Blank view, you can use Subview controls to re-use a view.

REUSING CREATE, READ, UPDATE, AND DELETE VIEWS

If you find yourself creating a complex Create, Read, Update, Delete (CRUD) view that may have a number of macro actions to validate or manage the data entry operations, it would be a shame to have to do them all again just because you needed a different configuration for a list pane, or because it needs to use a different recordsource. One way to avoid this difficulty is to only use Blank views to accept the data entry or modification, based on the underlying view. The key concept is that this Blank view will then be used in a Subview control as a source object to other views.

You can then use any other List views or Blank views that are based on any query that contains the primary key of the table that is used by the Blank view. You can use that as the linking field for the Subview control. You can then create many different List views or Blank views with different recordsources and reuse only a single CRUD view. In this way you can achieve a consistent experience for your users while enabling a greater variety of ways to present the data. You will see this used when we discuss query-by-form techniques. Furthermore, you could also use it as a popup view for Summary view and certain controls such as Related Items control or AutoComplete control. This would then mean you could use Datasheet view for quick browse while providing the CRUD operations in the popup view.

EFFECTIVE NAVIGATION DESIGN

First, you will examine how web view design is different from traditional form design. You need to identify situations where methods used in traditional form design won't apply in a web context, or which require modifications. We will review traditional techniques so you can see where you need to change your mind-set when you approach web design.

Because filtering also plays a large part in an effective navigation design, you will also consider how to design effective filtering mechanisms to make it easy for users to find relevant data with minimum effort. We strongly believe that once you design an app that's easy to navigate and find things, the rest of the application design will come more easily.

Traditional Navigation Patterns

Let's review three common techniques that you may already have used in previous databases:

1. A switchboard
2. An index form
3. A query by form

You may have different names for one or more of these methods and you may have implemented a few differences from what you see here, but you'll find our descriptions are conceptually similar. You will then learn how to create analogues to switchboards, index forms, and query by form navigation in the web environment.

Traditional Switchboards

Let's start our comparison of navigation patterns with what is arguably the most common form in Access databases, the switchboard. The switchboard in Figure 8-1 is from the Northwind database.

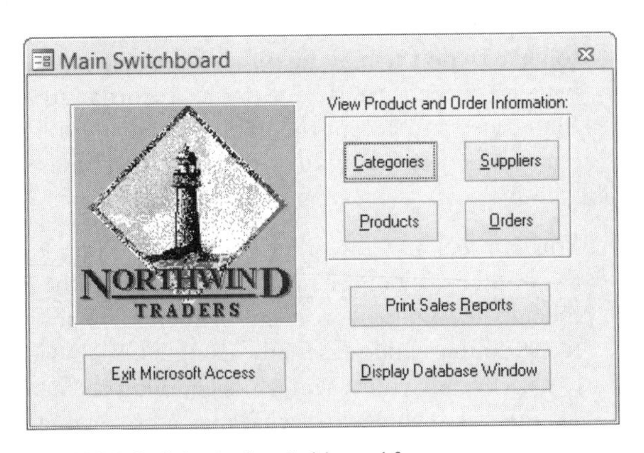

FIGURE 8-1: A typical switchboard form

The switchboard has been an Access feature since its inception and is probably the most familiar navigation pattern to seasoned Access developers, even if they do not use it in their own work. The layout of a switchboard is straightforward; an unbound form populated with command buttons provides a starting point to perform major tasks or start workflows. Users select buttons on the switchboard representing what they want to do and the switchboard takes them to that section of the database.

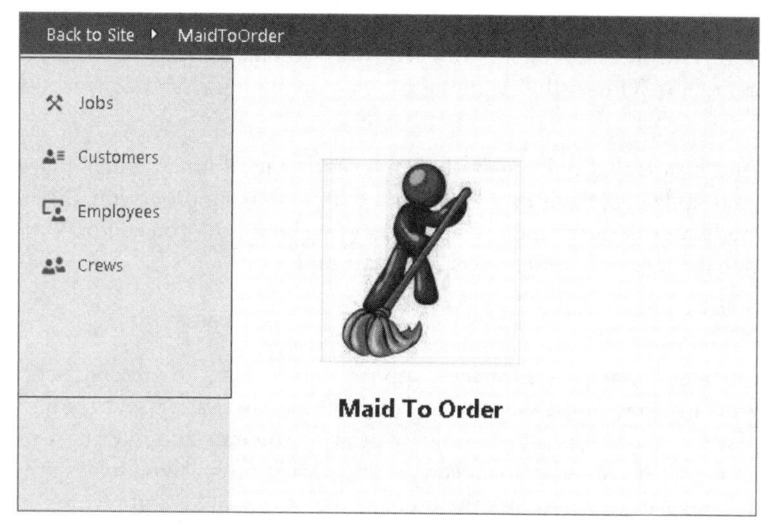

FIGURE 8-2: Web app's analogue of a switchboard

In a certain sense, the basic functionality of switchboards still exists in web apps. In the web environment, however, the buttons are replaced by tiles. Consider Figure 8-2, which illustrates how this functionality is implemented in web apps.

Tiles in a web app are presented to the user in a vertical column on the left side of the screen and can't be removed or relocated (although individual tiles can be hidden). And, of course, there is no separate, standalone form, as is the case with a switchboard. Navigation tiles are fixed in size and position on the screen. You'll learn more about the specific features of tile navigation later in this chapter.

In more complicated switchboards, it was common to change menu listings when certain buttons were clicked. This also continues to some extent in web apps. A number of links can be associated with each tile and can be used to navigate to a view, as shown in Figure 8-3.

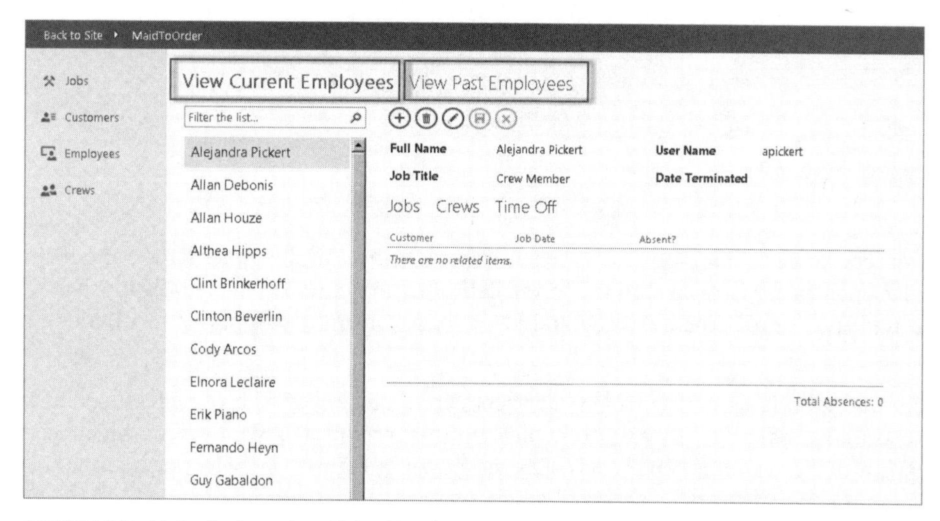

FIGURE 8-3: Links that can be clicked to change views

This layout presents us with an advantage over the traditional switchboard design — there is no need to use a Back button to return to the main menu; tiles are always visible and submenus (Links) are always visible on their parent view. This visibility allows for easy switching from one workflow to another.

Furthermore, the web app layout means that only one view can be active at all times, which plays right into the goal of keeping our app simple and avoiding issues that arise from processing different workflows from different points. Later in the chapter, you learn more about how you can maximize the power of tiles and links to make it easy for your users to get around.

Index Forms for Navigation

Many Access developers have created *index forms* for their applications in order to present users with a two-level, or summary-detail, view of the data. First, you have a form that presents only important, or summary, details of a record for users to quickly peruse. You may add filtering, either static or user-driven, but typically, an index form is read-only. Most often, these forms are implemented as continuous or datasheet views so that the user can select one of several records displayed. Clicking a record in the index form drills through to the related view with all the details for that record. The drill-through can be a separate form, or a subform on the same form, as in Figure 8-4, which is from the Northwind database.

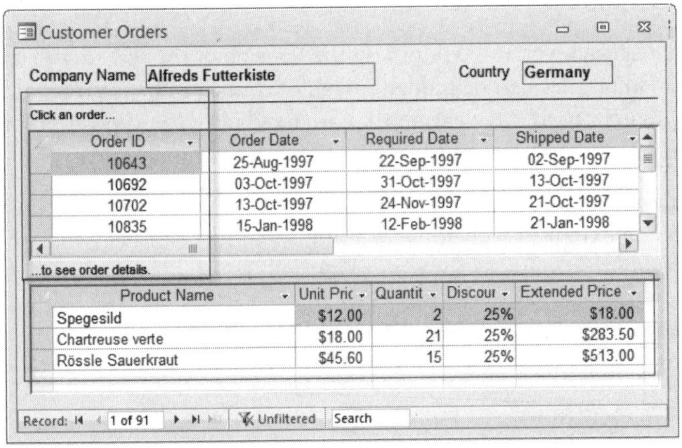

FIGURE 8-4: A typical index form

The full list of orders for each company is displayed in the datasheet in the upper half of the form. Clicking an order updates the datasheet in the lower half of the form to display details for that order. In other implementations, the details would be in a separate, editable, popup form, filtered to just those details.

An index form is also a good way to provide your users with a quick way to browse features in a web app. Microsoft now makes it very easy to implement this, providing a detail view, which as you saw in Chapter 4, provides an index on the left side, as shown in Figure 8-5. Selecting a name from the list enables you to navigate to the details for that employee.

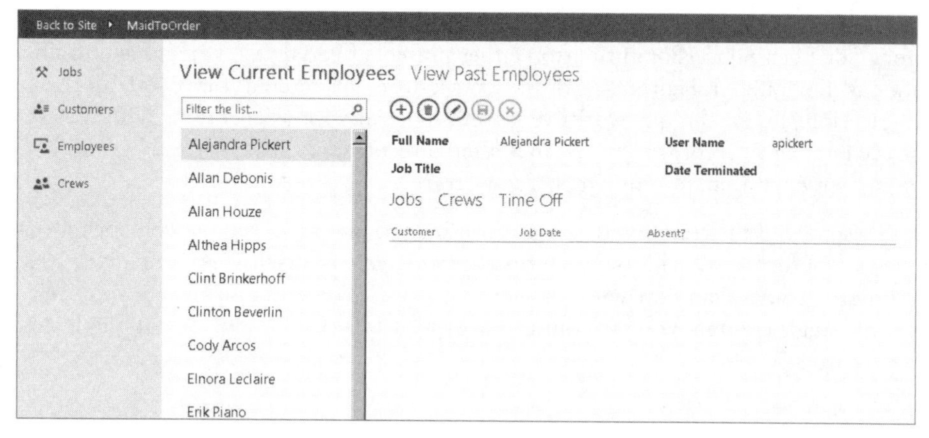

FIGURE 8-5: A web app index form

Although the mechanics of setting up the form and navigating the records are somewhat different in a web app index view, the concept and methods should be familiar to you. You'll learn more about creating index forms, or views, for your web apps later in this chapter.

Query by Form

Sometimes, an index form isn't appropriate, maybe because network resources are too critical or because users need more control over how they filter records for selection and editing. This is where you can use the query by form technique. Query by form, as you probably know, presents the user with a number of unbound controls that support different types of filtering, as illustrated in Figure 8-6, based on the Northwind database.

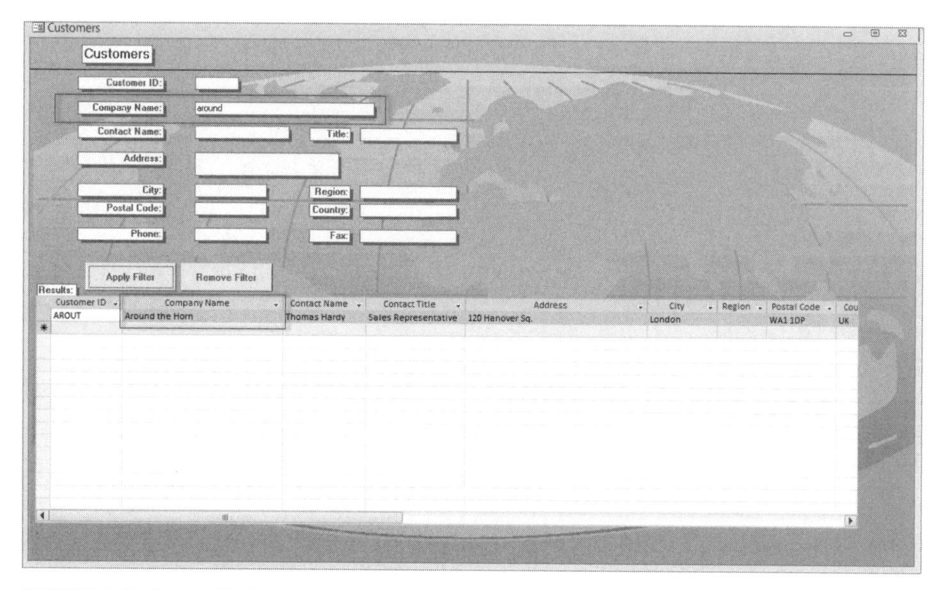

FIGURE 8-6: Query By Form in Access client

Users select options from drop-downs, or fill in the appropriate textboxes, and click an Apply Filter or Submit button. Code behind the Submit button either presents filtered results in a fashion similar to an index form, as illustrated in Figure 8-6, or presents a different, filtered, form with all the details for that selection. This technique works very well, especially for applications with remote servers because the number of records returned in a filtered recordset is generally the smallest possible for the current operation, minimizing network traffic.

Query by form is also one of the techniques you can continue to use effectively in web apps. Because web apps use views, not forms, we will use the term *query by view* to discuss designing views based on the same techniques you are familiar with for query by forms. For situations where you can't just filter or browse on a single column, you will want to use query by view, which you can implement in a web app, as in Figure 8-7.

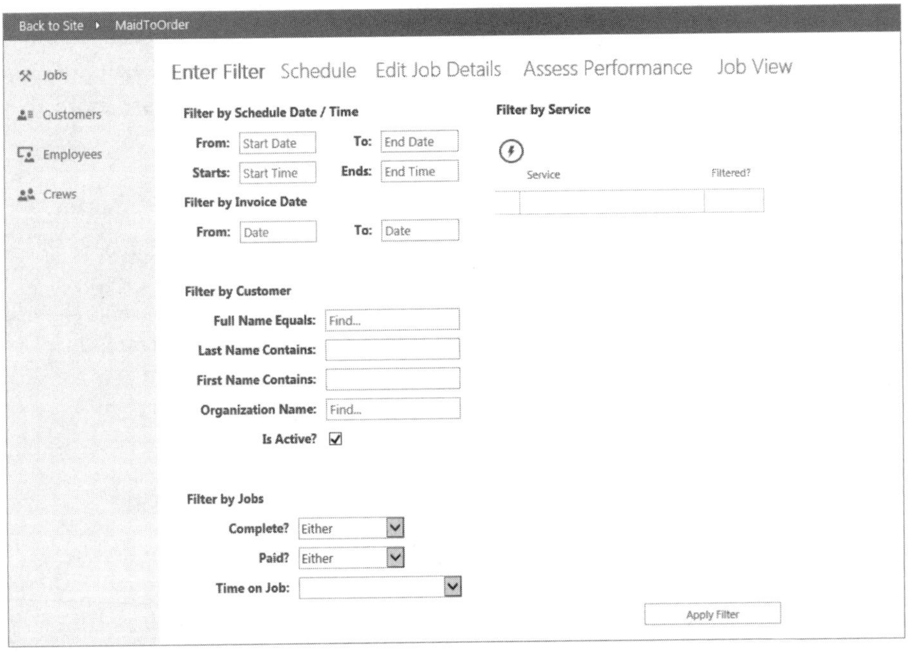

FIGURE 8-7: Query By view in a web app

The major change from your previous practice will be the coding process because query by form in a client database would typically be heavy in VBA and would probably use dynamic SQL to build the Where clause. On the web, you will need to adapt your query by form techniques to the fact that dynamic SQL can't be used in web apps. Again, you learn the specifics of using query by view techniques later in this chapter.

As you move to the details of designing views for web app navigation, let's start by reviewing the goals of web design and how the three navigation techniques you've seen can support those goals.

Web Design Principles

One of the goals of web design is to keep everything accessible and discoverable. A commonly repeated rule in web design is the "three-click rule," which posits that users should be able to do what they want to do within three mouse clicks. Although some may argue that this exact number of mouse clicks is not always practical, the underlying principle is sound. You want to lay out your site so that everything is easy to find with the fewest possible mouse clicks.

Organizing the Navigation List

You will probably want to organize your website according to the major tasks your users need to accomplish. The tiles on the Navigation list should be designed to present those tasks to your users in a logical sequence, the highest priority, or most frequently used, tasks at or near the top. That's highlighted in Figure 8-8.

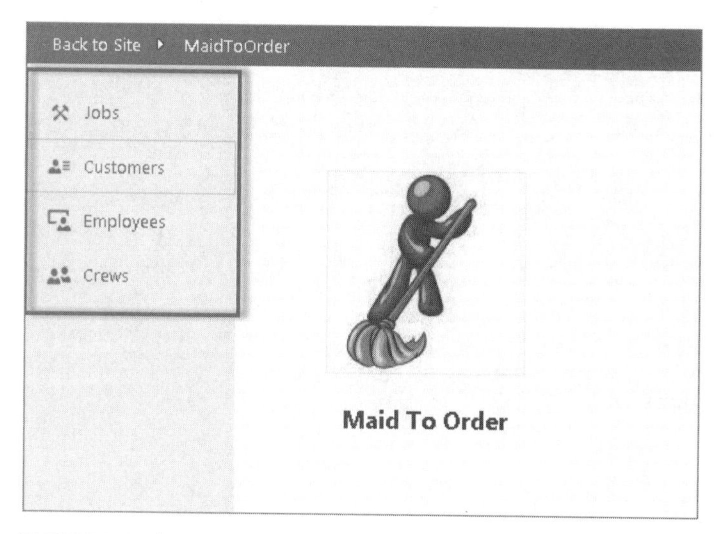

FIGURE 8-8: Organizing the navigation list

As you've learned in previous chapters, tiles are always bound to tables and to views on those tables. By default, when a web app launches, it will load the first view for the first tile at the top of the list. That can be convenient in getting users started quickly, especially if the view loaded represents the most common workflow users want to perform, as shown in Figure 8-8, for example, where managing jobs is the first selection.

Hiding Non-Working Tiles

Because each table in a web app has its own tile, which can't be deleted without deleting the table, you will need to hide tiles that don't fit into the overall navigation scheme for the app. For example, your apps will typically contain one or more lookup tables. The tiles for them should be hidden. Tiles for child tables that are edited only through subviews on a parent view should also be hidden.

Meaningful, User-Friendly Tile Names

You should also rename Tiles which are displayed using names that are more friendly and relevant to your users; we revisit renaming in more detail later in the chapter. You also want to group workflows that apply to an entity under Tiles. The individual workflow can then be a link associated with each tile. This gives you two clicks to get to a workflow you want to provide to your users.

Creating a Navigation List from the Tiles in a Web App

Let's take a closer look now at creating and organizing the tiles in a simple navigation list. Refer to Figure 8-9 to visualize how tiles and links will be organized.

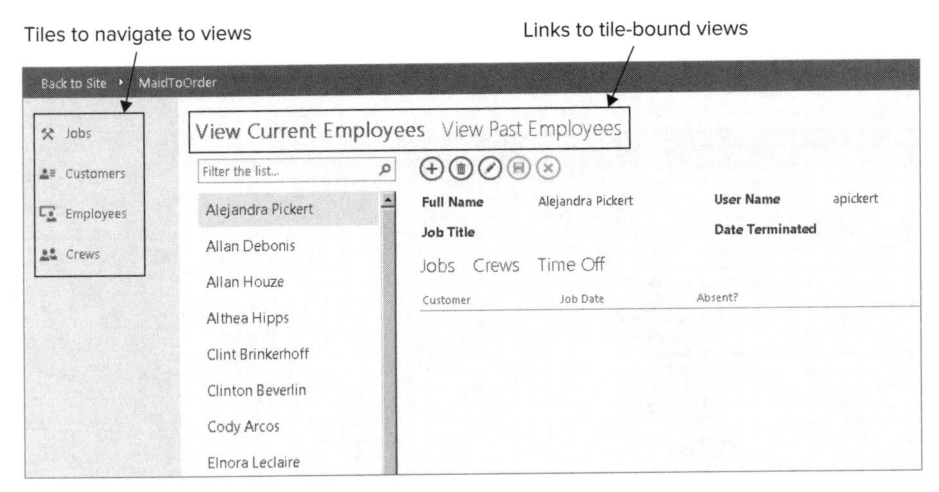

FIGURE 8-9: Click a tile to navigate to that view

In Figure 8-9, you can see that the logical groupings for the Maid To Order app are:

- Tasks that involve scheduled jobs
- Tasks that involve customers
- Tasks that involve individual employees
- Tasks that involve crews

Underneath those general categories, you'll find more specific tasks, reached by links on the views that belong to each task. This navigation list is organized around the major tasks the app is designed to support.

Clicking one of the other tiles navigates to the view associated with that function. You can see how that looks in Figure 8-9. Note that links on the view navigate to tasks within the category, allowing you to view current and past employees.

As you can see, the tile named "Employees" has been clicked and the app has navigated to the related view, in which tasks related to Employees are managed. This view supports managing active employees separately from past employees. Figure 8-9 shows the View Current Employees List view, which is presented by default because it is in the first position. Clicking the View Past Employees link navigates to the second view, which shows only past employees.

The view in Figure 8-9 also demonstrates use of static filters, which are more common in the web environment. Each view has a filter built into its recordsource so that only selected employees are shown in each view. You can reach either view in only two clicks. This approach works quite well for a small set of records where additional filtering is not typically needed.

Navigation Design Logic

Here's where your prior experience with Access client databases will be of significant value. As you saw in Chapter 3, the mechanics of designing the navigation list of tiles are pretty straightforward. The logic behind the structure of the list you create, on the other hand, depends on your understanding of the business rules and work functions on which the web app depends.

As previously noted, you should hide tiles linked to tables you don't want to expose in the web browser — things such as lookup tables or child tables that you edit only within a subview.

Grouping and Naming Tiles and Linked Views

You should group like functions in the list, and organize them from top to bottom in a priority order as the user is going to use them, either sequentially or by frequency of use. Within a group, use different views, linked on the main view, to show the user different elements of that task. For example, links to View Rosters and Assign Job are available on the Crews tile.

We also want to mention that tiles should be named with nouns that provide users with a context for using them. You should then use action phrases such as "View Schedule" for the links on that view. This noun-verb motif is crucial in making the navigation intuitive and accessible to users.

As you have just learned, creating the top-level navigation list in a web app is not entirely different, conceptually, from what you've always done with switchboards. Clicking a tile (or a button) navigates to the appropriate view where the user's work will be done. Of course, as you've also seen, the techniques you will use to construct the navigation list and the tiles themselves are quite different from client applications.

It's also worth noting that the primary navigation flow in a web app is different from switchboards in that the navigation list and the page layout remain static. The internal work surface in the page changes to the current task. Contrast that to the switchboard approach where one form closes and another replaces it on-screen. The user can easily lose his or her place in that environment, as screens come and go, or popups layer on top of other popups. We are convinced the navigation strategy in web apps will make users more confident in that regard.

Mapping Links

Now that you've seen how the navigation list works in the web app, let's take a look at the design surface in Access. Consider Figure 8-10, which illustrates what happens when you add a new table.

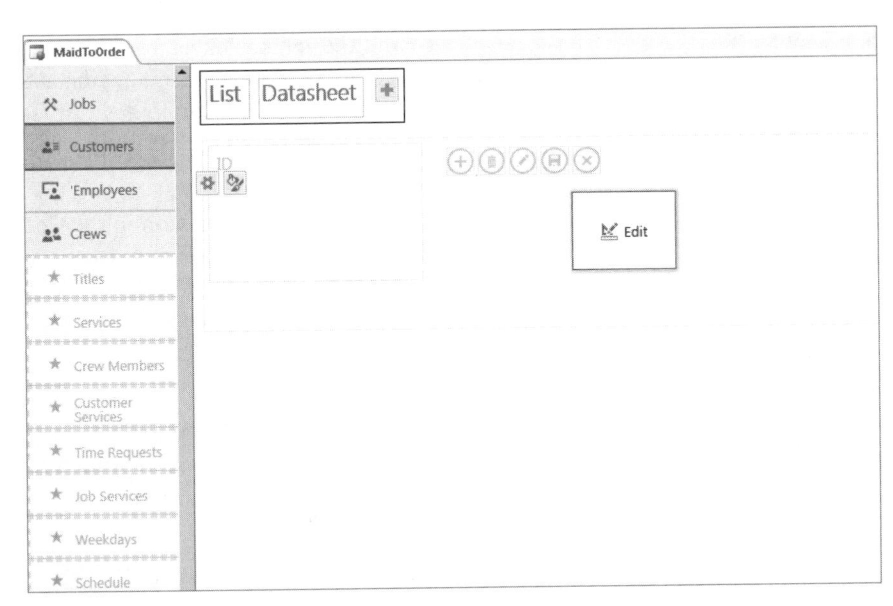

FIGURE 8-10: Default links on a new tile

By default, when you add a table to an Access web app, it auto-creates two views, a List view and a Datasheet view. The tile for that table will have two links to those views. This may be helpful in some cases, where you're prototyping a quick web app, for example. Because we have a particular design in mind for our client, however, we will create our views from scratch. So let's remove the clutter in the navigation pane by getting rid of the default views (see Figure 8-11).

1. If the navigation pane isn't shown already, click Navigation Pane on the ribbon's Home tab to bring it in focus.
2. Select the topmost form listed under the Forms group, and holding down the Shift key, select the bottommost form to select all forms.
3. Press delete or right-click the selection and select Delete; Then click Yes to the prompt that appears.

Now you have a blank slate and can start mapping custom views to your tables. At this point, you need to plan out the individual workflows you need to expose to the client. You'll also need to identify which workflow will be attached to which tile, and finally, you will need to decide what type of view is best for each workflow.

Planning for Navigation

The importance of that last point cannot be overstated: you can duplicate a view and reassign the duplicate to a different table or make it popup, but there is no way to *change* an existing List view to a Datasheet view or vice versa. Factor in the fact that you have no copy/paste facility to copy controls between views and you can see that prior analysis is crucial in planning out the correct type of view for each tile in advance.

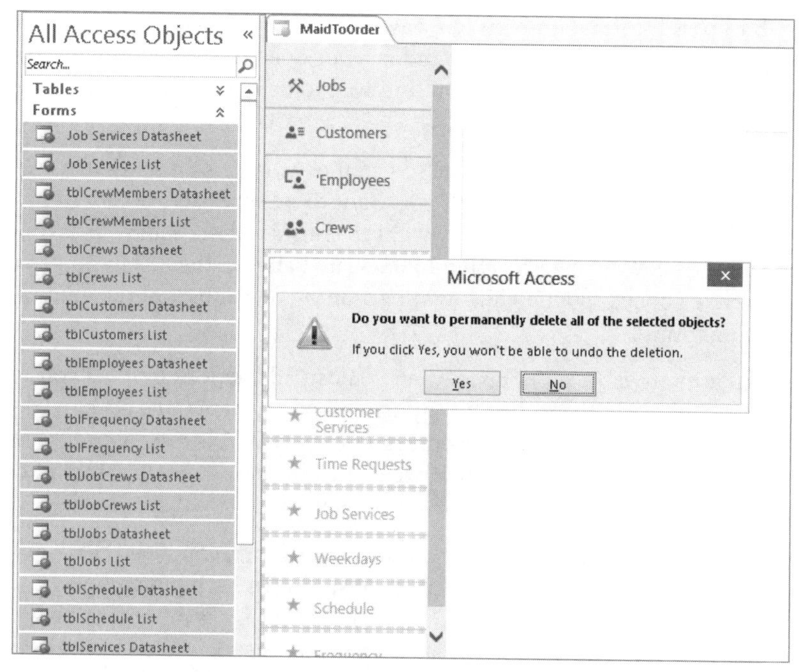

FIGURE 8-11: Delete a group of views

Types of Views Available

Let's review the four types of views available to you.

1. **Blank view** — Provides the most flexible layout option but no built-in filtering capability, ideal for unbound views.
2. **List view** — Provides filtering on one column and is rich and flexible.
3. **Datasheet view** — Has several more filtering options and can be applied to multiple columns, but layout is not as rich or flexible.
4. **Summary view** — Provides summary and drill-through information, which can be filtered but is very limited in layout design.

You will need to plan the ideal layout with your client before you begin creating the views. One thing to remember is that the user already has clicked a tile to reach a view, so links to other views will be the second click. The most common workflow for a tile should not require additional, explicit clicks. So ordering the links on a view is also important.

Tile-Bound View and Popup Views

One design principle you need to remember when working with web apps is that you can work with only one active view at a time in the browser context. Generally, you should *not* expect to be able to reference other views. Variables in apps that are set via the SetVariable macro action do have a global scope and can be used to pass information between views. However, views have no Close or Deactivate events that get fired when you change a tile-bound view or open or close a popup view. Because of the lack of Close and Deactivate events, you have no way to definitively act when a view unloads or loses focus.

A major ramification of this lack of events on views is that you cannot reliably refresh a form automatically when returning from a popup. Therefore, if you want to be sure users do not need to remember to manually refresh data frequently, you may want to consider designing your layout using tile-bound views and the ChangeView macro action to navigate between them. This approach will implicitly force a Load event or open a popup view to allow editing of a subset of the data that's not already shown on the calling form.

Do not be tempted to create a button to close a popup view so you can add actions to it (as you might have done with a client database); in the web environment, all popup views always have the X button in the upper-right corner to close the popup, and you can't remove it. Clicking it circumvents any macro actions you may have added to a button's Click event. Again, there is neither unloading nor change of focus events for you to trap the user's action on the popup.

You can open another popup from an already open popup view. Even so, we recommend that you don't rely on the OpenPopup feature in a popup view. The user must dismiss each popup opened in this manner and this can be frustrating, not to mention confusing if the user is more than two popups deep. As previously noted, in fact, this confusion has been one of the main drawbacks to the switchboard in client databases. Furthermore, deep popups are not as discoverable as links on the main surface, which leads to questions from users about where they need to go to perform their tasks.

Controlling Access to Views

A tile-bound view cannot be hidden, so if you need to control access to a view, you should use a popup view so you can check the user's access level before opening that view. A tile can be hidden via the design surface but it cannot be hidden or unhidden at run time.

To reach a view associated with a hidden tile, you can use the ChangeView macro action. However, when you navigate to the hidden tile, you get all of the links to each view bound to that tile.

CREATING A SPLASH SCREEN

By default, web apps drop the user onto the first view that happens to be associated with the topmost tile. As you saw earlier, designing the navigation list of tiles allows you to control that starting point just by positioning the tiles. That is adequate for some scenarios where you want the user to start right away, especially if they are going to perform the same task each time they log into the site. You can select a default view and place it in the priority position on the navigation list. However, most applications are available to a diverse user base, members of which don't always perform the same set of tasks. For this scenario, having a splash screen may be helpful. You've probably used splash screens in many of your client applications.

In this section, you learn the steps to create a splash screen for your web app.

To get started:

1. If you don't already have a table called `tblUtility`, create one. Click the Table icon in the ribbon to begin.
2. Click the link to create a new blank table, as highlighted in Figure 8-12. Add an image field to the table for the logo you want to display on the splash screen. Name it `LogoImage`.

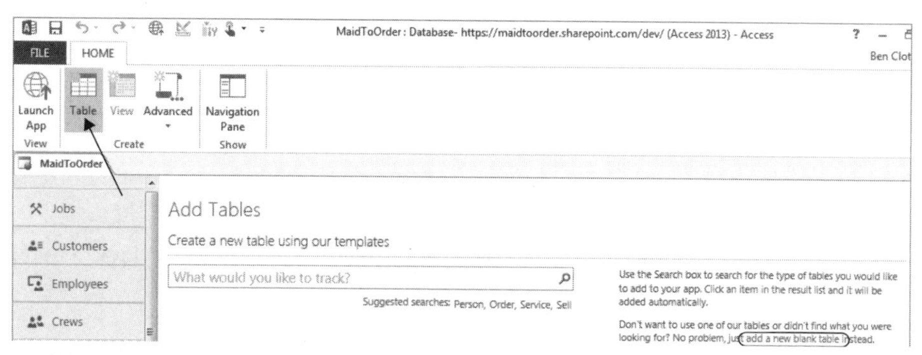

FIGURE 8-12: Add a new blank table

3. Add a second field to the table so you can add a record to it. You'll add other fields later.
4. Open the table in Datasheet view and add a single record, leaving the image field blank. You will load the image via the web browser. Save the record and close the table.
5. Click the `tblUtility` tile that was created when you created the table.
6. Click the + button, as shown in Figure 8-13, and provide the following parameters:
   - **View name:** `frmSplash`
   - **View type:** `Blank`
   - **Recordsource:** `tblUtility`
7. Click Add New View to save the new view.
8. Open the new view for Edit, illustrated in Figure 8-14.

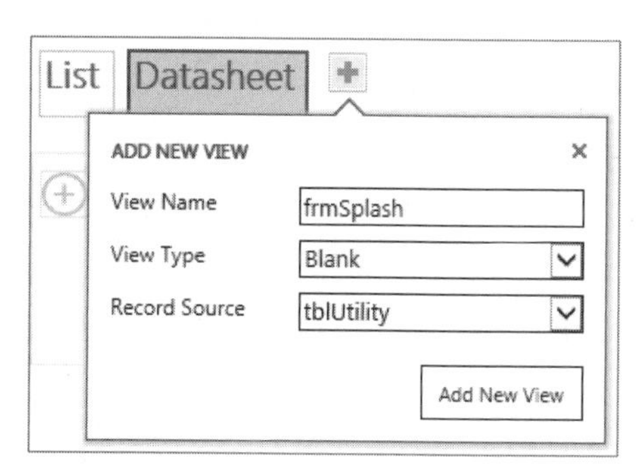

FIGURE 8-13: Add a view for the splash screen.

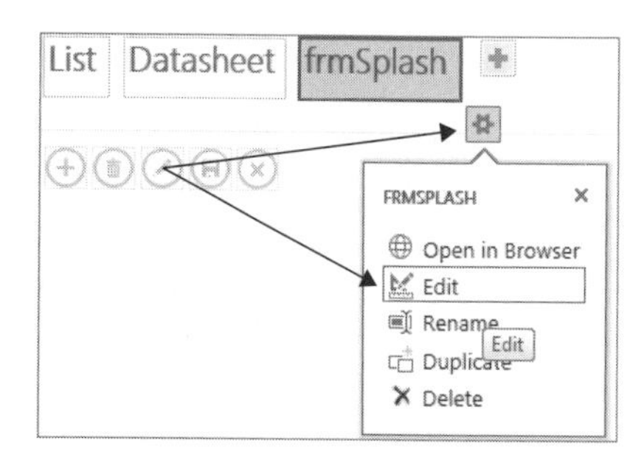

FIGURE 8-14: Edit splash view

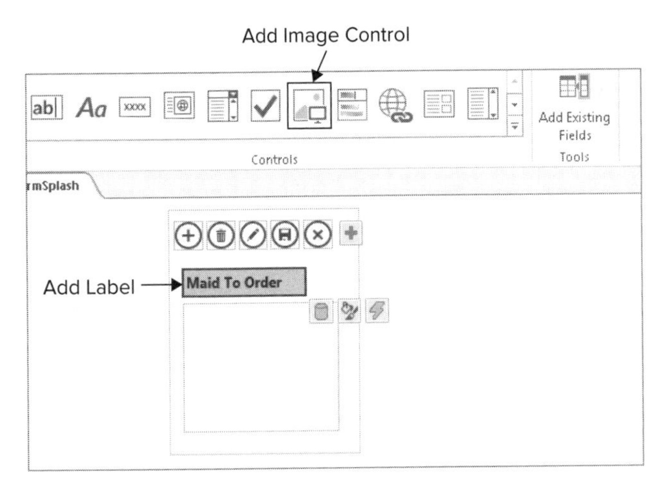

FIGURE 8-15: Add the Image field

9. Click the image field on the ribbon to add it to the form, as shown in Figure 8-15.

   You'll upload an image into the field from the web app later.

10. Click the label control from the ribbon, position it, and then select the Formatting button in the popout buttons.
11. Enter **Maid To Order** as the caption for the label and resize as needed.
12. Center the label under the image.
13. Click the , choose Rename, and put in a space to make the link invisible.
14. Save the form, naming it `frmSplash`, then close it.
15. Delete the default List and Datasheet views.
16. Hide the tile for the utility table.
17. On the ribbon's Home tab, click the Advanced menu and select On Start Macro.
18. Add a ChangeView action and enter the name of the utility table and the splash form.
19. Save the form and launch the app in the browser.
20. The initial view will load and be replaced by your new splash view.
21. From the web page, you can edit the image control to add the logo. Remember to click the edit button (the action button with the pencil icon).
22. Once the logo image is added, return to design view and set the form as Read-Only to prevent further editing. Do this by hiding the splash view's Action Bar, which will prevent editing in the browser, effectively making the view read-only.

> **NOTE** *Although Blank views, such as the one we used for the splash form, don't have a read-only property, you can take advantage of the fact that most views, by default, can't be edited unless you explicitly click the edit Action button. Removing the Action bar from the view effectively makes it read-only since the user has no way to enter the edit mode.*

DESIGNING AN INDEX FORM

If you've traditionally used an index form to browse records (see Figure 8-4), this is the place where you will need to make a more significant change in your approach. Actually, in a web app, List Views have built-in support for searching, which includes "contains" searching. Furthermore, these views are already optimized to load records only as needed, without requiring users to explicitly request a record or a set of records. In that sense, then, web app views are already very close to our traditional concept of an index form. As you'd expect, however, there are some differences.

We will consider three different kinds of index forms, which you can adapt to your web apps, listed here from simplest to most complex in terms of implementation:

1. List view
2. Summary view
3. Datasheet view

We will look at the functionality they offer without requiring coding on your part and what you can add to each one.

List View: Searching on a field

In a List view, search is based on the field you designate for that purpose. In other words, in a List view for employees, the Search field would be the appropriate key field for employees presented in that view. Figure 8-16 repeats the List view you first saw in Figure 8-3. Notice that the employee name is the Search field for this form. For workflows pertaining to employees, searching on the employee's name is typically all you need to get to the right record and get going on needed operations. As mentioned, the Search box uses "contains" matching, which makes it very flexible and does not require you to code anything beyond assigning the appropriate field in the view. You learned about the List pane and Search box Chapter 3.

For workflows where you perform some kind of browsing or searching, design the form around the most crucial column. The column you choose should reflect the kind of searching your users most often need to do, such as the name of a person or a date of service. With only a single search field available, it's important to consider the choice carefully.

Let's use the Crew Roster view to learn about the relevant components of a form in List view, which make it very suitable for use as an index form.

Start by selecting the Crews tile, as illustrated in Figure 8-17.

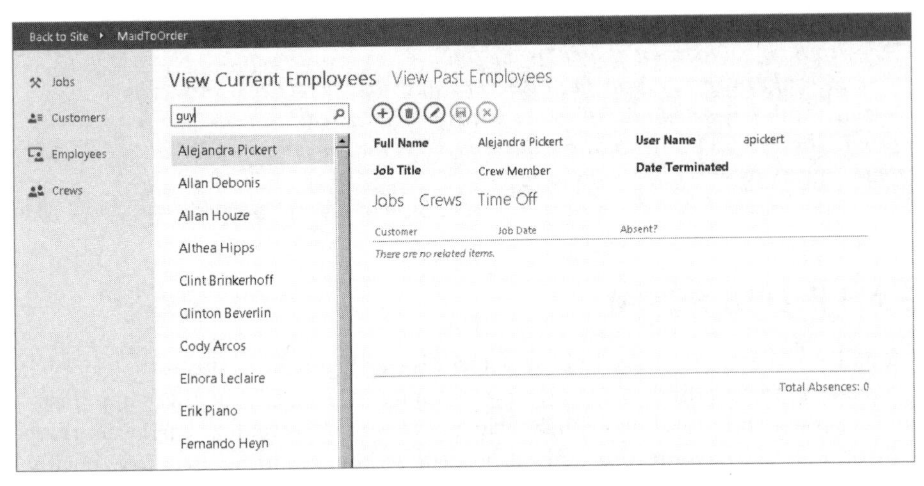

FIGURE 8-16: Web App view functioning as an index form

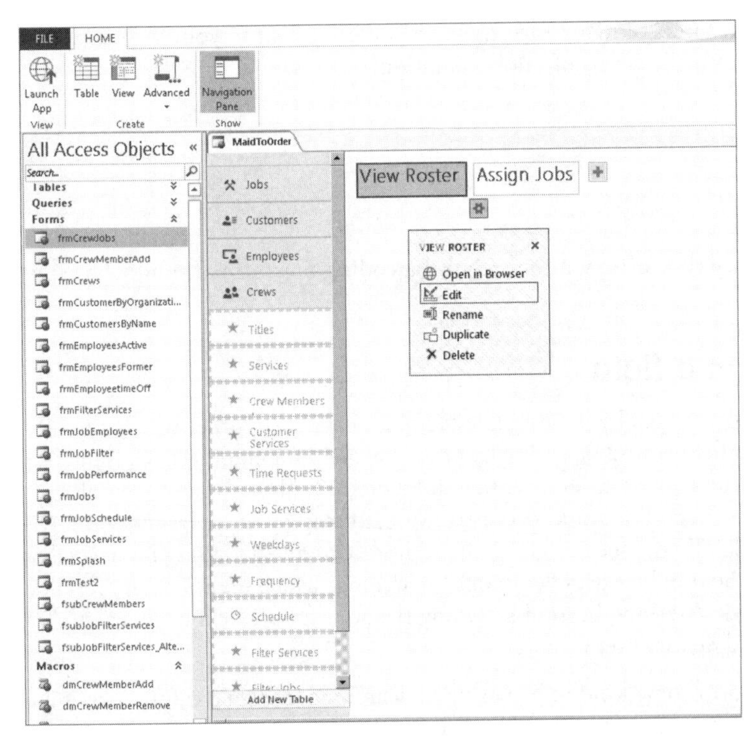

FIGURE 8-17: Select view for editing

The views available for crews include View Roster and Assign Jobs. Clicking the View Roster control reveals the ⚙ popup. Clicking it reveals the shortcut menu from which you will select the Edit option. As you can see in Figure 8-18, the form is loaded into the design surface for editing. The Field List sheet for the table to which the form is linked may also appear.

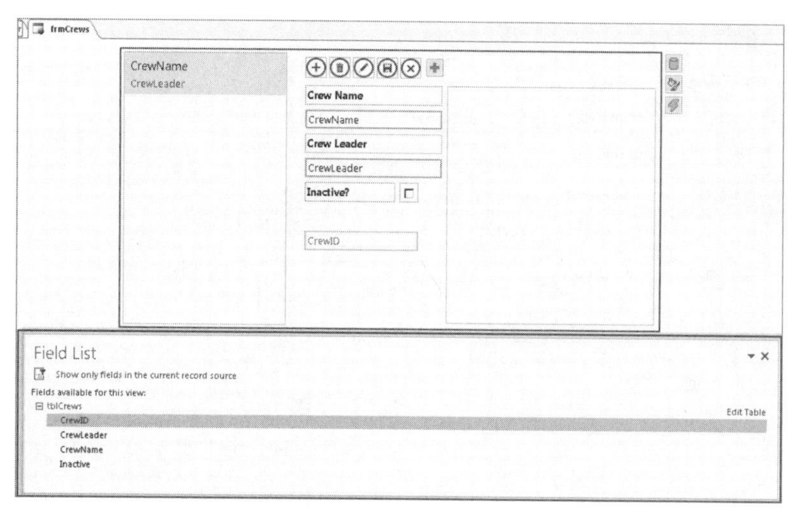

FIGURE 8-18: frmCrews ready for editing with Field List displayed

Because fields in the linked table are added to the view by default, you probably don't need the Field List, so you can dismiss it. Also, if you've previously added fields to the view for editing and are done with that step, you can dismiss the Field List when returning to make further edits.

Access Default Versus Human Intelligence

Access will make its best guess as to which field to use as the Primary Search field in the Search box. Much of the time, you can accept that default, but you should review Access's suggestions to be sure they meet your needs. Compare, for example, the selections in the existing Crew Roster form, called `frmCrews` (see Figure 8-19), with the selections offered in a new view for the same table (see Figure 8-20).

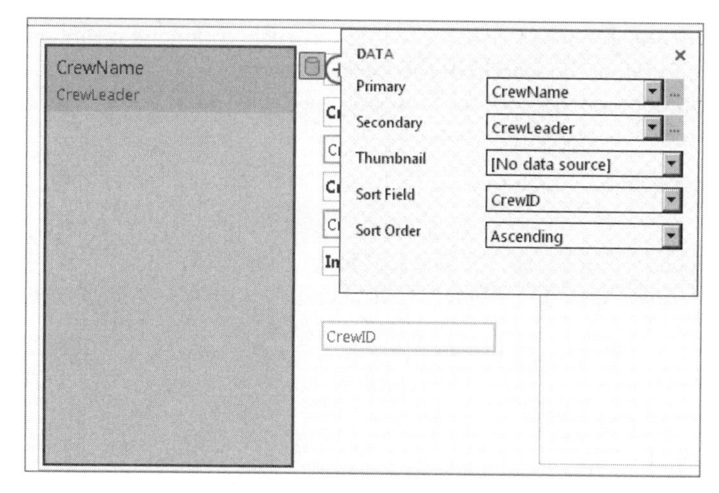

FIGURE 8-19: Search fields selected

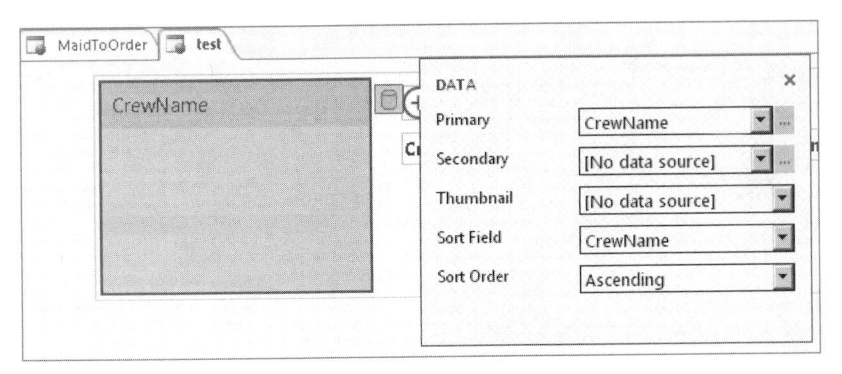

FIGURE 8-20: Search fields suggested

You can see that Access picked `CrewName` for the Search field. If you built the table similar to the way the customer table was built in Chapter 7, you might have defined the Display column as part of Lookup, which could be the `CrewName`. If the Lookup field had `CrewLeader` as the display name instead, Access would default to `CrewLeader` for the search field. You can always change the default field to get the results you need.

Also, you can see that you have the option of providing a Secondary Search field, in this case `CrewLeader`, to provide a more complete search experience. This illustrates once again how your experience as a developer is a crucial part of designing an intuitive, useful interface. Although Access does a great deal of plumbing work behind the scenes, it is still a piece of software without the level of intelligence needed to get the job completely done right.

Designing the Search Field

As you can see in Figure 8-19, the search field in a List view has several components that make it a perfect tool for an index form.

First, it uses a Primary field from the linked table to search existing records. Optionally it can also use a Secondary field from the table to refine the search; in this case, it presents a list of crews and the assigned crew leader. In this situation, having both the crew and the crew leader visible makes it a little easier for users to pick the crew they want to work with.

Second, it allows you to select both a field on which to sort the list and the sort order, ascending or descending.

The search field also supports the inclusion of icons, or images, along with the text name. Our sample application, Maid To Order, doesn't need such images, but Figure 8-21 has a screenshot of a web app that does use them.

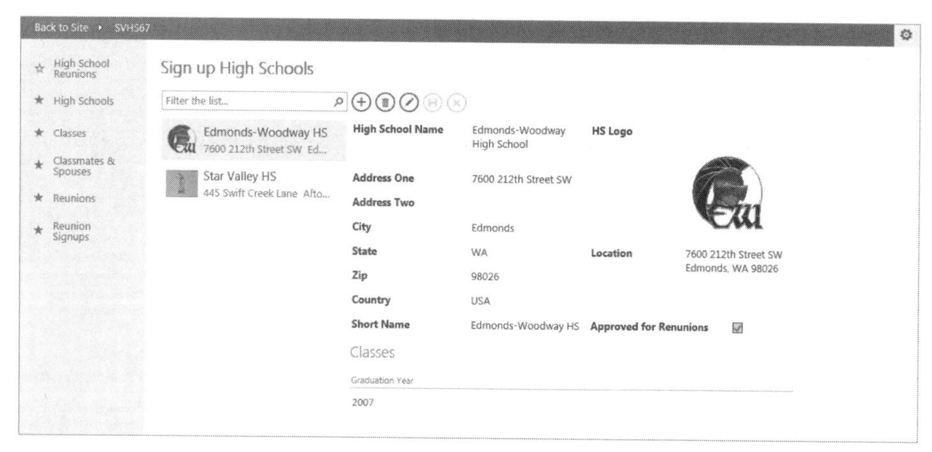

FIGURE 8-21: Icons supporting search terms

Summary View: Searching on an Aggregated Value

Occasionally, you need to find records that are based on some kind of total or a calculation. For example, you might want to identify your most popular products, which task has the highest rate of success, who sold the most items, and so forth. This is where a summary view is useful. While other view types can be based on queries that contain totals, Summary views allow you to view both the summary values and the individual records that contribute to the aggregated output. Furthermore, you can also add a popup view to enable detailed drill-throughs of the individual records, providing your users with a very easy way to assess the components that make up a given total.

The process of building the search list for a Summary view is very much like the process of building the List view so the same design considerations we discussed for List view apply. We will focus on additional considerations that come with choosing the right grouping and calculations.

For Maid To Order, a good use of a Summary view is to look at employees' off hours balance. Every year, Maid To Order allocates a fixed amount of hours for vacation and personal time to employees. To facilitate employees asking for time off, the app provides a view for employees to use when requesting time off, as shown in Figure 8-22.

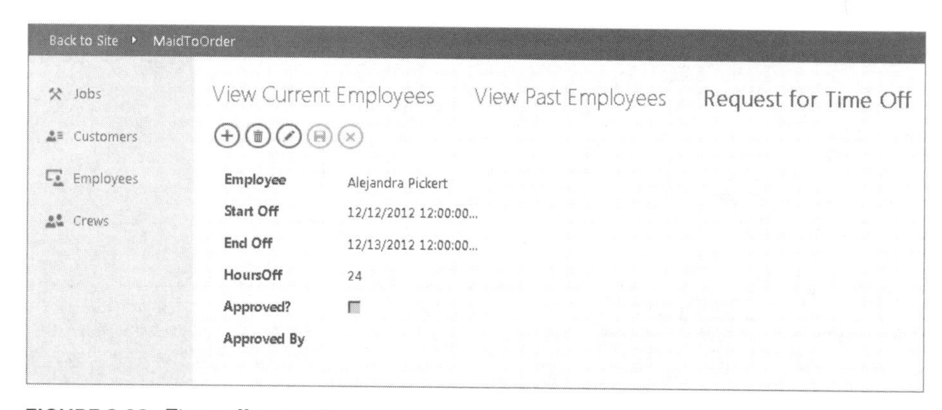

FIGURE 8-22: Time-off request

Managers, therefore, need to be able to quickly see the total hours an employee has requested since their last anniversary date. Having that information is crucial for managers to be able to manage employees' availability.

A new Summary view would provide limited options for its recordsource, as Figure 8-23 indicates.

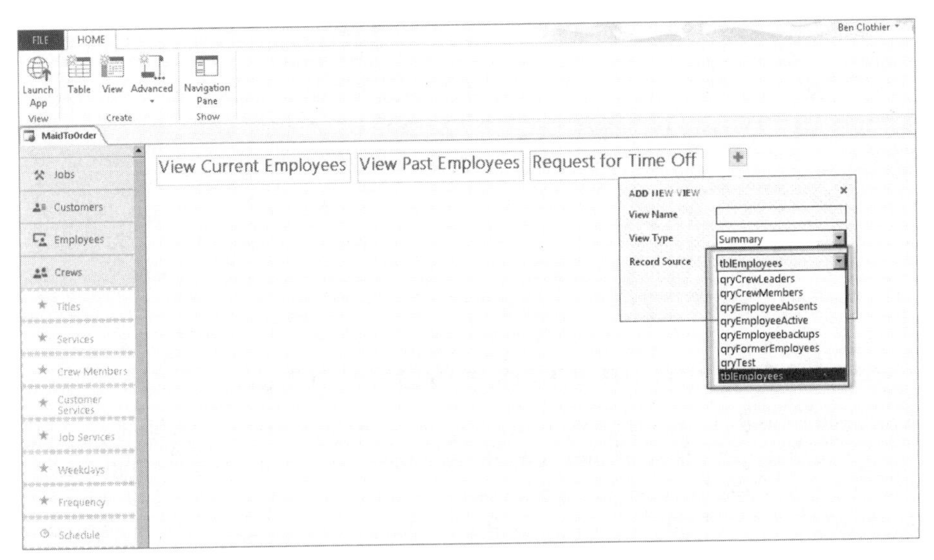

FIGURE 8-23: Available options for a new Summary view's recordsource

Two factors contribute to the limited choices. First, we chose to create a view bound to the Employee tile, which is based on the `tblEmployees` table. Therefore, the recordsource for the Summary view needs to be associated with that table in some way. Second, only queries that include the `tblEmployees` table are listed. However, the table we actually want for this view's recordsource is `tblTimeRequests`. Therefore, we need to create a new query that will join `tblEmployees` to `tblTimeRequests`. Even if we opted to create the Summary view on the tile bound to `tblTimeRequests`, we would need a query to filter the hours to only those within the current year because managers are interested in seeing how many hours have been accrued in a given year.

The query, shown in Figure 8-24, joins all of the information you will need for your new Summary view.

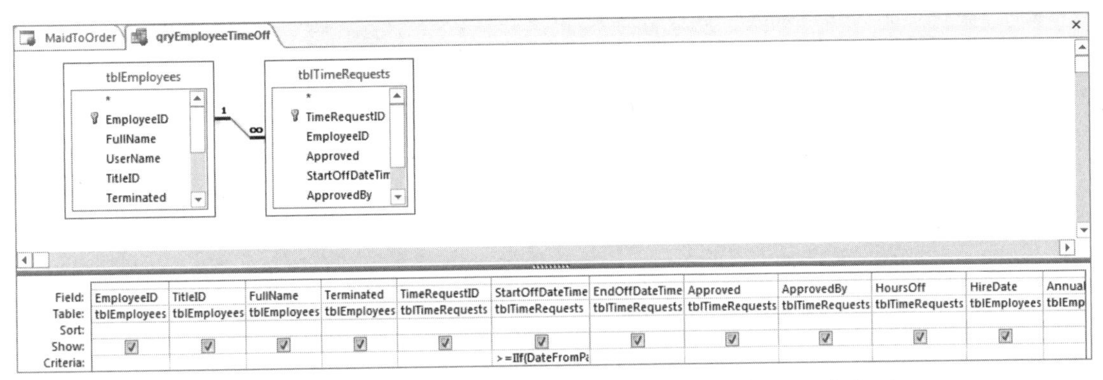

FIGURE 8-24: Query joining tblEmployees and tblTimeRequests and selecting needed columns

The query shown in Figure 8-24 contains a lot of detail that is hard to read, so let's look closer at the criteria you need to add to the query. As mentioned, the query only needs to include time requests within the *current year*, but Maid To Order is not considering a *calendar year*. The query must be based on the year from one anniversary date to the next for each employee, and that is based on the employee's hire date. Each employee could have a different anniversary date and, therefore, their time requests could be included or excluded on different dates. Because an anniversary date could fall anywhere in the calendar year, you need to check whether the filter needs to be based on the current year's anniversary date or the previous year's date, depending on whether you've already passed an employee's anniversary date in the current year. In other words, if today is the 12th of August and the employee's anniversary date is August 1, the filter is based on the current year going forward because the anniversary date has passed. If the employee's anniversary date is August 30, the filter is based on the previous year going back because the anniversary date has not yet passed.

Figure 8-25 shows how you can build the expression via the builder to describe this complex criteria.

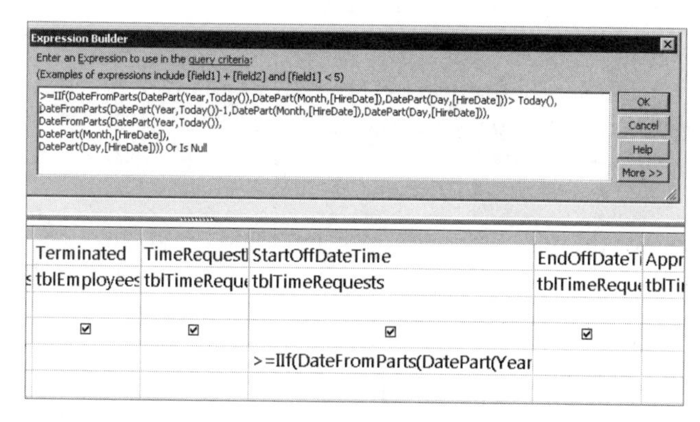

FIGURE 8-25: Expression Builder with criteria checking employees' anniversary dates

Here's the full expression so you can read it more easily:

```
    [tblTimeRequests].[StartOffDateTime] >= IIf(
      DateFromParts(
        DatePart(Year,Today()),
        DatePart(Month, [HireDate]),
        DatePart(Day, [HireDate])
      )>Today(), DateFromParts(
        DatePart(Year,Today())-1,
        DatePart(Month, [HireDate]),
        DatePart(Day, [HireDate])
      ), DateFromParts(
        DatePart(Year,Today()),
        DatePart(Month, [HireDate]),
        DatePart(Day, [HireDate])
      )
) Or [tblTimeRequests].[StartOffDateTime] Is Null
```

SARGABILITY AND EXPRESSIONS

You may notice the expression shown in Figure 8-25 is not necessarily the most optimized expression possible because we're doing calculations on a field that is not sargable. As you probably know, nonsargable queries can degrade performance. In this case, the number of employees and time requests are relatively small, so that may not be a concern. In a table with many more records, such as `tblJobs`, you may want to consider alternatives that can be optimized.

One possible performance enhancement you can add is a hard filter of `tblTimeRequests.StartDateTimeOff >= DateAdd(Year, -1, Today())` to restrict all time requests only to a one year period from today because no anniversary date can be more than a year away. Because that expression resolves to a static date, both the SQL Server and Access database engines are able to evaluate the filter using the static date first, and then scan the remainder using the original anniversary expression. This is relatively better than requiring it to scan the whole `tblTimeRequests` and testing if `StartOffDateTime` is later than the last anniversary date.

Another option is to add a calculated column to `tblEmployees` that provides the current anniversary date and index on it, simplifying the query. This is another area where your past Access experience will be an asset in designing good queries.

Save the query as `qryEmployeeTimeOff`. Once the appropriate query is built and saved, you can then return to the parent tile and add a new Summary view using the new query, as in Figure 8-26.

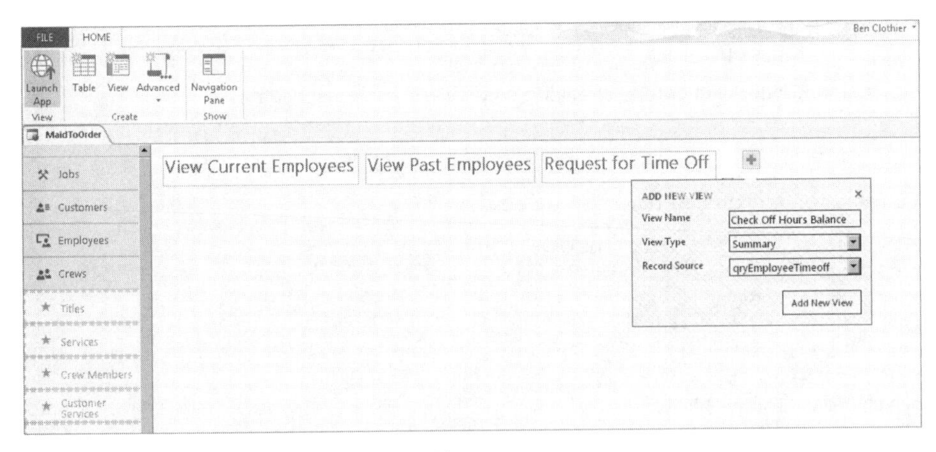

FIGURE 8-26: Creating a Summary view with a query

As with a List view, Access will attempt to guess what you want for your list pane and display. As you saw in Chapter 4, a Summary view looks somewhat similar to a Related Item control and you cannot add controls directly to it; you can only tell Access which fields you want displayed in the main area. Figures 8-27 and 8-28 show how Access set up the list pane and the main body, respectively.

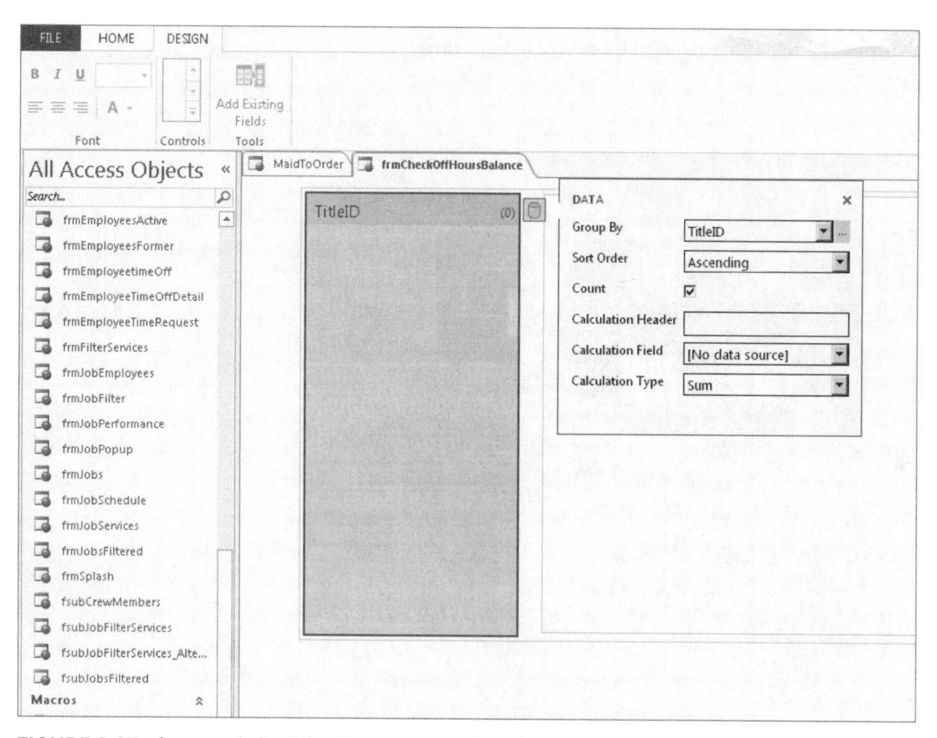

FIGURE 8-27: Access default for the summary list plane

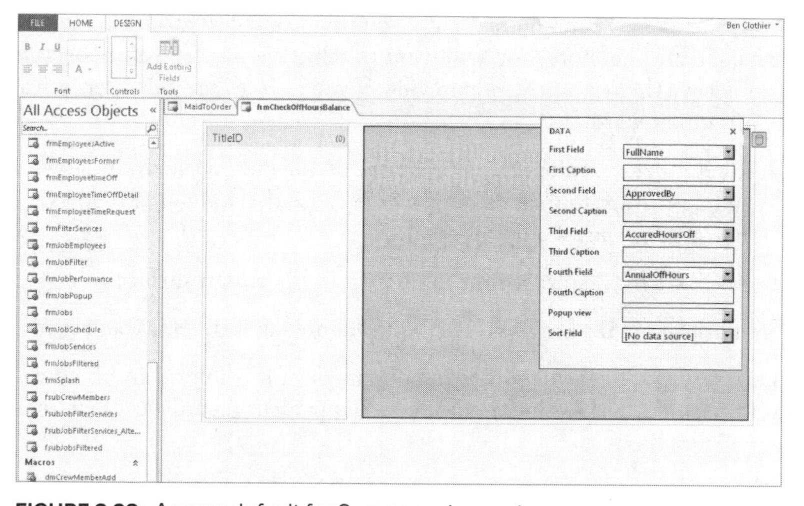

FIGURE 8-28: Access default for Summary view main area

As discussed in Chapter 4, on List views, this is also where you may want to revise the view to better suit the goals for the app. Because the goal here is to report on employees' accrued off hours since their last anniversary date, you'll use the employee's name as the grouping column and their accrued hours will be the calculated field using `Sum` as the expression. Figure 8-29 shows how you will set up the summary list pane to get the results you want.

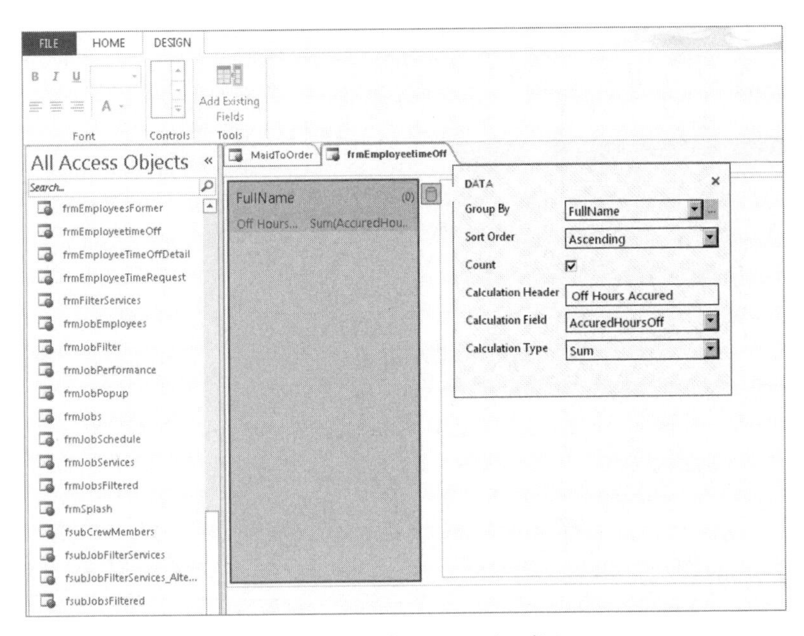

FIGURE 8-29: Selected fields for the Summary view list pane

Summary view allows only four fields in the main area, but also provide a facility to open a popup view just like the related item control. Therefore, you will want to select the four most important columns for the main area, and leave the rest to the popup view if you need to provide users a way to drill through for more details on a record.

You also need to be sure not to repeat the employee's name on the detail since it's already shown on the List pane. However, you might want to include off hours because the main area reports individual records whereas the List pane shows only the total.

Figure 8-30 shows a possible selection for display on the main area in the design surface.

Figure 8-31 shows this view as it displays in the browser. The four fields are numbered for your reference.

The last piece of the Summary view you'll learn about is the popup view. It is important to note that popup view selection is also restricted to views that are bound to equivalent recordsources in their parent view, as you can see in Figure 8-32.

Generally speaking, it's simplest to have the popup view use the same recordsource as its parent view so you would probably create a new blank view based on the same query, add the remainder of the fields missing from the Summary view, and provide a caption, as Figure 8-33 illustrates.

Do not expect to be able to edit the records even in a popup view. It's best to think of a Summary view and its popup view as an interactive report and use a separate view to edit the records. Even so, the capability to drill through is new to Access and we feel that this is very useful for many situations where users will ask, "Okay, what is this total made of?"

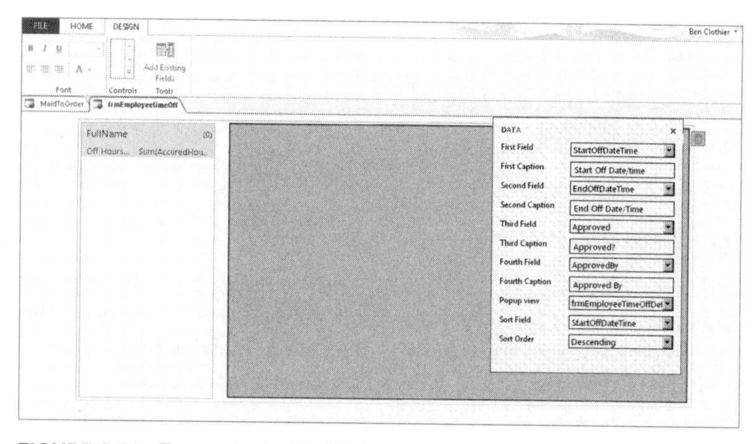

FIGURE 8-30: Four selected fields for Summary view main area

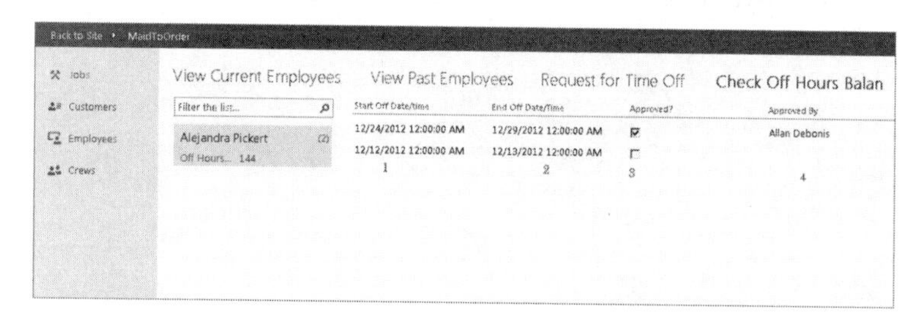

FIGURE 8-31: Summary view main area displayed

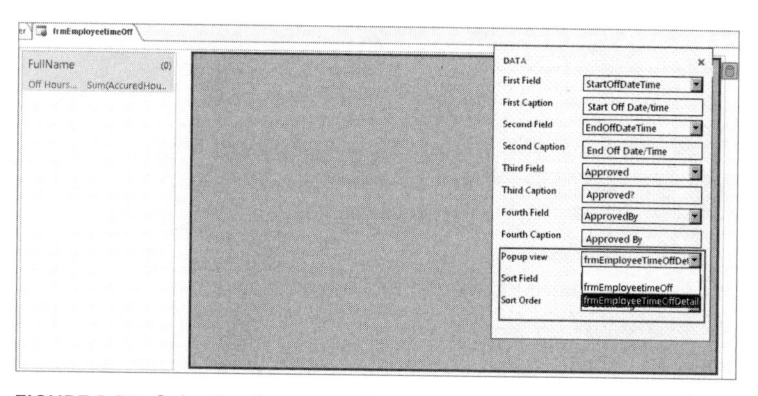

FIGURE 8-32: Selection for popup views

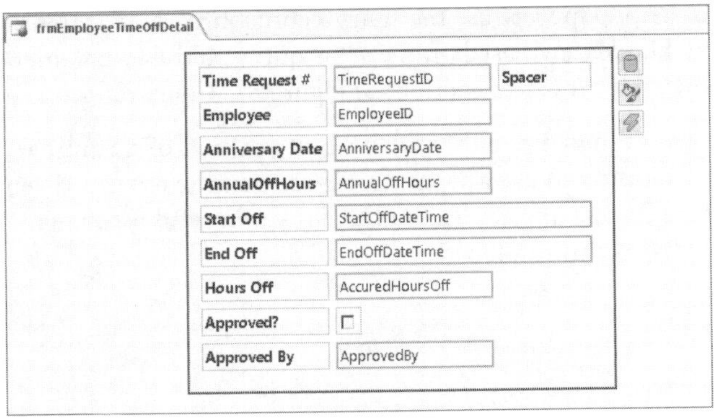

FIGURE 8-33: Popup view for Time Request details

Datasheet: Filtering Cumulatively

If you find that a single field, aggregated or not, is not adequate for comprehensive browsing in a particular situation, you may want to consider using the Datasheet view. Like their client counterparts, Datasheet views come with several filtering and sorting options built-in, as demonstrated in Figure 8-34. The list is about to be filtered on Organization name.

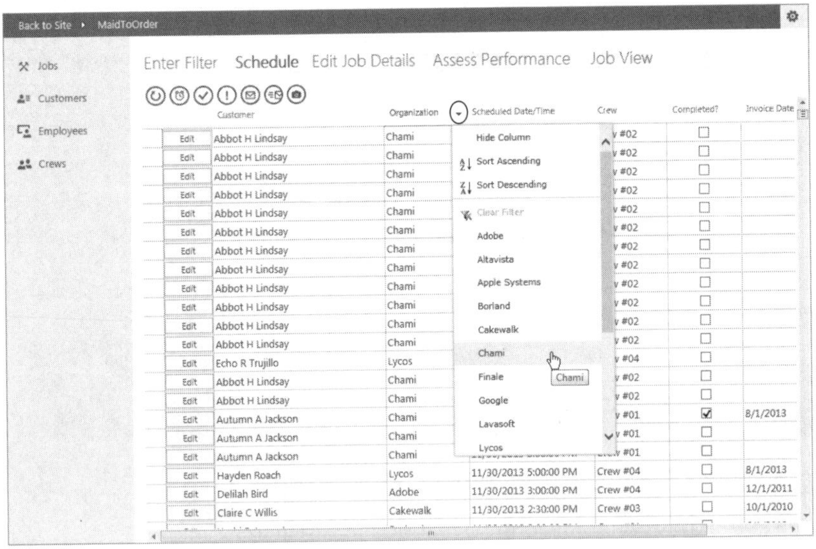

FIGURE 8-34: Schedule datasheet with right-click menu displayed

As shown in Figure 8-35, you can add more filtering by selecting additional columns and selecting other filter criteria — the Crew assigned to the job — which adds to the previously set criteria.

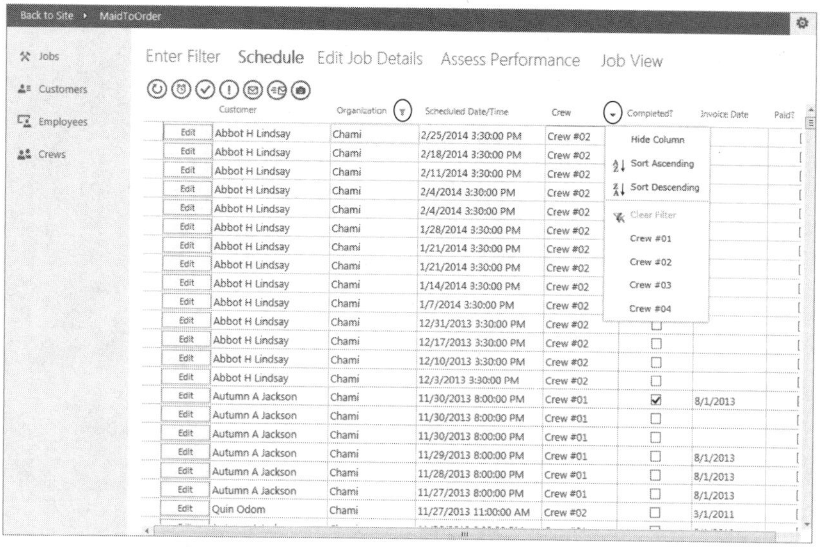

FIGURE 8-35: Adding second criteria to the datasheet with a filter already applied

This approach provides a very easy way to give users more complex filter criteria. Note, however, that all filter criteria can only be exact matches; there is no facility for wildcard matching on multiple columns. Furthermore, Figure 8-35 shows where an excessive number of possible values, such as the dates and times for scheduled jobs, may be problematic for filtering on the datasheet.

You can increase flexibility by adding custom action buttons on the schedule view to provide some common filtering options. For example, recognizing the difficulty of filtering by date and time for jobs, you could provide employees with an action button to filter the list to show only today's jobs. With that much smaller list, employees can more easily apply their own additional filtering. As Figure 8-36 shows, we provided an action button that will apply a static filter of `tblJobs.ScheduleDate=Today()` to the schedule List view.

Even though the filter itself is hard-coded, the results will change day-to-day, which makes it very well-suited as a custom Action Bar button.

Filtered Lists in Drop-Downs

Be aware, however, that filtering via action bars does not reduce the number of values available on any of the datasheet's filter drop-downs. Look at the date and time list in the filtered datasheet view in Figure 8-37. The list has been filtered to today's date, but all other dates are still available to be selected.

Thus, a datasheet provides you with a quick way to give your users a wide range of filtering choices with little or no coding on your part. However, when the range of choices is large and users need more than just exact matches, it's a good time to start looking at the query by view approach.

Back to Site • MaidToOrder

Jobs
Customers
Employees
Crews

Enter Filter Schedule Edit Job Details Assess Performance Job View

Show today's job

	Customer	Organization	Scheduled Date/Time	Crew	Completed?
Edit	Abbot H Lindsay	Chami	2/25/2014 3:30:00 PM	Crew #02	☐
Edit	Abbot H Lindsay	Chami	2/18/2014 3:30:00 PM	Crew #02	☐
Edit	Abbot H Lindsay	Chami	2/11/2014 3:30:00 PM	Crew #02	☐
Edit	Abbot H Lindsay	Chami	2/4/2014 3:30:00 PM	Crew #02	☐
Edit	Abbot H Lindsay	Chami	2/4/2014 3:30:00 PM	Crew #02	☐
Edit	Abbot H Lindsay	Chami	1/28/2014 3:30:00 PM	Crew #02	☐
Edit	Abbot H Lindsay	Chami	1/21/2014 3:30:00 PM	Crew #02	☐
Edit	Abbot H Lindsay	Chami	1/21/2014 3:30:00 PM	Crew #02	☐
Edit	Abbot H Lindsay	Chami	1/14/2014 3:30:00 PM	Crew #02	☐
Edit	Abbot H Lindsay	Chami	1/7/2014 3:30:00 PM	Crew #02	☐
Edit	Abbot H Lindsay	Chami	12/31/2013 3:30:00 PM	Crew #02	☐
Edit	Abbot H Lindsay	Chami	12/17/2013 3:30:00 PM	Crew #02	☐
Edit	Echo R Trujillo	Lycos	12/12/2013 3:00:00 PM	Crew #04	☐
Edit	Abbot H Lindsay	Chami	12/10/2013 3:30:00 PM	Crew #02	☐
Edit	Abbot H Lindsay	Chami	12/3/2013 3:30:00 PM	Crew #02	☐
Edit	Autumn A Jackson	Chami	11/30/2013 8:00:00 PM	Crew #01	☑
Edit	Autumn A Jackson	Chami	11/30/2013 8:00:00 PM	Crew #01	☐
Edit	Autumn A Jackson	Chami	11/30/2013 8:00:00 PM	Crew #01	☐
Edit	Hayden Roach	Lycos	11/30/2013 5:00:00 PM	Crew #04	☐
Edit	Delilah Bird	Adobe	11/30/2013 3:00:00 PM	Crew #04	☐
Edit	Claire C Willis	Cakewalk	11/30/2013 2:30:00 PM	Crew #03	☐

FIGURE 8-36: Additional filter under a custom action button

Back to Site • MaidToOrder

Jobs
Customers
Employees
Crews

Enter Filter Schedule Edit Job Details Assess Performance Job View

	Customer	Organization	Scheduled Date/Time	Crew	Completed?	Invoice Date
Edit	Autumn A Jackson	Chami	11/30/2013 8:00:00 PM			8/1/2013
Edit	Autumn A Jackson	Chami	11/30/2013 8:00:00 PM			
Edit	Autumn A Jackson	Chami	11/30/2013 8:00:00 PM			
Edit	Autumn A Jackson	Chami	11/29/2013 8:00:00 PM			8/1/2013
Edit	Autumn A Jackson	Chami	11/28/2013 8:00:00 PM			8/1/2013
Edit	Autumn A Jackson	Chami	11/27/2013 8:00:00 PM			8/1/2013
Edit	Autumn A Jackson	Chami	11/26/2013 8:00:00 PM			8/1/2013
Edit	Autumn A Jackson	Chami	11/25/2013 8:00:00 PM			8/1/2013
Edit	Ava N Yang	Chami	11/25/2013 10:00:00 AM			5/1/2011
Edit	Autumn A Jackson	Chami	11/24/2013 8:00:00 PM			8/1/2013
Edit	Autumn A Jackson	Chami	11/23/2013 8:00:00 PM			8/1/2013
Edit	Autumn A Jackson	Chami	11/22/2013 8:00:00 PM			8/1/2013
Edit	Autumn A Jackson	Chami	11/21/2013 8:00:00 PM			8/1/2013
Edit	Autumn A Jackson	Chami	11/20/2013 8:00:00 PM			8/1/2013
Edit	Autumn A Jackson	Chami	11/19/2013 8:00:00 PM			8/1/2013
Edit	Autumn A Jackson	Chami	11/18/2013 8:00:00 PM			8/1/2013
Edit	Autumn A Jackson	Chami	11/17/2013 8:00:00 PM			8/1/2013
Edit	Autumn A Jackson	Chami	11/16/2013 8:00:00 PM			8/1/2013
Edit	Autumn A Jackson	Chami	11/15/2013 8:00:00 PM	Crew #01		
Edit	Eagan Irwin	Chami	11/15/2013 2:30:00 PM	Crew #01	☐	2/1/2013
Edit	Autumn A Jackson	Chami	11/14/2013 8:00:00 PM	Crew #01	☐	8/1/2013

Hide Column
Sort Ascending
Sort Descending
Clear Filter
1/8/2010 4:30:00 PM
1/9/2010 4:30:00 PM
1/10/2010 4:30:00 PM
1/11/2010 4:30:00 PM
1/12/2010 4:30:00 PM
1/13/2010 4:30:00 PM
1/14/2010 4:30:00 PM
1/15/2010 4:30:00 PM
1/15/2010 5:30:00 PM
1/16/2010 4:30:00 PM
1/16/2010 4:30:00 PM

FIGURE 8-37: Full list of choices available in the Filter drop-down

Handling Filter Limitations on Datasheet Views

To put the query by view approach in context in web apps in perspective, let's look at some considerations you must take into account when designing Datasheet views, notably the difference in controls and programmability that are available on a Datasheet view. You will see what controls and techniques cannot be used in a Datasheet view and how to select appropriate columns.

The following controls are not available on a Datasheet view:

- Label
- Web browser
- Image
- Hyperlink
- Subview
- Related item

Note that you can work around the exclusion of labels and hyperlinks by using textboxes or buttons, formatted appropriately. We think that for the most part you would expect these controls to be excluded for the datasheet layout anyway.

On the other hand, you can use a popup view, which could contain the excluded controls. You can open the popup via a button on the datasheet, or use the ChangeView macro action to switch to a List or Blank view and filter it to the current row in the datasheet.

With those limitations and options of the Datasheet view in mind, we need to consider the difference in programmability between the different views.

First, on a Datasheet view, the After Update event is not available on any controls, which would have that event in any other kind of view. Thus, certain controls such as checkboxes and combo boxes will have no events to which you can attach a macro. Buttons and textboxes support the `Click` event, which you can continue to use in a datasheet view.

Next, the SetProperty macro action will generally not work for any kind of controls on a datasheet, with the exception of setting the value of Textbox controls. In effect, the layout of a Datasheet view is totally static. If you need to be able to toggle the visibility of a control, change formatting and so forth at run time, then you need to use a different view, such as the List view.

Let's look at how you can build the Schedule datasheet. You'll follow two previously discussed design principles: providing custom action buttons to provide additional filtering options and creating an Edit button to provide an easy way to get to the detail, which then can be edited.

Because you need some data from other tables, you need to base the Schedule datasheet on a query. Figure 8-38 shows the query, `qryJobsScheduled`, which is the recordsource for the Schedule datasheet.

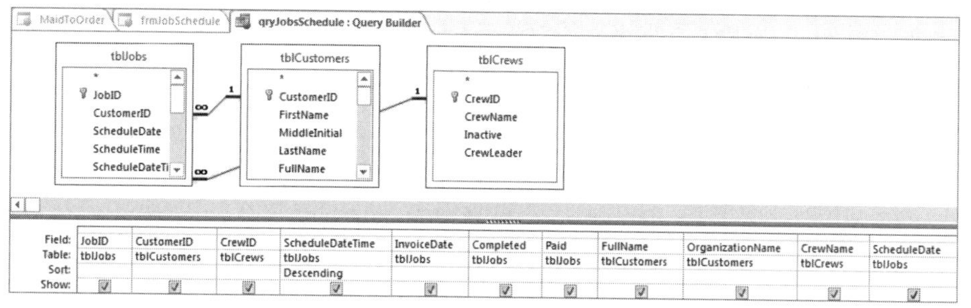

FIGURE 8-38: Query for Schedule datasheet's recordsource

In the Schedule datasheet view, you need to include the `JobID` field in order to enable the Edit button's functionality. However, the user doesn't need to see the `JobID` field. Thus, you will add the `JobID` field to the query and then hide it in the view, as shown in Figure 8-39.

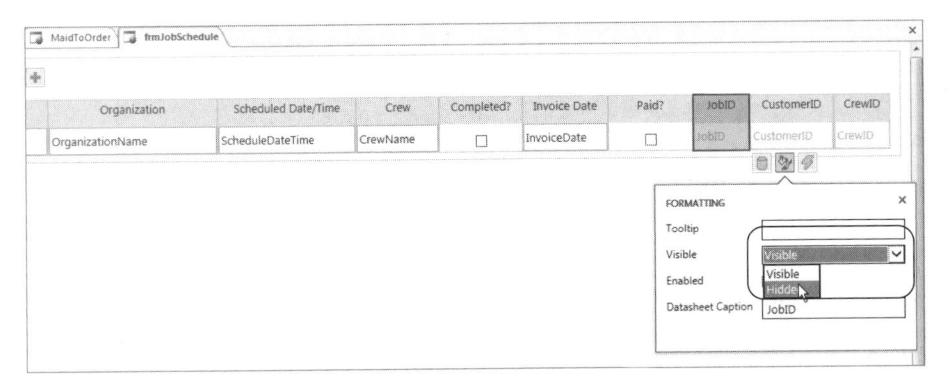

FIGURE 8-39: Hiding JobID field

Because this is meant to be an index form, which is typically read-only, you would tick the `Read Only` checkbox shown in the Figure 8-40.

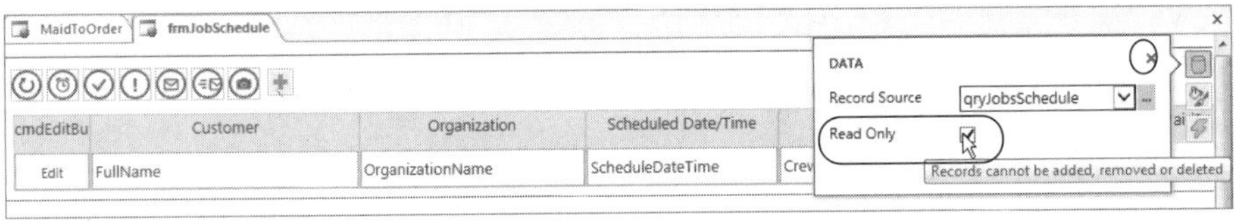

FIGURE 8-40: Making the view read-only

> **NOTE** *As you previously learned, most views don't have a read-only property, but the Datasheet view does. That's because values in Datasheet views can otherwise be edited without using an edit Action button. So, the view itself has the read-only property available.*

Next, let's look at managing the Action Bar. Because you made the form read-only, you no longer need the two default action buttons for adding and deleting records. Delete them, and then add a custom set of action buttons. Figures 8-41 and 8-42 show how default action buttons can be deleted and custom buttons added.

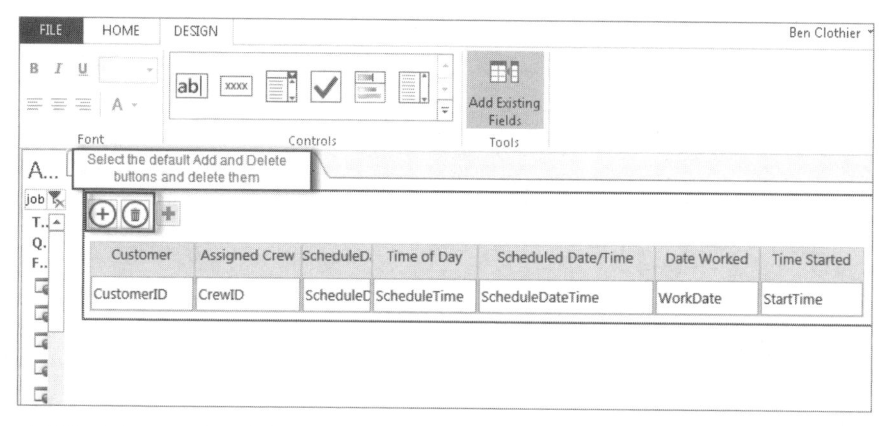

FIGURE 8-41: Deleting default action buttons

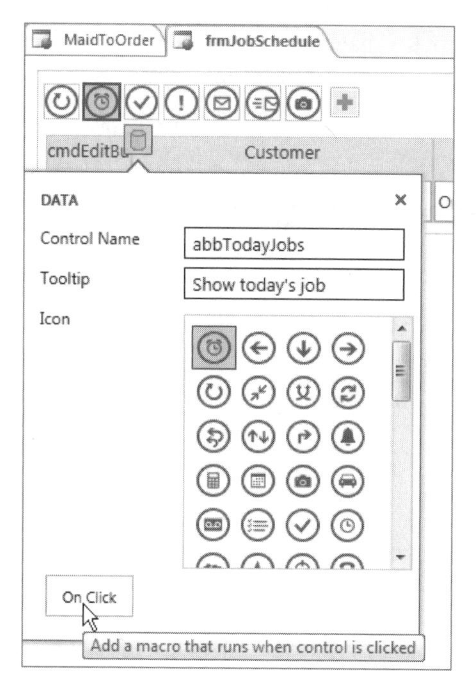

FIGURE 8-42: Adding custom action buttons

> **WARNING** *Modifying the default action buttons on the action bar is a one-way street. Once removed, they can't be added back. The only way to restore default action buttons is to delete the view and recreate a new view with a new action bar.*

Click the menu beside the action bar to open the action button menu, as shown in Figure 8-42.

When the action button menu opens, you can rename the action button, select an appropriate icon from the palette, and add the macro action for the action button's On Click event.

You can use Action Bar buttons to filter records, each with different criteria, so the macro content of each Action Bar's Click event is very similar. Let's look at the Click event handler for the Today action button shown in Figure 8-43.

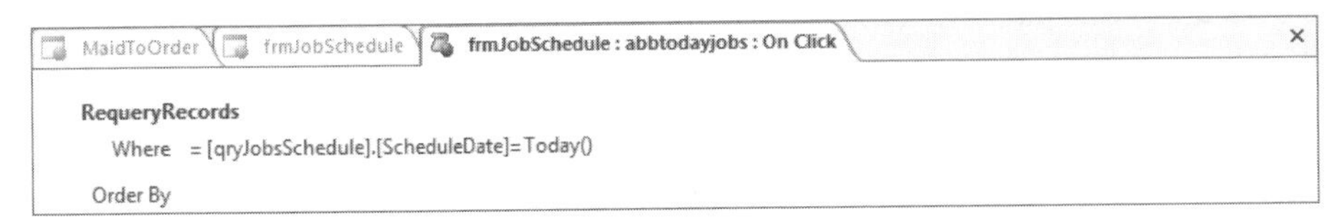
MaidToOrder
frmJobSchedule
frmJobSchedule : abbtodayjobs : On Click
RequeryRecords
Where = [qryJobsSchedule].[ScheduleDate]=Today()
Order By

FIGURE 8-43: Today action button click event handler

As you may expect, the only macro action needed is RequeryRecords, which provides an input of `[qryJobsScheduled].[ScheduleDate]=Today()` to the Where clause.

Assuming that you've already applied the appropriate filters for the rest of your custom action buttons, you can move onto the Edit button. Figure 8-44 shows the Edit button in the web app.

Again, the event handler behind the Edit button is quite straightforward, as you can see in Figure 8-45.

Back to Site ▸ MaidToOrder

Jobs
Customers
Employees
Crews

Enter Filter Schedule Edit Job Details Assess Performance Job View

	Customer	Organization	Scheduled Date/Time	Crew	Completed?
Edit	Venus Paul	Macromedia	6/9/2013 7:30:00 PM	Crew #03	☐
Edit	Justine N Emerson	Sibelius	6/9/2013 3:30:00 PM	Crew #03	☐
Edit	Delilah Bird	Adobe	6/9/2013 3:00:00 PM	Crew #04	☐
Edit	Yoshi R Acevedo	Borland	6/9/2013 2:00:00 PM	Crew #01	☐
Edit	Keaton V Holder	Cakewalk	6/9/2013 1:30:00 PM	Crew #04	☐
Edit	Cody Vazquez	Sibelius	6/9/2013 1:30:00 PM	Crew #04	☐

FIGURE 8-44: Edit action button in web app

MaidToOrder | frmJobSchedule | frmJobSchedule : cmdedit : On Click

ChangeView
Table tblJobs
View frmJobsEdit
Where = [qryJobs].[JobID]=[txtJobID]
Order By

FIGURE 8-45: Edit button click event handler

For this situation, we used the ChangeView action to move to a detail view and filter it to the same `JobID`, which is made available via the hidden control (refer back to Figure 8-39). Note that although we chose to use ChangeView here, you may have a scenario where the OpenPopup macro action would be a preferred solution. We chose ChangeView to guarantee that no requery on the original view will be needed after closing the popup view.

CREATING A QUERY BY VIEW

So far, we've reviewed the built-in options and simple approaches that provide your users a wide variety of navigation and filtering. We expect that for the bulk of your applications, these will be time-saving tools on your tool belt. However, just as a toolbox will never be complete if it's missing a hammer, we need to revisit our good old mainstay of Access programming — the query by form technique.

We will start with a review of the changes to SQL construction in web apps and then discuss how you can use macros and parameters to transmit complex filter criteria. We will then wrap up with a discussion of more advanced topics such as filtering on a related table and using tables to store filter results.

SQL Construction

Even though you only have macros to work with in web apps, you will be pleasantly surprised to find that you can build powerful query by views once you understand a few key points in your design. Let's start with SQL. As mentioned earlier in our discussion, a typical Access query by form would usually employ dynamic SQL, which was just a string assembled in VBA and submitted to the database engine (which may not necessarily be the Access database engine) to collect the matches, as demonstrated in Figure 8-46, taken from the Northwinds database.

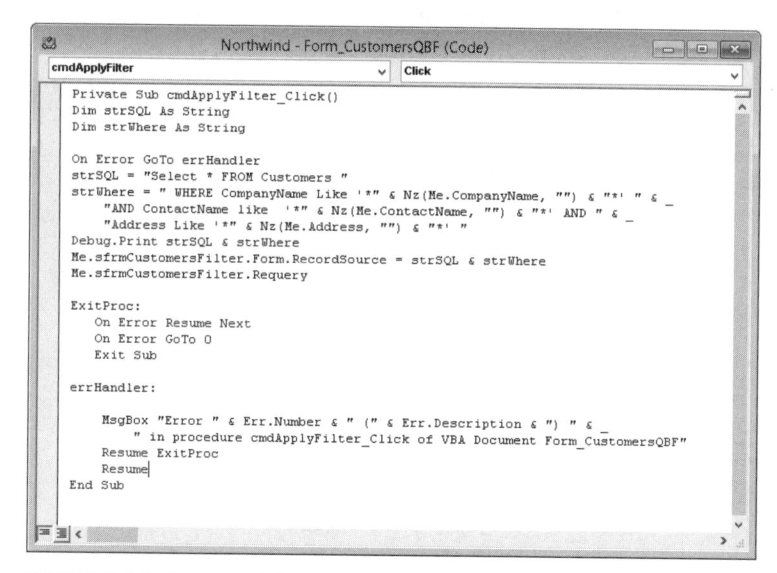

FIGURE 8-46: Dynamic SQL built in VBA

Partially because the Access database engine cannot execute multiple SQL statements and partially because an Access application is relatively isolated in comparison to a web application, this practice is far more common in Access databases, but in the context of web development, this practice is eschewed. The threat of SQL injection is ever present and you must guard against it, especially now that Access web apps are on a website. Consequently, Microsoft has designed various macro actions that contain Where clauses and Order By clauses to parameterize the SQL you will use. Refer back to the Where clause in Figure 8-45, where you see no dynamic strings at all.

SQL INJECTION?

SQL injection is a common threat against some big iron databases. Malicious users can issue arbitrary SQL commands by breaking out of the string concatenation that application code performs. It is arguably the number one reason why you should not concatenate SQL strings but use parameters instead. Access database engines cannot execute multiple statements so the usual approach of terminating a string and then appending an additional SQL statement to insert arbitrary SQL commands, followed by comments, will not work against Access. Even so, it is not immune to variants where a string is terminated and an expression inserted. Because Access web apps use SQL Server and are available online, this is a very important issue for you to understand and to account for.

It may be more useful to look at Figure 8-45 in very much the same way as you should look at what is typical in a SQL Server stored procedure. By using parameters as inputs to a stored procedure, you do not need to concatenate a number of strings together to form a SQL statement; you just write the SQL directly using the parameters. Figure 8-47 illustrates how SQL Server embeds the parameter in the stored procedure definition and expects calling code to pass a value as a parameter.

Some of you may be also familiar with the way Access allows parameters in queries, as shown in Figure 8-48; the parameter opens a small dialog box when the query runs. For various reasons, ranging from lack of ease of use to inconsistent performance, most seasoned Access developers have largely shunned this approach.

```
ALTER PROCEDURE [HumanResources].[uspUpdateEmployeeHireInfo]
    @BusinessEntityID [int],
    @JobTitle [nvarchar](50),
    @HireDate [datetime],
    @RateChangeDate [datetime],
    @Rate [money],
    @PayFrequency [tinyint],
    @CurrentFlag [dbo].[Flag]
WITH EXECUTE AS CALLER
AS
BEGIN
    SET NOCOUNT ON;

    BEGIN TRY
        BEGIN TRANSACTION;

        UPDATE [HumanResources].[Employee]
        SET [JobTitle] = @JobTitle
            ,[HireDate] = @HireDate
            ,[CurrentFlag] = @CurrentFlag
        WHERE [BusinessEntityID] = @BusinessEntityID;

        INSERT INTO [HumanResources].[EmployeePayHistory]
            ([BusinessEntityID]
            ,[RateChangeDate]
            ,[Rate]
            ,[PayFrequency])
        VALUES (@BusinessEntityID, @RateChangeDate, @Rate, @PayFrequency);

        COMMIT TRANSACTION;
    END TRY
    BEGIN CATCH
        -- Rollback any active or uncommittable transactions before
```

FIGURE 8-47: A typical SQL Server stored procedure with parameters

```
PARAMETERS
  [Beginning Date] DateTime,
  [Ending Date] DateTime
;
SELECT DISTINCTROW
  Employees.Country,
  Employees.LastName,
  Employees.FirstName,
  Orders.ShippedDate,
  Orders.OrderID,
  [Order Subtotals].Subtotal AS SaleAmount
FROM Employees
INNER JOIN (
    Orders
    INNER JOIN [Order Subtotals]
      ON Orders.OrderID = [Order Subtotals].OrderID
) ON Employees.EmployeeID = Orders.EmployeeID
WHERE Orders.ShippedDate Between [Beginning Date] And [Ending Date];
```

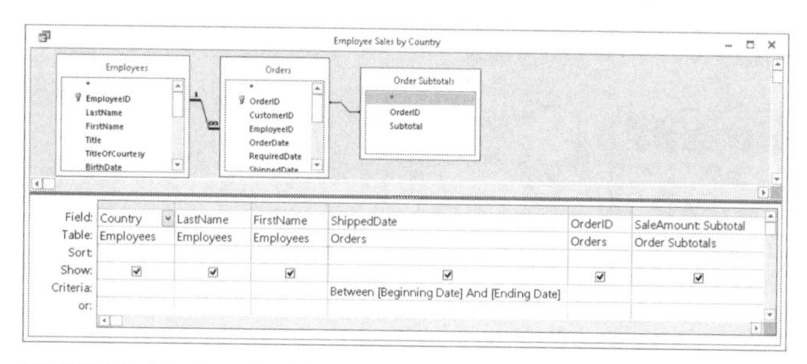

FIGURE 8-48: A typical Access query with parameters

Both Access queries with parameters and parameters passed to SQL Server stored procedures are conceptually similar to how you should treat the input in a macro action in a web app where SQL code is expected. Attempting to pass in a string representing a SQL snippet to a web macro, as in Figure 8-49, will fail because the string is not treated as a SQL statement, but rather as an input to a parameter.

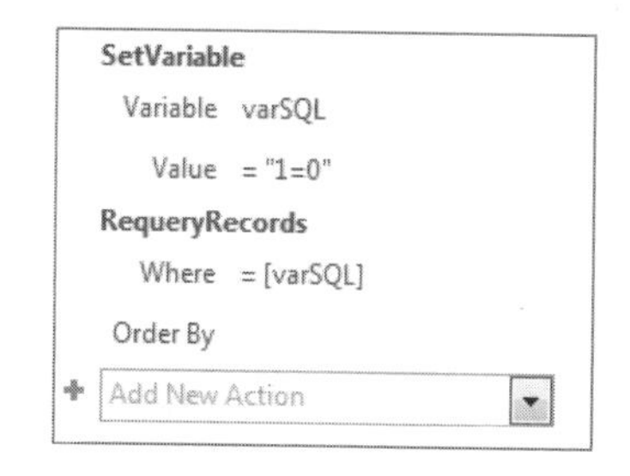

FIGURE 8-49: Passing in a string variable to a macro Where Clause results in errors

Therefore, you will need to modify your usual approach of writing dynamic SQL as a string and get used to writing SQL using parameters. You'll get used to using parameters liberally all over your applications. In doing so, you gain the advantages of being able to strong-type your input values and move away from complications arising from handling strings within strings, delimiting literals, and so forth.

Parameterized queries continue to exist in Access web apps and, as Figures 8-50 and 8-51 show, you can add parameters to a query.

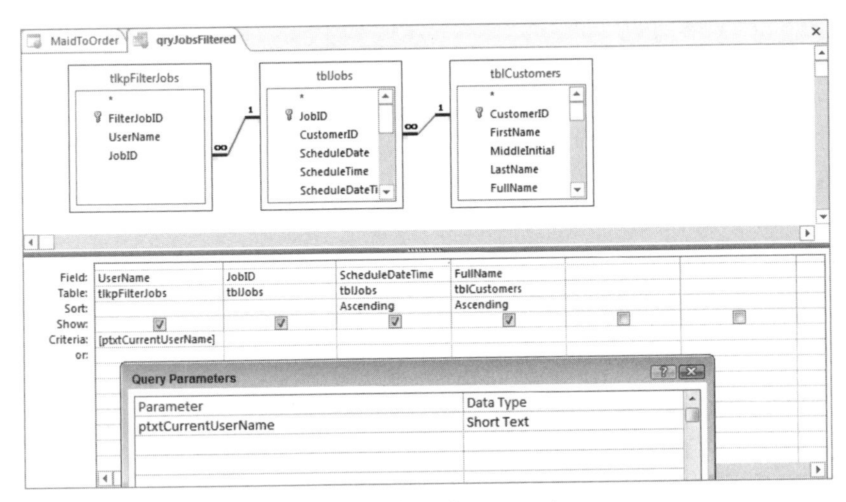

FIGURE 8-50: A parameterized query in an Access web app query

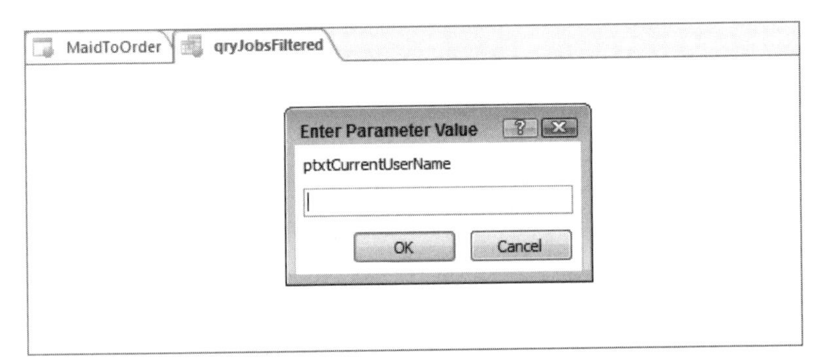

FIGURE 8-51: A parameter dialog box for an Access web app query

This provides you with additional options that may not be practical for those cases where you need to pass parameters via a Where clause argument in a macro action. For example, Where clauses are typically restricted to only 255 characters. No such restriction exists inside the query itself. Therefore, you could pass in a large number of parameters to a query that would far exceed the 255-character limitation for a Where clause.

However, as we alluded to earlier in this book, you are limited in how you can use a parameterized view. A tile-bound view cannot have a parameterized query as its recordsource because there is no means for passing the parameters to a view's recordsource.

However, you certainly can pass in parameters to a popup view via an OpenPopup action, as Figure 8-52 demonstrates.

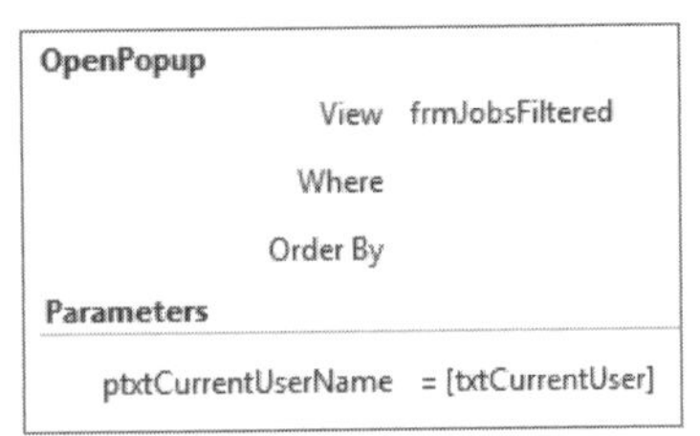

FIGURE 8-52: An OpenPopup macro action with parameters

At this point, you've covered the first steps toward building your own query by view in an Access web app. Because you will want to leverage parameters in web apps, let's go over techniques that will help you get the most out of parameters.

Techniques for Filtering

Because you will need to use parameters rather than build a dynamic SQL statement for your query by views, we'll review what techniques you would use to support a specific filtering requirement. You will then see those techniques applied in the query by view. But first we want to examine the technique in isolation so that you can see how it should be incorporated into your work.

Making a Parameter Optional

Often, seasoned Access developers would simply test a given control on the filtering form to determine if there is data in it and if so, add the new criteria to the SQL string being assembled. In web apps, parameters must be hard-coded and present at all times, whether you want to use them or not. This is similar to the difficulties that seasoned Access developers faced with the traditional parameter queries in the Access client. However, because the queries are executed against SQL Server and SQL Server has a much more developed query optimizer, it is able to make better choices than what we'd have seen with Access' parameterized queries and thus optimize parameterized queries.

You would probably want to use an expression similar to this:

```
([TableName].[FieldName] = [pvarParameter] OR [pvarParameter] IS NULL)
```

Whenever you do not want to supply a value for a given parameter, simply pass in a null value which will cause the condition to evaluate true based on the second predicate of `pvarParameter IS NULL`. This would return all rows. This technique can enable you to re-use a single query without having to create a copy of that query just to have different parameters.

Enabling/Disabling a Parameter With Another Parameter

For scenarios where you need to allow for filtering on nulls or use parameters with Yes/No data types, you cannot use the above technique. The alternative is to use two parameters; one to signal whether the filtering is requested and another to actually filter. Here is an example of how you can achieve this for a Yes/No field:

```
([TableName].[YesNoFieldName]=[pvarParameter] OR [pvarParameterExcluded]=Yes)
```

Note that both `pvarParameter` and `pvarParameterExcluded` parameters are of Yes/No data type. Similar to the previous technique, instead of checking whether the parameter is null, we can check if the second parameter signaling request to filter is No which then requires the first predicate to evaluate to true to return this row, effectively filtering those rows. This technique is also useful for when you want to filter on nulls:

```
(
  [TableName].[NullableFieldName] = [pvarParameter] AND
  [pvarParameterIsNull] = No
) OR (
  [TableName].[NullableFieldName] IS NULL AND [pvarParameterIsNull] = Yes
)
```

As you can see, `pvarParameterIsNull` determines whether the first outermost predicate or second outermost predicate should be used to evaluate the row. When `pvarParameterIsNull` is set to Yes, the second predicate will search for nulls in the field irrespective of whether `pvarParameter` has any values or not. Likewise, when it is No, only non-null values will be evaluated and, if it matches the `pvarParameter`, the row will be returned.

It is important to note that the given expression assumes you only want *either* null values or non-null values, in effect making this parameter required. If you want to support an optional parameter that also supports searching for nulls, you must provide additional predicates. You can do so by wrapping the original example and adding one more predicate:

```
(
  Same expression from above example
) OR (
  [pvarParameter] IS NULL AND [pvarParameterIsNull] = No
)
```

Optional Joins

Sometimes you need to filter based on values contained in another table but don't want to join the table if the filtering isn't requested. One approach you can employ is to use an outer join between tables with criteria on the outer table as shown in the following predicate:

```
(
  [OuterTableName].[FieldName] = [pvarParameter] AND
  [pvarFilterOnOuterTable] = Yes
) OR (
  [pvarFilterOnOuterTable] = No
)
```

Whenever a filter is applied on an outer table, the outer join effectively becomes an inner join and thus you get the filtering you need. When you don't want the filter on the outer table, setting the `pvarFilterOnOuterTable` to No will switch to the second predicate and allow all rows to be matched.

One complication you do have to deal with is that sometimes the joins can lead to duplicating of the inner table's row, which may not always be desirable. This typically will necessitate you solve the duplicating, possibly by either making the query result return distinct rows or using an aggregate query to roll up the multiple rows from the outer table into a single row so that there is a one-to-one ratio between the inner table's row to the outer query's rows and thus no unwanted duplicates. The particulars will determine which option is more appropriate for restricting unwanted duplicates.

Cascading Parameters

Sometimes, you may find that you need to apply a filter at different points and not all at once. When you have a query that needs to join to another parameterized query, you easily solve the need by passing along the parameters through the top-level query just as you could do in the Access client.

To illustrate, consider the query shown in Figure 8-53 which joins an aggregate query to a customer table.

Now suppose that you wanted to be able to count jobs performed for a customer within a certain date range. Had you filtered the same query shown in Figure 8-53, you may end up eliminating customers who did not have any jobs within a date range, a result which may be undesirable. Thus, to ensure that no customers are filtered out, you would make the aggregate query a parameterized query, with the criteria illustrated in Figure 8-54.

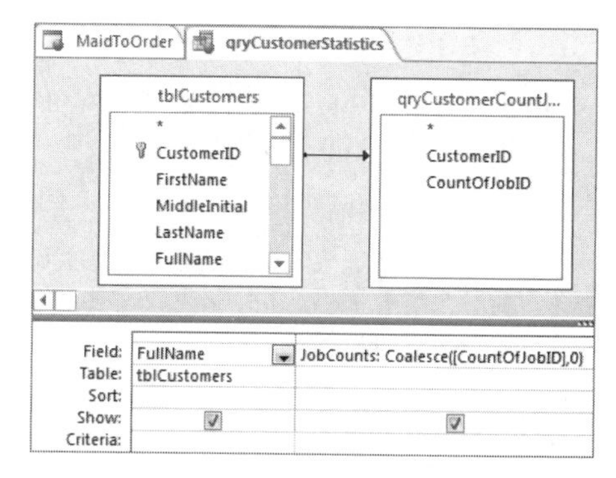

FIGURE 8-53: qryCustomersStatistics Query

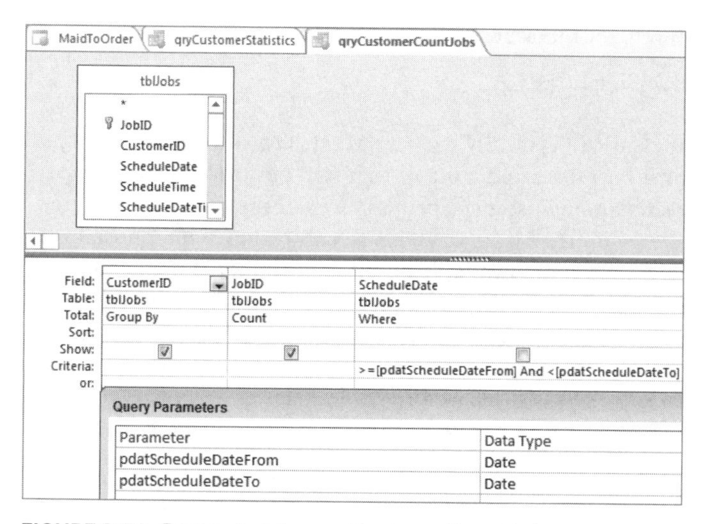

FIGURE 8-54: Parameterizing qryCustomerCountJobs query

However, since we won't open `qryCustomerCountJobs` directly, we need a means of supplying values to the parameters defined in the `qryCustomerCountJobs`. To do this, we add parameters of the same name and data types to the `qryCustomerStatistics` query. Even though the parameters are not used anywhere in the `qryCustomerStatistics`, we need to marshal the parameters forward into the `qryCustomerCountJobs` and thus achieve the counting of jobs only within a certain date range without eliminating any customers.

Naming Parameters

The naming of parameters is crucial to success. When you supply the parameter to the second query via an appropriate macro action, Access will also pass it forward to the underlying query without requiring you to reference it directly.

This technique opens up the potential for building more complex queries that can be initiated by a single OpenPopup macro action (or equivalent macro action). The view or data macros need to reference only the top-level query.

Filter Tables

In some situations, it's likely to be easier to create a special table to cache the matched rows. A filter table would typically have the following two fields in addition to the AutoNumber:

1. Lookup field to the primary key of table to filter upon
2. Session identifier, could be the user's name, user's e-mail address, or maybe some generated numeric code that is known to only one user, to prevent users from seeing results of other users' filtering

There may be a few reasons for wanting to create a filter table. Three possible reasons are:

1. Allowing you to use a popup view that can be updatable and thus enable users to edit records returned by filtering
2. Allowing users to cache the filters for quick reuse
3. Enable filtering on a many-many relationship

Should you choose to use a filter table, you will typically need a data macro(s) to clear and populate the table filter for each user requesting a new filter and a query that will perform the actual filtering. The query usually only needs to simply insert the primary key of the table to be filtered on into the filter table with the identifier supplied by data macro. Recall from Chapter 5 that `UserEmailAddress()` and `UserDisplayName()` are available in UI macros only and you must pass the results of those two functions into a data macro via a parameter. Even if you opted instead to use a numbering scheme to uniquely identify each user — or more likely, the session they are in — you'd still need to come up with a system of generating those numbers for each user's session. You could either generate them in a UI macro and pass them into the data macro, or you could generate them inside a data macro, which you should then return to the view invoking the data macro.

When you are ready to display the matched records, you can do so by using a query that joins the table with the filter table and matching on the filter table's session identifier. Due to the need for identifying the matched records from one user's filter to another user's filter, you will need to parameterize the query for the view. Thus, you will likely find that popup views are a good way to display the results specific to each user.

Handling Large Numbers of Parameters

Sometimes you may have a complex requirement and need more than just a few parameters. As you learned earlier, the Where Condition parameters in macro actions are limited to 255 characters, and you don't have SQL view to design in. If you need your queries to be available in a web browser, using a parameterized query will often involve large numbers of parameters. However, you will want to learn how to manage the query effectively. Due to the nature of the Query Designer, a criteria row is created for each possible filtering. To illustrate, compare the following T-SQL snippet with Figure 8-55 and see how Query Designer will expand those criteria into several rows:

```
WHERE (
  [tblCustomers].[Firstname] = @ptxtFirstName
  OR
```

```
        @ptxtFirstName IS NULL
    ) AND (
        [tblCustomers].[LastName] = @ptxtLastName
        OR
        @ptxtLastName IS NULL
    ) AND (
        [tblCustomers].[ActivationDate] = @pdatActivationDate
        OR
        @pdatActivationDate IS NULL
    )
```

Field:	CustomerID	FirstName	LastName	ActivationDate	[ptxtFirstName]	[ptxtLastName]	[pdatA…
Table:	tblCustomers	tblCustomers	tblCustomers	tblCustomers			
Sort:							
Show:	✓	✓	✓	✓	☐	☐	
Criteria:		[ptxtFirstName]	[ptxtLastName]	[pdatActivationDate]			
or:			[ptxtLastName]	[pdatActivationDate]	Is Null		
		[ptxtFirstName]		[pdatActivationDate]		Is Null	
				[pdatActivationDate]	Is Null	Is Null	
		[ptxtFirstName]	[ptxtLastName]				Is Null
			[ptxtLastName]		Is Null		Is Null
		[ptxtFirstName]				Is Null	Is Null
					Is Null	Is Null	Is Null

FIGURE 8-55: Excessive number of criteria rows

As you can imagine, a more complex query with several parameters can result in expansion of numerous criteria rows, far too many to manage manually; that's especially true when using techniques discussed above to allow for optional parameters similar to what is seen in Figure 8-55.

We want to reassure you that though the large amount of criteria rows appears inefficient, the underlying SQL is quite reasonable. You can prove that to yourself by viewing the SQL definition of the underlying table-valued function in SSMS connected to the web app's database. You will learn how to connect to the database from SSMS in Chapter 11.

One way to facilitate managing these queries is to save the SQL Where clause externally for easy reference. For example, when you need to build such queries so that the functionality is available on the web, you can save the SQL Where clause in a text document. Whenever you need to edit the query, simply delete all columns that are used for the parameters and replace them from your template. Refer to the section in Chapter 5 on manually copying queries for a refresher on selecting the columns. Keeping in the mind that each criterion cell has a limit of 1,024 characters, you can paste in the SQL snippet into the criterion cells for as many columns as you need. What you select for the column in the first row should actually be irrelevant because instead of using typical shorthand expressions such as `=[pvarParameter]` in the criterion cells, you'll be writing the complete predicate such as `[TableName].[FieldName] = [pvarParameter]`. When the predicate is complete, the Query Designer is intelligent enough not to apply this criteria to whatever column is selected and treats it independently. This is demonstrated in Figure 8-56.

Note how you do not start with an operator, such as `=<some value>` as you typically do in the Query Designer. You can see in Figure 8-56 that the expression must have a left-hand expression such as `[tblJobs].[CustomerID]`. The parameter is then assigned from the right hand of the expression. This should enable you to manage complex queries and make them available in web browsers.

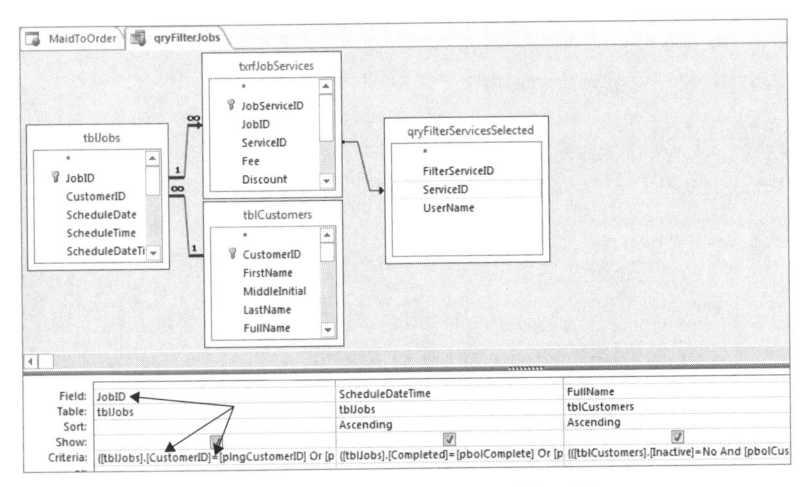

FIGURE 8-56: Complete predicates pasted into qryFilterJobs query

At this point, you've learned how to create the parameterized queries you'll incorporate into your query by views. Next, you'll apply that knowledge to some design requirements in a practical example of a query by view.

Design Requirements

To put the conceptual discussions in focus, we will go through an example and apply all the techniques discussed into a single query by form. As you can imagine, building a query by form can be a complex task, so to help facilitate the discussion, we've made available a sample that you can download that demonstrates all the capability discussed in this section. The materials are also available in the sample app, Maid To Order, available for download. To view the sample, you will need to provision the `.app` package to your SharePoint site. The instructions for provisioning an `.app` package can be found in Chapter 14.

For Maid To Order's jobs, the following criteria need to be filtered:

1. Range of job's scheduled date and time
2. Range of job's invoice date
3. Exact matching on customer's full name
4. Fuzzy matching on customer's first name
5. Fuzzy matching on customer's last name
6. Searching on customer's organization via a list
7. Showing active versus inactive customers
8. Displaying only jobs that are completed, paid, not paid, or either
9. Listing jobs that took a specified range of minutes to complete
10. Listing jobs that have specified services provided

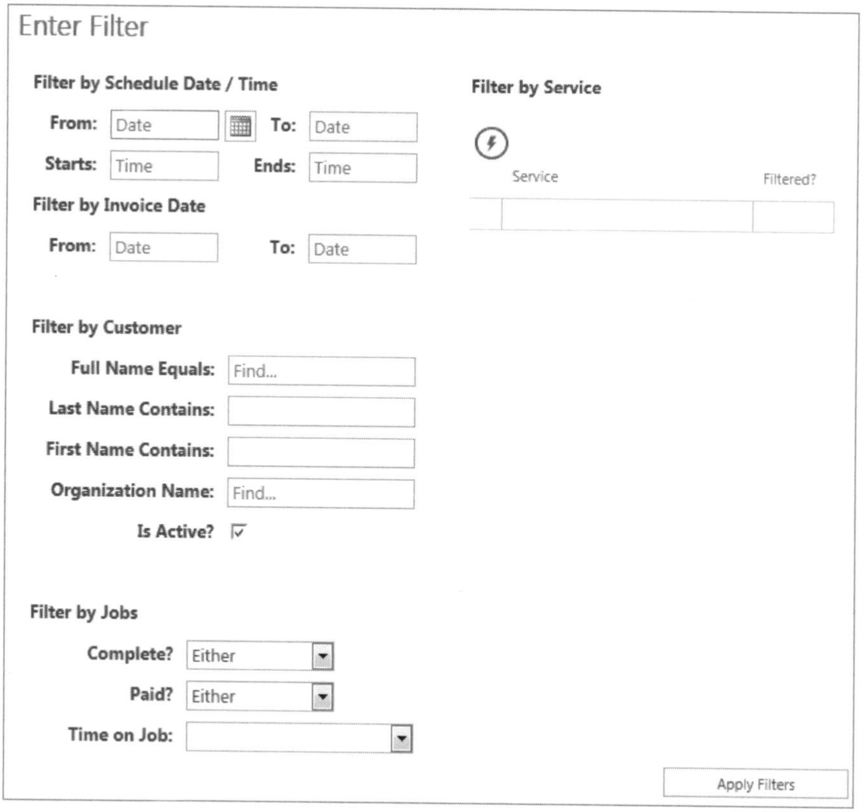

FIGURE 8-57: Layout of the query by form

Here's the layout of the query by view that supports all 10 filter criteria illustrated in Figure 8-57.

Let's think about what we need to have to support the required functionality. As you can see in Figure 8-57, we need two views to collect the inputs to the filters requested by the user. Like the traditional query by form, the main view is unbound, but the Filter By Service subview is bound to a filter table based on the `tblServices` table. The filter table for services is named `tlkpFilterServices`.

We need a query that will accept all the inputs from the main view and join to the `tlkpFilterServices` table. Because of the number of joins and complex criteria, the query will be non-updatable and since we want to enable editing of the matched records, we will insert the result of the query into a filter table for the jobs, called `tlkpFilterJobs`. In order to perform the inserts, we need a data macro to gather the parameters from the main form and run the query, then add the results into the `tlkpFilterJobs` table.

Once this is finished, we can display the results in a new popup view. Figure 8-58 demonstrates how the popup view should render the matched records and enable users to navigate through the records and perform any edits if desired.

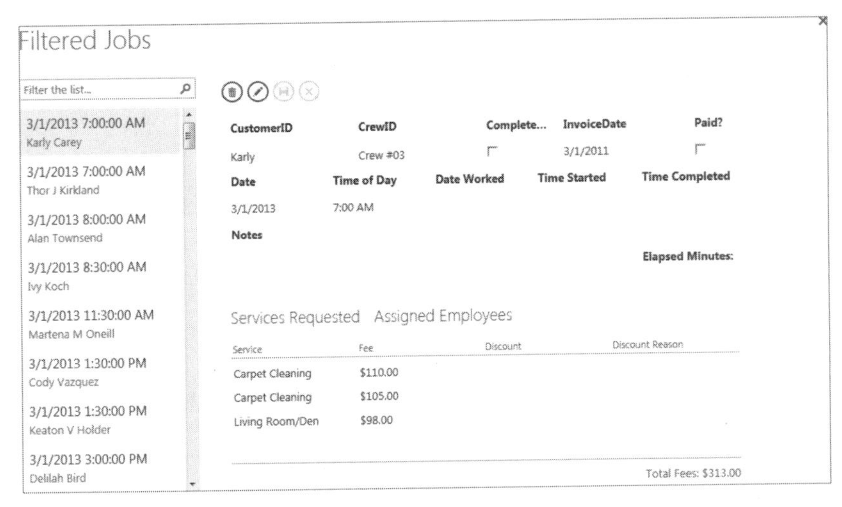

FIGURE 8-58: frmJobsFiltered popup view

So to recap, we need the following objects:

- Filter table for services (`tlkpFilterServices`)
- Filter table for jobs (`tlkpFilterJobs`)
- Query by View (`frmFilterJobs`)
- Filter by services view (`fsubFilterServices`)
- Filtering query for services by user (`qryFilterServicesSelected`)
- Filtering query for jobs (`qryFilterJobs`)
- Data macro to collect inputs, run the query and populate `tlkpFilterJobs` table (`dmFilterJobs`)
- Query for popup view's recordsource (`qryJobsFiltered`)
- Popup view to display matched records (`frmJobsFiltered`)

We will walk through each step necessary to build the query and we will point out to you when we use the techniques discussed in the previous section at each step and why we use them. This can seem like a big task but the intent is to demonstrate how far you can stretch the capability of web apps and give you a wide range of examples within a single context. With this background, let's get started.

Creating Filter Tables

Because we want to support both filtering on a many-many relationship, namely finding jobs based on what services are provided at the given job, and allow for editing of matched job records, we need two filter tables that correspond to the jobs and services table. They are structurally similar;

the only differences being that the Lookup fields reference their respective tables and the field names are "Job" and "Service" respectively. Figure 8-59 illustrates the design of the `tlkpFilterJobs` table.

MaidToOrder | tlkpFilterJobs

Field Name	Data Type
FilterJobID	AutoNumber
UserName	Short Text
JobID	Lookup

FIGURE 8-59: tlkpFilterJobs table design

The goal is to populate the `UserName` field with `UserEmailAddress()` supplied by a UI macro to identify which filter records belong to which users. You will see this in use when we build the `frmFilterJobs` view.

Creating Data Macro to Clear Selections

With a filter table, it is necessary to be able to clear the previous selections. Because filter tables may contain results from more than one user, we only want to clear all records associated with that user. You'd probably create a macro similar to `dmFilterServicesClear` which has the steps illustrated in Figure 8-60.

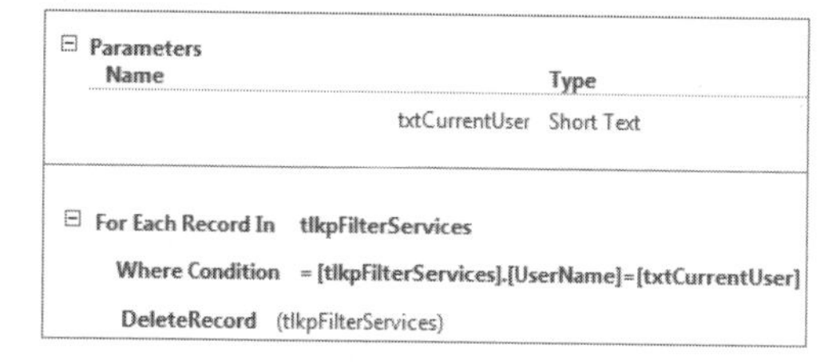
Parameters
Name
Type
txtCurrentUser
Short Text
For Each Record In tlkpFilterServices
Where Condition = [tlkpFilterServices].[UserName]=[txtCurrentUser]
DeleteRecord (tlkpFilterServices)

FIGURE 8-60: dmFilterServicesClear data macro definition

As you might expect, it's fairly straightforward; doing a ForEachRecord macro block, deleting each record matching the `UserName` field. Because `UserEmailAddress()` is only available in UI macro, it needs to be passed in as a parameter. We will pass that in the query by views.

Creating Query By View

We'll start with `fsubFilterServices` first and then see how it is used in `frmFilterJobs`'s subview and how it fits together with its parent view.

`fsubFilterServices` is a Datasheet view with `tlkpFilterServices` as the recordsource. The user can add new records to indicate they want a job that has one of those services indicated. The view should always start out empty. In order to achieve this, we need to run the `dmFilterServicesClear` data macro to delete any existing filter records on `tlkpFilterServices` for this user then filter the recordsource to an impossible criteria. Because the `UserName` field on `tlkpFilterServices` table is required, the Load event of the `fsubFilterServices` view will perform a RequeryRecords with the criteria `[tlkpFilterServices].[UserName] Is Null`. Both steps in the Load event are demonstrated in Figure 8-61.

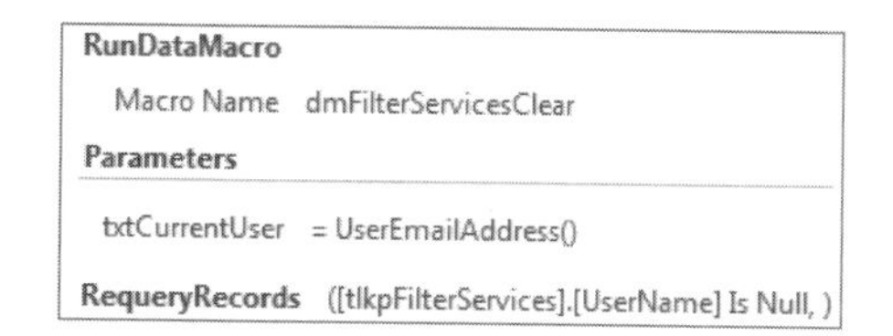
RunDataMacro
Macro Name dmFilterServicesClear
Parameters
txtCurrentUser = UserEmailAddress()
RequeryRecords ([tlkpFilterServices].[UserName] Is Null,)

FIGURE 8-61: fsubFilterServices view's Load event

The sole Action Bar button (`abbClearAll`) also provides a way for users to quickly clear all selections using the `dmFilterServicesClear` data macro. The macro actions behind `abbClearAll`'s click event are identical to the actions in the `fsubFilterServices` view's load event.

The `fsubFilterServices` has an AutoComplete control (`acmServiceID`) and a pair of textboxes (`txtFiltered` and `txtUserName`). The user would typically only need to interact with `acmServiceID` to select the service they want to filter the jobs on.

`txtFiltered` textbox is a non-editable textbox formatted as a hyperlink, which you can achieve by underlining the font and selecting blue as the font color from the ribbon as illustrated in Figure 8-62.

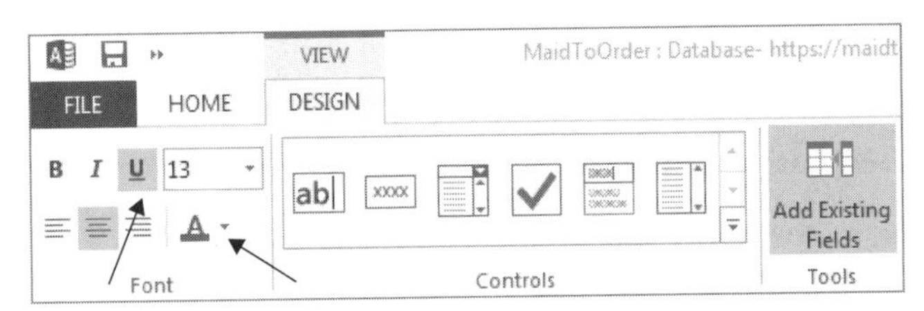

FIGURE 8-62: Underlining and coloring the fonts of a textbox

The calculation for the `txtFiltered` textbox is given as:

```
=IIf([acmServiceID] Is Null,"No","Yes")
```

The primary purpose of the `txtFiltered` textbox is to provide visual feedback to the user whether the selection the user made was actually saved or not. Recall from Chapter 4 that Datasheet view does not have a mechanism to force saving records or perform actions after updating. Generally, the user just needs to make the selection and the record is saved right away but it is possible to leave the edit in limbo by moving focus to one of the other controls outside the `fsubFilterServices` view. Though we could use a checkbox, the checkbox does not have a Click event. The button control does have a Click event but its caption cannot be set to a calculation. Thus representing a textbox as a hyperlink gives you the most flexibility in generating dynamic content that can be clicked to perform additional actions. The Click event can be used to either force a save of the unsaved selection or delete a saved record. The actions are listed in Figure 8-63.

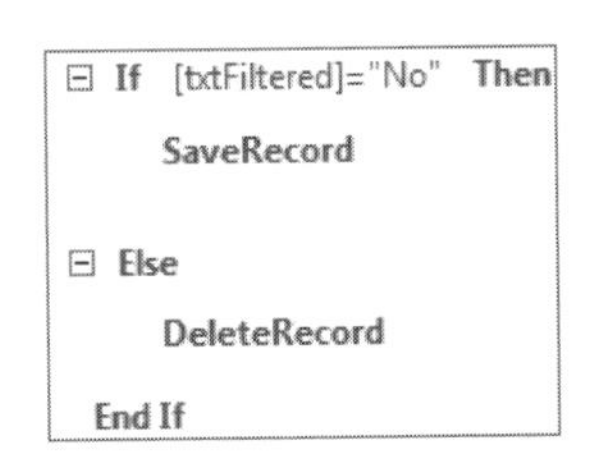

FIGURE 8-63: Macro actions behind txtFiltered textbox's Click event

The UserName textbox (`txtUserName`) is hidden from view and is there in order to allow us to supply a default value by reading the `UserEmailAddress()` into the textbox function whenever a new record is created, thus associating this service filter with the current user.

With this, we are ready to build the `frmFilterJobs` and then add `fsubFilterServices` as a source object for `frmFilterJobs`' subview control.

`frmFilterJobs` view is a Blank view with no recordsource. Figure 8-64 illustrates the layout in the design view.

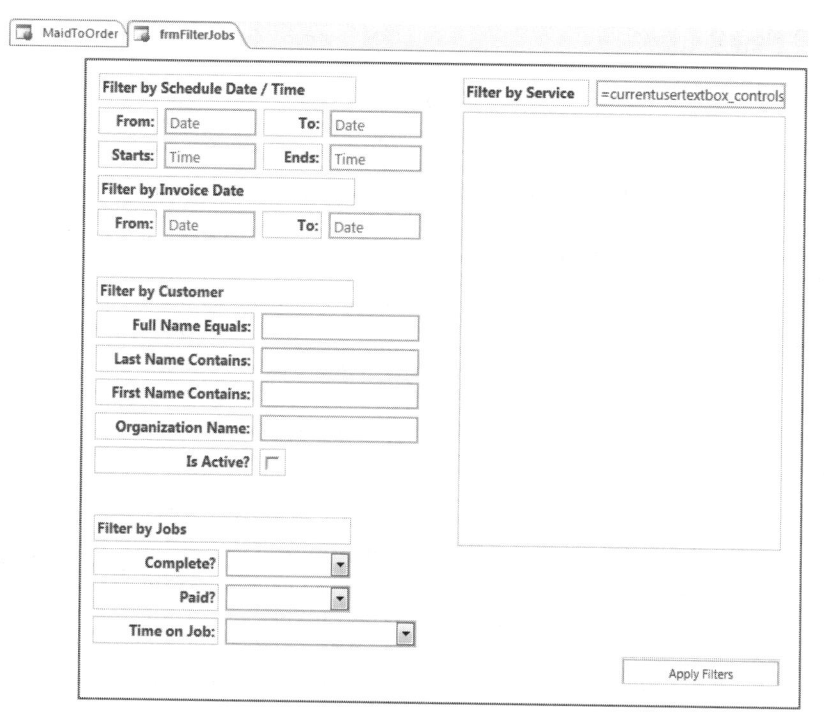

FIGURE 8-64: frmFilterJobs view in design view

The Format property needs to be changed so that textbox controls that accept date or time will have the appropriate date/time format. The textboxes accepting first name and last name need no special formatting.

There are two AutoComplete controls; one for the customer's full name (`acmCustomerFullName`) and another for the customer's organization (`acmCustomerOrganizationName`). Note that the `acmCustomerFullName` has its Bound Field property set to `CustomerID` though it will display the customer's full name for the user to select from. In contrast, `acmCustomerOrganizationName`'s Bound Field property is same as the Display Name property. This reflects the fact that the `OrganizationName` field on the `tblCustomers` table is a text field, not a Lookup field, and we want to search on the text of the organization name which may match a number of customers. Had it used `CustomerID` as the `acmCustomerFullName` did, it would only match a single customer, which is not how the `acmCustomerOrganizationName` should work.

The Completed combo box (`cboJobComplete`) and Paid combo box (`cboJobPaid`) both use the same value list which contains 3 options; "Either", "No", and "Yes". Both will have "Either" as the default. The combo box is used instead of a checkbox because it is more intuitive than a tri-state checkbox, which isn't available in the web app anyway.

The Time Elapsed combo box (`cboJobTimeElapsed`) is also a value list but has the following entries:

- Less Than 30 Minutes
- Less Than 1 Hour

- Less Than 1 1/2 Hours
- 2 Hours or more

Furthermore, there is no default for this control.

The `txtCurrentUserName` textbox on upper-right corner of the view is a hidden control with default value set to `=UserEmailAddress()` and will be used to provide the return value of `UserEmailAddress()` to be passed into the data macro for filtering by this user.

The subview control (`subFilterServices`) is not linked to the parent form. Though it is possible to link the subview to the `txtCurrentUserName` to filter the service selection by current user, at the time of writing, an error is raised if a new record is inserted in the subview when the subview control is linked. You already saw earlier that `fsubFilterServices` will automatically populate the `UserName` field with the return value of the `UserEmailAddress()` function.

Filtering Query

Before we can add macro actions to `frmFilterJobs`' Apply Filter button, we need to build the filtering query and the data macro to process the inputs from users and populate the `tlkpFilterJobs` filter table. The main filtering query will need a subquery, so we'll create the subquery, `qryFilterServicesSelected`. It takes a single parameter, `ptxtCurrentUserName`, which should be returned by `UserEmailAddress()`. Figure 8-65 shows how it should look in the Query Designer.

We then need to create the `qryFilterJobs` query that will use three tables and the `qryFilterServicesSelected` query. Because a job must have a customer, the join between `tblCustomers` and `tblJobs` can be an inner join. However, a job may not always have services selected already, so we'll left-join the `tblJobs` into `txrfJobServices`. This table is then joined to the `qryFilterServicesSelected`. You can see how it relates in Figure 8-66.

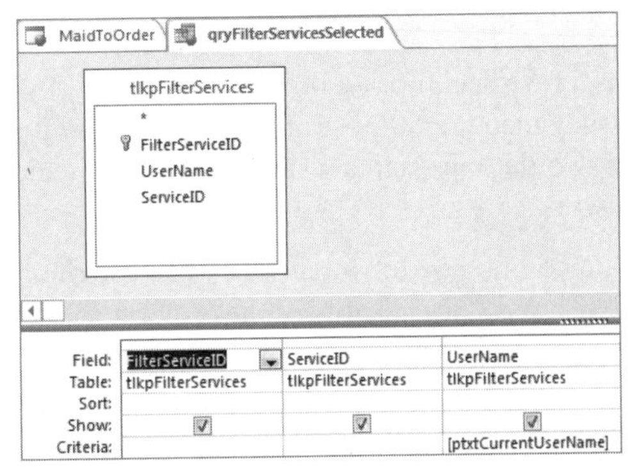

FIGURE 8-65: qryFilterServicesSelected query definition

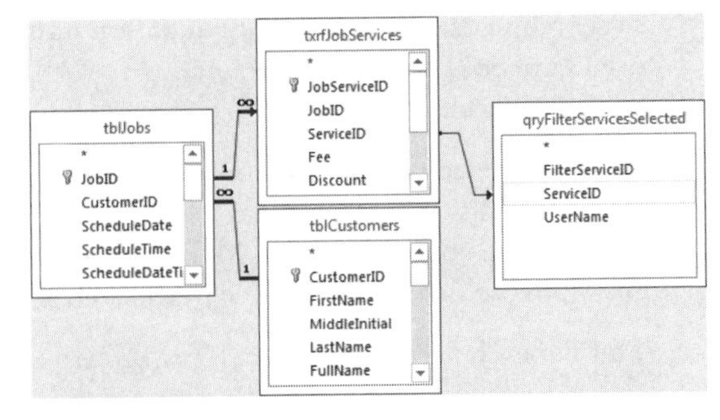

FIGURE 8-66: qryFilterJobs query's data sources

Next, because the query has potential to return duplicate records of jobs due to joining the `txrfJobServices` table, we'll use Unique Values to eliminate duplicate records. This works since we only need data from a single table, `tblJobs`. To ensure that the filter will have consistent results, we need also to apply ordering to the `qryFilterJobs` query, using the `tblJobs.ScheduleDateTime` and `tblCustomers.FullName` fields. Though we only need `JobID` field, we have to show both `ScheduleDateTime` and `FullName` because we chose to show unique values, requiring that the columns in the `ORDER BY` clause also appear in the `SELECT` clause. Furthermore, we want to ensure a maximum limit of rows is returned to ensure that users don't request more rows than they can intelligently browse. One hundred rows are entered in the Return textbox. Figure 8-67 shows how the query is configured for distinct and the maximum number of rows to return.

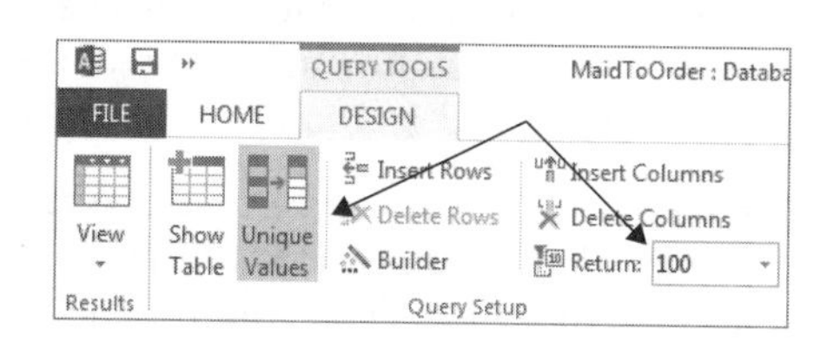

FIGURE 8-67: qryFilterJobs configuration

Note that when a query has a limit on how many rows may be returned, it becomes essential that the query itself be ordered to ensure that the results returned are consistent even when the number of matched rows exceeds the maximum value allowed. Applying order on the popup view would be too late because the popup view would display what is returned by the filtering query.

The `qryFilterJobs` query will need the following parameters to support all the criteria offered on the `frmFilterJobs` view:

- `plngCustomerID` - Number (No Decimal)
- `pdatScheduleDateFrom` - Date
- `pdatScheduleDateTo` - Date
- `ptimScheduleTimeStarts` - Time
- `ptimScheduleTimeEnds` - Time
- `pdatInvoiceDateFrom` - Date
- `pdatInvoiceDateTo` - Date
- `pbolComplete` - Yes/No
- `pbolCompleteExcluded` - Yes/No
- `pbolPaid` - Yes/No
- `pbolPaidExcluded` - Yes/No
- `ptxtFirstNameContains` - Short Text
- `ptxtLastNameContains` - Short Text
- `ptxtOrganizationName` - Short Text
- `pbolCustomerActive` - Yes/No
- `plngTimeSpentMin` - Number (No Decimal)

- `plngTimeSpentMax` - Number (No Decimal)
- `ptxtCurrentUserName` - Short Text
- `pbolFilterServices` - Yes/No

You may notice that some parameters are dependent on other parameters and when you build the UI macros to ultimately run the `qryFilterJobs` query, you will add actions to set the related parameters value accordingly. Some parameters should be self-explanatory to you.

First, `plngCustomerID` parameter filters on the `tblCustomers`' `CustomerID` field which is the primary key. This is useful when you also filter on a job's data such as schedule date ranges for only a single customer. This is mutually exclusive from the groups of parameters filtering on customers such as `ptxtFirstNameContains`, `ptxtLastNameContains`, and `ptxtOrganizationName`. It's a straightforward optional parameter; the snippet is:

```
([tblJobs].[CustomerID]=[plngCustomerID] Or [plngCustomerID] Is Null)
```

`pdatScheduleDate*` parameters enable us to search on a date range. Because there is a start and end parameter, we need to handle them together. If you have a similar requirement, you will find it much easier to use the >= and < operators instead of the `BETWEEN … AND …` operator because for the last day, we want to include the whole time during that last day. By advancing the last day to the next date, users will see results that have times other than midnight of the last day. For example, if the user specifies an end date of April 15th, 2013, the UI macro should increment it to April 16th, 2013 and use the < operator, ensuring that records containing data like April 15th 1:30 PM will be included in the results. Here is the snippet to set up the date range for schedule date:

```
(
  (
    [tblJobs].[ScheduleDate]>=[pdatScheduleDateFrom]
    OR
    [pdatScheduleDateFrom] IS NULL
  ) AND (
    [tblJobs].[ScheduleDate]<[pdatScheduleDateTo]
    OR
    [pdatScheduleDateTo] IS NULL
  )
)
```

Note that the outermost parentheses are needed to ensure that the date range will be evaluated as a single predicate separate from any other predicates. The syntax also allows the user to enter only one parameter and leave the other parameter blank, enabling search on date range with only a start date or with only an end date. Both the `ptimScheduleTime*` and `pdatInvoiceDate*` parameters are quite similar so we'll list the snippets:

```
(
  (
    [tblJobs].[ScheduleTime]>=[ptimScheduleTimeStarts]
    OR
    [ptimScheduleTimeStarts] IS NULL
```

```
    ) AND (
      [tblJobs].[ScheduleTime]<[ptimScheduleTimeEnds]
      OR
      [ptimScheduleTimeEnds] IS NULL
    )
  ) AND (
    (
      [tblJobs].[InvoiceDate]>=[pdatInvoiceDateFrom]
      OR
      [pdatInvoiceDateFrom] IS NULL
    ) AND (
      [tblJobs].[InvoiceDate]<[pdatInvoiceDateTo]
      OR
      [pdatInvoiceDateTo] IS NULL
    )
  )
```

You also can see how you would link together multiple parameters; for each optional parameter snippet, you need to wrap the snippet in a pair of parentheses and link them with `AND` operator. You can opt to use the `OR` operator if you don't want the filters to be cumulative. However, this is a decision that requires hard-coding so it is not something you can switch between in run time unless you are willing to maintain two versions of queries.

The next set of parameters use the technique of enabling/disabling filters based on other parameters. Both the `Paid` and `Completed` fields on the `tblJobs` table are a Yes/No field, and the parameters are Yes/No. Because none of those may be null, we need to use an extra parameter to signal whether we desire to filter on a Yes/No field:

```
  (
    [tblJobs].[Completed]=[pbolComplete]
    OR
    [pbolCompleteExcluded]=Yes
  ) AND (
    [tblJobs].[Paid]=[pbolPaid]
    OR
    [pbolPaidExcluded]=Yes
  )
```

Note how the values contained in `pbolCompleted` and `pbolPaid` are irrelevant if the `pbolCompletedExcluded` and `pbolPaidExcluded` parameters, respectively are set to Yes. Because the predicates are linked with an `OR` operator and there is only a single value for the `pbol*Excluded` parameter, the predicate will evaluate to true for all rows if those parameters are set to Yes. Only when the `pbol*Excluded` is set to No, does the row have to pass the more stringent test in the first predicate to be matched.

The next set of parameters demonstrates using the `LIKE` operator with wildcards. This is basically a variant of the optional parameter technique, with the difference being that instead of using the = operator, we wrap the parameter in wildcard metacharacters and evaluate it using the `LIKE` operator:

```
(
  [tblCustomers].[FirstName] LIKE Concat("%",[ptxtFirstNameContains],"%")
  OR
  [ptxtFirstNameContains] IS NULL
) AND (
  [tblCustomers].[LastName] LIKE Concat("%",[ptxtLastNameContains],"%")
  OR
  [ptxtLastNameContains] IS NULL
)
```

Note the use of SQL Server's metacharacters rather than Access' metacharacters, such as `%` instead of `*`. Also, as you can imagine, you could perform the concatenating within the UI macro if you want to support a wider variety of possible wildcard matches.

The Organization Name parameter is a straightforward optional parameter so we'll note that and move on:

```
(
  [tblCustomers].[OrganizationName]=[ptxtOrganizationName]
  OR
  [ptxtOrganizationName] IS NULL
)
```

The parameter for matching active or inactive customers is effectively a required parameter and cannot be omitted. To reflect this, different syntax is used:

```
(
  (
    [tblCustomers].[Inactive]=No
    AND
    [pbolCustomerActive]=Yes
  ) OR (
    [tblCustomers].[Inactive]=Yes
    AND
    [pbolCustomerActive]=No
  )
)
```

Instead of matching up the parameter, hard-coded criteria are used to evaluate each predicate; allowing only either active or inactive customers but not both.

The parameters for time spent on a job will also encompass a range, except that instead of dates or times, the range is numeric, however, the principle is similar:

```
(
  tblJobs.ElapsedTime >= [plngTimeSpentMin]
  OR
  [plngTimeSpentMin] IS NULL
) AND (
  tblJobs.ElapsedTime <= [plngTimeSpentMax]
  OR
  [plngTimeSpentMax] IS NULL
)
```

Though we could use BETWEEN … AND, the more verbose syntax of >= and <= allows us to choose whether we will use only one start or end point or both together.

This brings us to the last parameter used in the query, pbolFilterServices which allows us to optionally join in the results of the tlkpFilterServices table:

```
(
  (
    qryFilterServicesSelected.ServiceID IS NOT NULL
    AND
    [pbolFilterServices] = Yes
  ) OR
  [pbolFilterServices] = No
)
```

The pbolFitlerServices parameter will be evaluated within the data macro and you will see it later on. Note how we convert the outer join into an inner join by forcing the field from the qryFilterServicesSelected query to be non-null when the pbolFilterServices parameter is set to Yes. Otherwise, the result of the query is simply ignored and all rows from tblJobs will be returned.

As discussed before, the ptxtCurrentUserName parameter exists to accept the return value of UserEmailAddress() executed in a UI macro and though it is not used anywhere in qryFilterJobs, it will be useful to the qryFilterServicesSelected where you need to be able to identify services selected by the user, if any.

To put it all together, each predicate needs to be wrapped in parentheses and linked with an AND operator in between. Because each criterion cell has a limit of 1,024 characters, you need to break up the whole expression into 3 parts that can be pasted into each criterion cell. Figure 8-56 demonstrated how you would paste the snippets into each cell. Recall from the discussion about 8-56 that when a predicate has a field reference on the left hand of the expression, the Query Designer knows that it doesn't relate to the field specified in the same column.

It's important to note that ordering will be helpful in a filtering query, even if the only purpose is to return keys to match the field. You may find it necessary to limit the number of rows.

This completes the construction of your filtering query for the query by view. In your own web apps, you may not need to build a query as complex as this, but you should be able to cherry-pick from the many techniques demonstrated in this discussion to build your own filtering query to meet your particular requirements.

Building Data Macros to Populate Filter Tables

Though in principle, you could open a view based on the filtering query, and thus avoid the need for a data macro and a filter table, we have found that using a filter table helps avoid problems with using a filtering query directly as a recordsource. That is due to data type mismatches between the unbound controls on the query by view, which may be passed directly into the query's parameters as text. Furthermore, this facilitates creating views that are updatable. Should you choose to simply use the filtering query as the recordsource, you could skip this section.

With that said, the logical design of the data macro, to be named `dmFilterJobs`, is like this:

1. Set up variables to track the number of rows processed.
2. Clear any previous filter set by the same user.
3. Check whether the user has requested filtering by services.
4. Execute the filtering query (`qryFilterJobs`), and for each returned row:
    - Add the row into `tlkpFilterJobs` with the current user's identity.
    - Increment the numbers of processed rows.
    - Check if the maximum number of rows to process has been reached and if so, stop processing any further rows.
5. Return the numbers of rows processed to the calling macro.

The data macro will need these parameters, which are mostly similar to what is needed for the `qryFilterJobs` query.

- `plngCustomerID` - Number (No Decimal)
- `pdatScheduleDateFrom` - Date
- `pdatScheduleDateTo` - Date
- `ptimScheduleTimeStarts` - Short Text
- `ptimScheduleTimeEnds` - Short Text
- `pdatInvoiceDateFrom` - Date
- `pdatInvoiceDateTo` - Date
- `pbolComplete` - Yes/No
- `pbolCompleteExcluded` - Yes/No
- `pbolPaid` - Yes/No
- `pbolPaidExcluded` - Yes/No
- `ptxtFirstNameContains` - Short Text
- `ptxtLastNameContains` - Short Text
- `ptxtOrganizationName` - Short Text
- `pbolCustomerActive` - Yes/No
- `plngTimeSpentMin` - Number (No Decimal)
- `plngTimeSpentMax` - Number (No Decimal)
- `ptxtCurrentUserName` - Short Text

Note that the data macro will supply the `pbolFilterServices` parameter required by the `qryFilterJobs` query.

> **NOTE** *At the time of this writing, parameters of Time data types are problematic in passing from unbound controls on a view to a query even when correctly formatted. Thus, a workaround is to pass it to the data macro as a Short Text parameter. Within the data macro, it can be then passed into a Time parameter for query with no problem. You also can use* `TimeFromParts()` *function to help support passing around Time parameters between UI macros and data macros.*

There is really no benefit in returning more than 100 records to the users for browsing—most of the time users will find it hard to review that many. It's usually best that users be as specific as possible and adjust the filter if they find the initial result set too broad. Though we are already limiting the number of rows within the filtering query it is also useful to be able to return the count of rows. Because we are already looping in order to insert a new record, there is not much to gain by using a Count query so we'll use a local variable to track the number of inserts to be returned to the calling macro. You may also find it useful to have the limit also applied in the data macro to guard against situations where a coding error causes more insertions than you expected. Figure 8-68 illustrates the setup for the three variables, `vlngCurrentRecord`, `vlngMaxResults`, and `vbolFilterServices`. You'll see the first two used in the ForEachRecord macro block later and the last one used in a LookupRecord action.

```
SetLocalVar  (vlngCurrentRecord, 0)
SetLocalVar  (vlngMaxResults, 100)
SetLocalVar  (vbolFilterServices, No)
```

FIGURE 8-68: Setting up local variables in dmFilterJobs data macro

Before populating the new filter results into the filter table for the user, you need to ensure that any previous results are removed from the filter table. We can use a ForEachRecord macro block to delete the records found in the table, matching on the `UserEmailAddress()`'s result. This is shown in Figure 8-69.

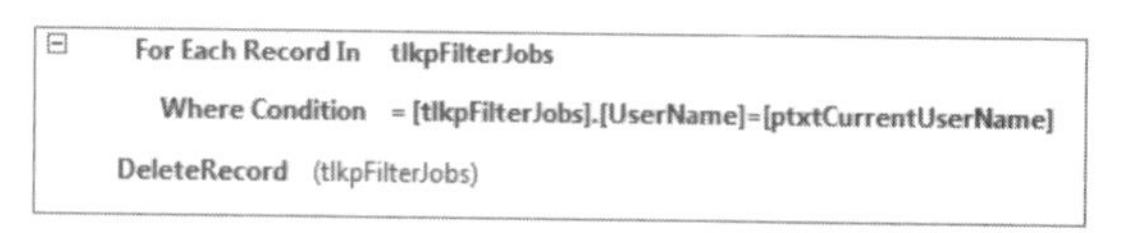

FIGURE 8-69: Removing user's previous results from tlkpFilterJobs table

Because we have an optional join with `tlkpFilterServices` to allow users to filter for any particular services, we need to determine if we want to enable the join or not and populate the `qryFilterJobs`' `pbolFilterServices` parameter accordingly. To make that determination, we would create a Count query that counts the records found in `tlkpFilterServices`, filtered to the user and use a LookupRecord macro block to get the result of the count to pass into the `qryFilterJobs` query via `vbolFilterServices` variable. Figure 8-70 shows how the `qryFilterServicesCountByUser` is designed, and Figure 8-71 shows how we use the LookupRecord macro action. Note the parameter used in the query.

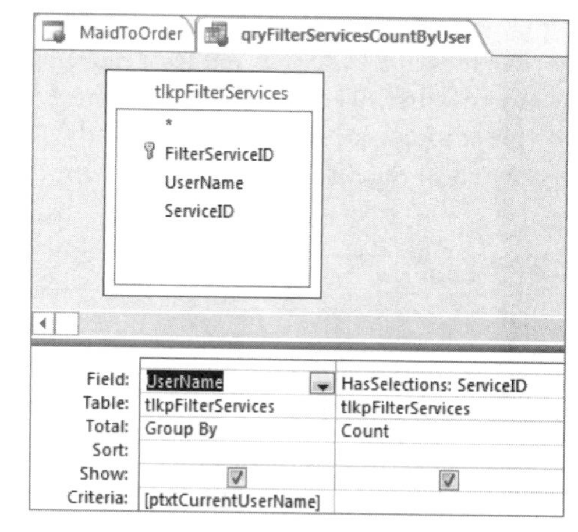

FIGURE 8-70: qryFilterServicesCountByUser query design

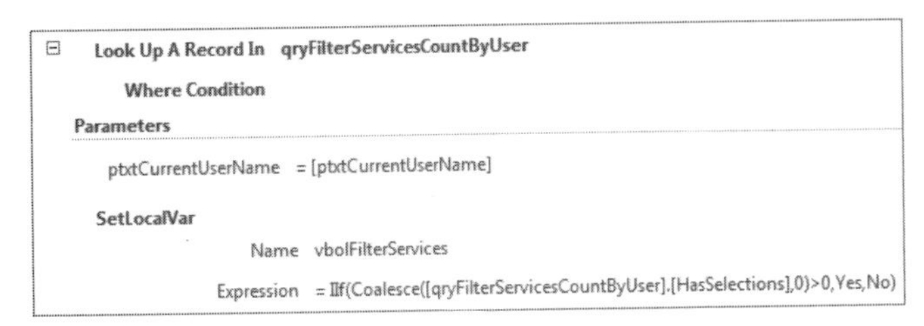

FIGURE 8-71: LookupRecord macro block in dmFilterJobs data macro

We now come to the centerpiece of the `dmFilterJobs` data macro; looping over the matched rows from the `qryFilterJobs` query and adding the row to the `tlkpFilterJobs`, along with the username. Note that for each iteration, we increment the `vlngCurrentRecord` variable. If it is 100 or greater, we use an ExitForEachRecord macro action to leave the loop early. Study Figure 8-72 to see how this pieces together.

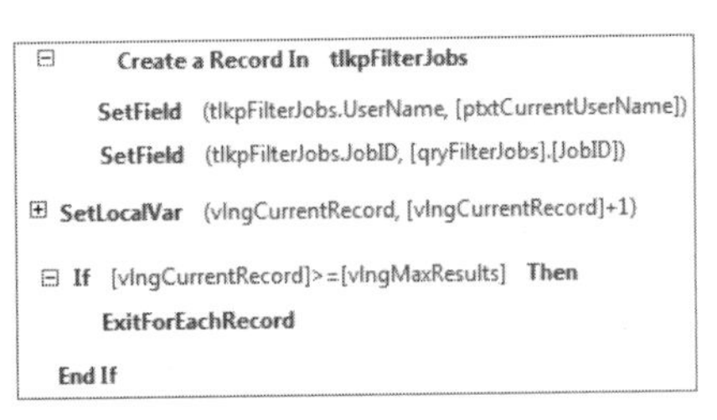

FIGURE 8-72: Body of ForEachRecord macro action iterating over the results of qryFilterJobs query

The last step in the `dmFilterJobs` is to return the number of rows matched. We will see this used in the UI macro that will call the `dmFilterJobs` data macro. You can see how SetReturnVar macro action is used in Figure 8-73.

```
SetReturnVar (rlngMatchedRecords, [vlngCurrentRecord])
```

FIGURE 8-73: SetReturnVar macro action

This completes the construction of `dmFilterJobs`. Before we can return to the query by view and add macro actions behind the `frmFilterJobs`' Apply Filter button, we need to create the popup view that will display the results.

Building a Popup View to Display the Filter Results

We'll need a List view, named `frmJobsFiltered`, to navigate through the matched records returned by the filter. We will assume that there is already a CRUD view that has all controls we want to use for editing a job so the List view only needs a single Subview control to display the CRUD view. The layout of the List view is illustrated in Figure 8-74.

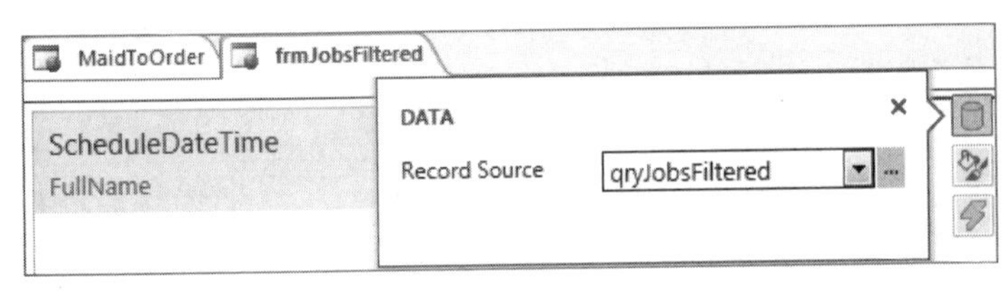

FIGURE 8-74: Layout of frmJobsFiltered view

The view will need to display the result of matches, filtered to the username. Because it will be a popup view, we can use a parameter query to supply the username. Figure 8-75 illustrates how we can design the `qryJobsFiltered` query which also contains sufficient information to sort and display jobs in the list pane in addition to providing the `JobID` primary key to join for the Subview control.

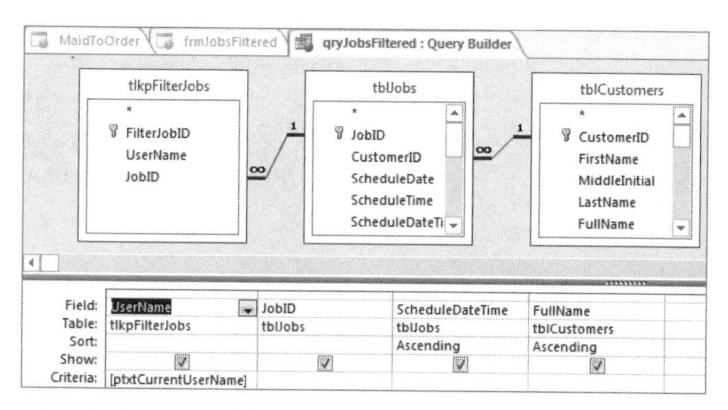

FIGURE 8-75: qryJobsFiltered query design

Figure 8-76 shows how you would fill in the Subview control's properties to link on `JobID` field between the `frmJobsFiltered` and `fsubJobs` views which is available via the button.

We will assume the `fsubJobs` view is already built. You can look in the sample web app to examine how the `fsubJobs` view is designed. You've now built the component parts you need for the query by view, so we can move on to the last step—building the event handler that will start off the whole chain of filtering and displaying the results.

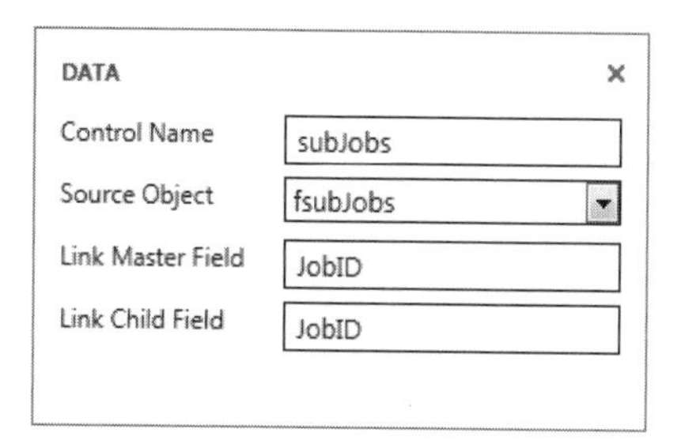

FIGURE 8-76: Data properties of the Subview control

Building a Click Event Handler

The last piece to connect all the pieces we've built so far is the Click event for the Apply Filter button on `frmFilterJobs` view. The macro will perform some conversions and reformat the inputs from the view. As you may recall, there are additional parameters that the user may not necessarily input directly so we need to handle those parameters in order to run the data macro as expected.

Because there are Time parameters, we want to perform an explicit cast of Time using `TimeFromParts()`, one of the few conversion functions available in UI macros, which enables us to validate that inputs for time before proceeding with the data macro. Figure 8-77 illustrates how the `gtimScheduleTime*` variables are populated from the textboxes via `TimeFromParts()` and `DatePart()` functions.

In Figure 8-77, you can only see part of the second SetVariable macro action, the one where `gtimScheduleTimeStarts` is set. Here's the part that you can't see:

```
TimeFromParts(
  DatePart(Hour, [txtScheduleTimeStarts]),
  DatePart(Minute, [txtScheduleTimeStarts]),
  DatePart(Second, [txtScheduleTimeStarts])
)
```

```
If [txtScheduleTimeStarts] Is Null Then
    SetVariable (gtimScheduleTimeStarts, Null)
Else
    SetVariable (gtimScheduleTimeStarts, Time
End If
If [txtScheduleTimeEnds] Is Null Then
    SetVariable (gtimScheduleTimeEnds, Null)
Else
    SetVariable (gtimScheduleTimeEnds, TimeF
End If
```

FIGURE 8-77: Populating Time parameters

The other expression not visible in Figure 8-77, where `gtimScheduleTimeEnds` is set, is similar, except that it acts on `[txtScheduleTimeEnds]` instead. The next part is to handle the Yes/No parameters, which also include an extra `*Excluded` parameter that should be populated. Because we are using a combo box, we need to evaluate the value of the combo box and set the parameter value accordingly. The process is shown in Figure 8-78.

The last part before running the data macro is setting the elapsed time parameter. This demonstrates how you can use a combo box to provide users with a list of common choices and populate the parameters within the UI macros. Only a part of the populating process is demonstrated in Figure 8-79; you can refer to the download sample web app for a complete example.

```
If [cboJobComplete]="Either" Then
    SetVariable (gbolCompleteExcluded, Yes)
    SetVariable (gbolComplete, Yes)
Else
    SetVariable (gbolCompleteExcluded, No)
    SetVariable (gbolComplete, IIf([cboJobComplete]="Yes",Yes,No))
End If
```

FIGURE 8-78: Setting Yes/No parameters

```
If [cboJobTimeElapsed]="Less Than 30 Minutes" Then
    SetVariable (glngTimeSpentMin, 0)
    SetVariable (glngTimeSpentMax, 30)
Else If [cboJobTimeElapsed]="Less Than 1 Hour" Then
    SetVariable (glngTimeSpentMin, 0)
    SetVariable (glngTimeSpentMax, 60)
Else If [cboJobTimeElapsed]="Less Than 1 1/2 Hours" Then
```

FIGURE 8-79: Setting Elapsed Time parameters

You can simply pass most parameters directly from the controls into the data macro parameters, using only variables that we populated from previous steps. You can see how we invoke the data macros and fill in the parameters in Figure 8-80.

Note that we get back the value of matched records from the data macro. This brings us to the last part of the event handler. We need to determine whether we had any matches and if so, open the popup view to display the filtered results and pass in the current username. In case there are no matches; we simply display the messagebox for the user to try a different filter. You can see how you'd build this in Figure 8-81.

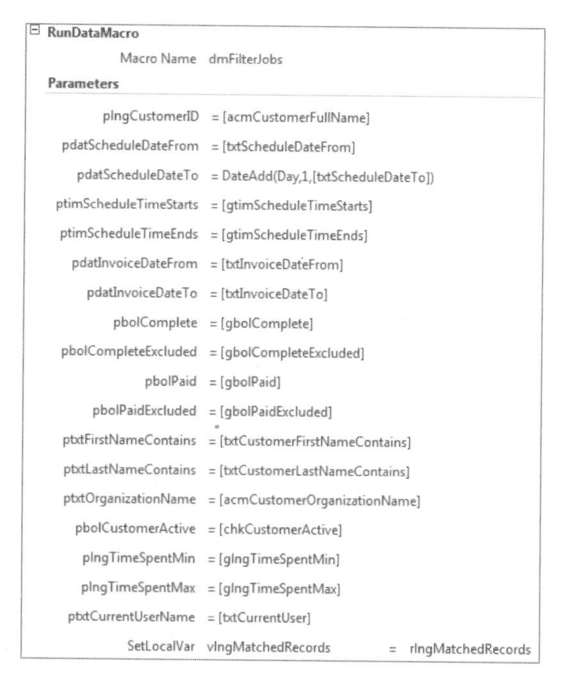

FIGURE 8-80: Invoking dmFilterJobs data macro

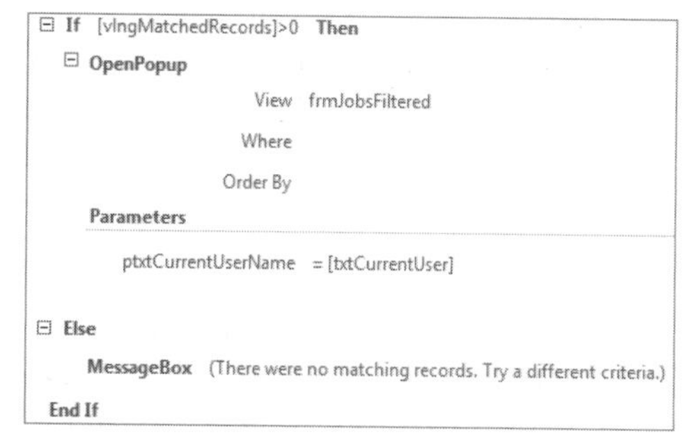

FIGURE 8-81: Evaluating the result of dmFilterJobs and acting upon it

With this last event handler in place, you have completed the link among several objects you created in previous steps to support a complex filtering requirement. As you can see, you have a great amount of power by combining various techniques we discussed for using parameters effectively. This is definitely a great improvement over previous Access 2010 web databases where even if you were to do something similar, it would have been far too slow and cumbersome to use. You now can provide your users with an option of using filters within their web browser. For Maid To Order, this enables maids to quickly answer various questions and make necessary adjustments out in the field about their jobs without having to be at a desktop computer or call someone at the office to get and update the information.

SUMMARY

In Chapter 4, you learned about many new tools made available in Access web apps and what they can do. In this chapter, we took this base knowledge and explored effective techniques you can employ with various design patterns to create rich, powerful web apps. You saw how you can translate traditional client design patterns such as switchboards, index forms, and query by views into the equivalent representations in Access web apps.

You studied the differences behind traditional form design and navigation controls and learned how the new tiles and links provide a convenient noun-verb motif to make navigation easy and accessible. You also considered the principles behind the web design and what it means in terms of minimizing clicks required to reach the desired workflow, empowering the user to do things without having to hunt for the right context.

You started a simple splash form, which also included consideration of the need to hide some tiles and expose the views associated with the hidden tiles.

You then took an in-depth look at how you can build an index form and three different approaches behind the design pattern. You saw that you can use a List view, a Summary view, or Datasheet view to provide the index form functionality, and you saw how they differ so you should be able to identify which is the best view for your particular workflow.

You took a deep dive into the query by view method, covering many changes required to design one effectively in the new environment. You saw how you should adapt your approach to SQL construction and leverage parameters to your advantage for controlling filtering. You then pieced together the building blocks for a simple query by view, a blank view for inputting criteria and a popup view for displaying the matched results.

You also saw how you can incorporate additional techniques, such as passing parameters into nested queries via the top-level queries and creating a filter table to enable optional joining.

Together with the information you will acquire in Chapter 9 you are well-equipped to come up with solid designs to support your users' workflows and enable them to do their work effectively. You will now turn to studying new capabilities you can add to your web apps by leveraging the power of macros.

Solving Business Problems with Macros

WHAT'S IN THIS CHAPTER?

- Examining the capabilities of UI and data macros and understanding how to use them together
- Effectively using table events to manage and enforce business rules
- Leveraging parameter queries and aggregate queries

WROX.COM CODE DOWNLOADS FOR THIS CHAPTER

The code and sample downloads for this chapter are found at `www.wiley.com/go/proaccess2013prog.com` on the Download Code tab. They are in the Maid To Order Sample App download. Refer to the Readme.txt for installation instructions.

You read in Chapter 6 about the new macro designer and how Access 2013 macros are different. In intervening chapters, you've read about how you can design tables and views, and with that information you are ready to consider the crucial questions all developers ask about their tool: "Is it the right tool for this job? Am I using it the right way?" In this chapter, we discuss some practical scenarios and quickly view some edge cases not only to show you what you can accomplish with macros, but also how to accomplish it easily and smoothly.

We will start by reviewing our toolkit, and then move to a discussion on typical scenarios where an Access application will have to fulfill the customer's requirements, and finally, work through some examples step by step. We will start with simple macros to insert a record into a table and copy a record, move on to using table events to automate maintaining a history of changes, and then turn to performing bulk updates to several records. You will then get a broader survey of other macro capabilities and get some idea of what you can do to adapt and expand the content to your specific business applications.

MACRO DESIGN CONSIDERATIONS

In traditional Access applications, you probably used VBA to enforce business rules and carry out processes in a typical workflow. You will find that several functionalities you have had via VBA exist within macros. You were introduced to different types of macros in Chapter 6: UI macros, data macros, and table events. We will now consider situations when you need to select the right kind of macro or if you need them at all.

When to Use Data Macros

One key feature of Access is enabling you to quickly build an application for managing data without significant upfront investment and programming. Many common tasks pertaining to *create, read, update and delete* (CRUD) operations are available out of the box, without additional programming. As you saw in earlier chapters, whenever you add a table you immediately get a pair of views to perform basic CRUD operations against that table. You learned that you can make use of validation rules and calculated fields to enforce common requirements and calculations at the record level. Finally, you saw how objects such as the Related Items control and the Summary view can provide easy access to managing related records and performing calculations. We cite those examples to help you establish when you need to start thinking about solving your business problem with a data macro. Generally speaking, you would want to turn to a data macro when you need to:

- Perform CRUD operations on more than a single record in a single action
- Automate system maintenance, such as recording an audit record when a record is updated, or updating a summary table
- Perform validations for scope wider than a record, and to block invalid data from being saved in a table
- Encapsulate a multiple step operation into a single action using parameters

Direct Access to Data

One significant consideration with regard to standalone data macros, especially those performing CRUD operations, is that you cannot always ensure users have access to data only through those data macros. You can remove the capability to add, edit, or delete records from a view or not present a view at all, but if users are allowed to connect to the database via the Access client and use a datasheet or Access client form to update the data, they will be able to circumvent data macros. Therefore, it is generally a more robust design to leverage out-of-the-box functionalities and use table events to ensure that business logic will be enforced at all times, regardless of how the user edits the data. The final choice depends partly on the customer's priorities, of course.

Using Table Events with Default Values

To put it in more concrete terms, let's say that Maid to Order wants to require that an initial job is created for every new customer at the same time this customer is added. You can certainly meet this requirement by using an unbound form and a data macro that collects all of the parameters needed to create both a new customer record and a new job record. However, you can also meet the requirement by using the Insert event on the customer table to add a new job record using default values for a new job. The Insert event on the customer table would always be fired regardless of how the customer's record got added, which means you can be assured that your requirement will be enforced at all times. On the other hand, using the table's Insert event means you cannot customize the default values for the job record. You would need to work out a good way to create a default — maybe by performing calculations for dates based on today's date. You almost certainly would have to display the newly created job for the user to further customize.

Inserting Customizable Defaults with Data Macros

On the other hand, if Maid To Order is more interested in streamlining its data entry and is not concerned about enforcing the addition of a job for each new customer, then it may see value in your creating an unbound form and a standalone data macro to encapsulate the inserts into two tables. Even so, you will almost certainly be investing more time and effort in building this functionality as opposed to using out-of-the-box functionality such as a subview or a Related Items control and a popup view. This is where your experience will help guide the customer to select the simplest approach that will also be robust and work well with the overall application design.

Handling Errors

Another consideration is the ability to handle errors. Within data macros, you can raise an error and send a custom error message back to the user, making them useful for performing complex validations, whether within a table event or a freestanding data macro. However, this is an all-or-nothing deal; you cannot opt to commit some of the changes performed in the data macro and discard others. An error will undo everything. This is generally a good thing as it guarantees that your application will not end up in an inconsistent state. However, this bears pointing out explicitly, especially when you call other data macros within data macros. If there are problems, such as an invalid value for a parameter, everything will be dropped and the user will be shown an error message. Therefore, it is even more important that you ensure, especially for table events, that the macros are robust and will work with all possible scenarios or that you have mechanisms in place to handle unexpected values or results.

ForEachRecord Macro Action and Queries

LookupRecord and ForEachRecord, as you may know, operate against the equivalent of a recordset. With LookupRecord and ForEachRecord actions, you can use either tables or queries, which raises some additional thoughts. Because data macros are fundamentally procedural, where the ForEachRecord action transforms into a cursor-type operation, it's usually a good idea to ensure that you use queries as much as possible, and not just to filter down the number of records that will be iterated in the macro actions. You should also use aggregate queries to quickly give you aggregate results where needed, instead of using the ForEachRecord macro action to aggregate across the records. In Chapter 8, as well as in later sections of this chapter, there are examples of how you can apply what you learned in Chapter 5 to use queries efficiently and how you can benefit from better performance for doing so.

In short, because the ForEachRecord macro action must iterate over a recordset, whereas queries can perform aggregate operations; when you find an opportunity to use a query instead of performing calculations over several records ForEachRecord macro action, you should pick the query most of the time.

When to Use UI Macros

Scope and context are important considerations when you work with macros. UI macros have a much narrower scope compared to data macros. As you will see later in the chapter, data macros can work with several objects at once. UI macros, on the other hand, can only operate in the context of the active view and its content. A UI macro can neither access other views — popup or not — nor can it manipulate a subview. For Blank and List views, you can manipulate the following six object properties at run time:

1. Enabled
2. Visible
3. ForeColor
4. BackColor
5. Caption
6. Value

When creating a freestanding UI macro, the onus is on you to ensure that, when it's called, the content within the UI macro is valid. For example, suppose that you wanted to have two buttons on four different forms that should behave similarly. You need to name the two buttons identically in each form in order for those forms to be able to call the freestanding macro without causing an error.

Furthermore, UI macros cannot contain parameters within themselves. However, you can address this limitation in a couple of ways. To parameterize a UI macro, you would use a SetVariable action to set a variable to the appropriate value before invoking the UI macro. The UI macro could then refer to that variable. Another possible method for parameterizing a UI macro is to call a RunDataMacro that returns a result to the UI macro, but this costs relatively much more than setting a variable, as the web browser needs to make a roundtrip to the server to get the output.

Because of these considerations, you will likely find that most of your UI macros will be written as event handlers for the events of various controls and views, and that you have only a handful, if any, freestanding UI macros.

Functions Exclusive to UI Macros

It's important to note that there is a pair of functions that is available only in UI macros:

- `UserDisplayName()`
- `UserEmailAddress()`

The results of those functions are not available within data macros. That is expected behavior because when running a data macro, which in actuality is a SQL module, the caller executing the SQL is actually Access, not the user. Thus, functions typically used in T-SQL cannot be used to determine the logged in user because of the impersonation. Therefore, if you have any data that is user-specific, it is necessary to pass the result of the `UserDisplayName()` or `UserEmailAddress()` function as a parameter into a query or data macro.

> **NOTE** *As you learned in Chapter 8, tile-bound views cannot be based on a parameterized query. Therefore, if you have data to which you need to manage access based on the logged-in user, you must use popup views in order to pass in the result of either function.*

On Start Macro

The On Start macro deserves a special mention. The On Start Macro offers immense value to you, the developer, because it gives you an opportunity to initialize local variables, ensure that your startup view is displayed, and get some information about the context.

One major use we quickly discovered for the On Start macro is to initialize variables. As mentioned earlier in this book, a variable used in UI macros has a global scope and therefore is subject to namespace pollution. For more complex applications, it can be a daunting task to track all possible variables.

Variable Declaration and Error Handling

If you refer to a variable that's not previously set via a SetVariable macro action, you will get the run time error illustrated in Figure 9-1.

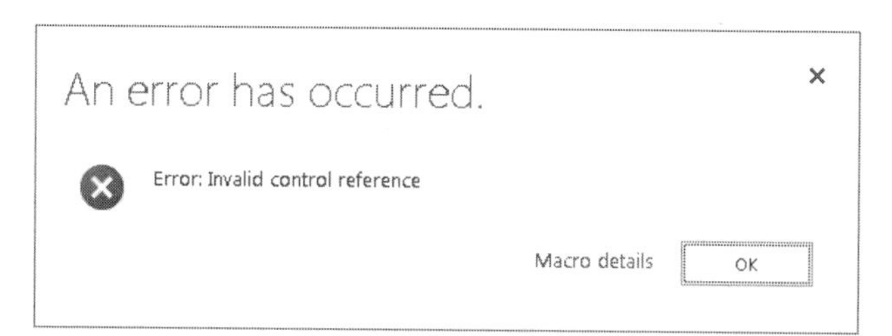

FIGURE 9-1: Uninitialized variable referenced in a macro

Thus, the On Start macro provides you with an ideal place to list all variables and initialize them to good default values as the partial list of variables in Figure 9-2 illustrates.

No function is available to determine whether a variable was declared or not, and with no ability to create error handling within UI macros, it is essential that you have initialized all of your variables before any single action references those variables. If you establish the practice of consistently declaring all new variables and initializing them via your app's On Start macro, managing variables will also be more documented. You also have a ready reference so you can ensure you are not creating redundant variables or struggling to ensure that all variables are initialized at the right time and re-used in the expected manner.

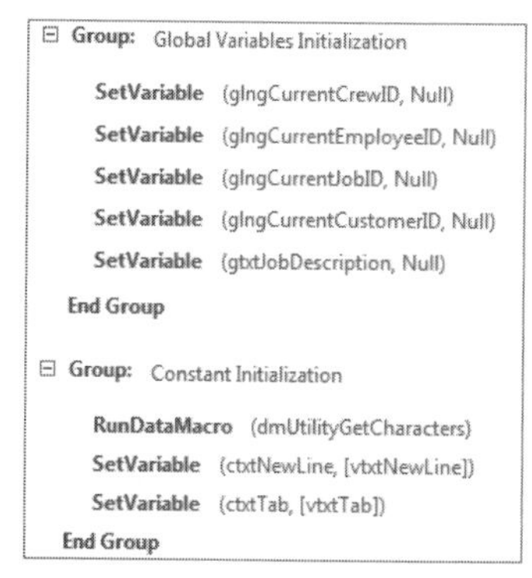

FIGURE 9-2: On Start macro initializing common variables

Look at the second group of the On Start macro, where a data macro runs to get two values — one for the new line character and one for the tab character. In the On Start macro itself, you can't retrieve values directly from a table; however, you can get them with the data macro. You'll learn more about these values and how they are used later in this chapter.

As you saw in Figure 9-2, we used null as the default value for variables initialized in this On Start macro. This makes it easy for us to check elsewhere in the application whether an expected value has been supplied or not, and in the latter case, provide a friendly message to the user, as illustrated in Figure 9-3.

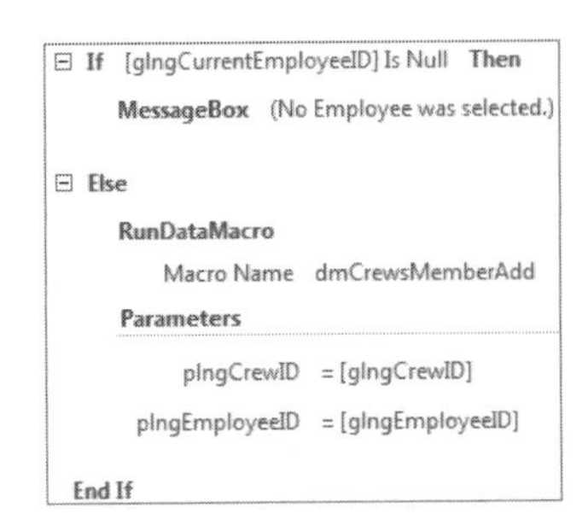

FIGURE 9-3: Testing whether a variable is null

The On Start macro is also a good place to manage any user defaults that may be stored in a table. Because users can leave the app at any time, the On Start macro offers you the opportunity to reset values to their original state as appropriate, our caveat regarding roundtripping notwithstanding.

USING FREESTANDING MACROS

In the next section, you will look at designing macros that are intended to be a part of a manual workflow where a user initiates the action, such as clicking a button to start off a series of operations encapsulated within one or more macros. You will start with a simple record copy workflow and escalate the process to a set of records and then into a set of tables.

Remember that because these macros are user-initiated, they can also be circumvented, and are, therefore, not appropriate for the task of enforcing validations or preventing unacceptable data from being saved in a table. It is more appropriate to approach them as tools to enable users to perform their tasks quickly and in the most efficient manner.

Cloning a Record

Maid To Order commonly has customers who ask for new jobs with the same services provided each time. While Maid To Order usually has a regular schedule with customers, there are times when customers want an extra job outside their regular schedule, perhaps to have maids come before or after a big party at their house. The only difference is the date being scheduled. Because of the trust the customers have built with the maids, it's typical that the same crew is assigned to the customer for each job, but there are times when this is not possible.

Instead of requiring the user to enter an entirely new job from scratch, you can offer the user an action button to clone a selected job for a new date, as shown in Figure 9-4.

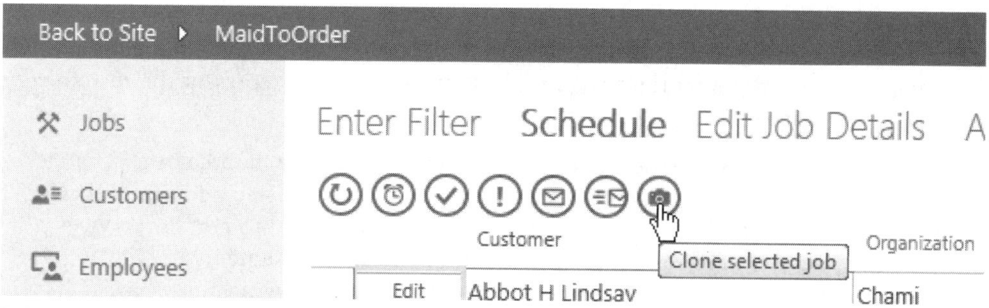

FIGURE 9-4: Action button to clone a job

Because you do not want every field in the cloned job to be identical, you need to customize certain parts, so it is not possible to simply fire off the data macro from this action button. Instead, you open a popup view using the OpenPopup macro action. You can see that in Figure 9-5.

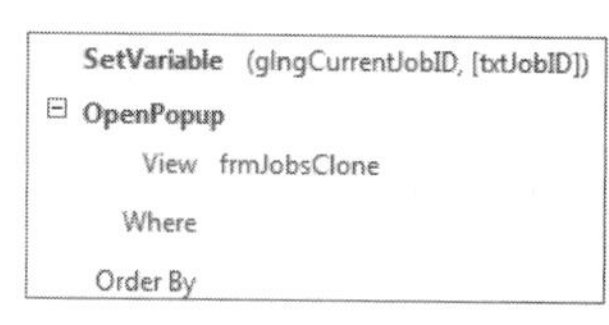
SetVariable (glngCurrentJobID, [txtJobID])
OpenPopup
View frmJobsClone
Where
Order By

FIGURE 9-5: OpenPopup macro action

When the popup opens, the default value for the job to clone is the one selected in the schedule when the action button was clicked. This is accomplished in the Load event of the popup, as shown in Figure 9-6. The user can accept the default or change to a different job.

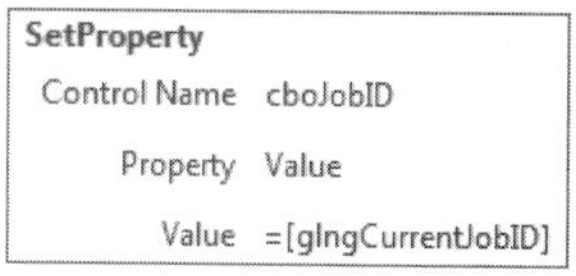

FIGURE 9-6: Load event of the Job Clone popup

Opening a popup form offers the user the opportunity to customize the commonly changed data when cloning jobs. Maid To Order has specified that users be able to customize jobs, as shown in Figure 9-7.

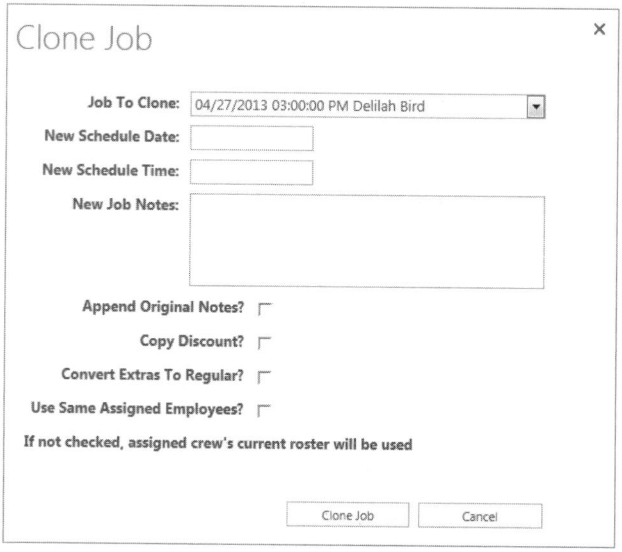

FIGURE 9-7: Popup form to accept input parameters for cloning a job

Note that the combo box in Figure 9-7 shows the cloned job as set in the macro that opened the popup. The main thing for us to note is that Users can select which job to copy, and enter a new date, time, and additional notes for the new job. Those three textboxes represent the customizations users may add to the cloned jobs.

However, Maid To Order doesn't stop there — they want to be able to handle other changes to customers' jobs as well. For example, the customer may have requested additional services for previous jobs and now wants those additional services to be converted to regular services on future jobs. Or you may need to reapply a discount, or assign the same listing of employees from the previous job rather than the current crew roster, which may have changed. Finally, you want users to be able to append the notes from the original job to the notes for the cloned job, making it easy to refer to notes that may be still relevant for the cloned job.

Let's look at the rowsource driving the combo box that selects the job. Although you are cloning a specific job, it's convenient for the user to see which customer's job they are cloning in the combo box. Thus, you use the `Concat()` function to display both the customer's name and the job's scheduled date and time in a single column. See the expanded Expression in Figure 9-8. When displaying date/time values, you have to use the `Format()` function to ensure they are rendered in readable format. Otherwise, dates will be shown in the format stored in SQL Server, typically `yyyy-mm-dd hh:mm:nn:ss`.

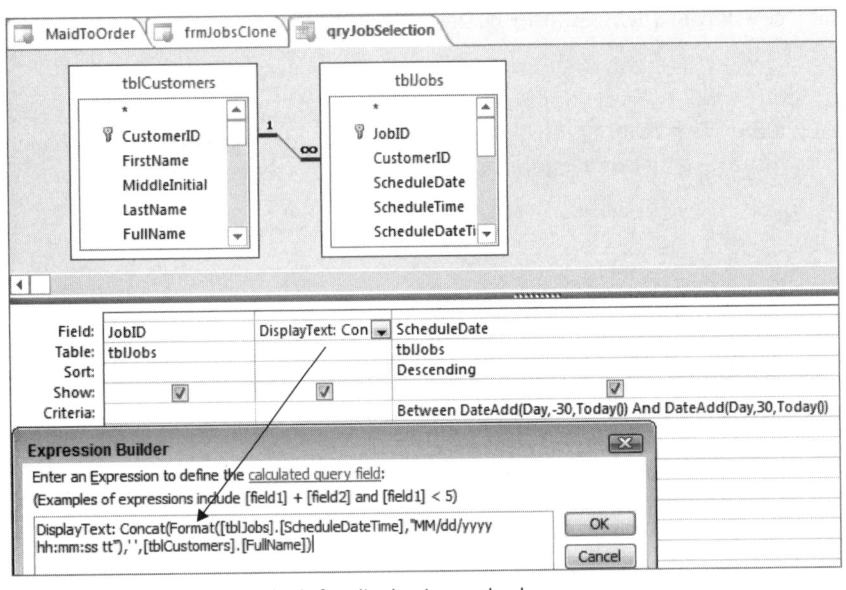

FIGURE 9-8: Concatenated job for display in combo box

NOTE *Note that the* `Format()` *function in web apps is significantly different from the one you knew in the Access client. Unlike the client version, lettercase matters because the function is implemented in SQL Server where case matters.* `D` *and* `d` *have different meanings and, if not used correctly, may provide unexpected output.*

NOTE *Recall that, unlike a client combo box, you cannot have multiple columns for a combo box in your web app, so concatenating will be necessary if you need to display values from more than one column. You may consider alternative approaches to displaying your data. Furthermore, sorting is determined by the displayed field irrespective of any sorting you may have designated in the underlying query. Finally, there is a limit of rows that can be returned. The AutoComplete control allows you to have more values, but it only works with fields and only one field can be searched. You cannot have it be bound to one field and display an expression. So, the combo box is your best choice if you want to use expressions. For this reason, you need to ensure that you have a way of filtering to a manageable number of rows that can be displayed.*

Looking at the popup view, as illustrated in Figure 9-7, there are no other macros beyond those behind the Clone Job and Cancel buttons. The Cancel button is straightforward, having only the ClosePopup action. However, the Clone Job button invokes several actions, including a data macro that needs some parameters. So, before you can build the event handler for the Submit button, you need to build the data macro it will call so that you can supply the parameters that you want to pass from this popup form into that data macro. Start by creating a new data macro using the Create Parameter link to add the nine parameters, as shown in Figure 9-9.

Parameters

Name	Type
plngSourceJobID	Number (No Decimal)
pdatNewScheduleDate	Date
ptimNewScheduleTime	Short Text
pbolCopyNotes	Yes/No
ptxtAdditionalNotes	Long Text
pbolCopyDiscount	Yes/No
pbolConvertExtraToPermanent	Yes/No
pbolCopyAssignedEmployees	Yes/No
pbolCopyJobServices	Yes/No

FIGURE 9-9: Parameters for the dmJobClone data macro

NOTE *In the following discussion, you'll be looking at different sections of a lengthy data macro. Fully expanded, this macro would fill multiple pages. In order to show you the relevant pieces of the macro for discussion, we've taken advantage of the fact that the macro designer allows you to expand and collapse elements within it.*

Because you want to allow users to append the notes from the original job to their new notes, and because there is no means of concatenating a carriage return using a constant such as `vbCrLf` as you would in VBA, you need to store the carriage return in a text field. You will use `tblUtility` table for this purpose. As mentioned earlier in the book, the `tblUtility` table is meant to have only one row. It is used to supply application-level features, such as this. Let's look at the table design in Figure 9-10 to see how you would add a field to store the carriage return.

MaidToOrder | tblUtility

Field Name	Data Type
UtilityID	AutoNumber
LogoImage	Image
CarriageReturnCharacter	Long Text
TabCharacter	Long Text

FIGURE 9-10: New field in tblUtility table

The simplest way to insert the carriage return into the tblUtility table is to save changes and switch from design to datasheet view. Now you can do a copy and paste from Notepad, for example into the field on the datasheet. Of course, you can't actually see the carriage return, which is a non-printing character, in the field, and you have to use Long Text to allow this character to be saved correctly.

Returning to the `dmJobClone` data macro, you can now look up the carriage return value from `tblUtility`, but do so only if you have added data for new notes and the user asks to append the original notes to that data. You wrap the lookup in the If/Then macro action to test both the parameter indicating whether the note is to be copied (`If [pbolCopyNotes] =Yes`) and whether there are any entries in the new notes (`If [ptxtAdditionalNotes] Is Not Null`). Figure 9-11 shows that part of the data macro.

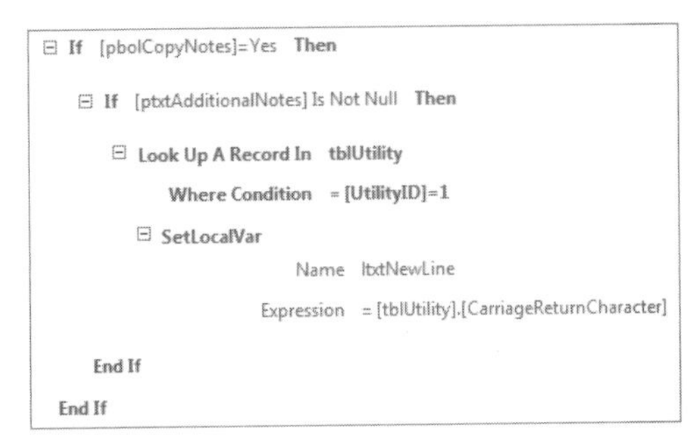

FIGURE 9-11: Looking up the carriage return when needed

NOTE *Figure 9-11 is a good example of how you can work to minimize processing. Using LookupRecord and ForEachRecord are much more expensive actions compared to evaluating a parameter or a variable. You also may find it beneficial to perform validations on parameters or variables as early as possible in the procedure to ensure that any problems are immediately detected and control is returned to the user sooner rather than later in the event of a problem with supplied values.*

Also, the On Start macro can call a data macro that sets a variable to do the same thing as this macro block to make it available for use within UI macros. Within data macros, a LookUpRecord will be needed to retrieve the special characters.

That concludes the setup portion of the macro, which you'll complete before you move into the actual copying part of the operation. In order to perform the copy, you first have to identify the target job, which you do using a LookupRecord against the parameter containing the `JobID` from the popup. Then you start the CreateRecord step inside the data block, also shown in Figure 9-12.

```
⊟ Look Up A Record In   tblJobs
      Where Condition   = [JobID]=[plngSourceJobID]
                Alias   tblJobs_Source

   ⊞   Create a Record In   tblJobs
                    Alias   tblJobs_New
```

FIGURE 9-12 LookupRecord macro action

Note the use of the alias, `tblJobs_Source` and `tblJobs_New` for the data block. Because you are copying a record from `tblJobs` and inserting the new record into the same table, aliasing disambiguates between the source job record and the newly created job record.

> **NOTE** *Recall from Chapter 6 that certain macro actions such as LookupRecord, ForEachRecord, CreateRecord, and EditRecord form a data block that also dictates its scope. In Figure 9-12, CreateRecord is within the LookupRecord block in order to allow for referencing between the lookup record and the created record. Had CreateRecord been created outside the LookupRecord's block, data from the LookupRecord would no longer be accessible for use within CreateRecord.*

Because you want to reference other fields in the lookup job record, you need to assign them to variables. Doing so makes the values available outside the scope of your LookupRecord data block. Once they are assigned to variables, you can reference the variable instead of the source field. Figure 9-13 shows two variables being set based on data in fields within the lookup record; you will see it again shortly in later steps.

Also, Figure 9-13 demonstrates the use of CreateRecord and SetField macro actions to assign either copied values or values from parameters into the newly created record. Note the use of `IIf()` to determine whether to use the original values or modified values supplied by parameters.

```
⊟   Create a Record In   tblJobs
                 Alias   tblJobs_New
    SetLocalVar  (lngCustomerID, [tblJobs_Source].[CustomerID])
  ⊞ SetLocalVar  (lngCrewID, [tblJobs_Source].[CrewID])
    SetField  (tblJobs_New.CustomerID, [tblJobs_Source].[CustomerID])
    SetField  (tblJobs_New.CrewID, [tblJobs_Source].[CrewID])
    SetField  (tblJobs_New.ScheduleDate, IIf([pdatNewScheduleDate] Is Null,[tblJobs_Source].[ScheduleDate],Try_Cast([pdatNewScheduleDate],Date)))
    SetField  (tblJobs_New.ScheduleTime, IIf([ptimNewScheduleTime] Is Null,[tblJobs_Source].[ScheduleTime],Try_Cast([ptimNewScheduleTime],Time)))
    SetField  (tblJobs_New.Notes, Concat([ptxtAdditionalNotes],[ltxtNewLine],[ltxtNewLine],IIf([pbolCopyNotes]=Yes,[tblJobs_Source].[Notes],'')))
```

FIGURE 9-13: CreateRecord and SetField macro actions

Figure 9-13 also shows the benefit of the alias; the source values (such as `[tblJobs_Source].[CustomerID]`) and target values (for example, `[tblJobs_New].[CustomerID]`) are disambiguated to clearly reference what goes where. You will want to get comfortable with two-part qualifier naming (as in `[tblJobs_Source].[CustomerID]`), as shown in Figure 9-13 to generate self-documenting macros.

One of the parameters you passed in was whether the macro should duplicate a particular job's customized services or use the default services specified by the customer. This is useful in cases where maids need to clone a special job that includes services that aren't a part of regular activity. Figure 9-14 shows an If/Then block, which allows you to choose whether to loop records within `txrfJobServices` or `txrfCustomerServices` depending on the value of the `pbolCopyJobServices` parameter.

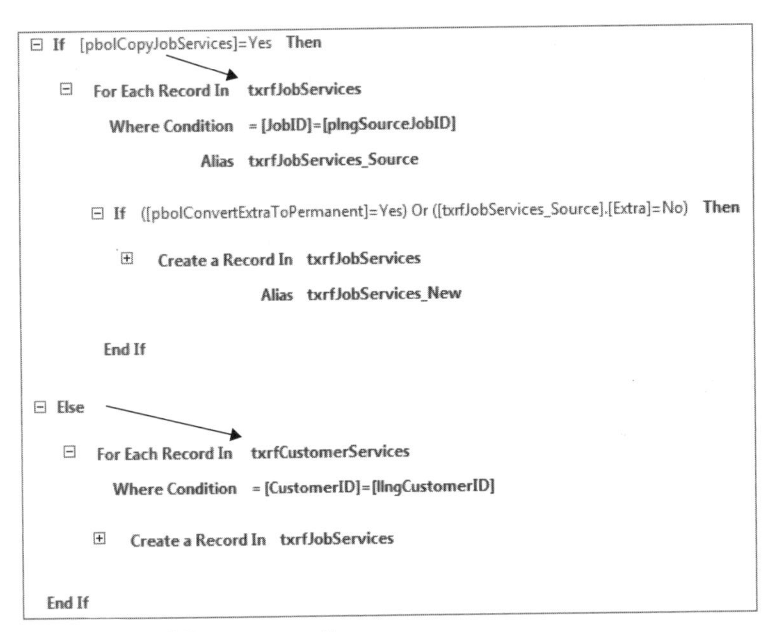

FIGURE 9-14: If/Then macro action

Let's expand the Create a Record action in the true part of the If/Then block from Figure 9-14 and look at what you need to do when copying services from a special job. Figure 9-15 shows the CreateRecord and associated SetField macro actions performed on the `txrfJobServices` in the True part of the block.

```
⊟ If ([pbolConvertExtraToPermanent]=Yes) Or ([txrfJobServices_Source].[Extra]=No) Then
    ⊟ Create a Record In  txrfJobServices
                    Alias  txrfJobServices_New
      SetField
                    Name   txrfJobServices_New.JobID
                    Value  = [txrfJobServices_Source].[JobID]
      SetField  (txrfJobServices_New.ServiceID, [txrfJobServices_Source].[ServiceID])
      SetField  (txrfJobServices_New.Description, [txrfJobServices_Source].[Description])
      SetField  (txrfJobServices_New.Notes, [txrfJobServices_Source].[Notes])
      SetField  (txrfJobServices_New.Fee, [txrfJobServices_Source].[Fee])
      ⊟ If [pbolCopyDiscount]=Yes Then
          SetField  (txrfJobServices_New.Discount, [txrfJobServices_Source].[Discount])
          SetField  (txrfJobServices_New.DiscountReason, [txrfJobServices_Source].[DiscountReason])
      End If
End If
```

FIGURE 9-15: CreateRecord for txtfJobServices table

Look closely at the two inner If/Then blocks. For the `Extra` field, you are factoring in the `pbolConvertExtraToPermanent` parameter so the value in the `Extra` field for the new job service record may not be same value as the source from which it came. Sometimes customers may want you to copy a special job. Sometime it's just a special job done one more time. But when the customer decides that it should be included in a new regular job, you want to convert the job service into a regular service. The `[pbolConvertExtraToPermanent]=Yes` condition for the If/Then block allows you not only to set the `Extra` field for the new service, but also to insert a new service into the customer's list of default services to ensure that any new job created for this customer has a full set of services, including this formerly extra service. On the other hand, if the same parameter is set to No, any job services that are extra will not be added to the cloned job.

> **NOTE** *In the context of a web macro, you should use the constants* `Yes` *and* `No` *instead of the* `True` *and* `False` *constants you may be used to using in VBA or client macros.*

Similarly, sometimes you may be obliged to offer the same discount from a cloned job to a new job once again, so you want to allow for this. This is accomplished by wrapping the discount selection in an If/Then macro action. Note that there is no Else block, which is perfectly fine because it just means that the `Discount` and `DiscountReason` fields will be `No` and `Null`, respectively.

You conclude the macro with similar logic regarding assigning employees to the new jobs, again choosing whether to clone from the job directly or use the crew roster. Figure 9-16 shows the block that switches between either table based on the `pbolCopyAssignedEmployees` parameter's input.

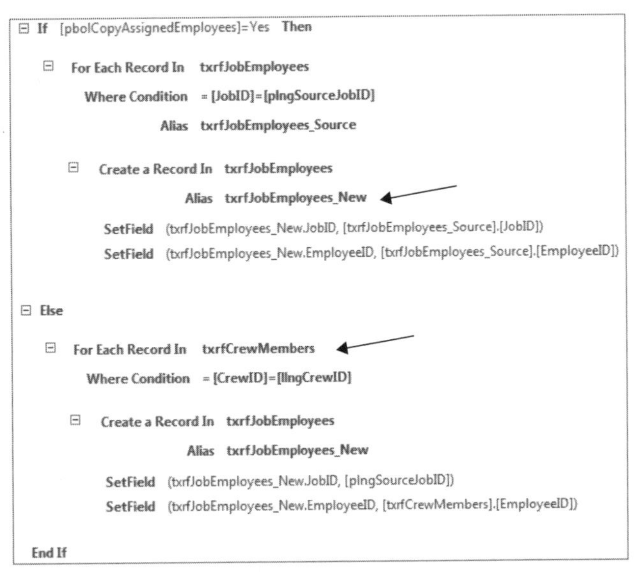

FIGURE 9-16: Final If/Then macro action choosing between txrfJobEmployees or txrfCrewMembers as the source for filling in a job's assigned employees

You have now seen how you can effectively manage several records and encapsulate a complex process into a simple call via RunDataMacro macro actions by passing in parameters. Within the process, you can see how you can branch your logic to handle a variety of scenarios.

Generating a Set of Records with Variable Parameters

Next, we want to consider a scenario where the customer would like to generate a schedule of new jobs for a specified interval. The complicating factor is that customers have different service frequencies; some want daily services, others weekly, and yet others some different period. Some want to schedule jobs only on a short-term basis, such as the next three times; others would rather schedule for the next year. However you put it, the basic problem for you to solve is to perform the same action, copying a record, the number of times specified by the users at run time.

The solution to this requirement is to use the ForEachRecord macro action. ForEachRecord allows you to loop a specific number of times in a data macro. However, you cannot specify an ad hoc number of iterations; it is determined solely by the number of records returned to the ForEachRecord macro action. Therefore, one solution to enable ad hoc iterations is to create a tally table that contains a range of sequential values, which can be used to determine the number of iterations needed for each operation where it is called. The user will not use this tally table directly, but it is used within macros to provide you with a loop construct.

First, you will learn to create a tally table, and then you'll circle back to the task of creating sets of records, taking advantage of this table.

> **TALLY TABLE AND QUERIES**
>
> While you may not have encountered tally tables in the Access environment, the tally table is a common feature used by SQL Server developers and can be very useful even in queries. Therefore, a tally table can provide value beyond simply supporting a loop construct for your data macros. For an in-depth discussion on other uses of tally tables, search on `www.sqlservercentral.com`.

Creating a Tally Table

When creating a tally table you need to take a few additional steps beyond those involved in creating data or lookup tables because, in the end, you need only one column, which is the original autonumbering ID column. This column is perfect for providing sequential values. However, as you are probably aware, you can neither insert into the autonumber column nor do an empty insert. Thus, the initial table design necessitates an initial seed value column, as Figure 9-17 shows.

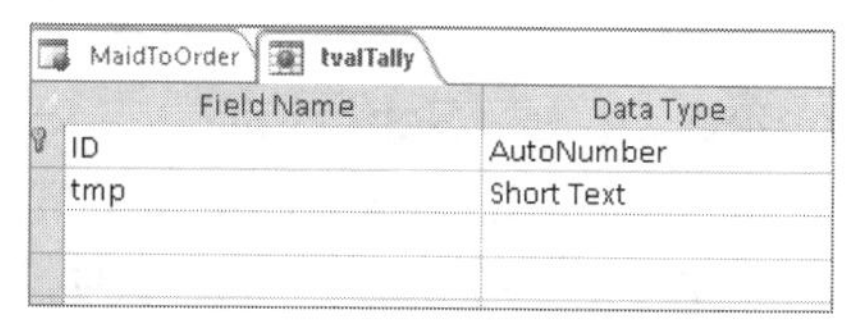

FIGURE 9-17: Initial tvalTally design

Because it's meant for programming purposes rather than to be used directly, name the table `tvalTally` using the `tval` prefix. You can name the seed value column `tmp` because, as the name implies, you will delete it later. The `tmp` column's only purpose is to facilitate the population of the records.

After saving the table, you need to insert values. Depending on the size and purpose of your app, you will want to insert as many as 10,000 records, as we've done; you may want less or more values in your tally tables. Even if you go as low as 100 rows, it can take quite some time to insert them one by one. If you don't want to import a source file, you could use a query using Cartesian joins, as in Figure 9-18.

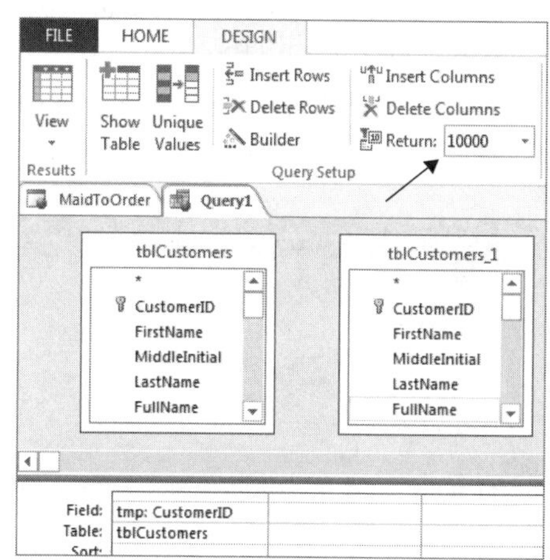

FIGURE 9-18: Using a Cartesian self-join with the biggest table in your database as the source

The idea is that you select the biggest table repeatedly, leveraging the fact that a Cartesian join generates a product of records between tables. If the biggest table in the database had just 100 rows, a Cartesian self-join would yield 100 × 100 = 10,000 records. As Figure 9-18 shows, you simply assign a constant value to the `tmp` column. The only point in inserting anything into the tally table is to simply generate 10,000 records, which causes the autonumber field to increment. To put a cap on the number of records to insert, set Return Records to a value, as shown in Figure 9-18.

Once you've run the query and inserted the needed number of rows into the `tvalTally`, whether using a data macro or a client query or pasting the query's datasheet into the table's datasheet, you can delete the `tmp` column. At this point, `tvalTally` is ready for use in the data macro and elsewhere in your app.

With the tally table, you can loop for so many times and when appropriate, use an additional condition to exit the loop earlier with the ExitForEachRecord macro action. Figure 9-19 demonstrates how you could specify the number of loops. The number of loops you need is passed into the macro as the `plngRecurrences` parameter, in this case, 25.

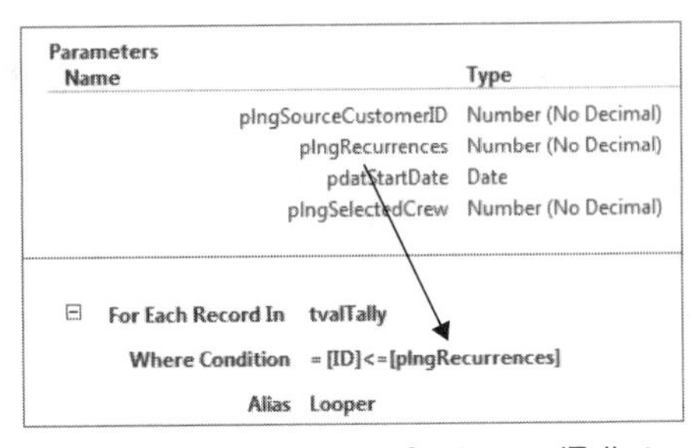

FIGURE 9-19: Example of using tvalTally to loop using a parameter (plngRecurrences)

Generating a Schedule

Now that you have your tally table present in the Maid To Order application, you can provide the requested functionality, in which customers want to schedule a specific, but variable, number of future jobs. Unlike the clone job functionality covered in the previous section, this task requires less customization; Maid To Order only wants to use the customer's requested services as the template to generate a new job; only two attributes are customized: the dates of the job, and the assigned crew, which may be different from previous jobs, to each future job.

Figure 9-20 shows the button that will open the popup to enter the parameters from `frmCustomerByName` view.

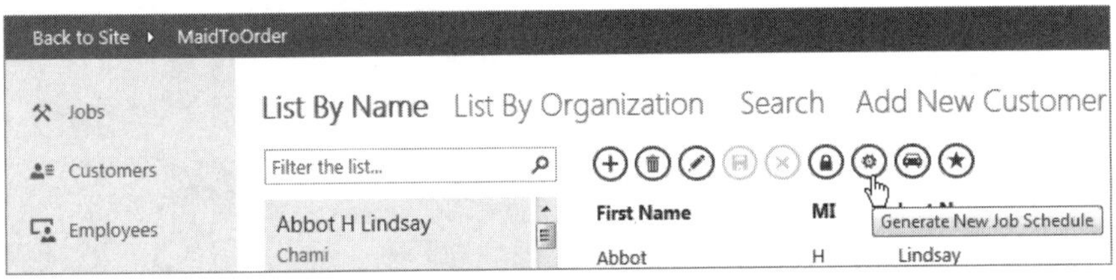

FIGURE 9-20: Button to generate a schedule

Like the button to clone a job shown in the previous section, this button simply performs an OpenPopup macro action. However, there's a twist — this popup form will have a recordsource, unlike the `frmJobsClone` shown in the previous section. In order to limit the records in that recordsource to those you want, you pass in the `CustomerID` as the parameter, as shown in Figure 9-21.

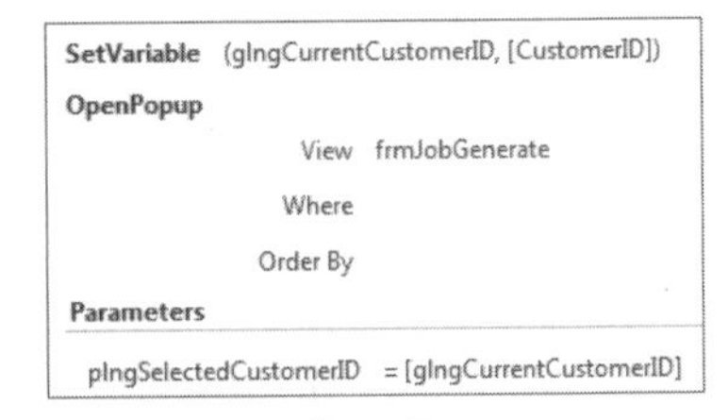

FIGURE 9-21: OpenPopup macro action with CustomerID parameter

You may be wondering why you would want to attach a recordsource to a popup view that is meant to take inputs. The reason is to provide default values to fill in the appropriate input controls. Figure 9-22 shows what the user would see when the user selects a customer who was last serviced on January 2, 2013 and who is on a weekly plan.

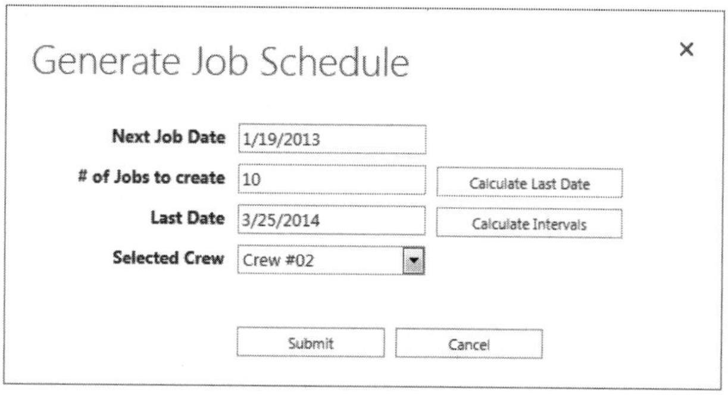

Generate Job Schedule

Next Job Date 1/19/2013

# of Jobs to create 10 Calculate Last Date

Last Date 3/25/2014 Calculate Intervals

Selected Crew Crew #02

Submit Cancel

FIGURE 9-22: User's view of frmJobGenerate with default values filled in

In order to be able to display 1/9/13 as the next start date, you need to look up the last job record for this customer. The data macro does that, but you also have to open a popup form. This shows how you can combine a pair of actions — looking up a record and opening a popup view — into a single step, offering users a better experience. Had you performed an OpenPopup macro action, followed by a RunDataMacro on the popup's Load event, the user would see the form open, and then be told to wait a second or two while the data macro runs, making it look slow. Even if the time taken to open a bound popup view is the same, the user sees only the form opening and thus experiences it as a bit quicker. Such subjective differences can be very important and should be factored in your application design.

Let's look at the query that will give you the parameters you want to fill in Figure 9-23.

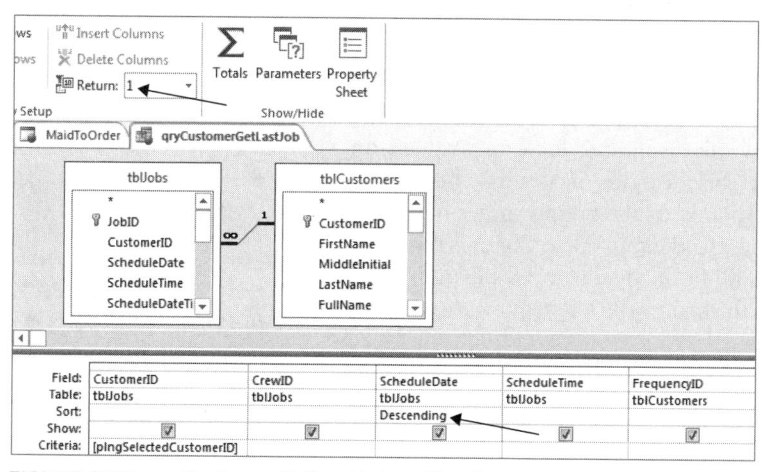

FIGURE 9-23: qryCustomerGetLastJob to filter form's recordsource and retrieve additional default parameters

Although getting a last job record could technically be done with a `Max(ScheduleDateTime)` action, you should specify that the query return one record and be sorted in descending order on ScheduleDateTime as illustrated in Figure 9-23. This allows you to select other columns from the job record. This is equivalent to doing a `SELECT TOP 1 … ORDER BY ScheduleDateTime DESC`. You define a single parameter, `plngSelectedCustomerID`, which is assigned a value in the data macro that opens the form. With this query, you can determine when the last job date was and which crew was assigned to it.

Let's look at how you use that information to open the `frmJobGenerate` view, shown in design view in Figure 9-24.

FIGURE 9-24: Design view of the frmJobGenerate popup view

You should note the following three things in Figure 9-24:

1. Visible fields, such as `Next Job Date`, where the user enters parameters, are all unbound.
2. All bound fields, highlighted, are hidden.
3. There is an On Current macro action

Binding the input controls in this view would be inappropriate — you don't want to have the user end up editing the last job or give the user a control that the user can't modify. You need hidden controls to receive the values so that you can pass the default values to the view for display to users.

The editable controls have a Default property, which also can be based on an expression. However, using it to look up a value from another control will not work because this occurs too early in the process and would show blank, as the bound values haven't been fetched when populating the default value. For this reason, you use the Current event to fill in the default values. Figure 9-25 shows the macro actions performed in the Current event.

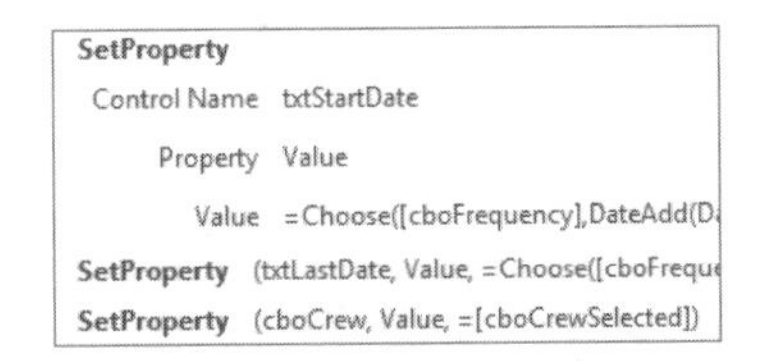

FIGURE 9-25: SetProperty macro actions in the frmJobGenerate Current event

Here are the complete expressions that were truncated from Figure 9-25, the first expression:

```
=Choose([cboFrequency],
  DateAdd(Day,1,[txtScheduleDate]),
  DateAdd(Week,1,[txtScheduleDate]),
  DateAdd(Week,2,[txtScheduleDate]),
  DateAdd(Month,1,[txtScheduleDate])
)
```

And the second expression:

```
=Choose([cboFrequency],
  DateAdd(Day,[txtRecurrence],[txtScheduleDate]),
  DateAdd(Week,[txtRecurrence],[txtScheduleDate]),
  DateAdd(Week,[txtRecurrence]*2,[txtScheduleDate]),
  DateAdd(Month,[txtRecurrence],[txtScheduleDate])
)
```

As you can see, you copy the values from hidden controls bound to the view's recordsource into unbound controls, which the user can edit. Note especially the manual addition of the equal sign in the Value expression. Without the equal sign, Access may interpret the expression as storing a string containing the name of the functions and the hidden controls into the unbound control.

Only one control does use a default value and that is the `txtRecurrence`, which has a value of ten stored, as shown in Figure 9-22 and repeated in design view in Figure 9-26. The Default Value property is accessible via the button.

Thus, you have provided maids with a popup form that gives starting default values, making it easy for maids to add a specific number of new jobs quickly. Whether a maid gets a request to add the next 25 job dates, or to add all job dates through the end of July next year, you need to support both. Therefore, the popup offers both a textbox that accepts an integer value representing recurrences and a textbox that accepts a date value representing an end date.

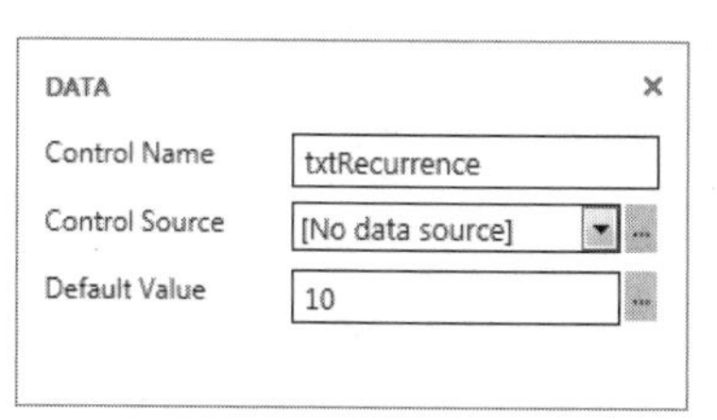

FIGURE 9-26: Default Value property of txtRecurrence Textbox control

You also provide a button so that, when one of those textboxes is changed, the correct value is recalculated for the other textbox. This behavior once again provides the maid with an easy way to see how many jobs would be created in a given date range or when the last job would be for a specified number of jobs. The maid can try several options before committing the final selection by clicking the Submit button.

WHY NOT DO IT IN AN AFTER UPDATE EVENT?

Some of you may be wondering why we use a button instead of automating the recalculation completely via the After Update event of the textbox. The answer is that unlike in the client environment, modifying the value of a textbox programmatically via a macro action triggers its After Update in a web app. Therefore, attaching an After Update event to both pairs of textboxes and modifying the other textbox's value on After Update would cause the other textbox's After Update event to fire, modifying the first textbox, re-triggering its After Update event again. At that point we have a runaway recursion. The user then will be presented with an error that the maximum number of recursions (19) has been reached, leaving the textboxes with incorrect values.

As you will see later, because the data macro uses recurrences as a parameter, and the ending date is meant to help in finding a recurrence using a date, you do use the After Update event for the ending date textbox only but require manual recalculating of the end date via a button when you modify the recurrence value.

Figure 9-27 illustrates how you recalculate the ending date when the `cmdCalculateLastDate` is pressed to execute its Click event.

The truncated expression in Figure 9-27 is similar to the second expression from Figure 9-26, except that instead of `txtScheduleDate`, it uses `txtStartDate`.

In order to avoid several If/Then macro actions, you can use the `Choose()` function seen in Figure 9-26 and 9-27 to select among possible formulas to calculate the end date. Because you are performing a `DateAdd()` function, and you cannot pass a variable into the DatePart argument, `Choose()` allows you to select the correct `DateAdd()` expression to use, based on how frequently a customer wants their service. The frequency comes from the `tvalFrequencies` table, shown in Figure 9-28.

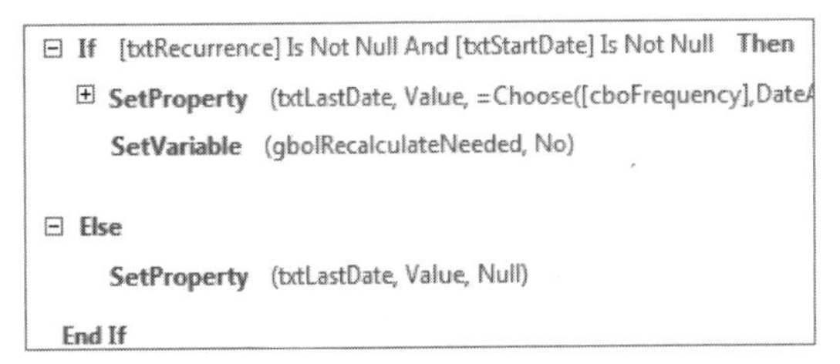

FIGURE 9-27: Macro actions behind the Click event of cmdCalculateLastDate

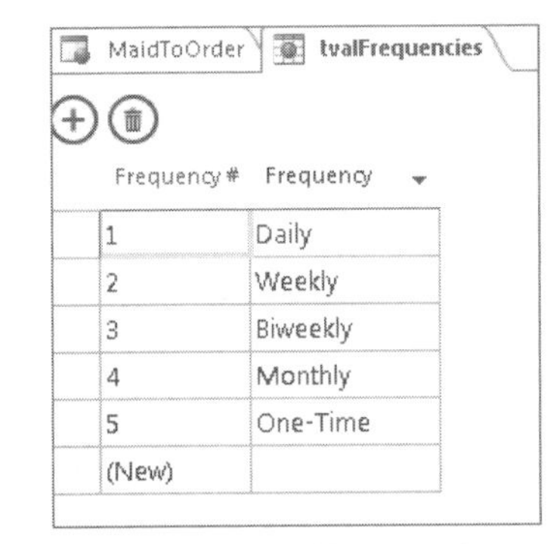

Frequency #	Frequency
1	Daily
2	Weekly
3	Biweekly
4	Monthly
5	One-Time
(New)	

FIGURE 9-28: tvalFrequencies table content

DATEPART ARGUMENT

In VBA, you specify the interval in a `DateAdd()` expression in a string, using something like `"d"` to indicate you want to add a number of days. In web apps, `DateAdd()` is much more like SQL Server's version of `DateAdd()` where you pass in a constant named `Day`, not to be confused with the function of the same name. To get help on the names of DatePart that you want, use Expression Builder to locate the DatePart category under the Constants listing. Intellisense in the Expression Builder will assist you.

The `tval` prefix for this table indicates that you use it to store constants. You basically have to promise never to change the values in the table because this is what macro actions will rely on to make correct choices.

The `Choose()` function makes its selection based on the value of the `FrequencyID` from the hidden bound `Frequency` control, so you arrange the possible formulas in the same order they are shown in Figure 9-29 to ensure that the correct DatePart argument is matched up. The following table shows how you want the `Choose()` function to evaluate the output.

WHEN FREQUENCYID IS . . .	YOU WANT . . .	SO YOU USE THIS FORMULA . . .
1	Daily	`DateAdd(Day, [RecurrenceTextBox], [ScheduleDateTextBox])`
2	Weekly	`DateAdd(Week, [RecurrenceTextBox], [ScheduleDateTextBox])`
3	Biweekly	`DateAdd(Week, [RecurrenceTextBox]*2, [ScheduleDateTextBox])`
4	Monthly	`DateAdd(Month, [RecurrenceTextBox], [ScheduleDateTextBox])`

Note that you don't evaluate the value 5 at all. Because it's a special one-time job, it makes no sense to try to schedule a set of jobs based on that non-regular interval. If the value 5 or any other value not listed in the table is passed to the `Choose()` function, the output will be null, which is appropriate. However, if in the future, your client decides to add one or more new intervals to the `tvalFrequencies` table, you would need to insert something like null output for the fifth argument in order to get to the sixth argument and beyond. Your experience and evaluation of the client's business rules will be helpful in deciding if you want to use the `Choose()` function or use a series of If/Then macro actions.

If you circle back to the Click event, you also see that in the Else block of the If/Then macro action, you set the ending date to null in case the user hasn't selected a starting date from which to calculate or a number of recurrences. That should provide you with ample coverage for different possible inputs based on the specified starting date, specified frequency, and the desired number of recurrences.

The last macro action is SetVariable, which sets `gbolRecalculateNeeded` to No. This will become clearer once we talk about the Click event for the Submit button. For now, let's turn to the Click event behind the `cmdCalculateIntervals`, shown in Figure 9-29.

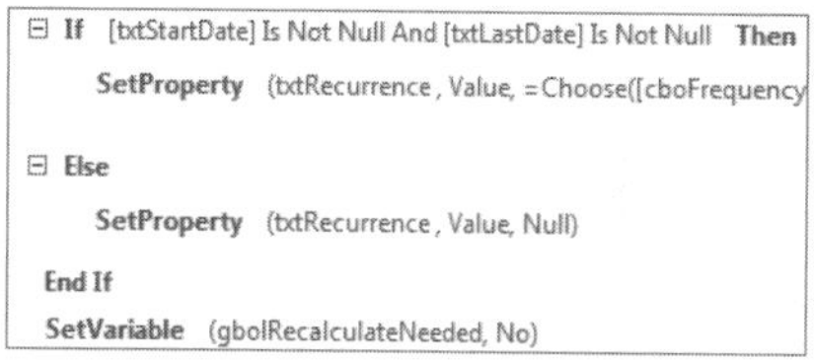

```
⊟ If [txtStartDate] Is Not Null And [txtLastDate] Is Not Null Then
      SetProperty (txtRecurrence, Value, =Choose([cboFrequency
⊟ Else
      SetProperty (txtRecurrence, Value, Null)
  End If
  SetVariable (gbolRecalculateNeeded, No)
```

FIGURE 9-29: Macro actions in the cmdCalculateIntervals Click event

The expression truncated from Figure 9-29 is given:

```
=Choose([cboFrequency],
  DateDiff(Day, [txtStartDate], [txtLastDate]),
  DateDiff(Week, [txtStartDate], [txtLastDate]),
  DateDiff(Week, [txtStartDate], [txtLastDate])/2,
  DateDiff(Month, [txtStartDate], [txtLastDate])
)+1
```

The implementation is very similar to calculating an end date, except that you change around the input values and use `DateDiff()` to extract the integer that will represent the number job recurrences that can fit in the range instead of `DateAdd()`. The only thing to note is that the ending date may not actually be the date of the last job because maids can enter an arbitrary date without having to conform to the constraints of the dates available based on the customer's desired frequency. For the sake of simplicity, you can assume that the maid knows that is the case and move on.

Also, contrary to what you do in the macro behind the `cmdCalculateEndDate`, you set the `gbolRecalculateNeeded` to `No`. Again, we visit this when you look at the Click event for the Submit button.

Sometimes a maid needs to generate a new schedule with a different starting date, perhaps because the customer wants to start services next month instead of next week or because the customer has been inactive for a while, which means the default date for their next job is actually in the past. Changing the start date may warrant updating the ending date to enable users to see the new ending date. Figure 9-30 shows how you would fill in the After Update event for the `txtStartDate`.

```
⊟ If [txtRecurrence] Is Not Null And [txtStartDate] Is Not Null Then
     SetProperty (txtLastDate, Value, =Choose([cbofrequency],DateA
⊟ Else
     SetVariable (pbolRecalculateNeeded, Yes)
     SetProperty
       Control Name  txtLastDate
           Property  Value
              Value  Null
End If
```

FIGURE 9-30: txtStartDate After Update event

The expression truncated from Figure 9-30 is same as the second truncated expression used in Figure 9-25.

This is similar to the `cmdCalculateLastDate`; this time calculating a new ending date and after doing so, setting the `gbolRecalculateNeeded` variable to `No`. This covers all macro actions on the form, leaving you with the two button events to build.

You would, of course, add a ClosePopup macro action to the Cancel button. Next, let's look at how you would program the Submit button in Figure 9-31.

```
⊟ If [gbolRecalculateNeeded]=Yes Then
     MessageBox (Please recalculate the intervals for the ending date.)
⊟ Else If [txtStartDate]<Today() Then
     MessageBox (Starting Date cannot be a past date. Enter a different starting date)
⊟ Else If [txtRecurrence] Is Null Then
     MessageBox (Please enter a number of recurrences or if there is an ending date, calculate the intervals by clicking Calculate Intervals button.)
⊟ Else If [cboCrew] Is Null Then
     MessageBox (A crew must be selected.)
⊟ Else
     RunDataMacro
               Macro Name  dmJobGenerateSchedule
     Parameters
        plngSourceCustomerID  = [glngCurrentCustomerID]
              plngRecurrences  = [txtRecurrence]
                pdatStartDate  = [txtStartDate]
             plngSelectedCrew  = [cboCrew]
     ClosePopup
End If
```

FIGURE 9-31: Macro actions in the Click event of the cmdSubmit button

Unlike the clone job functionality you made in the previous section, you need to perform validations on the various options. You should take the following into account.

First, to avoid nesting several If/Then blocks, you want to reverse conditions so that you can do an If/ElseIf/Else/End If at one level. Although it may be easier to read the condition `[txtStartDate]>Today()`, the total of four conditions to be met would require a four-level deep nested If/Then requiring you to handle all Else branches correctly, which would certainly not be as easy to read. Reversing the conditions is a good way to keep your macro actions readable.

You saw the `gbolRecalculateNeeded` variable in other event handlers. As noted earlier, you can't completely automate the calculations, but to ensure users don't enter a new ending date and forget to click the Calculate Interval button, you maintain the `gbolRealculateNeeded` variable at each step. Otherwise, users could get unexpected results because the `dmJobGenerate` data macro does not actually use the ending date at all. It only uses the starting date and recurrences as the parameters. Thus, you can see that if a user were allowed to enter a different end date but leave recurrences at the default 10, they'd end up with ten jobs when they were expecting fewer or more. By maintaining a variable, you also sidestep the problem of triggering a runaway recursion.

With two examples of input popup forms under your belt, you should be able to see how sophisticated you can make your logic in data macros, which makes it easy for users to get the necessary default values, perform validation before submitting changes, and automate the input process. You also may have noticed that different data macros repeat the expression used to evaluate either intervals and/or ending date. This is a potential place where you could further develop your macro into a freestanding UI macro and call that instead.

NAMING A FREESTANDING UI MACRO

One nice aspect about VBA modules is that you can have functions that are specific to a form or a module and be limited in scope to only that module. In UI macros, there is no such limitation and, in theory, any UI macro can be called anywhere. Were you to move the expressions used on the `frmJobGenerate` popup view into a freestanding UI macro, it could be hard to tell that it's meant to be used with the `frmJobGenerate` view only. An idea to help alleviate this problem is to consider embedding the view's name in the macro's name such as `mcr_frmJobGenerate_Validate` so that you can distinguish a view-specific macro from a macro that may be accessible by more than one form.

Next, let's examine the actual data macro, `dmJobGenerateSchedule`. To generate the schedule, you need the customer record, obtained via a LookupRecord macro action to provide you with all other relevant data about a customer as you construct a schedule. With the lookup, you can retrieve values such as the requested `TimeofDay`. You also need a variable to increment the current date of the job as you iterate. You initialize this variable via a SetVariable action, assigning the value of the `pdatStartDate` parameter passed into the data macro. And finally, your data macro enters a loop using ForEachRecord against the `tvalTally` table, using the `plngRecurrences` parameter to control the number of iterations. Figure 9-32 shows these macro actions, with the macro action, CreateRecord, collapsed for clarity.

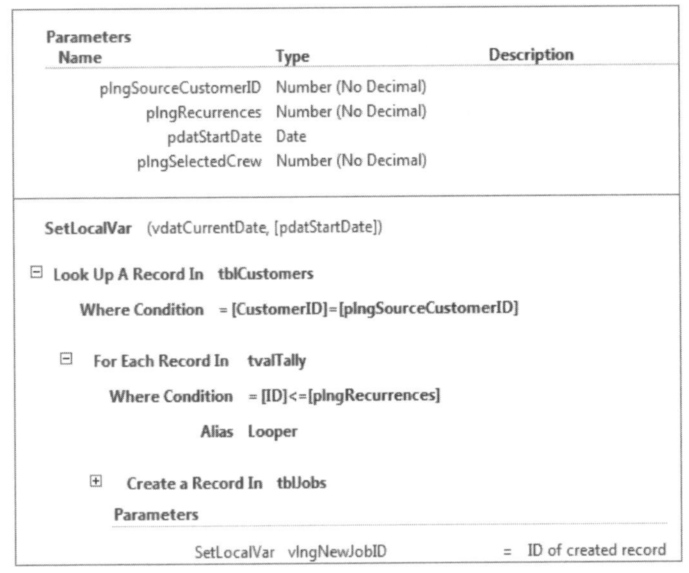
Parameters
Name
Type
Description
plngSourceCustomerID Number (No Decimal)
plngRecurrences Number (No Decimal)
pdatStartDate Date
plngSelectedCrew Number (No Decimal)
SetLocalVar (vdatCurrentDate, [pdatStartDate])
Look Up A Record In tblCustomers
Where Condition = [CustomerID]=[plngSourceCustomerID]
For Each Record In tvalTally
Where Condition = [ID]<=[plngRecurrences]
Alias Looper
Create a Record In tblJobs
Parameters
SetLocalVar vlngNewJobID = ID of created record

FIGURE 9-32: dmJobGenerateSchedule and the first macro actions to be performed

In Figure 9-32, you can see that the alias `Looper` was assigned to the tally table, so that it can be referenced in the loop. The loop will run as long as `Looper.ID` is less than or equal to the value of the `plngRecurrences` parameter. With each iteration in the ForEachRecord action, the macro creates a new record in the `tblJobs` with a CreateRecord macro action, using data from the customer's default job that was passed into the data macro via the parameter `tblCustomers` and the `vdatCurrentDate`, as illustrated in Figure 9-33.

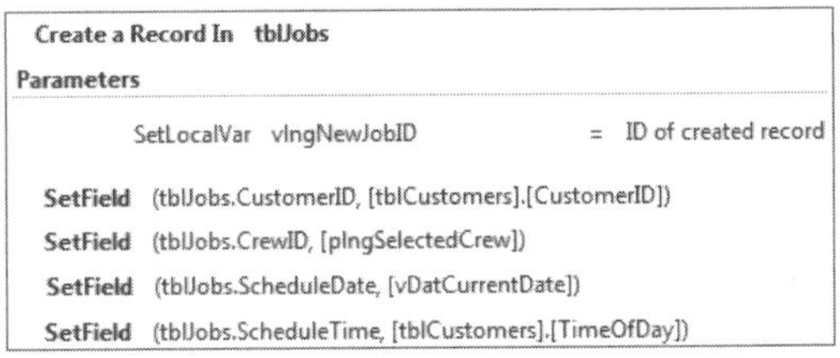

Create a Record In tblJobs
Parameters
SetLocalVar vlngNewJobID = ID of created record
SetField (tblJobs.CustomerID, [tblCustomers].[CustomerID])
SetField (tblJobs.CrewID, [plngSelectedCrew])
SetField (tblJobs.ScheduleDate, [vDatCurrentDate])
SetField (tblJobs.ScheduleTime, [tblCustomers].[TimeOfDay])

FIGURE 9-33: CreateRecord for tblJobs and its SetField actions

Unlike the `dmJobClone` data macro discussed in the previous section on cloning a job, there are no If/Then blocks to conditionally insert different values for the jobs in this case. Only the default values are needed for each new job; the only difference for each job is the date.

For each job created, you also insert the services to be provided in `txrfCustomerServicestable` and assign employees in the `txrfCrewMembers` table, using data from `txrfCustomerServices` and `txrfCrewMembers` to get the values, as demonstrated in Figure 9-34, which shows those sections of the data macro.

```
⊟ For Each Record In   txrfCrewMembers
    Where Condition   = [txrfCrewMembers].[CrewID]=[plngSelectedCrew]

  ⊟ Create a Record In   txrfJobEmployees
      SetField   (txrfJobEmployees.JobID, [vlngNewJobID])
      SetField   (txrfJobEmployees.EmployeeID, [txrfCrewMembers].[EmployeeID])

⊟ For Each Record In   txrfCustomerServices
    Where Condition   = [txrfCustomerServices].[CustomerID]=[plngSourceCustomerID]

  ⊟ Create a Record In   txrfJobServices
      SetField   (txrfJobServices.JobID, [vlngNewJobID])
      SetField   (txrfJobServices.ServiceID, [txrfCustomerServices].[ServiceID])
      SetField   (txrfJobServices.Fee, [txrfCustomerServices].[DefaultFee])
```

FIGURE 9-34: CreateRecords in the Job Employees table for the new job's assigned employees

This leaves you with one last step to perform in each iteration, calculating the next value of the `vdatCurrentDate` variable for the next iteration. This time, you use If/Then blocks primarily so that, for unexpected values, you can return a custom error message, which you can see for the value 5 and in the Else block in Figure 9-35.

```
⊟ Group:   Calculate Next Date

  ⊟ If   [tblCustomers].[FrequencyID]=1   Then
      /*   Daily
      SetLocalVar   (vdatCurrentDate, DateAdd(Day,1,[vdatCurrentDate]))

  ⊟ Else If   [tblCustomers].[FrequencyID]=2   Then
      /*   Weekly
      SetLocalVar   (vdatCurrentDate, DateAdd(Week,1,[vdatCurrentDate]))

  ⊟ Else If   [tblCustomers].[FrequencyID]=3   Then
      /*   Biweekly
      SetLocalVar   (vdatCurrentDate, DateAdd(Week,2,[vdatCurrentDate]))

  ⊟ Else If   [tblCustomers].[FrequencyID]=4   Then
      /*   Monthly
      SetLocalVar   (vdatCurrentDate, DateAdd(Month,1,[vdatCurrentDate]))

  ⊟ Else If   [tblCustomers].[FrequencyID]=5   Then
      RaiseError   (Cannot generate a schedule for customer with non-regular intervals.)

  ⊟ Else
      RaiseError   (Cannot generate a schedule for customer without a specified regular interval.)

    End If
End Group
```

FIGURE 9-35: Calculating vlngCurrentDate and RaiseError macro actions

There is an If or Else If condition for each standard frequency, starting with 1, for daily, and ending with 4, for Monthly. The data macro uses different versions of the `DateAdd()` function with the appropriate interval to generate the next schedule date for that option. And, when the frequency is ad hoc, or not provided, the appropriate error is raised.

WHETHER TO PRE-FIX OR TO POST-FIX, THAT IS THE QUESTION

Because the ForEachRecord macro action doesn't use a variable for incrementing, you have to perform it yourself. That leaves open the question of whether you should increment the variable as the first step inside the loop or as the last step. Your experience in looping recordsets in VBA will be helpful in determining which option would work the best in each situation. One handy way to help make the decision is to compare it to `Do Until <condition> ... Loop` versus `Do Until ... Loop <condition>`. The construction of the former expression means it may be executed zero to *n*th times whereas the latter construction executes one to *n*th times.

In this example of extending a variable schedule of jobs, you've learned additional ways to leverage data macros to enforce business rules. This concludes your introduction to the process of building and generating multiple records using arbitrary numbers. Let's now turn to another scenario where you need to populate records into different tables.

Generating Records in Different Tables

With the data macros `dmJobClone` and `dmJobGenerateSchedule`, you saw how you can clone new records from an existing record with some customization and also how you can generate a bulk amount of records using predetermined calculations to differentiate each record.

Although both operations worked with data from more than one table, let's now turn to a situation where you need to insert two records in two different tables. Maid To Order has said that, as a rule, no new customer should be added to their system without a first job being set up. To ensure users don't forget to add that job, Maid To Order wants a form that will allow the user to fill in both the new customer's data and the first job's data in one go.

To facilitate this requirement, you will use an unbound form that contains all of the controls that users fill in to set up a new customer and their first job. The values from those unbound controls will be fed to a data macro via parameters. Figure 9-36 illustrates how Maid To Order wants the form to appear in the web app.

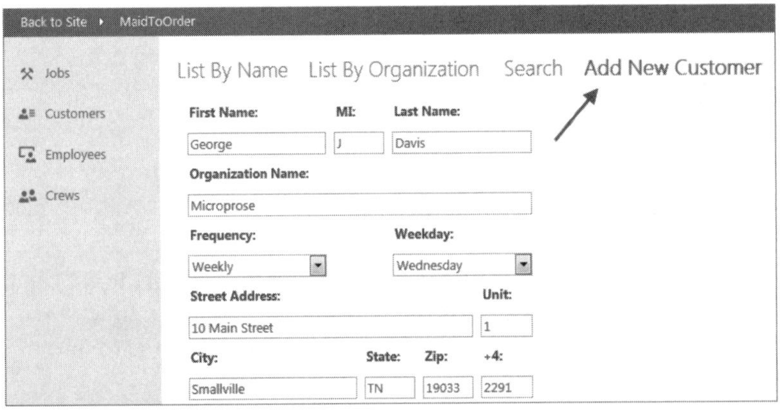

FIGURE 9-36: frmCustomerCreate view

Unlike previously implemented functions, which necessitated popup views, this is a crucial action for Maid To Order, so you can add it as a tile-bound view to the Customer's tile using the button. Figure 9-36 illustrated the placement of the `frmCustomerCreate` link on the Customer tile's View Selector.

Figure 9-37 shows how you have the subview reusing the `fsubFilterServices` you saw in Chapter 8 to allow for selection of services for the job.

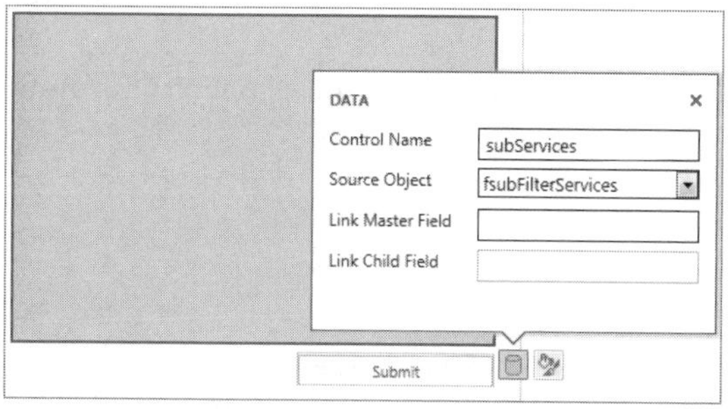

FIGURE 9-37: subServices Subview control's properties

> **NOTE** *Using a Subview control on a tile-bound view is also an example of how you can add parameters on a view bound to a tile. Although the Subview control allows you to filter related records using an unbound control, you can only do so on a single field. So, while you can't have parameters in tile-bound views, you can accomplish a similar purpose by using a Subview control.*

This functionality is an opportunity to illustrate how you can allow for multiple selections on a web form. You can use a filter table to store one or more services for the new job. In order to do so, of course, it is necessary to create that filter table to store the selections. You learned about creating a filter table in Chapter 8. Here you'll see how to use it.

To ensure the user always starts with an empty selection for the services to select for the customer, you need to clear the filter table of all records for the current user. You saw how to do this in Chapter 8.

One design assumption behind this approach is that you leave all validation up to the data macro invoked in the Submit button. If there is insufficient or invalid data, the data macro will fail and neither customer nor job will be added, and an error will be shown to the user, as demonstrated in Figure 9-38.

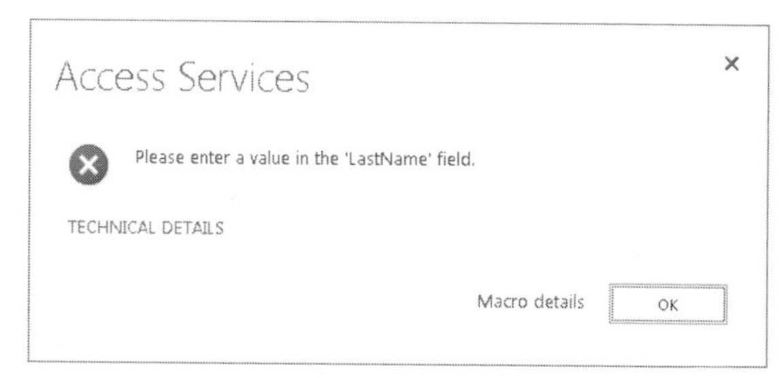

FIGURE 9-38: Error shown when the user does not fill in any values on the frmCustomerCreate

As Figure 9-38 shows, you don't necessarily have to write complex validation checks for the Submit button. There may be cases where it is actually needed which do warrant your valuable time and talent, but as you can see, the error is quite friendly in contrast to Access client databases where users get "helpful" error messages such as Type Mismatch or Invalid Use of Null.

Figure 9-39 shows the macro action behind the Click event of the Submit button with the first macro action collapsed.

RunDataMacro (dmCustomerCreate, [txtFirstName], [txtMiddleInitial], [txt
RunDataMacro
Macro Name dmFilterServicesClear
Parameters
ptxtCurrentUser = UserEmailAddress()
ChangeView
Table tblCustomers
View frmCustomerByName
Where = [tblCustomers].[CustomerID]=[vlngNewCustomerID]
Order By

FIGURE 9-39: Submit Button Click event

The Submit button copies all of the Customer values from the controls on the view and passes them as parameters to a data macro, `dmCustomerCreate`. Then the macro runs `dmFilterServicesClear` again to clear the filter table.

Note that the macro performs a ChangeView action to after running the two data macros. That allows you to place the user on the newly added customer's record for further editing. Note also that you obtain the new customer's ID via a return parameter from the `dmCustomerCreate` macro, which you will see how to set in the `dmCustomerCreate` data macro.

Let's start with the parameter list from the `dmCustomer Create` data macro that was previously collapsed in Figure 9-39. Figure 9-40 shows how you would build the list.

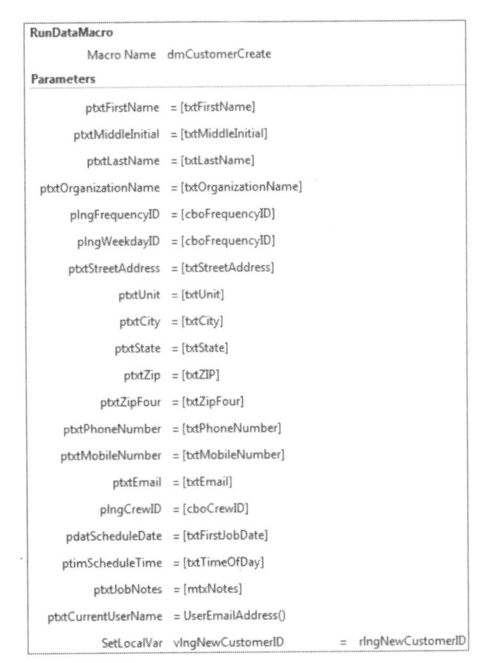

FIGURE 9-40: Parameter list for dmCustomer Create

As you would expect, most parameters shown in Figure 9-40 have a one-to-one correlation to the controls from the unbound `frmCustomerCreate`. The only parameter that doesn't correlate directly is `ptxtCurrentUserName`, which will be used for retrieving the user's selections of services from the subview.

You would add a CreateRecord action and, as before, you will need to retrieve `CustomerID` from the newly created record for the job. You enable this by clicking the Retrieve ID link on right side of the CreateRecord macro action. Note that the link is visible only when the CreateRecord has focus. The rest of the CreateRecord is quite straightforward, applying parameters to each control, as Figure 9-41 shows.

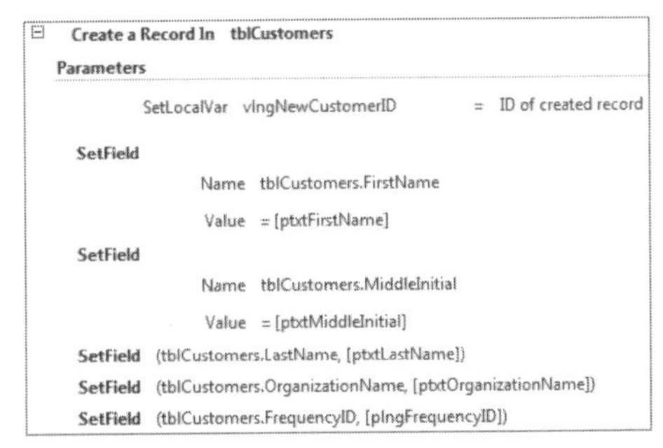

FIGURE 9-41: Setting a local variable for the ID and partially collapsed SetField macro actions

The new record is created in the Customer table, and then a variable is set to the ID of that new customer record. You'll need that variable in the next step. The SetField actions insert the values passed into the macro as parameters. The first two are expanded for you in Figure 9-41.

After adding the customer, you can turn to adding a job for that customer, via a second CreateRecord action. As you did for the customer record, you need to create the job and then obtain the new job ID, as shown in Figure 9-42. The macro can then add the job values from the parameters it receives.

Because you pass in a `CrewID` parameter, you can also populate the `txrfJobEmployees` table using the `txrfCrewMembers`, as shown in Figure 9-43.

You can now turn to handling the services for the first job. As you may recall, you used a filter table so users can make multiple selections. You would use a query that joins the `tlkpFilterServices` filter table with the `tlkpServices` table to provide all columns you need to build the service record, as shown in Figure 9-44.

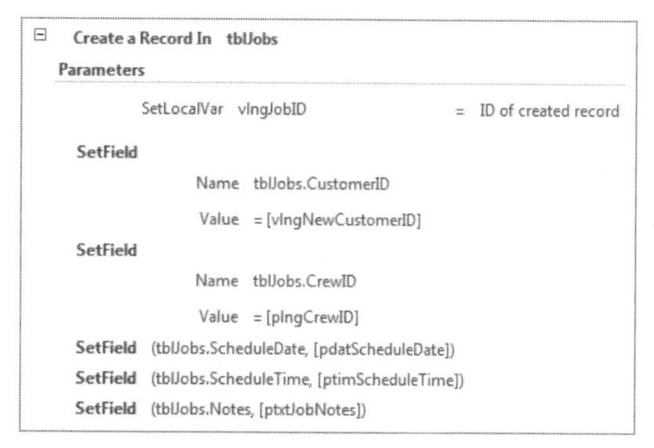

FIGURE 9-42: CreateRecord for the job record using parameters passed to the data macro from the view

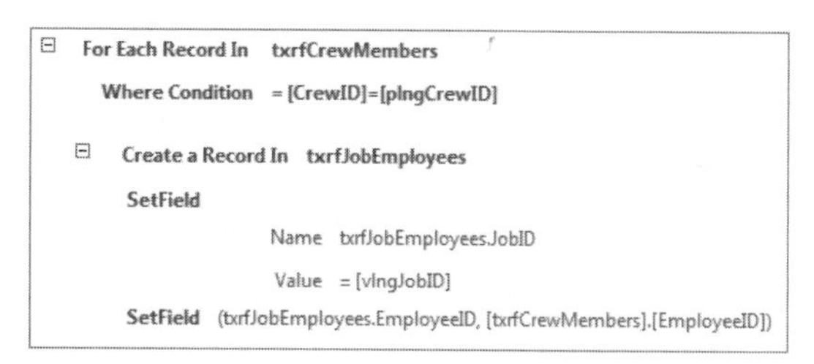

FIGURE 9-43: CreateRecord for the Job Employee record using parameters passed to the data macro from the view

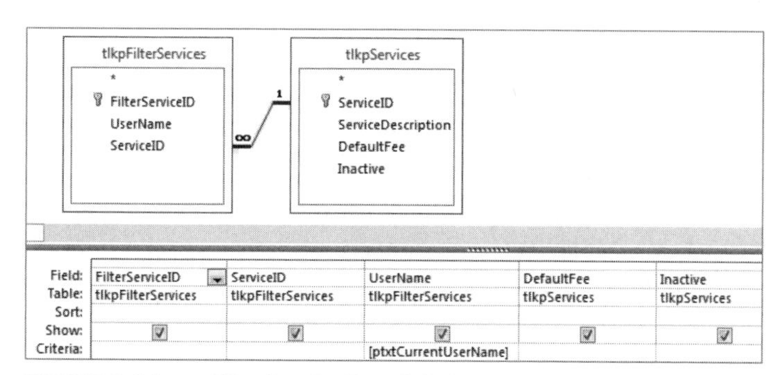

FIGURE 9-44: qryFilterServiceDetailsSelected design

You can perform a ForEachRecord macro action against the records returned by this query and retrieve the services from it into `txrfJobServices` to populate the services for the first job and also populate the default requested services for the customer in `txrfCustomerServices`. In this way, you can describe what services will be performed in the first job while simultaneously populating the default requested services for the customer for future jobs. You can then use both `vlngNewCustomerID` and `vlngNewJobID` to populate the foreign key in each table, as illustrated in Figure 9-45.

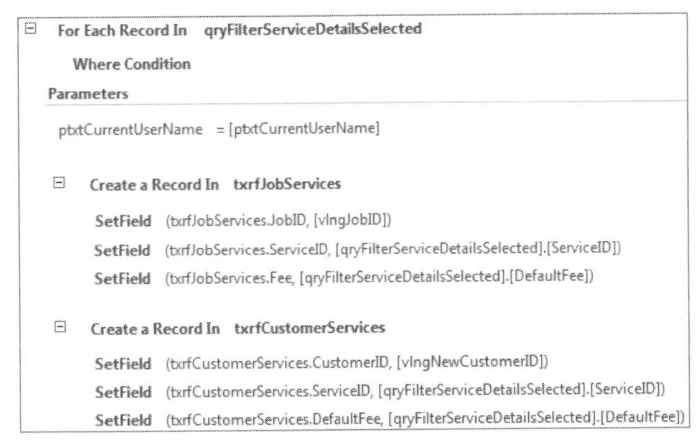

FIGURE 9-45: Adding services to the current job and to default services

You can conclude with a ReturnVar macro action, passing the new value for `CustomerID` back to the calling UI macro, as shown in Figure 9-46. This enables you to perform a ChangeView to focus on the newly added customer, as you saw in Figure 9-39.

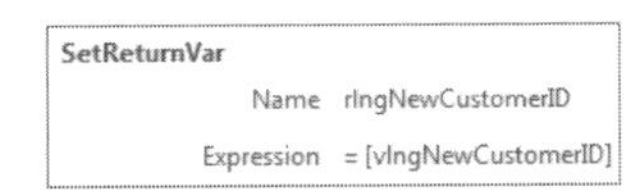

FIGURE 9-46: Return the new CustomerID

At this point, you have seen an example of how you can fulfill a customer request with an unbound form. In this case, you created a new customer record and an initial job for that customer in one function, and also populated supporting tables for that job in a single step.

Updating and/or Deleting Several Records

Thus far, the examples you've worked on dealt primarily with creating new records of some kind. Although you've had several glimpses of what kind of logic you can bring to bear upon in your data macros, let's consider an example where you can create a data macro that works on existing records.

Unfortunately, Maid To Order does have customers who drop out for some reason. It is necessary to either cancel or put on hold any future jobs scheduled for that customer. Because sometimes the customer may return after a pause in service, Maid To Order wants to have the option of retaining the job records. Other times, they may prefer to delete the records.

Thus, you would provide an action button on the `frmCustomerByName` view to initiate the process of either canceling or deleting the jobs, as in Figure 9-47.

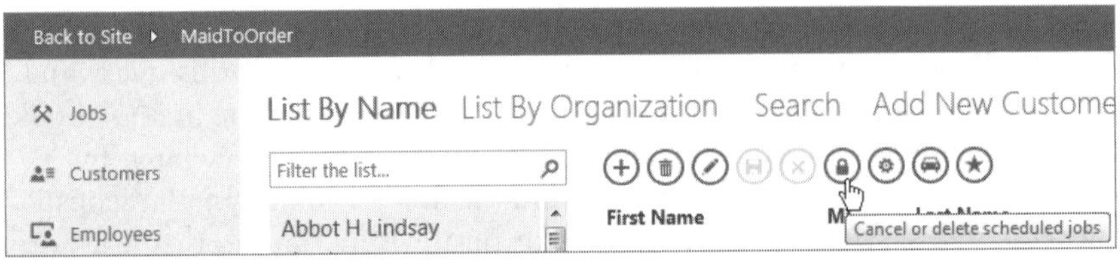

FIGURE 9-47: Action button to cancel jobs on frmCustomerByName

As you would expect, the button performs an OpenPopup action, which opens the `frmJobCancel` view. However, before the OpenPopup is performed, you need to set the variable `glngCurrentCustomerID` to contain the current customer ID, as illustrated in Figure 9-48, so you can pass it as a parameter to the popup.

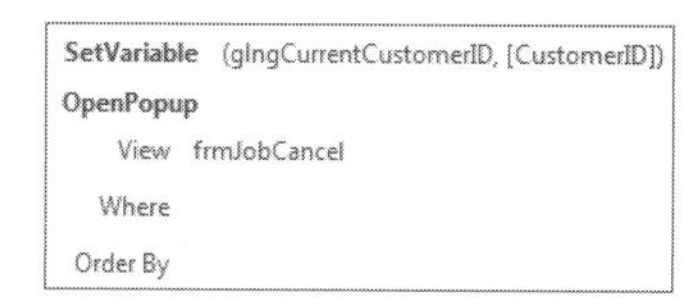

FIGURE 9-48: SetVariable and OpenPopup macro actions for the job cancellation macro

Figure 9-49 shows the design view for `frmJobCancel`.

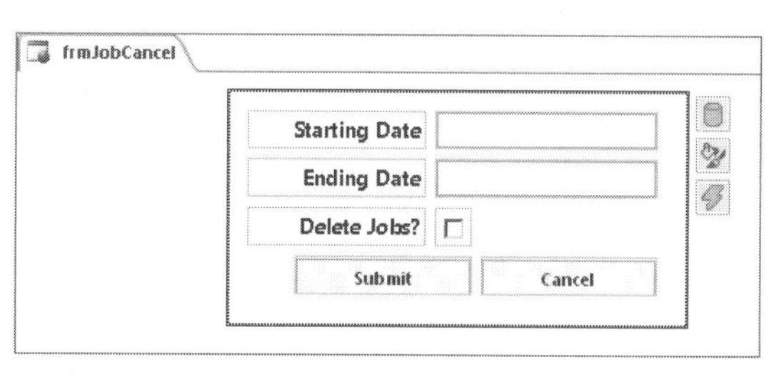

FIGURE 9-49: Design view of frmJobCancel

There are only three controls to parameterize: the starting date, the ending date, and the option to delete or cancel jobs. If the Delete Jobs checkbox is left blank, you will simply be canceling the jobs in the date range selected, which allows for quick restoration of services should a customer want the original schedule (or what is left of it) back.

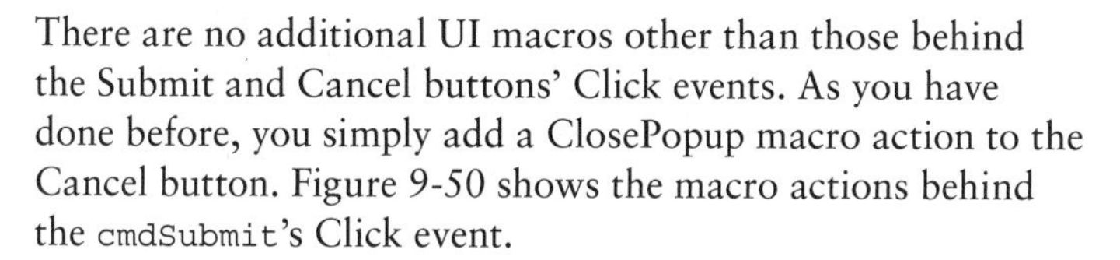

There are no additional UI macros other than those behind the Submit and Cancel buttons' Click events. As you have done before, you simply add a ClosePopup macro action to the Cancel button. Figure 9-50 shows the macro actions behind the `cmdSubmit`'s Click event.

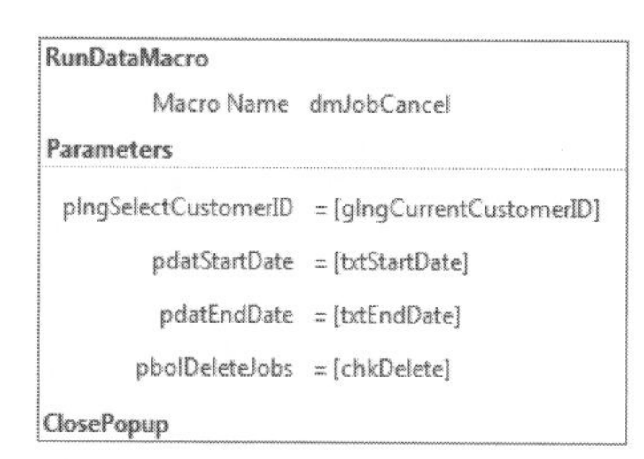

FIGURE 9-50: cmdSubmit Button Click event

The Submit button invokes `dmJobCancel` and passes four parameters to it. The actions in `dmJobCancel` are quite straightforward in contrast to previous data macros you've built so far in this chapter, so we don't need to discuss them in detail. Figure 9-51 demonstrates where you would use the If/Then block to determine whether you will be deleting records or just setting the `Cancel` field to `Yes` for particular jobs so they can be recovered later.

FIGURE 9-51: dmJobCancel data macro actions

The truncated expression for the Where Condition parameter in Figure 9-51 is given:

```
(
  [tblJobs].[CustomerID]=[plngSelectCustomerID]
  And
  (
    [tblJobs].[ScheduleDate]>=[pdatStartDate]
    Or
    [pdatStartDate] Is Null
  ) And (
    [tblJobs].[ScheduleDate]<[pdatEndDate]
    Or [pdatEndDate] Is Null
  )
) And [tblJobs].[Completed]=0
```

We opted to define the relationships between job, job services, and the job employee tables to allow cascade-deleting of related records in a job's services and assigned employees. Because of that, you don't need to explicitly loop the `txrfJobServices` and `txrfJobEmployees` tables to remove the related records, which saves you two additional ForEachRecord actions and a DeleteRecord action within each block.

BUT AREN'T CASCADE DELETES DANGEROUS?

One advice often given out within Access development has been to avoid the use of the Cascade Delete option in a foreign key constraint. This is quite understandable because there may be cases where you really don't want to delete child records but can't be sure that the existence of those records will be checked at all times, especially if someone goes directly to the table and deletes the record. If that happens, poof, everything's gone, regardless of whether you've written a nice VBA procedure to test the validity of deleting a record.

The factor that changes the rule here in the web app environment is that you now have a Delete table event to which you can attach your rules and therefore prevent unjustified deletes. Here, you are trading for speed and ease of development using Cascade Delete functionality with the understanding that, if you have a rule when a job should not be deleted, it will be checked at all times within the Delete table event and there is no way to circumvent this table event. Thus, unlike past versions, you now can "optionally" enable Cascade Delete on relationships and that can work out to your advantage. You will see this illustrated later in the chapter.

One other thing to note is the format of the Where clause in the ForEachRecord. It uses the starting and ending date and also makes either optional. The macro actions shown in Figure 9-51 are expanded in the text after the Figure so you can see it completely. This allows the user to use either date alone and thus affect all jobs before or after a given date. Lastly, there is a hard condition of `Complete=0`, which makes sense because you can't cancel or delete a job that has been completed.

You've now created a freestanding macro to add records to multiple tables in one controlled process. This concludes our coverage on building freestanding data macros to support functional requirements in a web app. You've seen how you can use UI macros and data macros together to form a powerful process and aid users in streamlining their workflow. The content here should go well with your experience in designing and building solutions for your customers. We'll now turn to table events.

USING TABLE EVENTS

In the following section, you learn how to use table events, which run automatically without requiring users to intervene manually. This is very useful for enforcing business rules that are not expressible in a validation rule at the field or record level. You will start with a simple validation check, move into creating a record of changes made, and conclude with gathering and maintaining metadata that does not work well in a relational model.

Performance Considerations

Because table events always fire when their respective triggering actions occur, and because the user has to wait for those events to finish processing, it becomes much more important that you design your table events to be as streamlined as possible. Three general design approaches you should undertake are:

1. Whenever your events deal with certain, specific fields within the table, you want to use `Update()` to check if those fields were actually changed by the triggering event before invoking an action. That provides for an opportunity to skip the extra processing when it's not needed.
2. Perform all validations as early as possible so that you can cancel out sooner, rather than later, to minimize the wait your users must tolerate. There is nothing more frustrating for a user than waiting a while only to be told there was an error, forcing them to start all over.
3. Do not try to depend on some context, such as determining which logged-in user is initiating the action, or getting a variable. This approach, even when it can be enabled, makes for fragile designs that may be circumvented by creative users, or can even create additional issues. If you cannot evaluate all dependent variables in a table event, it may not be appropriate as a table event.

Furthermore, and above all, you should be quite judicious about the need for the table event at all, asking yourself if the action must be completed and enforced at all times. If this action needs to be done only occasionally, consider if users would be happier using a button to run a freestanding data macro instead of paying the waiting cost every time they trigger a table event.

One more thing to note is that table events operate by rows, not by sets. As you might know, when you run a query, the query affects the entire table at once in a single operation — that's a set operation. The underlying SQL Server table triggers are also set-based, not row-based. However, when macro actions are attached via events in Access, a cursor is generated within the trigger to iterate over the individual records that are affected. On one hand, this greatly simplifies the thought process required to build a table event. This can be especially helpful for non-developers who aren't used to thinking about data in sets and who would be uncomfortable with SQL.

On the other hand, the design approach means more processing is involved, especially when a bulk operation is performed via the Access client or another mechanism where more than one row is affected. Therefore, if you anticipate performing bulk operations against the SQL database *outside the web application*, you should plan carefully whether table events will significantly slow down such operations. To be frank, this discussion may be beyond the reach of new developers not used to thinking seriously about the more advanced facets of database design. However, we anticipate that the more seasoned developers among us will find it useful to make this an important element of their design considerations.

Preventing Deletions of Completed Records

The simplest use of table events is preventing deletion of certain records. As mentioned in the previous section, it wouldn't be appropriate at all to delete a completed job.

To attach macro actions to a Delete event, you'd open `tblJobs` in design view and click Delete event on the ribbon, as shown in Figure 9-52.

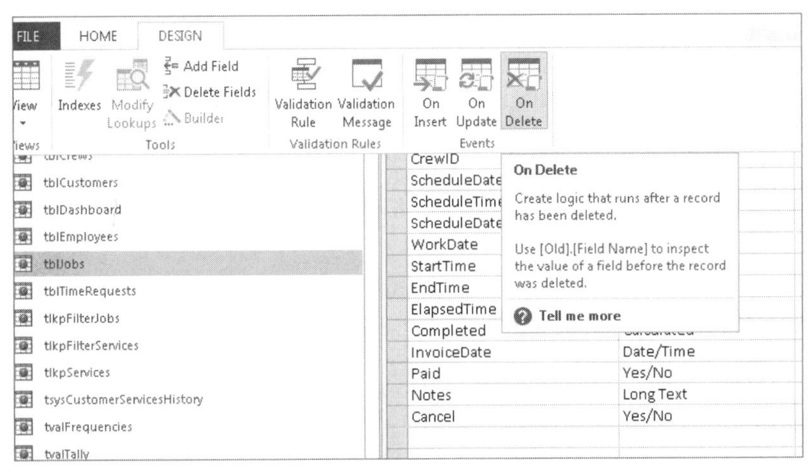

FIGURE 9-52: Delete event on the ribbon

Unlike data macros you've worked with so far, where you had to first perform a LookupRecord, ForEachRecord, and/or CreateRecord macro action in order to get a record to work with, a table event assumes that there is already a record to work with, and you can get started right away. Because this is a Delete event, you're going to use the `Old` virtual table, which would have identical structure to the active table being worked upon, which is `tblJobs` in this case.

You check whether `Completed` is `Yes` in the original record and, if so, you use a RaiseError macro action with description to communicate back to the user that the action can't be performed. Figure 9-53 shows the macro action behind the Delete event on the `tblJobs` table.

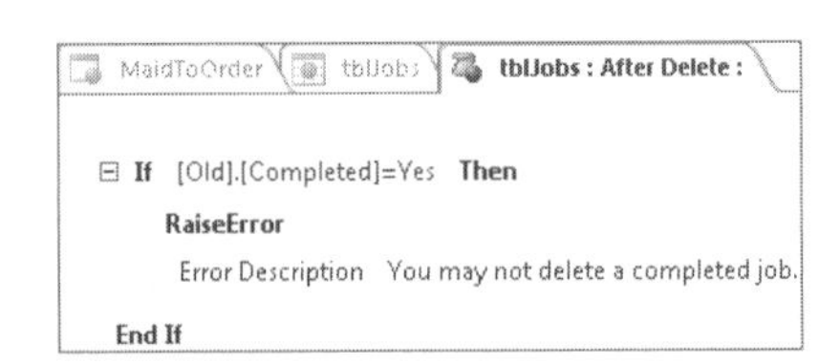

FIGURE 9-53: Macro actions in the tblJobs Delete event

If the user attempts to delete a completed job (`[Old].[Completed] = Yes`), the macro simply raises an error, which presents a message to the user and stops the delete. Figure 9-54 shows the error message the user will see when trying to delete a completed job.

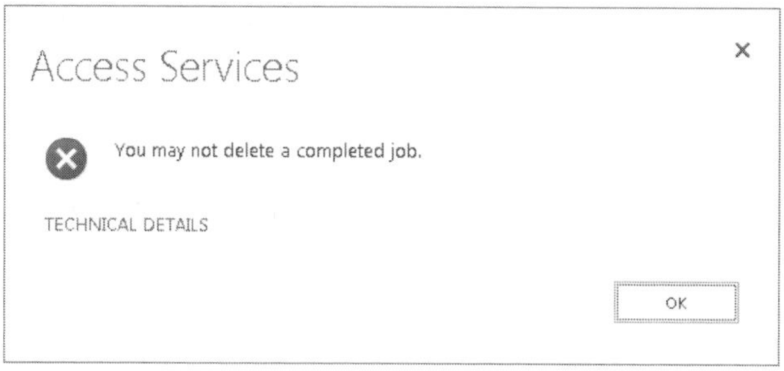

Access Services

You may not delete a completed job.

TECHNICAL DETAILS

OK

FIGURE 9-54: Error message displayed after inappropriate delete attempt

In a situation where the user might have goofed and indicated that the wrong job was completed, the user can correct the mistake by first editing the wrong job record to make it non-complete, saving those changes. At that point, the user is once again allowed to delete the job.

Note that a similar approach can be followed to prevent editing of a record by attaching the macro actions shown in Figure 9-52 to the Update event as well. However, this may prove to be too restrictive because there are times when editing a completed record may be legitimate, such as when entering the invoice date or checking off when the job has been paid for. Thus, additional checks would be necessary for validation of the Update event to allow edits in some circumstances but not in others.

Another thing to keep in mind is, that from the viewpoint of the database architecture, a "job" is actually a collection of three related tables. To the user, however, the services and assigned employees are logically just a part of a job record and they may not understand the implications of making changes. Therefore, to prevent inappropriate deletion or editing of the services and assigned employees for completed jobs, you need to attach macro actions to their respective Delete and Update events as well. The macro actions for the Delete and Update events are basically identical so we'll look only at macro actions in the Delete event of the `txrfJobServices` table, and leave to you the task of building the Update event similarly. Likewise, we'll just consider the `txrfJobServices` table and assume the `txrfJobEmployees` table has the same Delete and Update events, as shown for `txrfJobServices`.

In the macro illustrated in Figure 9-55, you used the `Old` virtual table to identify the deleted record. However, when working with the `txrfJobServices` table, you do not have the `Completed` field as a part of the `Old` virtual table because the `Old` virtual table in this context represents `txrfJobServices`, and not `tblJobs`. Because your table event needs to refer to the value of the `Completed` field in `tblJobs`, it needs to examine the value of the `Completed` field in that table before validating the delete action. Therefore, you first have to perform a LookupRecord into the jobs table, using `Old.JobID` to select the correct job, as demonstrated in Figure 9-55.

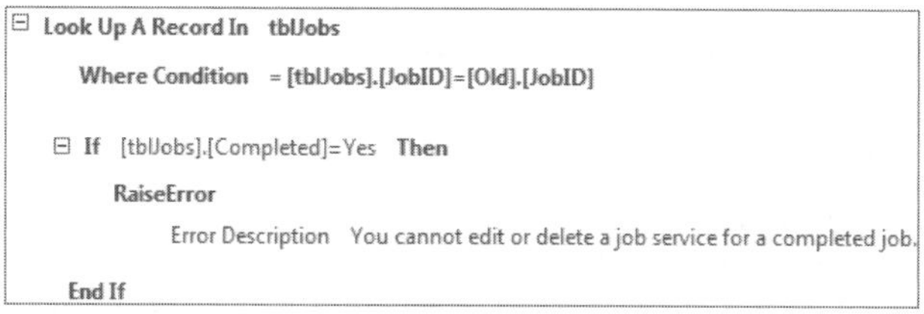

```
Look Up A Record In   tblJobs
    Where Condition  = [tblJobs].[JobID]=[Old].[JobID]

  If  [tblJobs].[Completed]=Yes  Then
      RaiseError
          Error Description   You cannot edit or delete a job service for a completed job.
  End If
```

FIGURE 9-55: Delete event for txrfJobServices

Once the `tblJobs` record is looked up, the actions are quite similar to what you saw for `tblJobs`: raising an error when `Completed=Yes`, stopping the delete action. As noted earlier, you will implement a similar Delete event for the Employees assigned to a completed job.

Unlike edits at the job level, it is not appropriate to edit services or assigned employees for a completed job. Thus, you can attach the same macro actions shown in Figure 9-54 to the Update events as well. Note that the `Old` virtual table is also available in the Update event, representing a copy of the record prior to editing the record that triggered the event.

Acquiring Default Values from Other Tables

As you saw in Chapter 2, you can supply a default value and provide a validation rule for a field in a table design. However, both are typically limited in their scope. You need to consider a situation where you want to acquire a default value from another table for use in a different table. Maid To Order maintains a list of default fees to charge for services in the `tlkpServices` table. Sometimes, a user may need to enter a specific fee that's different from the default fee. However, in all cases, Maid To Order does not want users to forget to enter some value for fees; they would rather have a default fee put into the record rather than none at all. The `DefaultFee` field in the `txrfCustomerServices` table is required; its Required property is set to `Yes`. But how does the user recall the current default fee that's stored in `tlkpServices` without having to look it up manually? While you certainly can provide the default via macro actions on the view (or via VBA in client forms), we're more interested in ensuring that you always supply a default fee in all possible situations, regardless of how the user enters the data. Remember from our earlier discussion that we are aware of, and want to guard against, problems arising from the possibility that users may connect to the database from a local Access database and enter records directly into tables. One possible approach is to make a convention that, where a fee of $0 is entered in any `txrfCustomerServices` record, you replace it with the current default fee from the `tlkpServices` for the same service. You can do this with a table event using the Insert event of the table.

You only need to enforce this convention when you insert a new service requested by a customer so you'll use the Insert event on `txrfCustomerServices`, as illustrated in Figure 9-56.

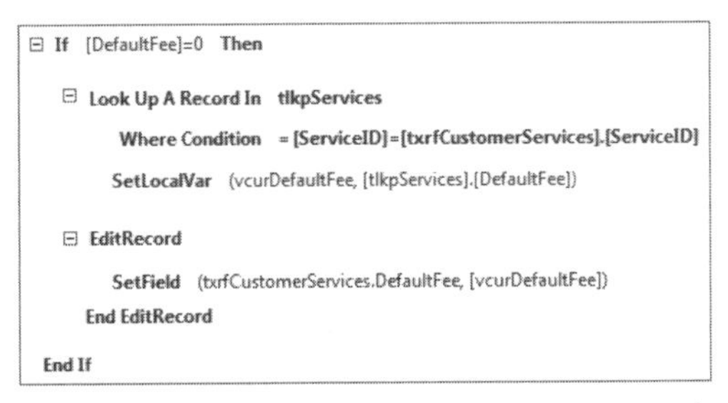

FIGURE 9-56: Macro actions in the Insert event for txrfCustomerServices

Because the default fee for a service is in `tlkpServices`, it's necessary to do a lookup into that table for the current service. In order to get the correct `ServiceID`, you need to refer to the newly inserted record in `txrfCustomerServices`.

In the following discussion, pay careful attention to the use, or rather non-use, of aliases, which you've seen in previous macros. Also pay careful attention to the scope in which various actions are performed. This can be a critical part of making your macros work as intended.

Unlike in previously discussed macros, where you added an alias to the CreateRecord macro block, you cannot provide an alias for the record in this situation. The syntax for referencing a new record being inserted in the table is in the form of *`table name.field name`*. LookupRecord, therefore, uses the expression `ServiceID = [txrfCustomerServices].[ServiceID]` in order to refer to the new record.

Within the LookupRecord data macro action, the macro reads the `tlkpServices.DefaultFee` value from the corresponding record looked up by its `ServiceID`, and then assigns that value to a `vcurDefaultFee` variable. Then, outside the LookupRecord action, the macro performs an EditRecord action.

Note that the alias for EditRecord is not given, and the macro changes the value of `txrfCustomerServices.DefaultFee` for the new record, using the variable `vcurDefaultFee`, which was previously set. The EditRecord had to be outside the LookupRecord to ensure it will refer to the record in the *current* table, which is the subject of the Insert event.

You can now see that unlike the Delete event where you had an `Old` virtual table to refer to the previous copy of the affected record, you need to use the table's name to refer to the current copy of the affected record. It's also useful to point out that the `Old` virtual table is not available at all in an Insert event, which is expected because there's no old anything to refer to.

Maintaining a History of Change

In some applications, it is desirable to have a complete history of all changes that have been made to the data. Some applications may go so far as to completely audit all kinds of changes in all tables. Because you can drive those audits from table events, you can ensure that complete records will be kept without any manual intervention.

Maid To Order has a limited audit requirement. They need to maintain a complete record of what services a customer has asked for in the past and when any changes to that list of services were made. This enables maids to answer customers' questions about services being rendered now or in the past, and also to make it easy for customers to ask to restore a service that was cancelled without requiring the maid to locate the last job where this service was rendered. Thus, a complete history is needed on the `txrfCustomerServices` table. You learn how to create an audit table in a web app later in this section of the chapter.

Audit Table Strategies

There are different ways to design an audit table; some applications may use a single audit table for the whole database and store each table's fields as a record so that the audit table can be used with any table, irrespective of the table's actual structure. Other applications may have one or more audit tables that are more or less a mirror of the original data tables.

Because Maid To Order is interested only in maintaining the history of customer services and changes to them, if any, you will use the latter approach. In addition to replicating the columns in the `txrfCustomerServices` table, you need additional columns to capture the date when the change was made and what kind of change occurred (for example, adding a new service, updating a service, or deleting a service no longer wanted) along with the ID of the service that was changed. Figure 9-57 illustrates the new audit table, `txrfCustomerServicesHistory`.

MaidToOrder | txrfCustomerServicesHistory

Field Name	Data Type
CustomerServiceHistoryID	AutoNumber
DateModified	Date/Time
Action	Short Text
DefaultFee	Number
AffectedCustomerServiceID	Number
CustomerID	Lookup
ServiceID	Lookup

FIGURE 9-57: txrfCustomerServicesHistory table design

With the table in place, the next step is to attach macros to each table event on the `txrfCustomerServices` table to place audit values into it, as needed. In this case, you need all three table events to record all possible changes. You'll start with the Insert event illustrated in Figure 9-58, starting after the first If/Then block, which we already covered.

```
SetLocalVar (vdatModifiedTimestamp, Now())
Create a Record In txrfCustomerServicesHistory
    SetField (txrfCustomerServicesHistory.AffectedCustomerServiceID, [txrfCustomerServices].[CustomerServiceID])
    SetField (txrfCustomerServicesHistory.Action, "Insert")
    SetField (txrfCustomerServicesHistory.CustomerID, [txrfCustomerServices].[CustomerID])
    SetField (txrfCustomerServicesHistory.ServiceID, [txrfCustomerServices].[ServiceID])
    SetField (txrfCustomerServicesHistory.DefaultFee, [txrfCustomerServices].[DefaultFee])
    SetField (txrfCustomerServicesHistory.DateModified, [vdatModifiedTimestamp])
```

FIGURE 9-58: The txrfCustomerServices Insert event after the initial If/Then block

The process is quite straightforward — you acquire a timestamp and place it into a variable, using the `Now()` function to get the current date and time for the change, and then create a new record in `txrfCustomerServices` and copy all fields from the current record, supplying the timestamp and indicating that it's an insertion event in the field called `Action`. Let's compare that action with the Update event, which is needed to capture current and changed values. Figure 9-59 shows the macro actions.

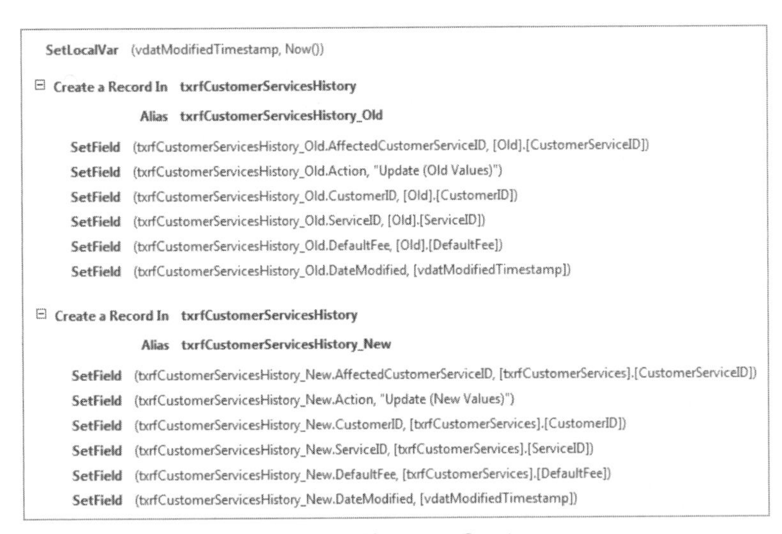

FIGURE 9-59: Update event for txrfCustomerServices

You can see clearly that because an Update event needs to save both a copy of the previous values and a copy of the modified values, and you have both the `Old` virtual table and the current record available to you, you can create the audit records using the same reference syntax you used for the Insert event. You also can see why you want to store the timestamp in a variable before creating the records. That way you can have a single time value in both records being created in `txrfCustomerServicesHistory`. Note also that you disambiguate between two paired records via `txrfCustomerServicesHistory`'s `Action` field: `Update (Old Values)` and `Update (New Values)`.

Figure 9-60 shows the Delete event for the `txrfCustomerServices` table, which is very similar to what you saw in Figure 9-58 for Insert, except that instead of referencing `txrfCustomerServices`, you reference the `Old` virtual table and record `Delete` as the action value.

```
SetLocalVar (vdatModifiedTimestamp, Now())
⊟ Create a Record In  txrfCustomerServicesHistory
    SetField (txrfCustomerServicesHistory.AffectedCustomerServiceID, [Old].[CustomerServiceID])
    SetField (txrfCustomerServicesHistory.Action, "Delete")
    SetField (txrfCustomerServicesHistory.CustomerID, [Old].[CustomerID])
    SetField (txrfCustomerServicesHistory.ServiceID, [Old].[ServiceID])
    SetField (txrfCustomerServicesHistory.DefaultFee, [Old].[DefaultFee])
    SetField (txrfCustomerServicesHistory.DateModified, [vdatModifiedTimestamp])
```

FIGURE 9-60: Delete event for txrfCustomerServices

With all three events covered, you now have a complete auditing process for changes to services in the `txrfCustomerServices` table. Best yet, this is all being done no matter how the users access the table — whether via the web views or via client Access forms, or even directly in tables in datasheet view.

SUMMARY

In Chapter 6, you learned about the basic workings of macros. Throughout this chapter, you have had opportunities to augment that knowledge with practical examples and discussion of the considerations that go into choosing one approach or another. You saw various considerations behind each type of macro and the ramifications for application design.

You then learned some different practical uses for macros and how to build those macros. We hope that you can now apply these skills to your own business problems. You should be able to identify which tool or tools will best meet your needs and be aware of performance ramifications, especially with table events. You saw how the On Start macro is an important tool to reduce errors relating to uninitialized variables.

You had opportunities to build freestanding macros and connect UI macros and data macros to form a workflow that users can initiate and that will enable them to perform more with less inputs. You saw a variety of possible designs to generate, edit, and delete record(s), and you used different views to provide input for parameters.

You moved onto table events and considered the performance impact and how you can maximize the use of table events to provide additional validation and enforce business rules, especially those not expressible at a record level. You saw how you can automate operations triggered by events irrespective of how a user initiated the event. You also saw how you can deploy a solution for managing custom calculations or a set of data that are not easily expressed in a relational model and use a mix of freestanding data macros and table events to facilitate the manual management of that data.

All in all, you've been exposed to a wide variety of scenarios in which you can use macros to build a rich and responsive web application and, most important, do so with far less effort on your part in comparison to more traditional web development tools. You now should have a clear vision of what you can do with the new macro actions for your web apps and how you can create powerful solutions. In the next chapter, you will go beyond Access and look at additional tools you can use to give additional functionalities not available from macros, centering around web browser control.

10

Extending Web Apps

WHAT'S IN THIS CHAPTER?

- Introduction to web services
- Using other SharePoint Apps
- Finding and configuring web services
- Integrating web services in your database

WROX.COM CODE DOWNLOADS FOR THIS CHAPTER

The code downloads for this chapter are found at `www.wiley.com/go/proaccess2013prog.com` on the Download Code tab. The code is in the Chapter 10 download and individually named according to the file names listed throughout the chapter.

> **NOTE** *A list of some of the potential issues you may encounter while working with web apps is available in the "What you need to use this book" section of the Introduction.*

In this chapter, you learn how to extend functionality in your Access databases by incorporating other web apps, web parts, and custom web pages into your Access web apps. You learn about two specific tools that you can use to create three different samples for your Access web apps. You learn how to add functionality to your web app by using third-party apps, and create custom pages to be used inside the web app. We also show you how to create a site mailbox so that users of your web apps can provide feedback and requests regarding the web app. We also show you how to integrate a custom page with JavaScript into your web app to extend its functionality. We then show you how to develop a charting application to provide Key Performance Indicators (KPI) for managers.

Unfortunately, a single chapter will not suffice to introduce you to everything you need to know about developing solutions using tools outside of Access. Much of the content in this chapter relies on SharePoint, SharePoint Designer, knowledge of JavaScript and HTML, and other tools pertaining to web development, such as the jQuery library. We don't expect that everyone will be comfortable with, or even necessarily familiar with, these tools at this stage. However, we are sure that successful web app development will call for using them. Therefore, we're including them in the discussions in order to establish a framework of knowledge for your future Access web app projects. The emphasis in this chapter is to introduce you to key concepts and point out how you can transition your programing skills to the new tools, supplemented with more complete tutorials acquired from your preferred learning sources.

The goal of the chapter is to help you understand what is possible outside of Access web apps themselves so that you can have a good idea of what is realistic when designing Access web apps, and whether you want to go outside the web app environment to augment the functionality requested by your customers.

It also bears pointing out that customizations discussed in this chapter may not be appropriate if you intend to distribute your web app via a public channel. Some of the additional installation requirements are not managed by the app installation process, making them unsuitable for that distribution path. For this reason, you may need to either design your web app so that it can run without the additional functionality with the instructions available to the consumers to obtain those extra functionalities or eschew the customization altogether. For bespoken development, you have more freedom and because bespoken solutions are typically more complex, you will find benefits in using additional tools beyond Access to develop the full solution.

Before we can get to specific examples, we will start with an overview of what you can do to build an integrated solution. You will learn about tools available to you and what you can look for to find solutions particular to your needs.

INTEGRATION OPTIONS

As you work through this chapter, you will learn about different methods you can use to extend your web application. We want to start out with the big picture to help you prepare for a change in how you previously may have done development. One great feature of the Access client is that the product allows you to achieve many things without ever leaving the Access environment. Because there were few things that VBA couldn't do, a great number of functionalities were made available in Access by applying some deft piece of code.

In web apps, your developmental platform is no longer Access, but rather SharePoint. When designing a web app in Access, you are working in the SharePoint environment, and many SharePoint features are available to your Access web apps. For this reason, you will find it beneficial to familiarize yourself with SharePoint as a development platform, especially when you want to be able to offer advanced and powerful capabilities that are not otherwise available out of the box.

One major objective of SharePoint is to offer people an environment where they can add new features without writing any code. You will see that the new app framework reinforces that goal. Of course, not all functionality can be expressed in a codeless way, so we encourage you to look at using other tools in addition to Access to design a complete solution. In particular, you will get a taste of using SharePoint Designer to help you create a custom web page. By the end of this chapter, you will know how you can use Access, your favorite web browser, SharePoint, and SharePoint Designer to build a complete solution. Of course, there are additional options such as Visual Studio, but we will not address those.

SharePoint allows you to customize pages and add extra functionality right in your web browser without any special tools or knowledge, as shown in Figure 10-1.

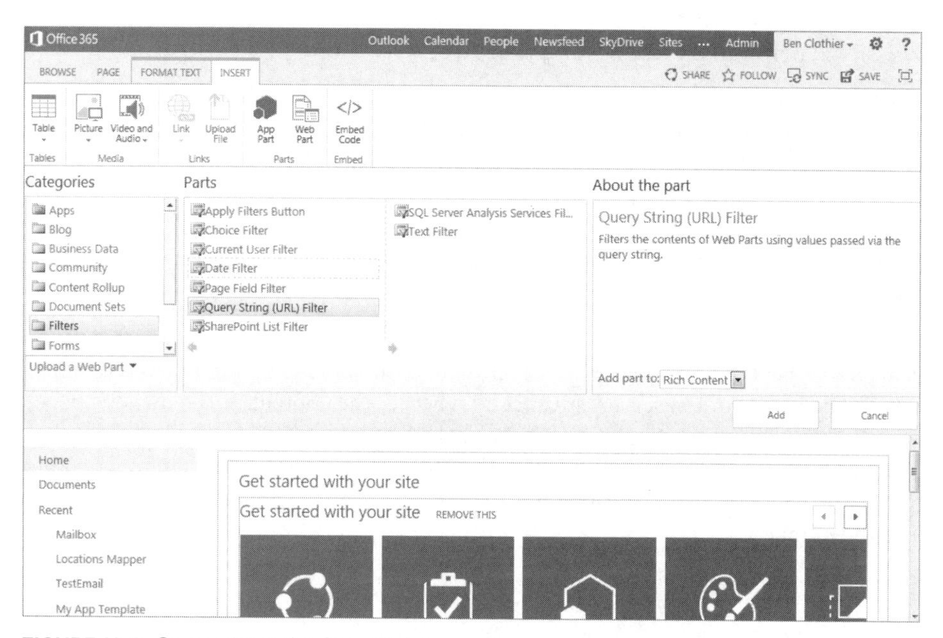

FIGURE 10-1: Customizing the SharePoint page in a web browser

With web parts and even app parts, it is possible to create complex pages without writing a single line of code. You also can embed some code in a limited fashion. In the context of building a rich Access web app, however, those pages cannot be easily inlined for direct consumption inside Access web apps. For this reason, this chapter walks you through the use of SharePoint Designer to enable inlining of custom pages.

Security Considerations

If you're not familiar with the concept of *inlining* pages, it refers to loading another page within a page, which is conceptually similar to how you could put a form in another form using a subform control. In web pages, this control is called an `iframe` element. The difference is that the subform might not reside in the same database, or even on the same network. It would be referenced by a URL at another location. In other words, the developer decided that this form, created and stored elsewhere, would make a good fit for his or her own project, and included it by referencing it. As long as the source of that form is reliable, that's not a problem, but it could happen that the provider of the form decides to add malicious code of some sort, or that the form falls into the hands of someone else who does that. If your database continued to use that subform, you might put your own clients at risk. The danger presented by inlined pages is similar for the same reason. Because the reality of the web is that pages can be inlined, this analogy should illustrate why inlining pages in a web browser is relatively more dangerous than using a subform control on an Access form. One reasonable response to this risk is to refuse to allow each host to manipulate the content that did not originate from the same host.

However, this does not mean you cannot use the SharePoint design experience available to you to build pages and enable inlining via SharePoint Designer. Furthermore, we encourage you to look for resources that discuss designing and customizing SharePoint pages. Resources of that kind can help you offer a professional polish to the site hosting your Access web app.

If you are new to web development, you will need to become familiar with two major security problems: cross-domain scripting and UI redressing. Consider this scenario — you want to make a purchase online and there's a Buy button right there on the web page. How do you know that button was actually rendered by the site owner and not by a malicious third party? The malicious third party could inline the original page and add some malicious JavaScript code to read your credit card numbers. In a scenario like this, you make an actual purchase with the original site owner while the third-party gets your credit card number. As a remedy, many vendors, including Microsoft, have agreed to adopt HTML5's new features that help control such scenarios.

One of those features is the `X-Frame-Options` header, which the server can add when returning an HTML request. The owner of the server can specify whether the content of the owner's page is allowed to be inlined in an `iframe` element and explicitly deny other sites from displaying their pages. Thus, you can be assured that when you click this Buy button, your information won't go to a third-party server that had inlined the original page in an `iframe` element with extra code to intercept your confidential data.

The other feature, while not new to HTML5, is the same-origin policy, which generally requires that scripting must be from the same origin as the HTML document was served. This ensures that when you read a page from `goodsite.example.com`, any JavaScript scripts loaded from this site can only access the content from `goodsite.example.com` or `example.com` and not from `badsite.com` or even `questionablecontent.example.com`. This ensures that a third-party JavaScript cannot just access content that's delivered from a different party and hijack it for malicious use.

One more consideration is that most modern browsers will not allow mixing of contents delivered over HTTP and HTTPS. If your Access web apps and your team site are hosted on Office 365, then it will always be delivered over HTTPS which means you must use only resources that are available over HTTPS. For an on-premises installation of SharePoint, the farm may allow HTTP, but in general, you probably don't want your sensitive data to be sent over the Internet unencrypted unless it's for intranet use. For this reason, you might find it easier to use only resources that have both HTTPS and HTTP protocol supported.

Thus, when you are developing a solution on the SharePoint platform, you must grapple with the fact that not everything can be trusted. A page won't oblige requests to run any piece of custom code handed to it willy-nilly. You saw in Chapter 4, in our discussion of the web browser control, that you had to address the security considerations in order for a web browser control to be able to render the content. This is still true even when developing a SharePoint solution. In a hosted environment, it is unlikely you can create and run ad hoc server-side code. For this reason, most custom code you will deal with will be either in an app or in a client-side form such as JavaScript. It is more likely you'll be able to provision forms of that sort successfully in a variety of environments. If you are fortunate to have enough rights and access to an on-premises deployment, you may find additional options otherwise unavailable on Office 365 or a hosted SharePoint site.

Implications for Access Developers

What this means for you as an Access developer is that, although you have a web browser control that functionally allows you to inline additional contents from outside your Access web apps, you must also be allowed to inline the external content from the security perspective. The decision of whether the content may or may not be inlined rests with the creator of the content. Therefore, if you want to inline a third-party app or page, there is nothing you can do short of obtaining permission from the creator to do so. In Chapter 4, for example, you saw how Google required you to pass in a parameter to allow you to inline Google's rendering of maps inside a web browser control.

When you create custom pages yourself and have them hosted on SharePoint, you, as the creator, can explicitly allow those pages to be inlined in your Access web apps. For those pages that you didn't create and over which you do not have direct control, you may need to consider opening them in a separate window or tab rather than inlining in your web app. You will see an example of opening a page in a popup form later in the chapter and you will also learn how you can allow inlining when you are the creator of a SharePoint page.

Using the XMLHTTPRequest Object

There is one more important distinction to note if you've created client-side solutions that interact with the web, such as using the `XMLHTTPRequest` object in VBA code. Asynchronous JavaScript And XML (AJAX) makes heavy use of the `XMLHTTPRequest` object to deliver rich content by submitting requests to the server and returning content and dynamically manipulating the rendered HTML document on your web browser. If you've used the `XMLHTTPRequest` object or its variant in VBA, you should know that you will have less freedom inside a web browser and JavaScript. In VBA or other client solutions, you had complete control over the `XMLHTTPRequest` object, and the object started with a completely blank slate. In a web browser, however, that is no longer true. When you instantiate an `XMLHTTPRequest` object in this context, it comes with various properties set by the browser, and some properties that you may have been able to manipulate via client solutions are either not available or invalid inside a web browser. As mentioned previously, this has to do with security. The goal is to prevent users of web browsers from being victimized by running malicious JavaScript code, which is a much more real risk compared to running malicious VBA code because users visit hundreds, if not thousands, of different sites owned by different parties. In contrast, they deal with only a handful of client programs and usually have a clear connection between the content delivered and who delivered it. On a web page, that connection is not as clear; it may be composed of multiple pieces from different sources.

The essential point is that what you know about programming for web services in the client context such as VBA and the `XMLHTTPRequest` object does not always translate to what you can do with the `XMLHTTPRequest` object within a web browser.

Introduction to Web Services

For those Access developers whose experience has not called for integrating web services into your applications, let's start with a brief overview of what they consist of.

Web services provide the means for one software application to connect to other software applications across the web using standard protocols that follow established specifications. Because web services must be architected to comply with standard protocols and conventions such as HTTP, REST, and SOAP, and data formats such as XML and JSON, your applications can access web services without having to account for how each web service is implemented. One example of a web service is a ZIP code service that returns information about a city and state, and additional data in some cases, from a ZIP code submitted to the web service. You learn about one web service of that type later in this chapter. There are many others, such as a service to calculate sales taxes or to validate American Bankers Association (ABA) routing numbers. Although many are free, some of the industry-specific web services require a fee for using them.

Requesting Data from a Web Service

Some web services can also be used to provide additional content. You will see an example of this in this chapter where we use a Google API to render a chart on the web page. Web services can be divided into two broad categories: those that accept input data via a GET request and others that expect data in a POST request. When you type in a URL on a web browser, you are performing a GET request, and for some web services, you can embed input parameters directly in the URL.

As you learned in Chapter 4, web services of the GET variety are very simple to use because it's just a matter of manipulating URL strings. However, URLs are limited to only about two thousand characters, and it can be problematic to express all of the needed data in that length, not to mention issues arising when invalid characters are encoded. For this reason, you will find that more-complex web services typically expect a POST request instead.

Web services of the POST variety basically mean you must format a document, typically an XML document or JSON document that contains the input data that you submit to the web service's server. Toward the end of the chapter, you will learn how to do this.

Getting Data Back from a Web Service

The next category you need to consider is the format in which the web services will return the data. Again, there are a couple of broad approaches to returning data.

Some web services return data in a format that is immediately useful, such as HTML or images, which makes it a simple matter to implement. Other web services may return data as XML or JSON documents, which require further processing on your end to transform the data into something that you can display in the web browser. JavaScript Object Notation (JSON), like XML, is a system of encoding data. One common use is to facilitate communication between server and client.

Thus, it is important to identify how to invoke each web service you want to use. Generally speaking, you will find that the web browser control for your Access web app is more amenable to web services that accept input via the GET request and query string parameters, and return

HTML or images. For other web services that expect a POST request, you may need to consider alternatives such as using JavaScript (specifically, AJAX) to submit requests and render the output appropriately.

SharePoint also supports web services that can be used in JavaScript, which enables you to interact with SharePoint objects such as adding a new list item to a SharePoint list or starting a workflow. Many major vendors including Microsoft, Google, and Yahoo also offer their own web services. Here are links to some of their APIs for you to look over:

- `http://msdn.microsoft.com/en-us/library/jj193034.aspx`
- `http://www.bing.com/developers/`
- `https://developers.google.com/products/`
- `http://developer.yahoo.com/everything.html`

Of course, there are many more third-party sources. You will want to get familiar with different sources, as you will discover that they have different implementations to offer the same or similar functionality, some of which may be more amenable to your particular needs.

In the next section of this chapter, we begin looking at some of the options available to you for extending functionality in your team website and apps, starting with a fairly simple third-party web app. As you gain experience with these elements, you'll also be preparing for a more advanced web service, which you'll explore later in the chapter.

LINKING A WEB APP FOR ADDITIONAL FUNCTIONALITY

One way to extend the functionality of an Access web app is to incorporate other web apps that can provide functions not available in the basic web app experience. To experience this sort of extension first-hand, you'll learn how to add a location mapping app to the Maid To Order web team site to supplement the Maid To Order web app. For example, crews can check a map showing pushpins for all of their customer locations and addresses for the day, prior to heading out for those jobs. While there are web services such as Bing Maps and Google maps which can locate single addresses, Maid To Order wants an app that shows all of the job addresses for a single day on one map. You'll learn how to do that, but as you read through this section, keep in mind that we're only able to show you some basic concepts and uses. We're sure that you'll be able think of additional ways to extend the mapping concept to fit your projects.

Locating and Adding the Locations Mapper App

As with other apps you've added to your team site, start by going to the Site Contents page and selecting Add an App. This takes you to the Your Apps page, where you select an app from those available to you. However, the one we want is offered through the SharePoint store, so we'll take a slightly different path here. When you get to the Add Apps page, use the Search box to look for "Locations." You should get a result like the one in Figure 10-2.

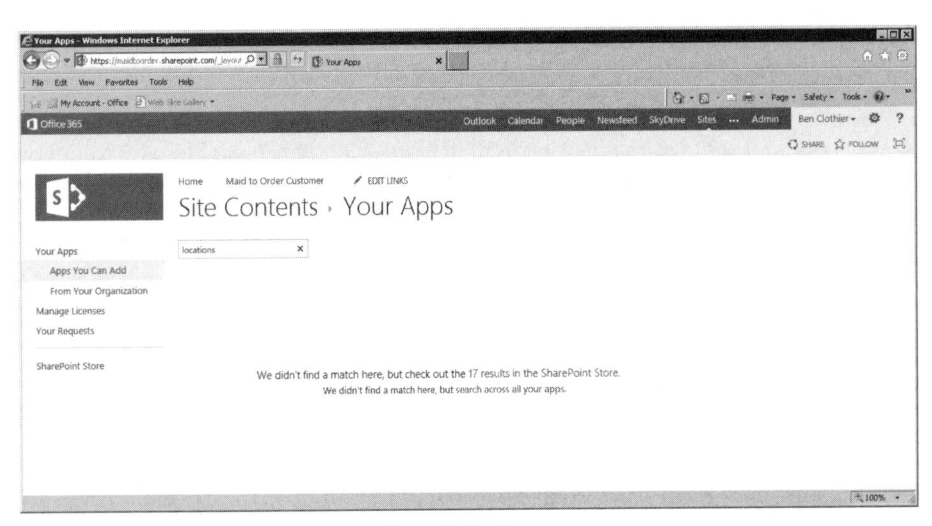

FIGURE 10-2: Locating an app on the SharePoint Store

You are looking for a specific app, created by a third party, called Locations Mapper. Because this is the first time you've used it in this context, it's not yet in your organization's app catalog. Clicking on the link to the SharePoint Store, however, will bring the choices to you. The one we want, Locations Mapper, is selected in Figure 10-3. As you can see, there is also a paid version of the mapper app from the same vendor, called Locations Map Plus, which offers more advanced features.

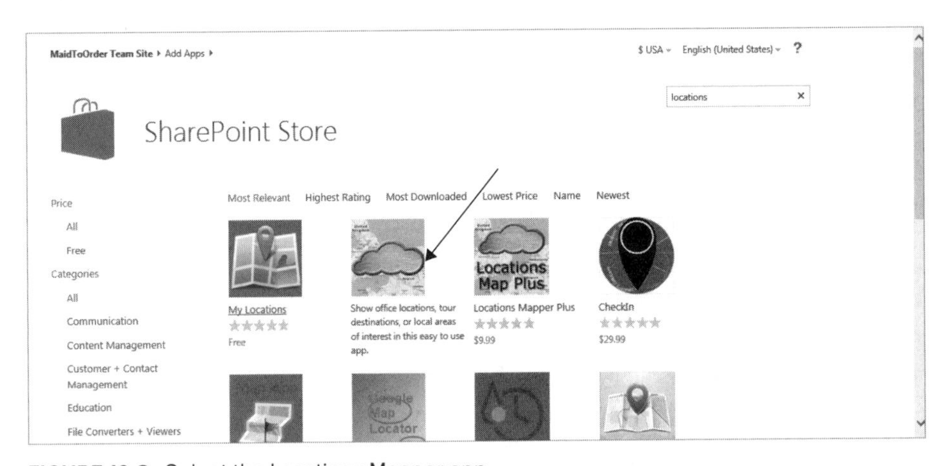

FIGURE 10-3: Select the Locations Mapper app.

Click the Locations Mapper app to select it. You'll be asked to confirm that you want to add it to your website. The next page looks like Figure 10-4.

FIGURE 10-4: Add the selected app to your site.

You can also check the website of the app's creator for more information. In this case, that website is quite useful because it provides details on using the app correctly. We'll show you that later, after you've added the app. Clicking Add It brings you to a confirmation screen, where you'll confirm that you want to add the app, shown in Figure 10-5.

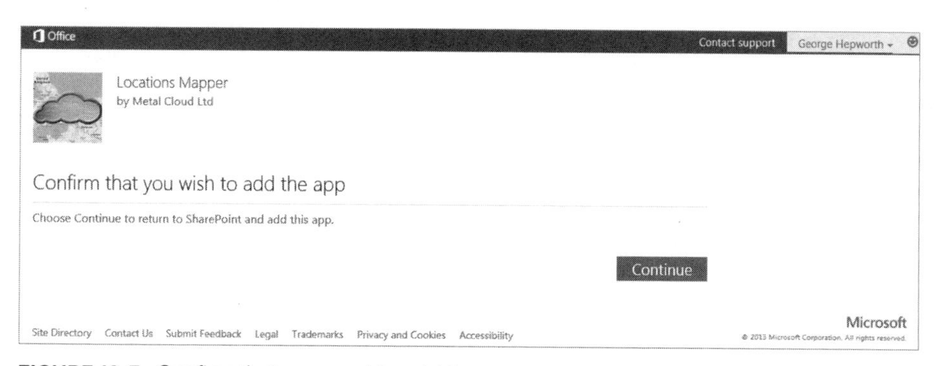

FIGURE 10-5: Confirm that you want to add the app.

Clicking Continue takes you to the next screen, Figure 10-6, where you should enable the app for all members of your organization.

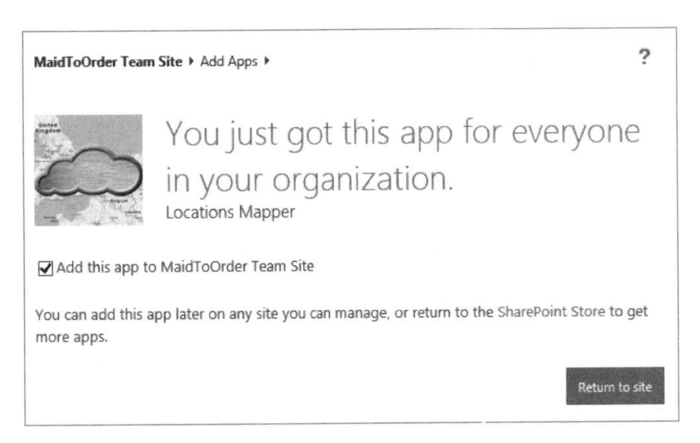

FIGURE 10-6: Enable the app for the team site.

Keep clicking, this time on Return to Site. The next confirmation, shown in Figure 10-7, enables the app by giving it access to basic information about the site and users of the site.

Trust the app. That will take you back to the apps page, as shown in Figure 10-8.

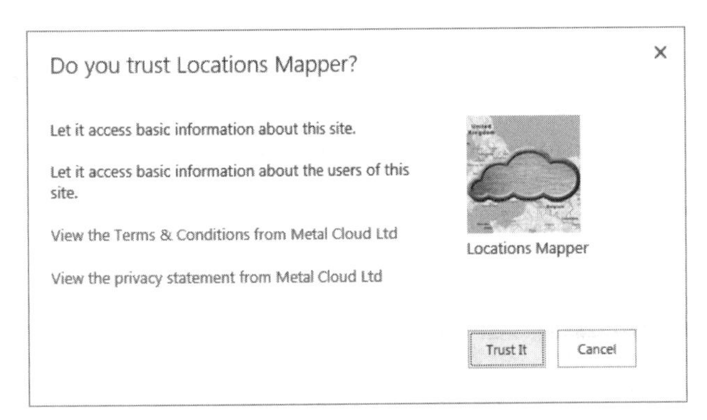

FIGURE 10-7: Trust the app, enabling it to use basic information about the site and users of the site.

FIGURE 10-8: Adding an app

Although the app is now among your other web apps, it still offers one final chance to cancel the addition. Once it's installed, however, it's ready to use.

> **NOTE** *You've walked through all of the steps required to obtain and install this particular app. Your experience may vary with other apps from different vendors. In all cases, however, the process should follow the same path from locating and selecting it, through adding and trusting it. If you select a paid app, there will be additional steps wherein you'll pay for the app.*

Configuring and Using the Locations Mapper App

The key to the usefulness of this app is that it is designed to display multiple locations as pushpins on a map. Configuring the app to show locations is not difficult, although it's not totally transparent, so let's dive into that now. Open the Locations Mapper from your team site, which will appear as in Figure 10-9.

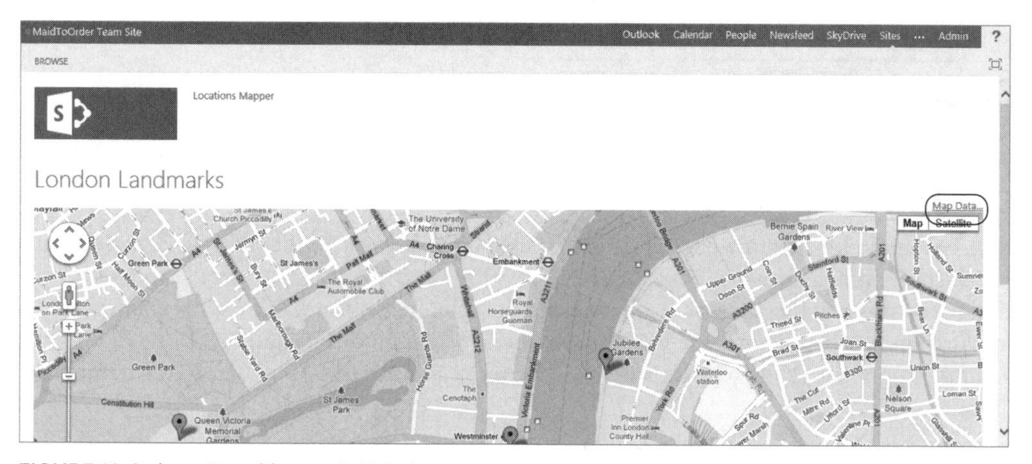

FIGURE 10-9: Locations Mapper initial view

The Locations Mapper defaults to a location in London, England; you'll change that to your own location.

Locate the link to Map Data on the top of the map at the right side; you can see it highlighted in Figure 10-9. Click it to open the configuration page. The mapper comes with three default locations defined as an example (see Figure 10-10).

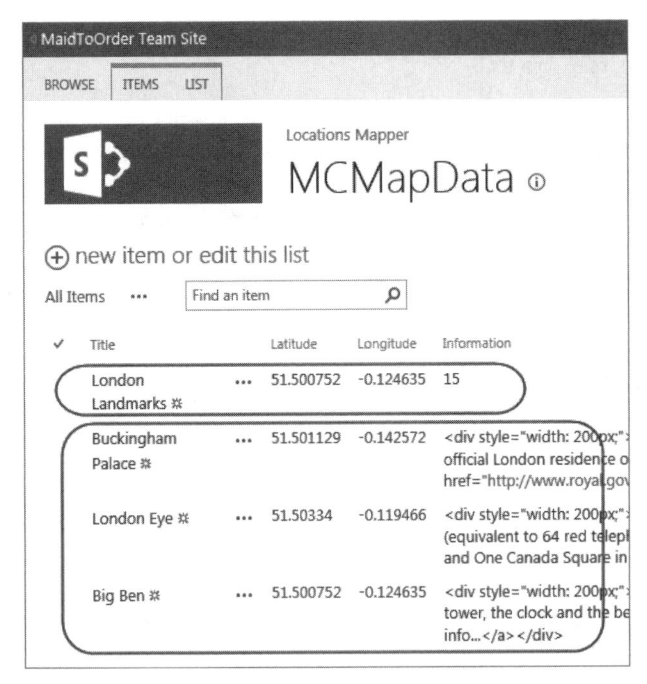

FIGURE 10-10: Mapped Locations

Initial Configuration in Line One

The first line in the list actually doesn't define a pushpin; it does two other things. First, it defines the title of the map, which, as you can see in Figures 10-9 and 10-10, is "London Landmarks." The coordinates on the first line center the map on that location when it opens. The number entered in the information field determines the initial zoom level for the map. The number 15 in Figure 10-10 results in the zoom level shown in Figure 10-9. Higher numbers zoom in closer; lower numbers zoom out.

Locations in Remaining Lines

The remaining lines define pushpin locations for the map. The title in these lines is used as the "hover" text. The latitude and longitude coordinates center the pushpin, and the Information text displays when the pushpin is clicked. As you can see, you can format the information text with HTML markup if you desire, but plain text displays fine as well.

You can add, delete, or edit pushpin locations in this list. Of course, once you've set it up for your team site, you'll want to remove the demo locations in London and replace them with locations appropriate to your own organization. The results might look something like Figure 10-11.

The pushpins shown in Figure 10-11 are generated by the list shown in Figure 10-12.

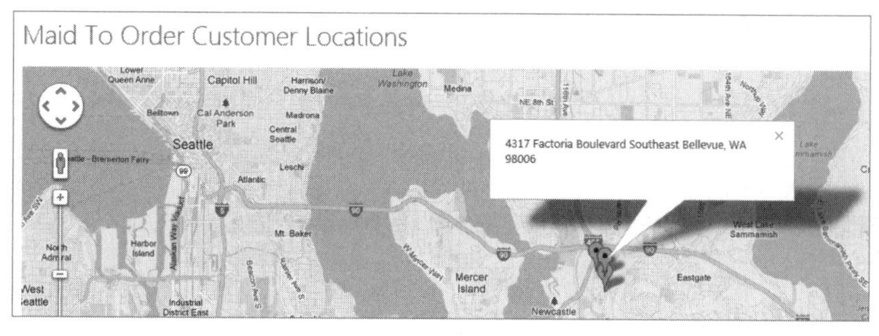

FIGURE 10-11: Maid To Order Customer Locations

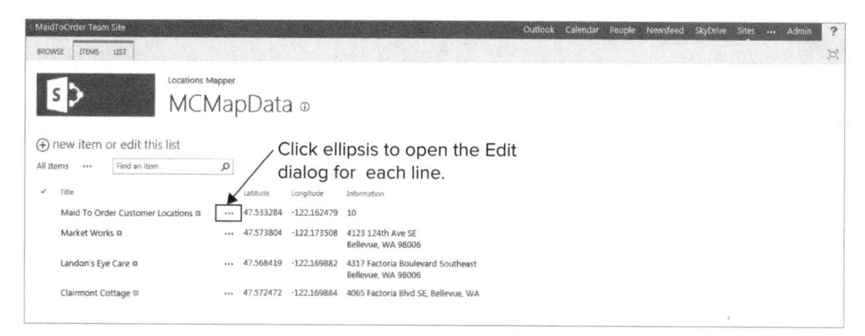

FIGURE 10-12: Maid To Order customer list for location mapper

You may be wondering how you'll go about determining the coordinates you need for your pushpins. Let's see one possible way to do that now. You can locate an address on Google Maps in your favorite browser, and use one of their built-in features to get the coordinates. Figure 10-13 shows that.

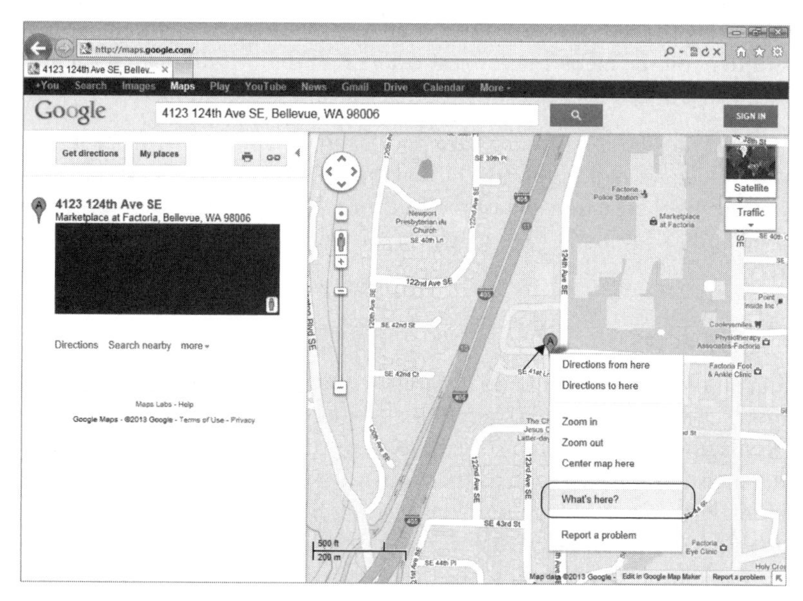

FIGURE 10-13: Obtain coordinates by clicking "What's here?"

Right mouse clicking on a pushpin opens the shortcut menu. Clicking "What's here?" returns the coordinates for that address, as illustrated in Figure 10-14.

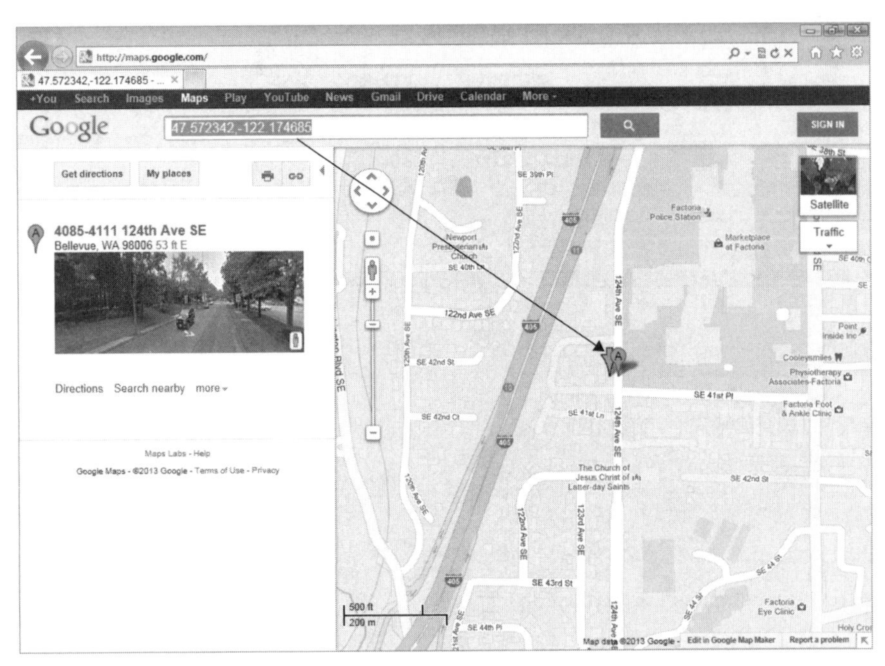

FIGURE 10-14: Obtain coordinates for an address.

You can now copy the latitude and longitude to the fields in the Location Mapper to add the new address to the list. To edit the fields in the Location Mapper, click on the ellipsis highlighted in Figure 10-12. Now click Edit Item on the menu that appears. The Edit dialog will open with fields for the required elements of the location: Title, Latitude, Longitude, and Description.

You've now seen just how easy it is to set up and configure a web app for your users. Once it has been set up, however, it can be much more useful than this basic map with multiple push pins. In the next section, you learn about one possible extension of the Location Mapper app. We're confident that you will be also able to identify additional ways in which you can use the information to extend and support your web apps.

Customer Locations for Daily Jobs

One possible use for the Location Mapper might be to generate a daily map of locations where jobs are scheduled for that day. Crew leaders could then pop open the map showing pushpins for all scheduled jobs to help decide how best to travel between jobs, or perhaps to coordinate travel to avoid known construction areas, or look up specific locations with which they are not familiar. Another possible use would be that office staff can use the Location Mapper from within their client database to locate addresses of new or potential clients to see where they are in relation to existing customers. Again, use your imagination as you follow the discussion of one of these potential uses.

Daily Job Map

To use the Location Mapper app within the Maid To Order office, the data in it must first be exposed in their `.accdb` file. Here's how you'll do that. Open the Location Mapper in your browser and copy out the URL. It contains information you'll need to link to the SharePoint list, which contains the coordinates for the pushpins. It will look something like Figure 10-15. The part you need is highlighted.

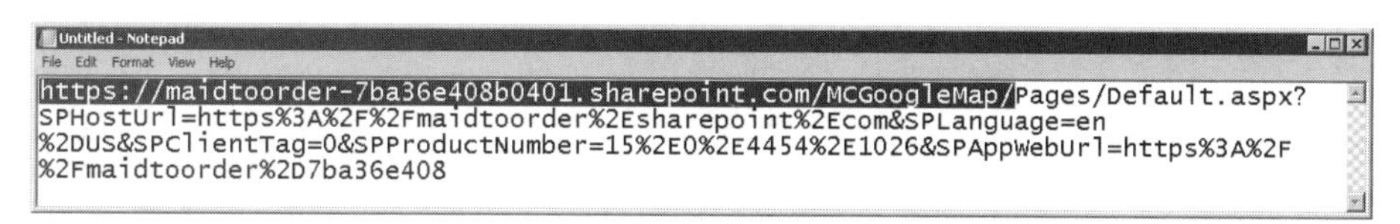

FIGURE 10-15: URL for the Location Mapper app on Maid To Order

Open your `MTOClient.accdb` file. You're going to link to the SharePoint list at the previous URL, and then you're going to create a form to work with it. You'll find the link to SharePoint in your Access client as shown in Figure 10-16.

Connecting to a SharePoint list should be familiar to you, but you can see the specifics for this list in Figure 10-17.

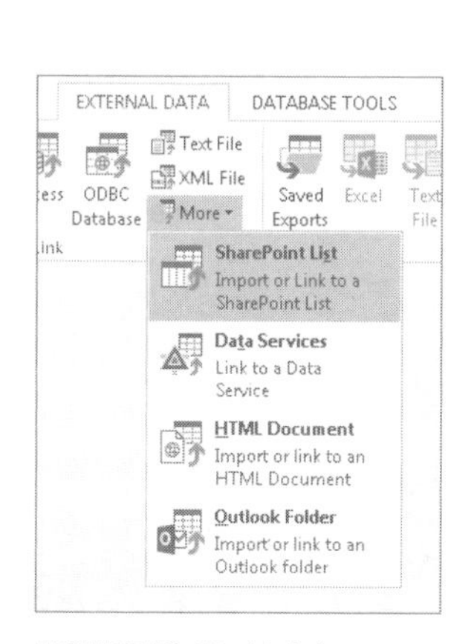

FIGURE 10-16: Link to a SharePoint List from `.accdb` file.

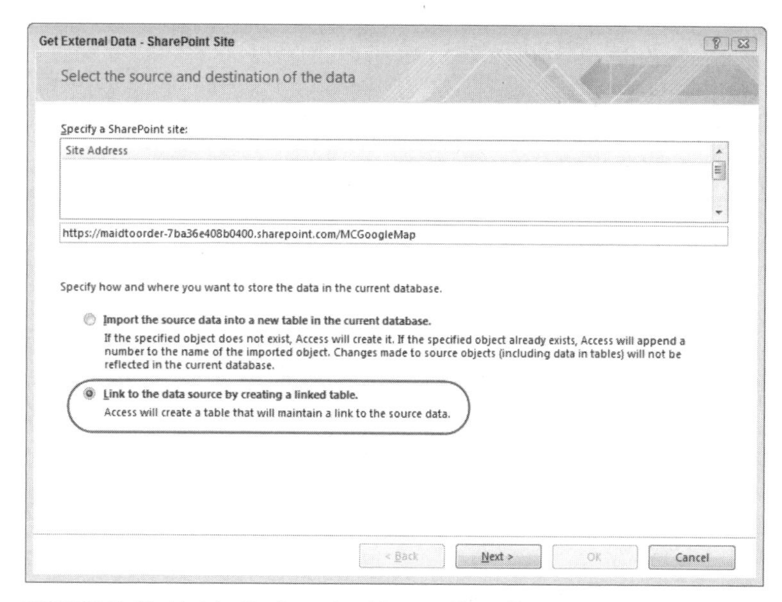

FIGURE 10-17: Link to the Location Mapper SharePoint list.

Make sure you enter the full path, including MCGoogleMap and that you link to the SharePoint list, not import it. When you click Next, you'll be offered a choice of two SharePoint lists; you want the one checked in Figure 10-18, called `MCMapData`.

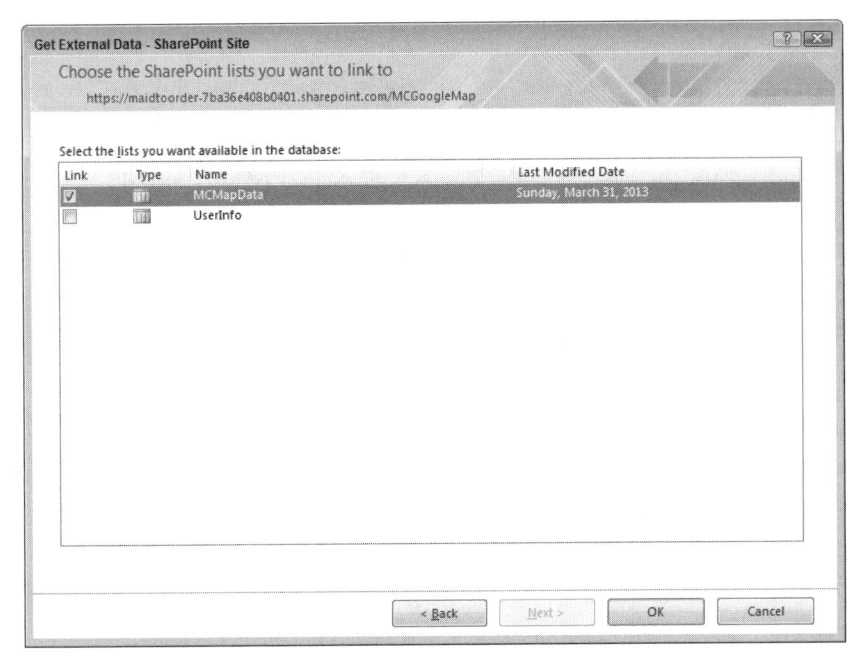

FIGURE 10-18: Link to the MCMapData list.

Clicking OK completes the link. The `MCMapData` SharePoint list is now linked into your `MTOClient.accdb` file. At this point, you now have the Location Mapper map data exposed in your `.accdb` file. You can build client Access forms, bound to that SharePoint list, with which you can easily edit the data in the list, perhaps creating a daily job location map for crew leaders, or as a lookup for staff to compare locations of new customers to existing customers for use in planning crew assignments, or for other purposes that you come up with. Let's just take a look at one such form as an example. It's shown in Figure 10-19.

MTO Daily Job Address Mapper

MTO Daily Job Address Mapper

Get Google Map Coordinates

Check Location Map on MTO

Do not change or delete the First Record

ID	Customer	Latitude	Longitude	Address
1	Maid To Order Customer Locat	47.533284	-122.162479	10
2	Market Works	47.573804	-122.173508	4123 124th Ave SE Bellevue, WA 98006
3	Landon's Eye Care	47.568419	-122.169882	4317 Factoria Boulevard Southeast, Be
4	Clairmont Cottage	47.572472	-122.169884	4065 Factoria Blvd SE, Bellevue, WA
(New)				

FIGURE 10-19: Daily Job Address Mapper

Note that the first record must remain as shown. The Address field (bound to the Information field in the list) specifies the initial zoom level for Location Mapper; you can increase or decrease the zoom level, as appropriate to your situation. The coordinates in the first record determine where it centers on opening. The other three records represent jobs scheduled for the day. The office staff will update job locations each day for the location Mapper app display. Crews can refer to the Location Mapper app for a visual of where their jobs are that day. Clicking the pushpin in the app confirms the address, stored as part of the pushpin. You may already have thought of this, but you can add quite a bit more text than just the address, so Maid To Order staff could include special instructions or comments about each job. Clicking that job's pushpin displays all of that additional content. Of course, MTO crews would need to be trained to consult the Location Mapper app to see any last-minute additions.

Also note that there are two hyperlinks on the form. One opens the web app in the browser, showing the pushpins for the day's jobs. The other is there to help the staff get the coordinates to put in the latitude and longitude fields for new customers. In this application, we expect to have a table of clients and their location coordinates. Adding clients to the Location Mapper list could be done using a drop-down of the records in that client location table, eliminating the need to look them up again. That's a fairly common Access task, which we assume most Access developers have done, so we'll leave it to you to create a client location table and combo box as an exercise.

The Google map link opens the Google Map tool, which you learned how to use previously (refer to Figure 10-13). The hyperlink on this form is set up to grab the address selected in the form for the coordinate lookup. We envision this hyperlink being used when a new client is signed up. The staff member types the client's address into the Address (Information) field and clicks the hyperlink to get the coordinates, which are then copy-pasted back into the form for that client and also added to the permanent client-location table. Again, because these are common Access tasks, we'll leave it to you to set up that part of the process.

We are also confident you'll find other ways to exploit the information exposed in the SharePoint list, such as creating a new pushpin to identify a specific location on the map where you want your crews to gather for a meeting. The information field allows you to put any comments you want into the pushpin, so this one could include a full description of the event as well as the address.

At this point, there's one more way we want to leverage the Location Mapper. You're going to learn how to expose it in the web app. Let's close the `.accdb` file and open the web app in Access. You'll put an action button on a view from which crew members can pop open the Location Mapper at any time.

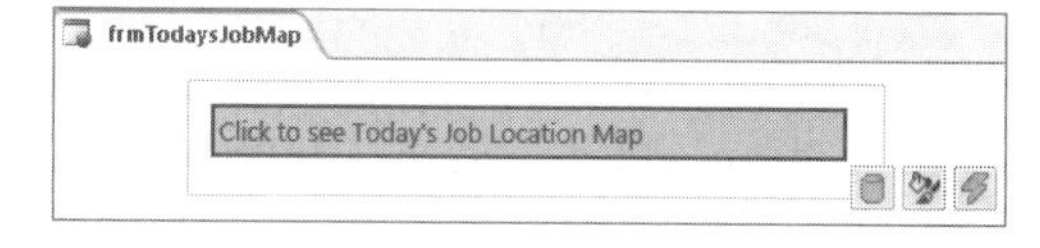

FIGURE 10-20: Blank Form with a Hyperlink control

Create a new blank view. Place a hyperlink control on it. See how this looks in Figure 10-20. Name this view `frmTodaysJobMap`.

You will want to set the Default URL property for the Hyperlink control via its button. The full URL is the same one you used earlier to connect from the `.accdb` file: `https://maidtoorder-7ba36e408b0401.sharepoint.com/MCGoogleMap/`.

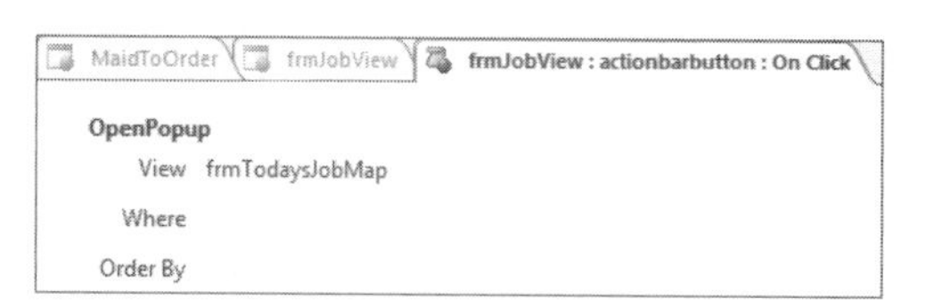

FIGURE 10-21: Action button macro to show popup with Today's Jobs hyperlink

Now, let's see how you're going to open this popup, using an action button in the Job view. The popup opens from the macro shown in Figure 10-21 behind the action button's click event.

Figures 10-22 and 10-23 show how this works in the browser.

FIGURE 10-22: Action button to launch Today's Job Location popup

Today's Job Location Map

Click to see Today's Job Location Map

FIGURE 10-23: Popup with hyperlink to launch Job Location Map

Clicking "Click to see Today's Job Location Map" opens the map with pushpins in a new browser window. Note that there is no code required in the web app extension other than the macro to open the popup with the hyperlink.

INLINING A WEB APP IN ACCESS WEB APP

In a previous section, you saw how you could build a hyperlink to open the web app in a new window or tab. As mentioned at the start of the chapter, the option to put the content in the web browser control directly on an Access web app must be explicitly allowed by the developer. Because the Location Mapper is developed by a third party, that developer decides whether it may be inlined or not; in this case, not.

Suppose you prefer being able to inline the Location Mapper rather than popping out a new window. Your option is to find an app that allows inlining. Fortunately, the same developer that offers Location Mapper also offers another app, Location Mapper Plus, which is, of course, a paid app. Among other more advanced features, the paid version allows the app to be added to other SharePoint pages as an app part. Let's look at how you can use this app and display it inside the Access web app.

> **NOTE** *In a SharePoint site, an App Part is a wrapper for an* `iframe` *which displays content, such as the Location Mapper Plus app, within the page.*

Adding an app part is not the same thing as setting a URL for the `iframe` element. For security reasons, SharePoint performs additional steps while rendering an app part to ensure that the content from the app isn't rendered in an uncontrolled manner or to unauthorized users. So, to accomplish our goal, we need an intermediate ASPX page that can accept an app part to provide a URL, which we can supply to the web browser control. You will learn how to do this next, and in the process, glimpse perhaps your initial experience of creating your custom pages in SharePoint.

Assuming you've already gone through the steps of adding the Location Mapper Plus app, following the steps you used to install the free Location Mapper app, you will go to the Site Pages library to create a new page. You can find the Site Pages library in the Sites Content page, as shown in Figure 10-24.

FIGURE 10-24: Site Pages library on the Site Contents page

In the Site Pages library, click the Files tab on the ribbon, click the New Document drop-down menu to select Web Part Page, as shown in Figure 10-25.

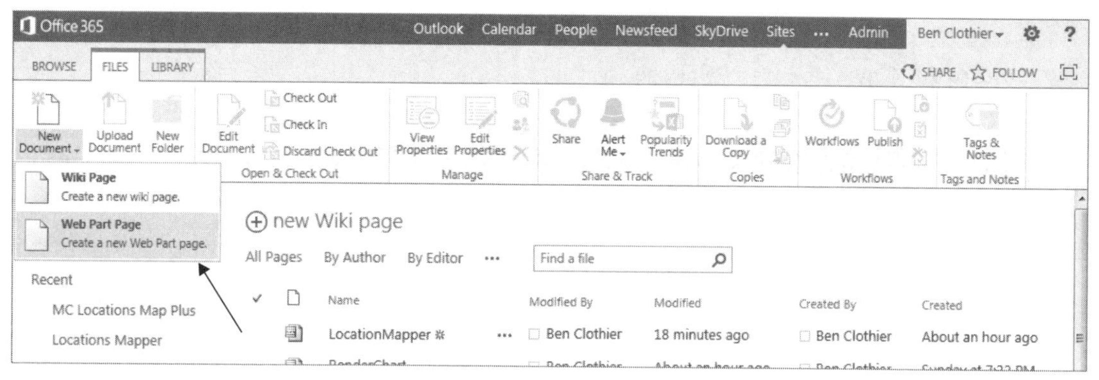

FIGURE 10-25: New Web Part Page

You'll be taken to a page to fill out the name and specify the layout for the web part; provide the name, `LocationMapper`, and specify Full Page, Vertical layout as in Figure 10-26.

Once you fill out and click the Create button, shown in Figure 10-26, you'll be taken to the new page in edit mode, which will look similar to Figure 10-27.

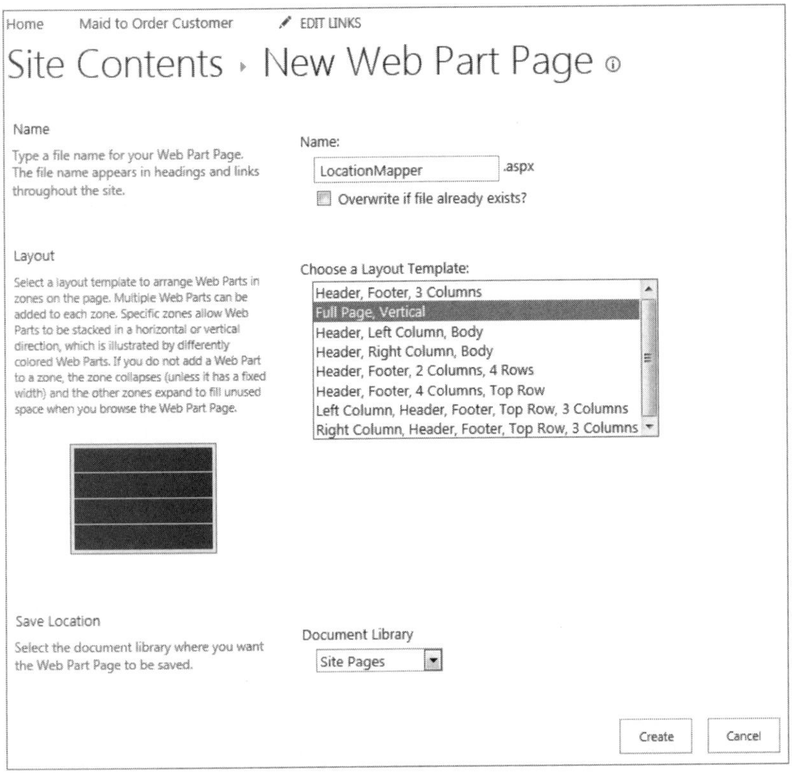

FIGURE 10-26: Create New Web Part Page

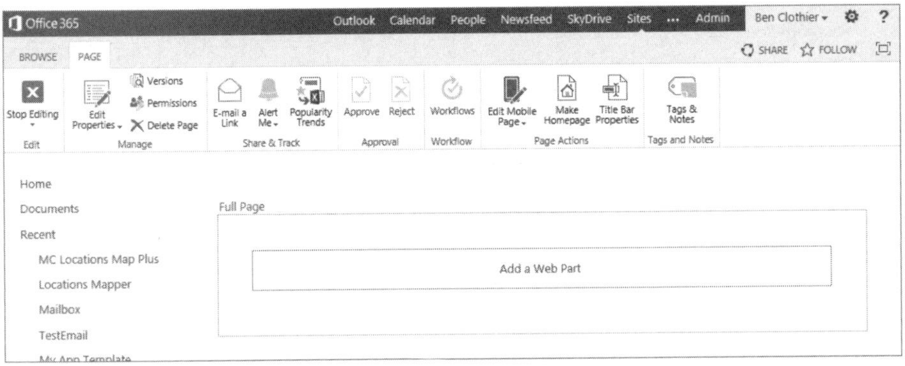

FIGURE 10-27: Edit page mode

Although a complete discussion of this design surface is beyond the scope of the book, you can see that SharePoint offers you an easy way of creating your custom content in a codeless manner. For now, let's add the app part to the page. Click the Add a Web Part hyperlink shown in Figure 10-27, which will pop up a dialog box listing all available app parts and web parts. Select the Apps folder and then select the Metal Cloud Locations Map Plus, as shown in Figure 10-28.

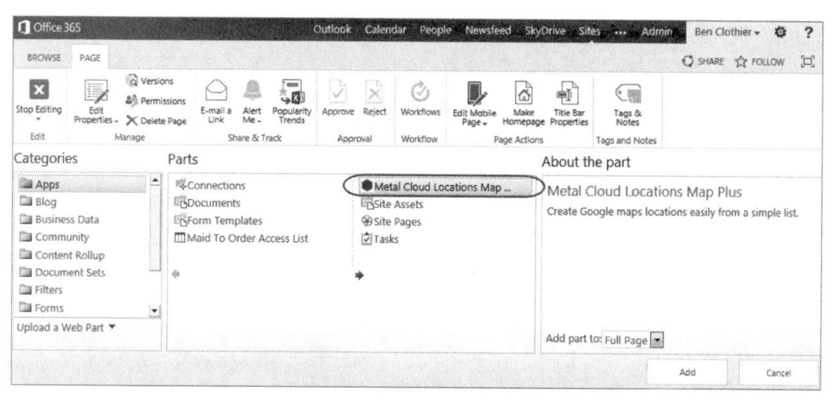

FIGURE 10-28: Adding an app part

> **NOTE** *In order to add this content, you may need to add* `*.microsoftonline.com` *as a trusted site in Internet Explorer. You'll find instructions on how to do that at* `http://support.microsoft.com/kb/2643142`.

Click Add to complete the dialog box. The new app part will then show on the page. You may want to remove the title and other chrome surrounding the app part. Click the drop-down and select Edit Web Part, as shown in Figure 10-29.

You'll want to re-name the title with a space and set Chrome Type to None, as in Figure 10-30, and click OK to save changes.

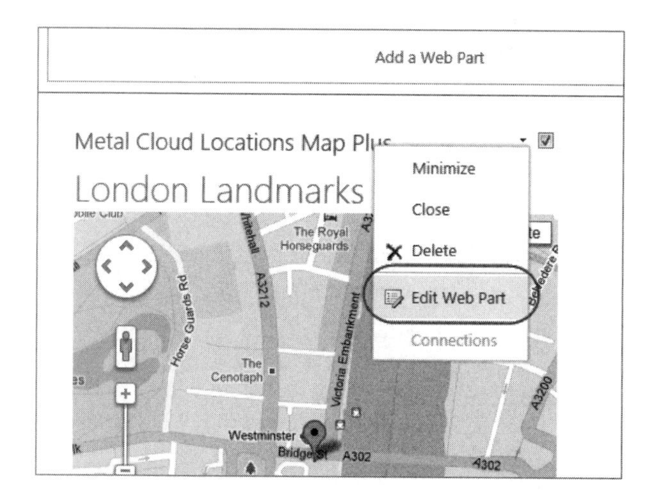

FIGURE 10-29: Editing web part properties

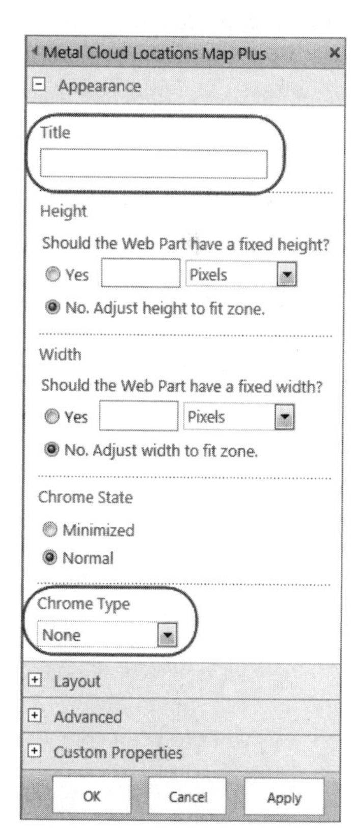

FIGURE 10-30: Editing properties

NOTE *If you do not put a space in the title property and delete it, it will automatically replace the title with "Untitled."*

CHROME, NOT THE SHINY KIND

You were introduced to the concept of chrome in Chapter 3. In the context of web browsers, chrome is where you have your back, forward, and refresh buttons, as well as the address bar and status bar. For SharePoint parts, it refers to menus that are associated with each object that enable closing or editing of the web part. By setting Chrome Type to None for this web part, you remove those menus and make it noneditable by end users. This is usually desirable when you want to use parts on a page without cluttering them up with unnecessary options.

At this point, you are done editing the app part; exit the edit mode by clicking the Stop Editing button on the ribbon, as shown on Figure 10-31.

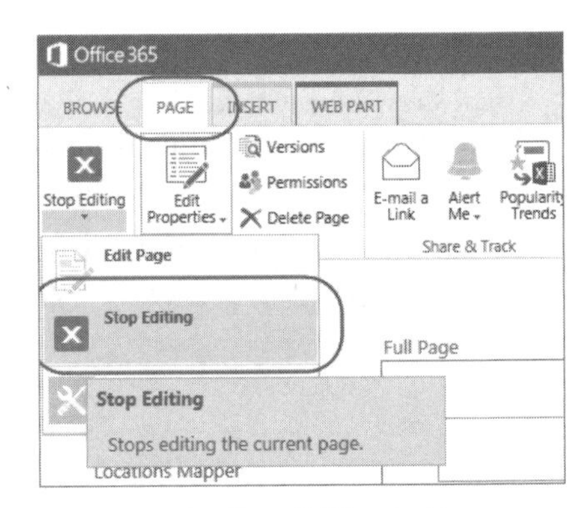

FIGURE 10-31: Stop Editing button

You've just created a brand new page that has the Locations Map Plus web app inlined, and you have a URL that you can supply to a web browser control in your Access web app to use this page.

Although the developer of this web app has allowed the web app itself to be inlined, the page containing the web app needs to be allowed to be inlined as well. Because you created the page, you can control this yourself. You use SharePoint Designer to do this.

INSTALLING SHAREPOINT DESIGNER

SharePoint Designer is an optional component, and is not always installed. However, it is free to download and install. Whenever you need advanced authoring capabilities, you will want to use SharePoint Designer, which is free to download and install. You can get a copy at `http://www.microsoft.com/en-us/download/details.aspx?id=35491`.

On the Page tab in the ribbon, click Edit Page and select Edit in SharePoint Designer, as in Figure 10-32.

This launches SharePoint Designer. You may get a security prompt asking for permission to launch it. Allow it to launch and you will be landed directly in the basic edit mode for this page in SharePoint Designer, as shown in Figure 10-33.

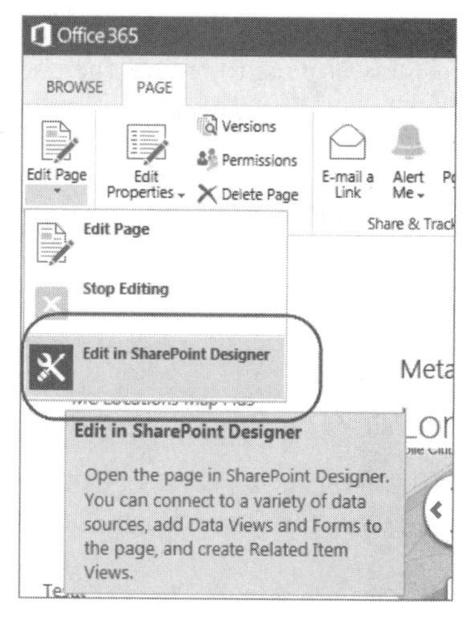

FIGURE 10-32: Edit In SharePoint Designer

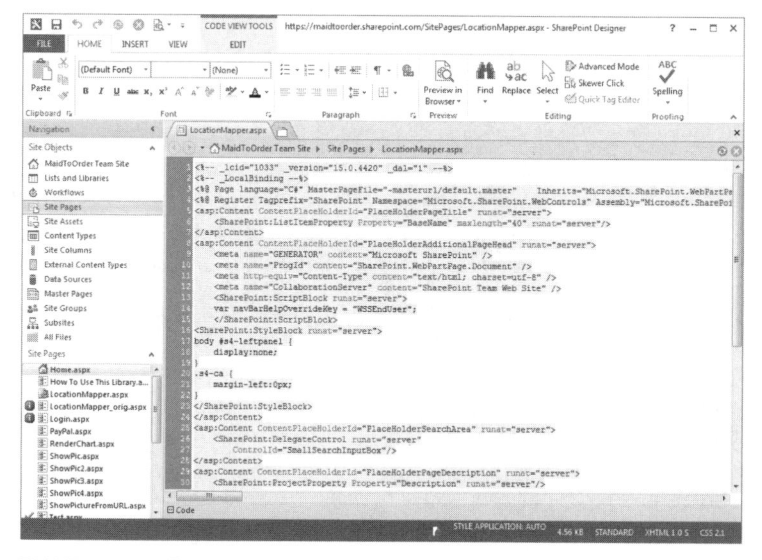

FIGURE 10-33: Page in basic edit mode

NOTE *Perhaps you're wondering why some code is highlighted yellow while other code is not. In the basic editing mode, SharePoint Designer highlights restricted content in yellow and makes those regions non-editable, enabling you to focus only on editable content. This roughly corresponds to the same design surface you saw when you were editing pages directly in the web browser.*

There are two things you need to do in SharePoint Designer; change the master page to a minimal master page to reduce the chrome around the web app and allow inlining of the page itself. To make those two changes, you need to work in Advanced mode.

Let's start with changing the master page. On the ribbon, click Advanced mode to allow you to edit additional properties, as shown on Figure 10-34.

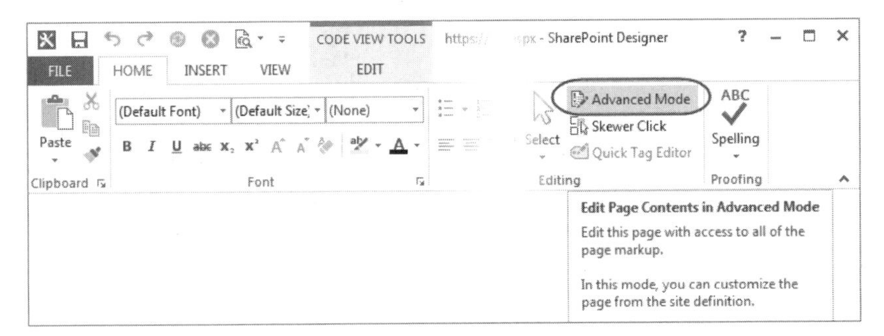

FIGURE 10-34: Edit in Advanced mode.

The ribbon will display additional tabs, one of them Style. Click it, and then click Attach drop-down and select `minimal.master`, as shown in Figure 10-35.

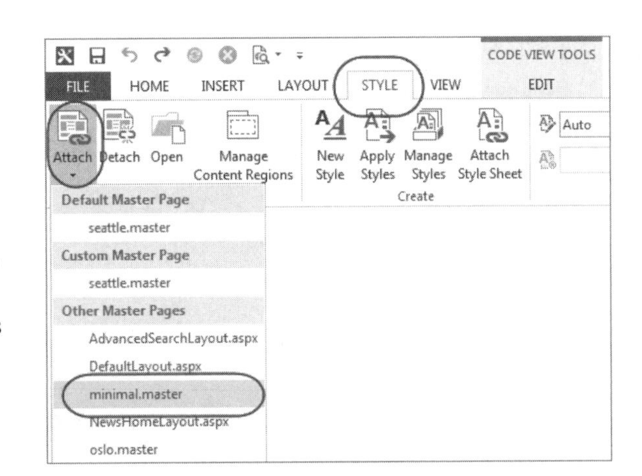

FIGURE 10-35: Attach a new master page.

A dialog box will pop up indicating a mismatch in the editable region of the page. Because you want to minimize and eliminate extraneous content, the only region to keep is the additional page head and main area, as illustrated in Figure 10-36. Use the Modify button indicated to set the other regions to (None), removing those extraneous regions.

This operation gives the page a new chrome, which will not only take less space but also ensure that the web app part is the only content displayed, without ribbons or any extraneous markup. However, you need to restore a referenced assembly that is not usually used in the new minimal master page to allow the framing. Add the following code on a line after the last `<%@ ... %>` element, as indicated in Figure 10-37:

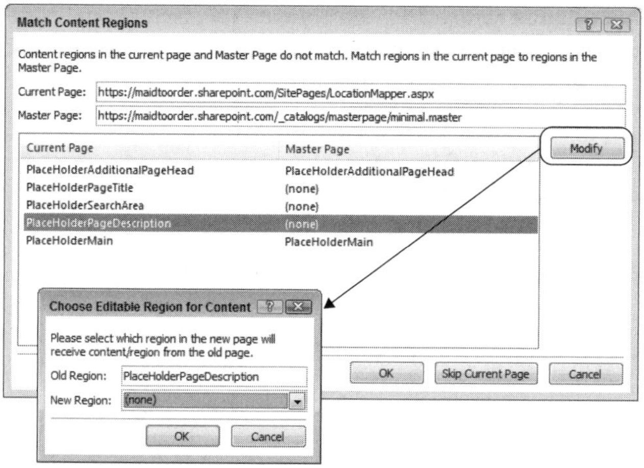

FIGURE 10-36: Edit content region.

```
<%@
  Register Tagprefix="WebPartPages"
  Namespace="Microsoft.SharePoint.WebPartPages"
  Assembly="Microsoft.SharePoint, Version=15.0.0.0, Culture=neutral,
PublicKeyToken=71e9bce111e9429c"
%>
```

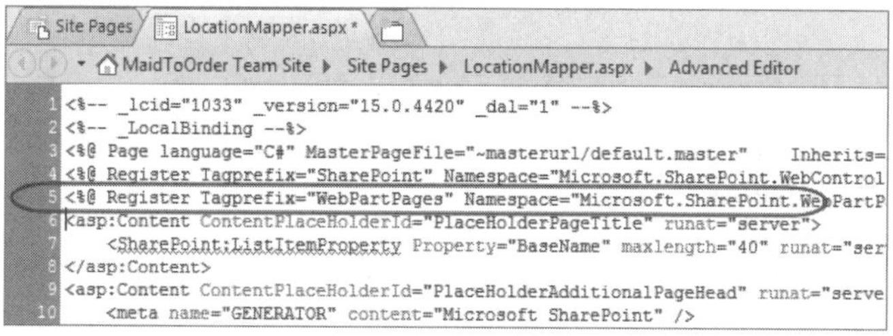

FIGURE 10-37: Add referenced assembly.

> **NOTE** *Normally you should see Version=15.0.0.0 in the directive, but some users have reported seeing Version=16.0.0.0, which may cause the page to render improperly. If you experience this problem, edit it to Version=15.0.0.0.*

The elements enclosed in `<%...%>` are directives to the server that describe how the server should handle the page you are creating. In this case, you are adding an assembly named `Micrsoft.SharePoint.WebPartPages`, which then enables you to reference objects within this assembly, analogous to how you would use References in VBA to add libraries to enable additional functionalities.

Consider the element you added and note how it has a prefix of `WebPartPages`; this references the `WebPartPages` from the second element. The `Tagprefix` attribute enables you to name your references and access objects or methods within the referenced library.

You'll need to add one more element. Look for an `asp:Content` element with `ContentPlaceHolderID` containing the value `PlaceHolderAdditionalPageHead`. If this does not exist, go ahead and add a new `asp:Content` right after the directives, as shown in Figure 10-38.

```
Site Pages / LocationMapper.aspx *
MaidToOrder Team Site ▸ Site Pages ▸ LocationMapper.aspx ▸ Advanced Editor
1  <%-- _lcid="1033" _version="15.0.4420" _dal="1" --%>
2  <%-- _LocalBinding --%>
3  <%@ Page language="C#" MasterPageFile="../_catalogs/masterpage/minimal.master"    Inh
4  <%@ Register Tagprefix="SharePoint" Namespace="Microsoft.SharePoint.WebControls" Asse
5  <%@ Register Tagprefix="WebPartPages" Namespace="Microsoft.SharePoint.WebPartPages" A
6  <asp:Content ContentPlaceHolderID="PlaceHolderAdditionalPageHead" runat="server">
7      <WebPartPages:AllowFraming runat="server" />
8  </asp:Content>
9  <asp:Content ContentPlaceHolderId="PlaceHolderMain" runat="server">
10     <div class="ms-hide">
```

FIGURE 10-38: Adding the asp:Content element

```
<asp:Content ContentPlaceHolderID="PlaceHolderAdditionalPageHead" runat="server">
    ...
</asp:Content>
```

> **NOTE** `asp:Content` *functions like a placeholder that refers to a certain part of the HTML page to be rendered. Thus,* `ContentPlaceHolderID` *is significant and can affect how the markup within the* `asp:Content` *is processed. Placing content that does not belong in the specified* `asp:Content` *can cause problems with rendering the pages.*

Within the `asp:Content` element, add the following line. If there are other lines already in this element, make it the first line within the element.

```
<WebPartPages:AllowFraming runat="server" />
```

The `WebPartPages:AllowFraming` element is what you need to enable the page to be inlined in an `iframe` element. `AllowFraming` is a server-side object, which will be initialized and will change the `X-Frame Options` header returned by the SharePoint server to allow framing of the content.

You're done editing the page. Save your work and preview the page using the Preview button on the ribbon's Home tab, as illustrated in Figure 10-39. Your result should be similar to what is shown in Figure 10-40.

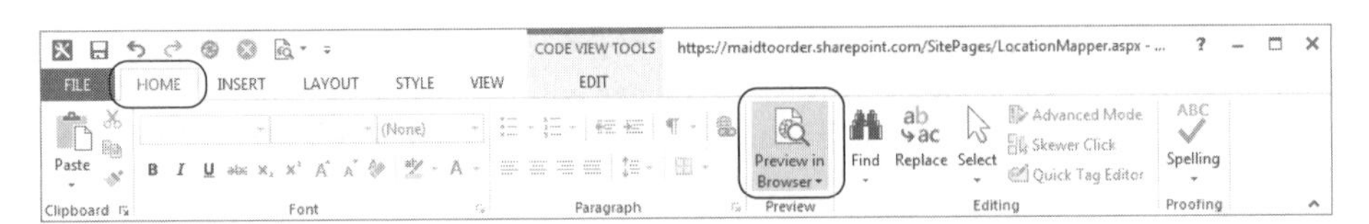

FIGURE 10-39: Preview button

The chrome around the Location Mappers is certainly much smaller but you still don't want any ribbon at all. To get rid of it, you simply need to edit the URL and append the `?` separator and a query string parameter `IsDlg=1` to the end of the URL, as shown here:

```
https://maidtoorder.sharepoint.com/SitePages/LocationMapper.aspx?IsDlg=1
```

This is recognized by SharePoint as a request to render the page in a dialog mode, transforming the result in Figure 10-40 to Figure 10-41.

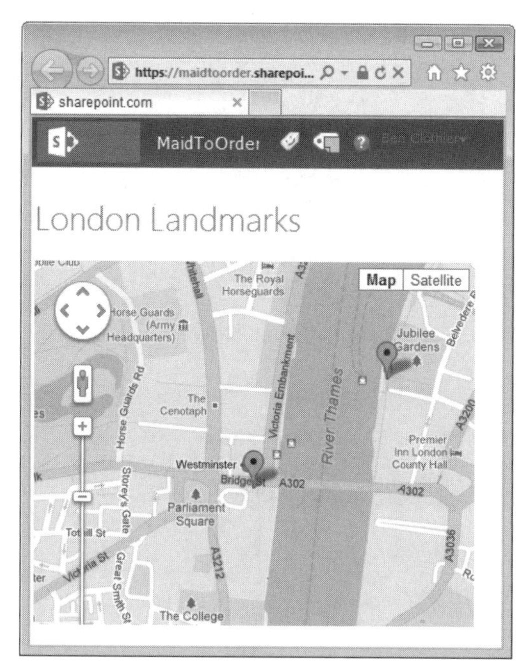

FIGURE 10-40: Rendered custom page

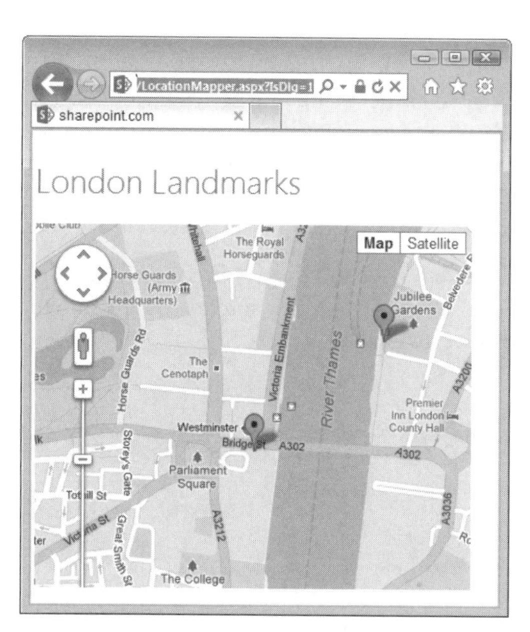

FIGURE 10-41: Page in dialog mode

WHAT WOULD HAPPEN IF YOU DIDN'T CHANGE MASTER PAGE?

With the default master page, it's possible that even with `IsDlg=1` appended, the ribbon markup will render and take up more vertical space than necessary.

WARNING *If your SharePoint or Office 365 has custom master pages or heavy customizations, there may be additional side effects rippling due to changing master pages or content that assumes a certain master page or layout is present or absent.*

At this point, you've successfully edited a page so that it is now ready to be consumed by a web browser control in your Access web app by passing in its URL and appending `?IsDlg=1` which also enables you to display content hosted somewhere on your SharePoint site without extraneous content such as the ribbon and sidebar being displayed. If you have additional query string parameters, you can add to end of the URL, separating with the `&` character.

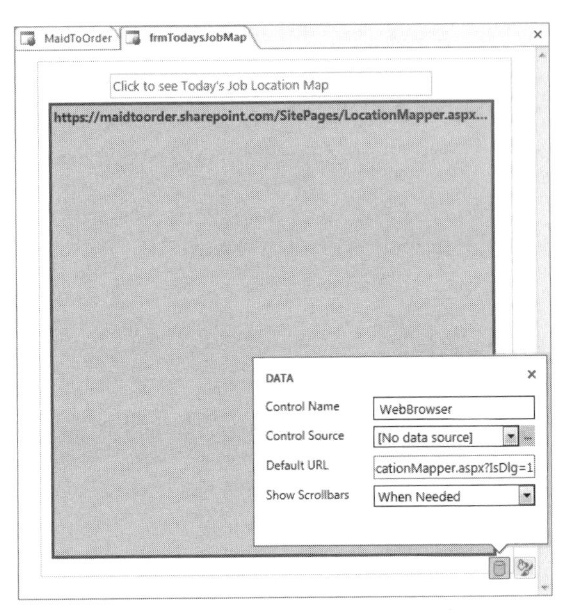

FIGURE 10-42: Adding web browser control

Return to the `frmTodaysJobMap` view that you created earlier using only a hyperlink control. You'll add a new web browser control to the form and set the default URL to point to your newly created page's URL with the `IsDlg` parameter appended, as shown in Figure 10-42.

Save the work and display it in web browser. You should get a result similar to that shown in Figure 10-43.

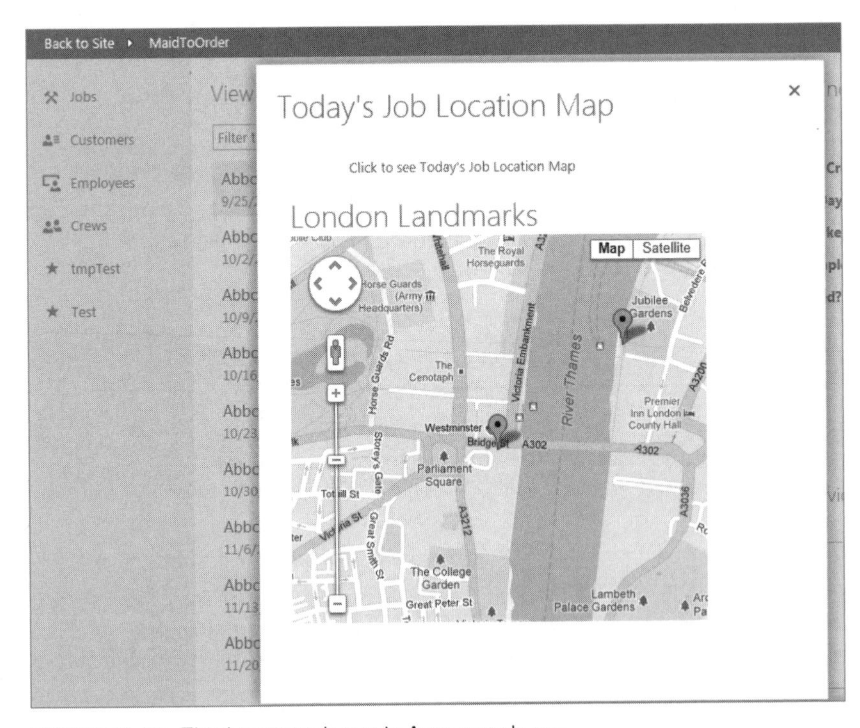

FIGURE 10-43: Third-party web app in Access web app

Congratulations, you've integrated a third-party web app into your Access web app. As you can see, adding SharePoint and SharePoint Designer to your toolbox has much to offer in the way of creating rich solutions. Later in the chapter, you will explore some more aspects of this extended design capability, such as creating a new page from scratch and using JavaScript. Although the process required to inline a web app is not entirely codeless because of the requirement to add the `WebPartPages:AllowFraming` element, we're confident that you will progressively get more comfortable with features found in SharePoint and SharePoint Designer to augment your Access web apps.

ADDING A PAYPAL BUTTON

Maid To Order wants to make it easy for their customers to sign up for automatic billing services; this adds an e-commerce component to their online application. As you can imagine, there are many ways to enable e-commerce and, indeed, there are many software vendors that sell various ecommerce software packages. For this exercise, you'll start with a relatively well-known, relatively easy-to-implement choice: PayPal. You'll deal with the challenge of folding HTML from PayPal into an Access web app.

Because you cannot write HTML directly in an Access web app, one way you can accomplish the e-commerce goal is to create a custom web page that you host on the SharePoint site which is also home to your web app. You will use SharePoint Designer for this task. The code file (title: `Chapter 10 - Paypal.aspx`) for this sample is available for download.

Getting the PayPal HTML

PayPal provides an easy way to add buttons to various sites and delivers it in the form of HTML. For this exercise, you must acquire the HTML markup generated by PayPal. Obviously, this means Maid To Order must have an account with PayPal. Furthermore, because Maid To Order has chosen to offer automatic billing services, they are required to sign up for the PayPal business package, rather than the basic package. The process of signing up for a PayPal account is outside the scope of our discussion, but note that this section assumes you have a business package. When logged into PayPal, you can go to Merchant Services to create custom buttons, as shown in Figure 10-44.

Click Create a button on the page, as shown in Figure 10-45.

You can choose from various buttons that have their own customization options. First, select Automatic Billing, as shown in Figure 10-46, to get the customizations relevant to this payment type.

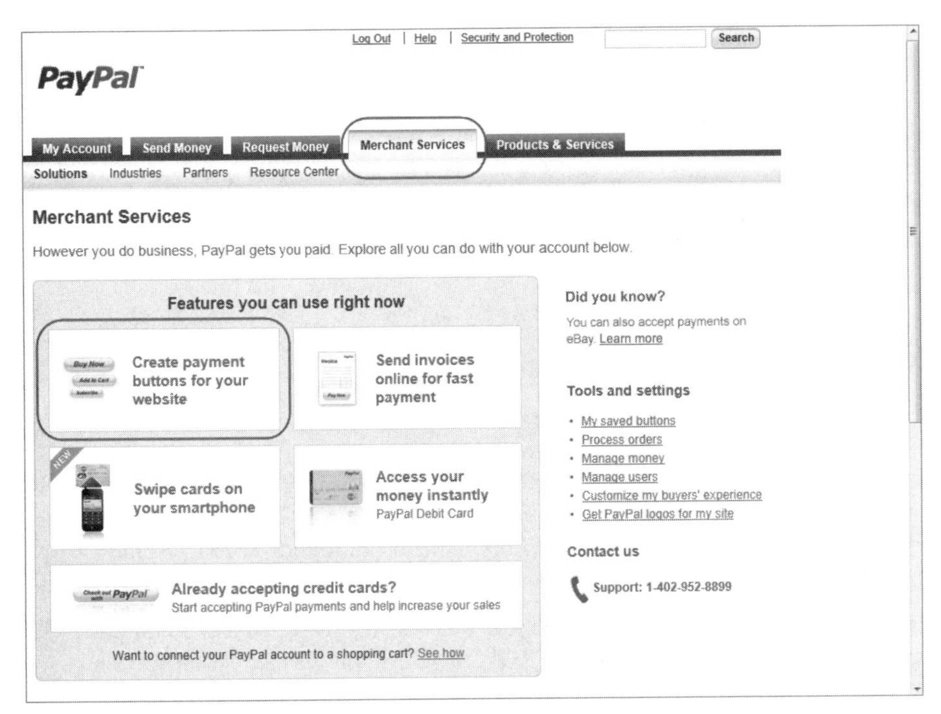

FIGURE 10-44: Merchant Services on PayPal account page

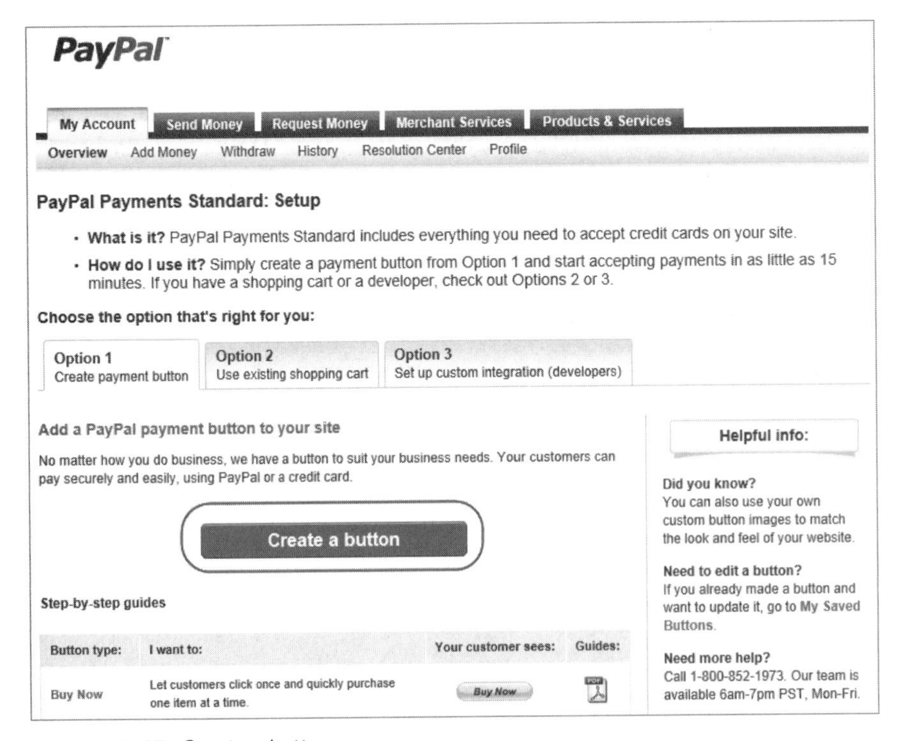

FIGURE 10-45: Create a button.

The page reloads. Fill out the rest of the customization options, as shown in Figure 10-47.

Once you're satisfied with your customizations, click Create Button, as shown in Figure 10-47, to take you to the last step where you can copy HTML markup (see Figure 10-48).

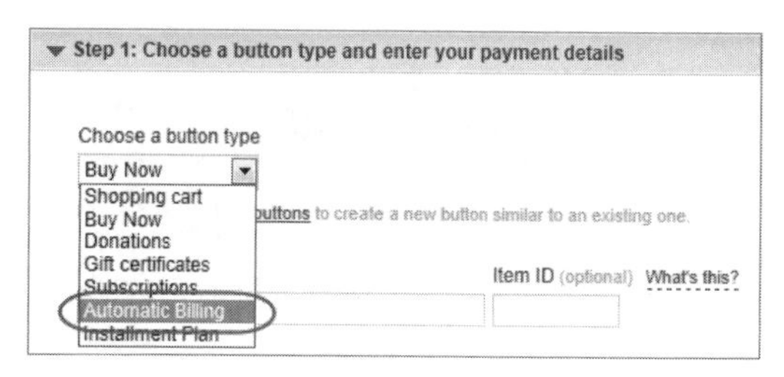

FIGURE 10-46: Selecting payment type

Step 1: Choose a button type and enter your payment details

Choose a button type

Automatic Billing

Which button should I choose?

Note: Go to My saved buttons to create a new button similar to an existing one.

Item name | Item ID (optional) What's this?

Maid To Order Automatic Billing | 1

Currency

USD

Set up your button

Set your billing limits What's this?

Let my customers choose their own maximum payment limits.

Description (optional)

For example, "Rent" or "Laundry Service".

Maid To Order Services

Minimum payment limit (optional) What's this?

USD

Done Clear

I'll set the payment limits.

Customize your button's text or appearance (optional)

PayPal button

Use smaller button

Display credit card logos

Country and language for button

United States - English

Use your own button image

What's this?

Your customer's view

Maid To Order Services

Enter the maximum amount you want to pay each month

$ USD

Sign up for

Automatic Billing

Merchant account IDs Learn more

Use my secure merchant account ID

Use your primary email address ben@maidtoorder.onmicrosoft.com

Step 2: Track inventory, profit & loss (optional)

Step 3: Customize advanced features (optional)

Create Button

FIGURE 10-47: Customizing a button

Website

```
<form action="https://www.paypal.com/cgi-bin/webscr" method="post" target="_top">
<input type="hidden" name="cmd" value="_s-xclick">
<input type="hidden" name="hosted_button_id" value="6454VVGV96LYN">
<table>
<tr><td>Maid To Order Services</td></tr><tr><td>Enter the maximum amount you want to pay each
month</td></tr><tr><td>$<input type="text" name="max_amount" value="">
USD</td></tr></table>
<table><tr><td align=center><i>Sign up for</i></td></tr><tr><td><input type="image"
```

Select Code   Go back to edit this button

FIGURE 10-48: Copy the generated HTML markup.

Copy the HTML markup and save it — Notepad might be a good place. You will need it when you build the custom page to hold the markup. You now are ready to start creating your own SharePoint pages to support your e-commerce solution. Unlike the task you completed in the previous section, you will create a new page directly in SharePoint Designer for your PayPal function.

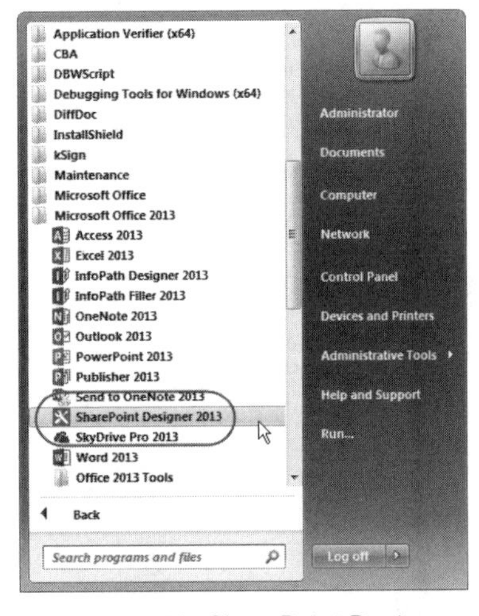

FIGURE 10-49: SharePoint Designer in the Start menu

Authoring a Custom Page in SharePoint Designer

Open SharePoint Designer via the Start menu, as shown in Figure 10-49. When launched, you click the Open Site button, as in Figure 10-50.

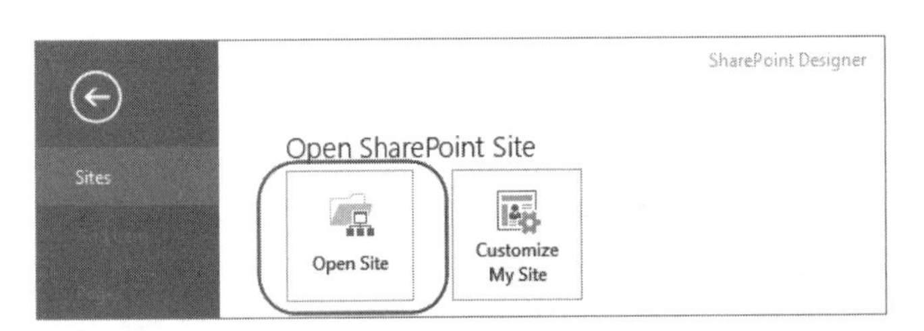

FIGURE 10-50: The Open Site button

In the dialog box, enter the team site's URL, as in Figure 10-51, and select Open.

You may be prompted to log in with your credentials. After you log in, you'll be dropped on the main screen, as shown in Figure 10-52.

To get started creating a new page, select Site Pages listed under the Site Objects displayed on the left pane, and create a new ASPX page, as shown in Figure 10-53.

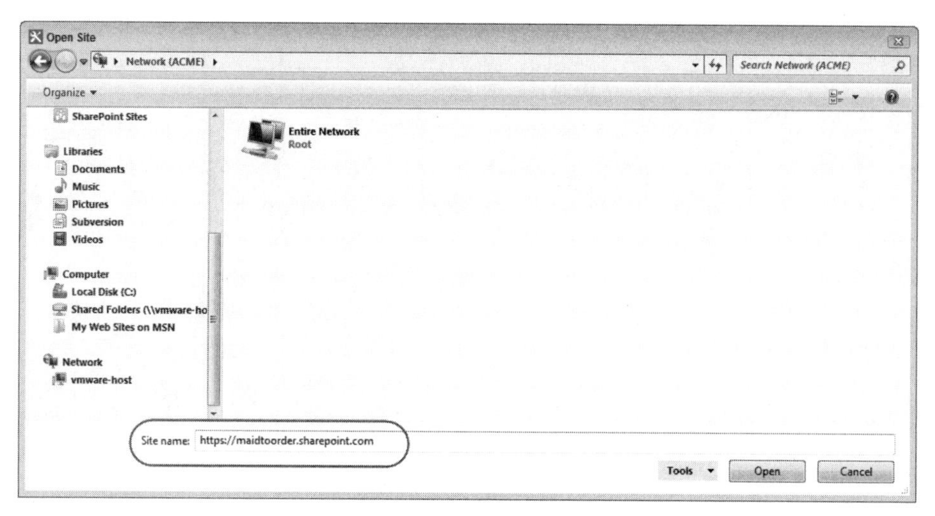

FIGURE 10-51: Entering a URL to open the site

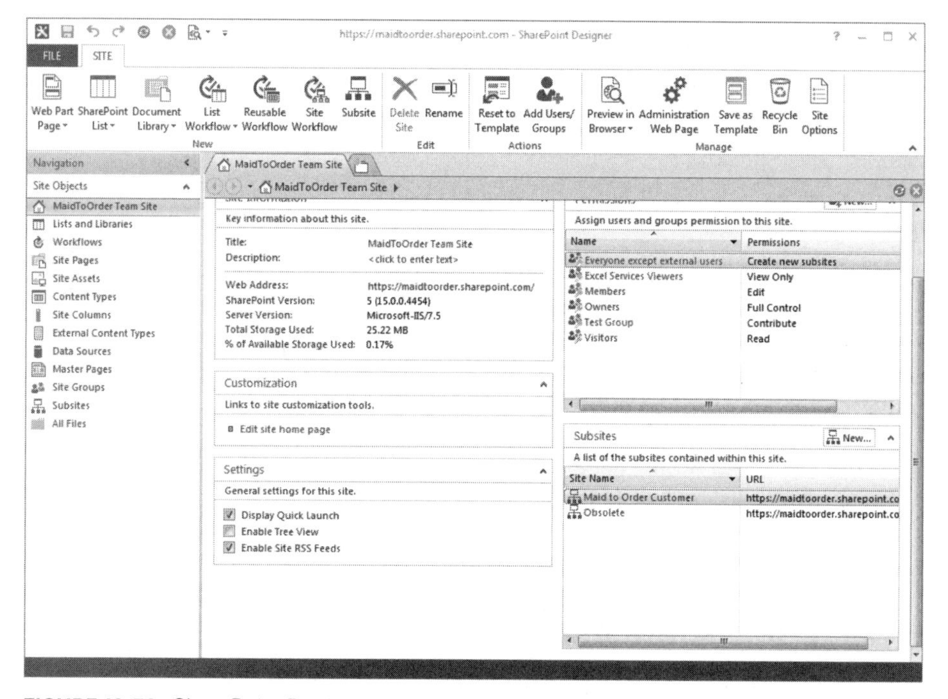

FIGURE 10-52: SharePoint Designer main screen

By default, the new page gets a name like `Untitled.aspx`. Rename the new page with a descriptive name, as illustrated in Figure 10-54.

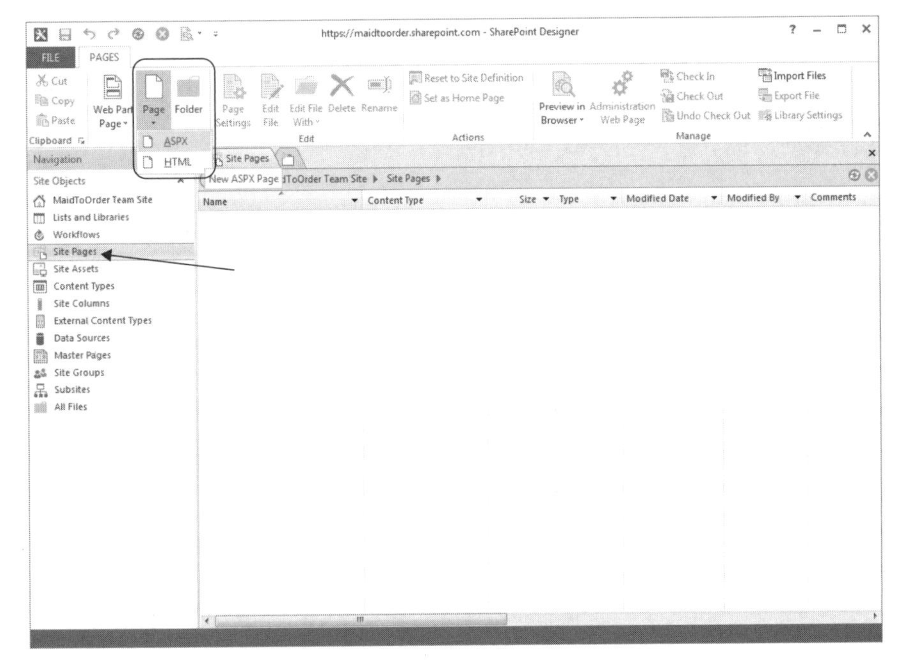

FIGURE 10-53: Creating a new ASPX page

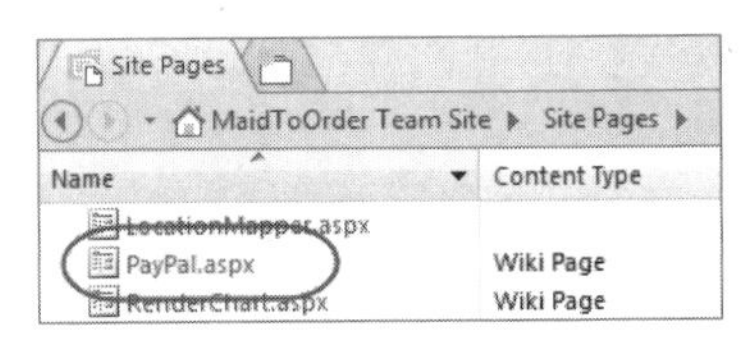

FIGURE 10-54: Renaming the ASPX page

Right-click the new page and select Edit File in Advanced mode, as shown in Figure 10-55.

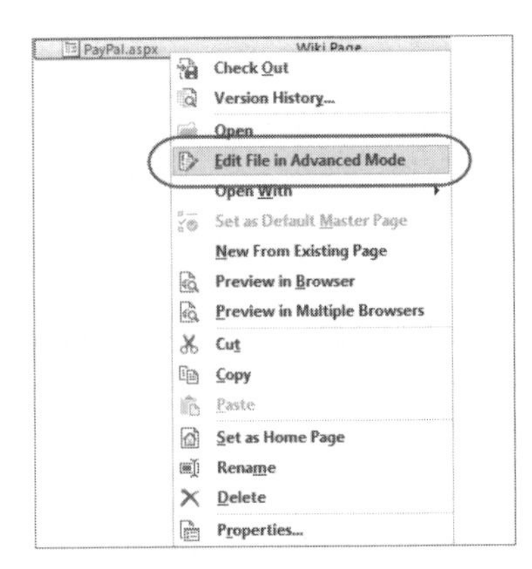

FIGURE 10-55: Edit File in Advanced mode

You are now ready to start creating your custom HTML and JavaScript code. Later you will learn how you can write a simple page with some JavaScript functions. One caution and a bit of encouragement are in order. You may find that this discussion — using JavaScript, HTML, and XML — is a bit challenging if you've not worked in this environment before. Giving you a complete picture, or even a good overview, is beyond our scope here. Nonetheless, we do expect seeing the power of the functionality described can be an incentive for you to begin studying the additional languages introduced.

Allowing Framing of Custom Page

Your objective is to create a page that can be inlined in an `iframe` element. If you've followed along with the instructions in the previous section on getting started in the SharePoint Designer, you know you'll be given a base template of an ASPX page. To help keep the example focused, let's start from scratch, so you will delete the entire HTML from the template and add the code step by step.

First, as discussed earlier in this chapter, you want to allow the page to be inlined in an `iframe` element. In order to do this, you need to tell SharePoint that this page may be inlined. Only the server can make that decision, so you need to provide a directive to the server. Paste the following code into the blank page:

```
<%@ Page language="C#" inherits="Microsoft.SharePoint.WebPartPages.WebPartPage,
 Microsoft.SharePoint, Version=15.0.0.0, Culture=neutral,
PublicKeyToken=71e9bce111e9429c" %>
<%@ Register Tagprefix="WebPartPages" Namespace="Microsoft.SharePoint.WebPartPages"
Assembly="Microsoft.SharePoint, Version=15.0.0.0, Culture=neutral,↵
PublicKeyToken=71e9bce111e9429c" %>
<WebPartPages:AllowFraming runat="server" />
```

> **NOTE** *Although you can indicate the page's language, that does not imply you can write ad hoc server-side code, nor should you try in this context. The* `runat` *attribute enables you to use custom functionality that is made available by the web server such as the user controls provided.*

You saw similar code earlier in the chapter associated with Figure 10-37. Because you are writing the page completely from scratch, you not only need to provide the directive but also the `AllowFraming` object.

Adding the PayPal HTML

Now that you've allowed framing of the page, you can create the body to contain the HTML that PayPal provided to you. Simply add the following elements to the page:

```
<html>
<body>

</body>
</html>
```

Within the `body` element, paste in the PayPal HTML markup you got from PayPal. The complete HTML should then look similar to this:

```
<%@ Page Language="C#" %>
<%@ Register
  tagprefix="SharePoint"
  namespace="Microsoft.SharePoint.WebControls"
  assembly="Microsoft.SharePoint, Version=15.0.0.0, Culture=neutral,↵
PublicKeyToken=71e9bce111e9429c"
%>
<WebPartPages:AllowFraming runat="server" />
<html>
<body>
<form action="https://www.paypal.com/cgi-bin/webscr" method="post" target="_top">
<input type="hidden" name="cmd" value="_s-xclick" />
```

```
<input type="hidden" name="hosted_button_id" value="39XM65QPUMDC4" />
<table>
  <tr><td>Maid To Order Services</td></tr>
  <tr><td>Enter the maximum amount you want to pay each month</td></tr>
  <tr><td>$<input type="text" name="max_amount" value="">USD</td></tr>
</table>
<table>
  <tr><td align=center><i>Sign up for</i></td></tr>
  <tr><td>
    <input
      type="image"
      src="https://www.paypalobjects.com/en_US/i/btn/btn_auto_billing_CC_LG.gif"
      border="0"
      name="submit"
      alt="PayPal - The safer, easier way to pay online!">
  </td></tr>
</table>
<img
  alt=""
  border="0"
  src="https://www.paypalobjects.com/en_US/i/scr/pixel.gif"
  width="1"
  height="1"
/>
</form>
</body>
</html>
```

> **NOTE** *The code generated by PayPal uses table elements, which result in additional code. As an exercise in pursuing web standards compliance and best practices, you may want to experiment with tweaking the generated code.*

Note that, when you save and close this page, SharePoint Designer may add some elements and reformat others. This is usually a good thing, and we encourage you to take note of changes it makes and, if needed, correct any markups highlighted in yellow and inked in red. As you gain experience using SharePoint Designer, you will recognize more appropriate patterns for designing custom pages to be used in SharePoint.

Showing a PayPal Button on an Access Web App

This is actually the easy part. You now have a page saved on your SharePoint site that will render the PayPal HTML, so now you need to point to it with a web browser control on your Access web app. Because the link is static and does not take any parameters, you can simply hard-code the link, as shown in Figure 10-56.

The resulting page would then look like Figure 10-57 when in a web browser.

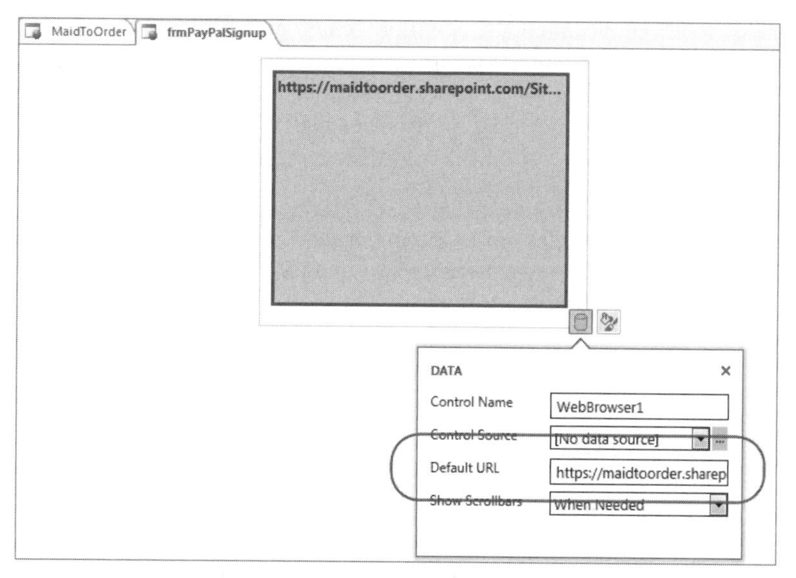

FIGURE 10-56: Hard-coding the PayPal page URL in a web browser control

Maid To Order's customers would not know that there was a separate page displayed. Although clicking the button would take them to PayPal to finalize the setup, the experience is much better than giving out a link and having them fill out a form for the product they want to buy.

At this point, you've learned how to add an inlined element into your web app. Plus, you've been exposed to some important concepts you need to understand when working with these elements. Next, we look at a more advanced technique: You learn how to add a team site mailbox and integrate it with your web app.

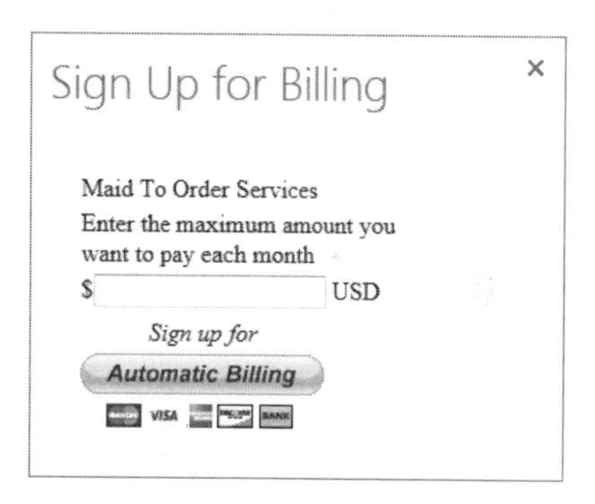

FIGURE 10-57: PayPal button on the Access web popup form

ADDING A SITE MAILBOX

One thing you might want to provide to users of your web apps is a shared mailbox, or *site mailbox*, where team members can exchange messages and share links to SharePoint document libraries. A site mailbox enables users to share both files and e-mail messages with other members of a team. Site mailboxes allow access to both Microsoft SharePoint 2013 documents and Exchange e-mail from the same client interface. It consists of three integrated components:

- An Exchange 2013 mailbox for e-mail messages
- A SharePoint 2013 site for documents
- A management interface that addresses provisioning and lifecycle needs

On our Maid To Order website, for example, a team site mailbox could give crews a way to report back to the MTO office from their work locations using their client e-mail application on a mobile device. One can imagine, for example, a report from a crew alerting MTO management to an incident on a customer's location involving personal injury or property damage with attached photos of the scene. When the e-mail is received by MTO risk managers, attachments can be saved to a SharePoint document library on the MTO team site.

Using e-mails to send images offers an advantage over using an Image control on Access web apps because a large number of mobile devices allow easy e-mailing of images, whereas uploading an image in a web browser is not supported on all mobile devices. Thus, although it would be simpler to use an Image control on your Access web apps, it would not be as accessible if you didn't set up a site mailbox. You will see later how you can ultimately associate the e-mailed images to a database record.

The site mailbox stores mail messages in Exchange, and provides access to those e-mail messages plus any attached documents through Outlook 2013. One key advantage you gain is that documents associated with those e-mail messages are stored in a document library, which allows site members to locate and work with those documents through SharePoint. Moreover, because SharePoint stores the documents, you can apply all of the relevant SharePoint tools — for example, coauthoring and versioning of stored documents.

So, let's learn how to plan for, set up, and use a site mailbox for Maid To Order.

Configuration for a Site Mailbox

Before we get into the specifics of setting up a site mailbox, you should be aware of the requirements for provisioning one, even though you typically won't be called on to do so yourself. In an on-premises installation, the following items are typically handled by the Site or Farm Administrator, whereas, in an Office 365 account, they are handled by Office 365 administrators; your involvement, if any, would normally be in communicating with the site admins regarding troubleshooting issues for your users. Nonetheless, in order to be able to communicate with the site admins, you should have some knowledge of what is required.

- Site mailboxes require Exchange Server 2013.
- Profile synchronization must be enabled for the site.
- The app management service application must be configured in the farm.
- The computer running SharePoint Server must have SSL configured.

Another key point is that SharePoint backups will not incorporate Exchange site mailboxes. To ensure your site mailboxes are being backed up, work with your Exchange administrator to ensure there's a backup protocol for your team site mailbox.

If you encounter difficulties in setting up a site mailbox for your team site, go ahead and contact the SharePoint Farm Administrator or Office 365 support and make sure all of these items are configured correctly for your needs.

Setting Up the Site Mailbox

You're ready to set up a site mailbox for the Maid To Order team site, so let's go there now, as shown in Figure 10-58. You need to install the Site Mailbox app for your site. As you've learned to do, go to Site Contents and select Add an App. That will bring you to the page showing the apps available, including the site mailbox highlighted in Figure 10-59.

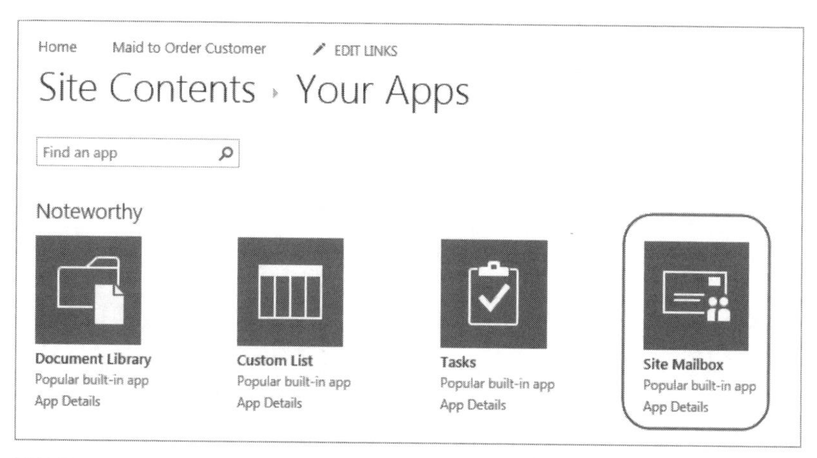

FIGURE 10-58: Navigate to the Add an App page and click the Site Mailbox app.

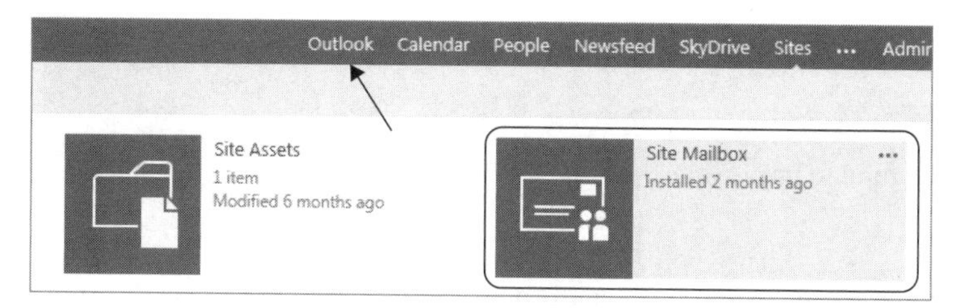

FIGURE 10-59: Open Outlook to add the site mailbox for your use.

> **NOTE** *Make sure you select Outlook web app from the team site, not your client Outlook application. Unless we specify otherwise, everything in this discussion refers to the Outlook web app.*

Select the Site Mailbox app. It will install like other apps you've previously added to your site. The app indicates that it may take up to half an hour or so to be fully provisioned for use, although our experience has been much better than that.

You'll come back later and look at the site mailbox itself, but in order to keep the setup path clear for you, let's move on to the next step in that process, which is to open Outlook. Confirm the site mailbox is available among your apps, and then select Outlook from the menu, as highlighted on the menu bar in Figure 10-59. Select your language and time zone for Outlook, if you haven't previously done that.

When Outlook opens, right-mouse-click on your mailbox to open the shortcut menu, as illustrated in Figure 10-60. Select the last option on the shortcut menu, add shared folder. That opens a dialog box to select the folder to share, as shown in Figure 10-61.

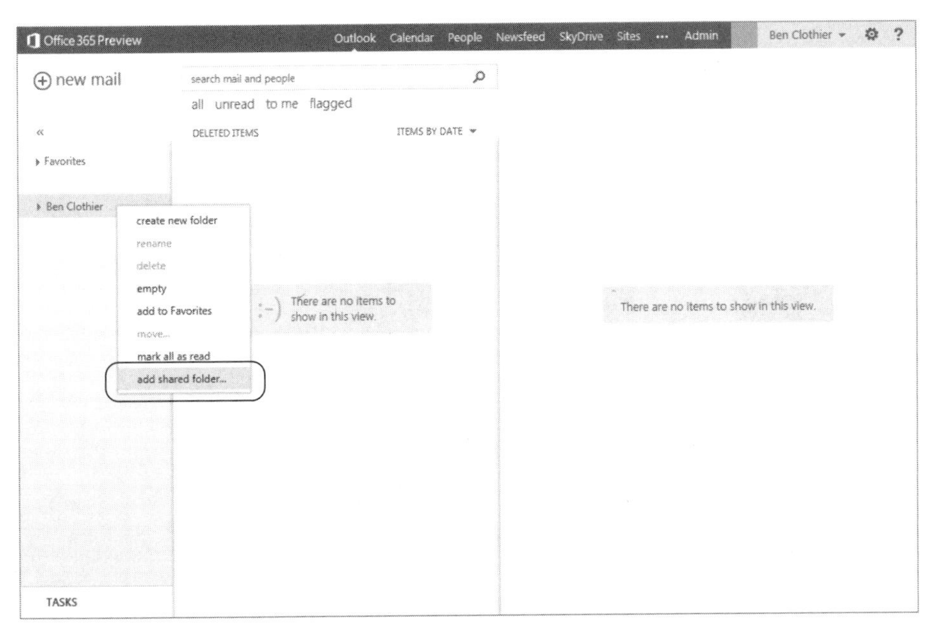

FIGURE 10-60: Add a shared folder for the team site mailbox.

In the dialog box that opens, enter the e-mail address for the team site mailbox you want to add. There is a search function in the dialog box that can assist you in selecting which team site mailbox you want to add, if more than one is available to you. You can see the match on "SMO" in Figure 10-61.

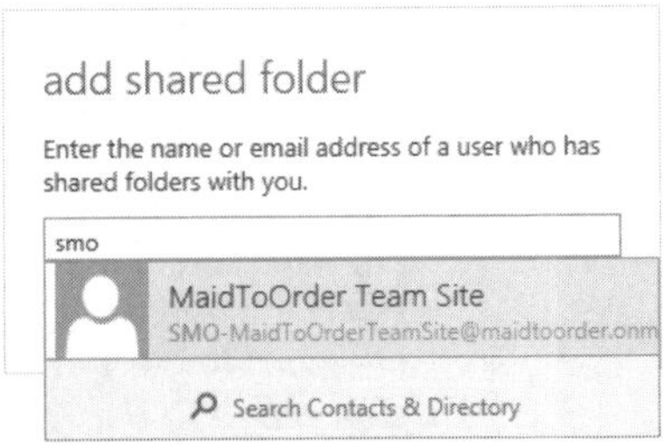

add shared folder

Enter the name or email address of a user who has shared folders with you.

smo

MaidToOrder Team Site

SMO-MaidToOrderTeamSite@maidtoorder.onm

Search Contacts & Directory

FIGURE 10-61: Enter the e-mail address for the shared team site mailbox.

Take a close look at the e-mail address in Figure 10-61. It has two important features you need to remember. First, the name begins with the letters SMO-. This prefix indicates that the e-mail address belongs to a team site mailbox. Second, the e-mail address contains the name of the team site mailbox to which it is installed, in this case, MaidToOrderTeamSite, rather than an individual name. As noted previously, you may have other shared folders available. This one is the team site mailbox for the Maid To Order team site.

When you click on the shared folder in the selection dialog box, SharePoint adds it to your Outlook mail account. You can see the new Maid To Order team site mailbox, highlighted in Figure 10-62.

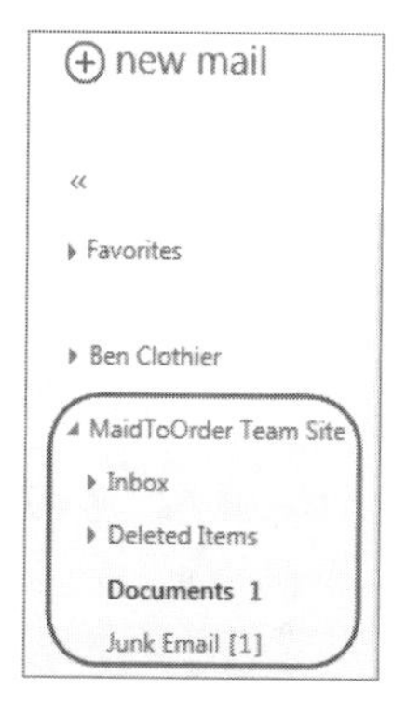

FIGURE 10-62: Team site mailbox available

All of the members of your team site need to repeat the process to add the team site mailbox as a shared folder to their own Outlook mail accounts. When they have done that, they can share both the messages in the Inbox and the documents in the shared folder from Outlook on the team site. As you can see in Figure 10-63, all of the documents in the team site Documents library are exposed.

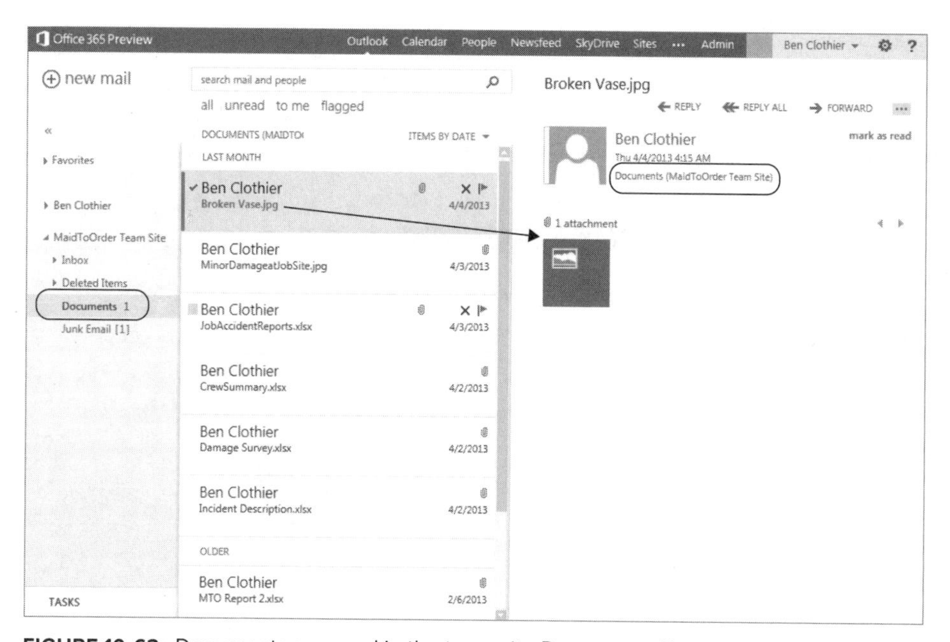

FIGURE 10-63: Documents exposed in the team site Documents library

From one location, then, team members can both read and share e-mail messages regarding jobs they work on for Maid To Order. In addition, they can locate and open any documents or images associated with their jobs. In the next section, you learn how to expose the documents and images from this shared folder in the Maid To Order web app, so team members can review them in that environment as well.

Before we transition to the web app, however, let's recap what you've learned so far. Setting up a team site mailbox is basically done in two steps. First, you, the site owner, install the Site Mailbox app for the team site. Then, you and the other members of your team site add it to your respective Outlook mailboxes. When you and the other members of your team have completed these steps you can share e-mail and documents through your Outlook mail accounts. If you elect to enable use of the team site mailbox in the Outlook client, your team members can also use it from their desktop Outlook. To get started on that setup, you need to select Options from the gear drop-down shown in Figure 10-64.

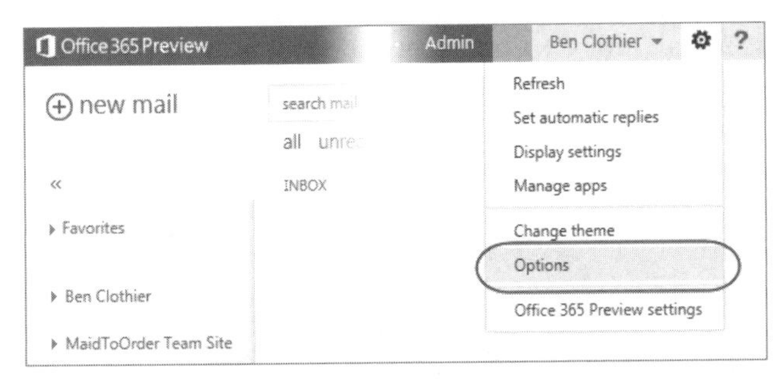

FIGURE 10-64: Options menu

That will take you to the options page, as illustrated in Figure 10-65.

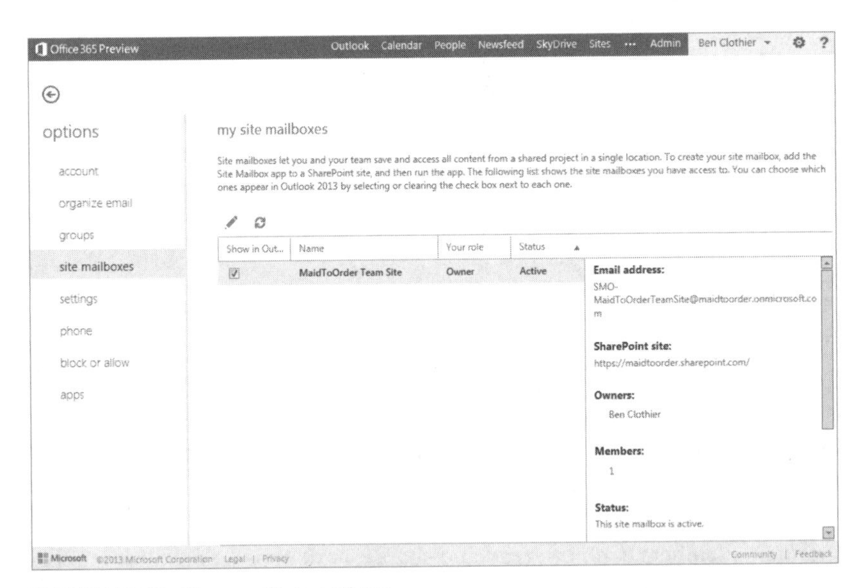

FIGURE 10-65: User mailbox options

Figure 10-65 shows the page where you can enable the option to have the team site mailbox exposed in client Outlook 2013. Note the e-mail address for this team site mailbox has the SMO- prefix.

As you can see in Figure 10-66, you may want to add the team site mailbox to the Quick Launch so that it is always available.

FIGURE 10-66: Opening the team mailbox

Also, we promised you a closer look at the site mailbox itself. Let's do that next. From the Team Site home page, you can select the Team Mail Box link, as shown in Figure 10-66 to go to the site mailbox, shown in Figure 10-67 on the team site page. Note the user display name change.

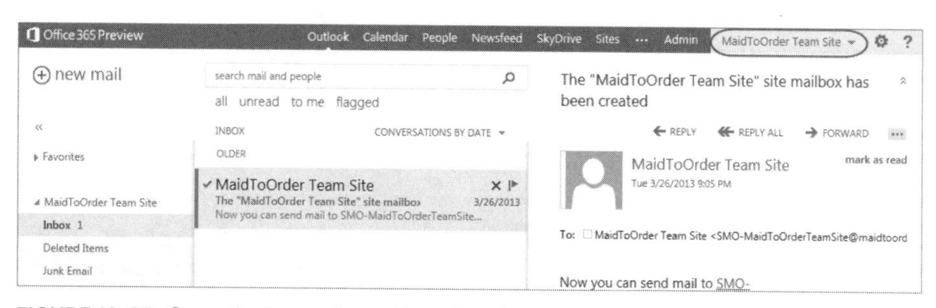

FIGURE 10-67: Open the team site mailbox directly.

Team Site Mailbox as a Shared Tool

In the previous section, you learned how to set up and use one of the SharePoint tools available to you, the team Site Mailbox app, to extend additional capabilities to the users of your web app. In the next section, you learn about extending those capabilities back into the web app, by exposing the documents from the shared folder to crew members.

As you learned in Chapter 2, you can link to SharePoint lists from an Access web app, if only as a read-only source. In this case, you will link to the Documents library used by your site mailbox and create a junction table within the Access web app to associate a document stored in the Documents library with a particular job in the Access web app. In the process, you will learn how to use SharePoint Designer to help create a custom web page to supplement a feature missing in Access web apps.

As you know, Access web apps have an Image control, which you can bind to an Image field of a table to display an image. It can also have a URL set at design time to point to a static image. However, when you link to the Documents library, the files are displayed as hyperlinks, not as images. Thus, you cannot bind an Image control to the documents' field directly. You also cannot change the URL property at run time so you cannot use an Image control to render pictures from the team's Documents library.

You may think you could just use a web browser control for this task, and indeed you will. However, you can't just point that control directly to the image. As you learned earlier, inlining an image inside an `iframe` element must be explicitly allowed. Furthermore, not all documents in a Documents library are images, so you need to handle this scenario as well.

It turns out the best solution is to create a custom page that you can host at Maid To Order's team site. You will use SharePoint Designer to create the new page and author the HTML and JavaScript code to create a page that can render an image based on a query string parameter. Then you can use the web browser control to supply the URL to be displayed as a picture inline. To complete this next task, you will also install jQuery, which provides a library to make it easier to write your custom JavaScript code for rendering the image and returning text when the URL does not point to a file.

Installing jQuery to Your Team Site

jQuery is a popular library, used by many web developers, which accomplishes two goals; it simplifies the process of executing AJAX queries and it provides an easy way to run code at the correct time. Many code samples you find when searching on the Internet for JavaScript will use functions or build upon functions exposed by jQuery. For this reason, it is usually desirable to add the jQuery library to your custom web pages. Let's add jQuery to your team site. Although you can also reference jQuery at a third-party repository, we want to demonstrate that you can build your custom JavaScript library by adding `.js` files to your SharePoint site.

> **NOTE** *In production, it is usually desirable to reference a library hosted on a content delivery network (CDN), which offers you the advantage of not having to host files on your own site. That helps gain some parallelism, and improves caching. As indicated, the example uses files uploaded to the SharePoint site to help demonstrate how you can add custom* `.js` *files that you might use when expanding on the common libraries delivered by CDNs. You will see an example of using a CDN later in this chapter.*
>
> *On the other hand, if you are using an on-premises SharePoint installation, you may have to consult with the local IT department's policies on using a CDN.*

To get the latest copy of the jQuery library, go to this URL and download it at
`www.jquery.com/download/`.

You may want to select the compressed production build. At the time of writing, it is 1.9.1, as shown in Figure 10-68. Take note of what browser versions are supported for a given jQuery version. If you need to support older browsers, you may opt for older jQuery version.

On your team site, select Site Contents and go to Style library, which is built-in, as shown in Figure 10-69.

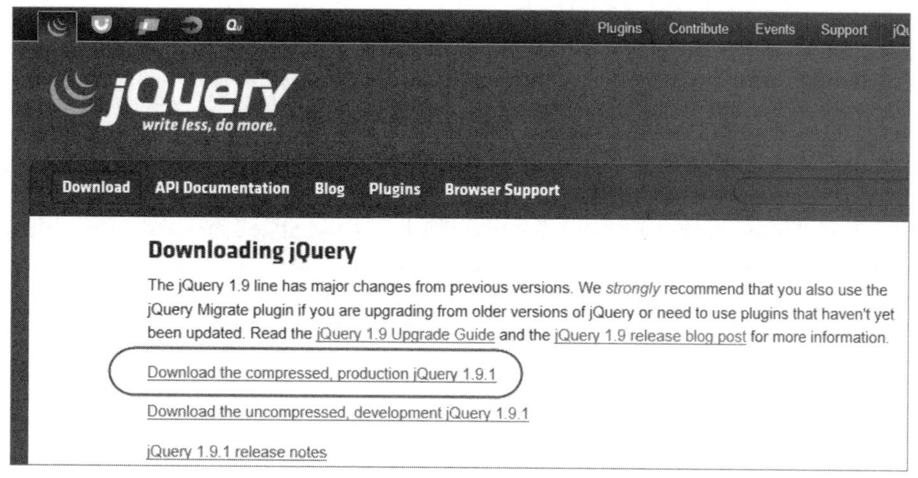

FIGURE 10-68: Download the jQuery Library.

At the Style Library, upload your `jQuery.js` file into the library. Note the icon for the jQuery indicating that it is a JavaScript file shown in Figure 10-70.

FIGURE 10-69: Style Library

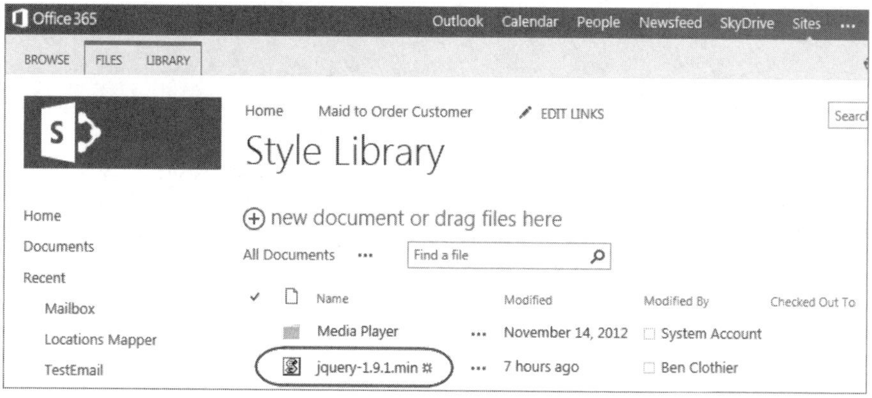

FIGURE 10-70: jQuery file uploaded

You're now done with the installation of jQuery. For any custom pages you author that need extensions from jQuery, you can now simply add a reference to `jQuery.js` contained in the Style Library. To refer to the jQuery in your custom pages, add the following script element:

```
<script type="text/javascript" src="../Style%20Library/jquery-1.9.1.min.js">
</script>
```

> **NOTE** *You can use the same process just demonstrated to upload your custom JavaScript libraries, enabling you to write a single* `.js` *file that may be shared among a number of custom pages you author for your SharePoint site.*

Note the use of a relative URL in the `src` attribute. This assumes that your custom pages are stored in the Site Pages library at the same site. Because Site Pages and Style Library are two different folders on the same site, it would be necessary to navigate one folder up to access content in the Style Library from Site Pages' pages. On the other hand, if the page you are editing is not in Site Pages but is on the team site's root folder directly, then you would not need the `../` snippet. You will see this later when you author your custom page.

VBA AND JAVASCRIPT CONTRASTED

If you're familiar with VBA but have never worked with JavaScript, two excellent resources to learn JavaScript are *JavaScript & JQuery: Interactive Front-End Web Development* by Jon Duckett (Wiley, 2013), and online courses offered for free at `http://www.codecademy.com/tracks/javascript`. For an in-depth discussion on JavaScript language features, consider *JavaScript: The Good Parts* by Douglas Crockford (O'Reilly, 2008).

That said, we want to quickly point out some key differences to help ease the transition.

Data typing

VBA and JavaScript both allow for weak typing of variables. However, unlike VBA, JavaScript has only one explicit data type; `var` and the specific type is determined at run time based on what value is assigned to it, similar to how VBA's `Variant` data type works. JavaScript's approach is known as *duck-typing* because if it walks and quacks like a duck, then it's a duck.

Object vs. prototype

VBA is object-based; you rely on having objects with certain attributes to do things. JavaScript also has objects, but they are more like a classless prototype. The essential difference is that once an object is defined in VBA, you can't change or add to this object; you must make another object that wraps around the first object. This is not needed in JavaScript; you can immediately extend anything, even the primitive data types.

Terminating statements

In VBA, you end a statement by entering a carriage return, which starts a new line. That means whitespace matters to VBA. You must use the line continuation character to extend a single statement over multiple lines. In JavaScript, the reverse is true. Whitespace does not apply and there is no need for line continuation. However, you must end each single statement with a semicolon.

Defining block scope

With VBA, you start a block of a procedure or a control flow with keywords such as Function...End Function, Do...Loop, If...End If, and so on. JavaScript has no distinctive pairs and instead uses the notation {...} to define the block. If we use the If/Then statement as an example, you only have if(a==1) {<true>} else {<false>}; no end keyword is required. Be sure to note which block a pair of {...} applies to so you know what context you are in.

Capitalization does matter!

In VBA, you do not have to worry about whether you capitalized your code. VBA is case-preserving and will run either MYFUNCTION() or myfunction() equally, even if the function is actually capitalized as MyFunction(). However, in JavaScript, those three different capitalizations are considered three distinct functions. Thus, it is imperative that you be very careful how you lettercase your JavaScript code. When using built-in methods or libraries, you must match their lettercasing exactly or you will get errors.

Events are functions

In VBA, when you want to handle an event, you typically use a specific event handler such as the Form_Load() procedure that has to conform to naming rules. You can call other functions from this procedure you authored. In JavaScript, events take JavaScript code or functions. There is no special procedure that must be named a certain way to get handled; you either assign a piece of JavaScript code, call a function defined somewhere, or define an anonymous function directly to the event property of the object.

Synchronous versus asynchronous

Many times when you invoke something in VBA, such as DoCmd.OpenForm, the calling code stops and waits for the code defined within the Form_Open event procedure to finish executing. In JavaScript, that is not true; everything runs asynchronously. This is far more compatible with how web browsers work; send a request to the

continues

continued

remote server and keep doing things until you get a response, which is typically raised via either an event or a callback function. For this reason, you will adapt your coding approach so there is no assumption of certain ordering among elements of your code.

References

In VBA, you add some references, and must rely on those references to exist before you can use them. Windows handles all the work of loading and accessing the library for you. In many cases, you probably relied on late-binding to avoid problems with versioning. In JavaScript, you can think of everything as being late-bound, but with an important addition that you must explicitly load the references before you attempt to access anything from the library.

Authoring a Custom Image Viewer Page

For the code used in this section, you can download the file titled `Chapter10 - ShowPictureFromURL.aspx`. Again, use SharePoint Designer to create the page. Refer to the "Adding a PayPal Button" section earlier in the chapter if you need a refresher on creating a new page. You need to create a new blank ASPX page and name it **`ShowPictureFromURL.aspx`**. You also need to allow framing of the page using the same steps covered in the section on creating a custom page earlier in the chapter. Once you've set up the page, the next thing to do is to define the HTML body itself. You can remove the default HTML markup completely and put in the following HTML snippet with an empty script block, which we will fill in shortly:

```
<%@ Page
  language="C#"
  inherits="Microsoft.SharePoint.WebPartPages.WebPartPage, Microsoft.SharePoint,➥
  Version=15.0.0.0, Culture=neutral, PublicKeyToken=71e9bce111e9429c"
%>
<%@ Register
  Tagprefix="WebPartPages"
  Namespace="Microsoft.SharePoint.WebPartPages"
  Assembly="Microsoft.SharePoint, Version=15.0.0.0, Culture=neutral,➥
  PublicKeyToken=71e9bce111e9429c"
%>
<WebPartPages:AllowFraming runat="server" />
<html>
<head>
<script type="text/javascript" src="../Style%20Library/jquery-1.9.1.min.js">
</script>
</head>
<body>
<script type="text/javascript">
   ...
```

```
</script>
</body>
</html>
```

You may be wondering where the HTML for displaying images will be. The answer is that the elements will be added dynamically at run time. You will be using JavaScript and jQuery to add new elements just in time. Let's consider why this is necessary.

Because it's possible to pass in a URL that points to a file that isn't a graphical file, or to an invalid URL, you want to ensure that the `img` element handles both scenarios. Furthermore, you have to deal with the fact that cached images may cause events to not fire. To accommodate these problems, you will use `load` and `error` events with the aid of jQuery to execute some JavaScript script. You will see how to do that shortly.

You may recognize the first `script` element from the previous section where you installed jQuery to your team site. Because you will want to use some of jQuery's functions, you need to reference the script. You can then write your custom JavaScript in the `script` element in the HTML body. Let's look at the JavaScript you will be inserting.

```
// Initialize queryString array
var queryString = { imgSrc: "" };

$(document).ready(function () {
  // Populate queryString object with values
  window.location.search.replace(/(\w+)=(.+)/g, function ( str, key, value ) {
    queryString[key] = value;
  });

  // Create a new image, and bind handlers to its events
  $("<img>").on({
    // If the image loads properly then
    load: function () {
      // Append it to the BODY element
      $(this).appendTo("body");
    },
    // If there is an error loading the image then
    error: function () {
      // Create an error message and append to BODY
      $("<p>").html("Path is not an image, or is missing.").appendTo("body");
    }
  // Set src attribute of image, and see if it loads
  }).attr("src", queryString["imgSrc"]);
});
```

> **WARNING** *As noted earlier, lettercase is significant. In the names of many functions, the first letter of the first word is lowercase, and the first letter of each subsequent word is uppercase. Some may call this camelCase, distinguished from PascalCase which you may be familiar with in VBA parlance. However, this convention is not universally true so you must take care to match lettercasing exactly.*

The jQuery library provides a custom event, the `ready` event, which guarantees that everything has been loaded at this point. You'll run your code inside that event using an anonymous function. The jQuery library exposes its extension via a `jQuery` object which also has a shorthand name, `$`. So we can refer to `jQuery`'s `ready` event handler given for the `document` object as follows:

```
$(document).ready(function(){
  ...
});
```

Let's start with the first function within the `ready` event procedure, which helps simplify the task of parsing the query string parameters from the URL.

```
window.location.search.replace(/(\w+)=(.+)/g, function ( str, key, value ) {
  queryString[key] = value;
});
```

The `window` object represents the browser session, and the `location` is the full URL for the page currently open in the `window` object. The `search` property returns the portion of the URL after the `?` separator, effectively giving us the full query string. The placement of `replace()` illustrates how there is really no distinction between primitive data types such as strings and integers versus objects; a string always has methods such as `len()` and `replace()`. In VBA, you use a separate function performing on a variable such as this:

```
Len("Hello, world")
Replace("Hello, world", "Hello", "Goodbye")
```

In contrast, to do the same thing in JavaScript, you invoke a method upon the object itself. This is true even when it's a simple string.

```
"Hello, world".length
"Hello, world".replace("Hello", "Goodbye")
```

You should now see that the `replace()` from the first function in the `ready` event is acting upon the string returned by the aforementioned `window.location.search`. Now we come to the next feature of JavaScript — the ability to use functions in a manner similar to how you use variables, enabling you to pass in a function as a parameter. The first parameter in the `replace()` function is a `RegEx` object which instructs the code to search for a pattern that matches a word divided by an equal sign with any number and kind of characters up to end of line.

```
...replace(/(\w+)=(.+)/g, function ( str, key, value ) { ... } )
```

Because the `RegEx` object has two pairs of `()`s which group the pattern and enable them to be used for backreferencing, the function needs two more parameters to receive the backreferences. Those parameters must be placed after the first parameter which returns the matched string. Note that the parameter names are user-defined and can be anything. What matters is that they are in correct ordinal position so that the first parameter receives the matched string, and the second parameter receives the first backreference, which is a word before the equal sign character, and the last parameter receives the second backreference, which is the rest of the string after the equal sign.

The last thing to note is that the function is an *anonymous function*, or unnamed. That would ordinarily be illegal in VBA, but JavaScript makes it easier for programmers to create any number of helper functions intended to be used in limited circumstances without having to come up with a name for every single helper function.

We now come to the actual function body itself which should be quite straightforward:

```
queryString[key] = value;
```

> **NOTE** *Note that unlike VBA, in JavaScript the* = *operator is always considered an assignment of value to the variable on the left-hand side and can never be used to test for equality. Furthermore, JavaScript allows you to use either* == *or* === *for equality comparison; the benefit of the latter syntax is that it disallows implicit conversion which is helpful in ensuring that you don't get a true result when comparing a number 1 with a string "1."*

Using the backreferences from the `RegEx` object within the `replace()`, we now have the name of the parameter and the value after the equal sign character, which you can now simply assign to the `queryString` array which was initialized already at the start of the script body. The `queryString` is used like an associative array where the indexer is the name of the parameter containing the value.

You've touched upon many new concepts that you will need to master when using JavaScript, and you now can see clearly the differences between VBA and JavaScript, which will be helpful in easing the transition should you choose to write your own JavaScript functions. With this, let's move onto the next function.

The `jQuery` object provides several other extensions; one is to simplify the dynamic HTML creation by passing in a HTML markup tag as a parameter to the `jQuery` object's default method. This is what `$("<img>")` does. It will return a reference to the newly created element. As you might expect, we are creating a new `img` element. We then use `jQuery`'s `on()` method, which simplifies the process of creating event handlers for the referenced HTML element, creating two event handlers for `load` and `error` events, respectively. Thus, with jQuery's help, you've simplified what usually are several lines of code to accommodate quirks and odd cases to ensure the code will run in a consistent fashion across different browsers.

```
$("<img>").on({
  load: function () {
    ...
  },
  error: function () {
    ...
  }
})...
```

We are counting on the fact that when we pass in the URL representing a potential graphical file, either one of the events will fire. When the URL does truly refer to a graphical file, then we will actually add the new `img` element to the HTML document. Otherwise, we will add a new p[aragraph] element to the HTML document notifying the user that it's not a graphical file. The `load` event procedure is basically a single line.

```
load: function () {
  $(this).appendTo("body");
}
```

`$(this)` returns the current object that is the subject of the event and, since we know from the `load` event firing that we do have a valid graphical file, we use `appendTo()` to actually insert the new `img` element into the HTML document's `body` element. Let's contrast this with the `error` event:

```
error: function () {
  $("<p>").html("Path is not an image, or is missing.").appendTo("body");
}
```

Since the `img` element doesn't have an image to display, there is no need to add an `img` element, so we don't add it. Instead, we create a new HTML element, again using jQuery's provided method, then we describe the HTML of this element which is to put in the text we want to show the user. Finally, we use the same `appendTo()` function to add the `p` element to the body element. This process also demonstrates how jQuery enables you to chain the calls upon the same objects, performing creation, formatting, and appending all at once. This is because several methods provided by jQuery will return the same object that was modified by the method.

The ability to chain calls upon the same object enables us to answer a question you may have about the original `img` element. You've seen how we add an `img` element and attach events, but how is its `src` attribute set? This is done after we complete the `on()` function for attaching events.

```
$("<img>").on({
  ...
}).attr("src", queryString["imgSrc"]);
```

As you might expect, this updates the `src` attribute of the `img` element to load the path to the document from the Documents library. It's done last so that event handlers are prepared by the time we assign the path to the `src` attribute. The path is derived from the `imgSrc` query string parameter, which you will pass from the Access web app, as you will see later on. Within the `ready` event, you change the `img` element's `src` attribute to whatever the value of the query string parameter may be. You could choose to look for a query string parameter named `imgSrc`, which means that you should expect the URL picture to be passed in like this:

```
http://maidtoorder.sharepoint.com/SitePages/ShowPictureFromURL
.aspx?imgSrc=<path to image's URL>
```

> **NOTE** *Some browsers may alter the encoding of URLs to be compliant with the specifications of allowable characters for URLs, such as converting a space into* `%20` *and so forth.*

At this point, you're done customizing your page and can save it in SharePoint Designer. Note that when you save your changes, Designer may insert additional code; this is expected. When you save your changes, Designer will sync it back to your team site's Site Pages folder. You can locate the new page by navigating to your Site Pages library.

Linking to the Documents Library in an Access Web App

Before you can use the new custom page, you need a means of obtaining the URL of the picture to render in your page. You will achieve this by linking to the Documents library in the web app. You learned how to link SharePoint lists in Chapter 2: Click Add New Table at the bottom of the tile list, then select SharePoint List. You can add a new table, like the one in Figure 10-71.

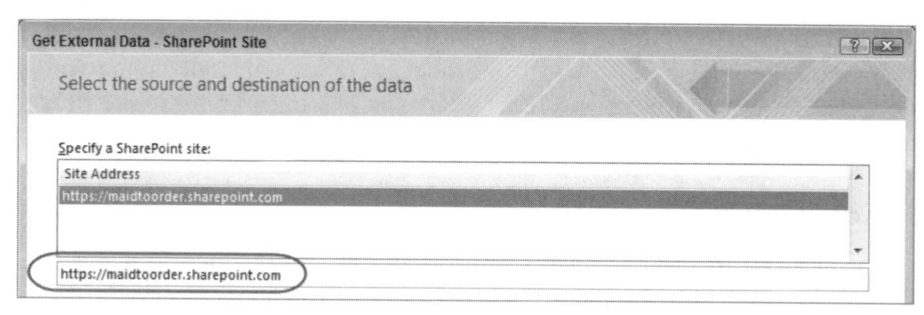

FIGURE 10-71: Linking SharePoint lists

Select the Documents library from the list and click OK, as shown in Figure 10-72.

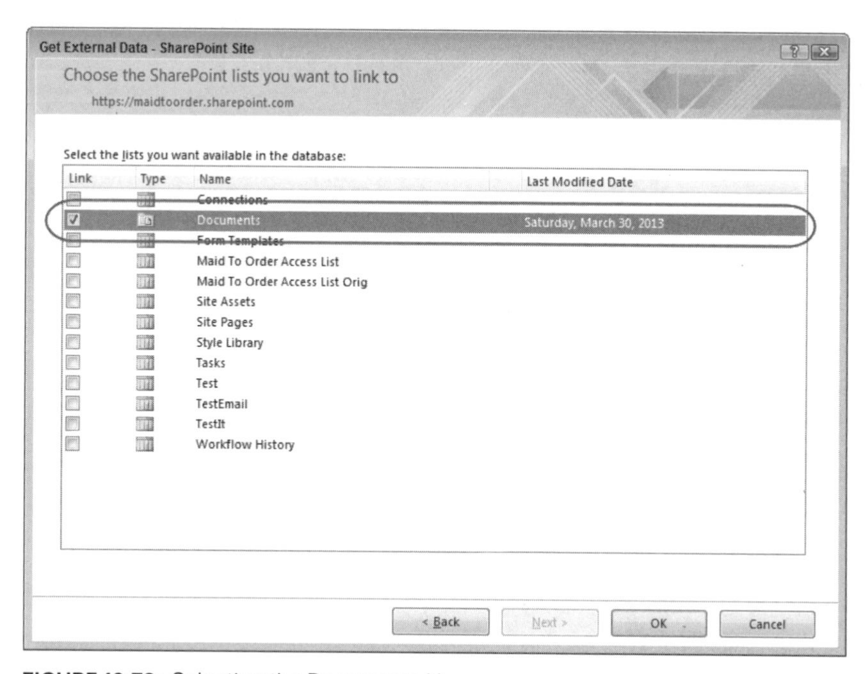

FIGURE 10-72: Selecting the Documents library

As you may recall from Chapters 4 and 8, you may want to delete the default views automatically created for this table and hide the Documents tile from your web app. Refer to Chapter 4 for detailed instructions.

You also need a junction table to connect the document record to a job. Create a new custom table with the field definitions shown in Figure 10-73.

MaidToOrder | txrfJobDocuments

Field Name	Data Type
JobDocumentID	AutoNumber
JobID	Lookup
DocumentID	Lookup

FIGURE 10-73: Creating junction table

`JobID` looks up values from the `tblJobs` table and `DocumentID` looks up values from the `ID` field stored in the Documents library.

You now have the tables you need to associate any given Job record with any number of documents. As you saw earlier with site mailbox setup, you can have your users move attachments into the Documents library. You need to provide an easy way to connect the documents uploaded to a specific job. You will build a form to do this. It will use a web browser control pointing to the custom page that you created in SharePoint Designer.

Inserting a Custom Page in an Access Web App

In order to use the document viewer to see documents associated with specific jobs, however, you'll need a popup view in the Access web app to make those assignments. You learn how to do this next. Before you go through these steps, you will see that the techniques you use are similar to those you might use in a `.accdb` file yet somewhat different, reflecting the constraints of the web environment.

You need a List view that contains a subview control which uses another List view as the source object. You've learned how to create both types of views in previous chapters. Refer to Chapter 4 if you want a refresher. The List view and its subviews will resemble Figure 10-74.

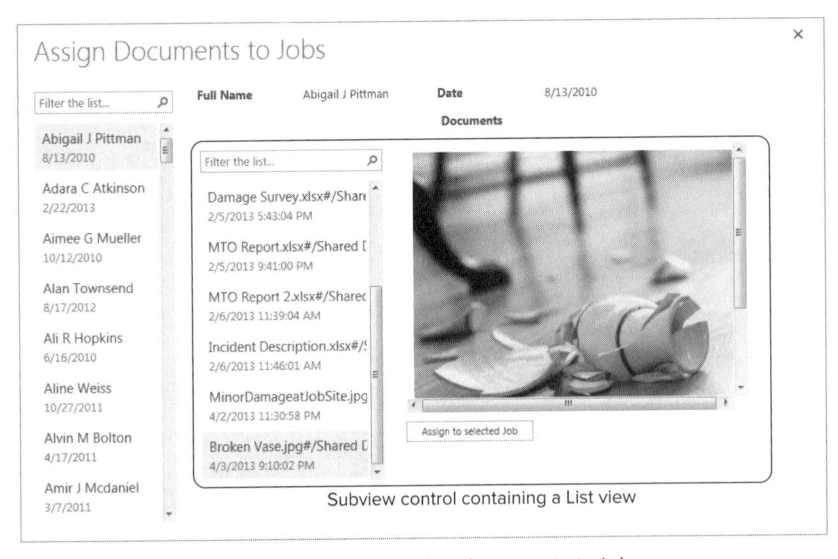

FIGURE 10-74: Popup view needed to assign documents to jobs

As Figure 10-74 reveals, the main view is a List view, with the names of customers and dates of jobs completed for them for the List pane. This allows you to find a particular job to which you need to assign a document. In the example, we're assuming these would be reports and images pertaining to an incident on that job.

The view is based on a query joining customers and jobs, so you can see all jobs for all customers. It's shown in the design view in Figure 10-75.

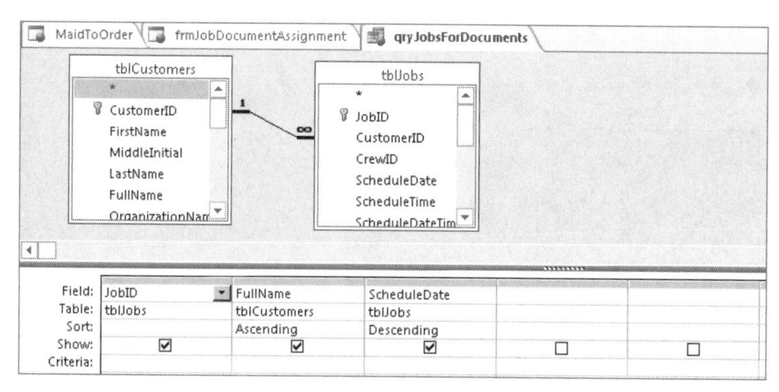

FIGURE 10-75: Jobs and customers query for Document Assignments

Note that the query is based on customer name, rather than organization; it could just as easily have been done the other way, however. The choice depends on whether you'll find it easier to search jobs by the contact person or the company.

The List pane is populated by the `FullName` and `ScheduleDate`, as you can see in Figure 10-76.

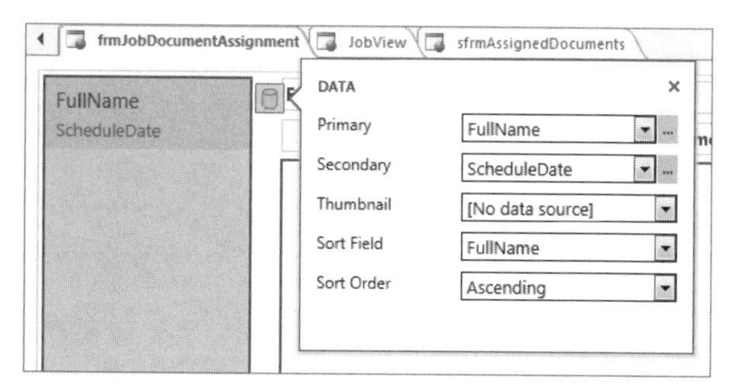

FIGURE 10-76: List pane for customer name and job date

The subview, which returns the documents from the SharePoint document list, is not linked to the main view with the master and child links because you want both views to operate independently.

At this point, however, you may be asking: If they aren't linked, how do you know which `JobID` to link the document with? The answer is that you use the Current event of the main view to set the value of a variable to the `JobID` of the current record. It's pretty simple, as you can see in Figure 10-77.

Each time you select a new job in the List pane, this macro sets `glngCurrentJobID` to that job's `JobID`. This variable can be called from any other macro, which is how you'll add it to the junction table for jobs and documents.

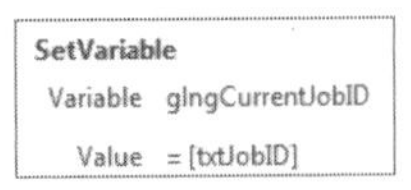

FIGURE 10-77: Set variable to the current JobID.

The `sfrmDocuments` subview shows all of the documents in the documents SharePoint list. You already learned how to link to that list. Create a List view linked to the documents list, and lay it out, as shown in Figure 10-78.

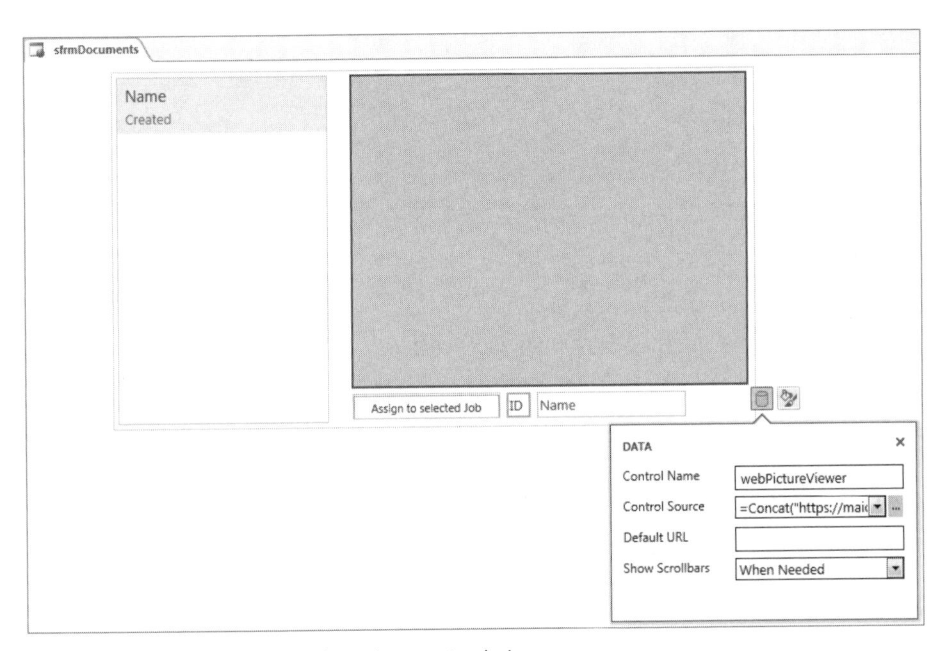

FIGURE 10-78: Document to job assignment subview

Remember that this subview is not linked to the main view with the master and child links because you want both views to operate independently. This subview shows all of the documents in the SharePoint list. As you scroll through the documents in this subview, you can quickly assign any of them to the current job by clicking the Assign button, shown in Figure 10-78. That button calls a data macro, as shown in Figure 10-79.

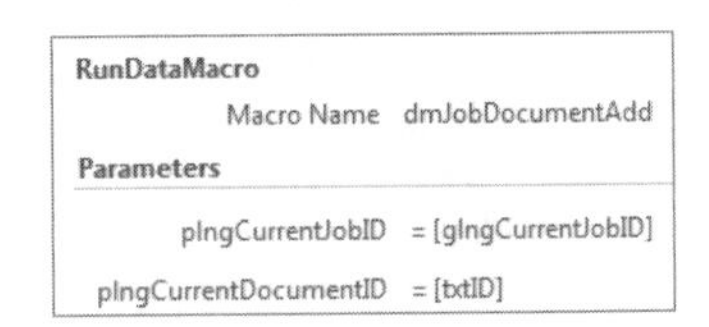

FIGURE 10-79: Calling a data macro from a UI macro

The data macro requires two parameters, the job's `JobID` field and the document's `ID` field. You get `glngCurrentJobID` from the value set in the parent view's Current event shown previously in Figure 10-77. You set the `plngCurrentDocumentID` with the value in the hidden `txtID` control, which is bound to the current document's `ID` field.

Here's the data macro that takes these values and inserts them into the job-document junction table in Figure 10-80.

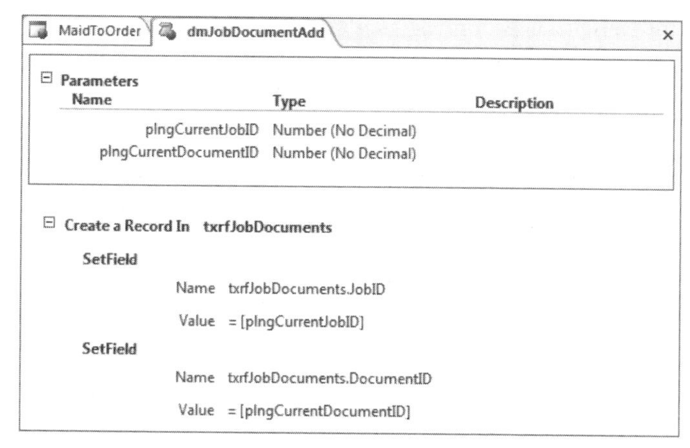

FIGURE 10-80: Data macro to create a record assigning documents to jobs

There's nothing new in this data macro that you've not done before, so let's just quickly note how it works. The data macro accepts two variables and creates a new record in the `txrfJobDocuments` table. It sets two field values, one for the document and the other for the job.

That's about it for the primary work needed to assign documents to jobs. In addition to the features described, you probably would want to add indications whether a document is already added, and whether users want to disassociate the document from a job in case of a mistake. It might also be useful to add additional coding to signal to the user that the assignment was successful. Another enhancement could be to filter out assigned images once they're assigned to the job. However, our space is limited, so we must leave those enhancements as exercises for you.

Now, as you know, some documents are just images. You made a new web page that renders images. Let's add a web browser control to the view and set the Control Source property, as shown in Figure 10-81.

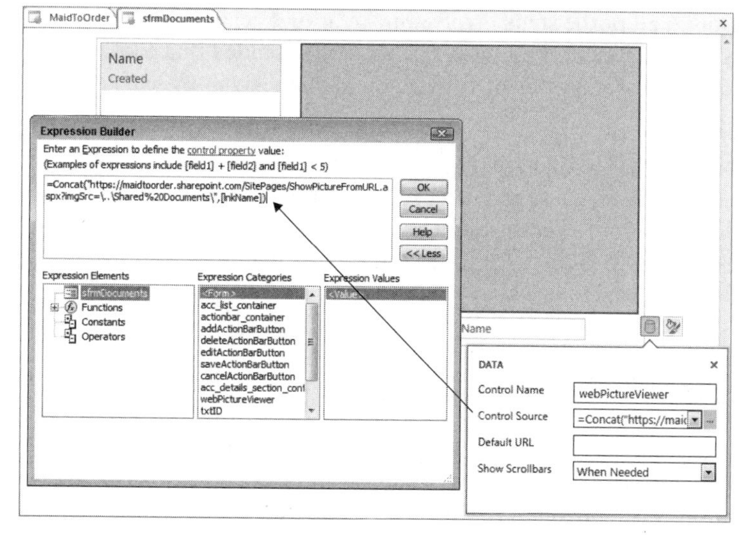

FIGURE 10-81: Customizing web browser control

The syntax for the expression to use for web browser control is:

```
=Concat("https://maidtoorder.sharepoint.com/SitePages/ShowPictureFromURL.aspx
?imgSrc=\..\Shared%20Documents\",[lnkName])
```

You can hide the hyperlink and the textbox controls, and you're done building the interface. You've achieved the result shown in Figure 10-82. When you load a document that's not a graphical file, you get the result illustrated in Figure 10-82.

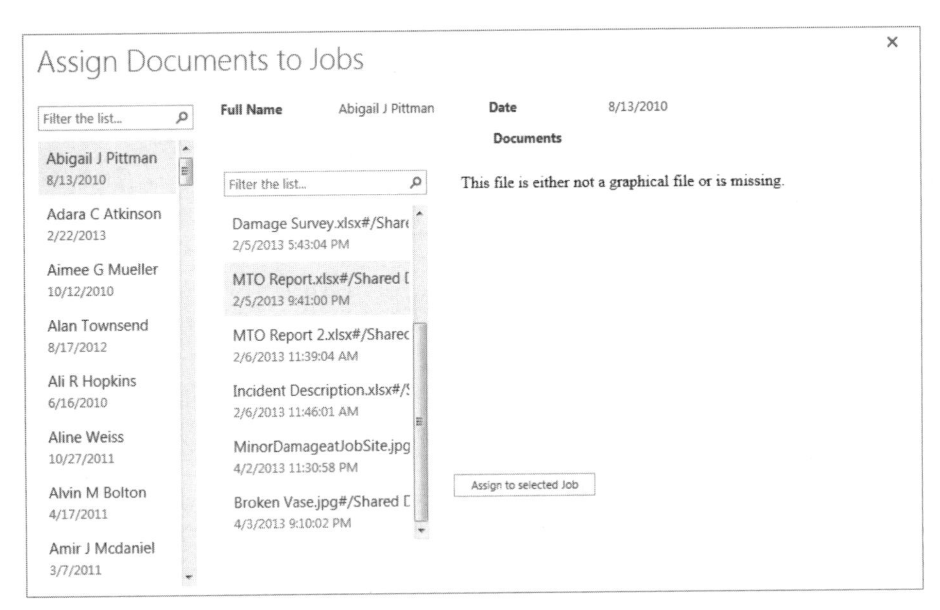

FIGURE 10-82: Non-graphical file selected

At this point, you've worked through all of the steps involved in creating a team site mailbox and using it to collect e-mail reports and documents from users. Then you extended that tool by linking your Maid To Order web app to that SharePoint list, exposing the documents in the web app so they can be assigned to one or more jobs.

All in all, you've successfully combined custom pages, designed for SharePoint using JavaScript, with native Access web app views. In the process, you reached out to the Documents folder on your SharePoint site to incorporate documents received through the team Site Mailbox app that you installed in your team site. In short, you've made a substantial start on integrating and extending your Access web apps to provide a rich experience to your users.

USING APIS WITH A WEB BROWSER CONTROL

As you learned earlier, you can consume some web services directly in a web browser control because they only need input via query string parameters. You saw an example of this in Chapter 4 where the Google Maps application was rendered in a web browser control. Later in this chapter, you learn how you can use another API to render a chart to provide a KPI experience for Maid To Order managers who want to see each day's progress at a glance on the splash page. Keep in mind that we're only suggesting one possible solution, intended to be an example of how you will approach this task. The code demonstrated in this section is available for download in the file named `Chapter 10 - RenderChart.aspx`.

Building a Page to Handle JavaScript Code

The great majority of web services available typically expect you to pass in data via a POST request or via an invocation of a method. You can do neither with Access's web browser control. Let's see an example of how this impacts the way you call web services in a web app using the web browser control.

Google offers an excellent API, which you can use to create charts and other visualization tools. It's located at `https://developers.google.com/chart/interactive/docs/quick_start`.

If you review Google's documentation, you can see that Google expects you to write custom JavaScript, which calls methods provided by Google's APIs and pass in data this way. Your data is contained in the web app database. So, how do you get the data from the database into JavaScript script? As you probably know, there are many ways to skin a cat. One way you can do this is to create a custom page where you can take in query string parameters and pass them to the JavaScript script. This enables you to easily pass in the raw data directly from your Access web app. Once again, you'll use the jQuery library in addition to Google's APIs and create a new page in SharePoint Designer. Using the same steps as before, create a new page and name it `RenderChart.aspx` with framing allowed.

This is the code you would write for `RenderChart.aspx`:

```
<%@ Page language="C#"
  inherits="Microsoft.SharePoint.WebPartPages.WebPartPage,↵
    Microsoft.SharePoint, Version=15.0.0.0, Culture=neutral,↵
 PublicKeyToken=71e9bce111e9429c"
%>
<%@ Register Tagprefix="WebPartPages" Namespace="Microsoft.SharePoint.WebPartPages"
  Assembly="Microsoft.SharePoint, Version=15.0.0.0, Culture=neutral,↵
 PublicKeyToken=71e9bce111e9429c"
%>
<WebPartPages:AllowFraming runat="server" />
<html>
<head>
<script type="text/javascript" src="//www.google.com/jsapi"></script>
</head>
<body>
  <!--Div that will hold the pie chart-->
  <div id="divChart"></div>
  <script type="text/javascript">
    // Options and Default Values
    var options = { title: "Today's Job Progress", width: 400, height: 300 };
    var queryString = { p: 0, w: 0, c: 0 };

    // Populate queryString object with values
```

```
      window.location.search.replace(/(\w+)=(\d+)/g, function ( str, key, value ) {
        queryString[key] = value;
      });

      // Load Google's Visualization module, and Corechart package
      // Once these are finished loading, call the drawChart function
      google.load("visualization", "1.0", {
        "packages": ["corechart"],
        "callback": drawChart
      });

      function drawChart () {
        // Important references
        var element = document.getElementById("divChart");
        var chart = new google.visualization.PieChart(element);
        var data = new google.visualization.DataTable();

        // Add columns, and define their value types
          data.addColumn("string", "Jobs");
          data.addColumn("number", "Status");

        // Populate DataTable with values from queryString
        data.addRows([
          ["Pending",   parseFloat( queryString["p"] )],
          ["Working",   parseFloat( queryString["w"] )],
          ["Completed", parseFloat( queryString["c"] )]
        ]);

        // Draw the chart
        chart.draw(data, options);
      }
    </script>
  </body>
  </html>
```

If you've already visited the link to Google's Chart API page, you'll notice that this code is based on the sample shown there. Let's break up the code and study how it fits together. We'll start with references in the `head` element:

```
<script type="text/javascript" src="//www.google.com/jsapi"></script>
```

> **NOTE** *Note the absence of the* `http` *or* `https` *protocol; this approach allows the reference to succeed regardless of whether it's requested with the* `http` *or* `https` *protocol.*

You need to reference Google's APIs in order to use their charting services. Google's Terms of Services require that you use the APIs hosted at Google, so you cannot download and self-host the web service as you did for the jQuery library for the location mapping application. This also demonstrates how you could reference any other APIs made available by CDNs as discussed earlier in the chapter.

Moving to the `script` element within the `body` element, you can see we're using the same function we used in the previous section to extract the query string parameter. Note, though, the `RegEx` object is different; instead of simply matching the whole string to the right of an equal sign, it will accept only numerical characters. Any non-numerical characters are ignored, thus preventing assigning invalid data to the parameters we will use for rendering the chart. In the next part of the code, we invoke the `google.load()` as shown:

```
google.load("visualization", "1.0", {
  "packages": ["corechart"],
  "callback": drawChart
});
```

The purpose of `google.load()` is to allow for asynchronous loading of the library responsible for drawing charts to help make the experience look faster. This is why you wouldn't reference the actual `.js` files that deal with the chart drawing, but rather let Google's `jsapi.js` deal with retrieving the code responsible for chart drawing and adding it just in time. However, because it has to be loaded, you can't just call the `drawChart()` function right after; you need to do so only when it has fully loaded and, for this, `google.load()` provides a callback method for you to pass in the `drawChart()` function.

We have the `drawChart()` function, which actually will do the work.

```
function drawChart () {
  var element = document.getElementById("divChart");
  var chart = new google.visualization.PieChart(element);
  var data = new google.visualization.DataTable();

  data.addColumn("string", "Jobs");
  data.addColumn("number", "Status");

  data.addRows([
    ["Pending",   parseFloat( queryString["p"] )],
    ["Working",   parseFloat( queryString["w"] )],
    ["Completed", parseFloat( queryString["c"] )]
  ]);

  chart.draw(data, options);
}
```

The first part of the function initializes variables that we'll need throughout the function. The chart uses a `div` element to dynamically format the HTML within the `div` element to draw the chart, so you'd pass in the initially empty `divChart` element when instantiating the chart in this line:

```
var element = document.getElementById("divChart");
var chart = new google.visualization.PieChart(element);
```

Before we can draw a chart, we need to describe the data and to do that, we need the `DataTable()` object instantiated as shown:

```
var data = new google.visualization.DataTable();
```

The middle part of the function deals with populating the `data` variable that will be used to model the chart, similar to how you would place data on an Excel spreadsheet to drive a chart, with columns and rows. Because JavaScript cannot connect directly to data sources as Excel can, you feed the data to it. You'll be doing that via the query string parameters you specify. As you can see, the table is set up as two columns with three rows, one listing the status of a job's progress and the other the count of jobs in the same status category. This page accepts three query string parameters: `p`[ending], `w`[orking], and `c`[ompleted].

Because query string parameters are strings, you need to convert them to a numeric data type in order for the values to be valid; hence, you would wrap it in a `parseFloat()` call. JavaScript also has a `parseInt()` function, which is useful if you don't want decimals, but assume for now that you want to allow for fractional percentages.

The next part of the `drawChart()` function then passes in the `data` and `options` to kick off the chart rendering. Because we don't need to modify the `options` dynamically, we initialized it at the start of the script as shown:

```
var options = { title: "Today's Job Progress", width: 400, height: 300 };
```

As you can see, you can specify custom formatting for your charts by passing in the option map. Refer to Google's documentation on what options are recognized because it can vary for different charting styles. For now, you only need to set the title and size of the chart.

At this point, you should be able to see how creating a custom page can enable you to extend Access web apps by converting parameters into a query string parameter, a format that is easy to use in a web browser control with the appropriate data type needed for the web service invocation. For this scenario, you are simplifying the template and accepting only three input parameters: a number representing pending jobs for today, another number for jobs that have been started, and a third number for jobs that are completed. Later, you'll create a query to return those three numbers, which you can then concatenate into the web browser control's URL.

Development Experience

After studying the code, you should have some idea of how this page will function, but undoubtedly, you're wondering to yourself: How do I find out about parameters and options for JavaScript? How do I use them? How do I experiment? Let's address the development experience. Many vendors, including Google, provide a means for you to experiment with web services. Google's Code Playground can be found at `https://code.google.com/apis/ajax/playground/`.

This playground offers you an easy way to play around with web services without needing to set up a sandbox for yourself, which can take some time. You built a pie chart in the previous section, and you may be wondering what a pie would look like if you wanted more data points. Refer to Figure 10-83 for an idea of how it may look in the Code Playground.

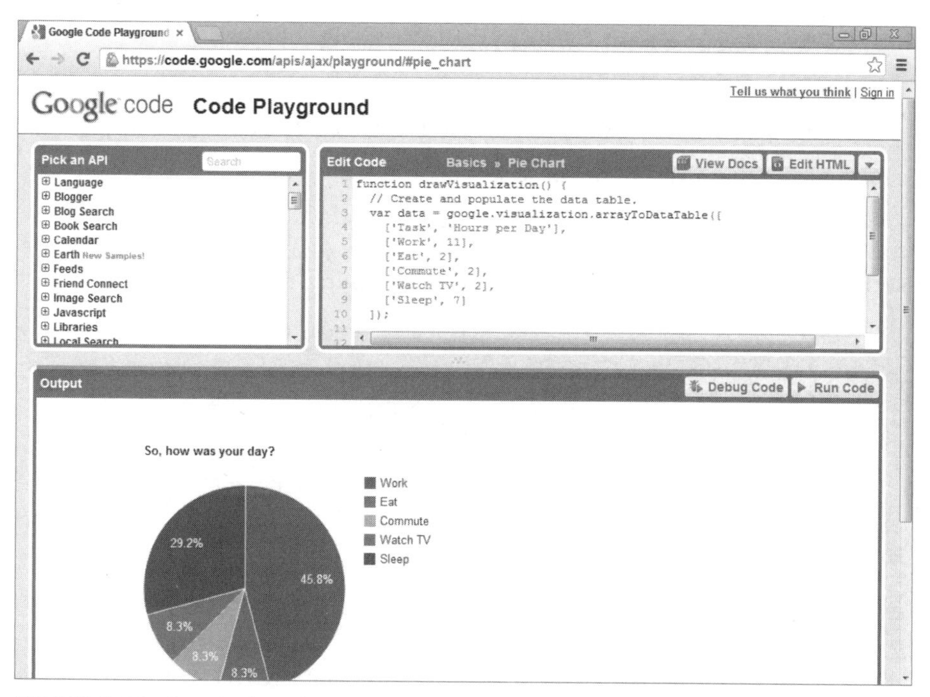

FIGURE 10-83: Google Code Playground

> **NOTE** *Google Code Playground works best in Google Chrome and Safari.*

Note that you have areas for both code and output. You can tweak the code and update to get immediate feedback. Once you've found the right parameters, it's a matter of copying the code and pasting into your own custom pages, and where needed, replacing the parameters. You've already learned how to use jQuery to give you a ready set of functions to extract the query string parameters.

The playground concept is not unique to Google; many vendors that offer web services typically also have a similar setup available for you to take advantage of.

Another aspect you will want to become familiar with when authoring your custom pages, especially when you have to support users who may use different mobile devices, web browsers, and so on is whether it will render as expected in X, Y, or Z browser? Several resources are available online that provide you with views of different browsers from a single web page. One possible resource is located at `http://browserstack.com`.

Loading the same page in each browser to be sure they all look the same saves you from needing to run several browsers concurrently.

You also need to become familiar with developer tools that come with various browsers. For example, pressing F12 on your Internet Explorer browser launches developer tools that allow you to:

- Inspect what resources a web page is using
- Locate and examine an element in the page
- Manually edit a loaded HTML document and get immediate feedback
- Put in breakpoints and watch JavaScript scripts
- Be told about errors in scripts and/or HTML rendering

You can see an active debug session with a watched variable in Figure 10-84.

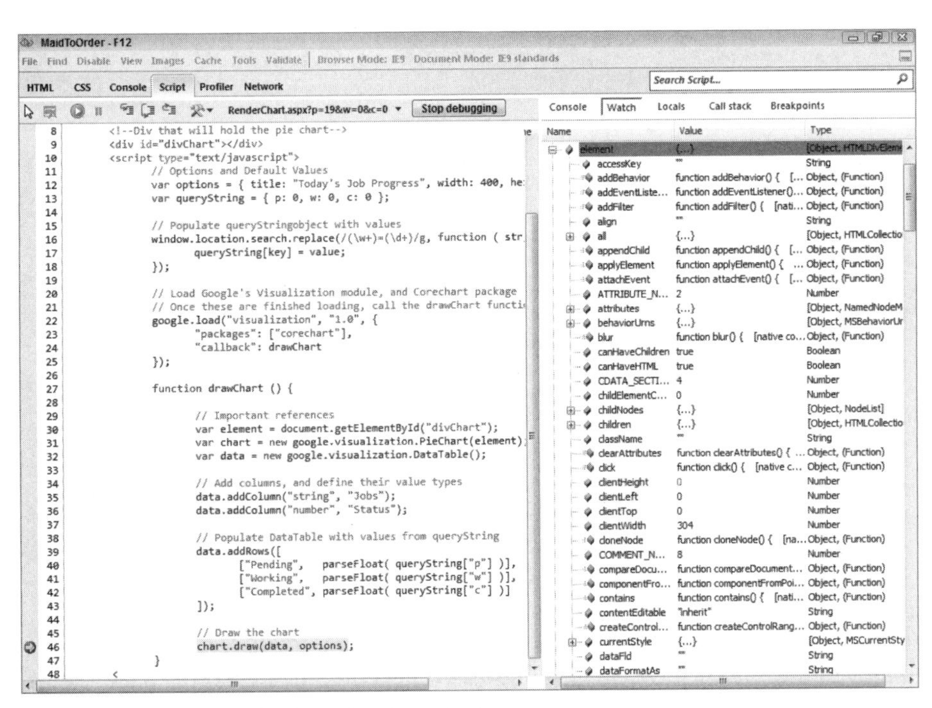

FIGURE 10-84: Internet Explorer developer tools

Many, if not all, major browsers have such tools included. An in-depth discussion on using those tools is beyond the scope of the book, but should you choose to delve further into authoring custom JavaScript scripts to augment your Access web apps, you will benefit from learning how to use those developer tools effectively.

Adding the Charting Page to Access Web App

You now have a means of dynamically generating a chart with three input parameters. In order to get the input parameters, you need to create a query and a subview to return the data for consumption in a web browser control. Let's start with the query. You may wonder why you would use a subview. The answer is that a subview is not loaded until it's made visible so you have a means of controlling the load experience. You want the splash page to load quickly but let chart data come in on its own sweet time without holding back everything else. As you saw in the previous code, much code is designed to run asynchronously, which is an advantage when the dataset is large or chart rendering complex.

However, that advantage is immediately lost if the whole web app must wait for the view to render. Including a subview means that you can partition the rendering, allowing the main content to load quickly and the additional content to come at a later time. Using the subview is a very simple way to achieve the perception of speedy loading. Otherwise, a view bound to the query is forced to wait for the query to return and must be refreshed in order to update the content. Furthermore, by using a subview that's hidden initially and made visible by the form's `Current` event, you don't have to refresh the whole form; update only the data returned from the data macro and the form itself can load quickly without forcing users to wait for additional calculations to complete. Of course, your experience will be useful in guiding you toward an optimal solution for your particular scenarios.

Create a new query, to be named `qryJobProgress`, which needs only one table similar to Figure 10-85.

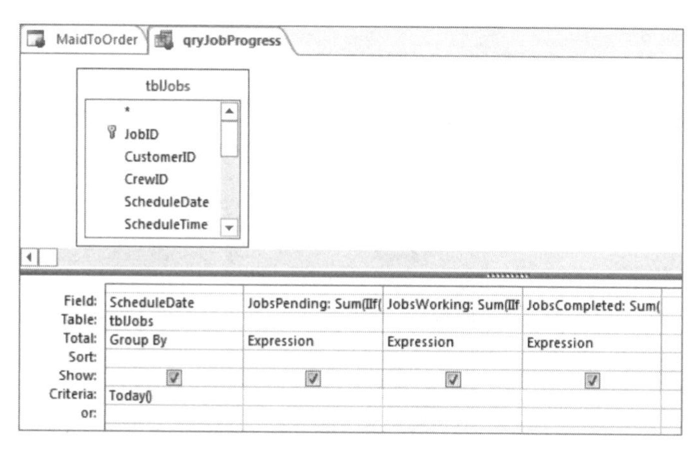

FIGURE 10-85: qryJobProgress query

The query will filter jobs to only today's jobs and perform aggregation on three columns. You need conditional counts to return the right counts for jobs that are not yet started, jobs that are started but not finished, and jobs that are finished. Here are the formulas for those three fields shown in Figure 10-85:

```
JobsPending: Sum(IIf([StartTime] Is Null And [Completed]=No,1,0))
JobsWorking: Sum(IIf([StartTime] Is Not Null And [Completed]=No,1,0))
JobsCompleted: Sum(IIf([Completed]=Yes,1,0))
```

Save the query and proceed. Create a brand new blank view and name it `fsubDashboard`. Bind this new view to the `qryJobProgress` query. Also, you need to add a web browser control and a textbox to the view. The textbox should be hidden. You might lay them out as shown on Figure 10-86.

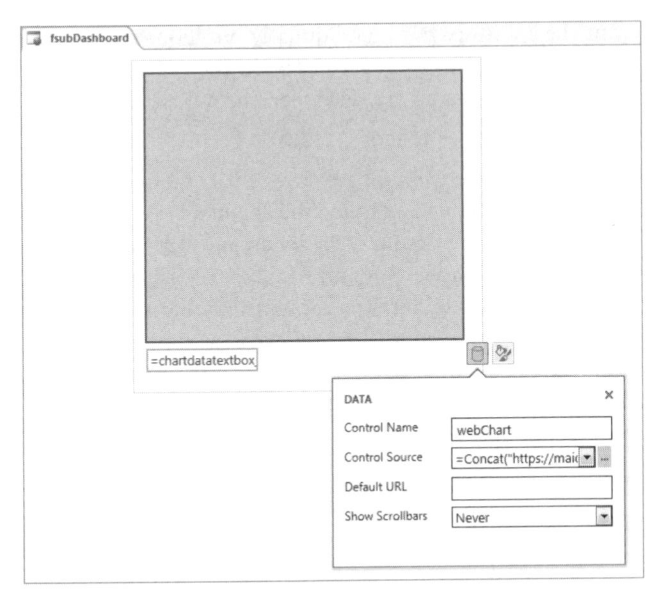

FIGURE 10-86: Layout of new fsubDashboard view

Because, initially, the complete URL won't be valid, there is no need to display the web browser control. Set it to hidden and set its `ControlSource` to the following expression:

```
=Concat("https://maidtoorder.sharepoint.com/SitePages/RenderChart.aspx?",
  [txtChartData])
```

As you see, the web browser has the address hard-coded; you only need to add the query string parameters. Let's add an expression to constitute the query string parameters from the recordsource to a textbox named `txtChartData`. Enter the expression as shown in Figure 10-87.

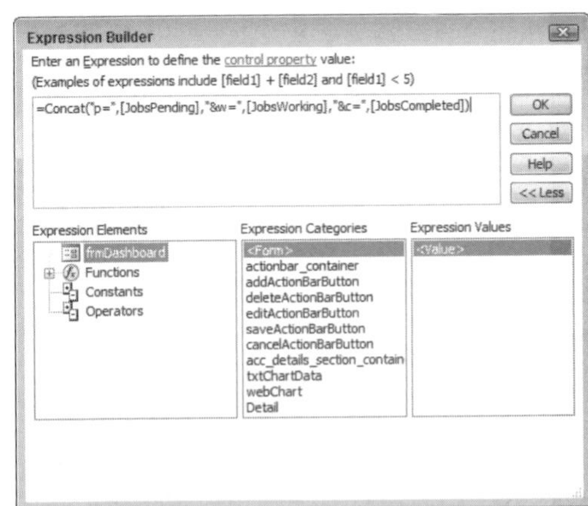

FIGURE 10-87: Expression for ChartDataTextBox

This is all you need to complete the subview construction. You'll want to add it to the `frmSplash` view, make it initially hidden, and add a Current event to make it visible (see Figure 10-88).

SetProperty	
Control Name	subDashboard
Property	Visible
Value	Yes

FIGURE 10-88: frmSplash's Current event

With this work completed, the Maid To Order manager is now able to see a chart visualizing today's progress on the front page of the web app. The final product should look something like Figure 10-89. Note how the pie chart provides a mouseover effect to provide additional information.

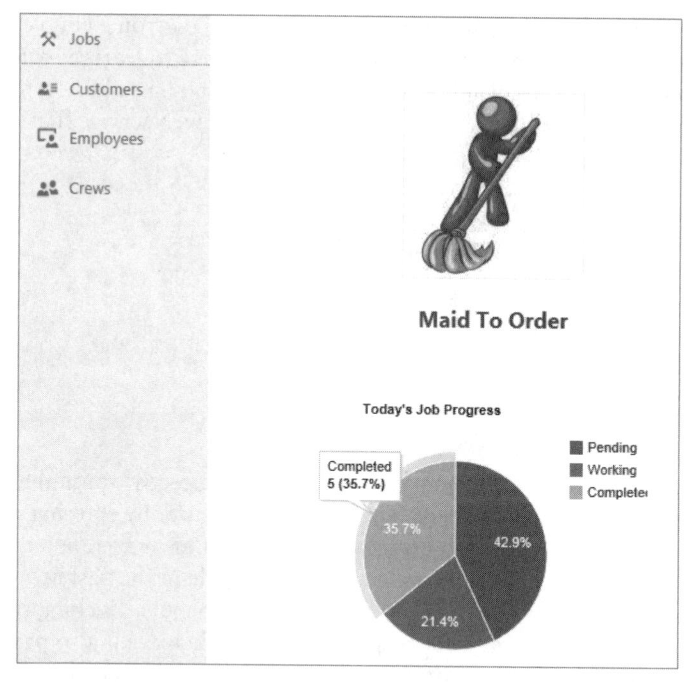

FIGURE 10-89: Chart rendered on the splash page

CONSUMING ZIP-LOOKUP WEB SERVICES IN THE CLIENT

Lest you think that the materials you've learned so far are good only for use inside a web browser, we think that you will also find tremendous benefit in using web services inside an Access client solution. Consider the problem of ZIP code lookup. Ideally, you would be able to identify the city, local region, and state/province from a ZIP code. Yet ZIP codes are not immutable. Some get split into two new ZIP codes. Some are never valid while others were once invalid but pressed into service later. In the past, some Access developers may have made do with acquiring a list of ZIP codes every so often from various sources. However, a static list can get out of date and, many times, there is a fee that discourages developers from keeping it updated. The code used in this section is available for download as a sample database file titled `ch10_ZIPLookup.accdb`.

Calling a web service is an excellent solution. Instead of being responsible for maintaining a current list of ZIP codes, you can pass that chore off to people who do nothing but maintain it and thus do it much better than what you could hope to do yourself. You don't have to worry about checking whether the information is valid; it is always up-to-date every time you look up the details. Furthermore, we think you'll be pleasantly surprised with the performance.

One word of caution is perhaps in order before we get much further. Consuming web services from within Access is probably not familiar to many Access developers. We don't expect everyone to jump right in and replicate this feature in their own databases right away, at least not without some amount of further study. However, we hope that seeing what can be done with a basic web service will encourage everyone to think about the possibilities in front of them.

With that said, let's learn how to consume one typical web service. First, we'll show you a couple of screenshots of the ZIP code web service in action, and then you'll have a chance to learn how it works. Figure 10-90 shows Maid To Order's setup form for new customers, which has a button to validate the ZIP code entered. This validation is actually a call to a Postal Code web service that returns valid city, state, and county for the ZIP code requested.

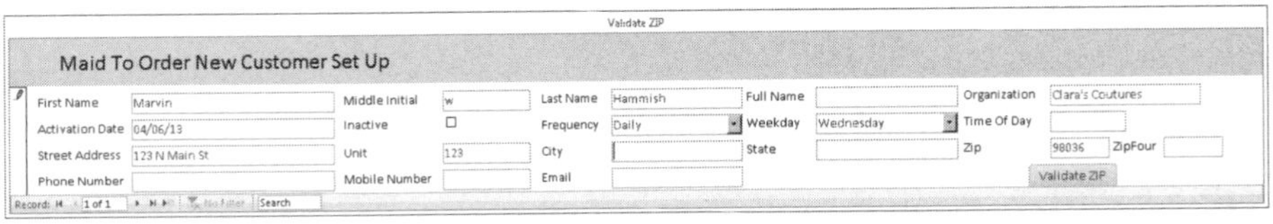

FIGURE 10-90: New Customer Set Up for Maid To Order

As you can see, Maid To Order's data entry person can enter the city and state directly or use the Zip code and validation process to look them up. Because data entry people are usually entering information provided from secondhand sources (for example, a sales rep or a hand-written note), and they can't just call the customers to verify the data, mistakes have been made in the past as information passed from customers to the data entry person via maids or sales people. Clicking the Validate ZIP button opens a form that runs the Postal Code web service. The Click event also passes in the value of the ZIP code entered for the customer's address so the data entry person can quickly validate the information. Figure 10-91 shows the result of the request. Although you can't see it in Figure 10-91, the possible address in the combo box displays immediately. You can imagine how long a search might take on a local table containing 40 or 50 thousand ZIP codes.

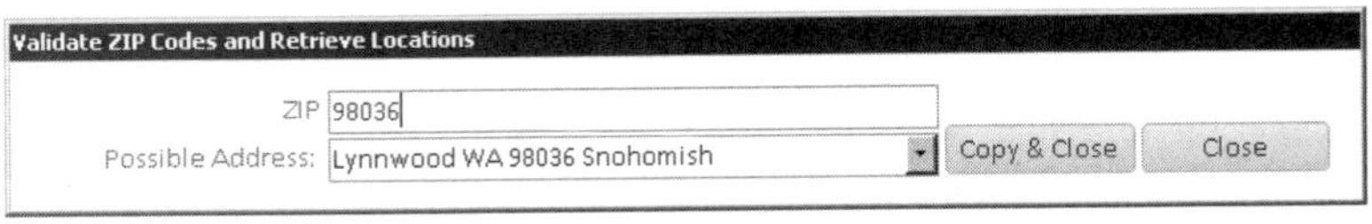

FIGURE 10-91: Address returned by the web service

When the form opens, the ZIP code passed to it is displayed and the web service is called to return the city, state, ZIP, and county. In the proposed usage for Maid To Order, there are a couple of scenarios. If the possible address is the same as the one already entered, the data entry person can just close the form and move forward. On the other hand, if the ZIP doesn't validate against the information provided by the client, the data entry person can use the Copy & Close button to update the city and state in the customer setup form from the most current values returned by the web service.

Creating a User Account for the Web Service

Although many web services are provided free by their owners, most require that you sign up and obtain a username before you can do so. The process may differ from web service to web service. In this example, we assume that Maid To Order has designated a developer to set up the web service account we'll be using. You'll need to do the same for any web service you choose to implement.

Library References and Code

So, let's review the code you'll write to implement this ZIP code verification. First, you need two library references, one to `Microsoft WinHTTP Services, version 5.1` and the other to `Microsoft XML, 3.0`. Locate and select these references as you normally do in your VBA IDE. Although you can late-bind the Microsoft XML library, you want to early-bind `WinHTTP Services` in order to subscribe to events raised by objects from this library, which is an important component in providing good performance.

The code itself is contained in a class module called `GeoName`, and in the code module of the validation form. The complete code from the class module follows.

> **NOTE** *Documentation for using the web service is available at* `http://www.geonames.org/export/web-services.html#postalCodeSearch`.
>
> *Courtesy* of `http://www.geonames.org/`.

Much of the code in the class module is needed to format the comma-delimited strings for the combo box which displays possible address matches for the selected ZIP code. However, to keep this discussion as short as possible, we'll assume you are familiar with the VBA concepts discussed, and we won't try to explain things like declarations or setting library references. Rather, we'll call out for your attention the elements that are unique to the code needed to call the web service. For example, you have probably defined `Enums` and created declarations for APIs many times. If you aren't comfortable with them, you can get a refresher in Chapter 16.

With that background regarding the code and your expectations, let's look at the code in the class module, `GeoName`, starting with the declarations. You'll find comments interspersed in the code as we show and discuss it.

The declarations section defines constants needed by the code in the class. Two of the declarations, `Private WithEvents objWinHTTP As WinHttp.WinHttpRequest` and `Private objDOMDoc As MSXML2.DOMDocument`, define objects for the HTTP call and the XML document, which passes requests to the web service. As noted, they assume the appropriate library references are in place. In case you're not familiar with the `WithEvents` keyword, using it allows methods defined within the class to be registered as event handlers for events raised by the object. As you will see later, enabling events for the `WinHTTPRequest` object will allow you to run the code asynchronously to provide better performance without hanging up the application. The first snippet of code follows:

```
Option Compare Database
Option Explicit

Private Const strModuleName As String = "GeoName Class"

Private WithEvents objWinHTTP As WinHttp.WinHttpRequest
Private objDOMDoc As MSXML2.DOMDocument

Private WithEvents frmSource As Access.Form
Private WithEvents txtZip As Access.TextBox
```

```
Private cboAddress As Access.ComboBox

Private bolASync As Boolean
Private bolLoaded As Boolean
Private intOrigColumnCount As Integer
Private strOrigColumnWidths As String
Private strOrigRowsource As String
Private strOrigRowsourceType As String
Private strResults() As String

Private lngExactPostalCodeLength As Long
Private lngMaxRows As Long
Private strCountryISOCode As String
Private lngOrdinalPositions() As Long
Private bolOrdinalPositionsValid As Boolean
Private lngResultsCount As Long
Private lngErrorNumber As Long
Private strErrorDescription As String

Public Enum GeoNameStyle
  gsShort
  gsMedium
  gsLong
  gsFull
End Enum

Public Enum GeoNameOperator
  gsAnd
  gsOr
End Enum
```

The `GeoNameColumns` enum defines the columns to be returned to the combo box on the validation form. It includes the `PostalCode`, `PlaceName` (i.e., city), `Country`, `Latitude`, and `Longitude` corresponding to the center of the ZIP code, and several "AdminCodes," which will, in fact, be populated with the state as an abbreviation and spelled out in full, among others. Here's the next snippet:

```
'Updating the enum requires maintaining
'the Min/Max property and FieldName property
'Ensure those are updated accordingly
Public Enum GeoNameColumns
  PostalCode = 0
  PlaceName = 1
  Country = 2
  Latitude = 3
  Longitude = 4
  AdminCode1 = 5
  AdminName1 = 6
  AdminCode2 = 7
  AdminName2 = 8
  AdminCode3 = 9
  AdminName3 = 10
  [_Min] = PostalCode
```

```
  [_Max] = AdminName3
End Enum

Private Const strLoading As String = "Loading..."
Private Const lngDefaultMaxRows = 10
Private Const strDefaultCountryISOCode = "US"
Private Const lngDefaultExactPostalCodeLength = 5
Private Const lngDefaultGeoNameStyle As Long = GeoNameStyle.gsMedium
Private Const lngDefaultGeoNameOperator As Long = GeoNameOperator.gsAnd
Private Const bolDefaultIsReduced As Boolean = False
```

You'll note a constant declared for UTF8 encoding and an API call for `WideCharToMultiByte`. They're included because your web service calls will be going to a specific URL. Because spaces and certain other characters aren't valid in a URI, you need to convert something like `foo bar` into `foo%20bar`. These two bits of code convert characters to UTF8 in order to handle the encoding and decoding of URIs for the call to the web service. This is the next snippet:

```
Private Const CP_UTF8 = 65001

Private Declare PtrSafe Function WideCharToMultiByte Lib "Kernel32" ( _
  ByVal CodePage As Long, _
  ByVal dwflags As Long, _
  ByVal lpWideCharStr As Long, _
  ByVal cchWideChar As Long, _
  ByVal lpMultiByteStr As Long, _
  ByVal cchMultiByte As Long, _
  ByVal lpDefaultChar As Long, _
  ByVal lpUsedDefaultChar As Long _
) As Long

Private Declare PtrSafe Sub Sleep Lib "Kernel32" ( _
  ByVal dwMilliseconds As Long _
)
```

The class module also defines several properties you'll use in the formatting process, such as the number of rows to display and the length of the postal code. Here's the next snippet:

```
Property Get DefaultMaxRows() As Long
  DefaultMaxRows = lngMaxRows
End Property

Property Let DefaultMaxRows(InputValue As Long)
  If InputValue <= 0 Then
     Err.Raise vbObjectError, strModuleName, "DefaultMaxRows cannot be zero " & _
    "or negative numbers."
  Else
    lngMaxRows = InputValue
  End If
End Property

Property Get ExactPostalCodeLength() As Long
  ExactPostalCodeLength = lngExactPostalCodeLength
```

```
End Property

Property Let ExactPostalCodeLength(InputValue As Long)
  If InputValue < 0 Then
     Err.Raise vbObjectError, strModuleName, "The Postal Code length cannot " & _
     "be zero or a negative number."
  Else
    lngExactPostalCodeLength = InputValue
  End If
End Property
```

Ordinal position is an important element in putting strings into the combo box on the validation form because you may have different formatting requirements in different usages. Specifying the ordinal position changes how the returned values should be formatted on the combo box. When you get a response back from the web service, it will come in the format of an XML document with nodes for parts of the location, such as place (city) or state. The code converts those nodes into items in an array called `lngOrdinalPositions()`. In later steps, the code references the values in that array to put values into the combo box.

The `Get` and `Let` properties in the class module retrieve and store those values like this:

```
Property Get OrdinalPosition(GeoNameColumn As GeoNameColumns) As Long
  OrdinalPosition = lngOrdinalPositions(GeoNameColumn)
End Property

Property Let OrdinalPosition(GeoNameColumn As GeoNameColumns, InputValue As Long)
  Dim colTestUnique As VBA.Collection
  Dim lngCount As Long
  Dim lngIterator As Long
  Dim lngValue As Long

  Select Case InputValue
    Case Is > (GeoNameColumns.[_Max] + 1), _
       Is < GeoNameColumns.[_Min]
      Err.Raise vbObjectError, strModuleName, "The ordinal position is " & _
     "out of bounds. You may set a number between " & (GeoNameColumns.[_Min] + 1) & _
        " to " & (GeoNameColumns.[_Max] + 1) & " or set to zero to indicate " & _
        "it will not be used."
  End Select

  On Error GoTo ErrHandler

  lngOrdinalPositions(GeoNameColumn) = InputValue
  bolOrdinalPositionsValid = False

  Set colTestUnique = New VBA.Collection
  lngCount = UBound(lngOrdinalPositions)
  For lngIterator = 0 To lngCount
    lngValue = lngOrdinalPositions(lngIterator)
    If lngValue > 0 Then
      On Error Resume Next
      colTestUnique.Add lngIterator, Format$(lngValue, "00")
      If Err.Number Then
```

```
          Err.Clear
          GoTo ExitProc
        End If
        On Error GoTo ErrHandler
      End If
    Next
    bolOrdinalPositionsValid = True

  ExitProc:
    On Error Resume Next
    Set colTestUnique = Nothing
    Exit Property
  ErrHandler:
    Select Case Err.Number
      Case Else
        VBA.MsgBox "Error " & Err.Number & " (" & Err.Description & ")"
    End Select
    Resume ExitProc
    Resume 'for Debugging
  End Property

  Property Get OrdinalPositionsValid() As Boolean
    OrdinalPositionsValid = bolOrdinalPositionsValid
  End Property

  Property Get ResultsCount() As Long
    ResultsCount = lngResultsCount
  End Property

  Property Get ErrorNumber() As Long
    ErrorNumber = lngErrorNumber
  End Property

  Property Get ErrorDescription() As String
    ErrorDescription = strErrorDescription
  End Property
```

Field names are defined for the `GeoNameColumns` enum to make it easy to convert an integer representing an enum value into the string of the same name. It will be used in the web service call when building the parameters for the request. Here is the next code snippet:

```
  Property Get FieldName(GeoNameColumn As GeoNameColumns) As String
    Select Case GeoNameColumn
      Case GeoNameColumns.PostalCode
        FieldName = "postalcode"
      Case GeoNameColumns.PlaceName
        FieldName = "name"
      Case GeoNameColumns.Country
        FieldName = "countryCode"
      Case GeoNameColumns.Latitude
        FieldName = "lat"
      Case GeoNameColumns.Longitude
        FieldName = "lng"
      Case GeoNameColumns.AdminCode1
```

```
        FieldName = "adminCode1"
      Case GeoNameColumns.AdminName1
        FieldName = "adminName1"
      Case GeoNameColumns.AdminCode2
        FieldName = "adminCode2"
      Case GeoNameColumns.AdminName2
        FieldName = "adminName2"
      Case GeoNameColumns.AdminCode3
        FieldName = "adminCode3"
      Case GeoNameColumns.AdminName3
        FieldName = "adminName3"
      Case Else
        Err.Raise 5, strModuleName, "The GeoNameColumn parameter " & _
           "is not a valid value."
    End Select
  End Property
```

As is the case with most classes, `GeoName` contains initialization code. It sets the `objWinHTTP` object as a new `WinHttp.WinHttpRequest`, and the `objDOMDoc` object as a new `MSXML2.DOMDocument`. You need those objects later when sending the request for address information to the web service and consuming the results. You also will want to use the undocumented `WizHook.SortStringArray()` function. In order to use this function, you have to provide a key to the `WizHook` object:

```
Private Sub Class_Initialize()
  bolASync = True
  Set objWinHTTP = New WinHttp.WinHttpRequest
  Set objDOMDoc = New MSXML2.DOMDocument
  WizHook.Key = 51488399

  lngMaxRows = lngDefaultMaxRows
  lngExactPostalCodeLength = lngDefaultExactPostalCodeLength
  strCountryISOCode = strDefaultCountryISOCode

  ReDim lngOrdinalPositions(GeoNameColumns.[_Max])
End Sub

Private Sub Class_Terminate()
On Error Resume Next
  Set cboAddress = Nothing
  Set txtZip = Nothing
  Set frmSource = Nothing
  Set objDOMDoc = Nothing
  Set objWinHTTP = Nothing
End Sub
```

You also need an error handler for the `objWinHTTP` object to handle the return from the web service. Remember that you are going outside the VBA world here, so you have to be prepared for unexpected results in the return. This also illustrates an advantage of using the `WinHTTP` object over, for example, the `MSXML2.XMLHTTPRequest` object; instead of checking different statuses and properties to determine there were no errors, you can have `WinHTTP` tell you that there is an error without having to know specifically what went wrong, and avoid writing specific error handlers for different cases.

Here is the next snippet of code:

```
Private Sub objWinHTTP_OnError(ByVal ErrorNumber As Long, _
  ByVal ErrorDescription As String)

  Const strOutput As String = "Error occurred"

  lngErrorNumber = ErrorNumber
  strErrorDescription = ErrorDescription

  If Not cboAddress Is Nothing Then
    With cboAddress
      If Not bolLoaded Then
        intOrigColumnCount = .ColumnCount
        strOrigColumnWidths = .ColumnWidths
        strOrigRowsourceType = .RowSourceType
        strOrigRowsource = .RowSource
      End If
      bolLoaded = True
      .ColumnCount = 1
      .ColumnWidths = vbNullString
      .RowSourceType = "Value List"
      .RowSource = strOutput
      .Value = strOutput
      .Locked = True
    End With
  End If
End Sub
```

With that preparation, you can start looking into the way things are processed by the remaining procedures. Here, you will be attaching controls and a form to the class, which allow you to listen for those control and form events from inside the class, reducing the need to write code in the calling form. This sub initializes the object references and sets properties for them to ensure that the class can listen to events raised by those objects. Take a look at the next snippet:

```
Public Sub AttachControls( _
  ZipCodeTextbox As Access.TextBox, _
  AddressSelectionComboBox As Access.ComboBox _
)
  Const Evented As String = "[Event Procedure]"
  Dim obj As Object

  Set txtZip = ZipCodeTextbox
  txtZip.AfterUpdate = Evented

  Set obj = txtZip
  Do
    Set obj = obj.Parent
  Loop Until TypeOf obj Is Access.Form
  Set frmSource = obj
  frmSource.OnCurrent = Evented

  Set cboAddress = AddressSelectionComboBox
```

```
    With cboAddress
      intOrigColumnCount = .ColumnCount
      strOrigColumnWidths = .ColumnWidths
      strOrigRowsourceType = .RowSourceType
      strOrigRowsource = .RowSource
    End With
  End Sub
```

Study the following procedure, `PostalCodeSearchAsync`, which contains the actual call to the web service. We'll pick up a discussion of its parts later.

```
Private Sub PostalCodeSearchAsync( _
  Optional PostalCode As String = vbNullString, _
  Optional PostalCodeStartsWith As String = vbNullString, _
  Optional PlaceName As String = vbNullString, _
  Optional PlaceNameStartsWith As String = vbNullString, _
  Optional CountryISOCode As String = strDefaultCountryISOCode, _
  Optional CountryBias As String = vbNullString, _
  Optional MaxRows As Long = lngDefaultMaxRows, _
  Optional Style As GeoNameStyle = lngDefaultGeoNameStyle, _
  Optional Operator As GeoNameOperator = lngDefaultGeoNameOperator, _
  Optional IsReduced As Boolean = bolDefaultIsReduced _
)

Const strURI As String = "http://api.geonames.org/postalCodeSearch?"
  Const strJoin As String = "&"
  Dim strParameters As String
  Dim strTmp As String

  Select Case True
    Case Len(PostalCode), _
       Len(PlaceName), _
       Len(PostalCodeStartsWith), _
       Len(PlaceNameStartsWith)
      'Parameters are okay, proceed
    Case Else
      Err.Raise vbObjectError, strModuleName, "You must supply either " & _
       "PostalCode, PostalCodeStartsWith, PlaceName, or " & _
       "PlaceNameStartsWith parameter; you cannot have all left blank."
  End Select

  If Len(PostalCode) Then
    strParameters = strParameters & "postalcode=" & URLEncode(PostalCode) & _
    strJoin
  End If
  If Len(PostalCodeStartsWith) Then
    strParameters = strParameters & "postalcode_startsWith=" & _
     URLEncode(PostalCodeStartsWith) & strJoin
  End If
  If Len(PlaceName) Then
    strParameters = strParameters & "placename=" & URLEncode(PlaceName) & _
     strJoin
```

```
    End If
    If Len(PlaceNameStartsWith) Then
      strParameters = strParameters & "placename_startsWith=" & _
        URLEncode(PlaceNameStartsWith) & strJoin
    End If
    If Len(CountryISOCode) Then
      strParameters = strParameters & "country=" & _
        URLEncode(CountryISOCode) & strJoin
    End If

    strParameters = strParameters & "maxRows=" & MaxRows & strJoin

    Select Case Style
      Case gsShort
        strTmp = "style=FULL"
      Case gsMedium
        strTmp = "style=MEDIUM"
      Case gsLong
        strTmp = "style=LONG"
      Case gsFull
        strTmp = "style=FULL"
    End Select
    strParameters = strParameters & strTmp & strJoin

    Select Case Operator
      Case gsAnd
        strTmp = "style=AND"
      Case gsOr
        strTmp = "style=OR"
    End Select
    strParameters = strParameters & strTmp & strJoin

    If IsReduced Then
      strTmp = "isReduced=true"
    Else
      strTmp = "isReduced=false"
    End If
    strParameters = strParameters & strTmp & strJoin

    strParameters = strParameters & "username=bgclothier"

    With objWinHTTP
      .Open "GET", strURI & strParameters, bolASync
      .send
    End With
  End Sub
```

Here's what the preceding code snippet does. First, the URI of the web service is supplied. It names the website hosting the service and a query string that identifies the service you want to use:

```
Const strURI As String = "http://api.geonames.org/postalCodeSearch?"
```

Next, the code checks whether any one of four optional parameters are supplied. The web service requires that one of those four parameters be supplied and, if none are included you cannot invoke the web service without an error. You abort the attempt if the calling code does not provide the required parameter.

```
Select Case True
  Case Len(PostalCode), _
     Len(PlaceName), _
     Len(PostalCodeStartsWith), _
     Len(PlaceNameStartsWith)
    'Parameters are okay, proceed
  Case Else
    Err.Raise vbObjectError, strModuleName, "You must supply " & _
    "either PostalCode, PostalCodeStartsWith, PlaceName, or " & _
    "PlaceNameStartsWith parameter; you cannot have all left blank."
End Select
```

Whenever the calling code supplies a parameter, you need to encode the parameter before adding it to the URL string. As noted previously, the `URLEncode()` function will convert UTF16 to UTF8 and insert the correct encoding to create a properly formatted URL. Now look at the next code snippet:

```
If Len(PostalCode) Then
  strParameters = strParameters & "postalcode=" & URLEncode(PostalCode) & _
  strJoin
End If
If Len(PostalCodeStartsWith) Then
  strParameters = strParameters & "postalcode_startsWith= " & _
    URLEncode(PostalCodeStartsWith) & strJoin
End If
If Len(PlaceName) Then
  strParameters = strParameters & "placename=" & URLEncode(PlaceName) & _
  strJoin
End If
If Len(PlaceNameStartsWith) Then
  strParameters = strParameters & "placename_startsWith=" & _
    URLEncode(PlaceNameStartsWith) & strJoin
End If
If Len(CountryISOCode) Then
  strParameters = strParameters & "country=" & _
    URLEncode(CountryISOCode) & strJoin
End If
```

We'll come back to the next step in `PostalCodeSearchAsync`, but for clarity before we go on, here's the function that converts the parameters shown in the preceding code snippets from UTF16 to UTF8:

```
Private Function UTF16To8(ByVal UTF16 As String) As String
  Dim sBuffer As String
  Dim lLength As Long

  If UTF16 <> vbNullString Then
    lLength = WideCharToMultiByte(CP_UTF8, 0, StrPtr(UTF16), -1, 0, 0, 0, 0)
```

```
        sBuffer = Space$(lLength)
        lLength = WideCharToMultiByte(CP_UTF8, 0, StrPtr(UTF16), -1, _
              StrPtr(sBuffer), Len(sBuffer), 0, 0)
        sBuffer = StrConv(sBuffer, vbUnicode)
        UTF16To8 = Left$(sBuffer, lLength - 1)
      Else
        UTF16To8 = vbNullString
      End If
    End Function
```

And here's the function that encodes the string passed to it as a properly formatted URL:

```
Private Function URLEncode( _
   StringVal As String, _
   Optional SpaceAsPlus As Boolean = False, _
   Optional UTF8Encode As Boolean = True _
) As String
  Dim StringValCopy As String
  Dim StringLen As Long

  StringValCopy = IIf(UTF8Encode, UTF16To8(StringVal), StringVal)
  StringLen = Len(StringValCopy)

  If StringLen > 0 Then
    ReDim Result(StringLen) As String
    Dim I As Long, CharCode As Integer
    Dim Char As String, Space As String

    If SpaceAsPlus Then Space = "+" Else Space = "%20"

    For I = 1 To StringLen
    Char = Mid$(StringValCopy, I, 1)
    CharCode = Asc(Char)
    Select Case CharCode
      Case 97 To 122, 65 To 90, 48 To 57, 45, 46, 95, 126
      Result(I) = Char
      Case 32
      Result(I) = Space
      Case 0 To 15
      Result(I) = "%0" & Hex(CharCode)
      Case Else
      Result(I) = "%" & Hex(CharCode)
    End Select
    Next I
    URLEncode = Join(Result, "")
  End If
End Function
```

As you have seen, postal codes are not the only parameters that may be passed in by the calling code so `PostalCodeSearchAsync` goes on to concatenate whatever additional parameters are passed onto the URL string. These parameters include the maximum number of rows to return, the style of the XML requested, the operator to use, and so on. Then, the final parameter is the username of the account which was set up to consume the web service.

```
strParameters = strParameters & "maxRows=" & MaxRows & strJoin

Select Case Style
  Case gsShort
    strTmp = "style=FULL"
  Case gsMedium
    strTmp = "style=MEDIUM"
  Case gsLong
    strTmp = "style=LONG"
  Case gsFull
    strTmp = "style=FULL"
End Select
strParameters = strParameters & strTmp & strJoin

Select Case Operator
  Case gsAnd
    strTmp = "style=AND"
  Case gsOr
    strTmp = "style=OR"
End Select
strParameters = strParameters & strTmp & strJoin

If IsReduced Then
  strTmp = "isReduced=true"
Else
  strTmp = "isReduced=false"
End If
strParameters = strParameters & strTmp & strJoin

strParameters = strParameters & "username=bgclothier"
```

With the entire set of parameters ready, `PostalCodeSearchAsync` makes the call to the web service. The code opens the `objWinHTTP` object, which was previously set to `WinHttp.WinHttpRequest`, and sends a GET request to the web service, with the URI and parameters just created as follows:

```
With objWinHTTP
  .Open "GET", strURI & strParameters, bolASync
  .send
End With
```

And that is how the `PostalCodeSearchAsync` procedure sends off the call to the web service. The next step is to consume the results of that call. Because the request is done asynchronously, there is nothing else for you to do in the procedure. You'll use events to provide visual feedback to the user and receive the response.

Look at the `objWinHTTP_OnResponseStart` event handler. Within it, you initialize the combo box to provide visual feedback to the users that the web service is being executed. You can see that the combo box is locked, its `RowSource` is cleared, and the string `Loading...` is put in the combo box so the user knows that it's working in background.

```
Private Sub objWinHTTP_OnResponseStart( _
  ByVal Status As Long, _
  ByVal ContentType As String _
```

```
)
  lngErrorNumber = 0
  strErrorDescription = vbNullString

  If Not cboAddress Is Nothing Then
    With cboAddress
      If Not bolLoaded Then
        intOrigColumnCount = .ColumnCount
        strOrigColumnWidths = .ColumnWidths
        strOrigRowsourceType = .RowSourceType
        strOrigRowsource = .RowSource
      End If
      bolLoaded = True
      .ColumnCount = 1
      .ColumnWidths = vbNullString
      .RowSourceType = "Value List"
      .RowSource = strLoading
      .Value = strLoading
      .Locked = True
    End With
  End If
End Sub
```

Note that the `objWinHTTP_OnResponseFinished` event handler assumes that the returned data is in the form of an XML document. When `objWinHTTP` detects a response and raises this event, you read the content of `objWinHTTP.responseText` into a XML document, and then parse for the nodes in it and — as they are found — assign their values to respective variables. When that step completes, the variables are concatenated into a delimited string. When that string is complete, the result is put into the combo box's rowsource as follows in this code snippet:

```
Private Sub objWinHTTP_OnResponseFinished()
  Dim lngCount As Long
  Dim lngIterator As Long
  Dim lngField As Long
  Dim lngValue As Long
  Dim lngMax As Long
  Dim varZip As Variant

  Dim objNode As MSXML2.IXMLDOMNode
  Dim objNodes As MSXML2.IXMLDOMNodeList

  Dim strFields(1 To GeoNameColumns.[_Max] + 1)
  Dim strDescription As String

  Dim strPostalCode As String
  Dim strPlaceName As String
  Dim strCountryCode As String
  Dim strLatitude As String
  Dim strLongitude As String
  Dim strAdminCode1 As String
  Dim strAdminName1 As String
  Dim strAdminCode2 As String
  Dim strAdminName2 As String
```

```
Dim strAdminCode3 As String
Dim strAdminName3 As String

On Error GoTo ErrHandler

objDOMDoc.loadXML objWinHTTP.responseText
With objDOMDoc
   If .hasChildNodes Then
   Set objNode = .selectSingleNode("//totalResultsCount")
   lngResultsCount = CLng(objNode.Text)
   If lngResultsCount Then
     If Not objNode Is Nothing Then
       Set objNodes = .selectNodes("//code")
       If Not objNodes Is Nothing Then
         lngCount = objNodes.length - 1
         ReDim strResults(lngCount)
         For lngIterator = 0 To lngCount
           Set objNode = objNodes.nextNode
           With objNode
             strPostalCode = .selectSingleNode("postalcode").Text
             strPlaceName = .selectSingleNode("name").Text
             strCountryCode = .selectSingleNode("countryCode").Text
             strLatitude = .selectSingleNode("lat").Text
             strLongitude = .selectSingleNode("lng").Text
             strAdminCode1 = .selectSingleNode("adminCode1").Text
             strAdminName1 = .selectSingleNode("adminName1").Text
             strAdminCode2 = .selectSingleNode("adminCode2").Text
             strAdminName2 = .selectSingleNode("adminName2").Text
             strAdminCode3 = .selectSingleNode("adminCode3").Text
             strAdminName3 = .selectSingleNode("adminName3").Text

             If bolOrdinalPositionsValid Then
               For lngField = GeoNameColumns.[_Min] _
               To GeoNameColumns.[_Max]
                 lngValue = lngOrdinalPositions(lngField)
                 If lngValue > lngMax Then
                   lngMax = lngValue
                 End If
                 If lngValue Then
                   strFields(lngValue) = FieldName(lngField)
                 End If
               Next

               strDescription = vbNullString
               For lngField = 1 To lngMax
                 If Len(strFields(lngField)) Then
                  strDescription = strDescription & _
                   .selectSingleNode(strFields(lngField)).Text & " "
                 End If
               Next
               strDescription = Trim(strDescription)
             Else
               strDescription = _
                 strPostalCode & " " & _
                 strPlaceName & " " & _
```

```
                  "(" & strLatitude & "," & strLongitude & ") " & _
                  strAdminCode1 & ":" & strAdminName1 & " " & _
                  strAdminCode2 & ":" & strAdminName2 & " " & _
                  strAdminCode3 & ":" & strAdminName3 & " " & _
                  strCountryCode
              End If

              strResults(lngIterator) = _
                strPostalCode & ";" & _
                strDescription & ";" & _
                strPlaceName & ";" & _
                strCountryCode & ";" & _
                strLatitude & ";" & _
                strLongitude & ";" & _
                strAdminCode1 & ";" & _
                strAdminName1 & ";" & _
                strAdminCode2 & ";" & _
                strAdminName2 & ";" & _
                strAdminCode3 & ";" & _
                strAdminName3
            End With
          Next
        End If
      End If
    Else
      Erase strResults
    End If
  End If
End With
WizHook.SortStringArray strResults

If Not cboAddress Is Nothing Then
  With cboAddress
    If Not bolLoaded Then
      intOrigColumnCount = .ColumnCount
      strOrigColumnWidths = .ColumnWidths
      strOrigRowsourceType = .RowSourceType
      strOrigRowsource = .RowSource
    End If
    bolLoaded = True
    .ColumnCount = 12
    .ColumnWidths = "0"";;0"";0"";0"";0"";0"";0"";0"";0"";0"";0"""
    .RowSourceType = "Value List"
    .RowSource = Join(strResults, ";")
    If Len(.RowSource) Then
      .Locked = False
      If .Value = strLoading Then
        .Value = Null
      End If
    Else
      .ColumnCount = 1
      .ColumnWidths = vbNullString
      .RowSource = "No Results"
      .Value = "No Results"
      .Locked = True
```

```
      End If
    End With
  End If

ExitProc:
  On Error Resume Next
  If lngResultsCount = 1 Then
    cboAddress.Value = cboAddress.ItemData(0)
  Else
    If lngResultsCount Then
      cboAddress.Dropdown
    End If
  End If
  Exit Sub
ErrHandler:
  Select Case Err.Number
    Case Else
      VBA.MsgBox "Error " & Err.Number & " (" & Err.Description & ")"
  End Select
  Resume ExitProc
  Resume 'for Debugging
End Sub

Private Sub frmSource_Close()
  On Error GoTo ErrHandler

  Set cboAddress = Nothing
  Set txtZip = Nothing
  Set frmSource = Nothing

ExitProc:
  On Error Resume Next
  Exit Sub
ErrHandler:
  Select Case Err.Number
    Case Else
      VBA.MsgBox "Error " & Err.Number & " (" & Err.Description & ")"
  End Select
  Resume ExitProc
  Resume 'for Debugging
End Sub
```

When the event is raised, you typically have a response from the server contained in `responseText`, which, in this particular case, is an XML document. To make it easier for you to parse the document, you want to load it into the `MSXML.XMLDocument` object.

```
objDOMDoc.loadXML objWinHTTP.responseText
```

You need to probe into the XML document to determine the data you got back from the web server. Because it is possible to have errors, such as a badly formatted parameter, which isn't necessarily returned as an error on the HTTP stack but may be returned as an XML document indicating that there was an error in resolving the client request, you need to validate that there is no error. One way you can do this is to look for elements that are usually associated with a successful response.

One such element is `totalResultsCount`, which you can attempt to find in the XML document. If it's not found, you should assume there was an error and give up at this point:

```
With objDOMDoc
  If .hasChildNodes Then
    Set objNode = .selectSingleNode("//totalResultsCount")
    lngResultsCount = CLng(objNode.Text)
    If lngResultsCount Then
...
    End If
  End If
End With
```

Note the use of `selectSingleNode` method, which expects an XQuery expression. The leading `//` indicates that you want to search the entire document for any appearance of an element of the given name.

> **NOTE** *If you want to learn more about XQuery, which is how you query an XML document — similar to using SQL against a database — you can go to* `http://www.w3schools.com/xquery/` *for free online tutorials.*

Once you've verified that you have data contained within the XML document, you need to iterate over all `code` elements and extract the data out of each `code` element, like this:

```
If Not objNode Is Nothing Then
  Set objNodes = .selectNodes("//code")
  If Not objNodes Is Nothing Then
    lngCount = objNodes.length - 1
    ReDim strResults(lngCount)
    For lngIterator = 0 To lngCount
      Set objNode = objNodes.nextNode
...
    Next
  End If
End If
```

As you can see, you extract the individual element's text and assign it to a set of VBA strings.

```
With objNode
  strPostalCode = .selectSingleNode("postalcode").Text
  strPlaceName = .selectSingleNode("name").Text
  strCountryCode = .selectSingleNode("countryCode").Text
  strLatitude = .selectSingleNode("lat").Text
  strLongitude = .selectSingleNode("lng").Text
  strAdminCode1 = .selectSingleNode("adminCode1").Text
  strAdminName1 = .selectSingleNode("adminName1").Text
  strAdminCode2 = .selectSingleNode("adminCode2").Text
  strAdminName2 = .selectSingleNode("adminName2").Text
  strAdminCode3 = .selectSingleNode("adminCode3").Text
  strAdminName3 = .selectSingleNode("adminName3").Text
...
End With
```

You now have all the text of an individual ZIP code; you need to determine how the text should be assembled for the display on the combo box.

```
With objNode
...
  If bolOrdinalPositionsValid Then
    For lngField = GeoNameColumns.[_Min] To _
                   GeoNameColumns.[_Max]
      lngValue = lngOrdinalPositions(lngField)
      If lngValue > lngMax Then
        lngMax = lngValue
      End If
      If lngValue Then
        strFields(lngValue) = FieldName(lngField)
      End If
    Next

    strDescription = vbNullString
    For lngField = 1 To lngMax
      If Len(strFields(lngField)) Then
        strDescription = strDescription & _
          .selectSingleNode(strFields(lngField)).Text & " "
      End If
    Next
    strDescription = Trim(strDescription)
  Else
    strDescription = _
      strPostalCode & " " & _
      strPlaceName & " " & _
      "(" & strLatitude & "," & strLongitude & ") " & _
      strAdminCode1 & ":" & strAdminName1 & " " & _
      strAdminCode2 & ":" & strAdminName2 & " " & _
      strAdminCode3 & ":" & strAdminName3 & " " & _
      strCountryCode
  End If
...
End With
```

Whenever the `GeoName` class has a valid group of `OrdinalPositions` — for example, there are no duplicates — you can loop over the `OrdinalPositions` to put all the elements' names in correct sorting order, and then loop over the sorted array of strings to extract the text from each element in the desired order. When there is no valid `OrdinalPosition`, you fall back to a default so that the function always returns data, even if not formatted nicely.

```
strResults(lngIterator) = _
  strPostalCode & ";" & _
  strDescription & ";" & _
  strPlaceName & ";" & _
  strCountryCode & ";" & _
  strLatitude & ";" & _
  strLongitude & ";" & _
  strAdminCode1 & ";" & _
  strAdminName1 & ";" & _
```

```
        strAdminCode2 & ";" & _
        strAdminName2 & ";" & _
        strAdminCode3 & ";" & _
        strAdminName3
      End With
```

You then build up the combo box's rowsource for an individual ZIP code and add it to an array. You will later sort the string array before you concatenate it and display it in the combo box using the `Join()` function.

Once the loop finishes, you'll have an array of strings to which you can apply `WizHook.SortStringArray` to put it in correct order; then, the rest of the procedure alters the formatting and data properties of the combo box, making it available to the user.

It's time to sum up what has happened. After the necessary objects are set up and initialized by the class, the call to the web service is made using `PostalCodeSearchAsync`. When `PostalCodeSearchAsync` is invoked, it marshals the parameters needed to send a properly formatted URL as a GET to the site that hosts the Postal Code web service. As the document is being sent, `objWinHTTP_OnResponseStart` changes the combo box to show `Loading` as a visual feedback to the user. When the response comes back, `objWinHTTP_OnFinish` prepares the combo box and places the results in it.

In the next section, we show you how to use the functions in the class to set up a form to use these functions.

Using Form and Control Events Inside the GeoName Class

The `GeoName` class has three objects: `frmSource`, `txtZIP`, and `cboAddress`, which can receive events. Instead of writing code in each form where you want to use `GeoName`, you can allow `GeoName` to listen to the form and control events and act upon them, simplifying the process of adding `GeoName` functionality to any form.

Consider the event handler `frmSource_Current`, which is invoked whenever any form that has `GeoName` running fires its own Current event. It initializes the `cboAddress` control, and then calls to the AfterUpdate event of the ZIP code box on the same form. Note that this assumes `txtZIP` is populated with a valid ZIP code when it opens. If it is not, nothing happens. If it is, `txtZip_AfterUpdate` calls the web service via `PostalCodeSearchAsync`, passing the value of the ZIP textbox and the ISO Country code. The Country code was declared as US by default in the declarations, as you may recall.

The result is that whenever the form opens or moves to a record with a ZIP code passed to it, `GeoName` immediately calls the web service to get the corresponding location, as follows:

```
Private Sub frmSource_Current()
  If bolLoaded Then
    With cboAddress
      .ColumnCount = intOrigColumnCount
      .ColumnWidths = strOrigColumnWidths
      .RowSourceType = strOrigRowsourceType
      .RowSource = strOrigRowsource
      .Value = vbNullString
```

```
    End With
    bolLoaded = False
  End If
  txtZip_AfterUpdate
End Sub

Private Sub txtZip_AfterUpdate()
  If Len(txtZip & vbNullString) Then
    If Len(txtZip.Value) = lngExactPostalCodeLength Then
      PostalCodeSearchAsync _
        PostalCode:=txtZip.Value, _
        CountryISOCode:=strCountryISOCode, _
        MaxRows:=lngMaxRows
    Else
      PostalCodeSearchAsync _
        PostalCodeStartsWith:=txtZip.Value, _
        CountryISOCode:=strCountryISOCode, _
        MaxRows:=lngMaxRows
    End If
  Else
    If bolLoaded Then
      With cboAddress
        .ColumnCount = intOrigColumnCount
        .ColumnWidths = strOrigColumnWidths
        .RowSourceType = strOrigRowsourceType
        .RowSource = strOrigRowsource
        .Value = vbNullString
      End With
      bolLoaded = False
    End If
  End If
End Sub
```

Loading the Validation Form with a Predetermined Value

Now that you have the pieces, let's learn how to put them into forms. Code like this is placed in the ZIP code validation form. It declares `gn As GeoName` and sets it to a new instance of the `GeoName` class, which makes all of the events and properties of the class available. It also checks the value of `OpenArgs` for a ZIP code passed to the form when it opens. When you call it from the new customer form, that ZIP code should be passed for validation. If there is a ZIP code, it's immediately inserted into the ZIP textbox. When the ZIP code is inserted into the textbox, the call to `txtZIP_AfterUpdate` is made, and the combo box populates. Performance can be quite surprising. Often, the values in the combo box are available at the same time the form becomes visible. You may refer back to the previous discussion of `txtZIP_AfterUpdate` to refresh your memory of how it functions.

```
Private gn As GeoName

Private Sub Form_Load()
  Dim strOpenArgs As String

  Set gn = New GeoName
  With gn
```

```
      .DefaultMaxRows = 100
      .OrdinalPosition(PlaceName) = 1
      .OrdinalPosition(admincode1) = 2
      .OrdinalPosition(PostalCode) = 3
      .OrdinalPosition(AdminName2) = 4
      .OrdinalPosition(Country) = 0
      .OrdinalPosition(Latitude) = 0
      .OrdinalPosition(AdminName1) = 0
      .OrdinalPosition(AdminCode2) = 0
      .OrdinalPosition(AdminCode3) = 0
      .OrdinalPosition(AdminName3) = 0
      .AttachControls _
        Me.txtZipCode, _
        Me.cboAddresses
  End With

  ' check the passed ZIP by inserting in the ZIP field

   If Len(Me.OpenArgs & "") > 0 Then
    strOpenArgs = Me.OpenArgs
    Me.txtZipCode = strOpenArgs

  End If
End Sub

Private Sub cmdClose_Click()
  DoCmd.Close objecttype:=acForm, objectName:=Me.Name
End Sub
Private Sub cmdValidateZip_Click()
Dim varopenargs As Variant
On Error GoTo ErrHandler
varopenargs = Nz(Me.Zip, "00000")
DoCmd.OpenForm FormName:="frmValidateZIP", view:=acNormal, datamode:=acFormAdd,_
 windowmode:=acDialog, OpenArgs:=varopenargs
ExitProc:
  On Error Resume Next
  Exit Sub
ErrHandler:
  Select Case Err.Number
    Case Else
      VBA.MsgBox "Error " & Err.Number & " (" & Err.Description & ")"
  End Select
  Resume ExitProc
  Resume 'for Debugging

End Sub
```

The return from the validation form can be from either a Close button that merely closes the form after the validation, or from a Copy and Close button that carries City and State values determined by the web service back to the customer setup form. Here's the code for the `cmdCloseAndCopy` button's `Click` event, which is quite straightforward:

```
Private Sub cmdCloseAndCopy_Click()
  Dim strCity As String
  Dim strState As String
```

```
    ' if we got a result back from the web validation,
    ' and if the user asked to pass it back to the customer
    ' set up form do so.
    If Len(Me.cboAddresses.Column(1) & "") > 0 Then

      strCity = Me.cboAddresses.Column(2)
      strState = Me.cboAddresses.Column(6)

      Forms!frmNewCustomerValidation.txtCity = strCity
      Forms!frmNewCustomerValidation.txtState = strState
    End If

    DoCmd.Close objecttype:=acForm, objectName:=Me.Name
  End Sub
```

Now that you've learned how to use one highly useful web service, we're confident that you'll be encouraged to seek out others. Granted, the code is a bit outside of the mainstays of VBA we all commonly use, but you can easily see that it's just a matter of gaining familiarity with that code and finding appropriate web services.

SUMMARY

In this chapter, you discovered how you can make your Access web app considerably richer by adding functionalities via SharePoint and SharePoint Designer, and authoring custom pages.

You learned about security considerations that may be new to you if you are coming from client development, and you saw how to work with new restrictions when writing code and how to accommodate those restrictions such as allowing framing of pages and using JavaScript to access only contents from the same origin.

You then saw how SharePoint offers you a built-in development experience, enabling you to create new pages and add contents directly in your web browser without any additional tools. You used that information to add a third-party app into a custom page in your Access web app.

You then learned how to use SharePoint Designer to further edit the custom pages in the basic mode and assign a different master page to change the styling of your page. You also saw how you can enable inlining of your page by adding the `WebPartPages:AllowFraming` element to your page. You also learned how to add your custom pages that are not based on any templates provided by SharePoint, and consume the web services provided by your custom web pages within your Access web app.

You then learned how to upload and reference JavaScript libraries for your site, which provide you with an easy way to expand and store your custom JavaScript for reuse. You also learned how to use JavaScript to dynamically manipulate your custom page, enabling you to dynamically render an image or display a custom error message.

You saw how you can use SharePoint Documents as another connection between the site mailbox and your Access web apps, making it easier to share images and, more importantly, provide your users with an easy way to send images from their mobile devices without having to deal with possible incompatibility with their mobile browser.

Finally, you went deeper with JavaScript and used that to call APIs delivered by Google to render a chart to add a KPI indicator to your Access web app. If the chapter has whetted your appetite and you want to learn more, consider *Beginning SharePoint 2013 Development* by Steve Fox, Chris Johnson, and Donovan Follette (Wiley, 2013). As you saw in the chapter, mastering JavaScript and becoming comfortable with web services will considerably broaden your ability to build rich solutions. More important, you don't necessarily have to build everything from scratch when authoring custom pages, offering an easy way to develop even on the web.

You got to see how you can also use web services inside your `.accdb` file by using the `XMLHTTPRequest` object and VBA to perform a ZIP lookup, which demonstrates the power of web services for solving a problem that is not easily managed with a static copy of ZIP codes.

All in all, you should have a clear idea of what options are available to you whenever you need more than what Access web apps have to offer right out of the box, and how you can leverage those tools with your Access web apps to deliver a richer solution.

Now that you've looked at tools you can use to deliver richer interface with your web apps, you will definitely want to learn about what else you can do with data contained in the web app's database. In the next chapter you will look at options available to you for connecting to the data and using it directly.

11

Connecting to Your Web App

WHAT'S IN THIS CHAPTER?

- Discovering and acquiring connection details
- Creating a connected Access desktop database
- Managing connections
- Using Excel to connect to the database
- Using SQL Server Management Studio to connect to the database

WROX.COM DOWNLOADS FOR THIS CHAPTER

The code and sample downloads for this chapter are found at `www.wiley.com/go/proaccess2013prog.com` on the Download Code tab. They are in the Chapter 11 download and individually named according to the filenames listed throughout the chapter. The app packages for the web apps in this chapter are called Maid to Order and Maid to Order Customer.

In this chapter, you learn about using other tools to enrich the web app you've developed. In preceding chapters, you've seen how the new approach to web app design enables you to build a rich and beautiful CRUD application, but you know that Access applications are not always simply CRUD applications. Microsoft recognizes the need to work with data beyond simple CRUD and has incorporated a built-in mechanism in web apps to allow you to not only use traditional Access desktop databases against the web app's database but also to use Excel, SQL Server Management Studio, and any other tool where ODBC connections are supported.

You start by learning how to get all the connection details you need to complete an ODBC connection string, after which you will learn how to use that string to connect to different ODBC clients.

After that, you will look at the familiar method of linking an Access desktop database to a remote database. You will learn how to apply best practices, accounting for differences in how you can manage objects within either an Access desktop database or SQL Server objects created by web apps.

You will then see how you can use Excel to provide a live view of the data using Office Data Connection (ODC, not to be confused with OD*B*C). This will provide you with an easy way to create charts and pivot tables for reporting. You will learn about keeping data refreshed in those workbooks and consider trust and sharing issues associated with using an Excel spreadsheet with an ODC connection.

You will finish your introduction by using the connection string in SQL Server Management Studio, creating a linked server object to make querying against the database easier. That enables you to integrate your existing SQL Server database with the web app's database objects.

> **NOTE** *A list of some of the potential issues you may encounter while working with Access web apps is available in the "What You Need to Use this Book" section of the Introduction.*

INFO BACKSTAGE

One of the new features in Access web apps is the addition of connection information for your web app as shown in Figure 11-1.

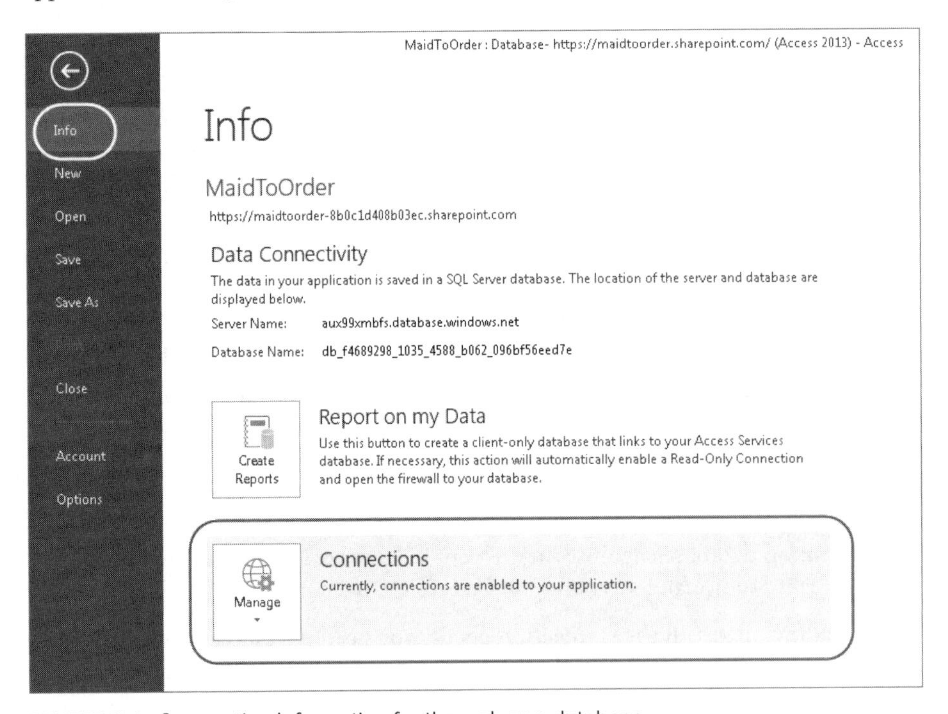

FIGURE 11-1: Connection Information for the web app database

The Info Backstage displays the name of your web app, the name of the server where it is located, and the name of the database itself. Take note that the database name is a long string of random characters, a GUID with a prefix.

There are two important actions you can take here. First, you can create a reporting version — an `.accdb` file — of your web app. Let's examine that now.

The result of clicking Report on My Data is an `.accdb` file, as shown in Figure 11-2. The resulting client database will be connected directly to your web app's tables. You can generate reports using the powerful Access reporting engine. However, your UserID and Password will be saved in the connection string, which may not be desirable. As you can see in Figure 11-2, including the configured `MSysConf` table in your database prevents saving the connection information. If you have the `MSysConf` table, or if a policy in your organization prohibits storing passwords, you will see a log in dialog, as shown in Figure 11-2. You'll learn more about the `MSysConf` table in Chapter 13.

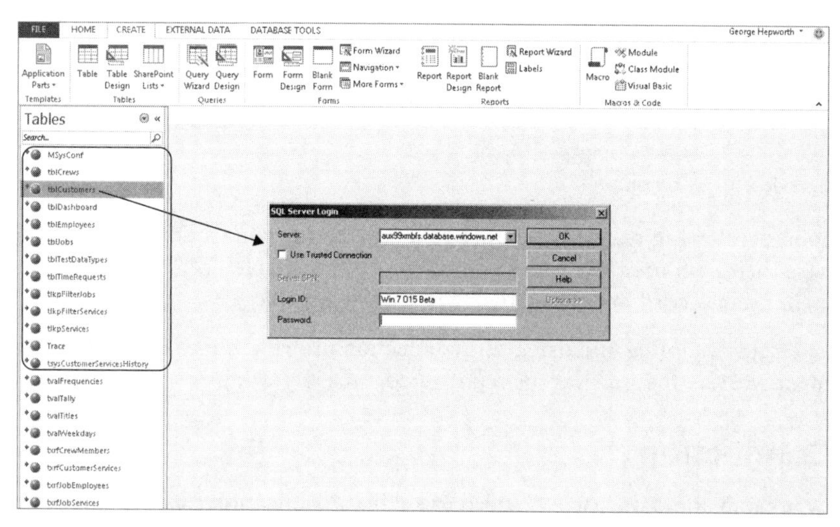

FIGURE 11-2: Reporting `.accdb` ready for connection to the web app database

You'll learn more about the `MSysConf` table in Chapter 13.

At this point, you may supply the login ID and password to complete the connection, if needed, and begin using the reporting database, so let's step back to the web app's Info Backstage, as shown in Figure 11-1, and learn how to manage that.

CONNECTIONS

When you first create the web app, external connections are not enabled. You enable them by clicking the other button, Manage Connections, in the Info backstage. That opens the connections page, as shown in Figure 11-3.

Here you manage connections to the web app database from external applications, such as Excel, Access, and SSMS. Note that you can allow connections either from only your current location or from any location. You choose an option depending on how the database will be used — by a single person or multiple persons at multiple locations.

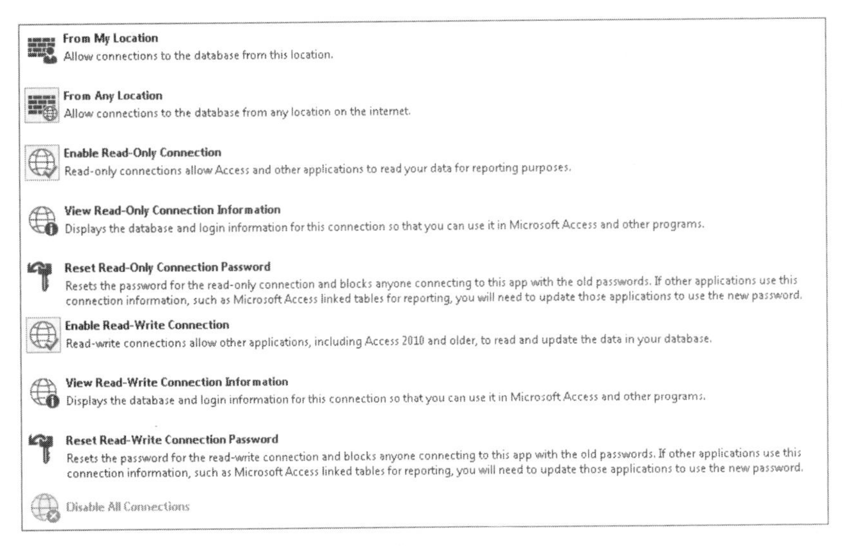

FIGURE 11-3: Connections page for web apps

Next, you have the option of allowing read-only connections, read-write connections, or both. Both types of connections have their own user ID and password so you can enable both and select which one to provide to different users according to how they will use the database.

In the next sections, we discuss enabling and using this connection information to connect to the web app database from an `.accdb` file, such as the reporting database.

Enable/Disable Connection

In order to connect to your web app database, you need to enable a connection to it. You do that by selecting the type of permissions you want to give, and then enabling one or both of the read-only or read-write options. Refer back to Figure 11-2. The pale pink rectangles around "From any Location," "Enable Read-Only Connection," and "Enable Read-Write Connection" indicate those options have been selected.

> **WARNING** *Each time you toggle one of the Enable Connections buttons, you reset the password associated with that option. For example, when you toggle the Enable Read-Only Connection on, the web app generates a password for the ExternalReader login. Toggling the Enable Read-Only Connection off, and then back on again, generates a new password for the ExternalReader.*
>
> *This seems like logical behavior. However, it can have unintended and negative consequences. If you have created an* `.accdb` *file for reporting purposes, and created a relinking method that depends on the original password, merely toggling the Enable Read-Only Connection off and on creates a different password that the reporting database won't have available. Your users would not be able to connect to the web app database, and may not have any idea what went wrong. Exercise caution and plan ahead to avoid problems like this.*

Getting Connection Details

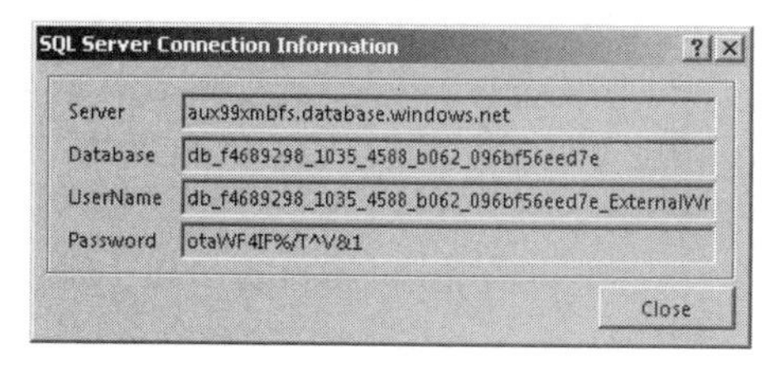

FIGURE 11-4: Connection Information for the MTO database

Figure 11-4 shows the connection information for the read-write user, called ExternalWriter (as opposed to ExternalReader). As you saw in Figure 11-3, you get this information by clicking the appropriate link for either the Read-Only user or the Read-Write user.

You might want to copy the connection information for your web app database into a text file so you can refer to it more easily when working with other external files, such as Access, Excel, or SSMS. You can always get to it through the Info Backstage page, but that takes several steps. Just be sure to treat that text file with appropriate caution. It contains everything anyone needs to connect directly to your web app database.

Reset Passwords

As noted, initially setting passwords is a matter of enabling the appropriate user. In addition, you can manually reset passwords by clicking the appropriate Reset buttons, as Figure 11-3 shows. You can also see that the Reset Password buttons include an explanation of the consequences of resetting a password, which applies to the silent reset caused by toggling the enabled status of the connection.

Now that you've seen how the web app supports external connections, you'll work through a couple of examples of using them, starting with the Access client.

USING THE ACCESS CLIENT

In this section, you learn how to connect to and use the database to which your web app connects from an Access client database. You just learned how to obtain the necessary connection information from the Info Backstage. This is one place you'll use that connection information. In this case, you'll create a small `.accdb` file for reporting. You'll use the Maid To Order database and create a report showing revenues generated by each crew during a given time period.

You can connect to your web app database from Access 2003, 2007, 2010, or 2013. Whichever Access version you use, however, you need to use the SQL Native Client 11.0 driver. The 11.0 driver is not supported on Windows XP. Using older SQL Server Native Client drivers may be possible but is not optimal. If you don't have SQL Server 2012 installed on your computer, you can download just the Native Client from the *Microsoft SQL Server 2012 Feature Pack*, which is located at `http://www.microsoft.com/en-us/download/details.aspx?id=29065` at the time of this writing.

The download page links to many other SQL Server tools, and to both 32-bit and 64-bit versions of those tools. Make sure you select the proper version for your OS: use the X86 Package (*sqlncli .msi*) for 32-bit operating systems, or the X64 Package (*sqlncli.msi*) for 64-bit operating systems. Download and install the SQL Native Client 11.0 driver you need from the download page for this exercise. A common mistake is to download the 32-bit driver for a 64-bit operating system on the assumption that you would only be running 32-bit Access. In fact, the 64-bit driver includes the 32-bit driver needed for 32-bit programs, including Access, to run on a 64-bit operating system.

Start by creating an `.accdb` file. You can do this from within the web app, the results of which are illustrated in Figure 11-2, or you can create a new `.accdb` file from scratch. The advantage of using the internal option, Create Reports, is that it inserts the links to the tables for you, although you still need to provide the connection string to use them.

You'll link this Access file to the web app database. In this demo, you'll start by creating a DSN to make the initial connection from a new empty `.accdb`. file Later, you learn how to convert the connection to a DSN-less connection for improved security.

If you have already installed the SQL Native Client 11.0 driver, you can either create the DSN using the ODBC Data Sources tool from the Windows control panel, or create the DSN within Access. You'll create this demo from within Access, using the 2013 version, even though in testing we have successfully created connections from within Access 2003, 2007, 2010, and 2013, and on both 32-bit and 64-bit versions of Windows 7, and Windows 8.

Use the ODBC Link icon in the Import & Link section of the ribbon as you would to connect to any remote database. In fact, except for the connection information, the process is already familiar to you. Let's pick up the process at the first place you may need to diverge from previous practice. We have found that trying to create a File DSN doesn't work. You'll need to create the DSN as a Machine Data Source, as in Figure 11-5.

There are some differences in behavior at this point, depending on whether you are using Access 2013 or Access 2010. If you start Access under Run as Administrator credentials, you will have the choice between User and System Data Sources. Under Access 2013, if you don't have Administrator privileges, you can create the System DSN, but it may not actually connect, although the User DSN will connect. Under Access 2010 and earlier you can create only a User Data Source for yourself.

Next, select the SQL Native Client 11.0, as shown in Figure 11-6.

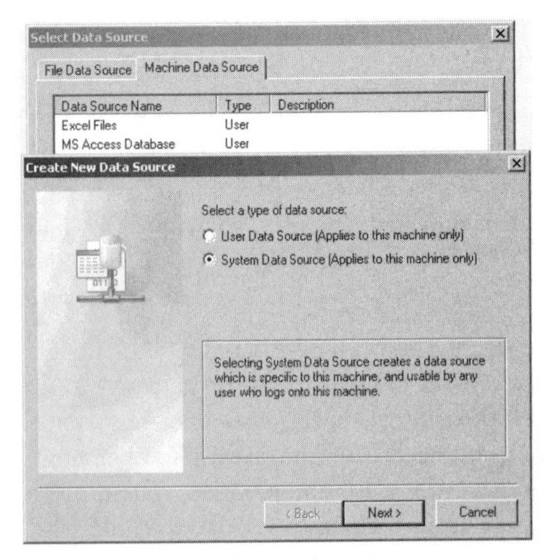

FIGURE 11-5: Create a System Data Source

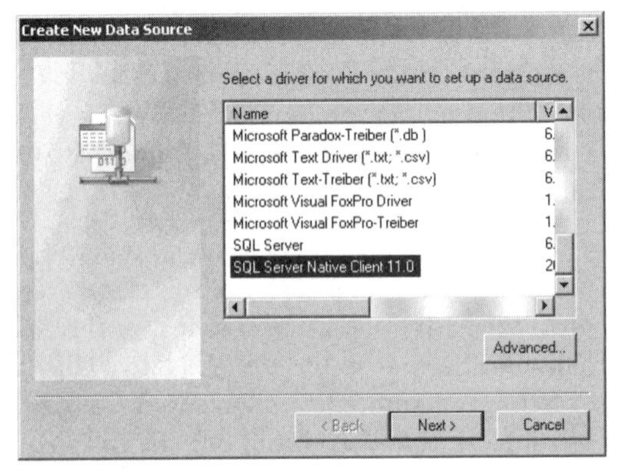

FIGURE 11-6: Select SQL Server Native Client 11.0

Clicking Next moves you to the next step in the wizard, where you'll start entering the connection information you previously obtained and saved from the connections section of the Info Backstage (see Figure 11-7).

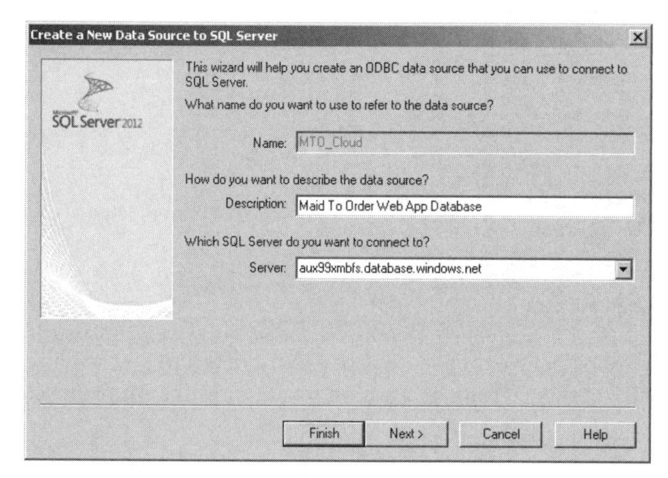

FIGURE 11-7: Enter a name and select the server.

Of course, you'll select SQL Authentication and enter the user login and password for the web app database (see Figure 11-8).

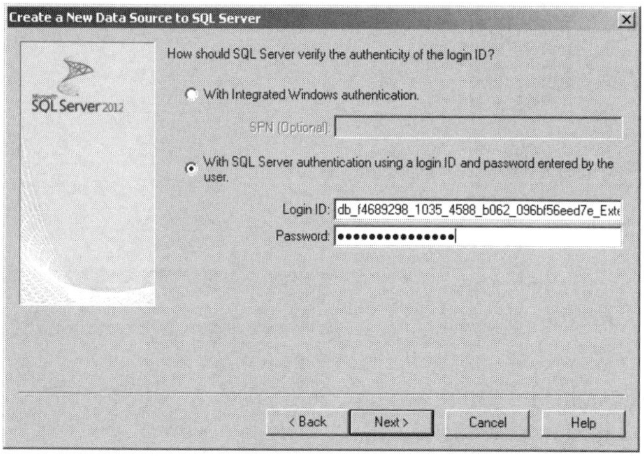

FIGURE 11-8: Login ID and password for the web app database

The next step is to select the web app database (see Figure 11-9).

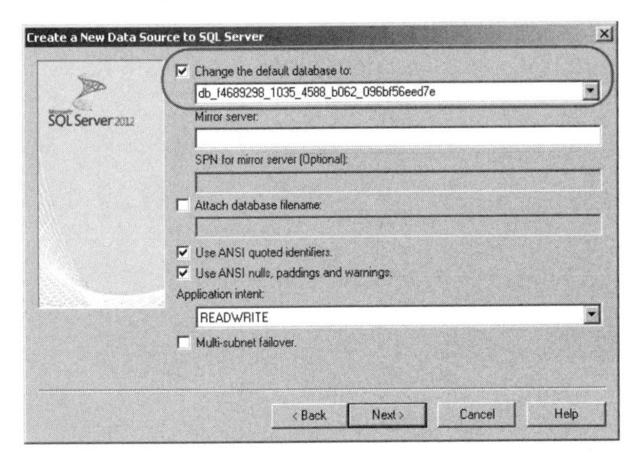

FIGURE 11-9: Enter the name of the web app database

The next step, again, is much like you've done before, but there is one extra detail to pay attention to. As shown in Figure 11-10, it's important to use strong encryption for data. Make sure you select the checkbox.

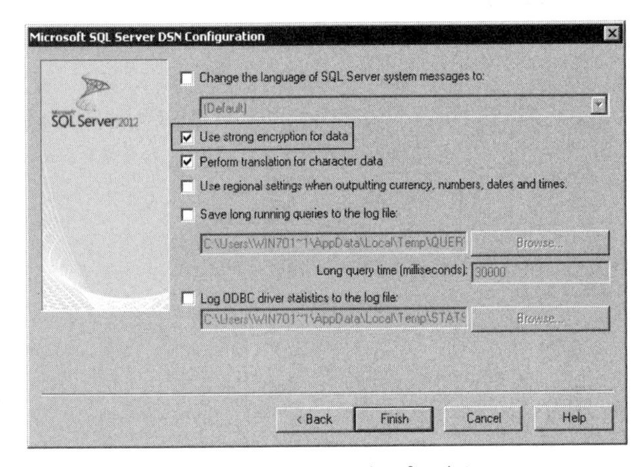

FIGURE 11-10: Use strong encryption for data

Clicking Finish completes the setup. You can verify the connection is complete by testing the connection, as shown in Figure 11-11.

At this point, your connection is complete and you can select tables from the web app database to link into your Access application. We assume you've had previous experience connecting to SQL Server from Access, so let's concentrate on the connection information. Select the DSN you just created, as shown in Figure 11-12.

The next step is to enter the appropriate password. In this case, you want to use the ExternalWriter Login, so you select the ExternalWriter password, as shown in Figure 11-13.

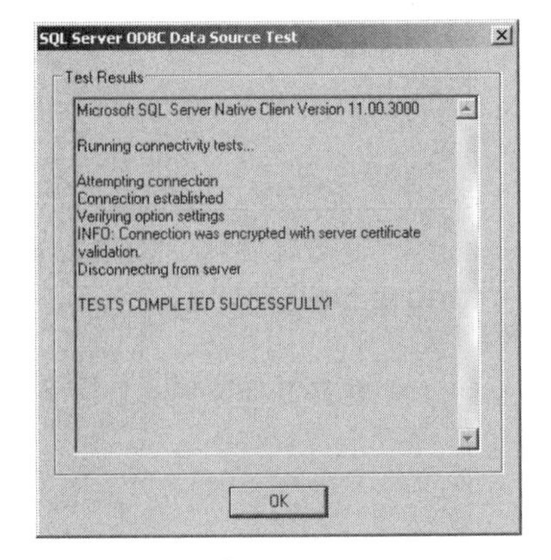

FIGURE 11-11: Success

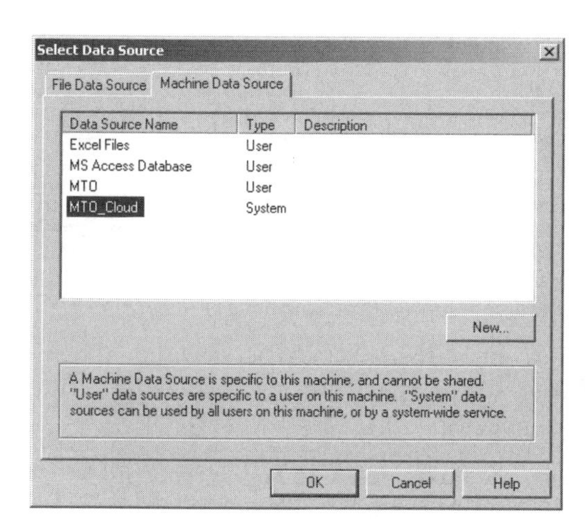

FIGURE 11-12: Select the web app DSN

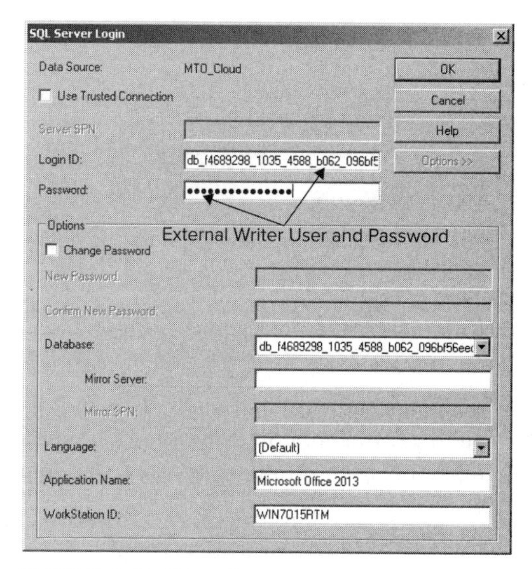

FIGURE 11-13: Enter the appropriate password

From here, you select all of the tables you need to create a local reporting tool for your web app. Proceed as you do with other SQL Server links. Figure 11-14 shows a couple of things that may not be familiar to you. First, the schema from which you'll link the tables is the `Access` schema, not the more common `dbo` schema with which you may be familiar.

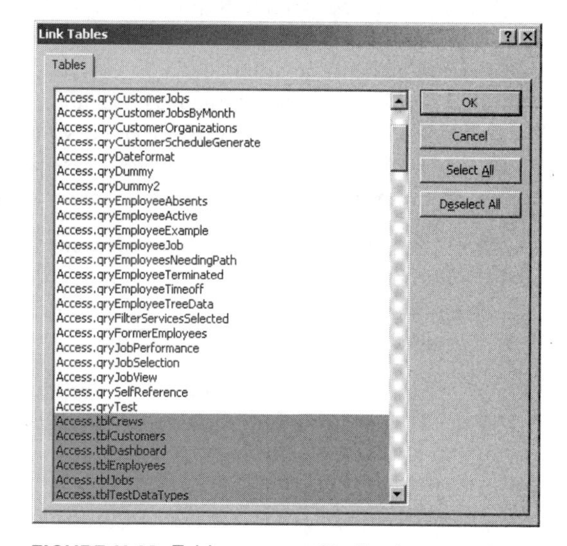

FIGURE 11-14: Tables exposed in the Access schema

Also, note that you do not link any of the queries (or views) from the web app database for our purposes here; they're designed for the web app. You could, if you wanted, go back to the web app and create additional queries to support reporting. These queries would be created as views on the web app database. You could then connect to those specific views for the reporting database. For better performance, you might wish to do that in some cases. Once again, your experience as an Access developer will guide your decision.

With the tables linked from your web app database, you can create as many reports as you need. In the next section you'll build a small example. The form shown in Figure 11-15 is typical of report launcher forms found in simple Access databases.

Clicking Show Report launches the report shown in Figure 11-16.

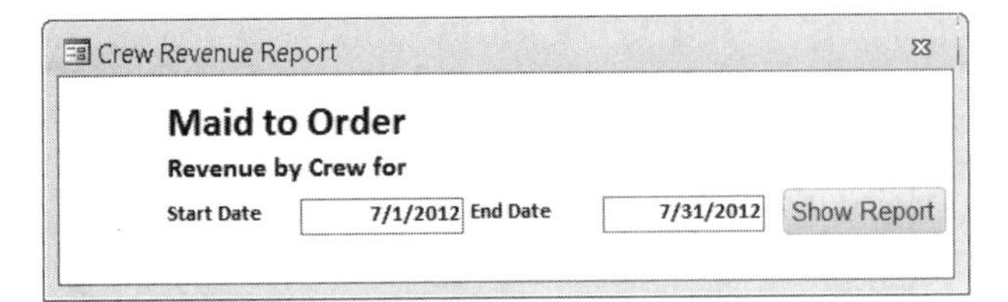

FIGURE 11-15: Report launch form in the Access reporting database

Maid to Order

Revenue by Crew for Time Period 7/1/2012 Through 7/31/2012

	Crew Leader	Sum of Fees
Crew #01	Elnora Leclaire	$25,271.00
Crew #02	Clinton Beverlin	$24,557.00
Crew #03	Margery Couvillion	$29,664.00
Crew #04	Allan Debonis	$23,841.00

FIGURE 11-16: Local Access Report using data from the web app database

Although the form and report shown in Figures 11-15 and 11-16 are very basic, they should serve as an illustration of how you can extend the reach of your web app databases to provide full-featured reporting in the familiar Access client database environment.

In the next section, you take a closer look at managing the linking of your Access reporting database in different ways.

Adding VBA Code to Relink

When you use the Create Reports feature, a nice thing about the client file it creates is that it uses a DSN-less connection string. However, it uses the ExternalReader user. If you had used that option to create a client `.accdb` instead of following the steps discussed in the previous section, you may find it necessary to switch the user to the ExternalWriter to enable update capability in the Access client — you can't use the Linked Table Manager because it works only with DSN connections. Even if you followed the previous steps to create your file from scratch, you need to be able to update the connection string easily in case there's a server move or a password reset.

There are many different ways to solve the problem of successfully connecting to the database behind the web app, some more complex than others. However, we want you to pay special attention to the elements required to implement a DSN-less option to the process you saw in the previous section.

We'll start out using one of the more commonly known solutions posted on the Internet by Access MVP Doug J. Steele for relinking tables using DSN-less connections.

> **NOTE** *The complete code sample for Doug's DSN-less connection string can be found at* `http://www.accessmvp.com/djsteele/DSNLessLinks.html`.
>
> *Also check out the DSN stripping utility written by Paul Litwin at* `http://access.mvps.org/access/modules/mdl0064.htm`.
>
> *Additionally, you can download the complete code samples in the file* `ch11_mdlODBCConnection.bas` *at* `www.wiley.com/go/proaccess2013prog.com`.

> **WARNING** *As Doug notes, this code assumes that all linked tables are still available in the source database. If a table is not found in the source database when the re-link is attempted, it will drop that* `tabledef` *from the local database. Therefore, it is important that you pass in valid server, database, user ID, and password values to avoid unintentionally deleting a link.*

In response to feedback from others, Steele added the ability to update passthrough queries in addition to linked tables to his code so that all tables and queries would function correctly when the connection string needs to be changed. This will be helpful when you have a number of passthrough queries.

The SQL Server ODBC driver was used as the driver in the original code sample:

```
strConnectionString = "ODBC;DRIVER={sql server};" & _
        "DATABASE=" & DatabaseName & ";" & _
        "SERVER=" & ServerName & ";" & _
        "UID=" & UID & ";" & _
        "PWD=" & PWD & ";"
```

Generally speaking, this is a good thing because the older SQL Server ODBC driver is already installed and widely available on different versions of Windows. However, for this scenario, you must use the newer SQL Server Native Client 11.0. Therefore, update the code to use the Native Client driver and pass in additional options. The code is also included in the `MTOClient.accdb` file available for download.

```
strConnectionString = "ODBC;DRIVER=SQL Server Native Client 11.0;" & _
  "SERVER=" & ServerName & ";" & _
  "DATABASE=" & DatabaseName & ";" & _
  "Trusted_Connection=No;" & _
  "Encrypted=yes;" & _
  "UID=" & UID & ";" & _
  "PWD=" & PWD & ";"
```

You can also see the additional argument to create an encrypted connection. The other change you need to make is to comment out the following line:

```
tdfCurrent.Attributes = typNewTables(intLoop).Attributes
```

Those two changes are all you need to apply to Doug's DSN-less connection string. You may find it necessary to further adapt the rest of the routine if you need to use a trusted connection with a different SQL Server, but we will not get into that alternative here.

You may be wondering why you should comment out the Attributes line and thus not save the password. The answer is that you want to have the user supply the password as a part of the application's startup. Access can cache the connection string so it is not necessary to store full details in the connection strings for all linked objects. Whenever possible, Access will try to reuse an existing connection that has similar parameters, such as driver, server, and database. This is true regardless of whether you're talking about a linked table or a passthrough query.

Therefore, you will execute VBA code as part of the application's startup to establish the initial connection, using the complete details. This code would be called either by the AutoExec macro or by the startup form's module, according to your preferences. The code simply needs to create a temporary `querydef` to make the initial connection; once its job is done, that `querydef` is discarded at the end of the procedure. The following function in the `MTOClient.accdb` shows how to do that:

```
Public Function InitConnect( _
  ServerName As String, _
  DatabaseName As String, _
  UserName As String, _
  Password As String, _
  FixConnectionsFlag As Boolean _
) As Boolean
' Description:  Should be called in the application's startup
'               to ensure that Access has a cached connection
'               for all other ODBC objects' use.
On Error GoTo ErrHandler
  Dim strConnectionString As String
  Dim dbCurrent As DAO.Database
  Dim qdf As DAO.QueryDef
  Dim rst As DAO.Recordset

  strConnectionString = "ODBC;DRIVER=SQL Server Native Client 11.0;" & _
    "SERVER=" & ServerName & ";" & _
    "DATABASE=" & DatabaseName & ";" & _
    "Trusted_Connection=No;" & _
    "Encrypted=yes;" & _
    "UID=" & UserName & ";" & _
    "PWD=" & Password & ";"

  Set dbCurrent = CurrentDb
  Set qdf = dbCurrent.CreateQueryDef("")

  With qdf
    .Connect = strConnectionString
    .SQL = "SELECT @@OPTIONS;"
    Set rst = .OpenRecordset(dbOpenSnapshot, dbFailOnError Or dbSQLPassThrough)
  End With

  If FixConnectionsFlag Then
    FixConnections ServerName, DatabaseName, UserName, Password
  End If
  InitConnect = True

ExitProcedure:
  On Error Resume Next
    Set rst = Nothing
    Set qdf = Nothing
    Set dbCurrent = Nothing
  Exit Function
ErrHandler:
```

```
    InitConnect = False
    MsgBox Err.Description & " (" & Err.Number & ") encountered", _
      vbOKOnly + vbCritical, "InitConnect"
    Resume ExitProcedure
    Resume
  End Function
```

When the linked tables already have correct connection strings, there is no need to fix the connection, so during startup you may determine that there is no change to the connection string and thus pass in `False` to `FixConnectionsFlag` to simply establish a connection. Regardless of whether `InitConnect` invokes the `FixConnections` procedure, no passwords are actually saved in the process, and at the end of `InitConnect`, there is no password to be discovered. Note that the connection string used in the `InitConnect` procedure mirrors the one that is used in the revised `FixConnections` procedure, with the addition of a user ID and password. Access is able to match the connection strings in linked tables and passthrough queries with the cached connection opened via the `InitConnect` procedure.

Of course, you still have to consider how you can safely store the username and password. We address this in Chapter 13 when we talk about security.

Best Practices

We want to list a few rules of thumb that will help ensure that your client applications function effectively in most scenarios.

Binding Reports to Passthrough Queries

Reports typically are quite complex, requiring multiple tables, and almost always need different ways to facilitate different user-specified filters. Access is smart enough to try and marshal as much of that work back to the server as it can, but sometimes you ask Access to do something that cannot be resolved into standard SQL and thus end up forcing Access to perform additional work when it could have been processed on the server.

Passthrough queries are your best bet for guaranteeing server-side processing. Because reports are read-only by definition, there is no problem with using a passthrough query, which as you know, is read-only. As discussed earlier, using a revised version of Steele's `FixConnections` procedure takes care of maintaining the passthrough queries' connection strings. Using passthrough queries also means you are free to use T-SQL's specific constructs, enabling you to leverage more functionality for your reporting than what you'd have to build yourself in Access.

Often, you will want to parameterize your passthrough queries. There is no built-in support for using parameters in passthrough queries; you must construct a SQL string with the literal values representing your parameterization for a specific invocation of the report. You may want to use tools such as J Street Tech's SQL Tools or FMS's Visual CodeTools to help with manipulating the SQL string.

> **NOTE** *You can get SQL Tools at* www.jstreettech.com/downloads *and buy FMS's Visual CodeTools at* www.fmsinc.com/microsoft access/VBACodingTools.html.

Binding Only One Data Source Per Form

When working with bound forms, which is Access's forté after all, it is good practice to link them to a single table, or a query based on a single table. Among the reasons for this, as you know, is to help ensure that the recordset in the form is updateable. Another consideration is the ability to limit records returned in a recordset to the smallest possible number to minimize performance hits. If you do need to populate a form with a more complex query with multiple joins, or with in-line functions, it is best to create a query specifically for that purpose in your web app, even though it won't be used by the web app itself. This allows you to link to this query in your client database, which should provide the best performance results.

Adding a Web Browser Control to Forms and Access Web Views

Introduced in Access 2010, the web browser control is another powerful tool to bring web pages directly into your Access database. In Chapter 4, you learned how to use the web browser control to enrich your web apps. You can also use them in your Access database. We want to identify this as one way to eliminate the need to switch back and forth from the web to the local database while you are working with the database. While creating reports in your Access database, you can keep a form open with the web app running for ready reference, rather than switch over to the browser. Consider Figure 11-17, where the Maid To Order web app is running in a web browser control embedded in a form.

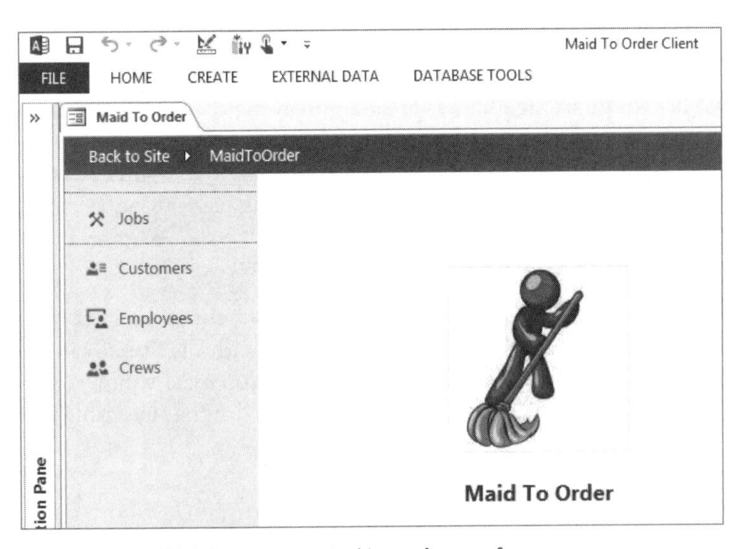

FIGURE 11-17: Web browser control in an Access form

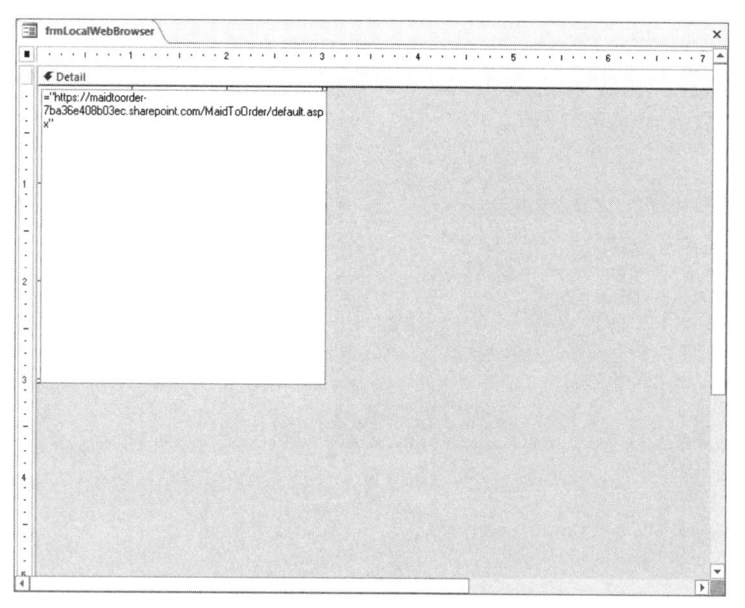

FIGURE 11-18: Static URL for a web browser control

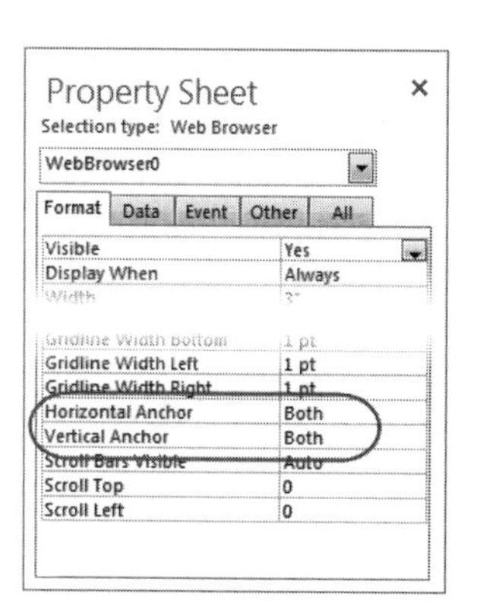

FIGURE 11-19: Property Sheet with anchoring properties

It's very simple to create a web browser control like this. Open the form in design view. Select the web browser control on the ribbon and draw the web browser control on the form. A static URL, like the one shown Figure 11-18, can be entered directly into the property sheet for the web browser.

Note that you don't have to bother with sizing the web browser. Simply set the Horizontal Anchor and Vertical Anchor properties shown in Figure 11-19 to allow it to resize automatically to fill up the form's space.

Furthermore, you can provide additional instructions, directing the web browser to load a specific view, and you can do this easily by taking note of the URL when you visit a view. For example, if you're on a view for Customers, the web browser's URL will show the following:

```
https://maidtoorder-7ba36e408b03ec.sharepoint.com/MaidToOrder/default.aspx#Tile=tbl
Customers&View=frmCustomersByName
```

In Chapter 4, you learned about query string parameters. There are two that are relevant: the Tile and the View, which represent the selected tile and view, respectively. You can supply the name of the tile and view as a parameter for your web browser by clicking the build button for the Control Source property, as shown in Figure 11-20, and the built-in HyperLink Builder helps make it easy. You could assign other Access controls or use VBA to change parameters at run time.

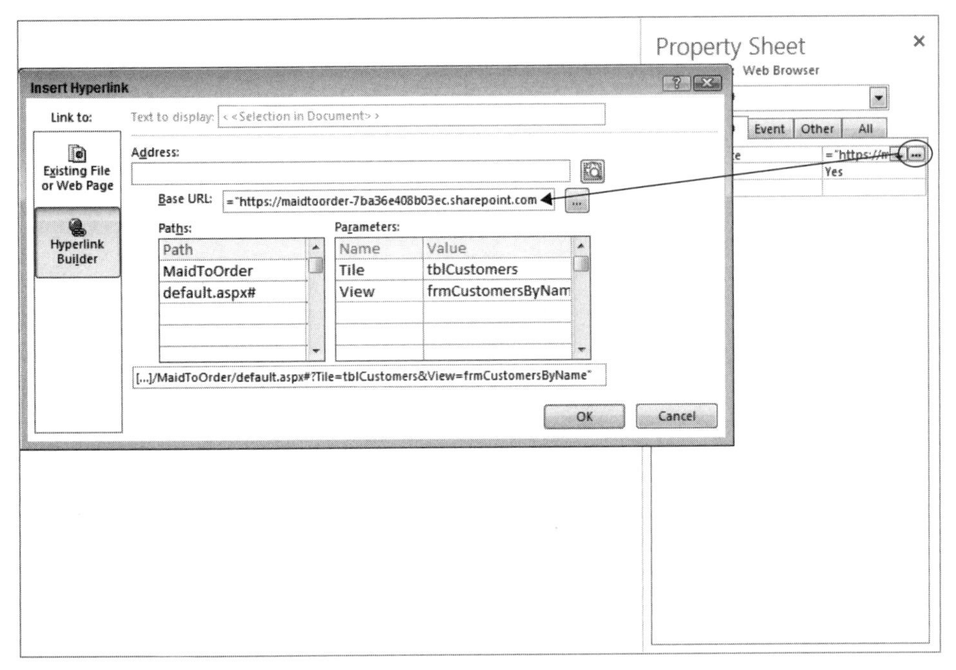

FIGURE 11-20: Parameterizing a web browser

While the focus in this chapter is on connecting to your web app from other applications, you can see that web browser control can be of substantial value even in a client database and not just for viewing web objects. That offers the same possibilities, such as a dynamic Bing map for customers' addresses. Refer back to Chapter 4 for a refresher.

USING EXCEL

Since Office 2007, Excel has had the capability to connect to various data sources and provide a live view of the data, which is a huge advantage when you need the output to be current and when you don't want to have to rebuild charts every time they are run. The code-less approach with Excel's ODC connection makes it very easy and timesaving to maintain complex charts and numeric-centric reports. You will start learning about creating an ODC connection and then see how it can be used for a variety of objects within an Excel spreadsheet for easy reporting.

Creating an ODC Connection

To get started, open Excel and use a blank worksheet. On the ribbon in Excel, select Data tab and choose Get External Data to get to the Data Connection Wizard, as shown in Figure 11-21.

> **WARNING** *Don't choose SQL Server. As shown in Figure 11-21, you need to use the connection wizard because you need to access advanced properties for the connection to succeed.*

> **NOTE** *If the data source buttons are disabled, you may need to set the focus on the cell in the Excel spreadsheet to enable the selection.*

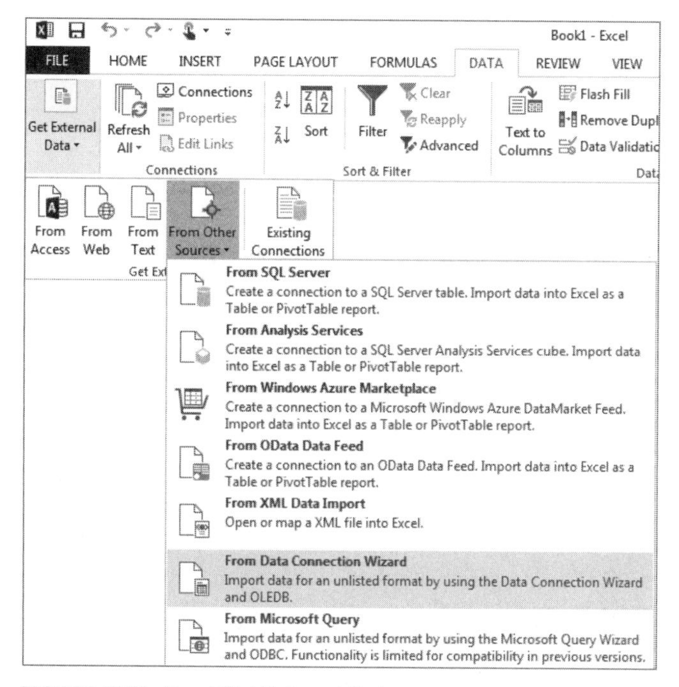

FIGURE 11-21: Excel Get External Data

The Data Connection Wizard will provide you with a list of providers. You want to choose Other/Advanced, as in Figure 11-22, and proceed to the next page. Although other options, including ODBC DSN, are listed, we are focusing on creating the ODC connection for this example.

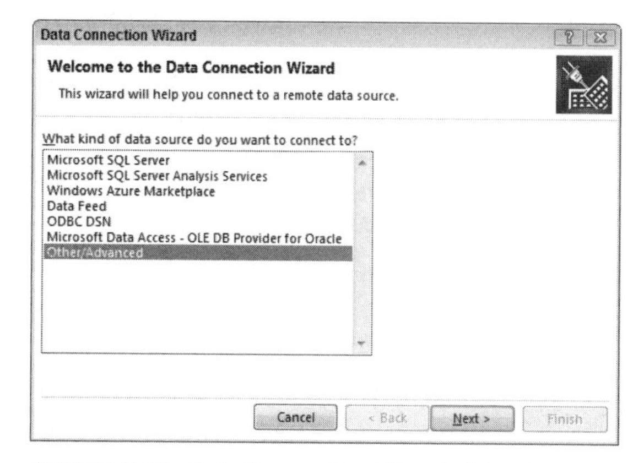

FIGURE 11-22: Data Connection Wizard dialog box

Next, select SQL Server Native Client 11.0; you may need to scroll down to locate it, as shown in Figure 11-23.

Clicking the Next button will take you to the Connection tab. There, provide the server name, specify SQL Server authentication, and supply the username and password. You should also input the database name. Figure 11-24 shows how it would look after you fill in the needed data.

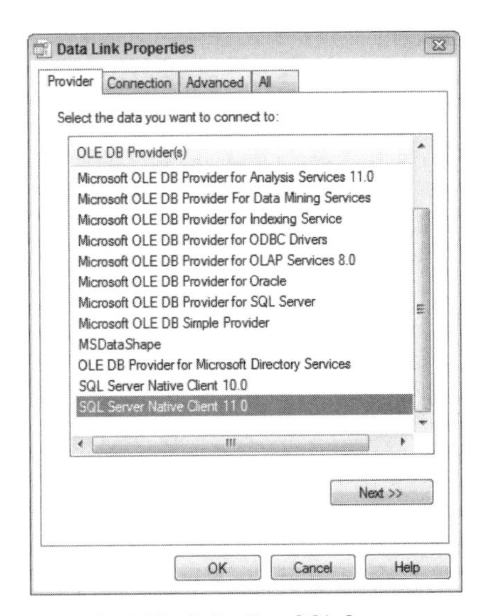

FIGURE 11-23: Selecting SQL Server Native Client 11.0

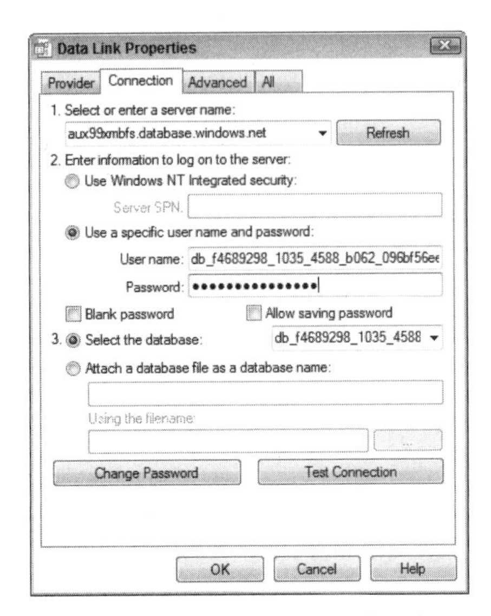

FIGURE 11-24: Filling in connection data

> **NOTE** *By default, Blank Password in Figure 11-24 is checked. Clear the checkbox to enable the Password field.*

Once you're done filling in the connection data, you can optionally test the connection using the Test Connection button shown in Figure 11-24. Finally, click OK to finish the process. The SQL Server client may then present a dialog box. If you do get the dialog box shown in Figure 11-25, simply clear Use Trusted Connection, provide the appropriate username and password if not already supplied, and click OK.

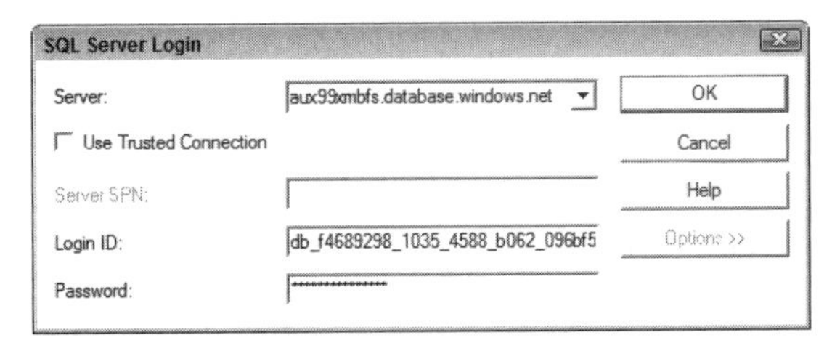

FIGURE 11-25: SQL Server client login

You will be presented with a list of tables to select from. However, you want to reuse the connection so you avoid selecting specific tables by clearing the Connect to a specific table checkbox, as in Figure 11-26.

Clicking Next takes you to the last page where you describe how the file should be named and other descriptive properties. Those are optional but it's usually a good idea to provide a meaningful name — one you'll remember, or at least recognize — and description to aid in reusing the ODC file. Figure 11-27 shows you how it may be filled out.

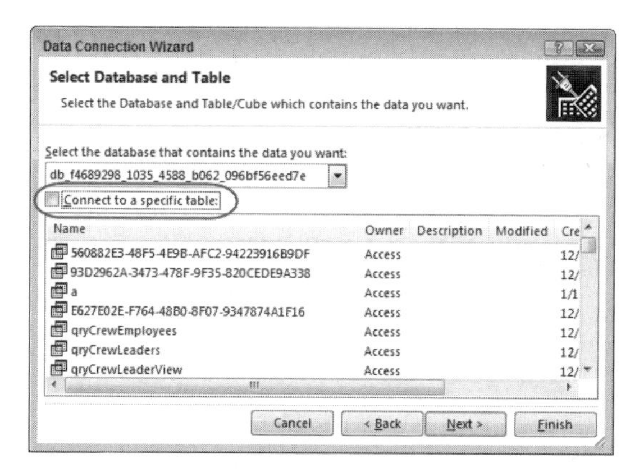

FIGURE 11-26: Select Database and Table pane

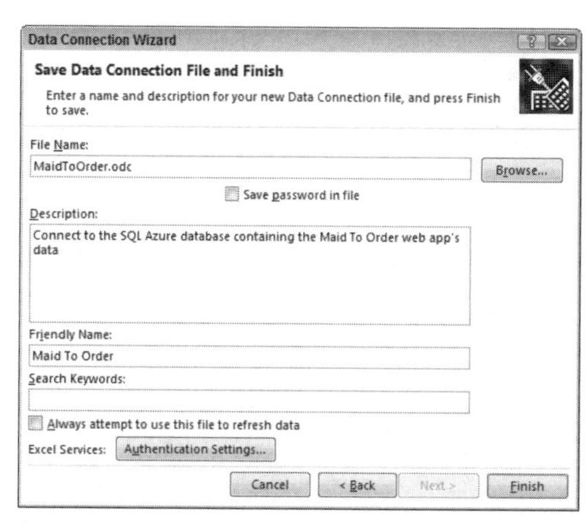

FIGURE 11-27: Data file properties

When you click OK, the ODC file will be created in the specified location and you will be presented with another dialog box to select tables. This is different from the one shown in Figure 11-26. Here, you have two checkboxes: one to enable selection of multiple tables and another to import relationships. You also have a button to select all related tables. You can see those in Figure 11-28. For now, check the Enable selection of multiple tables checkbox, so that you can use the same connection for other uses later in the chapter, and select `tblJobs` table.

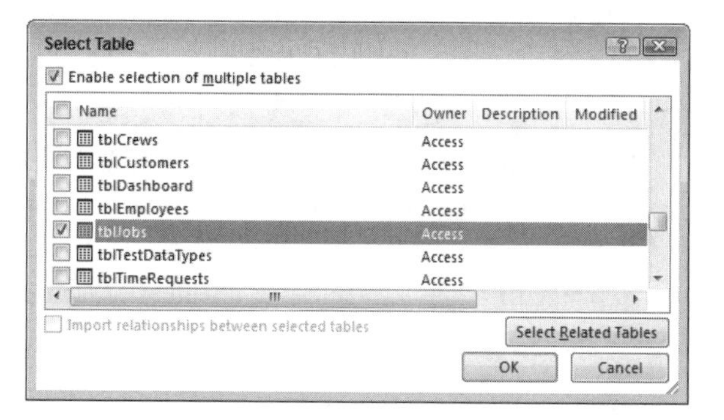

FIGURE 11-28: Select Table dialog box

At this point, you are ready to start creating tables, PivotCharts, and PivotTables in Excel. You will continue with the steps you've seen so far to create your first table.

Creating an Excel Table

In the context of Excel, a table is analogous to what you might think of as an Access datasheet view. It does not refer to an actual relational table at all, but it does provide an easy way to view and filter data.

Continuing from Figure 11-28, you only need to select a single table. Click OK, which takes you to the last dialog box. Ensure that Table is selected, as shown in Figure 11-29, and designate that it be placed on the existing worksheet at cell A1.

This returns the result shown in Figure 11-30.

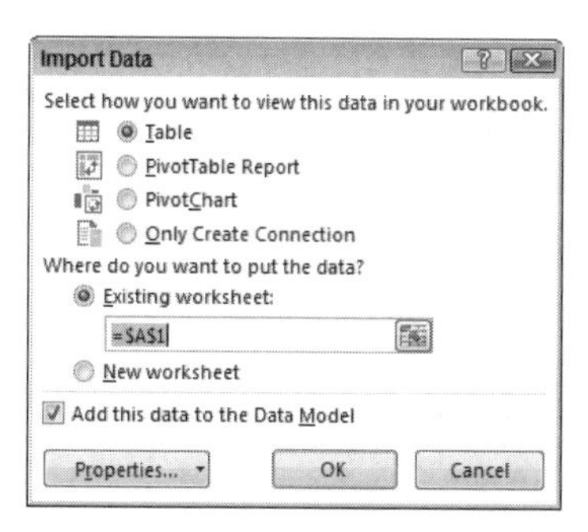

FIGURE 11-29: Import Data dialog box

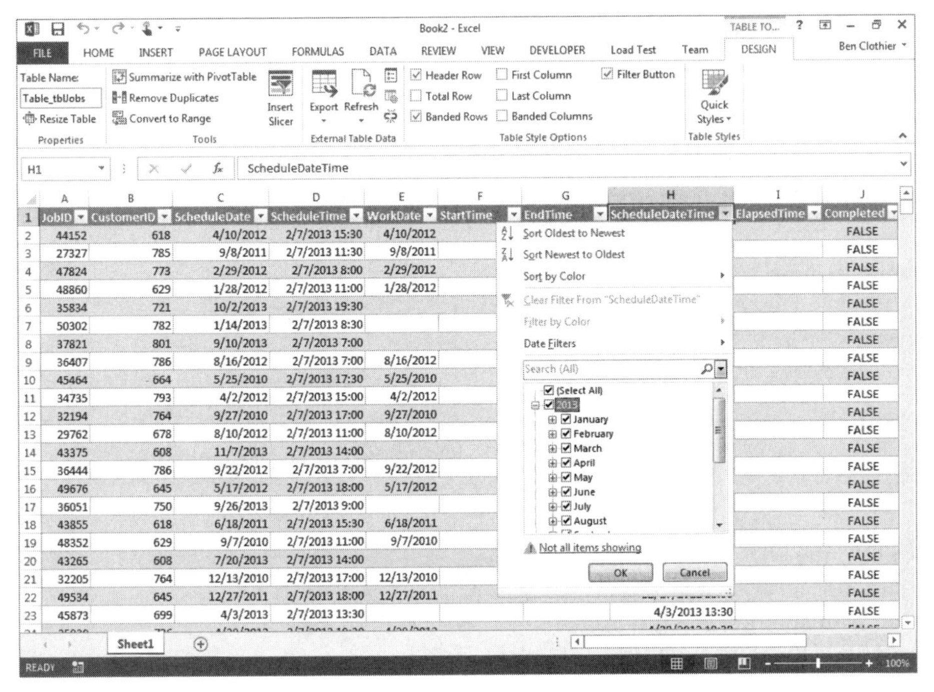

FIGURE 11-30: Excel Table based on tblJobs from the Maid To Order web app

As you can see, the Excel table has many features that are similar to an Access datasheet. Because it appears in a spreadsheet, though, it can be used in conjunction with other Excel tools such as formulas.

Creating an Excel PivotChart

Obviously, a simple table does not always make a report, and more graphics may be needed. Because you already created a connection that allows multiple tables for the workbook, you can reuse it. Create a new sheet on the current workbook and select PivotChart via the Insert on Excel ribbon, as in Figure 11-31.

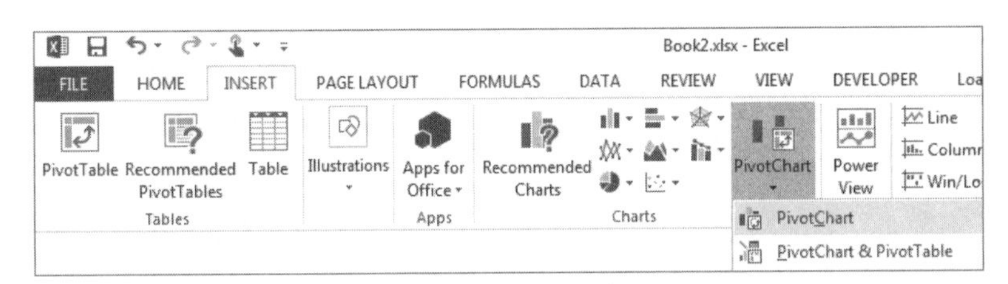

FIGURE 11-31: Insert PivotChart

You will be presented with a dialog box. Select "Use an external data source" and ensure that Existing Worksheet is selected and the address is the A1 cell, as illustrated in Figure 11-32.

Before you click OK, click Choose Connection; make sure you select the external ODC file you previously created, listed under Connections on this Computer section. You may be required to log in and, if so, refer to Figure 11-25 for the details you'll need to supply. You will get the same dialog box you saw earlier in Figure 11-28. This time, however, you want to select three tables — `tblCustomers`, `tblJobs`, and `txrfJobServices` — the first two of which are shown in Figure 11-33.

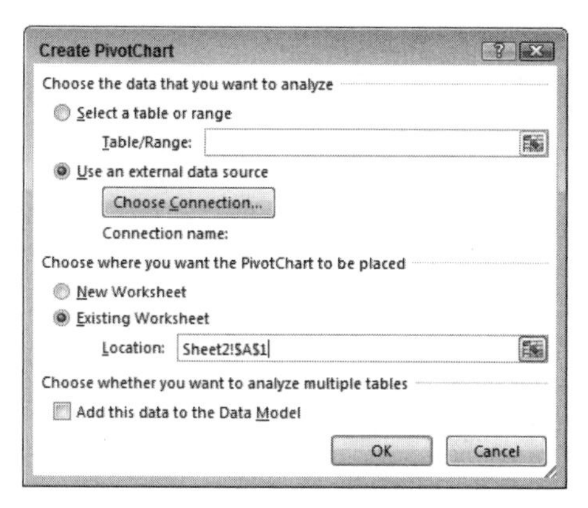

FIGURE 11-32: Create PivotChart dialog box

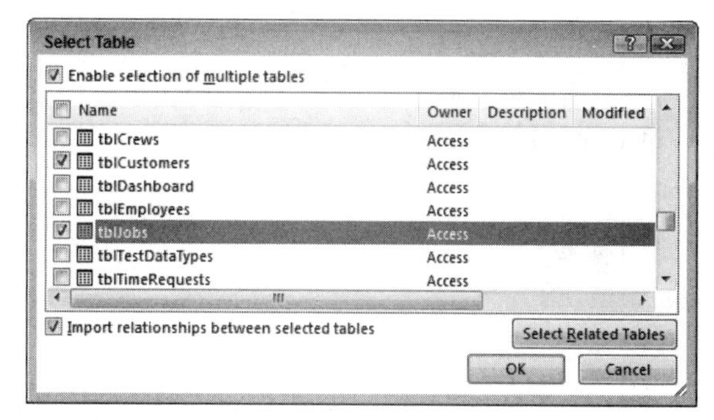

FIGURE 11-33: Selecting multiple tables

NOTE *If you are unable to select multiple tables, it may be that the connection is set to use only a specific table. Verify that the connection isn't restricted to a single table and that you didn't forget to clear the Connect to a specific table checkbox as shown in Figure 11-26.*

WARNING *If you select connections under the Connections in this Workbook section, you will not be able to select additional tables or change the selected table.*

Ensure that the Import relationships between selected tables checkbox is selected, as shown in Figure 11-33 and click OK to continue. You are then presented with a blank chart area and a pane to populate the fields, as shown in Figure 11-34.

The specifics of customizing PivotCharts are beyond the scope of this book, but we want to point out one gotcha you may encounter in building the chart. Consider Figure 11-35 where the chart returns the same output for all customers and note the yellow box in the pane indicating a relationship is needed.

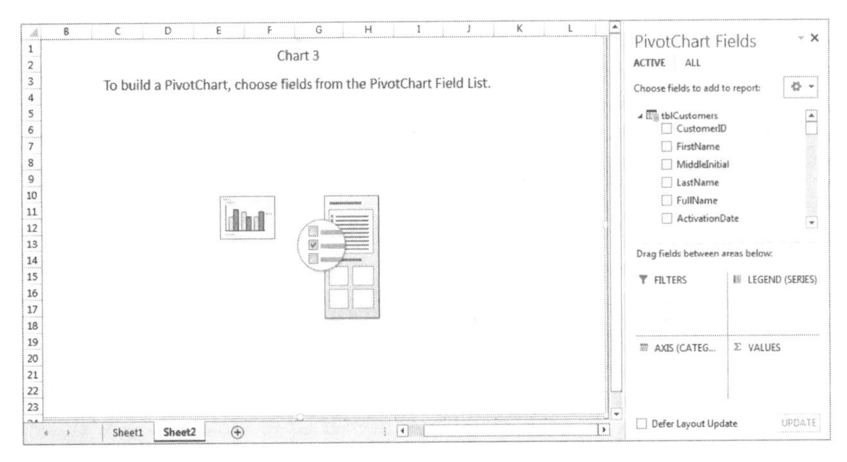

FIGURE 11-34: Blank chart and pane

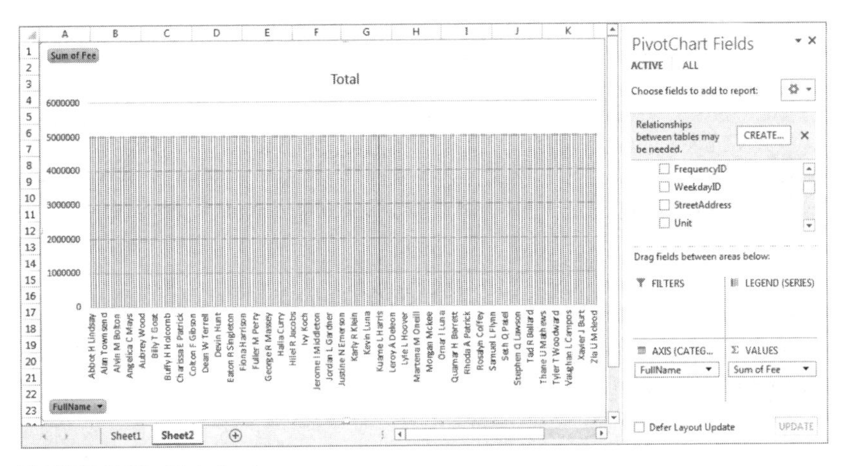

FIGURE 11-35: Flat chart

Click the Create button to bring up the Create Relationship dialog box. Fill in the same relationships that describe the three tables that you selected. You will need to repeat the process twice to designate the relationships between three tables, as shown in Figures 11-36 and 11-37.

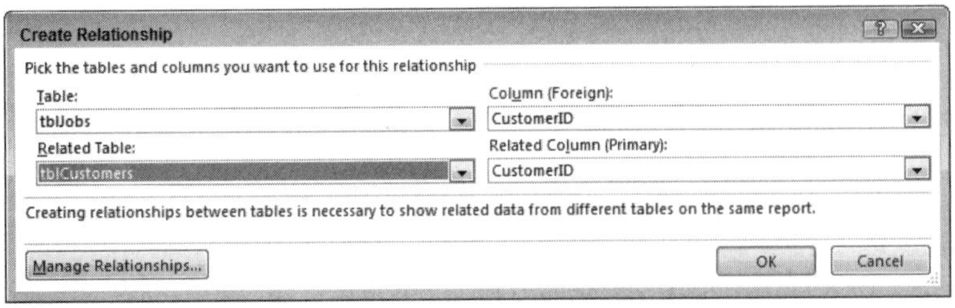

Create Relationship

Pick the tables and columns you want to use for this relationship

Table: tblJobs

Column (Foreign): CustomerID

Related Table: tblCustomers

Related Column (Primary): CustomerID

Creating relationships between tables is necessary to show related data from different tables on the same report.

Manage Relationships... OK Cancel

FIGURE 11-36: Create Relationship diagram

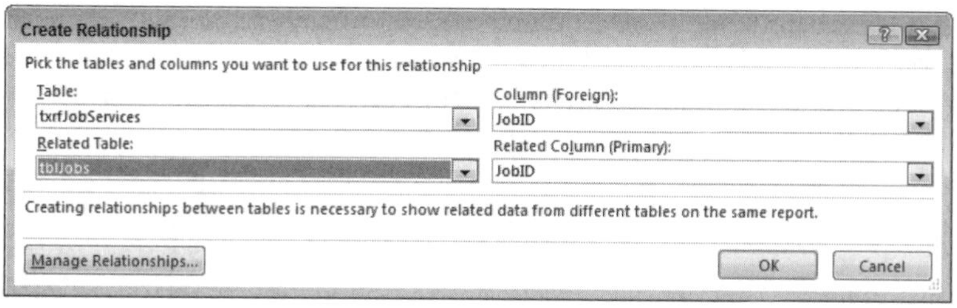

Create Relationship

Pick the tables and columns you want to use for this relationship

Table: txrfJobServices

Column (Foreign): JobID

Related Table: tblJobs

Related Column (Primary): JobID

Creating relationships between tables is necessary to show related data from different tables on the same report.

Manage Relationships... OK Cancel

FIGURE 11-37: Second relationship to create

Once you describe all relationships, the yellow bar will disappear and the PivotChart will now have varying output as desired, which is shown in Figure 11-38.

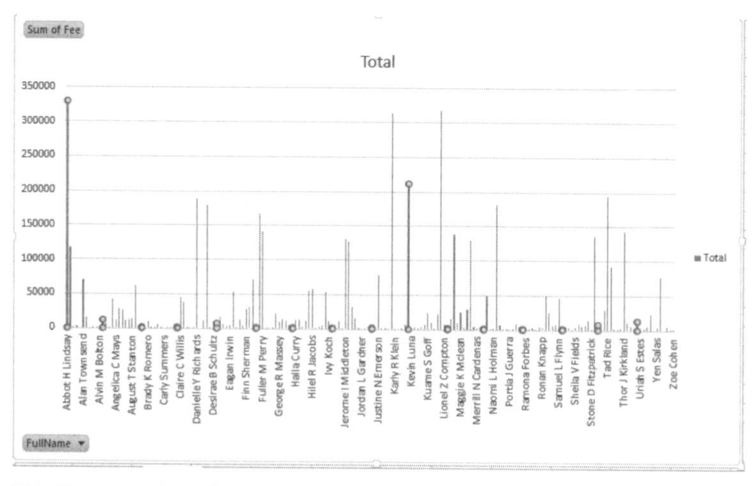

FIGURE 11-38: PivotChart with varying output

This leaves you with only one problem — you don't really want a chart of total revenue collected ever per customer. You want to filter down to a specific time period, such as a month. While you can use the Filter area, there is an easier way to manipulate filtering. On the Excel ribbon, select the Analyze tab under the PivotChart Tools contextual tab and click Insert Slicer, as shown in Figure 11-39.

A dialog box will be presented for you to select fields you want to slice on. Select the ScheduleDate field under tblJobs, as in Figure 11-40.

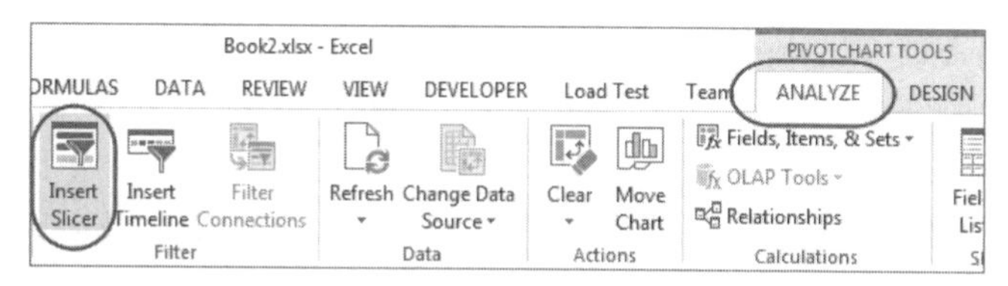

FIGURE 11-39: Insert Slicer

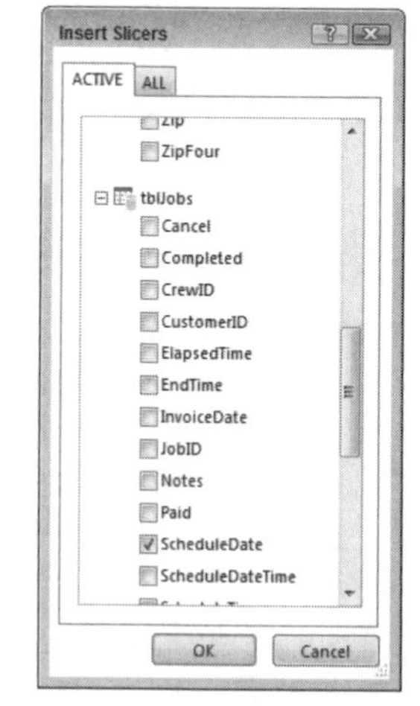

FIGURE 11-40: Selecting fields to slice on

A Slicer popup will display. Assume you want to see revenues by customers for the month of January 2013. To do so, select the first January 2013 date and locate the last January 2013 date, hold down the Shift key, and click the selection to highlight all January 2013 dates, as in Figure 11-41.

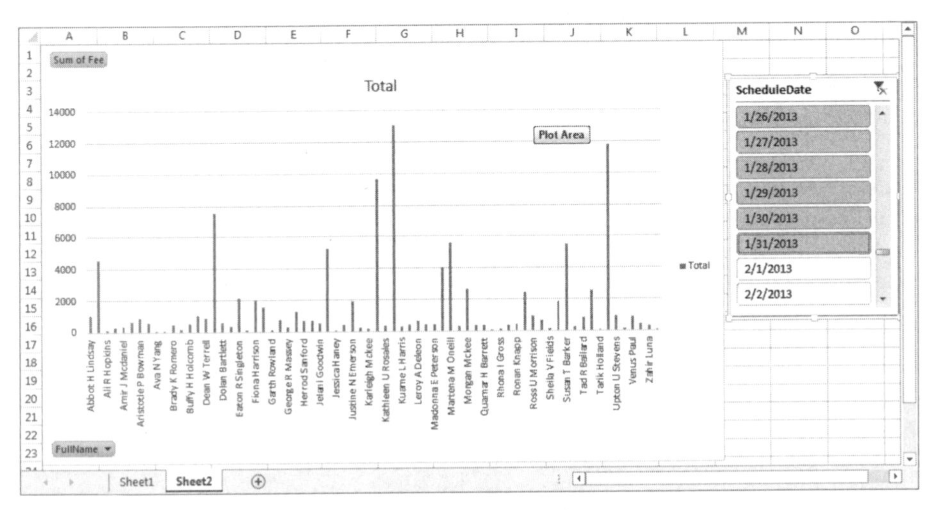

FIGURE 11-41: Sliced PivotChart showing only one month

Obviously, there are many other tools and approaches available to you in customizing and outputting the data in a chart but the discussion so far should give you grounds to effectively work with data from your web app databases and easily create beautiful Excel charts without writing a line of code.

> **NOTE** *Check out the TimeLine feature, shown in Figure 11-39, along with Slicer, which makes it easy to group dates for PivotCharts and PivotTables where you want to be able to report by months, quarters, or years.*

Creating an Excel PivotTable

As you saw in Figure 11-29, you can also use PivotTables as another method for displaying and reporting on your data. You will quickly look at the steps required to create a new PivotTable. Another thing you want to note is how to reuse data that you used for the example in the previous section, Creating an Excel PivotChart, for the PivotTable.

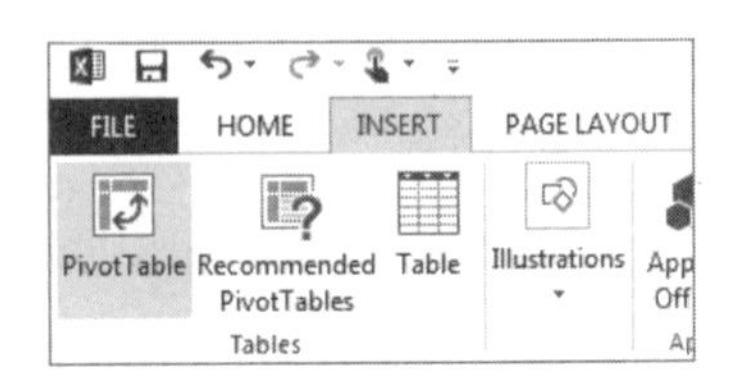

FIGURE 11-42: Insert PivotTable

To get started, create a new sheet in the same workbook and use the Insert tab to insert a new PivotTable, as in Figure 11-42.

This step is similar to what you did for PivotCharts and, as before, click Choose Connection. Note the difference in what connections are listed compared to the last time you saw that dialog box; this time, you will use the connection under Connections in this Workbook section, rather than the connection under Connections files on this computer section. So instead of using Maid To Order ODC, you can just reuse the existing workbook connection, as selected in Figure 11-43. As noted before, when you do that you cannot change table selections, but in this case you can save a step since the PivotTable can be based on the same selection as the PivotChart example.

This is all you need to get started building a PivotTable. As with the PivotChart, the particulars of building PivotTables are beyond the scope of this book, but one example of reporting that can be achieved with a PivotTable is shown in Figure 11-44.

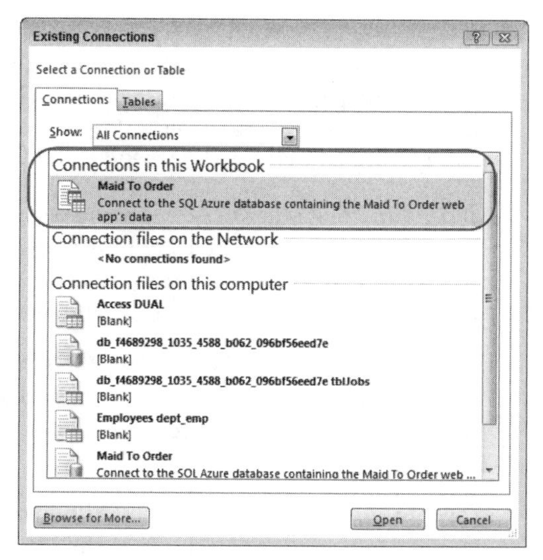

FIGURE 11-43: Selecting an existing workbook connection

Revenue	Column Labels								
Row Labels	1/1/2013	1/2/2013	1/3/2013	1/4/2013	1/5/2013	1/6/2013	1/7/2013	1/8/2013	1/9/2013
1	$1,802.00	$203.00	$203.00	$291.00	$1,288.00	$203.00	$203.00	$888.00	$203.00
2	$955.00	$557.00	$749.00	$961.00	$557.00	$557.00	$1,188.00	$955.00	$557.00
3	$2,029.00	$641.00	$691.00	$551.00	$512.00	$989.00	$647.00	$920.00	$1,335.00
4	$944.00	$944.00	$2,004.00	$944.00	$1,076.00	$944.00	$1,859.00	$944.00	$944.00
Grand Total	$5,730.00	$2,345.00	$3,647.00	$2,747.00	$3,433.00	$2,693.00	$3,897.00	$3,707.00	$3,039.00

Sheet1 Sheet2 Sheet3

PivotTable Fields
ACTIVE ALL
Choose fields to add to report:
ScheduleTime
WorkDate
StartTime
EndTime
ScheduleDateTime
ElapsedTime
Drag fields between areas below:
FILTERS
COLUMNS: ScheduleDate
ROWS: Crew #
VALUES: Revenue
Defer Layout Update
UPDATE

FIGURE 11-44: Finished PivotTable

External Data Considerations

Now that you've seen various ways Excel ODC can be used to aid in generating powerful reports, let's turn our attention to considerations behind managing those connections. We want to look at the issues surrounding the storage of passwords, trusting the external data, using it in an Excel web app context, and controlling frequency of data refresh.

Because you are using SQL Server authentication, it may not always be desirable to save the password inside either an ODC file or inside the workbook directly. For those who choose to do so, and who are willing to deal with the security ramifications, there are a few places to store the passwords. You may have noticed in your walkthrough that there are two places where connection data is stored: within the ODC file and directly inside the Excel spreadsheet.

Understand that regardless of whether you choose to store passwords within the Excel workbook or the ODC file, either approach will store passwords unencrypted. You could mitigate the risk by using the ExternalReader connection properties but that will not help when you have confidential data where reading data is simply unacceptable. In this situation, you need to secure access to the files.

So, realistically, the choice of using ODC versus embedding the connection data in the Excel workbook boils down to whether you find it more expedient to centralize your connection data so that changes made to connection data can be easily propagated to multiple Excel workbooks simply by changing the shared ODC file.

You can ensure that your Excel workbooks always use the ODC file. To do this, start with connection properties by checking the Data tab option shown on the ribbon, as in Figure 11-45. Click the Connections icon to see connection properties for all connections.

This will open up the dialog box; select the connection and click the Properties button as illustrated in Figure 11-46.

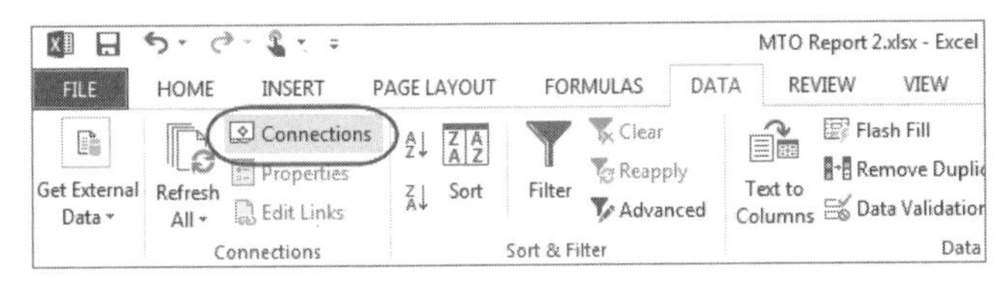

FIGURE 11-45: Connection properties

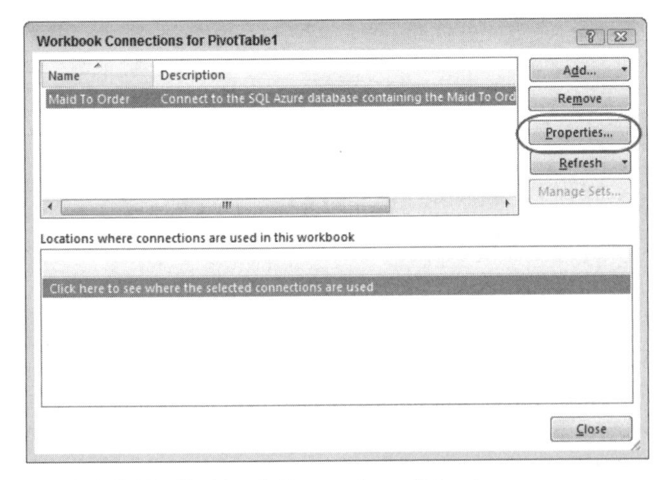

FIGURE 11-46: Workbook Connections dialog box

On the Connection Properties dialog box shown in Figure 11-47, choose the Definition tab and select the Always use connection file checkbox.

Note that this is also the same place where you can select Save password to embed the password as part of the Excel workbook. Furthermore, note that if you modify the connection string so that it no longer matches the ODC file, it will disassociate the workbook from the ODC and embed the connection string without any dependency on the ODC file, for better or worse.

The next consideration is the trust required for the document that contains connections. The next time you open an Excel workbook with those connections, you may get a yellow alert bar similar to Figure 11-48.

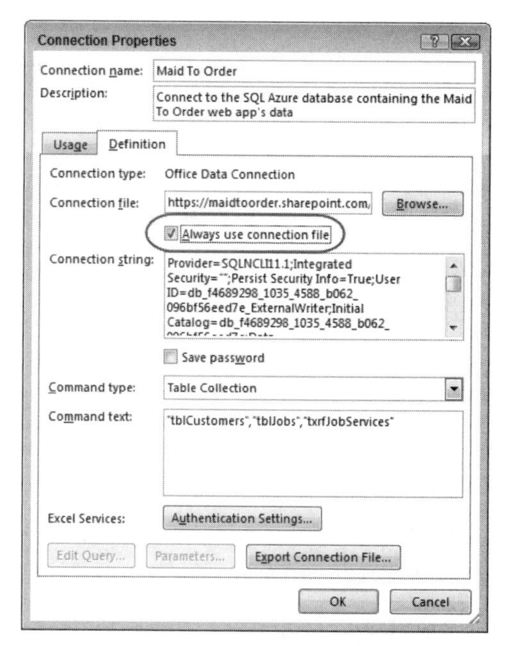

FIGURE 11-47: Connection Properties dialog box

To enable the connections without having to manually trust the document is very similar to the process you've seen with trusting VBA code and certain macro actions for an Access database; you can either make it a Trusted Document or place it in a Trusted Location. In addition, Excel's Trust Center has a setting for External Content, as shown in Figure 11-49.

SECURITY WARNING External Data Connections have been disabled | Enable Content

FIGURE 11-48: Security Warning bar

When the document is trusted, the data connections will be automatically made without prompting the users.

As you may know, SharePoint allows users to view Excel workbooks in a web browser. There are two editions: Excel Web Apps and Excel Services. Excel Services offer additional features beyond Excel Web Apps and is generally available only on SharePoint with enterprise licenses. You can use either option to upload your workbook to a SharePoint document for easy viewing in a web browser, similar to Figure 11-50.

Note that when you are using Excel Web Apps and not Excel Services, you can view the data that was current as of when it was last opened and refreshed in the Excel client. However, you cannot refresh it in the web browser.

The ability to connect and get live data inside the web browser requires that you use Excel Services, which may not be available on all Office 365 plans or SharePoint installations. If you look at Figure 11-50, you can see the yellow bar cautioning that External Data and BI features are not supported.

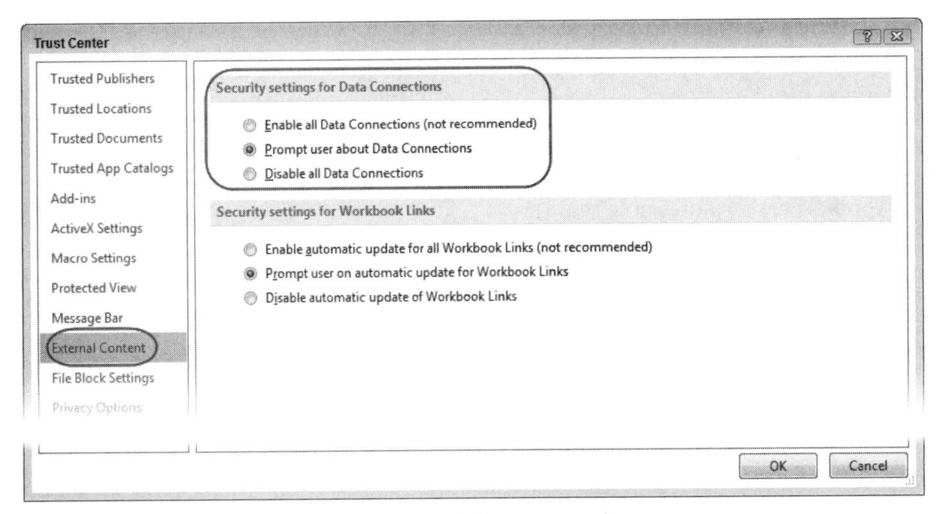

FIGURE 11-49: Excel Trust Center for External Data

MTO Report.xlsx - Windows Internet Explorer

https://maidtoorder.sharepoint.com/_layouts/15/WopiFrame.aspx?sourcedoc=/Shared%20Doc

MaidToOrder Team Site ▸ MTO Report.xlsx — Microsoft Excel Web App — ben@maidtoorder.onmicrosoft.com

FILE | EDIT WORKBOOK | SHARE | DATA | FIND

This workbook contains external data connections or BI features that are not supported.

	A	B	C	D	E	F	G	H	I	J	K	L	M	N
1	Sum of Fee	Column Labels												
2	Row Labels	1/1/2013	1/2/2013	1/3/2013	1/4/2013	1/5/2013	1/6/2013	1/7/2013	1/8/2013	1/9/2013	1/10/2013	1/11/2013	1/12/2013	1/13/20
3	1	$1,802	$203	$203	$291	$1,288	$203	$203	$888	$203	$596	$291	$270	$2
4	2	$955	$557	$749	$961	$557	$557	$1,188	$955	$557	$557	$557	$557	$5
5	3	$2,029	$641	$691	$551	$512	$989	$647	$920	$1,335	$1,168	$512	$1,486	$9
6	4	$944	$944	$2,004	$944	$1,076	$944	$1,859	$944	$944	$1,374	$944	$1,228	$1,3
7	Grand Total	$5,730	$2,345	$3,647	$2,747	$3,433	$2,693	$3,897	$3,707	$3,039	$3,695	$2,304	$3,541	$3,0

FIGURE 11-50: Excel Web App

> **NOTE** *It can be hard to tell whether you have Excel Services or only Excel Web Apps because both will display Excel Web App when starting up. One way of finding out is to look at the URL used when you open Excel workbook in a web browser. If you see* `xlviewer.aspx` *in the middle of your URL, then it's using Excel Services. If you see* `WopiFrame2.aspx` *in the middle, then it's using Excel Web Apps.*

Sharing Excel Workbooks on the Web

One thing you almost certainly will want to do is share reports with other people in an accessible manner. It may not always be practical to simply drop your Excel workbooks in a shared network folder. Even when you use Office 365 to host your Access web apps, your Office 365 or SharePoint account allows you to upload your Excel workbook and store it in a document library. You will look at two parts: uploading your ODC file and the Excel workbook.

As discussed previously in the External Data Considerations section, depending on your particular Office 365 subscription plan or your SharePoint server configuration, you also may be able to refresh the external data directly inside a web browser. Even if this is not supported by your specific environment, you can always use the document library as a convenient place to grab the latest workbook and the connection data and refresh it using the Excel client to get the current snapshot.

When you actually attempt to refresh an external data connection in Excel web app where it is not supported, you will get an error. Even in this case, however, the data from the last refresh is still available for viewing inside the web browser.

Should you choose to use an ODC file rather than embedding the connection in the workbook, you will almost certainly need your ODC file to be accessible, and this typically necessitates storing your ODC file in a document library. While there are different ways to accomplish it, we will show you one way, assuming you have a team site already set up on your Office 365 or SharePoint site. On your team site's Site Contents page, where you add an app, select Add an app and select Data Connection Library, as shown in Figure 11-51.

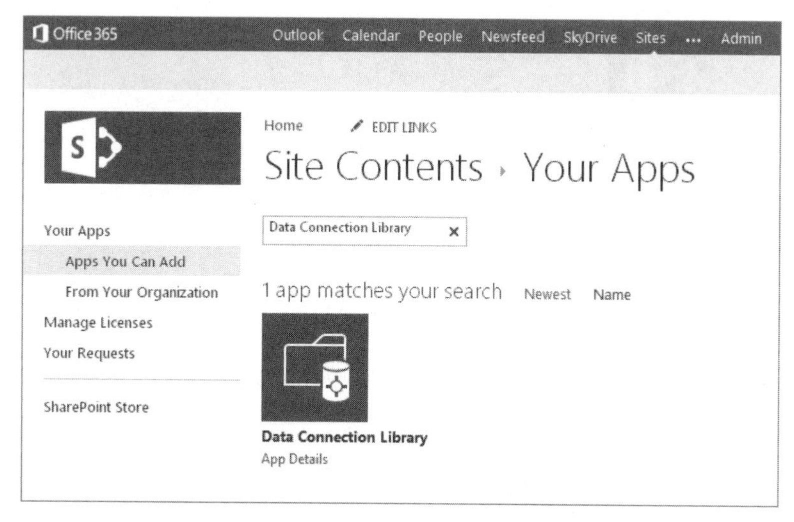

FIGURE 11-51: Data Connection Library

In the prompt, provide a name for your new Data Connection Library similar to Figure 11-52.

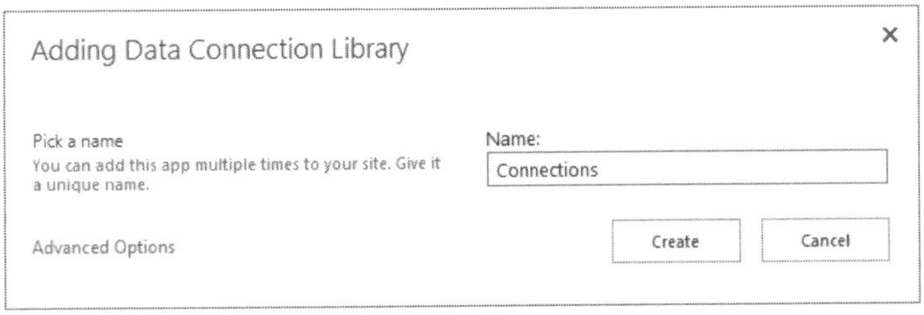

Adding Data Connection Library

Pick a name
You can add this app multiple times to your site. Give it a unique name.
Name:
Connections
Advanced Options
Create
Cancel

FIGURE 11-52: Naming a Data Connection Library

Click Create and the name will be added to your Site Contents. Click the new library in Figure 11-53 to open it.

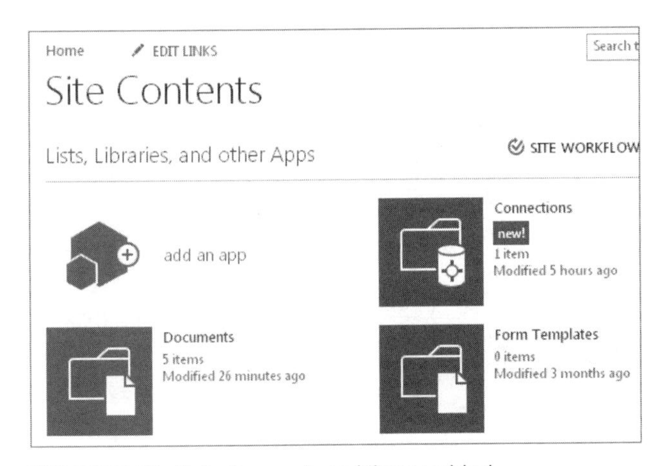

FIGURE 11-53: Data Connections Library added

On the library's page, click the Add new item link in Figure 11-54.

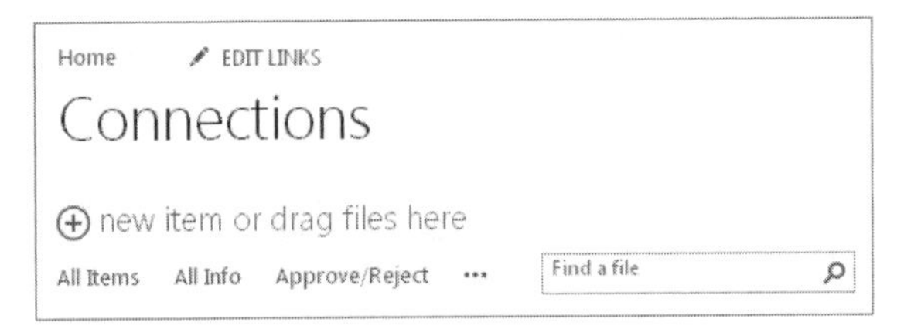

FIGURE 11-54: Adding a new file

In the prompt shown in Figure 11-55, provide the ODC file location either by typing it in or browsing for it. Then click OK.

SharePoint customarily shows another popup (see Figure 11-56) where you can further customize an uploaded document's properties, some of which are specific to the library. For now, accept the default and click Save.

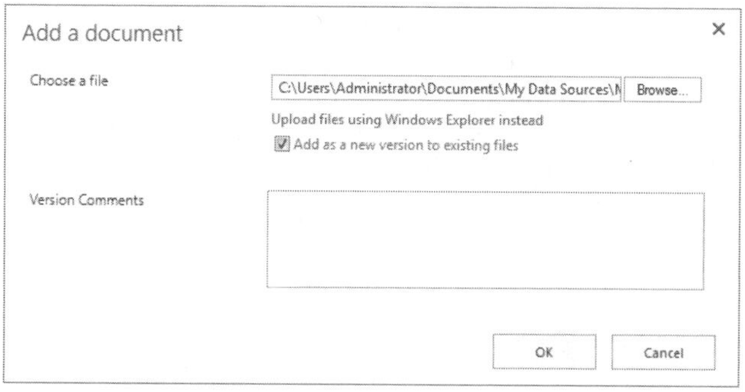

Add a document
Choose a file
C:\Users\Administrator\Documents\My Data Sources\M
Browse...
Upload files using Windows Explorer instead
Add as a new version to existing files
Version Comments
OK
Cancel

FIGURE 11-55: Adding a document popup

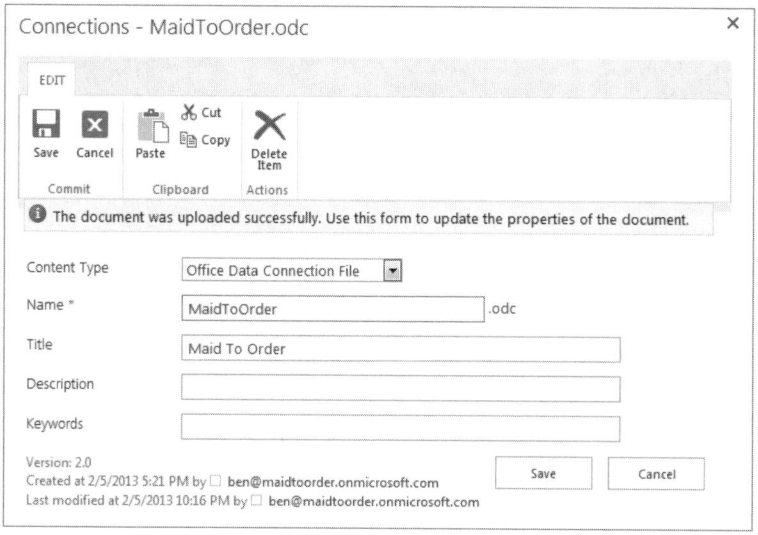

Connections - MaidToOrder.odc
EDIT
Save
Cancel
Paste
Cut
Copy
Delete Item
Commit
Clipboard
Actions
The document was uploaded successfully. Use this form to update the properties of the document.
Content Type
Office Data Connection File
Name *
MaidToOrder
.odc
Title
Maid To Order
Description
Keywords
Version: 2.0
Created at 2/5/2013 5:21 PM by ben@maidtoorder.onmicrosoft.com
Last modified at 2/5/2013 10:16 PM by ben@maidtoorder.onmicrosoft.com
Save
Cancel

FIGURE 11-56: Document properties popup

When the ODC file is uploaded, you'll see it listed, as in Figure 11-57.

Connections
new item or drag files here
All Items
All Info
Approve/Reject
Find a file
Title
Name
Description
Modified
Maid To Order
MaidToOrder
2/5/2013 5:27 PM

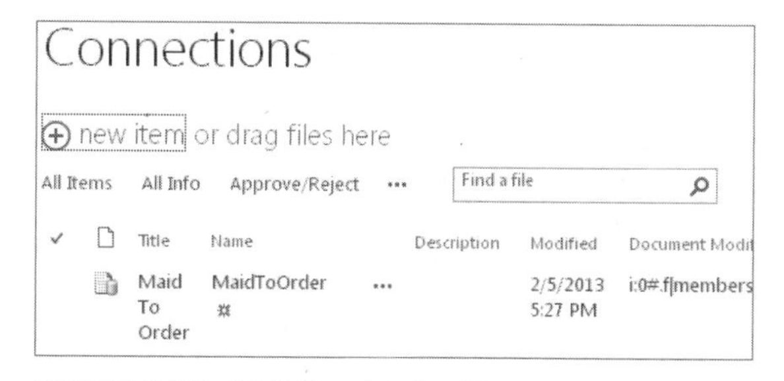

FIGURE 11-57: ODC file added to library

At this point, you have an ODC file that can easily be accessed by anyone who has access to the library you used. Note that you can further secure that library by making it read-only to simplify the administration of the ODC files.

However, it is necessary to ensure that the Excel workbook will reference the uploaded ODC file rather than the local ODC file before you upload your Excel workbook for others' consumption. To do that, you need to open the Excel workbook in the Excel client and return to the Workbook Connections dialog box that you saw in Figure 11-46 and use the Add button, which will open the Existing Connections dialog box you saw from Figure 11-43. On Existing Connections dialog box, use the Browse button provided on that dialog box. By default, you get File Picker opening to one of your local directories. Enter the URL pointing to your new Data Connection Library, as demonstrated in Figures 11-58 and 11-59.

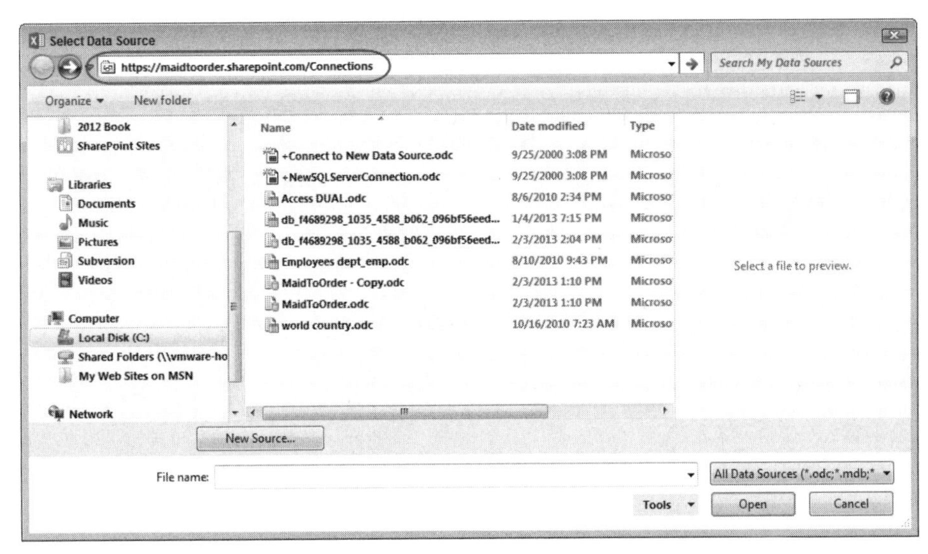

FIGURE 11-58: Navigating to the Data Connections Library

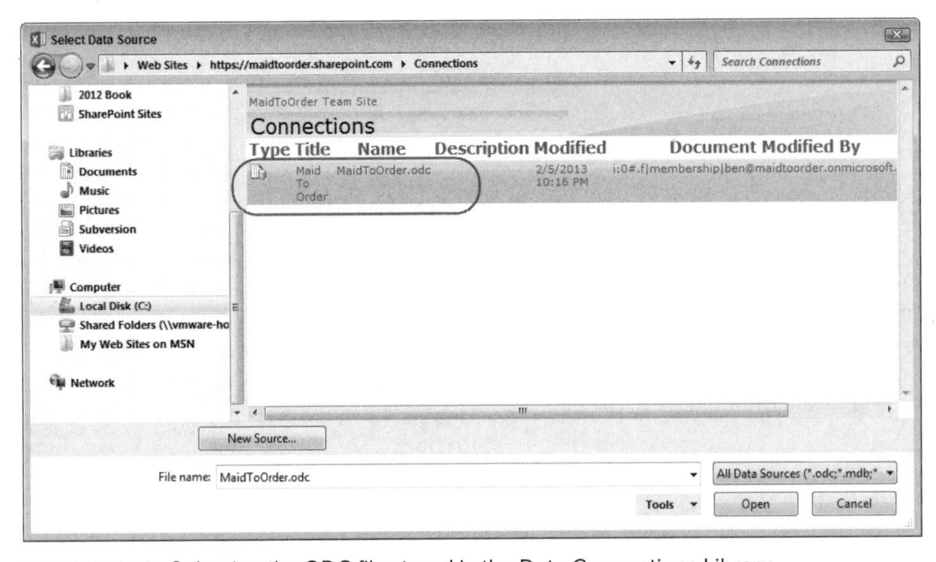

FIGURE 11-59: Selecting the ODC file stored in the Data Connections Library

> **WARNING** *The protocol matters; using* `http` *instead of* `https` *may return errors. Ensure that you have the URL correct when navigating. You can simplify the navigation by adding the website to your favorites.*

> **NOTE** *When browsing to a website address where you enter the URL by hand rather from a saved location, it may take a while for Windows Explorer to list contents, so you may need to allow a bit more time when navigating to such locations. Once saved, the navigation is usually faster because Windows Explorer already has the needed metadata to effectively navigate.*

Save the changes to your workbook. You can now upload an Excel file to a document library, typically on your team site, using the same process you used to upload the ODC file to the data connections library, as shown in Figure 11-60.

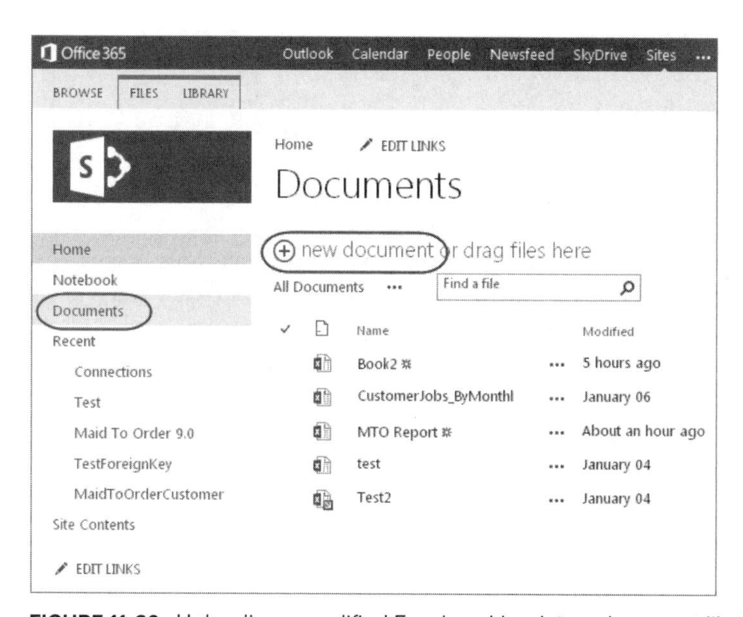

FIGURE 11-60: Uploading a modified Excel workbook to a document library

At this point, it's a simple matter of providing the URL for the workbook to people who have access to the document library. They can then open it in Excel Web App or Excel Services, and also download it to open in their Excel client. Because the ODC file is accessible, users can easily refresh data in the workbook from anywhere. If you want to get the URL, you can click the build button to the right of the file in the document library, as illustrated in Figure 11-61.

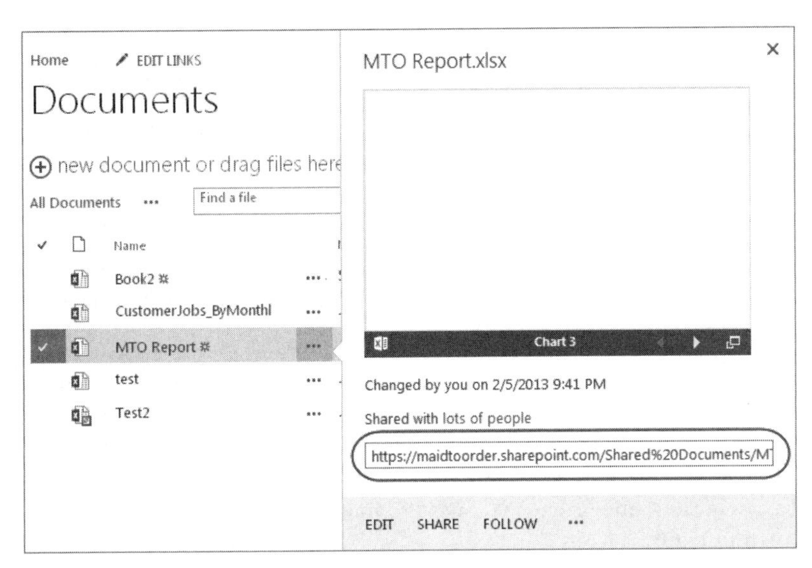

FIGURE 11-61: Getting a file's URL

> **NOTE** *Don't forget to also share the libraries with the users if they are not already a member of the site.*

With those steps completed, you now can see how you may be able to leverage Excel Web Apps as an easy way to distribute your reports. Because you can design your workbooks using a live connection, you don't have to worry about saving multiple versions to take snapshots of data every so often. With many new reporting and business intelligence features added to Excel, you will come to appreciate the new potentials you can reach by joining Access with Excel.

USING SSMS

Because web apps use SQL Server, it should naturally follow that you can use SQL Server Management Studio to connect to the web app's database. In this section, you will look at two approaches: connecting to the database directly or creating a linked server to access the database.

Generally speaking, when you want to perform primarily administrative tasks, it usually suffices to connect to the database directly. However, if you have an existing SQL Server database, and you want to work with data from both that local SQL Server database and your web app's database, you will appreciate the benefits a linked server has to offer you.

Connecting to a Web App Database

If you've used SSMS before, then the process of connecting to your web app database should be quite familiar to you. When you open up SSMS, you are prompted with a login screen to connect to a server, usually the one used most recently by default. As you may expect from earlier chapters, you fill in the server name, select SQL Authentication, and provide the username and password, as in Figure 11-62.

If you went ahead with only those details, you may get an error similar to the one shown in Figure 11-63, especially when you are using Office 365.

Unlike local SQL Server instances, SQL Azure has additional security requirements, which require additional configuration beyond simply pointing at a server and giving it a username and a password. In this case, you should click the Options >> button shown in Figure 11-62. This will expand the dialog box similar to what you see in Figure 11-64.

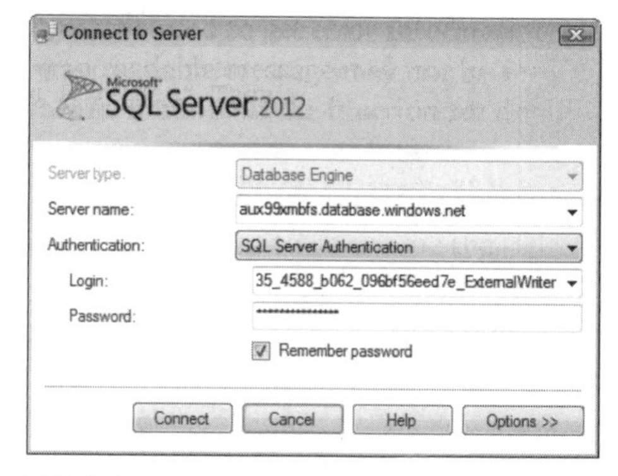

FIGURE 11-62: Login dialog box

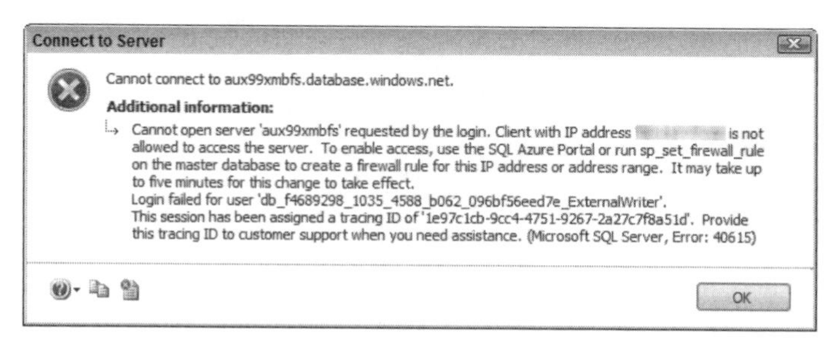

FIGURE 11-63: Error displayed after default login

FIGURE 11-64: Expanded Login dialog box

> **NOTE** *Remember to enable From Any Locations in the Connections page in Access web apps in order to connect to the database behind the Access web app.*

You click Connection Properties, identified in Figure 11-64, and then you need to provide the database name and select the Encrypt connection checkbox, as demonstrated in Figure 11-65.

As you can see, connecting to a SQL Azure database will always require that connections be encrypted, and you must connect to a specific database for which you have permissions. Once you've made the changes, you can complete the login; the database will be made available in Object Explorer. As you can see in Figure 11-66, you can browse SQL objects created by the web app in your web app database.

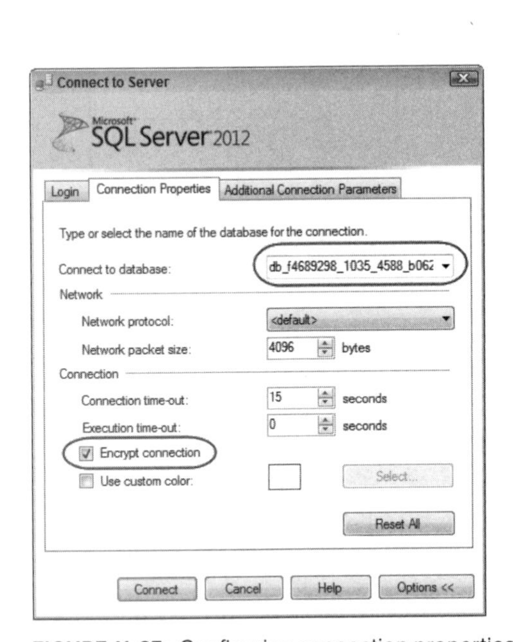

FIGURE 11-65: Configuring connection properties

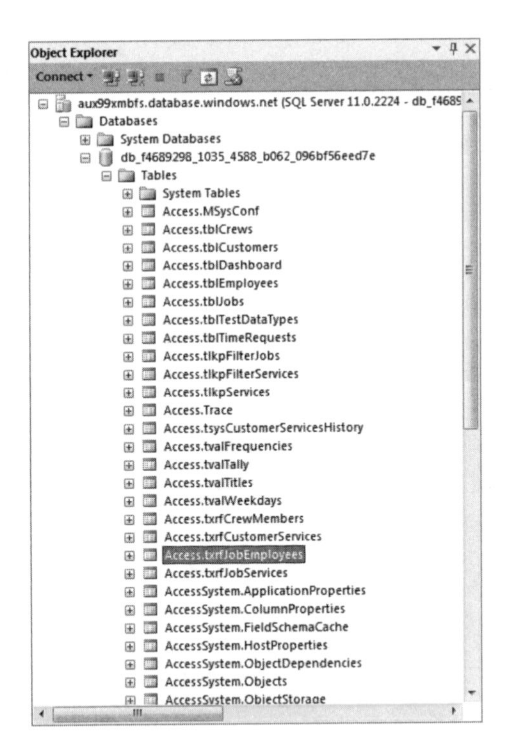

FIGURE 11-66: Object Explorer

As we alluded to earlier in the book, all objects you create via a web app are stored in the `Access` schema. Those are the objects you should be interested in primarily. If you use the ExternalWriter user to connect to the web app database, you are also allowed to read data from objects contained in `AccessSystem` and read and write data to the `AccessRuntime` schema. However, generally speaking, you wouldn't really want to use `AccessRuntime`, which is used primarily for design-time experience and is usually a modified view of a pre-existing object in the `Access` schema. It's best to ignore the `AccessRuntime` schema. ExernalWriter users will not have permission to write to `AccessSystem`; some of its data may be changed as a part of manipulating the Access UI when designing a web app.

Because the ExernalWriter user has full read and write permissions to any base tables within the Access schema, you can write T-SQL queries to read and modify data from SSMS.

Adding a Linked Server on the Web App Database

Sometimes it's not enough to be able to use SSMS and do administrative work. If you have existing SQL Server databases and you want to make it easy to work with data from both a local SQL Server database and a web app's database, then you will surely appreciate the linked server feature. Although the linked server feature is not new, the web app makes it much more relevant for you in your development work.

> **NOTE** *We recommend that you use SQL Server Management Studio 2012 to leverage the linked server approach discussed in this section.*

You will learn how to create a linked server graphically, and then get a T-SQL script to simplify the automation during your work. To get started, locate the Linked Servers folder under Server Objects, as shown in Figure 11-67, and right-click to bring up the context menu.

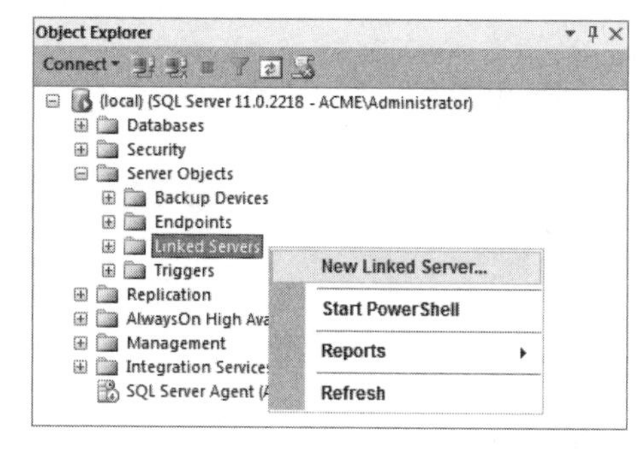

FIGURE 11-67: Queries to reference objects in the Linked Servers folder and context menu

Selecting New Linked Server will provide you with this dialog box. Similar to the login issue you learned at the start of the section, you cannot simply use the SQL Server option to short-circuit the process. You want to provide a descriptive name for the new linked server and select SQL Server Native Client 11.0 as the provider, as illustrated in Figure 11-68.

> **NOTE** *Note that the dialog box forces the linked server name to be in uppercase. If you don't want the name in all caps, use a T-SQL script, as described later, instead.*

Two more properties you need to fill in on this page are the Data Source, which needs to be the server name, and the Catalog, which is the name of the web app's database, as illustrated in Figure 11-69.

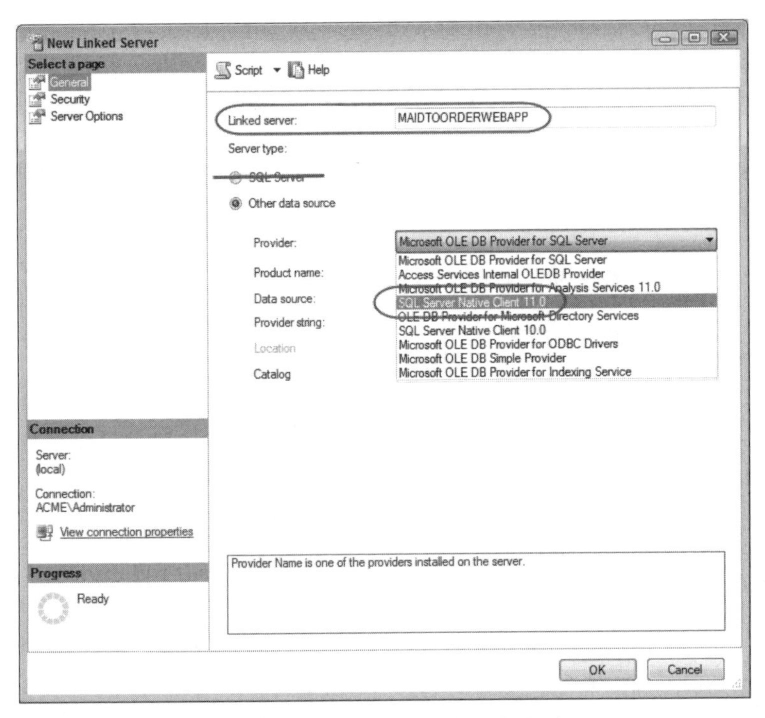

FIGURE 11-68: Providing name and provider for a linked server

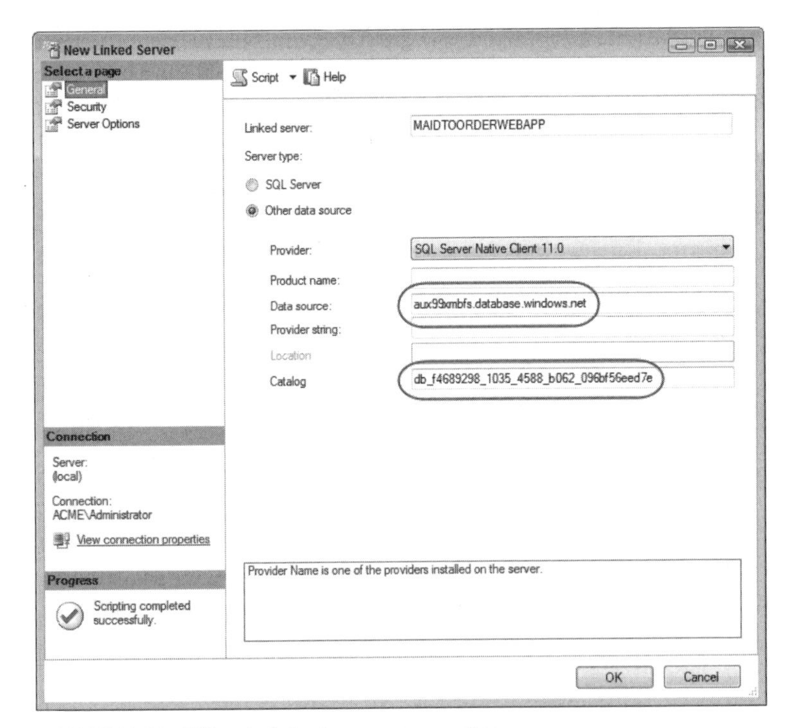

FIGURE 11-69: Filling in linked server properties

The next step is to add an authorized remote user to use for credentials when connecting to the linked server. For simplicity, you will embed the remote user credential and make it available to anyone who wants to access the linked server. To do so, click the Security pane, choose Be made using this security context, and provide the username and password, as in Figure 11-70.

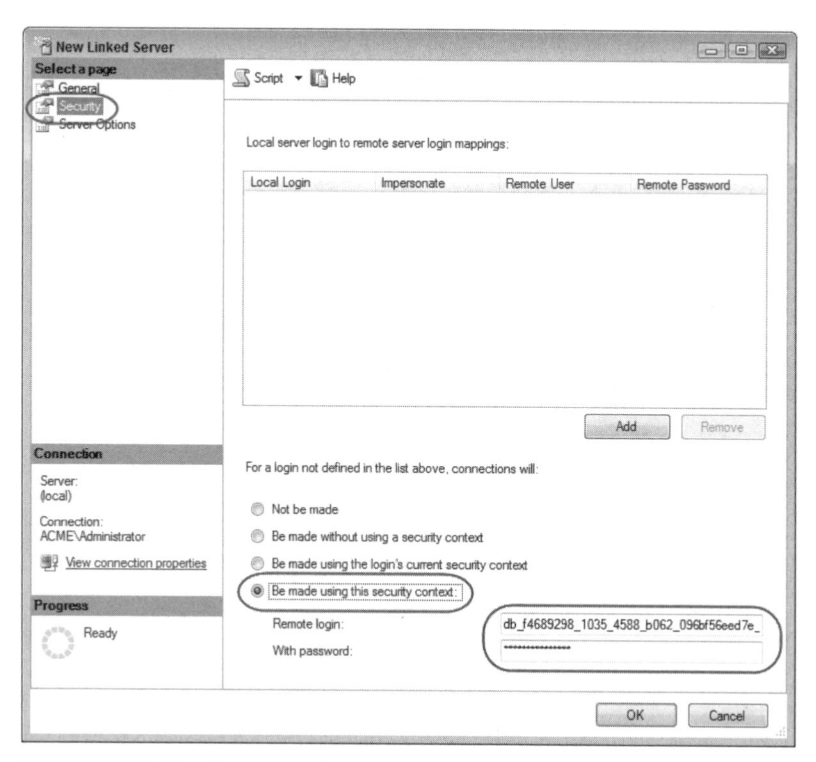

FIGURE 11-70: Creating a remote user

> **WARNING** *This configuration is not necessarily secure and should not be used indiscriminately in production. You learn more about security in Chapter 13. For now, keep in mind that you can restrict access by mapping only certain local users to authorize them to login using the ExternalWriter credentials.*

You've filled in the minimum details needed to successfully create a linked server. You can click OK to finish creating the linked server. However, if you anticipate a need to repeat the steps, you may find it convenient to create a T-SQL script that you can customize for repeated use. As with most SSMS dialog boxes, you can easily script out the changes via the Script menu, as in Figure 11-71.

The script creates several T-SQL statements, which you can incorporate, especially if you want to change the default setting, but at the minimum, you need only two T-SQL statements:

```
USE [master]
GO
EXEC master.dbo.sp_addlinkedserver
  @server = N'Maid_To_Order_Web_App',
  @srvproduct=N'',
  @provider=N'SQLNCLI11',
  @datasrc=N'aux99xmbfs.database.windows.net',
  @catalog=N'db_f4689298_1035_4588_b062_096bf56eed7e'
;
EXEC master.dbo.sp_addlinkedsrvlogin
  @rmtsrvname = N'Maid_To_Order_Web_App',
  @locallogin = NULL,
  @useself = N'False',
  @rmtuser = N'db_f4689298_1035_4588_b062_096bf56eed7e_ExternalWriter',
  @rmtpassword = N'DM&5qe#BoAjKZzx'
;
GO
```

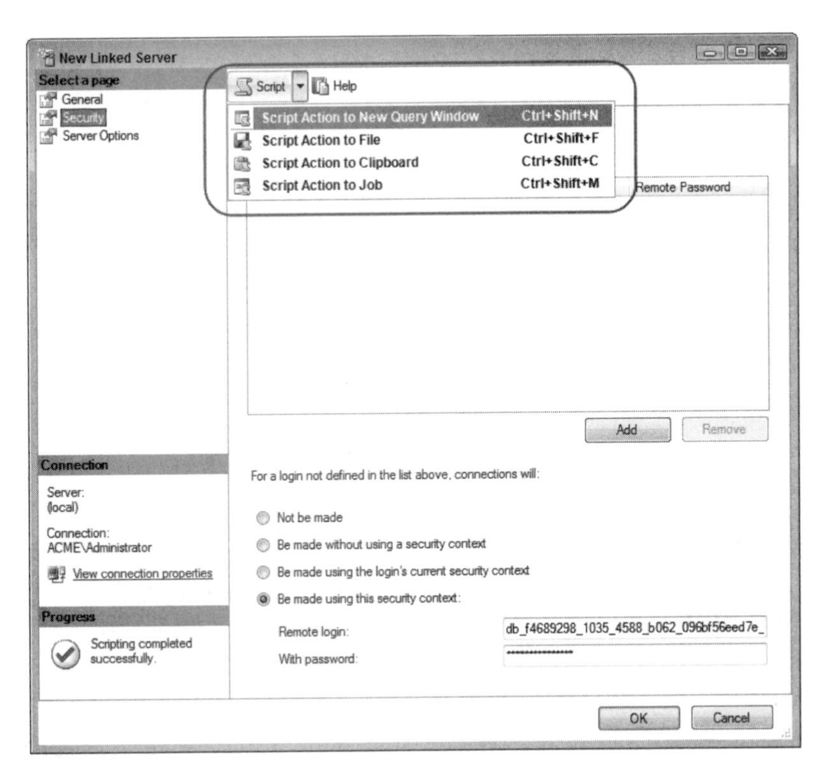

FIGURE 11-71: Script menu

Note that the `@rmtsrvname` parameter was modified from the all caps name shown in Figure 11-68. Once you either click OK or execute the T-SQL script, you can browse the linked server in a somewhat similar but limited fashion to a regular SQL Server instance, as Figure 11-72 demonstrates.

There are a few differences between what is listed in a linked server and when you connect to the same server directly. First, a linked server lists only tables and views. Any other objects, such as stored procedures or functions, are not directly browsable via the linked server drop-down. Next, you cannot navigate to a more granular level beyond object level and therefore cannot get a list of columns and their data types as you would via the tables.

Now that you have a linked server, you will look at how you can use it as part of T-SQL queries.

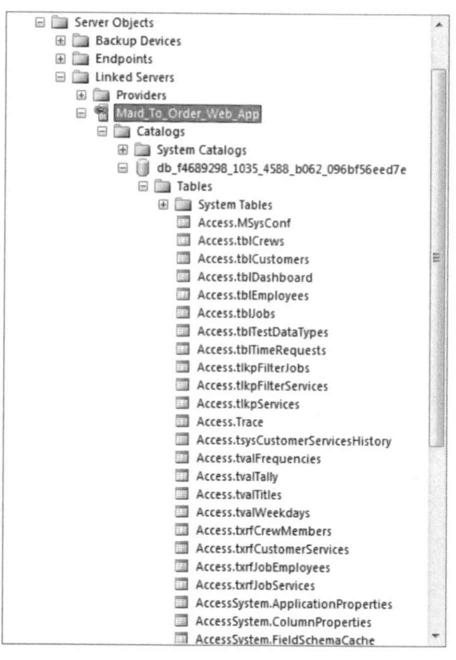

FIGURE 11-72: Browsing a linked server

Querying Data in a Linked Server

By far the easiest way to write a T-SQL query against a linked server is to take advantage of the scripting functionality in SSMS. To do that, right-click a table or view in a linked server and choose Script Table As, select the desired action such as `SELECT`, and finish by selecting the desired output. Figure 11-73 shows the scripting of a `SELECT` SQL statement that will be output into a new query window.

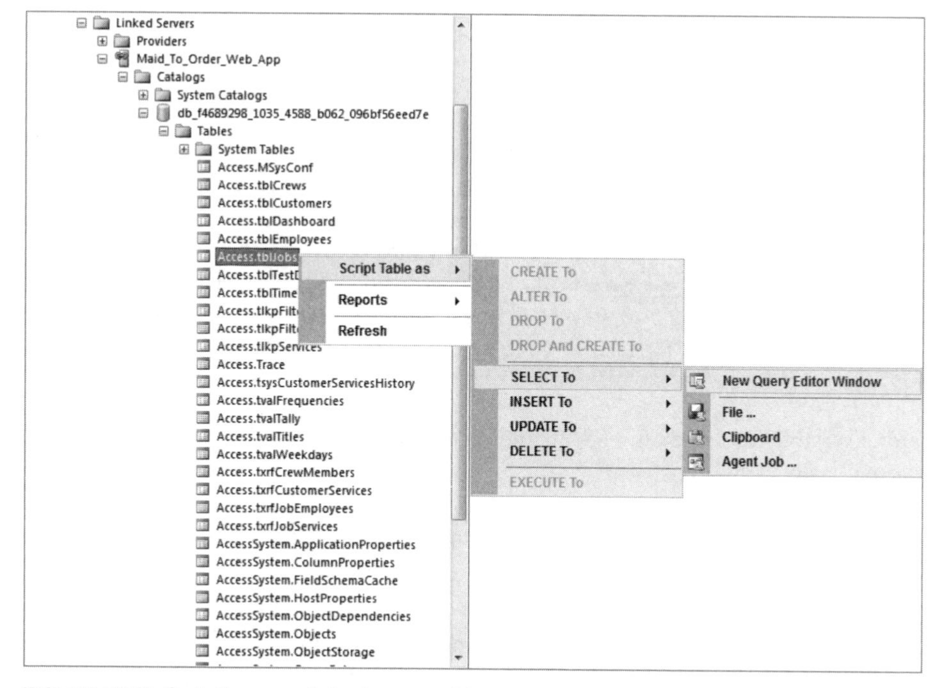

FIGURE 11-73: Scripting on a linked server object

Selecting this option provides you with the following T-SQL output:

```
SELECT [JobID]
      ,[CustomerID]
      ,[ScheduleDate]
      ,[ScheduleTime]
      ,[WorkDate]
      ,[StartTime]
      ,[EndTime]
      ,[ScheduleDateTime]
      ,[ElapsedTime]
      ,[Completed]
      ,[Paid]
      ,[InvoiceDate]
      ,[Notes]
      ,[CrewID]
      ,[Cancel]
  FROM
[Maid_To_Order_Web_App].[db_f4689298_1035_4588_b062_096bf56eed7e].[Access] ➥
.[tblJobs]
GO
```

Consider the `FROM` clause. If you've worked with SQL Server, you may be familiar with how you can use two-part qualified names or three-part qualified names to disambiguate objects that may come from different places but might have the same names. When you use a linked server object, you must always use four-part qualified names representing:

```
<linked server name>.<catalog name>.<schema name>.<object name>
```

Omitting any part of the four-part qualified name will cause SQL Server to assume that the object is a local object. As you can see, the requirement to use a four-part qualified name can get quite unwieldy very fast and especially when you need to work with multiple objects.

> **NOTE** *When linking to another SQL Server instance, you can presume that catalog is equivalent to a database. Note that when you link to a different type of data source, the syntax may be different. For example, if you link to an Access database, which does not use either catalog or schema, the syntax becomes* `[Northwinds]...[Employees]` *to select the Employees table from a Northwind Access database file.*

One simple option available for use within SSMS and certain environments is to use synonyms. You can create a synonym using T-SQL:

```
CREATE SYNONYM dbo.tblEmployees FOR
[Maid_To_Order_Web_App].[db_f4689298_1035_4588_b062_096bf56eed7e].[Access]➥
.[tblEmployees];
```

You can then use the synonym, `dbo.tblEmployees`, as if it were an actual table, performing `SELECT` on it or any modifications such as `INSERT`ing or `UPDATE`ing into the table. Unfortunately, synonyms do not work for all scenarios; for example, Access cannot list the synonyms to be linked in a Link Table operation. However, synonyms are listed when you use Excel to connect to SQL Server.

Perhaps your scenario requires that you be able to easily work with both linked server objects and local server objects within and outside the SSMS. For example, you may have an Access client that links to both a local SQL Server instance and the instance for your web app. Let's also say that this Access client needs to do some heterogeneous operations. In another scenario, you might want to control access to the web apps and you might need more granular access than the ExternalWriter user provides. You will learn more about security in Chapter 13, but for now note that permissions for synonyms cannot differ from the base objects on which they depend, so you may want to create a view on one or more linked server objects in order to gain granular security control over the underlying web app objects. If you prefer to use views rather than linking directly to tables in the web app and pay for the extra overhead, you can execute a T-SQL script to generate scripts for the view definitions. You can use the following T-SQL script to gather the needed metadata to help you build the views. You will need to adjust the two `SELECT INTO` statements to refer to the correct four-part qualified name from your own linked server:

```
DECLARE @PL nvarchar(3) = N']@[',
    @NL nvarchar(2) = CHAR(13) + NCHAR(10),
    @CreationSQL nvarchar(MAX) = N'',
    @LinkPath nvarchar(MAX) =
N'[Maid_To_Order_Web_App].[db_f4689298_1035_4588_b062_096bf56eed7e]↵
.[Access].',
    @SchemaName nvarchar(20) = N'web';

SELECT t.*
INTO #tmpTables
FROM
Maid_To_Order_Web_App.[db_f4689298_1035_4588_b062_096bf56eed7e]↵
.INFORMATION_SCHEMA.TABLES AS t
WHERE t.TABLE_TYPE IN ('BASE TABLE', 'VIEW')
  AND t.TABLE_SCHEMA = 'Access';

SELECT c.*
INTO #tmpColumns
FROM
Maid_To_Order_Web_App.[db_f4689298_1035_4588_b062_096bf56eed7e]↵
.INFORMATION_SCHEMA.COLUMNS AS c
INNER JOIN #tmpTables AS t
  ON c.TABLE_CATALOG = t.TABLE_CATALOG
  AND c.TABLE_SCHEMA = t.TABLE_SCHEMA
  AND c.TABLE_NAME = t.TABLE_NAME;

SELECT @CreationSQL =
  N'BEGIN TRANSACTION;' + @NL +
  N'--COMMIT;' + @NL +
  N'--ROLLBACK;' + @NL +
  @NL +
  N'GO' + @NL +
  @NL + 'CREATE SCHEMA ' + QUOTENAME(@SchemaName) + N' AUTHORIZATION dbo;' + @NL +
  @NL +
  N'GO' + @NL +
  @NL + REPLACE(STUFF((SELECT @PL + REPLACE(
  N'CREATE VIEW [web].' + QUOTENAME(t.TABLE_NAME) + N' AS' + @PL +
  N'SELECT' + @PL + N'    ' +
```

```
    REPLACE(STUFF((SELECT N',' + QUOTENAME(c.COLUMN_NAME) + @PL
      FROM #tmpColumns AS c
      WHERE c.TABLE_CATALOG = t.TABLE_CATALOG
        AND c.TABLE_SCHEMA = t.TABLE_SCHEMA
        AND c.TABLE_NAME = t.TABLE_NAME
      ORDER BY c.ORDINAL_POSITION
      FOR XML PATH(N'')),1,1, N' '),@PL,@PL + N'    ') + @PL +
    N'FROM ' + @LinkPath +
      QUOTENAME(t.TABLE_NAME) + N';',@PL + N'    ' + @PL,@PL) + @PL +
    @PL +
    'GO' + @PL
    FROM #tmpTables AS t
    ORDER BY t.TABLE_NAME
    FOR XML PATH(N'')),1,3,N''),@PL,@NL);

  SELECT @CreationSQL;

  DROP TABLE #tmpTables;
  DROP TABLE #tmpColumns;
```

The script performs the following tasks:

1. Acquires metadata on tables and queries and their columns
2. Inserts that metadata into temporary tables
3. Concatenates all columns for a specific table or view into a formatted `SELECT` list
4. Concatenates each table into a formatted `CREATE VIEW` statement, receiving the column list from step 3
5. Concatenates all `CREATE VIEW` statements together
6. Outputs the final T-SQL

When you execute the script, you get the T-SQL output as a single column, which you can then right-click to copy the content, as in Figure 11-74.

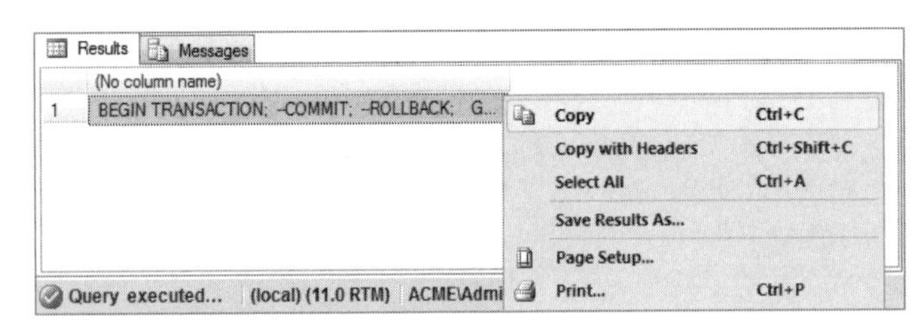

FIGURE 11-74: Copying the output

You then paste the content in a new query window and examine the output to your satisfaction. Note the first three lines generated the following:

```
BEGIN TRANSACTION;
--COMMIT;
--ROLLBACK;
```

The script runs in a transaction but will not actually end the transaction, which offers you an opportunity to evaluate the results and decide to finalize the result by highlighting either `COMMIT` or `ROLLBACK` and executing those commands, taking care to not also highlight the `--` comment delimiter.

> **WARNING** *Don't forget to actually commit or roll back the open transaction! Forgetting means other users may be locked out if they try to query affected objects and must wait for the lock to be released.*

This provides you with an easy way to populate your local SQL Server database with a mirror object of the web app's database objects. Those local objects are generally more accessible and provide you with the detailed metadata and some level of access control. The script also creates all objects within a new schema named `web` to keep it separate from other schemas in your local database server. Of course, you may want to modify the `@SchemaName` parameter if you want to name it something other than `web`.

In cases where you need to re-synchronize or delete all objects generated in this script, the easiest way to accomplish the task is to drop all created views and then drop the schema. You can execute the following T-SQL script to generate the `DROP` statements:

```
DECLARE @PL nvarchar(3) = N']@[',
    @NL nvarchar(2) = NCHAR(13) + NCHAR(10),
    @SchemaName nvarchar(20) = N'web';

SELECT
  N'BEGIN TRANSACTION;' + @NL +
  N'--COMMIT;' + @NL +
  N'--ROLLBACK;' + @NL +
  @NL +
  N'GO' + @NL +
  REPLACE((
  SELECT N'DROP VIEW ' + QUOTENAME(@SchemaName) + N'.' +
    QUOTENAME(v.TABLE_NAME) + N';' + @PL + N'GO' + @PL
  FROM INFORMATION_SCHEMA.VIEWS AS v
  WHERE v.TABLE_SCHEMA = @SchemaName
  ORDER BY v.TABLE_NAME
  FOR XML PATH(N'')),@PL,@NL) +
  N'DROP SCHEMA ' + QUOTENAME(@SchemaName) + N';'
;
```

You can use the same steps shown in Figure 11-74 to copy the output into a new query window. As before, the script has a transaction that is left open to provide you with the opportunity to review and make a decision based on the result of running the script.

With those two scripts, you now have an easy process for automating creation and removal of mirrored objects from your web app database into a local SQL Server database. You can then use the views to present the web app database objects as if they originated from the same local SQL Server and simplify your other T-SQL scripting when working with objects from the web database. In Chapter 13, you will circle back to the discussion about securing web app objects for client consumption and options.

Using Linked Server Programmability Objects

So far, you saw how you can query data, but you may be wondering about how to reuse all that hard work you've invested in building data macros and parameterized queries, which are represented as stored procedures and table-valued functions in your web app database. Before you can get started, there are additional configuration steps you need to perform. Return to the Linked Server dialog box by right-clicking the linked server and selecting properties (see Figure 11-75).

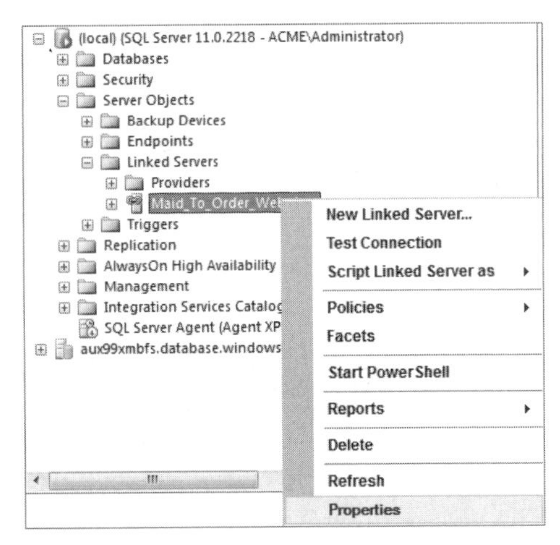

FIGURE 11-75: Linked server properties

Select the Server Options pane and make two changes to RPC and RPC Out, setting both to True, as shown in Figure 11-76.

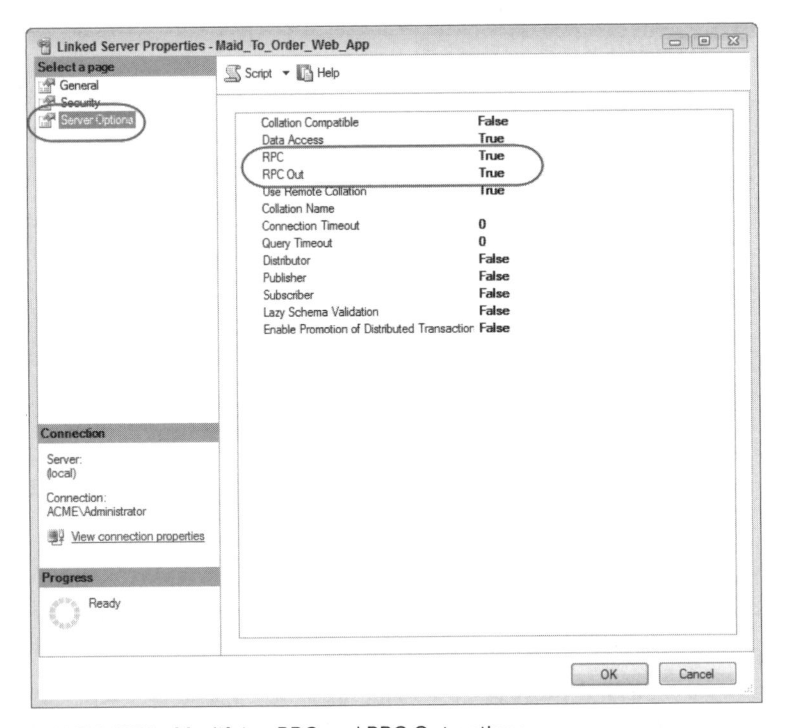

FIGURE 11-76: Modifying RPC and RPC Out options

Take note of the Enable Promotion of Distributed Transaction option, which defaults to True. You will see it again when we talk about using temporary tables later in this section. With those changes, you are now ready to use a linked server's stored procedures and functions.

As you saw in Figure 11-72, you can only browse tables and views, but you can actually also execute programmatic objects such as stored procedures via a linked server. If you have a scenario where you would want to invoke such objects on the web app's database, the best method for doing so is to use `EXEC ... AT`.

To avoid problems with writing dynamic SQL and potential SQL injections, we strongly recommend that you parameterize the `EXEC` statement. Let us suppose that you want to add a new customer to the web app's database and there's already a data macro that performs the job — you saw the `dmCustomerCreate` data macro in Chapter 9. You can invoke the data macro as a stored procedure. A T-SQL script to create the customer may look like this:

```
DECLARE
  @NewCustomerID Int = NULL,
  @FirstName NVarChar(4000) = 'Billy',
  @MiddleInitial NVarChar(4000) = 'T',
  @LastName NVarChar(4000) = 'Goat',
  @OrganizationName NVarChar(4000) = 'Pixar',
  @FrequencyID Int = 1,
  @WeekdayID Int = 2,
  @StreetAddress NVarChar(4000) = '100 A Street',
  @Unit NVarChar(4000) = NULL,
  @City NVarChar(4000) = 'Hollywood',
  @State NVarChar(4000) = 'CA',
  @Zip NVarChar(4000) = '91601',
  @ZipFour NVarChar(4000) = NULL,
  @PhoneNumber NVarChar(4000) = '1301234567',
  @MobileNumber NVarChar(4000) = NULL,
  @Email NVarChar(4000) = 'billy@goat.com',
  @CrewID Int = 1,
  @ScheduleDate Date = '2013-03-04',
  @ScheduleTime DateTime2(3) = '13:00',
  @JobNotes NVarChar(Max) = NULL,
  @CurrentUserName NVarChar(4000) = 'ben@maidtoorder.onmicrosoft.com';

EXEC('EXEC Access.dmCustomerCreate
  @NewCustomerID = ? OUTPUT,
  @FirstName = ?,
  @MiddleInitial = ?,
  @LastName = ?,
  @OrganizationName = ?,
  @FrequencyID = ?,
  @WeekdayID = ?,
  @StreetAddress = ?,
  @Unit = ?,
  @City = ?,
  @State = ?,
```

```
    @Zip = ?,
    @ZipFour = ?,
    @PhoneNumber = ?,
    @MobileNumber = ?,
    @Email = ?,
    @CrewID = ?,
    @ScheduleDate = ?,
    @ScheduleTime = ?,
    @JobNotes = ?,
    @CurrentUserName = ?',
    @NewCustomerID OUTPUT,
    @FirstName,
    @MiddleInitial,
    @LastName,
    @OrganizationName,
    @FrequencyID,
    @WeekdayID,
    @StreetAddress,
    @Unit,
    @City,
    @State,
    @Zip,
    @ZipFour,
    @PhoneNumber,
    @MobileNumber,
    @Email,
    @CrewID,
    @ScheduleDate,
    @ScheduleTime,
    @JobNotes,
    @CurrentUserName
  ) AT [Maid_To_Order_Web_App];
  SELECT @NewCustomerID;
```

Note the `AT [Maid_To_Order_Web_App]` predicate, which instructs the SQL Server to marshal the statement to the linked server as opposed to simply executing it locally. You can see that you don't have to insert the parameters into the SQL string. However, you must provide the parameters in the same order they should appear within the SQL string because there are no named parameters. That means the position of parameters matters. Also note that `@NewCustomerID` needs to have `OUTPUT` in two places: within the SQL string itself and as a part of the `EXEC ... AT` statement to ensure that the output values all make their way back from the linked server to you.

> **NOTE** *For programmatic objects with many parameters such as* `dmCustomerCreate`*, you may want to connect to the web app's server directly and use scripting, as shown in Figure 11-73, to quickly list the parameters you need to work with for your T-SQL scripting within the local SQL Server database.*

A web app database may contain other programmatic objects: table-valued functions, which can be accessed via an `EXEC ... AT` statement as well.

```
DECLARE @SelectedCustomerID int = 700;
EXEC ('SELECT * FROM [Access].[qryCustomerGetLastJob](?)',
  @SelectedCustomerID
) AT [Maid_To_Order_Web_App];
```

Note that unlike stored procedures, you cannot pass a named parameter to a table-valued function, which also makes the requirement to have correct position for each single parameter much more important.

For ad-hoc querying and to allow heterogeneous joins, you could use OPENQUERY as shown here:

```
SELECT * FROM OPENQUERY(
[Maid_To_Order_Web_App],
'SELECT * FROM [Access].[qryCustomerGetLastJob](700);'
);
```

However, OPENQUERY, along with its sibling functions OPENROWSERT and OPENDATASOURCE, cannot accept parameters, which makes them ill-suited for managing objects that require parameters. For this reason, we recommend that if you need to perform heterogeneous operations, you should consider alternatives such as inserting the output of EXEC ... AT into a temporary table, as demonstrated in this script:

```
CREATE TABLE #tmpCustomers (
  CustomerID int,
  CrewID int,
  ScheduleDate date,
  ScheduleTime time,
  FrequencyID int
);
DECLARE @SelectedCustomerID int = 700;
INSERT INTO #tmpCustomers
EXEC ('SELECT * FROM [Access].[qryCustomerGetLastJob](?)',
  @SelectedCustomerID
) AT [Maid_To_Order_Web_App];
SELECT * FROM #tmpCustomers;
DROP TABLE #tmpCustomers;
```

DISTRIBUTED QUERY TRANSACTION

The script provided requires a distributed transaction because it inserts data from a remote source. You may get an error similar to this:

```
OLE DB provider "SQLNCLI11" for linked server
"Maid_To_Order_Web_App" returned message
"The partner transaction manager has disabled
its support for remote/network transactions.".
Msg 7391, Level 16, State 2, Line 9
The operation could not be performed because
OLE DB provider "SQLNCLI11" for linked server
"Maid_To_Order_Web_App" was unable to begin a
distributed transaction.
```

continues

continued

This can happen when the remote server will not allow distributed transactions. If you are not concerned about enforcing integrity across servers, you can disable the default option of promoting to a distributed transaction using the following T-SQL script:

```
USE [master]
GO
EXEC master.dbo.sp_serveroption
  @server=N'Maid_To_Order_Web_App',
  @optname=N'remote proc transaction promotion',
  @optvalue=N'false'
```

Alternatively, you could use DAO transactions to execute heterogeneous queries which simplify the process of distributing a transaction among servers but with less assurance than a true distributed transaction.

Generally speaking, we feel that it's usually best to use temporary tables when you need to perform joins to ensure you do not consume excessive network bandwidth in processing the data.

All in all, you've learned a new array of tools available to you to make it easy to work with your web app database and manage it effectively along with your existing SQL Server databases.

The significance of being able to do this should not be lost on Access developers. To those who have questioned the limitations of web apps as a viable tool for Line-Of-Business apps, it should be clear that the ability to use standard SQL Server tools enables you to work with your web app's database effectively. In fact, you can easily see that the accessibility of the web app database means you can program against it with any number of existing programming languages. At this early stage, the process is still a bit rough around the edges. Nonetheless, there is a clear path forward for Access developers who are willing to adopt a more versatile approach toward development.

NOTE *If you want to script out mirroring objects for stored procedures and functions similar to what you saw earlier in the section, "Querying Data in a Linked Server," you can use* `INFORMATION_SCHEMA.ROUTINES` *and* `INFORMATION_SCHEMA.PARAMETERS` *to provide you with the needed metadata on the objects.*

SUMMARY

You've learned about a lot of new opportunities that epitomize what Access is all about: making data accessible. Although the data is now in the cloud, it is still easy to access the data, and Microsoft has provided you with tools to make a client file quickly and simply with options for you to dig deeper.

You learned about effectively managing your connections, both within the web app and within the client. The code provided illustrates one possible method out of several to make it easy to maintain the client's link to the database behind the web app with minimum effort. You will learn more about some of these aspects in Chapter 13 when we delve into security in more detail.

You've now seen examples of how you can use the new tools in Excel to provide reporting options for your web apps. In the last sections of this chapter, you looked at how you can manage your web database in SSMS. You saw how you can support scenarios where you have a pre-existing local SQL Server to facilitate cross database querying using linked servers and scripting creation to provide an easy interface to the linked servers. All in all, you now have more tools available to you for delivering a professional solution to your consumers that combines the power of your familiar Access client tools with the ability to deploy web apps using the same database. You will see more possibilities when you consider enterprise solutions in Chapter 12.

12

Web Apps in the Enterprise

WHAT'S IN THIS CHAPTER?

- Creating a library to hold Access templates in an app catalog
- Creating an Access client template
- Customizing an app package
- Synchronizing data between app databases

WROX.COM CODE DOWNLOADS FOR THIS CHAPTER

The code and sample downloads for this chapter are found at `www.wiley.com/go/proaccess2013prog.com` on the Download Code tab. They are in the Chapter 12 download and individually named according to the filenames listed throughout the chapter. The app packages for the web apps in this chapter are called Maid to Order and Maid to Order Customer.

In this chapter, you learn how to more fully incorporate your Access web apps, and the databases behind them, into your enterprise environment. In many organizations, Access developers have struggled with the fact that their database applications have been relatively isolated from the rest of the IT infrastructure. Access web apps, deployed in the SharePoint app catalog, can go a long way toward closing that gap. In this chapter, we show you some ways that can be done.

First, you learn how to create a SharePoint library to store Access client templates for deployment to authorized developers in the organization. Under the control of the SharePoint admin, Access files in the Access Template Library can be used to start everyone off on the same baseline.

Then, you learn how to customize your app packages with a corporate logo, branding them for your corporate use.

And finally, you learn some techniques for synchronizing data between web app databases, as well as creating a differential backup of data from an app database. For the local backup, we assume you have a local SQL Server instance to which you have admin rights. Your web app databases need not be on-premises for the backup process, however.

Although this is a fairly limited list of features to begin with, we believe it will help get you started in the direction of integrating your Access web apps and Access client databases into an enterprise environment.

> **WARNING** *All of the material in this chapter assumes you are using Access 2013, SharePoint 2013, and SQL Server 2012, as you would expect. Although some VBA functions would be similar in earlier versions, we do want to remind you that you may experience unexpected results if you attempt to use earlier versions of Access, especially when working with SharePoint features.*

> **NOTE** *A list of some of the potential issues you may encounter while working with web apps is available in the "What You Need to Use this Book" section of the Introduction.*

CREATING A DOCUMENT LIBRARY

In this section, you learn about sharing your Access files with others in the enterprise. You will need a document library to hold templates of Access files, which may be either `.accdb` or `.accdt` files, depending on your specific requirements. Because these files will typically be used with web apps, it may make sense to store them in your app catalog so there is a uniform location for you and other developers to go to when downloading app packages from an app catalog. One possible place is to create a document library on the same site where the app catalog is hosted. Maid To Order's account is a Microsoft Office 365 Small Business Premium plan; the app catalog is located at this URL:

```
https://maidtoorder.sharepoint.com/sites/appcatalog
```

Not all Office 365 plans support App Catalogs. If you are not sure what your plan supports, you can search for "app catalog." Several SharePoint pages have a search box on the upper-right corner; enter App Catalog in the search box and hit enter. If one is found it will look like Figure 12-1.

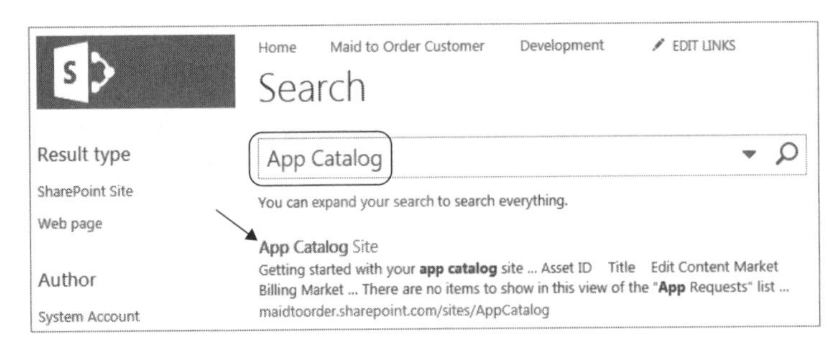

FIGURE 12-1: Search returns a list of App Catalog pages

If you cannot find it, you may want to check the Admin pane to see whether you can create an app catalog, as shown in Figure 12-2

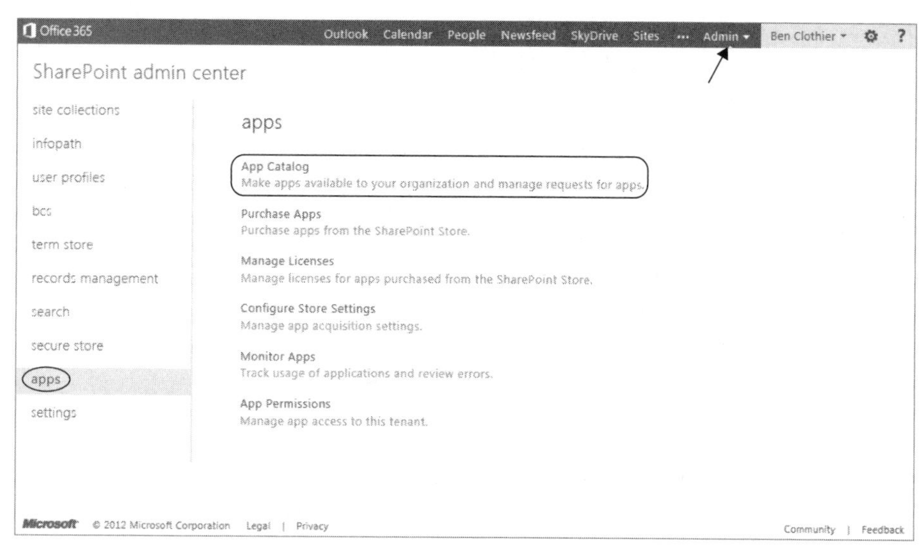

FIGURE 12-2: Create App Catalog

If you can find neither, then you probably do not have the App Catalog feature available in your site. If your plan has the option to create an App Catalog, as illustrated in Figure 12-2, then you may need to create a site for App Catalog via the Admin pane. If you need to place the App Catalog in a subsite, refer to Chapter 13 for a refresher on creating subsites.

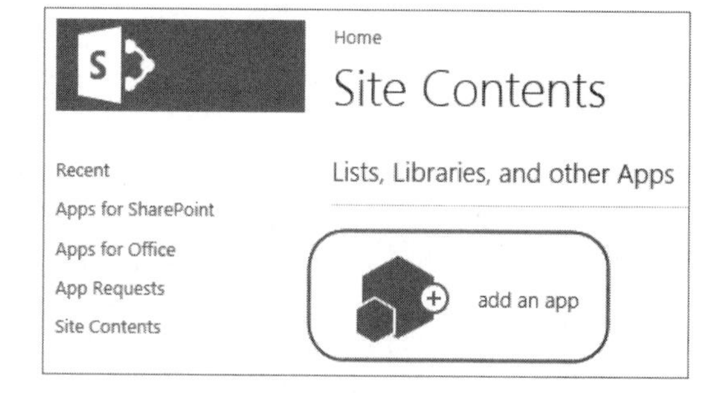

FIGURE 12-3: Site Contents page

We put the document library in the app catalog on the assumption that most organizations would prefer to make it available to designated developers. Due to different rights requirements, you might prefer to use your team site so more people can use it. Because we are putting it in an app catalog site, which has a separate permission hierarchy, you might need to refer to Chapter 13 for more information on how to grant permissions to designated users who should be able to get the templates.

FIGURE 12-4: Document Library app

Because the document library should also hold Access files and templates, you'll want to customize the library a bit so that it's easy to create new files using a common baseline. To get started, go to the app catalog URL as indicated, and within that page select the Site Contents link, click "add an app" and select Document Library, as shown in Figures 12-3 and 12-4.

Give this app a descriptive name that fits your environment and create it; Figure 12-5 shows one possible name.

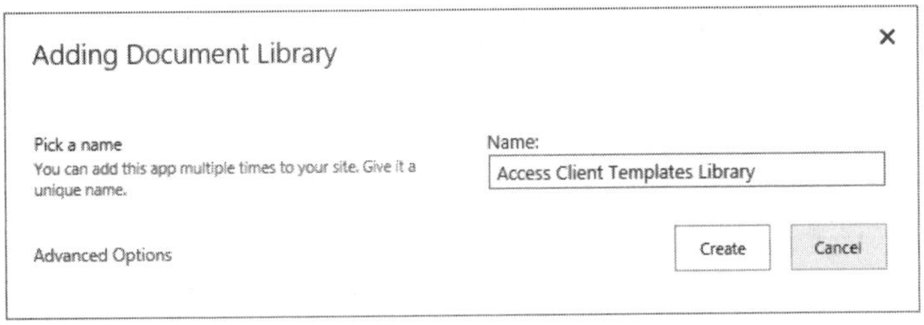

Adding Document Library

Pick a name
You can add this app multiple times to your site. Give it a unique name.

Name:
Access Client Templates Library

Advanced Options

Create Cancel

FIGURE 12-5: Naming and creating a document library

On the Site Contents page, click the newly created library to go to the library's page. On its page, open the ribbon and select Edit Library, as shown in Figure 12-6.

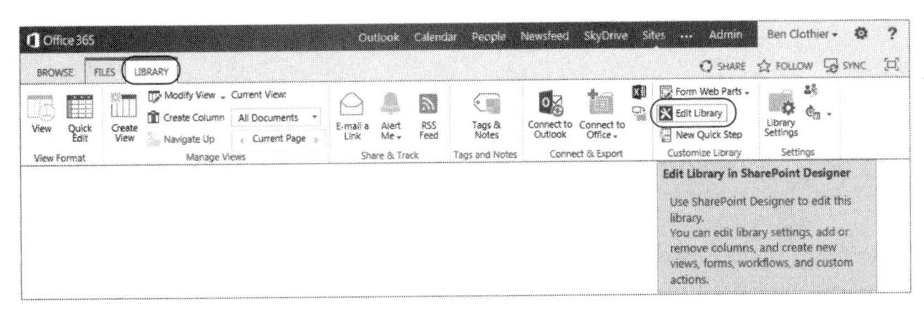

FIGURE 12-6: Edit Library in SharePoint Designer

> **NOTE** *If the Edit Library button shown in Figure 12-6 is disabled, it may mean that SharePoint Designer is not installed, or that using Designer is not allowed on this site. In the former case, refer to Chapter 10 for instructions on installing SharePoint Designer. In the latter case, consult with the site owner to enable the Designer, which you can do via the Site Settings page.*

Within SharePoint Designer, you will do the following:

- Create a custom content type representing an Access file
- Import image files that you will use for custom buttons you create
- Change the library's template to point to an Access file that you upload
- Customize the library's ribbon to open this new template

This makes it easier for people using the library to create a new file based on the same template, and you can upload edits to the template as you need to. This gives you an easy way to maintain standard client files for use across the organization.

Creating a Custom Content Type

In SharePoint Designer, open the Content Types via the Navigation pane, as shown in Figure 12-7.

When you are on Content Types, the ribbon should show a New group with Content Type, as illustrated in Figure 12-8. Select it to create a new content type.

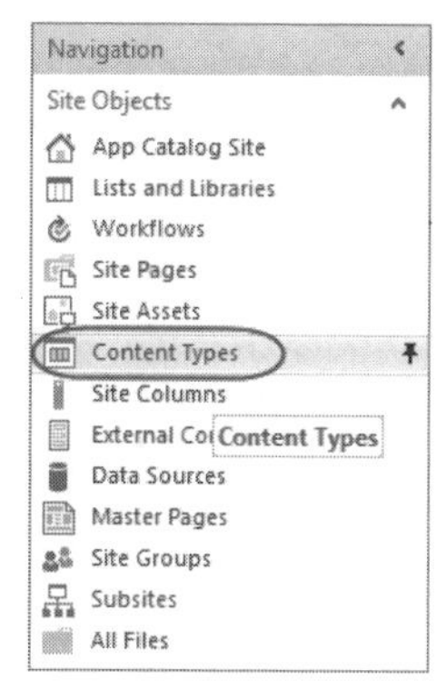

FIGURE 12-7: Clicking Content Types

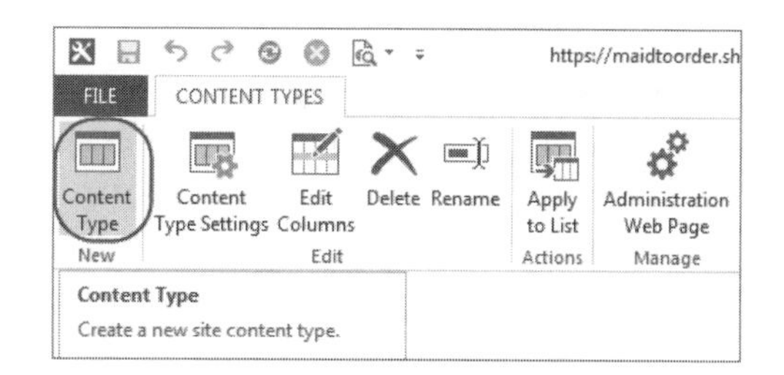

FIGURE 12-8: New Content Type button

Provide a name, and, because it should be based on Access files, you want it to inherit from the Document content type. You may want to create a new group to keep your templates organized should you have multiple templates. Figure 12-9 illustrates how you could fill out the dialog box to create the new content type.

If you create a new group, the Content Types tab lists your brand new content type under the new group that you also created, similar to what you see in Figure 12-10.

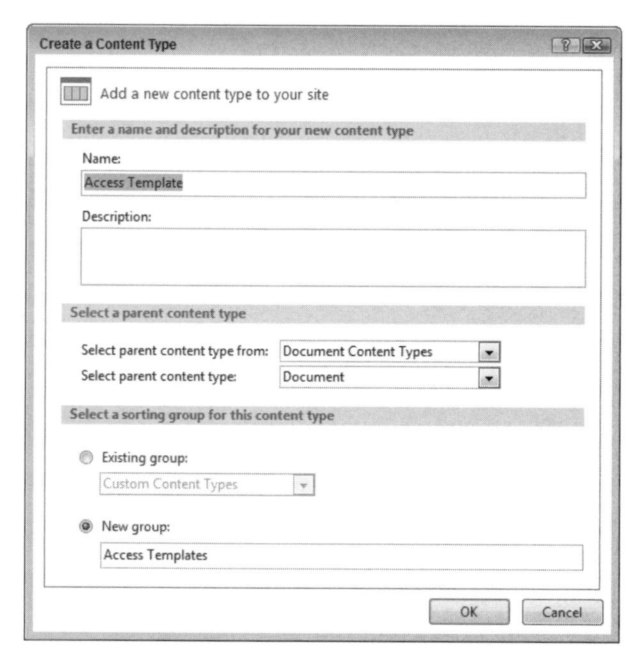

FIGURE 12-9: Creating a Content Type dialog box

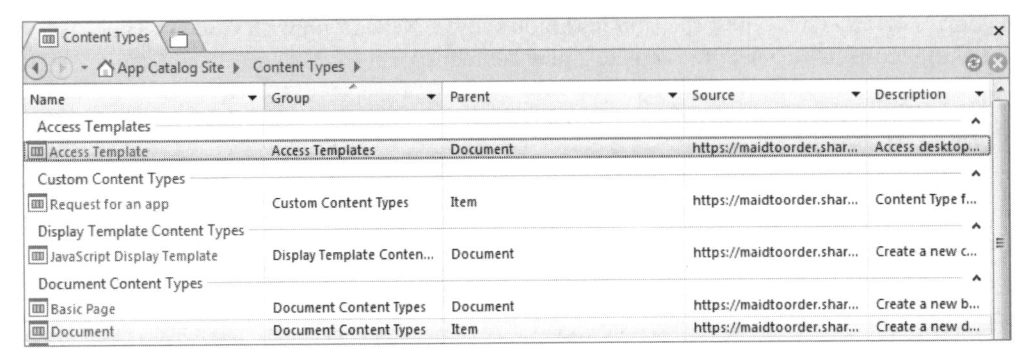

FIGURE 12-10: New content type added

A template for this content type has to be uploaded in SharePoint, not via the SharePoint Designer. To do this, go to the ribbon and select Administration Web Page, as shown in Figure 12-11.

On the web page in your web browser, click the Advanced Settings link, as depicted in Figure 12-12.

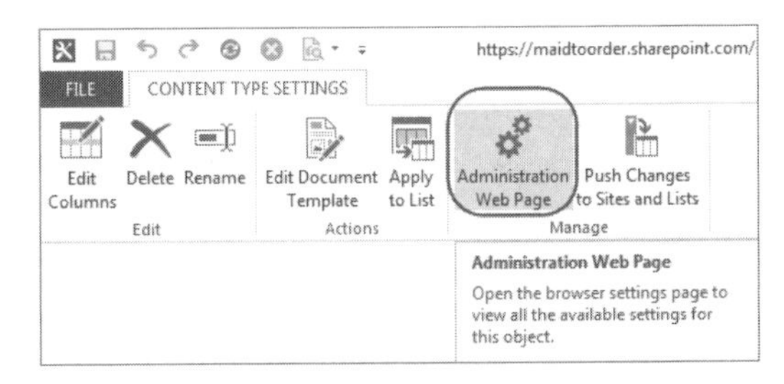

FIGURE 12-11: Administration Web Page button

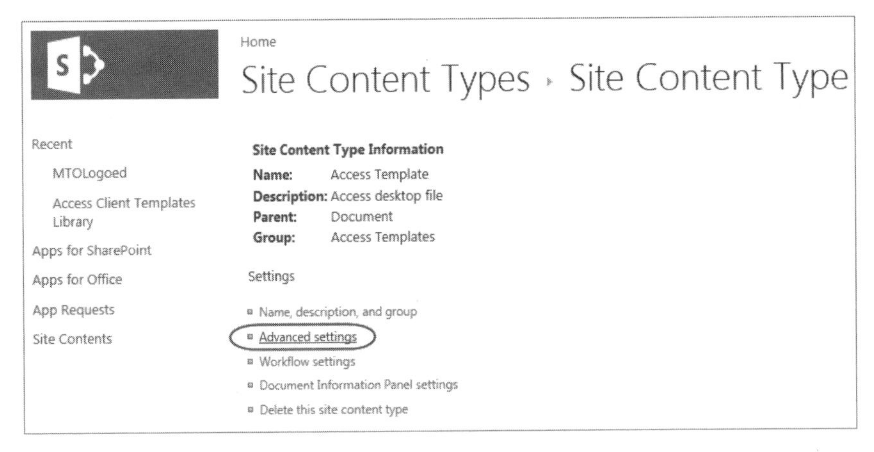

FIGURE 12-12: Advanced Settings link

On the page illustrated in Figure 12-13, you can upload an Access `.accdb` as a template. You could choose to use an `.accdt` file instead if it suits your needs. The template you prepare for your organization should include standard elements that you want all databases to have, such as a splash form, menu system, AutoExec macro, standard VBA functions, and other objects you want developers to use in all databases, and so on. The exact content depends on your organization's standard. Click Browse and select the Access client file to upload. Once uploaded, click OK to save the changes.

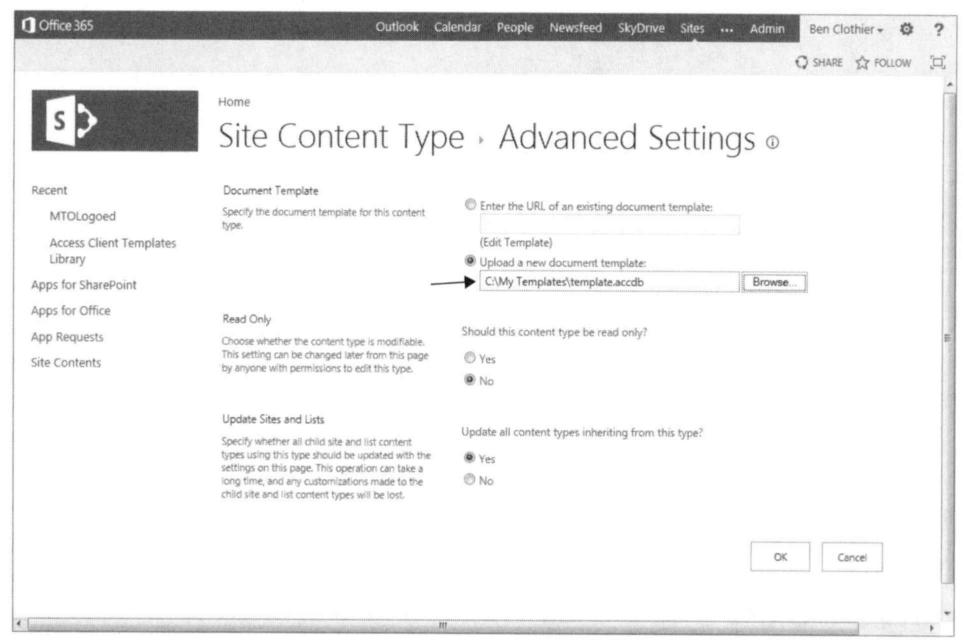

FIGURE 12-13: Advanced Settings page

Importing Image Files

After uploading the template file, return to SharePoint Designer. You'll also want to upload images that you will use later for custom buttons you create for your library. You can upload both 32x32 and 16x16 graphical files. One way to do this is to select All Files in the Navigation pane and select the images folder, as shown in Figure 12-14.

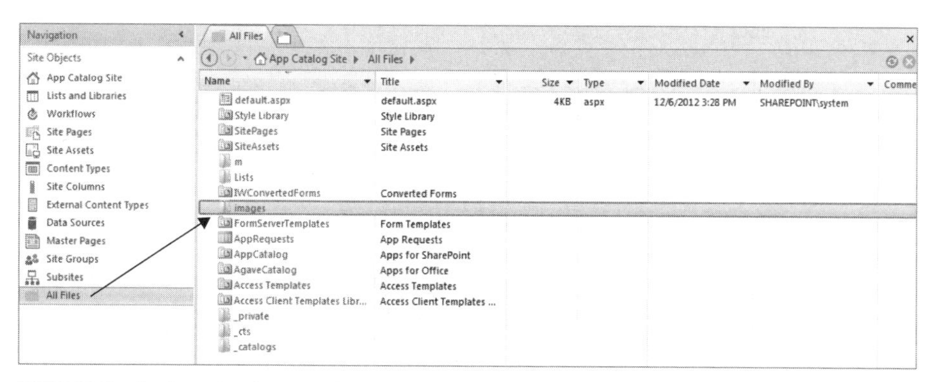

FIGURE 12-14: Opening images folder

The image folder may be initially blank. On the ribbon, select Import Files, as illustrated in Figure 12-15.

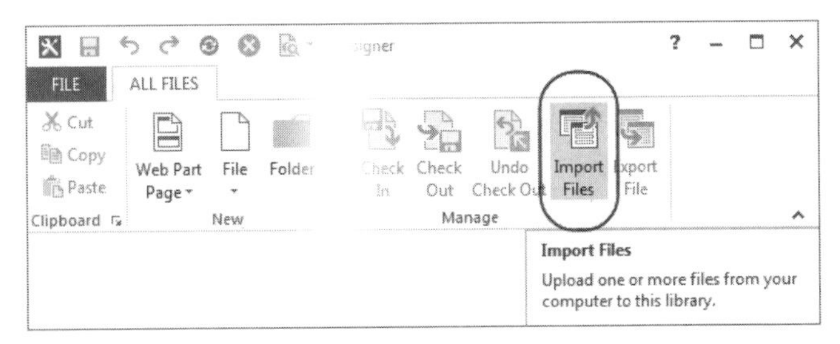

FIGURE 12-15: Import Files button

In the dialog box shown in Figure 12-16, add your two image files sized at 16x16 and 32x32 using the Add Files button. Then click OK to complete the import.

Once the import process completes, you should see the files listed in the images folder. You will need them later on when you create a custom action.

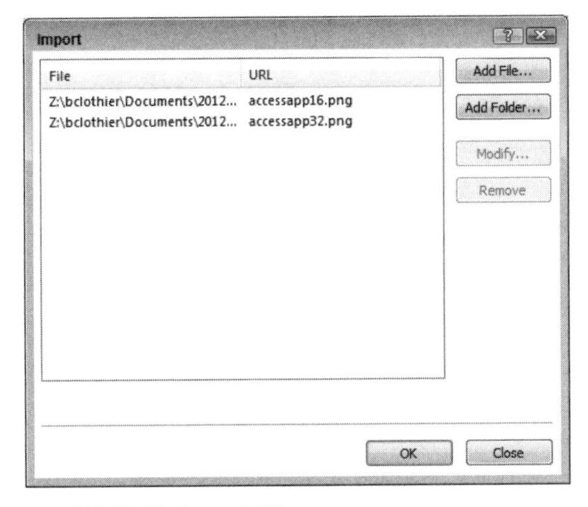

FIGURE 12-16: Import Files

Customizing a Library

Select List and Library in the Navigation pane in Designer to return to the new library you created previously and click once on the new library's name, as demonstrated in Figure 12-17.

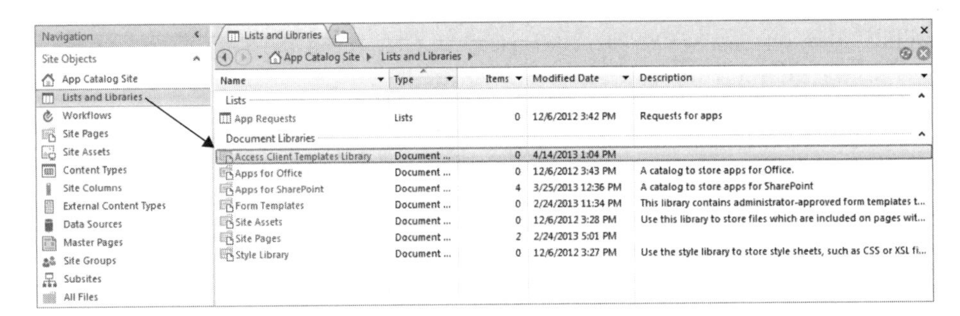

FIGURE 12-17: Lists and Libraries pane

You should land on the configuration sheet for your library, which contains a number of panes. You'll start with the Settings pane by selecting Allow management of content types, as shown in Figure 12-18.

Next, on the Content Types pane, click the Add button to add a new content type to the library, as shown in Figure 12-19.

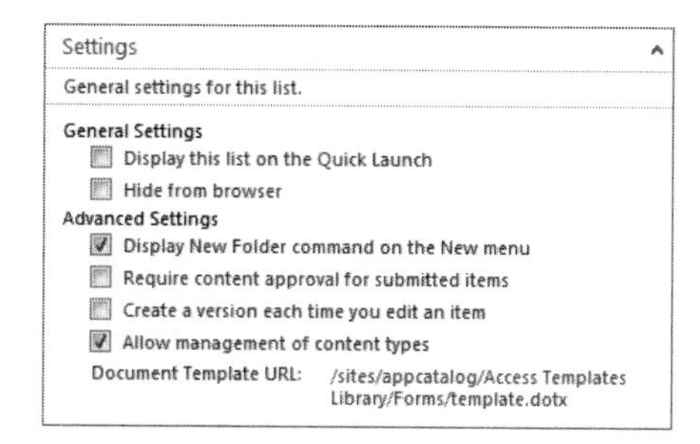

FIGURE 12-18: Settings pane

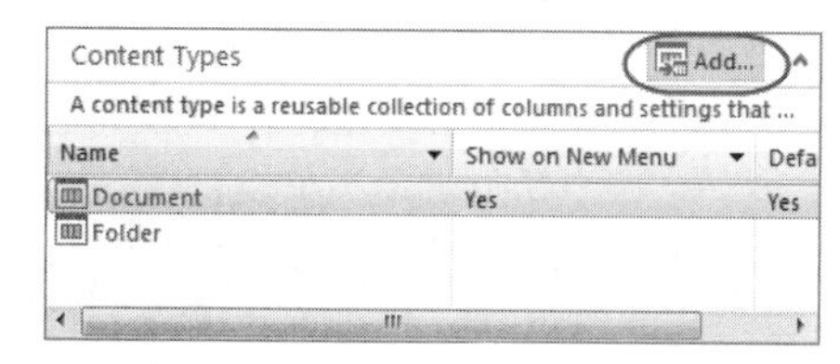

FIGURE 12-19: Add button on the Content Type pane

A dialog box will appear to select a content type; select the custom content type that you created previously, similar to what is shown in Figure 12-20.

Back on the Content Types pane, select two other content types that are there by default — Document and Folder — and press delete to delete those content types, leaving you with only a custom content type, as shown in Figure 12-21.

Return to the Settings pane and clear the Allow management of content types checkbox.

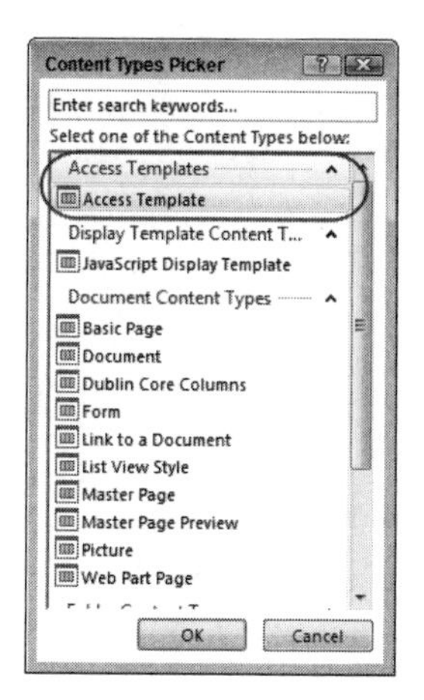

FIGURE 12-20: Selecting a content type

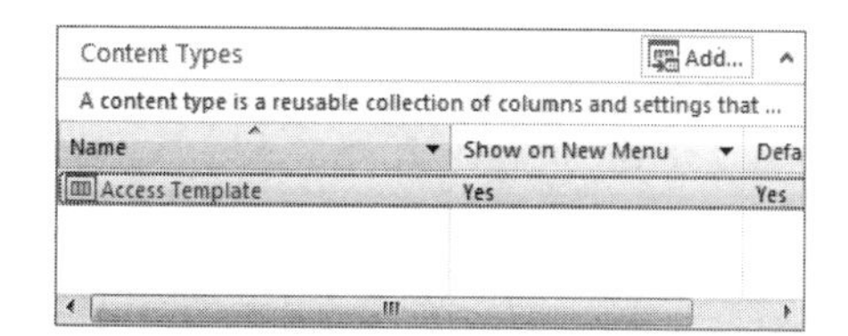

FIGURE 12-21: Other content types removed

> **NOTE** *Although you've removed other content types and disallowed management of content types, that will not prevent the uploading of wrong file types to the library.*

Customizing a Library Ribbon

On the ribbon's List Settings tab, select View Ribbon from the Custom Actions drop-down as shown in Figure 12-22.

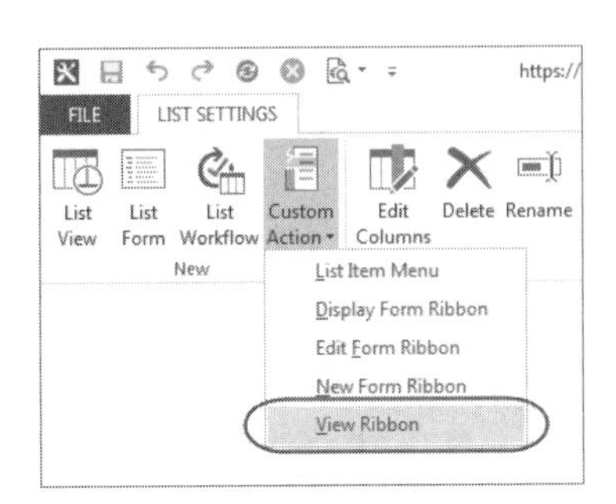

FIGURE 12-22: New Custom Action

A Create Custom Action dialog box appears, as shown in Figure 12-23. Fill in a name and description, and then scroll down the dialog box, if needed.

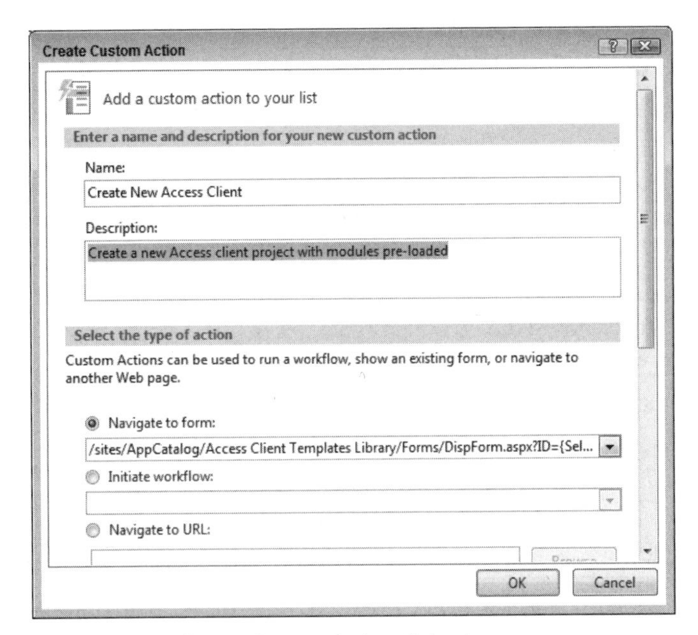

FIGURE 12-23: Create Custom Action dialog box

Look at Figure 12-24, which depicts the bottom part of the same dialog box that you'll need to fill out.

For the action itself, select the Navigate to URL radio button and browse to the template `.accdb` file you previously uploaded to the library. If you've been following our path, the address would be located at:

```
https://maidtoorder.sharepoint.com/sites/AppCatalog/Access Client Templates
Library/Forms/Access Template/template.accdb
```

You can add images to the action to use in displaying the action on the ribbon. You will set URLs for images using the same path that you set in the previous section. For example, the URLs for the two images are:

```
https://maidtoorder.sharepoint.com/sites/AppCatalog/images/accessapp16.png
https://maidtoorder.sharepoint.com/sites/AppCatalog/images/accessapp32.png
```

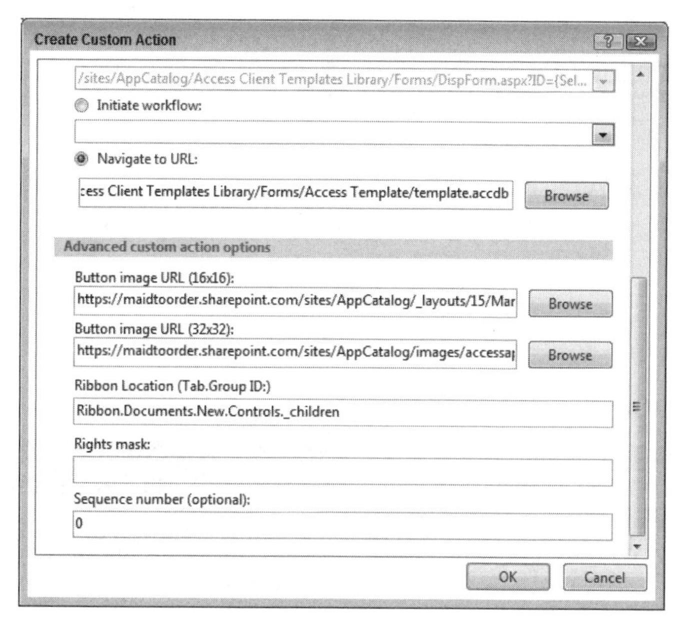

FIGURE 12-24: Bottom portion of the Create Custom Action dialog box

Finally, you need to set the location where the custom action should appear. You want it to appear in the New group of the ribbon, so enter the following directive:

```
Ribbon.Documents.New.Controls._children
```

Ensure that the sequence is set at 0, which makes the custom action appear leftmost in the group. Click OK to save the changes so far. This provides you with a custom button that will download the template and, depending on the browser's configuration, open it in Access directly. However, the steps taken so far do not actually eliminate the built-in buttons to create a new document. This can be a problem because the built-in button will attempt to open Word unless users remember to use the drop-down menu to explicitly select the custom content type. To avoid this stumbling block, you need to hide the built-in button, allowing the custom action you just created to replace it entirely.

To do this, select All Files from the Navigation pane, similar to what you did for uploading images. This time, however, open the folder representing your custom document library and then the Forms folder within it. You should get a list like the one shown in Figure 12-25. Note the breadcrumbs shown in the image.

FIGURE 12-25: Complete listing of the library's forms

As Figure 12-26 shows, select `AllItems.aspx` and open it in advanced mode. Locate the `asp:Contents` element that contains an attribute-value pair `ContentPlaceHolderId=PlaceHolderMain`. Inside this element, add a `style` element as the first child element:

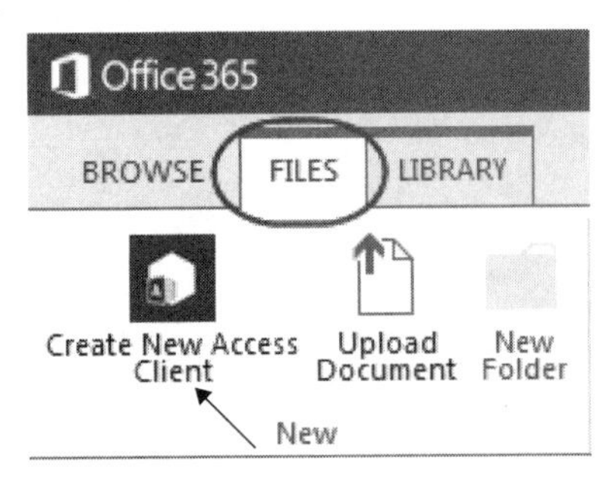

FIGURE 12-26: Customized Library ribbon

```
<style type="text/css">
#Ribbon\.Documents\.New\.NewDocument-Large {
    display:none;
}
#Ribbon\.Documents\.New\.NewDocument {
    display:none;
}
</style>
```

If you are unfamiliar with CSS, the style indicates that, for an element with an `id` attribute set to `Ribbon.Documents.New.NewDocument-Large`, the attribute `display:none;` should be applied. The backslash is used to escape the period character while the pound sign signifies that CSS is to select by an element's `id` rather than by the element's type or class. You can discover the `id` of an element by using a web browser's developer tools to inspect the elements and discover its `id` and `class` attribute to use for CSS selection. Refer to Chapter 10 for a brief overview on using developer tools in your web browser.

Save the change; you will get a dialog box warning that the change no longer matches the site definition. Click Yes and proceed. Open the new library in the browser. The final result should look similar to Figure 12-26.

Version Control

A significant advantage of storing Access files in a SharePoint document library is that you also gain some version control, which you traditionally have with Source Code Control (SCC). While it is not as granular as an SCC plugin where you can check in/out individual objects, for some scenarios versioning may be sufficient to manage the file without tracking the individual objects. Thus you will find many advantages in configuring versioning for the library. The configuration is best done on SharePoint where you have more options than in SharePoint Designer. In SharePoint Designer, navigate to the library and select the Administration Web Page button on the ribbon, similar to what you saw in Figure 12-11. That will take you to the page for List Settings as shown in Figure 12-27.

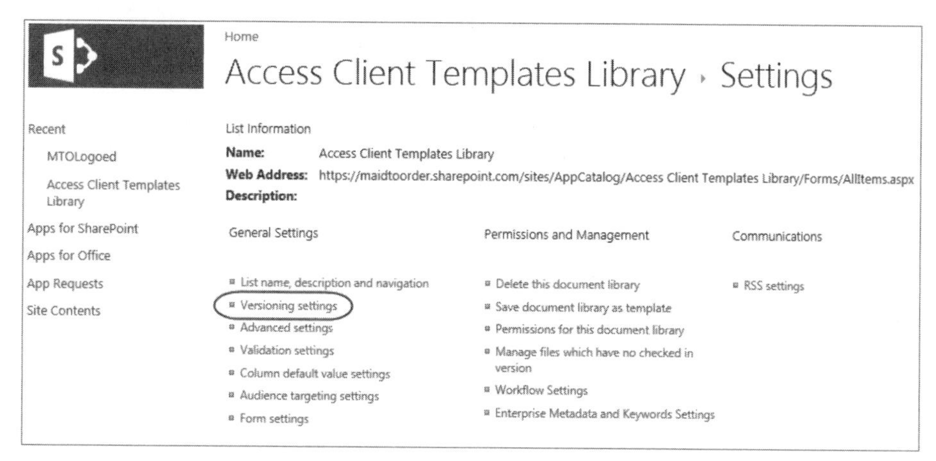

FIGURE 12-27: List Settings page

Click the Versioning settings link, which will take you to the page depicted in Figure 12-28.

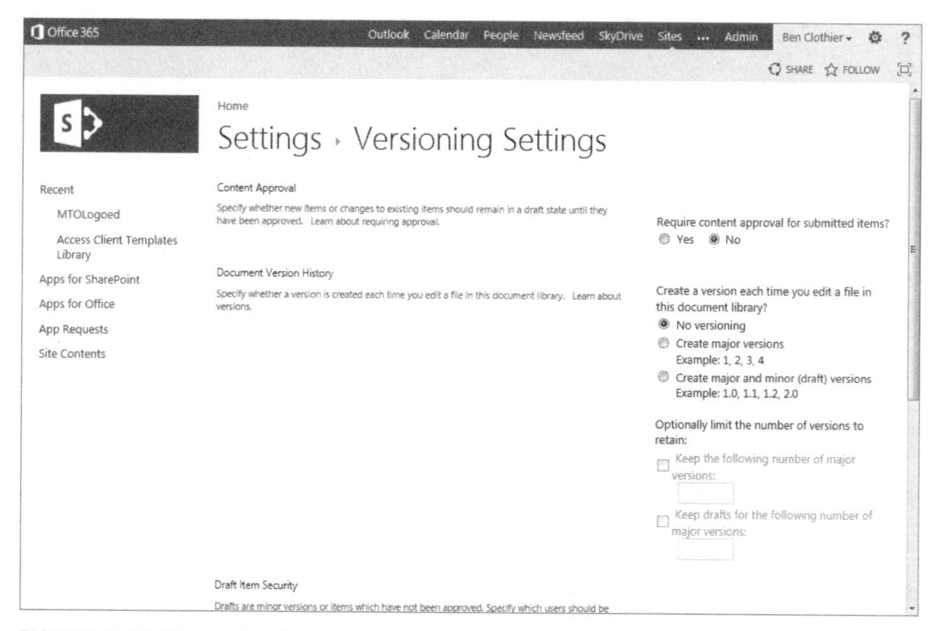

FIGURE 12-28: Versioning Settings page

On this page, you can choose whether you want to:

- Require approval for any submitted items
- Version a document every time it is edited
- Restrict visibility of items to non-creators
- Require that a document be checked out before editing it

You can customize as needed to meet your particular needs. When you have versioning enabled, you can access the history of edited files via Version History on the ribbon shown in Figure 12-29, which provides you with the popup shown in Figure 12-30 where you can view, restore, or delete versions.

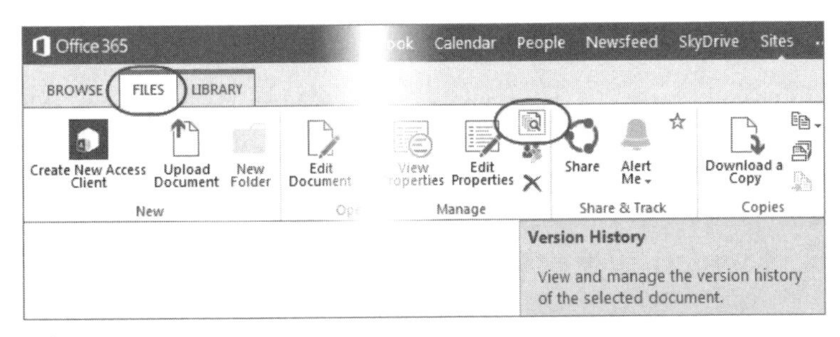

FIGURE 12-29: Version History button

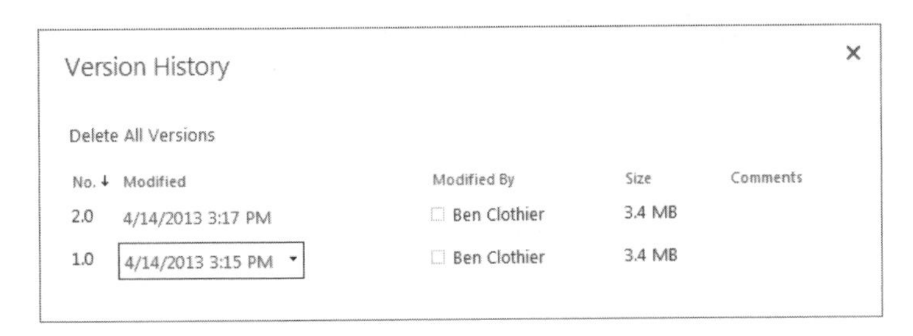

FIGURE 12-30: Version History dialog box

Although a SharePoint document library is not as full-featured as traditional source code control software, the fact that it comes built-in to any SharePoint installation is quite a compelling case for storing your Access template files with it if they are not a part of traditional source code control projects. Of course, you need to plan storage requirements and management for maintaining multiple versions.

CUSTOMIZING AN APP PACKAGE

In previous chapters, you've learned how to create a web app; how to save it as a local app package, both for backup and for deployment to other SharePoint sites; and how to install the app package into a site. In all of those examples, the app has appeared with a generic Access icon when installed. In Chapter 10, you learned how to install third-party apps, which have their own logos, and you probably wondered if you couldn't do the same for the apps you deploy into your enterprise app catalog. We'll show you how to do that now.

The process is very straightforward, if not entirely obvious at first.

Begin by creating a local app package as you learned how to do in Chapter 3, and for which you will get more details in Chapter 14. As a refresher, you can see this process illustrated in Figures 12-31 and 12-32.

As you can see in Figure 12-31, we gave this app package a different name so we can more easily identify it in the app catalog.

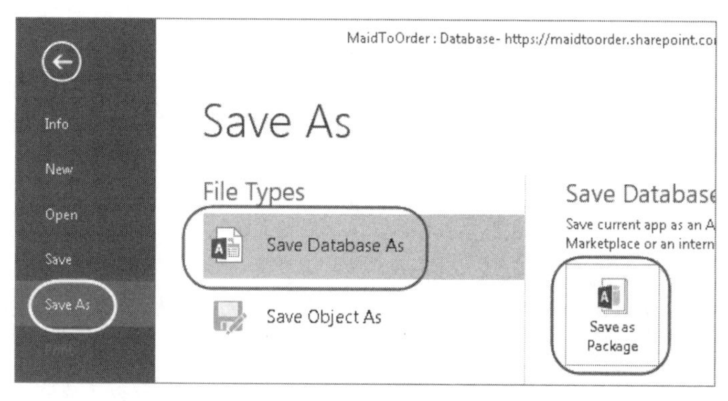

FIGURE 12-31: Creating an app package

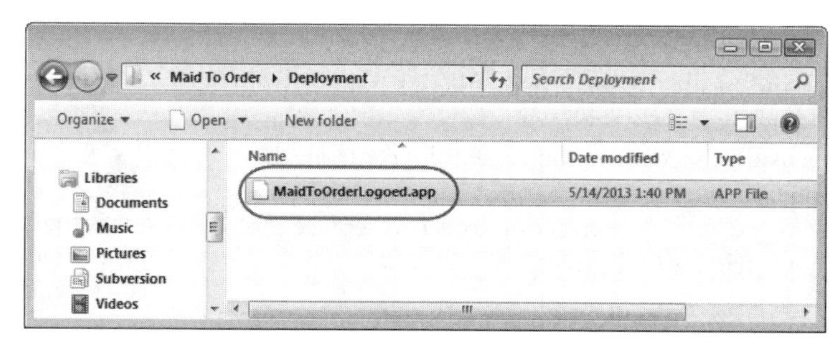

FIGURE 12-32: Local app package

The next step is to rename the app package, changing the extension from `.app` to `.zip`, so you can handle it as a Zip file. In fact, app packages are Zip files. With the renamed app package, right-click the file and select "extract" from the shortcut menu. You'll be asked for a destination folder and offered a default name. Go ahead and use that folder and name as shown in Figure 12-33.

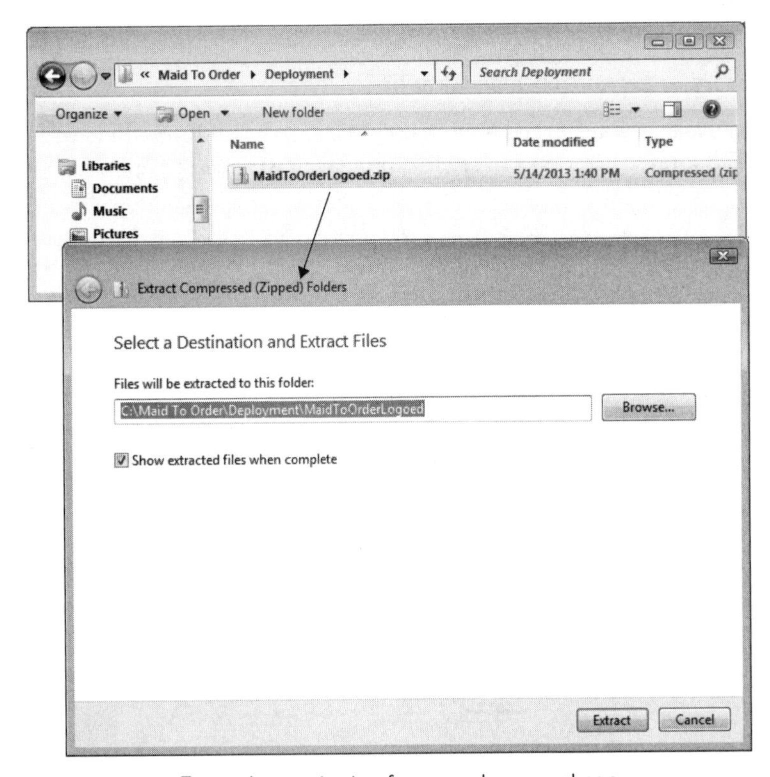

FIGURE 12-33: Extracting contents of renamed app package

Now, open the extraction folder and locate the image icon file. It's named `accessapp.png`. You'll be replacing this image with your own. Your image needs to have the same name and dimensions, so remove the current image from the extraction folder. Locate your own image file and rename it to `accessapp.png`, if you haven't already done so. Copy it into the extraction folder to replace the original image. Figure 12-34 shows what it looks like.

FIGURE 12-34: Maid To Order icon to replace the generic image

The next step is to gather the files in the extraction folder and create a new Zip file from them as illustrated in Figure 12-35.

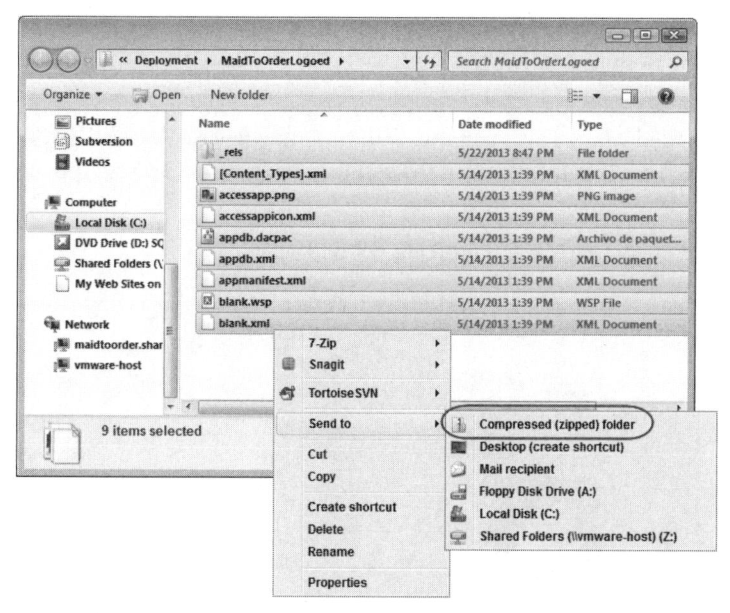

FIGURE 12-35: Creating a new Zip file from the extraction folder contents

> **WARNING** *A common mistake made is to try to zip the folder containing the files. Doing so will create an invalid .app package because the Zip file would contain the folder with files within, rather than putting all files directly in the Zip file.*

Be sure to create a new Zip file; don't reuse the old one. The new Zip file will end up in the extraction folder, but you can move it out of that folder to complete it for upload to your app catalog. You can see that in Figure 12-36

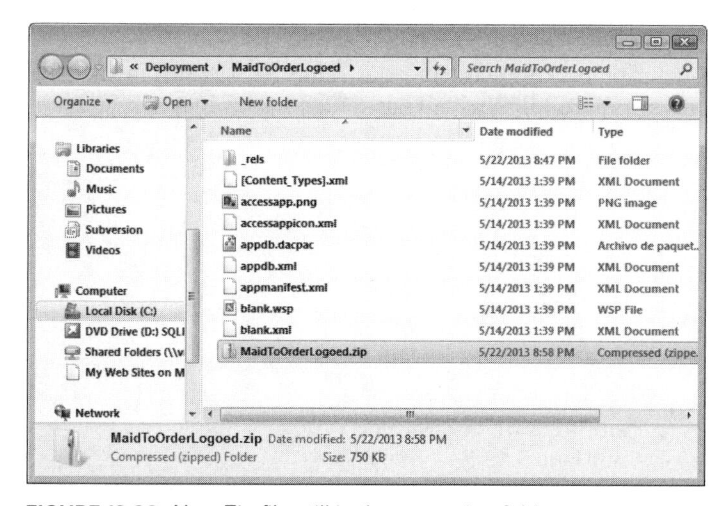

FIGURE 12-36: New Zip file still in the extraction folder

Move the new Zip file out of the extraction folder and rename it with the original `.app` extension. It is now ready for upload to your app catalog. You learned how to do this in a previous chapter, but as a refresher, refer to Figure 12-37.

As you can see, the previously uploaded Maid To Order apps still have the generic Access icon. Click on "add an app" and browse through the available apps until you find the generic Access App icon, shown in Figure 12-38.

Click the Access App icon. The dialog box shown in Figure 12-39 will open.

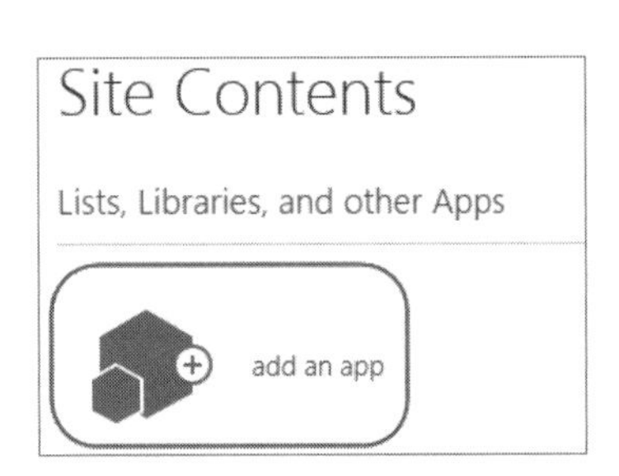

FIGURE 12-37: Adding an app

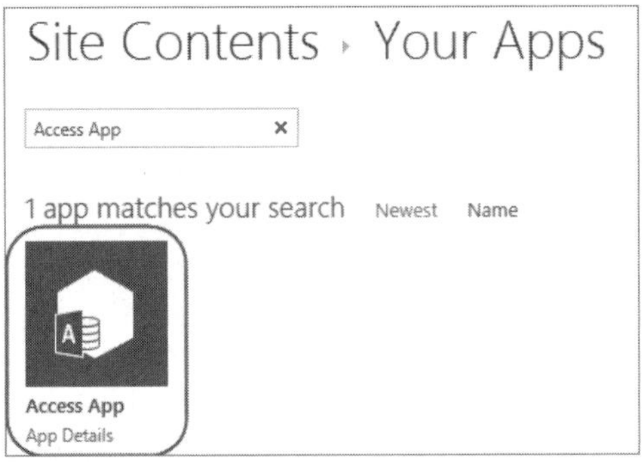

Site Contents › Your Apps

Access App ×

1 app matches your search Newest Name

Access App
App Details

FIGURE 12-38: Access App icon to add an app

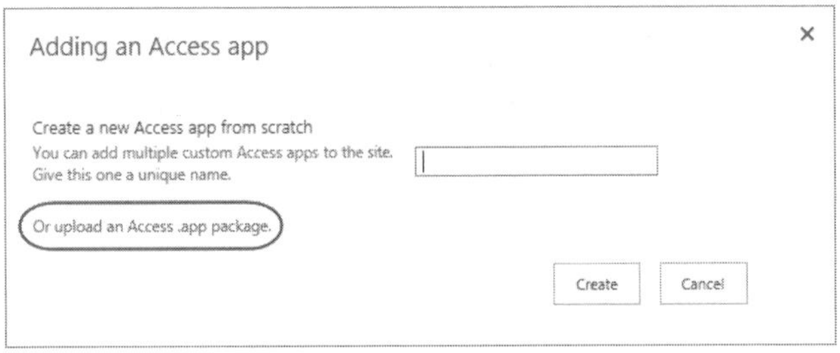

Adding an Access app ×

Create a new Access app from scratch
You can add multiple custom Access apps to the site. Give this one a unique name.

Or upload an Access .app package.

Create Cancel

FIGURE 12-39: Uploading an app package

Use the Browse button to find your new app package and upload it. Click the Create button and wait for the app package to be uploaded and installed, as in Figure 12-40. This may take a few minutes, so just be patient.

The final result will be like the one shown in Figure 12-41.

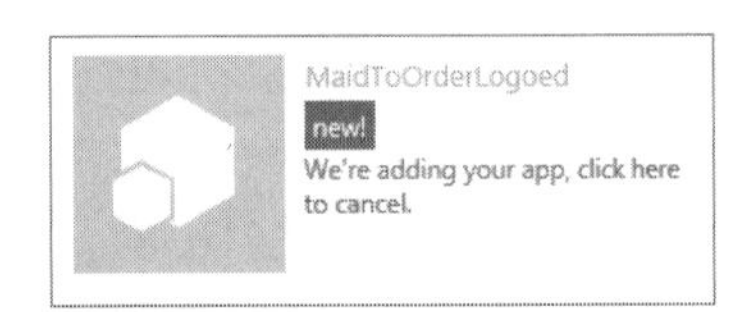

FIGURE 12-40: Installation of the new app in progress

FIGURE 12-41: Installed app with logo

You can see how easy it is to put your organization's logo in each app you deploy, whether in an enterprise setting or in a small site on Office 365.

LINKING TO A TEMPLATE FILE

When creating your custom Access web apps where you expect to need a client counterpart, it may be desirable to make it easier to link to the Access template (`.accdb` file in this example) you added to the document library in the previous section so you can download a template with all of the customizations you want or require in a client file. This is useful when you need to support different app packages that may need different clients and want to ensure there is a single point of distribution. You will create a web app template file with a blank view that contains a hyperlink pointing to the Access database template file you pointed to for the document library's custom action, as illustrated in Figure 12-42.

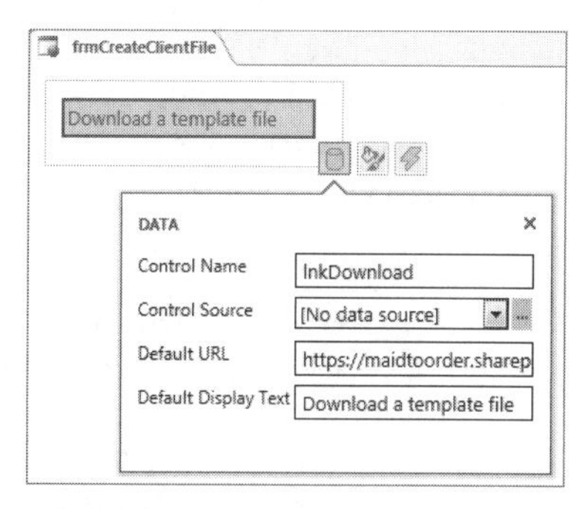

FIGURE 12-42: Template hyperlink

You can save the Access web app as a package and add it to the app catalog, making it available for reuse or for distribution to other developers. To start a new project using the same template, they choose the Access web app template added to the app catalog, as illustrated in Figure 12-43.

Thus, as Figure 12-44 shows, users are now just a click away from downloading the client file. They can customize and use it in conjunction with the new Access web app.

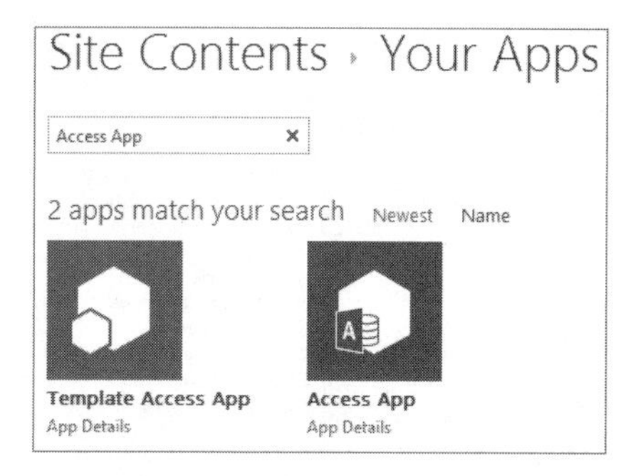

FIGURE 12-43: Adding Template Access app

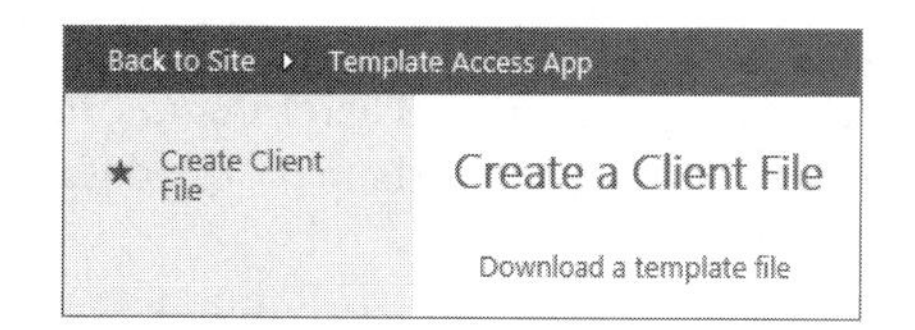

FIGURE 12-44: Template file hyperlink

SYNCHRONIZING DATA BETWEEN APP DATABASES

In this section, you learn a technique for synchronizing data between two different web app databases using familiar Access queries and VBA techniques. In addition, you learn about a method by which you can create a local, differential backup of the data in your web app databases to a local SQL Server installation. In all cases, we assume you have a local SQL Server instance to which you have sufficient rights in order to implement the methods demonstrated. Let's start with a simple method which involves Access client queries and VBA. If you wish to follow along, the code is available for download at `www.wiley.com/go/proaccess2013prog.com` in the file named `MTODailySynch.accdb`

> **NOTE** *There are many ways to implement functions in Access; backup and data synch are no exception. We only selected a possible method to show you here. You may very well prefer other methods of your own. Our point is primarily to make it clear that synchronizing and backing up the databases for your Access web apps should be a standard part of your maintenance plans.*

Local Differential Backup

To begin, you'll need to create a database on your local SQL Server installation. This database will be the local backup for the data in your web app database. You can call the database anything you like, but, of course, the name should reflect its relationship to the web app database to which it is created. Ours is called `MTOLocal`, reflecting its relationship to the Maid To Order web app database as illustrated by Figure 12-45.

Note that for the sake of clarity, we've set up only one table for this example. Your scenarios would normally include all tables for which you need to create backups. You can also see that you'll add two new fields to the table to support the backup process. Because both the local backup table and the web app database table have primary keys with identity specification, the primary keys on the local backup tables will differ from those in the web app database. Therefore, in order to link local records to their counterpart in the web app database, you need to store the primary key from the table in the web app database in a new field called `CustomerLinkID` in the local database. You can see that additional field in Figure 12-45.

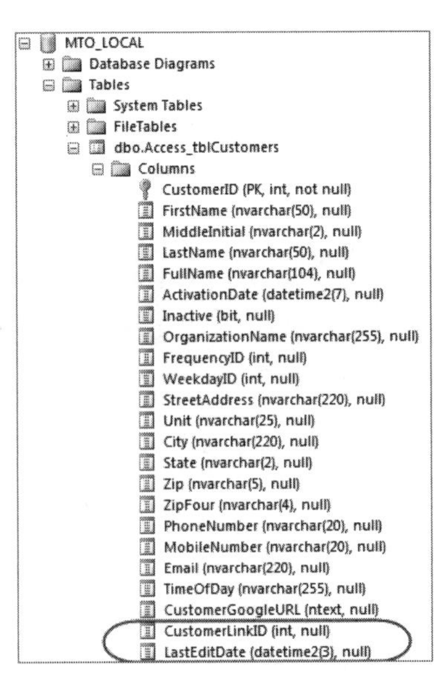

FIGURE 12-45: Local copy of table to be backed up

You'll also need a `datetime` field in the local table to store the `LastEditDate` (and time) for records. That gives you a value on which you can filter updates so that your backup only copies records in the web app database that were edited after the last backup. That allows you to do differential backups, updating only new and changed values from the web app. Figure 12-46 shows the same table in the database behind the web app.

The web app table in our example, `tblCustomers`, has the `LastEditDate` (Date and Time) field to capture the date and time of changes to this table. You'll create a data macro on this table to capture that information. Let's look at that step next. Consider the macro in Figure 12-47.

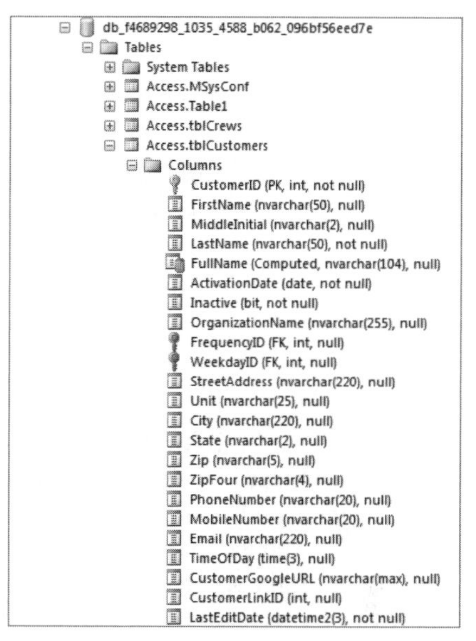

FIGURE 12-46: Web app table to be backed up

This macro is pretty simple. In order to prevent an endless loop, it first checks whether the field updated is the `LastEditDate` field, and if not, it sets the value of that field to `Now()`. Note that in a web app database, which is running on SQL Server, the precision of that time will be to milliseconds, which may present a problem later, when we reference that field in Access. You'll see that in a few moments.

The data macro that runs on inserts is even simpler, as you don't need to worry about triggering an endless update. See Figure 12-48.

The first web app table is now set up for differential backups and synchronization. Of course, you'll need to create the same table in your second web app, with the same fields and data macros to complete the synchronization. We'll leave that to you as an exercise. Our second web app is a customer-only version of the web database for a customer app, which needs to be kept in synch with the main web app for maids.

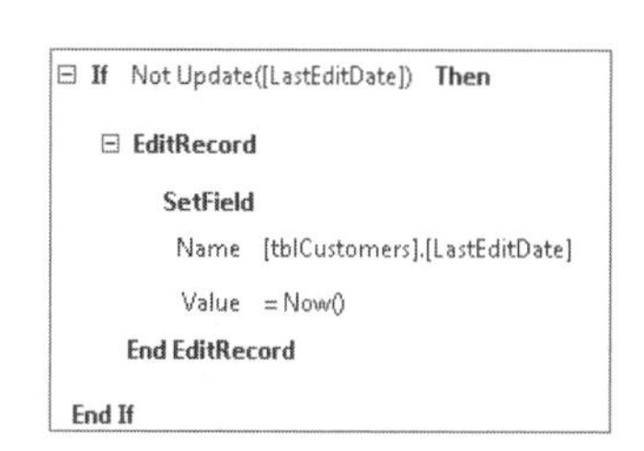

FIGURE 12-47: Macro to set LastEditDate on record updates

Now that you have the setup in place, let's look at the VBA which handles both the differential backup for the primary web app databases and the synchronization between the two web app databases.

Create an `.accdb` to host the VBA and link to the three tables in your three SQL Server, or SQL Azure, databases: the local database into which backups are retrieved from the web database, and the two databases for the respective web apps. In our example, we used code to check credentials of the user and re-create the links to the web app databases when the client `.accdb` opens. You'll explore how to create this code for your databases, in considerable depth, in Chapter 13. For now, Figure 12-49 shows only the tables, queries, and code modules you need for the task at hand.

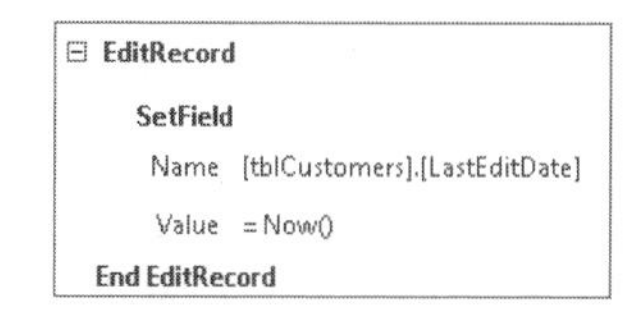

FIGURE 12-48: Macro to set LastEditDate on record inserts

As you can see, we've only linked to the three tables for your first demo. In a real application, of course, you'll link to all of the tables you want to keep backed up and synchronized.

Here's an overview of the process, in which the first step is to run the differential backup to the local SQL Server database. Then, the synchronization runs to move new records into the Customer version of the web app, update existing records in the customer version of the web app, and finally to update the employee Maid to Order database with changes in the customer version.

Here are the details of the process. Two Insert queries copy new records from the employee Maid To Order web database. The first one copies them into the customer web database and the second one copies them into the local backup SQL Server instance. Next, there are three Update queries to synchronize changes in existing records.

FIGURE 12-49: Tables, queries, and code for backup and synchronization

Because you know that customer records can change in both the employee and the customer apps, you need to synchronize both ways, using `LastEditDate` to determine which version holds the newer values. In addition, you use the same date field to create a differential update into the local backup database whenever you detect changes in the employee web database.

> **NOTE** *We've made several simplifying assumptions in order to keep this discussion reasonably concise. First, as already mentioned, we're only working with a single table out of many in the web app. Second, we assume that new customers are added only through the employee web app and that customers won't appear in the customer version of the web app until they've been processed on the employee side, eliminating one synchronization direction. Also, we assume the local database is exclusively a backup and that we therefore don't need to synchronize from it back to the web databases. In any scenario you develop for your customers, all of these possibilities must be considered.*

Pay close attention to the naming conventions adopted for this backup and synchronization process. The linked tables deviate from our standard convention of prefixing tables with `tbl_`. There is a good reason for that in this scenario. You need to coordinate between three versions of the same table: the local backup version of `tblCustomer`, the version of `tblCustomer` in the employee web app, and the version of `tblCustomer` in the customer web app. To keep them straight, it's simpler to adopt a naming convention that identifies the source of the tables: MTOLocal, MTOCustomer, and MTOEmployee. You'll see that we did keep the standard `tbl` prefix on each table within its full name.

If you've worked with ODBC linked SQL Server tables before, you know that Access prepends `dbo_` to linked tables, reflecting the schema from which the tables come. In this case, we're just using a variation of that approach to identify the database source instead of the schema.

Insert and Update Queries

Let's turn our attention next to the first of the insert queries, `qryEmployeeCustomerstoLocalCustomers`. It's the first one we run. It copies new records from the employee version of Maid To Order's web database into the local SQL Server database. Figure 12-50 is the query grid view of this query. The SQL is shown immediately after it.

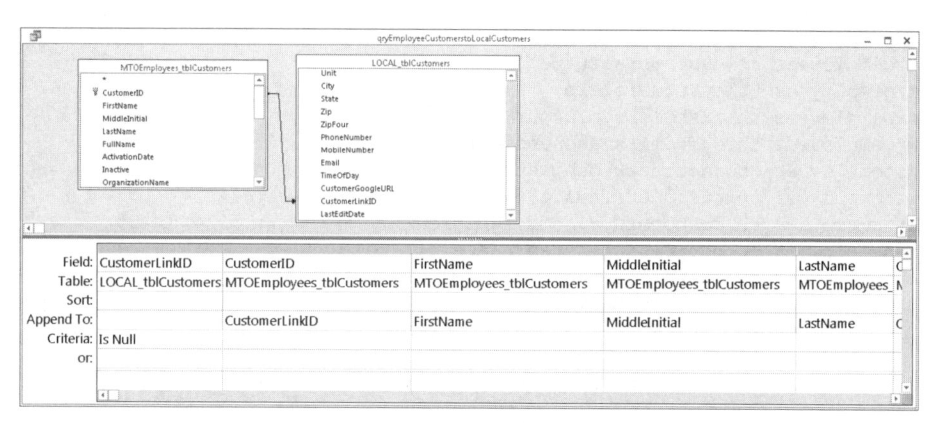

FIGURE 12-50: Query grid view of qryEmployeeCustomerstoLocalCustomers

```
INSERT INTO mtolocal_tblcustomers
            (customerlinkid,
             inactive,
             firstname,
             middleinitial,
             lastname,
             organizationname,
             activationdate,
             frequencyid,
             weekdayid,
             timeofday,
             streetaddress,
             unit,
             city,
             state,
```

```
            zip,
            zipfour,
            phonenumber,
            mobilenumber,
            email,
            customergoogleurl,
            lasteditdate)
SELECT mtoemployees_tblcustomers.customerid,
       mtoemployees_tblcustomers.inactive,
       mtoemployees_tblcustomers.firstname,
       mtoemployees_tblcustomers.middleinitial,
       mtoemployees_tblcustomers.lastname,
       mtoemployees_tblcustomers.organizationname,
       mtoemployees_tblcustomers.activationdate,
       mtoemployees_tblcustomers.frequencyid,
       mtoemployees_tblcustomers.weekdayid,
       mtoemployees_tblcustomers.timeofday,
       mtoemployees_tblcustomers.streetaddress,
       mtoemployees_tblcustomers.unit,
       mtoemployees_tblcustomers.city,
       mtoemployees_tblcustomers.state,
       mtoemployees_tblcustomers.zip,
       mtoemployees_tblcustomers.zipfour,
       mtoemployees_tblcustomers.phonenumber,
       mtoemployees_tblcustomers.mobilenumber,
       mtoemployees_tblcustomers.email,
       mtoemployees_tblcustomers.customergoogleurl,
       mtoemployees_tblcustomers.lasteditdate
FROM   mtoemployees_tblcustomers
       LEFT JOIN mtolocal_tblcustomers
              ON mtoemployees_tblcustomers.[customerid] =
                 mtolocal_tblcustomers.[customerlinkid]
WHERE  ((( mtolocal_tblcustomers.customerlinkid ) IS NULL ));
```

This is an ordinary "frustrated join" query, in which all records from the left-side table are returned if they do not have a matching record in the second table. The query was created, in fact, using the Query Wizard to find unmatched records. In this case, we're looking for records in the web app table that don't have a corresponding record in the backup table. The only difference here, of course, is that the join is *not* on the `CustomerID` fields in both tables, but on the `CustomerID` field in the web app table and the `CustomerLinkID` field in the backup table. Linking on the `CustomerLinkID` field means you're matching on the Primary Key field in the web app database and its counterpart in the local backup table.

This query was then converted into an Insert query to copy any new records into the backup.

The next query is similar to the previous one, except that the insert is from the employee web app table into the customer web app table. There are fewer fields in the customer web app version, so the insert only copies that subset of fields into the customer web app's customer table. You can see this query in Figure 12-51.

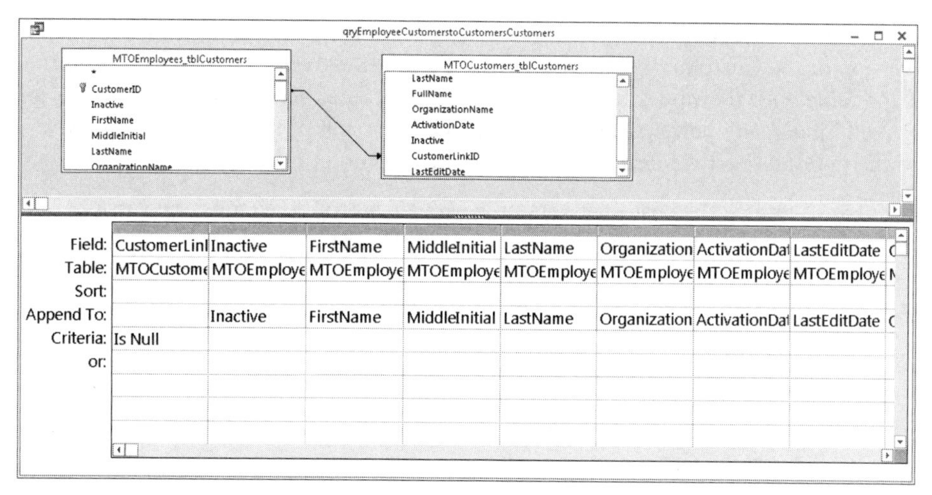

FIGURE 12-51: Query grid view of qryEmployeeCustomerstoCustomersCustomers

Here's the SQL.

```
INSERT INTO mtocustomers_tblcustomers
            (inactive,
             firstname,
             middleinitial,
             lastname,
             organizationname,
             activationdate,
             lasteditdate,
             customerlinkid)
SELECT mtoemployees_tblcustomers.inactive,
       mtoemployees_tblcustomers.firstname,
       mtoemployees_tblcustomers.middleinitial,
       mtoemployees_tblcustomers.lastname,
       mtoemployees_tblcustomers.organizationname,
       mtoemployees_tblcustomers.activationdate,
       mtoemployees_tblcustomers.lasteditdate,
       mtoemployees_tblcustomers.customerid
FROM   mtoemployees_tblcustomers
       LEFT JOIN mtocustomers_tblcustomers
              ON mtoemployees_tblcustomers.customerid =
                 mtocustomers_tblcustomers.customerlinkid
WHERE  ((( mtocustomers_tblcustomers.customerlinkid ) IS NULL ));
```

When these two queries have run, all three tables have the same records in them. However, it is possible that changes to some fields have been made either in the employee web app or in the customer web app. Those changes need to be synchronized back and forth. This time, however, the task is a bit more complex. We need to update values in each table using the newer of the two records, when they are different, in the two web app tables. The first two queries synchronize the employee and customer web app tables. For the local backup, synchronization is only one way, from the web app table to the local backup table. The backup must be synchronized last, from the values in the employee web app database.

So, the processing order is to update the customer web app table with the values from records in the employee version of the Customer table that have a newer `LastEditDate`, then to update the employee web app table with the values from records in the customer version of the Customer table that are newer. And finally, any newer values in the employee version of the Customer table are carried back to their counterpart records in the local backup version of the Customer table.

Let's create the query to update the customer version with values from the employee version. `qryUpdateCustomerCustomerChanges` does that (see Figure 12-52).

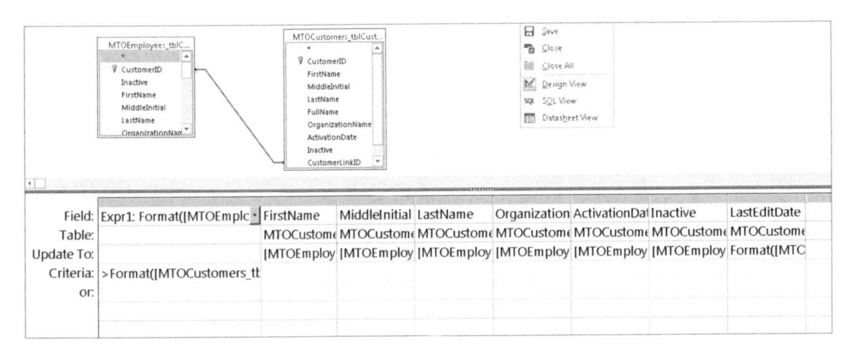

FIGURE 12-52: Updating the customer version of a table with newer values in the employee version

Here's the SQL for this query:

```
UPDATE mtoemployees_tblcustomers
       INNER JOIN mtocustomers_tblcustomers
              ON mtoemployees_tblcustomers.customerid =
                 mtocustomers_tblcustomers.customerlinkid
SET    mtocustomers_tblcustomers.firstname =
       [mtoemployees_tblcustomers].[firstname],
       mtocustomers_tblcustomers.middleinitial =
       [mtoemployees_tblcustomers].[middleinitial],
       mtocustomers_tblcustomers.lastname =
       [mtoemployees_tblcustomers].[lastname],
       mtocustomers_tblcustomers.organizationname =
       [mtoemployees_tblcustomers].[organizationname],
       mtocustomers_tblcustomers.activationdate =
       [mtoemployees_tblcustomers].[activationdate],
       mtocustomers_tblcustomers.inactive =
       [mtoemployees_tblcustomers].[inactive],
       mtocustomers_tblcustomers.lasteditdate = Format(
       [mtoemployees_tblcustomers].[lasteditdate], "mm/dd/yyyy hh:nn:ss")
WHERE
((( Format([mtoemployees_tblcustomers].[lasteditdate], "mm/dd/yyyy hh:nn:ss") )
 > Format([mtocustomers_tblcustomers].[lasteditdate], "mm/dd/yyyy hh:nn:ss") ));
```

When this query runs, all values for newer records in the employee version of the table are written over the values in the same record(s) in the customer version. Take note of a couple of things about this query and the logic in it. First, we don't know which field or fields got changed, only that `LastEditDate` was updated. Therefore, we just update all of the fields, knowing that any changed values will overwrite the old values in the same field. Any values that are the same will just be overwritten with the same value. Second, you may be wondering why we formatted the `LastEditDate` field to return values down to the second. In testing, we found that Access wasn't always able to detect differences to the same millisecond precision used in the web app database fields. We formatted to the nearest second instead for the match to ensure Access can handle it.

As you'd expect, the synchronization back in the other direction is just the reverse of Figure 12-51. That query, `qryUpdateEmployeeCustomerChanges`, is shown in Figure 12-53 with the query grid view followed by the SQL.

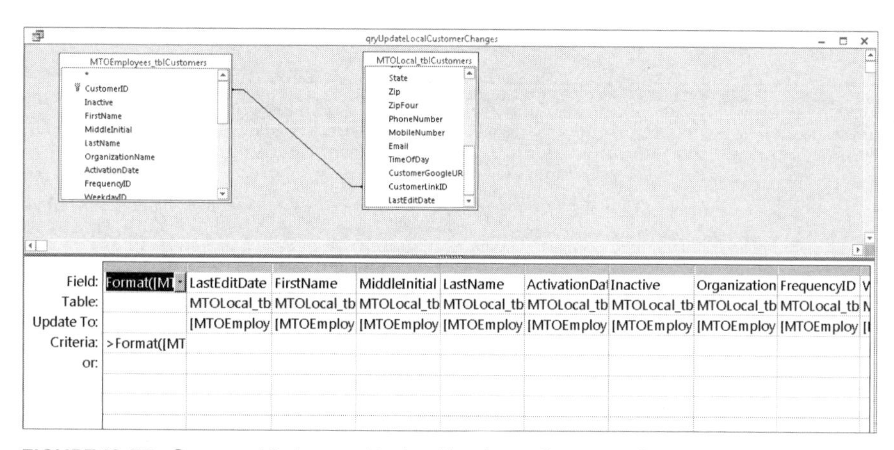

FIGURE 12-53: Query grid view qryUpdateEmployeeCustomerChanges

And again, the SQL from the query is as follows:

```
UPDATE mtoemployees_tblcustomers
       INNER JOIN mtocustomers_tblcustomers
               ON mtoemployees_tblcustomers.customerid =
                  mtocustomers_tblcustomers.customerlinkid
SET    mtoemployees_tblcustomers.firstname =
       [mtocustomers_tblcustomers].[firstname],
       mtoemployees_tblcustomers.middleinitial =
       [mtocustomers_tblcustomers].[middleinitial],
       mtoemployees_tblcustomers.lastname =
       [mtocustomers_tblcustomers].[lastname],
       mtoemployees_tblcustomers.organizationname =
       [mtocustomers_tblcustomers].[organizationname],
       mtoemployees_tblcustomers.activationdate =
       [mtocustomers_tblcustomers].[activationdate],
       mtoemployees_tblcustomers.inactive =
       [mtocustomers_tblcustomers].[inactive],
       mtoemployees_tblcustomers.lasteditdate =
       [mtocustomers_tblcustomers].[lasteditdate]
WHERE  (((
Format([mtocustomers_tblcustomers].[lasteditdate], "mm/dd/yyyy hh:nn:ss") )
> Format([mtoemployees_tblcustomers].[lasteditdate], "mm/dd/yyyy hh:nn:ss") ));
```

And the final query in this set synchronizes the changes back to the local backup table. Again, the structure of the query is the same, except for the tables involved. You can see `qryUpdateLocalCustomerChanges` in Figure 12-54.

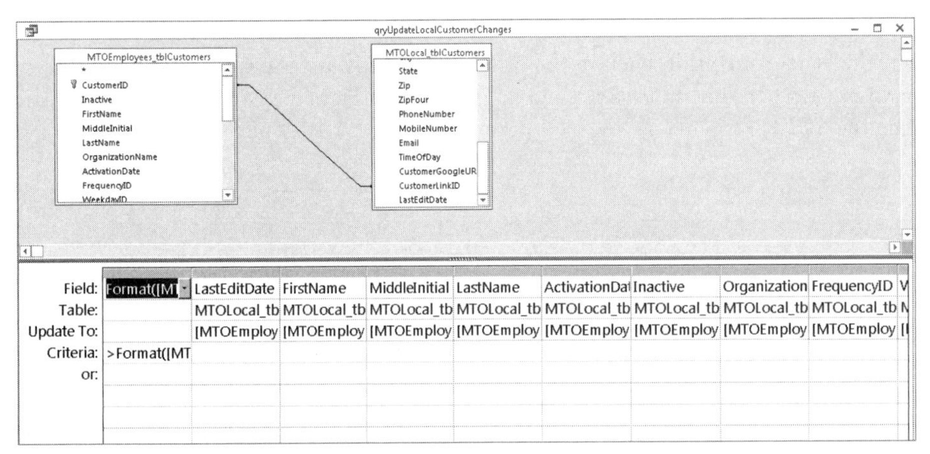

FIGURE 12-54: Query grid view of qryUpdateLocalCustomerChanges

The SQL for this query is as follows:

```
UPDATE mtoemployees_tblcustomers
       INNER JOIN mtolocal_tblcustomers
              ON mtoemployees_tblcustomers.customerid =
                 mtolocal_tblcustomers.customerlinkid
SET    mtolocal_tblcustomers.lasteditdate =
       [mtoemployees_tblcustomers].[lasteditdate],
       mtolocal_tblcustomers.firstname =
       [mtoemployees_tblcustomers].[firstname],
       mtolocal_tblcustomers.middleinitial =
       [mtoemployees_tblcustomers].[middleinitial],
       mtolocal_tblcustomers.lastname = [mtoemployees_tblcustomers].[lastname],
       mtolocal_tblcustomers.activationdate =
       [mtoemployees_tblcustomers].[activationdate],
       mtolocal_tblcustomers.inactive = [mtoemployees_tblcustomers].[inactive],
       mtolocal_tblcustomers.organizationname =
       [mtoemployees_tblcustomers].[organizationname],
       mtolocal_tblcustomers.frequencyid =
       [mtoemployees_tblcustomers].[frequencyid],
       mtolocal_tblcustomers.weekdayid =
       [mtoemployees_tblcustomers].[weekdayid],
       mtolocal_tblcustomers.streetaddress =
       [mtoemployees_tblcustomers].[streetaddress],
       mtolocal_tblcustomers.unit = [mtoemployees_tblcustomers].[unit],
       mtolocal_tblcustomers.city = [mtoemployees_tblcustomers].[city],
       mtolocal_tblcustomers.state = [mtoemployees_tblcustomers].[state],
       mtolocal_tblcustomers.zip = [mtoemployees_tblcustomers].[zip],
```

```
        mtolocal_tblcustomers.zipfour = [mtoemployees_tblcustomers].[zipfour],
        mtolocal_tblcustomers.phonenumber =
        [mtoemployees_tblcustomers].[phonenumber],
        mtolocal_tblcustomers.mobilenumber =
        [mtoemployees_tblcustomers].[mobilenumber],
        mtolocal_tblcustomers.email = [mtoemployees_tblcustomers].[email],
        mtolocal_tblcustomers.timeofday =
        [mtoemployees_tblcustomers].[timeofday],
        mtolocal_tblcustomers.customergoogleurl
        =
        [mtoemployees_tblcustomers].[customergoogleurl]
WHERE
((
( Format([mtoemployees_tblcustomers].[lasteditdate], "mm/dd/yyyy hh:nn:ss") )
> Format([mtolocal_tblcustomers].[lasteditdate], "mm/dd/yyyy hh:nn:ss") ));
```

When this last query has run, all three tables are synchronized.

VBA Module

Let's turn our attention next to the VBA module needed to run them. This should be familiar to everyone, except possibly for the use of the transaction. Take a look at the following function and then you'll learn about the logic in it:

```
Public Function BackupAndSynch() As Boolean
Dim ws As DAO.Workspace
Dim in_trans As Boolean
Dim db As DAO.Database

On Error GoTo errHandler
   Set db = CurrentDb
   Set ws = DBEngine.Workspaces(0)
   in_trans = True
   ws.BeginTrans
   'Append new customer records to the local backup table
   db.Execute "qryEmployeeCustomerstoLocalCustomers", dbSeeChanges
   'Append new customer records from the employee Maid to Order
   'to the Customer Maid to Order  database
   db.Execute "qryEmployeeCustomerstoCustomersCustomers", dbSeeChanges
   'Update Changes from the Employee web site database to the customer
   'web site database
   db.Execute "qryUpdateCustomerCustomerChanges", dbSeeChanges
   'Update changes from the customer Maid to Order database to the
   'employee Maid to Order databae
   db.Execute "qryUpdateEmployeeCustomerChanges", dbSeeChanges
   'Update local customers with any changes from the web site
   db.Execute "qryUpdateLocalCustomerChanges", dbSeeChanges
   'Repeat for all other tables that must be kept in synch
   ws.CommitTrans
   in_trans = False
   BackupAndSynch = True

Cleanup:
    On Error Resume Next
```

```
        Set ws = Nothing
    Trans_Exit:
        Exit Function
    errHandler:
        If in_trans = True Then
            ws.Rollback
            MsgBox prompt:="Something went wrong. Sorry." & vbCrLf & _
                "No backup was made and no synch occurred." & vbCrLf & _
                "Make sure the connections to all three databases " & vbCrLf & _
                "are correct and try again.", _
                buttons:=vbOKOnly, title:="Back up and Synch Not Completed"

        End If
        Resume Cleanup
        Resume
    End Function
```

As previously noted, we assume that all new customer records will be created in the employee version of the table. That means you can safely assume that starting the process with a backup from the web app database will obtain all new customers for the backup. If that were not the case, of course, you'd have to do the synchronization between the two web app databases first, adding a step to insert new customers from the customer web app into the employee web app before doing the backup. Of course, you could also move the local backup to the next to last step anyway. It's really up to you, as long as you give careful consideration to the logic involved and the business rules that apply.

After the initial backup, this function synchronizes the two web app databases and uses the new values in the employee web app databases to synchronize the local backup.

As you saw in the design of the queries, each of these steps depends on the combination of linking a `CustomerID` field and `LastEditDate` to complete only a differential insert or update, minimizing the impact of the actions.

Using a Transaction

You have, no doubt, noticed that the backup and synchronization process is wrapped in a transaction. Although it would not be as critical as an interrupted bank transfer transaction would be, we do not want to let some of the inserts and updates happen when others don't complete. So, with the transaction, we ensure all of the actions complete, or roll them all back if one of the steps fails. During testing for this example, in fact, we had reason to do just that. A spelling error in one of the queries caused it to fail. Fortunately, we'd already put in the transaction logic to roll back that test so there was no messy inconsistency to unravel.

Why Not a Full-Featured Audit Trail?

There is a difference between the previous backup/synchronization scenario and a full-featured audit trail. In a full-featured audit trail you want to identify which field or fields got changed, what the old and new values are, and probably who changed them and when. While a full audit trail is beyond our scope here, we're confident you can see how the methods touched on here can be expanded to accommodate that requirement. One difference is that you'd need one or more audit tables. Additional data macros would be created to insert values from changed records into the audit table in the web app database, which could later be copied down into a local SQL Audit database for retention. After the audit records are copied down in the Audit database, the Audit tables in the web app database could be flushed to keep it smaller and better performing.

Choosing Approaches

You have learned how to set up just one possible approach to handle synchronization between a web app database and other databases, whether it is local, another web app database, or other remote sources. There obviously are more approaches, such as using T-SQL and passthrough queries to leverage features of SQL Server for synchronizing or some other options. You may be wondering how to choose between those two approaches. We feel that the primary consideration is purely stylistic and will depend primarily on what you are more comfortable with. The first approach allows you to take advantage of the Access query designer to graphically maintain the queries and provide concrete steps that are easy to test in isolation while the second approach gives you the full benefit of T-SQL's greater power and better performance but also additional coding and an opaque process. Your experience will be helpful in guiding you to an ideal combination that will meet your particular needs.

SUMMARY

In Chapter 12, you pursued your journey beyond the departmental silo, which has too often been a boundary for many Access developers. You learned about tools and techniques available to you to help facilitate the management of Access solutions. You saw how you can create a document library to host your Access client files, which your Access web apps can then link to, using a URL hyperlink for easy download and configuration of a client database to connect to the given web app using the same template prescribed by the organization.

You also learned what SharePoint has to offer in terms of version control and you looked at customizing your app package so you can provide branding for it. You learned how to set up and use the existing SharePoint infrastructure to do this.

In the latter part of the chapter, you learned about ways you can synchronize related databases across different platforms. You learned how to implement two different methods available to you for supporting synchronization between a web app database and another database, whether a local database or another web app database, and you learned about design requirements to support synchronization and how you can implement them.

Those tools and techniques will be very helpful when you need to coordinate multiple Access web apps and client databases and establish a standard among those files. Used in conjunction with Audit and Control Management Server and IT support, the story for developing and enforcing a development standard is definitely improved.

With this new knowledge, you are ready to look into the subject of security and how you can create secure applications both in the web browser and when connecting to the web app database. You will do this in Chapter 13.

13

Implementing Security Models for the Access Web App

WHAT'S IN THIS CHAPTER?

- Recognizing differences in security architecture
- Reviewing traditional security methods in client `.accdb`s
- Learning about SharePoint security
- Designing a secure web app

WROX.COM CODE DOWNLOADS FOR THIS CHAPTER

The code and sample downloads for this chapter are found at `www.wiley.com/go/proaccess2013prog.com` on the Download Code tab. The code is in the Chapter 13 download and individually named according to the names listed throughout the chapter. The app packages for the web apps in this chapter are called Maid to Order and Maid to Order Customer. Refer to the Readme.txt file also located there for installation instructions.

In this chapter, you learn about securing your applications. Because a complete application will often include both a web app component and a client database component, our discussion covers both environments. We start with a review of the different architectures involved. You then investigate the design elements required for a successful security implementation. You learn what features are available to you out of the box and what you need to do to augment those out-of-the-box features.

You learn about managing SharePoint accounts, which are needed to access, read, modify data, and design the web app hosted on the site. Once you master the essential operations to manage users, we turn to embedding security in your web app and discuss strategies for enforcing it effectively.

The chapter concludes with information about designing a secure front-end `.accde` file that can connect to the web app database and effectively enforce additional security requirements you may want to put in place. You will learn strategies that will enable you to avoid sharing the password to connect to your web app database with your users.

SECURITY CONSIDERATIONS

Let's start with a look at the big picture regarding security and think about how you might need to revise your typical approaches to security now that you're dealing both with a web application and an application file that may link to the database for your web app. To help frame the discussion for the rest of this chapter, we want to start with two analogies that we think will be helpful in visualizing the steps you should consider, and not consider, in the process of securing your solution.

File-Based Security

Access client solutions are file-based. You store your data in a file (or, in some cases, multiple files). Those physical files reside on a local hard drive or a network share. This means, of course, that anyone with access to that file could copy it to a different location, including a jump drive. You could opt to store the data in an encrypted file. However, because it's still a physical file, this is equivalent to putting confidential documents in a safe, locking it, and taking the safe outside your house. The misconception of the safety of encrypted files is the assumption that anybody who knows the combination to the safe can get to the data inside it, while a casual passerby is not able to see the data because they don't have the combination, making the data safe.

But with the safe outdoors, anyone who can get to it can simply pick it up and take it to another location where they can apply a blowtorch to the safe at their leisure and eventually break in and get the data within. As you already know, this is a fundamental problem with file-based security, and it cannot be avoided.

Agent-Based Security

A web application, on the other hand, is akin to a bank vault. Before you can get to your safe deposit box, an agent of the bank has to identify you and give you access to the box. You can't just walk into a vault without an agent. Some banks are a bit more lax than others and simply have the agent walk into the vault with you while you pull out the safe deposit box. Others are more strict and will not allow you to even see the front door of the vault. Instead they direct you to a waiting room while they retrieve your box and deliver it to you in the designated waiting room.

With this analogy in mind, you can see that some security processes which may make sense for file-based security, such as encrypting content, do not have quite the same relevance with a web application because of the insertion of an agent into the process. You will learn that you don't need to be so concerned about restricting access to tables based on user role as you would with a traditional SQL Server and Access solution. Rather, you'd enforce the restrictions by programming the views in the web apps and within the client application accordingly.

Normally, that would be unacceptable when talking about Access front-end applications because one could simply bypass the Access application and connect to the SQL Server directly via SSMS or another software tool, circumventing any logic embedded in the application. It goes back to the fact that an Access front-end file isn't the same thing as a bank agent in terms of controlling access to the data because the user has direct access to the SQL Server database.

On the other hand, when you have secured your web app so that only trusted people have design rights to it, there is no way for regular users to simply circumvent the logic you've embedded in your web apps. To do so, they would need to access the web app's database directly. Obviously, however, as you've seen in previous chapters, direct access can be enabled. We'll talk about securing access for scenarios where you need both.

We hope the analogies we've provided will help you appreciate why suggestions in this chapter about securing the web app for online use are quite different from those we'd offer for securing an Access client file to connect to the database.

FIX PEOPLE, NOT COMPUTERS

Above all, we should not forget that security remains fundamentally a people problem. Technology could never adequately fix the shortcomings of people. It's more likely that you will find it more efficient to secure sensitive resources by having a competent Human Resources department than to encrypt data, require logins, and various other technological solutions. Effective security is commonly achieved by simply preventing access to sensitive resources as opposed to restricting the use of the sensitive resources.

Securing Web Apps on SharePoint

Before we continue with details on securing web apps, we should set out the terms of what is available to you. In this section, we'll cover user groups, connection options, and access types.

User Groups

By default, only users who have design rights to your web app have access to the database behind your web app. They can be given that access via both the web app and the Access client. Anyone who is not an administrator or owner of the SharePoint site where the web app is hosted simply does not have access via either method.

A SharePoint site has three default groups:

1. Owners
2. Members
3. Visitors

Each group has different default rights. Owners can design the web app. Members can open the web app and modify data, but they cannot modify the app itself. Visitors can open the web app and view the data but cannot modify any data. You will learn more about customizing permissions later in this chapter. Note for now, however, when speaking of Access web apps, you cannot selectively grant access to some tiles and views to only one group and deny access to others. Access, the ability to read and modify data, and the ability to make design changes, is granted to the web app as a whole.

External Connections

Turning next to external connections for your web apps, you have a couple of options. You learned how to enable external connections in Chapter 11.

The first option is to enable connections only from your current location. That means that even if others had the appropriate credentials, they would be denied the ability to connect to your web app's database because all connections must come from the same IP address you use.

Alternatively, you can turn on external connections for any IP address in the world. Of course, in that case, they still have to have the credentials to connect. In other words, it's a combination of location and credentials that grants or denies access. Depending on whether and how you want others to use the web app, you will enable one type of external connection or the other.

Security Access Type

You also have two choices of access type, read-only and read-write. ExternalReader can read any data from any table but cannot modify data for any table. External Read-Write (also referred as ExternalWriter) can read the data, and can also modify any data in any table. Again, you cannot customize these permissions unless you also have administrative access to the SQL Server hosting your web app database. This is unlikely in most hosted scenarios but may be feasible for an on-premise scenario.

Security in the Application Layer

Now that we've defined all of the options that are available to you in managing access to your web app, let's delve into the specifics of providing selective access and controlling access both in the web browser and in the Access file, which you create as a front end to your web app's database. We offered the bank agent analogy because most security mechanisms you learn about rely on the fact that an effective agent exists, performing operations on your users' behalf.

Because you cannot define security at a more granular level beyond the database level, it is necessary to embed granular security into the application level. This can be undone by accessing the database directly. Therefore, you learn how you can restrict direct access to the database without limiting your users' freedom to perform their jobs intermediated by an agent, whether the agent happens to be the web app in the browser or the `.accde` front-end file later in the chapter.

SHAREPOINT SECURITY

SharePoint security is one of the advantages that comes with using web apps and also when using linked SharePoint lists in a client app. SharePoint supports a granular system of permissions where you can assign different permission levels to groups and/or individual users. In the context of an Access web app, there is a general relationship between users' permission on the site and what users can do on the web app. For example, in order to edit data on a web app, they first must have permission to edit data on the site containing the app.

There are a number of objects within SharePoint that can be secured and that may or may not inherit permissions from their parent. Those objects are considered *securable objects*:

- Site collection
- Site (which may be a subsite of another site)
- List
- List item/folder

> **NOTE** *In the context of a SharePoint list, everything is an item in a list, even a folder, which is just a special kind of list item.*

Note that apps are not on the list because apps have their own permission scheme. Following the agent analogy, an app performs much like an agent and thus has a specific set of permissions that it may or may not require from the SharePoint site. The permissions are distinct and limited to ease the process of distribution and deployment of web apps. In Chapter 2, you saw how an app had to be trusted, as in Figure 13-1, showing a trusted app.

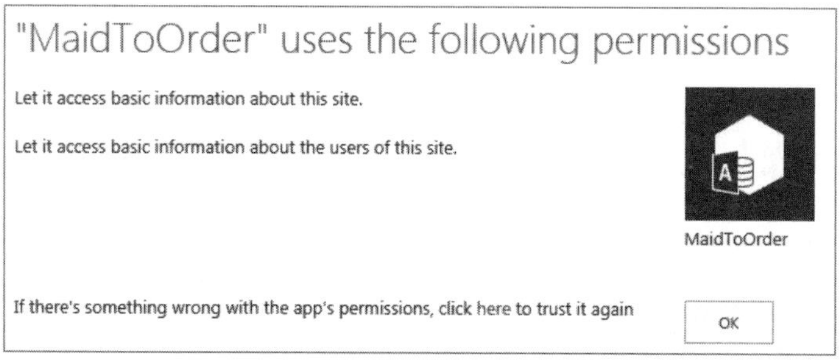

"MaidToOrder" uses the following permissions

Let it access basic information about this site.

Let it access basic information about the users of this site.

MaidToOrder

If there's something wrong with the app's permissions, click here to trust it again

OK

FIGURE 13-1: Permissions for an app

For this reason, the level of granularity between a user's permission on the site and permission on the app hosted at the same site is not necessarily the same. It is a compelling reason why you need to manage permissions via the site containing the app and not directly on the app. The app acts as an agent for the users and, depending on the permission level, permits the user to do things with the app, be it reading the data, editing the same data, or opening it in design view.

As we return to the SharePoint security model, it is helpful to remember that generally, permissions are inherited between the containing and contained securables. You can choose to break inheritance and you will see an example of breaking the inheritance later in the chapter. This is a necessary step whenever you need to provide a different level of permissions for different securable objects in the site. As you can see, you need to work with SharePoint objects if you need to fine-tune permissions for your apps; you will learn about creating a subsite to achieve this goal.

Team Sites and Personal Storage

When you create an Office 365 account, you get a personal storage location and a team site. Within your Office 365 account, this is a private storage location for your own documents and apps. It's relevant to a discussion of web apps because you can install web apps in this location. However, these web apps can't be shared, so you'd limit your use of this personal storage area to those apps you want to keep private. Don't confuse this personal storage location for apps with your SkyDrive Pro folder, which is a sync to your personal documents.

Web apps installed on a team site, on the other hand, can be shared with others. This is the place for apps you want to make available to others in your group, or invited external users. Later in this chapter, you learn how to secure a subsite, under your team site, to isolate a web app for use by a group of specific users.

Managing User Accounts

In this section, we introduce you to user accounts and show you how they work to secure your Office 365 or SharePoint sites. For this discussion, keep in mind that user accounts are an admin function on your SharePoint site. While our primary focus is always on Access web apps, you do need to have some basic understanding of SharePoint functions to work with them effectively.

In this section, you learn how to manage users within your Office 365 or SharePoint site. Note that we are talking about SharePoint users, who will have access to the full range of SharePoint features to which you give them permissions. Later in this chapter, you learn about adding external, or invited, users to specific web apps on your site.

> **NOTE** *The discussion that follows is based on the "P1" plan for Office 365. There are multiple plans available. If you are on one of those plans, in particular one of the "E" or Enterprise plans, your admin pages might be somewhat different from ours. In addition, an on-premises installation of SharePoint may differ. In this case, consult with the SharePoint administrators.*

Adding Users

You will add users through the Admin function on the header. Click Admin and then select users & groups, as shown in Figure 13-2. This will display the page of user accounts.

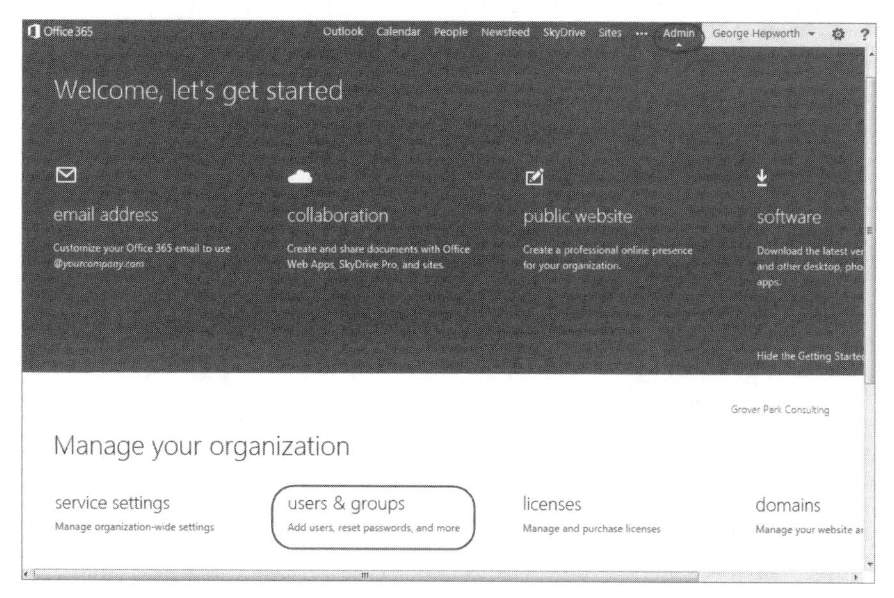

FIGURE 13-2: Manage users and groups

> **NOTE** *Note that Figure 13-2 displays the Getting Started pane, which can be hidden (the blue area). If you've previously visited the Admin page and hidden the Getting Starting pane, you would only see the bottom portion, with the highlighted link.*

Click the plus sign to start the process of adding a new user highlighted in Figure 13-3. Make sure the user's link is highlighted. Figure 13-4 shows the second step in the user setup dialog.

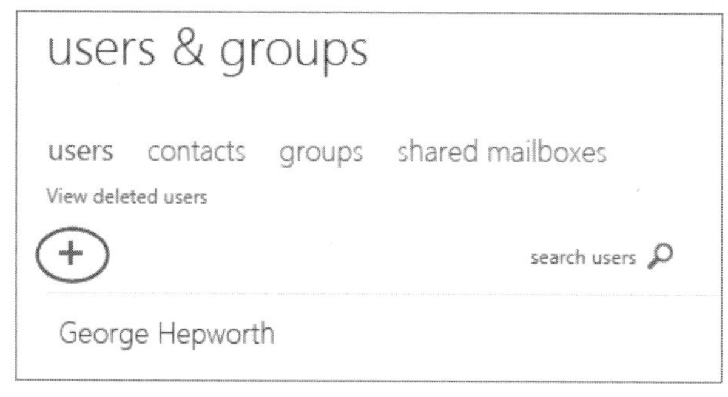

FIGURE 13-3: Add a user.

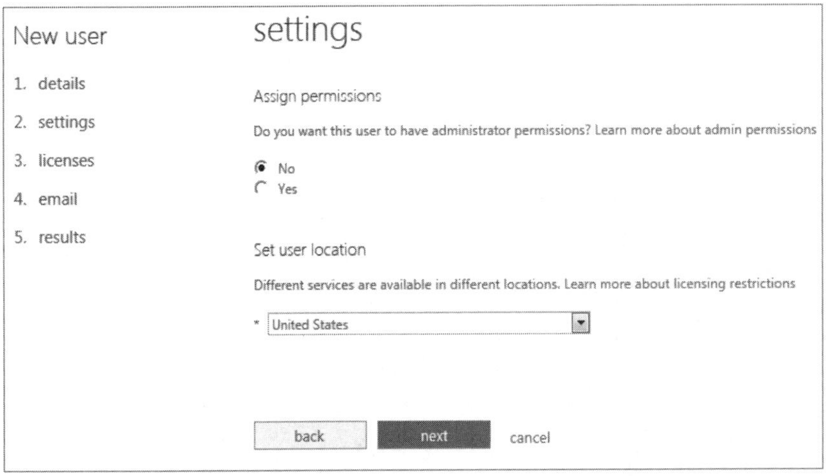

FIGURE 13-4: Assign permissions and a location for the new user.

In this context, there are only two options for permissions: should the new user be an administrator or not? You'll probably want to limit the number of administrators to keep tighter control.

Users assigned to accounts in your Office 365 site may need to use one or more Office client applications. While they can obtain client installs of those applications, you can allocate one of the licenses from your Office 365 package. As you can see in Figure 13-5, 10 licenses are available in the current version of the Small Business Premium package.

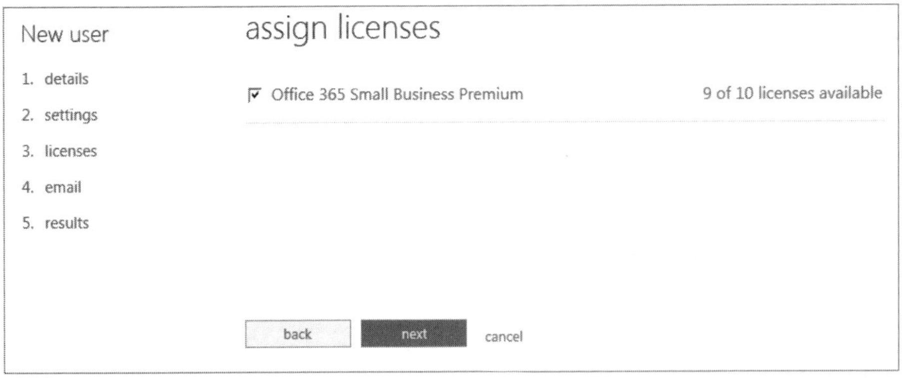

FIGURE 13-5: Assign licenses to the new user.

The next step is to decide whether to send e-mail notifications to new users, as illustrated in Figure 13-6. Most of the time, it would seem to be a logical thing to do. However, there may be situations where you are provisioning accounts for anticipated users as part of a setup protocol, where you wouldn't necessarily need to send out e-mails.

New user

1. details
2. settings
3. licenses
4. email
5. results

send results in email

The new users and any corresponding temporary passwords will be displayed on the next page. You can also email these results to up to five recipients, including yourself. Enter the email addresses separated by semicolons.

Send email

ben@maidtoorder.onmicrosoft.com; george@maidtoord

Note: Passwords are sent in clear text through email.

back create cancel

FIGURE 13-6: Notify the user and Cc yourself.

The last step, depicted in Figure 13-7, presents the results, including both the new username and temporary password. You can verify the setup was successful by seeing the new user listed in the user list, as shown in Figure 13-8. Depending on your workflows, you might want to take note of the temporary password to be able to support the user should they experience problems signing in.

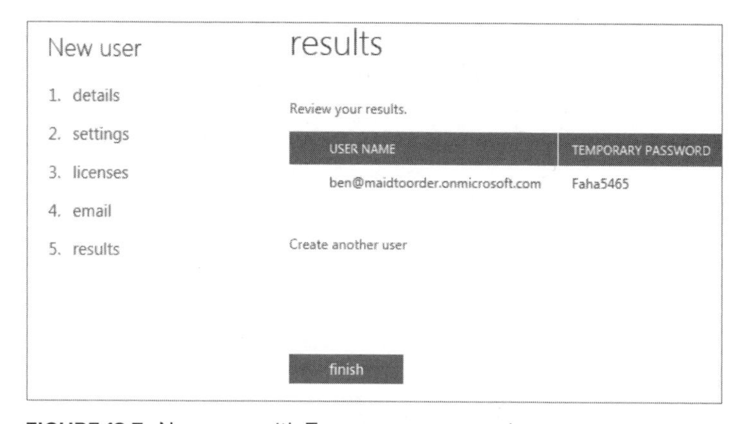

FIGURE 13-7: New user with Temporary password

users & groups

users contacts groups shared mailboxes

View deleted users

\+ search users

Ben Clothier

George Hepworth

FIGURE 13-8: User list with two users

Editing

Editing an existing user is done from the same place. Select the user you want to edit and click the pencil icon to open the editing page, as in Figure 13-9.

FIGURE 13-9: Change user settings.

You can change a user's status to administrator or remove that status. Note that you can block a user temporarily or permanently, meaning you can control access to your site without having to delete an account completely. In addition, you can add or remove Office licenses for the user. You may reallocate licenses from one user to another to balance usage as needed.

> **WARNING** *Keep in mind that an Office license is not necessary for a user to work with Access web apps; you can invite those users as external users. You typically would assign an Office license to a user who also needs a full install of Office.*

Deleting Users

Of course, you may want to completely remove a user. This is straightforward as well. Select the user and click the trashcan icon seen in Figure 13-9. Confirm that you want to delete the user and reuse the licenses previously assigned, as you can see in Figure 13-10.

You have 30 days to recover a deleted user and any of their data.

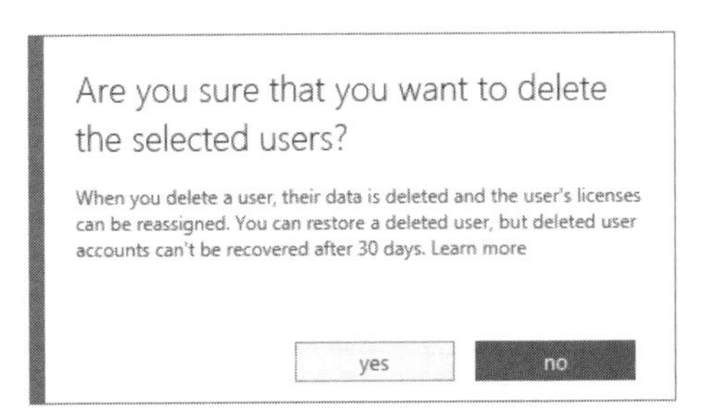

FIGURE 13-10: Delete users and reuse their licenses.

Extending Permissions

In order to share your web apps with other users, you need to extend permissions to them. As noted, some users will be internal users who have accounts on your site. They can be assigned to one or more apps internally. So they may need to be given specific permissions on your site. Let's take a quick look at that process. We added Ben Clothier earlier. Now you'll give him permission to use the Maid To Order web app.

Navigate to the Team Site where the Maid To Order web app is installed. You'll give the new user permission to use that site and the web apps on it. Click the Share link in the header, as highlighted in Figure 13-11.

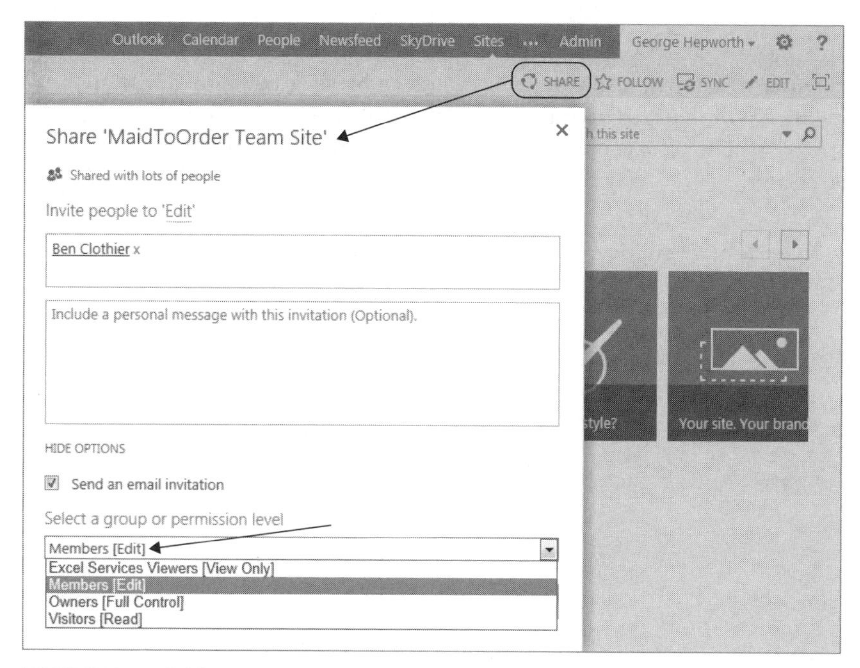

FIGURE 13-11: Add a user to a site.

We're putting Ben Clothier in the Member group, with full design and edit permission on all of the objects in the Team Site, including the Access web apps. In the following section of this chapter, on inviting external users, you learn how to add invited external users to other, more restricted, groups so they can use the app, but not change its design. You can see that the new user was successfully added in Figures 13-12 and Figure 13-13.

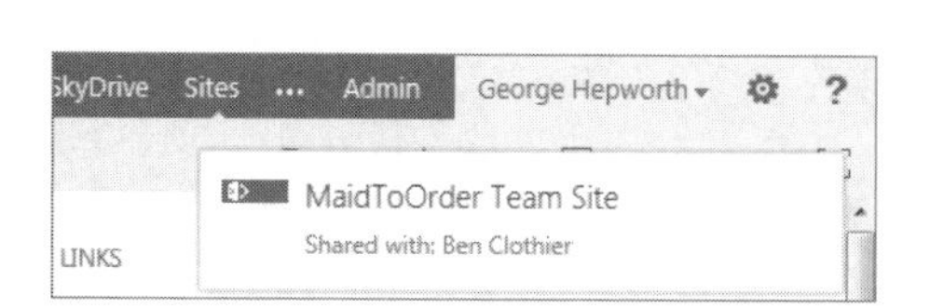

FIGURE 13-12: Confirmation that the user was added to the site

FIGURE 13-13: New user in the Member group

External User Accounts

In order to share your web apps with external users, you need to invite them to the site. We go into more detail about external invitations in a later section, when we show you how to implement a secured subsite for a specific web app for a restricted group of users. An external user does not count toward your license limit and you can invite up to 500 guests and enable them to use your site and the resources within it, including your web apps. Of course, an external user wouldn't be able to use the Office client products and would need to have their own licenses should they want to use the client products.

Inviting

When you wish to add a user to a site or a subsite, you can do so by clicking Share at the appropriate level. You can see in Figure 13-14 that this invitation is to the MaidToOrder Team Site. Later, when you learn how to create a subsite for a specific web app, the importance of making sure to select the appropriate site will be clearer.

Share 'MaidToOrder Team Site'

Shared with lots of people

Invite people to 'Read'

DonJohnson@CarriageHouse.com

Include a personal message with this invitation (Optional).

HIDE OPTIONS

Send an email invitation

Select a group or permission level

Visitors [Read]

Share Cancel

FIGURE 13-14: Inviting an external user

The invited user will get an e-mail at the address you entered. If they elect to use your web app, they will accept the invitation and create a sign-in for themselves. You'll walk through this process in more detail later in the chapter.

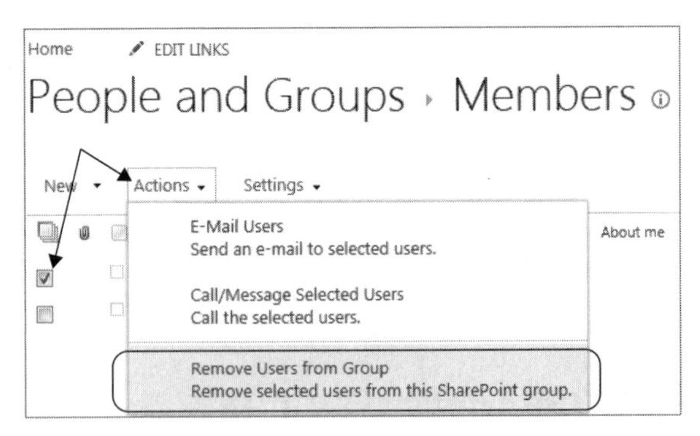

FIGURE 13-15: Revoking permission from an invited user

Revoking Invitations

Revoking an invitation is just a matter of finding the group(s) in which a user is included and removing them as shown in Figure 13-15.

Anonymous Access

Sometimes you have a scenario where you do want to allow anonymous access to your web app. Access web apps allow for anonymous access in an indirect fashion. It must be provisioned on a SharePoint site where anonymous access is allowed. Anonymous users cannot have custom permissions so they can have read-only permissions. If you want to grant individuals permissions beyond read-only, you will need to invite them and set them up as external users.

The simplest way to implement anonymous access to your app is to make use of your public website, which comes by default with Office 365. For those using on-premises SharePoint, you may need to contact your farm administrator and plan the deployment. If you have administrative rights to your Office 365 account, you can discover where your public website is located by going to the Admin pane. As shown in Figure 13-16, under the service settings, you can click the link `Manage public website`.

FIGURE 13-16: Manage public website link

> **NOTE** *Figure 13-16 assumes that you've dismissed the Getting Started pane. Clicking 'public website' on the Getting Started pane has additional steps to help you get set up. For the purpose of this discussion, we will focus on enabling the public website and leave the details of setup to you.*

This will take you to another page where you can see the address and click the link to go and design the public website, as shown in Figure 13-17.

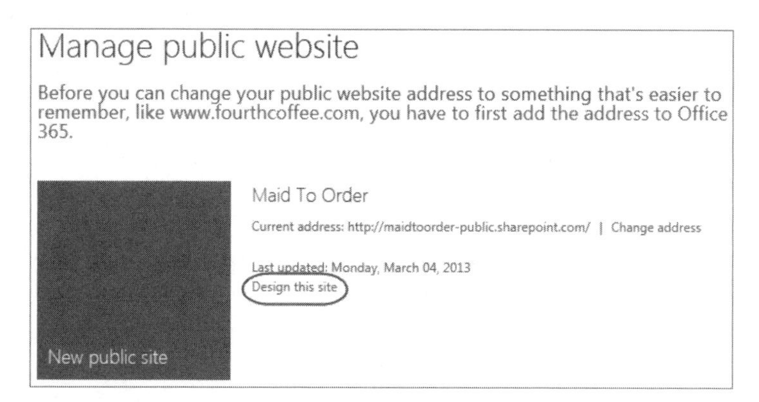
Manage public website
Before you can change your public website address to something that's easier to remember, like www.fourthcoffee.com, you have to first add the address to Office 365.
Maid To Order
Current address: http://maidtoorder-public.sharepoint.com/ | Change address
Last updated: Monday, March 04, 2013
Design this site
New public site

FIGURE 13-17: Design public website page

You now design your public website and, when you are ready, bring it online. The link to bring it online is highlighted in Figure 13-18.

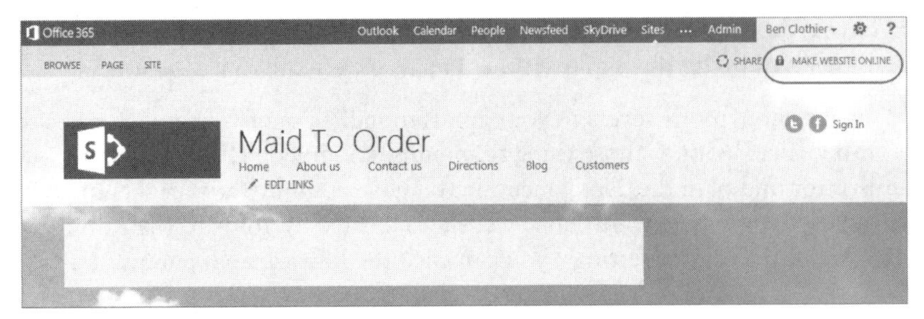

FIGURE 13-18: Make Website Online link

You can then add an Access web app using the same process you have already used throughout the book to add apps on the public website. Any Access web app created on the public website will be available to anonymous users for read-only access without any other special modifications.

Note that when anonymous users are permitted, the two expressions used to identify signed-in users will return different results on your public site. `UserEmailAddress()` will return null while `UserDisplayName()` will return Anonymous User. You can reliably identify whether you have an anonymous user or not by using the expression of `UserDisplayName() = "Anonymous User"`. You can use that information to enable or disable features on your public-facing web apps. If you provide a way for anonymous users to request and receive access to the team site via the public website, they can gain additional permissions such as writing to the app on the public website.

Note that there is currently no out-of-the-box mechanism to allow anonymous users to register themselves as external users and thus gain additional permissions. This can be only done via an invitation.

SECURING WEB APPS IN THE WEB BROWSER

As previously discussed, most security you may want to implement for your web apps essentially will be embedded in the application logic itself, meaning that you will supply the UI macros and view objects to enforce security. In the following sections, you learn how you can use the action bar and popup views to effectively restrict access and check the user's privileges using the `UserEmailAddress()` functions. The example is to provide a mechanism for creating a restricted section within the web app in a web browser. For additional security, you should consider using a client application in conjunction with a security mechanism such as Active Directory which is discussed later in the chapter.

We want to emphasize that using the `UserEmailAddress()` function is not a complete solution because in some scenarios, users have the ability to change their e-mail addresses. Thus, while it may be an acceptable way of disambiguating users in some scenarios, it should not be assumed to be a secure method of identifying the user.

In this situation, your best option is to implement security at the application level and allow non-trusted users access to only the web interface and withhold the access to the client application or to the database behind the web app. However, to support scenarios where you need to allow access to restricted information in a web browser, you will learn how to make use of macros to implement a custom login form and use that to manage access to other views.

Generally speaking, if you want to implement a restricted area of your site, it is best implemented as a popup view rather than a tile-bound view. This is due to the fact that, at the time of this writing, you cannot hide tiles or links at run time with a UI macro. Furthermore, you can always navigate to a tile-bound view, even when its tile is hidden, by entering its URL directly. For example, a view named myView associated with table myTable could be reached by appending the parameters to the base URL, which is `www.exampleapp-xxxxxxxxxxxxxx.sharepoint.com`:

```
https://exampleapp-xxxxxxxxxxxxxx.sharepoint.com/default
.aspx#Tile=myTable&View=myView
```

You may notice the `#` is used instead of `?` in this URL. A full discussion is beyond the scope of this book. It is used in conjunction with AJAX. Thus, it can be hard to control whether a user has gone through the log in process before they arrive at the tile-bound view. All in all, we think you will find it much more straightforward to restrict access by using popup views, which can be opened after a successful login.

Suppose, for example, that you want to create an app that MTO's customers will use to make schedule requests, which is a separate app from the app used by the maids. Customers need to log in and see only their own profile. Recall that the customer has already had to log into SharePoint; the only purpose of creating a login within the app is to ensure the user has not left the computer unattended, thus identifying themselves in order to access the information specific to them.

On a new app, you need four components to demonstrate the concept behind rolling out a custom security system within a web app:

1. Customer table
2. Tile-bound view
3. Macros to perform the login and validation
4. Popup view

You can refer to earlier chapters for detailed steps on creating each component, or refer to the sample available for download. Here we will focus more on what each component should contain. The Customer table should contain the username and password. There is no simple mechanism to hash the password so it will be stored as plaintext.

> **WARNING** *Be aware that some jurisdictions may have requirements regarding securing the data at rest and may have specific requirements for password storage. If the data is under such regulation (examples include, but are not limited to, personal healthcare data, which falls under HIPAA in the United States, or personal identifying data under the European Union's Privacy laws). It is your responsibility to verify compliance with applicable laws and regulations.*

As you can see in Figure 13-19, two columns identify a user based on their login and password. You need to create a tile-bound view that will contain two textboxes and a button to log the user in. Figure 13-20 provides an example of such a view.

You may want to note two things that are not apparent from Figure 13-20. First, there is no password mask for the password textbox but you can achieve a similar result by modifying the textbox's forecolor to be the same as the backcolor, demonstrated in Figure 13-21.

MTOCustomer | tblCustomers

Field Name	Data Type
CustomerID	AutoNumber
FirstName	Short Text
MiddleInitial	Short Text
LastName	Short Text
FullName	Calculated
OrganizationName	Short Text
ActivationDate	Date/Time
Inactive	Yes/No
LogOn	Short Text
PWD	Short Text

FIGURE 13-19: Customer table

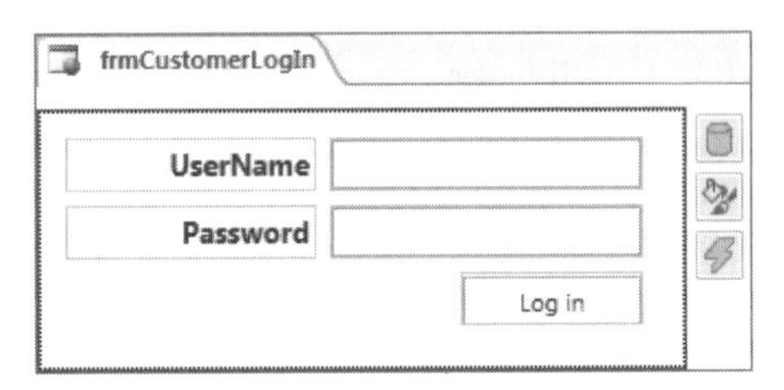

FIGURE 13-20: frmCustomerLogin view

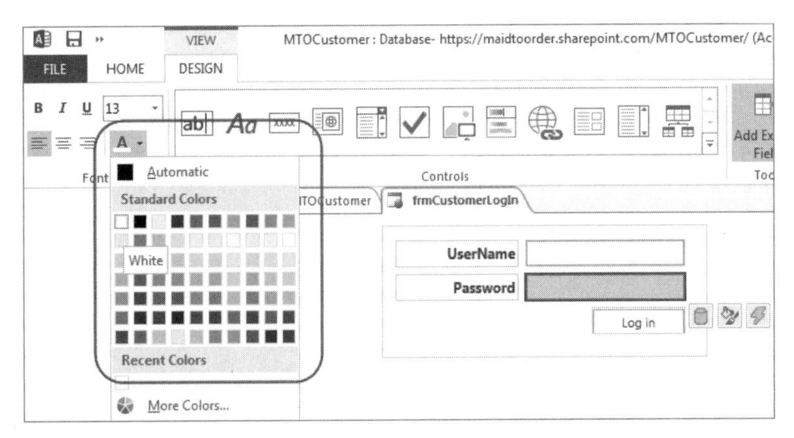

FIGURE 13-21: Modifying a textbox's forecolor

Second, to make entry a bit easier, we auto-populate the `UserName` field with the `UserEmailAddress()` function via the Default Value. Figure 13-22 shows that.

Now you need a data macro to validate that the user is who they claim to be, which can be done with a LookupRecord action as illustrated in Figure 13-23.

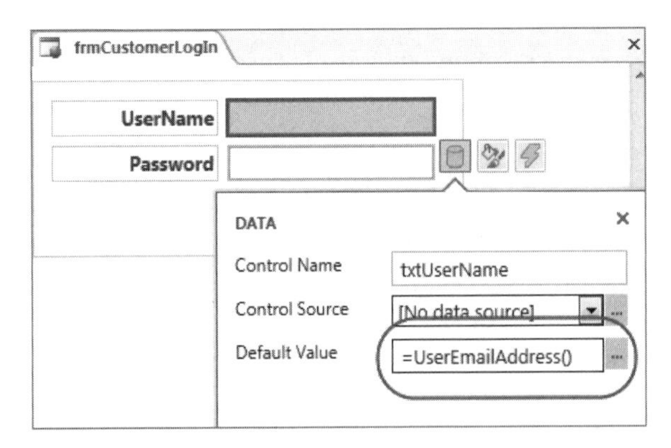

FIGURE 13-22: UserEmailAddress ( ) Default Value

```
MTOCustomer   dmLogin

Parameters
Name                 Type          Description
ptxtUserName         Short Text
ptxtPWD              Short Text

⊟ Look Up A Record In  tblCustomers
    Where Condition  = [tblCustomers].[LogIn]=[ptxtUserName] And [tblCustomers].[PWD]=[ptxtPWD]
    SetReturnVar
        Name        rlngCustomerID
        Expression  = [tblCustomers].[CustomerID]
```

FIGURE 13-23: dmLogIn Data Macro

You then need to provide the macro actions placed behind the Log In button's `Click` event to call the data macro and check the return value. As you can see in Figure 13-23, if there is no match for the given parameters, null will be returned. Figure 13-24 shows how to check for this.

```
⊟ RunDataMacro
    Macro Name  dmLogin
  Parameters
    ptxtUserName  = [txtUserName]
    ptxtPWD       = [txtPassword]
    SetLocalVar   vlngCustomerID        = rlngCustomerID
  SetProperty
    Control Name  txtPassword
    Property      Value
    Value         =Null
⊟ If  [vlngCustomerID] Is Not Null  Then
    OpenPopup
        View      frmCustomer
        Where     = [tblCustomers].[CustomerID]=[vlngCustomerID]
        Order By
⊟ Else
    MessageBox  (Invalid username or password)
  End If
```

FIGURE 13-24: UI macro to call dmLogin and check results

We want to step aside and remind you that although this is a simple example, you are also free to further augment the process for additional security. For example, you could have `dmLogin` return a timestamp, which you then use within UI macros to ensure that nobody has left a session idle for too long. Or you may also want to generate a session ID or similar concept. The finished product would look like what is shown in Figure 13-25. Figure 13-26 shows the popup view.

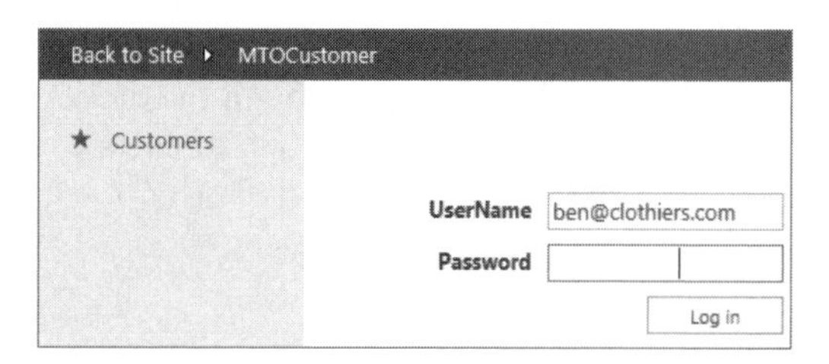

FIGURE 13-25: Login in web browser

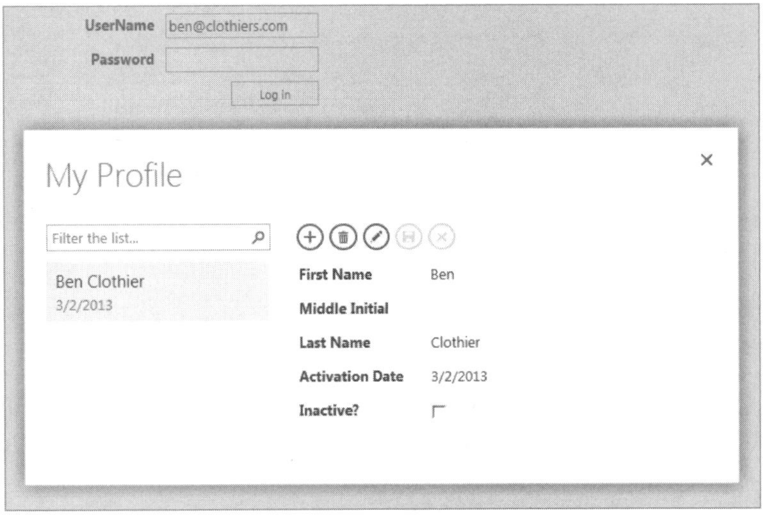

FIGURE 13-26: Secured popup view

We want to point out that one primary reason for logging in from a tile-bound view instead of using a popup view is that popup views can always be dismissed by clicking the X button and there is no reliable method of intercepting when a popup view is closed. Thus, implementing a login form as a popup view can be problematic. Once the popup view is open, however, you are free to open other popup view or customize the popup view to handle navigation in whatever method you prefer.

You now have a basic working concept for enabling restricted sections within your web apps. It is worth emphasizing that for situations where security matters and is subject to audits, you may be better off using client applications where you can leverage security mechanisms such as Active Directory to manage access.

Using Subsites to Restrict Users to Specific Apps

Because SharePoint permissions determine what actions users can perform on a site and any subsites under it, and because different User Groups have different permissions, you can manage your site, subsites, and web apps to which different users have access through the proper combination of User Groups and permissions. In this manner, you can restrict certain users to a single app. You'll walk through the process in this section. At the end of the process, you will have a web app for a selected group of users who will not have access to any other areas of your site. This group of users will include you, the administrator, as well as one or more external users who have been invited to share it.

Sites and Subsites

You'll need to be logged in as an administrator to complete the following steps. Before you can create the subsite and load the restricted app to it, you'll need to make the app available in the app catalog. For this discussion, we'll assume you've done that. You can refer to Chapter 14 for a review.

The first step in creating a restricted web app is to define a subsite under the main site in which the web app will be installed for a restricted group of users. Navigate to the Site Contents page in your SharePoint site. Take a look at Figure 13-27 showing Site Contents for the Maid To Order app.

Click the new subsite link, highlighted in Figure 13-27, to create a subsite for the app. Fill in the fields in the definition page, as shown in Figure 13-28.

The Title of the subsite should reflect its intended use. In this case, it will be the home of the customers-only web app. The description is optional, but completing it will be helpful to others who may be called on to maintain the subsite and web app in the future.

The URL for the subsite is required and it is quite important. Choose a name that is both relatively easy to remember and meaningful. This URL will lead your users to the proper pages in your subsite. Select the other options as indicated in Figure 13-28.

Because the intended use for this subsite is to support a secure location for a web app, you'll assign it unique permissions for specific groups, not inherited from the parent site. You can change that later as well, but you'll start out with the proper inherited permission settings for this subsite because you already know that it will be unique.

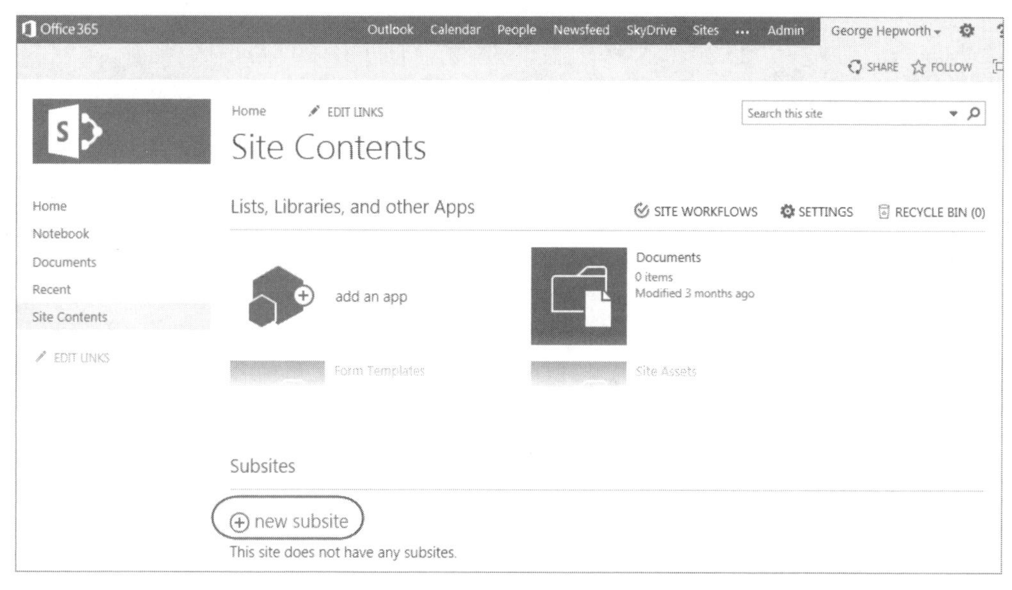

FIGURE 13-27: Site Contents page

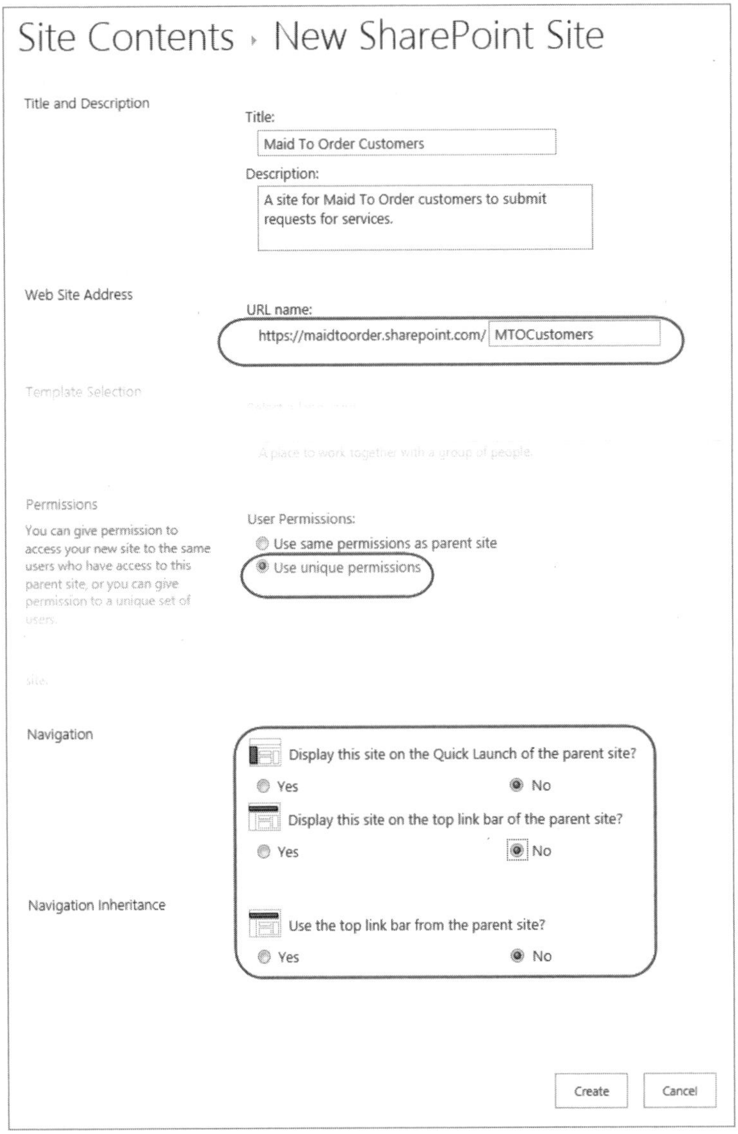

FIGURE 13-28: Create a subsite for the web app.

If you want the subsite to be available to all users on the parent site, you can leave the link on the top link bar and Quick Launch. That is not what you want to do, however, because the goal is to provide a restricted site for the app and its users.

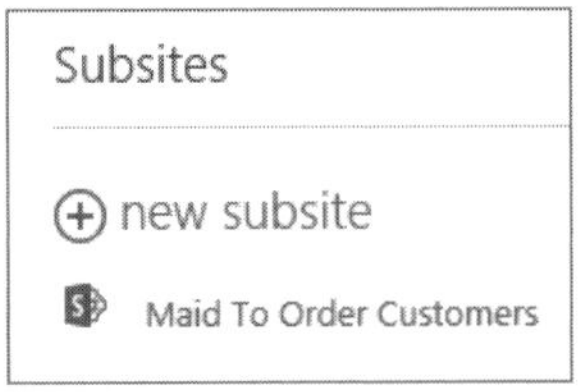

Click Create to accept the changes. Because you chose "Use unique permissions," you will have one more step, shown in Figure 13-29, to create new groups or use an existing group to set up the permissions. For this exercise, accept the default which is to create a brand new

FIGURE 13-29: Creating new groups for the subsite

group for Owner, Member, and Visitor groups. Doing so means the Visitors group will be empty. Only you will be in the Owner and Member groups. However, you won't be using either the Member or Visitor groups because by default they map to either a too high or too low permission level. You will perform this step after you install the app to the subsite.

The next step is to install the app in the subsite. Click the link, identified in Figure 13-29, to launch the subsite. It will look like Figure 13-30.

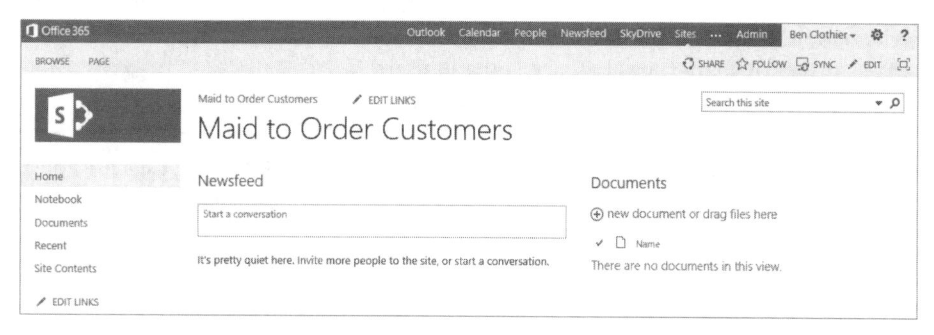

FIGURE 13-30: Default layout for new Maid To Order Customers subsite

Because of its intended use as a secure location for a single web app, you'll want to remove all elements from the page that don't apply. You'll also drop in a link for the web app. But first, let's install the customer's web app so we may drop the link to that web app here. Click Site Contents in the links list on the left to get to the next page, shown in Figure 13-31.

When you click the link to add an app, you'll be presented with all of the apps available in your app catalog. For this exercise, we are assuming that the MTO Customers Access web app is uploaded to the app catalog. Choose the one you want to add to the subsite, as shown in Figure 13-32.

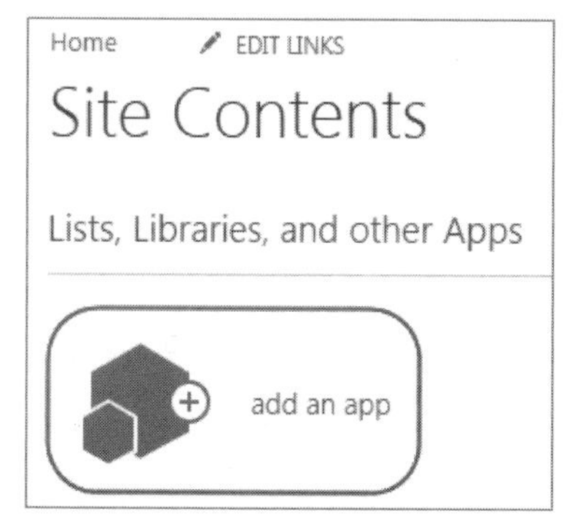

FIGURE 13-31: Add an app to the subsite.

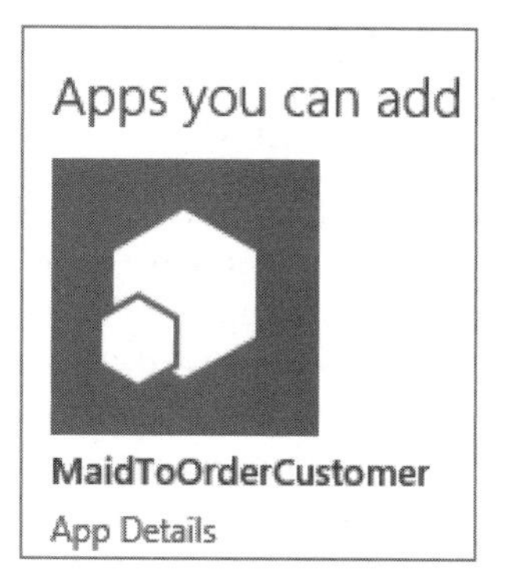

FIGURE 13-32: Select and add your app.

You will be asked to trust the app before continuing. Do so in the dialog box. The app will be added to the subsite. It may take a few moments to set it up, as indicated in Figure 13-33.

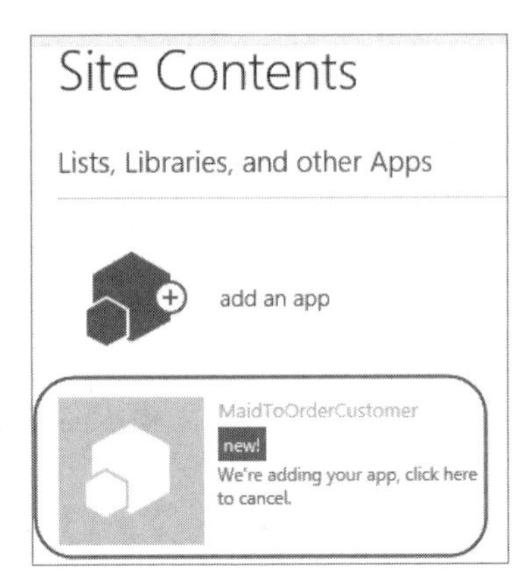

FIGURE 13-33: Office 365 adding a new web app

At this point, the subsite is ready and the app is installed; and you're ready to create the permissions needed to restrict this new app to the selected users. You need to define a group into which the users will be added, give that group contributor rights so they can read and write data but not change the app itself, and also set permissions on the subsite for that group. Later, you'll add users to the group. Let's change the settings for the subsite first. Click the Settings link, as shown in Figure 13-34.

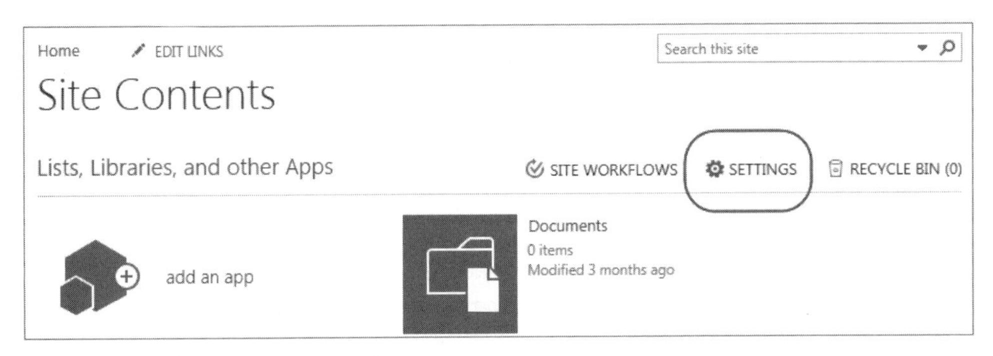

FIGURE 13-34: Change settings for the subsite.

On the Site Settings page, you can define various settings dictating how a site should operate. Take care that you are on the correct site as each site has its own Site Settings. For this task, you need to edit permissions, so click on Site Permissions shown in Figure 13-35.

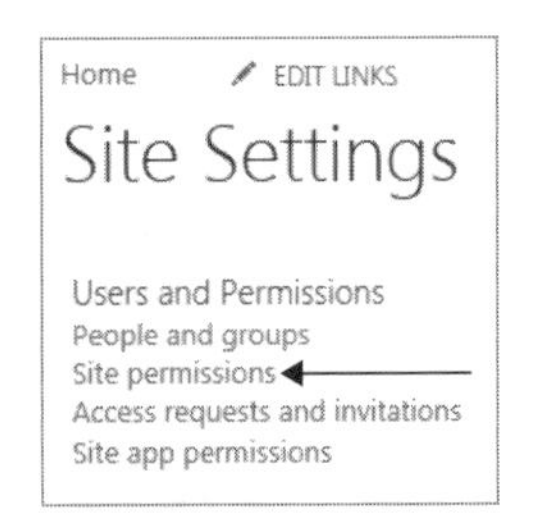

FIGURE 13-35: Users and Permissions for the subsite

Click the link for the subsite permissions. You may see different groups from those in our sample app, but the three shown are typical: members, owners, and visitors. You'll want to create a new group that only has contributing rights to prevent them from making design changes to the app. You cannot use Members because the default is to allow members to have design rights which also enable them to customize Access web apps. Note that you can fine-tune permissions by creating a new permission level and associate a group to your custom permission level, but this is beyond the scope of book. For now, we'll create a new group and call it Maid To Order Customers Contributors. To do so, start by clicking Create Group as shown in Figure 13-36.

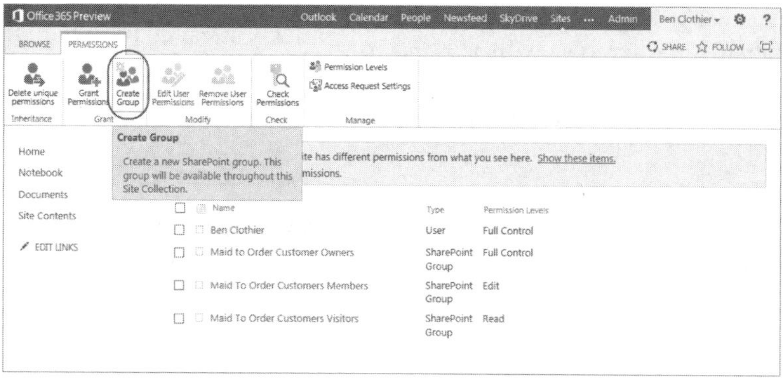

FIGURE 13-36: Create Group button to create a new group

Provide the name "Maid To Order Customers Contributor" for the group. Ensure that requests to join or leave the group are not allowed, as shown in Figure 13-37. You will also see permission levels listed. Check the Contribute permission and taake note of its description and compare it to other permission levels shown in Figure 13-38. Click Create to finish the group creation. You will typically add users to this new contributor group and perhaps reserve Members for other employees who should be able to perform patches or updates to the applications. Of course, if you need to provide read-only access, you can use the visitor group for this purpose.

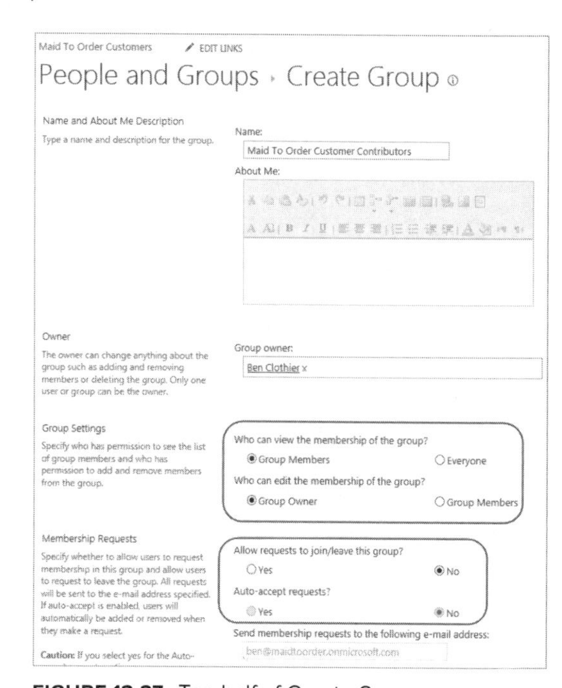

FIGURE 13-37: Top half of Create Group page.

Give Group Permission to this Site

Specify the permission level that you want members of this SharePoint group to have on this site. If you do not want to give group members access to this site, ensure that all checkboxes are unselected.

View site permission assignments

Choose the permission level group members get on this site: https://maidtoorder.sharepoint.com/MTOCustomers

- [ ] Full Control - Has full control.
- [ ] Design - Can view, add, update, delete, approve, and customize.
- [ ] Edit - Can add, edit and delete lists; can view, add, update and delete list items and documents.
- [x] Contribute - Can view, add, update, and delete list items and documents.
- [ ] Read - Can view pages and list items and download documents.
- [ ] View Only - Can view pages, list items, and documents. Document types with server-side file handlers can be viewed in the browser but not downloaded.
- [ ] Create new subsites - Can create new subsites

Create | Cancel

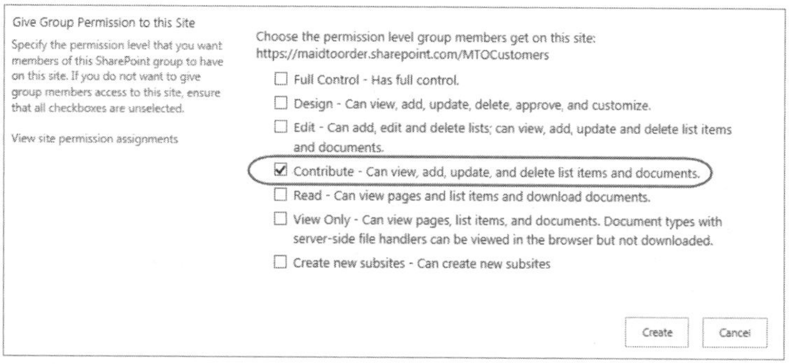

FIGURE 13-38: Bottom half of Create Group page

Let's add users next. You can either create new users, or you can add existing users to the group. If you want users with accounts to be able to use the subsite, you can just add them. See Figure 13-39. Because this web app is intended for external users, the process is a bit more extended.

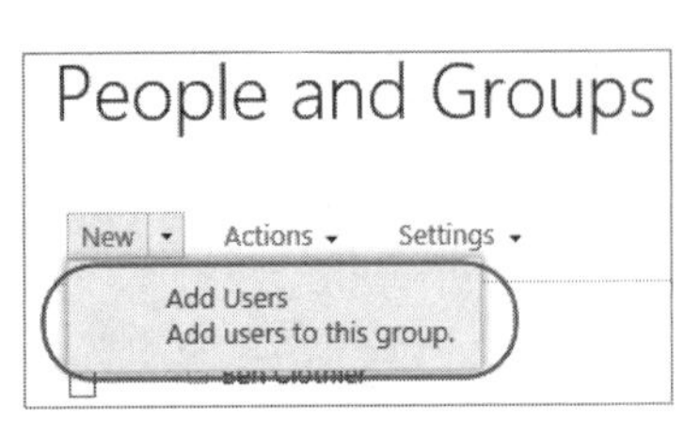

FIGURE 13-39: Add Users

First, let's invite a new user to the site. To do this, you need to use the Share button available on the upper-right of the site's menu which will open the Share dialog. Enter the e-mail address of the invitee as in Figure 13-40.

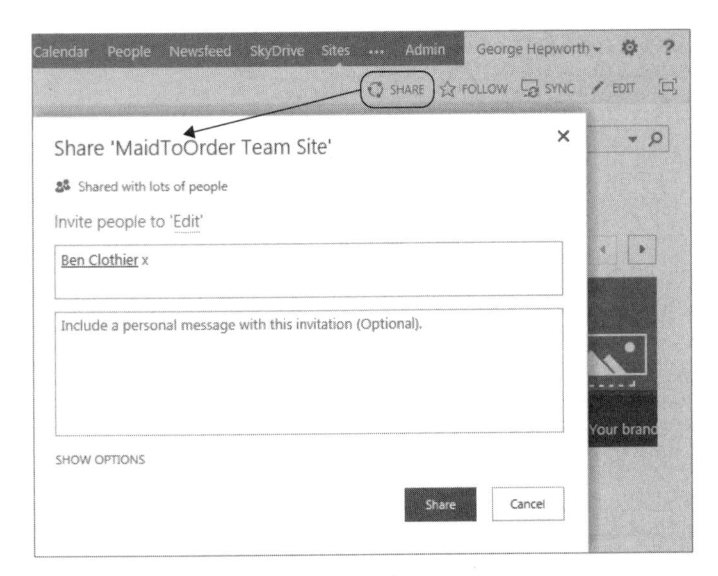

FIGURE 13-40: Share the site by inviting new users.

Enter the invited user's e-mail address and a short message. As you would anticipate, the e-mail addresses you enter here are those you obtain from new customers as they sign up for your services. In a different app, you might be inviting coworkers to an organizational app. The point is that you need to know the e-mail address of the invited user so you can enter it here.

Clicking the Share button sends the invitation. When the invited user receives and accepts the invitation, he or she will need to create a Microsoft Account, or Windows Live ID, with which to sign in. Figure 13-41 shows the invitation as your invited users will see it.

> **NOTE** *In this section, we're describing steps taken by invited users, who are most likely not under your direct control or guidance. You'll want to create and share good instructions with them, at least the first time you invite them to one of your web apps. The steps needed are not difficult, but they may prove to be confusing to novices.*

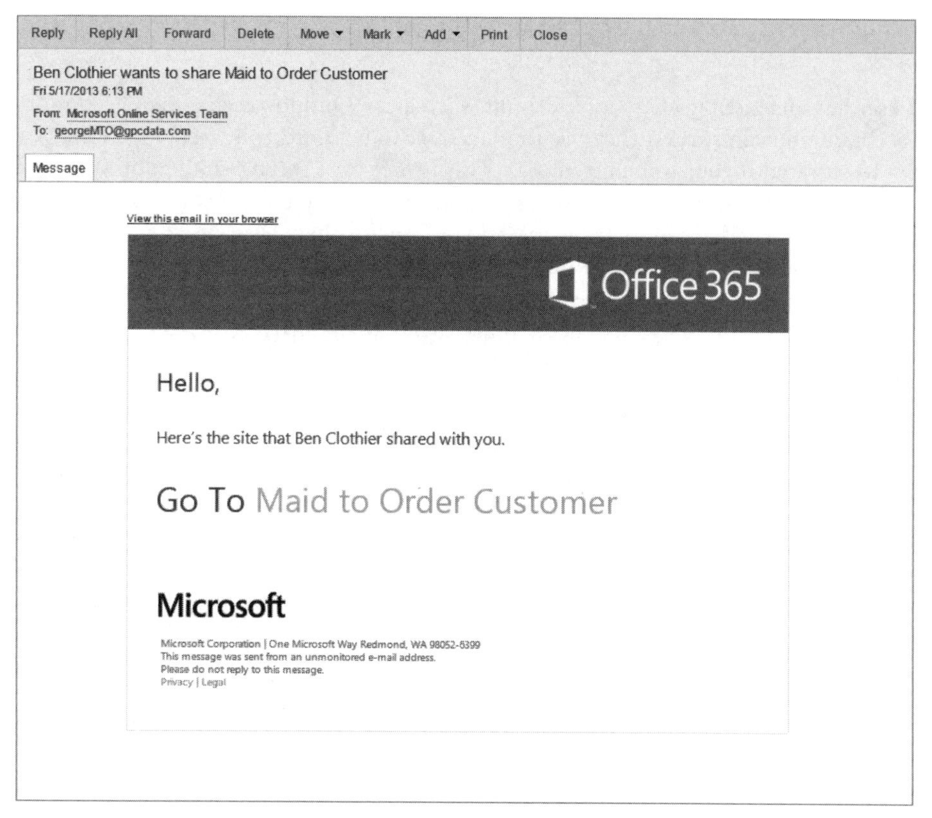

FIGURE 13-41: Invitation received by an invited user

Replying to the invitation by clicking the link in the invitation e-mail brings the invited user to the Welcome page in your site, as shown in Figure 13-42.

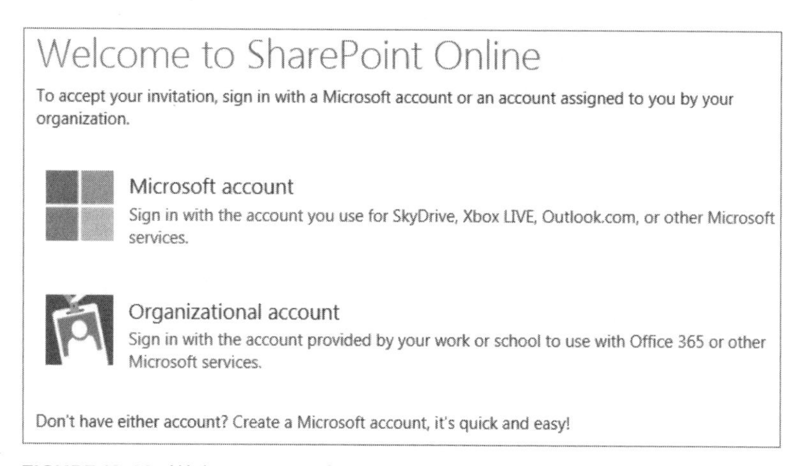

FIGURE 13-42: Welcome page for a new user

Consider the options on this page carefully. It's potentially confusing, especially to someone who's new to the process.

If your invited user has an existing Microsoft account, such as an Outlook.com e-mail account or an Xbox Live account, you can suggest they use that account to log in to your web app. They'll use that account to work with your web app subsite. This is true even if the e-mail address used to invite those users were not the same e-mail address associated with such Microsoft accounts. Or, if your organization has created accounts for its users, you can ask them to use that account. You may have to provide information to them regarding that organizational account separately. In this case, because you're inviting external customers to use the app on Office 365, the Organizational Account option won't apply. Your users will need to use their existing Microsoft account or create a Microsoft account.

If your users are using an Office 365 account supplied by their organizations, they may have an Organizational Account with their organizations. In that situation, they should give preference to that account because it is associated with the company they work for rather than the person.

The last option, creating a new account, is the most appropriate for the situation where the user has not previously set up an account, such as a Hotmail or Outlook e-mail account. They'll be asked to create one as part of the sign-in process.

So, assuming your user does have an organizational Account, tell your user to click that link to go to the sign-in page (see Figure 13-43).

FIGURE 13-43: Cropped view of login page

You need to be aware of a couple of important elements of this sign-in page that may not be immediately apparent, and which can, once again, potentially be misleading to your invited users. If this is the first time they've visited your site, they'll see a sign-in like Figure 13-43. However, on return visits, they may see a page like Figure 13-44. The difference is caching.

Office 365 remembers the last used sign-in from the computer. In this case, it's the owner of the site, which we show as an example. Caching the last used sign-in can be very handy, of course, because it saves you the trouble of typing it in again. However, it can be somewhat confusing, especially on a shared computer. The cached sign-in could be the sign-in information for another user who shares this computer. It could also be a sign-in for an entirely different account, if the user happens to have more than one. Just remember to tell your users to sign in to your web app with the e-mail address and password associated with your web app. You'll learn how to make that association next.

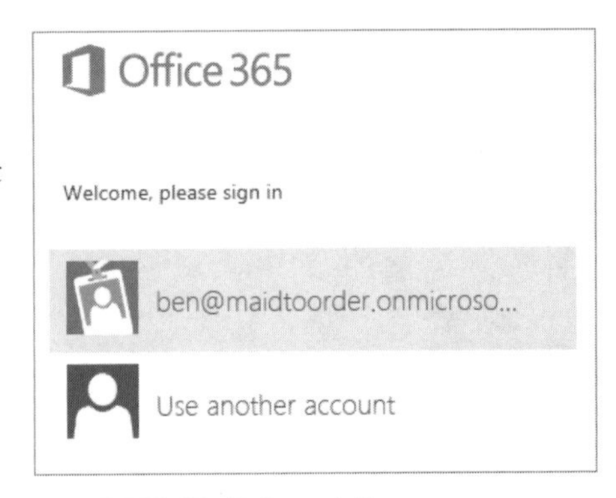

FIGURE 13-44: Return visit

Because not everyone has a Microsoft account, the experience may differ when users are invited using their non-Microsoft accounts. Suppose that we sent an invitation to someone with a Gmail account. They'll start on the same login page as shown in Figure 13-43 but as soon as they complete typing in their Gmail address, they will be redirected to a different page to complete the sign-in process. Figure 13-45 shows the redirect message.

FIGURE 13-45: Entering a non-Office 365 account causes redirects

When your invited user is redirected to the page depicted in Figure 13-46, the user can continue to use their Gmail account only if it is already linked to a Microsoft account. Otherwise, the user may need to create a Microsoft account and link it to their preferred e-mail address. The user can then complete the sign-in and return to your website.

FIGURE 13-46: Redirected Sign-in Page

When the invited users have provided credentials, they will be taken back to the site they were invited to and are free to do whatever they are permitted to do in that site.

We need to look at one more scenario for sites where Access Requests is enabled. When a user who is not a site owner uses the Share button from Figure 13-40 to invite other users, access will not be immediately granted. Rather, it is treated as an access request which must have the approval of the site owner. The requesting user will be shown the notification depicted in Figure 13-47 that the access request was sent to the site owner.

FIGURE 13-47: Notification regarding access request

The site owner can provide approval by going to the Access Request and Invitations link exposed on Site Setting, as depicted in Figure 14-35, under the called out link. This will then take the site owner to the page shown in Figure 13-48 where the site owner can then grant or deny the request by the requesting user to give access to other users specified by the requesting user. Furthermore, note that only the site owner can determine the permission to be given to the recipient of the access request.

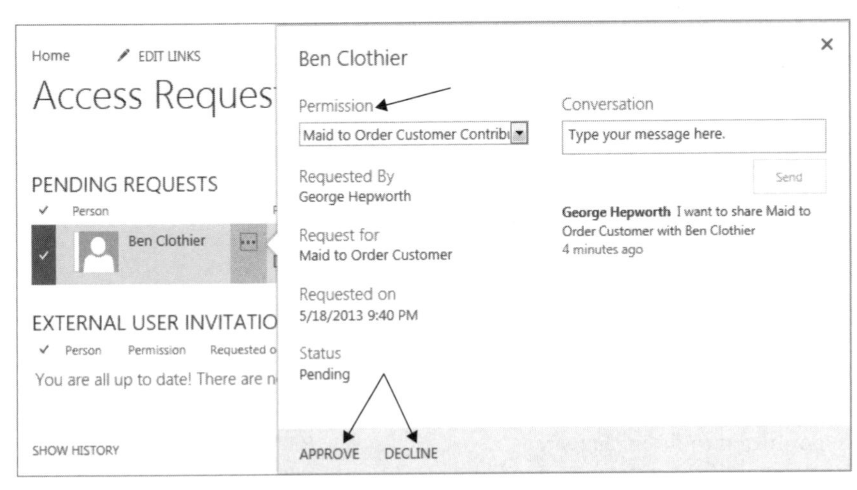

FIGURE 13-48: Access requests and invitation page

Two things happen when you click Approve in the Pending Request. The invited user is added to the appropriate user group. As you can see in Figure 13-47, you want to add the invited customer to the contributors group so that they have rights to add, modify, and delete only data, not change the app in any way.

The second action is sending an e-mail to the invited user, letting them know the process is complete and that they can now use the subsite and the app on it. When the invited users get the approval e-mail, they can click the link in it and go to the sign-in page again. This time, signing in takes them to the subsite page, from which they can launch the MTO customer app. Figure 13-49 shows that.

FIGURE 13-49: Maid To Order Customer app

We didn't flesh out a complete web app for Maid To Order customers, just enough to show you how it works. There are two very important features to take note of, one you can see, the other you won't see until you click Back to Site.

You may already have noticed in Figure 13-49 that the "gear" is missing in the upper-right corner. This prevents your invited users from designing the web app in Access. They are in a contributors group that has rights only to work with the data. You can also see in Figure 13-49 that the user's name does not appear in the upper-right corner. Users in this group are not permitted to get to About Me, which would open up a path into the team site.

The other important point in the security discussion is that clicking Back to Site returns you to the subsite, not the Team site. Essentially, users of this app are "in a box."

If you've worked with SharePoint before, you may be thinking that the users can "break out" of the box by altering the URL to go directly to a page on the team site directly into the browser. Figure 13-50 shows you what happens when they try that.

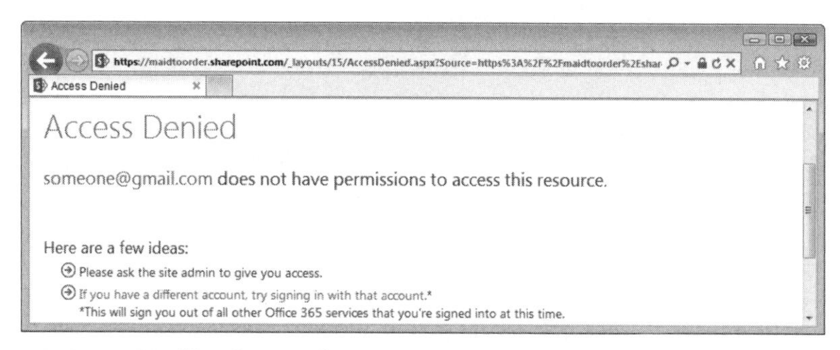

FIGURE 13-50: "Breaking out" is not permitted.

The user can, of course fill out and submit the request for permissions to the Team Site if requests are permitted, but you don't have to accept that request. You can deny the request and keep the user in his or her box.

In this section, you learned about one method for securing a specific app to a specific group of users, while at the same time, limiting the members of that user group from seeing other elements of your site. You could extend this method to two or more subsites, each with its own unique app and set of users. With two or more related, but separate, subsites you could deal with synchronizing the data between them, which is touched upon in Chapter 14.

TRADITIONAL METHODS FOR SECURITY IN CLIENT SOLUTIONS

When you link a client `.accdb` file to the database behind the web app, many traditional security methods with which you may be familiar continue to be available. In fact, if you are planning on managing security at the application level, some traditional features must be used for the security to be effective. As discussed, both ExternalReader and ExternalWriter users have quite a broad set of permissions and when you want to achieve a more granular level, it is necessary to separate the user from the database and use the Access client in conjunction with VBA as the agent. However, to avoid circumventing the VBA programming, the file must be compiled into an `.accde` file format to remove the source code and lock the VBA project. However, security is also achieved through depth; instead of relying on one feature to secure the resources, you can use more than one feature in conjunction to make it harder to bypass. Your experience will be helpful in guiding you to decide how much security a given project will need.

For the sake of completeness, we want to list traditional approaches that you may be familiar with we want to list traditional approaches you may be familiar with:

- Hiding the navigation pane and default ribbon
- Disabling the Shift bypass key
- Using runtime mode
- Password-protecting the VBA project or converting to `.accde`
- Customizing the ribbon and Quick Access Toolbar (QAT)
- Using the `MSysConf` table to prevent saving passwords
- Using Windows filesystem permissions or Active Directory

The first three methods should be familiar and are documented in various places, and there are several samples available in a web search. For a quick reference, here is the minimum VBA code required to hide the navigation pane and ribbon, typically done at startup:

```
DoCmd.RunCommand acCmdWindowHide
DoCmd.ShowToolbar "Ribbon", acToolbarNo
```

The Shift bypass can be also disabled by setting the property at startup:

```
CurrentDb.Properties("AllowBypassKey")=0
```

> **NOTE** *The* `AllowBypassKey` *property does not exist by default; you'll need to create it before setting it on a given* `.accdb`.

The first three methods make it harder to access the design surface but are not foolproof. There are some methods in VBA that may show the navigation pane or ribbon as a side effect. On the other hand, they are very simple to implement as a part of a startup routine and are usually sufficient for simply keeping people that you trust honest. The next method, using the runtime mode, is a bit less likely to be circumvented by accidental programming. Simply changing the file extension to `.accdr` enables runtime mode.

Using runtime mode disables many design features and prevents user-driven customization of the ribbon and QAT. In addition, runtime mode is immune to Shift-key bypass. However, you need to re-implement ribbons, QAT, and shortcut menus in a runtime mode when you want to allow users to use features such as copy and paste, filtering commands, and so forth.

To truly prevent any unwanted changes to source code, you have the option of password-protecting the VBA project or compiling the database into an `.accde` file. While you can do both, it is not helpful to do so since compiling into an `.accde` file removes the source code, leaving nothing to password protect. Using an `.accde` file is a fairly effective method for making it much less likely that your security logic will be compromised.

The next two methods are relatively less common and merit some more discussion. You may already know that you can specify a custom Ribbon XML to customize the ribbon, QAT, and the backstage. When your custom Ribbon XML specifies the `startfromscratch="true"` attribute, you also prevent any possible customization of the UI, which can be effective, in conjunction with runtime mode, in preventing people from reaching design features and gaining more access than you may want them to have. Furthermore, it is the only way to remove unwanted options that are present by default in runtime mode such as the Privacy Options button that appears whenever runtime mode is used. For your convenience, here is a minimal ribbon XML that you can use in the `USysRibbons` table to strip out all default buttons that may be available in runtime mode and prevent any UI customizations:

```
<customUI xmlns="http://schemas.microsoft.com/office/2009/07/customui">
  <ribbon startFromScratch="true">
  </ribbon>
  <backstage>
    <button idMso="ApplicationOptionsDialog" visible="false"/>
    <button idMso="FileExit" visible="true"/>
  </backstage>
</customUI>
```

> **NOTE** *For a primer on ribbon customization, we recommend* RibbonX: Customizing the Office 2007 Ribbon by *Robert Martin, Ken Puls, and Teresa Hennig (Wiley, 2008). You can also augment the information with Access-specific information from Gunther Avenius's excellent site,* `http://www.accessribbon.de/en/`.

You can then use the appropriate references to add the desired functionality, whether built-in or custom, to the base XML. Note that if you choose to not use runtime mode, you have more built-in elements that you may need to hide.

Next, a `MSysConf` table is actually not a new feature. It can be used with the database behind the web apps as well as other ODBC databases. The table is implemented on the ODBC database, and is read by the Access client during initial login. It has two purposes; it can be used to disable the Save Password feature on ODBC-linked tables and to control the refresh interval for background data fetching. We are primarily interested in the Save Password aspect. As you know, when you link to an ODBC database, you may see the checkbox shown on the Link table in Figure 13-51.

FIGURE 13-51: Link Tables dialog box with the Save password checkbox

With a database that contains a configured `MSysConf` table, the Save Password option is not available, as you can see in Figure 13-52.

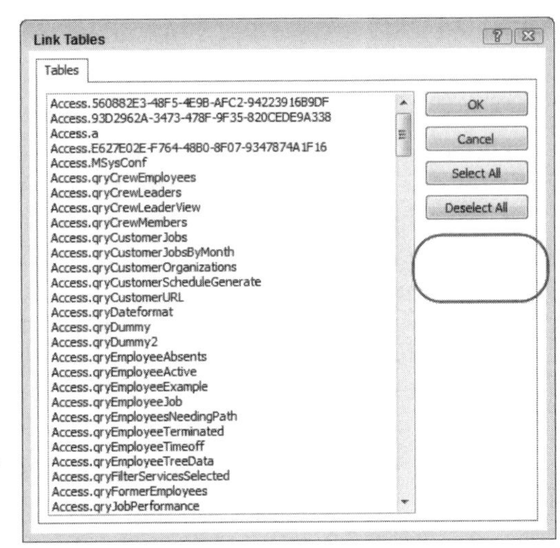

FIGURE 13-52: Link Tables dialog box without the Save password checkbox

More importantly, having an `MSysConf` table also prevents any programmatic export of the linked tables with the password saved. For example, `DoCmd.TransferDatabase` has a parameter to save the login that will copy the password into a new `.accdb` file; it is ignored when `MSysConf` prohibits this. Thus, you may find additional value in implementing the `MSysConf` table in your web app's database. The name is important — the Access client will search specifically for a table by this name so you must ensure it is named `MSysConf`. Figure 13-53 shows how you should define `MSysConf` within your web app's design surface. Field names and their data types must be exactly as shown here.

MaidToOrder | MSysConf

Field Name	Data Type	Description (Optional)
ID	AutoNumber	Required by web app
Config	Number	Whole Number (no decimal places)
chValue	Short Text	255 characters long
nValue	Number	Whole Number (no decimal places)
Comment	Short Text	255 characters long

FIGURE 13-53: MSysConf table definition in web app

For this example, we only need to prevent saving passwords so you need to add only one row. You would fill it in as shown in Figure 13-54.

ID	Config	chValue	nValue	Comment
1	101		0	Disallow saving
(New)	0		0	

FIGURE 13-54: Populating MSysConf table

A value of 101 in the `Config` field indicates that the `nValue` field should modify the behavior of whether Access should allow saving passwords or not.

Next, the ExternalWriter user has broad permissions and thus can write to the `MSysConf` table, which we don't want. You can prevent this by setting up triggers for all three table events, as in Figure 13-55.

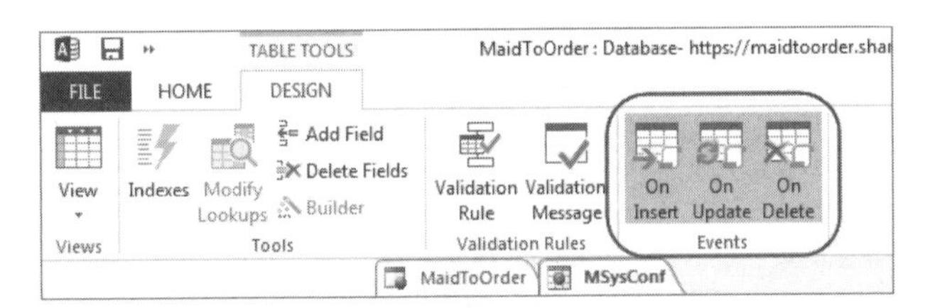

FIGURE 13-55: Enabling table events for MSysConf

All three events will have identical macro actions, which is just a single action, raising an error, as shown in Figure 13-56 when a user tries to alter data.

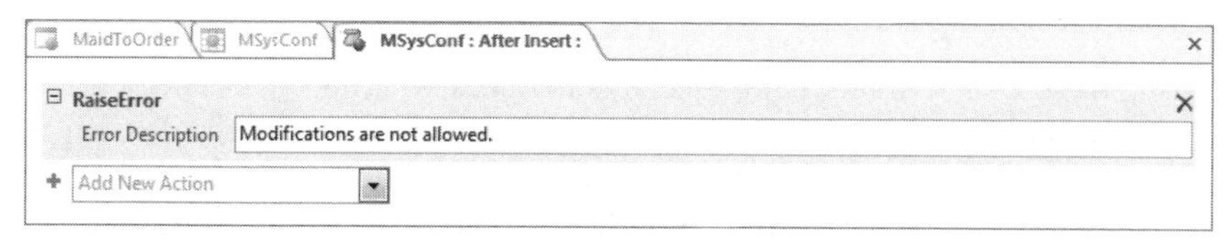

FIGURE 13-56: Raising an error to prevent modifications

> **NOTE** *For reference on how to create table events, refer to Chapter 9.*

This effectively prevents the ExternalWriter user from being able to modify data in the table, and the ExternalWriter user does not have the rights to deactivate the table events; it can be only done via the web app design surface. These properties make this is an effective mechanism for preventing unauthorized changes to the `MSysConf` table and ensure that the option to disallow saving passwords will be enforced at all times.

Finally, you always can augment the security with Windows filesystem or Active Directory permissions. This is a simple yet effective method of keeping non-users out. Where there is an Active Directory or equivalent mechanism in place, you can check to ensure that the client application was opened on a domain-joined computer and thus ensure it is not running outside of the domain. You may want to use VBA code to call into WMI or API to determine whether a computer is joined to a domain. Here is an example using WinNTSystemInfo object:

```
Public Function GetDomainName() As String
    Dim objSys As Object
    Set objSys = CreateObject("WinNTSystemInfo")
    GetDomainName = objSys.DomainName
End Function
```

Obviously, you are limited only by your own imagination in how you implement security. The discussion here should help you with deciding which traditional features you will want to leverage when implementing security for your client applications that should work with the web app database. You will now turn to the next problem of keeping the password for either the ExternalWriter or ExternalReader account from the user in order to make your Access client application an effective agent. This will not be possible without making an `.accde` file or, at least, password-protecting the VBA project. The other features you just reviewed will make it more effective.

WEB APP LINKED FILE SECURITY

As discussed earlier, an `.accde` front-end file cannot be an effective security agent if the users already know the password for the database and thus can just simply log into the SQL Server using Excel or a different Access database file. Therefore, if you need to use an `.accde` file as an agent in order to enforce security built in the application layer, your users should not know the password used to connect to the web app database. In the following section, you learn different ways to handle this part of the security puzzle. As you learn about each, you can choose which is more suited to the needs of your specific solution.

One option for restricting the use of an `.accde` file format is to check whether it's opened on a computer that's joined to a certain domain. If the `.accde` file format can contact the domain controller and verify it is on the right domain, then it can decrypt the password stored within the `.accde` file and allow the user to use the application. Another option for securing the password so that it does not need to be stored inside the `.accde` file is to store it on a SharePoint list on the same site where the web app is. The ability to access a SharePoint list requires that the user first authenticate via SharePoint, making it a great way to store the password so that the `.accde` front-end file can connect to the appropriate list without the user's intervention or knowledge of the password to connect to the back-end database. You will learn more about how you can implement those two options and make an informed decision as to which works the best for you.

DSN-Less Linking and Relinking

Once you have linked your `.accdb`/`.accde` file to the web app's database with a *data source name* (DSN) file, you have the option of redefining the connection as a DSN-less connection. You learned how to do that in Chapter 11. Let's just quickly review the components involved and add some additional considerations from the security perspective.

As you learned in Chapter 11, when using the relinking code to make DSN-less connections, you do not use the option to store the password in the tables' connections. This allows you to require that users provide the password each time they launch the `.accdb` /`.accde` file and ensure that anyone who doesn't have it can't get to the data in the tables.

The choice to use a DSN or not isn't directly a security question but more of an administrative question. The advantage of using a DSN-less connection is greater predictability in how you can manage your connection. You can thus secure the connection string. With a DSN, there are relatively more hiding places for the password. DSNs typically are stored in the registry, which makes distribution problematic. A file DSN makes it easier to distribute but also requires that you manage a second file in addition to the client. Using a DSN-less connection gives you more flexibility in how you can gather the information you need to construct the connection string and how you should be able to obtain it in a secure manner.

For an example of creating DSN-less connections, refer to Doug J. Steele's code, which is freely available online at `http://www.accessmvp.com/djsteele/DSNLessLinks.html`., which was also discussed in Chapter 11.

In addition, when creating linked tables or passthrough queries, there is typically no reason to store the full connection string. It is sufficient to store only the driver, server, and the database parameter in a connection string. During startup, you call a temporary passthrough query that contains the full connection string. Here's an example procedure you'd use during an application's startup. The code is available in `MTOClient.accdb` in the Chapter 13 folder:

```
Private Function CheckConnection(Token As String) As Boolean
    Dim qdf As DAO.QueryDef
    Set qdf = CurrentDb.CreateQueryDef(vbNullString, "SELECT NULL;")
```

```
    qdf.Connect = _
        "ODBC;DRIVER={SQL Server Native Client 11.0};" & _
        "DATABASE=db_f4689298_1035_4588_b062_096bf56eed7e;" & _
        "SERVER=aux99xmbfs.database.windows.net;Encrypt=yes;" & Token
    On Error Resume Next
    qdf.OpenRecordset (dbOpenSnapshot)
    CheckConnection = (Err.Number = 0)
End Function
```

Even though the `querydef` object is discarded at the end of the procedure, Access will cache the initial connection that `querydef` object opens. As long as a linked table's or passthrough query's `Connect` property matches the first three parameters, Access will be able to marshal all those linked tables and passthrough queries through the cached connection.

It is worth noting that there is no programmatic access to the cached connection, and also that the cached connection does not go away when you close only that database without closing Access itself. Therefore, to maximize security, we recommended that you design your client application to quit Access when the last form is closed. An easy way to implement this is to hide the startup form rather than closing it and, within its Close event, add the code to quit the application:

```
Private Sub Form_Close()
    Application.Quit acQuitSaveNone
End Sub
```

This works regardless of how a user attempts to close the database.

The DSN-less connection strategy allows you to eliminate DSN files completely. This removes one path through which unauthorized users could theoretically get to the data from a different source, such as an Excel file.

Another consideration is that, should you want to eliminate the requirement that users log in each time they open the application, you can store the password to the web app's database as part of the relinking code in an `.accde` file with a reasonable level of confidence that it won't be seen by ordinary users because they can't get to the code. However, as noted in our initial analogy, the determined attacker who gets possession of a copy of your file can remove it and work on cracking it at their leisure. Because it is possible, though not easy, to reverse-engineer an `.accde` file, this should be considered a higher level of security than an open `.accdb`, but not an absolute level of security.

Instead of relying on Access for security, then, let's look at the full range of options open to you.

Password Storage/Non-Storage

Although encryption is a good way to remove some risk from the security equation, the fundamental problem with storing a password, especially if you need to secure it from direct use, is that encryption simply moves the problem one step further back without eliminating it.

To effectively encrypt a message and then decrypt it back to the original message, you must use a key. A key is just another password. The primary reason to encrypt the password is so that your users do not need direct knowledge of that password to connect to the web app database. This means you can focus on managing the key. The key used to encrypt and decrypt the password can then be managed some other way, including but not limited to:

- A password that users enter in a login form in `.accde` file format; the password they use is not the same one that connects to the database.
- A constant fact that is known and should be available to authorized users; an example is the domain controller's machine name and GUID.

Using encryption to secure the key itself is not appropriate because it is more effective to restrict access to the key by storing it in a secured resource such as a network share on a domain of which a machine must be a member, or in a SharePoint list, which requires users to sign in. For this reason, you may not want to store the encrypted output of the password inside the `.accde` file; otherwise, you're back to the analogy of the portable safe in the front yard.

Another important consideration here is that, once the password is decrypted and retrieved, it should be used only long enough to connect successfully to the web app database, and then it should be discarded immediately. In other words, as far as a normal user knows, the web app database password doesn't even exist. The app retrieves and uses it without revealing it or saving it anywhere the user could see it.

Setting Up a SharePoint List

In order to manage access to keys, you need to create a custom SharePoint list, as highlighted in Figure 13-57, to act as the repository. You also want to customize the list a bit to partition the keys between users and to set up a notification system for requesting and granting access. Furthermore, you will be creating a SharePoint workflow so that e-mails will be sent whenever a user adds a new record to the list.

The process to grant access will work as follows:

1. A user tries to log in and is told they don't have access.
2. The client application inserts a new record into a SharePoint list containing the key to be used for encryption.
3. The workflow on the SharePoint list reacts to the insertion and sends an e-mail to the administrator.
4. The administrator encrypts the ExternalWriter's password using the given key and updates the record.
5. The update triggers the same workflow again, causing it to e-mail the user a notice that access has been granted.
6. The user returns to the client application and logs in successfully.

> **NOTE** *If you are unfamiliar with SharePoint workflows, it may be useful to read up on them and how they work. You can learn more about workflows at the MSDN site:* `http://msdn.microsoft.com/en-us/library/jj163986.aspx`.

To get started, go to the team site, and add an app, selecting a new custom list via the Site Contents – Your Apps page, as shown in Figure 13-57.

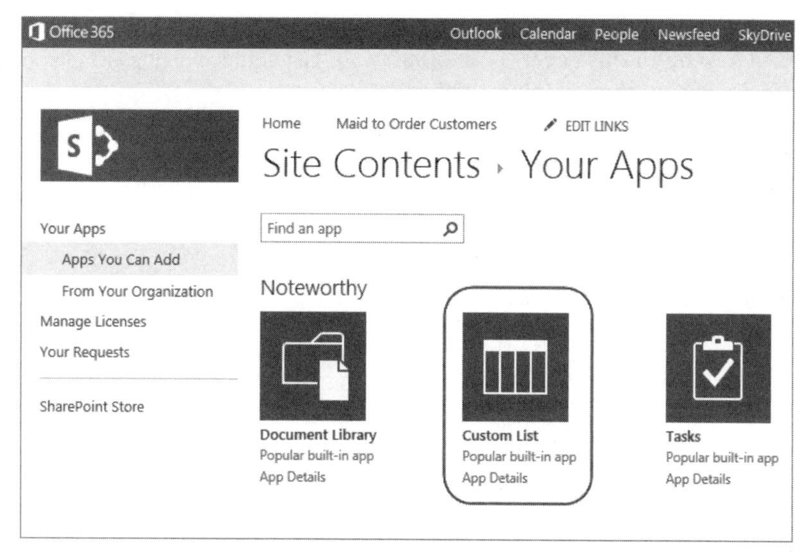

FIGURE 13-57: Add a New Custom List

In the following prompt, name the list. You might name it "`MaidToOrderAccessList`," as in Figure 13-58.

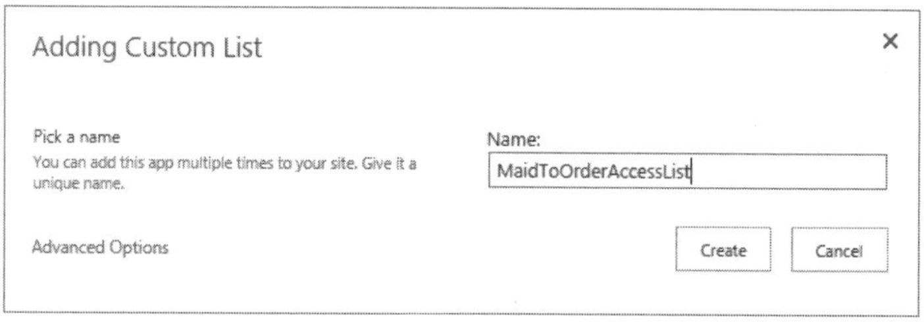

Adding Custom List

Pick a name

You can add this app multiple times to your site. Give it a unique name.

Name:

MaidToOrderAccessList

Advanced Options

Create Cancel

FIGURE 13-58: Name the new custom list.

> **NOTE** *Although you may see spaces in names of SharePoint objects, it's good practice to avoid spaces just as you would with Access objects. Doing so makes programming against such objects easier, but you can then rename it with spaces afterward to look nice on the page without affecting the underlying programmatic name which is set exactly once at the time of creation and cannot be changed afterwards.*

Once the list is created, click the new list to go to its page. Click the List tab to show the ribbon and select List Settings, as shown in Figure 13-59.

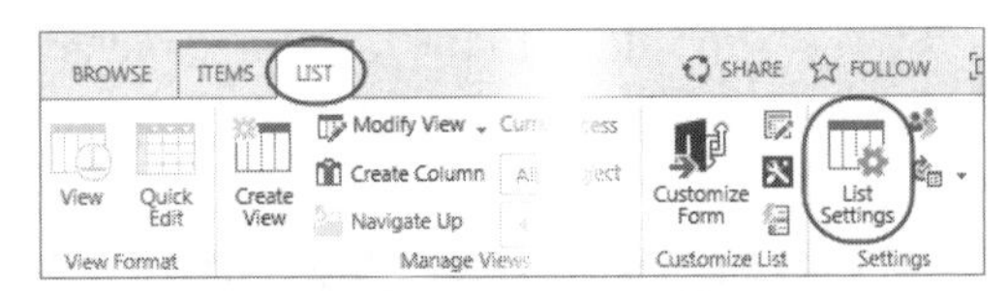

FIGURE 13-59: List Settings on the List tab on the ribbon

The List Settings page describes several list options and attributes. You may need to refer to this page while customizing the list. Take note of the following tasks you need to perform, and refer to Figure 13-60 to locate the appropriate link as you follow through the subsequent steps:

1. Rename the list to include spaces.
2. Change user permissions so that users can view only their own list items.
3. Disable folders and attachments for this list.
4. Add columns.
5. Add workflow.

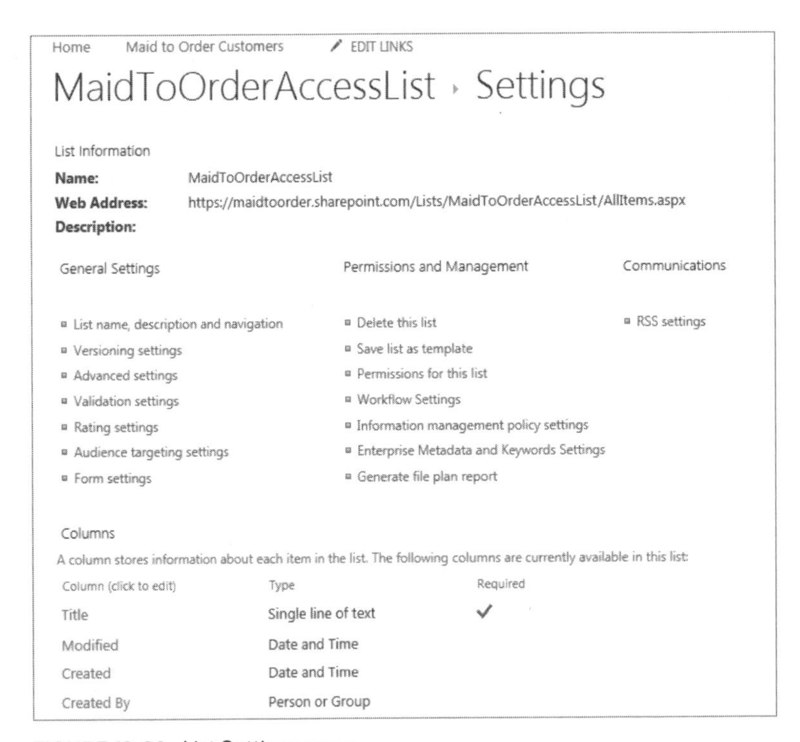

FIGURE 13-60: List Settings page

Click the `List name, description and navigation` link shown in Figure 13-60. Rename the list to contain the spaces, as shown in Figure 13-61, and then save and return to the List Settings pages.

Click the Advanced Settings link shown in Figure 13-62. You will customize several options on it.

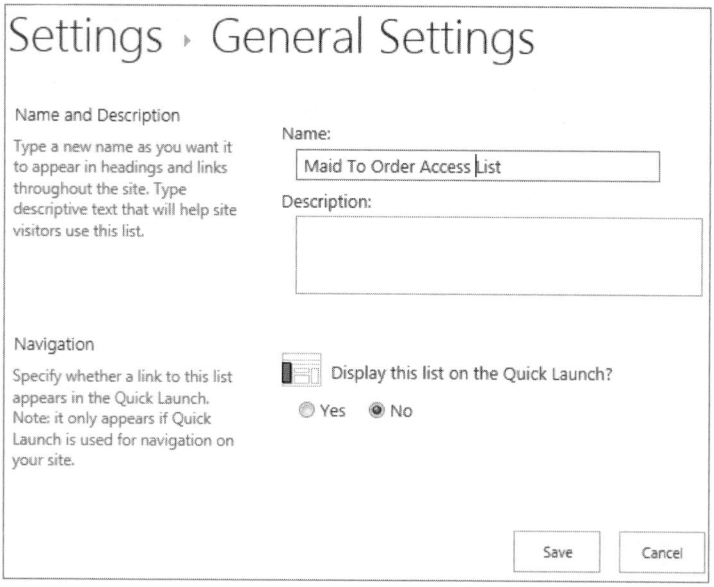

Settings › General Settings

Name and Description

Type a new name as you want it to appear in headings and links throughout the site. Type descriptive text that will help site visitors use this list.

Name:

Maid To Order Access List

Description:

Navigation

Specify whether a link to this list appears in the Quick Launch. Note: it only appears if Quick Launch is used for navigation on your site.

Display this list on the Quick Launch?

Yes No

Save Cancel

FIGURE 13-61: Renaming a list

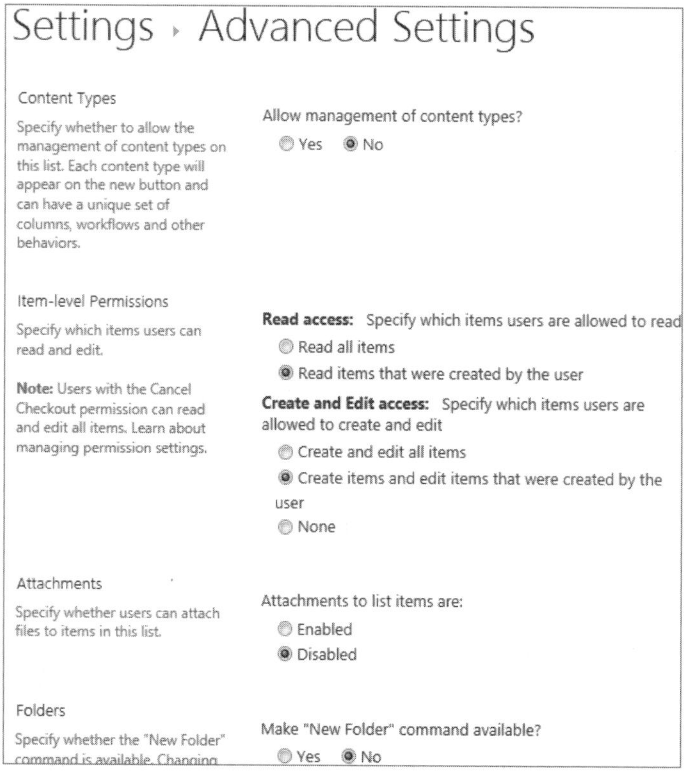

Settings › Advanced Settings

Content Types

Specify whether to allow the management of content types on this list. Each content type will appear on the new button and can have a unique set of columns, workflows and other behaviors.

Allow management of content types?

Yes No

Item-level Permissions

Specify which items users can read and edit.

Note: Users with the Cancel Checkout permission can read and edit all items. Learn about managing permission settings.

Read access: Specify which items users are allowed to read

Read all items

Read items that were created by the user

Create and Edit access: Specify which items users are allowed to create and edit

Create and edit all items

Create items and edit items that were created by the user

None

Attachments

Specify whether users can attach files to items in this list.

Attachments to list items are:

Enabled

Disabled

Folders

Specify whether the "New Folder" command is available. Changing

Make "New Folder" command available?

Yes No

FIGURE 13-62: Advanced Settings page

In the Item-Level Permission section, under Read Access, select the radio button labeled Read items that were created by the user. Under Create Access, select the radio button labeled Create items and edit items that were created by the user. Those two radio buttons ensure that users can see only their own list items. Users with Manage List permissions (typically a member of the Owner group) will always be able to see all list items.

On the Attachment section, select the Disable radio button to turn off attachments for this list. For the rest of the page, select the No radio button for every section. You would have a result similar to what is shown in Figure 13-62.

Once you click OK and return to the List Settings page, scroll down a bit and click the Title column to edit it. On the Edit Column page shown in Figure 13-63, change the name of the column from “Title” to “Token” and click OK.

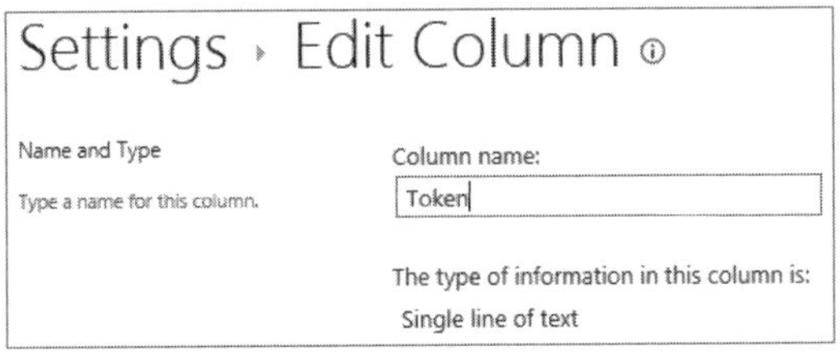

FIGURE 13-63: Edit Column page

On the List Settings page, click the `Create Column` link to add a new column. Provide Key as the name, and under Require that this column contains information, select the Yes radio button, as illustrated in Figure 13-64.

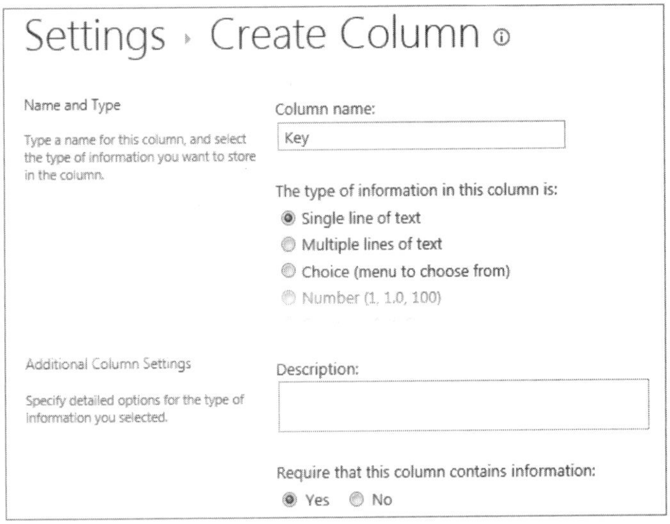

FIGURE 13-64: The Create Column page

Click OK to save the change and return to List Settings. You need one more column, so click the `Create Column` link again. Provide Status as the name and choose Choice for the data type, as shown in Figure 13-65.

Scroll down the page and click the Yes radio button to ensure that it is set as required. Then set four choices, as shown in Figure 13-66, and ensure that the Default value is set to the first entry.

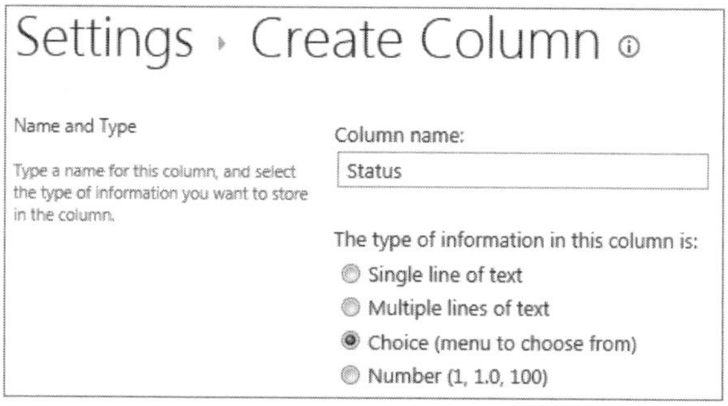

Settings › Create Column

Name and Type

Type a name for this column, and select the type of information you want to store in the column.

Column name:

Status

The type of information in this column is:

Single line of text

Multiple lines of text

Choice (menu to choose from)

Number (1, 1.0, 100)

FIGURE 13-65: Creating a Choice column

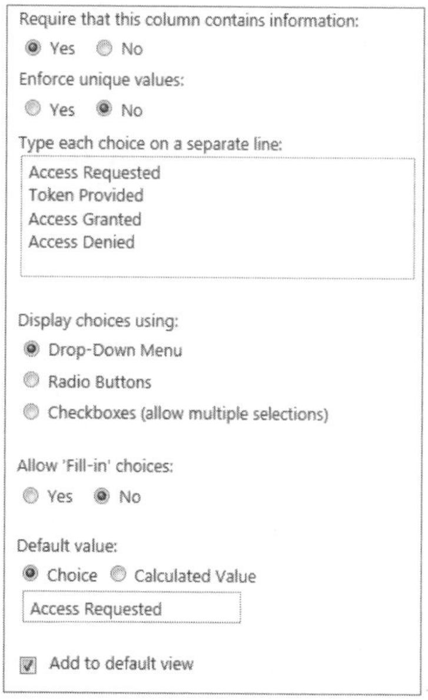

Require that this column contains information:

Yes No

Enforce unique values:

Yes No

Type each choice on a separate line:

Access Requested
Token Provided
Access Granted
Access Denied

Display choices using:

Drop-Down Menu

Radio Buttons

Checkboxes (allow multiple selections)

Allow 'Fill-in' choices:

Yes No

Default value:

Choice Calculated Value

Access Requested

Add to default view

FIGURE 13-66: Choice entries

Click OK to save the changes and return to the List Settings page. You now have the list structured the way you need it to support the storage of the key that provides access to the password. Take note that while you could edit the permissions for the list, we've already restricted access at the site which the list will inherit also. To help support a scenario where you have new users who do not have an entry yet in this list, you want to have a notification system so that when a new user requests access to your client application, you will get an e-mail and grant (or deny) access, a step which also notifies the user of your action. To do this requires a workflow. On the List Settings page, click the `Workflow Settings` link.

SharePoint provides a number of workflows for different kinds of content and you must choose the correct one; you want Three-State workflow, which is attached to workflow Items. Therefore, you need to select Item from the drop-down in Figure 13-67.

Click the `Add a workflow` link. On the Add a Workflow page, select Three-State workflow and provide a name such as AccessRequest, as shown in Figure 13-68.

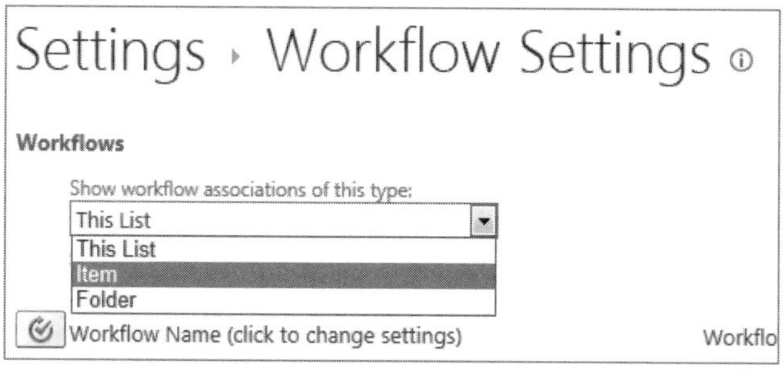

Settings › Workflow Settings

Workflows

Show workflow associations of this type:

This List

This List

Item

Folder

Workflow Name (click to change settings)

Workflo

FIGURE 13-67: Select a workflow association.

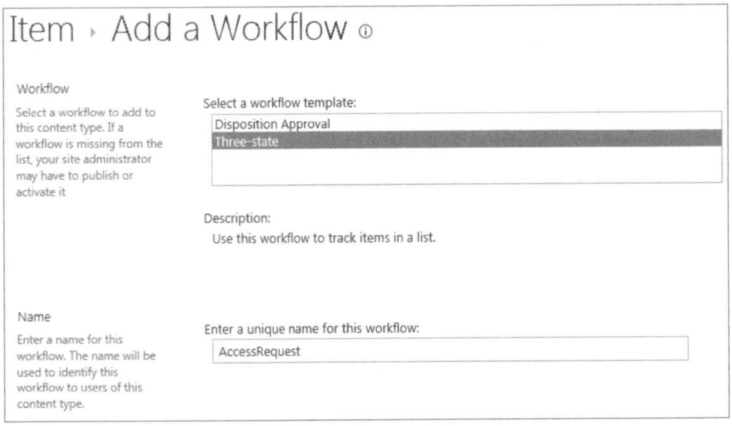

FIGURE 13-68: Add a Workflow page

Accept the default for the Task List and History List section and clear the checkbox labeled "Allow this workflow to be manually started by an authenticated user with Edit Item permissions" checkbox, and then select the Creating a new item will start this workflow checkbox, as shown in Figure 13-69.

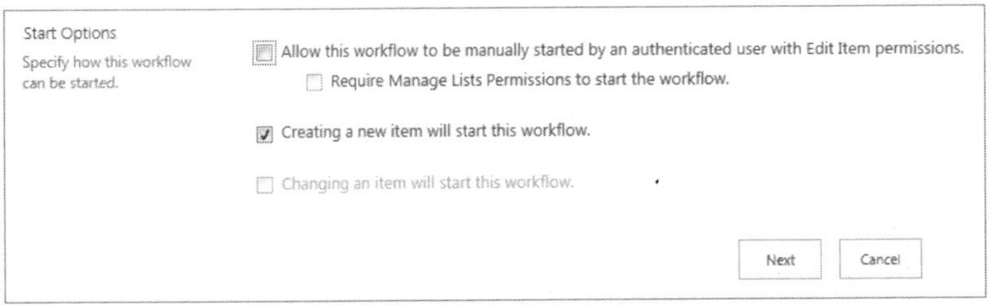

FIGURE 13-69: Start Options

Click Next and verify that the Workflow status has the expected values, similar to what you see in Figure 13-70.

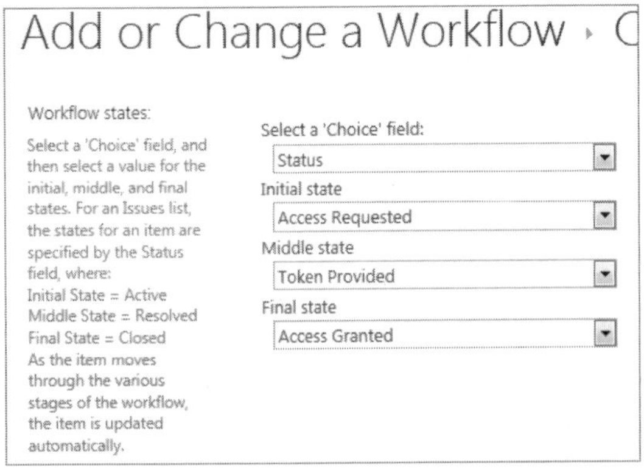

FIGURE 13-70: Workflow Status options

Next, you will customize and format the task so an e-mail will be generated and sent when a request is made. The objective is to send an e-mail to the administrator of the site notifying him or her that an access request has been made by a particular user. Customize the fields as shown in Figure 13-71.

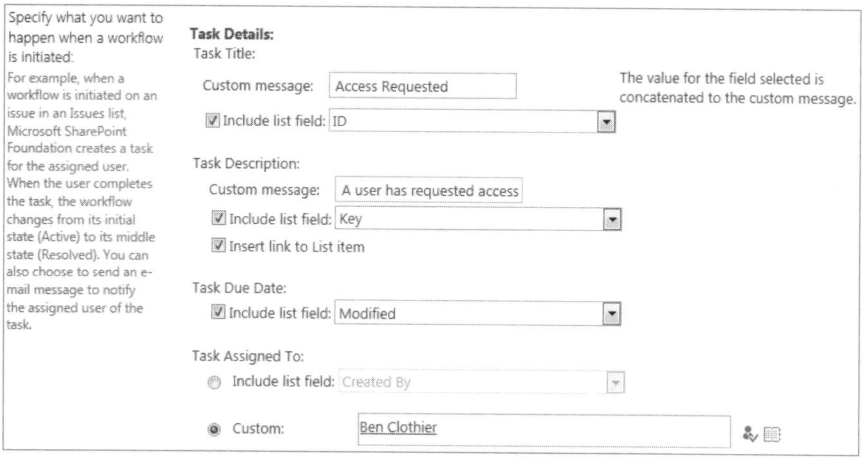

FIGURE 13-71: Task parameters for Access Requested state

The custom message sent in the e-mail, shown in Figure 13-71, is too long to be shown in the image; the full text is, "A user has requested access to Maid To Order client application." Note that the task is assigned to Ben Clothier, who is the designated site administrator and will be responsible for granting access to the users who want to use the client application. The e-mail will be sent whenever the user adds a new list item, which you will see later in the section.

Assigning a task is not sufficient. You also want to send an e-mail, so you customize the E-mail Message Details section. Several of the settings can be inherited from the Task settings you customized in the step illustrated in Figure 13-71 so you can leave fields blank where there is a checkbox to read values from the Item List, as shown in Figure 13-72.

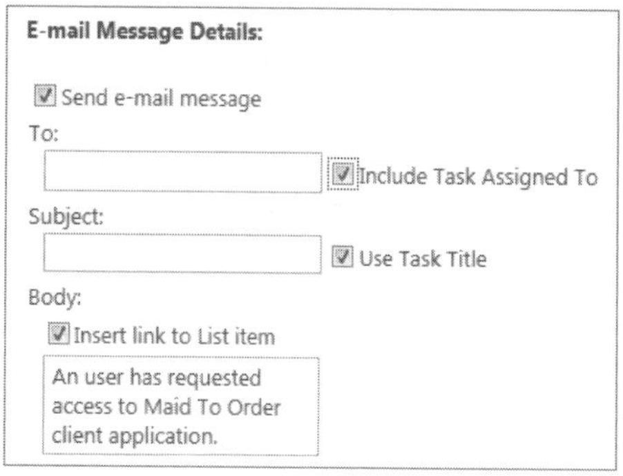

FIGURE 13-72: E-mail Message Details

This sets up the actions that should happen when a user adds a new item to the list. In a later section of this discussion, we'll explain how a user adds that item in order to request access to the client program. The administrator will get an e-mail notifying him or her that a user has requested access to the client program. Of course, it would do little good to grant access without also notifying the user of that. Fortunately, you can do just that. The next two sections about providing notification to the user are similar to what you just saw for the steps illustrated in Figures 13-71 and 13-72.

Unlike the first task and e-mail, you shouldn't need to provide a user with any data so you would clear checkboxes and customize the message to simply indicate that access was granted, as illustrated in Figure 13-73.

Specify what you want to happen when a workflow changes to its middle state:
For example, when an issue in an Issues list changes to Resolved status, it creates a task for the assigned user. When the user completes the task, the workflow changes from its middle state (Resolved) to its final state (Closed). You can also choose to send an e-mail message to notify the assigned user of the task.

Task Details:
Task Title:
Custom message: Access Granted
Include list field: Token
The value for the field selected is concatenated to the custom message.
Task Description:
Custom message: Access to client application h
Include list field: Token
Insert link to List item
Task Due Date:
Include list field: Modified
Task Assigned To:
Include list field: Created By
Custom:

FIGURE 13-73: Task parameters for Access Granted state

Tasks get assigned to the user in the `Created By field`, who is the original user that created the list item in the first place. The full text for the Custom Message field is "Access to client application has been granted." You also want to send an e-mail to this user, but you don't need to send the user back to the list; the user can go to the client application directly after receiving the e-mail. Because the task is already assigned to the user who started the process, we can simply leave both To: and Subject: blank while keeping the checkboxes checked to indicate that the e-mail is to go to the user using the same title as the task, as in Figure 13-74.

E-mail Message Details:
Send e-mail message
To:
Include Task Assigned To
Subject:
Use Task Title
Body:
Insert link to List item

FIGURE 13-74: E-mail Message Details for returning e-mail

Once you complete this section of the Workflow setup, you can click OK to save the Workflow. At this point, you are done with configuring the list. You can now move on to creating the login routine within the Access client application, which you will learn about in the next section.

Storing Passwords in a SharePoint List

As discussed earlier, you want to store encrypted content containing the ExternalWriter password in a secure resource. SharePoint lists require authentication at all times so they are a good place to secure the data and restrict it only to users who should be able to access the client program. We want to step aside and remind you that SharePoint lists can be linked in an Access client solution and, more importantly, support caching for offline access. Normally this is a desirable feature, but for this security purpose you want to ensure that your users aren't reading an offline list with potentially stale data. Therefore, you will link to the list at run time and delete the link when you finish. This also supports the scenario where you want to link to other SharePoint lists and use them in an offline setting. This ensures both that your List must be online to be used, and that it not be available to an offline client, as discussed in the previous section.

For the purpose of illustration, let's assume that you use your user's domain name and username as the key to decrypt the password. This is not the best possible key; we leave it up to you to come up with a better key for your environment; the attribute used should be a fact known to both the administrator and the user so they can encrypt and decrypt using the same key and get the original message, which is the ExternalWriter password.

In the sample presented in this section, you will be using a VB implementation of the BlowFish algorithm graciously provided by David Ireland, which is available online at his site: `http://www.di-mgt.com.au/crypto.html#BlowfishVB`. The full code is too large to include in the book; the relevant functions are `blf_Initialise`, `blf_BytesEnc`, and `blf_BytesDec`.

To get started, you need a VBA function to obtain the domain name and username (available in the `MTOClient.accdb` file):

```
Public Function GetUserName() As String
    Dim objSys As Object
    Set objSys = CreateObject("WinNTSystemInfo")
    GetUserName = objSys.DomainName & "\" & objSys.UserName
End Function
```

Next, you need to write a function that is called as a part of a startup routine, perhaps via an AutoExec macro or in a startup form's Open event. The function needs to handle those scenarios:

- The user already has access and can use the token to obtain the password.
- The user is new and needs to request access.
- The user was denied access and no token is available.

Only the first condition should allow the user to continue opening the client application and use the rest of the program; the other conditions should cause the program to quit as there is nothing else for the user to do besides perhaps nagging the administrator to provide access. Here is the complete procedure also available in the `MTOClient.accdb` file. We will dissect parts of it as we progress:

```
Public Function CheckAccess() As Boolean
  Dim db As DAO.Database
  Dim tdf As DAO.TableDef
  Dim rs As DAO.Recordset

  Dim strToken As String
  Dim strKey As String
  Dim bytKey() As Byte
  Dim bytToken() As Byte
  Dim bolQuit As Boolean

  Const tblName As String = "MTOAccessList"
  Const strNoAccess As String = _
```

```
    "You currently do not have access to the client " & _
    "application. Do you want to send a request for access?"
  Const strPending As String = _
    "You do not have access yet; the request is still pending. " & _
    "Please contact the administrator if the request has not " & _
    "been fulfilled. The application will quit now."
  Const strRequested As String = _
    "Access request has been submitted. You will receive an " & _
    "email when the access has been granted. Application will " & _
    "quit now."
  Const strFailed As String = _
    "The login was not successful. Contact an administrator." & _
    "The application will quit now."
  Const strDenied As String = _
    "You were denied access to the client application. " & _
    "Please contact the administrator if you believe you should " & _
    "have access. The application will quit now."
  CheckAccess = False
  Set db = CurrentDb

  On Error Resume Next
  db.TableDefs.Delete tblName
  On Error GoTo 0
  Set tdf = db.CreateTableDef
  tdf.Name = tblName
  tdf.Connect = _
    "ACEWSS;HDR=NO;IMEX=2;ACCDB=YES;" & _
    "DATABASE=https://maidtoorder.sharepoint.com;" & _
    "LIST={D6AF2651-F48C-4CA4-9608-B564B1978E08};" & _
    "VIEW=;RetrieveIds=Yes"
  tdf.SourceTableName = "Maid To Order Access List"
  db.TableDefs.Append tdf

  bytKey = GetUserName
  blf_Initialise _
    StrConv(bytKey, vbFromUnicode), _
    LenB(StrConv(bytKey, vbFromUnicode))

  Set rs = db.OpenRecordset( _
    "SELECT TOP 1 * " & _
    "FROM " & tblName & " " & _
    "WHERE Key = '" & GetUserName & "' " & _
    "ORDER BY ID DESC;", dbOpenDynaset)
  If Not (rs.BOF And rs.EOF) Then
    Select Case rs.Fields("Status")
      Case "Access Request Pending"
        MsgBox strPending, vbInformation, "No Access granted"
        bolQuit = True
      Case "Token Provided", "Access Granted"
        bytToken = GetUserName
        bytToken = blf_BytesEnc(StrConv(bytToken, vbFromUnicode))
        blf_Initialise _
          StrConv(bytToken, vbFromUnicode), _
          LenB(StrConv(bytToken, vbFromUnicode))
        strToken = blf_BytesDec(rs.Fields("Token").Value)
```

```
        strToken = StrConv(strToken, vbUnicode)
        If CheckConnection(strToken) Then
          If rs.Fields("Status").Value = "Token Provided" Then
            rs.Edit
            rs.Fields("Status").Value = "Access Granted"
            rs.Update
          End If
          CheckAccess = True
        Else
          bolQuit = True
          MsgBox strFailed, vbCritical, "Unable to continue"
        End If
      Case "Access Denied"
        MsgBox strDenied, vbCritical, "Access Denied"
        bolQuit = True
    End Select
  Else
    If vbYes = MsgBox( _
      strNoAccess, vbYesNo, "No Client Access Available" _
    ) Then
      bytToken = GetUserName
      strToken = blf_BytesEnc(StrConv(bytToken, vbFromUnicode))
      rs.AddNew
      rs.Fields("Token") = strToken
      rs.Fields("Key") = GetUserName
      rs.Update
      rs.Bookmark = rs.LastModified
      MsgBox strRequested, vbInformation, "Access Request Submitted"
    End If
    bolQuit = True
  End If
  rs.Close
  Set rs = Nothing
  On Error Resume Next
  db.TableDefs.Delete tblName
  If bolQuit Then Application.Quit acQuitSaveNone
End Function
```

Regardless of the outcome, the first step is always to access the SharePoint list to determine whether access is available. To relink to a SharePoint list at run time, you can use either `DoCmd.TransferSharePointList` or append a `DAO.TableDef`. First delete any old copy left behind because of an application crash or such. Then relink the table using the URL provided:

```
On Error Resume Next
db.TableDefs.Delete tblName
On Error GoTo 0
Set tdf = db.CreateTableDef
tdf.Name = tblName
tdf.Connect = _
  "ACEWSS;HDR=NO;IMEX=2;ACCDB=YES;" & _
  "DATABASE=https://maidtoorder.sharepoint.com;" & _
  "LIST={D6AF2651-F48C-4CA4-9608-B564B1978E08};" & _
  "VIEW=;RetrieveIds=Yes"
tdf.SourceTableName = "Maid To Order Access List"
db.TableDefs.Append tdf
```

> **NOTE** *An easy way to find the connection string and GUIDs for a SharePoint List is to use the UI to link to a SharePoint List and then read the* `Connect` *property of the created* `DAO.TableDef`.

With the SharePoint list linked, your next step is to initialize the BlowFish algorithm by supplying the key using the user's full account name. The account name, as you recall, is the domain name and username of the currently logged on user. It's stored in the SharePoint list:

```
bytKey = GetUserName
blf_Initialise _
  StrConv(bytKey, vbFromUnicode), _
  LenB(StrConv(bytKey, vbFromUnicode))
```

> **NOTE** *If you are familiar with low-level programming languages, you may already know that a string is just an array of bytes. Thus, it's no surprise that in VBA you can assign a string variable to an array of bytes and vice versa. However, you need to factor in the Unicode versus ASCII-encoding, which you can handle with the* `StrConv()` *function.*

The `blf_Initialise` routine prepares the BlowFish algorithm using the specified key. Anything that is subsequently encrypted using this key can then be decrypted if the same key is used. Otherwise, it comes out as gibberish.

The next step is to determine if the user already has an entry in the SharePoint List. Normally, there should only be one list item per user but you cannot explicitly block additional items from being added, so you use the next best thing — a query that selects the last item matching the user's full username stored in the Key column, which is ordered on the ID column in descending order. This returns the last list item created by this user:

```
Set rs = db.OpenRecordset( _
   "SELECT TOP 1 * " & _
   "FROM " & tblName & " " & _
   "WHERE Key = '" & GetUserName & "' " & _
   "ORDER BY ID DESC;", dbOpenDynaset)
```

You have used the If/Then condition to determine whether there is a record for this user or not:

```
If Not (rs.BOF And rs.EOF) Then
  'There is a record found
Else
  'There's no record
End If
```

Let's think about what you did so far. You set up a SharePoint list and associated a workflow with it so that you can send notifications. So, although this code looks like it simply adds a new list item and nothing else, all the magic behind the notification is happening on the SharePoint side. The case of a new user with no record is more relevant right now. Let's look further into the code in that part of the conditional:

```
If vbYes = MsgBox( _
   strNoAccess, vbYesNo, "No Client Access Available" _
) Then
  bytToken = GetUserName
  strToken = blf_BytesEnc(StrConv(bytToken, vbFromUnicode))
  rs.AddNew
  rs.Fields("Token") = strToken
  rs.Fields("Key") = GetUserName
  rs.Update
  rs.Bookmark = rs.LastModified
  MsgBox strRequested, vbInformation, "Access Request Submitted"
End If
```

If the user chooses to request access, a new entry is created in the SharePoint list and the encryption key for that record is stored in the `Token` column. This Token is temporary until the administrator grants access, which will update the `Token` column. There is nothing else left to do for a new user, so the application quits.

> **WARNING** *It's worth remembering that in order for the user to be able to insert a record in this list, the user must first have permission to access the list. You usually do that by inviting the user to the site where the web app is hosted. Therefore, a user that cannot browse to the site because he or she is denied access will be unable to request access.*

The next time the code runs after the administrator has granted access, the code will step into the true part of the outer `If...Then` section. Within this section, you have to evaluate the state of the list item, which you can do by checking the Status column. The Status column allows four possible states:

```
Select Case rs.Fields("Status")
  Case "Access Request Pending"
    ...
  Case "Token Provided", "Access Granted"
    ...
  Case "Access Denied"
    ...
End Select
```

The "Access Request Pending" and "Access Denied" states cause the application to quit after displaying a message to users notifying them about their standing on the access request.

"Token Provided" and "Access Granted" are similar except that when an administrator initially grants the token, Status will have the former value and after a successful login, the Status is updated to the latter value:

```
bytToken = GetUserName
bytToken = blf_BytesEnc(StrConv(bytToken, vbFromUnicode))
blf_Initialise _
  StrConv(bytToken, vbFromUnicode), _
  LenB(StrConv(bytToken, vbFromUnicode))
```

```
strToken = blf_BytesDec(rs.Fields("Token").Value)
strToken = StrConv(strToken, vbUnicode)
If CheckConnection(strToken) Then
  If rs.Fields("Status").Value = "Token Provided" Then
    rs.Edit
    rs.Fields("Status").Value = "Access Granted"
    rs.Update
  End If
  CheckAccess = True
Else
  bolQuit = True
  MsgBox strFailed, vbCritical, "Unable to continue"
End If
```

Again, we caution that we are using the user's full account name as the key for the purposes of illustration. This is not the best choice for an encryption key, but we used it here so you can see how you would initialize BlowFish to use a new key. The key is the encrypted output of the user's account name using the user's account name key. You will see later on that the administrator received the encrypted output of the user's account name and used that as the key to encrypt the actual password. For the user to decrypt the content from the administrator, you have to re-initialize the BlowFish algorithm to use the encrypted output of the account name rather than the plaintext value.

Once you decrypt the content, the next step is to test if that content will enable you to connect to the database. To check this, call the `CheckConnection` routine:

```
Private Function CheckConnection(Token As String) As Boolean
  Dim qdf As DAO.QueryDef
  Set qdf = CurrentDb.CreateQueryDef(vbNullString, "SELECT NULL;")
  qdf.Connect = _
    "ODBC;DRIVER={SQL Server Native Client 11.0};" & _
    "DATABASE=db_f4689298_1035_4588_b062_096bf56eed7e;" & _
    "SERVER=aux99xmbfs.database.windows.net;Encrypt=yes;" & Token
  On Error Resume Next
  qdf.OpenRecordset (dbOpenSnapshot)
  CheckConnection = (Err.Number = 0)
End Function
```

This function creates a temporary `querydef` object that is made a passthrough by assigning the ODBC connection string. You can see that the `Token` parameter is then concatenated to the connection string in order to complete it. The only thing you have to check is whether you can open the query successfully and return a result.

If the `Status` is Token Provided and `CheckConnection` returns True, you perform one final update of the record to change the `Status` column to Access Granted. That then will complete the workflow.

This concludes our overview of constructing a function to check and obtain access from a secure resource. Clearly, you are free to come up with a different implementation, perhaps a simpler one, or one that's more complex and that uses different resources where appropriate. The point of this exercise is that, by storing the key in a secure resource, you have efficiently used SharePoint as your agent in granting access and the user need not have direct knowledge of the password for the ExternalWriter. Also, because the password is stored outside of the client application, stealing the client application file would accomplish exactly nothing. Plus, you can easily change the password every so often without disrupting the users' activities.

Tasks for the Administrator

The user's part of the process is only half of the story. You saw how to manage access from the user's end. You also need to look at how you would grant access from the administrator's end. Generally speaking, you would probably want to have the code for granting access in a separate `.accdb` file to ensure that nobody can grant themselves access to the database by calling the routine. You may also recall from the Setting Up a SharePoint List section, when you created the workflow for e-mail notification, the administrator received a link with the ID embedded in the e-mail. The administrator can use the ID value to select the row to grant access to. Here's the sub that grants access, available in the `MTOClient.accdb` file:

```
Public Sub GrantAccess(ID As Long)
  Dim db As DAO.Database
  Dim tdf As DAO.TableDef
  Dim rs As DAO.Recordset

  Dim strToken As String
  Dim strKey As String
  Dim bytKey() As Byte
  Dim bytToken() As Byte

  Const tblName As String = "MTOAccessList"

  Set db = CurrentDb

  On Error Resume Next
  db.TableDefs.Delete tblName
  On Error GoTo 0
  Set tdf = db.CreateTableDef
  tdf.Name = tblName
  tdf.Connect = _
    "ACEWSS;HDR=NO;IMEX=2;ACCDB=YES;" & _
    "DATABASE=https://maidtoorder.sharepoint.com;" & _
    "LIST={D6AF2651-F48C-4CA4-9608-B564B1978E08};" & _
    "VIEW=;RetrieveIds=Yes"
  tdf.SourceTableName = "Maid To Order Access List"
  db.TableDefs.Append tdf

  Set rs = db.OpenRecordset( _
    "SELECT * " & _
    "FROM " & tblName & " " & _
    "WHERE ID = " & ID, dbOpenDynaset)
  If Not (rs.BOF And rs.EOF) Then
    blf_Initialise _
      StrConv(rs.Fields("Token").Value, vbFromUnicode), _
      LenB(StrConv(rs.Fields("Token").Value, vbFromUnicode))
    bytToken = _
      "UID=" & _
      "db_f4689298_1035_4588_b062_096bf56eed7e_ExternalWriter;" & _
      "PWD=V/x^QC715w9gGcc;"
```

```
        strToken = blf_BytesEnc(StrConv(bytToken, vbFromUnicode))
        rs.Edit
        rs.Fields("Token").Value = strToken
        rs.Fields("Status").Value = "Token Provided"
        rs.Update
      Else
        MsgBox "ID not found.", vbCritical, "No matching record"
      End If
      rs.Close
      Set rs = Nothing
      On Error Resume Next
      db.TableDefs.Delete tblName
    End Sub
```

You might note that the start and end of this procedure are similar to the `CheckAccess` routine where you add and delete the linked SharePoint list at run time. In production, the procedure would not be in the same `.accde` file you distribute to your users. Note, however, that the `WHERE` criteria is different, taking in the `ID` parameter as opposed to looking up the user's name:

```
Set rs = db.OpenRecordset( _
  "SELECT * " & _
  "FROM " & tblName & " " & _
  "WHERE ID = " & ID, dbOpenDynaset)
```

When the correct record has been located, the administrator takes in the value of the `Token` column, which is the encrypted output of the user's account name, and uses it as the key for the BlowFish algorithm to encrypt the ExternalWriter's username and password:

```
blf_Initialise _
  StrConv(rs.Fields("Token").Value, vbFromUnicode), _
  LenB(StrConv(rs.Fields("Token").Value, vbFromUnicode))
bytToken = _
  "UID=" & _
  "db_f4689298_1035_4588_b062_096bf56eed7e_ExternalWriter;" & _
  "PWD=V/x^QC715w9gGcc;"
strToken = blf_BytesEnc(StrConv(bytToken, vbFromUnicode))
rs.Edit
rs.Fields("Token").Value = strToken
rs.Fields("Status").Value = "Token Provided"
rs.Update
```

The last step in the process is to update the `Status` column. Updating the `Status` column prompts the workflow to send an e-mail back to users to notify them that they have been granted access. The next time the users open the client application, they will be able to log in successfully.

You have now learned how to use a SharePoint list as your secure resource for storing a key to control access to your web app database, and how to use SharePoint to authenticate your users. This opens up the ability to secure your application when used in conjunction with traditional best practices for securing a client file.

Local SQL Server

We've touched on how you can use your local SQL Server to interact with your web apps and you saw examples of working with a remote SQL Server database in Chapter 11. You also saw how you could create a linked server and map a local user to a remote user.

If you want to ensure there is no direct access to the linked server and control access, you will find it necessary to create procedures with `EXECUTE AT` in conjunction with the `EXECUTE AS` statement (not to be confused with the `EXECUTE AS` clause) so you can segregate the local user from the remote user.

As you saw in Chapter 11, when you create a linked server, you can create a security context for any users not listed. To restrict access to the linked server, you choose not to create a security context available to any users, and map the remote login only to a certain SQL Login, similar to Figure 13-75.

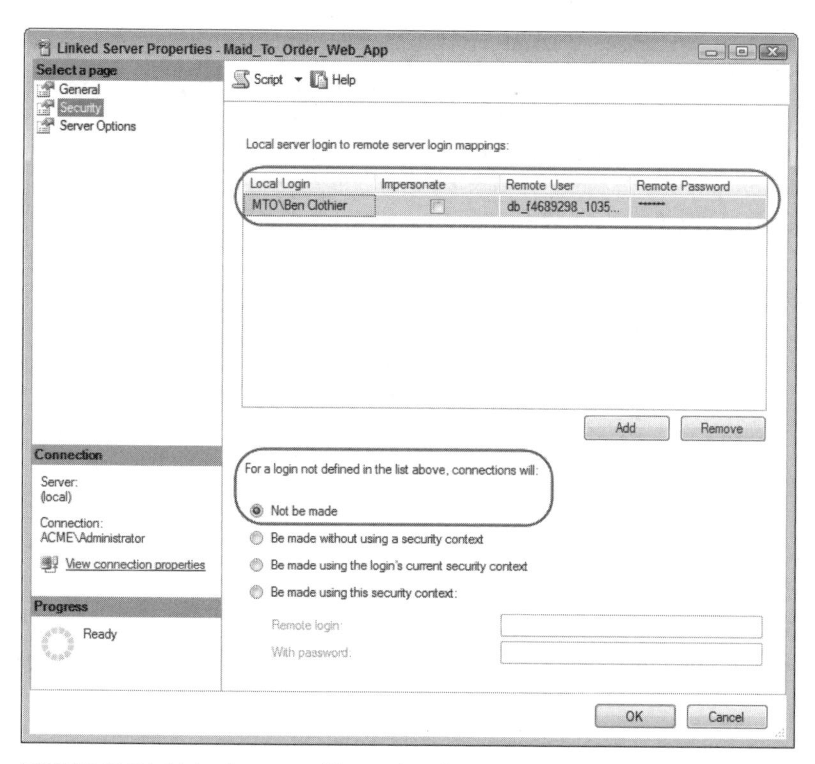

FIGURE 13-75: Linked server with restricted access

The method illustrated in Figure 13-75 is a simple way of ensuring that only your trusted users can access the linked server. However, those users would have a broad set of permissions. Granular access is not trivial to implement because linked servers and login mapping reside at the server level and thus deal with server permissions, not database permissions. Although SQL Server has provided many new features to make it easier to transfer the scope from database to server, it is generally recommended that you restrict the permissions to only trusted users and consider using jobs to move data between local and remote SQL Server as a simple way to segregate the permissions.

However, if you have a requirement to enable users to invoke select procedures against a web app's database at a lesser level of permissions than a ExternalReader or ExternalWriter, this can be done by taking a few steps. In general, you need the following:

- A certificate created on both the `master` database and the local database for the user to execute a stored procedure
- A local login that is mapped to the remote server's user
- A local login mapped to the certificate which is allowed to impersonate the local login with access to a remote server
- A stored procedure that is both signed by the certificate and contains the `EXECUTE AS` statement

> **NOTE** *A full treatise on how SQL Server manages permissions at different scopes and how permissions are chained is beyond the scope of the book. However, for an excellent discussion, we recommend reading SQL Server MVP Erland Sommarskog's thorough discussion found at his website:* `http://www.sommarskog.se/grantperm.html`.

To get started, you will need a certificate, which needs to be created in the `master` database. It will later be copied to the database where you want your users to execute against a web app database. It has to be created on the master in order to enable chaining of server permissions. The following T-SQL snippets are provided in `Chapter 13 - Create secured Stored Procedure using Certificate.sql`:

```
USE [master];

CREATE CERTIFICATE MTO_Server_Certificate
  ENCRYPTION BY PASSWORD = 'MTO_Server_Certificate'
  WITH SUBJECT = 'MTO_Server_Certificate',
  EXPIRY_DATE = '2020-01-01';
GO
```

The next step is to create a SQL Login mapped to the certificate. While still on the `master` database, execute the following statements:

```
CREATE LOGIN MTO_Agent
FROM CERTIFICATE MTO_Server_Certificate;
```

In order to enable the SQL Login `MTO_Agent`, impersonate the SQL Login `MTO\Ben Clothier`. The `MTO\Ben Clothier` Login which as you saw in Figure 13-66 has mapping to the web app's database, grant permission as follows:

```
GRANT IMPERSONATE ON LOGIN::[MTO\Ben Clothier] TO MTO_Agent;
```

The next step is to copy the certificate from the `master` database to the local database. This allows server permissions to be chained to a database user. You also need to create a master key in the process. While still on `master`, execute the following batch:

```
DECLARE
  @public_key varbinary(MAX) =
    certencoded(
```

```
            cert_id('MTO_Server_Certificate')
        ),
    @private_key varbinary(MAX) =
        certprivatekey(
            cert_id('MTO_Server_Certificate'),
            'MTO_Server_Certificate',
            'MTO_Server_Certificate'
        )
;

USE [LocalMTO];

CREATE MASTER KEY ENCRYPTION BY PASSWORD = 'MTO_Server_Certificate';

DECLARE @sql nvarchar(MAX)
SELECT @sql =
  N'CREATE CERTIFICATE MTO_Server_Certificate
    FROM BINARY = ' + CONVERT(nvarchar(MAX), @public_key, 1) + '
    WITH PRIVATE KEY (BINARY = ' + CONVERT(nvarchar(MAX), @private_key, 1) + ',
    DECRYPTION BY PASSWORD = ''MTO_Server_Certificate'',
    ENCRYPTION BY PASSWORD = ''MTO_Server_Certificate'')'
;
EXEC sp_executesql @sql;
```

> **WARNING** `certencoded()` *and* `certprivatekey()` *are new functions added to SQL Server 2012. If you are running a script on previous versions, it is necessary to save the certificate to the filesystem and read it back. Refer to Erland Sommarskog's article for the syntax on bouncing it over the filesystem.*

Dynamic SQL is necessary because the `CREATE CERTIFICATE` statement does not allow for variable assignment to the parameters. Note the procedure changes the database to `LocalMTO` after taking in values from the certificate in `master`. Once this is done, you can create a database user mapped to the same certificate on the `LocalMTO` database:

```
CREATE USER MTO_Agent FOR CERTIFICATE MTO_Server_Certificate;
```

> **WARNING** *Be aware that SQL Login and SQL User are not interchangeable; SQL Login is at server scope whereas SQL User is at database scope.*

This provides you with all the chaining you need to enable the association of a server-level permission to a database object, namely a stored procedure, so you can allow users to execute the stored procedure but not give those users access to the web app's database directly. Create a new stored procedure that performs the `EXECUTE AS` to change context:

```
CREATE PROCEDURE dbo.uspRemoteQuery (
  @ServiceID int
```

```
) AS
BEGIN
EXECUTE AS LOGIN = 'MTO\Ben Clothier';
EXEC (
  N'SELECT [ServiceID]
          ,[ServiceDescription]
          ,[DefaultFee]
         ,[Inactive]
    FROM [db_f4689298_1035_4588_b062_096bf56eed7e].[Access].[tlkpServices]
    WHERE ServiceID = ?;',
 @ServiceID
) AT [Maid_To_Order_Web_App];
REVERT;
END;
```

Note that it is also necessary to do an `EXEC(...) AT ...` instead of using four-part qualifier syntax to reference linked tables or views. This is because context is determined before the stored procedure is executed, whereas an `EXEC` statement defers the context evaluation to run time. Using the four-part qualifier syntax would be considered to be executed in the caller's context even if it is between the `EXECUTE AS … REVERT` statements.

Now suppose a user is granted `EXECUTE` permission on the stored procedure `dbo.uspRemoteQuery`; the user will fail to get any results because the user does not have `IMPERSONATE` permission on `MTO\Ben Clothier`. You certainly do not want to grant `IMPERSONATE` permissions because that would give the user the same permission level as `MTO\Ben Clothier` and thus allow that user ad hoc access to the web app database. This is where the certificate comes in.

You want to sign the procedure with the certificate as shown here:

```
ADD SIGNATURE TO dbo.uspRemoteQuery
BY CERTIFICATE MTO_Server_Certificate
WITH PASSWORD = 'MTO_Server_Certificate';
```

Now the user with `EXECUTE` permission on the `dbo.uspRemoteQuery` will be able to get results with the certificate acting as the intermediary and enabling impersonation of `MTO\Ben Clothier` *only* when the stored procedure is used. If a user were to attempt to directly impersonate `MTO\Ben Clothier` by doing an ad hoc script containing `EXECUTE AS LOGIN = 'MTO\Ben Clothier'`, that user would be denied permission, which is what you want.

> **WARNING** *Every time you* `ALTER` *a procedure, you must re-sign the procedure in order for certificate mapping to be effective.*

You can see that it is possible to secure the web app database as a linked server provided that you are willing to take some steps to create the necessary components and deal with the required maintenance of signing your stored procedures every time a change is made.

SUMMARY

In Chapter 13, you learned a different way to think about security. You saw why you may want to use an agent-based system to achieve more granular permissions. You learned how SharePoint secures its objects and how apps act as an agent, using broad permissions to secure objects. Then you saw how you can add users, both licensed and external users, and grant them permissions. You got to learn about managing groups and users within SharePoint, which impacts the users' freedom of action on the web app. You also saw how you can enable anonymous access to your web apps.

You learned about techniques for creating restricted sections of your web apps using security driven by application logic within the web browser. You should be able to describe why you need to use popup views to display secured content and use tile-bound views to provide a login interface. Furthermore, you learned why you cannot use `UserEmailAddress()` nor `UserDisplayName()` as reliable security methods although you can reliably identify anonymous users using `UserDisplayName()`.

Next, you turned to the client side and reviewed traditional security methods available to you in previous versions of Access and saw how it continues to be relevant to your client application. You also explored possible ideas for securing access to the web app's database by not storing the password directly in the client application, preventing the user from extracting the full connection parameters, which would give them the same permission level of the ExternalWriter user, which may be too broad for your scenarios. You also looked at how you can secure the remote linked server in your local SQL Server by making use of certificates and impersonation.

While this whirlwind tour of security touched on many important concepts, we are well aware that there is a good deal more to be considered in the security realm. We encourage you, therefore, to continue your study of sound security practices and policies.

In the next chapter, you will continue your exploration of web apps and how to go about deploying them effectively in your organization.

14

Deploying Access Web Apps

WHAT'S IN THIS CHAPTER?

- Deploying Access web apps
- Versioning Access web apps
- Storing an app on a SharePoint site
- Controlling distribution
- Monetizing Access web apps

WROX.COM CODE DOWNLOADS FOR THIS CHAPTER

The code and sample downloads for this chapter are found at `www.wiley.com/go/proaccess2013prog.com` on the Download Code tab. They are in the Chapter 14 download and individually named according to the file names listed throughout the chapter. The app packages for the web apps in this chapter are called Maid to Order and Maid to Order Customer. Refer to the ReadMe.txt file for installation instructions.

You've learned how to build a web app, and now you want to distribute it. In this chapter, you learn how to do that. You may appreciate the fact that, once it's been deployed, distributing a new version can be as easy as updating the web app. There is no file copying to do. Of course, you may also want to maintain a separate test and production environment for proper lifecycle management over your apps, releasing updates to your web apps when you are ready to do that. Thus, in this chapter, you learn how you can provide a form of version control for releasing your web apps.

You will also deal with another aspect of app management that has never been done up to now — distributing your application via a public channel such as the Office Store and possibly monetizing it in the process. You will learn how to handle some new challenges you face when you distribute and update your web apps to a large number of people who may download and/or purchase your web app. You'll also learn how you can manage the licensing.

As part of the process, you will learn more about app catalogs and how they can be used as your tool for managing the development lifecycle and how they fit with distributing via the Office store.

DEPLOYING ACCESS WEB APPS

To be shared, Access web apps need to be placed in a location where others can access them. Unlike Access client files, you can't simply copy a file from one location to another. Nor can you use an automated deployment tool, such as Tony Toews Auto FE Updater. Access web apps need to be exposed for your users in a SharePoint team site or SharePoint personal site to which potential users have access via their browser. In this chapter, you'll learn about the locations and processes by which you can deploy your web apps for others. Note that we've discussed some aspects of this deployment in previous chapters. In this chapter, we consolidate and summarize the processes that relate specifically to the deployment process.

As you read the discussions in this chapter, you'll see that much of the information pertains to SharePoint, whether it's on-premises or hosted. We're sensitive to the fact that experienced Access developers may not have had a large amount of previous SharePoint experience. Like the authors, therefore, you may find yourself thinking about some of these considerations for the first time. It's well worth the effort to gain confidence in working with SharePoint in addition to developing your web apps.

Web Apps and App Catalogs

As we alluded to earlier in the book, you can essentially create a brand new Access web app directly on a SharePoint site without going through an app catalog. Any web apps created in this manner are not a part of an app catalog and cannot be redistributed. This is a good way to design and develop a prototype of your app. However, for the purpose of lifecycle management, you will also want to create an app package from it that can be added to an app catalog. This can be true regardless of whether you will be distributing the web app for on-premises deployment, in the cloud, or for public consumption.

There are several issues to be aware of when planning for distribution or reuse of your web apps. Let's review a couple of the more important ones.

Packaging for Distribution

When you create a web app outside of an app catalog, you can always package it up and add it to an app catalog, but the original app is neither upgradable nor redistributable. Therefore, when you create a brand new Access web app that you intend to distribute, you will need to use the Save As Package function to generate an app package. You can then upload that app package into an app catalog. Your original app, of course, is retained for further development, as needed.

Your knowledge of good lifecycle management will come into play as you decide how to implement this functionality for your web apps. You'll see more on this later in the chapter.

Creating a Template of Your Apps

As you learned in Chapter 12, you may want to save an app package containing your base customizations and then use it as your template when starting a new Access web app project to ensure that all of your web apps are managed and easily redistributable. You can upload an app package easily by adding an Access web app and clicking the hyperlink, as shown in Figure 14-1.

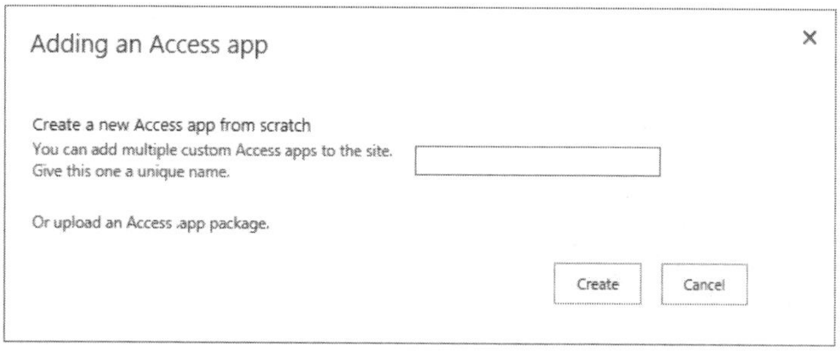

Adding an Access app

Create a new Access app from scratch
You can add multiple custom Access apps to the site.
Give this one a unique name.

Or upload an Access .app package.

Create Cancel

FIGURE 14-1: Adding an Access package via Site Contents

While this is an easy way to add a new Access web app from a package, it merely creates a web app that is still not redistributable and, perhaps more importantly, not upgradable. The only way to create an upgradable web app is to actually add it to an app catalog directly. In later sections of this chapter, you learn the steps to do this.

On-Premises SharePoint Server

When your organization deploys an on-premises SharePoint server, your choice of deployment locations is essentially limited to the app catalog for your *tenancy*. Although tenancy is somewhat outside the scope of our discussion here, to understand deployment, you do need to know a little bit about "tenancy" as it relates to both on-premises and online SharePoint installations. In this context, tenancy refers to logical partitioning of data and properties among multiple client organizations (tenants) within a single SharePoint site.

Tenancy

Each tenancy in SharePoint can have only one app catalog, whether on-premises or in the cloud. Also, the deployment method you may choose for your web apps in an on-premises environment is related to tenancy. So let's take a very high-level look at some of the salient factors.

In SharePoint Online, a tenant consists of the site collections under one account. As noted previously, each tenant will have one app catalog. That's pretty much all you really need to know about it for your Office 365 accounts. Your tenant has an app catalog to which you deploy your web apps.

In an on-premises installation, tenancy can be a bit more involved because tenancy refers to a set of site collections, which can be all of the site collections in the SharePoint installation, a subset of them, or site collections from across different web applications on the server farm. The key point here is that there may be more than one tenancy and, therefore, more than one app catalog in the on-premises installation.

Apps deployed to an app catalog in a tenancy can have "web scope" or they can have "tenant scope". When you upload a web app to the app catalog of a tenancy, it is immediately available to be installed on all websites within that tenancy. Apps that are installed this way are said to have *web scope*.

Tenant administrators, however, can limit installation of apps to a subset of websites within a tenancy. Installing apps this way gives them *tenant scope*. Such, "batch-installed" apps consist of a single web app, which is shared by all the host websites on which the app is installed. It is located in the site collection of the corporate app catalog, but accessible by users in all of the tenants to which it is installed. Tenant scope, therefore, can be more limited if you choose.

Now that you have a general idea of how web apps are installed in app catalogs, let's look closer at the specifics of deploying them to a given app catalog.

Using the App Catalog

We've talked about using them, so now let's see what *app catalogs* are. An app catalog is a SharePoint site in which an organization can place apps for use by the people in their organization. Apps in the app catalog are available to anyone in your organization who can access the catalog and find the apps in it. Adding an app to an app catalog does not constitute an installation. Rather, your users can select the app from the app catalog and add it to their own site. That's important because it means that you will install apps in the catalog only when you want those apps to be freely available across your organization. As you learned in Chapter 13, there will also be web apps that you don't want to expose to everyone. Those shouldn't be in the app catalog.

Creating the App Catalog for Enterprise Plans or On-Premises SharePoint

If you are using an Office 365 enterprise account or an on-premises SharePoint installation, the site administrator must set up the app catalog, so most Access developers in that environment won't need to be involved in that process. In the interest of completeness, however, here are the steps you would take to create an app catalog — as outlined on the Microsoft support site — should you be called on to do so:

1. Sign in to the Office 365 admin center with your SharePoint Online admin username and password.
2. Go to Admin ➪ SharePoint.
3. Click Apps on the left, and then click app catalog.
4. Select Create a new app catalog site, and then click OK.
5. On the Create app catalog Site Collection page, enter the required information, and then click OK.

Once the app catalog is set up, you, or other developers in your organization, can deploy apps in it for others to use. You can also install apps from it into your own site or sites.

In the future, you can then reach the app catalog, as shown in Figure 14-2, by selecting Admin, then SharePoint, and clicking the apps link in the SharePoint admin center.

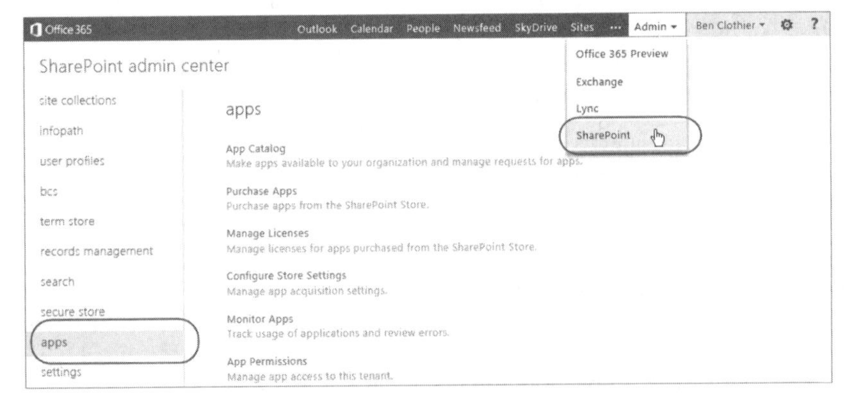

FIGURE 14-2: Navigate to the App Catalog for your site.

Make a note of the URL of your app catalog; you'll need it again when you proceed with deployment later in the chapter.

Accessing an App Catalog in Small Business Plans

If you are using Office 365 small business plans, it may not be obvious where to locate your app catalog. As you saw for enterprise plans, there is an Admin page that enables you to create and manage an app catalog but this is not available in small business plans. Rather, certain small business plans have their default app catalog, which will be located at the following address:

```
https://your domain.sharepoint.com/sites/AppCatalog
```

You can enter the URL manually to reach the app catalog. Or, you can use the built-in search facility on your Sharepoint site and search for "app catalog." If you do not find it, the particular plan may not support app catalog.

Whether you are on an enterprise plan or a small business plan, you may also want to customize your team site to add a link for easy access to the app catalog as there is no link to the app catalog out-of-the-box, necessitating manual navigation for first-time use. You will need the app catalog's URL later in the chapter.

Getting an App Ready to be Installed in the App Catalog

Let's take a closer look at how you add apps to an existing app catalog because you, the developer, will be doing that. Obviously, you need to have an app created and ready to upload to your site, so let's switch the discussion from the app catalog and learn how to do that with a test version of a web app being developed for Maid To Order customers. The Maid To Order sample app available for download will help walk you through the examples. You want to make this web app available for testing by other members of your organization while you continue development on the original.

Start Access and open your web app. Go to the backstage and select Save As, which you can see in Figure 14-3.

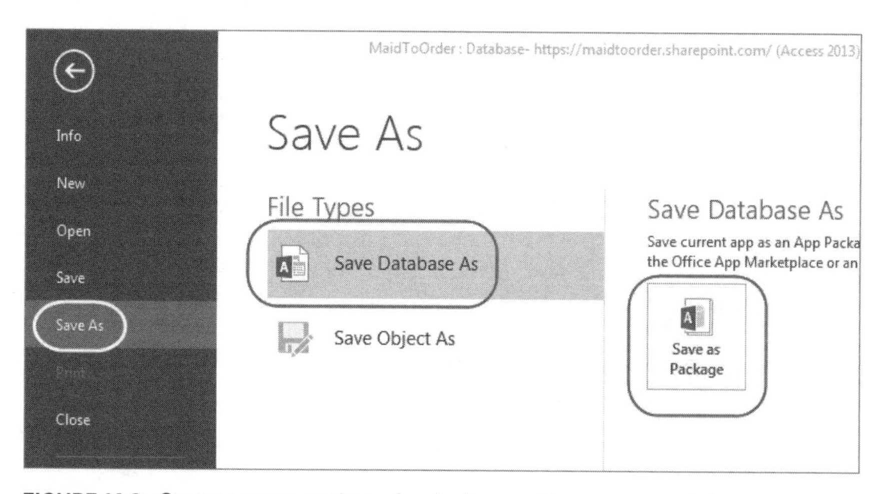

FIGURE 14-3: Create an app package for deployment in your app catalog

The option tells you that the app package you are about to create can be submitted to the Office Store or to an internal catalog. You'll be taking the second option for this exercise. When you are ready to distribute apps to the world, you'll create them the same way, but you'll need a vendor account to submit apps to the Office Store.

Give the App Package a Meaningful Name

Click the icon to start the packaging process. When you see the dialog box that asks you for the title of the app package, give it a short, meaningful name. Give careful consideration to the name. The web app will begin its journey to your organization's app catalogue from here, and it may be deployed in the Office Store later. It makes sense to give this app package a name that is detailed enough to make sure you remember what it's all about when you revisit it later (see Figure 14-4).

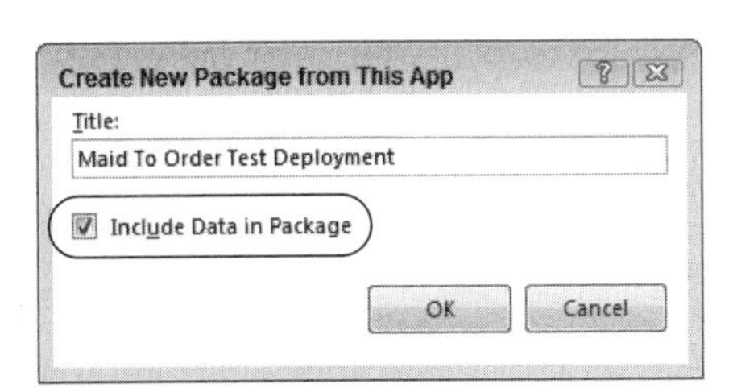

FIGURE 14-4: Name the app package

Include or Exclude Data

You'll need to make an important decision here regarding data. You can choose to save the app package with existing data or without it. Most likely, when you are deploying an app for others to use, you'll not include test data you used in the development of the web app. However, many databases include one or more lookup tables. If your web app has lookup tables, you want to include that data. Therefore, the decision about including data depends on the experience you want your users to have. Let's assume that the test data in all of the working tables was deleted, but there is still some data from the lookup tables you want to provide along with the web app.

> **NOTE** *One factor in deciding whether to include data is the storage limit of an app package, which is 100 MB. While it's unlikely that most of your Access web apps will become that large, you need to be aware of the limit and plan accordingly.*
>
> *While we're on the topic of storage limits, there is a 1 GB limit on the size of your web app's database in Office 365. This is a hard limit. On-premises, this is the default limit, although it is configurable. Again, this seems like a reasonable size limit for the majority of Access web apps you're likely to build or encounter. Also, as you've already learned, each web app has its own database, and the 1 GB limit is per database. Later in this chapter, in the section on Upgrading and Maintaining Access Web Apps, we'll introduce you to some strategies for backing up the data in your web app databases outside the app package.*

Click OK to save the app package. In the dialog box that opens, browse to the folder where you keep app packages. Figure 14-5 shows that folder for the Maid To Order web apps.

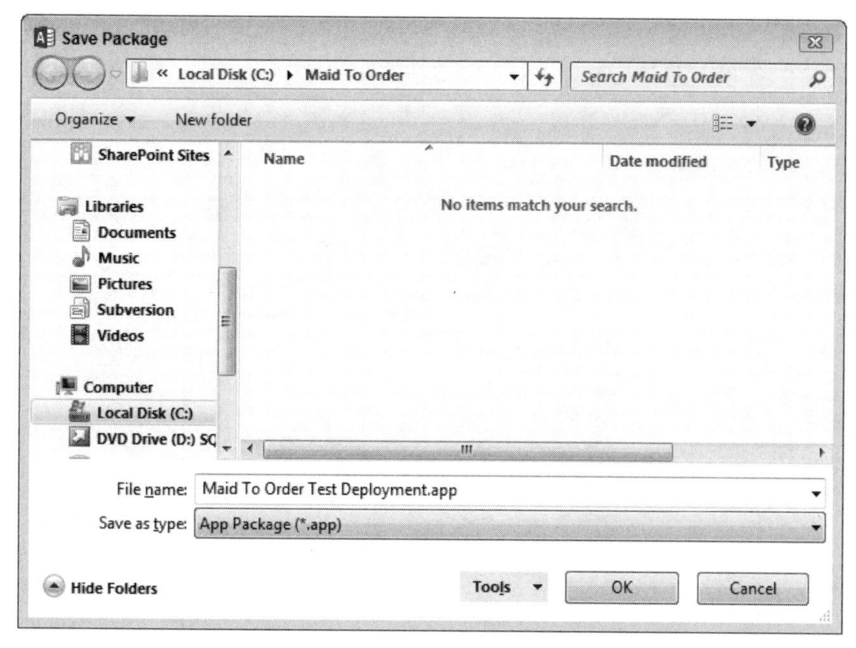

FIGURE 14-5: Save the app package in the proper folder.

Click OK to save the app package. It's now ready for deployment to your app catalog.

Version Control

Let's assume that this won't be the last version of this web app that you'll want to deploy. In other words, this is a test version of this app, so you'll be making further changes to it in your development copy based on feedback from your testers, and you'll want to update the deployed web app with those changes. You'll need GUIDs from the app package to do that. Here are the steps you need to follow to get to, and record, those GUIDs.

First, make a backup copy of the app package. Change the extension to `.zip` so you can edit it. Figure 14-6 shows this.

At this point, we're interested in only two of the files shown in Figure 14-6: the `appmanifest.xml` and the `appdb.xml`. They contain GUIDs you need to identify the app package for later versions. Figure 14-7 shows the two GUIDs you need.

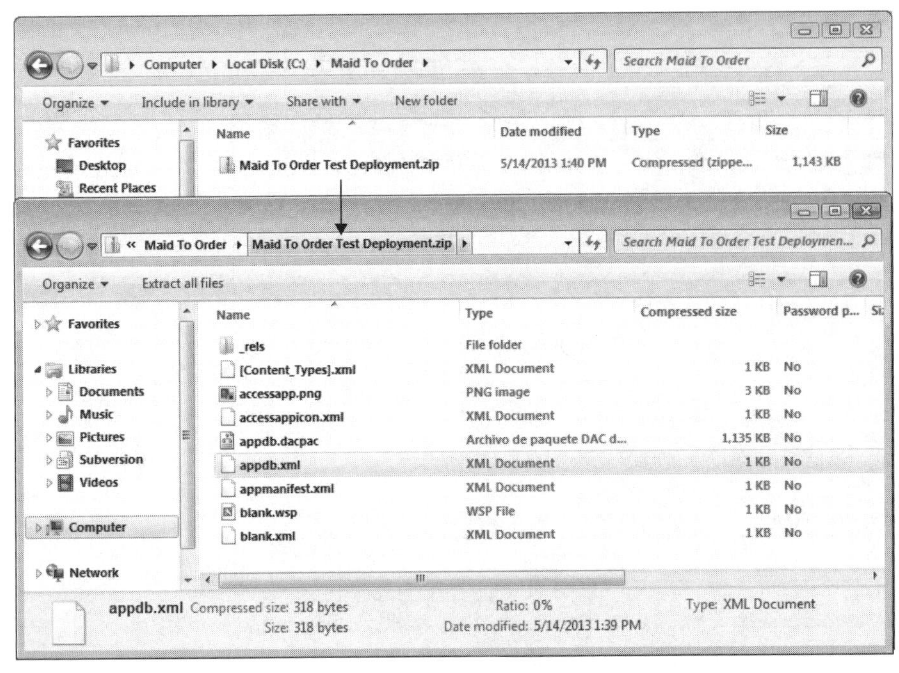

FIGURE 14-6: Change the extension to .zip so the app package can be edited.

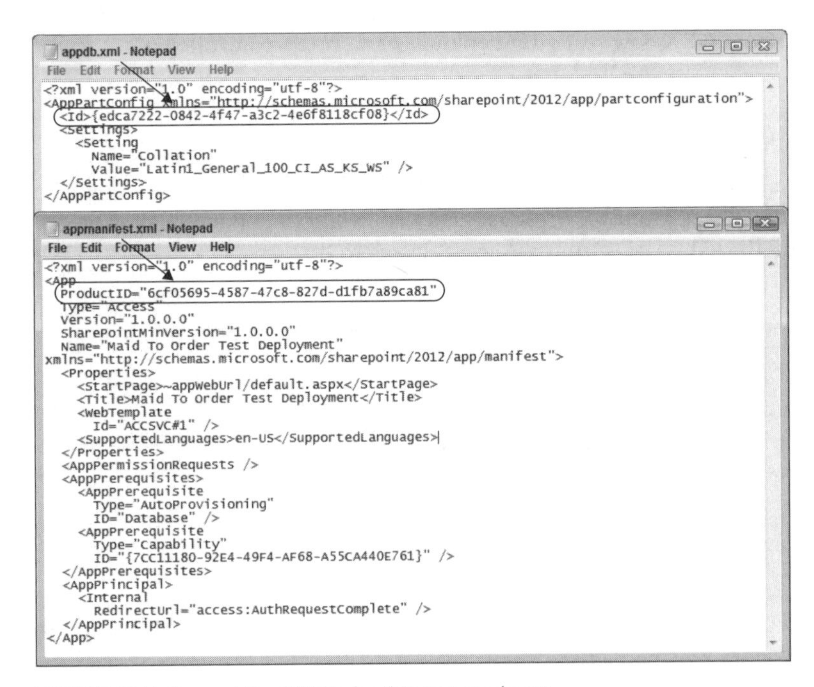

FIGURE 14-7: Record the GUIDs for this app package

From the `appmanifest.xml` file, record the `App` element's `ProductID` attribute. From the `appdb.xml` file, record the `AppPartConfig` element's child element named `ID`.

Close the zip version of the app package for now.

Now your app is ready to be uploaded to your SharePoint app catalog to be deployed for others in your organization. Let's move on to that process next.

Adding Apps to the App Catalog

Any custom app created by you or another person in your organization can be added to your app catalog. To do so, you, or other developers in your organization, will follow the steps outlined here. In this exercise, you learn how to install the test web app you just created for your testers to use.

Navigate to the App Catalog site for your account at the URL you recorded earlier.

What you see in Figure 14-8 is basically the default appearance of the app catalog site, which you can customize to suit your own needs. It has separate pages for Apps for SharePoint, Apps for Office, and requests for apps. This page can be customized. The Recent links list on the left side of the page also has links to the two catalogues for Office and SharePoint. You will use the Apps for SharePoint page to host your Access web app packages.

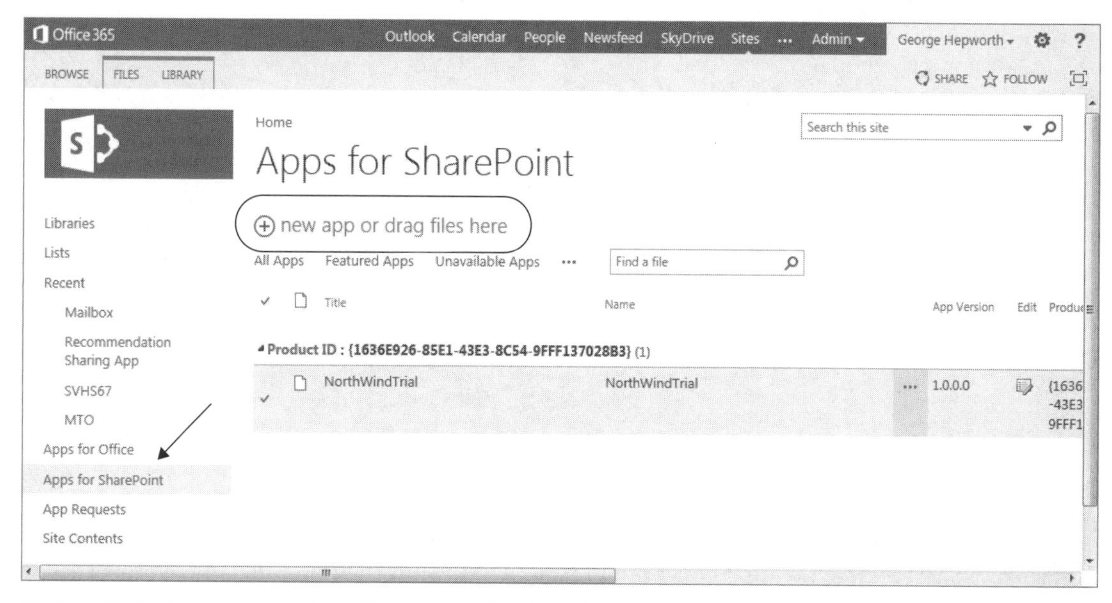

FIGURE 14-8: Selecting apps for Office or apps for SharePoint

WHY ISN'T IT APPS FOR OFFICE?

You may recall Apps for Office mentioned in Chapter 1; they are small apps that can be integrated into certain Office client products such as Excel or Outlook using only HTML5 and JavaScript. Even though Access is an Office product, Access web apps are actually Apps for SharePoint, which can do much more.

At this point, there is already an app in the app catalog shown in Figure 14-8. It is identified by both a product ID and a title. The ProductID, which is a GUID, is universally unique, but SharePoint doesn't require the title for an app to be unique. We have found this to be a potential source of confusion. It is easy to end up with two or more apps with similar, or even the same, names. Knowing which is which is not simple. So, beware when adding new apps. Give them names you'll recognize later and consider whether you want to include a version number as part of the name.

Click the new app link from Figure 14-8. In the dialog box that opens, use the browse button to find your app package (see Figure 14-9). Make sure you grab the `.app` version, not the `.zip` version.

In the Add a document dialog box, add any optional comments you'd like about this version of the app, and then click OK. Figure 14-9 shows an example.

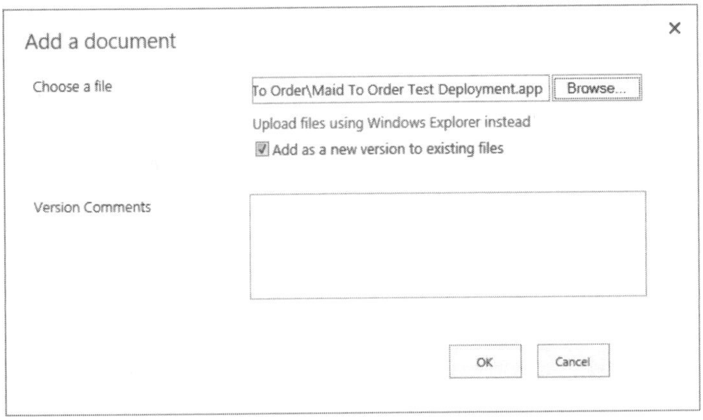

Add a document

Choose a file | To Order\Maid To Order Test Deployment.app | Browse...

Upload files using Windows Explorer instead

☑ Add as a new version to existing files

Version Comments

OK | Cancel

FIGURE 14-9: Add the app to the app catalog

In the properties dialog form, review or update the name for the app. You can also specify things such as a Short Description or a Description. Not all of the information listed in the properties dialog box is required to upload the app; you'll be prompted for required properties. Follow the instructions on the screen for things such as image size if you include an icon. If you have an icon you want to use for the app, you can provide a URL for that in the Icon URL field. Figure 14-10 shows some of these properties; the page has several fields and is quite tall so you may want to scroll through the page and learn about properties provided there.

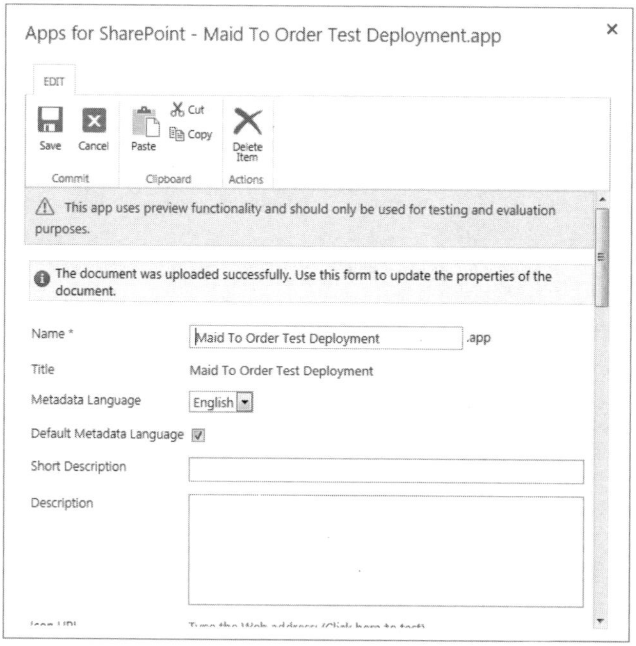

Apps for SharePoint - Maid To Order Test Deployment.app
EDIT
Save
Cancel
Paste
Cut
Copy
Delete Item
Commit
Clipboard
Actions
This app uses preview functionality and should only be used for testing and evaluation purposes.
The document was uploaded successfully. Use this form to update the properties of the document.
Name *
Maid To Order Test Deployment
.app
Title
Maid To Order Test Deployment
Metadata Language
English
Default Metadata Language
Short Description
Description

FIGURE 14-10: Add app properties and save

Once the app is uploaded, you can further modify its properties. Click the edit icon to display the properties page highlighted in Figure 14-11 which then navigates to the page shown in Figure 14-12.

Admin overview
Apps for SharePoint - All A...
Office 365
Outlook
Calendar
People
Newsfeed
SkyDrive
Sites
Admin
Ben Clothier
BROWSE
FILES
LIBRARY
SHARE
FOLLOW
Home
Apps for SharePoint
Search this site
Recent
Apps for SharePoint
Apps for Office
App Requests
Site Contents
new app or drag files here
All Apps
Featured Apps
Unavailable Apps
Find a file
Title
Name
App Version
Edit
Product ID
Metadata Language
Default Metadata Language
Product ID : {6CF05695-4587-47C8-827D-D1FB7A89CA81} (1)
Maid To Order Test Deployment
Maid To Order Test Deployment
1.0.0.0
{6CF05695-4587-47C8-827D-D1FB7A89CA81}
English - 1033
Yes

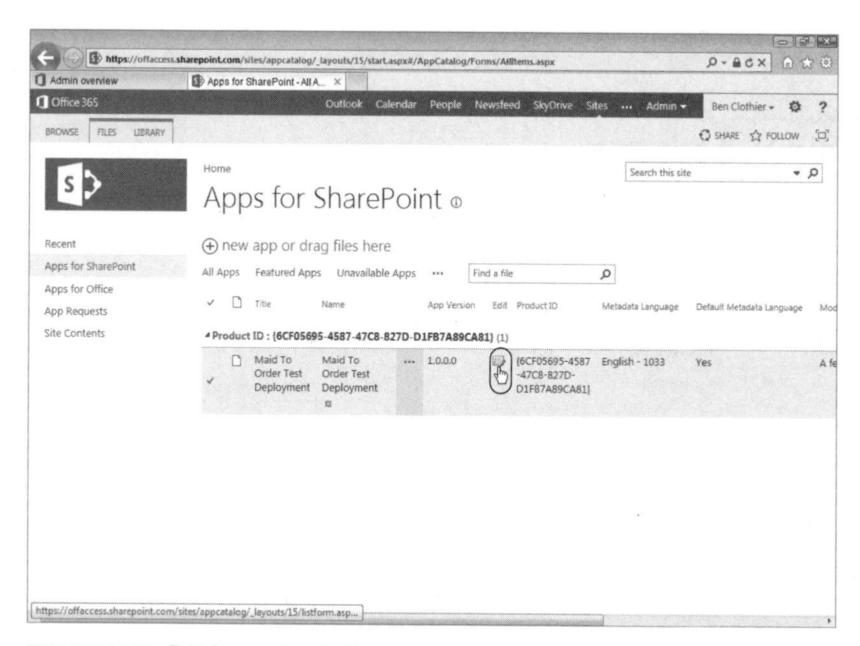

FIGURE 14-11: Edit Properties button

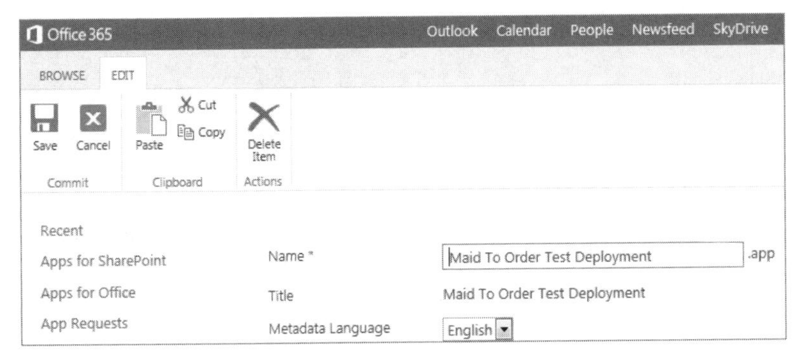

FIGURE 14-12: Modify properties for your web app.

The page is too long to fit in an image, so we elected to show part of it and encourage you to explore the page in full. For example, if you want to categorize the app so that it is appears under a specific category, select or specify a Category.

If there is a site or location where app users will be able to access Help for the app, you can provide a URL for that in the Support URL field. Make sure the Enabled checkbox is selected so that users will be able to add this app to sites. If you want the app to be listed in the Noteworthy content view of the app catalog, select the Featured checkbox.

In the Hosting Licenses box, specify the number of licenses you think you will need; the initial allocation for this web app is 10. Finally, Click Save. You've now added the test version of the Maid To Order Customer web app to the site catalog so your test users can install and use it, as shown in Figure 14-13.

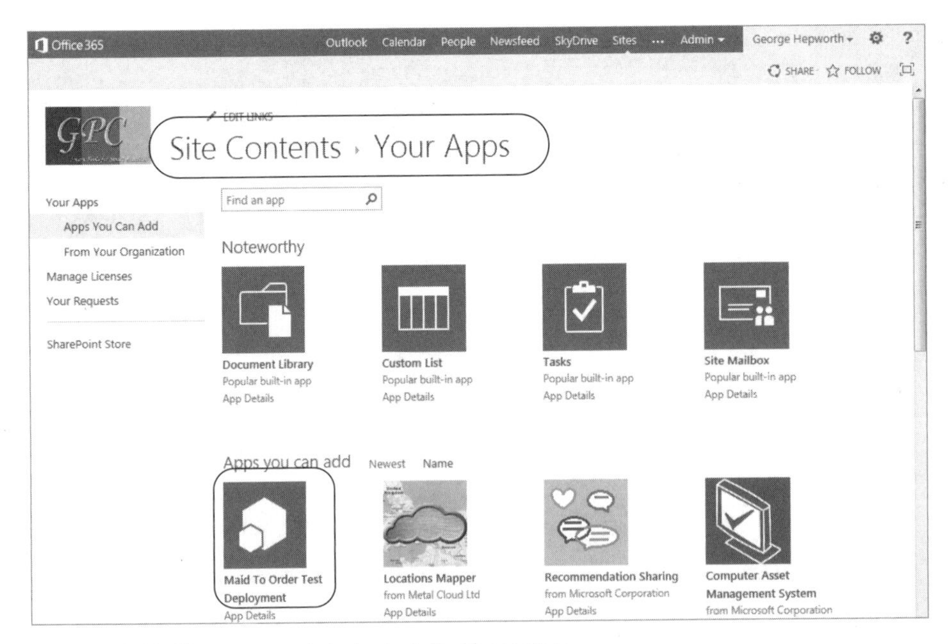

FIGURE 14-13: New app ready to be installed by testers

You learned how to install web apps in a site in Chapter 13, so you can refer to that chapter for instructions on installing the web app from your app catalog.

Inter-Site Portability

You may have noticed that the example shows the installation of the Maid To Order Customer Test Deployment web app, which originated on the Maid To Order site, onto a totally different site. We did this partly to illustrate the portability of the app package as a deployment method across sites, should the need arise. Normally, of course, you'd be deploying an app package onto a site within your organization's or client's sites.

Versioning Web Apps

Earlier, you learned that you can open the app package for your web app and record the GUIDs from it for use later in updating the app package. Let's learn how to update the app package next.

Let's assume, for this exercise, that you've gotten feedback from your testers, used it to make updates to your web app, and are now ready to deploy the final test version. Make a new app package from your development web app as before. Refer back to Figure 14-3 if you need a refresher.

This time, however, you may not want to include the data. You're only going to update the interface elements. If you do include the data from your development version, you'll overwrite any test data. All user data will be erased from the target database and the data in your app package will be added to the database. Should you do that? It depends. If your testers need to continue working with any sample data they previously added, you should not replace it. On the other hand, if the testers need to start over, you can replace the data. Here's another place where your previous experience managing the lifecycle of your Access databases can pay off.

As before, create a copy of the app package for safety. This time, you're going to convert the master copy to a `.zip` file so you can edit it. In order to update the contents of the app package, you'll first need to extract them from the Zip file into another folder where you can edit it. Within the folder, you can edit and save the `appmanifest.xml` and `appdb.xml` files.

Double-click the `appdb.xml` file to open it. Change its GUID to the one you recorded in the original app package. Figure 14-14 shows the updated GUID replacing the one saved in the app package.

Save and close the `appdb.xml` file. Next, open the `appmanifest.xml` file. You'll need to make two changes in it, as identified in Figure 14-14.

As indicated, update the GUID to the one previously recorded for the original version. Also, give this version a new version number. Save and close the `appmanifest.xml` file. Next, you'll need to move the updated files back into the `.zip` file from which they came. Rename it back to the `.app` extension so you can upload it to your site. Give the app package the same name as the original if you want it to appear in the list of apps with the same name. Keep the new version name if that is more appropriate for your situation. If you keep the same app package name and leave the Add as new version to existing files checkbox shown in Figure 14-10 checked, it will replace the original package as the new version. Attempting to overwrite a file without the checkbox checked will result in an error. You will learn more about versions shortly. If you give it a new name, it will be added as a separate package. In this example, you want this version to show up as a new version of the original. As you can see in Figure 14-15, the version name (from inside the app package) is new and the app version has increased. If we had uploaded it with a different name, it would appear as a separate package under same product ID, as in the bottom portion of Figure 14-15.

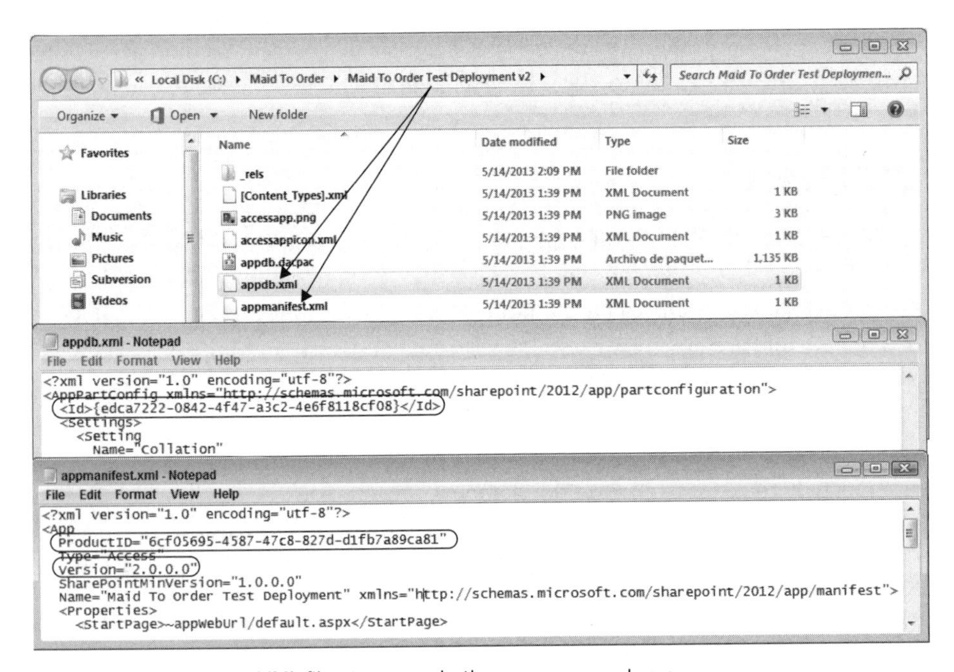

FIGURE 14-14: Edits to XML files to upgrade the new app package

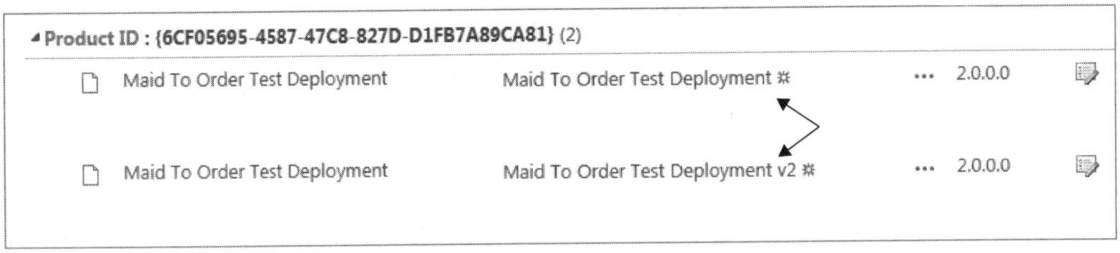

Product ID : {6CF05695-4587-47C8-827D-D1FB7A89CA81} (2)

Maid To Order Test Deployment — Maid To Order Test Deployment — 2.0.0.0

Maid To Order Test Deployment — Maid To Order Test Deployment v2 — 2.0.0.0

FIGURE 14-15: Version two of the test web app replacing the web app of the same name

Note that when you choose to use the same name for your app package and replace the original version, you still can review the history and thus extract the previous version via this dialog. You can access it via the ribbon button shown in Figure 14-16, which then displays a version history dialog box illustrated in Figure 14-17.

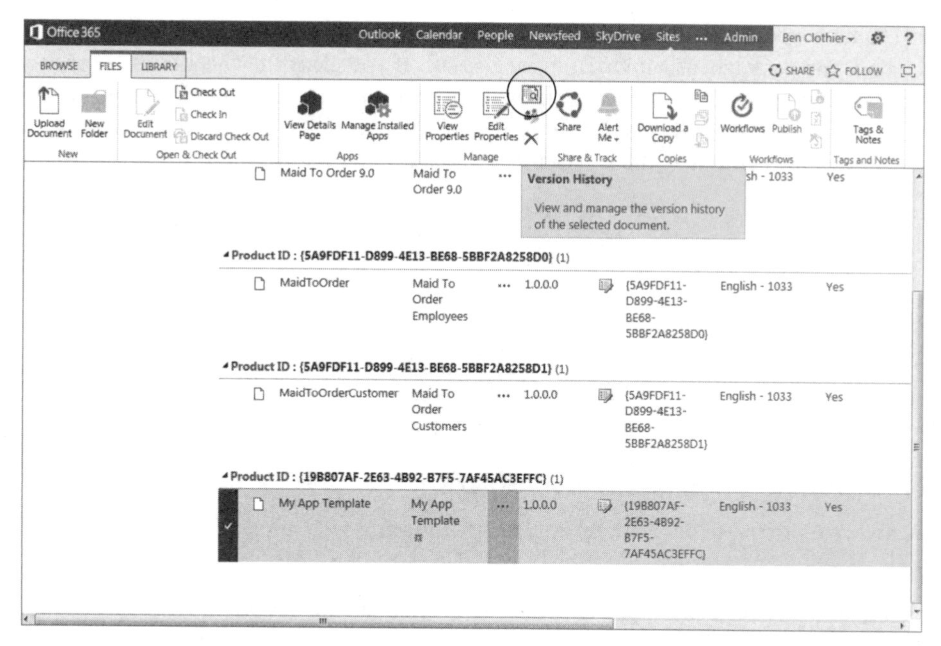

FIGURE 14-16: View Version on the File tab

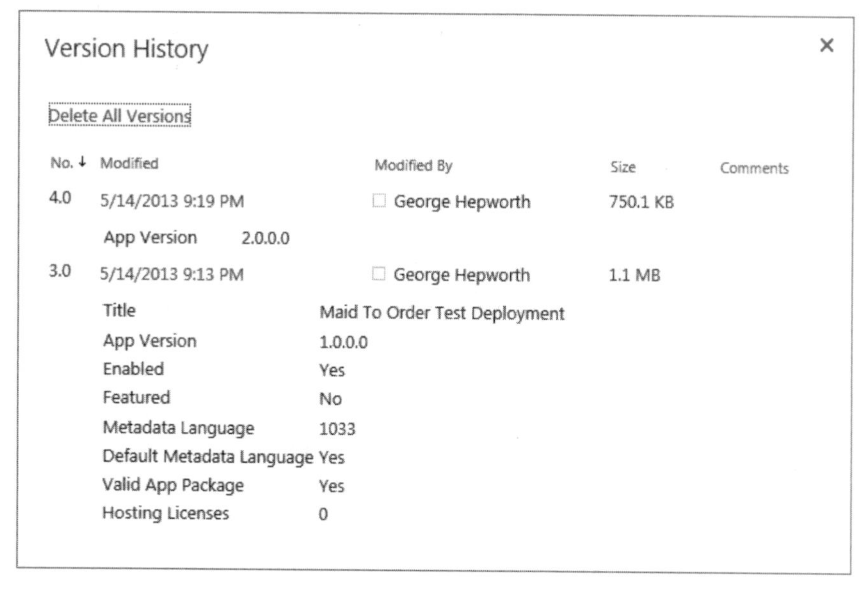

FIGURE 14-17: Version History dialog box

You do not need to be concerned with overwriting the original version that is selected by default when you add a new app package, as shown in Figure 14-10. If you clear the checkbox and try to upload an app package of same name, you will get an error preventing the overwriting because the app catalog enforces versioning at all times. You do need to be concerned about how you name your app packages, however, to ensure that the versioning will be correct for your app packages.

For app catalogs, this option defaults to being true if you use different methods of adding app packages such as dragging the files into the web browser.

With a new version of the web app available, you can inform your users that they should go to your app catalog and update it from the new version. They also will be notified about updates in the Site Contents page. You can see that in Figure 14-18.

FIGURE 14-18: New version of the web app available to update

Cautions When Updating an Existing Web App

You need to be aware of a couple of cautions regarding updating web apps with a new app package.

First, renaming a field or table in your app will result in a delete/create action on that field or table upon upgrade. You may lose data as a result. App versioning, therefore, should be done only when the table architecture is frozen, or in conjunction with a process to back up and restore the data as a separate, coordinated step. You will consider this later in the chapter.

Views and queries in the updated app package will overwrite any views or queries in the target application on upgrade. If users are allowed to make changes and have customized their copy of the app, those customizations will be lost during the upgrade. On one hand, this is no different from traditional deployment when replacing the front-end `.accdb` file. On the other hand, when you intend to distribute your app to the public via the Office Store, you must carefully consider whether those customizations need to be preserved and communicate your intentions to your users.

In the preceding section you've learned how to deploy your web apps into app catalogs for your users. In the following sections, you learn how to control distribution to groups and users you choose.

Office 365

In the Office 365 location, you can publish your apps to three places; directly on a site, to the publicly available app catalog, or to the personal site which is usually private. The options allow you to share your web apps with an audience of your choosing. You've already seen the option to publish your app to the team site and from there to the app catalog. Let's take a look at the personal site option next. Start Access and select the option to create a new web app. Note the wording in the dialog box in Figure 14-19. It doesn't actually refer to your personal site, but to Personal Apps, on your Office 365 site.

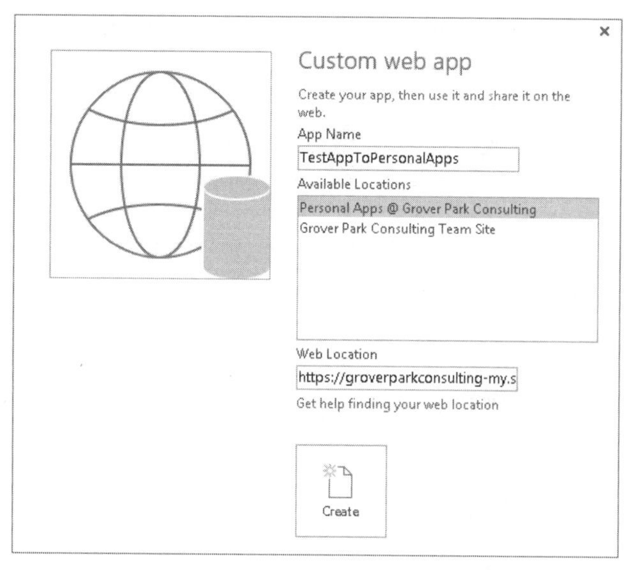

FIGURE 14-19: Select Personal Apps to publish to your personal site

Click OK to create the web app and proceed to build it. When it is ready, you can find it in your personal site. Note the -my suffix to your domain which indicates that you are on your personal site. You would use the Sites link on the Office 365 bar to get there. However, finding the Site Contents link is not necessarily very obvious. Consider Figure 14-20.

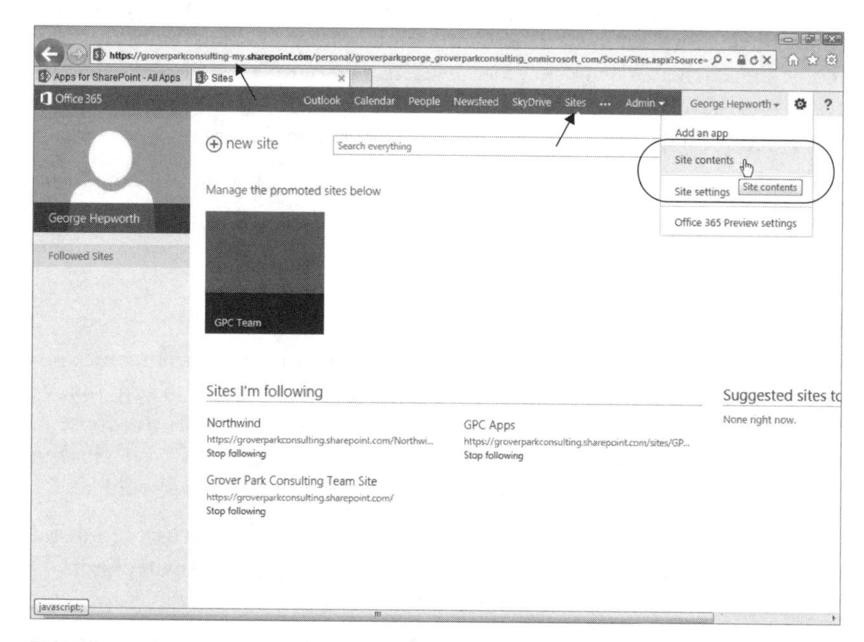

FIGURE 14-20: Locate web apps in your site's site contents

Clicking Site contents takes you to the page listing all of the web apps installed in your personal site. See Figure 14-21, which shows the web app we just created.

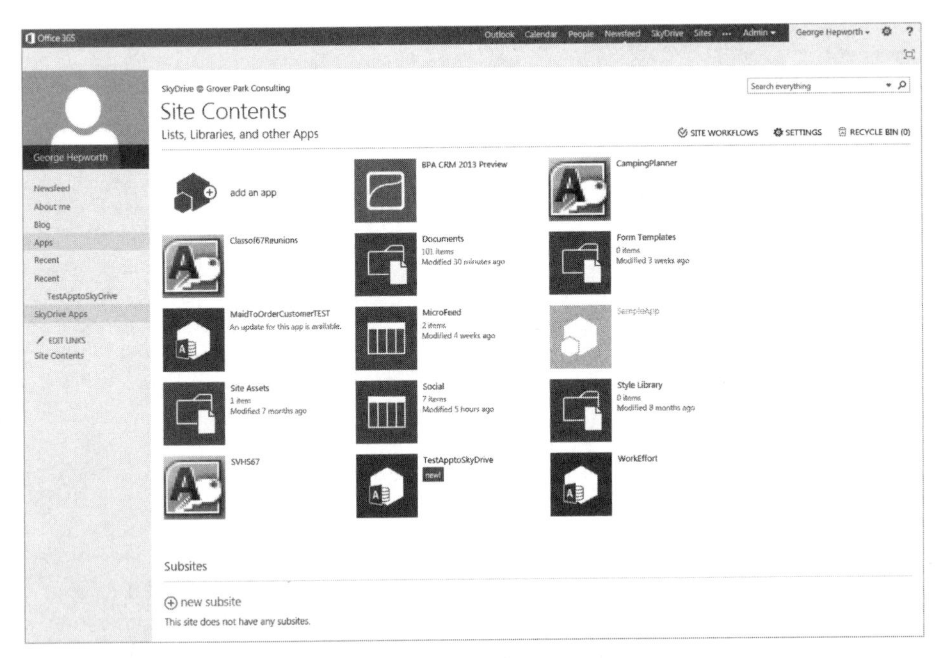

FIGURE 14-21: Web apps available in the personal site location

Note that you still can share your web apps off your personal site. A major difference is that nobody has rights to your web apps by default; you must give them permission by sharing. Publishing a web app directly to a SharePoint site, such as a team site, means users have same level of permissions to the web app as they have to the SharePoint site. As you saw in Chapter 13, anyone who is a member of the site has member-level rights, and others who are merely visitors can only read.

When you add to an app catalog, you are no longer installing an app but rather provisioning it for distribution, even if it's going to be consumed by only one site. Only via the app catalog can you control the updating and licensing.

Controlling Distribution

As you've learned, SharePoint makes it relatively easy to install and update web apps in your app catalog. Let's look at how you can control that distribution. When you publish a web app, following the steps you learned in the previous chapter, one of the options you can set is whether to expose the web app to others. You saw a part of the property page in Figure 14-12; Figure 14-22 is a close-up of the relevant section of that page, where you can adjust how exposed the web app should be.

Uncheck the option to expose the web app to end users. You can still invite specific users to install the web app, using the sharing options you learned about in the previous chapter. Invited users would otherwise not be aware of an app for which this option is disabled.

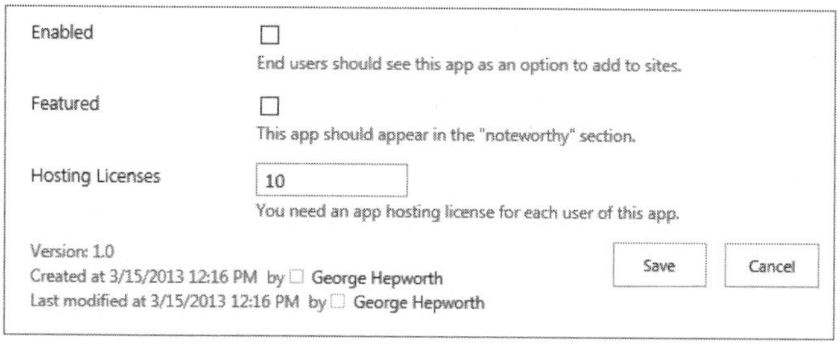

Enabled
☐
End users should see this app as an option to add to sites.

Featured
☐
This app should appear in the "noteworthy" section.

Hosting Licenses
10
You need an app hosting license for each user of this app.

Version: 1.0
Created at 3/15/2013 12:16 PM by George Hepworth
Last modified at 3/15/2013 12:16 PM by George Hepworth

Save Cancel

FIGURE 14-22: Disable the option to expose the app to users

Making Web Apps Publicly Available

In addition to the members of your own organizations, you can make your web apps available to the public by submitting them to the Office Store. Let's see how the Office Store works.

Office Store

Access developers who want to monetize a web app can do so by submitting it to the Office Store. Microsoft's Office Store is a place where developers can offer their products to a worldwide audience. Although most aspects of the Office Store are currently settled, other elements are still developing at the time of this writing. The following description represents our best understanding of the Office Store at this time. Please check the Microsoft store site at `http://office.microsoft.com/en-us/store/dashboard.aspx?AssetId=PN102957641` for examples of web apps available for you to install. The offerings will grow rapidly, so checking back frequently is a good idea.

The Office Store accepts apps submitted by developers who have completed an application and been approved as a seller. Once you've signed up to be part of the Office Store, you can begin submitting your Access web apps for distribution to the public. As noted previously, the program may still be evolving in the near future so the following guidelines should be taken as general guidance. Look for current information at the websites noted in the material that follows.

To add your own apps, you'll need to apply to be a provider. Here's an outline of the process as it currently works. These guidelines, as well as the links that follow, are subject to evolution as the Office Store matures.

We recommend you start at `http://office.microsoft.com/en-us/downloads/list-your-products-or-services-through-office-com-search-HA102846640.aspx?CTT=5&origin=HA001047828`. You'll get the most current information on listing your products on Office.com. Also, read the overview at `http://office365.pinpoint.microsoft.com/en-US/Guidelines` for guidance on how to create a viable Profile for yourself as a seller.

Once you're ready to go, you apply to be a seller through the Office Store. The process of signing up involves multiple steps. We won't try to guide you through the entire process; we'll point you to the starting point for creating a seller account: `https://sellerdashboard.microsoft.com/Registration`. As noted before, we can't provide specifics, which are not only beyond the scope of our discussion here, but which may also evolve between the time of this writing and when you read this chapter. However, if you do anticipate selling or distributing your apps through the store, you might as well set up a seller account now.

In addition to creating an account, you'll provide payment information so you can get paid for apps which the Office Store sells on your behalf. Even if you only intend to offer apps free, you'll need to provide your tax information. You may choose to have payments deposited into a checking or savings account, or you can use PayPal. In either case, of course, you'll need to provide account information. You also provide tax information, as appropriate.

A Paid Developer Site is Required

One additional requirement applies to publishing apps. You need a paid Office 365 subscription that includes a Developer Site collection. This can be an individual Developer Subscription, or an enterprise Office 365 account. You must sign up for that separately from your seller account.

You'll be able to start adding apps as soon as your seller account is approved by Microsoft. But because apps must pass Microsoft certifications to be approved, we recommend that you don't start adding apps prematurely. Submit apps only when you are confident they'll be accepted.

Once your seller account has been approved — a process that may take up to three days — you're ready to start submitting apps. As noted previously, this step involves having Microsoft review and certify the app, so it's a good idea to do so only when you're sure your app is ready.

Requirements for Posting an App to Office Store

As of the time this was written, the following requirement applies to apps submitted to the Office Store to be offered as SharePoint apps: Your application must be compatible with an Office 2010 or Office 2013 component.

In addition to the basic compatibility requirement, apps submitted to the Office Store will be reviewed for compliance with a series of verification checks to ensure your app adheres to the app content and behavior guidelines. For example, Microsoft checks whether the app manifest is valid and complete. It checks to be sure that items included in the app do not contain elements that aren't allowed for SharePoint. It checks that SharePoint Features don't have a scope that is broader than Web scope. The package is also inspected for objectionable content, although that term is not specifically defined. If the app package passes all tests, it's wrapped into a file and signed by Microsoft.

We touch on licensing in the next section.

Supported Licensing Model

SharePoint and the Office Store do not specify license terms, nor do they enforce license terms you implement in your app. That's up to you, the developer. However, the Office Store does provide a framework for licensing so that you can include code logic in your app to enforce whatever licensing restrictions you need. This licensing framework applies only to apps obtained through the Office Store, or from an app catalog hosted on Office 365. It doesn't reach apps you deploy on other locations, such as an on-premises app catalog.

The Office and SharePoint 2013 app license framework includes the following features and functions:

- The Office Store handles payments and issues licenses for apps that are sold on your behalf. As previously noted in our discussion of creating a seller account, you specify the payment mechanism for your account, which can include PayPal.

- It handles storage of licenses and renewal of app license tokens for your apps. Your responsibility is primarily in setting up licensing and monitoring activities in your seller account.
- The Office Store provides APIs you can use to get license information for an app. It also supports a web service you can use to verify whether a license is valid.
- SharePoint 2013 provides an administration user interface for app license management. In this way, the purchaser of an app can assign the license to themselves or another user, or delegate management of licenses to other users.

All of these license management features are available to you as a seller in the Office Store. You decide how to implement them for each app you submit.

You specify the attributes of the license you want to offer users who download it, such as whether you are offering your app for free, on a trial basis with the option to purchase, or for purchase. You also specify whether your app can be acquired on a per-user or site basis.

With the Office Store, you can freely monetize apps you have produced. Or you can use the Office Store as a way of putting your apps in front of many potential clients as marketing tools for your other products and services. Partnering with the Microsoft Office Store allows you to reach many more potential customers with a limited investment, other than the investment in developing the original web app.

Upgrading and Maintaining Access Web Apps

In wrapping up our discussion of deployment, we're going to revisit the task of upgrading and maintaining your Access web apps. Previously in this chapter, we discussed the process of installing and updating an Access web app. You learned how to open the app package and update it to maintain the version history of your app.

From a planning point of view, the primary considerations reflect the need to account for the version control over the interface as well as back up for the data. You will also find that you need a different approach for managing updates between apps that are deployed in-house, where you have control, versus publicly distributed apps, where customers may choose to perform updates on their own time and on their site. The latter holds many more consequences so we will go through both scenarios.

Updating the Interface

Upgrading a production web app means that you must solicit and track feedback from users regarding features and functions in the web app. You would then judiciously apply changes to the development copy of the app which you maintain in your developer site. As you reach stability on a new version of the web app, you can create the app package for that version and, following the steps outlined earlier in this chapter, upgrade the deployed web app for your users and notify them to install the update. It is, of course, important that such changes do not include data from your developer version. The current mechanism for this task is still a bit raw, requiring editing of the XML files in the app package as you learned to do earlier. Nonetheless, it is a viable way to implement upgrades and even bug fixes in a production web app.

Obtaining Data Backups

Although there is no out of the box method of backing up only the data from your production database, it is possible to manage backups of your data in a few different ways, some primarily manual, the others possibly more automated.

First, as you just learned, you can create an app package that includes data. The process is manual and it requires that the manager of the web app perform the task on a regular schedule, so it's not ideal. In addition, this type of backup can only be done from the Access client. Nonetheless, it is a viable way to keep backups.

In addition, you can also create a client `.accdb`, which connects to the SQL Server or SQL Azure database behind your web app. From that client, you can implement custom backup methods by which a copy of the data can be saved locally. A series of queries can be used to differentially back up each table. A VBA module can be set up to run those queries. If you or your customer wants regular data-only backups, you can create a Windows scheduled task setup to open the Access database and run the backup function on an overnight schedule.

Alternatively, you can install a free SQL Server Express Edition and then create a linked server, as demonstrated in Chapter 12. You can then create a SQL script to be executed via a `sqlcmd` command client line using Windows task scheduler. If your app is running on a local SQL Server or you have a licensed edition of SQL Server, you can implement a SQL Server Agent Job to execute a backup command. Experienced Access developers will have experience with one or more of these approaches, so we'll limit the discussion to one simple example of how you can collect the data for local backup by using the built-in stored procedure `sp_tables_ex` to gather information about table structures from the linked server. Refer to Chapter 12 for a refresher on creating a linked server and querying against it. The code is available in the file named `Chapter 14 - Generate Local Copies.sql`.

```
DECLARE @sql nvarchar(MAX);

CREATE TABLE #tmp (
  TABLE_CAT nvarchar(255),
  TABLE_SCHEM nvarchar(255),
  TABLE_NAME nvarchar(255),
  TABLE_TYPE nvarchar(255),
  REMARKS nvarchar(255)
);

INSERT INTO #tmp (TABLE_CAT, TABLE_SCHEM, TABLE_NAME, TABLE_TYPE, REMARKS)
EXEC sp_tables_ex
  @table_server='Maid_To_Order_Web_App',
  @table_type='TABLE',
  @table_schema='Access';

SET @sql = (
  SELECT CONCAT(
    'IF EXISTS(SELECT NULL
            FROM sys.objects
            WHERE objects.name = ''' + TABLE_NAME + '''
              AND objects.schema_id = SCHEMA_ID(''tmp''))
        DROP TABLE tmp.',
    QUOTENAME(TABLE_NAME),
```

```
        '; SELECT * INTO tmp.'
        ,QUOTENAME(TABLE_NAME),
        ' FROM ',
        QUOTENAME(TABLE_CAT),
        '.',
        QUOTENAME(TABLE_SCHEM),
        '.',
        QUOTENAME(TABLE_NAME),
        ';'
      )
      FROM #tmp
      FOR XML PATH ('')
    );

    EXEC sp_executesql @sql;

    DROP TABLE #tmp;
```

The script illustrates how you can gather data from all tables within a web app's database and copy it to a local SQL Server database. You definitely would want to expand on this prototype, perhaps adding additional columns to copy only new data added since the last copy or select only certain tables for copying. You can also save this as a `.sql` file, which can be then executed via `sqlcmd` if you cannot create a SQL Server job.

You also can see that you can reverse the process and write from local copy back to the web app's database. This approach gives you an option for managing destructive changes to the data such as renaming columns where data may be lost. The general process you would want to adopt for processing an upgrade that includes schema changes would have a pattern similar to this:

1. Perform a differential backup of data that will be affected by changes in schema.
2. Update the app.
3. Run SQL scripts to restore the backed-up data to the upgraded app's database.

At the time of this writing, there is no easy way to automate the process and thus it is necessary to perform the upgrade manually or at least automate the first and third step using either a helper `.accdb` file or SQL scripts. You would still have to manually perform the second step.

In scenarios where you chose to publicly distribute apps, and want to perform schema changes, you may need to consider the need to distribute the versions directly to your consumers so that you can perform the update for your consumers or provide them with the instructions. Otherwise, they may risk losing their data were they to proceed with an upgrade the next time one becomes available. More importantly, there is no simple way to warn them of the extra steps that are necessary to bring their data forward to the next version.

Admittedly, there is no "great" backup and lifecycle story for the databases behind your web apps, but we have pointed out at least a couple of ways you can perform your regular data backups and use that to help you manage the lifecycle of your web apps.

SUMMARY

In this chapter, you've learned how to package an Access web app for deployment to a SharePoint App Catalog. The process involves creating an app package containing the `appmanifest` and `appdb` XML files. You may or may not include data in that app package. The app package can then be uploaded to your SharePoint site and deployed to users. Deployment can be directly on a SharePoint site or in the app catalog, where all users have access to the app, or to your personal site if you want to restrict its use.

If you wish to restrict the web app to invitation-only sharing, you can either disable the property that makes it visible to all users or install it to your personal site. Otherwise, anyone who can get to your app catalog is free to install the web app. You also learned how an app catalog enables distribution of your apps to other people, whereas an app that's directly installed on a SharePoint site is not redistributable unless an app package is created and added to an app catalog.

You also learned how to monetize your web apps by establishing a seller account on Microsoft's Office Store through which you can sell or give away your apps. The Office Store handles the financial transactions for your apps and provides a payment mechanism for selling licenses to your apps.

Finally, you learned some techniques, effective albeit somewhat unrefined at this point, by which you can manage versions of your apps and create regular backups of the interface and data.

PART II
Client-Server Design and Development

- ▶ **CHAPTER 15:** Managing Data Sources
- ▶ **CHAPTER 16:** Programming Using VBA, APIs, and Macros
- ▶ **CHAPTER 17:** Creating Intuitive Forms
- ▶ **CHAPTER 18:** Creating Powerful Reports
- ▶ **CHAPTER 19:** Automating and Integrating with Other Programs
- ▶ **CHAPTER 20:** Securing, Deploying, and Maintaining Access Applications
- ▶ **CHAPTER 21:** Maximizing SQL Server Capabilities

15

Managing Data Sources

WHAT'S IN THIS CHAPTER?

- The importance and benefits of RDBMS normalization
- The process of importing and linking to different file formats and data sources
- Considerations and techniques when using and managing data sources

WROX.COM CODE DOWNLOADS FOR THIS CHAPTER

The wrox.com code downloads for this chapter are found at `www.wiley.com/go/proaccess2013prog.com` on the Download Code tab. The code is in the Chapter 15 download and individually named according to the code filenames listed throughout the chapter.

Microsoft Access is a very versatile tool. In addition to being a powerful rapid development tool for database applications combined with a management suite with a native file server database (ACE), Access is also a portal that enables you to manage a variety of data sources, ranging from other database engines, such as SQL Server, to flat files like Excel spreadsheets and text files.

In this chapter, you learn how to manage and work with various data sources using Access. Following a brief discussion about table structure and normalization, you will see how to link to local flat files and how to use ODBC to connect to external databases, whether they are on a server or a file server.

NORMALIZATION

A database development book would not be complete without discussing normalization. One of the cornerstones of *relational database management systems* (RDBMS) is the proper design of the structure, by identifying how to store the data in a way that promotes data integrity and ease or reporting. A properly designed database not only ensures that the information is captured and collected with minimal (optimally with no) data duplication but also enables you to efficiently query and report the data.

One goal of normalization is to eliminate duplicate entry and storage of the same data. When you enter client information (client ID, first name, last name, salutation, address, and so on), you will enter the information once into the appropriate table with each record being assigned a unique ID. This ID will be used to associate that record with related data in other tables, allowing you to retrieve, display, and manage client information as needed. The unique ID is the *primary key* (PK) field in the Client table and it is used as a *foreign key* (FK) in related tables. This is the cornerstone of a relational database structure.

The guidelines for normalization are referred to as Normal Forms. The normalization levels are numbered from 1 to 5, and are referred to as First Normal form through Fifth Normal Form (1NF through 5NF). In most cases, normalizing the data in your database application to a *third normal form* (3NF) will suffice. If you want an in-depth lesson on normal forms, countless references are available. The following brief review is intended to create a common ground for building the examples and discussions in this book.

Normalization is the process of organizing the data in a database. You establish this by creating tables and relating them to each other according to normalization rules designed to eliminate redundancy in the data stored and to maintain data integrity. The process also makes the database more flexible and supports expansion of data and additional business modules.

While disk space is much cheaper today, storing redundant data takes more storage space and, if you are using ACE as your back-end database engine, you need to be aware of the 2GB file size limit. It can also wreak havoc when you are maintaining the data. Once the same data value is stored in more than one table, when you are changing that value, you must ensure you changed it in all the locations. Changing the last name of a student once in the Students table is much easier than changing it also in the Classes table, Grades table, and so on. Poor maintenance due to poor design will adversely impact the data integrity and may render the database useless.

Because it is always good to remember why and how you normalize databases, let's review the first three normalization forms.

First Normal Form: Eliminate Repeating Groups

When you normalize your table to the first normal form, you eliminate duplicate fields (also referred to as repeating groups) from the table. Because you still need to capture and report the data, you will end up creating a separate table for each of the groups of the related data. The first normal form does the following when you normalize:

- Eliminates repeating groups in individual tables.
- Creates a separate table for each set of related data.
- Identifies each set of related data with a primary key.

Avoid using multiple fields (repeating groups) in a single table to store similar data. For example, a student attends a few classes. The Schedule table may contain fields for Class 1 and Class 2. What happens when you add a third class? Changing the table design to add a field is not the right answer. Modifying a table after the database solution is deployed impacts both the back-end and the front end of the solution and can require a lot of the programmer's attention and time. To top it off, it doesn't support a dynamic number of classes for each student. What happens when you need to add a fourth class? Instead, create a separate table for the class information — Class table and then link the Student table and the Class table to each other using the keys of each table.

Second Normal Form: Eliminate Duplicate Data

The second normal form builds on the 1NF and continues the process of eliminating duplicate or repeating data. It places subsets of data that apply to multiple rows of a table in separate tables and creates relationships between the tables. Normalizing the database to 2NF does the following:

- Meets all requirements for 1NF
- Places sets of values that apply to multiple records in separate tables
- Creates a relationship between these tables using a foreign key

Records in a table should not depend on anything other than a table's primary key. For example, consider a patient's address in a billing system. The address is needed by the Appointment table, but also by the Claims, Referrals, Lab, and Invoices tables. Instead of storing the patient's address as a separate entry in each record in each of these tables, you store it in one place — Patient table — or if appropriate to the design, in Address table, and use the primary key from that table in the tables that need that information.

Third Normal Form: Eliminate Fields That Do Not Depend on the Key

The third normal form continues to build on the second normal form and will bring you to the normalization level of most database solutions. The 3NF eliminates fields from a table that do not depend on the key of that table. When you normalize the data to 3NF, you remove values in a record that do not depend on that record's key from the table and place them in a separate table or tables.

For example, in a Class Schedule table, a professor's name and degree may be included. But you need a complete list of the professors for group mailings. If the professor's information is stored in the Class table, there is no way to list professors without classes for the current semester. By creating a separate Professor table and linking it to the Class Schedule table with a professor's primary key value you can generate a mailing list for all professors, not only the ones who are scheduled to teach.

Other Normalization Forms

There are two additional normalization levels:

1. Fourth normal form, also called Boyce Codd Normal Form (BCNF)
2. Fifth normal form

While the two additional normalization levels are defined, they are rarely considered in practical database solution design. Although when you disregard these two forms you may create a less than "perfect" solution design, it should have no impact on the functionality of the solution you are designing.

NORMALIZATION EXAMPLES

Using the information discussed previously, you will go through the steps to normalize the following sample data. Additionally, you will add a PK and change the filenames to use the proper naming convention. The table will show the minimal number of fields needed for this example. Typically tables will include an additional number of fields.

Un-Normalized Table

The following table is our starting point. It shows a list of students with classes they registered for and with the names of the advisor for each student. The table has a layout you typically can find in a spreadsheet file.

CLASS SCHEDULE

```
StudentID  Student Name  Advisor Name  Room#  Subj 1   Subj 2  Subj 3
1022       Carey         Budreau       41     Engl01   Psyc202 CS101
4123       Keller        Tamam         67     Math201  Eng205  Phys301
```

First Normal Form: Eliminate Repeating Groups

Tables in a database solution should be two dimensional. Because one student can take several subjects in school, these subjects should be recorded in a separate table. Fields Subj1, Subj2, and Subj3 in the preceding code record are a sign of a future design problem.

At times, you will be building a database solution based on an existing spreadsheet file. Often, the spreadsheet data uses the third data dimension, but that doesn't mean the table should. Another way to look at this: When you are using a one-to-many relationship, do not put the two sides, the one and the many, in the same table. Instead, eliminate the repeating columns (`Subjects`) and create another table in first normal form, as shown in the code that follows:

1NF

```
StudentID   AdvisorName   Room  Subject
    1022      Budreau     41    Engl01
    1022      Budreau     41    Psyc202
    1022      Budreau     41    CS101
    4123      Tamam       67    Math201
    4123      Tamam       67    Eng205
    4123      Tamam       67    Phys301
```

Second Normal Form: Eliminate Duplicate Data

Note the records showing multiple Subject values for each Student value in the preceding 1NF table. Because Subject is not dependent on Student, this table does not conform to second normal form. To normalize the data to 2NF, you will create the following three tables:

TABLE STUDENTS

StudentID	StudentName	AdvisorName	Room
1022	Carey	Budreau	41
4123	Keller	Tamam	67

TABLE CLASSES

SubjectID	CourseNo	Subject
1	Eng101	English Level 101
2	Psyc202	Psychology Level 202
3	CS101	Computer Science Level 101
7	Math201	Mathematics Level 201
9	Eng205	English Level 205
12	Phys301	Physicis Level 301

TABLE REGISTRATION:

StudentID	SubjectID
1022	1
1022	2
1022	3
4123	7
4123	9
4123	12

Third Normal Form: Eliminate Fields That Do Not Depend on the Key

In the last example, the Room Number is functionally dependent on Advisor, not on the Student, and each Advisor has an office number. The solution is to move that attribute from the Students table to the Advisors table:

TABLE STUDENTS

StudentID	StudentName	AdvisorID
1022	Carey	1
4123	Keller	2

TABLE ADVISORS

AdvisorID	AdvisorName	Room
1	Budreau	41
2	Tamam	67

Notice how we changed some of the field names as we were normalizing the data to adhere to a basic naming convention. We removed spaces: Advisor Name is now AdvisorName. We also removed special characters from the field name: Room# is now Room. Additionally, we added a primary key to each table and used it as a foreign key in the related tables.

Depending on your naming convention schema, field names can end up being non–end user friendly. While you understand what `lngVisitNo` is, the users may not. There are a few ways to resolve that. You can alias the fields when you create the queries. In Access query designer it's as simple as what you see in Figure 15-1.

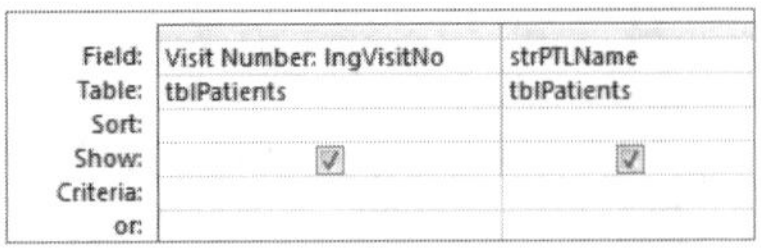

Field:	Visit Number: lngVisitNo	strPTLName
Table:	tblPatients	tblPatients
Sort:		
Show:	☑	☑
Criteria:		
or:		

FIGURE 15-1: Aliasing a field in QBE

In forms and reports, you can change the text in the label for the reported field. Additionally, you can use the `Caption` property of the field when you build the table. The caption value will show when you are viewing the table in query outputs, forms, and reports. Using the `Caption` property is useful in a web-based solution where it's called `Label Text`. You can read more about it in Chapter 2.

The output of a query when you use either of the methods is shown in Figure 15-2.

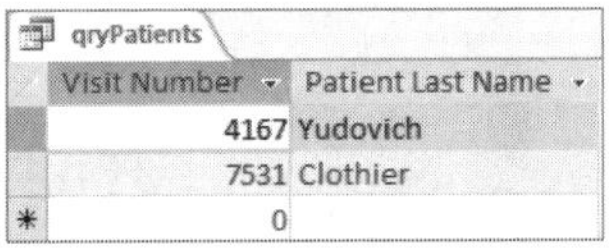

qryPatients

Visit Number	Patient Last Name
4167	Yudovich
7531	Clothier
0	

FIGURE 15-2: Output of Aliasing or Caption Methods

While normalization is paramount to a properly designed database solution that deals with user data entry, you may encounter instances where breaking the rules is appropriate. It is not to be done lightly, nor should it be done because you'd rather not work through the normalization process. Identifying a case for breaking the rules requires you to articulate to yourself and in your documentation why it is beneficial to not normalize the specific value. You will also need to call out the repercussions of not normalizing and how it will be handled throughout the application. Going through this process you will find out that in most cases, proper normalization (at least to third normal form) is the way to go.

When you design a reporting solution only — usually one that links to other data sources or imports data from various sources — you do not have to worry about normalization. In fact, when using Access as the front-end interface for a reporting tool, or even as a data warehouse, you will typically find that de-normalizing, or flattening the tables will enable the users to generate the reports faster. Depending on the size of the recordset you are using in the reporting solution, you and the users may also benefit from using summary tables with the data already aggregated.

PRIMARY KEYS

As mentioned previously, every table should have a primary key field. As the developer, you will need to make the decision of what values to use as primary keys in the tables. You will evaluate the options and choose during the design phase of the database. When you look at your data, you will begin to identify fields that are candidates for that selection. However, there are certain guidelines you need to look at before you make your choice.

When you evaluate a candidate field for a primary key, you should ask the following questions:

- Will it be unique for the life of the database?
- Is it applicable to all records (rows)?
- It is minimal?
- Will it be stable over time?

If any of the answers is no, the field has failed the test and should not be used as a primary key.

The uniqueness of the value in the field ensures that no two records will have the same value throughout the life of the database solution. This guarantees that every record in the database is unique when you look at the values it represents.

It must be applicable to all records in the database. You need to identify that every record entered to the table will have a value in that field. Although a `NULL` can mean something in a database record (the lack of value) because the value must be unique, you can have only one `NULL` value in the table. Every other record must have a value.

A primary key should be minimal — a single field in the table. Creating a composite primary key from multiple fields will lead to challenges when you join the table to other tables. You can address the need for the composite uniqueness by creating a unique index across multiple fields. The index does not need to be the primary key index.

The stability of the values in the field is important. Will the values change over time from a numerical value to a string or vice versa? A stable primary key field safeguards the data integrity of the database solution.

You are most likely aware of the debate between developers about using natural primary keys or surrogate primary keys. Some developers will use only a surrogate primary key while others will look at the fields already designed into the table and will try to identify and select one or more fields to be the primary key index.

There is merit in both approaches. A surrogate key will do the job 100 percent of the time and it takes basically no time to add it to your table. All you need is to add a field with an `AutoNumber` data type to your table and set it as the primary key. A surrogate key adds a field to your table, and it may make it harder to report and query the data because you will need to join the table that holds the actual values. On the other hand, natural keys already exist, and you do not need to add a field to the table. Selecting a natural key can take time on your end because you want to make sure you select the right one, should it exist in the table.

Most transaction tables will benefit from a surrogate primary key. Very few, if any, will have an appropriate field that can be used as a natural primary key. Some reference or lookup tables do not need a surrogate primary key and will be more useful to you with a natural primary key.

If you look inside a hotel reservation database solution, chances are there is a table that holds information about the rooms, including the room number. The room number field can be used as a natural primary key because it meets the requirements of the four questions earlier in this chapter. It is unique: Each room must have its own number. It is applicable to all rows: Each guest room record will have a room number. It is minimal: A room number field is a single field identifying the room. It will be stable over time: Room numbers do not change after being assigned. Room 41 will stay Room 41 throughout the life of the hotel and, by extension, the database solution that supports that hotel.

There are rare and extreme cases where you will need to change the primary key value for a record. Should that happen, your best line of defense to ensure data integrity in the database is to check the Cascade Update Related Fields option when you set the referential integrity.

OVERVIEW OF ACCESS FILES AND THE DATABASE ENGINE

Microsoft Access comes with its own database engine from the get-go. The database engine is called ACE, and it's a file server database file. ACE is the newer database engine, replacing the JET database engine as of Access 2007. You are reading this book so you already know that one reason that Access is a favorite development tool is the ease of development and administration when compared to other databases.

The access shell file (`.accdb`) is the management suite for the database engine. Through it you can create, modify, and remove objects such as tables, queries, forms, and reports. While each `.accdb` file has a separate database engine, you can link the tables from one `.accdb` file to the other.

Both ACE and the access file have limitations that you, as a developer, need to learn how to work around and maximize the benefits of each solution you develop. One of the most known, if not *the* most known, limitations is the size limit of 2GB for an `.accdb` file. That size limit includes the data stored in ACE and the objects stored in Access, such as forms and reports and system objects.

This size limit must be considered when you are designing a database solution to evaluate the appropriate back end for the solution. That being said, 2GB is a lot of space. You can store and manage millions of records in a properly designed and maintained database. You can also work around this limit by linking to tables in other `.accdb` files.

There are additional limitations, such as total number of fields in a single table (255), total number of objects in a single `.accdb` file (32,768), and number of actions in a macro (999). All this and much more information can be found by typing **specifications** in Access Help, or by going to the Microsoft Office web page at `http://office.microsoft.com/en-us/access-help/access-specifications-HP005186808.aspx`.

Don't let the fact that there are limitations scare you. Every database engine and every development tool out there has limitations. The specifications will vary from one product to the other. Some you won't care about and some will be the determining factor in choosing that product. Knowing and understanding the Access specifications enable you to build a better database solution. Most of the limits are high and you should not reach them during development.

OTHER DATA SOURCES

Access offers you, as the developer, flexibility by enabling you to connect to data sources external to Access. In addition to being able to import data from Excel files and text files, both delimited and fixed length, into a table in Access, you can also link the files to the `.accdb` file and use the data the same way you would use any other link table.

Not all linked data sources are updatable. For example, when you link an Excel file or a text file to Access, you can read the data, but you cannot update it.

There are benefits to lining the files versus importing them into the database. First, importing the file will also import the size of the data in the file into the database. With the 2GB size limit on an `.accdb` file, you can save space by linking. Another benefit to linking the files is that you can replace the text file with an updated version of the data, and as long as the new file is named the same and is located in the same folder, the data in the `.accdb` file will reflect the updated values. There is no need to truncate the existing tables and reimport the data into them. This is useful, especially when you are using Access as a reporting tool for external data.

To link your files to the database, you will need to use the External Data ribbon shown in Figure 15-3. Under the Import & Link option, you will see the different data source types you can use to import or link to the database.

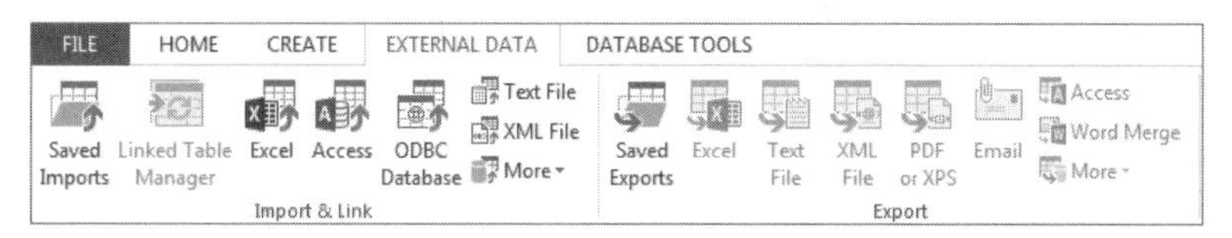

FIGURE 15-3: External Data ribbon

As you can see, the prominent data sources are Excel, Access, and ODBC database. Also listed as options are Text file and XML file. When you click the More button, you will see SharePoint Lists and Outlook Folders among other data sources.

After you select the data source type appropriate to your solution, you will use the wizard to either add data into a new table, append data into an existing table, or link the data to your database solution.

With the exception of another `.accdb` as the data source, you will be asked to identify the data type and field names of the imported or linked data. Don't rely on Access to guess the right data type. The wizard uses the first few rows of data to identify the data set, and it may not be as accurate as you need it to be.

Data in linked `.accdb` tables are fully editable from your database solution. To change the table properties, you will need to open the originating `.accdb`.

After you have successfully linked the text data file, you can use it as an almost regular, linked table in your database. While you cannot edit the existing records in the text file, you will be able to add records if needed.

The capability to import and link different data sources into one database solution portal is part of what makes Access a robust and flexible front-end solution development tool.

Overview of ODBC Linking

Access is a very flexible development tool. Not only can you link to various flat files as we discussed earlier, but you can also link to databases and use Access as the front-end tool to work with the data stored on the server. The tool of choice for the task is the Open Database Connectivity (ODBC).

Open Database Connectivity (ODBC) is an interface allowing you to access data stored in various relational and non-relational database management systems such as SQL Server, ORACLE, dBase, Excel, and Text. The ODBC provides a vendor-neutral, open means of accessing data stored in personal computers and different databases. An ODBC is based on a Call Level Interface (CLI) specification of the SQL Access Group. The ODBC interface was first created in 1992 and became a part of the national SWL standard in 1995.

The strength and benefit of ODBC is that is it provides a universal data access interface and allows you to use different database environments without the need to learn different application programming languages. With ODBC, you can simultaneously access, view, and modify data stored in an assortment of database platforms because the ODBC re-codes the SQL queries you write in Access and translates them to the specific "dialect" of the database you are accessing.

As you can see in Figure 15-4, it takes three components to create a solution that uses ODBC:

- An ODBC-enabled front end or client
- The ODBC driver
- A server database that supports ODBC

Given that you are reading this book, you likely already have an ODBC client at your disposal — Microsoft Access. Access is one of the top options when you are looking to develop a solution based on a database server. You can also use a .NET solution or an ODBC-enabled solution from other vendors. Additionally, Access also takes care of the second component of an ODBC solution, the driver for the back-end database you are planning to use. Because Access comes preloaded with ODBC drivers, connecting to a server is a matter of a few clicks through a dialog wizard. And last but not least, you will need a server database. SQL Server is one of the more popular ones; however, you can use a variety of database platforms such as Oracle, My SQL, AS/400, and so on.

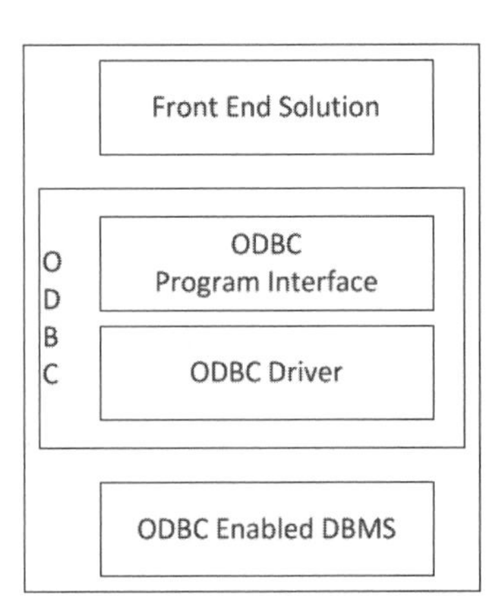

FIGURE 15-4: Open Database Connectivity (ODBC)

> **NOTE** *To obtain an ODBC Driver Catalog, call the Microsoft Order Desk at (800) 360-7561. If you are outside the United States, contact your local subsidiary. To locate your subsidiary, see the Microsoft World Wide Offices website at* `http://www.microsoft.com/worldwide.`

How Does the Process Work?

The ODBC client uses a collection of commands (which is referred to as "ODBC") to request data from, or to send data to, the back-end DBMS server. The commands are written and communicated in the client's language. However, for the DBMS to understand the client request, the command needs to pass through the ODBC driver for that specific DBMS. The ODBC driver is located on the front-end tool. The ODBC driver translates the command into a format that the DBMS Server can understand. When the ODBC Server responds, it responds to the ODBC driver, which in turn translates the response into a format that the front-end ODBC client can understand.

Why Is ODBC a Good Thing?

There are a few great things about ODBC. To begin with, you, as a database solution developer, don't need to change the tool you are using to access the data from different back ends. As long as you have an ODBC driver for the back-end platform you want or need to use, you are good to go. Additionally, you can connect to an ODBC-enabled back-end database with any available ODBC client as long as you have the ODBC driver for that particular DBMS.

Examples of Using ODBC

You can use ODBC in different ways with different front-end and back-end combinations. A few examples are listed in the following list:

- Microsoft Access front-end solution accessing data from a SQL Server back end using the SQL Server ODBC driver, which ships with Access
- VB.net front-end solution accessing data from a dBase back end using the dBase ODBC driver; the driver comes with a Microsoft ODBC Database Drivers Pack

There is a possible drawback to using ODBC drivers. Connecting your front-end solution to a large number of ODBC back-end DBMS may impact system resources negatively. One way that the ODBC driver vendors addressed that potential issue was to design a Multi-Tier ODBC driver. While a single tier driver, shown in Figure 15-5, processes both the ODBC functions and the SQL statements; a multi-tier driver, shown in Figure 15-6, processes the ODBC function while sending the SQL statements to the database engine to be processed. An example of a single tier driver is the Microsoft Access ODBC driver.

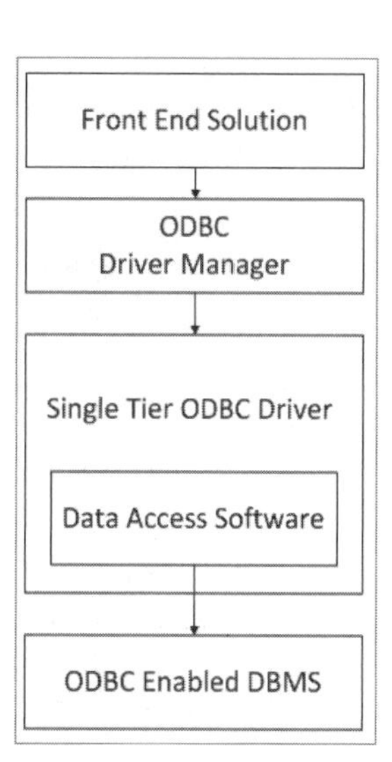

FIGURE 15-5: Single Tier ODBC

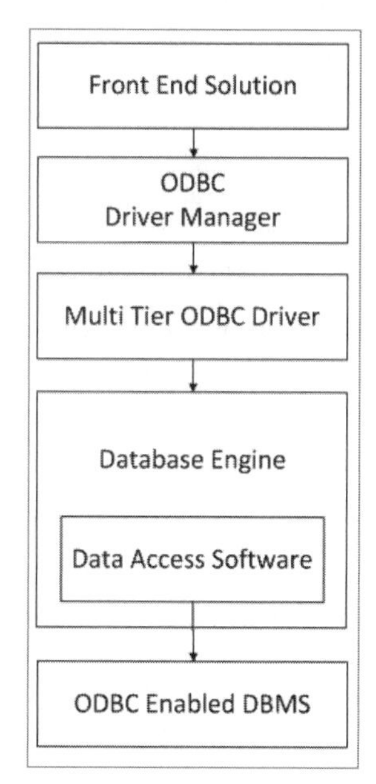

FIGURE 15-6: Multi Tier ODBC

As with all things related to database solutions design, you will need to pay attention to the performance of the front-end client you are designing. Use your smarts to evaluate what is needed, and try to shy away from the "super solution." If you pay the same attention to the solution connection design that you give to the database design, your solution will work like it should.

Managing Linked Objects

You can use Access in different ways. The most obvious way is to develop a database solution to meet your business needs. Additionally, you can use Access as a data management tool that gets data from other data sources — other databases, spreadsheets, text files, and so on — and has them all available to you in a central portal to manage and provide information to your business.

ETL — Extract, Transform, Load

ETL stands for extract, transform, load — three database functions that you can use to pull data out of one data source and send to another database.

The three steps of the process are:

1. Extract: Reading data from a data source.
2. Transform: Converting the extracted data from its current format to the format needed.
3. Load: Writing the data into the target database.

The ETL process is used to migrate data from one data source — be it another database or a flat file — into another database. It's commonly used when you load data to a data warehouse, or into a reporting solution. It is also used when you need to normalize data from an external source before importing it to your database solution to ensure data quality.

The extraction process can be as simple as linking or importing a file or a table to Access. If you decide to import the data into your Access database, and it does not conform to the format you need, you will want to use a temp table to store the initial data set.

After you extracted the data set, you will transform it so it can be written into another database. The transformation process uses other data tables, lookup tables, and rules to parse the data or combine it with other data available to you.

When the transformation is completed, the new formatted data is written to the target database to be used as needed. Depending on the destination of the data, you can use an Append query or you can export it using Access's data export process.

There are ETL tools on the market that will help you work with the data. The cost will vary, depending on the product; some tools can carry a price tag in the $100,000 range. When you are going through the build or buy process, consider that there are cases where Access is the right tool for you to create your own ETL solution. For added strength, you can use it with a SQL Server back end.

Managing Import and Export Spec

As we discussed earlier in the chapter, you use the import wizard to link or import data to Access. During the process, you will be able to save the import specifications. At the end of the process, you will be able to save the import steps. While the two may sound similar, they are two different tools Access offers you to manage data import and export.

Saving the import specification is done while you are in the process of setting the fields data types and identifying the file type: `delimited`, `fixed length`, and so on. The saved specifications can be called the next time you are using the import wizard, either manually or through VBA code. You can apply the specification to any file with the same field layout and format (code file: `DataSources.txt Import spec in VBA`):

```
DoCmd.TransferText acImportDelim, "MyDataFile_ImportSpec", "tblMyData", _
    "D:\Users\DougY\Desktop\MyDataFile.txt", True
```

At times, you will get multiple files from the external source that you will need to load into your database. When this happens, you can loop through the files and load them in a single process.

Saving the import steps is a different way to create a shortcut to the import or export process that can help you save time and automate importing and exporting data. Unlike saving the specification, this feature saves the whole process and when you run the saved import, the process will look for a file with the name and the location to match the steps you saved. You can call the saved step via code (code file: `DataSources.txtSaved Import Export in VBA`):

```
DoCmd.RunSavedImportExport "MyDataFile_SavedImport"
```

Additionally, you can create a task in Outlook to remind you to run the import or export process and let you run it from Outlook.

Before running either of the two methods, `DoCmd.TransferText` or `RunSavedImportExport`, you should make sure that the source file exists and that it's ready for import. You should be aware that the process will overwrite an existing table. It may be the desired results, but if it's not, you need to compensate for it.

If you need to make changes to the specifications of the import process, you will run the import manually. Change the parts you need to change and save the new specifications of the new import steps. You can overwrite the existing specifications or save the new specifications with a different name.

Temp Tables

When you load data to Access from a different data source, chances are that the data structure and format do not conform to the format and data types your solution needs. Loading the initial data set into a temp table as is will allow you to create queries to manage the data and convert it to a format consumable by your solution.

Temp tables accept the data without worrying about the content of it. In the majority of cases most, if not all, the data type for the fields in a temp table is `Text`. The sole purpose of the temp table is to contain the data and have it under your control.

One down side of the temp table in the ACE database engine is that it can cause the file to bloat if it is not compacted periodically. Unlike SQL Server, ACE will retain the space allocated to a table until you run Compact and Repair (C&R). While you were able to run only the repair portion of the process, as of Access 2000, both compact and repair, are run together. The repair switch is kept for backward compatibility.

Views to Clean the Data

Now that you have the data loaded into your database solution, you can transform and conform it to the specific needs of your reporting or data management solution. To do that, you can use queries and, if needed, user-defined functions.

> **NOTE** User-defined functions *(UDF) are discussed in more detail in Chapter 16.*

A well-crafted `SELECT` query can be used as a view of the data and as the base for a report, or as an action query to append the data to one of the tables in your solution. In that query, or a set of queries, you can change the data type of the fields, parse existing fields in the temp table into many fields, or combine fields from the temp table into one.

Parsing data and converting the results to the desired format is not the only purpose of the transformation. You may need to assign values to the existing records to maintain data integrity of the stored data. Converting and adding a foreign key value based on the text value in the record is a common task.

When the number of values you need to convert is low, you may be tempted to hard-code the crossover into the formula or the code you are writing. We strongly recommend you avoid it and instead create a lookup table, even if it includes only one or two records. As time goes by, additional values may be needed, and having a table will make the maintenance an easy task.

Date Conversion of Data from SQL

One specific data type conversion to call out is date fields between SQL and Access. SQL Server's `Datetime` field stores the value differently than Access: It can record and report nanoseconds, while Access stops at seconds.

```
SQL Datetime Value: 2013-05-29 00:00:00.000
Access Datetime value: 5/29/2013 00:00:00
```

When you load the date field to Access, the import process will not recognize it as a date, and if the destination table expects a date value, you will receive an error message.

There are a couple of ways to handle that. The first is to load the value into a text field in the temp table, and convert it to a date value Access can consume. Depending on the detail level of the date value you need, it can be as simple as parsing the value to the date part and using the `CDate()` function (code file: `DataSources.txt Convert T-SQL date to Access date`):

```
MySQLDate = 2013-05-29 09:09:25.333
CDate(Left(MySQLDate,10)) --> 5/29/2013
```

If you need to capture the `Time` part of the date value in the same field as the `Date` part, the formula will vary a bit (code file: `DataSources.txt Convert T-SQL date to Access date II`):

```
MySQLDate = 2013-05-29 09:09:25.333
DateTime: CDate(Left([MySQLDate],19)) --> 5/29/2013 9:09:25 AM
```

The following code will work if you have control over the SQL script that generates the data file for you. The script can be changed to parse the date part from the `Datetime` field and deliver the clean value to you (code file: `DataSources.txt Convert T-SQL date to Access date in T-SQL`):

```
MySQLDate = 2013-05-29 09:09:25.333
CONVERT(VARCHAR(10), MySQLDate, 101) --> 5/29/2013
```

As you can see, transforming the dates from SQL to Access is not as simple as it looks up front. Knowing the differences and how to accommodate for them will make the process work well with your solution.

QUERYING EXTERNAL DATA EFFECTIVELY

Now that you have the data linked into your Access solution, let's look at how to work with it and get the most out of it. We will overview how to optimize the queries and explore passthrough queries in Access. We will discuss the differences between Access SQL and T-SQL. Chapter 21 provides deeper coverage of those topics as they relate to the SQL Server back end.

Linked Object Performance and Query Optimization

When you query linked data files in your Access solution, the data is processed locally. In most cases, the processing power of today's PCs is strong enough that processing the data locally is a non-issue. However, sometimes you will be dealing with a very large data file and the response time from your query will be less than satisfactory to you or your end users.

If you are linked to data tables from a different database, you can work with the *database administrator* (DBA) who oversees that database and identify potential indexes that can be created in the originating table. Proper indexing will make queries process faster. Because you cannot edit the properties of linked text files of Excel files, you cannot add indexes to them.

When you are using linked objects, you cannot change the design of the linked table, so adding or modifying indexes in the linked objects is not an option. However, you can create local tables to store initial returned results for faster processing in subsequent queries. The trick is to cast a wider net in the initial query and insert it into a local table. After you have stored the data, you can refine the resulting data set further by using the local table as a data source.

You can go about it in two ways. The first is to create the table on the fly by running a Make Table query (code file: `DataSources.txt Make Table Query`):

```
SELECT LinkedFile.PatientName, LinkedFile.BirthDate, LinkedFile.Notes
INTO LocalDataFile
FROM LinkedFile
WHERE LinkedFile.BirthDate = #4/1/2009#;
```

The resulting table will not be indexed; depending on the size of the data set and your subsequent needs, it may not be a factor you care about. In your code, you will want to destroy (delete) the table object when you are done with the whole process by using `DoCmd.DeleteObject` (code file: `DataSources.txt Delete Object`):

```
DoCmd.DeleteObject acTable,"LocalDataFile"
```

If you prefer not to delete the table in your code, running the `Make Table` query again will overwrite the existing table. Depending on how you run the query, you may get a warning that you will need to accept in order for the query to complete. You will not get the warning if you use `CurrentDB.Execute` in your code.

The second way to store data locally is to create the table in advance, and use an Append query to insert the data into that table (code file: `DataSources.txt Apppend query`):

```
INSERT INTO LocalDataFile (PatientName, BirthDate, Notes)
SELECT LinkFile.PatientName, LinkFile.BirthDate, LinkFile.Notes
FROM LinkFile WHERE LinkFile.BirthDate = #4/1/2009#;
```

Using this method, you can create indexes on the local file to help you with the subsequent queries and reports.

When you are done with the current data set, you can truncate the table and have it ready for the next time you are processing the data (code file: `DataSources.txt Delete query`):

```
DELETE * FROM LocalDataFile;
```

Passthrough Query and T-SQL

When your database solution uses linked tables from a server DBMS such as SQL, ORACLE, or MySQL, you can write a query in Access that will be sent to the server, processed there, and that will return the results to you. This type of query is called a passthrough query and it is available to you from within Access.

A passthrough query takes advantage of the server processing powers. When you execute a passthrough query, Access sends the request to the server. The query is processed on the server side, and not locally, and the server will send back the resulting data set to the desktop.

Because the query is processed on the server side, you will need to write the query in the native SQL dialect of the server DBMS, and not ACE SQL. As you set the query type to passthrough query, the QBE grid will not be available to you, and you will need to write the query by typing it into the SQL pane in Access as shown in Figure 15-7.

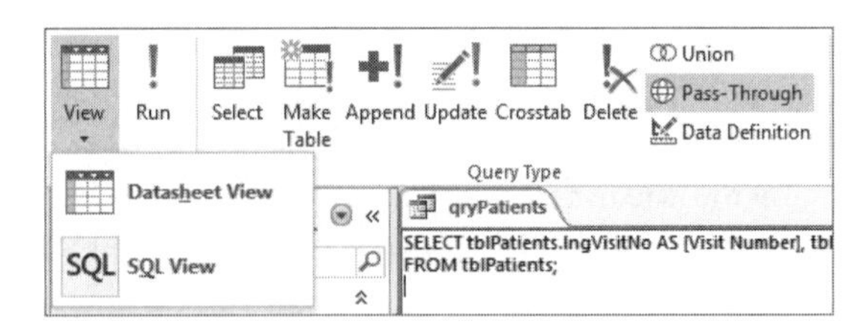

FIGURE 15-7: Access SQL pane

SQL, the query language, not the server, comes in many flavors. Oracle SQL syntax is slightly different than T-SQL. The same applies to MySQL and Access. Overall, they read the same. If you know how to read Access SQL, you will be able to read T-SQL. The differences in syntax mainly come into play when you want to use functions in your script.

Comparing Access SQL and T-SQL

Sometimes, especially when you are starting to write SQL, it is easier to convert scripts and learn by trial and error. Let's compare the Access SQL script that follows (code file: `DataSources.txt Access SQL`) to the T-SQL script it was converted to so it can run on the server (code file: `DataSources.txt T-SQL`):

ACCESS SQL

```
SELECT
  "1,""Transaction""" AS 1
, "100,""1""" AS 100
, "202,""" & Left([strPatientName],3) & """" AS 202
, IIf(IsNull([lngCSN]), "212,""P/F"""
, IIf(Len([lngCSN])<7,"212, ""P/F""","207," & """" & [lngCSN] & """")) AS 207_212
, "230,""" & Format(Month([dtDOS]),"00") &
   Format(Day([dtDOS]),"00") & Right(Year([dtDOS]),2) & """" AS 230
, "290,""" & IIf(IsNull([DEPARTMENT_ID]),
   IIf(Left([strMRN],1)='U','2020','2021'), [DEPARTMENT_ID]) & """" AS 290
, IIf(DateDiff("d",[dtDOS],[dtSignDate])>29, "510,""30D""", Null) AS 510
FROM
  dbo_tblVisits
LEFT JOIN
  dbo_tblTransactions_ENC_DE
ON
  dbo_tblVisits.lngCSN = dbo_tblTransactions_ENC_DE.PAT_ENC_CSN_ID;
tblVisitstblTransactionsENCtblVisitstblTransactionsENC
```

T-SQL

```
SELECT
  '1,"Transaction"' AS [1]
, '100,"1"' AS [100]
, '202,"' + LEFT(C.strPatientName, 3) + '"' AS [202]
, CASE WHEN [strEncounterNo] IS NULL THEN '212,"P/F"'
    WHEN LEN([strEncounterNo]) < 7 THEN '212,"P/F"'
    ELSE '207,"' + [strEncounterNo] + '"'
  END AS [207_212]
, '230,"' + REPLICATE('0', 2 - LEN(CAST(DATEPART(mm, C.dtDos) AS NVARCHAR)))
    + CAST(DATEPART(mm, C.dtDos) AS NVARCHAR)
    + REPLICATE('0', 2 - LEN(CAST(DATEPART(dd, C.dtDos) AS NVARCHAR)))
    + CAST(DATEPART(dd, C.dtDos) AS NVARCHAR)
    + RIGHT(CAST(DATEPART(yy, C.dtDos) AS NVARCHAR), 2) + '"' AS [230]
, '290,"'
    + CASE WHEN ISNULL(CAST([DEPARTMENT_ID] AS VARCHAR), '') = '' THEN
        CASE WHEN LEFT([strMRN], 1) = 'U' THEN '2020'
            ELSE '2021'
        END
      ELSE CAST([DEPARTMENT_ID] AS VARCHAR) END + '"' AS [290]
, CASE WHEN DateDiff([d], [dtDOS], [dtSignDate]) > 29 THEN
    '510,"30D"' ELSE NULL END AS [510]
FROM
  dbo.tblVisits AS C
```

```
LEFT OUTER JOIN
  dbo.tblTransactions_ENC_DE AS D
ON
  C.lngCsn = D.PAT_ENC_CSN_ID
tblVisitstblTransactionsENC
```

For reference, the resulting data out of the scripts will be the following (shown vertically for clarity):

```
1, "Transaction"
100, "1"
202, "YUD"
212, "P/F"
230, "052913"
290, "4167"
510, "30D"
```

Both scripts will return the same output when they are executed against the same base data set. You can also see that while there are some differences between the two, if you can read one, you can read, or at least understand, the other.

The first difference you will notice is that T-SQL uses a single quote to identify a string, while in Access you can use either one, and by default the system will use double quotes.

While Access uses the Immediate `IF` function `IIF()`, T-SQL does not. To get similar functionality you use `CASE`, `WHEN`, `ELSE`, `END`. Much like `IIF()`, you can nest `CASE` statements.

In T-SQL you will need to `CAST()` data types when you want to add them together. In the preceding script, you used `CAST()` to format the date parts to `navchar` to concatenate them. You did not need to do that in Access. Additionally, in T-SQL you must use the plus (+) sign to concatenate values. In Access, you can use the ampersand (&) or the plus (+) sign, although the two will behave differently depending on the values in the fields you concatenate.

As you develop more, you will run into additional differences between the syntaxes that aren't covered in the preceding query. A great source of information about T-SQL is Books On Line (BOL), which comes with the SQL Server software.

The ability to use passthrough queries in Access can give your solution the extra power it needs to provide you and the users the right data management tool. Combining Access and SQL Server into a single solution allows you to benefit from the rapid development and rich development tools Access has to offer, and the power and security of SQL Server. Chapter 21 explores the relationship between Access and SQL Server in greater detail.

SUMMARY

In this chapter you read and refreshed your knowledge about normalization and primary keys. You reviewed the steps to normalize a database to third normal form, and what factors to consider when you identify what field to use as a primary key for a table.

The discussion about using various data sources from within Access provided you information about ODBC and how to use it in your database solutions. Additionally, you learned about linking to different file types, such as text files or Excel files, and what you can do with the linked data.

The review of the ETL process showed what you can do with Access to transform and load external data into your database. You read about how to use temp tables to manage the process of converting the data to fit into the format and layout of the tables in your solution. It focused on Date conversion because it is one of the main points when loading data from a SQL server into Access.

After the data is linked, you read how to query it and insert it to local tables when you need to improve performance. Another method you learned about is using Passthrough queries to have the server process the data request. In the discussion about Passthrough queries you learned about the differences between Access SQL and T-SQL. A more in depth discussion about the differences is presented in Chapter 21.

In the next chapter, you will read about how to use VBA to enhance your database solution by creating *user defined functions* (UDFs) and by using a robust error handling and using API calls. You will learn a few advanced query techniques to help you manage your data, and how to create Query by Form to let your users select what records they want to view.

16

Programming Using VBA, APIs, and Macros

WHAT'S IN THIS CHAPTER?

- Using VBA to maximize your database solution
- Using enhanced query techniques
- Leveraging APIs from fundamentals through tips

WROX.COM CODE DOWNLOADS FOR THIS CHAPTER

The wrox.com code downloads for this chapter are found at `www.wiley.com/go/proaccess2013prog.com` on the Download Code tab. The code is in the Chapter 16 download and individually named according to the names listed throughout the chapter.

In this chapter, you will briefly review some VBA fundamentals before you delve into writing VBA procedures and user-defined functions to support your business rules. As you proceed, you will review how to enhance queries and how to create queries on the fly using VBA.

This chapter then provides a brief review of APIs and how you can use them to expand the reach of your Access solutions. The discussion uses a real-world example to explain the steps required to create and implement a Windows API call. It also includes valuable tips and techniques to assist developers already familiar with APIs.

Finally, the chapter reviews how data macros can offer new toolsets that can be effective for performing data validation and maintaining data integrity. You will see a few scenarios where data macros are superior to the traditional approach of using VBA in form events and validation rules.

VBA

When developing an application, you rely on events to perform actions based on user actions. Some of the commonly used events are `OnLoad`, `Click`, `Enter`, `BeforeUpdate`, `AfterUpdate`, `Dirty`, and so on. When a user clicks a control or the cursor moves into or out of a textbox, you expect the event to be triggered to run the specified code (or macro) so it is helpful to be familiar with the available events and the order in which they fire.

As you read through this chapter, you'll review some of the fundamentals of working the VBA. You'll also benefit from some tips and techniques gleaned from experienced developers on leveraging procedures, user-defined functions, and queries. With this, you will be better equipped to choose the appropriate event, and write the procedure, functions, or both as needed to satisfy the business rules.

Procedures

Procedures in Access VBA, and any other programming language, do something. They perform a task or a process in response to an event or a request.

You can use procedures to help the user navigate the database solution, move between forms, open and close forms, open reports, and so on. Additionally, you can use the procedures to process the data the user enters in the form and do something with it. You can refresh the recordset the user is viewing or trigger a query based on the criteria the users selected. You will read about queries and codes later in this chapter.

User-Defined Functions

As you just read, you use procedures to perform an action, and now you'll see how you use functions to return something. Even if you haven't been writing VBA, you have benefited from the many functions that are built-in to Access, such as `Left();` `Right();` `InStr();` and `DateDiff()`.

Most functions require you to pass arguments when you are using them; for example, `UCase(string)` and `Left(string,length)`. Depending on the function, however, some of the arguments are optional and you can omit them when you use the function. In Table 16-1, optional arguments are indicated by brackets.

TABLE 16-1: Using Functions

FUNCTION	USAGE	OUTPUT
InStr([start,]string1,string2[,compare])	`instr("Access 2013","2013")`	8
DateDiff (interval,date1,date2, [firstdayofweek],[firstweekofyear])	`DateDiff(("d",#2/18/2013#, #1/1/2014#)`	317

You can also have one function invoke other functions to return the value needed by the business rules: for example, `UCase(Left(string,length))`.

Sometimes, especially when the solution you are building is supporting complex business rules, the built-in functions are not enough. When this happens, you will want to build your own functions to accommodate the business needs. The good news is that you can. Access and other office products support the development of your own functions.

When you create your own function, it is referred to as UDF — user-defined function. The UDF can, and will need to, use system functions and, at times, other user-defined functions that are available to you. If you created the UDF as a public function, you will be able to use it throughout your database solution.

While in some cases you can, and should, consider using a formula in the query or form instead of creating a UDF, the power of the UDF is that you have the business logic in one centralized location, and you can use it anywhere in your database solution, and even in other database solutions. This way, if the business logic has changed, you will only need to make the change in the UDF.

You can create your own library with your own custom user-defined functions. When you do, other database solutions can reference that library file and have access to the function you created. To do so, you will need to convert the `.accdb` file to an `.accde` file. After the library is created, you can reference it by going through the Tools ➪ References dialog box in the VBA editor. Browse to the location of the `.accde` file and add it to your database solution as shown in Figure 16-1 with `Doug_BI_Lib.accde`.

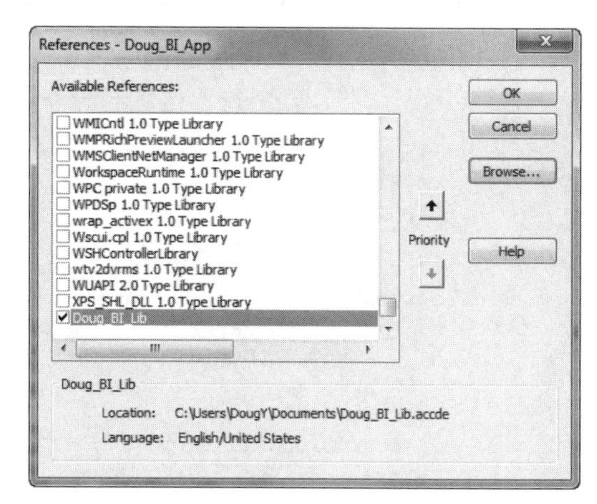

FIGURE 16-1: UDF Library Reference

When you create your own library, you need to make sure that all of your functions and subroutines have tight error handling. An unhandled error will cause the code to end abruptly. You will read more about error handling later in this chapter.

Creating a UDF

When you decide to create a UDF, you will go through the following steps:

1. Identify need.
2. Write down business rule(s).
3. Model the algorithm.
4. Write the code.

After you write the code for the UDF, the standard test cycle applies, as shown in Figure 16-2.

The code that follows illustrates examples of user-defined functions and how they are used in a database solution. The first UDF was used in a reporting solution; the second, more complex example was used in a data processing solution.

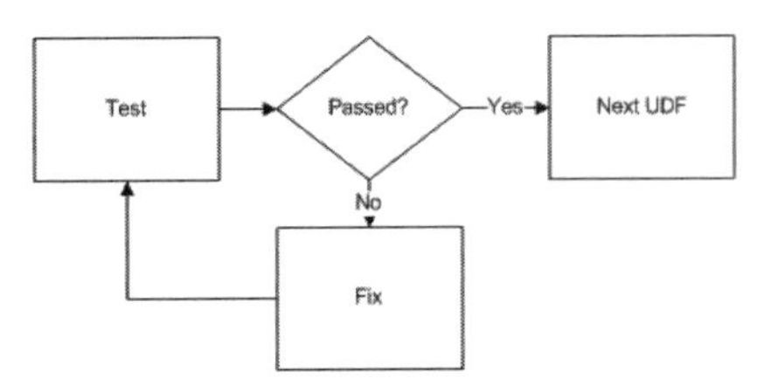

FIGURE 16-2: UDF development cycle

The reporting solution was getting a data feed from a main billing system, and the data was de-normalized in the ETL process discussed in Chapter 15. One of the challenges was to add a custom grouping that was not available in the originating system. The baseline for the grouping was a lookup table cross-referencing the insurance to the group name. However, there were a couple of exceptions: medical specialty of the doctor and specific denial type on the record. For this scenario, all factors are available for each record, which means that there is one less thing to worry about (code file: `UDF.txt Public Function pfGroup`):

```
Public Function pfGroup(strDept As String, _
    strPayor As String, strDenial As String) As String

'-------------------------------------------------------------------
' Function   : pfGroup
' Author     : DougY
' Date       : 4/1/2013
' Purpose    : Return the group name for the denial reports
' Arguments  : strDept = Clinical department = provider specialty
'              strPayor = Insurance company
'              strDenial = Denial type
'-------------------------------------------------------------------

    Dim strGroup As String
    strPayor = Replace(strPayor, "'", "")

    'assign payor team
    strGroup = Nz(DLookup("TeamName", "tblTeamsPayor", "PayorName = '" _
        & strPayor & "'"), "Commercial Non Contracted")

    'check the department for specialty specific group override
    strGroup = Nz(DLookup("TeamName", "tblDeptOverride", "Dept = '" _
        & strDept & "'"), strGroup)

    'check the denials for denial specific group override
    strGroup = Nz(DLookup("TeamName", "tblDenialOverride", "Denial = '" _
        & strDenial & "'"), strGroup)

    pfGroup = strGroup

End Function
```

The UDF was used in a query (see Figure 16-3) providing the data source for a report showing the data grouped by the values from the UDF:

```
SELECT Dept, Payor,Denial, pfGroup([Dept],[Payor],[Denial]) AS Team ...
```

The second example is from a database solution that gets data feeds from external vendor systems and needs to load them into a table for reporting. Although the files are pipe delimited text files, the challenge is that the number of fields in each record in the file will vary from 26 to 34 within the same file. Additionally, not all the data from the record is needed in the reporting solution, only selected fields.

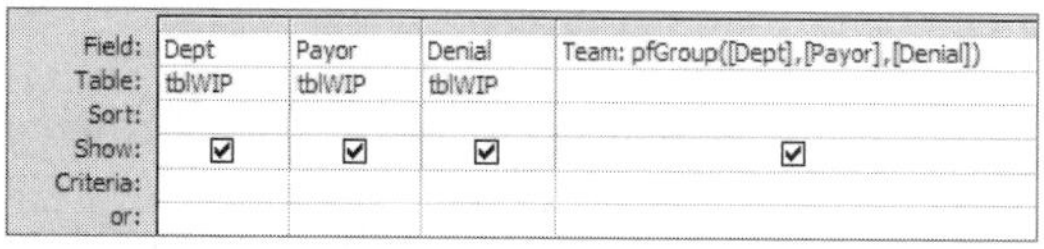

Field:	Dept	Payor	Denial	Team: pfGroup([Dept],[Payor],[Denial])
Table:	tblWIP	tblWIP	tblWIP	
Sort:				
Show:	☑	☑	☑	☑
Criteria:				
or:				

FIGURE 16-3: Using UDF in QBE

The UDF reads, processes, and appends the text file one record at a time to the table (code file: `UDF.txt Public Function ImportInvoice(strRec, strChr)`:

```
Public Function ImportInvoice(strRec, strChr)

'---------------------------------------------------------------------------
' Function   : ImportInvoice
' Author     : DougY
' Date       : 5/29/2013
' Purpose    : Return the values to be appended to the reporting table
' Arguments : strRec = A single record from the text file
'             strChr = The delimiter for the record
'---------------------------------------------------------------------------

    Dim intLen As Integer
    Dim intCounter As Integer
    Dim intLoop As Integer
    Dim arrChr() As Integer
    Dim arrValues(12) As String
    Dim varValues As Variant
    Dim strSQL As String


    'get the length of record from text file
    intLen = Len(strRec)
    'reset value of counter
    intCounter = 0

    'this loop counts how many delimiters are in the record
    For intLoop = 1 To intLen
        If Mid(strRec, intLoop, 1) = strChr Then intCounter = intCounter + 1
    Next intLoop

    ReDim arrChr(1 To intCounter)

    'reset values of variables
    intLoop = 0
    intCounter = 0

    'identify the position of the delimiters in the record
    For intLoop = 1 To intLen
        If Mid(strRec, intLoop, 1) = strChr Then
            intCounter = intCounter + 1
            arrChr(intCounter) = intLoop
        End If
```

```
Next intLoop    'intLoop = 1 To intLen

'capture the values needed from the record
'we don't need to capture all the data from the text record
'based on the specifications we know what fields we want to capture
'we use the position of the delimiters to read the value we need
arrValues(1) = "'" & _
    Mid(strRec, arrChr(3) + 1, arrChr(4) - arrChr(3) - 1) & "'"
arrValues(2) = "'" & _
    Mid(strRec, arrChr(4) + 1, arrChr(5) - arrChr(4) - 1) & "'"
arrValues(3) = "'" & _
    Mid(strRec, arrChr(10) + 1, arrChr(11) - arrChr(10) - 1) & "'"
arrValues(4) = "'" & _
    Mid(strRec, arrChr(17) + 1, arrChr(18) - arrChr(17) - 1) & "'"
arrValues(5) = "'" & _
    Mid(strRec, arrChr(18) + 1, arrChr(19) - arrChr(18) - 1) & "'"
arrValues(6) = "'" & _
    Mid(strRec, arrChr(20) + 1, arrChr(21) - arrChr(20) - 1) & "'"
arrValues(7) = "'" & _
    Mid(strRec, arrChr(21) + 1, arrChr(22) - arrChr(21) - 1) & "'"
arrValues(8) = "'" & _
    Mid(strRec, arrChr(22) + 1, arrChr(23) - arrChr(22) - 1) & "'"
arrValues(9) = "'" & _
    Mid(strRec, arrChr(23) + 1, arrChr(24) - arrChr(23) - 1) & "'"

'in EDI, the record terminates if there is no data in the
  'last field(s) without delimiters
'the following code blocks test to see if there are additional fields we
 'need to capture into the table
If UBound(arrChr) = 32 Then
    arrValues(10) = "'" & _
        Mid(strRec, arrChr(31) + 1, arrChr(32) - arrChr(31) - 1) & "'"
    arrValues(11) = "'" & _
        Mid(strRec, arrChr(32) + 1) & "'"
End If  'UBound(arrChr) = 32

If UBound(arrChr) = 33 Then
    arrValues(10) = "'" & _
        Mid(strRec, arrChr(31) + 1, arrChr(32) - arrChr(31) - 1) & "'"
    arrValues(11) = "'" & _
        Mid(strRec, arrChr(32) + 1, arrChr(33) - arrChr(32) - 1) & "'"
    arrValues(12) = "'" & _
        Mid(strRec, arrChr(33) + 1) & "'"
End If  'UBound(arrChr) = 33

If UBound(arrChr) > 33 Then
    arrValues(10) = "'" & _
        Mid(strRec, arrChr(31) + 1, arrChr(32) - arrChr(31) - 1) & "'"
    arrValues(11) = "'" & _
        Mid(strRec, arrChr(32) + 1, arrChr(33) - arrChr(32) - 1) & "'"
    arrValues(12) = "'" & _
        Mid(strRec, arrChr(33) + 1, arrChr(34) - arrChr(33) - 1) & "'"
End If  'UBound(arrChr) > 33
```

```
        'concatenate the values captured above into a single string for the
        'append query
        varValues = arrValues(1) & ", " & arrValues(2) & ", " & _
                        arrValues(3) & ", " & arrValues(4) & ", " & _
                        arrValues(5) & ", " & arrValues(6) & ", " & _
                        arrValues(7) & ", " & arrValues(8) & ", " & arrValues(9)

        'test for additional fields if thet exist
        If Nz(arrValues(10), "") = "" Then      '25
            varValues = varValues & ", '', '', ''"
        ElseIf Nz(arrValues(12), "") = "" Then  '32
            varValues = varValues & ", " & arrValues(10) & ", " & _
                arrValues(11) & ", ''"
        Else                                    '33
            varValues = varValues & ", " & arrValues(10) & ", " & _
            arrValues(11) & ", " & arrValues(12)
        End If 'arrValue(#) values

        'create the SQL to insert teh records to teh table
        strSQL = "INSERT INTO tblInvoiceData" & _
                        " (SaleDate, InvoiceDate, Company," & _
                        " ClientID, ClientFirstName, ClientLastName," & _
                        " SaleFromDate, SaleToDate, InvoiceAmount," & _
                        " ErrorCode, ErrorMEssage, ErrorData)" & _
                    " SELECT " & varValues & ";"

        CurrentDb.Execute strSQL, dbFailOnError

    End Function
```

Although this UDF does not return a value to the user, it returns the values of the data that need to be appended to the reporting table.

As you can see from the two examples, UDF is a powerful tool you can deploy to make your solution powerful and useful for your business. Your ability to develop complex UDFs in Access to support the business rules will ensure that the solution does right by you and the users.

Error Handling

Despite your best efforts, errors will happen, whether they are due to less than optimal design, changes to programs, devices or the network, or a myriad of other factors. Whatever the reason for the error, you need to handle it properly in your code to avoid or minimize impact to the users and data.

When an error occurs in your Access database solution without an error handling routine, the user will typically get an error message similar to the one in Figure 16-3. While the error numbers and descriptions vary, the option of debugging is there, which allows the user to get to the code behind the solution (see Figures 16-4 and 16-5).

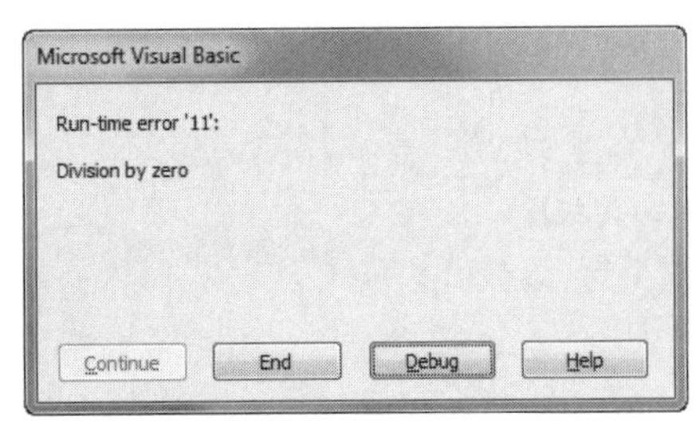

FIGURE 16-4: Un-handled error message

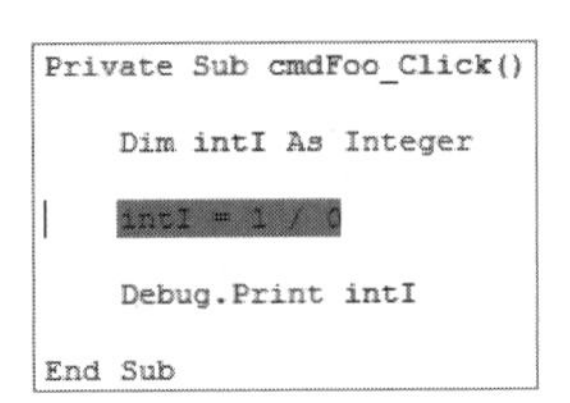

FIGURE 16-5: Highlighted error in VBA

This is an undesired result that can lead to serious consequences. Users should not be in the code of the database; they should only be interacting through the user interface that you provided.

To handle an error, you need to add an error handling routine to your code. Every procedure and every function should have the routine in it because you never know where an error can happen. Depending on the situation, routines can include several features in addition to error trapping. They can provide a message to the user, log the error, send a message to the developer or other party, move the user to a different part of the application, and in rare events, they can even be used to graciously close the program.

The error handling routine can be as simple as exiting the current code gracefully (code file: (`ErrorHandling.txt Private Sub cmdFoo_Click 1`):

```
Private Sub cmdFoo_Click()

On Error GoTo ErrorTrap

    Dim intI As Integer
    intI = 1 / 0
    Debug.Print intI

ErrorTrap:
    Exit Sub

End Sub
```

In the preceding sample, when an error occurs (and it will, you cannot divide by 0), the code will go to the label ErrorTrap and it will perform the code written immediately after it to exit the subroutine.

> **NOTE** *You create a label by adding a colon after the label name (for example,* `ErrorTrap:`*). The VBE will left-align the label name with the procedure header and footer.*

While this error handling routine will prevent the users from seeing any error messages, it is not useful for either you, as a the developer, or the user. From the user's prospective, everything went well, but nothing happened. That will cause frustration and eventually lead to help tickets that are scanty on details yet filled with irritation. From your perspective, you do not know what error has occurred and where exactly. Without that information you cannot fix the code or modify it to support changes outside of the control of your solution.

The code snippet that follows shows a more robust error handling routine. The code for the `ErrorTrap` label will let the user know about the error, and it will provide instructions on what to do next. In this case, contact the support department with the information about the error. Figure 16-6 shows what the custom messagebox looks like to the user (code file: `ErrorHandling.txt Private Sub cmdFoo_Click 2`):

```
Private Sub Foo_Click()

10     On Error GoTo ErrorTrap

           Dim lngI As Long
20         lngI = 1 / 0
30         Debug.Print lngI

ExitMe:
40         Exit Sub

ErrorTrap:
50         MsgBox "An Error occurred" & vbCrLf _
           & "Please send an Email to the Support Department:" & vbCrLf _
           & "Support@BeInformedConsulting.com" & vbCrLf _
           & "Include the error, the code segment, and the line number" _
           & vbCrLf _
           & vbCrLf _
           & "Error:  " & Err.Number & " -- " & Err.Description & vbCrLf _
           & "Code Segment:Test - Form_frmTestMe - cmdFoo_Click" & vbCrLf _
           & "Line number:  " & Erl, _
           vbOKOnly + vbInformation, "Error Information"

       60    Resume ExitMe

End Sub
```

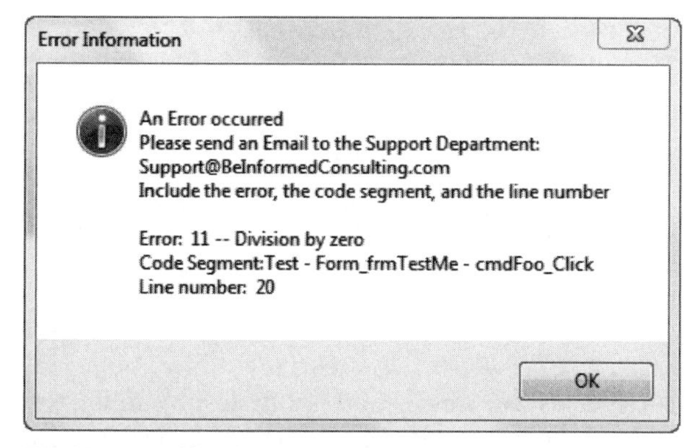

FIGURE 16-6: Handled error message

> **NOTE** *No doubt you noticed the line numbers in the code. VBA is a descendant of BASIC. As such, it retained some of the features of BASIC, such as line numbering. Unlike BASIC, you are not required to number the code lines in VBA. However, it is a handy feature that will help you pinpoint where the error occurred. If you want the* `Erl` *in the code to return a value other than 0, you must use line numbers in your code. You can read more about tools that will help you with line numbering and other coding features in the section after the error handling.*

Receiving e-mails from users with information about the error, helps you support the solution. However, unless you log every error you get from the users, it will be hard to analyze the database solution to see if there is a hot spot that requires extra attention.

The code sample that follows shows an error handling routine that logs the information about the error in a table. Storing the data allows you to review and analyze it to identify patterns (code file: `ErrorHandling.txt Private Sub cmdFoo_Click 3`):

```
Private Sub cmdFoo_Click()

10     On Error GoTo ErrorTrap

           Dim lngI As Long
20         lngI = 1 / 0
30         Debug.Print lngI

ExitMe:
40       Exit Sub

ErrorTrap:

           Dim strErrSQL As String
50         strErrSQL = "INSERT INTO tblErrors(ErrorNumber, " & _
                 "ErrorDescription, CodeSegment, LineNumber)" & _
                 " SELECT " & Err.Number & ", '" & _
                     Replace(Err.Description, "'", "") & "', '" _
                     & Me.Name & "|" & Me.ActiveControl.Name & "', " & Erl
60         CurrentDb.Execute strErrSQL, dbFailOnError

70       MsgBox "An Error occurred and had been logged" & vbCrLf _
         & "Please notify the Support Department:" & vbCrLf _
         & "Support@BeInformedConsulting.com", _
         vbOKOnly + vbInformation, "Error Information"

80     Resume ExitMe

End Sub
```

The code stores the data in a table with the seven fields listed here. This is a basic table to log errors. You can use additional fields and values to meet your needs, such as User ID, PC Name, IP address, and so on.

- Primary key
- Error Number
- Error Description
- Code Segment
- Line Number
- Error Date — defaults to `Date()`
- Error Time — defaults to `Time()`

The code segment is a concatenation of the form name and the active control name.

You can also have an e-mail sent to you, or to the help desk, indicating that an error has occurred in the solution. This ensures that you know there is an error and that you don't have to rely on the users to notify you (code file: `ErrorHandling.txt Private Sub cmdFoo_Click 4`):

```
Private Sub cmdFoo_Click()

10    On Error GoTo ErrorTrap

          Dim lngI As Long
20        lngI = 1 / 0
30        Debug.Print lngI

ExitMe:
40       Exit Sub

ErrorTrap:

          Dim strErrSQL As String

50        strErrSQL = "INSERT INTO tblErrors(ErrorNumber, " & _
                "ErrorDescription, CodeSegment, LineNumber)" & _
                " SELECT " & Err.Number & ", '" & _
                    Replace(Err.Description, "'", "") & "', '" _
                    & Me.Name & "|" & Me.ActiveControl.Name & "', " & Erl
60        CurrentDb.Execute strErrSQL, dbFailOnError

70        DoCmd.SendObject acSendNoObject, "", "", _
                "Support@BeInformedConsulting.com" _
               , , , "Training Tracking - Error Alert", _
                "Error:  " & ErrorNumber & " -- " & ErrorDescription & vbCrLf _
               & "Database: " & CurrentDb.Name & vbCrLf _
               & "Form Name: " & Me.Name & vbCrLf _
               & "Procedure Name:  " & Me.ActiveControl.Name & vbCrLf _
               & "Line number:  " & Erl, True

80    Resume ExitMe

End Sub
```

You should add the error handling routine after you have designed and tested your code. When you test run your solution and you encounter an error, you need to be able to debug the code, and error handling circumvents that option. If you already added the error handling, it will gracefully exit you from the subroutine without allowing you to enter a debug mode to identify the error and the solution.

Another way to handle error handling routines is to create an error handling process UDF. In your code, you will call the error handling UDF and pass the parameters you want to capture to the function. You can also include an argument to tell the process how to handle an error.

Third-Party Tools

As mentioned, you can use third-party tools to help you code faster and to access features such as line numbering that otherwise will be tedious to add. Two popular tools that can provide valuable functionality and time-saving support are MZ-Tools and FMS Inc.'s Total Access CodeTools. Both tools offer some similar features like line numbering, naming convention, and code template, which are useful for adding error handling routines and other common functions into your code and much more. A major difference is that one is freeware and the other is a commercial product. MZ-Tools is a freeware add-on you can download and install on your PC. Total Access CodeTools is a commercial product that you will need to purchase. You can read more about each product on their prospective websites:

- `http://www.mztools.com/index.aspx`
- `http://www.fmsinc.com/MicrosoftAccess/VBACodingTools.html`

Debugging

As you develop your database solution, you will test your code to make sure it's performing to your expectations. If it doesn't, you will go through the debugging process to identify the errors and correct them. There are a few debugging methods and tools available to you in Access VBE. This section provides a brief review to both refresh your knowledge and, we hope, to add some techniques to your repertoire.

You can write to the Immediate window in VBE as part of your code by either using the `Debug.Print` command or typing directly in it. When your code is in break mode, you can use `?MyVariableName` to see the value of the variable. And, if you are creating a query on the fly using VBA, a good way to see and test the query script is to break the code after the SQL variable is valued. Then, print the SQL to the immediate window using `?strMySQL`; you can then copy the SQL string and paste it into the QBE to see if you parsed the query correctly.

In addition to the `Debug.Print`, you can use the `Debug.Assert` command in your code. `Debug.Assert` conditionally suspends the execution of your code at the `Debug.Assert` line. Even though it's a good debugging tool, you should make sure to remove the `Debug.Assert` command before putting a solution into production. `Debug.Assert` will halt the program abruptly and without an explanation.

Breakpoints enable you to pause the code execution. They are particularly useful for checking the values of variables at a given point. While the code is paused, you can test and review what the code is doing. You can set a breakpoint on any line of code with the exception of lines with `Dim` statements and comments.

While in debug mode, pressing the F5 key will continue the code execution to its completion or to the next breakpoint. Pressing F8 will step through the code allowing you to review each step.

Pressing the F8 key executes the code one line at a time for executable lines. That includes any procedures or functions the current procedure calls. If you want to stay in the current routine, pressing Shift+F8 enables you to skip the steps of the called routine. If your code has one procedure calling another one or you have nested procedures, you may benefit from using the Call Stack dialog box. The Call Stack displays the list of the current active procedures while you are in break (debug) mode. This can be helpful if you are trying to determine where the (wrong) data may be originating from.

When you are dealing with a large volume of variables, stepping through the code may not be the most efficient way to debug. This is where the Locals window can be handy. The Locals window displays all the variables in a procedure along with their values. Using the Locals windows, you can see the value changes in the variable as you step through the code. The Locals window retains the values of the variables until the code has been executed.

The Watch window is also helpful when debugging. Using the Watch window enables you to keep an eye on a variable in your code routine. You can use it to automatically switch to debugging mode when there is a change to the value of the variable or when the variable is `True`. You can also use it to watch the expression without pausing the code, much like the Locals window, except the Watch window will only display the selected variable.

LEVERAGING QUERIES

Any database solution that you design will include queries to support collecting, displaying, and manipulating the data. Being able to effectively query the data is arguably as important as creating the proper table structure. Understanding how to improve your queries will go a long way toward being able to provide an efficient, useful solution to your users.

In this section, you will read about enhancing the query efficiency, complex query concepts, and how to let your users generate the filter to the queries using forms. You will also read about creating a query on the fly in VBA using values in the UI and system values.

Enhancing Query Techniques

You can quickly turn a relative straightforward query into a powerful, customized tool just by adding the right criteria, recordsources, and joins. The following examples show how to create and modify various types of queries to fit a variety of real-world scenarios. The discussions explain how you can modify the queries and SQL statements to fit your business rules.

Sargable Query

Sargable is an old term referring to the query efficiency. Your query is sargable if the database engine you are using can take advantage of the indexes to execute the query faster. Like a lot of terms in the computer world, sargable is a contraction, in this case contracting the words Search Argument.

Although today's computers are much more powerful than they were years ago, the concept is still applicable. When you create a query, you want the results as fast as possible. You don't want your users to have a sense of lag.

While creating a sargable query is beneficial in any database, the benefits are more noticeable with passthrough queries.

There are two general rules you should pay attention to when creating the `WHERE` clause:

- Avoid using `NOT`.
- You should put the column by itself on the left side of the operator. For example, `MyDate Between #1/1/2013# and 1/31/2013#`.

Here is an example of a non-sargable query even though the criteria is on the indexed field, `RecordDate`:

```
SELECT *
FROM     MyTable
WHERE    Year(RecordDate) = 2013;
```

When the RDBM engine executes that query, it cannot take advantage of the index on `RecordDate` and it will not be able to perform an indexed search. Modifying the `WHERE` clause slightly will return the same results much faster (code file: `Queries.txt Sargable`):

```
WHERE    RecordDate Between #1/1/2013# And #12/31/2013#;
```

In addition to `BETWEEN`, other sargable operators are: `=`, `>`, `<`, `>=`, `<=`, and `LIKE` with a trailing wildcard. Non-sargable operators include `<>`, `NOT IN`, `OR`, and other `LIKE` conditions.

You can experience the difference by testing with the following examples — using your own data and field names. If you change the `WHERE` clause to use a sargable operator, `>=`, the second query will be faster (code file: `Queries.txt Sargable2`):

```
SELECT * FROM MyTable
WHERE DATEDIFF("d", RecordDate, Date()) <= 7;

SELECT * FROM MyTable
WHERE RecordDate >= DATEADD("D",-7,DATE());
```

While it may not always be possible to make your query sargable, you should try. Sargable conditions can be low-hanging fruit that will help you offer your users a fine-tuned solution. It is worth your time to pay attention to it as you develop the queries to your solution or when you are investigating performance issues with it. You took the time to add indexes to your table, so take the time to use them and write your queries to take advantage of them.

> **NOTE** *If you are writing queries directly in SQL Server Management Studio, you can use the Estimated Execution Plan to identify bottlenecks in the query execution.*

Frustrated Join

Although "frustrated join" may not be common terminology, it is recognized as describing a join or query that has certain types of restrictive criteria, such as `NOT IN`. Now that we've introduced it, we will continue to use it when discussing such scenarios. There are the times when you want to report all the records from one table that do not have a matching record in another table. One way to do this is to use a query such as this one (code file: `Queries.txt FrustratedJoin`):

```
SELECT
PatientID
, PatientName
FROM
  tblPatients
WHERE
  PatientID NOT IN
 (SELECT PatientID
  FROM   tblAppointments);
```

It can work, and in a smaller dataset it may even perform adequately. However, run this kind of a query against a medium or larger size dataset and you will experience the slow performance consequences of using the `NOT IN()` clause, making it a non-sargable query. A better way to get the data is to use an outer join between the tables (code file: `Queries.txt OuterJoin`):

```
SELECT
  P.PatientID
, P.PatientName
FROM
  tblPatients P
Left Join
  tblAppointments A
ON
  P.PatientID = A.PatientID
WHERE
  A.PatientID IS NULL;
```

The left join indicates that you want all the records from `tblPatient` with or without a matching record in the `tblAppointment`. You "frustrate" the join by using a `WHERE` clause to limit the records the query is returning to those where there are no matching records in `tblAppointments`.

Sometimes you can get better performance by using `NOT EXISTS()`, as shown here (code file: `Queries.txt Exists`):

```
SELECT
  PatientID
, PatientName
FROM
  tblPatients
WHERE
  NOT EXIST
  (SELECT NULL
   FROM tblAppointments
   WHERE tblAppointment. PatientID = tblPatients.PatientID);
```

The NOT EXISTS() operator usually performs better than the NOT IN() operator, and it may show a slight improvement over the frustrated join. It varies by scenario, so you should test your data to see which is better suited for a given situation.

Complex Queries

Complex queries can be invaluable for collecting, compiling, and manipulating data from multiple tables. They are particularly helpful in situations where it is not possible to collect the data with just one query. You'll use them with financial reports, invoices, grouping and reporting data by region/contact/salesperson, and a myriad of other places. In some cases, they can be used in lieu of a work table. One of the common questions that a business might ask is: "What were the most widgets produced per day in each month of the last quarter?" Not a complex question, and it can be computed using an aggregate query, grouping by month or production date, and looking for the MAX() number of widgets, as shown here (code file: Queries.txt Complex1):

```
SELECT
  Month(ProductionDate) AS ProductionPeriod
, Max(Widgets) AS Produced
FROM
  tblWidgetProduction
WHERE
  ProductionDate >= DATEADD("q",-1,Date());
GROUP BY
  Month(ProductionDate);
```

What if, in addition to the highest number of widgets produced, you need to report the employee name and the date that employee produced the most widgets? This is where things become a bit trickier.

You cannot just aggregate by employee, as that will return the maximum widgets produced each month by each employee. Although that is valuable information, it is not what the user requested. Nor can you aggregate by production date; you will return a record for each date of production, which again is not what was requested.

One way to provide the information is to use the aggregate query you wrote previously and join it to the transaction data to get the detail record associated with the data the aggregate query returned, as shown in the following SQL statement. In the chapter download files, you can also see a version of this query in query design view. The graphic display makes it easy to see that this is a complex query that uses an aggregate query as part of the data source (code file: Queries.txt Complex2):

```
SELECT DT.*
FROM
(SELECT
  Month(P.ProductionDate) AS ProductionPeriod
, P.ProductionDate
, E.FullName
, P.Widgets AS Produced
FROM tblWidgetProduction AS P
INNER JOIN
  tblEmployees AS E
```

```
ON
  P.EmployeeID = E.EmployeeID
WHERE
  ProductionDate >= DATEADD("q",-1,Date())) AS DT
INNER JOIN
(SELECT
    Month(ProductionDate) AS ProductionPeriod
  , Max(Widgets) AS Produced
 FROM tblWidgetProduction
WHERE
  ProductionDate >= DATEADD("q",-1,Date())
 GROUP BY
    Month(ProductionDate)) AS Mx
ON  DT.ProductionPeriod = Mx.ProductionPeriod
AND DT.Widgets = Mx.Produced;
```

Another way to accomplish the same results is to use a query with a frustrated self-outer join. The query does not use any aggregate function but rather joins the transaction table to itself in order to identify the record to report (code file: `Queries.txt Complex3`):

```
SELECT
  Month(P.ProductionDate) AS ProductionPeriod
, P.ProductionDate
, E.FullName
, P.Widgets AS Produced
FROM
  (tblWidgetProduction AS P
INNER JOIN
  tblEmployees AS E
ON P.EmployeeID = E.EmployeeID)
LEFT JOIN
  tblWidgetProduction AS W
ON (P.Widgets < W.Widgets)
  AND (Month(P.ProductionDate) = Month(W.ProductionDate))
WHERE
  ProductionDate >= DATEADD("q",-1,Date())
AND
  W.Widgets IS NULL;
```

The query uses a frustrated join to itself, matching each record to all other records in the table on the same month of activity. When the periods match, the query joins the data on the number of widgets produced, looking for an inequitable value, in this case less than (<). The `WHERE` clause filters out all the records where the number of widgets is less than the record you are evaluating. The record with the most widgets in each month is retained and reported back.

The two methods shown can be used to report the record with the most (`MAX()`) or with the least (`MIN()`) value of widgets per the desired grouping. You can modify and incorporate this into your solutions.

Exists () Subquery

You use the `Exists()` subquery to check for the existence of values in a resulting dataset. (See the snippet that follows.) It is a `Boolean` data type so it will return a value of `True` or `False` to indicate if any records contain the value (`True`); otherwise, it will be `False`. Keep in mind that it will not return data or even tell you how many records meet the criteria (code file: `Queries.txt Exists1`):

```
SELECT
  PatientID
, PatientName
FROM
  tblPatients AS P
WHERE
  EXISTS
  (SELECT
     PatientID
   FROM
     tblClaims C
   WHERE
     P.PatientID = C.PatientID);
```

> **NOTE** *A subquery joined to the main query, as in the preceding code, is called a correlated query.*

You can reverse the `Exists() Boolean` by using the `NOT` operator in front of the `Exists()` subquery. If we continue with the earlier scenario, the following snippet will return a list of patients that do not have a claim in the system (code file: `Queries.txt ExistsNot`):

```
SELECT
  PatientID
, PatientName
FROM
  tblPatients AS P
WHERE
  NOT EXISTS
  (SELECT
     PatientID
   FROM
     tblClaims C
   WHERE
     P.PatientID = C.PatientID);
```

The Cartesian Product

The Cartesian product join can be used with a `Select` query to return all possible combinations of all rows in all tables in the query. For example, if you query the two tables, `tabPatients` and `tblClaims`, without any `WHERE` clause qualification or any join between the tables, the result (all patient records combined with all claim records) will be a Cartesian product. The SQL example is shown here; if viewed in query design grid (QBE), you will notice that there is no join line between the two tables (code file: `Queries.txt Cartesian`):

```
SELECT
  P.PatientID
, P.PatientName
, C.ClaimDate
, C.ClaimAmount
FROM
tblPatients AS P
tblClaims AS C;
```

There are several scenarios where it is beneficial to generate a Cartesian product. If you are testing, you can create a large volume of test data in an expedited manner or stress test your database solution. In production or sales, a Cartesian join can be used to list each product with each color, size, or other feature. However, as a rule, it is not a good thing and is more often inadvertent than by intent. The resulting dataset can overwhelm the system and the user. Even with intentional use, it is important to always properly qualify both the joins and filtering criteria. A Cartesian join on two tables, each with one thousand records, will return one million rows.

Upsert Operation

The `Upsert` operation updates records in a table based on a defined `WHERE` clause, or inserts new records if the `WHERE` clause is not met using a single SQL statement.

You can use an outer join query to perform an `Upsert` operation against the outer table. This operation is handy when you want to synchronize records between two tables while also inserting new rows because it essentially handles both processes simultaneously.

> **NOTE** *As you can see from the word* `UPSERT`*, the operation's name is a combination of* `UPDATE` *and* `INSERT`*, referring to the dual action performed by the query.*

One of the preferred approaches for using the `Upsert` operation is to test for the existence of the records before updating them. If the records do not exist, you will insert the data (code file: `Queries.txt Upsert 1`):

```
If DCount("*", "tblAppointments", "PatientID = 41") = 0 Then
    CurrentDB.Execute "SQL for Insert Query", dbFailOnError
Else
    CurrentDB.Execute "SQL for Update Query", dbFailOnError
End If
```

With the `Upsert` operation, you can perform the two steps in one query by using a left join between the two tables, as shown in the following snippet using `tblPatients` and `tblAppointments` (code file: `Queries.txt Upsert 2`):

```
UPDATE
  tblPatients
LEFT JOIN
  tblAppointments
ON
```

```
    tblPatients.PatientID = tblAppointments.PatientID
  SET
    tblAppointments.AppointmentDate = #5/29/2013#
  , tblAppointments.PatientID = [tblPatients].[PatientID]
  WHERE (((tblPatients.PatientID) In (17,41,42,105)));
```

If patients have an appointment date, the query will update the date. If the patient does not have an appointment, the appropriate records will be added with the appointment date.

The `Upsert` query will work only if you are using Access tables. You cannot run it against linked SQL Server tables. However, if you are writing T-SQL queries and you are using SQL Server 2008 or higher, you can use the `MERGE` command, as shown in the snippet that follows, to have essentially the same functionality as the Access `Upsert` operation (code file: `Queries.txt Upsert3`):

```
USE [MyDatabase]
GO
MERGE INTO tblAppointments as Target
USING tblPatients as Source
ON Target.PatientID = Source.PatientID
WHEN MATCHED THEN
UPDATE SET Target.AppointmentDate = '2013-05-29'
WHEN NOT MATCHED THEN
INSERT (PatientID,AppointmentDate) VALUES (Source.PatientID, '2013-05-29')
```

Query by Form

In most Access solutions, you do not want the users to have direct access to the structure of the database: tables and queries. That's why you create intuitive forms and reports to allow users to navigate through the data. You can further empower the user by giving them tools to query and filter the data to meet their needs. A query that is managed via a form is called, not surprisingly, Query by Form, also known as QBF. In addition to allowing users to select the values they want to filter on, the QBF also allows you to control and validate the data the users enter.

The user interface controls for the Query by Form can be any control that allows the user to either enter or select a value. This can be a textbox, a list box, combo boxes, checkboxes, or radio buttons. If you'd like, you can also use a toggle.

When creating the QBF, it is a good practice to show users the available data values for them to filter or select from. This ensures that there will be records in the returned dataset after they submit the query. This in turn alleviates frustrations and the perception that the database is not working just because no data is returned.

List boxes and combo boxes are two of the best controls for allowing users to view and select data filters. You can further manage the data displayed by tailoring the query used for the Row Source of the control. Depending on the scenario, you can show additional fields to help with the user selection, adjust the sort order, show or hide active/inactive records, or whatever meets your needs. Of course, this is another place to leverage the benefits of foreign keys; you can show the users the description from the lookup table while passing the actual ID value to the query.

Both types of controls work well with the cascading controls concept. You will usually hear the term "cascading combo boxes," but the concept applies equally to the List box control, as well as other control types. And you can also use a combination of control types in the cascading chain. Essentially, after you select the value, or values, in the first control, the data returned from the `row-source` of the second control is cascaded to show only values based on what is selected in the first control.

This is accomplished by creating the `rowsource` of the second control on the fly using the value from the first combo box. As you can see in Figures 16-7 and 16-8, selecting the value in the Filter/Search By combo box will show the available Document Type values in the Select A Filter Val combo box.

FIGURE 16-7: Cascading combo boxes — before selecting Filter/Search By value

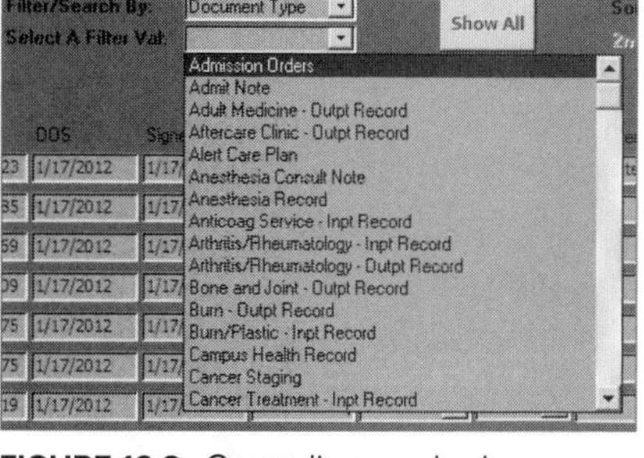

FIGURE 16-8: Cascading combo boxes — available Document Type values

The basic code for cascading controls is shown here. It uses `tblColors` and `tblCars`. `tblCars` has an FK field with `ColorID`. The code will filter the values available in the `cboCars` based on the value of the color chosen from `cboColors` (code file: `Querie.txt CascadeBoxes`):

```
Private Sub cboColors_AfterUpdate()

    Dim strRS As String

    strRS = "SELECT [CarID], [CarName] " & _
        "FROM tblCars WHERE [tblCars].[fkColorID] = " & _
        Me.cboColors.Column(0) & " ORDER BY [CarName];"

    Me.cboCars.RowSource = strRS
    Me.cboCars.Requery

End Sub
```

Another benefit of QBF is that you can use the UI to communicate to the users about the data they are selecting, thereby allowing users to quickly preview and modify their search criteria. Figure 16-9 shows a form that allows users to select data for their report by choosing between current data, records up to one year old, and archived data. Because users typically want to see reports on current data, there is no need to query several years of records every time. This method eliminates performance issues by allowing the user to limit the records retrieved to just the current year.

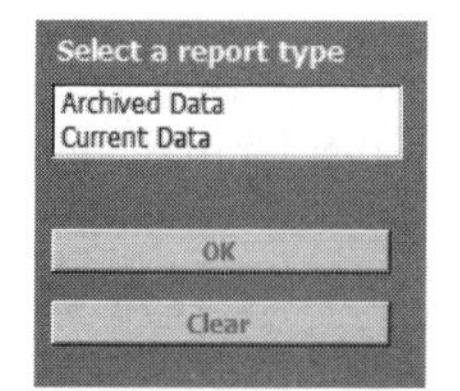

FIGURE 16-9: Filtering the dataset

You can further enhance the QBF by indicating the minimum or maximum of what is available — such as the latest sales week, the oldest month, and so on. For example, if the user needs to select the date range for a report, you can inform them of the earliest date available, as shown in Figure 16-10. The date is displayed in the upper-right corner, and appears in red font in the actual solution.

Although you cannot always use cascading controls, you can use other methods to allow users to display, filter, and select data. One way to reduce user anxiety is to let users know when the values they selected will not return any records. The list boxes in Figure 16-10 show all possible values the users can filter on, but that does not guarantee that their criteria will result in having anything to report. In that case, the solution will return a messagebox informing the user that no records were found.

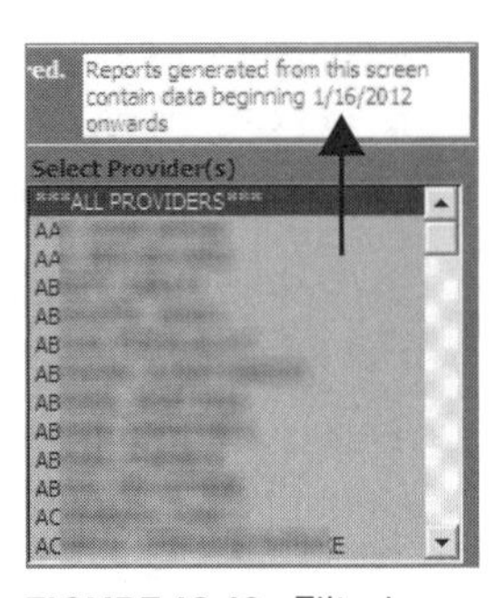

FIGURE 16-10: Filtering the dataset

The following snippet shows how to do this by testing for the number of records, using the domain aggregate `DCount()`. If the result is `0`, it will generate a messagebox telling the user that no records were found (code file: `Queries.txt_CascadeBoxes 2`):

```
Private Sub cboColors_AfterUpdate()

    Dim strRS As String

    strRS = "SELECT [CarID], [CarName] " & _
        "FROM tblCars WHERE [tblCars].[fkColorID] = " & _
        Me.cboColors.Column(0) & " ORDER BY [CarName];"

    If DCount("[CarID]", "tblCars", "fkColorID = " & _
        Me.cboColors.Column(0)) = 0 Then
        MsgBox "No Records Found. Please select another color"
        Exit Sub
    End If

    Me.cboCars.RowSource = strRS
    Me.cboCars.Requery

End Sub
```

As you can see, QBF is a powerful tool that you can use, customize, and apply to a myriad of scenarios. When you provide the users with QBF and filtering options, it makes their interaction with the data effective and productive. The more the user can do, the more opportunities they will see. It is amazing what you can accomplish by incorporating various tools and techniques as you enhance the database and the user experience.

Creating a Query On the Fly Using VBA

Sometimes you will want or need to construct a query on the fly based on the data the user enters in the forms or on system event information, such as from an error handling routine. When constructing the query SQL, you will need to write the framework for the script and fill it with the variables you want to capture and use.

If you look at the snippet that follows from the last error handling example, you will notice that the code is creating a query to append the error data into a table for future analysis:

```
<...snip>
          Dim strErrSQL As String

50        strErrSQL = "INSERT INTO tblErrors(ErrorNumber, " & _
                 "ErrorDescription, CodeSegment, LineNumber)" & _
                 " SELECT " & Err.Number & ", '" & _
                   Replace(Err.Description, "'", "") & "', '" _
                   & Me.Name & "|" & Me.ActiveControl.Name & "', " & Erl
60        CurrentDb.Execute strErrSQL, dbFailOnError
<...snip>
```

As you see in the following code snippet, the framework of the query includes literal text values in the double quotes:

```
"INSERT INTO tblErrors(ErrorNumber, " & _
"ErrorDescription, CodeSegment, LineNumber)" & _
" SELECT "
```

This is the actual text you are typing to create this query. The literal test will not change when you execute the routine unless you go back to the VBA code and change it.

The second part of constructing the query is to add the variables to the SQL you are creating (code file: `Queries.txt QueriesOnTheFly`):

```
& Err.Number & ", '" & Replace(Err.Description, "'", "") & _
 "', '" & Me.Name & "|" & Me.ActiveControl.Name & "', " & Erl
```

Each of those variables can hold a different value for the different errors that occur on different forms and from different lines of code. You will add the variable to the SQL script along with concatenating the appropriate delimiters for the data type to each variable.

Each data type requires a specific delimiter to indicate the data type to the RDBMS engine. In VBA, you need to use the delimiters in Table 16-2.

TABLE 16-2: Data Delimiters in VBA

DATA TYPE	DELIMITER
`String`	'
`Date`	#
Number (any)	None

> **NOTE** *Although Access QBE uses doubles quotes in the* `WHERE` *clause to indicate a text value, it will accept single quotes. In VBA, double quotes are reserved to indicate to the system that you are passing a literal value. Additionally, in VBA you use a single quote in the beginning of a sentence to indicate a comment.*

Looking at the preceding example of the error handling code, you will see that the `Err.Number` and `Erl` variables are not surrounded by delimiters, while `Err.Description`, `Me.Name`, and `Me.AdctiveControl.Name` are surrounded by single quote delimiters.

When the error handling routine for the sample procedure is executed by the error (division by zero), the SQL string your code creates will look like this:

```
INSERT INTO tblErrors(ErrorNumber, ErrorDescription, CodeSegment, LineNumber)
SELECT 11, 'Division by zero', 'frmTestMe|cmdFoo', 20
```

You can use these methods to construct different queries to support error trapping. The second UDF is another good example to use as a model. You can modify the function to our scenario and identify the values that you need to append to a table and concatenate them into a single variable. When the values are set, you can use the variable with the query framework to execute the append query.

One of the best ways to learn, experiment, and see what is happening is to use the QBE. With query design view, you can quickly add tables, adjust joins, set criteria, and preview the results. Then, you can view the SQL view. When you have things set, you can copy and paste the SQL into the code. This gives you a jump start, and will get you to where you need to parse the literal text and insert the variables you want to use to collect and pass the values to the final query.

You will also find examples using QBF in Chapters 17 and 18 on Forms and Reports, respectively. Each chapter includes a different technique that leverages QBF to allow the user to select and customize reports. These examples demonstrate how powerful QBF and a little code can be.

API

Application Programming Interfaces (APIs) allow you to extend VBA code by using external libraries that are not part of native VBA. The term "API" can be used to refer to nearly any library or framework. The Windows operating system APIs, the Google Maps API, ESPN's API for gathering sports information, and the entire .NET framework are all examples; the .NET framework in and of itself can be considered an API or as sets of APIs. APIs come in a few different flavors, such as those provided as COM components and used through ActiveX controls or other object types, those that are used via HTTP Requests, and those that reside in DLL, EXE, and LIB files and require a special syntax to declare and run from your VBA code.

The power of the API is that it provides nearly endless opportunities to extend the reach of your Access solution. The Windows APIs allow you to manipulate windows, controls, devices, and system parameters. Using APIs, in addition to controlling window properties such as size and position, you can even control the transparency of an Access form by combining several API functions. Driver software for printers must use Windows API functions to interact with the system for print jobs, so by extension, you have this and other low-level functionalities available to you as well. Other APIs provided by companies such as Google, Yahoo, Weather Underground, or VideoLAN may allow you to manage maps, documents, profiles, weather data, or playback and recording of media. You can even write your own powerful code in languages such as C++ and expose that code as an API, which you can then call from VBA.

This section walks you through the style of API programming that calls external functions from library files such as DLLs. In the context of Access development, these types of function calls are typically APIs provided by Windows, but the information can be applied to any properly created DLL, LIB, or EXE files. By working through the following examples, you will gain the experience of creating and implementing a few real-world API calls. With that foundation, you can leverage other resources to experiment, build confidence, and have another technique in your developer toolset.

You will learn where to find detailed documentation on Windows functions, how to declare external functions from VBA, and how to map data types from one language to another. You will also learn some common constructs and techniques required for leveraging external library functions. As you work through the examples, you will build a module that can be used to open a window in Windows Explorer, programmatically find and reference that window, retrieve system information about that window, and finally specify the size and location of that window. These examples expose a very small portion of functionality that can be obtained through the API, but they give you the foundation to delve deep into the Windows OS functions and other library file–related functions.

Before working with the examples, you need some background concepts to apply. You can start by learning how to find documentation, how to map data types from one language to another, and how VBA's user-defined types and C-style `structs` work together; you then move on to a discussion about pointers and handles. After these conceptual overviews, you will be prepared to start declaring and using API functions.

Obtaining Documentation for API Functions

Documentation of API functions varies by the provider of the functions. For the following examples, you can use the Microsoft Developer Network (MSDN) documentation. All Windows API functions are fully documented in the MSDN and provide the function syntax, return type, parameter information, and usage remarks, as well as the library and function name that must be called.

An easy way to find documentation for a Windows function is to use Google or Bing and type the function name. The official MSDN documentation will usually be the first or second result listed.

Mapping Data Types

In many cases, APIs are written in a different language than VBA. Because of this, the data types used by the API must be correctly mapped to VBA data types. Most Windows API functions are written in C or C++, so you need to start by determining the target data type required by the API. You can then identify which VBA data type correctly maps to it. The MSDN documentation will prove an invaluable tool for that. One feature of the C++ language is that custom data types can be created based on the core C++ types. Windows defines many custom data types, which, like other custom data types, must be mapped to a C++ type before mapping to the appropriate VBA type.

> **NOTE** *The term "mapping data types" means that you will examine the type and range of two separate data types — usually from different languages — and determine which data type from one language has the same range and base type as the other. For example, the VBA* `Long` *data type is defined as a 32-bit signed integer, and the C++* `int` *data type is also defined as a 32-bit signed integer. Thus, the two types map to each other.*

You can find a complete list of Windows data types with their descriptions and C++ mappings:

```
http://msdn.microsoft.com/en-us/library/windows/desktop/aa383751(v=vs.85)
.aspx
```

The next link provides information on the core C++ types:

```
http://msdn.microsoft.com/en-us/library/s3f49ktz(v=vs.110).aspx
```

For example, you often work with the Windows `BOOL` type as it is a common return type for Windows API functions. By examining the MSDN documentation for `BOOL`, you can determine that the type is defined as the C++ `int` data type. Looking at the C++ types, you can then determine that the C++ `int` type is a 32-bit signed integer ranging from –2,147,483,648 to 2,147,483,647. You may recognize this as VBA's `Long` type, which is the correct mapping to use in this case.

It is important to note the variances in data types between languages. You may know that a `Boolean` data type is, generally speaking, a 0 or 1, but in order for your API calls to work correctly with the Windows `BOOL` type, the mapping needs to be precise, so you must use VBA's `Long` data type.

VBA User-Defined Types and C-Style Structs

When reviewing MSDN documentation for a function, you'll often find that one or more of the parameters require a `struct`. A `struct` is the C/C++ equivalent of a VBA *user-defined type* (UDT). To make API calls for functions requiring a `struct`, the equivalent UDT must be defined in VBA. The name of the UDT and its members do not matter, but the member data types must be correctly mapped and they must appear in the same order within the UDT as they appear in the MSDN documentation for the `struct`. The Windows API relies on those sizes and positions to determine where each value starts and ends; thus, correct mapping and order is of utmost importance.

> **NOTE** *The MSDN documentation is arguably the most important resource for API programming. It is the only reliable reference that provides complete information on all API functions. Indeed, many developers will have the MSDN documentation open as they create and modify API calls.*

Many API `structs` require that a member of the `struct` represent the overall size of the `struct`. To determine the size of a UDT before sending it to the API, use `Len(YourUDTVariable)`. As you work through the examples later in the chapter, you will make use of three different `structs` required by the API, one of which requires the size to be set before calling the API.

Pointers and Handles

Many C++ functions rely heavily on *pointers* and *handles*, so in order to be proficient with APIs, you must have a conceptual understanding of them. Although a detailed discussion of pointers is beyond the scope of this book, you will learn the basics here and can easily find additional information on the Internet.

A pointer is an address to a block of memory. When you declare a VBA object type, VBA allocates a block of memory large enough to represent the object and assigns your variable an address at the start of that block of memory. This address points to the object in memory, ergo the term "pointer." As you may be aware, assigning the value of one object variable to another object variable does not duplicate the object, but instead it creates two separate references to the same object. The pointer to the object is copied to a new variable, but a new memory block is not allocated as it would be for an entirely new object. Understanding the concept of pointers will be a tremendous help as you work with the Windows API.

Handles are similar to a pointer in that they use the same data types. For example, you would use the `LongPtr` data type to declare a window handle parameter. However, pointers are used to identify a memory address, whereas handles are used as a unique identifier to an object such as a window, file, or some other system resource.

It is especially important to understand how pointers are used by 32-bit and 64-bit systems. In 32-bit applications, a pointer is a 32-bit memory address, allowing just over 4.29 billion possible values. In 64-bit applications, a pointer is a 64-bit memory address, providing double the space and exponentially more possible values than its 32-bit counterpart.

To deal with the transition from 32-bit architectures to 64-bit and the requirement to mix both together between applications and OS, VBA7 provides two special keywords: `PtrSafe` and `LongPtr`. `PtrSafe` simply asserts that the API declaration is suitable for use in 64-bit Office. The `LongPtr` data type is converted at run time to a `Long` data type in 32-bit Office or a `LongLong` (64-bit integer) for 64-bit Office. By using `PtrSafe` and `LongPtr`, your code will be usable by both 32-bit and 64-bit installations of VBA7. However, if you are using VBA6 in versions up to and including Office 2007, you must omit the `PtrSafe` keyword and use the `Long` type to represent a pointer. The issues with 32- and 64-bit platforms are discussed in more detail in the next section.

32-Bit vs. 64-Bit

The Microsoft Office 2013 system, including Access 2013, is available in both 32-bit and 64-bit versions. The 64-bit version of Office enables you to work more efficiently with much larger sets of data; especially when analyzing large datasets using Excel.

If you need to use Access 2013 64-bit to design solutions, you must update the existing Declare statements in the Windows Application Programming Interface, API. Additionally, you will need to update the display window handles and the address pointers in the statements. You will encounter two major issues when you use the 64-bit version to run existing 32-bit solutions:

1. The Office native 64-bit processes cannot load 32-bit binaries. You can expect to run into that issue if you have existing Microsoft ActiveX controls and existing add-ins.
2. 32-bit VBA does not have a Pointer data type and because of this, developers used 32-bit variables to store pointers and handles. These variables now truncate 64-bit values returned by API calls when using Declare statements.

While there are some benefits in installing the Office 2013 64-bit version, at this time they are not related to Access, so you will not currently shortchange yourself by installing the 32-bit version. Using the 32-bit version of Access enables you to use database solutions built in previous versions without needing to modify the code.

Along with the 64-bit version of Access, Microsoft released a new version of VBA Code Base, VBA 7, to work with both 32-bit and 64-bit applications. The code base provides two conditional compilation constants: `VBA7` and `Win64`. The `Win64` constant is used to test what version you are using — 32-bit or as 64-bit. The `VBA7` constant tests the version of VBA in your solution, VBA 7 or an earlier version of VBA.

One of the main challenges you will have with 64-bit solutions is that they are not compatible with existing 32-bit Active-X controls regardless of whether they are supplied by Microsoft or by a third party vendor. The possible solutions for this problem are:

- If it's your control, or you have the source code, you can create your own Active-X for 64-bit.
- Check with the vendor about updated versions.
- Search for alternative controls, or work-around solutions.

> **NOTE** *The* `Win32API.txt` *provided by Microsoft is for 32-bit only. If you want to use it in a 64-bit solution, you need to update it using the* `Win32API_PtrSafe.txt` *file. The file is available at* `http://www.microsoft.com/en-us/download/details.aspx?id=9970`.

As mentioned, you can use two new conditional compilation constants: `VBA7` and `Win64`. In most cases, you will use the `VBA7` constant to ensure backward compatibility with previous versions of Access and other Office products. You use it to prevent code specific to 64-bit from running in a 32-bit solution. You will use the `Win64` constant to handle code that is different between the two versions. One of the examples is the math API. In the 64-bit version, it uses the `LongLong` data type and in 32-bit it uses `Long`. Here is an example of using the `Win64` constant (code file: `API32-64.txt Private Sub VBA7`):

```
#If Win64 Then
   Declare PtrSafe Function MyMathFunc Lib "User32" _
    (ByVal N As LongLong) As LongLong
#Else
   Declare Function MyMathFunc Lib "User32" (ByVal N As Long) As Long
#End If
```

To ensure the code you wrote in `VBA7` will run on previous versions of VBA, you will use the `VBA7` constant:

```
#if VBA7 then
   Declare PtrSafe Sub MessageBeep Lib "User32" (ByVal N AS Long)
#else
   Declare Sub MessageBeep Lib "User32" (ByVal N AS Long)
#end if
```

If you are unsure about needing a 64-bit Access, chances are high you don't need it. So go ahead and install Access 32-bit. However, if you do proceed to use Access 64-bit and you want your code to be used in a previous version of Access, you will need to use the two new constants, VBA7 and Win64.

Putting It All Together: Create and Manage an Explorer Window

It is time to implement what you've been learning by working through a real-world scenario. The task is to create and reference an Explorer window, then specify size and position. You'll create the Explorer instance by using the built-in `Shell` function. Because the `Shell` function does not provide a handle to the window that is created, you'll first check all open windows and record any existing Explorer window handles. After the new Explorer window is created, you will identify it by checking all open windows again to determine which Explorer window handle was added.

After identifying the target Explorer window, you will instruct the API to provide a set of the window's system properties. Next, you will modify those properties to specify the new size and position. Finally, you will call another API function that passes the complete set of properties — all of the original ones with a few modifications — for the system to reposition and resize as indicated.

The block of code presented and discussed in this section represents the entire process (code file: `API.txt Create and Manage an Explorer Window`). The steps are enumerated in the comments so that you can easily refer to the specific block as you review the explanation and work through the detailed instructions that follow.

Note that the code example has been organized to help with the flow of instructions while maintaining its integrity as usable code. Even so, the steps may be out of order. Although the organization may not adhere to your conventions, it will, we hope, provide a valuable reference tool. And, as you know from working with VBA, the placement of certain code entities, such as those in the declarations section of the module, or the order of procedures is largely a developer preference. For your convenience, you can find this version of the function (`APIExamples`) as well as a more conventional layout (`APIExamplesFormatted`) in the Chapter 16 download files.

The following process will open Windows Explorer and get its handle (Task 1), and then place the Explorer window (Task 2). As mentioned above, each tasks requires numerous steps, which are enumerated here to make it easier for you to follow along.

Task 1 — Steps 1 through 10: Open Explorer and get its Handle. After step 10, you should stop and test your code.

1. Get the Desktop Window Handle. Use this to check all of its children and determine which might be an instance of Windows Explorer.
2. Declare the `Sleep` API to allow your code to pause while Explorer fully opens.
3. Declare the `EnumChildWindows`, the API that will be used to instruct the system to enumerate all desktop windows.
4. Declare the `EnumChildProc` callback. The system will call that one time for each window it finds.
5. Declare the `GetClassName` API. You'll use this to determine if the window is an Explorer instance by checking if the class name is either `CabinetWClass` or `ExploreWClass`, the two class names assigned to Windows Explorer.
6. Define the `GetClassName` wrapper. This is a user-defined function to handle the string buffering and return from the GetClassName API.
7. Define the module-level constants and variables. The constants direct the `EnumChildProc`, and the variables store static information between calls to `EnumChildProc`.
8. Fill the `EnumChildProc` with logic required to examine the windows.
9. Create the main `OpenAndPlaceExplorer` procedure.
10. Stop and test your code.

After you have tested your code and resolved all issues, you are ready to proceed with Task 2. This takes the Explorer window that you just opened and makes it the size and position that you speficified.

Task 2 — Steps 11 through 14: Place the Explorer window.

11. Define the UDTs required by `GetWindowPlacement` and `SetWindowPlacement`.
12. Declare the `GetWindowPlacement` and `SetWindowPlacement` APIs.
13. Create the `PlaceWindow` procedure. This uses `GetWindowPlacement` and `SetWindowPlacement` to read window information and allow you to specify size and location of the new window.
14. In `OpenAndPlaceExplorer`, add the call to `PlaceWindow`. Once you clean up the module-level variables, you're done.

Now that you've reviewed the steps in quasi-code, it will be easier for you to understand the actual code that makes it all happen. Each of the numbered steps above correlates directly to the step numbers that are commented in the following code:

```
Option Compare Database
Option Explicit
'Task 1 - Steps  1 through 10 - Open Explorer and get its Handle
'Task 2 - Steps 11 through 14 - Place the Explorer window
'The steps are not in numerical order but are numbered to facilitate
'working through the process.



'Step 1: Get the Desktop Window Handle
Private Declare PtrSafe Function apiGetDesktopWindow _
  Lib "User32" Alias "GetDesktopWindow" () As LongPtr

'Step 2: Declare the Sleep API
Private Declare PtrSafe Sub Sleep Lib "Kernel32" (ByVal ms As Long)

'Step 3: Declare the EnumChildWindows API
Private Declare PtrSafe Function apiEnumChildWindows _
  Lib "User32" Alias "EnumChildWindows" _
  (ByVal hWndParent As LongPtr, ByVal lpEnumFunc As Long, _
   ByVal lParam As Long) As Long

'Step 5: Declare the GetClassName API
Private Declare PtrSafe Function apiGetClassName Lib "User32" _
      Alias "GetClassNameA" _
  (ByVal hWnd As LongPtr, ByVal lpClassName As String, _
   ByVal nMaxCount As Long) As Long

'Step 7: Define the module-level Contsants and Variables
Const ECP_GETEXISTING = 1
Const ECP_GETNEW = 2
Private m_ExistingExplorers As String
Private m_NewExplorer As LongPtr

'Task 2 - Steps 11 through 14 - Place the Explorer window


'Step 11: Define the UDTs required by the WindowPlacement API
'This step immediately follows testing your code.

Public Type apiPOINT
  X As Long
  Y As Long
End Type

Public Type apiRECT
  Left As Long
  Top As Long
  Right As Long
  Bottom As Long
End Type

Public Type apiWINDOWPLACEMENT
  length As Long
  flags As Long
```

```
  ShowCmd As Long
  ptMinPosition As apiPOINT
  ptMaxPosition As apiPOINT
  rcNormalPostion As apiRECT
End Type

'Step 12: Declare the GetWindowPlacement and SetWindowPlacement APIs
Private Declare PtrSafe Function apiGetWindowPlacement _
  Lib "User32" Alias "GetWindowPlacement" _
  (ByVal hWnd As LongPtr, lpwndpl As apiWINDOWPLACEMENT) As Long

Private Declare PtrSafe Function apiSetWindowPlacement _
  Lib "User32" Alias "SetWindowPlacement" _
  (ByVal hWnd As LongPtr, lpwndpl As apiWINDOWPLACEMENT) As Long

'Step 13: Create the PlaceWindow procedure
Private Sub PlaceWindow( _
    hWnd As LongPtr, Top As Long, Left As Long, Bottom As Long, Right As Long)
  Dim wp As apiWINDOWPLACEMENT
  wp.length = Len(wp)
  apiGetWindowPlacement hWnd, wp
  With wp
    .rcNormalPostion.Top = Top
    .rcNormalPostion.Left = Left
    .rcNormalPostion.Bottom = Bottom
    .rcNormalPostion.Right = Right
  End With
  apiSetWindowPlacement hWnd, wp
End Sub

'Step 4: Declare the EnumChildProc callback
Public Function ECPGetExplorer( _
    ByVal hWnd As LongPtr, ByVal lParam As Long) As Long

 'Step 8: Fill the EnumChildProc callback with logic
  Dim ret As Long
  ret = -1
  If lParam = ECP_GETEXISTING Then

If (Classname(hWnd) = "CabinetWClass") Or _
    (Classname(hWnd) = "ExploreWClass") Then
      m_ExistingExplorers = m_ExistingExplorers & ";" & CStr(hWnd) & ";"
    End If
  ElseIf lParam = ECP_GETNEW Then
    If (Classname(hWnd) = "CabinetWClass") Or _
        (Classname(hWnd) = "ExploreWClass") Then

      If InStr(1, ";" & Classname(hWnd) & ";", m_ExistingExplorers & ";") = 0 Then
        m_NewExplorer = hWnd
        ret = 0
      End If
    End If
  End If
  ECPGetExplorer = ret
End Function
```

```
'Step 6: Write the GetClassName Wrapper
Private Function Classname(hWnd As LongPtr) As String
  Dim s As String
  s = String(255, 0)
  apiGetClassName hWnd, s, 255
  Classname = Replace(s, Chr(0), "")
End Function

'Step 9: Create the main OpenAndPlaceExplorer procedure
Public Sub OpenAndPlaceExplorer()
  Dim hWndDesktop As LongPtr

  hWndDesktop = apiGetDesktopWindow()
  apiEnumChildWindows hWndDesktop, AddressOf ECPGetExplorer, ECP_GETEXISTING

  Shell "Explorer.exe", vbNormalFocus
  Sleep 500
  apiEnumChildWindows hWndDesktop, AddressOf ECPGetExplorer, ECP_GETNEW

  'Step 10: Stop and test your code
  Debug.Print "Existing Explorer Handles: " & m_ExistingExplorers
  Debug.Print "New Explorer Handle: " & m_NewExplorer

  'Step 14: Add the call from OpenAndPlaceExplorer to PlaceWindow and
  '         clean up the module-level variables
  PlaceWindow m_NewExplorer, 200, 200, 800, 800

  m_ExistingExplorers = ""
  m_NewExplorer = 0

End Sub
```

The first task is to get a list of all windows currently open and identify the Explorer windows. These windows are children of the Desktop window and will be enumerated using the `EnumChildWindows` API function. By reading the MSDN documentation about the function, you can determine that they require a handle to the desktop window and a callback function used for the enumeration. You begin by declaring the `GetDesktopWindow` API function in your VBA project. This will provide a handle to the desktop window, which the `EnumChildWindows` function will use for enumeration.

API Declaration

Declaring API functions requires a special syntax in VBA. All API declarations must be placed in the declarations portion of the module. They also have a few required sections that are not seen elsewhere in VBA. Step 1 in the code sample demonstrates a standard API declaration, as shown here:

```
Private Declare PtrSafe Function apiGetDesktopWindow _
  Lib "User32" Alias "GetDesktopWindow" () As LongPtr
```

The function can be declared as Public or Private. The VBA name of the function, `apiGetDesktopWindow`, follows the `Private Declare PtrSafe Function` portion of the declaration. You will also use this name to call the API. The VBA name can be whatever you wish as long as it does not interfere with the rest of the project's naming. These examples prefix API functions with "api" so that they are easily identifiable and you avoid name conflicts.

The `Lib` portion of the statement is required as it tells the API which library to use. In some cases, you may be required to use the extension as well as the library name (i.e., – `Lib "User32.dll"`). Most libraries are registered and are located in the system or system32 directory. If a library is not registered, the `Lib` portion will need to include the full path to the file.

The `Alias` portion is only required when the VBA function name you declare is different than the function name declared by the DLL. In this case, the Windows function name is `GetDesktopWindow`. Because the VBA declaration is `apiGetdesktopWindow`, the Alias is required in order to tell the system what function to find.

Following the `Alias` is a list of parameters — or a set of empty parentheses to indicate that there are no parameters. The declaration line is ended with the API return data type — in this case, `LongPtr`.

Another API that you will use in this example is the `Sleep` API, as shown in Step 2. This will pause the execution of code for a specified amount of time so that you can ensure that the new Explorer window instance is fully opened before proceeding. The `Sleep` API subprocedure, is one of the rare instances that an API is used as a sub rather than a function. The declaration is still similar in both uses.

Note that this does not have a return type because this is a sub and not a function, and subs do not return data (as noted by the VOID return within the MSDN documentation). Also note the lack of an alias. As you'll recall, if the VBA declared name is the same as the API declared name, an alias is not required.

One thing that you may find when working with text-based API functions such as the `GetClassName` function later in the examples is that the MSDN will list both an ANSI and Unicode version of the function name at the bottom of the documentation. The ANSI version will end with an `A` and the Unicode version with a `W`. When using text-based functions from VBA, you will use the ANSI version of the function. You'll notice this later when you declare `GetClassName` and see `GetClassNameA` as the Alias.

Declaring the Enumeration Function

After the `GetDesktopWindow` function is declared, you will declare the `EnumChildWindows` function (Step 3 in the preceding code). The declaration syntax is the same as `GetDesktopWindow`. This instance has some additional parameters as required per the MSDN documentation.

> **NOTE** *Determining when to use* `ByVal` *or* `ByRef` *in API declarations can be tricky, especially because using the wrong one will crash your application. See the "Using ByRef and ByVal" discussion in the "Tips and Techniques" section later in the chapter.*

Declaring the Callback Function

The EnumChildWindows function requires a callback function that will be called one time for each window found. A callback function is a public function that the API will invoke as many times as it needs to, passing information as parameters. Per the MSDN documentation for EnumChildWindows, your project will require the EnumChildProc callback. Because you will pass a pointer to the callback when calling the API, the name you give the callback does not matter except in the context of your project. What is important is that the *function signature* matches the specification and the parameter data types are mapped correctly. A callback function must be declared as Public and reside in a standard module. When you call the EnumChildWindows function, you will use the VBA statement AddressOf to pass the pointer of your function to the EnumChildProc callback.

> **NOTE** *A procedure's* signature *is the line that defines the input and outputs for a procedure, such as the type of procedure, the type of the return, and the argument list and their respective types. With API programming, the names given to these signature definitions seldom matter, but the signature itself must correlate to the required API signature. The return type and the argument list order and types must all match.*

Each time the callback is invoked, the system will pass the handle to the next window in the hWnd argument, and the lParam argument will contain what you specify when calling the EnumChildWindows lParam parameter. With the lParam argument, you can create a logical flow of code based on how the function was called.

The next step is to create the callback function, as shown in Step 4. The name in the example is ECPGetExplorer to signify that it is an EnumChildProc whose purpose is to obtain Explorer instances. You will leave this function blank for now. In a few more steps, you will fill it with the required logic.

Determining the Class Name of a Window

The next API required is GetClassName. This function accepts a handle to a window and returns the Windows class name. From your callback function, check the class name of the current window to find one of two possible Windows Explorer class names: CabinetWClass or ExploreWClass. If the window is determined to be an Explorer window, the window's handle will be added to a module-level variable for later comparison. You are building a list of existing Explorer window handles so that you can determine the handle of the new instance of Explorer when it is added.

In Step 5, you declare the GetClassName API function in your module declarations. After the API function is declared, you will need a small utility function to convert the returned class name from the API's C-style buffered string into something more easily used with VBA. The user-defined function from Step 6 will provide a wrapper for your apiGetClassName function.

> **NOTE** *The Windows API uses strings much differently than VBA does. Because of this, working with API strings require certain techniques that aren't usually used in native VBA. For more information, see the "String Buffers" topic in the "Tips and Techniques" section.*

With that completed, you have declared API functions to get all child windows of the desktop and have the tools to determine which are Explorer windows. Next, you'll start filling in some native VBA code for handling the tracking.

Preparing the EnumChildProc for Two Different Uses

Because you will enumerate the desktop windows twice — once before and once after opening the new Explorer window — you will need a way to tell the `EnumChildProc` what to look for. This is accomplished by passing a value through the `EnumChildWindows` call, which is then forwarded by the API to the `EnumChildProc` as the `lParam` argument. You also need to declare two module-level constants to indicate the before and after routines. The `callback` will read the values and act accordingly.

Next, you will need two module-level variables for tracking explorer instances. The first will be a string of delimited Explorer handles for existing instances, and the second will be a `LongPtr` to indicate the handle of the new instance. Step 7 demonstrates the creation of the two constants and variables.

Now you have sufficient definitions to make use of the `EnumChildWindows` and its `EnumChildProc` callback. Refer to Step 8 ("Fill the `EnumChildproc callback` with Logic") in the example code and add that code to the body of the `ECPGetExplorer` callback function.

Note that the `callback` function returns a –1 by default (`True`), and a 0 if a new instance is found. In many cases, enumeration callbacks can be halted by returning `False` and instructed to continue by returning `True`. You should consult the function's documentation for details.

Creating the Main Procedure

You now have enough API code and supporting procedures to create the main sub. Although this is only the first task — determining the Explorer windows — it is an opportune time to stop and debug your work. Once everything works as expected, it is time to proceed with creating the procedure.

You need to create a public sub to use as the main entry point to the task, as described in Step 9. At present, you will only fill it with the first half of the logic — determining the Explorer instances. You can view the handles for the existing and new Explorer windows by using the immediate window and the `Debug.Print` statements, as shown in Step 10. (Note that you should omit the code for Step 14 at this point.)

At this point, you should compile, save, exit, and back up your database. Then re-open it and run the `OpenAndPlaceExplorer` sub and examine the printed values. Pointers typically look like large random numbers, and a pointer value of 0 typically indicates that a window was not found. You will find additional information on this topic in the "Tips and Techniques" section.

> **NOTE** *Debugging and handling errors in API programming are different than in native VBA. See the "Error Handling" and "Preparing for Crashes" topics in the "Tips and Techniques" sections for more information.*

Retrieving Window Information

Now that you have a handle for the newly created Explorer instance, it's time to retrieve the current window information, modify the placement, and feed the modifications back into the system. This requires two more API function declarations, and they both require some *user-defined type* (UDT) declarations. The `GetWindowPlacement` and `SetWindowPlacement` APIs make use of the `WINDOWPLACEMENT struct` as noted in the MSDN documentation. Additionally, three members of the `WINDOWPLACEMENT struct (ptMinPosition`, `ptMaxPosition`, and `ptNormalPosition)` require two additional `structs`: the `POINT struct` and the `RECT struct`. First you need to define the required UDTs to map to the `structs`. Then, you will make the declarations for the two API functions.

To declare the UDTs, you need to map the VBA data types to the `struct` data types using the same methods that you used in previous examples to map API parameters and return values. This is shown in the declarations section, Step 11, in the example module. When you complete the UDT declarations, you can proceed with Step 12 to declare the `GetWindowPlacement` and `SetWindowPlacement` API functions.

In the process, you will create an empty `apiWINDOWPLACEMENT` variable to pass to the `GetWindowPlacement` API. The API will fill your `apiWINDOWPLACEMENT` type with the current settings for the Explorer window. You will then adjust the `rcNormalPosition` members to represent the screen position and size that you want the window to show. After making those adjustments, you need to call the `SetWindowPlacement` API, and pass the entire `apiWINDOWPLACEMENT struct` to it. The API will read all of the settings defined in the `struct` and make any necessary adjustments to the settings that you defined.

As a good practice, you will want to create a private sub to handle the logic for these API calls so that they do not clutter the main entry sub. This is demonstrated in Step 13, where you create and implement the `PlaceWindow` procedure. Note that per the MSDN documentation, the `length` member of the UDT must be set before calling the API.

The final step is to add a call to the `PlaceWindow` sub in your main `OpenAndPlaceExplorer` sub. The call should be placed after the last enumeration added to the procedure. You can see this at the end of the code sample in Step 14. Additionally, you need to clear the two member-level variables so that they do not interfere the next time the example runs.

Of course, you should replace the hard-coded size and position values with whatever you like by setting them up as arguments of the procedure and letting the database or users supply the parameter information.

Tips and Techniques

As you've experienced in other areas of development, it is great to be able to work through basic processes and to be able to create and customize functions and routines. But there is a lot more to it if you want to master an area, especially in today's dynamically changing environment. The following tips and techniques are based on lessons learned over the years by several developers. You can benefit from their experiences as you refer to and integrate these techniques into your solutions.

You can find all of the code snippets in the download text file for this chapter (code file: `850832_ch16_CodeSnippets.txt`).

Passing Nulls

`Null` values in API calls are different than VBA Nulls. The C/C++ languages generally define `Nulls` as either 0 or a character whose value is 0, whereas in VBA, a `Null` value is an unknown and is most commonly seen before a field has data entered. In most cases, a `Null` can be passed to the API by passing the value of 0 in the correctly mapped type, using either a variable or a type-declaration character such as this (code file: `API.txt Tip_Nulls`),

```
EnumChildWindows hWndDesktop, AddressOf MyCallback, 0&
```

or this:

```
Dim lptr As LongPtr
lptr = 0
EnumChildWindows lptr, AddressOf MyCallback, 0&
```

Note that the `vbNullChar` constant provides a character whose value is `0`, and the `vbNullString` constant provides a `Null` pointer — that is, a pointer that has no value (it doesn't point anywhere) as opposed to a pointer that has a value but points to a `Null` address.

Preparing for Crashes

Unless you happen to be an API programming prodigy, you *will* crash your application during testing. Before running any code, you should save your project, close it, and back it up. In many cases, the crash will cause a loss of work from the last time the database was opened, despite the project being saved in the interim.

Error Handling

Debugging and error handling for APIs often require a different approach than with conventional VBA. In many circumstances, it will not be possible to step through the code. Often, attempts to step through the code will result in the application crashing. An alternative recommendation is the liberal use of `Debug.Print` statements.

Most Windows API functions will return a value that indicates the success of the call. The value varies depending on the function. You should consult the MSDN documentation for details of function returns.

The Windows API defines a `GetLastError` function, which can be used to get error information. Regretfully, is isn't necessarily intelligible and getting a human readable message may not be very straightforward. Here again, you can refer to the MSDN documentation on the function for details:

```
http://msdn.microsoft.com/en-us/library/windows/desktop/ms679360(v=vs.85).aspx
```

The VBA `Err` object provides a `LastDLLError` property, which can be used to determine the last DLL error that was encountered for DLL functions called from VBA. Refer to the MSDN documentation on the `LastDLLError` property for more information:

```
http://msdn.microsoft.com/en-us/library/office/gg278794.aspx
```

For some API functions, the MSDN documentation will direct you to make use of the `GetLastError` API function, and for others you may find better results with VBA's `Err.LastDLLError` property.

String Buffers

In most cases that the Windows API returns textual data, it will expect a buffered string of null characters passed to it, which it will then fill and return. This is typically filled to a maximum amount of characters — usually 255 or 256 characters — with each character having a value of 0 (`vbNullChar`). When the API returns, you will most often look for the first null character and trim the string to that point. This type of string is called a null-terminated string.

APIs may also require that a null-terminated string be passed to the function. In this case, add the null character `vbNullChar` to the end of your string before sending it to the API. For multiple returns, such as multiple files selected with `GetOpenFileName` API, the list will be delimited by a single null character and terminated by a double-null character.

Using ByRef and ByVal

It can be confusing to determine when to use `ByRef` or `ByVal` for API declarations. The frustration can quickly be compounded because using the wrong one will result in a crash of the application. This confusion is mainly due to the fact that VBA handles data types differently behind the scenes, using pointers that you do not have access to on the surface. For example, when a string is handled by VBA, there is an underlying pointer that indicates the start address of the string. Even though you may require `ByRef`-like use of the string for the API call, the API declaration must be declared as `ByVal` because it is the `ByVal` pointer that actually gets passed into the API.

Generally speaking, most API parameters will be declared as `ByVal` except when passing UDT variables, which must always be passed `ByRef`.

Avoiding Expressions as Parameters (Using Sustainable Pointers)

When you call directly upon the API function, the best practice is to avoid any use of expressions to send the parameter to the API, especially in the case of strings. Look at the following example, which intends to write a formatted date to an `ini` file using the API:

```
WritePrivateProfileString "MyApp", "MyKey", _
    Format(Date(), "yyyymmdd"), strIniFilePath
```

Any expression used to pass a value to an API call risks causing an error. This will result in an error because the `Format()` function is used to create the value string, as it does in the last line of the API call above. Instead, the value should be assigned to a variable and then passed to the API, as you'll see next.

The API expects an `LPCSTR` (long pointer to a constant string), and VBA will provide the pointer on your behalf. However, because the pointer that will be passed is the result of an expression, VBA disposes of the pointer as soon as the expression is evaluated, thinking that it's no longer required. By putting the string into a variable before sending it to the API, the pointer is sustained throughout the API call because the variable does not go out of scope until the calling procedure is complete. The following snippet shows the correct method of calling the function (code file: `API.txt Tip_SustainablePointer`):

```
Dim strFormattedDate As String, strIniFilePath As String
strIniFilePath = "C:\MyProject\myapp.ini"
strFormattedDate = Format(Date(), "yyyymmdd")
WritePrivateProfileString "MyApp", "MyKey", strFormattedDate, strIniFilePath
```

Working with Flags

Many API functions make use of flag values. Flags are bitwise values that are put into a single integer type variable (typically a `Long`) where each bit represents one setting (with a `Long`, 32 bits are available to set). A familiar example of a flag value in VBA is the `VbMsgBoxStyle` constants used with `MsgBox()`. The values of the constants are 1, 2, 4, 8, 16, 32, and so on, and can be added or subtracted to set the desired flags. Use the bitwise `AND` and `OR` operators when working with API flags to determine and assign bitwise values to flag variables. You can find some additional information about the `AND` and `OR` operators in the VBA Help file. Another good resource, for this and many other support topics is the Utter Access wiki, `http://www.utteraccess.com/wiki/index.php/Category:Access_Wiki_Index`.

Avoiding "Any"

VBA provides a type that can be used for API declarations called `Any`. This does not mean that the API will accept any type of data, only that VBA will not perform type-checking before it passes the value to the API. You should avoid using `Any` unless there is specific reason to use it.

INTRODUCTION TO DATA MACROS

Introduced in Access 2010, data macros offer you a new set of tools that you may find quite effective for performing data validation and maintaining data integrity. In this section, you see a few scenarios where data macros are superior to the traditional approach of using VBA in form events and validation rules. Data macros were originally built to offer additional functionalities in Access web databases for Access 2010. For compatibility purposes, they were also made available to the client. Even though Access web databases are now replaced by Access web apps, data macros continue to be supported in the client, affectively making Access the only desktop file-based database product to have triggers and stored procedures. On the other hand, Access web apps have a different set of macro actions from client data macros. Access web apps also store macros differently, so what you learned about data macros in the web section of this book does not necessarily apply in the context of the client's data macros. However, the design surface for data macros will be largely the same. We examine the differences in the macro actions and functionality made available in the client data macros next.

Why Use Data Macros?

Traditionally, whenever you needed to perform data validation or some kind of additional data processing, you would use VBA attached to events in a module behind a form, primarily the form's `BeforeUpdate` or `AfterUpdate` events. One downside to that approach was that if multiple forms used the same table, perhaps to provide a different view for different processes, it was necessary to use the same VBA code, either by copying the code to the other form or by calling a common routine. Either way, it was extra maintenance, which also meant that you had to remember to include the code in every new form added to the project. In a large project, it is too easy to forget that validation and data processing routines must be performed in all of the appropriate places and the proper code implemented.

Validation Rules and Check Constraints

Validation rules are a partial solution because you can set them at the table level and have them enforced in all forms bound to that table. However, at most, the scope of a validation rule is at the record level; you cannot look up other tables, which limits the usefulness of a validation rule. Access also supports check constraints, but they were never surfaced in the UI. That was problematic because there was no facility to trap for check constraint violations and accurately diagnose the error in order to provide a friendly and helpful error message. Users were stuck with highly technical error messages about a check-constraint violation, which were utterly meaningless to them. Although data macros aren't meant to have any UI components either, they do have a mechanism for raising a descriptive error message, which Access will then happily display as a messagebox. In other contexts, data macros errors may not be displayed but will be logged.

Application Independence

This brings us to another reason data macros can be quite useful. If an Access database can be used by different applications, data macros on the tables in that database can uniformly enforce validation and data processing regardless of which application is using the data. For example, if there is a .NET service that accesses and updates the Access database, data macros will fire even in this context. This will happen even though the service may not even open the Access application itself and instead use OLEDB to connect directly to the database engine. In other words, data macros are truly application-independent processes that you can leverage to enforce business logic at all times, in all places.

Differences in Client and Web Data Macros

When Access 2010 came out, both the client and the web counterpart had an identical working set of macro actions available in data macros. Because Access 2013 web apps are provisioned on a SQL Server, Microsoft had to revise the set of data macro actions to work with SQL Server's underpinning; as a consequence, the web app's data macro catalog is not identical to the client's counterpart. If you've used data macros in 2010, you will find they remain compatible with the Access 2013 client. That said, let's quickly list key differences between client data macros and Access web app data macros:

- Client data macros are associated with a table, whereas web data macros are standalone.
- Client data macros can be based on five table events: Before Delete, Before Change, After Insert, After Update, and After Delete. Web data macros have only three table events.
- In client data macros, only the set of Before* table events can be cancelled. In web data macros, all table events can be cancelled.
- Errors with data macros in the client are logged to the USysApplicationLog system table, whereas web data macros errors are not recorded, although they can be traced in a trace table.

Also, if you did not work with data macros in 2010, there are a few important restrictions to keep in mind. These limitations still apply to client data macros in 2013:

- You cannot perform a CreateRecord macro action within a ForEachRecord block.
- You can only do EditRecord or DeleteRecord on the record from the outermost ForEachRecord block.
- You cannot recursively run a data macro or a set of data macros more than 19 times.

One thing that may trip up unwary users is running a data macro that does a ForEachRecord block and within that block, calling another data macro that performs a ForEachRecord within the called data macro. If the called data macro performed an EditRecord, it would appear to comply with the rules because EditRecord is associated with the outermost ForEachRecord block for this data macro. But that's not strictly true because it is being called within the first data macro's ForEachRecord. That means the EditRecord action fails. Thus, it is a good habit to treat a RunDataMacro action as if it was simply an expansion of the content inside the calling data macro rather than a separate stack.

Use Cases for Data Macros

As alluded to earlier, there are two distinct uses for data macros:

1. Perform validation that cannot be done within the scope of one record.
2. Perform additional data processing.

The validation part is fairly straightforward; it's something you might have run into before. You might have a scenario where you needed data from another table to make a decision about whether an action on the first table is permissible. A common example of that sort of validation is prohibiting deletion of an order that has been shipped in parts. When shipping has already started, and one or more shipments are already recorded in the separate shipping table, you can't delete the order record. In order to know about any shipments, you need to look at the shipments table to see if any part of the order was included in any shipments already sent. Should this be the case, you cannot delete the order because some of the goods in the order are already on their way and must be marked as a loss or recorded for recall.

As you can see, the ability to run a data macro that checks data from other tables helps protect against changes that would leave you with inconsistencies such as a quantity of a product that is missing because products have already shipped based on a non-existent order.

Data processing, on the other hand, is not as straightforward. Although it can be tempting to use code to enable certain processes in which data is manipulated in several steps, it is usually the case that those processes should be resolved by normalization instead. Nonetheless, there are three situations where it does make sense to perform additional actions with data macros:

- Improving Query Performance
- Maintaining Audit Trails
- Creating Supplemental Records

We'll consider each in the following sections.

Query Performance Considerations

The first possible use is to improve query performance where you use calculated values as the criteria in the query. Consider the scenario where a company wants to know which orders had sales of $10,000 or more in a given time period, perhaps in order to allocate bonuses, or to identify its best customers. In a properly normalized database, you would have an order table and an order detail table. You can use an aggregate query to sum up the total from order details to get the order total, and you shouldn't have to store the order total as well. In a large enough dataset, however, the cost of calculating all order details and summing them up for each order can become very expensive, slowing the query's performance. In the past, some Access developers may have chosen to denormalize and store the order totals in the Order tables so that the total field could be indexed for better performance. That also eliminates the need to run an aggregate query over the order details table and filter out the aggregated values less than $10,000 to get the result. However, this approach creates a maintenance problem, especially with a form where users can potentially interrupt the query or leave the calculation incomplete. Ultimately, you might need to manually recalculate the totals every so often, particularly before running the query to search for orders totaling $10,000 or more, so that it will be correct.

Calculated Values

Data macros can substitute for the traditional summing of values in an aggregate query. Although Access 2010 also introduced calculated data types, calculated fields cannot be indexed unlike in 2013 web apps. So, there is very little benefit in using calculated data types for this task. Moreover, the calculated field cannot calculate outside the scope of the current record. Thus, a data macro is an excellent fit. You will see two examples of storing a calculated value later in the chapter.

Audit Trails

The second scenario pertains to audit trailing, where a copy of a record is made in a separate audit table. Auditing is a special case as the purpose of auditing typically is to record changes in data, rather than storing facts about data. Audit trailing is most useful in scenarios where you have the ability to identify what changes were made to data, when the change occurred, and who made it. One example that comes to mind is a series of financial transactions where accountability is required. Data macros can be implemented to ensure the audit trail is maintained regardless of how changes to the data occur, as you learned in the introduction to this section.

Potential for Misuse

While some may be tempted to use a similar approach with data tables, this may cause more problems than it solves. Consider the scenario where you need to update a customer's address. Suppose that a data macro copies the customer's old address to a history table. On the surface, that might look like a neat solution because you don't have to complicate your queries by joining your customer table with the address table and deciding which address you should use. However, if you call up a past invoice, it now appears that it was sent to the customer's new address when in actuality, it was sent to the old address. You've lost the record of the change, which would have enabled you to resolve the discrepency. Using an address table and indicating a current address from the customer table enables you to avoid this problem without involving data macros at all.

Creating Supplemental Records

Our third example is probably the most esoteric use: creating a new record based on an event. Later in the chapter, you will see an example of creating a new receiving batch to represent the quantity that was returned to the warehouse. The creation is done indirectly via increasing the quantity on hand for this product. This is done in reaction to a retroactive correction and depends on specific business rules, which do not generalize well. However, the ability to edit or create new records can be useful, provided you implement it in a way that does not deviate from the normalization, introducing far more maintenance problems than it solves.

CREATING DATA MACROS

In this section, we'll show you how to create and use data macros to address the objectives previously outlined. In the first two examples, you'll be using data macros and aggregate queries. First up is a data macro to address performance issues by creating a calculated field that can be indexed.

Maintaining Calculated Values to Support Indexing

For this section, you'll be using an inventory and ordering database. The relationship diagram is shown in Figure 16-11.

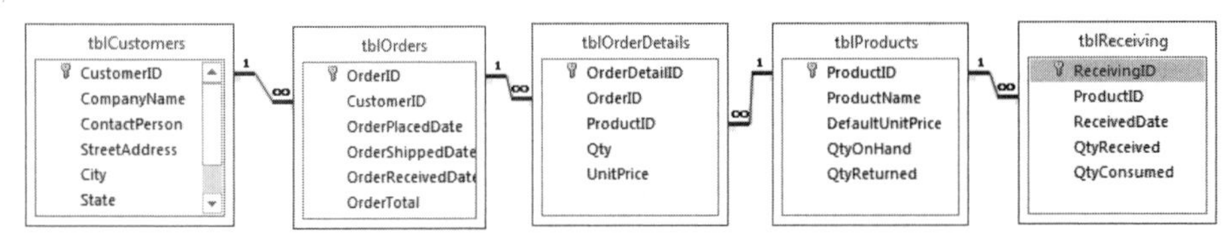

FIGURE 16-11: Inventory and Ordering Database relationship diagram

The first example demonstrates how to maintain an order total by storing the calculated value in a field in the order table every time an order's details are edited. Recall that the goal of storing the calculated value is to improve query performance when determining which orders have $10,000 or more in sales without requiring an aggregation over the details table.

You'll need a query that will sum the details for a particular order and give out the total. Build a new query and name it `qryOrderTotals`, as shown in Figure 16-12.

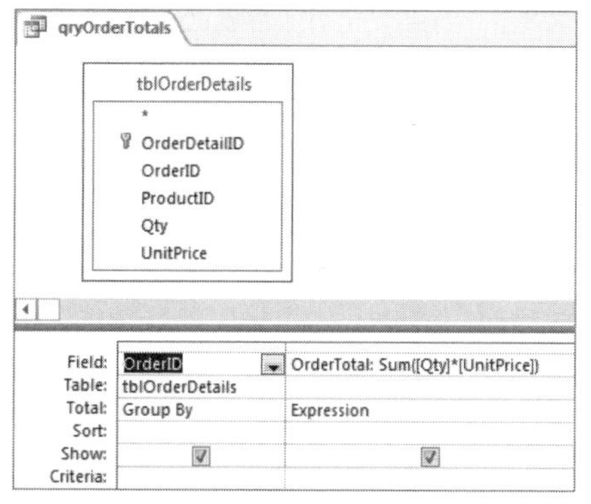

FIGURE 16-12: qryOrderTotals definition

USING QUERIES AS THE RECORDSOURCE FOR A FOREACHRECORD BLOCK

If you've been developing Access solutions for a long time, you've probably been advised to use queries instead of looping over a recordset in VBA. This advice still applies to data macros. Although it is possible to do a ForEachRecord over the entire order detail table and sum up the totals this way, it is much more expensive. Even using a ForEachRecord on an aggregate query would be superior to doing a ForEachRecord on a table. Thus, if there is an opportunity to use a query to do some aggregating, filtering, or sorting, take advantage of it and use the query as the source instead of the table.

As you might recall, client data macros must be associated with a table. In order to create a new data macro, you must open a table in design view. Open the `tblOrders` table in design mode and, on the ribbon, select Create Named Macro as illustrated in Figure 16-13.

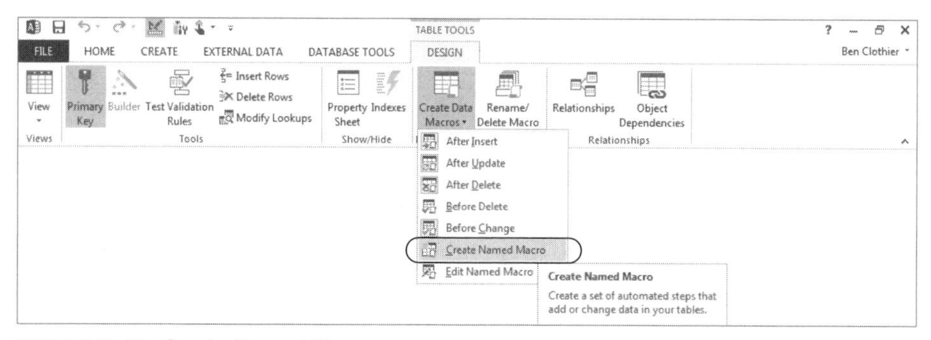

FIGURE 16-13: Create Named Macro

Within the data macro, you'll create a parameter, `plngOrderID`, to pass in the order for which you need to get the total; perform a LookupRecord macro action on the `qryOrderTotals` query to get the total; and then assign that value into the `OrderTotal` field on `tblOrder`, as shown on Figure 16-14. Save and name it `dmUpdateOrderTotals`.

```
Parameters
 Name                                   Description
                      plngOrderID

SetLocalVar
          Name  pcurOrderTotal
    Expression  = 0

⊟ Look Up A Record In  qryOrderTotals
    Where Condition  = [OrderID]=[plngOrderID]
  SetLocalVar
            Name  pcurOrderTotal
      Expression  = [qryOrderTotals].[OrderTotal]

⊟ Look Up A Record In  tblOrders
    Where Condition  = [OrderID]=[plngOrderID]
  ⊟ EditRecord
      SetField
              Name  tblOrders.OrderTotal
             Value  = [pcurOrderTotal]
    End EditRecord
```

FIGURE 16-14: dmUpdateOrderTotal definition

The next step is to call this named data macro from the three `After*` events on the `tblOrderDetails` table. Each table event will have a single action, RunDataMacro, which passes in the current `OrderID` of the edited order detail. Figure 16-15 shows how you can set the action for each After table event.

```
tblOrderDeta... | tblOrderDetails : After Insert :                    ×

RunDataMacro
  Macro Name  tblOrders.dmUpdateOrderTotal
 Parameters
   plngOrderID  = [OrderID]
+ Add New Action
```

FIGURE 16-15: RunDataMacro in a table After event

Note that you need to add the same data macro to the other two After* events.

Timing of the actions is important in understanding how the data macro works. The data macro runs in any one of three After table events, after the edit in the `tblOrderDetails` is already saved. This means the sum returned from the query, `qryOrderTotals`, will be correct when it is recorded into the associated order's record. Regardless of how the order details were edited — whether via a form, a query or even by another application — you can count on the `OrderTotal` field being current. All of this is done to enable indexing of the `OrderTotal` field, as shown in Figure 16-16.

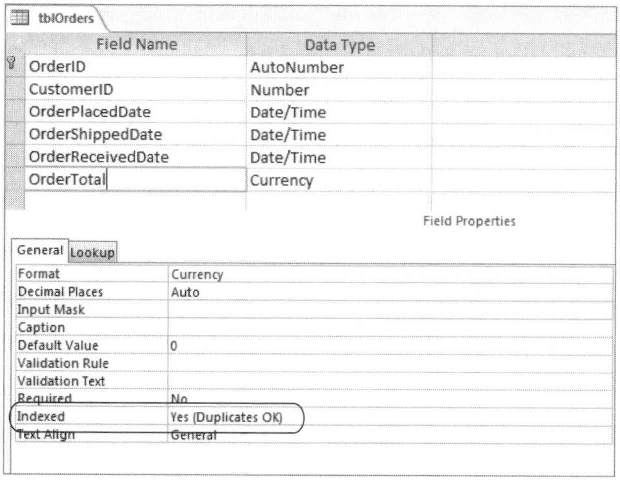

tblOrders

Field Name	Data Type
OrderID	AutoNumber
CustomerID	Number
OrderPlacedDate	Date/Time
OrderShippedDate	Date/Time
OrderReceivedDate	Date/Time
OrderTotal	Currency

Field Properties

General | Lookup

Format	Currency
Decimal Places	Auto
Input Mask	
Caption	
Default Value	0
Validation Rule	
Validation Text	
Required	No
Indexed	Yes (Duplicates OK)
Text Align	General

FIGURE 16-16: Indexing the OrderTotal field

Thus, any queries that filter or sort by the total sales on an order will be much improved because they can use the indexed `OrderTotal` field instead of calculating on the fly.

Maintaining Quantity On Hand to Support Business Logic

The next example involves maintaining quantity on hand for inventory items. The objective is to ensure that you only fill orders for an inventory item when there is enough quantity for that item in the warehouse to do so.

As you saw in Figure 16-11, you need a Receiving table and an Order Details (aka shipping) table, both related to the Product table. The Product table has a `QtyOnHand` field while the Receiving table has `QtyReceived` and `QtyConsumed` fields. The Order Detail table simply has a `Qty` field to indicate the quantity needed to fill this order for a given product. The business logic here is that an order cannot be fulfilled if there isn't sufficient `QtyOnHand` in the product table. Furthermore, the quantity on hand can be spread across multiple received batches. For example, you can have three received batches of 50 units, 75 units, and 100 units, respectively. Assuming nothing has been used for other orders, that would add up to a quantity on hand of 225 units. The first order that requires 75 units should consume 50 units from the first batch and then 25 from the second batch. The second order that needs 100 should then consume the 50 from the second batch and 50 from the third batch, leaving the quantity on hand at 75.

With the specifications for the on-hand calculation defined, you'll want to start adding the quantity whenever a new batch arrives. You will now create a data macro to make that happen. Open the `tblProducts` table in design view and create a new named macro on that table. Just to be clear, a Named macro must be attached to the table, but not to one of the events on that table. Within the macro, the process is fairly straightforward; each time an event occurs that impacts quantities of a product, your macro needs to look up the product in the `tblProducts` table and update the `QtyOnHand` column with that quantity. The steps are illustrated in Figure 16-17. You might name this macro `dmProductChangeQtyOnHand`.

```
Parameters
  Name                                   Description
                         plngProductID
                         plngQtyChange

Look Up A Record In  tblProducts
    Where Condition  = [ProductID]=[plngProductID]

    EditRecord
        SetField
                 Name  tblproducts.QtyOnHand
                 Value = Nz([tblproducts].[QtyOnHand],0)+Nz([plngQtyChange],0)
    End EditRecord

SetLocalVar
         Name  vbolDone
   Expression  = False
```

FIGURE 16-17: Definition of dmProductChangeQtyOnHand

Note the usage of two parameters, `plngProductID` and `plngQtyChange`, to pass in the `ProductID` and the change quantity. You can see this in Figure 16-17. As you see, the calculation is set up so that you can pass both increasing and decreasing quantities simply by passing in either a positive or negative number, respectively.

Next, you wire this data macro up to all three of the After table events on `tblReceiving`, similar to what is shown in Figure 16-18.

```
tblReceiving | tblReceiving : After Update :

If Updated("QtyReceived") Then
    RunDataMacro
        Macro Name  tblProducts.dmProductChangeQtyOnHand
    Parameters
        plngProductID  = [ProductID]
        plngQtyChange  = [QtyReceived]-[Old].[QtyReceived]
End If
If Updated("QtyConsumed") Then
    RunDataMacro
        Macro Name  tblProducts.dmProductChangeQtyOnHand
    Parameters
        plngProductID  = [ProductID]
        plngQtyChange  = ([Old].[QtyConsumed])-([QtyConsumed])
End If
```

FIGURE 16-18: tblReceiving's After table event definition

This should set you up for receiving new quantity into the product's on-hand field.

> **NOTE** *When designing and testing data macros, you might need to reset values between tests. One easy way to reset values without firing off the data macros is to open the table being changed in design view, which will prevent macros from running.*

Next you need to set up a macro for quantity shipped. However, before you can create the macro you need to define the queries it will use. You'll be working with batches in this step, so you need queries to present quantities in those batches. When the queries are ready, you can return to the design view of `tblProducts` and create another named macro called `dmProductChangeConsumedQty`.

> **NOTE** *If you're familiar with standard accounting, what you're about to do with this data macro is often referred to as the FIFO — or First In, First Out — method of inventory accounting.*

Unlike the previous data macro, where you can simply add and subtract from the on-hand quantity, you have multiple batches of received quantities to consider. When taking away from the quantity on hand, you want to work from the oldest batch until the order is fulfilled. On the other hand, for the sake of simplicity when you have quantities returned, you add those to a new batch rather than trying to track which batch they originally came from.

Name the first query `qryAvailableQtys`. The objective is to get a listing of batches of product that have available quantities that you can consume, sorted from the oldest batch to the newest batch. In order to match up to the order to be shipped, you need to work only on products that are contained in the order details. Because an order may have multiple products associated with it, it is necessary to use a ForEachRecord block so you can iterate for every product included in the order.

When you factor in the restriction that only the outermost ForEachRecord block can be edited, which precludes even doing a LookupRecord macro action inside a ForEachRecord block to edit the looked up individual record, it is necessary to ensure that you can get only products used by this order without impacting the query's updatability. If you joined the `tblReceiving` table with the `tblOrderDetails` table, you would have a non-updatable query and thus couldn't do an EditRecord macro action within the ForEachRecord block.

With this understanding, `qryAvailableQtys` should have only one data source: the `tblReceiving` table. Add a parameter, named `plngOrderID`, of Long Integer data type. Figure 16-19 shows the table and parameter dialog box. Note that `plngOrderID` is also selected and the last column is too long to fit and will be explained in the following text.

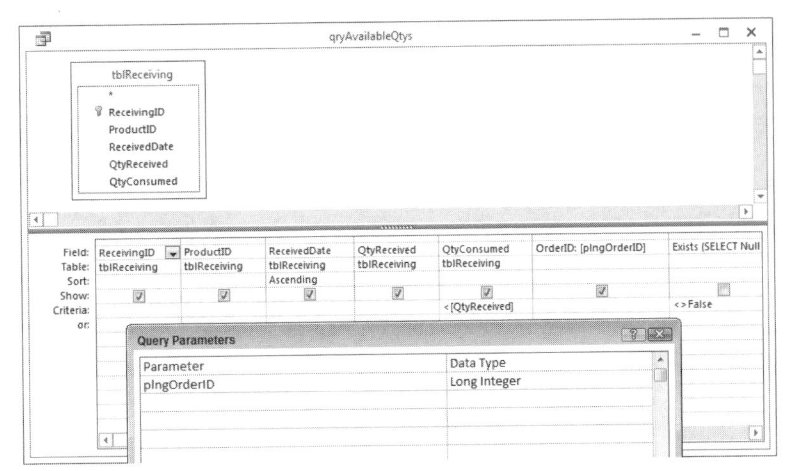

FIGURE 16-19: qryAvailableQtys with parameter dialog box

In addition to selecting the `plngOrderID` parameter, you should select all fields from the `tblReceiving` table. Add a criteria of `<[QtyReceived]` for the `QtyConsumed` column. This ensures that you do not select any batches that have been used up already. Add a sort on `ProductID` and then `ReceivingDate`, descending from oldest batch to newest.

You're probably wondering how you are going to filter out the products that aren't used in the orders. The answer is to add one more column, which was shown partially in Figure 16-19, that will perform an `Exists()` check. Enter the expression:

```
Exists (
  SELECT Null
  FROM [tblOrderDetails]
  WHERE [tblOrderDetails].ProductID = [tblReceiving].[ProductID]
    AND d.OrderID = [plngOrderID]
)
```

Note how the function uses the parameter `plngOrderID` to filter the order details table based on a certain order, and then consider how you also link the order details table back to the receiving table on the `ProductID`. This affectively gives you a way to filter the `tblReceiving` table down to only products that relate to an order. Most important of all, you do not lose the query's updatability.

> **NOTE** *If you're unfamiliar with the* `Exists()` *function, you might be wondering why the subquery is selecting nulls. Unlike the* `In()` *function, which you might have used before to return a list of possible values from another table,* `Exists()` *returns only a boolean value;* `true` *if there is a matching record anywhere in the table; or* `false` *if there is no matching record even once in the table. Thus, what you select is completely irrelevant and, because the function returns just a boolean value, it's more performant than an* `In()`*, which returns a table that must be evaluated separately. An easy way to demonstrate this is to do a* `SELECT 1 FROM aTable WHERE EXISTS (SELECT 1/0 FROM aTable);` *and note that you do not get a division by zero error when running the query.*

Save qryAvailableQtys and create another one, named qryConsumedQtys. This one is more straightforward because in this case, you're creating a brand new receiving record for each returned quantity so you only need to get enough details to create a new receiving record. For this query, use tblOrder-Details and tblProducts as the source with the columns selected as shown in Figure 16-20.

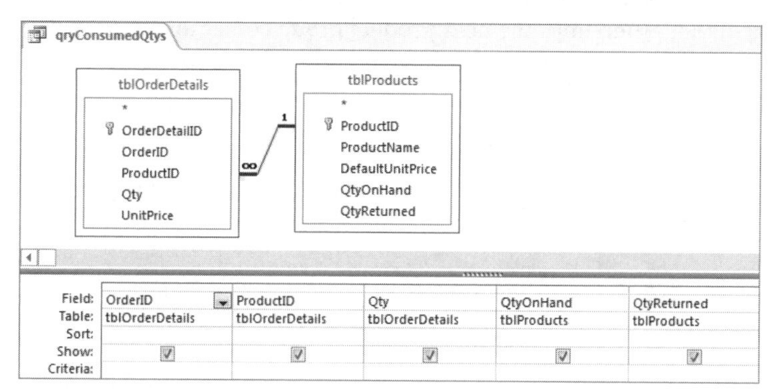

FIGURE 16-20: qryConsumedQtys definition

Save the query and close it. You need to make a third and final supporting query that you should name qryOrderProductTotalQtys. As the name implies, it should sum the quantity grouped by product and by orders, as illustrated in Figure 16-21.

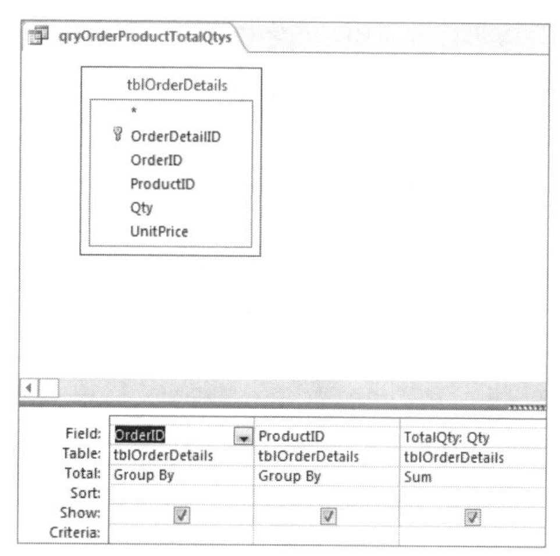

FIGURE 16-21: qryOrderProductTotals definition

Save and close the query and return to tblProducts design view. Create another named macro called dmProductChangeConsumedQty. As you saw, you have two queries designed to handle both consumption and restoration of quantity. For this reason, you need to split the parts with an If/Then block to determine whether the process will be consuming the quantity or restoring the previously consumed quantity, as shown in Figure 16-22.

The outer If/Then Block, as you can see, branches processing depending on whether pbolConsumeQty is true (the If branch) or false (the Else branch). As you can also see in Figure 16-22, you need two parameters for this data macro: one to indicate which order you need to work on and the other to indicate whether you are consuming quantity on hand or restoring it. The latter parameter is used to determine which branch of the If/Then block should be executed. Let's examine the steps to be performed when you consume the quantity.

```
Parameters
 Name                          Description
        plngOrderID
        pbolConsumeQty

SetLocalVar (vlngProductID, Null)

⊞ If [pbolConsumeQty]=True Then

⊞ Else

End If
```

FIGURE 16-22: Outer If/Then block

Within the true part of the If/Then block, you'll loop over the qryAvailableQtys query, passing in plngOrderID to its parameter. Because the query will return all available batches for a product and you don't necessarily want to consume all the available quantities, you need a system of taking only as much quantity as needed, from the right product. Recall that you sorted the query on `ProductID` and then `ReceivingDate`, assuring all products are grouped together when you iterate over a given product. You update only the batches where there are quantities that need to be consumed and once this is fulfilled, skip the rest of the records in that group until the next product group comes up. To achieve this goal, you need two If/Then blocks within the ForEachRecord block, as illustrated in Figure 16-23.

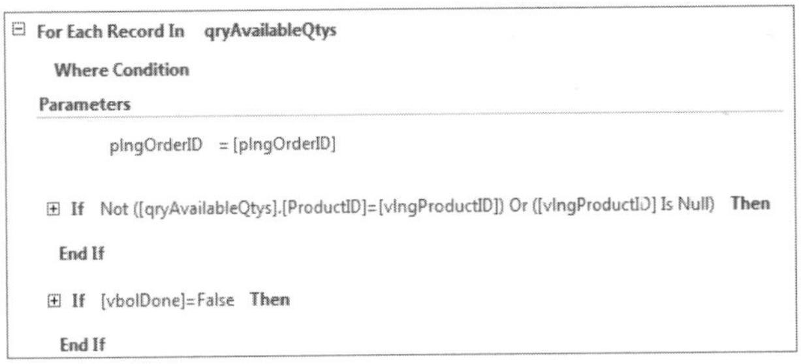

```
⊟ For Each Record In   qryAvailableQtys
    Where Condition
   Parameters
          plngOrderID   = [plngOrderID]

   ⊞ If   Not ([qryAvailableQtys].[ProductID]=[vlngProductID]) Or ([vlngProductID] Is Null)   Then
     End If
   ⊞ If   [vbolDone]=False   Then
     End If
```

FIGURE 16-23: Expanded ForEachRecord block with two collapsed If/Then Blocks

The first If/Then block should be executed whenever you enter a new group of batches of that product, which will also always happen on the very first iteration of the ForEachRecord. You will use this block to reset variables to maintain the amount of quantities consumed so far between each iteration for a given product. You also need to know the quantity you need to satisfy the order's product quantity, which you do with a `LookupRecord` against `qryOrderProductTotals`. Set up the block as shown in Figure 16-24.

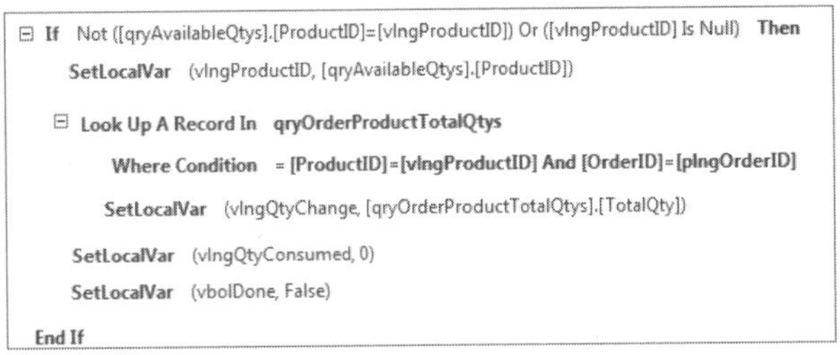

```
⊟ If   Not ([qryAvailableQtys].[ProductID]=[vlngProductID]) Or ([vlngProductID] Is Null)   Then
      SetLocalVar   (vlngProductID, [qryAvailableQtys].[ProductID])
    ⊟ Look Up A Record In   qryOrderProductTotalQtys
          Where Condition   = [ProductID]=[vlngProductID] And [OrderID]=[plngOrderID]
          SetLocalVar   (vlngQtyChange, [qryOrderProductTotalQtys].[TotalQty])
      SetLocalVar   (vlngQtyConsumed, 0)
      SetLocalVar   (vbolDone, False)
  End If
```

FIGURE 16-24: First If/Then block

Note the `vlngProductID` being set; you will refer to the `vlngProductID` in the outer If/Then block to help track whether you are on a record of another batch for the same product or a batch belonging to another product.

In each iteration for the same product's batch, you need to check how many items you've consumed so far, check how much quantity is still available to consume in this batch, and consume accordingly. When you've consumed all quantities that you need for this product, you can skip the rest of the batches belonging to the same product. Using variables you set in the previous If/Then block, you inspect the data in the current record and update the variables, as demonstrated in Figure 16-25.

```
If [vbolDone]=False Then
    SetLocalVar (vlngQtyAvailable, [qryAvailableQtys].[QtyReceived]-[qryAvailableQtys].[QtyConsumed])
    SetLocalVar (vlngQtyChange, [vlngQtyChange]-[vlngQtyConsumed])
  EditRecord
            Alias qryAvailableQtys
    If [vlngQtyChange]>[vlngQtyAvailable] Then
        SetLocalVar (vlngQtyConsumed, [vlngQtyConsumed]+([qryAvailableQtys].[QtyReceived]-[qryAvailableQtys].[QtyConsumed]))
        SetField (qryAvailableQtys.QtyConsumed, [qryAvailableQtys].[QtyReceived])
    Else
        SetField (qryAvailableQtys.QtyConsumed, [qryAvailableQtys].[QtyConsumed]+[vlngQtyChange])
        SetLocalVar (vbolDone, True)
    End If
  End EditRecord
End If
```

FIGURE 16-25: Second If/Then block

As you see, the EditRecord block may either set the field `QtyConsumed` to the value of `QtyReceived`, consuming it completely, or increase `QtyConsumed` to the quantity that is needed to fulfill the order. When you have exhausted all quantities needed to satisfy the order, the `vbolDone` variable is set to `true`. That allows you to skip the remaining batches belonging to the same product without editing them.

This concludes your introduction of setting up a process to consume quantities when shipping the order. Next you need to deal with a scenario in which an order is returned. This example assumes that whenever an order is returned, the quantities can always be restored to inventory, and do not have to be disposed of otherwise. With returns, however, the process is easier because you only need to create a new receiving batch to receive the returned quantities, which will also restore the on-hand quantity. Within the outermost If/Then block's Else branch, loop over the `qryConsumedQtys` and write values into the `QtyReturned` field. If you recall from earlier in the chapter, a CreateRecord action cannot be executed inside a ForEachRecord block. However, you can circumvent this restriction by doing an EditRecord action inside the ForEachRecord and attaching an After Update table event to perform a CreateRecord action. Figure 16-26 shows how you would program the ForEachRecord block.

```
For Each Record In qryConsumedQtys
    Where Condition = [OrderID]=[plngOrderID]
  EditRecord
      SetField (qryConsumedQtys.QtyReturned, [qryConsumedQtys].[Qty])
  End EditRecord
```

FIGURE 16-26: ForEachRecord block

> **NOTE** *Keeping tables open while running data macros so you can inspect the results of data macros gives you immediate feedback on edited records; however, you need to close and reopen tables to see newly created records.*

Note that you update the `QtyReturned` field in `tbl-Products`. Use `tblProduct's` After Update event to do so only when the `QtyReturned` field was the field that was updated; the `Updated() expression` tells you that. Perform a `CreateRecord` in the `tblReceiving` table. Because you need to use variables from `tblProducts`' fields, you need to perform a `SetLocalVar` action before entering the CreateRecord, which loses the current record's scope. The actions would be arranged similar to what you see in Figure 16-27.

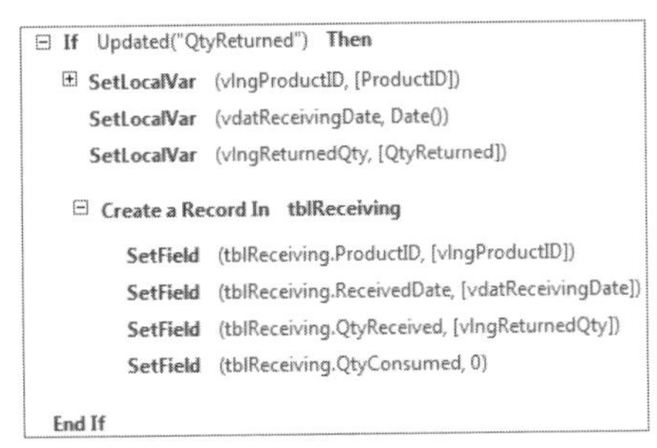

FIGURE 16-27: After Update event for tblProducts

> **NOTE** *The LogEvent macro action can be very helpful in tracing the progress of your data macro and reporting values to validate that those variables are getting expected values.*

Let's recap what you just built. The requirement was to maintain an accurate quantity on hand for any given product when handling returns. You adjust the on-hand quantity whenever a new receiving batch is added in the `tblReceiving` table, using its After table event. New records, increases to the `QtyReceived` field, and decreases to the `QtyConsumed` field all add more to the current on-hand quantity. Likewise, deletion of records, decreases to `QtyReceived`, and increases to `QtyConsumed` fields reduce the on-hand quantity.

You then ship the order by filling in the `OrderShippedDate` field, which increases the `QtyConsumed` fields of receiving batches, starting with the oldest batch first until as many as needed to fulfill the order. In the next section, you'll create the macro to do this.

A change to the `QtyConsumed` field in turn decreases the on-hand quantity of the product. When the order is returned, you update the `QtyReturned` field in `tblProducts`, which in turns creates a new record in `tblReceiving` to represent a new batch, which subsequently increases the on hand quantity.

Creating Validation Checks

As you can see, you can build a complete system to automate the tracking process, which can be very useful, especially when the dataset is either too large or changes so rapidly that using frequent aggregate queries becomes a problem. However, there is one other major factor to account for. You certainly do not want to kick off the process of consuming quantities only to find that you do not have enough to fulfill the order. Thus, it is prudent to check inventory levels before you start the process. In the next section, you will learn about building validations using Before table events.

Once again, you'll use a query as a recordsource to help you validate whether the action should be allowed. Create a new query named `qryCheckQtys`, using `tblOrderDetails` and `qryOrderProduct-TotalQtys` as the source. To filter the records, you need to select `OrderID` and `ProductID`. Finally, you'll need an expression to indicate whether there are sufficient quantities on hand to cover the total quantity requested in this order: `[TotalQty] - [QtyOnHand]`. The expression should be filtered to return only records with nonzero quantities. The query would look similar to what is depicted in Figure 16-28.

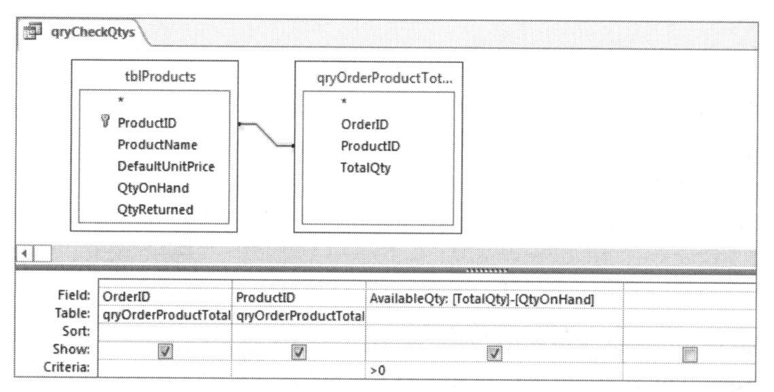

FIGURE 16-28: Query definition for qryCheckQtys

This query simply needs to check whether there are any records where the expression is positive, indicating a shortage that prevents a new order from being fulfilled. This means you simply look up whether there are any records or not, in a similar fashion to how the `Exists()` function was used previously. The `Before Change` table event for the `tblOrders` simply needs to check this query whenever the `OrderShippedDate` field is updated and use the RaiseError action to cancel the operation inside the LookupRecord, as demonstrated in Figure 16-29, if there is a shortage.

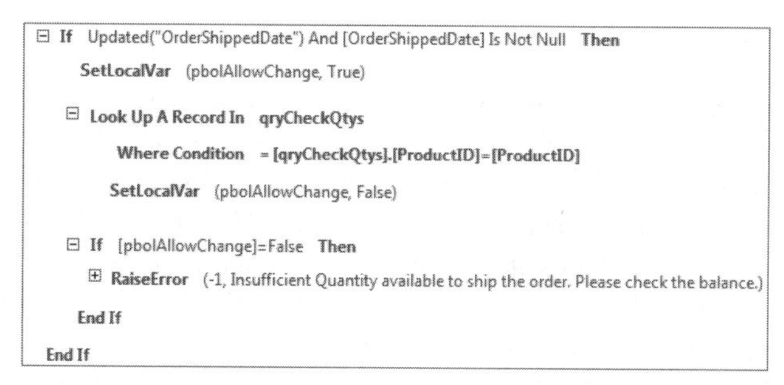

FIGURE 16-29: tblOrders' Before Change table event

The `qryCheckQtys` query checks for all products used by a given order so you can immediately decide if the order can be shipped. This also fits within the constraint placed on the `Before` table events where you cannot use the ForEachRecord block at all because LookupRecord is the only block available to you in this context.

Another example of using the Before Change table event is to ensure that nobody edits an order that has already shipped. While it's easy enough to check for and prevent edits to the order record itself as the shipping date is recorded on this record, there is no record of the shipping date on the order details level. Because you can perform a LookupRecord action in the Before Change table event, you can use that to check the order table and determine whether the order was shipped before allowing the change to the order details. The macro is quite straightforward; you just need a LookupRecord action with a RaiseError action, as shown in Figure 16-30.

```
SetLocalVar (vlngOrderID, [OrderID])

⊟ Look Up A Record In tblOrders
     Where Condition = [tblorders].[OrderID]=[vlngOrderID]

   ⊟ If [tblOrders].[OrderShippedDate] Is Not Null Then
        RaiseError (-1, Cannot edit order details for an order that has been shipped.)
     End If
```

FIGURE 16-30: tblOrderDetails Before Change table event

As you may remember, you can simply press Ctrl+A and then Ctrl+C to select all and copy the macro actions. You can then create a new Before Delete table event and use Ctrl+V to paste the actions to enforce the same rule within the Before Delete table event.

As you can see, Before table events offer you a new level of flexibility in managing validation in your web apps; with the `LookupRecord` action combined with a query, you can check for complex conditions all at the table level without being concerned about how the data is modified. In conjunction with After table events to initiate additional data processing, maintenance is more consistent where you have found a need to denormalize some data, such as storing calculated values. Obviously, these techniques can be misused to enable solutions that fall short of best practices in database design. That's where your experience will be valuable in guiding you toward a reasonable balance.

Data Macros and VBA

Because data macros were originally designed to be compatible with web databases in Access 2010, and because they are meant to be application-independent, there is no direct support for using VBA within data macros. However, you can choose to use VBA with the caveat that doing so means the tables can be used only when your Access application is running with the same VBA project loaded. Any other programs would be unable to modify the data within the tables You should take precautions to ensure that the VBA does not perform data access or modification. Strictly speaking, while there are no restrictions against VBA doing either data access or modification when called from a data macro, you cannot assume that such actions will be done in a predictable manner given that this method is outside the original design scope of the data macros. With that caveat in mind, let's look at how you can access VBA from a data macro. You have two possible routes available to you: via a query using Expression Services and in SetField macro actions.

Calling VBA Expressions in a Query

As you probably know, you can use VBA expressions within a query. To get a value from a VBA function into a data macro, you can create a query containing SQL such as `SELECT MyVBAFunction();` and save the query. You can reference the value from the query in a LookupRecord macro action and assign the content to a local variable.

Calling VBA Expressions in a Macro Action

Whenever you create a new record or edit an existing record with CreateRecord or EditRecord, respectively, you can set the value of the SetField macro action to an expression that evaluates to a VBA function because the expression also uses Expression Services to reach into the VBA project and access the function. You saw an example of this method in the audit trail section covered in Chapter 20.

As you can see from the preceding discussions, additional options are available to you in situations where you cannot adequately express your needs using only macro actions and when you are willing to forego the application independence that data macros can offer. Using VBA indirectly via Expression Services enables you to create even more powerful solutions using data macros. Because it was not part of the original scope of the tool, it is prudent to carefully and thoroughly test any solution you create. Prepare for unexpected results, especially as concurrency becomes important.

SUMMARY

This chapter provided the opportunity for you to refresh and update your skills in several key areas for working with VBA. The examples are based on real-world scenarios so that they will be applicable and extendable to a wide variety of industries and needs.

Keeping in mind that you may be proficient in one area, but may not have encountered or worked with several others, the chapter is designed to provide value to developers with a variety of experiences and areas of expertise.

The discussion on user-defined functions armed you with several examples along with explanations of how and why to create and modify them to implement business rules. From the review of error handling, you have several examples with features that include custom message boxes, e-mail notifications and error logging. The functions are provided in the companion documentation so that you can easily copy, paste, and modify them to enhance your solutions.

As you worked through the query examples, you learned about several powerful query techniques and saw how effective they can be for collecting, updating, and compiling data. This is particularly true with the query by form techniques. You completed that section by seeing ways to create queries on the fly.

The chapter then moved to leveraging Windows API calls. In this section, you found some valuable tips, along with coverage of the fundamentals and cautions about potential conflicts and issues due to varying versions of Windows and programs. The discussion centered on a demonstration of how to create and manage a Windows Explorer window. Having completed the example, you should feel confident that you can not only understand API calls, but that you're also able to incorporate them into your solutions.

In the Macros section you learned how to use macros, especially data macros and table events, to perform different validation and data management tasks. Because table events are triggered by changes at the table level, you are assured that they are fired regardless of how the data get updated. That allows you to use macros to help support query performance by maintaining calculated values which can be indexed, maintain an audit history in which crucial values are saved regardless of how changes are made, and create supplemental records in related tables.

Now that you've refreshed and augmented your programming skills, you are in a good position to see how some of the techniques can be incorporated into your solutions. The next two chapters are about Access forms and reports. You'll be working with a contacts database based on a real-world scenario. The focus is on giving you some techniques and tools that add some professional touches to your solutions.

17

Creating Intuitive Forms

WHAT'S IN THIS CHAPTER?

- Creating intuitive and professional forms
- Built-in functionality you can leverage
- Managing images, attachments and MVFs
- Report Runner tool

WROX.COM CODE DOWNLOADS FOR THIS CHAPTER

The code and file downloads for this chapter are found at `www.wiley.com/go/proaccess2013prog.com` on the Download Code tab. The code is in the Chapter 17 download folder in the files named:

- `850832_ch17_Team_CodeSnippets.txt`
- `850832_ch17_ReportRunner_CodeSnippets.txt`
- `850832_ch17_MVF_CodeSnippets.txt`

The files include the code snippets from their respective database examples, sequentially from throughout this chapter. The download folder also contains the associated databases `2013Team.accdb` and `MVFDemo.accdb` and their support files so that you can easily follow the discussion and expand on the examples.

> **NOTE** *As with most downloaded files, you may need to specifically trust and enable these files and their locations for them to function properly. To display some of the images, you will also need to store the image folder as directed or update the links to their location on your computer. For more information, please read the "What you Need" section in the book's Introduction.*

Forms will make or break your user's experience with the database and it's important they are not only functional but that they also look great. You can have the best program in the world but if it looks like it was written by an amateur, that's the level of respect that it will get. Although an in-depth discussion on UI design (*user interface*) is beyond the scope of this chapter, it is a critical aspect of both the functionality and the acceptance of a database solution.

Whether you are a UI expert or expanding your focus by venturing into designing forms, you will find some new ways to incorporate, leverage, and apply the features that Access provides for creating powerful forms. As you design the forms, you need to focus on people who will be using them and ensure that the information, layout, and flow through the form(s) will be as intuitive and efficient as possible for each user or user group. Consider the user background, the work environment, and the flow of the data. You also need to minimize the opportunity for errors and to provide whatever verifications are necessary to avoid reporting data incorrectly.

From a functional standpoint, forms are the operation center of the database. They provide the path for entering, retrieving, editing, and reporting data. The success or failure of your solution can be contingent on how quickly and easily users adapt to using the forms that you create. So, the focus of this chapter is to demonstrate some techniques that you can use to create powerful, intuitive forms. And, true to real-world form (no pun intended), the effort has been invested in providing clear examples to demonstrate functionality rather than on customizing the look and flow of the forms. As you incorporate the objects into your applications, you can apply the theme and other design properties as appropriate.

The examples are based on real-world scenarios to show you how to design and incorporate the techniques and tools into your solutions. Using the scenario of tracking people at a conference, you will see how to work with images, create attendee lists, print badges, and look up speaker profiles. You will also see how to leverage `Datasheet` view to create powerful search and filter forms, and how to organize data so that it is easy for users to navigate and manage. The examples and techniques can easily be adapted to support a myriad of other industries and needs, from parts or product lists, to restaurant menus or construction projects.

You'll also work with a tool for designing reports. This approach allows users to customize their reports by not only selecting the report and record source, but also to select which fields should be filtered and to specify the filter criteria. In addition to creating the forms, the discussion will explain the tables that are required and the programming involved. As you go through the process, you will learn about the associated objects, events, and properties. And, you will find out how you can incorporate this amazing tool in your Access solutions.

CREATING INTUITIVE FORMS

Forms simplify the navigation through the database by guiding users through entering, validating, and retrieving data. Without a properly designed *user interface* (UI), most users will be quickly overwhelmed, particularly if they are required to use the Navigation Pane to find what they need in order to add data, run queries, and view reports. It is much better to guide the user by providing navigation through menus, the ribbon, the Navigation window, and controls and events on the forms and reports themselves. You will see a variety of techniques as you work with the examples and other forms and reports in the database files. By creating an intuitive UI, you can make it easy for users to quickly and efficiently find, enter, and report data. And you can also control when and how users can view and manipulate various parts of the data.

As in the past, you can choose from a variety of approaches for creating forms, ranging from using a blank form to deploying a wizard to provide a functional result that you can tailor to meet your needs. By working with real-world examples, the discussions will cover some of the fundamentals, suggest alternative approaches, and demonstrate how you can leverage the features and techniques to provide powerful tools for your users.

The ultimate goal is for you to provide robust, reliable, effective and intuitive solutions. One approach will not fit all, but by having a variety of options, you can combine them to match the scenario and environment. With that in mind, our discussion will start with the general and work through some commonly used controls and end up with a very complex solution. So, the first step is to review some tips shared by several Access MVPs.

Clean Layout

Appearances make lasting impressions, and this also applies to the look and actions of the forms and reports in your database. If forms are too busy, the user may get confused, make mistakes, get unduly frustrated, or become alienated from the program. Some of the key aspects of having a clean look include:

- **Start and end with timed screens** — Most people agree that an attractive, informative splash screen provides a professional introduction as a program opens. Similarly, you can have a closing screen that assures the user that all files are properly saved and closed.
- **Color and font** — You can keep the tones appropriate for the environment and consider the size of the screen, the work environment, and the activities involved. Most important, you can focus on users, and particularly their eyes. Use color and font, type, size, and weight to convey information. Unless the application is for entertainment purposes, bright colors and lots of action will be a distraction.

Use various types of forms and controls to organize data and provide it when needed. Find the right combination for the situation, such as combining cascading combo boxes with subforms and a tab or treeview control, or to expand on the functionality of `Split Form` and `Datasheet` views.

Guiding the User Through the Process

There are several features and properties that you can combine to guide a user through the process. As you are placing the textboxes and other controls on the forms, consider the user's hand movements as well as how and where they are getting the raw data. In some cases, you may need to minimize use of the mouse; at other times mouse clicks may be nearly all that is required.

Leverage the tab order in conjunction with show or hide, and enable controls based on the user, the current process, how the form was opened, and other criteria. At points where the user must be led in a certain direction, you can use a dialog form, or a pop-up style modal form to prevent any other processing until the form is closed, as explained in the upcoming section about these types of forms. You can expand on this by incorporating validation processes, events, and the `Tag` property to enable, hide, and otherwise change the appearance of a control. You'll read more about these techniques later in this chapter.

Showing and Verifying Data in a Timely Manner

It isn't enough to collect data; you need to ensure that users are able to efficiently enter, retrieve, and edit records. In many instances, it may not be clear which record the user really needs. For example, the user may be looking for Sam Jones but there are 10 records with that name. There are several ways to help the user make informed selections. Depending on the specific scenario, you might use an enhanced combo box, cascading combo boxes, a `Split Form`, or `Datasheet` view, or some combination of these and other controls. You will find several variations mentioned and demonstrated in the chapter.

Data entry can encompass a wide spectrum of tasks and environments, and it is incumbent upon you to create a solution that manages the processes as efficiently, effectively, and effortlessly as possible. That includes ensuring that the data is valid, complete, and not duplicated. Fortunately, there seems to be an endless variety of techniques to help both you and the user. This discussion will focus on what you can do at the form level. This complements and builds on techniques you learned in other chapters, such as working with data macros which is covered in Chapters 9 and 16.

There are several properties and resources you can leverage when creating your forms. Some of the key ways to validate or manage data include using `Validation Rules` and setting the `Required` property. You can also use the `Tag` property to designate required fields, stipulate criteria, and take specific actions. For example, you can use code with the `Tag` property to check for values and, if something is amiss, intervene before the record is updated to highlight the errant fields and put the cursor in the first field to be corrected.

There are seemingly endless combinations of techniques to guide the user through their tasks. You can also use prompts, default values, Smart Tags, control tips, conditional formatting, show/hide/enable controls, the tab order, and numerous other clues to help users efficiently and accurately work with the data. Several of these techniques are discussed and demonstrated in the examples for this chapter.

User-Friendly Messages and Tips

Courtesy is one of edicts of professionalism. The messages and instructions that the user sees should follow that guidance.

Let the user know where they are by using clear captions and labels on forms, reports, and controls. It's important to remember to change the control name as well; this makes it much easier to identify and work with the desired item using VBA or macros.

Trap error messages and provide your own words that are easy to understand — give the user the necessary information and instructions. This might include the form name, instructions to contact tech support (you), what needs to be fixed, which field is missing data, and so on. And remember, it is not polite to shout, so exclamation marks and bold should be used very judiciously.

On forms that may be complicated or unfamiliar to the user, you can include information labels that provide the appropriate background and instructions. There are more and more options for how to convey the information. You might include it on form itself, in tips, or in pop-ups, or via a video or PowerPoint demo that is opened from a command button.

Keep these types of ideas in mind as you read through the chapters. This will help you to build correlations between the examples and your projects and make it easier for you to modify and incorporate the techniques into your solutions.

LEVERAGING BUILT-IN FUNCTIONALITY

The form controls that are supplied with Access 2013 are robust and are relatively easy to implement. These controls are much more than textboxes and labels typically used to display, add, or edit data. There are formatting controls such as the `Line` and the `Rectangle` controls for drawing, the `Image` and the `Unbound Object Frame` to display pictures or objects, and `Hyperlinks` and `Web Browser` controls. You'll work with these in several of the examples in this chapter.

When designing forms, there are always multiple ways to implement the same functionality, having a rich toolbox of controls, and understanding what they do and how they work, makes it easier for a developer to design a form the way the customer, be it either a commercial client or an internal user within your organization, wants the data presented.

> **NOTE** *You can toggle the control wizard feature on or off. Although not all controls offer wizards, most of the more complex ones do. As with other types of wizards, in addition to creating the object (control), you can use the control wizard to gain insights into how a control works and how you can modify or create it manually. You can turn the control wizards on or off by using the toggle button,* `Use Control Wizards`*. You'll find that button by opening a form or report in* `Design` *view, and then going to the ribbon's* `Design` *tab; in the* `Controls Group`*, click the* `More` *button and you should see it.*

Textbox

The `Textbox` is by far the most prevalent control. It is so heavily used that you might think everyone has mastered all of its properties. But reality is far different. There are so many properties and ways to combine properties that most barely scratch the surface of the possibilities. Although textboxes are typically bound to a record source, you have probably also used them as unbound controls and perhaps changed the record source at runtime.

As you work through the examples in this chapter, you'll see all three approaches and much more. You will see how to use events and properties of forms and controls to not only customize the visual effects, but also provide guidance and direct user actions, such as using the `Tag` property to change the appearance of a control to help collect data in required fields.

In addition to the features demonstrated in the chapter and examples, there are countless controls and properties that you can find and explore. For example, you can use conditional formatting to change the background color of a control based on the data. This could draw attention to preferred customers or past due or overdrawn accounts, or could even indicate required fields that are empty. You can quickly create the conditional formatting rules using the features in the `Control Formatting` group on the ribbon's `Format` tab, which is available when a form is in `Design` view or `Layout` view.

> **NOTE** *You can also apply conditional formatting to controls on reports. Similar to working forms, the* `Conditional Formatting Rules Manager` *is found in the* `Control Formatting` *group on the ribbon's* `Format` *tab, which is available when the report is in* `Design` *or* `Layout` *view.*

If the textbox is bound to a `Long Text` (`Memo`) field, you can set the `Text Format` property to `Rich Text` to allow users to apply additional formatting directly to the text itself.

Label

Labels are usually static and used to identify the content or purpose of another control. When you add a control to a form, it typically includes an associated label that will follow the control wherever it is moved, and it will also be deleted if the associated control is deleted. An associated label can be deleted separately from the primary control and conversely, a new label can be associated with a control that does not already have an associated label.

When a label is not associated with a control, it will have a small green triangle in the upper-right corner label, indicating that it is an unassociated label. This indicator may seem like a nuisance, but sometimes such indicators are helpful warnings about significant issues that need to be addressed.

> **NOTE** *When a green triangle appears in a control, it indicates some type of error, ranging from minor issues such as, an unassociated label to major issues such as, being bound to a nonexistent control source.*

The captions and formatting of labels can also be set at runtime by changing the label's properties. Using this in conjunction with changing the control source of a textbox allows the user to identify what values are being displayed in the control. Although a label does not have any `Data` properties, it has a large selection of `Format`, `Event`, and other properties, most of which can be manipulated at runtime thru VBA. This means that you can use the label's colors, font weight, visibility and other features, to provide scenario-based guidance to the user. You can also use the label's `Event` properties to run code or macros. However, labels for `Option Button` and `Check Box` controls do not have events because their event is used to change the value of the control itself. You might be tempted to use an invisible label to initiate an event. And although an invisible control is not enabled, you can use a combination of property settings to make a label appear to be invisible, and the event will still fire, as illustrated in Figure 17-1.

With this technique, you can strategically locate areas that will trigger events without relying on the traditional command button. For example, you could put several labels on a logo or image so that different events are triggered based on where the user clicks. You can also use this technique to hide a control so that only select people will know how to open a set of forms or reports. Obviously, this is not intended to replace true security, but it is a relatively easy way to provide secret doorways to additional forms.

FIGURE 17-1: Click event for a transparent label

Command Buttons

Using a *Command Button* is the most common way to have a user initiate an action, be it to open a form, preview a report, exit a form, or exit the application. The `On Click` event is probably the most used event for this control. Most computer users are familiar with clicking objects to initiate tasks, so your focus should be to make your command buttons as intuitive as possible. That means you need to consider the look, the size, and the location, and you should be as consistent as possible.

You can use a combination of properties to help guide users through a form or process in the order that you want things to occur. For example, by setting a command button's `Enabled` property to `False`, it will be visible but grayed out and its events will not fire. Users will interpret this to indicate that some actions need to be completed before they can use the command button. Of course, you will want to provide guidance about what actions need to be completed. How you do that should be based on the scenario and users. Once the necessary actions are completed, you can use code or a macro to enable the command button.

You can also hide the command button by setting the `Visible` property to `No`. Hiding controls is often done to prevent users from seeing commands and/or implementing actions based on their permissions or because certain conditions have been met. For example, you can hide a command button until acceptable values have been entered into all of the required fields.

> **NOTE** *A similar approach can be used to provide a hidden doorway to objects, whether for you or specified users. You can strategically place a command button, then set its* `Transparent` *property to* `Yes` *and use the* `double-click` *event to open the door.*

Some of the most common uses of command buttons are to open and close forms, save records, or go to a specified record or value. However, they can also include a series of processes that allow for different outcomes depending on the results. For example, the events behind a `save record` button could be used to confirm that all required fields have acceptable values, that it is not creating a duplicate record, and that any number of other requirements are satisfied before the record is actually saved.

Split Forms

`Split Forms` were introduced in Access version 2007, but they were not widely accepted right away. Many developers hesitate to work with the 2007 `Split Form` due to some inconsistencies with its object model. However, it is time to recognize the benefits and functionality that the `Split Form` has to offer.

Creating a Split Form

The `Split Form` allows you to create a form that displays the data in both an overall and a detailed datasheet format at the same time. This is easily accomplished with the help of a wizard. And, as you can see in Figure 17-2, the `Split Form` created by a wizard looks a lot like a form with a subform.

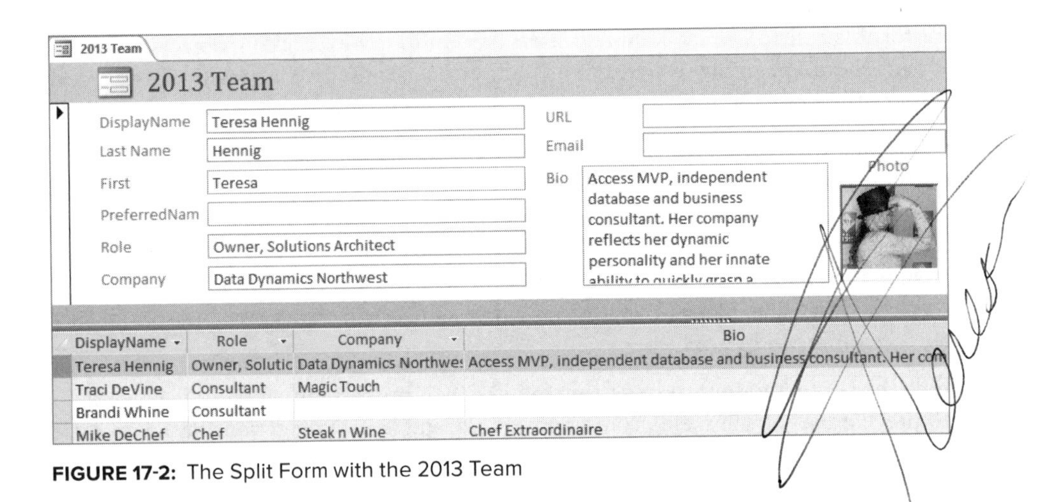

FIGURE 17-2: The Split Form with the 2013 Team

As you can see, the `Split Form` simultaneously displays data in both form and grid-style views. Although Figure 17-2 shows the single view on top, there are actually four configuration options:

1. Datasheet on top
2. Datasheet on bottom
3. Datasheet on left
4. Datasheet on right

As the user navigates through the records in either the form or datasheet section, the data remains synchronized and both views are based on the same record. One aspect that may not be obvious is that you can selectively hide fields in either view. This means that you can limit the fields on the form view and also organize the datasheet columns into a logical tab order or to have the most frequently searched fields on the far left.

Split forms have the advantage of having only a single object in your database as compared to having to maintain both a main form and one or more associated subforms, each with their own record source and master-child link.

Splitter Bar

The area of the single form and the datasheet can be adjusted by moving the `splitter bar`, shown in Figure 17-3.

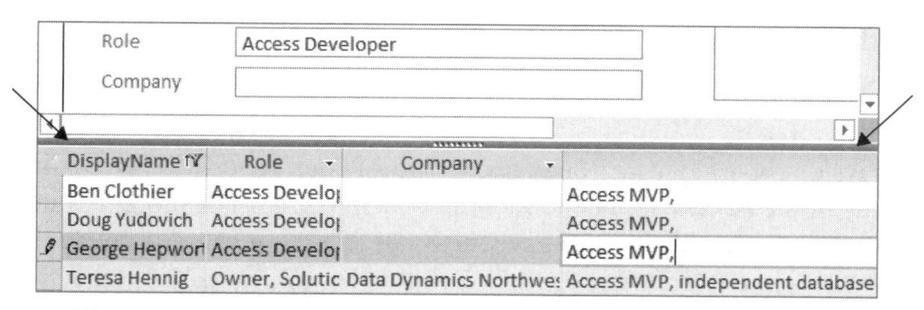

FIGURE 17-3: The Split Form splitter bar

By dragging the `splitter bar` up or down (or left or right for side-by-side configurations), you can control the amount of data or space displayed on each section. Once you are satisfied with the placement of the splitter bar and to prevent the user from moving it, you can set the `Split Form Splitter Bar` property to `No` to hide the splitter bar. Alternatively, you can allow users to move the splitter bar; they may want to maximize the search grid when they need it and then minimize the grid to work with the selected records in form view.

Some developers prefer to actually hide the traditional form portion and opt instead to provide users with a pop-up form to display the details about the data. Using this technique, the developer is able to display more records in the datasheet portion, as shown in Figure 17-4, and still having the form header to provide some functions that you cannot usually do with a datasheet form.

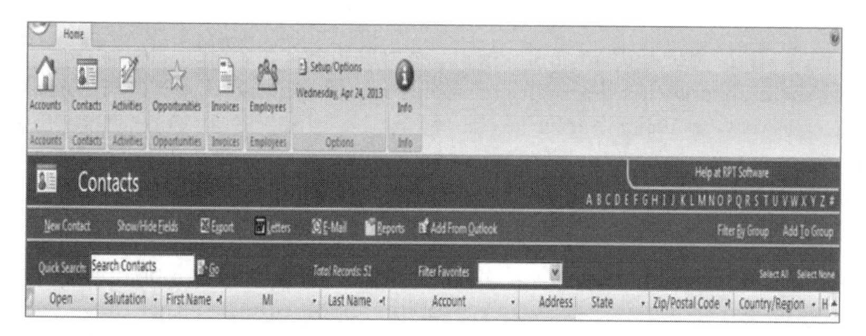

FIGURE 17-4: Header for a Split Form using only a datasheet view

You will also find several more tips for working with `Datasheet` views as you read through Appendix A. The examples can be applied to the datasheet sections of the `Split Form` as well as to the `Datasheet` view of a form or subform.

Pop-up, Modal, or Dialog Forms

Access forms can be opened within your application in three different window modes: `Popup`, `Modal`, or `Dialog`. These can be set manually using the property sheet or programmatically using VBA or macros. Each mode behaves differently and can be used for different purposes. You can also combine the modes to have even greater control over the way the user can interact with the form and the entire application when the form is open.

Pop-up

A *pop-up* form opens and stays on top of all other open forms within your application (actually, the pop-up form opens outside of the Access application window). Although it is on top of other objects, the pop-up form does not necessarily have to have the focus. This can be quite helpful when you want to present the user with some reference information that needs to be available while they are using or entering data on another form. A pop-up form also allows the user to access the ribbon buttons and menus.

You can create a pop-up form by setting its `PopUp` property to `Yes`. This property is often used in conjunction with setting other properties such as `Modal`, `Cycle` (of records) and `Border Style`.

Modal

A *modal* form opens and keeps the focus until it is closed (or hidden). When a modal form opens, the user will not be able to use other forms or even go to the ribbon (it won't even let you click the `Exit` button to quit Access). This mode is useful when you want to control the user's workflow by opening each modal form in sequence based on the task they're doing.

You can create a modal form by setting the form's `Modal` property to `Yes`. If you use both the `PopUp` and `Modal` properties, you can make the form behave both as a pop-up (stays on top) and a modal (keeps the focus) form by setting them both to `Yes`.

Dialog

A *dialog* form opens on top of all the other forms and also keeps the focus until it is closed (or hidden). There is one major difference with a dialog form's behavior as compared to a form with its `PopUp` and `Modal` properties set to `Yes`. When a form is opened in dialog mode, all code execution is also "suspended" until the dialog form is closed. This type of behavior is very useful when you need user input before proceeding with the next logic in your code. Some examples of dialog forms are the "warning" messages from Access or the `MsgBox()` and `InputBox()` functions.

You can only open a form in dialog mode using code (VBA or macro). The form can be opened in dialog mode regardless of the `PopUp` and `Modal` property settings. You can use either of the following lines of code to open a form in dialog mode,

```
DoCmd.OpenForm "FormName", , , , , acDialog
```

or:

```
DoCmd.OpenForm "FormName", WindowMode:=acDialog
```

There are several other properties that you can use to help guide users through the application. The next example introduces you to the `Tag` property.

THE DEMO FORMS

To provide clear examples of some of the features, properties, and controls, the 2013 Team database includes a few forms that have the single purpose of demonstrating the specific functionality that is being discussed. These forms start with the prefix `frmDemo` and aren't intended to be integrated with other processes of the database. The data source may be specifically structured to support features being discussed and should be considered as a slice of a solution or a temporary work table rather than representing fully developed, normalized tables, forms, or reports. As you go through the following examples, you can supplement the discussion by exploring the forms that are referenced.

Tag Property

Most of the controls on a form have a `Tag` property. It is a general purpose property that you can take advantage of to enhance the functionality of a specific form or apply it globally throughout the application. The `Tag` property accepts any text value that you assign, so you can adjust the designation depending on the purpose. For example, you can use the `Tag` property to ensure that certain fields are "read-only" by using the text value "`readonly`," as you will see in this demonstration. Another common use of the `Tag` property is to show or hide controls based on the user, the data, or some other condition.

The form `frmDemoTagReadOnly` is specifically designed to provide a demonstration that you can easily expand on and incorporate into your solutions. You can see how it works as you follow the discussion. The database also contains the form `frmDemoTagRequiredData` as an example of how you can use the `Tag` property to direct user actions when specific data is required based on a scenario. On this form, the `Tag` property is used to provide an easy-to-understand message to the user; it also changes the background color of the applicable controls and places the cursor in the field needing data. The technique can also be used to provide user-friendly messages for fields that are required at the table level. You will see additional ways to use the `Tag` property later in this chapter when you review the code to reset column widths in `Datasheet` view as well as when you are working with the Report Runner.

The current example could likely apply to a lot of your projects, as many solutions require a method to have users log in, and then use that information to identify their permission level or user role, which then dictates what they can do within the database. The form `frmDemoTagReadOnly`, shown in Figure 17-5, demonstrates how to use the `Tag` property in conjunction with a user role to allow users to see or edit fields depending on having either an `Admin` or `User` role. In this case, Admins are allowed to make any changes to the data, while Users can only change certain fields in the database.

FIGURE 17-5: Using the Tag property to enforce user permissions

Where you would normally use a login form or some other means to determine the current user's role, `frmDemoTagReadOnly` uses a combo box to simulate this process. It then uses the following code in the form's `Open` event to set the read-only fields based on the role selected:

```
Private Sub Form_Open(Cancel As Integer)
'Initiate the user's role in memory based on the combobox value
TempVars.Add "UserRole", Me.cboUserRole.Value

'Set read-only fields based on current user's role
Dim ctl As Control
Dim blnAdmin As Boolean

'Check user's role
If Nz(TempVars("UserRole"), "User") = "Admin" Then
  blnAdmin = True
Else
  blnAdmin = False
End If

For Each ctl In Me.Controls
  If ctl.Tag = "readonly" Then
    Select Case ctl.ControlType
      Case acTextBox
        Ctl.Enabled = blnAdmin
    End Select
  End If
Next

End Sub
```

Looking back at the code, you can quickly review what it does. At the beginning of the code, an object variable is declared to represent the controls on the form. Then, after establishing the current user's role using a `TempVar`, the code loops through all the controls on the form checking the `Tag` property.

If any control has "`readonly`" in its `Tag` property, the code sets that control's `Enabled` property according to the role.

> **NOTE** *Some controls, such as the* `checkbox` *and* `Option Button`*, do not have a* `Backcolor` *property, so an additional check for the* `ControlType` *property is necessary. You can see an example of this in the* `BeforeUpdate` *event on* `frmDemoTagRequiredData` *in the code following the comment: '*`Some controls don't have a Backcolor property`*'. For those controls, you might change the color of the associated label.*

You may also want to include code to confirm values or take other actions. And of course, your forms will have the full suite of controls and navigation appropriate for the situation.

Displaying Images

When designing forms, you can use images, such as logos, to enhance a form's appeal to the user and to convey critical information. Proper use and placement of images can make the form look more interesting and professional. There are several ways you can include images on a form, including bound and unbound objects, the image control, and attachment fields. `FrmDemoImage`, shown in Figure 17-6, demonstrates the effects of some of the settings. It also demonstrates the benefits of including an image within the instructions to provide helpful guidance to the users.

Bound Object Frame

This control is used to display Object Linking and Embedding (OLE) objects stored in your database table. OLE objects can be an image or any other file on your computer. If the content of the object cannot be rendered by Access in the control, an icon is displayed instead.

When storing OLE objects in your table, you have the option of linking the record to the file or embedding the file into the record. Linking the record will cause Access to check the original file for any changes and automatically update the record when a change is detected.

Displaying Images

Using image files can enhance and provide a professional polish to forms and reports.
There are several ways to incorporate image files.
And, a few things to avoid - such as JPG and PNG files.

The first two image controls use the Bound Object Frame and the Control Source is the field with the photo.
The Size Mode property is set to Zoom - so that the photo will fill the control but maintain its proportions.

The Size Mode property of the second control is set to Stretch, so the image will shrink or stretch as needed to fit the frame.

The third and fourth pictures uses the Image control.
They both have an embedded picture - so the default image will remain the same for all records.
The third picture also has a control source, and will disply the picture from the image path if it is available

C:\Flowers\Ts_Hat.bmp

The fourth picture does not have a control source- so the image will remain the same for all records.

You can use this technique to provide a background or default image when the preferred image is not found.

The final example uses an Attachment field.
Note: If there are multiple attachments, it will display the first one. To see the other attachments, click on the control and use the popup navigation control .

TIP: notice that an image control is used to show navigation control in the instructions.

FIGURE 17-6: Ways to display images on a form

When displaying images using the `Bound Object Frame`, three display size modes are available: `Clip`, `Stretch`, and `Zoom`. `Clip` will display the object at actual size and clip the image if the control is smaller than the object. `Stretch` will size the image to fill the entire control that could result in distorted proportions. And `Zoom` will display the entire image within the control while preserving its aspect ratio.

`Bound Object Frames` are extremely powerful. For example, they allow you to edit a Word object in place. As a consequence, it is also a very "heavy" object, taking up a lot of memory and processing power, so use it judiciously.

Unbound Object Frame

The `Unbound Object Frame` control is similar to the `Bound Object Frame`, except that the unbound control is primarily used to display objects that are not stored in the database. When using this control, you have the option to use an existing file or to create a new file.

Image Control

The `Image` control is primarily used to display image files. For example, if you want to display a company logo on the form, you would typically use the `Image` control. It has similar properties to the bound and unbound object frame controls, such as the ability to link or embed the image and adjust the size displayed in the control.

One very useful property of the `Image` control is the `Control Source` property. This property allows you to "`bind`" the control to a field in your table that stores the full path to an image file. For example, you could create a profile form in your employee database to display a photo of each employee by using image files stored on the company's server. This approach can also be used to include logos on labels, envelopes, invoices, etc. The image control can also be an ideal approach for displaying a QR (Quick Response) code.

> **WARNING** *Anytime you link to items stored outside the database, there is a risk that the item will not be found, whether it is due to the file or the folder not being available as specified. When evaluating what approach to use for managing images, attachments, or any external object, you need to consider the files, the computer/network configuration, and the controls that are in place. A common approach is to store additional files in the same directory as the data file. You can also check for their existence during the startup process.*

Attachment Control

The `Attachment` control is used primarily to display and manage an `Attachment` field on your form. It is similar to a `Bound Object Frame` in that it can contain images and other files. However, the main advantage of an `Attachment` field over an `OLE Object` field is that an Attachment field can contain more than one object in one record. As a result, the `Attachment` control includes a small navigation toolbar that pops into view when the `Attachment` control has the focus.

`Attachment` and multi-value fields require special handling, particularly when you need to copy or move records or tables that contain them. You'll learn how to do that a little later in this chapter.

List and Combo Boxes

List and combo boxes are typically used to provide users with lists of values to select from. Whether the purpose is to fill in a value or to find an existing record, it is typically easier and more accurate to allow users to select from a list rather than to type freeform. There are numerous ways to customize the controls to fit the specific needs. For example, when possible you can minimize the potential for entry errors by setting the `Limit To List` property to `Yes`. If you do that, you can also specify what list to use, such as selecting a `Field` or setting the `Row Source` property to display the unique values of the underlying field. Additional features make it easy for users to add values to the list. For example, you can use the `NotInList` event to accept new values from the user or you can select an appropriate data entry form in the `List Items Edit Form` property.

Combo boxes and cascading combo boxes are often used to allow users to search for a record or records that meet the criteria. With very little effort, you can greatly enhance the user's experience by adding additional fields to the record source or dropdown list. Some fields are displayed to help make informed selections, and other fields can be hidden but still used to organize or limit the records or used to populate fields after the selection is made.

For example, if you have 5,000 people registered for an event, you will likely need more than a first and last name to distinguish each person. So in designing the combo box, you would use industry knowledge to add additional fields to help the user make the correct selection, as demonstrated on form `frmDemoComboBox`. In this case, it seems reasonable to include their company and their position or title, as shown in the first combo box of Figure 17-7. In the lower part of the figure, you can also see that the record source includes additional fields that are used to filter and organize the records.

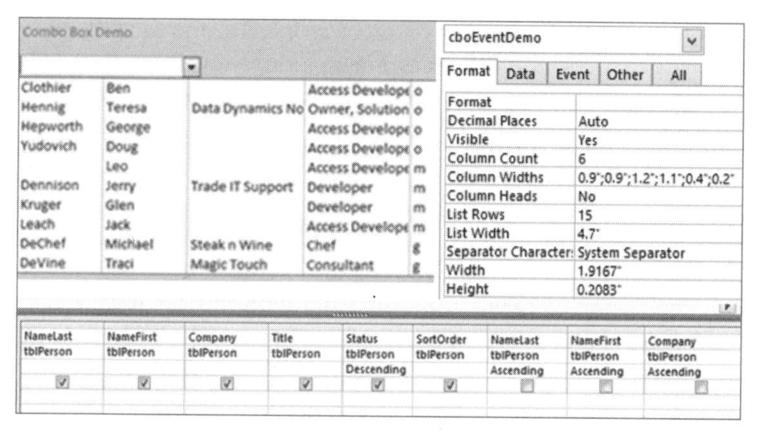

FIGURE 17-7: Enhanced combo box techniques

If you look at the query grid, you'll notice that the first sort field is the `Status` field, followed by `LastName` and other fields that have been designated for sorting. As the records are displayed, they are first grouped by the Status, and then sorted by the last name. The record source also includes a specifically designated sort order field. That can be tremendously helpful when you are dealing with categories or items that you might include in a list but that don't lend themselves to alpha/numeric sorting.

> **NOTE** *Using a specifically designated Sort field can provide significant benefits when organizing and sorting data, particularly in look-up tables. Consider a list of colors; you certainly can't use an alpha sort on colors to group and sort them by color. Another tip is to allow large gaps between initial increments so that new records can be inserted in the desired display order. You may also find it helpful to use a field to indicate inactive records and move them to the bottom of their lists.*

These are the types of UI enhancements that were discussed earlier in this chapter. You can provide similar benefits to those using your applications by including standard sort and status fields in your tables. You may not always need them, but it is easier to have them included but unused than it is to add fields to tables, forms, and control sources after a solution has been deployed.

As you work with combo boxes, you will likely become adept at setting the properties to best suit the scenario. But as you're experimenting and learning which combinations work best for specific situations, you may find it helpful to create and preserve some examples with write-ups, similar to the demo combo box provided here. You might include notes about the importance of the column order and widths, the order in which columns are filtered and grouped, and other comments that may be useful when you are incorporating the example into a future project.

Datasheet View Search Forms

Earlier, you looked briefly at a `Split Form` in a discussion of a few of the options and benefits associated with having a single source that simultaneously provides both a form and grid layout. Although not a `Split Form`, the datasheet search example demonstrates some of the techniques that you can use with the form's `Datasheet` view to give users powerful, informative search capabilities. You can follow the example by using `frmSearchPersonEvent`. This has the form as a main form, but you can also apply a similar approach to use this as a subform and have additional controls in the main form.

The main purpose of this demonstration is to show you how quickly and easily you can give users a powerful search tool that displays valuable information to help them quickly and accurately filter to the desired record or records. Once they have identified the records, you can offer any number of custom or built-in options, such as sending them to Excel, transmitting them by e-mail, or using them as the record source to open a form or report. You can also put specific actions behind each textbox and even vary the actions based on the user. As you work with this example, you'll recognize the vast potential for uses and benefits.

To get started, you can create a complex query that includes all of the desired information. You will want to ensure that you've used the correct join properties to ensure that records are not eliminated as is often the case if you use an inner join instead of a right or left join. Figure 17-8 shows the design view of `qrySearchPersonEvent`, the record source for the search form.

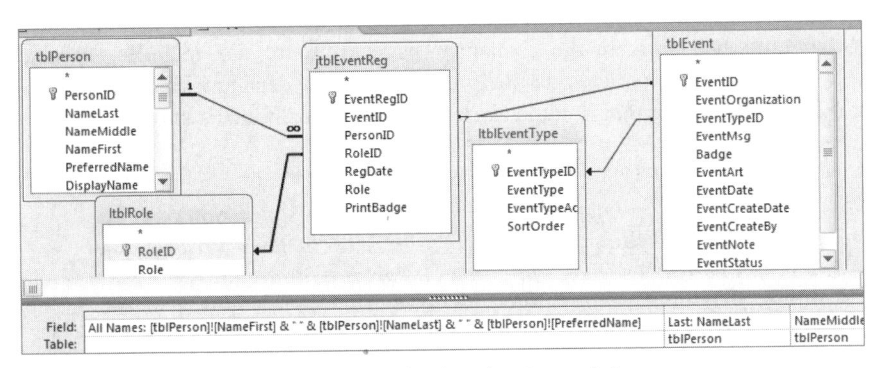

FIGURE 17-8: Record source query for the datasheet search form

You'll notice that it has a field called `All Names`. This was created to facilitate searches across the first, last, and nickname or preferred name fields. Many times, the user may not know how the name was entered, so rather than have them conduct three searches, you can create an expression in your query and search that. The `All Names` field uses the following expression: `All Names: [tblPerson]![NameFirst] & " " & [tblPerson]![NameLast] & " " & [tblPerson]![PreferredName]`, as shown in the preceding query.

After you create the query, the next step is to create the form. The easiest way is to select the query and then use the ribbon's `Create` tab and click the `More Forms` button; then click `Datasheet`. This will automatically create the `datasheet` form with all of the fields in the order that they appear in the query, as shown in Figure 17-9.

qrySearchPersonEvent

All Names	Last Name	Midd	First	AKA	DisplayName	Company	Org	
Teresa Hennig	Hennig		Teresa		Teresa Hennig	Data Dynamics Northwe:	Pacific Northwest Acce	Use
Traci DeVine Traci	DeVine		Traci	Traci	Traci DeVine	Magic Touch	Pacific Northwest Acce	Use
Jerry Dennison	Dennison		Jerry		Jerry Dennison	Trade IT Support	Pacific Northwest Acce	Use

FIGURE 17-9: Datasheet view as created

You can adjust the fields and make other changes. One of the first tasks should be to give the form a correct name. It is also helpful to use the properties to only allow `Datasheet` view and to specify whether or not users can update or add data. If this is to be strictly a search form, you use the property settings to prevent users from making any changes but still allow them to open other forms so that they can add and edit records. You can also open pop-up forms from either the record selector or a control (field) on the form to provide users with additional details and options.

> **NOTE** You can use a pop-up form to allow the user to view and edit individual fields, such as lengthy text fields. Users often appreciate the added benefit of using a larger font size for the display, much like being able to zoom in.

One of the benefits of using the `Datasheet` view is that a lot of people are used to working with Excel so they feel comfortable and confident working with this view in Access. Users may also be familiar with searching and filtering within spreadsheets, so a nice tip to share with them is the built-in feature to perform complex searches in a single column. The most intuitive approach is to use the search and filter drop-down at the top of the column. `If you need multiple` criteria across several fields, you can use the `Filter by Form` feature that is on the ribbon's `Home` tab, in the `Sort and Filter` group. You can also include this control in custom ribbons. Note that Filter by Form is not available in Access Runtime solutions.

For the purpose of this example, consider that you want to search the `All Names` column. Using the search tool at the top of the column, you can quickly select items from the list of unique values, or choose one of the text filters. If you are searching for a single value, you merely select the appropriate filter, such as Equals, and type the value into the custom filter form. You can also search for multiple values, such as all names that start with `de` or `te`. You would need to use `Text Filters` and `Contains` because the name can be anywhere in the field. In the `Custom Filter` window you need to type: `*de* or *te*` — with no quotes, as shown in Figure 17-10.

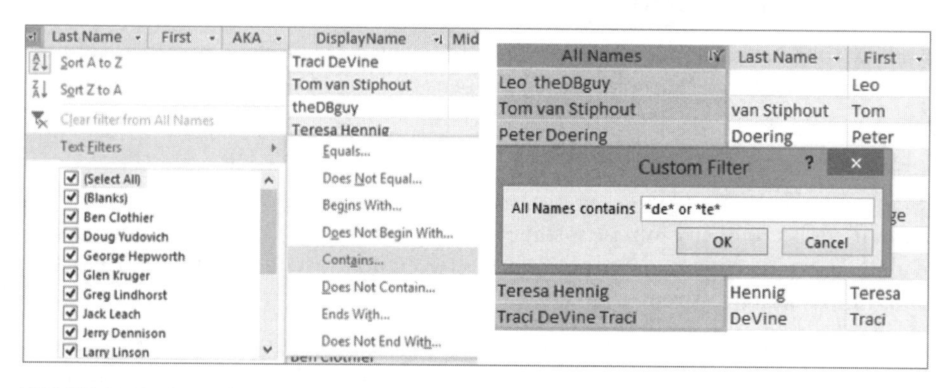

FIGURE 17-10: Steps for creating a complex custom text filter

As mentioned earlier, after you have located the desired records, you can take any number of actions, such as opening a form or report by using the form's double-click event. In the next example, you will see how to take that one step further, and open multiple instances of a form. Plus, you will see how to use the `Collection` property to limit it to one instance per person. But first, let's look at an approach that might help you resize or hide columns after a user has dragged them out of place:

```
Called in the Current event of the form  =ResetDataSheetColumns([Form])
 You will need to rename and modify to your application.
Public Function ResetDataSheetColumns(frm As Form) As Boolean
'------------------------------------------------------------------------------
' Procedure : ResetDataSheetColumns
' Author    : GPG - ' with modifications
' Purpose   : Reset column widths
'------------------------------------------------------------------------------
On Error GoTo errHandler
Dim ctl As Control
For Each ctl In frm.Controls
  If ctl.Tag = "Hidden" Then

    If ctl.ColumnHidden = False Then ctl.ColumnHidden = True
  ElseIf ctl.Tag = "Fixed" Then
    ctl.ColumnWidth = -2 ' -2 sets column width to fit displayed text exactly
  End If
Next ctl

exitProc:
  Exit Function
errHandler:
  Call GlobalErrorMessage(iNum:=Err, iLn:=Erl, sCtl:= _
"procedure ResetDataSheetColumns of Module modUtils")
   Resume exitProc
   Resume
End Function
```

Multiple Instances of a Form

Access usually allows only one instance of a given form to be open at one time, regardless of how many times the form is called. For example, this code opens the form only once, despite it being executed twice:

```
DoCmd.OpenForm "frmMyForm"
DoCmd.OpenForm "frmMyForm"
```

However, you can use VBA to open multiple instances of the same form. One of the common scenarios is to allow users to compare details or select between items, such as parts or products, menu items, or as in this scenario, event speakers.

In order for the form to be opened multiple times, the `Has Module` property must be set to `Yes`. With that set, you can open multiple versions of the same form by simply creating a new instance of the form using a form object. You could start with the following code:

```
Dim frm As frm

Set frm = New Form_frmMyForm

frm.SetFocus
```

In the preceding code, a form object is declared and assigned an instance of the original form by using the `New` keyword. However, the usefulness of that code (and life of the form) depends on where the object variable was declared. As soon as the variable goes out of scope, the form will automatically close. To prevent that, you need to use a more persistent object variable. For the purpose of this demonstration, a global `Collection` object will be used to contain each instance of the form to keep it available until it is no longer needed.

The download file included in this chapter supports the premise that the user would like to see the profile of each event speaker (or attendee) in a separate form. This allows users to compare speakers as a factor in choosing which sessions to attend. By making the profile (`frmAbout`) available from the search form, `frmSearchPersonEvent`, the user can look up available information about anyone that is registered. This example uses the form's `DoubleClick` event, but you can also place the code behind specific fields. Regardless of the placement, you will also need to inform the users how and why to open this or any other forms that you include.

To open the speaker's profile, the following code can be used in the search form's `DoubleClick` event:

```
DoCmd.OpenForm "frmAbout", , , "PersonID=" & Me.PersonID, , acDialog
```

That code would open the profile form in dialog mode filtered to the speaker info on the current record. However, using dialog mode will not allow any further user interaction on the main form until the profile form is closed. If you don't use dialog mode, which sets the `Modal` and `PopUp` properties to `No`, the user can double-click on another record to view the speaker's profile. When they do, Access will replace the data on the already opened copy of `frmAbout`, so the user will still only be able to see one profile at a time.

To allow users to simultaneously view multiple instances of `frmAbout`, you can use the following code in a standard module:

```
Option Compare Database
Option Explicit

Public collAbout As New Collection 'Instances of frmAbout

Public Sub OpenAbout(ByVal PersonID As Long)
'Open an independent instance of frmAbout

Dim frm As Form
Dim var As Variant
Dim blnAlreadyOpen As Boolean

'Check if same person is already in collection
For Each var In collAbout
  If var.PersonID = PersonID Then
    Set frm = var
    frm.SetFocus
    blnAlreadyOpen = True
    Exit For
  End If
```

```
Next

'Open new person form
If Not blnAlreadyOpen Then
  Set frm = New Form_frmAbout
  frm.Visible = True
  frm.Filter = "PersonID=" & PersonID
  frm.FilterOn = True

  'Add to collection
  collAbout.Add frm, CStr(PersonID)
End If

Set frm = Nothing
Set obj = Nothing

End Function
```

As you review the code, you can see that it starts by creating a `Collection` object that will store each instance of the form. Because each speaker could appear on the search form multiple times, the code also checks to see if a profile form is already open for the selected person. If not, a new instance of the profile form is opened, as shown in Figure 17-11 .When a new instance of the form is created, it is added to the collection to keep it available.

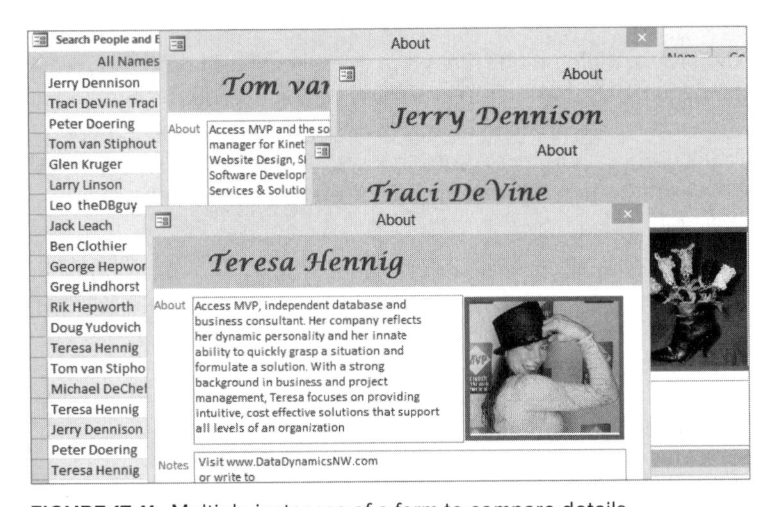

FIGURE 17-11: Multiple instances of a form to compare details

Using this technique allows you to open and preserve a form, but you are responsible for managing this and tracking when forms are closed. When the profile form is closed, it needs to be removed from the collection. To do that, you can use the following code in a standard module:

```
Public Sub CloseAbout (ByVal ID As Long)
'Remove form instance from collPerson collection

Dim var As Variant
Dim bool As Boolean

'Check if form instance is in collection
```

```
For Each var In collAbout
  If var.PersonID = ID Then
    bool = True
    Exit For
  End If
Next

'Remove instance from collection
If bool Then collAbout.Remove CStr(ID)

End Sub
```

You would then use the following code in the `Close` event of `frmAbout` to remove the current instance of that form from the collection:

```
Private Sub Form_Close()

'Remove form instance from public collection
Call CloseAbout(Me.PersonID)

End Sub
```

With that, there is one step remaining for you to manage multiple instances of the profile form rather than one. You need to replace the original `DoubleClick` event code with the following code snippet. So the following code goes behind `frmSearchPersonEvent`, in the form's `DoubleClick` event procedure:

```
Private Sub Form_DblClick(Cancel As Integer)

'Open profile form for this person
Call OpenAbout(Me.PersonID)

End Sub
```

When you use attachments, such as the image files, you will also encounter new challenges if you need to copy records or files. So the next example provides a process that you can use to copy, insert, or add records and tables that have MVFs or attachments.

MULTI-VALUE FIELDS

Every seasoned developer is familiar with the "evils of lookup fields at the table level." So when Microsoft added the *multi-value field* (MVF) feature to easily display child records in one field, it sparked some interesting discussions among Access developers. The primary concern was that storing multiple values in one field is considered against established normalization rules, and therefore, might be a likely source of programming challenges and data discrepancies.

However, the way the MVF was implemented in Access doesn't necessarily violate the rules on normalization — at least there is a valid argument that it doesn't. The MVF uses an internal table to store the child records separate from the parent table, and it maintains the one-to-many relationship between the records. As the use of MVFs has become more prevalent, you may need to know how to manage the data, particularly how to transfer records from one database to another.

That being said, this demonstration provides both the background and a tool to help you manage and manipulate records that contain MVFs. You will learn about their benefits, limitations, and special handling requirements. You will see that using MVFs has several similarities to handling other special controls, such as a multi-select `listbox`. This example uses the chapter download database file named `MVFDemo.accdb`, and the code is available in the file named `850832_ch17_MVF_CodeSnippets.txt`.

Appending MVFs

As you may already know, you can't use a simple make-table or append query to move or copy multi-value fields from one table into another. This is one of its limitations. The more important limitation is that MVFs are not supported by most *relational database management systems* (RDBMS). So, if you are planning to upscale your database into an enterprise system, then you will need to use a different approach or make specific arrangements to accommodate the MVF data.

To append the data from a multi-value field into another table, you must loop through its recordset. The following VBA example demonstrates one way to accomplish that. You can find the code and example in the database file `MVFDemo.accdb`:

```
Private Sub cmdAddMVFs_Click()

On Error GoTo errHandler

Dim rs As DAO.Recordset
Dim strSQL As String

'Check for records first
If DCount("*", "tblNewTable") > 0 Then
  'Open table with MVF
  strSQL = "SELECT RecordID, MVFs.Value As NewMVF " _
    & " FROM tblOldTable WHERE MVFs.Value Is Not Null ORDER BY RecordID"
  Set rs = db.OpenRecordset(strSQL, dbOpenSnapshot)

  'Loop through all records and insert MVF into new table
  With rs
    Do While Not .EOF
      strSQL = "INSERT INTO tblNewTable (MVFs.Value) VALUES ('" _
        & !NewMVF & "') WHERE RecordID=" & !recordid
      db.Execute strSQL, dbFailOnError
      .MoveNext
    Loop
    .Close
  End With

  'Refresh new table subform
  Me.frmNewMVF.Requery

Else
  MsgBox "Please add records first.", vbInformation, "No Records"

End If

errExit:
  'Cleanup
```

```
    Set rs = Nothing
    Exit Sub

errHandler:
    Select Case Err.Number
      Case 3022
        MsgBox "MVFs were already added.", vbInformation, "Done!"
      Case Else
        MsgBox Err.Number & ": " & Err.Description
    End Select
    Resume errExit

End Sub
```

As you read the code, you see that the MVF values are being copied from `tblOldTable` into `tblNewTable`. The first step is to create a recordset based on `tblOldTable`. Then the code loops through the records and inserts each record into the multi-value field in `tblNewTable`. It uses the `RecordID` field to maintain the correct associations.

The `recordset` object in the code contains all the child records in the multi-value field. You get that by using the `Value` property, which is rather unique to MVF. Using the `Value` property, you can refer to the child records in the MVF from the recordset produced by the SQL statement.

Appending Attachments

It may not be obvious but `Attachment` fields are also considered a special type of MVF. As such, make-table and append queries will not work for moving or copying records with attachments. You might think that because it is an MVF, you can use the same technique shown previously to manipulate its records.

However, that is not the case. `Attachment` fields have additional properties that also require special handling. Instead of using a simple SQL statement, you will need to create a separate recordset for each `Attachment` field and loop through its content. The following VBA example demonstrates one way to accomplish that:

```
Private Sub cmdAddAttachments_Click()

On Error GoTo errHandler

Dim rs1 As DAO.Recordset 'Table with attachments to be imported
Dim rs2 As DAO.Recordset 'Table to import attachments into
Dim rs3 As DAO.Recordset2 'Attachments to be imported
Dim rs4 As DAO.Recordset2 'Recordset to accept the new attachments
Dim strSQL As String

'Open table with attachments
strSQL = "SELECT RecordID, Attachments FROM tblOldTable " _
  & " WHERE Attachments.FileName Is Not Null ORDER BY RecordID"
Set rs1 = db.OpenRecordset(strSQL, dbOpenSnapshot)

'Loop through all the records to be imported
Do While Not rs1.EOF
  'Open table to be appended
```

```
    strSQL = "SELECT RecordID, Attachments FROM tblNewTable " _
      & " WHERE RecordID=" & rs1!RecordID
    Set rs2 = db.OpenRecordset(strSQL, dbOpenDynaset)

    'Recordsets for the attachment fields
    Set rs3 = rs1!Attachments.Value
    Set rs4 = rs2!Attachments.Value

    'Table to be appended must be in edit mode
    rs2.Edit

    'Add all new attachments (Note: Access automatically adds the file type)
    Do While Not rs3.EOF
      rs4.AddNew
        rs4!FileData = rs3!FileData
        rs4!FileName = rs3!FileName
      rs4.Update
      rs3.MoveNext
    Loop

    'Update parent record
    rs2.Update

    'Go to next record with attachment to import
    rs1.MoveNext

  Loop

  'Refresh new table subform
  Me.frmNewAttachment.Requery

  errExit:
    'Cleanup
    rs2.Close
    rs1.Close
    Set rs4 = Nothing
    Set rs3 = Nothing
    Set rs2 = Nothing
    Set rs1 = Nothing
    Exit Sub

  errHandler:
    Select Case Err.Number
      Case 3021
        MsgBox "Please add records first.", vbInformation, "No Records"
      Case 3820
        MsgBox "Attachments were already added.", vbInformation, "Done!"
      Case Else
        MsgBox Err.Number & ": " & Err.Description
    End Select
    Resume errExit

End Sub
```

As in the previous example, the code uses `tblOldTable` as the table with the attachments to copy or move. And it copies the attachments to `tblNewTable`.

As you can see, this requires four `recordset` variables to deal with the `Attachment` field. To avoid any confusion and to ensure that this clearly shows which recordset is being manipulated, the code purposely does not use any `With/End With` code block.

As you follow through the code, you will discern that `rs1` represents the table with the attachments, and `rs2` represents the table where the attachments are being appended. `rs3` represents the records in the `Attachment` field of `tblOldTable`, and `rs4` represents the records that will be inserted into the `Attachment` field in `tblNewTable`. As with the MVF code in the earlier example, this code uses the `Value` property of the `Attachment` field to instantiate `rs3` and `rs4`.

There are two more properties that you need to handle for Attachment fields: the `FileData` and `FileName` properties. A third property, `FileType`, will be handled automatically by Access, so it is not included in the code.

In a nutshell, the code loops through all the records that have an attachment and then loops through each attachment and copies it to the new table by adding a new record.

Add Attachment from File

You can use the preceding method to copy an `Attachment` field from another table, but you can also add individual attachments. The DAO method called `LoadFromFile` allows you to add singular attachments from a file. It uses the following syntax:

```
Recordset.Fields("FileData").LoadFromFile(<filename>)
```

So, continuing with the previous example, if you wanted to add a new attachment from a file, you could use code such as this:

```
rs4.AddNew
  rs4!FileData.LoadFromFile "c:\foldername\filename.ext"
rs4.Update
```

Save Attachments to File

You may be thinking that what comes in, must go out. So, if you can create an attachment from a file, you should also be able to save an attachment to a file. And, you would be correct. There is also a DAO method to save an attachment to a file. It is called `SaveToFile` and uses the following syntax:

```
Recordset.Fields("FileData").SaveToFile(<filename>)
```

You can take that a step further with the following code that will check to make sure the correct attachment is being saved to a file:

```
If rs4!FileName = "filename.ext" Then
'Save current attachment to a file
rs4!FileData.SaveToFile "c:\foldername\filename.ext"
End If
```

And applying it to the current scenario, the code might look something like this:

```
'Save current attachment to a file
rs4!FileData.SaveToFile "c:\foldername\filename.ext"
```

As you work with `MVFDemo.accdb`, you can see how the code is structured and how you can use it to manage attachments.

That wraps up the individual examples. In the next example, you will learn about and leverage several controls and properties of forms as you create a power tool that allows users tremendous flexibility and control for creating customized reports.

REPORT RUNNER

Most users think of forms primarily as a means of entering and viewing data or navigating between forms. While this is certainly true, forms can also provide users with a powerful mechanism for launching reports. Rather than opening the report to show all records, you can use a form to allow users to filter and select the exact records that fit their current needs. And that's what you're about to learn how to do.

This section will cover a host of tools and techniques that you can incorporate into your solutions so that your users will have the ability to not only filter their reports but to predefine which fields they will use as filters.

In the process, you will review how to iterate through a form's `controls collection` and how to use the hidden system tables. You will also see how to use a report's recordsource to determine which fields the user might wish to include in his filter sets, and use a form control's `Tag` property to clear the control based on the type of control it is. The code snippets for this section are found in the chapter download file named `850832_ch17_ReportRunner_CodeSnippets.txt`. The code is listed sequentially by heading and task.

Creating the Foundation

The first step is to build the tables to hold the information about your reports. For this example, you will use two tables, `tblReportCriteria` and `tblReportCriteriaDetail`, shown in Figures 17-12 and 17-13 respectively.

tblReportCriteria

Field Name	Data Type	Description (Optional)
ReportCriteriaID	AutoNumber	Autonumber Primary Key
ReportID	Number	Report ID from MSysObjects
ReportDisplayName	Short Text	Report Display Name/Description
Notes	Short Text	Additional notes about this report

FIGURE 17-12: tblReportCriteria in design view

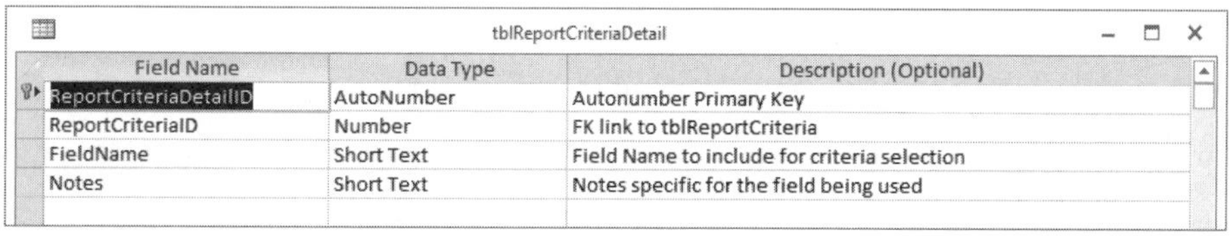

tblReportCriteriaDetail

Field Name	Data Type	Description (Optional)
ReportCriteriaDetailID	AutoNumber	Autonumber Primary Key
ReportCriteriaID	Number	FK link to tblReportCriteria
FieldName	Short Text	Field Name to include for criteria selection
Notes	Short Text	Notes specific for the field being used

FIGURE 17-13: tblReportCriteriaDetail in design view

These two tables, together, play a critical role in allowing users to establish the criteria selection fields for their reports. So when you incorporate this functionality into your applications, you will need to use the same table structure. As you can see, `tblReportCriteria` has four fields: an autonumber primary key, a field that is a foreign key linked to the system ID of the report, a field to give the user a friendlier display name for the report (other than its actual name, which is often not very descriptive), and notes the user may wish to give others about how to use the report.

Table `tblReportCriteriaDetail` also has four fields: an autonumber primary key, a foreign key to `tblReportCriteria`, the field name, and notes specific to the criteria fields the user is given. It is a good idea to create a relationship between these two tables and enforce referential integrity with `Cascade Delete`. This will prevent orphaned detail records should the parent record be deleted. You can also add `MSysObjects` to the `Relationships` window by selecting "`Show System Objects`" in `Navigation Options` . You can then create the relation with the `ReportID` field, but since this is a system table you cannot enforce referential integrity.

Now that you have your tables, you're ready to build your forms. You will use three forms. Two of the forms will be bound to the tables. One will be an unbound form that will use the information from the tables to let the user choose which report they want to run and apply any criteria they want (within the constraints defined by the criteria records) to the report.

> **NOTE** *The tables and forms described and illustrated here are included in the 2013 Team database. They are designed for optimum portability and can be incorporated into your files without requiring modifications.*

Setting Up the Report and Its Criteria Fields

The report criteria setup form and subform provide a user-friendly and easy-to-apply method of building the criteria fields for your user's reports. By allowing the user to define which field's criteria may be applied for each report, you remove the burden from you, the developer, of trying to anticipate how each report would be filtered. Often, you would use parameter queries or specialized individual forms to allow the user to choose which records to report on. As the user's needs change, you are usually forced to create new reports or to change or add parameters to the report's query. The same holds true if users start building reports on their own and then find that these new reports need to be filtered to specific records as well.

The tables that mange the reports utilize information from system tables, so any new reports that are added will automatically be available for criteria field selection by the user.

There are a few caveats that need pointing out:

- The tables for the reports will be maintained in the front-end files.
- To provide user-friendly data for filtering, many of the lookup fields store the actual data rather than the PK value.
- To avoid having to deal with raw SQL statements, all reports must be based on a named query or table — the filtering cannot be done within the report's record source.
- A report only has one set of report criteria; your users can change the criteria as needed.
- Fields can be used as criteria selection only once.
- The current process is not designed to use attachment, multi-value, or memo (`Long Text`) fields as criteria fields. If desired, you can modify the code to prevent fields with those data types from being available as report filtering criteria. In that case, you may benefit from moving some of the code into modules.

It is also helpful to understand the benefits related to some of the deviations from normal practices. Although some developers may argue that it isn't necessary, these tables use an `Autonumber` for their primary key. The `ReportID` has a default value to support a process for determining if an empty record has been created. You will also see that each variable in the modules is dimensioned as a `Variant` rather than an `Integer`. This allows you to leverage the ability for a `Variant` to be null and use that to pinpoint failure modes.

The next step is to examine the process for setting up a report to accept criteria selections. You begin with `frmReportCriteriaSetup`, shown in Figure 17-14. This form is bound to `tblReportCriteria`.

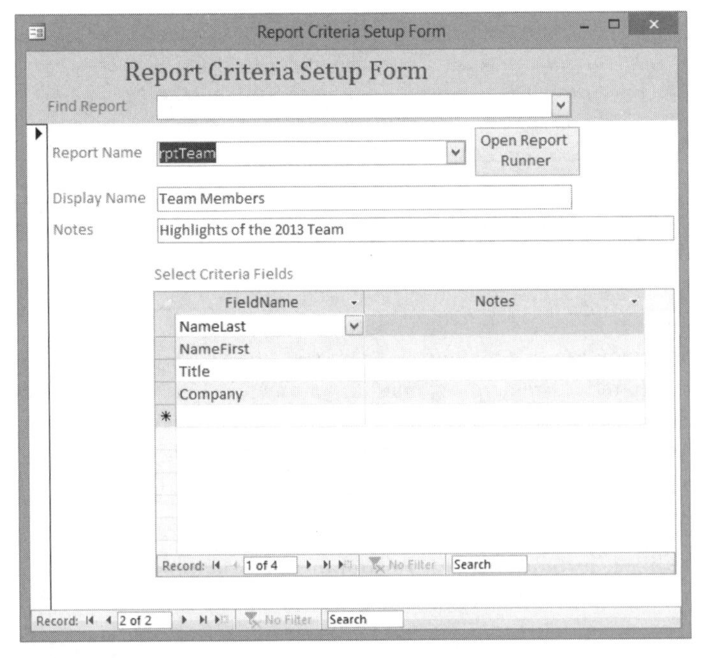

FIGURE 17-14: The report criteria setup form

The main body of this form has one `ComboBox` control, two `TextBox` controls, and a `SubForm` control. They are for the `ReportID`, `DisplayName`, `Notes`, and the `SubForm` for the criteria field names, respectively.

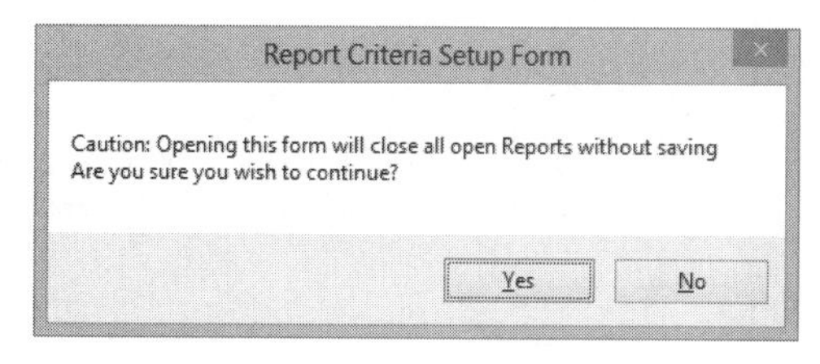

FIGURE 17-15: The flash screen for the report criteria setup form

You will notice that when you open the form, a flash screen (similar to a splash screen) pops up to warn you that opening the form will close any open reports without saving. As shown in Figure 17-15, this form gives you the option of canceling the action so that you can close any open reports in a more controlled manner.

The reason that all of the reports need to be closed is so that you can open them again later. As the user selects a report, or does a search for a report that has already been set up, the code will open a hidden instance of the report in design view. This is done so that you can extract the report's `RecordSource` and get the field list for the Report Runner's subform. You use the following code in the form's `On Open` event to display a flash screen (aka splash screen) and to close any open reports:

```
Private Sub Form_Open(Cancel As Integer)
  'Display message and close any open reports then
  On Error GoTo TrapError:

  Dim obj As AccessObject
  Dim db As Object
  Dim varResponse As Variant

  varResponse = MsgBox("Caution: Opening this form will close all open " _
  & "Reports without saving" & vbCrLf & "Are you sure you wish " _
  & "to continue?", vbYesNo, "Report Criteria Setup Form")

  If varResponse = vbNo Then
    Cancel = True
    GoTo ExitSub
  End If

  Set db = Application.CurrentProject

  For Each obj In db.AllReports
    If obj.IsLoaded Then
      DoCmd.Close obj.Type, obj.Name, acSaveNo
    End If
  Next

ExitSub:
  'clean up objects
  Set obj = Nothing
  Set db = Nothing
  Exit Sub
```

```
TrapError:

  MsgBox "Error number: " & Err.Number & vbCrLf & "Error Description: " _
& Err.Description & vbCrLf, vbCritical, "Unkown Error"
Resume ExitSub
End Sub
```

Once the criteria setup form is open, you use code to control various aspects of what is displayed in certain controls as well as the opening and closing of the hidden reports as the user navigates through existing records or creates new ones. You also control the choices in some of the combo boxes to prevent error messages if the user tries to create records that already exist, and to prevent unauthorized choices (reports with record sources not based on a saved query or table).

You can review all of the code behind this form at your leisure, but for now it is worth discussing the form's `On Current` event. This event contains some useful code for setting the `RowSource` property of the `cboReportIDComboBox`. The code for the event is listed here:

```
Private Sub Form_Current()

  On Error GoTo TrapError
  Dim strReportIDSQL As String

  'Set rowsource for cboReportID
If Me.NewRecord Then
    strReportIDSQL = "SELECT MSysObjects.Id, MSysObjects.Name, " _
  & "MSysObjects.Type " _
  & "FROM MSysObjects LEFT JOIN tblReportCriteria " _
  & "ON MSysObjects.Id = tblReportCriteria.ReportID " _
  & "WHERE (((MSysObjects.Type)=-32764) AND " _
  & "((tblReportCriteria.ReportID) Is Null));"
  Else
    strReportIDSQL = "SELECT MSysObjects.Id, MSysObjects.Name, " _
  & "MSysObjects.Type " _
  & "FROM MSysObjects LEFT JOIN tblReportCriteria " _
  & "ON MSysObjects.Id = tblReportCriteria.ReportID " _
  & "WHERE (((MSysObjects.Type)=-32764));"
  End If
  Me.cboReportID.RowSource = strReportIDSQL
  Me.cboReportID.Requery

  'Hide search if in data entry mode
  If Me.DataEntry Then
    Me.cboFindReport.Visible = False
  Else
    Me.cboFindReport.Visible = True
  End If

  Dim obj As AccessObject
  Dim db As Object
  Dim strReportName As Variant

  'Close any hidden reports that may have been opened by this form
```

```
    'This closes reports that may be in memory and prevents multiple instances
    Set db = Application.CurrentProject

    For Each obj In db.AllReports
      If obj.IsLoaded Then
        DoCmd.Close obj.Type, obj.Name, acSaveNo
      End If
    Next

    'open current report as hidden to get current recordsource
    strReportName = Me.cboReportID.Column(1)
    strSQL = ""
    Me.txtSQL = ""

    If Not strReportName = "" Then
      DoCmd.OpenReport strReportName, acViewDesign, , , acHidden
      strSQL = Reports(strReportName).RecordSource
      Me.txtSQL = strSQL
  'Next: display the fields in this query using combobox RowSourceType = FieldList _
  'The control is hidden, but can be visible to show the SQL for troubleshooting.
      Me.sfrmReportCriteriaDetail.Form.cbofieldname.RowSource = strSQL
    End If

  ExitSub:
    'clean up objects
    Set obj = Nothing
    Set db = Nothing
    Exit Sub

  TrapError:

    MsgBox "Error number: " & Err.Number & vbCrLf & "Error Description: " _
  & Err.Description & vbCrLf, vbCritical, "Unkown Error"
    Resume ExitSub
  End Sub
```

There are several factors being addressed by the section of code under the comment 'Set rowsource for cboReportID' that is used to set the RowSource property of the cboReportID combo box. One of the challenges is to ensure that a report is only in the list one time — a user can change the criteria, but they can only have one set of criteria per report. You might consider enforcing this at the table level using a unique index (such as a primary key), but that still allows the user to select the report and then presents an error if it already has a record. It is more considerate to not show reports that have already been selected, such as accomplished with this approach.

Selecting the Criteria and Running the Report

Now that you've created your records that give you a description of the report and the fields that can have criteria applied to them, you're ready to select the criteria and run your report. To do this, you will create an unbound form to facilitate the report and criteria selection process. Your form will allow up to three criteria fields to be chosen from those that have been set up for that report. This can be expanded by adding more controls and code as needed.

In this example, you allow the user to choose how subsequent criteria fields are used. As in a query, you can use either `And` or `Or` to join the criteria. Using `And` indicates that each record must contain all of the criteria chosen for all fields. In contrast, using `Or` between two or more fields' criteria will return all records that meet at least one of the criteria. Your Report Runner form is intrinsically simple yet very powerful. In the header of the form, you have four usable controls: a `ComboBox` for selecting the report to be run, a `CheckBox` for selecting if the report is to be previewed or printed directly to the default printer, a `CommandButton` for launching the report, and a `CommandButton` for clearing all of the criteria selections.

In the detail section of the form, you have the controls for first selecting the criteria field and then selecting the value(s) from those fields to filter the report. These controls work as a group and use a combo box to select the field and a list box to select the criteria. Between criteria fields 1 and 2 and between 2 and 3 you have an `OptionGroup` with two `Radio Buttons`. These allow the user to choose whether to combine the criteria (using `And`) or to get records that meet both criteria (using `Or`).

You'll also find three command buttons. These allow users to clear the selection criteria, one list at a time. You can get a better understanding of the form by looking at the `Design` view in Figure 17-16, or by working with the form itself.

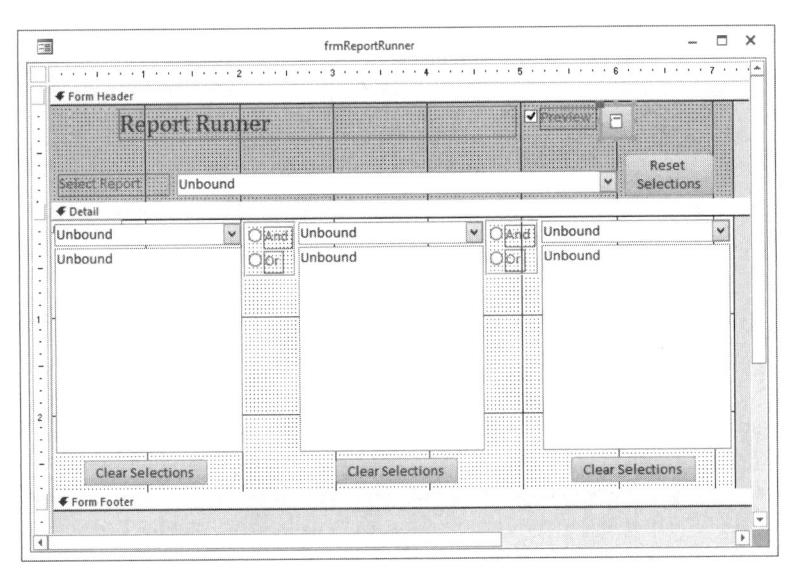

FIGURE 17-16: Design view of the Report Runner form

You will notice that the form itself and the controls are unbound — they do not have a `RecordSource`. To display the data, you use the `RowSource` property of each `ComboBox` control. The combo boxes for the three criteria fields are cascading, so each `RowSource` is filtered based on the report selected as well as on the choices made in each of the previous criteria fields. This prevents the user from choosing the same criteria field more than once. You can see the rowsource of the three combo boxes in Figures 17-17, 17-18, and 17-19.

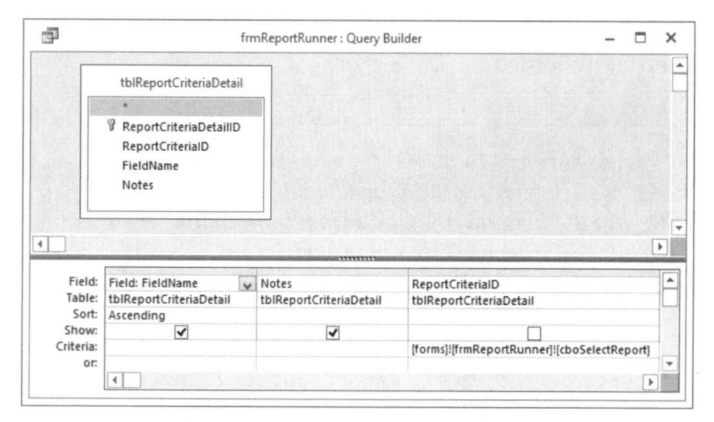

FIGURE 17-17: Criteria 1 Row Source

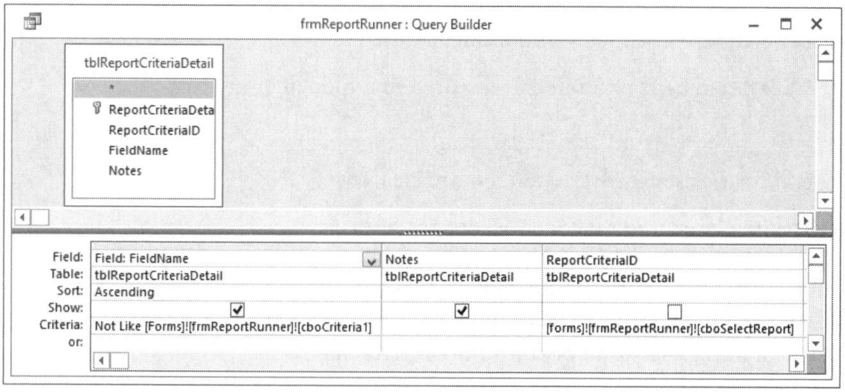

FIGURE 17-18: Criteria 2 Row Source

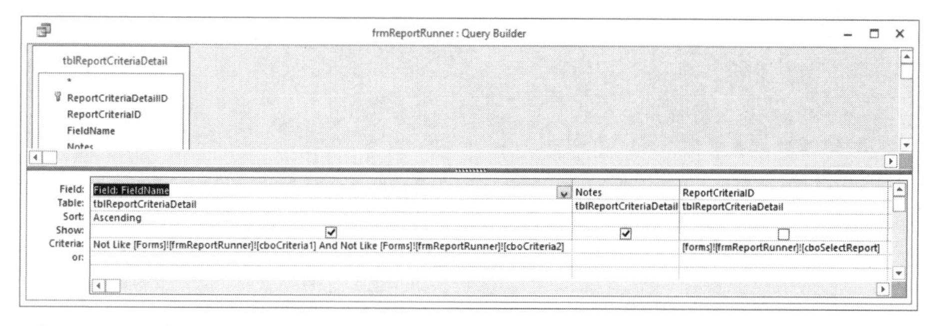

FIGURE 17-19: Criteria 3 Row Source

Note that for the first criteria field, the only filter used is the report selected. This is also used for the other criteria fields. The second criteria field also now uses the `Not Like` criteria stipulation with a pointer to the first criteria field to prevent the choice from that field from being available for the second criteria. The third criteria field uses the same method but includes pointers to both the first and second criteria fields. If you wanted to allow the user even more fields to choose from, then duplicate this method for as many controls as needed.

> **NOTE** *The use of* `Like` *is typically limited to filters that require wildcards. However, it is an expeditious and effective method for filtering the* `RowSource`. *Keep in mind that this is filtering the field names, so the maximum number of options is 255, whether the* `RowSource` *uses a table or a query.*

The next step for allowing your user to actually choose criteria values is to populate the `ListBox` control under each criteria field with values from the report's `RecordSource`. To make this process easier, most of the work is done behind the scenes and it uses a hidden `TextBox` to store the SQL statement in the event that it is needed for troubleshooting.

When the user chooses the report to run, several activities take place behind the scenes, including:

- The report is opened in `Design` view and hidden.
- The report's `RecordSource` is extracted and stored in a hidden `TextBox`.
- All of the criteria `ComboBoxes` are cleared.
- All of the criteria for the `ListBox` `RowSource` are cleared.
- All open reports are closed and all code objects are released.

The code described in the preceding text is triggered by the report selection's `After Update` event, as shown in the following code. It could be placed in a module, but it is kept behind the form so that the forms are self-sufficient and easier to import into other databases:

```
Private Sub cboSelectReport_AfterUpdate()
  On Error GoTo TrapError

  'Open current record's report in hidden mode to get current SQL source
  On Error GoTo TrapError
  Dim obj As AccessObject
  Dim db As Object
  Dim strReportName As Variant
  Dim strSQL As String
  Dim ctl As Control

  'Close any hidden reports that may have been opened by this form
  Set db = Application.CurrentProject

  For Each obj In db.AllReports
    If obj.IsLoaded Then
      DoCmd.Close obj.Type, obj.Name, acSaveNo
    End If
  Next

  'Open current report as hidden to get current recordsource
  strReportName = Me.cboSelectREport.Column(3)
```

```
    strSQL = "" 'initialize variable
    Me.txtSQL = "" 'initialize hidden text box

    If Not strReportName = "" Then
      DoCmd.OpenReport strReportName, acViewDesign, , , acHidden
      strSQL = Reports(strReportName).RecordSource
      Me.txtSQL = strSQL 'put report record source in hidden text box
    End If

  ExitSub:
    'Clean up objects, clear selections, and close reports
    For Each obj In db.AllReports
      If obj.IsLoaded Then
        DoCmd.Close obj.Type, obj.Name, acSaveNo
      End If
    Next
    For Each ctl In Me.Controls
      Select Case ctl.Tag
        Case "Clear"
          ctl.Value = Null
        Case "ClearSQL"
          ctl.RowSource = ""
          ctl.Value = Null
          ctl.Requery
      End Select
    Next
    strCriteria = ""
    Set obj = Nothing
    Set db = Nothing
    Exit Sub

  TrapError:

    MsgBox "Error number: " & Err.Number & vbCrLf & "Error Description: " _
  & Err.Description & vbCrLf, vbCritical, "Unkown Error"

    Resume ExitSub

  End Sub
```

You now have at your disposal the actual values for each of the criteria fields that are available in the report. You use the `After Update` event of each criteria control to change the `RowSource` property of its corresponding `ListBox`. Although the delimiters are strings, this code uses a `Variant` for the `Public Variables`; which avoids issues in the event that a `Null` is used. It is worth it in order to smoothly handle unexpected values — and we all know that can happen.

> **NOTE** *The choice of variable type is often based on personal style and experience since more than one type can work in many situations. This example uses a* `Variant` *to provide additional options for testing, troubleshooting, and trapping logical errors, such as when the* `Public Variable` *is assigned a value that is unexpected or not accepted. It also won't error-out if it is inadvertently assigned an object.*

The following code is used for the AfterUpdate event:

```
Private Sub cboCriteria1_AfterUpdate()

  'Determine and set SQL for Criteria list box
  Dim strSQL As String
  Dim strWHERE As String
  Dim strSQLTemp As String
  Dim strFieldName As String
  Dim strSourceName As String
  Dim intType As Integer

  strSourceName = Me.txtSQL
  strFieldName = Me.ActiveControl

  'Get the Query Field's DataTypeEnum Integer value to use to get
  'the correct Delimiters.
  intType = GetFieldDataType(strFieldName, strSourceName)

  'Get the correct Delimiter for the Field Data Type and store it
  'in a hidden text box.
  varDelimiter1 = GetDelimiter(intType)

'The following line could use SELECT DISTINCT instead of SELECT with GROUP BY:
strSQL = "SELECT " & Me.ActiveControl & " FROM " & Me.txtSQL & " GROUP BY " _
       & Me.ActiveControl & ";"
  Me.lstCriteria1.RowSource = strSQL

End Sub
```

To insure there are no errors when applying criteria, you must determine the DataType of the criteria field selected. Once you determine the DataType, you need to use the correct delimiter for that DataType. For example, text must be enclosed in single quotes while dates must be enclosed with '#'. You use two functions to determine and use the correct delimiters; Function GetFieldDataType and Function GetDelimiter. (Special thanks to Patrick Wood for these functions.)

Function GetFieldDataType accepts two variables: strFieldName and strSourceName. These are the field name and table or query name linked to the criteria field selected. The function returns the numeric value of the data type associated with the field. This value is passed to the function GetDelimiter, where the delimiter associated with that data type is determined. This delimiter is stored in a publicly declared variable for use by the subSetCriteria sub routine for building the criteria used when opening the report:

```
Public Function GetFieldDataType(ByVal strFieldName As String, _
        ByVal strSourceName As String) As DataTypeEnum
'Purpose: Get the DataTypeEnum value of the specified Field.

On Error GoTo ErrHandle

  Dim db As DAO.Database
  Dim fld As DAO.Field

  'Cannot just use CurrentDb to set the fld Object
  'because it causes an error when trying to get the fld.Type.
```

```
  Set db = CurrentDb

  On Error Resume Next
  Set fld = db.QueryDefs(strSourceName).Fields(strFieldName)
  If Err.Number = 3265 Then
    'This is not a Query field.
    Err.Clear
    On Error GoTo ErrHandle
    Set fld = db.TableDefs(strSourceName).Fields(strFieldName)
  ElseIf Err.Number <> 0 Then
    'Unknown Error. Trap it.
    GoTo ErrHandle
  End If

  If Not fld Is Nothing Then
    GetFieldDataType = fld.Type
  Else
    GetFieldDataType = 0
  End If

ExitHere:
  On Error Resume Next
  Set db = Nothing
  Set fld = Nothing
  Exit Function

ErrHandle:
  GetFieldDataType = 0
  MsgBox "Error #" & Err.Number & " " & Err.Description _
  & vbCrLf & "In Procedure GetFieldDataType"
  Resume ExitHere

End Function

Public Function GetDelimiter(ByVal intType As DataTypeEnum) As String
'Purpose: Get the delimiter needed to build the Criteria.

On Error GoTo ErrHandle

  Dim strDelimiter As String

  Select Case intType
    Case dbBoolean
      strDelimiter = vbNullString  'Boolean (True/False or Yes/No) Data Type
    Case dbByte, dbInteger, dbLong, dbCurrency, dbSingle, dbDouble, dbBigInt
       strDelimiter = vbNullString  'Numeric Data Type.
    Case dbDate
       strDelimiter = "#" 'Date and/or Time Data Type.
    Case dbText, dbMemo, dbChar
      strDelimiter = "'"  'Text Data Type.
    Case Else
      strDelimiter = "'"  'Assume text Data Type.
```

```
    End Select

    GetDelimiter = strDelimiter

  ExitHere:
    Exit Function

  ErrHandle:
    'Don't bother the user with an error in this Procedure.
    GetDelimiter = "'" 'Assume a text data type.
    Debug.Print "Error #" & Err.Number & " " & Err.Description _
    & vbCrLf & "In Procedure GetDelimiter"
    Resume ExitHere

  End Function
```

Now the user is ready for the criteria value selection process. To give your users the greatest flexibility in choosing values, you will want to set each `Listbox`'s `Multi Select` property to `Extended`. This will give them the functionality most of them have come to expect when selecting items in a `ListBox`. That is the use of Ctrl+Click and Shift+Click for selecting multiple items in the list.

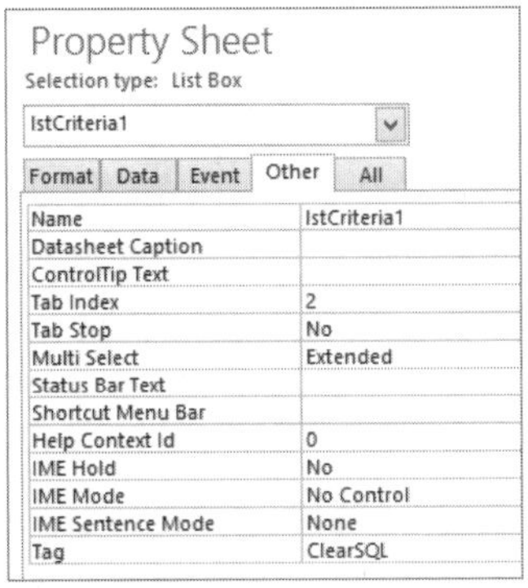

Notice the `Tag` property at the bottom of the property list displayed in Figure 17-20. As you've seen in other examples, the `Tag` property can be remarkably helpful when you need to execute the same code across multiple controls on a form or report. Here, you use two `Tag` values: `Clear` and `ClearSQL`. You may have noticed that they are used in the `cboSelectReport_AfterUpdate` event to clear the criteria `ComboBoxes` and `ListBoxes` respectively.

Property Sheet

Selection type: List Box

lstCriteria1

Format | Data | Event | Other | All

Name	lstCriteria1
Datasheet Caption	
ControlTip Text	
Tab Index	2
Tab Stop	No
Multi Select	Extended
Status Bar Text	
Shortcut Menu Bar	
Help Context Id	0
IME Hold	No
IME Mode	No Control
IME Sentence Mode	None
Tag	ClearSQL

FIGURE 17-20: Property sheet showing MultiSelect and Tag Properties

NOTE *The* `Tag` *property can be used for many purposes. It is often much easier to use the* `Tag` *property when iterating through control collections than it is to use the control's intrinsic properties. For example, if you attempt to set the* `RowSource` *property, it will generate an error when it gets to a* `TextBox` *control because that type of control does not have a* `RowSource` *property. So you would first have to test each control to determine if it was the correct type. It is much easier to use the* `Tag` *property.*

You can also use multiple values in the `Tag` *property. This will allow you to easily apply multiple rules and/or formatting options to each control based on your individual needs.*

To tie all of the choices together and open a filtered report, you will use a named `SubRoutine` and a command button. The `SubRoutine` is triggered by the `AfterUpdate` event of each `ListBox` control.

> **NOTE** *It is a good practice to ensure that you have defined your global options of* `Option Compare Database` *and* `Option Explicit`*. The first global option is to ensure that certain intrinsic string functions work as expected. For example, the* `Instr()` *function is designed to return the position of a substring in a larger string.* `Option Compare Database` *ensures text comparisons happen using the same rules the database engine is using. Omitting this statement leads to binary text comparisons which most likely will lead to unexpected results.* `Option Explicit` *ensures that you fully* `Dimension` *your variables and helps prevent you from misspelling a variable name and thereby creating an unintended variable. These are usually defined at the beginning of any code module. This is also where you would* `Dimension` *any public variables for use by other procedures within that module.* `Option Explicit` *can be set for all new modules by selecting Tools ➪ Options ➪ Require Variable Declarations from the VBA editor menu.*

The following code builds a SQL criteria statement that is used when opening the report. Although the `GetDelimiter` function returns a string and the delimiters are all strings, this code also uses a `Variant` for the `Public Variables` in the event that a `Null` is used, as previously explained:

```
Option Compare Database
Option Explicit
Public strReportSource As String
Public strCriteria As String
Public varDelimiter1 As Variant '\
Public varDelimiter2 As Variant ' } Dimension delimiter variables
Public varDelimiter3 As Variant '/

Public Sub subSetCriteria()
  On Error GoTo ErrorHandler

  Dim ctlListBox As Listbox
  Dim varItem As Variant
  Dim strCriteria1 As String
  Dim strCriteria2 As String
  Dim strCriteria3 As String
  Dim strDelimiter As String

  strCriteria = "" 'initialize criteria variable

  If IsNull(Me.cboSelectReport) Then Exit Sub

  Set ctlListBox = Me.lstCriteria1 'Get primary category selections if any

  'Get the Delimiter for the lstCriteria1 List Box Field Data Type.
  strDelimiter = Nz(varDelimiter1, "'")

  For Each varItem In ctlListBox.ItemsSelected
    strCriteria1 = strCriteria1 & strDelimiter _
    & ctlListBox.ItemData(varItem) & strDelimiter & ", "
  Next

  If Len(strCriteria1) < 2 Then
```

```
    'if no criteria selection force criteria to empty string
    strCriteria1 = ""
  Else
    'remove trailing comma
    strCriteria1 = Left(strCriteria1, Len(strCriteria1) - 2)
  End If

  Set ctlListBox = Me.lstCriteria2 'Get secondary category selections if any

  'Get the Delimiter for the lstCriteria2 List Box Field Data Type.
  strDelimiter = Nz(varDelimiter2, "'")

  For Each varItem In ctlListBox.ItemsSelected
    strCriteria2 = strCriteria2 & strDelimiter _
    & ctlListBox.ItemData(varItem) & strDelimiter & ", "
  Next

  If Len(strCriteria2) < 2 Then
    'if no criteria selection force criteria to empty string
    strCriteria2 = ""
  Else
    'remove trailing comma
    strCriteria2 = Left(strCriteria2, Len(strCriteria2) - 2)
  End If

  Set ctlListBox = Me.lstCriteria3 'Get secondary category selections if any

  'Get the Delimiter for the lstCriteria3 List Box Field Data Type.
  strDelimiter = Nz(varDelimiter3, "'")

  For Each varItem In ctlListBox.ItemsSelected
    strCriteria3 = strCriteria3 & strDelimiter _
    & ctlListBox.ItemData(varItem) & strDelimiter & ", "
  Next

  If Len(strCriteria3) < 2 Then
    'if no criteria selection force criteria to empty string
    strCriteria3 = ""
  Else
    'remove trailing comma
    strCriteria3 = Left(strCriteria3, Len(strCriteria3) - 2)
  End If

  'Build criteria string if any
  If Not Len(strCriteria1) = 0 Then
    strCriteria = strCriteria & "[" & Me.cboCriteria1 _
                 & "] In (" & strCriteria1 & ") " _
                 & IIf(Me.optCriteria2 = 1, " AND ", " OR  ")
  End If
  If Not Len(strCriteria2) = 0 Then
    strCriteria = strCriteria & "[" & Me.cboCriteria2 _
                 & "] In (" & strCriteria2 & ") " _
                 & IIf(Me.optCriteria3 = 1, " AND ", " OR  ")
  End If
  If Not Len(strCriteria3) = 0 Then
    strCriteria = strCriteria & "[" & Me.cboCriteria3 _
```

```
                  & "] In (" & strCriteria3 & ") "
    End If

    If Len(strCriteria) > 5 Then
      If Right(strCriteria, 5) = " AND " _
      Or Right(strCriteria, 5) = " OR  " Then
          strCriteria = Left(strCriteria, Len(strCriteria) - 5) 'remove ending
      End If
    Else
      strCriteria = "" 'set length to 0
    End If

    Exit Sub

  ErrorHandler:

    MsgBox "There was an unexpected error" & vbCrLf _
           & "Please report the following to the database developer" _
           & vbCrLf & "Error: " & Err.Number & vbCrLf & "Description: " _
           & Err.Description & vbCrLf & "In Procedure subSetCriteria " _
           & "of Form_frmReportRunner", vbCritical

    Exit Sub
    Resume
  End Sub
```

The preceding code builds a SQL criteria statement that will be used when opening the report. The code iterates through each `ListBox`'s `ItemSelectedCollection` and concatenates the selected items together inside a SQL `IN()` clause. An example looks like this: `[FieldName] IN (Value1, Value2,...,ValueN)`. The different fields are then linked together with either an `AND` or `OR` depending on the choice of the user. Once the full criteria has been built, any extraneous `AND` or `OR` is removed. The completed criteria statement is stored in the public variable `strCriteria` for use later when opening the report.

Because the criteria selection is based solely on the `ListBox` controls and `Radio Buttons`, you only call the *`subSetCriteria`*`Sub Routine` from the `AfterUpdate` event for each of these controls:

```
Private Sub lstCriteria1_AfterUpdate()
  Call subSetCriteria
End Sub

Private Sub lstCriteria2_AfterUpdate()
  Call subSetCriteria
End Sub

Private Sub lstCriteria3_AfterUpdate()
  Call subSetCriteria
End Sub

Private Sub optCriteria2_AfterUpdate()
  Call subSetCriteria
End Sub

Private Sub optCriteria3_AfterUpdate()
  Call subSetCriteria
End Sub
```

The final piece of the puzzle is running the report. This is controlled via the *cmdOpenReport* command button, by using the following code:

```
Private Sub cmdOpenReport_Click()

  On Error GoTo ErrorHandler

  Dim strReportCriteria As String
  Dim strReportName As String
  strReportCriteria = "" 'initialize criteria

  If IsNull(Me.cboSelectREport) Then
    MsgBox "Please select a report to print", vbCritical
    Exit Sub
  Else
    strReportName = Me.cboSelectREport.Column(3)
  End If

    strReportCriteria = strCriteria

  If Me.chkPreviewReport Then
    If Len(strReportCriteria) Then
      DoCmd.OpenReport strReportName, acViewPreview, , strReportCriteria
    Else
      DoCmd.OpenReport strReportName, acViewPreview
    End If
  Else
    If Len(strReportCriteria) Then
      DoCmd.OpenReport strReportName, acViewNormal, , strReportCriteria
    Else
      DoCmd.OpenReport strReportName, acViewNormal
    End If
  End If

  Exit Sub

ErrorHandler:
  If Err.Number = 2501 Then Exit Sub

  MsgBox "There was an unexpected error" & vbCrLf _
& "Please report the following to the database developer" _
& vbCrLf & "Error: " & Err.Number & vbCrLf & "Description: " _
& Err.Description, vbCritical

  Exit Sub

End Sub
```

As you can see there are other `Command Buttons` on the form for clearing selections made by the user. The code behind these has not been covered, but it should be easy to figure out.

And that wraps up the discussion of the Report Runner. It provides an impressive foundation for a custom report designer. Now that you have the functionality and concepts, you can tailor it to work with your projects.

SUMMARY

Forms are the primary way that users work with data and navigate the database. And as the database designer, it is incumbent upon you to make it as efficient, intuitive, and easy as possible for users to manipulate, manage, and report their data. You also need to ensure that the data is accurate, valid, and correctly reflects the user's criteria and purpose.

This chapter covered a lot of tips and techniques to help you create a user-friendly interface. It also included several tools that you can incorporate into your projects, such as the Report Runner, using datasheet searches to open detail records, and managing attachments.

The examples were designed to represent a slice of real-world scenarios to provide you with multiple approaches to find and display data. You can combine and adapt the techniques to best fit whatever project you are working on.

Many of the techniques, such as working with images, are also applicable to reports. And of course, the Report Runner tool, itself, will certainly prove invaluable when you want to allow users to customize their selection criteria. And that is an excellent segue to Chapter 18, "Creating Powerful Reports."

In Chapter 18, you will cover many of the fundamentals as you create some reports that respond to business needs. You will also create another report customization tool. This one will allow users to determine the grouping and level of detail that they want to see. That means that you can create one report and then enable users to modify the criteria to suit their current needs. For example, users can retrieve summary level reports across all departments or a detailed report for just one group.

18

Creating Powerful Reports

WHAT'S IN THIS CHAPTER?

- Customizing reports
- Using subreports
- Giving users greater control
- Adding professional polish to reports

WROX.COM CODE DOWNLOADS FOR THIS CHAPTER

The code downloads for this chapter are found at `www.wiley.com/go/proaccess2013prog.com` on the Download Code tab. The chapter download file includes five database files:

- `2013Team.accdb`
- `ReportExamples.accdb`
- `ReportExamplesNW.accdb`
- `PDFDemo.accdb`
- `PDFDemo.mdb`

Also included are the code snippets for this chapter, which are all located in the file named `850832_ch18_CodeSnippets.txt`. You will also find PDFDemo.pdf to use with the PDF examples.

> **NOTE** *As with most downloaded files, you may need to specifically trust and enable these files and their location for them to function properly. To display some of the images, you will also need to store the image folder as directed or update the links to their location on your computer. For more information, please read the "What you Need" section in the book's Introduction.*

The built-in report writer in Access has always been one of the most powerful and popular features of Access. In addition to the powerful wizards that can create formatted reports in a matter of minutes, Access has an easy-to-learn interface used to create, revise, and customize reports. You can use built-in Macros and VBA, or a combination thereof to modify reports on the fly at run time, either from user input or from values within the database.

Whether you have been working with Access reports for years or are just venturing into reports, you can easily find an abundance of good tips and examples. So the focus of this chapter is to point out some built-in features and fresh ideas to demonstrate how you can quickly benefit by leveraging them in your reports. It provides some powerful tools and examples that you can incorporate into your solutions to give your users more flexibility and control over the content selection, organization and display of their reports.

In addition to the techniques, features, and tips that are covered in the chapter, you can delve into the code and get more ideas by working with the forms and reports in the database files that accompany the chapter. You can use these, in whole or in part, to quickly add features and functionality that will improve the user interface and give your Access solutions a more professional presentation.

As with any solution, the style and visual enhancements of the final design is based on the project and developer. With that in mind, the examples are kept relatively plain so that you can easily extract portions and apply your choice of formatting to them, include them in templates, or use them in other manners.

INTRODUCTION TO REPORTS

Storing information in a database is only part of the challenge. You must also make it easy to enter, retrieve, review, and report in ways that are usable and meaningful to the consumers of the data. Just because the data is contained in well-designed tables does not mean that anyone but the application developer can see the data. Queries, forms, and reports are the principal methods used to deliver and present meaningful information to the consumer. This chapter focuses on reports, and builds on information about queries, macros, and forms that you may already know or was covered in earlier chapters.

Queries are at the heart of most reports and forms. Queries are used to return specific sets of data that will be displayed in a report. Having good query building skills is a big plus when designing reports. Chapter 16, "Programming using VBA, APIs, and Macros," includes discussions and examples that will help you enhance and leverage queries to retrieve precisely the data that you want and expect.

To give you a common foundation for working with subsequent examples, this chapter starts with a brief overview of some of the fundamentals for creating reports. The examples in the first part of the chapter leverage built-in features, such as the wizards and various properties of the report itself. You will see how to leverage these features to quickly give users the ability to create event badges and personalized session schedules that incorporate multiple subreports in one report.

Later in the chapter, the examples focus on leveraging events properties to give users control over the content and layout of the reports. You will again start with simple examples that become the foundation for creating a form that allows users to specify the way the data is grouped and summarized in their reports. The discussion wraps up with some tips on providing professional polish. But it doesn't stop there. As an added bonus, you will also find an example that demonstrates how to use Access to fill in PDF forms. You get the complete package, database, code, and demo PDF files.

CREATING REPORTS

This section is designed to establish a common foundation to support the rapid progress through the examples presented later in the chapter. Whether your expertise is working with other areas of Access or you are interested in a quick review, you can often find helpful nuggets by starting from a fresh perspective.

The discussion and examples are intended to build on each other and to give you a variety of options to use in your solutions. Some examples are demonstrated techniques that can save you time or add professional polish, other examples provide code and features that can be incorporated into your solutions to provide greater flexibility and control for your users.

You will start with examples using the `Report Designer` on a blank report. Then, you'll use the `Report Wizard` and the `Label Wizard`. Even if you typically don't use these wizards, it is good to see how they work as they tend to provide insights into approaches that you may not have thought about. After that, the examples will use the reports that you created to demonstrate how to modify the reports to fit your specific requirements. Some of the techniques will be familiar, but they serve multiple purposes here. In addition to providing alternative approaches for accomplishing a task, they may also help you troubleshoot or update a solution created by someone else.

Fundamentals

Although you may do some heavy lifting to ensure you're presenting the correct data, the majority of your time may easily be spent customizing the layout so that the end result achieves the desired look. You'll want to invest a little extra effort to ensure that your reports present the level of professionalism that adds to, rather than detracts from, the information being conveyed. The property sheet is a great resource for managing both the content and presentation of reports.

Property Sheet

Three of the most common approaches to customizing layouts include using a template (or copying objects from one), using the Property Sheet, and using the tools on the `Design ribbon`. Quite often, it will be a combination of all three. For now, the emphasis will be on the `Property Sheet Format` tab. You can open the `Property Sheet` from the `Design ribbon` or by right-clicking the report and selecting `Properties` at the bottom of the list. Figure 18-1 is a composite figure showing the `Format` tabs for both the `Report` and the `Detail` sections, as well as `Group and Sort` window. It is helpful to be familiar with the location of some of properties as you will use them extensively as you follow the examples and create your own reports.

As you are looking at the `Format` tab, you'll be familiar with most of the properties; but the focus here is to identify ones that you can leverage most effectively to create a professional presentation in your reports. With that in mind, there are a few properties that you'll most likely use, based on the part of the report or the control type.

FIGURE 18-1: Property sheet tabs and group and sortcontrol

Key Format Properties applicable to all objects include:

- `Caption` should be used to display user friendly names.
- `Font` selection should focus on making the content easy to read, and on judicious use of script or fancy styles.
- `Font Size` and `Weight` selections should be used to enhance clarity, purpose and readability. Use bolder and/or larger sizes in headings and totals to make them stand out. And, perhaps most importantly, be consistent.
- `Color` choices should stay with a schema and be used to help convey the message or to provide intuitive clues, but it should not be distracting. Access makes this easy by offering several theme-related colors in the dropdown.
- `Back Color` can be useful to communicate purpose, status, or importance of a field, section, tab, or other object.
- `Can Grow` and `Can Shrink` are very helpful properties for text that varies in length. Using `Can Grow` will allow the text field to expand down the page or form.
- `Hide Duplicates` can improve readability and clarity by eliminating the repetitious display of data.
- `Display When` is a convenient way to show a control only on screen or in print. This technique can be ideal for obtaining and printing user input without storing it, such as for a one-time use to print a name tag.

- Border Style and other related properties can be used effectively to draw attention to textboxes and labels, whether it is to make them transparent, bold, or to change based on conditional formatting.

Key Properties of Report include:

- All of the Data tab properties can be effectively leveraged.
- Caption should be used to give the report a user friendly name.
- Border Style can be used to control user actions, such as using a dialog style to require a user response.
- Page Header typically displays the headings and other information one time per page.
- Page Footer should provide a consistent display of page number, print/data date, report identifier, and other such items.
- On No Data Event should be used to provide a polite message for the user to replace the system message.
- Pop-up and Modal should be used judiciously to help guide or control user actions.
- Cycle can be used to specify what records a user can/will see and is particularly useful in conjunction with on-screen viewing and interactive reports.

Header and Footer Properties (for various sections) include:

- Name should be changed and follow your established naming conventions so that you can easily identify and work with them in code and macros.
- Visible can be used to show or hide the header based on specific criteria. It can be used in conjunction with showing or hiding detail sections to quickly use one report and provide either a summary or detail display.
- {Group} Keep Together can be used to avoid displaying orphan records or headings on a page. You can quickly add a professional touch just by controlling the way data is split across page breaks and by starting major groups on a new page.
- Force New Page can be used to insert a page before or after a section. By choosing Before Section, you can start each heading on a new page. Used judiciously, this provides an excellent mechanism to organize and separate data to meet specific needs.

Layout View

It can save time to start with a wizard or report designer, but you'll almost always need to move some controls and customize the features. When you are moving controls, Layout View will quickly become either a help or a hindrance. It can be a handy tool for keeping controls neatly arranged as you work with several in a group, and it allows you to see the actual data in the controls. But it can quickly become a thorn if you are trying to move just one of the controls in a group.

The key is to recognize the benefits of using Layout View and learn to use the layout features to your advantage. The two layouts are Tabular or Stacked. So, when you want the controls neatly arranged and aligned in either pattern, you can select the controls and apply the layout. Conversely, if the controls are already in a layout grid, you can select the controls that you want to work with independently and remove the layout just from them. You can use the `Ribbon` control, but you can also use the right-click menu tool. `Layout` is just below the `Insert` and `Merge` options, and has a flyout that allows you to select `Tabular`, `Stacked`, or `Remove Layout`, as shown in Figure 18-2.

FIGURE 18-2: Right-click layout options

Calculated Fields

Before starting on the examples, there is a data type that is worth mentioning as it can be particularly beneficial when creating various types of reports. It is the `Calculated Field` data type, and it can be used with both text and numeric values. You will see it momentarily as the `Display Name` in the examples for creating badges and printing personalized conference session schedules.

The `Calculated Field` data type may seem somewhat of an exception to the rules about not storing calculated values or repeating data in tables. To reiterate, it is a built-in exception to the rule — which is not to say that just because it is *built-in* it is good. But, in this case, it does seem to be an exception worth keeping and using.

To demonstrate this, consider a common scenario that most developers can relate to: storing and working with names. You frequently need fields for first name, last name, and preferred name. But just because a table has all three fields, doesn't mean that a record will have data in each field.

On the name tag, you likely want to show a person's preferred name with their last name, but if the preferred name is blank, it needs to use the first name with the last name. But if neither the preferred or first name is available, it needs to provide the last name. That sounds straightforward. However, you also need to consider the space before and after the names. Meaning, if there is a first name but no last name, don't include the extra space that would otherwise follow the first name. Wow, your eyes may spin as you work to envision the `IIf` statement needed to implement that logic. Plus, if you do this on a report or query, you'd have to write it for every report that uses that name combination.

That's where the beauty of the calculated field starts to shine. You can incorporate that type of logic at the table level and then use the calculated field in forms and reports. When any of the underlying values are updated, the calculated field will automatically be updated. Figure 18-3 shows the calculated field, `DisplayName`, along with the expression.

tblPerson

Field Name	Data Type
PersonID	AutoNumber
NameLast	Short Text
NameMiddle	Short Text
NameFirst	Short Text
PreferredName	Short Text
DisplayName	Calculated
Title	Short Text
Company	Short Text
Photo	OLE Object
ImagePath	Short Text
ImageAttach	Attachment

Expression Builder

Enter an Expression to calculate the value of the calculated column:
(Examples of expressions include [field1] + [field2] and [field1] < 5)

```
Trim((IIf([PreferredName] Is Null,[NameFirst],[PreferredName])+" ") &
[NameLast])
```

OK | Cancel | Help | << Less

Expression Elements: tblPerson, Functions, Constants, Operators
Expression Categories: PersonID, NameLast, NameMiddle, NameFirst
Expression Values: <Value>

FIGURE 18-3: Calculated field and expression builder

The Expression Builder will help you create the expression by providing the prompts and syntax framework based on the functions and fields that you select. This example uses Is Null to display the First Name only if there is no Preferred Name. Then it uses the plus sign (+) instead of the ampersand (&) to add a space after the name to separate it from the last name. If there is neither a first or preferred name, there won't be a space (see note about propagation of nulls). However, if it was left at that with no last name, it would still have a space after the first name. This could throw off the spacing in letters, greeting lines, or other such items. That is why Trim is added to the expression — it will remove all leading and trailing spaces from the final results:

```
Trim((IIf([PreferredName] Is Null,[NameFirst],[PreferredName])+" ")&[NameLast])
```

NOTE *It is very important to understand how to use the "propagation of nulls" in expressions and functions. It is very helpful when parsing or building strings of data, plus it can be used in query criteria and expressions as well as in VBA and macros. The key is to remember that the ampersand (&) preserves existing values that are added to null, and the plus (+) preserves or propagates null. For example:*

```
Null + "Teresa" = Null
Null & "Teresa" = "Teresa"
```

These are just a few of the fundamentals for creating and working with reports. The following examples will help solidify the concepts and open the door to more variations and possibilities.

Creating and Customizing Reports

There are several ways to start the process of creating a report. Among the easiest is to select the data source, typically a query or table, and then use the tools provided on the Create Ribbon. Report, Report Wizard, and Labels will start with a data source that you specify. The Report Design and Blank Report options essentially start with an empty sheet, except that Report Design has the grid and the page header and footer sections.

Regardless of how you get started, it is a good practice to save the new object immediately after creating it — before adding fields or making significant customizations. And, of course, you should follow good naming conventions — not just for the report itself, but for the controls within the reports. Most often, you will need to make at least a few modifications, such as changing the title and field captions, adjusting the placement and sizes of fields, and inserting a logo and image controls with custom graphics.

NOTE *You can also incorporate a standard header or footer by copying and pasting the controls (or the entire section) from another report. Or, better yet, create a few template reports and forms and use them in total or in part to quickly provide custom features and consistency throughout the application. You can start a template from scratch, use the* Normal *report template, or select from countless templates available for download.*

Using the Report Wizard

If you are building a report that requires a subreport, the `Report Wizard` can be an excellent place to start. This wizard allows you to select fields from multiple record sources, both tables and queries. If you select record sources that do not have an established relationship, the wizard will prompt you to create the relationship or select a different record source.

If you choose to create the relationship, it will open the relationship window for you. You can then add the appropriate tables and establish the join properties. Figure 18-4 shows the message and subsequent table relationships that will support creating the subreport to display an individual's conference sessions in an upcoming example.

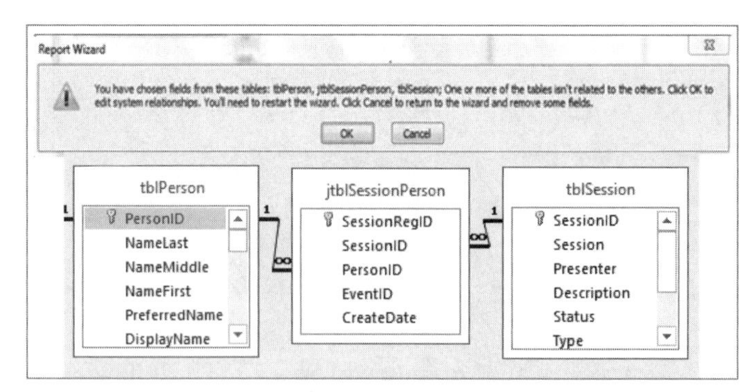

FIGURE 18-4: Report Wizard message and the relationships window

Using the Label Wizard

To quickly review the basic steps and some good practices, you can start by creating a report to print event badges. This will use the built-in features for labels to get a preset size. You will also customize the look by formatting the company name, using the person's preferred name if it is provided, and formatting the fields to emphasize the person's name and company. You might also include conditional formatting, such as designating a color based on the person's role. You could also include a company or event logo, a barcode, or other event specific fields. You can use a similar approach for envelopes, address labels, and a myriad of other purposes.

Start by selecting query `qryEventPerson` as the record source. Then on the `Create Ribbon`, go to the `Reports` tab and click the `Label` button. This opens the `Label Wizard`. To quickly create a name badge that will fit in most badge holders, you might choose `Avery 4168`, continuous feed, to create name badges that are 2 1/6 inches tall by 4 inches wide. After clicking `Next`, you can customize the font. This example uses `Calibri`, size `10`, `Medium` weight in the default black color. After clicking `Next`, you will begin selecting the fields to appear on the badge.

> **NOTE** *As you are looking at the custom labels, you should notice that there are several standard sizes, such as Avery 8387, 4 1/4" X 5 1/2", which sets perfect margins for printing postcards four-up on a page. These are excellent for sending event directions, collecting session surveys, and countless other tasks.*
>
> *It is important to realize that most continuous feed designs will not appear in your printer and page default options. So when you preview these types of special reports, you will see one-up on a page, surrounded by an abundance of white space.*

One of the handy features of the label wizard is the ability to move up and down the badge as you select fields and put them on the line that you want. This is just the initial layout and you will have the opportunity to rearrange fields, add formatting, and apply more complex criteria shortly. For the purpose of this demonstration, you can start adding fields by clicking at the top of the `Prototype label` window, which will create a gray area to indicate where your field selections will be placed.

Select the `DisplayName` for the first line, then click in the area for the second line and select the field `Title`. On the third line, select `Company`. Leave the next two lines blank, and select `EventOrganization` on the sixth line. On the next line, first select `Role` and then use the space bar to move the cursor to about the middle of the badge and then select `EventDate`.

At this point, the prototype will be similar to the image on the left in Figure 18-5. When you see it later in `Design View` it will be similar to the image on the right.

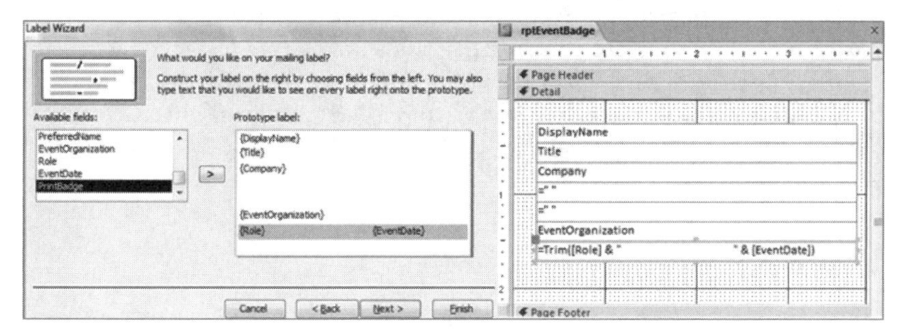

FIGURE 18-5: Label wizard and event badge prototype

After clicking, `Next`, you can select the field(s) to sort by, such as `LastName` and then `FirstName`. Notice that you can sort by fields that are included even if they do not appear on the badge. In this case, you may want to print badges in alphabetical order by last name, so that it is easy to include them with other conference material that is compiled by last name. Regardless of the print order, the badge will show the `DisplayName` because that uses the preferred name with the last name.

Next, you are prompted to save the report — this example is named `rptEventBadge`. You can then look at the report in `Design View`, (shown in Figure 18-5) and as you review the controls you should rename each `TextBox` to follow good naming standards, such as `txtDisplayName`. The practice of properly naming controls is important when you use code and macros to manipulate the controls or their content.

> **NOTE** *When naming controls, it is important to also select and name the container or object itself, such as the container for the subreport or* `tab` *control. This becomes more important as the complexity and programming increases. As you may have experienced, correctly naming these objects can be critical to managing cursor movement, particularly in forms. So it is best to develop and practice good naming conventions throughout your projects.*

You'll also notice that the wizard does not allow you to use `IIf` statements to customize the name or to wrap text to another line. You will need to make those adjustments later. However, if you have a long line of text or otherwise exceed the width or height of the label, you will receive a nice little reminder about the text wrapping — by way of a messagebox that pops up to indicate that there may be blank pages. This can often be the result of putting multiple fields on one line or of a header or footer that was magically added. Fortunately, these types of issues are easily fixed in design view.

This quick demonstration gives you a good place to start on creating event badges, and it offers several opportunities to mention tips and features. That is a nice segue into customizing the reports, in this case badges, to your needs.

> **NOTE** *When working with custom layouts that have smaller dimensions, objects can easily exceed the designated print area and cause extra pages to print. Some of the common culprits include extra headers or footers, lines or other objects exceeding the width, and forgetting to readjust the print areas after reducing the size or repositioning objects.*

SubReports

Subreports are merely Access reports (or forms) that are embedded in another report. The subreport uses the properties `Link Master Fields` and `Link Child Fields` to link the master report and the child (subreport), as shown in Figure 18-6, which includes both the `Design View` and `Property Sheet` of the subreport.

You'll also see that the `Source Object` for the subreport is named `srptPersonSideSession`, but the container itself is named `sRptSideSession`. The container, like the report itself, has its own properties. You can change the `Source Object` to change what is displayed within the subreport. This is essentially the same look and functionality that you've used with subforms and tab controls. You can use subreports to display details, show charts, or to include a variety of other objects.

You can have multiple subreports on one report. Typically they are displayed sequentially down the page, even with a subreport within a subreport. But you can also have two subreports that are displayed side by side. This could be an effective way to display a chart on the left and the data in a grid on the right. You would also need to work with the properties to allow them to shrink or grow as needed.

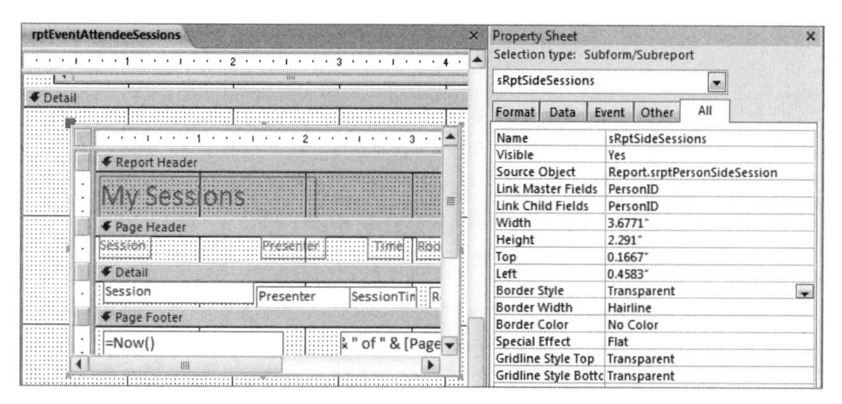

FIGURE 18-6: Subreport links master and child fields

In a completely different scenario, you might include an unbound subreport so that the information does not change based on the content of other reports. If you think about conferences, there are typically plenary sessions as well as concurrent sessions that people select. To allow attendees to print their schedule for the day, they might have a printout that includes their name and company at the top along with the information about plenary sessions. Then the body of the schedule would be split into two subreports to show information about the side sessions.

On the left the report would show the schedule of the attendee's side sessions — this would use a master-child link. On the right you could use an unbound report to display a diagram showing the location of the conference rooms. Figure 18-7 shows the subreport with the meeting room diagram along with the `Property Sheet` to illustrate that this does not have a master-child relationship between the main report and the subreport containing `rptRoomDiagram`. You can again see that the container has a distinct name, `sRptDiagram`.

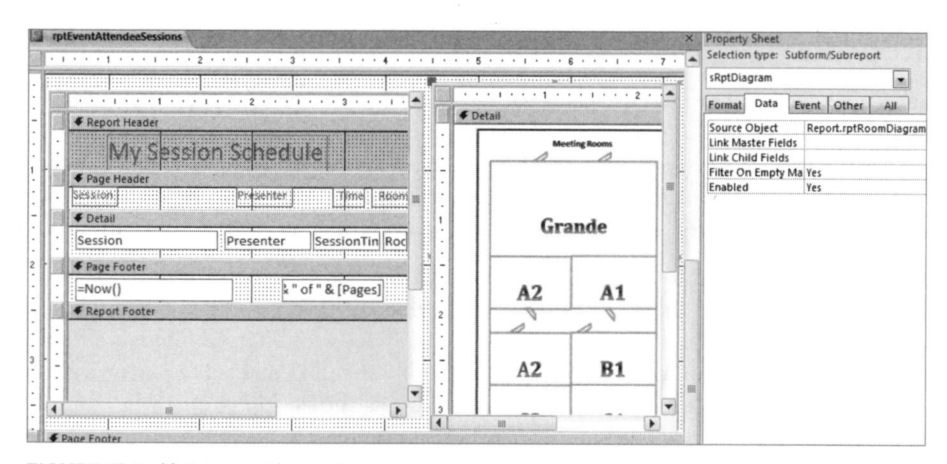

FIGURE 18-7: Using an unbound subreport

Finally, you can see the end result: a personalized schedule for the "*Access 2013 Conference*" complete with the attendee's name, general sessions, side session schedule, and room diagram, as shown in Figure 18-8. This will print one page per attendee. You can use the forms and reports in the sample database (`2013Team.accdb`) provided on the website to experiment with the settings and adopt them to use in your applications.

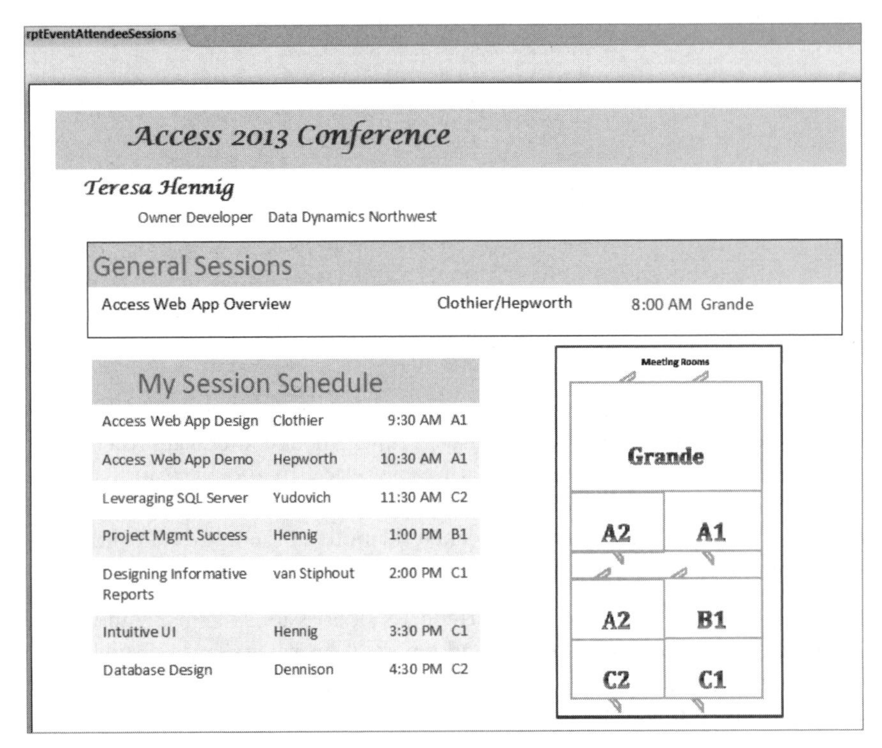

FIGURE 18-8: Personalized conference schedule with three subreports

Drill Down Reports

Taking the conference scenario one step further, you may want to help personalize the experience for both the attendees and the presenters. Many of the side sessions will have a lot of discussion, so it can be helpful for the presenters to recognize and know a little bit about the participants. With that in mind, you can easily provide them with an attendee list that is both a nicely formatted report for printing and a convenient tool for *drilling down* (looking up) information about the attendees.

You can do that by adding an event to the record or field on a report. When displayed in `Report View` (rather than `Print Preview`), the user can click (or double click) to open the related report or form. To demonstrate this, you can open the report `rptAttendees` and have it filtered to events. That will show the people registered for the *Access 2013 Conference*. If you click a person's name, it will open the *About Form* to show their picture, bio and notes, as shown in Figure 18-9. You can see how helpful this would be for event organizers, instructors, presenters, et al. This technique can be incorporated to benefit countless other situations. For example, in sales, users could look up products, or in a production scenario, users could look up parts.

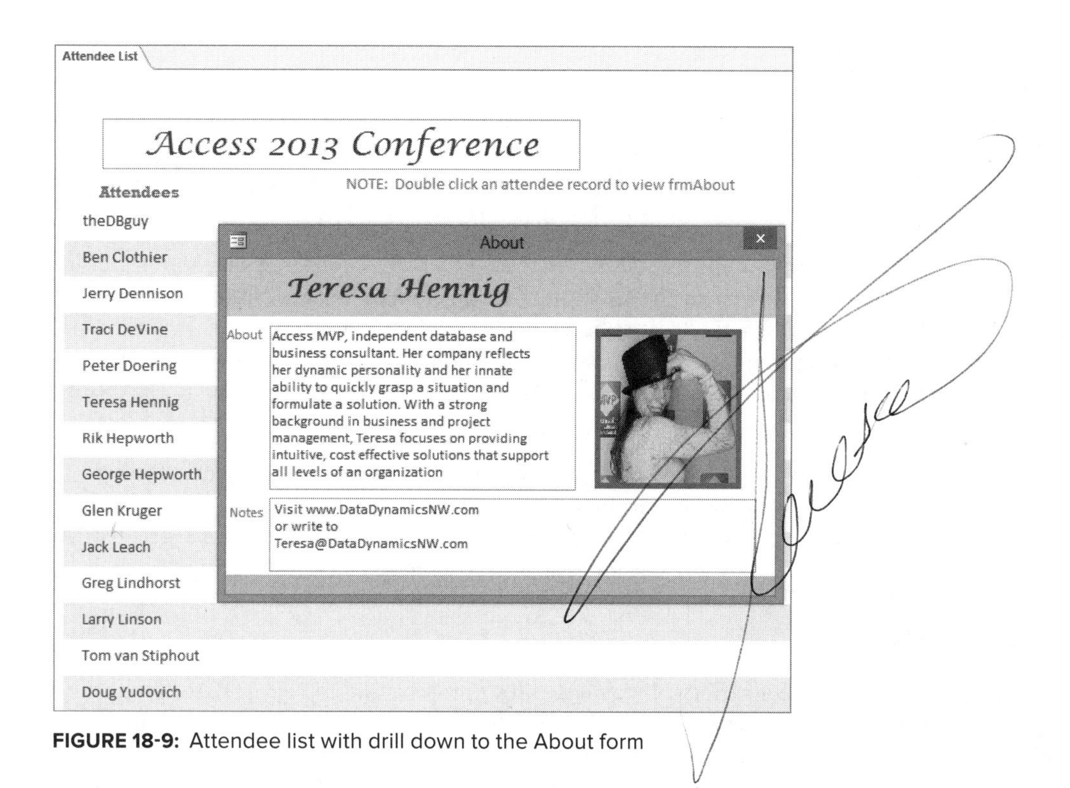

FIGURE 18-9: Attendee list with drill down to the About form

It is very easy to add this feature to your applications. You can use a macro or event procedure to open a form or report. Typically, you will want to open the item to a specific record. In this case, the field `PersonID` was used to link the records so that the form opened to show only the record for the person selected. The following code is behind the `Click` event for the `DisplayName` field:

```
Private Sub DisplayName_Click()
DoCmd.OpenForm "frmAbout", acNormal, , "[PersonID] = " & Me.PersonID, _
  acFormReadOnly, acDialog
End Sub
```

The field that is used to link the detailed display to the report needs to be on both objects, but it does not have to be visible on either one. As you can see on this report, the `PersonID` field is included in the report `Detail` section, however it does not appear to the user because the `Visible` property is set to `No`. The form opens in dialog mode so that the user will need to close it in order to move elsewhere in the report or application. You will find more information about working with forms, including the images, in Chapter 17.

These examples have focused on leveraging built-in features and functionality to meet the needs of real-world scenarios. Of course, you will want to fine-tune the formatting and layout to fit your needs. And, as with most aspects of database design, there are several other approaches that you might use to achieve comparable results. Soon you will have even more options to choose from. The next set of examples will help you leverage criteria forms and record source options to give users more flexibility and control with their reports.

REPORT EXAMPLES

By now, you have significant experience with Access both from your own projects and from some of the techniques in this book. That gives you a strong foundation for creating more complex solutions. The next few examples are aimed at giving you some powerful report techniques that you can incorporate into your own solutions to give your users greater control over the granularity and layout of their reports.

Unless otherwise noted, examples in this section are based on the file `ReportExamples.accdb` found in the chapter download. This file uses the tables and data from Microsoft's Northwind sample database as the foundation; it is a freely distributed demo file that many developers are familiar with. In this case, it provides the tables with a sufficient amount of data to demonstrate report techniques and results. For your convenience, all of the Northwind objects are included in the chapter download file `ReportExamplesNW.accdb`.

To make it easy to distinguish the forms, queries, and reports that were added to support the examples in this chapter, their names have a prefix and start with an underscore (`_`), such as `_rptOrders`. This also makes them easy to find since they sort to the top of an alphabetic list, and you can type " _" in the `Search` field of the `Navigation` pane to see all new objects.

Grouping Data

It is good to know how to use a variety of techniques for grouping and reporting data. That way, you can select and tailor the techniques to your current needs. With that in mind, the first example uses the Northwind application which includes a form, `Sales Reports Dialog`, found in the chapter download file `ReportExamplesNW.accdb` to provide users with a grouping dialog, as shown in Figure 18-10. Although this allows the user to select the way they want the data displayed in the reports, it requires a separate report for each selection option. Creating that many reports can be quite time-consuming and costly to develop and test, and it can become a maintenance nightmare.

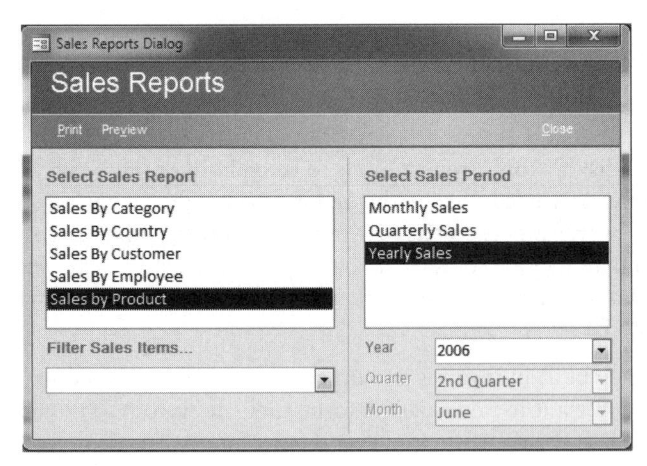

FIGURE 18-10: Criteria form for user determined grouping

However, this dialog invokes different reports based on the selected option, and there is no real grouping level. Instead, it uses the `WhereCondition` to filter the data, as shown in the following code:

```
' Determine report filtering
If Nz(Me.lstReportFilter) <> "" Then
    strReportFilter = "([SalesGroupingField] = """ & Me.lstReportFilter & """)"
End If

' Determine reporting time frame
Select Case Me.lstSalesPeriod
Case ByYear
    strReportName = "Yearly Sales Report"
Case ByQuarter
    strReportName = "Quarterly Sales Report"
Case ByMonth
    strReportName = "Monthly Sales Report"
End Select

DoCmd.OpenReport strReportName, ReportView, , strReportFilter, acWindowNormal
```

When you have a finite number of variables, this type of approach can let you quickly create the reports and provide a solution for your users. However, it becomes very labor and maintenance intensive if the needs or complexities grow or change. This brings you to the next series of examples. As you go through the following examples, you will look at an assortment of report options and learn how to create a single report that will group and display data in a variety of ways based on the criteria selected by the users.

Reports with Simple Criteria

You have probably seen Access applications with many reports. Some of them are very similar. There may be several for a date range, such as:

- `SalesReport_2011`
- `SalesReport_2012`
- `SalesReport_Q1_2013`

Each selection is bound to its own query. So for the three reports listed, you might use the following three queries, respectively:

- `qrySalesReport_2011`
- `qrySalesReport_2012`
- `qrySalesReport_Q1_2013`

You already know this is not a good idea from a maintenance perspective. Copying a query just to change the date range is very wasteful, and invariably over time the queries and reports will be just a little bit different. For example, one year is using only Active customers, while the other years are using all customers, causing confusion for the users of the reports.

You also already know how to fix this problem. You can create a single report with a simple date criteria form, such as the one as shown in Figure 18-11.

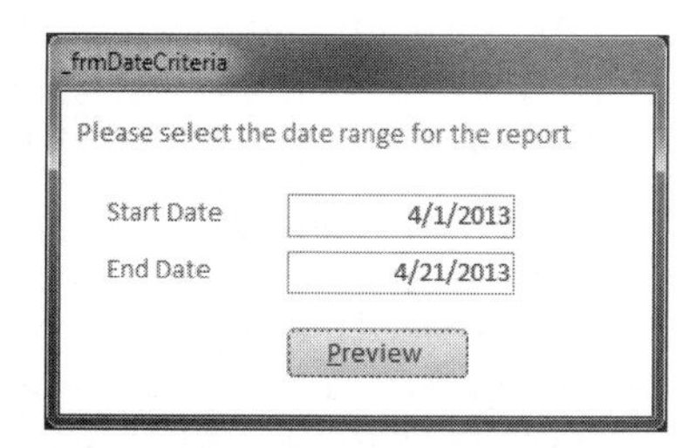

FIGURE 18-11: Simple date criteria form

The two text boxes have the `Format` property set to `Short Date` and the `Show Date Picker` property set to `For Dates`, so calendar buttons automatically appear when the fields have focus. In the preview's `Click` event you write:

```
DoCmd.OpenReport "_rptOrders", acViewPreview, _
  WhereCondition:= "[Order Date] between #" & Me.txtStartDate & _
    "# And #" & Me.txtEndDate & "#"
```

Reports with Simple Groupings

Another way reports can be similar is by the way they group the data. Even if you are only working with two types of groups, there can be an extensive list of variations based on the criteria used in each group and the way the data needs to be displayed within the groups. A few of the examples for reporting sales by rep and status include:

```
SalesReport_BySalesrep
SalesReport_ByStatus
SalesReport_BySalesRep_ByStatus
SalesReport_ByStatus_BySalesRep
```

Combine this with the date range reports you just worked with, and you can see that creating separate reports for each variation can quickly become unmanageable. This is clearly a time to create a single query, a single criteria form, and a single report. The upfront investment in writing some VBA will pay significant returns for the life of the project. In the next section, you will learn how to create this type of functionality.

One Flexible Report

If you need to provide multiple ways of displaying the same data, it is often more efficient to use an approach that builds flexibility into the process, than to use an ever increasing number of similar reports and queries. In this section, you will create a single query and report and learn how to use them to create a variety of report configurations.

The example uses a list of orders that can be grouped in different ways. You can easily apply the same techniques to an infinite number of scenarios, such as people in organizations, manufacturing processes, and more.

There is only a single query that simply selects all orders and the names for the various ID values, as well as the total amount per order. The criteria form shown in Figure 18-12 builds on the simple date criteria form used previously, and adds several options for filtering and grouping the data.

The Scope group allows the user to specify whether the report will show or hide the `Report Detail` section. By selecting `Summary`, the report will hide the details so only the group headers and footers are displayed, as shown in Figure 18-13.

Per the requirements for the `Orders` report, it should always be grouped by `Order Date`, and optionally by another grouping level like `Salesrep`, `Shipper`, or `Status`. Even with that, users may want to see the data grouped by the first criterion and then by the second, or vice-versa, depending on how they intend to use the data. Users control the order by selecting from the `Group` options. With these few controls, you have given the users the ability to create 48 distinct reports and filter them for any given date range. Not bad for about 50 lines of code.

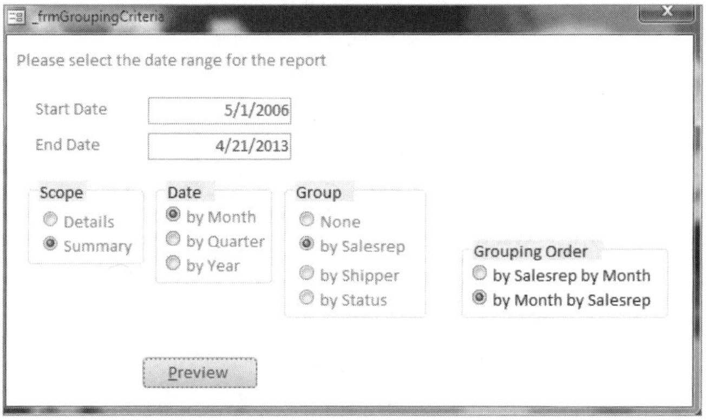

_frmGroupingCriteria

Please select the date range for the report

Start Date 5/1/2006

End Date 4/21/2013

Scope: Details, Summary (selected)

Date: by Month (selected), by Quarter, by Year

Group: None, by Salesrep (selected), by Shipper, by Status

Grouping Order: by Salesrep by Month, by Month by Salesrep (selected)

Preview

FIGURE 18-12: Flexible grouping criteria form

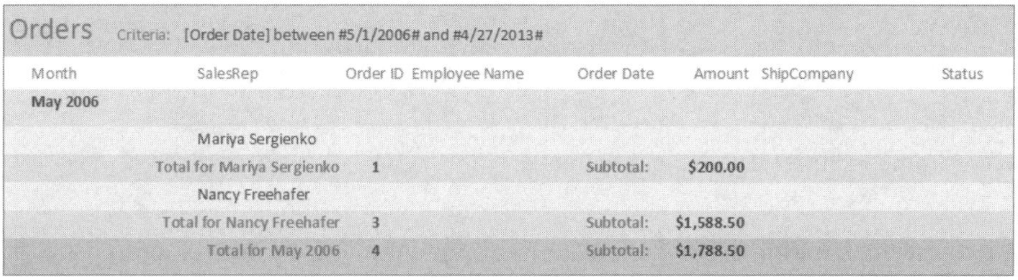

Orders Criteria: [Order Date] between #5/1/2006# and #4/27/2013#

Month	SalesRep	Order ID	Employee Name	Order Date	Amount	ShipCompany	Status
May 2006							
	Mariya Sergienko						
	Total for Mariya Sergienko	1		Subtotal:	$200.00		
	Nancy Freehafer						
	Total for Nancy Freehafer	3		Subtotal:	$1,588.50		
	Total for May 2006	4		Subtotal:	$1,788.50		

FIGURE 18-13: Summary report shows only group headers and footers

The next examples show the same grouping along with the data. Figure 18-14 shows sales grouped by `Date` and `Salesrep` and then Figure 18-15 shows the data by `SalesRep` and by `Date`. You should also note that the report header is used to display the date range that was selected by the user. This technique of showing the criteria in the report helps people have a better understanding of exactly what they are reviewing so they can make informed decisions.

Orders Criteria: [Order Date] between #5/1/2006# and #4/27/2013#

Month	SalesRep	Order ID	Employee Name	Order Date	Amount	ShipCompany	Status
May 2006							
	Mariya Sergienko						
		67	Mariya Sergienko	5/24/2006	$200.00	Shipping Company B	Closed
	Total for Mariya Sergienko	1		Subtotal:	$200.00		
	Nancy Freehafer						
		71	Nancy Freehafer	5/24/2006	$736.00	Shipping Company C	New
		70	Nancy Freehafer	5/24/2006	$800.00	Shipping Company C	New
		69	Nancy Freehafer	5/24/2006	$52.50	Shipping Company A	New
	Total for Nancy Freehafer	3		Subtotal:	$1,588.50		
	Total for May 2006	4		Subtotal:	$1,788.50		

FIGURE 18-14: Orders grouped by date then sales rep

Orders Criteria: [Order Date] between #5/1/2006# and #4/27/2013#

SalesRep	Month	Order ID	Employee Name	Order Date	Amount	ShipCompany	Status
Andrew Cencini							
	June 2006						
		79	Andrew Cencini	6/23/2006	$2,490.00	Shipping Company C	Closed
	Total for June 2006	1		Subtotal:	$2,490.00		
	Total for Andrew Cencini	1		Subtotal:	$2,490.00		
Anne Hellung-Larsen							
	June 2006						
		77	Anne Hellung-Larsen	6/5/2006	$2,250.00	Shipping Company C	Closed
		76	Anne Hellung-Larsen	6/5/2006	$660.00	Shipping Company A	Closed
	Total for June 2006	2		Subtotal:	$2,910.00		
	Total for Anne Hellung-Larsen	2		Subtotal:	$2,910.00		
Mariya Sergienko							
	May 2006						
		67	Mariya Sergienko	5/24/2006	$200.00	Shipping Company B	Closed
	Total for May 2006	1		Subtotal:	$200.00		
	June 2006						
		75	Mariya Sergienko	6/5/2006	$510.00	Shipping Company B	Closed
	Total for June 2006	1		Subtotal:	$510.00		
	Total for Mariya Sergienko	2		Subtotal:	$710.00		

FIGURE 18-15: Orders grouped by sales rep then by date

Before delving into the explanation of how to create the report, it might be helpful to take a look at it in design view, as shown in Figure 18-16.

You can create the report by using the report wizard and selecting the query `_qryRptOrders` as the record source. You will need to add two arbitrary grouping levels which will become level `0` and `1`. In this example we used `ShipCompany` and `OrderDate`. And, of course, you will need to apply appropriate formatting to tailor the look to your project.

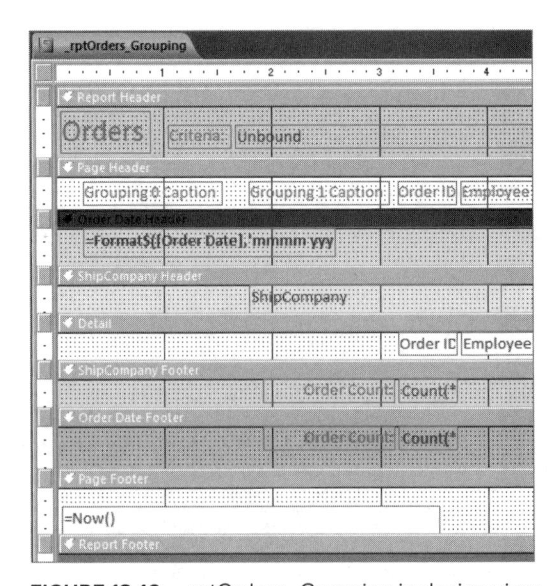

FIGURE 18-16: _rptOrders_Grouping in design view

In this example, the grouping labels and text fields have control names that are easy to use programmatically, such as `lblGroupLevel0` and `lblGroupLevel1`. It also uses background color to indicate the `outer` (purple) and the `inner` (green) grouping level. These are, of course, among the items that you will want to adjust according to your project needs.

It only takes one line of code to launch the report: `DoCmd.OpenReport`.

The heavy lifting occurs in the `Report_Open` event. This is where the report retrieves the criteria from the criteria form and formats the report accordingly. The following four tasks are accomplished based on the criteria:

1. Group by `Date` and another field, or vice versa.
2. Set the grouping level captions in the page header.
3. Bind the `level0` and `level1` header controls to the fields they are grouped by.
4. Bind the grouping levels to the fields based on the grouping.

You can apply this technique in numerous scenarios to quickly give users significant flexibility and control for both the selection and layout, such as reporting on production by plant, division and model, or perhaps it is restaurants by region, state or city.

To implement Step 1, you use the variables `nDateLevel` and `nGroupLevel`. Depending on which `Group` option is chosen, they can be level `0` and `1`, or if the other option is chosen, level `1` and `0`. The following line of code is used to bind the grouping level to the correct field:

```
Me.GroupLevel(nDateLevel).ControlSource = "Order Date"
```

To implement Step 2, you can take advantage of the specifically designed naming convention for labels by using the following line of code to set `Me.lblGroupLevel0` or `Me.lblGroupLevel1` to `Month`. The Date options "`by Quarter`" and "`by Year`" are handled very similarly:

```
Me("lblGroupLevel" & nDateLevel).Caption = "Month"
```

Step 3 is implemented in a similar way to Step 2, only this time by setting the text boxes' `ControlSource` property, as shown in the following code:

```
Me("txtGroupLevel" & nDateLevel).ControlSource = _
  "=Format$([Order Date],'mmmm yyyy')"
```

If you are using the second grouping level, and the user chose "`by Salesrep`" it would create this:

```
Me("txtGroupLevel" & nGroupLevel).ControlSource = "=[Employee Name]"
```

If the user chose "`by Shipper`" this would be created:

```
Me("txtGroupLevel" & nGroupLevel).ControlSource = "=[ShipCompany]"
```

Finally, if the user chose "`by Status`" it would create this:

```
Me("txtGroupLevel" & nGroupLevel).ControlSource = "=[Status Name]"
```

The last Step, #4, sets the `ControlSource` of the grouping level itself. This actually includes several actions to accommodate the options that are covered in the example. To follow the example, you can start with this code:

```
Me.GroupLevel(nDateLevel).ControlSource = "Order Date"
```

Then, if the user chose "`by Salesrep`" it would create this:

```
Me.GroupLevel(nGroupLevel).ControlSource = "Employee Name"
```

The Group options "`by Shipper`" and "`by Status`" are handled very similarly.

At this point, the `Order Date` needs to be set to group by `Month`, `Quarter`, or `Year`. Access has built-in support for Date grouping by `Month`, `Quarter`, and `Year`. So if the user chose "`by Month`" it would create this:

```
Me.GroupLevel(nDateLevel).GroupOn = 4     ' 4=Mon
```

If the user chose "`by Quarter`" this would be created:

```
Me.GroupLevel(nDateLevel).GroupOn = 3     ' 3=Qtr
```

Finally, if the user chose "`by Year`" it would create this:

```
Me.GroupLevel(nDateLevel).GroupOn = 2     ' 2=Year
```

Finally, you set the `Order Date` filter for the report equal to the values in the `Start Date` and `End Date`. That completes the process for creating the *flexible report.*

An alternative approach is to specify the date range in the `WhereCondition` property of `DoCmd.OpenReport`, as you did for the simple report with date range criteria. However, since the flexible selection criteria required additional code, you might as well write it all in the `Report_Open` event. It is often preferable to keep your code in one place so that it is easier to maintain and for someone else to work on the project.

Calling the Criteria Form from the Report

In many scenarios, there are benefits in calling the criteria form from the report, instead of using the criteria form to select and open a report, such as:

- It makes the report more self-contained.
- It is a more object-oriented approach.
- The report can't be run without criteria being set.

The Northwind sample app, which is the foundation for the `ReportExamples.accdb`, already shows how to implement this approach. So you can investigate and experiment with the reports in the chapter database. If you look at the `Monthly Sales Report`, you'll see the following code in the `Report_Open` event:

```
    If IsNull(TempVars![Display]) Or IsNull(TempVars![Year]) Or
IsNull(TempVars![Month]) Or IsNull(TempVars![Group By]) Then
        DoCmd.OpenForm "Sales Reports Dialog"
        Cancel = True
        Exit Sub
    End If
```

This code tests several elements of the `TempVars` collection. These elements are only set by getting values from the criteria form. If any of elements are `null`, then the form has not been completed, so the criteria form is opened and the report opening is canceled by setting `Cancel` equal to `True`.

Reports that Compare Values

Many reports need to compare actual values with expected or estimated values. For example, you may want to compare actual factory production figures with their goals or projections, or actual employee production with their quota. This technique can address needs across a wide spectrum of industries and departments, from auditing to sales, and from appointments booked to those kept on time. But, as with all reports, if you want to report the statistics you need to ensure that you have collected and stored the underlying data.

In this example each salesperson has a monthly quota. As in many real-world scenarios, tracking the quota adds a new requirement to the database. So the original specifications do not incorporate all of the requisite data in the table and fields. Therefore, you need to add a `MonthlySalesQuota` field to the `Employees` table in order to store this data. As all salespersons have a quota, you make it a required field.

> **NOTE** *When making changes to the table structure, it is important to consider both the immediate and long term ramifications — including normalizations, maintenance, likelihood of future changes, and such. In the* `ReportExamples` *file, which uses the tables and data from Microsoft's Northwind database, it is a focused, simplified scenario. So in this case all employees have sales quotas. Even so, this still doesn't address the likelihood of quotas changing over time, which would require maintaining an association between person, quota, and timeframe.*

The next step is to add the new field to the existing `_qryOrders` query. While this query is selected in the `Navigation Pane`, you select the `Report Wizard` from the ribbon and create a report with grouping levels by `Employee Name` and `Order Date`. For this example, save the report with the name `_rptOrders_SalesQuota`.

To compare the `Actual` value (the monthly sales) to the `Expected` value (the sales quota), you use `Conditional Formatting`. If `Actual >= Expected`, the `Monthly Sales` field will be green, otherwise it will be red. To apply the conditional formatting you select the `Monthly Sales` field in the `Order Date Footer`, and select `Conditional Formatting` from the `Format` tab on the ribbon. You enter two rules — one for green and one for red — comparing the value of this field to the `MonthlySalesQuota` field, as shown in Figure 18-17.

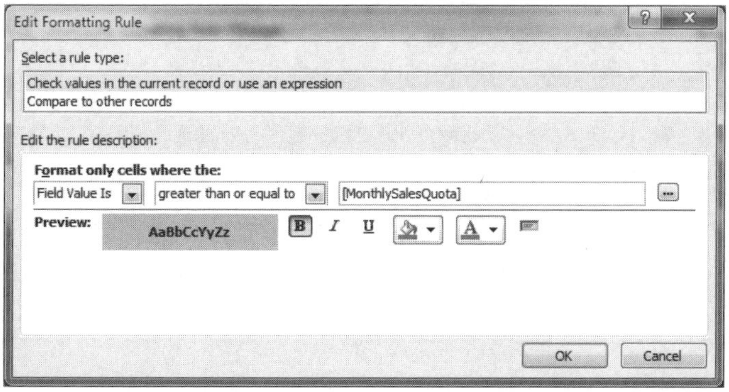

FIGURE 18-17: Applying conditional formatting

As expected, the report now indicates for each month if the salesperson met the quota, as shown in Figure 18-18.

Sales Quota

Employee Name	Order Month	Order Date	Order Total	Cumulative	Company	Status
Andrew Cencini						
	April 2006					
		4/3/2006	$127.50	$127.50	Company F	Closed
		4/25/2006	$380.00	$507.50	Company D	New
		4/25/2006	$0.00	$507.50	Company C	New
Sales Quota	$2,000.00	Total for April 2006	$507.50			
	June 2006					
		6/23/2006	$2,490.00	$2,490.00	Company F	Closed
Sales Quota	$2,000.00	Total for June 2006	$2,490.00			

FIGURE 18-18: _rptOrders_SalesQuota with conditional formatting

This report also shows another often-used technique: cumulative amounts. You might think this would require a complicated SQL query, but fortunately the Access report engine is doing all the work. You simply add a second `Order Total` field and set the `Running Sum` property to `Over Group`. Access will calculate the cumulative values and restart the count for the next month. If you like, you can add conditional formatting to this field comparing the value to the monthly quota. You will see that initially the field is red, to indicate that it has not met the quota. Once the cumulative value exceeds the quota, it will be green.

Another very interesting use of `Running Sum` is to provide line numbering. If the new requirement is to number each order line starting at 1 each month, you can add a text field and set its `Control Source` to "`=1`" and set its `Running Sum` to `Over Group`. You can then view the results and adjust the layout to suit your preferences, as shown in Figure 18-19. This is all done with features in the report design, so the query remains unchanged.

Sales Quota

Employee Name	Order Month		Order Date	Order Total	Cumulative	Company	Status
Andrew Cencini							
	April 2006						
		1	4/3/2006	$127.50	$127.50	Company F	Closed
		2	4/25/2006	$380.00		Company D	New
		3	4/25/2006	$0.00	$507.50	Company C	New
Sales Quota	$2,000.00	Total for April 2006		$507.50			

FIGURE 18-19: _rptOrders_SalesQuota

PROFESSIONAL POLISH

When you write reports, you are mostly focused on presenting accurate data. However, a pleasing and consistent style is important as well. You can setup a Normal template with the basics. This section covers some of the other aspects that you can leverage to give your reports a professional polish.

Report Criteria

Reports are basically intended to be standalone documents, often saved or printed and viewed separately from the database. At that point, the criteria form is a thing of the past, so you — and more importantly the people viewing the report — will not have the criteria form to indicate the selections used for a given report. That's why in many cases it is remarkably helpful to repeat the criteria in the report header.

When you make it easy for readers to see which criteria were used to produce the report, you should be as complete as possible, so the report is not ambiguous. For example, you may have a criteria form that prompts for a date range, so the criteria field should display similar information, as shown in Figure 18-20. As you can see, this report shows the selected beginning and ending dates in the report header.

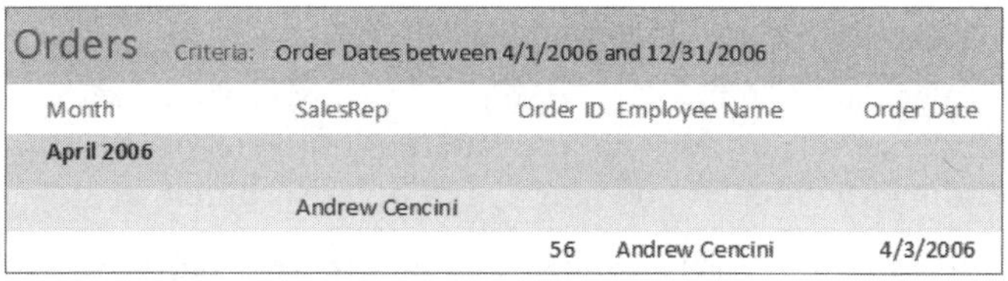

Orders Criteria: Order Dates between 4/1/2006 and 12/31/2006

Month	SalesRep	Order ID	Employee Name	Order Date
April 2006				
	Andrew Cencini			
		56	Andrew Cencini	4/3/2006

FIGURE 18-20: Including report criteria in the report header

In this case, the expression in the criteria field includes the subject (order date) as well as the start and end dates. You can apply this technique of providing informative headings and labels to other areas of your reports — and forms, too, for that matter. The following expression was used to create the information line in the header of this report. In the declaration section at the top of the report, include this code:

```
Public m_strCriteria As String
```

In `Form_Open` event, include the following code, using `m` to indicate that this is a public variable and used across multiple procedures:

```
m_strCriteria = "Order Dates between " & frm.txtStartDate & _
  " and " & frm.txtEndDate
```

In `Form_Load` event, include the following code:

```
Me.txtCriteria = m_strCriteria
```

The reason you want to set `m_strCriteria` in `Form_Open` is because that's where all formatting takes place. It is best practice to keep all of the code together in one place.

You may also be wondering why to use `Form_Load` instead of `Form_Open`. The reason you use `Form_Load` to set the text is because `Form_Open` is too early in the creation of the report and the field value cannot be set at that time.

However, you may have other criteria to consider. For example, if your query also restricts the orders to only those for active customers, or any other relevant criteria, you could include those in the report header as well.

> **NOTE** *Alternatively, if there are several criteria and perhaps other caveats for the report, you may use an information page at the end of the report. In some cases, the report footer can be used to create a standalone page that contains a listing of report criteria, company caveats, and other information that is too extensive or distracting to include in the front of the report, but too critical to omit. You can still include critical criteria in the report header and even repeat it in the footer.*

You can further customize the string to provide proper syntax. For example, if your date criteria form allows the start date or end date to be empty indicating "all dates," then you should write the criteria text accordingly. You can enhance the professional presentation of the report by using proper grammar and matching the wording for singular and plural, and other such items.

The following code uses the order dates. You can use this example and modify the code to work with your scenarios:

```
If IsNull(Forms!frmCriteria!txtStartDate) _
  And Not IsNull(Forms!frmCriteria!txtEndDate) Then
    Me.txtCriteria = "Order Dates up to " & frm.txtEndDate
ElseIf Not IsNull(Forms!frmCriteria!txtStartDate) _
  And IsNull(Forms!frmCriteria!txtEndDate) Then
    Me.txtCriteria = "Order Dates from " & frm.txtStartDate
Else
  'Both dates exist
  Me.txtCriteria = "Order Dates between " & frm.txtStartDate & _
    " and " & frm.txtEndDate
End If
```

There are many other factors that might improve the delivery of the information being reported if they were pointed out to the reader. For example, if it is not obvious and relevant to the type of report you are creating, you should also state how the report is sorted.

These are just a few of the factors that you can leverage to create a professional report tailored to the specific criteria that it is displaying. In addition to the data, there may be other corporate, legal, or routine matters that need to be conveyed with the reports. These can be addressed in the report header, footer, or both.

Confidentiality Statement

Your reports often contain sensitive information, and many organizations have a confidentiality statement that should appear on each report. You could use a label for that in the footer, but what if the statement changes? Then you have to fix all your reports.

It's much better to make this a data-driven element. One solution is to have a `SystemSettings` table with a `ConfidentialityStatement` field. You can then use a `textbox` in the footer of each report and set the `ControlSource` to:

```
= DLookup("ConfidentialityStatement", "SystemSettings")
```

Be sure to set the `CanGrow` property of this field to `True` so that the entire statement will be displayed, extending down multiple lines if necessary.

Page Numbers and Report Date

The Access report wizard adds page numbers and the report date to all reports. If you design a report from scratch, you should always add these. Page numbers should appear in the format "`Page X of Y`" so the user knows not just the current page number, but also the total number of pages.

Report Name

In some organizations the report name is a required field in the footer of any report. Often the name will be assigned by the department requesting the report. Sometimes it is followed by a sequential number for each revision, which you will have to maintain.

If you simply want to state the name of the Access report, you can use a textbox and set the `ControlSource` to `=Me.Name`. Of course, it would be more professional to use a nicely formatted name, such as you might store in a table so that it can easily be used for the report title, footer, and other places. You've seen this technique mentioned and used in both this chapter and Chapter 17.

Using Work Tables

Creating a temporary or work table can provide benefits to performance and a significant relief to development challenges in cases that involve a series of calculations or work with very large amounts of data. It particularly makes sense when you are working with historic data rather than data that is subject to ongoing changes.

There are differing schools of thought and approaches to working with temporary tables. Some developers prefer to create the tables when and as needed, and others prefer to have a permanent structure and then delete the records just before or after using the table. The benefit of keeping the records until the next use is that you can rerun the report or research anomalies. However, deleting the records and compacting the file after use takes a smaller footprint. Either way, it is preferable to use linked rather than local work tables to avoid undue database bloat.

And that brings this to a good point to wrap up the polish and share one final bonus example, the PDF tool.

FILLING OUT PDF FORMS USING ACCESS

Portable Document Format (PDF) files seem to be nearly ubiquitous. More and more organizations use PDF forms for requisitions, routing slips, tax forms, invoices, receipts, registration, and legal forms. They are easily distributed online and via e-mail, and they provide a structured format for collecting and presenting data. Given that PDF files are such an effective way to request data, it is important to have an efficient way to fill them out, which you'll soon learn how to automate.

As PDF files have become more prevalent, their specifications have also changed. Although there are a variety of formats available, developers recognize Adobe's PDF specification as an industry standard for producing and distributing official documents in electronic format. So that is the format used for this example.

Fortunately, as techniques for completing PDF files continue to evolve, they have become easier to automate and incorporate into Access solutions. Whether the PDF is produced internally or provided by an outside entity, you can use an Access data file as the source data for filling out the forms.

A PDF file is essentially a report as much as it is a form. So the focus here is to provide some approaches that you can use to print a PDF file. The methods range from emulating the original form to actually inserting data into specific fields. The following techniques are just a few of the options that are currently available. You can select and modify the techniques to correspond with the specifics of your scenario.

You will find a working example of this in the database named `PDFDemo.accdb`, which is available on the book's website. As an extra bonus, you'll see that an `.mdb` version is also provided so that you can easily incorporate the techniques into legacy solutions.

Using Reports

The traditional method of filling out a PDF form using Access is by duplicating the PDF form's structure and format in an Access Report. In some scenarios, this can include shading, numerous font sizes, and even inserting images of text that use special fonts or sizes that are not available due to network or printer limitations. As you can imagine, replicating a PDF form in this manner can be very tedious.

It can also become problematic when you have to modify the report in response to changes in the form, or require multiple versions to correspond to specific date periods, such as with tax forms. In many cases, it might be better to start fresh and create a new report from scratch. However, a notable benefit of this approach is it produces a high quality replica of the PDF form.

One other method that could save time when using a report as a PDF form is to scan the original PDF form and then use the scanned image as a background for the report. In this case, all the developer has to add to the report are the data fields from the Access table. This is not as simple as it might sound. This technique requires that each textbox control be precisely aligned with the background image on the report. In addition, the final outcome of the report is heavily dependent upon the quality of the image as well as the capabilities and settings of the printer itself.

These techniques work, but fortunately for developers, Adobe provides tools that can spare developers all the pain of duplicating a PDF form in an Access report.

Using an XFDF file

XML Forms Data Format (XFDF) is an XML-based specification for working directly with the data used in PDF forms. Although you don't need Adobe Acrobat to create XFDF files, you do need a PDF reader application to view the final result.

The Essentials

The XFDF file is an XML-based document, so it requires both a header and a body section that follow strict formatting rules. Specific tags have to be used to describe the path to the PDF form being populated with the data, to specify the names of the fields in the PDF form, and to designate the values of the data coming from your Access database.

The following is an example of an XFDF file format. In this example, `MyPDF.pdf` is the name of the PDF form to be filled out and `FirstName` and `LastName` are the names of the fields in the PDF form:

```
<?xml version="1.0" encoding="UTF-8"?>
<xfdf xmlns=http://ns.adobe.com/xfdf/ xml:space="preserve">
<f href="MyPDF.pdf" />
<fields>
    <field name="FirstName">
        <value>DB</value>
    </field>
    <field name="LastName">
        <value>Guy</value>
    </field>
</fields>
</xfdf>
```

> **NOTE** *There is actually a third way to fill out a PDF form using Access, and that is to use Acrobat DLL automation. However, this technique is a lot more complicated, and it adds third-party dependencies to your application.*

It is important to remember that XFDF is an XML-based file, so certain characters have special meaning when the file is parsed by the PDF reader. If your data contains any of these characters, you must convert them into XML entity references. The following table shows the five predefined entity references in XML.

XML ENTITY REFERENCE	CHARACTER	MEANING
<	<	less than
>	>	greater than
&	&	ampersand
'	‘	apostrophe
"	“	quotation mark

Sample Code

The following example shows how you could create an XFDF file that the PDF reader will use to fill out the PDF form. You can also find this code in the download file for this chapter.

```
Option Compare Database
Option Explicit

Private Sub cmdPDF_Click()
'theDBguy@gmail.com
'www.accessmvp.com/thedbguy
'04/10/2012 - Original version (v1)
'06/13/2012 - Update (v1.1)
'04/14/2013 - Update (vW1)

' - XML parsing will fail if the field contains either an ampersand (&)
'   or a less than symbol (<)
' - One approach is to replace "&" with "&amp;" and "<" with "&lt;"

'This demo creates a XFDF file to merge with a fillable PDF form.
'Tthis method avoids the need to use an Acrobat DLL to manipulate the PDF file.
'This method relies on the capabilities of the installed PDF reader.

'Declare the PDF file to be filled and assume it's in the
'same directory as the database.
Const strPDF As String = "theDBguy.pdf"

'Declare the XFDF file to use
Const strXFDF As String = "theDBguy.xfdf"

Dim strPath As String
Dim intFile As Integer

strPath = CurrentProject.Path
intFile = FreeFile

'Create XFDF file
Open strPath & "\" & strXFDF For Output As #intFile

Print #intFile, "<?xml version=""1.0"" encoding=""UTF-8""?>"
Print #intFile, "<xfdf xmlns=""http://ns.adobe.com/xfdf/"" xml:space=""preserve"">"
Print #intFile, "<f href=""" & strPDF & """/>"
Print #intFile, "<fields>"
Print #intFile, "<field name=""fname"">"
Print #intFile, "<value>" & Me.txtFName & "</value>"
Print #intFile, "</field>"
Print #intFile, "<field name=""lname"">"
Print #intFile, "<value>" & Me.txtLName & "</value>"
Print #intFile, "</field>"
Print #intFile, "<field name=""notes"">"
Print #intFile, "<value>" & Replace(Replace(Me.txtNotes,_
   "&", "&amp;"), "<", "&lt;") & "</value>"
Print #intFile, "</field>"
Print #intFile, "</fields>"
```

```
Print #intFile, "</xfdf>"

Close #intFile

'Open the PDF file
ShellEx strPath & "\" & strXFDF

End Sub
```

> **NOTE** `ShellEx` *in the preceding code sample is in the Standard Module of the PDF database demo file. It is a modified version of the* `ShellExecute API`.

SUMMARY

Although reports are primarily used to create customized layouts for printing, they can also be used for on-screen viewing. One of the greatest benefits in that area is the opportunity to leverage interactive features — such as allowing users to do their own sorting and filtering. Combining this with the increased mobility and portability of devices, you can use reports to preview, select, and print specific items, such as the example with printing event badges, personalized schedules, or PDF files.

Access 2013, as well as previous versions of Access, allows developers with skills ranging from novice to expert to quickly create customized professional reports. It is arguably the most versatile, robust, and easy-to-use reporting tool available, particularly if you need to combine data from multiple sources.

In Chapter 17 and this chapter you worked with forms and reports based on data stored in Access tables. You now have several new database files to contain the forms, reports, and queries that you've been working with, along with several other examples that demonstrate techniques that will allow you to quickly add features and style to improve the user interface. You can incorporate these into your projects to give your Access solutions a more professional presentation.

In the next chapter, you will learn how to extend the reach of Access by integrating with and automating other Office programs.

19

Automating and Integrating with Other Programs

WHAT'S IN THIS CHAPTER?

- Taking advantage of automation using menus, macros, VBA, and more
- Leveraging features in other Office applications from within Access
- Leveraging Access with third-party applications

WROX.COM CODE DOWNLOADS FOR THIS CHAPTER

The code downloads for this chapter are found at `www.wiley.com/go/proaccess2013prog.com` on the Download Code tab. The code is in the Chapter 19 download in the file `530832_ch19_CodeSnippets.txt`. Each snippet is listed sequentially and under the respective chapter heading. You can also get the code from the chapter's demo database, `ch19Automation.accdb`.

OVERVIEW OF INTEROPERABILITY

Many Access developers have become experts in working with Access for specific purposes but have little or no experience with using Access to automate other programs. However, as work processes become more integrated, many developers are seeing more and more opportunities to expand their business and better serve their clients by using Access to leverage the functionality in other programs. Fortunately, one of the main features making Access and the entire Office Suite so popular is the increased integration between applications within the Suite itself — not just to share data, but to literally open and manipulate the program with all of the features and benefits of working directly with its user interface.

You've seen how to take advantage of Access's data integration features in Chapter 15. In this chapter, you will take that much further and see how Access's features are integrated with other applications. You will also learn how to use interoperability to integrate your Access solutions with other applications

When creating database applications, it is quite common to use Access as the main environment, or platform, and to create forms and reports to maintain data stored in an Access or SQL Server back-end database. Using interoperability, you can create powerful "office-wide" applications that enable you to easily create extensive Office documents using Access data, with intricate formatting that originally was only doable using the native application.

The following are some examples of tasks using Access and Office applications:

- Using your Access solution to create a formatted Excel workbook using data in Access, and then e-mailing that workbook to the recipient
- Creating a Word document generated from Access that has Word tables embedded in it, with other text included
- Maintaining sales contacts within Access, and monitoring e-mail that is stored in Outlook from those sales contacts
- Dynamically creating a PowerPoint presentation based on data in your Access database

You will see how to accomplish some of these tasks as you go through the examples in this chapter and work with the download files.

Interoperability provides various ways to control one application (server) from another (controller). Some of the ways that Access uses interoperability include:

- **Ribbon commands** — Whenever you use any of the `EXTERNAL DATA` ribbon items for exporting data to another application such as Excel, interoperability controls that application for tasks such as opening the newly created worksheet with the Access data formatted while still in Access.
- **Macro actions** — When you use macro actions such as `EmailDatabaseObject`, interoperability will create an e-mail with the provided data, and then either send the e-mail or open an Outlook Email form for you to edit.
- **Automation** — Coding VBA, you can create other applications' objects, such as Word documents or Excel worksheets, and then manipulate those objects using the same properties and methods that are provided for by the application's object model.

These areas will be covered in the following pages. After that, you will move on to a detailed explanation of automation. Although it is more complicated, automation provides even greater flexibility and power. Using automation, you can programmatically perform most tasks that otherwise could only be accomplished through the application's user interface.

> **WARNING** *When using the first two modes of interoperability mentioned previously, there is nothing you really need to worry about as far as versioning when working with different applications. Access takes care of that for you. The last type, automation, takes more consideration when working with various applications and moving from one version to another. Versions after Access 2007 handle this better than earlier versions, but you can avoid or minimize versioning issues by using late binding. To avoid issues with versioning, be sure to read the section, "Early Binding vs. Late Binding."*

GETTING STARTED WITH AUTOMATION

When coding in VBA using Access and data objects, you are working with the Access and DAO object models. With automation, you will be working with these same object models, as well as working with properties and methods of objects of whichever application you are going to automate.

A few basic steps are involved with automating other applications:

1. Set a reference to the application's type library.
2. Declare and initiate variables for various objects in the object library that are required for your solution.
3. Use the objects' classes, properties, and methods as necessary.

Although this may seem vague at this point, you gain an understanding of what is involved as you go through the examples in the chapter.

> **NOTE** *Not to be confused with the database concept of client server, when an application such as Excel or Word is being automated, that application is known as the "server" and the application executing the automated code, such as VBA in Access, is the "controller." Access is controlling Excel or Word using the objects, properties, and methods of the application's object model, which are available after setting a reference to the application's object library.*

To use another application's objects, you first need to set a reference to that application's object library, sometimes referred to as *type library*. You do this using the References dialog box shown in Figure 19-1.

Follow these steps to add a reference to the Excel library:

1. While in the VBA editor, from the Tools menu, select `References`.
2. Scroll down and locate the `Microsoft Excel 15.0 Object Library`.
3. Place a checkmark in the checkbox next to the object library's name.

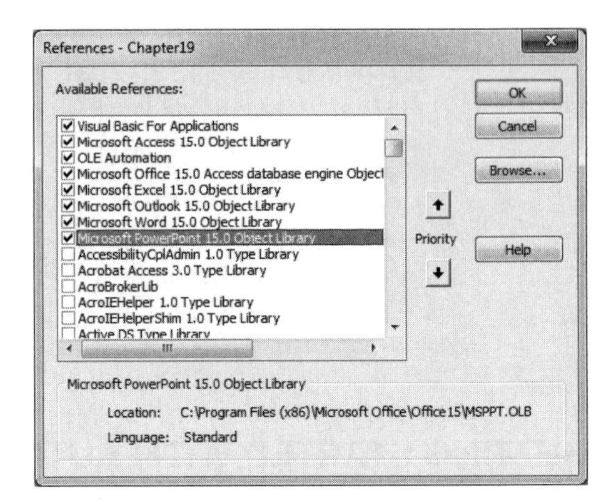

FIGURE 19-1: Using the References dialog box to set references

By adding a reference to a library, the objects for that application are now available for you to:

- Use throughout the code in this project
- Use IntelliSense, to show the syntax to use for methods available to the object model's classes
- View in the Object Browser

Using the Object Browser is a great way to learn how to use an application's object model, especially when there is no other documentation. To show the Object Browser, as displayed in Figure 19-2, press F2 while in the Module editor.

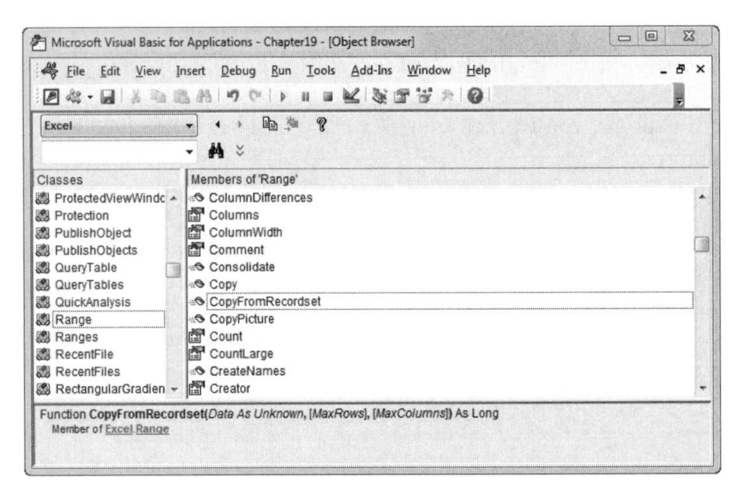

FIGURE 19-2: Using the Object Browser to view properties and methods

Once you have specified the object library, you can use the classes, collections, properties, and methods of the application's object model just as you do when using VBA from within that application. You will occasionally face additional hurdles because some applications make you jump through more extensive hoops to use their objects. For example, while Microsoft provides object libraries for Microsoft OneNote, you need to be comfortable working with XML and scripting in order to take advantage of them. Fortunately, with most Office products you just need to be able to work your way through their object models. You will find that it gets easier with practice and truly appreciate that the knowledge is transferable between products.

Declare and Instantiate Variables

For most applications, once you have set a reference to the application's object library, you can then declare variables and set references to objects within the application's object model starting with the Application level. As an example, when using the Excel object model, you will start with `Excel.Application` as shown here:

```
Public appExcel As Excel.Application
```

Once the variable is declared, you will then set a reference, also called "instantiation," using that variable by using the `Set` command:

```
Set appExcel = New Excel.Application
```

NOTE *Using* `Public` *to declare a variable to be used for an Application object versus* `Private` *or* `Dim` *can be important. Indeed, it is critical if you need the variable to survive after the routine is exited. If you don't specify* `Public`*, the routine is exited and the server application will be closed because the life of private and undeclared variables is limited to the life of the routine. For example, if you create a new Word document and want the user to view or edit the document when the routine is completed, you would need to declare the variable as* `Public` *in a public module.*

NOTE *In case there is an existing instance of the Application object, you can make use of the instance with this code:*

```
On Error Resume Next
Set appExcel = GetObject(, "Excel.Application")
If Err.Number <> 0 Then
    Set appExcel = New Excel.Application
End If
```

Once you have declared a variable and set a reference to the Application object in an object model, you can then work your way through the other objects and collections, depending on how the object model is structured. These objects don't typically need to be declared `Public`, but can be declared as necessary in the routines where they are used. The following code shows some additional examples of various objects being declared for use in the Excel object model:

```
Dim wbk As Excel.Workbook
Dim wks As Excel.Worksheet
Dim rngCurr As Excel.Range

On Error GoTo Err_CreateExcelWSAndPopulate

'-- Open Excel, then add a workbook, then the first worksheet
```

```
Set appExcel = New Excel.Application

Set wbk = appExcel.Workbooks.Add
Set wks = wbk.Worksheets(1)
```

In setting the references to the various objects in the Excel object model, you can also see examples of a new workbook being created, and a reference to the first worksheet created in the workbook. Remember that, by default, Excel creates three worksheets in each new workbook. For the most part, applications will behave in automation as they do when using the application's user interface.

> **NOTE** *When trying to find solutions to tasks you want to perform using automation from VBA, you can usually find them using Bing, Google, or another engine along with the search term 'VBA' and the name of the task to complete. The results list should point you in the right direction with regard to the classes, properties, and methods that you will need. You will have to add the Application object assignment to the code and modify lines of code to use it.*
>
> *If it doesn't seem to make sense when you try to use the suggested code, or if you get too many results in the search, you can narrow the results by adding "From Access" to the search string.*

Early Binding Versus Late Binding

Early binding refers to setting a reference to an object library, and then declaring and instantiating a variable using an object from that object library. You need to keep in mind that using early binding with different versions of applications can cause problems, such as creating untrappable errors at run time. For example, you create a database application in Access 2013 with references set to the same version of Word 2013, and then open the same database in Access 2007. You will get a reference error when the database is opened, not because it is an earlier version of Access, but because 2007 uses an earlier version of Word and the reference is for Word 2013.

You can avoid this issue by using late binding with error trapping. With late binding, you can declare various objects that you will be using from the object libraries as an `Object` data type, and then use the `CreateObject` function to instantiate a variable to pass a string that specifies which application you are creating.

For example, if you wanted to use the Excel object model, you would use the following declaration for the variable,

```
Public appExcel As Object
```

and then use the `CreateObject` syntax as follows:

```
Set appExcel = CreateObject("Excel.Application")
```

This syntax will open whichever version of Excel is installed on a system. If multiple versions of the application are installed, it will open the most recently installed version. Otherwise, if you want to open a specific version, perhaps to use version-specific features, you can specify the version, as shown here:

```
appExcel = CreateObject("Excel.Application.15")
```

> **NOTE** *Since Access 2000, the different versions of Access can no longer be determined by version number. This is because all versions share the same CLSID Registry. As a consequence, on systems with multiple versions of Access the most recently opened version will always be used, independent of version number.*

Using the `CreateObject` function creates a new instance of the application. You can then open a current file — for example, a document (Word) or worksheet (Excel) — using the appropriate methods for opening existing files. You can also instantiate an existing file by using the `GetObject` function and pass in the path string and class. For example, if you want to open an existing Excel worksheet located in a specific folder on the system, you model your code after the following snippet:

```
Set wbkExcel = GetObject("c:\test\example.xlsx". "Excel.Application")
```

The downside of using late binding is that, because the variables being used are of the `Object` data type, IntelliSence is not available for those objects. The way to work around this is to use early binding when developing, and then change the code to use late binding before distributing the application. Additionally, instead of constants, the actual value of the constant has to be used, for example, -4157 instead of xlSum. Further information on distributing your Access application can be found in Chapter 20.

Following is an example of a simple routine for populating a worksheet using late binding:

```
Option Compare Database
Option Explicit

'-- Late Binding for Excel Application
Public appExcelLB As Object


Function CreateExcelWSAndPopulateLateBinding()

   Dim rsProducts As DAO. Recordset

   Dim wbk As Object
   Dim wks As Object
   Dim rngCurr As Object

   On Error GoTo Err_CreateExcelWSAndPopulate

   '-- Open Excel, then add a workbook, then the first worksheet
   Set appExcelLB = CreateObject("Excel.Application")

   Set wbk = appExcelLB.Workbooks.Add
   Set wks = wbk.Worksheets(1)

   '-- Other code that will used whether Late or Early binding is used.

   '-- Clean up
   rsProducts.Close
   Set rsProducts = Nothing
```

```
    Exit Function

Err_CreateExcelWSAndPopulate:

    Beep
    MsgBox "The following error has occurred:" & vbCrLf & _
                        Err.Description, vbCritical, "Error Occurred"
    Set appExcelLB = Nothing
    Exit Function

End Function
```

This code is a modified portion of the code you'll see in the section, "Using Automation to Send Data to Excel," later in this chapter.

For the preceding example, the first change is in declaring the variable *appExcelLB* using the data type of `Object` in the Module Declaration section of a public module. Within the `CreateExcelWSAndPopulateLateBinding` function, the *wkb*, *wks*, and *rngCurr* variables are also declared as Object variable types although these variables are actually used as Excel Workbook, Worksheet, and Range objects.

Once declared, the *appExcelLB* variable is assigned using the `CreateObject` function. The other variables are actually assigned just as they were in the original function. With late binding, you can use error handling to safely trap any errors that occur, and use the line of code `Set appExcel = Nothing`, to prevent Excel from becoming hung up by any errors.

> **NOTE** *Use error handling extensively in your VBA code. As a standard, it is a good thing to develop routines with error handling in place but commented out; this is more convenient when you need to debug the code. Once you feel the code is complete, uncomment the error handling and thoroughly test the code again. Error handling is covered in detail in Chapter 16.*

One last difference to recognize between early and late binding is that applications using late binding take a performance hit, but the hit is really so miniscule, especially as processors improve, as to not be a concern.

AUTOMATING OFFICE PROGRAMS

When automating Microsoft Office applications, Microsoft provides the object libraries for various Office applications, from the full Office Suite to specialized programs such as OneNote. In addition to supplying the object libraries for various Office applications for use with automation, Microsoft has integrated the applications so that the tasks that are most often needed between the various products can be accomplished without writing a line of code. That is when the other methods of using automation come in, such as the ribbons, menus, and macros.

The demonstrations throughout the rest of this chapter will be launched from the form called frmAutomation, displayed in Figure 19-3.

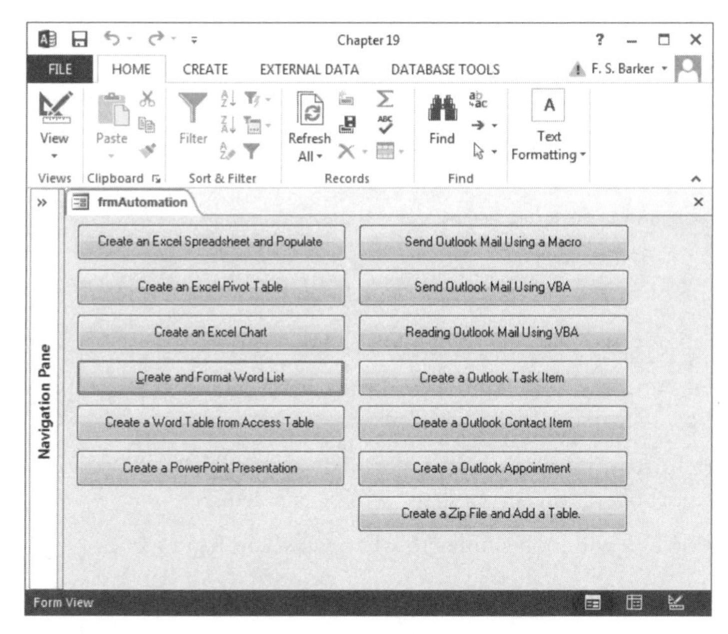

FIGURE 19-3: Switchboard form for automation demonstrations

MICROSOFT EXCEL INTEGRATION

Excel is integrated through ribbons, (right-click) menus, macros, and VBA automation. You can easily accomplish many tasks through the commands on the ribbon (for example, the External Data Ribbon) and by using macros.

Automation can also be used for more extensive tasks such as importing and exporting data from specific cells, formatting data, creating calculated cells, creating Pivot Tables and Charts, pushing and pulling data from template worksheets, and much more.

Integration with Excel Using Ribbons, Menus, and Macros

When using ribbons, menus, and macros to work with Excel from Access, the main purpose is to simplify transferring data back and forth between the two applications. Such tasks might be to:

- Import data from Excel worksheets into Access tables
- Export Access objects, including data generated from tables, queries, forms, and reports, creating new Excel worksheets
- Link to Excel worksheets from Access and having the worksheets display as linked Access tables

Exporting a Table to Excel Using the Ribbon and Menus

You can see the Import and Export sections on the Access External Data ribbon, which contains buttons for importing and exporting data, shown here in Figure 19-4.

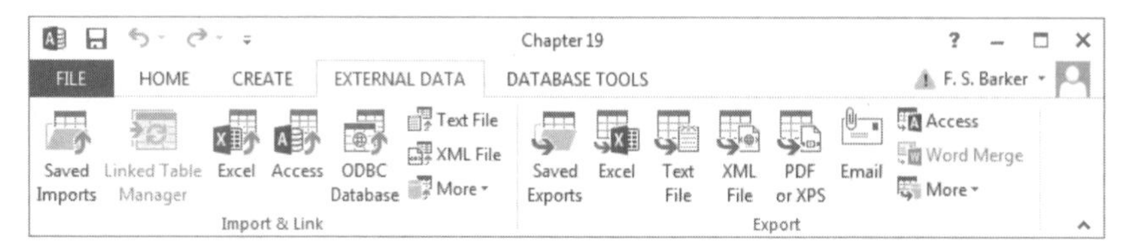

FIGURE 19-4: Ribbon used to import, link, and export

To export the table called `tblProjects` located in the chapter database, follow these steps:

1. Highlight the table called `tblProjects` in the navigation pane.
2. In the Export section of the `EXTERNAL DATA` ribbon, click the Excel button. The Export – Excel Spreadsheet dialog box appears.
3. Select the Export data with formatting and layout option. The option labeled "Open the destination file after the export operation is complete" will be enabled.
4. Select this option. The dialog box will look similar to what you see in Figure 19-5.
5. Click OK.

Export - Excel Spreadsheet

Select the destination for the data you want to export

Specify the destination file name and format.

File name: C:\Users\FSBarker\Documents\tblProjects.xlsx Browse...

File format: Excel Workbook (*.xlsx)

Specify export options.

Export data with formatting and layout.
Select this option to preserve most formatting and layout information when exporting a table, query, form, or report.

Open the destination file after the export operation is complete.
Select this option to view the results of the export operation. This option is available only when you export formatted data.

Export only the selected records.
Select this option to export only the selected records. This option is only available when you export formatted data and have records selected.

OK Cancel

FIGURE 19-5: Exporting a table to Excel from Access

The spreadsheet will then be created and displayed in Microsoft Excel. You can perform the same task by highlighting the table, then pressing the right mouse button, and choosing `Excel` from the `Export` menu off the right-click menu.

Exporting a Table to Excel Using a Macro

You can automate the process to export a table to Excel using a macro or VBA code. This can provide a more robust and customizable alternative to using the ribbon or right-click options described previously.

Using a macro to perform the same tasks described can be an efficient method to accomplish exporting and importing data. This is especially true if the same task will be repeated, you want the user to only have to click a button from a form, or if the task is just one step within a larger group of tasks.

You can create a macro to export the table called `tblProjects` with the following steps. From Access's Create ribbon:

1. Choose `Macro` from the `Macros and Code` ribbon section. A new macro will be generated and opened in the design view.
2. Select `ExportWithFormatting` as the macro action to perform.
3. Select `Table` for the Object Type.
4. Select `tblProjects` for the Object Name.
5. Select `Excel Workbook` (*.xlsx) for the Output Format.
6. Select `tblProjects.xlsx` for the Output File.
7. Select `Yes` for the Auto Start. The dialog box will now look similar to what you see in Figure 19-6.
8. Click the `Run` button.

You will then be asked to save the macro. When you save and run the macro, it will open a new spreadsheet. Additional actions can be added to this macro to further customize the process to your needs. And, to make it easy for the user, you can add a button to a form to call the macro.

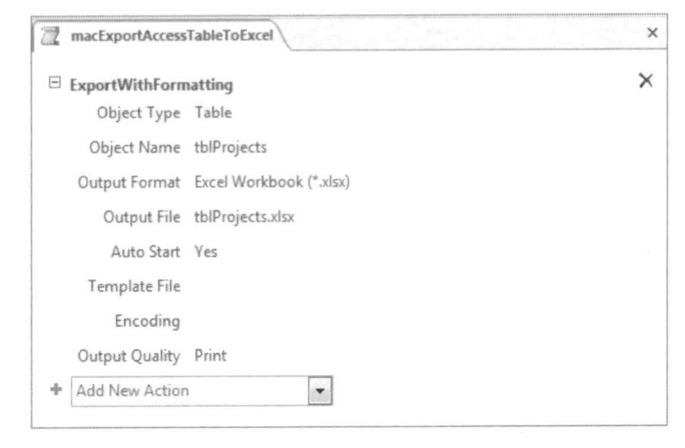

FIGURE 19-6: Exporting a table to Excel using a macro

Another way to use this macro is to call the macro from VBA code using the `DoCmd.RunMacro` statement. Alternatively, you can use the `DoCmd.RunCommand` statement, using the `acCmdExportExcel` command.

There are additional ribbon and menu commands, and macro actions that can be used for exporting and importing data between Access and other applications. As you work through the chapter examples, you will also learn how to use VBA to customize the worksheet with column names, using ranges, adding calculations, and much more.

Referencing the Excel Object Library

If you want to work with Excel or view the Excel object model, you need to set a reference to the Excel object library as discussed in the first section of, "Getting Started with Automation. "You can select the approach that is appropriate for your scenario. If you are using Excel 2013, you will use the `References` dialog box to set a reference to `Microsoft Excel 15.0 Object Library`. After the library is referenced, you can begin automating processes.

Working with the Excel Object Model

As you prepare to go through some examples that demonstrate how to automate Excel, it is good to keep in mind that you will be working with the Excel object model rather than the Access object model. Like most object models, the Excel object model is set up in a hierarchical format.

Before you actually manipulate the workbooks and worksheets you will typically start with the following steps to create Excel files:

1. Set a reference to the Application object.
2. Set a reference to the Workbook object returned by the `Add` method of the `Workbooks` collection.
3. Set a reference to a worksheet or worksheets in the referenced `workbook` object.

At this point, you can work with individual cell objects or use the Range object to work with a group of cells. These steps are the base for the majority of the Excel examples provided in this chapter.

> **NOTE** *Another great way to see example code for a task you are trying to accomplish in Excel from Access is to go into Excel and record an Excel macro to perform the task. Take VBA code that is generated by the Excel Macro recorder and use that in the code that you are creating in Access to automate Excel. You will usually be able to get the code working by adding the* `appExcel` *variable on the front of the objects that are being used, or by replacing* `Me` *with* `appExcel`.
>
> *In some cases the code generated is not always the most efficient way to code, but it will point you the right direction. At least, it will be a good guide to show you how the task can be completed.*

Using Automation to Send Data to Excel

There are a myriad of scenarios for sending data to Excel. Whether it is for additional manipulation, ease of sharing, providing a safe sandbox for users, or to support a personal reporting preference, it can be a powerful and beneficial technique to master. Whatever your needs, you can extrapolate from and model after the following example.

The data source for this example is an Access query, but you could choose a table or other object. The goal is to take the data from Access and push it into Excel. You can add formatting, specify the location, and incorporate other features as appropriate for your purposes. Using the query displayed in Figure 19-7, the process will send the Date, Product, and Cost for items ordered and delivered to Excel. You can also view this by using this chapter's download files.

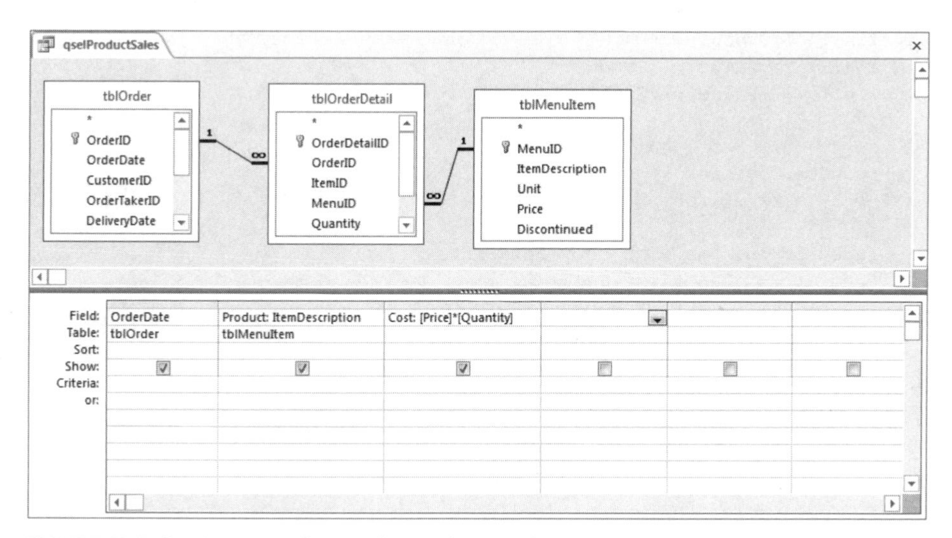

FIGURE 19-7: Design view of query for products ordered

Exporting the results of this query can be accomplished just by using a command on the Access `EXTERNAL DATA` ribbon, but additional tasks are being accomplished with the `CreateExcelWSAndPopulate` function shown here:

```
Function CreateExcelWSAndPopulate()

   Dim rsProducts As DAO. Recordset

   Dim wbk As Excel.Workbook
   Dim wks As Excel.Worksheet
   Dim rngCurr As Excel.Range

   On Error GoTo Err_CreateExcelWSAndPopulate

   '-- Open Excel
   Set appExcel = New Excel.Application

   '-- In order to see the action!
   appExcel.Visible = True

   '-- Add a workbook, then the first worksheet
   Set wbk = appExcel.Workbooks.Add
   Set wks = wbk.Worksheets(1)
```

```
    '-- Open the product sales query
    Set rsProducts = CurrentDb.OpenRecordset("qselProductSales")

    With wks

        .Name = "Raw Data"

        '-- Create the Column Headings
        .Cells(1, 1).Value = "Date"
        .Cells(1, 2).Value = "Product"
        .Cells(1, 3).Value = "Cost"


        rsProducts.MoveLast
        rsProducts.MoveFirst

        '-- Specify the range to copy data into.
        Set rngCurr = .Range(wks.Cells(2, 1), _
                .Cells(2 + rsProducts.RecordCount, 3))

        rngCurr.CopyFromRecordset rsProducts

        '-- Create the calculation that sums up the Duration Column
        .Cells(2 + rsProducts.RecordCount, 3).Value = _
                "=SUM(C1:C" & LTrim(Str(rsProducts.RecordCount) + 1) & ")"

        '-- Format the columns
        .Columns("A:C").AutoFit
        .Columns(3).NumberFormat = "$ #,##0"
     End With

     '-- freeze the top row
     appExcel.ActiveWindow.SplitRow = 1
     appExcel.ActiveWindow.FreezePanes = True

     '-- Clean up
     rsProducts.Close
     Set rsProducts = Nothing

     Exit Function

Err_CreateExcelWSAndPopulate:

     Beep
     MsgBox "The following error has occurred:" & vbCrLf & _
                    Err.Description, vbCritical, "Error Occurred"
     Set appExcel = Nothing
     Exit Function

End Function
```

The function is behind the `Create an Excel Spreadsheet and Populate` button on the form named `frmAutomation`. If you click that button, you will see the results, as displayed in Figure 19-8.

With a quick review of the `CreateExcelWSAndPopulate` function, you will see that it covers a lot more than just creating a new workbook and inserting data into it. The following lists the key Excel-specific concepts in the order that they were introduced.

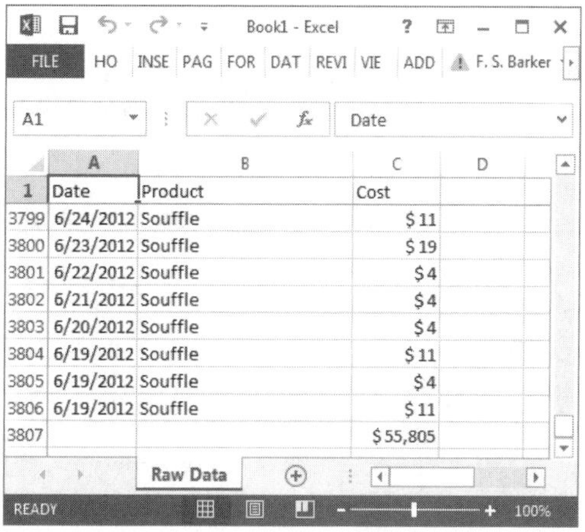

- Excel is displayed by setting the `Visible` property of the *`appExcel`*, the `Application` object, to `True`.
- The worksheet `Name` property is used to specify "`Raw Data`" as the title of the worksheet.
- Setting the `Value` property of `Cells` provides the capability to specify custom column titles for the data.
- The `Range` object is used to calculate where to place the data in the worksheet. The number of rows to be used as the max limit is derived from the `RecordCount` property of the `Recordset` object.
- The data is pulled into the worksheet using the `CopyFromRecordset` method of the `Worksheet` object.
- A calculated cell is created, summing up the third column of data using Excel's `SUM` function again using the `RecordCount` property of the `Recordset` object.
- Formatting is applied using the `Columns` collection of the `Worksheet` object.
- The first row is frozen in place so you can scroll down to the last row.

FIGURE 19-8: Sending data to Excel using automation

The `CreateExcelWSAndPopulate` function is also used as a base for the next example.

Creating an Excel `PivotTable` from Access

For a number of versions, Microsoft included two features in Access called `PivotTable` and PivotChart, available as views of tables, queries, forms, and reports. As of Access 2013, the `PivotTable` and PivotChart are no longer features within Access. However, you can use automation to create pivot tables and charts in Excel.

The following example continues working with the concepts and code from the previous section. In this case, you will use the worksheet that was just created to provide the range of results to the `PivotTableWizard` in order to create a `PivotTable` object in Excel.

For the most basic `PivotTable`, you just need to select the cells that you want to include in the range of data that you want to use, and then call Excel's `PivotTableWizard` to create the `PivotTable` object. By starting with the routine used in the last section, you will need to add only two additional lines of code, as shown here:

```
CreateExcelWSAndPopulate

appExcel.Range("A1").Select
appExcel.ActiveSheet.PivotTableWizard
```

When the complete code is executed, it will create the Raw Data worksheet of product information. Then it will create a new worksheet with the `PivotTable`. It will automatically include the three fields, as shown in Figure 19-9.

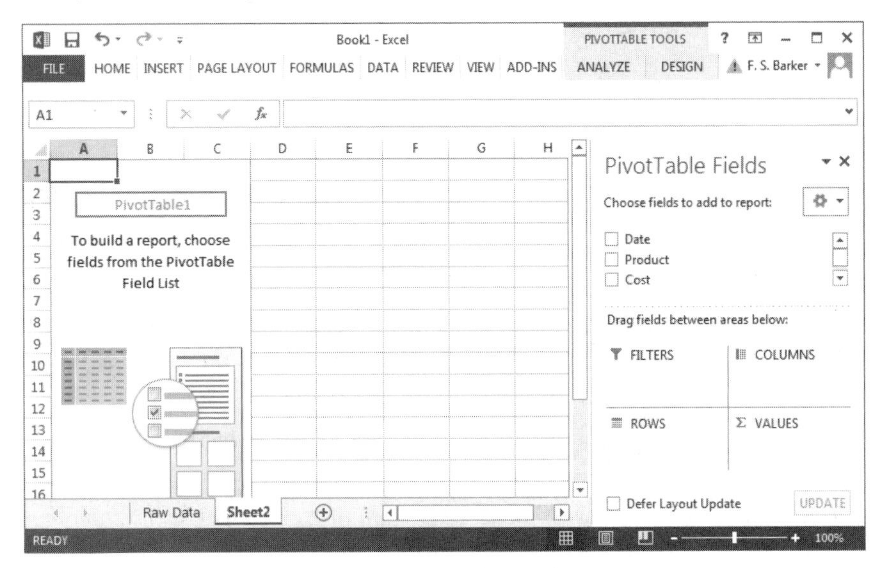

FIGURE 19-9: Minimal `PivotTable` created

The code snippet just displayed is not actually on `frmAutomation`, but it is part of the next code snippet, called `AccessToExcelPivotTableAutomation`. This code is a bit more extensive as it specifies additional features to use such as formatting cells and fields to use by default:

```
Function AccessToExcelPivotTableAutomation()

    Dim pf As PivotField

    '-- Creates a worksheet with the products information.
    CreateExcelWSAndPopulate

    On Error GoTo Err_AccessToExcelPivotTableAutomation

    '-- Select the range of data to use.
    appExcel.Range("A1").Select

    With appExcel.ActiveSheet.PivotTableWizard

        '-- Specify the Date field for Row summary.
        .AddFields RowFields:="Date", ColumnFields:="Product"

        '-- Alternate way of specifying fields, and formatting
        Set pf = .PivotFields("Cost")
```

```
            pf.Orientation = xlDataField
            pf.Function = xlSum
            pf.NumberFormat = "$ #,##0"

         End With

         appExcel.ActiveSheet.Name = "Products Pivot Table"

      Exit Function

   Err_AccessToExcelPivotTableAutomation:

      Beep
      MsgBox "The Following Automation Error has occurred:" & _
                   vbCrLf & Err.Description, vbCritical, "Automation Error!"
      Set appExcel = Nothing
      Exit Function

   End Function
```

To have the code initially display a more complete `PivotTable` for the user, you can add fields to the `PivotTable` for Row, Column, and Page use. As you review the preceding code, you can see how it accomplishes tasks in the following order:

1. Use the `With` command, using the `PivotTable` returned by calling the `PivotTableWizard`.
2. The `AddFields` method is used when assigning the `RowFields` parameter to use the `Date` field, and the `ColumnFields` parameter to use the `Product` field.
3. An alternative way to assign a field, a `PivotField`, declared at the top of the routine, was set and specified as the `DataField`, using `Sum` as the function, and formatting the value as currency.
4. The worksheet title is specified by setting the Name property to "Products Pivot Table."

When the `PivotTableWizard` method is called, the new worksheet is populated and set as the active worksheet. It then displays the results in a `PivotTable`, as shown in Figure 19-10.

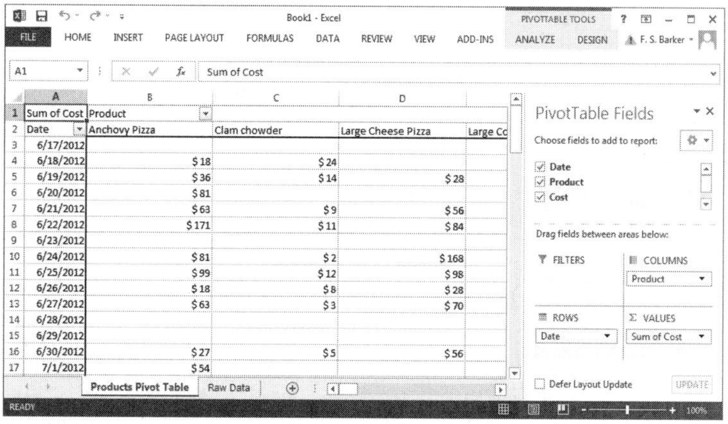

Sum of Cost	Product			
Date	Anchovy Pizza	Clam chowder	Large Cheese Pizza	Large Cc
6/17/2012				
6/18/2012	$ 18	$ 24		
6/19/2012	$ 36	$ 14	$ 28	
6/20/2012	$ 81			
6/21/2012	$ 63	$ 9	$ 56	
6/22/2012	$ 171	$ 11	$ 84	
6/23/2012				
6/24/2012	$ 81	$ 2	$ 168	
6/25/2012	$ 99	$ 12	$ 98	
6/26/2012	$ 18	$ 8	$ 28	
6/27/2012	$ 63	$ 3	$ 70	
6/28/2012				
6/29/2012				
6/30/2012	$ 27	$ 5	$ 56	
7/1/2012	$ 54			

FIGURE 19-10: Generated `PivotTable` using automation

Generating an Excel Chart from Access

Charts can be a powerful way to quickly summarize and convey complex data. They also have broad appeal in presentations and reports. Fortunately, it is relatively easy to create a variety of charts in Excel by using the PivotChart object.

If you wanted to create the chart from a `PivotTable` in prior versions of Excel, you would first have to create a `PivotTable`. But now, you can take data from Access and show it directly in a PivotChart, without having to create a `PivotTable`. This is especially convenient if you are generating the workbook from Access and want to e-mail it to someone.

The following example demonstrates how to create an Excel chart based on an Access query. The recordsource, `qselProductSalesSummary`, is a query that summarizes the costs for each product. Similar to the `PivotTable` and other Excel objects, it requires only minimal code to take advantage of the feature, and you can add additional code as required to set the properties to meet your needs. The current scenario requires two columns of information, `Products` and `Code`. Once the worksheet containing the two columns is created, the following code is used to create the actual chart in Excel:

```
'-- Specify the range to chart
Set rangeChart = appExcel.ActiveSheet.Range("A:B")

'== Add a chart to Excel
Set chartNew = appExcel.Charts.Add

'-- Create the chart by specifying the chart's source data.
With chartNew
    .SetSourceData rangeChart
    .ChartType = xl3DColumn
    .Legend.Delete
End With
```

In this code, a `Range` object is passed to a new `Chart` object created using the `SetSourceData` method, the `ChartType` is set to `xl3DColumn`, and the legend removed using the `Delete` method of the `Legend` object.

The following code combines the steps taken to create a worksheet from Access, and then uses that worksheet to create the new Excel chart:

```
Function AccessToExcelChartAutomation()

    Dim rsProducts As DAO. Recordset
    Dim wbk As Excel.Workbook
    Dim wks As Excel.Worksheet
    Dim rngCurr As Excel.Range
    Dim rangeChart As Range
    Dim chartNew As Chart

    On Error GoTo Err_AccessToExcelChartAutomation
```

```
    '-- Open a recordset based on the qselProductSalesSummary query.
    Set rsProducts = CurrentDb.OpenRecordset("qselProductSalesSummary")

    '-- Open Excel, then add a workbook, then the first worksheet
    Set appExcel = New Excel.Application
    Set wbk = appExcel.Workbooks.Add
    Set wks = wbk.Worksheets(1)

    '-- In order to see the action!
    appExcel.Visible = True


    With wks
        .Name = "Raw Data"
        '-- Create the Column Headings
        .Cells(1, 1).Value = "Product"
        .Cells(1, 2).Value = "Cost"

        rsProducts.MoveLast
        rsProducts.MoveFirst

        '-- Specify the range to copy data into.
        Set rngCurr = .Range(wks.Cells(2, 1), _
             .Cells(2 + rsProducts.RecordCount, 3))

        rngCurr.CopyFromRecordset rsProducts

        '-- Format the columns
        .Columns("A:B").AutoFit
        .Columns(2).NumberFormat = "$ #,##0"

    End With

    rsProducts.Close
    Set rsProducts = Nothing

    '-- Specify the range to chart
    Set rangeChart = appExcel.ActiveSheet.Range("A:B")

    '== Add a chart to Excel
    Set chartNew = appExcel.Charts.Add

    '-- Create the chart by specifying the chart's source data.
    With chartNew
        .SetSourceData rangeChart
        .ChartType = xl3DColumn
        .Legend.Delete
   End With

   Exit Function

Err_AccessToExcelChartAutomation:

   Beep
   MsgBox "The Following Automation Error has occurred:" & _
             vbCrLf & Err.Description, vbCritical, "Automation Error!"
```

```
        Set appExcel = Nothing
        Exit Function

    End Function
```

You can also view that code in the chapter's demo database. To execute the code, simply click the `Create an Excel Chart` button located on the `frmAutomation` form. This will create a new workbook in Excel with a worksheet labeled Raw Data, which will contain the following data:

PRODUCT	COST
Anchovy Pizza	$ 3,555
Clam Chowder	$ 558
Large Cheese Pizza	$ 5,264
Large Coke	$ 313
Large Diet Coke	$ 348
Large Hamburger Pizza	$ 4,099
Large Pepperoni Pizza	$ 4,716
Large Sprite	$ 271
Lasagna	$ 1,916
Last Try	$ 1,149

Another worksheet is also created that contains the chart shown in Figure 19-11.

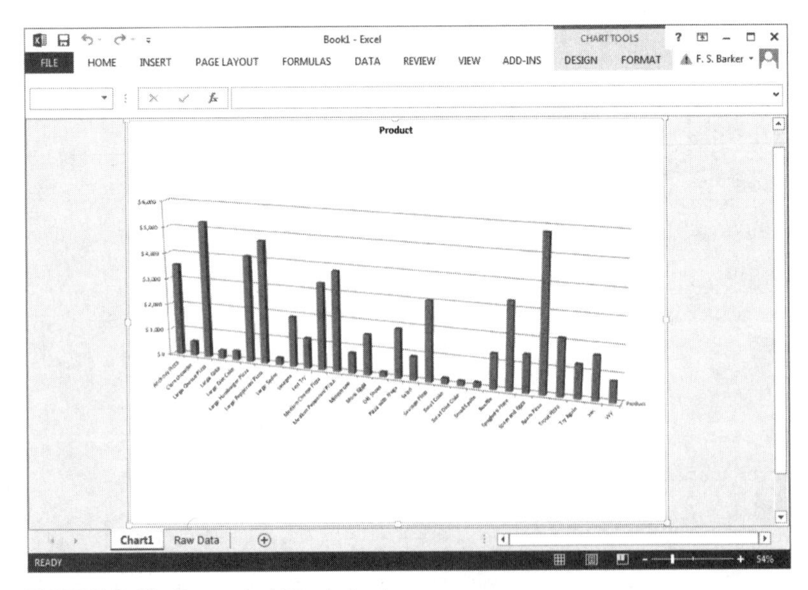

FIGURE 19-11: Generated Excel chart

As you become comfortable with manipulating workbooks, worksheets, ranges, and cells it is relatively straightforward to extend those techniques to accomplish other tasks.

WORD INTEGRATION

As with Excel, you can integrate Word by exporting data using ribbons, menus, macros, or automation. When data is exported to Word using ribbons, menus, and macros, Access generates documents with the .rtf extension, which stands for Rich Text Format.

The formatting of the document is based on the type of object that you are exporting. If you export tables or queries, the data will be put into tables within a document. However, if you want the documents to be formatted similar to the report, you can export a report or form. These straightforward techniques may suffice a majority of the time, but as your users come to expect more they may request more polished and customized presentations. This is likely to expand exponentially after they see what can be done with automation.

Unlike Excel, you can't import data from Word documents using the ribbons, menus, or macros. But, you can use automation to read data from Word documents.

Integration with Word Using Ribbons, Menus, and Macros

The ribbon provides a few options to export tables, queries, forms, and reports to Word. To view these, open the `EXTERNAL DATA` ribbon, and in the Export section choose More, then Word. The Export - RTF File dialog box opens and lists options for exporting the data. The Export section also contains the `Word Merge` command. This is can be a powerful tool for incorporating Access data into Word documents. Fortunately, it is relatively intuitive and there are ample guides and tutorials to help you master these tools.

Another method you can use for exporting objects is to select the object in the navigation pane, right-click the mouse on the object you want to export, and then choose Word RTF File from the Export menu.

If you prefer to use a macro, you can use any of the macro actions that export data to create `Rich Text Format (*.rtf)` for `Format Type`. Depending on the task at hand, you might use either `EMailDatabaseObject` or `ExportWithFormatting`. You can also use the macro command `WordMailMerge`.

Referencing the Word Object Library

As with Excel, in order to work with the Word object model you need to set a reference to the Word object library as discussed in the first section of "Getting Started with Automation;" you can follow the process to fit your needs and select Word object library.

If you are using Word 2013, you would use the References dialog box to set a reference to `Microsoft Word 15.0 Object Library`.

Working with the Word Object Model

Using automation, you can manipulate Word documents any way you need to, much like you can through Word's user interface. The main object you will use is the `Document` object. Quite often, you will also use the `Range` object, which looks similar to the `Range` object that you just worked with in Excel.

The `Range` object in Excel is made up of columns and cells of an Excel worksheet, along with the data contained in those cells. The `Range` object in Word is made up of "ranges" of text within a Word document. It can include paragraphs and formatting. Both Word and Excel objects allow you to work with data or text in memory at run time.

Sending Access Data to Word with Automation

When exporting Access objects to Word using the `Access Export` command, you have limited control and choices about how the data gets put into the document. With the built-in export process, a table is created, data placed into it, and there is minimal formatting. That works for some scenarios, but it doesn't provide the polish or versatility that you and your users may be accustomed to. It is more common to want the data inserted into an existing document, to have some attractive formatting, or to manipulate the document after the data has been added. You will learn how to accomplish those goals as you work through the next example.

> **WARNING** *The path assigned to the `strTemplate` variable is the path of the Office templates on the local machine. This path could vary on other installations. Additionally, the .thmx extension is new to Office 2013. This extension may vary based on the referenced version of Office.*

The demonstration uses the data in `tblProjects` to create a report in a Word document. As you read through the function that follows, you will see the steps used to create a simple report header. After that, the code goes through the records in the table to group and display the tasks for each resource:

```
Function AccessToWordAutomation()

   Dim strTheme As String
   Dim strCurrResource As String
   Dim rsProjects As DAO. Recordset
   Dim docWord As Word.Document
   Dim rngCurrent As Word.Range

   On Error GoTo Err_AccessToWordAutomation

   '-- Open the projects table
   Set rsProjects = CurrentDb.OpenRecordset( _
            "Select Resource, Task from tblProjects Order By Resource")

   Set appWord = New Word.Application
   appWord.Visible = True
```

```
    strTheme = _
         "C:\Program Files\Microsoft Office\Document Themes 15\Slice.thmx"

    '-- Create the document variable
    Set docWord = appWord.Documents.Add()
    docWord.ApplyDocumentTheme strTheme

    '-- Set Range object to current document
    Set rngCurrent = docWord.Content


     With rngCurrent

         '-- Add a report header

         .InsertAfter "Project Task Report"
         .InsertAfter vbCrLf
         .InsertAfter Date
         .InsertParagraphAfter
         .Collapse Direction:=wdCollapseEnd


         '-- Loop through projects, breaking on each resource
         Do Until rsProjects.EOF

             '-- If new resource, write out the resource information
             If strCurrResource <> rsProjects!Resource Then
                 .InsertParagraphAfter
                 .Collapse Direction:=wdCollapseEnd
                 .InsertAfter "Tasks for Resource: " & rsProjects!Resource
                 .InsertParagraphAfter
                 .Collapse Direction:=wdCollapseEnd
                 strCurrResource = rsProjects!Resource
             End If

             '-- Write out the task, formatting it as a bullet.
             .InsertAfter rsProjects!Task
             .InsertAfter vbCrLf
             .ListFormat.ApplyBulletDefault

             rsProjects.MoveNext

         Loop

     End With

     Set docWord = Nothing

    Exit Function

Err_AccessToWordAutomation:

    Beep
    MsgBox "The Following Automation Error has occurred:" & _
                vbCrLf & Err.Description, vbCritical, "Automation Error!"
```

```
        Set appWord = Nothing
        Exit Function

    End Function
```

Once again, you can view the code in the chapter's demo database. To execute the code, click the `Create and Format Word List` button located on `frmAutomation`. Once the code is executed, you will see the document created, as shown in Figure 19-12.

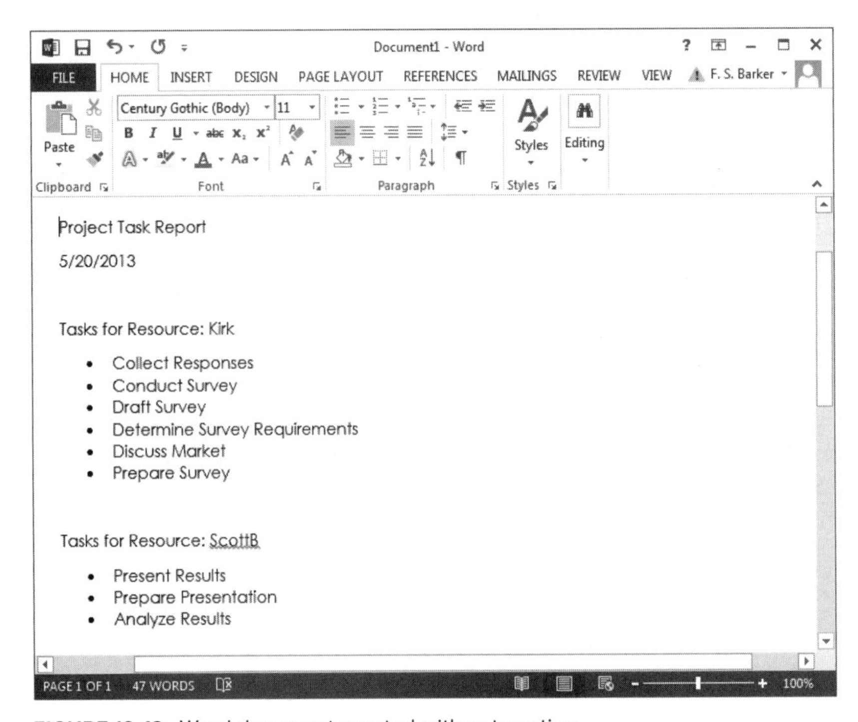

FIGURE 19-12: Word document created with automation

The code begins by assigning the report title and date created as the heading. Then, each resource is displayed with a label "`Tasks for Resource:`" along with a bulleted list of the tasks performed. The data is derived from the records in `tblProjects`. The following explains the purpose of each step in the code. As you read through it, you will gain a better understanding of how to create and modify the code to fit specific needs:

- The *`strCurrResource`* `String` variable is declared to track which resource and tasks are currently displayed.
- The *`rsProjects`* `Recordset` variable is declared.
- The Word document object called *`docWord`* and a `Range` object called *`rngCurrent`* are declared.

- After setting the error handler to the code `Err_AccessToWordAutomation`, the *`rsProjects`* is set using the `OpenRecordset` method of `CurrentDb`.
- *`appWord`* is set to `Word.Application`, which is next made visible setting the `Visible` property of the *`appWord`* to True.
- A document is created and assigned to the *`docWord`* document variable by calling the `Add` method of the `Documents` collection. The Theme is also applied using the `ApplyDocumentTheme` method of the `Document` object.

  Note that the theme file location is based on the machine used to create this demonstration, so you may need to specify a different file location. Also, Office 2013 uses theme files with a .thmx extension. Prior versions use different extensions, so you may need to determine and select a theme and extension type that is compatible with the Office version that you are using.
- The current text in the document is assigned to the *`currRange`* variable by assigning the `Content` property of the `Document`, which is of the type `Word.Range`. Although there isn't anything in the `Content` at this point, it is required for the rest of the routine as the *`currRange`* variable will be used for adding additional text and various tasks to be performed.
- The `InsertAfter` method of the `Range` object is used to add a title on one line of the document, and the *`vbCRLF`* is used to put the carriage return line feed characters in the document and then add the current date using the `Date` function.
- The `InsertParagraphAfter` method of *`currRange`* is called to add a couple of lines of text.
- The `Collapse` method of the `Range` object is used to collapse the range down to either the start or the end of the current `Range` so that you can work with new data. In this case, `Direction:=wdCollapseEnd` specifies the end of the current range.
- Within the `Do Until` loop, you can see the same `Range` object using various method calls to add the individual tasks to each of the resources. The tasks are formatted to use bullets by the code calling the `ApplyBulletDefault` method `Range.ListFormat` object. Notice that the `Collapse` method is used to make sure that only the tasks are bulleted.

At this point, you should be able to walk through the code displayed and see how the data is added to the document using the methods described.

Using Access Automation to Create Word Tables

In some cases, you may want to create a Word table using automation instead of using the user interface to export the data. You can accomplish this by starting with the previous example and adding some code.

After creating the document and adding the appropriate title information, you will use the `Word.Table` object's `Cells` collection and `Cell` object, as well as the `AutoFormat` method. You can do that with the following lines of code:

```
'Create the Word table.
Set tableWord = docWord.Tables.Add(rngCurrent, rsProjects.RecordCount, 2)

With tableWord

    .Cell(1, 1).Range.Text = "Resource"
    .Cell(1, 2).Range.Text = "Task"

    '-- Populate the cells with data from the Access table.
    For intRow = 1 To rsProjects.RecordCount
        For intCol = 1 To 2
            .Cell(intRow + 1, intCol).Range.Text = rsProjects(intCol - 1)
        Next
        rsProjects.MoveNext
    Next

    '-- Format the table.
    .AutoFormat Format:=wdTableFormatList1

End With
```

The preceding code adds a Word table to the *docWord* `Tables` collection, and then uses the `Cell` object to assign text as headings. Then, it loops through records and fields in the Access database to add the data from the *rsProjects* results. The code is completed by using the `AutoFormat` method of the *tableWord* object, using the same formatting as it would if you specified the table autoformat using Word's ribbon commands.

> **NOTE** *By using the* `Format` *parameter name of the* `AutoFormat` *method and then the assignment using ":=", IntelliSense will display all the enumerations for the available formats. Using* `Named` *parameters with the assignment operator, ":=", alleviates the need to ensure that parameters are in a specific position.*

You can see the complete code for the example in the following function:

```
Function CreateWordTableFromAccessAutomation()

    Dim rsProjects As DAO. Recordset
    Dim docWord As Word.Document
    Dim rngCurrent As Word.Range
    Dim tableWord As Word.Table
    Dim intRow As Integer
    Dim intCol As Integer

    On Error GoTo Err_CreateWordTableFromAccessAutomation

    '-- Open the projects table
    Set rsProjects = CurrentDb.OpenRecordset( _
            "Select Resource, Task from tblProjects Order By Resource")

    Set appWord = New Word.Application
```

```
        appWord.Visible = True

        '-- Create the document variable
        Set docWord = appWord.Documents.Add()

        Set rngCurrent = docWord.Content

        '-- Add report header

        With rngCurrent
            .InsertAfter "Project Task Report"
            .InsertAfter vbCrLf
            .InsertAfter Date
            .InsertParagraphAfter
            .Collapse Direction:=wdCollapseEnd
        End With

        '-- Create the Word table
        Set tableWord = docWord.Tables.Add(rngCurrent, rsProjects.RecordCount, 2)

        With tableWord

            .Cell(1, 1).Range.Text = "Resource"
            .Cell(1, 2).Range.Text = "Task"

            '-- Populate the cells from the Access table
            For intRow = 1 To rsProjects.RecordCount
                For intCol = 1 To 2
                    .Cell(intRow + 1, intCol).Range.Text = rsProjects(intCol - 1)
                Next
                rsProjects.MoveNext
            Next

            '-- Format the table
            .AutoFormat Format:=wdTableFormatList1

        End With

      Exit Function

  Err_CreateWordTableFromAccessAutomation:

      Beep
      MsgBox "The Following Automation Error has occurred:" & _
                  vbCrLf & Err.Description, vbCritical, "Automation Error!"
      Set appWord = Nothing
      Exit Function

  End Function
```

To execute the code from the chapter's demo database, click the button Create a Word Table from Access Table, located on `frmAutomation`. You will see the completed document, as displayed in Figure 19-13.

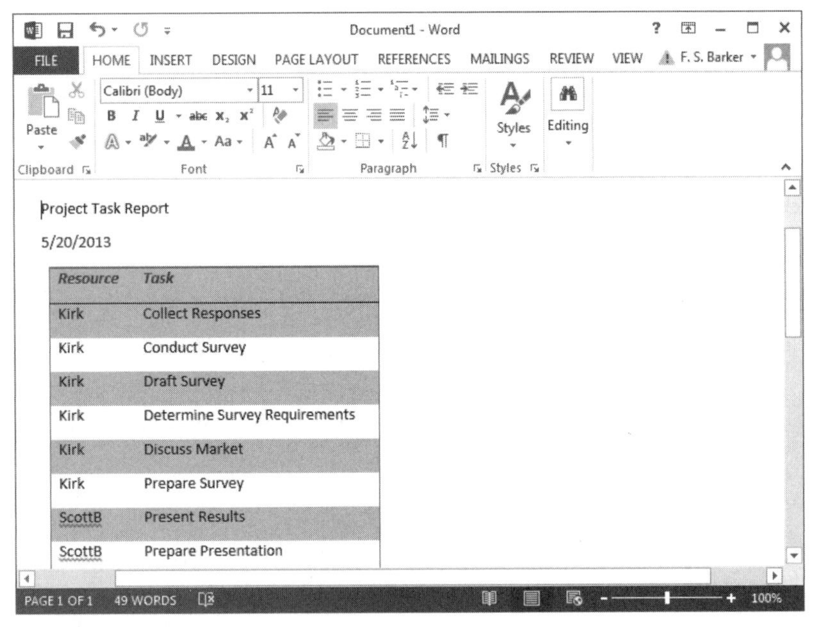

FIGURE 19-13: Generated Word table using automation

As you walk through the code, you can see that Word adds the cells in the table as you assign the text, and it does not require code to specify the number of columns and rows. The use of the `AutoFormat` method makes it relatively easy to create attractively formatted tables.

> **NOTE** *There are a number of other tasks you can accomplish by working with other classes in the Document object. In particular, you will benefit by experimenting with the* `Bookmark` *class along with the corresponding collection* `Bookmarks`*. These work well when you want to expand on or move specific areas within an existing document. Remember that the* `Range` *class, while extremely useful, is only effective while the document is open in memory for that specific instance of the objects being used.*

POWERPOINT INTEGRATION

PowerPoint is one of the most impressive applications in the Office suite, but it is also one of the least automated. When working with day-to-day tasks, most people will use Word, Outlook, or Excel, whereas PowerPoint is more likely to be used by managers or assistants to create presentations. This is rarely a day-to-day activity, so most workers have little or no experience with PowerPoint.

However, there are a number of reasons you could have for automating PowerPoint and providing data into those presentations from Access. Some scenarios that benefit from automating the transfer of data from Access to PowerPoint include:

- **Dynamically updating narrative content** — A company that provides content for online training could generate the PowerPoint slides and then dynamically update the content from the Access database. This content (data in Access tables) is maintained using Access forms.
- **Dynamically updating project status reports** — A development company that has people (resources) working on various project needs to track/report people, projects, tasks, and schedules. Management presentations can be created so that the slides can be dynamically updated to report the status at a specified time.

These examples should correlate well with many of your projects. The last example should sound familiar as it is based on the tblProjects table that you've been working with. You will continue using that table with the following demonstration.

Setting a Reference to the PowerPoint Object Library

In order to work with the PowerPoint object model, you need to set a reference to the PowerPoint object library as discussed in the first section of "Getting Started with Automation." For PowerPoint 2013, you will use the `References` dialog box to set a reference to `Microsoft PowerPoint 15.0 Object Library`.

Working with the PowerPoint Object Model

As with the other applications, getting comfortable with automating PowerPoint is a matter of understanding its object model and which objects you need to work with in order to accomplish the tasks you are completing. Initially, the two classes you will work with are the Presentation class and the `Slide` class, along with their respective properties and methods.

Creating a Presentation from an Access Table

The purpose of this section is to demonstrate how to create a new presentation, and then how to apply a template, provide text for a title slide, and populate the other slides from an Access table. The complete code is provided in the following snippet, followed by a discussion of the PowerPoint objects:

```
Function CreateAPowerPointPresentation()

    Dim rsProjects As DAO. Recordset
    Dim strCurrResource As String
    Dim strTemplate As String
    Dim strSlideText As String

'Create the presentation -- , title slide and new slides from the template.
    Dim ppPresentation As PowerPoint.Presentation
    Dim slideTitle As PowerPoint.Slide
    Dim slideNew As PowerPoint.Slide
```

```
On Error GoTo Err_CreateAPowerPointPresentation

'-- Open the projects table
Set rsProjects = CurrentDb.OpenRecordset( _
          "Select Resource, Task from tblProjects Order By Resource")

'-- Open the PowerPoint application and make it visible
Set appPowerPoint = New PowerPoint.Application

With appPowerPoint
    .Visible = True

    '-- Specify the template to use.
    strTemplate = _
          "C:\Program Files\Microsoft Office\Document Themes 15\Slice.thmx"
    .Presentations.Open strTemplate, False, True, True

    '-- Add a title for the presentation
    Set slideTitle = .ActivePresentation.Slides( _
                          .ActivePresentation.Slides.Count)
    slideTitle.Shapes(1).TextFrame.TextRange.Text = _
            "Presentation Generated From Access"
    slideTitle.Shapes(2).TextFrame.TextRange.Text = _
            "For Professional Access 2013 Programming" & vbCrLf & _
                        "By F. Scott Barker"
    strCurrResource = rsProjects!Resource

    '-- Loop through the tasks and resources.
    Do Until rsProjects.EOF

        '-- Add a new slide, activate it, and set a reference to it.
        .ActivePresentation.Slides.Add _
                (.ActivePresentation.Slides.Count + 1), ppLayoutText
        .ActiveWindow.View.GotoSlide .ActivePresentation.Slides.Count

        Set slideNew = .ActivePresentation.Slides( _
                        .ActivePresentation.Slides.Count)

        '-- Set the title for the slide
        slideNew.Shapes(1).TextFrame.TextRange.Text = _
                    "Activities Performed By " & rsProjects!Resource

        '-- Loop through the tasks for the current resource
        Do While strCurrResource = rsProjects!Resource

            If strSlideText <> "" Then
                strSlideText = strSlideText & vbCrLf
            End If

            strSlideText = strSlideText & rsProjects!Task

            rsProjects.MoveNext

            If rsProjects.EOF Then
                Exit Do
            End If
```

```
                Loop

                '-- Add the string of tasks to the slide
                slideNew.Shapes(2).TextFrame.TextRange.Text = strSlideText

                If Not rsProjects.EOF Then
                    '-- Set the new resource
                    strCurrResource = rsProjects!Resource
                    strSlideText = ""
                End If

            Loop

            Set slideNew = Nothing

        End With

        Exit Function

    Err_CreateAPowerPointPresentation:

        Beep
        MsgBox "The Following Automation Error has occurred:" & _
                    vbCrLf & Err.Description, vbCritical, "Automation Error!"
        Set appPowerPoint = Nothing
        Exit Function

    End Function
```

You can also view this code in the chapter's demo database. To execute the code, click the button `Create a PowerPoint Presentation`, located on `frmAutomation`. This will create the title slide (displayed in Figure 19-14) as well as the slide for each resource along with their assigned tasks, as shown in Figure 19-15.

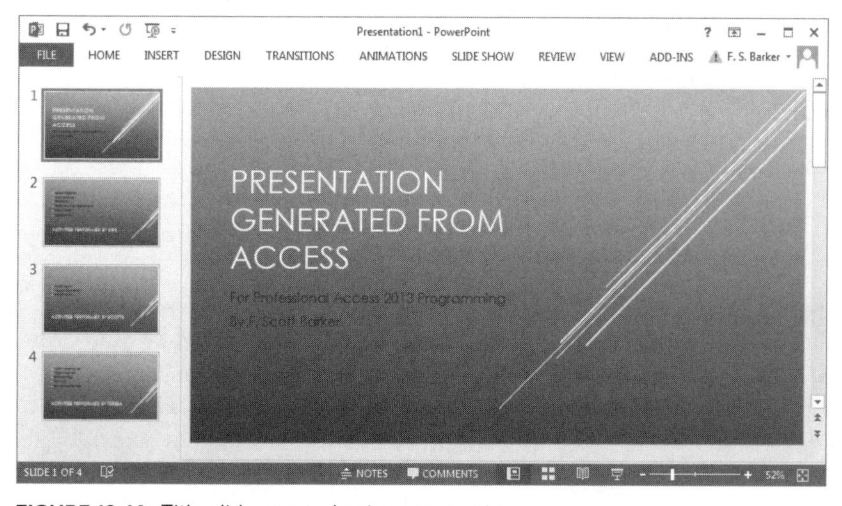

FIGURE 19-14: Title slide created using automation

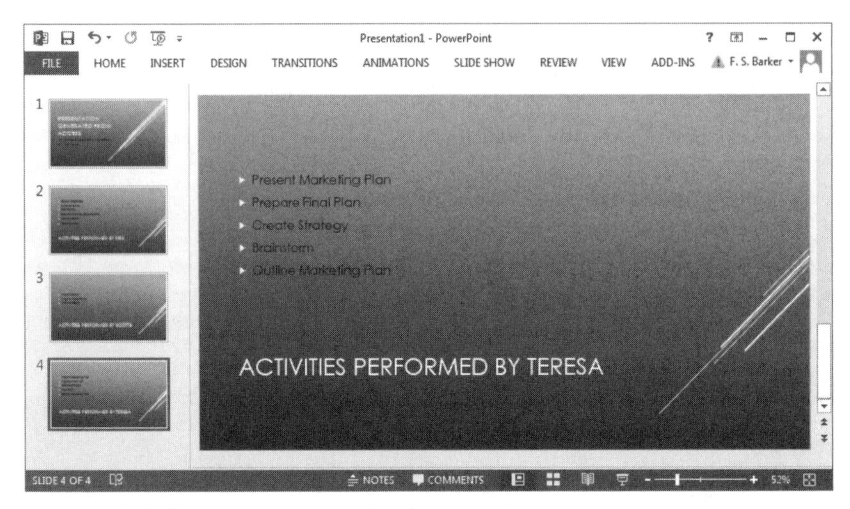

FIGURE 19-15: Project resource and tasks created

After the `Recordset` variable and other support variables are declared, three PowerPoint objects are declared: one `Presentation` object and two `Slide` objects. As discussed previously, it also requires the following three Dim statements:

```
Dim ppPresentation As PowerPoint.Presentation
Dim slideTitle As PowerPoint.Slide
Dim slideNew As PowerPoint.Slide
```

Next, the `PowerPoint.Application` object is assigned to the *`appPowerPoint`* object, and its `Visible` property is set to `True`. A `Presentation` object is then created by passing in the name of the template you want to use:

```
'-- Open the PowerPoint application and make it visible
Set appPowerPoint = New PowerPoint.Application

With appPowerPoint
    .Visible = True

    '-- Specify the template to use.
    strTemplate = _
        "C:\Program Files\Microsoft Office\Document Themes 15\Slice.thmx"
    .Presentations.Open strTemplate, False, True, True
```

> **WARNING** *The path assigned to the* `strTemplate` *variable is the path of the Office templates on the local machine. This path could vary on other installations. Additionally, the *.thmx extension is new to Office 2013. This extension may vary based on the referenced version of Office.*

By using the specified template, a title slide is created with two Shape objects, one for the title and one for the body text of the slide:

```
Set slideTitle = .ActivePresentation.Slides( _
                    .ActivePresentation.Slides.Count)
slideTitle.Shapes(1).TextFrame.TextRange.Text = _
        "Presentation Generated From Access"
slideTitle.Shapes(2).TextFrame.TextRange.Text = _
        "For Professional Access 2013 Programming" & vbCrLf & _
                "By F. Scott Barker"
```

These lines deserve a closer review to ensure that you understand the way that the objects and properties are being used. The first line assigns the *`slideTitle`* `Slide` object, using the `ActivePresentation.Slides` collection of the `Presentation` object. It uses the `Count` property to make sure that the slide is the last slide in the collection. The next two lines of code assign the title and then the subtitle for the title slide, using the `Slide` object's `Shape.TextFrame.TextRange.Text` property.

The next step is to add, activate, and assign text to a new slide. The big difference is that a new slide is added by using the `Add` method, along with the `ppLayoutText` constant to make sure that the slide is designed for text. The title for the slide is assigned by using Shape in the `Shapes` collection, and then assigning the *`Resource`* field of the `rsProject Recordset` variable to the `TextFrame.TextRange.Text` property.

Next, the data in the `Task` field is added to the string variable called `strSlideText` based on the records associated with the current Resource.

After you work through the code, it becomes fairly straightforward to create the slides. This can provide a tremendous benefit to the users, not only saving time but improving accuracy and consistency in the reports. Users and managers will be amazed by how great the slides look and how quick and easy it is for them to have up-to-date reports.

OUTLOOK INTEGRATION

Microsoft has taken great strides to make Outlook's objects more accessible for automation. Early versions had numerous hurdles to overcome before you could even "see" Outlook's objects. Even today, there are a couple of extra steps required with some objects because Outlook uses MAPI to store its objects in folders.

Fortunately, most of the automation tasks that you'll implement are relatively straightforward. As with other Office applications, you can accomplish most of the actions that can be performed through Outlook's user interface. This includes creating or reading items such as:

- **Mail items** — This can include sending and reading mail, or maintaining folders. This is useful if you want to send e-mail from the database, monitor e-mail, or even store messages in records within the database.

- **Task items** — You can maintain tasks in the database applications and ensure those tasks are assigned to someone.
- **Contact items** — You can maintain contacts in the database and then share them with Outlook — for example, in a sales application.
- **Appointment items** — When creating an office-wide management system, you can create a scheduler in your application and then post the appointments to Outlook.

The following section discusses how you can incorporate automating each of these items into your Access solutions. You can find the code in the chapter's demo database behind `frmAutomation`. The code resides in the public module called `modOutlookRoutines`.

Sending Outlook Mail Using a Macro Action

Before jumping into using VBA to automate Outlook, it is good to consider the ease and benefits of using a macro. The macro action EMailDatabaseObject enables you to mail any of the database objects, and it allows you to convert them to various output formats such as Excel workbooks, Rich Text Format (Word), and even Adobe PDFs.

Other arguments in the `EMailDatabaseObject` macro action allow you to specify if you want to include Recipients, Subject Line, and Body of the e-mail, as well as whether or not to display the e-mail for editing before sending. Figure 19-16 shows an example of using the `EmailDatabaseObject` to send a table, `tblCustomer`, as a PDF. If you execute this macro from the frmAutomation form by clicking the button `Send Outlook Mail Using a Macro`, it will create the e-mail displayed in Figure 19-17.

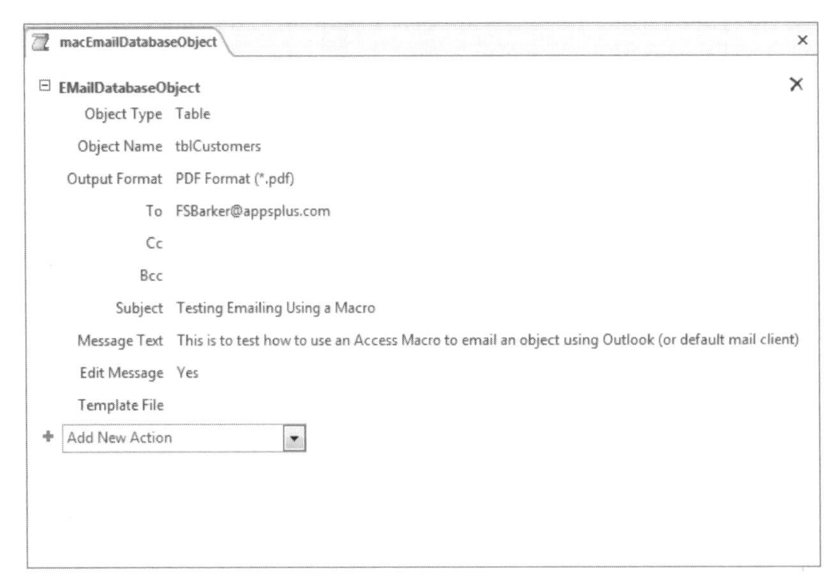

FIGURE 19-16: E-mailing a database object

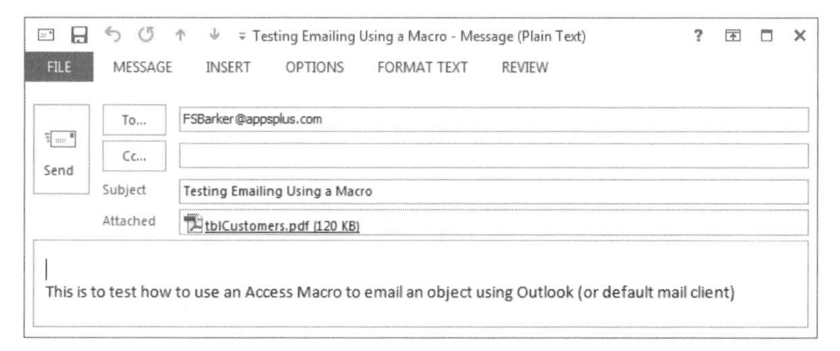

FIGURE 19-17: E-mail generated by the EMailDatabaseObject macro action

> **NOTE** *In VBA, if you only need to send e-mails, you can do so by using the* `DoCmd.RunMacro` *command to run the macro displayed in the preceding text. Alternatively, you can use the* `DoCmd.SendObject` *command, which provides the same abilities and arguments as the macro action* `EMailDatabaseObject`.

If the automation tasks are more extensive, you will need to use a combination of automation and VBA.

Referencing the Outlook Object Model

In order to work with the Outlook object model, you will need to set a reference to the Outlook object library. You can follow the process described in the first section of "Getting Started with Automation," and use the Outlook object library. If you are using Outlook 2013, you will set a reference to `Microsoft Outlook 15.0 Object Library`.

You can then declare variables for the `Outlook.Application` object and the `Outlook.Namespace` object:

```
Public olkApp As Outlook.Application
Public olkNameSpace As Outlook.Namespace
```

The `Namespace` type variable is declared to work with MAPI folders in the Outlook object model.

Sending Mail Using VBA and Automation

This first example is a straightforward approach that creates an e-mail item and then opens the item in Outlook. The following line of code is used to call the `CreateOLMailItem` routine. This code is attached to the Send Outlook Mail Using VBA button, located on `frmAutomation`:

```
Private Sub cmdOutlookMailVBADemo_Click()

        CreateOLMailItem "test@microsoft.com", "Subject is Testing", _
                "This is a Test"

End Sub
```

Three parameters are passed: the recipient, the subject line, and the body of the e-mail. The complete code for the `CreateOLMailItem` routine is provided here, followed by a brief explanation of each part.

```
Sub CreateOLMailItem(strRecipient As String, strSubject As String, _
                            strBody As String)

    Dim objMailItem As Outlook.MailItem

    Set olkApp = New Outlook.Application

    Set objMailItem = olkApp.CreateItem(olMailItem)

    With objMailItem
        .To = strRecipient
        .Subject = strSubject
        .Body = strBody
        .Display
    End With

    Set objMailItem = Nothing
    Set olkApp = Nothing

End Sub
```

The routine `CreateOLMailItem` performs the following:

- Three arguments are declared to receive the recipient, subject line, and body of the e-mail. They are `String` variables called *`strRecipient`*, *`strSubject`*, and *`strBody`*.
- *`objMailItem`* is declared as a type of `Outlook.MailItem`.
- *`olkApp`* is assigned to a new instance of Outlook.
- *`objMailItem`* is assigned using the `CreateItem` method of the `Application` object.
- The properties `To`, `Subject`, and `Body` are assigned to the *`objMailItem`* object.
- The `Display` method is used to display the e-mail to the user in Outlook.
- Both the *`objMailItem`* and *`olkApp`* variables are set to `Nothing` to clean them up before leaving the routine.

If you click the button Send Outlook Mail Using VBA, located on `frmAutomation`, you will see the e-mail message shown in Figure 19-18.

You can incorporate this code into your Access solutions to create an e-mail message. With the next examples, you'll see how easily you can modify the code to handle more complicated needs.

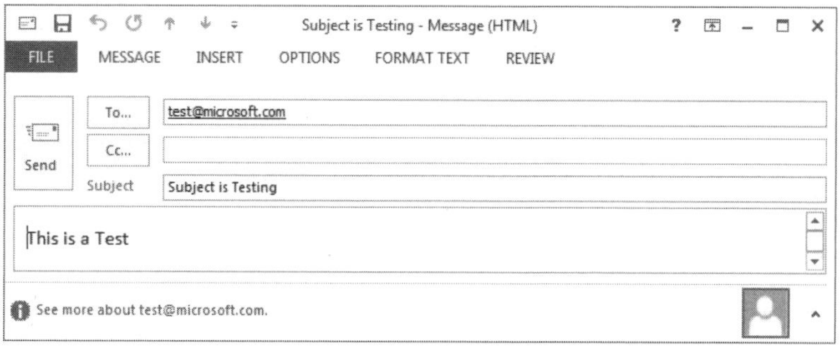

FIGURE 19-18: Outlook e-mail created using automation

Reading and Moving Mail Using VBA and Automation

Another common scenario for automation is to read an e-mail and move it into a folder and/or to transfer data from the mail into an Access database.

> **NOTE** *The code in this section processes mail in the Inbox and moves the e-mail into a folder called "Processed Mail." Before using this code, you will need to create a folder named "Processed Mail" as a subfolder of the Outlook Inbox. The name and location of the folder are critical; if the specified folder is not found, the code will generate an error.*

In addition to the `MailItem` class introduced in the last section, you will now use `MAPIFolder` class and the `Item` collection, which is a collection of `MailItems`. The next code snippet shows how they are used, and the explanation that follows will give you a better understanding of each step in the process:

```
Function ReadingAndMovingOutlookMailItems()

    Dim rsProcessed As DAO. Recordset
    Dim olkInboxFolder As Outlook.MAPIFolder
    Dim olkProcessedFolder As Outlook.MAPIFolder
    Dim olkItems As Outlook.Items
    Dim olkMail As Outlook.MailItem

    Set rsProcessed = CurrentDb.OpenRecordset("tblProcessedMailItems")

    Set olkApp = New Outlook.Application
    Set olkNameSpace = olkApp.GetNamespace("MAPI")

    Set olkInboxFolder = olkNameSpace.GetDefaultFolder(olFolderInbox)
    Set olkProcessedFolder = olkInboxFolder.Folders("Processed Mail")

    Set olkItems = olkInboxFolder.Items
```

```
    Do Until olkItems.Count = 0

        Set olkItems = olkInboxFolder.Items

        For Each olkMail In olkItems

            If olkMail.UnRead = True Then
                olkMail.UnRead = False 'Mark mail as read
                rsProcessed.AddNew
                    rsProcessed!From = olkMail.SenderName
                    rsProcessed!MailDate = olkMail.ReceivedTime
                    rsProcessed!Subject = olkMail.Subject
                    rsProcessed!Body = olkMail.Body
                rsProcessed.Update
     End If
     olkMail.Move olkProcessedFolder

        Next

    Loop

    MsgBox "All Mail Items Processed", vbOKOnly

End Function
```

Although many of the steps may be familiar to you, the details may make it easier for you to modify and implement the code in your solutions. As you read through the code, notice that it is accomplishing the following tasks:

- The `Recordset` type variable called *`rsProcecessed`* is declared. This variable will be set so that records can be added as mail is read from Outlook.
- Two `Outlook.MAPIFolder` type variables are declared: *`olkInboxFolder`* and *`olkProcessedFolder`*.
- A variable called *`olkItems`* is declared as `Outlook.Items` for referencing the `Items` collection of the `Inbox` folder.
- The *`olkMail`* is declared as `Outlook.MailItem`. This variable will be used to read individual e-mails.
- The *`rsProcessed`* variable is set, which opens the Access table called `tblProcessedMailItems`.
- After assigning the *`appOutlook`* variable to open Outlook, the *`olkNamespace`* object is assigned using the `GetNamespace` method.
- The two `MAPIFolder` type variables, *`olkInboxFolder`* and *`olkProcessedFolder`*, are assigned using the `GetDefaultFolder` (which would be the Inbox folder) and the Processed Mail folder (located in the `Folders` collection).
- A reference variable called *`olkItems`* is set to the `Items` collection. This will be used to retrieve the latest e-mails, and make sure any that come in will be seen, when this variable is updated.

- After opening a loop to verify there are items to process, the variable is referenced once again. Then, it assigns each of the items in the Inbox (*olkItems*) to a MailItem object to process.
- It then checks to see if the item has been read by testing the UnRead property of the mail item. If it has been read, it updates the UnRead property to False, and then adds a new record to the *tblProcessedMailItems* table using the Recordset variable called *rsProcessed*.
- Next, it uses the MoveTo method to move the e-mail to the Processed Mail folder, passing the MAPIFolder type variable *olkProcessedFolder*.
- After looping through all of the items, it displays a message to let the user know that the process is completed.

You can see from the code and explanation presented here that manipulating mail in Outlook using automation and VBA is not as difficult as you would think. Take a look now at how other items are just as straightforward as mail items are.

Creating Other Outlook Items Using VBA and Automation

Creating the other Outlook items, such as a Task, Contact or Appointment, follow essentially the same steps as the ones you just reviewed for creating mail items. The next example will create an *appointment*. You can modify the code and use it to create the type of item that you need, such as to add a task or contact.

Appointments

The following example demonstrates how to add appointments (AppointmentItems) to Outlook by adding records from the table, *tblProjects*. The Categories property is assigned so that the appointment can be removed later by running the ClearOLAppointments routine, found at the end of this section.

You start with the following code to get the appointment information from Access and create the appointment in Outlook:

```
Private Sub cmdOLCalendarItemsDemo_Click()

    Dim rstProjects As DAO. Recordset

    Set rstProjects = CurrentDb.OpenRecordset("tblProjects")

    With rstProjects

        Do Until .EOF

           AddOLAppointment !Task, !Start, _
                    DateAdd("d", !Duration, !Start)

           .MoveNext
```

```
            Loop

            .Close

        End With

        Set rstProjects = Nothing

    End Sub
```

The code populates a `Recordset` variable called *`rstProjects`*, based on data in the table *`tblProjects`*. It then calls the routine, `AddOLAppointment`, and passes data in the `Task` and `Start` fields. It calculates the end date by adding the Duration value to the `Start` field.

The `AddOLAppointment` routine is shown here, followed by an explanation of the steps:

```
Function AddOLAppointment(strSubject As String, varStart As Variant, _
                varEnd As Variant)

   Dim olkNameSpace As Outlook.Namespace
   Dim olkCalendar As Outlook.MAPIFolder

   Set olkApp = New Outlook.Application

   Set olkNameSpace = olkApp.GetNamespace("MAPI")
   Set olkCalendar = olkNameSpace.GetDefaultFolder(olFolderCalendar)

   With olkCalendar.Items.Add(olAppointmentItem)
      .AllDayEvent = True
      .Subject = strSubject
      .Start = CVDate(varStart)
      .End = CVDate(varEnd)
      .ReminderSet = False
      .Categories = "Access Appointment"
      .Save
   End With

   Set olkApp = Nothing

End Function
```

The `AddOLAppointment` routine performs the following steps:

- It creates three arguments, a `String` variable called *`strSubject`*, and two Variants to handle the date values called *`varStart`* and *`varEnd`*.
- `olkNameSpace` is declared as the type `Outlook.Namespace`, and *`olkCalendar`* is declared as a type `Outlook.MAPIFolder`.
- *`olkApp`* is assigned to a new instance of Outlook.

> **WARNING** *For the purposes of the demos in this chapter, the assignment of the application to its variable is performed with the loop of adding the records. However, when incorporating these examples into your solutions, you should adhere to the preferred practice of placing the application assignment outside of the loop.*

- `olkNameSpace` is assigned using the `GetNamespace` method of the `Application` object.
- `olkCalendar` is set to the calendar folder by calling the `GetDefaultFolder` method of the `olkNameSpace` and passing `olFolderCalendar`.
- The `Add` method of the `Items` collection is used to create a new appointment item, and then all of the appropriate properties are assigned.
- The `Categories` property is assigned "Access Appointment." This will be used in the next routine to remove an appointment.
- The `Saved` method is used to save the appointment in Outlook.
- The `olkApp` variables are set to `Nothing` to clean them up before leaving the routine.

When you click the `cmdOLCalendarItemsDemo` button, the appointments are created. You can find them in your Outlook calendar, as displayed in Figure 19-19.

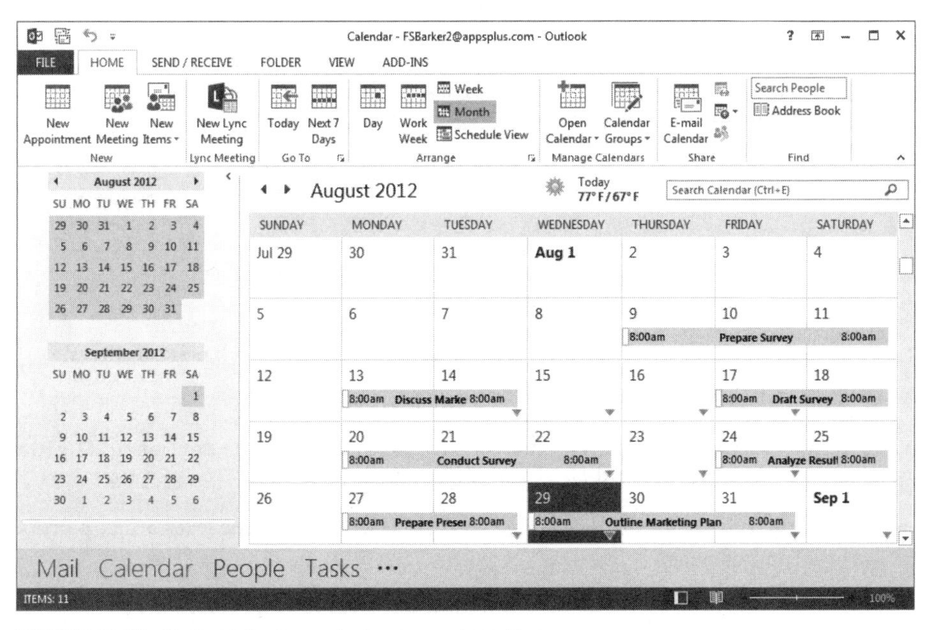

FIGURE 19-19: Outlook task created using automation

When you are ready to remove the appointments that were added to the calendar, you can run the `ClearOLAppointments` routine, shown here and then explained. Be aware that this will delete *all* of the appointments from Access where the `Categories` property was set to "Access Appointment." If you want to keep any appointments, you will need to incorporate selection criteria as described in the note following the code and explanation:

```
Sub ClearOLAppointments()

   Dim olkFolder As Outlook.MAPIFolder

   Application.Echo True, "Deleting Access Appointments in Outlook..."

   Set olkApp = New Outlook.Application
   Set olkNameSpace = olkApp.GetNamespace("MAPI")

   Dim intCurrAppointment As Integer

   Set olkFolder = olkNameSpace.GetDefaultFolder(olFolderCalendar)

   '-- Delete starting from the last of the list
   For intCurrAppointment = olkFolder.Items.Count To 1 Step -1

      '-- Delete the entry if it came from Access
      If olkFolder.Items(intCurrAppointment).Categories = _
                           "Access Appointment" Then
         olkFolder.Items.Remove (intCurrAppointment)
      End If

   Next

   Set olkApp = Nothing

   Application.Echo True

End Sub
```

The `ClearOLAppointments` routine performs the following steps:

- Declares *`olkFolder`* as `Outlook.MAPIFolder`
- Uses `Application.Echo` to display a message to tell the user know what is happening
- Sets the *`olkApp`* and *`olkNameSpace`* variables to their respective objects
- Declares the *`intCurrAppointment`* variable as `Integer`, then uses the `GetDefaultFolder` method to retrieve the Calendar folder in Outlook by passing *`olFolderCalendar`*
- Iterates through the *`olkFolder`* `Items` collection and tests to see if the `Categories` property equals "Access Appointment"
- If the property matches, it uses the `Remove` method to delete the `AppointmentItem` from the `Items` collection
- Sets *`olkApp`* to `Nothing`, and then uses the `Application.Echo` statement to clear the status bar

In the chapter's demo database, the form, `frmAutomation`, provides additional examples, including some that work with `TaskItems` and `ContactItems`. You can use these examples to learn more about automating Outlook and as models for incorporating automation into your Access solutions. If you want to see the list of Microsoft products that Access is "ready" to work with, you can view them in the VBA Editor. From the Tools menu, open the Reference dialog box and scroll down to the object libraries list to the ones starting with Microsoft. You can modify and apply the techniques and code from the previous examples to help get you started. In the next section, you will have a brief overview of integrating with third-party products.

INTEGRATING ACCESS WITH OTHER APPLICATIONS

Similar to how you worked with Office products, you can also integrate Access with other applications, as long as those applications are designed to work through automation. As before, the focus of these examples is to demonstrate how to use VBA to implement the automation.

There are a number of ways that you can determine if an application can be automated using VBA. Some of the more common approaches include:

- **Searching the Internet, such as with Bing or Google, to look up "VBA," "Automation," or the name of an application** — You don't have to specify Access in the search string because the product shouldn't care where it is being automated from.
- **Going to the application's home website to search the support or developers pages** — A good example of this is the Intuit website, owner of QuickBooks. It has an entire site dedicated to outside developers and integration with QuickBooks. It even addresses how to automate its product using various developer languages.

Search developer and product communities for help. You may find a thread that discusses and provides solutions that fit your needs. If not, you can post a question to seek help in solving the problem or discover where else to look. You will find invaluable assistance from community forums, such as `www.utteraccess.com`, which is dedicated to helping Access developers and users. Once you find information on the product or technology you want to automate, you should be able to adapt the sample code to work in your applications. You may need to experiment and tweak a few things, but like most tasks, the more you work with it the easier it gets to extend your experiences to work with other products.

Common automation tasks include being able to compress and un-compress files from within Access. PKZip was one of the first compression utilities used, and it still has the most popular format for compression. Plus, it has been integrated into Windows.

Utilizing compression is as simple as adding a couple more references, knowing how to work with the object models, and using the correct parameters to call the `Shell` command. The following example walks you through the process to automate PKZip.

The code for this example is located in the chapter's demo database. You can view and work with it in the module `modCompressionAutomation`.

The first task is to set up the reference to PKZip. You will follow the same steps you used to set references to the object library of an Office application. However, in this case there are two libraries that need to be referenced:

1. `Microsoft Scripting Runtime`
2. `Microsoft Shell Controls and Automation`

The following steps walk you through the process of setting a reference to the application's class libraries using the References dialog box. After the references are set, you will be ready to use the new object models in your code:

1. While in the VBA editor, from the Tools menu, select `References`.
2. Scroll down and locate the two specified libraries.
3. Place a checkmark in the checkbox next to the object libraries' names.

In order to show how to manipulate compressed folders, you will find the following code on `frmAutomation`, attached to the button `Create a Zip File and Add a Table`:

```
Private Sub cmdPerformZipFile_Click()

        MakeZipLibrary CurrentProject.Path & "\mycompressedfolder.zip", _
                                        CurrentProject.Path & "\mytextfile.txt"

End Sub
```

The `MakeZipLibrary` routine takes the name of the zip file you want to create and the file you want to add to that zip file.

In addition to using new object models, you will need to set the `Option Base 0`, to tell the code to start arrays as 0 instead of 1. You also need to use a Windows API to call the `Sleep` routine. The following code shows you how to write these statements as well as the code that calls the `MakeEmptyZipLibrary` and `AddFileToZip` routines. After that, you see the code for each routine along with a brief explanation of the steps:

```
Option Explicit
Option Base 0

'-- PtrSafe is for 64 bit.
Declare PtrSafe Sub Sleep Lib "kernel32" (ByVal lngMS As Long)

Public Sub MakeZipLibrary(strZipPath As String, strFilePath As String)

    '-- Create an empty zip file
    MakeEmptyZipLibrary strZipPath

    '-- Add the file.
    AddFileToZip strZipPath, strFilePath

End Sub
```

The first routine, `MakeEmptyZipLibrary`, is shown next, with the zip file path, including the extension passed to it. An example of a path and filename to use could be "C:\temp\mycompressedfolder.zip." Note that if this folder exists, then it would be deleted:

```
Private Sub MakeEmptyZipLibrary(strZipPath As String)

    '-- File system object allows user to work with zip file
    Dim fso As Scripting.FileSystemObject
    Set fso = CreateObject("Scripting.FileSystemObject")

    '-- Delete zip file if already exists
    If fso.FileExists(strZipPath) Then
        fso.DeleteFile strZipPath
    End If

    '-- Create zip file
    fso.CreateTextFile(strZipPath).Write "PK" & _
Chr(5) & Chr(6) & String(18, Chr(0))

    Set fso = Nothing

End Sub
```

The `MakeEmptyZipLibrary` routine performs the following tasks in this order:

1. Receive the parameter *`strZipPath`* as a `String` variable. This will be used as a name for the compressed folder.
2. A variable called *`fso`* is declared as a `FileSystemObject` object and then assigned using the `CreateObject` method. This will be used to allow the code to perform system I/O commands, in this case, create a file with the name provided.
3. Using *`fso`*, the `FileExists` method is called to see if the file specified in the *`strZipPath`* already exists, and if it does, delete it using the `DeleteFile` method.
4. The `Write` method of the `CreateTextFile` class is called, with *`strZipPath`* passed to the `CreateTextFile`. The PKZip format is specified by the argument, `"PK" & Chr(5) & Chr(6) & String(18, Chr(0))`.
5. The variable *`fso`* is set to `Nothing` to clean up.

After the compressed folder is created, you can add the files using the `AddFileToZip` routine shown here:

```
Private Sub AddFileToZip(strZipPath As String, strFilePath As String)

    Dim strShellApp As Shell32.Shell
    Dim strFolder As Shell32.folder
    Dim intCount As Integer

    '-- Create and open zip file
    Set strShellApp = CreateObject("Shell.Application")
    Set strFolder = strShellApp.Namespace(strZipPath)
```

```
        '-- Copy items into zip folder
        intCount = strFolder.Items.Count

        strFolder.CopyHere strFilePath, 4 + 16 + 1024

        Do
            Sleep 1000
        Loop Until intCount < strFolder.Items.Count

        Set strFolder = Nothing
        Set strShellApp = Nothing

    End Sub
```

This code uses the Shell class to copy files into the compressed folder by first opening the folder using the `NameSpace` class, and then using the `CopyHere` method to copy the individual file into the compressed folder. The `Sleep` command is used to give the system enough time to copy the file into the folder.

If you wanted to copy more than one file into this folder, you could pass a string array into the routine and within a loop call the `CopyHere` method with the individual items.

You can further enhance the code to have it read the files as well.

SUMMARY

Access has long been known for its ability to integrate with other applications. Just in terms of sharing data, Access is able to import, export, and link to more file formats than most other database products on the market. Access established this position with version 1.0, and it has increased its compatibility and reach ever since.

But working with data is just one area of integration; even greater benefits can be realized by coupling that with automating other programs. Automation enables Access developers to create seamless applications using various technologies, including other Office applications, such as Excel, Word, and Outlook, as well as products from other companies. If you have worked with VBA, the Access object models, and DAO, you can build on that experience as you work with other products. It becomes a matter of getting familiar with their object models and how they behave.

As with many areas of programming, working with different versions of a product can cause problems, so it is helpful to learn when and how to use both early and late binding. You can get a quick refresher from the discussion in the chapter, which explained how to use both and when to switch. You can use early binding to take advantage of IntelliSense and then switch to late binding before deploying if there are concerns that different versions of referenced products are or may be used.

You also saw that you can use essentially the same process to automate non-Microsoft products as you used for Office applications. You just need to find the necessary documentation and send the appropriate references to their object libraries.

You can further enhance your Access solutions by distributing them in customized deployment packages. You learn about that in the next chapter.

20

Securing, Deploying, and Maintaining Access Applications

WHAT'S IN THIS CHAPTER?

- Review how to track and identify users and changes to the data in the databases solution
- Walk through development lifecycle environments
- Look at different deployment methods
- Learn how to maintain your database solution

WROX.COM CODE DOWNLOADS FOR THIS CHAPTER

The wrox.com code downloads for this chapter are found at `www.wiley.com/go/proaccess2013prog.com` on the Download Code tab. The code files are in the Chapter 20 download, and are individually named according to the code filenames noted throughout the chapter.

In this chapter you will read about methods to secure who can access your solution and how to set permissions to the users who access the database. You will also learn about different methods to set an audit trail to capture and log changes users make to the data once they are allowed into the database.

The chapter discusses the development cycle and the different environments you need to support development and your database solutions. You will read how to update and maintain the database and the *front-end* (FE) file once you deploy the solution to your users.

USER LEVEL SECURITY AND AUDIT TRAIL

Some of the database solutions you design will require you to include security features. The types of features will range from setting different permission levels and access limits for different users, to creating an audit trail to capture who did what with the data.

It can be important to a company to control who gets to access the solution. Not every employee needs to be able to log into the database. Additionally, even when a user is authorized to log into the database, permission to specific data elements may be restricted. For example, only users who work in payroll should see the salary information for the company's employees.

The following discussion points will help you and the business owner identify and set up the permissions:

- Who can open a specific form/report?
- Who can edit the data in a form?
- What fields do they need to see or edit?

The security matrix you design for each database can vary in complexity. It can range from setting permissions to specific forms and reports, to setting permissions to specific controls on a form, to showing a defined or custom ribbon. Additionally, you can set read-only or read-write permissions for the different users. The sample database, `Security.accdb`, included in the online material, has sample code for you to review the techniques.

Figures 20-1 and 20-2 show you what a form, `My Profile`, looks like to an Admin and to a User.

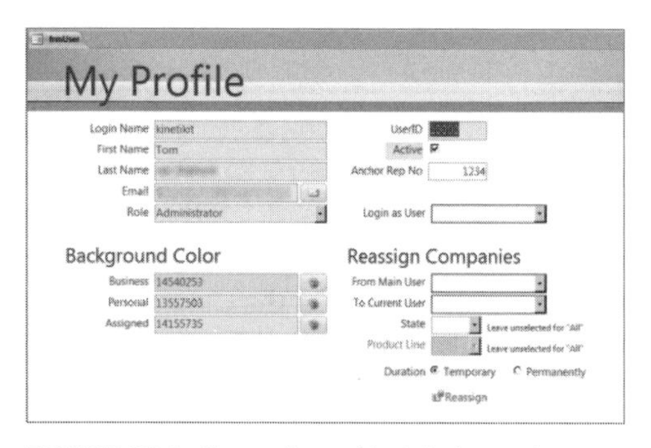

FIGURE 20-1: Form viewed in Admin mode

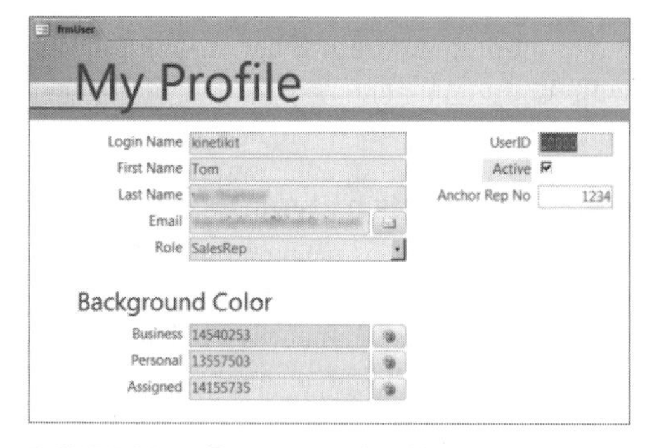

FIGURE 20-2: Form viewed in User mode

There are a couple of ways for you to set a security matrix: user-based, and role-based.

The first method is user-based — each user is listed along with what he or she can see or do in the database solution. This method allows you to customize the access level per user. Although it may sound like a good way to set up the security matrix, it is not a recommended way to go.

As you enter the users and the various permissions, you will find out that you are duplicating security records. Additionally, when a user changes jobs within the same company, you end up with a heavier maintenance load when you change that user's security profile.

The second method is role-based security. In this method, you create different roles — for example: Administrator, Data Entry, Read Only, and so on. You designate what each role can access and do in the database solution. When you add users to the database, you assign the user to a role.

Because a user must be attached to a role, the role-based security method provides for a consistent security matrix with much simpler maintenance. When a user changes jobs within the company, all you need is to change the role of the user. Additionally, if the system is audited, as some systems are, it is easy to generate an audit report to show who can do what in the database solution.

In the following sections, you will read about different ways to set the security matrix in your database applications. The discussion uses the role-based method because it's considered to be the better way to set up a security matrix.

Local User Table

In each database solution you design, you include additional tables to store information about users, roles, and the different form, report, and control objects in the database.

> **NOTE** *This method somewhat mimics the now deprecated* `User Level Security`.

When you, or the database solution administrator, add users to the solution, you first set up a username and a password for each user before you assign the user to a role. When a user wants to log into the database, he needs to use the username and password you created. Most database solutions offer users an option to change the password once they are logged in.

The benefit of this security method is that it works in any environment: network with domain, network without domain, and standalone.

The list of downsides of this method is longer. Users need to remember yet another user ID and password. The user ID and the password are stored in a table in Access. If someone gets into the tables, they can use the information to log into the database as someone else. Additionally, when users leave the company, they need to be deactivated in the database along with other systems.

> **NOTE** *If the database solution is designed to capture a user ID as part of the data it stores, it is better to deactivate users in the database than to delete them from the database. Deleting the user can create orphan values in the table that will impact reporting.*

This method can work well in small, standalone environments with a low employee turnover rate. It also works for environments where a few users with different access levels to the solution share the same workstation with a common login.

> **NOTE** *It is never a good idea to store passwords in plain text in a database. If you choose to use this security method you should encrypt, or better yet hash the password before storing it.*

Network Identity

Most companies use Active Directory (AD) to manage the network domain and the users. AD lets you set various groups and assign users to one or more groups. You can leverage that feature and create the different group levels for the database solution in the AD. After the groups are set, you can assign the security matrix in the database file to each group.

After you create the security groups in the AD, you assign the users to the group they belong to. If the security matrix is not hierarchical, a user may belong to more than one group.

When the user tries to open the database solution, the system will identify the Windows user ID and, based on the group the user belongs to, the solution will open, or the system will provide a message to the user that he's not authorized to open the solution. Similarly, you will test users' permissions to forms and controls as they navigate the database solution.

Using this method does not require the users to log into the database. As long as they are logged into the workstation, the solution recognizes them. The users' information is stored in a central location that is already managed by IT. Additionally, if the solution you design uses SQL as a back end, this method works well with the server's security. Another benefit of this method is the ability to use the same groups across multiple database solutions as long as the roles and the users in each role are the same.

You will need to work with IT to set up this method. In most companies, the IT department is responsible for creating the groups in the AD and managing the users in each group. After deployment, the database business owner will work with IT to manage the users in each group.

This method relies on each user logging into a workstation under his or her own Windows network ID. If a few users that belong to different security groups share the same workstation without logging in and out, it will not work.

> **NOTE** *This online article by Access MVP Tom van Stiphout is a good reference for how to use AD to manage database security:*
>
> `http://www.accesssecurityblog.com/post/2011/02/05/Securing-Access-databases-using-Active-Directory.aspx.`

Network Identity with a User Table in Access Database

This method is a hybrid of the two you read about in the previous pages. It combines the use of the users' network IDs to validate who logs into the database, but the security matrix and the roles are stored locally in the database.

This method is good when you use a hierarchical model for security. In the hierarchical model, each group can access or do everything the previous group can, plus additional permissions. For example, the "Reporting" group can only run reports in the database solution; "Read Only" can run reports and view data using the forms; "Data Entry" can do everything "Read Only" can do, plus edit data; and so on, all the way to the "Administrator" group, which can do everything, including add and inactivate users.

The benefits of this method are also a combination of the benefits from the previous two methods: Users do not need an additional login for the database; it uses the Windows network ID. Control over the groups and the users stays with the database business owner. There is no need to work with IT when you add a new user or change permissions for an existing user. Although you are storing the user ID in a table, you are not storing the passwords in the database. Passwords are managed by IT on an enterprise level.

In systems using Windows 2000 or newer, even if there is no domain, you can read the user's Windows login name using the `fOSUserName()` function written by Dev Ashish: `http://access.mvps.org/access/api/api0008.htm`.

Much like the previous method, this method relies on each user logging into a workstation under his or her own Windows network ID.

Different Front-end Files for Different User Roles

Another method you can use to ensure a different level of access for different users is to create and distribute different FE files. For people who only need to run reports, the FE will offer only the reporting menu and the reports. For the users who only need to view the data, the FE version will have the forms' properties set to `Read Only` in advance, and it can offer a specific set of forms based on the business rules.

It's a good way to deploy a reporting-only version for users who do not need to edit data in the database. The reporting FE provides a simpler UI and, in many cases, does not need to be updated as frequently as the full version of the FE file.

This method can be very simple to implement: after you create the full FE solution, you make copies of the file and modify the objects to support the different users. It can be an effective method if the solution requires only two or three different user group levels. Additionally, it can also be cost effective for small organizations where the ongoing maintenance is minimal because this method does not rely on any other factor outside of the content of the FE file.

The downside of this method is maintenance. If you need to go back and make revisions to the FE solution, you may need to make the same revisions in multiple FE files. This can cause a duplication of effort and increase in maintenance cost.

Security Summary

There is no one right way to implement a security matrix. Each security method described earlier has its pros and cons. Your role as the developer is to work with the business during the design phase of the database solution to identify the method that best fits the business model and resources available.

Make sure to interview the appropriate people from the IT department to learn the processes and procedures they use to manage the users and groups. This will help you analyze the best way to create and implement the security matrix for the database solution.

Converting from .mdb with User Level Security to .accdb

Access `.mdb` files provide a User Level Security (ULS) feature. ULS uses `.mdw` files to record and maintain the permissions for users and groups. After the database administrator added users to the database and assigned them to a group, users needed to log in to the database with the assigned username and password. Microsoft deprecated the ULS feature when it came out with `.accdb` files in Access 2007. Although you can run `mdb` files utilizing ULS in newer versions of Access, ULS cannot be used with `.accdb` files.

Although ULS sounds like a powerful and easy-to-use security feature, in practice it is a very advanced topic that few developers implement correctly, and it is vulnerable to password crackers and hacks.

To upgrade an `mdb` file that has ULS to an `accdb` format, your first step is to unsecure the database. You will need to upgrade both the FE and *back-end* (BE) files, including all of the necessary database objects.

Essentially, you have two options. The easiest approach is to use the backup file, usually named `DatabaseName.bak`, and convert it to `.accdb`. The backup file was created when the ULS was added to the `.mdb` database solution. It is a copy of the database file without the ULS. You can either open the backup file in Access 2013 and use the Save As option to create the `DatabaseName.accdb` file, or create a new `.accdb` file and import the database objects from the backup file.

An alternative approach is to use the Access 2003 (or earlier to match the file format) to remove the ULS before you import the objects into an `.accdb` file.

You can use the following steps:

1. Open the database file using Access 2003 (or earlier as appropriate) and log in to the secured `.mdb` database file as an administrator.
2. Use the User Level Security Wizard to change the Users group permissions to `Administer` for all database objects (see Figure 20-3).

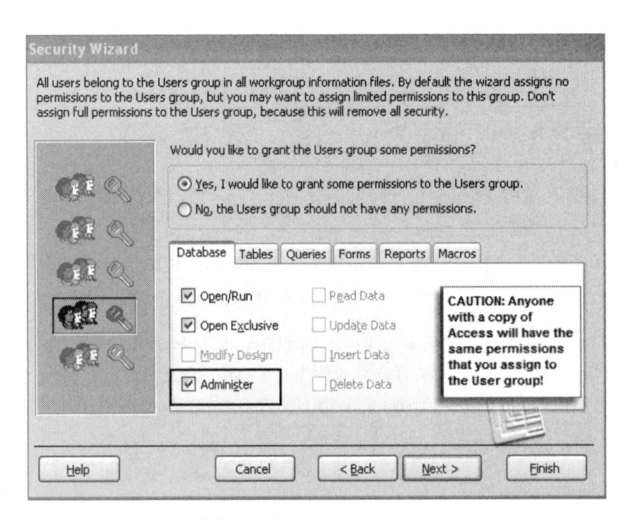

FIGURE 20-3: ULS Wizard

3. When done, exit the `.mdb` file and Access.
4. Open Access 2013, create a new `.accdb` file, and import the desired objects.

The new `.accdb` file is devoid of ULS and is unsecured. The database objects can be modified and you can proceed to implement a different method of security to the database solution.

Audit Trail

Depending on the specifications of the database solution you design, you may need to add an audit trail module. In its core, an audit trail collects and stores information about changes made to the data, the user who made them, and the time the changes were made. It typically does not store information about read-access to the data and who viewed it.

> **NOTE** *Some industries are subjected to regulatory guidelines, such as PCI and HIPAA, that require them to be able to report who viewed the data. You should discuss with your client what regulations govern their business.*

If you develop the database solution with SQL Server Enterprise Edition as the database engine, the audit trail option is available to you on the server side. When you or the Database Administrator (DBA) set the database, you can set the audit trail options and the server will take care of the process.

Access, on the other hand, does not offer a built-in audit trail tool. It is up to you to design and implement it in the database solution. In versions prior to Access 2010, you could only design an audit trail for changes performed through the forms. Changes made directly in the tables, through manual entry or the execution of an action query through the `QBE`, could not be tracked.

With the data macros available to you since Access 2010, you can build the audit trail to capture changes wherever they occur, including changes made directly in the table.

When you use VBA to design the audit trail, the code needs to fire on the `Before Update` event of the form. This allows you to capture both `Control.OldValue` and the `Control.Value` of any bound control and store them in the audit trail table as the `Before` and `After` values.

When you use data macros, you use the `After Change` event to capture the values the user changes in the table. Data macros retain the `Old.FieldName` value after the record is changed for you to use as the `Before` value.

The actual data components you capture in the audit trail record can vary based on the business rules and relevant regulatory guidelines. At the least, to make the audit trail an effective tool, you should record and store the following data elements:

- Table name
- Record primary key value
- Field name
- Field value before change

- Field value after change
- Date and time of change
- User ID making the change

Optional values you can capture if they add benefit to the audit trail are:

- Changed through (the name of the form used)
- PC IP Address used to access the solution (may not work in all environments)
- Record inserted (new) or record updated

The Audit Trail sample database accompanying this book, `AuditTrail.accdb`, has sample code for an audit trail using the VBA method and the data macro method in the tables.

Using VBA

To create an audit trail module for your database, you start by designing the table to store the information you want to track. After the table is ready, you will create a module in your FE file. In your code, you will call that module in the `Before Update` event of the form (code file: `Deploy_Maintain.txt CaptureAuditTrail`):

```
'-----------------------------------------------------------------------------
' Function   : CaptureAuditTrail
' Author     : DougY
' Date       : 4/1/2013
' Purpose    : Insert data into the audit trail table
' Arguments  : strTableName = Name of table
               frmName = Name of the form used
               strRecordPK = Primary key value of the record that was changed
'-----------------------------------------------------------------------------

Public Function CaptureAuditTrail(strTableName As String, _
                                  frmName As Object, _
                                  strRecordPK As String)

    Dim ctl As Control
    Dim rst As DAO.Recordset

    Set rst = CurrentDb.OpenRecordset("tblAuditTrail")

    For Each ctl In frmName.Controls

        Select Case ctl.ControlType

            'not all controls have ControlSource property
            'acControl ID below are: 106, 111, 110, 109, 122
            Case acCheckBox, acComboBox, acListBox, acTextBox, acToggleButton

                If Not IsNull(ctl.ControlSource) Then
                    If ctl.Value <> ctl.OldValue Or IsNull(ctl.OldValue) Then
```

```
                    If Not IsNull(ctl.Value) Then
                        rst.AddNew
                        rst("ChangedThrough") = frmName.Name
                        rst("TableName") = strTableName
                        rst("RecordPK") = strRecordPK
                        rst("FieldName") = ctl.ControlSource
                        rst("BeforeValue") = ctl.OldValue
                        rst("AfterValue") = ctl.Value
                    End If
                    rst("ChangeUser") = fOSUserName()
                    rst("ChangeTime") = Now()
                    rst.Update
                End If
            End If

        Case Else
            'do nothing

    End Select

  Next

  'clean up
  rst.Close
  Set rst = Nothing

End Function
```

When called, the `CaptureAuditTrail()` function cycles through the controls on the form, compares the control's value to the control's old value. If the values are different, the code will insert a new record to the audit trail table with the data components you decided to capture (code file: `Deploy_Maintain.txt Call Audit Trail`):

```
If Me.Dirty Then

    Call CaptureAuditTrail("tblClass", Me, Me.txtSubjectID)

End If
```

Using Data Macros

If you go the data macro route, you will add an `After Update` macro for each table you want to track. In the macro, you will list the condition it will meet to activate, and the values to be recorded in the audit trail table. Figure 20-4 shows you the audit trail data macro being set.

After the macro is set and saved, every time a record is added or modified in the table, the information is recorded into `tblAuditTrail`.

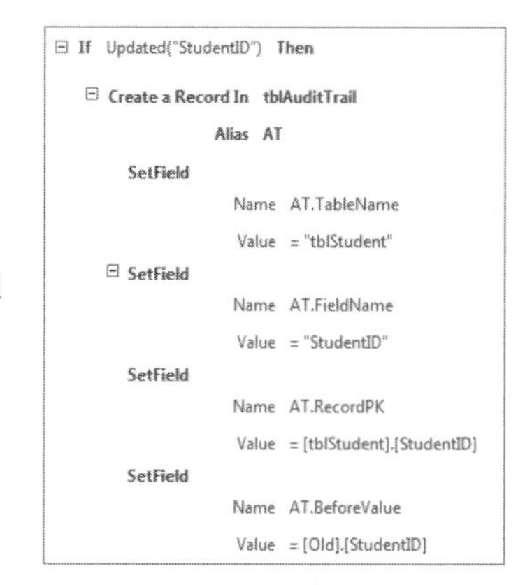

FIGURE 20-4: Setting audit trail with data macro

Although the setup of the audit trail with data macros is more cumbersome than the VBA function, the benefits may outweigh the extra work. Data macros enable you to capture data changes in situations where VBA cannot be used, for example, when the data is changed directly in the table.

Remote Query

In some cases, the audit trail data can be highly sensitive. When this is the case, consider taking an extra step to hide the table from possible prying eyes. Instead of linking the audit trail table to the FE file, use a remote query technique to append the data to the audit trail table in the BE database or a different database file altogether. The following SQL script shows you the syntax of a remote append query (code file: `Deploy_Maintain.txt Remote Query`):

```
INSERT INTO tblAuditTrail
  (TableName
, RecPK
, FieldName
, BeforeValue
, AfterValue
, ChangeTime
, ChangeUser )
IN '\\COFFEE\MyFolder\MyDatabase.accdb'
SELECT <list of values to insert>;
```

The line `IN '\\COFFEE\MyFolder\MyDatabase.accdb'` tells the query to find the table `tblAuditTrail` in the database file `MyDatabase.accdb` without the need to link the table to the FE file. If you use the QBE to construct the query, you change the query property `Source Database`, as shown in Figure 20-5.

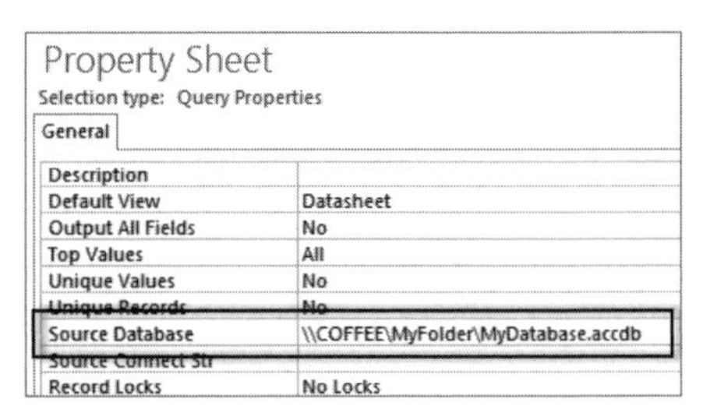

FIGURE 20-5: Setting remote query in QBE

You cannot use the remote query option if you use data macros. The audit trail table needs to be either local in the FE or linked to the FE file.

Audit trail can be an important feature of the database solution you design for your clients. However, it is not a replacement tool for tables that hold historical data, such as changes in product price, or changes in salary for staff. It is meant to help you and the business to track changes, and if needed to reverse erroneous or malicious change.

DEPLOYMENT CONSIDERATIONS

After you are done with the development phase of the database solution, it is time to deploy it to the users. The initial deployment step is usually different from subsequent deployment of updated versions. In the following sections you will read about both deployments and the different methods you can use for each of them.

When you review deployment options you look at a few key factors:

- **Size of company** — Large companies usually have an IT department with resources, both systems and personal, to manage and support a large deployment.

- **Number of users** — It can be faster and cheaper to manually install the solution on a handful of workstations versus using a commercial deployment solution.
- **Location of users** — If users are in remote locations, it may be easier and more cost-effective to use a deployment solution instead of traveling to the different locations. Alternately, you can e-mail the deployment files to the remote users for them to deploy.

Based on those factors, you can choose the method that best fits your process and the environment of your clients. There is no right way or wrong way; as long as the method works for you efficiently it's the right one.

Depending on where you work and your agreement with the client, you may choose to deploy an `accde` FE file instead of an `.accdb` file. An `.accde` file secures the design of forms, reports, and code from the user. If you do that, remember to safeguard the original copy of the `.accdb` file; you will need it to maintain and update the FE file.

If your solution uses your own reference library (you can read about creating a reference library in Chapter 16), you should store the reference library file in a centralized location on the network, accessible to the users and to the FE file. This allows you to update the code in the library file and still retain the reference link to the FE files.

We recommend you review the code before you deploy the solution to look for hard-coded values of paths, file folders, and so on — for example, `strPath = "C:\Users\Doug"`. You and your users will be better served if you use configuration tables within the database solution to store the information and call it from the code. For example: `strPath = Dlookup("Path", tblPath", "PathType = SaveReports")`. If the path needs to be changed after the solution is deployed, you change the value in the table without the need to edit and test the code itself.

Additionally, it is better to use *Universal Naming Conventions* (UNC), sometimes referred to as *Uniform Naming Convention*, when storing the path of folders and files. It is possible for different workstations to map to various drives using different letters. For example, the network drive `\\Coffee\Data` can be mapped to drive `Y:\` on one machine, and to drive `S:\` on another. If you use `Y:\Data` in your database solution, it will generate an error on the workstation using `S` as the letter for the same drive.

> **NOTE** *In Windows OS, the format for UNC is* `\\servername\sharename\path\filename`.

If different versions of Access are installed on different workstations, it is best practice for you to develop in the lowest version available to the users. This ensures that the users can open the FE solution and that you did not use features available in newer versions of Access, including the file format `.mdb` or `.accdb`.

Deploying Front-end Files

When you deploy the solution, you deploy the FE file to the users. The BE file, which holds the database tables, remains on a network location available to all users, and it is not deployed to the users' workstations.

Usually, the FE file is deployed to the workstation hard drive. However, depending on the business rules, you may need to deploy the FE to the user's personal network drive space. This option prevents data breach if someone removes the workstation from the premises because the file is not stored on the workstation. In either scenario, each user ends up with a separate FE file connected to the BE database engine.

Although different users may get different flavors of the FE solution, it is important that they use the same release version of the FE for each flavor. It's easier and less hassle to support one version of a solution throughout the organization. It also ensures that users have the latest features for the FE file they use.

Although the actual location of the FE file can vary, it is common practice to place a shortcut to open the solution on the workstation desktop. Ideally, that shortcut is placed in the `C:\Users\Public\Desktop` folder, so it appears for all users on the machine. Make sure that you copy the files to a folder on the workstation that all users have access to. In previous operating systems that would be `C:\Program Files`, but in modern versions of Windows, a folder below `C:\Users\Public` is a safe place.

Much like other topics we discussed, there is more than one way to accomplish the initial deployment task. In the following sections you will read about two methods, manual and automated. Because each deployment can be different, you, as the developer, are best positioned to decide which one to use.

Manual Install

If you need to deploy the system to a small number of users located in the same office, one of the options at your disposal is to go around the office and copy the FE file to each user workstation.

In a small office environment, or for a small department within an organization, this is a simple and effective way to deploy the FE solution. It also allows you to verify that the solution starts properly on each workstation.

What you copy to the workstation depends largely on how you plan to publish FE updates to the workstations. If you use a batch file to get updated versions, you copy the batch file only to the appropriate folder. If you use an auto-updater tool, you may need to copy the FE solution file along with the tool.

Consider creating a deployment folder on the network drive. In the folder, you have all the files you need to deploy the solution to the workstation.

Push to Workstation

Deployment of the FE solution to a large number of employees may require a different approach. Although doable, it is not efficient to go around and manually install the FE file on 50 or more workstations.

In larger companies, the IT department usually has network and workstation management tools. One of the features in those tools is the ability to remotely push files to the workstations connected to the network.

When you use this method to deploy, you work with the IT department to identify the users who need the database solution and the location of the files. The management tool will do the rest. After the FE is deployed, it is prudent to walk around and test a few different workstations to make sure the solution is deployed properly.

Many network and workstation management tools are available. In most cases, the IT department has already chosen the tool they want to use. As a developer, you work with the tools available in each client's site and with the IT department to push the new FE solution to the users.

In smaller companies, you may need to revert to manual deployment if the client does not have an IT department with network management tools. One possibility is to e-mail the users instructions about what files to copy from the network drive and the location where they can save the FE files.

Automation of deployment can also be accomplished with the use of deployment packages. Access comes with a built-in tool to create a Package Solution. The package generates a Windows Installer Package you distribute to the users. Additionally, there are third-party deployment tools that will create the package you will provide to users. The following are a couple of tools for you to review if you want to take this route.

- **Inno Setup** — `http://www.innosetup.com/isinfo.php`
- **Sagekey** — `http://www.sagekey.com`

Auto-Updating the Front End

Now that the FE file is deployed, you may be asked to work on enhancements and updates to the database solution. When the new version of the FE file is ready, the next step is deploying it to the users.

Either of the two methods described for the initial deployment can do the job for subsequent updates. However, there are better ways to update the FE on a user workstation. The auto-updating methods allow you to automatically update the FE file, even multiple times during the day. All it takes for the user to get the latest version is to exit the database solution, if they are using it, and open it using the shortcut icon you provided.

Auto-Updater Tool

The main concept of the auto-updating process is using an *auto-updater* (AU) tool to check the version of the FE file located on the user's workstation and compare it to the master version of the FE file located on the server.

When the user double-clicks the shortcut to the database solution, the shortcut opens the AU tool first. The tool validates that the local version matches the version on the network. If the versions match, it proceeds to open the local database solution file. If the version number is different, the AU tool will copy the FE file from the server to the designated location on the user's workstation and then proceed to open the file.

There are a few AU tools and products available for you to download and use. Some have a cost associated with the license, and some are free. The following is a list of some AU products for you to review to see which one is right for you:

- **Auto-FE-Updater by Tony Toews** — `http://autofeupdater.com/`
- **DBUpdate by Gunter Avenius** — `http://www.avenius.de/?Produkte:DBUpdate`

- **mdb-Loader by Henry Habermacher** — `http://www.dbdev.org/down42.htm`
- **UtterAccess Code Archive** — `http://www.utteraccess.com/forum/Easy-Front-Autoupdater-t304808.html`

Batch File

Another approach is to use a Windows batch file. In this method, when the user clicks the shortcut icon, it executes a `.bat` file with a code to copy the FE file from the server to the user's workstation.

The code that follows copies the `Octothorp.accde` file from the location on the server, `\\JavaHut\Data\MathDB\`, to the user's personal network folder, `\\Coffee\MathDB\`. The code opens the database file after it is copied over (code file: `Deploy_Maintain.txt Batch file to Copy FE`):

```
@echo off

@echo.

@echo Please wait The NEW database is updating...
@echo.

xcopy /Y /Q /H \\JavaHut\Data\MathDB\Octothorp.accde \\Coffee\MathDB\
\\Coffee\MathDB\Octothorp.accde
:End
```

> **NOTE** *To prevent errors when using paths or file names with spaces in them (e.g. Java Hut), you need to add double quotes around the entire path string.*

With this method, the user always gets a fresh copy of the FE file, even if it's not an updated version. This method not only assures that the user has the most recent version of the database FE solution, but it also takes care of the need to manage the `Compact and Repair` process for the FE file located on the user's workstation. As long as you compact and repair the network copy of the file before you release it to production, the users get the compacted file every time they open the database solution. You will read more about `Compact and Repair` later in this chapter.

Deploying Back-end Changes

In some cases the changes you are asked to do will involve changes to the database structure. You may need to modify existing tables or add new tables to the database. Deployment of a revised back end requires a different approach from deployment of FE files. The data stored in the database must be the same after the update as it was before it to ensure the integrity of the database solution.

You apply the same development cycle principles to the BE changes as you do to the FE. You gather the requirements and make the changes based on the specifications you design for the new BE database.

After you complete the changes to the database in the development environment and you test the changes, it is time to promote the revised back-end file to the production environment. To do so, you need to take full control of the BE file for the duration of the update.

The first step is to make sure all users are out of the database solution. Common practice is to notify the users in advance of the system downtime. The date and time for the update are determined in cooperation with the business owners to allow for minimal disruption to the workforce. In many cases, the update is done overnight, or over a weekend.

To ensure users cannot connect to the BE during the downtime, you can change the FE file on the server to a file that is not connected to the BE, and use a startup form with a message to the users that the system is down for maintenance. The auto-updater tool will copy the temporary FE file to the users' workstations should they try to open the file. You will release the new production FE version after the deployment of the BE is completed.

When you have control of the BE file, the next step is to make a backup of the current production version. Before you make any changes to the database structure, you want to ensure you can revert back without data loss should anything go sideways.

After the backup is done and the copy is secured, you can proceed in one of two ways: modify the database structure and reapply the changes you made in the development copy to the tables in production, or append the data from the current production database into the updated database. If you choose to append the data, you need to be extremely careful with the values in the `autonumbers` fields. If not done correctly, you may break the relationship between tables and render the database useless.

When you are done with updating the new production database, your next step is to validate that all the records from the production tables are still there, or were appended properly to the new database. To do so, consider using a checksum.

> **NOTE** *A checksum, also known as a hash sum, is a value calculated from an arbitrary set of data to identify accidental errors that may have occurred during data transmission. The integrity of the data is validated by calculating the checksum on both the pre-transmitted and the post-transmitted data sets and comparing them. If the checksum values match, it is highly likely the data is the same between the two sets.*

For the checksum, you should total not only fields that store amounts, such as Price, Cost, and so on. Look at other fields that hold numerical values and add them. A good example is to sum the value of the table primary key if you are using an autonumber (long data type) for it. Be creative with selecting the various checksum fields; it will help you succeed with the validation of the data migration.

If the database engine is SQL Server, you can use the `CHECKSUM_AGG()` function to compare the values in the tables.

After you validate the data in the new BE, you promote the new file to production, along with an updated FE file that has the tables linked to the new BE, and the UI to expose the new data components to the users.

MAINTAINING DIFFERENT ENVIRONMENTS

Throughout your career as a developer, you design new database solutions and maintain and update existing solutions. When you work on the database solution, it is best practice to use different environments for different stages of the development cycle.

A standard development cycle consists of the following stages:

- Requirements
- Analysis
- Development
- Testing
- User Acceptance
- Deployment

The standard development cycle calls for at least three different environments for you and other developers to work in when you develop:

1. Development (DEV)
2. Testing (TST or QA or UAT)
3. Production (PROD)

Some companies have additional environments, such as Adhoc, Support (SUP), Proof of Concept (POC), and so on. You will read more about the optional environments further in this chapter.

DEVELOPMENT, TEST, AND PRODUCTION ENVIRONMENTS

> **NOTE** *There is a joke amongst developers: "I don't always test my code, but when I do, I test it in production." Don't be that guy. It is essential that you do not develop or test using the production environment. A single module with an erroneous code can cause a negative impact on the production data, business productivity, and your longevity with the company or the client.*

Development Environment

After you collect the requirements and get the specification approved both by you and the business owner, you start the development of the solution or the requested changes in the DEV environment. This environment is usually accessible only to developers, and end users do not have permission to access it. If there are only three environments, this is also the environment you use to experiment with new concepts and test new approaches for the system you maintain.

When you are done with your development and tests, it's time for users to test the new solution in the Test environment.

Test Environment

The Test environment may have different names in different companies: Test, QA (Quality Assurance), or UAT (User Acceptance Testing). User testing, also known as User Acceptance Testing (UAT), should be done in the QA environment. Using a separate testing environment allows you to have the users test a specific feature while you keep on developing the next feature without a conflict.

Unlike the DEV environment, the QA environment usually has more recent data for the user to test with. This helps users identify issues more easily because they can compare the results to the data in the production environment.

When users finish the tests and approve the changes, the next step is to move the application to the PROD environment.

Production Environment

The PROD environment is the most important one of all environments. When you promote the database solution to this environment, it is as ready as it can be for primetime. It is also the environment that gets the most attention from those who support the network, usually the IT Department.

The main focus of the IT department is to support the production environment. The health of the PROD environment is related directly to the operational health of the business and the productivity of the staff. If there are issues with the PROD environment and with another environment, the highest priority for resources goes to the PROD environment. Test or QA can wait for the next available analyst after PROD is up and running.

Additional Environments

The additional environments are usually copies of PROD with varied data refresh cycles to allow you to support the system, experiment with proposed changes to the database solution, and to help define the scope for new projects. They are optional, and the business may not have the infrastructure or the resources to support the multiple environments on top of the basic three. Additionally, some of the environments can be collapsed into a single environment.

> **NOTE** *An environment does not mean a different server. A different environment is simply a copy of an FE linked to a specific BE database available to different users in the company.*

Adhoc

When you or the business analysts need to data mine the database, an Adhoc environment eliminates the processing overhead to the PROD environment. The database solution may support built-in reports; however, analysts may need to create and run queries to analyze data. A large number of complex adhoc queries executed against the production environment may impact the performance of the PROD database and slow down users' productivity.

An Adhoc environment for data analysis will alleviate this problem and allow the analysts to do their job without interfering with the resources of the production environment.

To be effective, the data in the Adhoc environment needs to match the data in PROD as much as possible. Usually, a nightly refresh should do because the Adhoc system is usually used for analysis versus operational reports. Most of the solutions you develop will have operational reports in them as part of the design specifications.

Support

The Support (SUP) environment provides you or the support analyst with an environment to try to reproduce errors reported by the users, and it does so without requiring changes to the production data.

When users encounter errors or issues as they perform their daily tasks, they report it to the helpdesk. After you or the helpdesk log the help ticket, someone from the support team needs to investigate. When you re-create the steps the user performed when the error occurred, you may need to edit data in the process. The SUP environment provides you with a safe dataset to perform the support.

Proof of Concept

The Proof or Concept (POC) environment allows you to test different concepts to evaluate if they're worth pursuing. It differs from DEV because not everything you experiment with in the POC environment will make it out of the conceptual stage. It's a good place to test different "what-if" scenarios.

You can test proposals from users to improve the system before starting the analysis phase of the development cycle. Having an environment to experiment in can be beneficial as it can save time from further analysis or projects that may not mature properly.

Back-end Data Refresh Cycles

After the various environments are created and named, you will identify and implement the refresh cycle that best meets the business needs for each of the environments. The settings can vary from a shadow server with near real-time refresh rate to the other side of the spectrum, an environment set to be refreshed on demand every so often.

The guidelines that follow are just that, guidelines. It is up to you to work with the business and the IT department, if there is one, to find the balance of resources to refresh cycles.

> **NOTE** *A shadow server is an optimal setting for an Adhoc environment where you can query and report on the same data stored in the production environment without impacting the production servers and the users. It can take a lot of resources, hardware, and personnel to support both production and shadow servers. You must safeguard the production server performance while ensuring that the shadow server is robust enough to support the instantaneous data load and querying.*

One of the popular settings for refresh cycles, usually for the Adhoc and SUP environments, is to make a full copy of PROD, overwriting any changes to the environment nightly. This method allows decision support analysts and system support analysts to use production-like data to perform their respective tasks.

The DEV environment refresh cycle can vary to meet the development needs. You may decide that a regularly updated copy of PROD is best to support your development, or maybe you prefer a snapshot of the data before you start the design phase of the changes that will allow you to see how the changes you make behave over time.

The QA environment is usually refreshed before handing over the system to the UAT testers. This allows the users to start the test using a production-like data. It also enables you and the testers to see the differences between PROD and QA as the new features are tested.

The POC environment can be updated as needed. Not all suggested changes can be tested in one day. Some involve processes that may take a few days or even longer to fully cycle in the system. It is better to not update too frequently to allow the developers and analysts to evaluate the new concepts over the needed time period.

Front-end Environments

When you have multiple back-end environments, it also means you have multiple front-end versions at your disposal. Each version of the FE is linked to the related BE database. You can also, in some of the cases, have a single FE file with an option to switch the linked tables from different BE files as needed.

First on the list is the master copy of the production version. The one that is safely stored in the version control tool available to you. This copy is not changed until any revisions go through the proper design cycle phases and are approved to be pushed to production by the business owner.

The development copy is the one where you and your fellow developers work to implement any changes and enhancements requested by the users. It, too, should be stored in a version control tool and checked in at least at the end of each day. This will ensure that any changes made are saved and available to the team the next day. Using a version control tool also allows you to roll back changes made in case of an error.

Leading the “top three” environments is the QA copy of the FE. You distribute this file to the UAT users who are assigned to test the changes to the database solution. Much like the previous two versions, it should be stored in a version control tool to allow consistency and safe keeping.

The Adhoc, SUP, and POC versions are usually copies of the current PROD version. Because those versions are used by a selected few, the FE may be open as an `.accdb` format, allowing the analysts more access to the different database objects and options, such as creating `UDF` for the adhoc queries for analysis. If the analysts are only creating queries, you can keep the FE as an `.accde` file.

Switching Between Back-end Environments

As you work with different FE environments, you need to connect them to the matching back-end environments. Additionally, as mentioned earlier, you may utilize one front end to connect to different back ends. You can switch between linked back ends by using the Linked Table Manager in Access — you will find it on the External Data ribbon. Choose the tables you want to refresh and select the Always prompt for new location checkbox, and the process will ask you for the location of the linked tables you want to update.

If you select linked tables from different sources, you will be prompted for a new location for each table, not each source. You can handle that situation by refreshing all linked tables from one source at a time, even if you end up connecting to a single BE environment when you are done with the relink process.

You can save yourself the manual linking steps if you create a module with a code to enable you to switch environments at the click of a mouse. Additionally, there are tools already developed by others that you can use to relink the FE file to a different BE file.

Review the following tools to see which one works for you:

- **Dev Ashish** — Relink Access tables from code at `http://access.mvps.org/access/tables/tbl0009.htm`
- **J Street Technology** — J Street Access Relinker at `http://www.jstreettech.com/cartgenie/pg_developerDownloads.asp`
- **Peter Vukovic** — Reconnect attached tables on startup `http://allenbrowne.com/ser-13.html`
- **Utter Angel** — Boilerplate database at `http://www.utterangel.com/UtterAngel/utterangel.aspx?cat=acc` (scroll down)
- **UtterAccess Code archive** — ReLinker with multi-BE, Label Table description to show connect info at `http://www.utteraccess.com/forum/ReLinker-multi-BE-Label-t1680238.html`
- **UtterAccess Code archive** — Relink/swap between Live, Test, and Local data at `http://www.utteraccess.com/forum/Relink-Swap-Live-Test-t1328573.html`

It's important that you know the environment you are working in. Entering test data into the production environment is, to put is nicely, less than desirable.

Visual cues in the FE files provide an effective flag for you and other users. For example, you can change the caption and the background color of a label on UI forms when the FE file is connected to a non-production environment. The visual cues can be a single color scheme (Red = Non-PROD), or you can use a color system (Red = DEV; Yellow = QA; and so on).

One method is to read the value of "database name" from a configuration table in the database and display it in the caption of every form. Or, using the value, you can code for the background color of a textbox or a label. The following code is an example of changing the backcolor of a textbox based on the value of the textbox bound to the configuration table (code file: `Deploy_Maintain.txt Change Textbox BackColor based on Textbox value`):

```
Select Case Me.txtBE
    Case "Prod"
        Me.txtBE.BackColor = vbGreen
    Case "Test"
        Me.txtBE.BackColor = vbYellow
```

```
    Case "Dev"
        Me.txtBE.BackColor = vbRed
    Case Else
        Me.txtBE.BackColor = vbBlue
End Select
```

Another way to determine the environment you're working in is for you is to find the location of a linked table. Either one of the three code samples that follow will work, depending on the information you want to use.

CODE FILE: DEPLOY_MAINTAIN.TXT PF_FINDPATH

```
Option Compare Database
Option Explicit

Public Function pf_FindPath(ByVal strTableName As String) As String

'---------------------------------------------------------------------------
' Function   : pf_FindPath
' Author     : DougY
' Date       : 4/1/2013
' Purpose    : Return the full location of the BE for a linked table,
'              including the name of the BE file
' Arguments : strTableName = Name of linked table
'---------------------------------------------------------------------------



pf_FindPath = _
    Mid$(DBEngine.Workspaces(0).Databases(0).TableDefs(strTableName).Connect, 11)


End Function
```

CODE FILE: DEPLOY_MAINTAIN.TXT PF_FINDFOLDER

```
Public Function pf_FindFolder(ByVal strTableName As String) As String

'---------------------------------------------------------------------------
' Function   : pf_FindFolder
' Author     : DougY
' Date       : 4/1/2013
' Purpose    : Return the folder of the BE for a linked table
' Arguments : strTableName = Name of linked table
'---------------------------------------------------------------------------

    Dim strPath As String
    Dim lngCNT As Long

strPath = _
        Mid$( _
```

```
            DBEngine.Workspaces(0).Databases(0).TableDefs(strTableName).Connect, 11)

        For lngCNT = Len(strPath) To 1 Step -1

            If Mid(strPath, lngCNT, 1) = "\" Then
                pf_FindFolder = Left$(strPath, lngCNT)
                Exit For
            End If 'Mid(strPath, lngCNT, 1) = "\"

        Next lngCNT

    End Function
```

CODE FILE: DEPLOY_MAINTAIN.TXT PF_FINDNAME

```
Public Function pf_FindName(ByVal strTableName As String) As String

'---------------------------------------------------------------------------------
' Function   : pf_FindName
' Author     : DougY
' Date       : 4/1/2013
' Purpose    : Return the name of the file for a linked table
' Arguments  : strTableName = Name of linked table
'---------------------------------------------------------------------------------

    Dim strPath As String
    Dim lngCNT As Long

    strPath = _
      Mid$( _
       DBEngine.Workspaces(0).Databases(0).TableDefs(strTableName).Connect, 11)
    pf_FindName  = Mid(strPath, InStrRev(strPath, "\") + 1)

End Function
```

You can change the backcolor of a label or even the form based on the returned value from any of the preceding functions.

Either of the two methods to determine the environment you are working in, using configuration table or using the code, will help you and other developers and analysts to know which BE environment is linked to the FE file you open.

Promoting Files from Test to Production

The final stage of the project is promoting the database solution to the production environment. Depending on the magnitude of the changes, if it's the initial release or a release of a major upgrade, it can be referred to as a "go-live" event.

Regardless of the magnitude of the release, before you move a new version to the production environment, you must have your client's (the business owner's) approval.

You want to ensure you have the approval for a few reasons. The first is that the approval of the business owner also means the business agrees that all changes you made meet the specifications approved in the requirement and analysis stages of the project.

Additionally, depending on the nature of the business, your client may be subjected to an annual audit by external auditors to meet regulatory requirements. Auditors look closely at the implementation of checks and balances to protect the integrity of financial data of the business. The fact that developers can make changes to the system is balanced by the fact that there must be testing and explicit approval by the business to move the changes to production.

As the developer, you should document the requests for the changes and the source for the requests. You should also document the testing phases both by you and by the UAT testers. Finally, you should have the approval to promote the revised files to production well documented for each project.

With smaller clients, you benefit from the same procedures even if the company is not subjected to regulatory audits. It will help you maintain a good relationship with your client and allow the client to be in control of the promotion schedule.

Version Control

Version control, also known as *revision control*, is a way to manage changes to your solutions. Although always an important concept, it is downright necessary when you work with a team of developers on the same project.

The version control tool allows you to track the changes made to the solution or to the database, and to prevent a conflict between developers who try to work on the same file at the same time.

The version control software will allow only one person to check the file out at a time to make changes. Some version control systems work on the object level. Developers can check an object from the file and work on the same file but different objects. The file — be it an object, the database, or the front-end solution — will need to be checked in before someone else can check it out. You can have one project broken down to a few files to allow different developers to work on different features of the project concurrently.

Many types and styles of version control applications are available. The tools are split among three main categories:

1. **Local data** — The developers need to use the same computer system. This type of software often manages single files individually.
2. **Client-server** — The developers use a single, shared file repository.
3. **Distributed** — Each developer works with her local repository. Sharing the changes between the repositories is a separate step.

Each category has open source or proprietary tools you can choose from to meet your needs and your budget. Some are free and some require you to purchase a license, either for the company or for each user.

Here are a few tools for you to review. Although Microsoft Visual SourceSafe (VSS) is listed, you should be aware that it is not supported any longer. Its out-of-mainstream support and extended support is scheduled to end July 11, 2017. If you choose to use VSS, you may need to download it from a source other than Microsoft, such as CNET.

- **Microsoft Team Foundation Server** — `http://msdn.microsoft.com/en-us/vstudio/ff637362`
- **OASIS-SVN** — `http://dev2dev.de/changelang-eng.html`
- **TortoiseHG** — `http://tortoisehg.bitbucket.org/`
- **Vault** — `http://www.sourcegear.com/vault/`
- **Microsoft Visual SourceSafe** — `http://msdn.microsoft.com/en-us/library/ms181038%28v=VS.80%29.aspx`

> **NOTE** *Access used to have a Source Control add-in, but the feature was deprecated in Access 2013. Before proceeding with purchasing a version control solution, make sure it can work with Access without needing the Source Control Add-in.*

DATA MAINTENANCE

After the database solution is deployed, it needs to be maintained. Maintenance of a database solution includes regular backup for both the database and the FE files, and periodic execution of the Compact and Repair (C&R) tool for Microsoft Access database to reclaim any space no longer needed.

You can perform both tasks, backup, and Compact and Repair manually. It is preferable that no user is in the database while the backup process is executed. Users must be out of the database when you perform the C&R process.

It is better, and easier, to have both tasks automated. They can be scheduled to run during the non-business hours of the business so they don't interfere with the users during normal business hours.

In the following sections, you will read about different options to automate the backup and the database maintenance processes.

Automating Backups

In large companies, the IT department is responsible for the backup process of the whole network. That means that if you place the database BE file and the master FE file on the network, it will be backed up without your having to do anything else.

You want to confirm with the IT department that the location you selected for the files is one that is included in the backup process. You will also want to work with them to identify the recovery process as it can vary from one company to another.

Even without an IT department, smaller companies may already have a backup process in place. You should work with the client to identify the process, and how you can include the database files in it.

If there is no process in place, it is up to you to help the business to create a backup process. The process may be limited to the database solution, or you can take the opportunity to help the business establish a process to back up all files important to the business.

Local Backup Versus Cloud Services

The backup files can be stored locally, on another network drive, on an external hard drive, or on a PC dedicated to the backup process and storage, or they can be stored in the cloud.

There are many backup applications suited for local backup processes. Windows computers come with a backup application from the get-go or you can download and use one of the many tools available online. All of the tools share some common features, including the ability to schedule the process, set the folder and files to back up, and set the location of the backup files.

You may want to add the security of an off-site backup location to the process. This way, if a disaster were to strike, and the physical location of the business were also impacted, a copy of the backup files are available to start the business recovery process.

Nowadays, a few cloud-based options are available to consumers and businesses alike. There are different types of services with different price points, starting at no cost at all for a small storage space. When you evaluate the products, consider also the security of the data on the cloud servers. The data should be encrypted and protected from prying eyes.

The following are cloud-based tools to get you started. Entering the search term, "cloud based backup solutions" into your favorite search engine will yield more results for you to review:

- **Carbonite** — `http://www.carbonite.com`
- **Mozy** — `http://mozy.com/`

Although not exactly intended as cloud backup solutions, both Microsoft SkyDrive and Google Drive allow you to save files to the cloud. You can sync files from a selected folder on your PC or laptop to the cloud and have the files available to you when needed, including in case of a catastrophic failure of your local machines.

- **Microsoft SkyDrive** — `http://windows.microsoft.com/en-US/skydrive`
- **Google Drive** — `https://www.google.com/intl/en_US/drive/start/features.html`

Batch File on Windows Task Scheduler

One way to automate a backup process for the database solution is to use a batch file along with the built-in Windows Task Scheduler.

The VB Script that follows copies the specified database file to a specified location, in this case the same folder, and compacts the database. You will read more about Compact and Repair in the following section (code file: `Deploy_Maintain.txt Copy Compact Repair`):

```
Option Explicit

Dim WshShell
Dim objFile
Dim objFSO
Dim objAccess
Dim strPathToDB
Dim strMsg
```

```
Dim strTempDB
Dim strFile
Dim strPath
Dim strDate

strPathToDB = "\\COFFEE\Users\Shakshoka\Desktop\Test\CnR_Test.accdb"
strTempDB = "\\COFFEE\Users\Shakshoka\Desktop\Test\CompTemp.accdb"
strPath = "\\COFFEE\Users\Shakshoka\Desktop\Test\"
strFile = "CnR_Test"
strDate = Year(Date) & MonthName(Month(Date)) & Day(Date)

Set WshShell = WScript.CreateObject("WScript.Shell")
Set objFSO= CreateObject("Scripting.FileSystemObject")
Set objFile = objFSO.GetFile(strPathToDB)

' For Access 2013, use Application.15
Set objAccess = CreateObject("Access.Application.14")
' Perform the DB Compact into the temp accdb file
' (If there is a problem, then the original accdb is  preserved)
objAccess.DbEngine.CompactDatabase strPathToDB ,strTempDB

If Err.Number > 0 Then
    ' There was an error. Inform the user and halt execution
    strMsg = "The following error was encountered while compacting database:"
    strMsg = strMsg & vbCrLf & vbCrLf & Err.Description
Else

    ' Back up the original file as FilenameDATE.accdb. In case of undetermined
    ' error, it can be recovered by simply renaming the file
    objFSO.CopyFile strPathToDB , strPath & strFile & "_" & strDate & ".accdb",
True
    ' Copy the compacted accdb by into the original file name
    objFSO.CopyFile strTempDB, strPathToDB, True

    objFSO.DeleteFile strTempDB

End If

' Clean up
Set objAccess = Nothing
Set objFSO = Nothing
```

You create a task with the Windows Task Scheduler to execute the VBScript file at a time when it works for the business. This method requires the machine with the task file to remain powered on. Although for most Scheduler tasks the machine does not need to be logged in, you should test it to make sure when you create a new task.

Using a Zip File

Another method for you to explore is to zip the files into a compressed folder, using the default Windows Zip program, 7-Zip, or WinZip. You can call either of the programs via VBA-code to send files to a compressed folder or to retrieve files from the compressed folder.

With this method, you can have multiple backup copies of the database file. If you need to restore the file, you can select which file to use. Additionally, because the file is saved in a Zip folder, even if users can see the folders, chances are high they will not accidently use the backup file instead of the production copy.

Ron de Bruin, an Excel MVP, provides good sample code for all three programs on his site: `http://www.rondebruin.nl/win/section7.htm`. It is worth reading through the samples to choose the one that works for you best if you decide to use Zip files.

Although the default Windows Zip program and 7-Zip are free to use, remember that to use WinZip you need to have a registered copy of the program.

Automating Maintenance

Unlike SQL Server, ACE database does not self-compact to release unused disk space. To reclaim the space, you run the Compact and Repair (C&R) process in Access.

The C&R process is actually two processes. In older versions of Access, you could run them separately. Beginning with Access 2000, both processes run together when you use Access to start the Compact process. You can still run each process separately if you use the command line to execute the tasks. You can read about the command line switches in this Microsoft KB article: `http://support.microsoft.com/kb/209207`.

As time goes by, both the FE and the BE may gain size, especially if you included temporary tables in the solution that you load and truncate on a regular basis. The C&R process will shrink the size of the Access file. Because Access has a file size limitation, the process is important for proper maintenance of the file and for improving the performance of the solution.

The C&R process does the following to the database file:

- Recovers space used by deleted or renamed objects and records.
- Updates both table and index statistics. This helps the query optimizer to choose the most efficient query plan when executed.
- Physically re-orders the records in the tables in accordance with the clustered index set for the table.
- If the process finds structural inconsistencies in the database, it repairs it.

A regularly scheduled C&R will help minimize database corruption, and will provide you and your users with a better experience when you use or support the database solution.

Compact on Close

Access offers you the ability to `Compact on Close`. Every time you close the database file, the C&R process will kick in. Although it may sound like a great solution, it is better if you avoid this feature.

When the database is set to `Compact on Close`, it can add significant time to the closing process of the database. It can also use a large chunk of the workstation resources. The added time and the load on the system resources will slow users from moving on to the next task and will impact productivity; something businesses frown upon.

Additionally, `Compact on Close` only works on the FE file. It does not work on the linked BE database file. You need to manage the maintenance of the BE independently of the maintenance of the FE file.

Remote Compact and Repair

Another method you can use is to compact and repair the database remotely. This section discusses two possible ways based on code developed by fellow Access developers.

You can find the first tool in UtterAccess forums Code Archive: `http://www.utteraccess.com/forum/Auto-compact-backup-t678947.html`. This tool allows you to list the database files you want to compact and repair and set different options, including creating sequential copies of the compacted database.

Because it's a code sample, you may need to clean it after you download the file to make it work for you. But with a little effort, you can have a tool to manage and maintain your database solutions.

The second option is to use an Access add-in to help you perform the tasks. The `.mda` file, `Compactor.mda` is available to you at `http://access.mvps.org/access/modules/mdl0030.htm`. The original `.mda` was written by Dev Ashish. This version works only in Access versions up to Access 97. The second, newer `.mda` file, available on the same web page, was modified by Peter Doering, Access MVP, and can be used with newer Access versions.

Both use the same concept. You save the `.mda` file in a folder — for example \\Coffee\MyMDA — and you execute the following code in VBA (code file: `Deploy_Maintain.txt Call MDA file`):

```
Call Application.Run("\\Coffee\MyMDA\Compactor2003.DoCompact", True)
```

To use it in a distributed database solution, add the preceding code somewhere in your code. Make sure that it is the last line of code in the procedure because anything after may not be executed. What the add-in does is close your current database file, run the Compact and Repair on it, and open it again. You may have to wait for a few seconds before it starts the job, depending on the size of your database. Make sure you've saved all Dirty objects before the line is executed to avoid data loss.

Descriptive. Edited. DougWindow Scheduler

Much like the backup process, you can use the same VBScript from the previous section to compact only the selected database file.

This section of the code is the one that compacts the database into a temp database:

```
' Perform the DB Compact into the temp accdb file
' (If there is a problem, then the original accdb is  preserved)
objAccess.DbEngine.CompactDatabase strPathToDB ,strTempDB
```

When the C&R is done, this section of the code will copy the temp database file over the original database file with the same name:

```
    ' Copy the compacted accdb by into the original file name'
objFSO.CopyFile strTempDB, strPathToDB, True
```

When you execute this script, you can take care of both tasks, backup and C&R, in one task. If the backup is handled by another process or tool, you can modify the VBScript to keep only the C&R steps *sans* the backup.

Third-Party Solutions

You can also use third-party solutions to help you maintain the database files. Much like other tools mentioned in this book, you should do your own research to identify the tool that fits best with your or your client's business.

Review the following tools to see if they fit your business needs:

- **Access Autopilot** — `http://www.databasedev.co.uk/compact_and_repair.html`
- **FMS Total Visual Agent** — `http://www.fmsinc.com/microsoftaccess/DatabaseCompact.html`

> **NOTE** *In the section about auto-updating the FE files, the option of using the batch file to copy the FE file to the user's workstation also eliminates the need to C&R the FE located on the workstations. As long as the master copy is compacted, users will always get a compacted copy when opening the solution. You will still need to manage the backup for both FE and BE, and the C&R for the BE.*

How to Kick Users Out of the Application

Sometimes you may need to have all users log out of the database solution in the middle of the workday to perform maintenance. In a small office environment, it is pretty easy to ask everyone to log off until further notice. However, in a larger environment, perhaps one that spans over multiple locations, that may not be feasible.

The knowledge base article at `http://support.microsoft.com/kb/304408` walks you through the steps of shutting down an Access database solution gracefully. After everyone is out, you can continue with the tasks you need, like the C&R process, or updating the BE file.

You can use the same approach when you want to close a database solution that was left open overnight.

OWNERSHIP OF CODE

This section provides you with high-level information about what's involved when you develop a database solution as an employee or as an independent contractor, and the possible implications on intellectual property rights. This information is meant only as talking points, not as legal advice. It is always wise to consult a lawyer in your area for legal advice about your specific situation.

You will also read about how to deploy a trial solution to allow potential clients to evaluate the product you designed.

Intellectual Property Rights

As a developer, you might work in various employment statuses. You may be an employee for a company, or you might be an independent contractor, either self-employed or through a placement company.

As you develop database solutions, the question that often needs to be addressed is who owns the *intellectual property rights* (IPR) to the database solution. Each employment status will trigger different discussion points and can lead to a different owner of the IPR.

Employee

In most cases, when you work for a company as an hourly or salaried employed, the code you develop during work hours belongs to the company you work for. Some companies will have you sign an agreement stating that fact when they hire you; some may not. However, even without a signed agreement, the company still maintains rights to the code. Any exceptions will need to be addressed explicitly by both the company and the employee and preferably up-front before there is a need to address a potential problem. For example, no one on the Access Development Team working for Microsoft owns the IPR for Access. Because they are employed by the company, everything they develop on company time is owned by Microsoft. The EULA you sign when you install Access is with Microsoft, not the Access Development Team.

Independent Contractor

Things can get interesting when you are contracted to develop a database solution for a client. As a contractor, you are your own company (putting the actual legal structure of your business aside) so you may own the products you develop. However, when a client hires you to build a database solution, the client has a reasonable expectation of ownership of the product.

Here are a few questions to ponder as you embark on negotiating a contract with a client:

- Can the client modify the code after you deploy the solution?
- Can the client hire another developer to modify the solution?
- Can the client sell or give a copy of the database solution to someone else?
- Does the client need to pay an annual licensing fee?

The answers to those questions will help you define the terms of the contract and set a clear expectation of ownership up-front. Whatever you and the business client agree on should be part of the written contract.

It can be beneficial to consult a lawyer before you start talking with prospective clients to help you create a standard contract for you and your company.

Trial Version

Not all the database solutions you design will be a custom application. Sometimes you develop a database solution as a product that you can license or sell to many potential clients.

If that's the case, you may want to offer potential clients the option to try the product before they commit to the purchase. There are two ways you can limit the usage of the database solution: time-based and record-based.

Whichever way you choose to use, remember that in most jurisdictions, the data in the trial version belongs to the users and you cannot prevent them from keeping or retrieving it.

Record Limited Preview

You can limit the demo product to allow only a certain number of records in a table or tables. For example, if you develop a Contact database, you can set it so that the potential client can enter no more than 10 records in the main table.

You can control that by checking for the number of records when the form is loaded. If it reached the maximum number you set for it, the solution will close or be set as read-only. You can use a `DCount()` function on a startup event to test for the number of records (code file: `Deploy_Maintain.txt Trial - Number of records`):

```
'Place the variable in a standard module

'Set this number as appropriate for each product type or customer
Public Const lngMaxRecordsAllowed as long = 5

'Place this code in the startup code

If dcount("ContactID", "tblContacts")> lngMaxRecordsAllowed Then
    MsgBox "The preview period has ended.", vbCritical
    <code to quit, open solution as read only, or take them to "buy me" page>
End If
```

In this way, you can allow the user to edit current records but prevent him from using the database solution to its full capacity.

Time Limited Preview

The other method is to set a time limit on using the database solution. In its simplest way, the application compares the current computer date to a fixed start date embedded in the application. If the date is past the fixed expiration date, the code will set the application to read-only or will close it. The code snippet that follows illustrates this method (code file: `Deploy_Maintain.txt Trial - Timed`):

```
'Place the variable in a standard module

'Set this date as appropriate for each customer
Public Const dtEndOfPreview as Date = #5/29/2013#

'Place this code in the startup code

If Date > dtEndOfPreview Then
    MsgBox "The preview period has ended.", vbCritical
    <code to quit,  open solution as read only, or take them to "buy me" page>
ElseIf Date > DateAdd("d", -10, dtEndOfPreview) Then
    MsgBox "Warning: Preview is about to expire.", vbIconExclamation
End If
```

> **NOTE** *Instead of hardcoding the date in your solution, you can code the database solution to write the trial expiration date to the registry or to a database property the first time it is opened. Exercise caution when writing to the registry, you don't want to negatively impact your potential client's computer.*

Releasing the Full Version

If the client decides to purchase the database solution product, the simplest way to unlock the trial version is to send the client a full-version FE file without the use-limitation code. Depending on your setup, the client may be able to download the FE file from your website.

There are other, more elaborate, ways to unlock a trial solution, including having the database file connect to your server to verify the status of the application: Trial, Expired, or Full. Either way you choose to limit the trial version, make sure to communicate to the user that it is a trial version and that is will expire when the limits are reached.

SUMMARY

In this chapter, you read about how to evaluate and create a security module in your database solution. The module enables different users to have different experiences with the same solution to meet and accommodate business needs and rules. The design and implementation of an audit trail can also be part of the security feature of your solution. Not all databases require audit trails. The ones that do may require different levels of granularity, depending on the industry, regulations, and business rules.

You also read about various deployment techniques and methods to update a revised FE file on users' workstations to ensure a unified version in production and an easier support for the solution.

You reviewed what different environment you should establish to support the development cycle. We discussed the benefits of multiple environments and how to go promote the files from one environment to the other at the end of each development stage. Optional environments such as SUP, Adhoc, and POC offer you additional options to provide support and to have analysts create adhoc queries and reports to support the business.

The discussion about database maintenance presented ways for you to provide ongoing support to your product. Responsibility to the maintenance plan can be an integral part of your role in the company. Automation of tasks allows you to focus on enhancements and user support while ensuring the health of the database solution.

You read through a high-level review of the intellectual property rights issue, and you now have the basic information you need to begin a discussion about how you want to provide services to a client. As mentioned, it is wise to consult a lawyer in your area to make sure you understand and secure your rights.

Next, you will read about how to work with SQL Server. As we mentioned a few times, Access and SQL work well together and you will find that by working with both, you can develop robust and powerful database solutions that can support a large number of users. Chapter 21 discusses the upsizing process and techniques to help you when you work with SQL Server.

21

Maximizing SQL Server Capabilities

WHAT'S IN THIS CHAPTER?

- Understanding the reasons to upsize a database to SQL Server
- Walking through the upsizing process
- Reviewing techniques and methods when using a SQL Server

WROX.COM CODE DOWNLOADS FOR THIS CHAPTER

The wrox.com code downloads for this chapter are found at `www.wiley.com/go/proaccess2013prog.com` on the Download Code tab. The code is in the Chapter 21 download and individually named according to the code filenames listed throughout this chapter.

As you read in an earlier chapter, Access works well with SQL Server. When you use SQL Server as the back-end database engine for your solution, you tap into a powerful server-based system. Using Access as the front end allows you to design a robust and feature-rich user interface. Combining the two together in your database solutions enables you to create a solid, high-performing database solution for your clients.

UPSIZING

This section focuses on existing Access solutions that utilize Access data files rather than SQL Server. Although a few of those may have been designed with upsizing in mind, a relatively small portion of the others may need and benefit from using a SQL Server database engine as the *back end* (BE).

There are a variety of reasons for choosing to upsize to SQL Server. This chapter helps you evaluate your solutions to determine if they will benefit from upsizing, what the upsizing process entails, and what to look for as you are going through the process.

When to Upsize

It is important for you to recognize that not all Access database solutions need to be, or even should be, upsized. Access, with its ACE database engine, is the right platform for the majority of the solutions. When approaching the upsizing evaluation, you should start from the position of "there is no need to upsize until business operational and regulatory needs require changing the database platform." As long as your solution works consistently and meets the business threshold for scalability, reliability, and security, you have no reason to upsize it.

Web-Based Access Solutions

If you need your solution to be accessed over *wide area network* (WAN) or over the web, you should consider upsizing the back end to SQL Server. Access is a great platform for *local area network* (LAN). However, if you try to use the desktop database solution on a WAN, the performance will degrade quickly and you may experience an increase in data corruption.

Access 2013 offers the capabilities to develop and publish web-based solutions. To take advantage of that, you are required to use SQL as the back end of your solution. Access does not offer you the option of an ACE database engine for web-based solutions. When you are creating a web database, the SQL database will be created for you, either in Office 365 or on your own server if it's set up for Access Services.

While this is not strictly an upsizing issue, it is a consideration you should be aware of when you are in the requirements gathering phase of a development project. You can learn about Access web apps from the first part of this book.

Access Application Limitations

When you work through the decision-making process regarding which database engine to use, Access's limitations will be your primary considerations. You may determine that one or a combination of the following may warrant upsizing your data file.

Maximum Database Size

The maximum size of an Access `.accdb` file is 2GB. That includes space for the system objects, so in reality you have a little less than that to store the data. 2GB of space is quite a lot of space and can support a large number of records. However, you may need to deal with very large data sets in some of your solutions that ACE cannot accommodate space-wise or cannot process efficiently. If you cannot effectively use multiple Access BE files to compensate for the data volume, you should look at SQL Server. Using SQL Server offers you virtually unlimited space; essentially, it is only limited by the hardware. It also offers you scalability and the option to increase the capacity as needed.

Number of Concurrent Users

When you read the Access specifications, you will see that you can have up to 255 concurrent users. In reality, you will find out that a well-designed LAN solution can effectively support around 25 concurrent data entry users and still retain good performance levels. A read-only reporting solution can support more users. Access can run up to 100 concurrent reports without causing noticeable lag.

When using SQL Server, you can support an unlimited number of concurrent users. The database engine was designed for a large number of users editing data at the same time without having a noticeable impact on performance.

Scalability

You cannot scale the ACE (or JET if you are using an older version of Access) database engine well. By design, the database engine is limited to running in a single thread only. Additionally, when you execute the queries in the front end, they run locally on the client computer rather than on the server. Although today's personal computers are robust and can provide strong processing power at the desktop level, they are still not a match to a server designed purely to process data.

When you design a solution with a SQL Server back end, you can take advantage of both the server's processing power and its multi-threaded capabilities. You also benefit from the superior locking mechanisms. The bottom line is that processing larger data sets takes less time on the server than using ACE.

Features

SQL Server offers many powerful features that are not found in Access. If your solution requires any of these features, you should consider using SQL Server as your back-end database engine. At times, just one can justify upsizing. Some of those features are:

- **Data warehousing** — Analysis server is a special version of SQL Server optimized for this task.
- **Reporting Services** — SQL Server comes with SQL Server Reporting Services (SSRS) to provide a robust reporting tool that can also be used online.
- **Full Text Index** — This is the ability to store pages of text in the database and index them in a special way, so you can find keywords, including verb conjugations, single/plural forms of nouns, and synonyms.
- **.NET assemblies** — These code libraries can run in the SQL Server address space and be called from a stored procedure to very quickly perform arbitrary calculations.
- **Special data types** — SQL Server supports natively special data types, such as XML data and spatial data.
- **Replication** — While older versions of Access supported a form of replication, SQL Server implements replication with enterprise-level reliability.

Reliability and Availability

Reliability should be a key factor when you evaluate the need to upsize a database engine. Reliability can mean different things to different businesses, so you will need to define it first. Some points to consider when discussing reliability are:

- What is the needed uptime of the database solution?
- What is the acceptable downtime?
- Backup and recovery cycles — how much data or time can you afford to lose?

For some business, having the solution up and running for 10 hours a day will be sufficient, allowing plenty of downtime for maintenance and support. Some business will need the solution to run all the time. When you design solutions at this level, reliability becomes the top consideration in your analysis.

Database Corruption, Backup, and Recovery

Data can be lost and databases can become corrupted for many reasons, such as a sudden loss of power, a hiccup in the network traffic, hardware failure, and so on. Access databases are particularly sensitive to these issues. When designing a new database or evaluating an existing solution, consider how to recover both the application and the data, as well as what is acceptable in terms of data loss and downtime — for you or your clients.

You should always have a backup plan for the data files, including whether it is you or someone else that is responsible for implementation and follow-up. When disaster strikes, and it will, you need to be able to recover the lost data and get the solution back up and running quickly. How much loss is acceptable is a business decision that needs to be made sooner rather than later.

Backing up an `.accdb` database file is much like backing up Word or Excel files. Usually, you run a nightly process that backs up the files on the network drives. Depending on the business decision, the backup file, or a copy of it, may be sent off-site.

Although you can back up the database files when users are using it, it is not advisable, at least as the first option. So if the system needs to be accessible around the clock, you may not have a time window to close it for maintenance and to create a copy of the data. And even if you do make a nightly backup, if the system crashes at noon, the recovery will cause you to lose the data that was entered between the time the backup process was executed and the time of the crash.

SQL Server Transaction Log files allow you to set the backup frequency up to the minute. It also can perform the backup while users are accessing the system. Even though one-minute backups may be the extreme, the ability to set the time interval enables you to strike a balance between performance and acceptable data loss. Using the transaction log in SQL Server is also handy when you want to roll back the data to a previous state.

Servers Versus Workstations

Server machines often include hardware features that are too expensive for workstations. This is one of the reasons that they are more reliable. A server typically includes:

- **Several hard drives managed in such a way that one disk can fail without data being lost (for example, RAID 10)** — In fact, the server can keep running while the bad disk is swapped out (hot-swappable).

- **Multiple CPUs** — Not only does it allow for faster processing, if one fails, the machine will keep running.
- **Redundant power supplies** — Having more than one keeps the server working while you replace a faulty power supply.
- **UPS** — An uninterruptible power supply sufficient for a temporary power outage or until the server is gracefully shut down.

Server machines also require a server-level operating system, which supports higher levels of system management and security.

Security

Security means different things in different places. In addition to securing who can do what in the *front end* (FE) of the solution, you need to protect access to the back end and to the data itself. The level of security is related to the type of data. For example, using a database solution to generate invoices does not require as high a level of security as a system that stores bank or credit card numbers used to pay invoices or that stores medical information. The latter is also subject to government regulations that you will need to adhere to when designing the solution. Identifying the requirements will help you in deciding whether or not to upsize the database.

With an Access data file, the best method for securing the database is to use the Windows network filesystem permissions on the folder where the files reside or on the file itself. When you create an Access solution, the database is stored on the file server. For the users to be able to use the solution, they also need read/write permissions to the folder containing the data file. That means that if users know where the BE resides, they can also copy the file.

SQL Server is designed with enterprise security features. The security is more powerful and allows more granularity than Access. Similar to Access, it can also use Windows authentication and leverage the Active Directory to assign users to different roles. The data files in SQL Server are not available to users because they are not stored on the file server and they are exclusively locked by the SQL Server service. Only users with the highest level of access permissions can manage the SQL Server data files.

SQL Server Versions

When you are ready to upsize a database, you can choose from several approaches and platforms. The following material discusses several of the SQL Server platforms. They are listed in order of complexity and cost.

SQL Server Express

Using SQL Server Express (SSE) with Access as the FE user interface is a good way to increase the capabilities of your database solution without incurring an additional expense. SQL Server Express is available for free from Microsoft. SSE is a great product enabling you to power and run desktop, web, and small server applications. It's also good for redistribution. Additionally, it's a great way for you to become familiar with SQL Server and to learn how to develop with SQL Server. You can find the download information at `http://msdn.microsoft.com/en-us/evalcenter/hh230763.aspx`.

SQL Server Express has some limitations compared to what the full version of SQL Server has to offer, primarily the maximum memory utilized and the database file size. However, it is a significant step up from an ACE database engine and a great migration option. You can find more about the differences between the various SQL Server 2012 editions at `http://msdn.microsoft.com/en-us/library/cc645993(v=SQL.110).aspx`.

SQL Server Azure

You can use the Microsoft SQL Azure platform, which is also available through Office 365. Although it is a cloud-based database platform, use of SQL Azure is not limited to the web solutions that you learned to build in earlier chapters.

The Azure platform offers you a SQL database service running in Microsoft data centers. The hardware is owned, hosted, and maintained by Microsoft so you don't have to worry about those tasks. In some cases, it may not be as feature-rich as a local installation of SQL Server, but SQL Azure offers you more than SQL Express because it has the additional benefit that you do not need to worry about maintaining the infrastructure.

Azure services come with a subscription cost that needs to be evaluated and matched to the budget. However, as you explore the cost associated with the service, you may find out that it's cheaper to host the service with Azure than to host SQL Server. You can find more about the pricing structure of SQL Azure at `http://www.windowsazure.com/en-us/pricing/details/sql-database/`.

SQL Server Enterprise

Of all the SQL Server editions, SQL Server Enterprise offers you the most power and the most scalability. Using a local installation of SQL Server is another option, particularly if the infrastructure is already in place. If the infrastructure is not in place, you will need to consider the cost of both setting it up and maintaining it. If it is in place, you can work with the current caretaker to identify the possible increase to work and cost. Fortunately, that will often be negligible in an IT shop that supports a server farm.

Much like the previous two SQL Server options, you can upsize the back-end database engine and link the tables to the FE. You will also need to make some changes to the FE in order to take advantage of the server's processing powers. However, you should be able to preserve most of the FE, making it more cost effective to modify an existing well-built solution rather than building a replacement from scratch.

.NET Framework

Although this is a book about Access development, we would be remiss if we did not mention the .NET option. The most complex, costly, and time-consuming option for upsizing a database solution is to migrate the back end to a SQL Server platform and develop the front end of the solution with .NET or ASP.NET. With .NET you can develop rich, robust applications that can be deployed anywhere. However, it is not a rapid development platform, and the cost associated with developing .NET solutions can be prohibitive for many businesses.

The Tradeoffs for Upsizing

In database development as in life, there are trade-offs. If you decide you need to upsize the database engine to SQL Server, you need to understand the requirements, the timing, and all of the associated costs for both hardware and software.

First, you need a server. If you or the client does not have one already, you will need to spec out the hardware configuration and purchase a server. If you are working with a company that already has servers, you will need to work with the IT department to set up the space for the database in one of the existing servers.

You, or the network team, will also need to manage the server. Before installing the SQL Server software on the server, you need to install an operating system. Chances are that the server will come preloaded with an *operating system* (OS), but if not, you will need to buy and install an OS.

Last but not least, when it comes to software, you need to buy and install SQL Server. There are different editions of SQL Server as well as different license types to choose from. You can find information on the Microsoft site to help you choose the one that best fits the environment at `http://www.microsoft.com/en-us/sqlserver/get-sql-server/how-to-buy.aspx`.

After the server is set up, someone needs to manage the server hardware and software. In many larger companies, this is included in the responsibilities of the IT department, along with updates, patches, maintenance, and backups. So, if you offer hosting to complement your development services, you also need to provide the reliability and maintenance yourself or through another support service.

On top of server support, you need a Database Administrator (DBA) to manage the SQL Server database. The DBA is responsible for the health and proper functionality of the database engine. The functions include creating the database files, ensuring proper and timely backups, setting up the various system jobs, researching and resolving errors, and so on.

In some IT shops, the DBA is the person responsible for creating the database and the various database objects in the production environment. You, as the developer, will work with the DBA and provide the schema. You should have access to the DEV environment to help you design and develop the database objects that you need, but the DBA will be the one to push it to production after approving the changes from the technical aspect, for example making sure the queries are optimized, etc. It is appropriate for the business users to approve promotion to production after they have tested the new or revised solution. You learn more about this in the discussion on deployment in Chapter 20.

You can manage it all yourself depending on your skill set, the client, the environment, and the complexity of your database solution and of your database schema. However, doing so will take considerable time away from development and maintenance of your solutions. Some of the previous options can help you mitigate the management aspect of the development — for example, by using the Azure platform.

Summary of When to Upsize

When you evaluate the database solution for possible upsizing, you should consider a number of different factors. It is up to you, in cooperation with the business users, to review the needs of the business and identify the best development platform for the solution. In your role as the technical advisor, you should provide the business with the pros and cons of the proposed approaches and help your clients make the best decision. Doing so will go a long way toward a successful project and a happy client.

The Upsizing Process

There is more than one way to upsize your database from Access to SQL Server. You can re-create the database structure in SQL Server and append the records to the tables. You can use SQL Server Integration Services (SSIS) to transfer the tables from Access to SQL Server. Or, you can export the tables from Access to SQL Server and use an ODBC connection.

The SQL Server Migration Assistant (SSMA) is one of the best ways to migrate an Access database to SQL. The SSMA is a free tool provided by Microsoft that is specifically designed to migrate databases to SQL Server, including: Oracle, MySQL, Sybase, and of course, Access. It is available to download from `http://www.microsoft.com/en-us/download/details.aspx?id=28763`. After you install the SSMA, you will need to register it to get the license. When you first open the SSMA, it will provide a link to the registration page.

If the target database does not exist, SSMA will prompt you to create it. Alternatively, you can create the database in SQL Server before you start the process. Either way, you need to allocate space and provide a name for the database. SQL Server takes care of the rest, at least to the extent of creating the database container and the system database objects. It is up to you to add the rest.

The Migration Wizard will guide you through six steps, as shown in Figure 21-1. As you gain experience with the SSMA, you can skip using the wizard and walk through the steps on your own to achieve the same results.

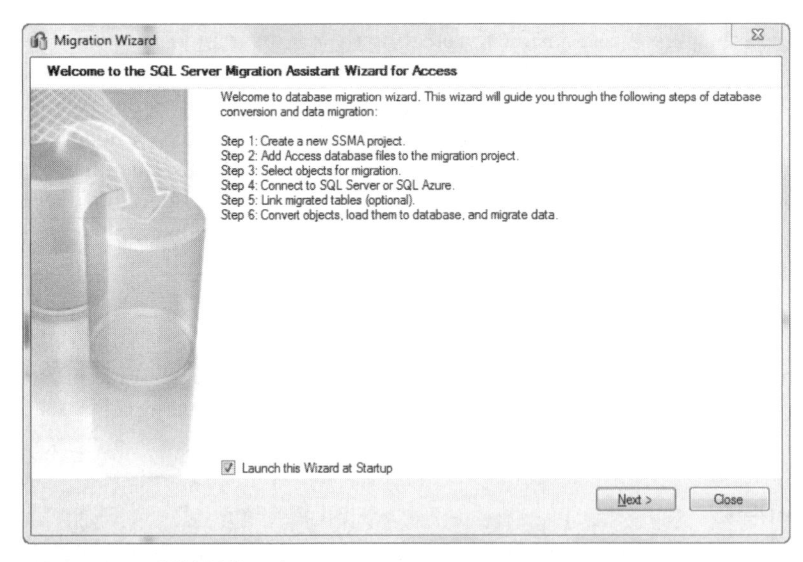

FIGURE 21-1: SSMA Wizard

When you open SSMA, it will start the Migration Wizard. The first step is to create a project and add a source database that will migrate to SQL Server, as shown in Figure 21-2. Using the dialog box, navigate to the folder the .accdb file is stored in and add it to SSMA. The tool will allow you to select the objects you want to migrate: tables and queries. You do not need to migrate every object in your .accdb database, only the ones that you want to upsize.

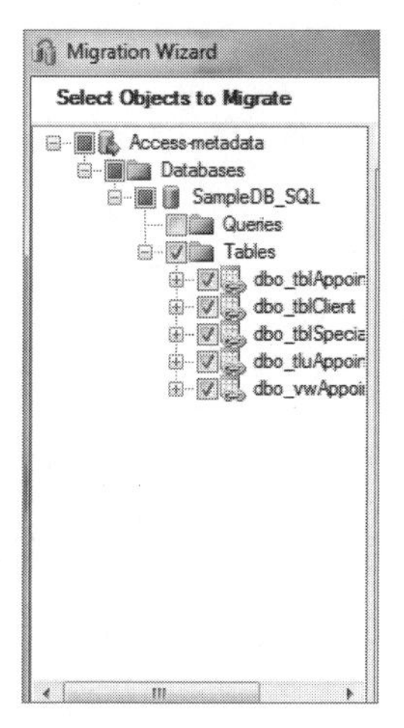

FIGURE 21-2: Objects in source file

The next step is to connect SSMA to the SQL Server database you created earlier, as shown in Figure 21-3.

When the two databases, Access and SQL Server, are connected to the SSMA, you are ready to start the migration process. The wizard will give you an option to link the tables from SQL Server to your .accdb file. You do that by selecting the checkbox in the wizard dialog box, something that is easy to miss. You can achieve the same result later by SSMA, Tools ➪ Link Tables, or within Access using External Data ➪ ODBC Database from the Access ribbon.

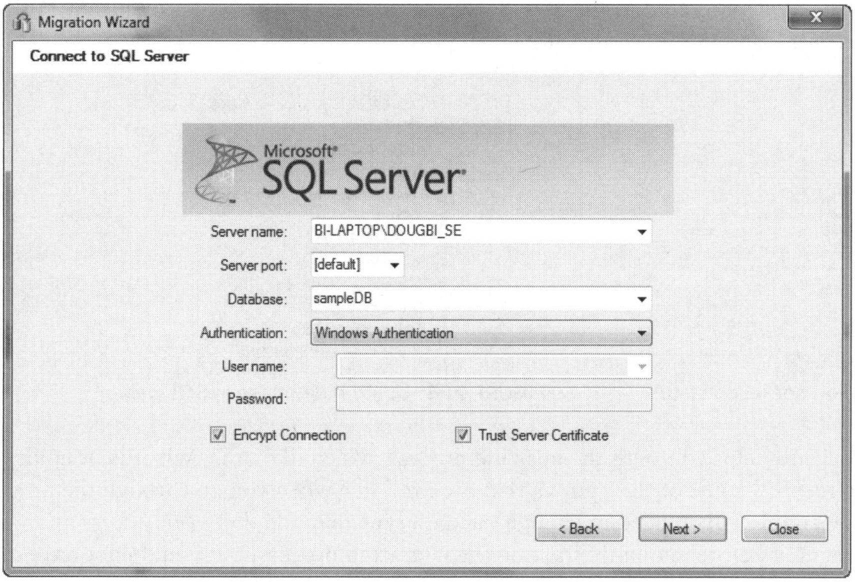

FIGURE 21-3: SQL Server connection dialog box

When you are done selecting the options, just click Next, and the SSMA Wizard will start the migration process. You will see the progress on the screen as it goes through the various stages, as shown in Figure 21-4.

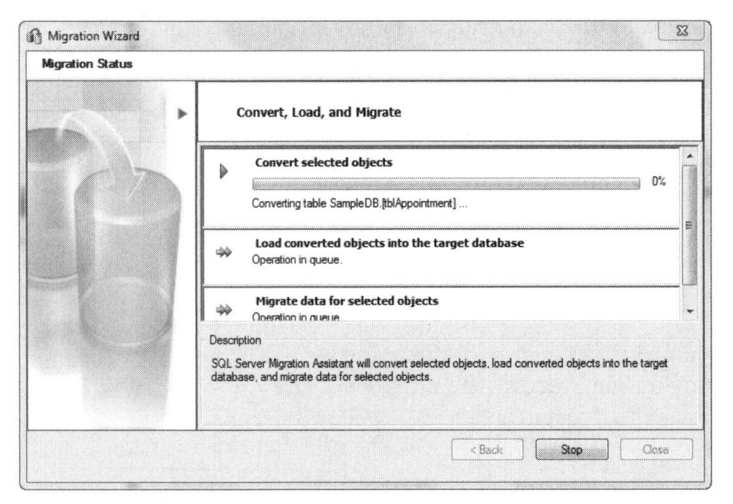

FIGURE 21-4: SSMA progress dialog box

If all goes well, SSMA will let you know the final status of the migration, as shown in Figure 21-5. The Access database will be migrated to the SQL Server database, and you will see the new tables and queries in your SQL database, as shown in Figure 21-6.

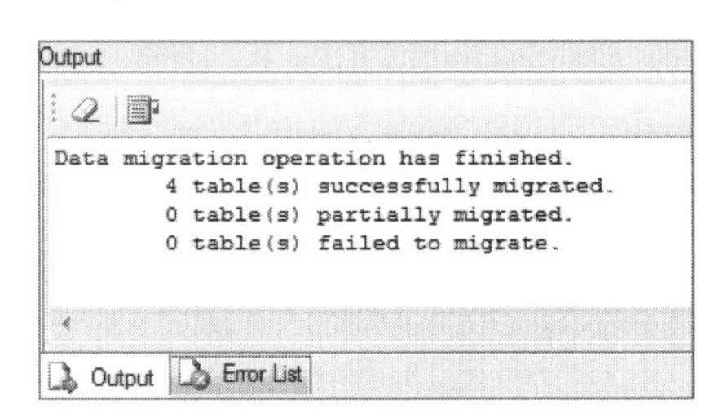

FIGURE 21-5: Migration operation status

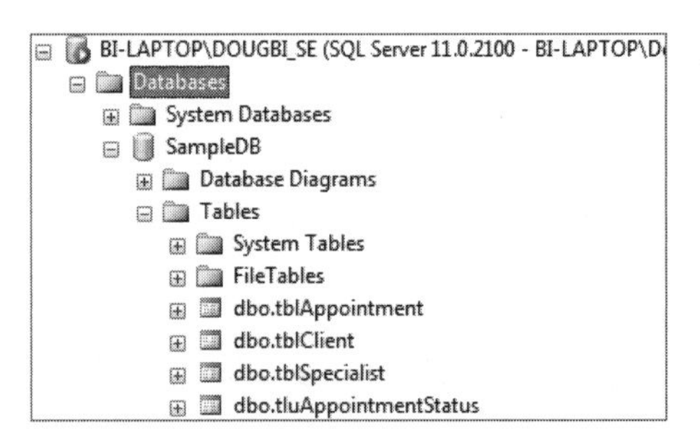

FIGURE 21-6: Upsized database in SQL Server

Working with the wizard helps you with the upsizing process. Much like other wizards, it holds your hand but also restricts some of the options that are available when you go through the process independently. For example, if you need to change the data type mapping between Access and SQL Server, you can do it before manually starting the migration process, but you do not have the opportunity when you are using the wizard.

> **NOTE** *Standard data type mappings include* `date` ➪ `datetime2`. *However, like all data types that Access cannot handle,* `datetime2` *will be treated as* `Text` *after linking the migrated table. It is advisable to change the mapping to* `date` ➪ `datetime` *prior to migration.*

The next step is to start the upsizing process. You do that by clicking the Convert, Load, and Migrate button in the toolbar or by right-clicking the Access database in the Access Metadata Explorer in SSMA and then selecting the same option from the context menu.

Not all migration will go smoothly, so you will need to resolve the errors. The most common issues are associated with data types and indexes. In the following sections, you learn what to watch for and how to resolve some common issues.

If you need or want to rerun an existing migration project, you can do so by selecting File ➪ Open Project from the SSMA menu and navigating to your saved migration project file. When the file is open you can change some of the settings, such as the data type mapping, before running the migration process.

Things to Watch for When Upsizing

Much like in other development phases, there are things you should be watching for when you upsize your database. As the saying goes: an ounce of prevention is worth a pound of cure. Paying attention to the details and mitigating issues when possible will help with the migration process.

Bumpy Migration Process

Even with your best efforts in preparing to upsize, there is no magic formula that will guarantee a smooth process. In some cases, the migration process will work without a hitch. However, chances are that the data will not upsize smoothly the first time, the second, or maybe even the third time. In the words of Douglas Adams: Don't panic. Work through the process to figure out the reasons for the errors, fix them, and try again. You can also use a multi-pronged approach such as using the SSMA for the bulk of the migration combined with creating selected tables by yourself.

Mapping Data Types Between Access and SQL

As you prepare to use SQL Server, it's helpful to know how the data types are mapped between the two platforms. If you are using SSMA, the wizard will, for the most part, handle the data type incompatibilities. You can read more about the data types later in this chapter.

Index Differences Between Access and SQL

When you are using SSMA to upsize your database, it will usually convert the majority of the indexes properly. However, you should be aware of a few exceptions:

- If your table does not have a primary key field, or at least one unique index, the SSMA will add an identity field to that table. The Access Upsizing Wizard may fail to upsize the table altogether. Adding a unique index (for example, an autonumber) to your table before upsizing will avoid that issue.
- SQL Server does not support multiple null values in a unique indexed field. If one of your tables has multiple null values in a unique indexed field, you cannot upsize that table. You can either remove the unique index from the field or limit it to no more than one null value before upsizing.

Date Limits

Access and SQL Server support different date limits. In Access, you can have dates from 01-JAN-100 through 31-DEC-9999; in SQL you can only have dates from 01-JAN-1753 through 31-DEC-9999. The SSMA will migrate the tables with out-of-bound dates. However, it converts them to the SQL limit and uses 01-Jan-1753 for any date before 1753. If the date requires dates prior to 1753, you will need to convert the field to text and create expressions to use it as date values. Otherwise, you can delete the values or use the SQL date bound.

You can test the date values in your records before upsizing by using the following (code file: `SQL.txt Check out of bounds dates`):

```
WHERE MyDateField < #1-1-1753#
```

Expressions

Expressions in queries and code can create problems when you upsize the database. Many characters are not compatible between Access and SQL. While the SSMA Wizard tries its best to handle the differences, you can help the process by changing the expressions before you start the migration process.

- In Access, you can use either single quotes (`'`) or double quotes (`"`) as a string terminator. SQL uses single quotes only (`'`). You will need to review your queries, code, and macros in Access and replace the double quote characters with single quotes.
- Look for embedded single quotes characters in field values and replace them with two single quotes. For example, `O'Neill` becomes `O''Neill`. The second instance of the name uses two single quotes, not a double quote. This distinction is critical, but it may not be visually apparent.
- Access uses the pound sign as a date identifier: `#05/29/2013#`. SQL uses single quotes: `'05/29/2013'`. You should replace the pound sign with a single quote when identifying a date.
- In Access, you can concatenate with the ampersand character (&). For example: `"Seattle" &" " & "Sounders"` will return `"Seattle Sounders"`. In SQL, you need to use the plus (+) sign. For example: `'Seattle' + ' ' + 'Sounders'`. Here again, you should replace the ampersand with the plus sign.

Access Functions That Do Not Upsize to SQL

There are differences between Access SQL and T-SQL used in SQL Server. Not everything written in Access can be translated to T-SQL, as there are functions that are not supported by T-SQL. You need to review your queries before you upsize and identify the incompatibilities. The following Access functions are not compatible with T-SQL:

- `DateValue()`
- Domain aggregate functions
- `First()`
- `Last()`
- `NZ()`
- `StrConv()`

- `Switch()`
- `Time()`
- `TimeSerial()`
- `TimeValue()`
- `Val()`
- `WeekDayName()`

Upsizing Large Data Sets

Access databases can hold a lot of records, upwards of a few million records. And, as you might anticipate, transferring a large number of records to SQL Server can take a long time. If the lengthy process causes problems, you can copy the table structure only and upsize the empty tables. When you are satisfied with the table structure in SQL Server, you can append the Access data using SQL Server Management Studio (SSMS) or SQL Server Integration Services (SSIS).

WORKING WITH SQL SERVER AS THE BACK END

One of the attractions of Access is that it is a single product that offers both a database engine (or actually two: JET for `.mdb` and ACE for `.accdb`) as well as a rapid development environment with powerful tools to design and deploy a robust user interface — a full complement of macros, queries, forms, and reports. In contrast, SQL Server offers capacity, reliability, and security to simultaneously support a multitude of demands and scenarios. However, it does not offer a development environment for creating a custom user interface. The best it offers in that area is the SSRS (SQL Server Reporting Service).

If you are just getting started with SQL Server, you may want to have your own playground, so to speak. Fortunately, it can be very simple and cheap. You can start with SQL Server Express. Just download the free Express Edition with Tools from Microsoft, at `http://www.microsoft.com/en-us/sqlserver/editions/2012-editions/express.aspx`.

If you run the setup program and use the default installation options, you will have everything to start exploring SQL Server. Although a few things will be different, you will see that there are many parallels between the two platforms.

SQL Server Management Studio

SQL Server Management Studio (SSMS) is the most important tool you will use to maintain SQL Server databases. When you first start it, you will be prompted to connect to the database server, as shown in Figure 21-7.

FIGURE 21-7: SSMS Connection dialog box

You can connect to any server that you have credentials for, whether they are in your network or on the Internet. The network databases will be listed if you use the Server Name drop-down and choose Browse for more. For databases outside your network, for example at an *Internet service provider* (ISP), you will need to get credentials from the owner of the database. For Access 2013 web databases, you can find connection information under File ➪ Info ➪ Connections.

The two authentication options to the database are Windows Authentication and SQL Server Authentication. The options you selected during the setup will dictate whether or not the latter is available to you. Windows Authentication means that you're using your Windows login to connect to the SQL Server. Typically, this is the best idea because you are already logged in to Windows and you don't need to remember another set of credentials. It also enables the server administrator to use Active Directory to set up groups of users with different levels of access.

SQL Server Authentication uses an account setup in SQL Server itself, under Logins. One built-in account that always exists is the system administrator's account named, `sa`. During the setup, you gave this account a password. Using SQL Server authentication accounts makes sense for web-based applications where the user, impersonated by the IIS, is connecting to the server: You set up a SQL Server login for the web application and use the credentials in the `ConnectionString` used by the application to connect to the database. You can read more about setting SQL Server authentication modes in this MSDN article: `http://msdn.microsoft.com/en-us/library/ms144284.aspx`.

For now, you can accept the default values in the *Connect to Server* dialog box and connect to your local server.

When the SSMS opens, you will see the Object Explorer, shown in Figure 21-8 , and quickly recognize the similarity to the navigation pane in Access.

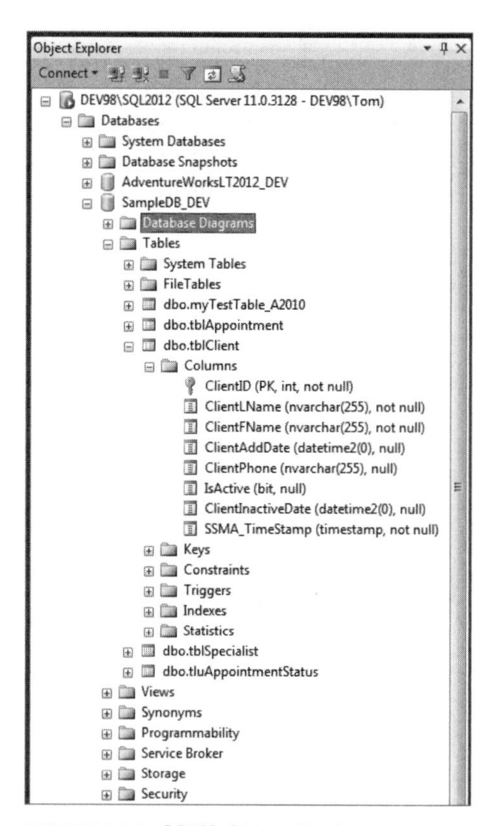

FIGURE 21-8: SSMS Object Explorer

Using the Object Explorer, you can drill down in the available databases and inspect their objects and properties. You can also review server-wide options such as security and management features.

Despite being a powerhouse data server, searching for an object by name in SQL Server is a relatively crude process compared to the simplicity of the Access search bar. With Object Explorer, you have to right-click a container node, choose Filter, and then enter a filter expression.

For now, you may want to ignore many of the objects in Object Explorer and proceed to restore the sample database that comes with this book.

Restore Database

To follow along with the examples in this chapter and to have a database ready to go for you to experiment, we recommend you download the sample database provided in the sample files for this chapter.

More comprehensive sample databases can be downloaded from CodePlex: `http://msftdb prodsamples.codeplex.com/releases/view/55330`.

Although Access has no built-in support to back up and restore databases, SQL Server has two options to restore a database. You can either use a SQL command or the SSMS user interface. To use a SQL command, use File ➪ New ➪ Query with Current Connection. Then enter this script (code file: `SQL.txt Restore database`):

```
RESTORE DATABASE [SampleDB_DEV] FROM  DISK = N'C:\myFolder\SampleDB_DEV.bak'
```

Note that the `N` before the filename indicates that it is a Unicode string. It is not strictly needed but it's a good practice to add it because there are a few areas in SQL Server programming where Unicode strings are required.

Replace the path with your path. Hit the Execute button in the toolbar to execute the script. If you have multiple statements in the query window, like the ones shown in Figure 21-9, highlight the one(s) you want to run and click the Execute button or press F5.

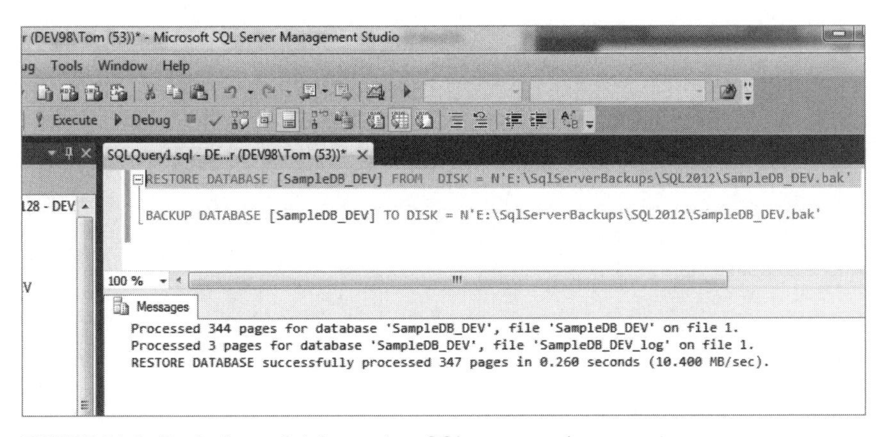

FIGURE 21-9: Restoring a database via a SQL command

After that, right-click the Databases node and click Refresh. The new database node should be listed.

You can also restore the database by using the SSMS user interface shown in Figure 21-10. Right-click the Databases node and choose Restore Database from the context menu. In the Source section, select Device and locate the backup file. The other fields are filled out automatically and when you click OK, the database will be restored. Note that the Restore command will overwrite a possibly existing database without warning. It is a powerful command and SQL Server assumes that if you are allowed to run it, you know what you are doing.

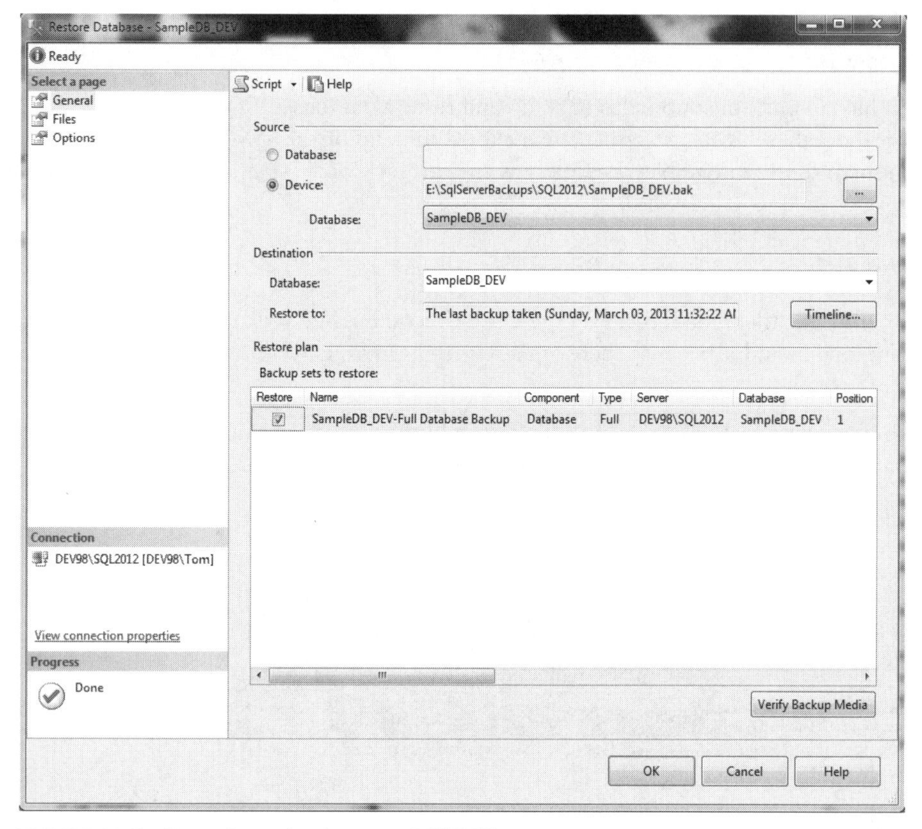

FIGURE 21-10: Restoring a database via SSMS UI

Backup Database

You can use two similar methods to back up a database. One method uses a SQL statement (code file: `SQL.txt Backup database`):

```
BACKUP DATABASE [SampleDB_DEV] TO DISK =
N'E:\SqlServerBackups\SQL2012\SampleDB_DEV.bak'
```

The other method is to right-click the database node and choose Tasks ⇨ Backup.

You will notice that a backup file can contain multiple backups. As a test, execute the preceding script multiple times, each time checking the size of the backup file. When restoring a database, you can select which backup you want to use. This is a handy feature should you want to restore to an older backup point than the most recent one, as mentioned earlier.

If you want to make backups every night, you can set up a maintenance plan. You start with the Expand the Management node, right-click the Maintenance Plans node, and choose the Maintenance Plan Wizard. It is common to set up at least two plans: one to make backups every night and another one to perform more elaborate database maintenance tasks once a week.

Like most other topics discussed in this chapter, there is a lot more to discover about backups. You'll want to learn about backing up transaction logs, recovery models, partial backups, backing up to tape, and so on. The SQL Server help system named "Books Online" is an excellent resource for further study.

SQL Server Files

SQL Server stores the data in `.mdf` files. These files are locked by SQL Server so they cannot be copied by anyone. This is a security improvement over Access files, which can be copied while in use. Only authorized personnel assigned to the appropriate role can make SQL Server backups or restore the database.

You will also see `.ldf` files, which are the transaction log files — one of the ways SQL Server ensures inconsistent data cannot occur. They are not lock files like Access has (`.ldb`, `.laccdb`) because lock files are not needed. The server handles locking issues internally without an external file. If you want to see where the data files are located, right-click the database node in Object Explorer and choose Properties ➪ Files from the context menu.

In addition to these two file types, you will also see `.bak` and `.trn` files. These are created by SQL Server during the backup process for the database files and the transaction log respectively.

Database Diagrams

As you know, Access has a single Relationships window for each database file. In SQL Server, you can create as many relationship diagrams as you like for the same database. Right-click the Database Diagrams node and choose New Database Diagram.

If you get an error message about Database Diagram support, right-click the database node, select Properties, Files page, and enter `sa` (the built-in account for System Administrator) as the database owner. Once installed, you can create as many diagrams as you like; for example, you might want one for each functional area of your database. Diagrams offer automated arrangement of tables and multiple views of the fields: Right-click a table and choose Table Views. In Figure 21-11, you can see a database diagram with four tables.

In SQL Server, you can use the Database Diagrams as your main work area for creating new tables, adding indexes, adding constraints, and so on. When you save the changes made in the Database Diagram, they are applied to the tables as well.

Tables

Overall, you will see that SQL Server tables are very similar to Access tables. One difference is that in the SQL Server each table belongs to a "schema," which plays a role in security. You can think of "schema" as a container of objects, and "dbo" (database owner) as the default container. The SQL Server security model includes options to set permissions for an entire schema, rather than one object at a time.

When linking SQL Server tables to Access, the tables will appear in `[schemaName]_[tableName]` format. For example, "`dbo_tblClient`" indicates that the Client table is in a schema named dbo.

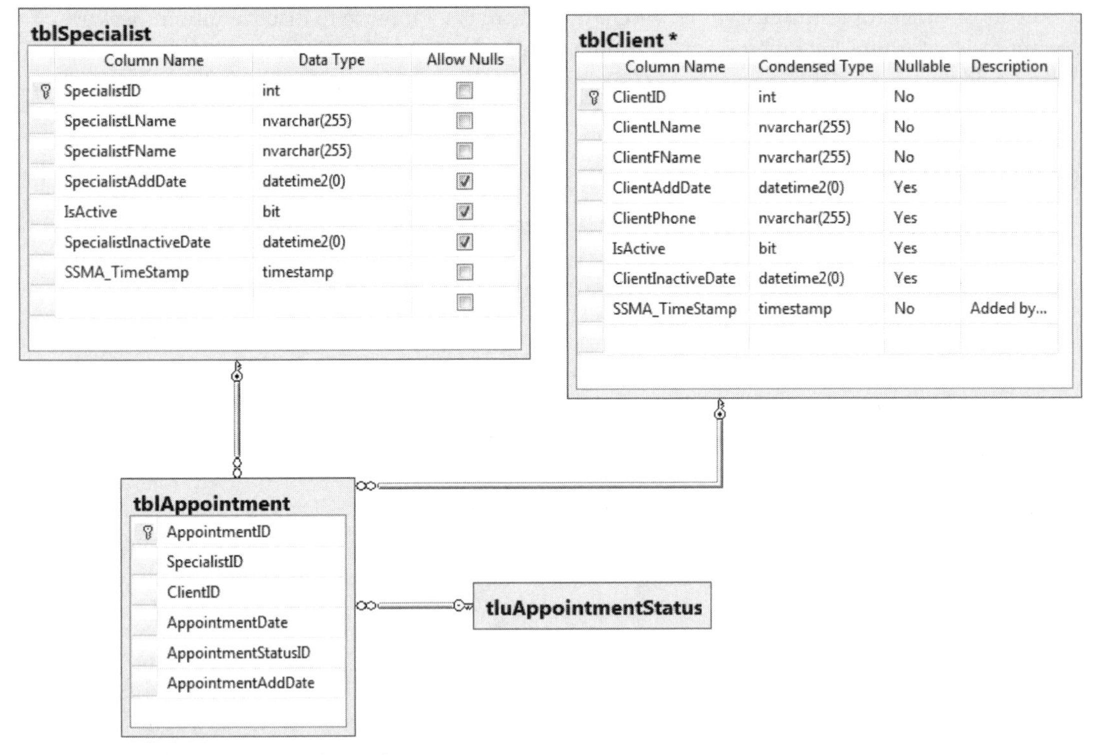

FIGURE 21-11: SQL Server database diagram

When you are in Object Explorer and choose a design from the table context menu, you will see that many of the options presented are very familiar to you: a list of field names with their data type and other more detailed options. The table designer toolbar offers additional options, as shown in Figure 21-12.

FIGURE 21-12: SQL Server Table toolbar

Available Data Types

As in Access, each field has a data type. The types in SQL Server are mostly equivalent but may be named differently. Table 21-1 compares the most common data types in Access and in SQL Server.

TABLE 21-1: Most Common Data Types Comparison

ACCESS	SQL SERVER	COMMENTS
`Integer`	`smallint`	In Access, an `integer` is 16-bit for legacy reasons. In SQL Server, an `integer` is 32-bit.
`Long Integer`	`int`	
`Single`	`real`	32-bit precision.

Double	float	64-bit precision.
Short string	varchar, nvarchar (for variable-length strings) char, nchar (for fixed-length strings)	The "n" prefix is for Unicode data that can store any language. In Access, all strings are variable-length Unicode under the hood.
Long string	varchar(max), nvarchar(max), varbinary(max)	SQL Server's text and ntext are deprecated.
Date/time	datetime, smalldatetime	SQL Server also has date, time, and other data types, but they are harder to work with from Access.
Currency	money, smallmoney	
Yes/No	bit	In SQL Server, Yes or True is 1; No or False is 0. In Access VBA, True is -1.
OLE Object	varbinary(max)	
Hyperlink	Will be converted to text	Handle in front-end application.
Attachment	Not supported	
Calculated	Will be converted to base data type	Re-create the formulas in SQL Server Computed Column Specification.
Lookup Wizard	Not supported	

> **NOTE** *Note that the "n" in* nvarchar, *and* nchar. *stands for the* Unicode *version of that data type, while the version without the "n" is the* ANSI *version. In Access, text data is always stored as* Unicode.

SQL Server also supports user-defined data types; for example, OrderNumber could be created as a custom data type defined as nvarchar(25).

When creating your own database, it is good to keep a few guidelines in mind:

- Every table should have a primary key. Not only is it good database design, but it is also required for linked tables in Access to be updatable. Additionally a timestamp or uniqueidentifier field helps with concurrency. When upsizing an Access database using SSMA, the tool will add this field for you if needed.
- Use data types that are compatible with Access, as indicated in Table 21-1.
- Avoid using Reserved Words and special characters such as the space character and $ sign for any database object.

- When creating relationships, consider also creating indexes on the many-side of the relationship. Access does this automatically for you, but in SQL Server you need to create the indexes yourself.
- Use Check Constraints at the table level like you use Validation Rules in Access at the field level.

SQL Server Objects

In this section, you will find information about the most important SQL Server objects you will use on a daily basis. You will read about views, stored procedures, T-SQL user-defined functions, and triggers.

Views

Views in SQL Server are similar to select queries in Access. They select rows and columns from one or more base tables or other views. Just like in Access, the view contains a select statement, although the syntax includes more elaborate options. One of these options is an explicit indexing option, using the `with schemabinding` clause, as indicated in the example that follows. The `with (nolock)` clause is another example; it is a locking hint that can improve performance and can be used in situations where data does not frequently change.

SQL Server views have two limitations that are not found in Access:

1. Views cannot be sorted (but there is a work-around using `select top N` queries).
2. Views do not accept parameters.

Since views are virtual tables, you can link to them from Access just like you can with standard tables. Much like with linked tables, if the order of the records is important, you will need to manage it in your solution. If a view has a unique index, Access will use the index. If not, Access will prompt the user when the view is being attached (see Figure 21-13).

FIGURE 21-13: Unique Identifier prompt dialog box

In this case, `AppointmentID` should be chosen because it is the primary key in the underlying table. Without a unique index Access will treat the table as read-only.

The following is a simple example of a view syntax (code file: `SQL.txt SQL Server view`):

```
--PURPOSE: List all appointments with status of Show
CREATE VIEW [dbo].[vwAppointments_Show]
WITH SCHEMABINDING
AS
  SELECT AppointmentID,
         SpecialistID,
         ClientID,
         AppointmentDate,
         AppointmentStatusID,
         AppointmentAddDate
```

```
  FROM dbo.tblAppointment
  WHERE (AppointmentStatusID = 4)
GO

CREATE UNIQUE CLUSTERED INDEX uidx_vwAppointments_Show_AppointmentID
  ON [dbo].[vwAppointments_Show](AppointmentID)
GO
```

In the preceding example, GO is the "Batch Separator." This means that if you execute the entire set of statements on the page, everything up to the first GO will be executed first; then the next batch will be executed.

Stored Procedures

Stored procedures are often the workhorse of the database. They are superior to Access queries because they can contain a rich syntax with multiple statements. They accept input and output parameters, and can return a status value to the calling procedure. They can contain both Action queries and Select queries, as well as DDL (Data Definition Language) statements that may, for example, create a temporary table.

The following is a simple example of a stored procedure (code file: `SQL.txt Stored Procedure`):

```
--PURPOSE: List all appointments with the given status
CREATE PROCEDURE dbo.spGetAppointmentsForStatus
    @statusID int
AS
BEGIN
  -- SET NOCOUNT ON added to prevent extra result sets from
  -- interfering with SELECT statements.
  SET NOCOUNT ON;

  SELECT AppointmentID,
         SpecialistID,
         ClientID,
         AppointmentDate,
         AppointmentStatusID,
         AppointmentAddDate
  FROM dbo.tblAppointment WITH (NOLOCK)
  WHERE (AppointmentStatusID = @statusID)

  RETURN 0
END
```

Stored procedures cannot be linked to from Access, but you can execute them in a couple of different ways. You can use a passthrough query in your database solution. See `testRunRecordsetReturningStoredProcedure` in the sample database, `SampleDB_SQL.accdb`, as an example of this method. The beauty of this method is that the statement is passed on to the server without any interpretation by Access, thus eliminating the overhead of Access SQL statement parsing. When you are sending a `SELECT` statement to SQL, the server still has to interpret it and calculate an execution plan. If you are sending a stored procedure call to the server, the execution plan has already been calculated and performance is improved.

The following is the main part of the VBA function to call a passthrough query. You can find further details such as the `GetConnectionString` function in line 20 in the sample database (code file: `SQL.txt Calling stored procedure via VBA`).

```
'PURPOSE: Generic function to run a recordset-returning stored procedure.
'NOTE:    Passthrough queries are always readonly,
'         not just because we're using dbOpenSnapshot here.
Public Function RunRecordsetReturningStoredProcedure(ByVal strSQL As String) _
                As DAO.Recordset
          Dim qd As DAO.QueryDef

10        Set qd = CurrentDb.CreateQueryDef("")       'Create temporary querydef
20        qd.Connect = GetConnectionString()
30        qd.SQL = strSQL
40        qd.ReturnsRecords = True

50        Set RunRecordsetReturningStoredProcedure = _
            qd.OpenRecordset(dbOpenSnapshot, dbSQLPassThrough)

60        qd.Close
70        Set qd = Nothing
End Function
```

Alternatively you can use ADO to achieve the same goal. The performance differences between the two methods are likely to be minimal so you should choose the method that works best for you. However, because OLEDB has been deprecated, you are better off using ODBC.

User-Defined Functions

Much like in Access (see Chapter 16) you can create a user-defined function in SQL Server. A user-defined function is a SQL routine that accepts parameters, performs calculations, and returns the result of that calculation as a value. The return value can either be a scalar (single) value or a table with multiple records. They can be used in the `SELECT` clause of a SQL statement. The following is a simple scalar user-defined function code sample (code file: `SQL.txt SQL UDF`):

```
--PURPOSE: Return quotient of Numerator by Denominator, handling division by zero.
CREATE FUNCTION dbo.fnDivideFloat(
  @Numerator float
  , @Denominator  float)
RETURNS float
AS
BEGIN
  DECLARE @ReturnValue float

  IF @Denominator = 0 --catch divide by zero
  SET @ReturnValue = 0
  ELSE
     SET @ReturnValue = @Numerator/@Denominator

  RETURN @ReturnValue
END
```

You can call this function from a `SELECT` statement such as (code file: `SQL.txt Calling UDF I`),

```
SELECT dbo.fnDivideFloat(12.3, 45.67)
```

or using a table, such as (code file: `SQL.txt Calling UDF II`):

```
SELECT dbo.fnDivideFloat(Cost, Price) AS ProfitMargin FROM myTable
```

Triggers

SQL Server tables can have triggers, which are procedures that run when records are inserted, updated, or deleted. They are somewhat equivalent to data macros in Access. Triggers are available only for actionable events; you cannot set up a trigger on a "Select" event.

The classic reason for a trigger is an audit trail feature: The trigger runs at each insert, update, and delete and can write information about who accessed what data to an audit trail table.

Another use is for enforcement of referential integrity. Typically, we would apply relationships declaratively at design time, just like in Access, by drawing lines between related objects in a designer. However in some database designs, that does not work: for example, if an ID value could come from one table or another, but not from anywhere else. Because triggers are essentially stored procedures that allow for a rich syntax, you can code this unusual rule using T-SQL statements. For example, the `Insert` trigger will test if the given ID value occurs in Table1 or Table2, and if it doesn't the trigger raises an error, which prevents the Insert from completing. You would need to put a corresponding `Delete` trigger on table1 and table2 to ensure the record to be deleted does not occur in the related table.

When you are using an application, it is not always readily apparent that a trigger is executing. Keep that in mind when you see some unexplained behavior when editing data in the application.

SQL Server also supports triggers at the database level, but they are rarely used in normal business applications. You can find the list of triggers using this SQL statement (code file: `SQL.txt Getting list of triggers`):

```
SELECT * FROM sys.triggers
```

Catalog Views

In SQL Server parlance, the "Catalog" is the database, and Catalog Views are built-in views you can use to find out more about the objects in the database. We just saw one of them in action in the previous section, to find a list of all triggers.

Here is another example, showing that these queries can be quite powerful. In this case, we want to find all bit fields in the database that don't have a default value. These fields are suspect because the lack of a default value causes the bit fields to have three states: true, false, and null, which is usually not desirable (code file: `SQL.txt Using built-in view`):

```
--PURPOSE: Find bit fields that are not required.
SELECT OBJECT_NAME(object_id) as theObjectName, *
FROM sys.columns
WHERE system_type_id = (select system_type_id from sys.types where [name] = 'bit')
AND object_id in (select object_id from sys.tables)    --Only user tables
AND is_nullable = 1
```

Troubleshooting

When you first use SQL Server you may run into some issues that take getting used to. In this section, we will cover some common errors and mistakes and how to resolve them.

Unable to Connect to the SQL Server

When you are unable to connect to the SQL Server, it can be for different reasons. Table 21-2 shows some of the most common reasons.

TABLE 21-2: SQL Server Troubleshooting

REASON	RESOLUTION
The server is not running.	Use SQL Server Configuration Manager to check.
The server does not have the right protocols enabled.	In Configuration Manager, expand SQL Server Network Configuration and ensure that Named Pipes and TCP/IP are enabled. Set the same options under SQL Native Client 11.0 Configuration and Client Protocols. It should be noted that in SQL Server Express versions, TCP/IP is disabled by default.
Firewall	If you are setting up a server outside of your normal network (for example in a DMZ), the SQL Server port (1433 by default) may need to be unblocked. Note that to access an instance of SQL Server that is not the default instance (such as Servername\SQLExpress vs MSSQLServer), the SQL Server Browser Service must be running on the server and port 1434 UDP should be unblocked.
You're not sure of the server name.	Use the Browse for more option in the Server name drop-down.
You're using Windows Authentication and cannot connect.	Try again when logged into Windows as a member of Administrators or Domain Administrators. They automatically have full access to the server.
You're using SQL Server Authentication and cannot connect.	Try again with the `sa` user who automatically has full access to the server.

If none of the these help, search the web for the exact error message you are receiving, you should get plenty of leads to help you connect. You can also post a question on online forums such as the MSDN forums.

If your Access application cannot connect to the SQL Server, make sure you have the correct connection string. `http://www.connectionstrings.com/sql-server-2012` has excellent information about the various connection strings.

You can also take a step back and first try connecting to the server using an Access built-in method: From the External Data tab on the ribbon, choose ODBC Database, create a Data Source Name in the ODBC applet, and use it to connect.

Unable to Access the Database

Once you are connected to the database server, you don't necessarily have the right to access the database or certain database objects. As stated previously, you can log in with specific built-in accounts and get access to all database objects.

SQL Server security is an advanced topic. You should study it thoroughly before making any changes. Once you do, consider making changes for all members of an Active Directory group rather than for individuals, and to all objects in a schema rather than to individual objects. Working with these collections is less work and easier to understand for yourself and your successor.

Performance Issues

One of the reasons you may upsize an Access database to SQL Server is that it promises better performance. You may instead find out that some parts of your application are faster, and others slower.

Indexes help queries run faster, so you should check that you have indexes on the fields that are used in the `WHERE` clause of a SQL statement. Additionally, SQL Server does not automatically create indexes on the many-side of a relation; you need to do that yourself.

Sometimes it makes sense to create a View in SQL Server, especially if it is a complex indexed view, rather than a similar query in Access. You can then link to this view just as you link to a table. Because the view statement is evaluated on the server, it may be able to select the records much more quickly.

For the same reason, you can move some processing into stored procedures and user-defined functions and execute them from the Access application.

SQL Server has several tools to assist with performance issues:

- SQL Server Profiler shows all SQL statements being run on the database and how long they take to execute.
- Database Engine Tuning Advisor takes a look at all objects in the database and suggests optimizations.
- You can analyze an individual query or SQL statement by turning on the Execution Plan in the SSMS toolbar.

SQL Language Differences

The version of the SQL language used by Access and SQL Server is similar but not identical. If you are using ODBC-attached tables and local queries that is not a problem: Access and the ODBC driver will provide the necessary translations. If, however, you are using SQL passthrough queries, you have to use the T-SQL language.

Here are some of the differences:

- In T-SQL, literal date values are wrapped in single quotes, not in # signs.
- The `JOIN` statement is different when multiple tables are involved.
- Access uses a syntax with nested parentheses as follows (code file: `SQL.txt Access Inner Join`):

```
SELECT
  dbo_tblClient.ClientID
, dbo_tblAppointment.AppointmentID
, dbo_tblSpecialist.SpecialistID
FROM
```

```
   (dbo_tblAppointment
INNER JOIN
   dbo_tblClient
ON dbo_tblAppointment.ClientID = dbo_tblClient.ClientID)
INNER JOIN
  dbo_tblSpecialist
ON dbo_tblAppointment.SpecialistID = dbo_tblSpecialist.SpecialistID;
```

- T-SQL is more linear (code file: `SQL.txt T-SQL Inner Join`):

```
SELECT
  tblClient.ClientID
, tblAppointment.AppointmentID
, tblSpecialist.SpecialistID
FROM
  tblAppointment
INNER JOIN
  tblClient
ON tblAppointment.ClientID = tblClient.ClientID
INNER JOIN
  tblSpecialist
ON tblAppointment.SpecialistID = tblSpecialist.SpecialistID
```

- You prefix object names with their schema name (for example, `dbo.tblClients`).
- T-SQL has a different set of built-in functions. For example, `NZ()` does not exist, `ISNULL()` is a good replacement for it; `MID()` does not exist and `SUBSTRING()` is its replacement.
- Access and VBA are very liberal with implicit type conversions; T-SQL often requires an explicit conversion using `Convert` or `Cast`. For example, while in Access you would simply write `select "Value of x = " & x from SomeTable` and the system would perform the type conversion from integer to string for you. In T-SQL, you will need to write the following code (code file: `SQL.txt SQL data type conversion`):

```
declare @x int
set @x = 5
print 'Value of x = ' + cast(@x as varchar)
```

SUMMARY

As you read in this chapter, most of your solutions will prosper in the Access world; however, some may need to be upsized to keep meeting your business needs. Upsizing your database solution to SQL Server is not a task to be taken lightly and you should consider the reason you and/or your business clients want to use SQL Server as the database engine.

After you decided to upsize, you learned what it takes to manage your database in SQL Server. The transition requires a learning curve. This chapter introduces the different tools in SQL Server and discusses how to create programming objects such as stored procedures and SQL user-defined functions.

Access and SQL Server are a good match. One provides a good home for the data; the other provides great tools for developing the front-end interface. Combining the two enables you to design and deploy robust and professional database solutions.

INDEX

INDEX

Symbols & Numbers

A

D

E

G

H

I

J–K

L

M

N

O

P

Q

R

S

T

U

V

W

X

Y–Z